Mergent



# HANDBOOK OF DIVIDEND ACHIEVERS

## Fall 2011

MERGENT

# Mergent's Dividend Achievers

## Mergent, Inc.

Jonathan Worrall
Publisher

John Pedernales
Executive Managing Director

Thomas Wecera
Managing Director of Print Products

Charlot Volny
Director of Print Products

Mohamed Hanif
Director of Equity Research Data

Wayne Arnold
Quality Assurance Editor

Andrew J. Kalinski
Editor

## Index Department

Kevin Heckert
Director-Global Index Operations

Bill Rogers
Director-Global Index Development

Thomas Rash
Financial Analyst

David Lukowski
Manager, Index Operations

Mergent's Dividend Achievers is published quarterly by Mergent Inc.

# TABLE OF CONTENTS

# Total Return on $10,000 Investment

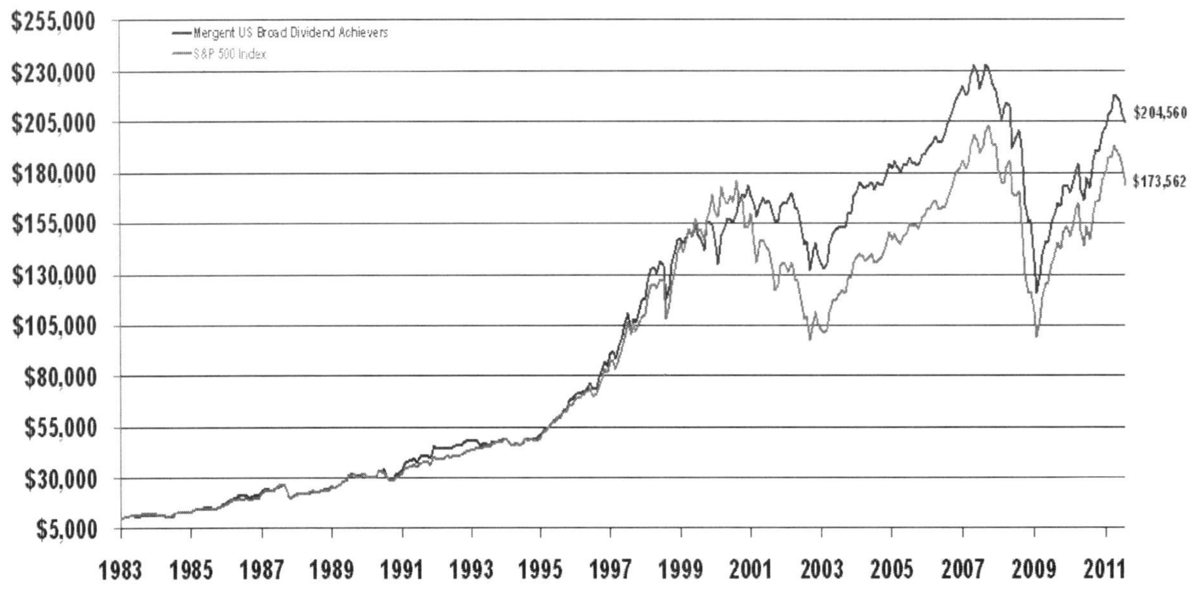

# Longest Records of Dividend Achievement

*These Dividend Achievers boast 25 or more years of consecutive dividend increases.*

| Rank | Years | Company | Ticker | Rank | Years | Company | Ticker |
|---|---|---|---|---|---|---|---|
| 1 | 57 | AMERICAN STS WTR CO | AWR | 47 | 37 | CENTURYLINK INC | CTL |
| | 57 | DIEBOLD INC | DBD | | 37 | MCGRAW HILL COS INC | MHP |
| | 57 | PROCTER & GAMBLE CO | PG | | 37 | RPM INTL INC | RPM |
| 4 | 55 | DOVER CORP | DOV | 50 | 36 | ARCHER DANIELS MIDLAND | ADM |
| | 55 | NORTHWEST NAT GAS CO | NWN | | 36 | CONSOLIDATED EDISON INC | ED |
| 6 | 54 | EMERSON ELEC CO | EMR | | 36 | KIMBERLY CLARK CORP | KMB |
| | 54 | GENUINE PARTS CO | GPC | | 36 | TELEPHONE & DATA SYS INC | TDS |
| | 54 | PARKER HANNIFIN CORP | PH | 54 | 35 | AUTOMATIC DATA | AUD |
| 9 | 52 | 3M CO | MMM | | 35 | MGE ENERGY INC | MDSN |
| | 50 | CINCINNATI FINL CORP | CINF | | 35 | VECTREN CORP | VVC |
| 11 | 49 | LOWES COS INC | LOW | | 35 | WAL MART STORES INC | WMT |
| 12 | 48 | COCA-COLA CO | KO | | 35 | WALGREEN CO | WAG |
| | 48 | COLGATE PALMOLIVE CO | CL | 59 | 34 | CARLISLE COS INC | CSL |
| | 48 | ILLINOIS TOOL WKS INC | ITW | | 34 | CLOROX CO DEL | CLX |
| | 48 | JOHNSON & JOHNSON | JNJ | | 34 | FAMILY DLR STORES INC | FDO |
| 16 | 47 | TOOTSIE ROLL INDS INC | TR | | 34 | HELMERICH & PAYNE INC | HP |
| 17 | 46 | ABM INDS INC | ABM | | 34 | MCDONALDS CORP | MCD |
| | 46 | CHUBB CORP | CB | | 34 | PENTAIR INC | PNR |
| 19 | 45 | ALTRIA GROUP INC | MO | | 34 | RLI CORP | RLI |
| 20 | 44 | HORMEL FOODS CORP | HRL | | 34 | SYSCO CORP | SYY |
| 21 | 43 | CALIFORNIA WTR SVC GROUP | CWT | | 34 | WGL HLDGS INC | WGL |
| | 43 | FEDERAL REALTY INVT TR | FRT | 68 | 33 | MEDTRONIC INC | MDT |
| | 43 | FULLER H B CO | FULL | 69 | 32 | VALSPAR CORP | VAL |
| | 43 | SJW CORP | SJW | 70 | 31 | PIEDMONT NAT GAS INC | PNY |
| | 43 | STANLEY BLACK & DECKER | SWK | | 31 | QUESTAR CORP | STR |
| | 43 | STEPAN CO | SCL | | 31 | SHERWIN WILLIAMS CO | SHW |
| 27 | 42 | COMMERCE BANCSHARES INC | CBSH | 73 | 30 | CLARCOR INC | CLC |
| 28 | 41 | LANCASTER COLONY CORP | LANC | | 30 | NORDSON CORP | NDSN |
| | 41 | WASHINGTON REAL ESTATE | WRE | 75 | 29 | EATON VANCE CORP | EV |
| 30 | 40 | MINE SAFETY APPLIANCES CO | MSA | | 29 | OLD REP INTL CORP | ORI |
| | 40 | UNIVERSAL CORP VA | UVV | | 29 | SIGMA ALDRICH CORP | SIAL |
| 32 | 39 | BARD C R INC | BCR | | 29 | UNITED BANKSHARES INC | UBSI |
| | 39 | BLACK HILLS CORP | BKH | 79 | 28 | AFLAC INC | AFL |
| | 39 | GRAINGER W W INC | GWW | | 28 | AIR PRODS & CHEMS INC | APD |
| | 39 | LEGGETT & PLATT INC | LEG | | 28 | CINTAS CORP | CTAS |
| | 39 | NATIONAL FUEL GAS CO N J | NFG | | 28 | ENERGEN CORP | EGN |
| | 39 | PEPSICO INC | PEP | | 28 | EXXON MOBIL CORP | XOM |
| | 39 | PPG INDS INC | PPG | 84 | 27 | BEMIS INC | BMS |
| | 39 | TARGET CORP | TGT | | 27 | NACCO INDS INC | NC |
| 40 | 38 | ABBOTT LABS | ABT | | 27 | PITNEY BOWES INC | PBI |
| | 38 | BECTON DICKINSON & CO | BDX | | 27 | SONOCO PRODS CO | SON |
| | 38 | GORMAN RUPP CO | GRC | 87 | 26 | AT&T INC | SBC |
| | 38 | MIDDLESEX WATER CO | MSEX | | 26 | BRADY CORP | BRC |
| | 38 | NUCOR CORP | NUE | | 26 | BROWN FORMAN CORP | BF.B |
| | 38 | TENNANT CO | TNC | 91 | 25 | HCP INC | HCP |
| | 38 | V F CORP | VFC | | | | |

# Dividend Achievers Arrivals

***The following companies are classified as new Dividend Achievers as they have recorded at least ten consecutive years of dividend increases and satisfied the liquidity requirements.***

CARBO CERAMICS INC
CONOCOPHILLIPS
SCANA CORP
UNISOURCE ENERGY CORP

# Dividend Achievers Departures

***The following former Dividend Achievers did not increased their regular cash dividends in 2010-2011.***

BANCORPSOUTH INC
BANK HAWAII CORP
BLOCK H & R INC
DENTSPLY INTL INC NEW
ENERGY TRANSFER PARTNERS LP
FEDERATED INVS INC PA
FIRST FINL BANKSHARES
GALLAGHER ARTHUR J & CO
HOLLY CORP
HOME PROPERTIES INC
INTEGRYS ENERGY GROUP INC
LAKELAND FINL CORP
LILLY ELI & CO
MARTIN MARIETTA MATLS INC
PAYCHEX INC
PROGRESS ENERGY INC
S Y BANCORP INC
SUPERVALU INC
TELEFLEX INC
WASHINGTON TR BANCORP
WOLVERINE WORLD WIDE INC
WSFS FINL CORP

## *The following former Dividend Achievers have been acquired or are in the process of being acquired since January 1, 2011*

Beckman Coulter, Inc.

Wesco Financial Corp.

## *The following companies have increased their dividend for at least 10 consecutive years but did not meet volume/liquidity requirements for inclusion in Mergent's US Dividend Achievers Index*

1ST SOURCE CORP
ALERUS FINL CORP
ARROW FINL CORP
ARTESIAN RESOURCES CORP
BANK UTICA N Y
BOWL AMERICA INC
CAMBRIDGE BANCORP
CB FINL SVCS INC
CCFNB BANCORP INC
CITIZENS FINL SVCS INC
CITIZENS HLDG CO MISS
COMPUTER SVCS INC
CONNECTICUT WTR SVC INC
EDUCATIONAL DEV CORP
FARMERS & MERCHANTS BANCORP
FIRST CAPITAL INC
FIRST KEYSTONE CORP
FIRST NATL BK GROTON N Y
FIRST ROBINSON FINL CORP
GREENE COUNTY BANCORP INC
HARLEYSVILLE SVGS FINL CORP
HEARTLAND BANCCORP
HERSHEY CREAMERY CO
JUNIATA VALLEY FINL CORP
KILLBUCK BANCSHARES INC
MUNCY BANK FINANCIAL INC PA
NATIONAL BANKSHARES INC VA
NEWFIELD BANCORP INC
NORTHEAST IND BANCORP INC
NORTHUMBERLAND BANCORP
NORWOOD FINANCIAL CORP
OHIO VY BANC CORP
ORANGE CNTY BANCORP INC
ORRSTOWN FINL SVCS INC
REPUBLIC BANCORP KY
SOLVAY BK CORP SOLVAY N J
SOMERSET TR HLDG CO
SPAN AMER MED SYS INC
THOMASVILLE BANCSHARES
TOMPKINS FINANCIAL CORPORATION
TORRINGTON WATER CO
TRI CITY BANKSHARES CORP
WEYCO GROUP INC
YORK WTR CO

# Dividend Achiever Name Changes

No new name changes

# Top 20 by 10 Year Compounded Annual Dividend Growth Rate (CAGR)

*Companies are listed by the 10-year average annual compound growth of their dividends. Also shown are the total number of years of consecutive annual dividend growth.*

| Rank | Company | CAGR | Years of Increases |
|---|---|---|---|
| 1 | FASTENAL CO | 43.27% | 12 |
| 2 | STRYKER CORP | 31.10% | 18 |
| 3 | CENTURYLINK INC | 30.66% | 37 |
| 4 | LOWES COS INC | 26.71% | 49 |
| 5 | MCDONALDS CORP | 25.95% | 34 |
| 6 | C H ROBINSON WORLDWIDE INC | 25.89% | 13 |
| 7 | FACTSET RESH SYS INC | 24.43% | 11 |
| 8 | NUCOR CORP | 24.19% | 38 |
| 9 | CARDINAL HEALTH INC | 23.45% | 14 |
| 10 | HUDSON CITY BANCORP | 23.40% | 11 |
| 11 | EXPEDITORS INTL WASH INC | 23.11% | 16 |
| 12 | EOG RES INC | 22.91% | 11 |
| 13 | ROSS STORES INC | 21.74% | 16 |
| 14 | MERIDIAN BIOSCIENCE INC | 20.73% | 18 |
| 15 | TJX COS INC NEW | 20.61% | 14 |
| 16 | LINEAR TECHNOLOGY CORP | 19.89% | 18 |
| 17 | APTARGROUP INC | 19.62% | 17 |
| 18 | AFLAC INC | 19.47% | 28 |
| 19 | STANCORP FINL GROUP INC | 19.08% | 11 |
| 20 | MINE SAFETY APPLIANCES CO | 18.59% | 40 |

# Top 20 by Return on Equity

*Based on latest available year-end information. Ratios determined using net income.*

| Rank | Company | R.O.E. | Rank | Company | R.O.E. |
|---|---|---|---|---|---|
| 1 | LINEAR TECH | 99.6 | 11 | MCDONALDS | 33.2 |
| 2 | ALTRIA GROUP | 91.1 | 12 | KIMBERLY-CLARK | 32.7 |
| 3 | COLGATE-PALMOLIV | 74.4 | 13 | NORDSON | 31.5 |
| 4 | INTL BUS MACH | 58.8 | 14 | CH ROBINSON | 31.4 |
| 5 | POLARIS INDUST | 43.4 | 15 | MCGRAW-HILL | 31.0 |
| 6 | EATON VANCE | 41.3 | 16 | FAMILY DOLLAR | 29.0 |
| 7 | AVON PRODUCTS | 40.0 | 17 | RAVEN INDUSTRIES | 28.5 |
| 8 | ROSS STORES | 38.4 | 18 | SHERWIN-WILLIAMS | 28.2 |
| 9 | QUESTAR | 37.9 | 19 | FACTSET RESEARCH | 28.1 |
| 10 | GRACO | 36.9 | 20 | BARD C R | 26.7 |

# Top 20 by Return on Assets

*Based on latest available year-end information. Ratios determined using net income.*

| Rank | Company | R.O.A | Rank | Company | R.O.A |
|---|---|---|---|---|---|
| 1 | LINEAR TECH | 34.9 | 11 | EATON VANCE | 16.7 |
| 2 | FACTSET RESEARCH | 22.4 | 12 | T ROWE PRICE | 15.6 |
| 3 | RAVEN INDUSTRIES | 21.9 | 13 | NORDSON | 15.2 |
| 4 | LANCASTER COLONY | 19.7 | 14 | MCDONALDS | 15.1 |
| 5 | CH ROBINSON | 19.4 | 15 | BARD C R | 14.3 |
| 6 | GRACO | 19.3 | 16 | POLARIS INDUST | 13.7 |
| 7 | COLGATE-PALMOLIV | 19.1 | 17 | BADGER METER | 13.6 |
| 8 | FASTENAL | 18.1 | 18 | SEI INVESTMENTS | 13.6 |
| 9 | MERIDIAN BIOSCI | 17.7 | 19 | 3M COMPANY | 13.3 |
| 10 | ROSS STORES | 17.5 | 20 | BROWN-FORMAN B | 13.3 |

# Top 20 by Current Dividend Yields

*Based on latest available Prices*

| Rank | Company | C.D.Y | Rank | Company | C.D.Y. |
|---|---|---|---|---|---|
| 1 | GETTY REALTY | 10.1 | 11 | UNIV HEALTH RLTY | 6.5 |
| 2 | VECTOR GROUP | 8.6 | 12 | BUCKEYE PARTNERS | 6.3 |
| 3 | CENTURYLINK | 8.0 | 13 | CORP OFFICE PROP | 6.2 |
| 4 | PITNEY-BOWES | 7.3 | 14 | MERCURY GENERAL | 6.1 |
| 5 | SUBURBAN PROPANE | 7.2 | 15 | ALTRIA GROUP | 6.0 |
| 6 | OLD REPUBLIC | 7.0 | 16 | AT&T INC | 6.0 |
| 7 | TC PIPELINES LP | 6.9 | 17 | CINCINNATI FINL | 5.8 |
| 8 | INVESTORS RE TR | 6.7 | 18 | URSTADT BIDDLE | 5.8 |
| 9 | KINDER MORGAN EN | 6.6 | 19 | ENTERPRISE PROD | 5.7 |
| 10 | PLAINS ALL AMER | 6.5 | 20 | NATL RETAIL PROP | 5.6 |

# Highest Price/Earnings Ratios

*Based on latest available year-end information. Ratios determined using net income.*
*Based on closing prices as of August 31, 2011*

| Rank | Company | P/E Ratio | Rank | Company | P/E Ratio |
|---|---|---|---|---|---|
| 1 | KINDER MORGAN EN | 39.0 | 11 | PEOPLES UTD FINL | 29.4 |
| 2 | STEPAN | 37.8 | 12 | TENNANT | 29.3 |
| 3 | CARBO CERAMICS | 36.7 | 13 | HCP | 28.7 |
| 4 | CASEYS GEN STORE | 36.0 | 14 | CH ROBINSON | 28.2 |
| 5 | WILEY JOHN | 34.9 | 15 | MERIDIAN BIOSCI | 26.4 |
| 6 | FASTENAL | 31.6 | 16 | EXPEDITORS INTL | 26.0 |
| 7 | NORTHEAST UTIL | 31.5 | 17 | ATLANTIC TELENET | 25.5 |
| 8 | EOG RESOURCES | 30.9 | 18 | TANGER FACTORY | 24.9 |
| 9 | WEST PHARMACEUT | 30.9 | 19 | UNIV HEALTH RLTY | 24.9 |
| 10 | ERIE INDEMNITY | 29.4 | 20 | ENTERPRISE PROD | 24.8 |

# Lowest Price/Earnings Ratios

*Based on latest available year-end information. Ratios determined using net income.*
*Based on closing prices as of August 31, 2011*

| Rank | Company | P/E Ratio | Rank | Company | P/E Ratio |
|---|---|---|---|---|---|
| 1 | STANCORP FINL | 6.8 | 11 | MEREDITH | 9.1 |
| 2 | AFLAC | 6.9 | 12 | INVESTORS RE TR | 9.2 |
| 3 | HUDSON CITY BANC | 6.9 | 13 | UNIVERSAL CORP | 9.3 |
| 4 | NACCO INDUST | 7.7 | 14 | GETTY REALTY | 9.5 |
| 5 | QUESTAR | 7.8 | 15 | HARLEYSVILLE GRP | 9.6 |
| 6 | TRANSATLANTIC | 7.9 | 16 | CONOCOPHILLIPS | 9.7 |
| 7 | CHEVRON | 8.6 | 17 | ARCHER-DANIELS | 9.8 |
| 8 | PITNEY-BOWES | 8.6 | 18 | HCC INSUR HLDGS | 10.1 |
| 9 | SOUTHSIDE BANCSH | 8.8 | 19 | CORP OFFICE PROP | 10.3 |
| 10 | GEN DYNAMICS | 9.1 | 20 | TELEPHONE & DATA | 10.3 |

# Highest Price/Book Ratios

*Based on latest available year-end information. Ratios determined using net income.*
*Based on closing prices as of August 31, 2011*

| Rank | Company | P/B Ratio | Rank | Company | P/B Ratio |
|---|---|---|---|---|---|
| 1 | COLGATE-PALMOLIV | 13.7 | 11 | CARBO CERAMICS | 6.4 |
| 2 | ALTRIA GROUP | 12.1 | 12 | TJX | 6.3 |
| 3 | LINEAR TECH | 11.4 | 13 | MCDONALDS | 6.1 |
| 4 | CH ROBINSON | 8.9 | 14 | RAVEN INDUSTRIES | 6.0 |
| 5 | POLARIS INDUST | 8.5 | 15 | ROSS STORES | 5.7 |
| 6 | INTL BUS MACH | 8.2 | 16 | EATON VANCE | 5.6 |
| 7 | FASTENAL | 7.1 | 17 | MERIDIAN BIOSCI | 5.5 |
| 8 | FACTSET RESEARCH | 6.9 | 18 | MCGRAW-HILL | 5.5 |
| 9 | GRACO | 6.8 | 19 | ECOLAB | 5.3 |
| 10 | TANGER FACTORY | 6.4 | 20 | FAMILY DOLLAR | 5.1 |

# Lowest Price/Book Ratios

*Based on latest available year-end information. Ratios determined using net income.*
*Based on closing prices as of May 31, 2011*

| Rank | Company | P/B Ratio | Rank | Company | P/B Ratio |
|---|---|---|---|---|---|
| 1 | OLD REPUBLIC | 0.7 | 11 | HARLEYSVILLE GRP | 1.0 |
| 2 | TELEPHONE & DATA | 0.7 | 12 | ARCHER-DANIELS | 1.0 |
| 3 | HUDSON CITY BANC | 0.7 | 13 | UNIVERSAL FOREST | 1.0 |
| 4 | STANCORP FINL | 0.7 | 14 | BLACK HILLS | 1.1 |
| 5 | TRANSATLANTIC | 0.7 | 15 | COMMUNITY TRUST | 1.1 |
| 6 | PEOPLES UTD FINL | 0.8 | 16 | CHUBB | 1.1 |
| 7 | CINCINNATI FINL | 0.9 | 17 | BANCFIRST CORP | 1.2 |
| 8 | UNIVERSAL CORP | 1.0 | 18 | MURPHY OIL | 1.2 |
| 9 | HCC INSUR HLDGS | 1.0 | 19 | PROSPERITY BANCS | 1.2 |
| 10 | CENTURYLINK | 1.0 | 20 | MERCURY GENERAL | 1.2 |

# Top 20 by Revenues

*Based on latest available year-end information (US$ in millions)*

| Rank | Company | Revenues | Rank | Company | Revenues |
|---|---|---|---|---|---|
| 1 | WAL-MART STORES | $421,849 | 11 | TARGET CORP | $67,390 |
| 2 | EXXON MOBIL | $383,221 | 12 | JOHNSON JOHNSON | $61,587 |
| 3 | CHEVRON | $204,928 | 13 | PEPSICO | $57,838 |
| 4 | CONOCOPHILLIPS | $198,655 | 14 | UNITED TECH | $54,326 |
| 5 | AT&T INC | $124,280 | 15 | LOWES COMPANIES | $48,815 |
| 6 | INTL BUS MACH | $99,871 | 16 | CATERPILLAR | $42,588 |
| 7 | CARDINAL HEALTH | $98,503 | 17 | SYSCO | $37,243 |
| 8 | PROCTER & GAMBLE | $82,559 | 18 | ABBOTT LABS | $35,167 |
| 9 | ARCHER-DANIELS | $80,676 | 19 | COCA-COLA | $35,119 |
| 10 | WALGREEN | $67,420 | 20 | ENTERPRISE PROD | $33,739 |

# Top 20 by Net Income

*Based on latest available year-end information (US$ in millions)*

| Rank | Company | Net Income | Rank | Company | Net Income |
|---|---|---|---|---|---|
| 1 | EXXON MOBIL | $30,460 | 11 | MCDONALDS | $4,946 |
| 2 | AT&T INC | $19,864 | 12 | ABBOTT LABS | $4,626 |
| 3 | CHEVRON | $19,024 | 13 | UNITED TECH | $4,373 |
| 4 | WAL-MART STORES | $16,389 | 14 | 3M COMPANY | $4,085 |
| 5 | INTL BUS MACH | $14,833 | 15 | ALTRIA GROUP | $3,905 |
| 6 | JOHNSON JOHNSON | $13,334 | 16 | MEDTRONIC | $3,096 |
| 7 | COCA-COLA | $11,809 | 17 | TARGET CORP | $2,920 |
| 8 | PROCTER & GAMBLE | $11,797 | 18 | CATERPILLAR | $2,700 |
| 9 | CONOCOPHILLIPS | $11,358 | 19 | GEN DYNAMICS | $2,624 |
| 10 | PEPSICO | $6,320 | 20 | AFLAC | $2,344 |

# Top 20 by Market Capitalization

*Based on latest available year-end information (US$ in millions )*
*Based on closing prices as of August 31, 2011*

| Rank | Company | Current Value | Rank | Company | Current Value |
|---|---|---|---|---|---|
| 1 | EXXON MOBIL | $359,893 | 11 | MCDONALDS | $93,285 |
| 2 | INTL BUS MACH | $205,312 | 12 | ABBOTT LABS | $81,737 |
| 3 | CHEVRON | $197,977 | 13 | UNITED TECH | $67,471 |
| 4 | WAL-MART STORES | $184,708 | 14 | 3M COMPANY | $58,874 |
| 5 | JOHNSON JOHNSON | $180,318 | 15 | CATERPILLAR | $58,795 |
| 6 | PROCTER & GAMBLE | $174,980 | 16 | ALTRIA GROUP | $56,316 |
| 7 | AT&T INC | $168,772 | 17 | COLGATE-PALMOLIV | $43,770 |
| 8 | COCA-COLA | $161,760 | 18 | MEDTRONIC | $37,209 |
| 9 | PEPSICO | $101,967 | 19 | ENTERPRISE PROD | $35,844 |
| 10 | CONOCOPHILLIPS | $93,460 | 20 | TARGET CORP | $34,888 |

# Bottom 20 by Market Capitalization

*Based on latest available year-end information (US$ in millions )*
*Based on closing prices as of August 31, 2011*

| Rank | Company | Current Value | Rank | Company | Current Value |
|---|---|---|---|---|---|
| 1 | MIDDLESEX WATER | $284 | 11 | BANCFIRST CORP | $547 |
| 2 | SHENANDOAH TELE | $327 | 12 | MCGRATH RENTCORP | $582 |
| 3 | SOUTHSIDE BANCSH | $328 | 13 | UNIVERSAL FOREST | $596 |
| 4 | COMMUNITY TRUST | $389 | 14 | GORMAN-RUPP | $613 |
| 5 | FIRST FINL CORP | $408 | 15 | INVESTORS RE TR | $629 |
| 6 | SJW CORP | $434 | 16 | GETTY REALTY | $635 |
| 7 | UNIV HEALTH RLTY | $471 | 17 | NACCO INDUST | $644 |
| 8 | URSTADT BIDDLE | $496 | 18 | AMER STATES WATR | $664 |
| 9 | ATLANTIC TELENET | $511 | 19 | MERIDIAN BIOSCI | $760 |
| 10 | BADGER METER | $529 | 20 | STEPAN | $772 |

# Top 20 by Total Assets

*Based on latest available year-end information (US$ in millions )*

| Rank | Company | Total Assets | Rank | Company | Total Assets |
|---|---|---|---|---|---|
| 1 | EXXON MOBIL | $302,510 | 11 | PEPSICO | $68,153 |
| 2 | AT&T INC | $268,488 | 12 | CATERPILLAR | $64,020 |
| 3 | CHEVRON | $184,769 | 13 | HUDSON CITY BANC | $61,166 |
| 4 | WAL-MART STORES | $180,663 | 14 | ABBOTT LABS | $59,462 |
| 5 | CONOCOPHILLIPS | $156,314 | 15 | UNITED TECH | $58,493 |
| 6 | PROCTER & GAMBLE | $138,354 | 16 | NEXTERA ENERGY | $52,994 |
| 7 | INTL BUS MACH | $113,450 | 17 | CHUBB | $50,249 |
| 8 | JOHNSON JOHNSON | $102,908 | 18 | TARGET CORP | $43,705 |
| 9 | AFLAC | $101,039 | 19 | ARCHER-DANIELS | $42,193 |
| 10 | COCA-COLA | $72,921 | 20 | ALTRIA GROUP | $37,402 |

# About Total Return

Total return represents one of the best measures of how well an investor of a given stock has fared as it reflects both dividend income and price appreciation. Mergent calculates total return for each Dividend Achievers company on the basis that cash dividends were reinvested on the ex-dividend date of each dividend payment. The following table demonstrates the effect of compounding as well as each stock's performance and the level of dividends paid. Total returns have been adjusted for splits, stock dividends and spin-offs. In the case of a spin-off, shares in the spun-off company were assumed to be converted to cash and reinvested in the original company's stock.

How to read the rankings: On the following pages, the Dividend Achievers companies are listed alphabetically with their respective total returns and rankings over trailing one, three and five year periods ending August 31, 2011. For example, an investor who purchased shares of Abbott Laboratories on August 31, 2010, and sold them on August 31, 2011 would have realized a total return of 10.32% on their original investment. Following each company's one-year total return are its three-year and five-year annualized total returns and their respective rankings for each period. The three-year annualized total return is based on an investment made on August 29, 2008, and the five-year annualized total return represents an investment made on August 31, 2006. Thus an investment made in Abbott Laboratories on August 29, 2008, would have generated an annualized total return of .38% during the three year period ended August 31, 2011. If an investor had bought shares in Abbott Laboratories on August 31, 2006, and sold them on August 31, 2011, their annualized total return would have been 4.60%.

# Ranking the Dividend Achievers by Total Return

*Based on the 1, 3, and 5 year periods ending August 31, 2011*

| Ticker | Name | Tot Ret. 1 Year | Rank 1 Year | Tot Ret. 3 Year | Rank 3 Year | Tot Ret. 5 Year | Rank 5 Year |
|---|---|---|---|---|---|---|---|
| MMM | 3M CO | 8.29% | 141 | 8.08% | 75 | 5.76% | 93 |
| ABT | ABBOTT LABS | 10.32% | 129 | 0.38% | 132 | 4.60% | 108 |
| ABM | ABM INDS INC | 6.65% | 150 | -5.64% | 161 | 5.08% | 103 |
| AFL | AFLAC INC | -18.22% | 185 | -10.26% | 178 | -1.28% | 160 |
| APD | AIR PRODS & CHEMS INC | 13.26% | 112 | -1.18% | 141 | 6.76% | 83 |
| ALB | ALBEMARLE CORP | 27.94% | 46 | 10.15% | 61 | 14.62% | 26 |
| MO | ALTRIA GROUP INC | 29.39% | 43 | 16.65% | 21 | 13.37% | 34 |
| AWR | AMERICAN STS WTR CO | 9.85% | 132 | -0.57% | 137 | 1.25% | 139 |
| ATR | APTARGROUP INC | 23.10% | 65 | 9.57% | 65 | 16.24% | 18 |
| WTR | AQUA AMERICA INC | 14.18% | 110 | 9.73% | 64 | 1.33% | 138 |
| ADM | ARCHER DANIELS MIDLAND CO | -5.68% | 177 | 5.93% | 91 | -5.46% | 176 |
| T | AT&T INC | 11.53% | 121 | 2.32% | 112 | 3.57% | 120 |
| ATNI | ATLANTIC TELE NETWORK INC | -20.10% | 187 | 1.95% | 114 | 15.00% | 23 |
| ATO | ATMOS ENERGY CORP | 23.62% | 64 | 12.03% | 47 | 8.01% | 71 |
| ADP | AUTOMATIC DATA PROC. INC | 33.54% | 36 | 7.46% | 79 | 6.19% | 87 |
| AVP | AVON PRODS INC | -19.79% | 186 | -16.59% | 187 | -2.07% | 162 |
| BMI | BADGER METER INC | -4.65% | 176 | -7.40% | 167 | 7.35% | 77 |
| BANF | BANCFIRST CORP | -1.61% | 170 | -7.36% | 166 | -3.54% | 167 |
| OZRK | BANK OF THE OZARKS INC | 25.65% | 54 | 28.95% | 4 | 9.23% | 63 |
| BCR | BARD C R INC | 24.91% | 59 | 1.46% | 118 | 5.64% | 97 |
| BDX | BECTON DICKINSON & CO | 21.79% | 70 | -0.43% | 136 | 4.91% | 106 |
| BMS | BEMIS INC | 10.86% | 126 | 7.11% | 81 | 2.36% | 133 |
| BKH | BLACK HILLS CORP | 5.50% | 151 | 2.08% | 113 | 2.12% | 134 |
| BRC | BRADY CORP | 9.13% | 138 | -6.87% | 164 | -4.30% | 170 |
| BRO | BROWN & BROWN INC | 11.94% | 119 | 2.67% | 109 | -5.56% | 178 |
| BF B | BROWN FORMAN CORP | 21.04% | 75 | 10.53% | 58 | 6.07% | 88 |
| BPL | BUCKEYE PARTNERS L P | 9.71% | 134 | 21.67% | 8 | 15.50% | 21 |
| CHRW | C H ROBINSON WORLDWIDE INC | 10.59% | 128 | 12.71% | 43 | 10.90% | 48 |
| CWT | CALIFORNIA WTR SVC GROUP | 12.16% | 116 | 1.91% | 117 | 3.05% | 126 |
| CRR | CARBO CERAMICS INC | 112.93% | 1 | 40.30% | 1 | 33.65% | 1 |
| CAH | CARDINAL HEALTH INC | 44.77% | 13 | 4.45% | 101 | -1.17% | 159 |
| CSL | CARLISLE COS INC | 42.16% | 20 | 8.85% | 68 | 0.12% | 151 |
| CASY | CASEYS GEN STORES INC | 21.21% | 74 | 17.14% | 19 | 14.99% | 24 |
| CAT | CATERPILLAR INC DEL | 42.25% | 18 | 12.11% | 46 | 9.32% | 62 |
| CTL | CENTURYLINK INC | 7.27% | 143 | 6.25% | 89 | 3.68% | 117 |

| Ticker | Name | Tot Ret. 1 Year | Rank 1 Year | Tot Ret. 3 Year | Rank 3 Year | Tot Ret. 5 Year | Rank 5 Year |
|---|---|---|---|---|---|---|---|
| CVX | CHEVRON CORP NEW | 37.73% | 30 | 8.40% | 71 | 12.57% | 40 |
| CB | CHUBB CORP | 15.17% | 105 | 11.93% | 50 | 7.02% | 80 |
| CHD | CHURCH & DWIGHT INC | 44.13% | 15 | 12.83% | 42 | 18.74% | 9 |
| CINF | CINCINNATI FINL CORP | 10.31% | 130 | 3.82% | 103 | -5.27% | 175 |
| CTAS | CINTAS CORP | 27.69% | 47 | 3.24% | 105 | -1.29% | 161 |
| CLC | CLARCOR INC | 39.68% | 25 | 6.42% | 87 | 10.34% | 52 |
| CLX | CLOROX CO DEL | 11.13% | 125 | 9.25% | 66 | 6.23% | 86 |
| KO | COCA-COLA CO | 29.76% | 42 | 14.15% | 35 | 12.73% | 39 |
| CL | COLGATE PALMOLIVE CO | 25.22% | 57 | 8.54% | 70 | 11.10% | 46 |
| CBSH | COMMERCE BANCSHARES INC | 19.06% | 84 | 3.16% | 106 | 2.56% | 131 |
| CBU | COMMUNITY BK SYS INC | 15.36% | 104 | 8.08% | 74 | 7.08% | 79 |
| CTBI | COMMUNITY TR BANCORP INC | 0.03% | 169 | -4.95% | 159 | -4.30% | 171 |
| COP | CONOCOPHILLIPS | 34.52% | 35 | -2.44% | 149 | 4.78% | 107 |
| ED | CONSOLIDATED EDISON INC | 23.85% | 62 | 17.26% | 15 | 9.59% | 60 |
| OFC | CORPORATE OFFICE PPTYS TR | -22.18% | 188 | -7.65% | 169 | -6.87% | 180 |
| CFR | CULLEN FROST BANKERS INC | 2.83% | 160 | 0.47% | 131 | 0.29% | 148 |
| DBD | DIEBOLD INC | 14.38% | 108 | -6.90% | 165 | -4.32% | 172 |
| DCI | DONALDSON INC | 42.24% | 19 | 11.65% | 51 | 13.31% | 35 |
| DOV | DOVER CORP | 30.99% | 40 | 7.96% | 76 | 5.73% | 95 |
| EV | EATON VANCE CORP | -3.80% | 175 | -9.79% | 176 | 0.30% | 147 |
| ECL | ECOLAB INC | 14.61% | 106 | 6.91% | 83 | 5.07% | 104 |
| EMR | EMERSON ELEC CO | 2.44% | 163 | 3.02% | 107 | 5.45% | 99 |
| EGN | ENERGEN CORP | 16.21% | 100 | -3.02% | 151 | 3.48% | 121 |
| EPD | ENTERPRISE PRODS PARTNERS L | 20.52% | 77 | 20.87% | 9 | 17.18% | 14 |
| EOG | EOG RES INC | 7.25% | 145 | -3.25% | 153 | 8.03% | 70 |
| ERIE | ERIE INDTY CO | 83.17% | 3 | 17.22% | 16 | 9.65% | 59 |
| ESS | ESSEX PPTY TR INC | 40.53% | 22 | 11.96% | 49 | 6.95% | 82 |
| EXPD | EXPEDITORS INTL WASH INC | 15.89% | 101 | 9.12% | 67 | 3.58% | 118 |
| XOM | EXXON MOBIL CORP | 28.29% | 44 | -0.16% | 135 | 4.03% | 114 |
| FDS | FACTSET RESH SYS INC | 20.76% | 76 | 13.39% | 39 | 16.07% | 19 |
| FDO | FAMILY DLR STORES INC | 26.50% | 49 | 31.11% | 3 | 17.91% | 11 |
| FAST | FASTENAL CO | 51.39% | 10 | 11.39% | 53 | 14.87% | 25 |
| FRT | FEDERAL REALTY INVT TR | 18.00% | 89 | 10.27% | 60 | 7.83% | 72 |
| THFF | FIRST FINL CORP IND | 10.61% | 127 | -6.68% | 163 | 1.55% | 137 |
| FELE | FRANKLIN ELEC INC | 37.25% | 31 | 1.26% | 119 | -0.96% | 157 |

| Ticker | Name | Tot Ret. 1 Year | Rank 1 Year | Tot Ret. 3 Year | Rank 3 Year | Tot Ret. 5 Year | Rank 5 Year |
|---|---|---|---|---|---|---|---|
| BEN | FRANKLIN RES INC | 25.30% | 56 | 6.73% | 84 | 5.49% | 98 |
| FUL | FULLER H B CO | 18.28% | 87 | -3.91% | 157 | 4.19% | 113 |
| GD | GENERAL DYNAMICS CORP | 17.61% | 92 | -9.18% | 173 | 1.04% | 141 |
| GPC | GENUINE PARTS CO | 35.90% | 33 | 13.63% | 36 | 9.92% | 58 |
| GTY | GETTY RLTY CORP NEW | -17.66% | 183 | 5.28% | 99 | -1.05% | 158 |
| GRC | GORMAN RUPP CO | 43.66% | 16 | -1.77% | 145 | 15.43% | 22 |
| GGG | GRACO INC | 44.34% | 14 | 3.83% | 102 | 3.20% | 125 |
| GWW | GRAINGER W W INC | 48.24% | 11 | 21.98% | 7 | 20.40% | 6 |
| HGIC | HARLEYSVILLE GROUP INC | -2.17% | 171 | -2.43% | 148 | -0.29% | 153 |
| HSC | HARSCO CORP | 17.79% | 90 | -22.15% | 188 | -8.46% | 184 |
| HCC | HCC INS HLDGS INC | 18.21% | 88 | 7.22% | 80 | -0.31% | 154 |
| HCP | HCP INC | 11.60% | 120 | 7.58% | 78 | 10.81% | 49 |
| HP | HELMERICH & PAYNE INC | 54.65% | 8 | 0.52% | 129 | 19.04% | 7 |
| JKHY | HENRY JACK & ASSOC INC | 26.02% | 52 | 15.25% | 29 | 10.34% | 53 |
| HRL | HORMEL FOODS CORP | 30.36% | 41 | 18.12% | 12 | 10.67% | 50 |
| HCBK | HUDSON CITY BANCORP | -43.66% | 189 | -27.28% | 189 | -10.65% | 189 |
| ITW | ILLINOIS TOOL WKS INC | 15.76% | 102 | 0.78% | 126 | 3.75% | 116 |
| IBM | INTERNATIONAL BUSINESS MACHS | 42.05% | 21 | 14.36% | 33 | 18.28% | 10 |
| IRET | INVESTORS REAL ESTATE TR | 2.66% | 161 | -2.59% | 150 | 2.67% | 129 |
| JNJ | JOHNSON & JOHNSON | 19.52% | 81 | 1.14% | 122 | 3.47% | 122 |
| KMB | KIMBERLY CLARK CORP | 12.00% | 118 | 8.37% | 72 | 5.67% | 96 |
| KMP | PARTNERS | 11.44% | 122 | 14.71% | 31 | 17.19% | 13 |
| LANC | LANCASTER COLONY CORP | 36.27% | 32 | 23.46% | 6 | 9.39% | 61 |
| LEG | LEGGETT & PLATT INC | 21.41% | 72 | 5.42% | 95 | 4.22% | 112 |
| LLTC | LINEAR TECHNOLOGY CORP | 3.02% | 159 | -1.06% | 139 | -0.55% | 155 |
| LOW | LOWES COS INC | 0.25% | 168 | -5.11% | 160 | -4.49% | 173 |
| MATW | MATTHEWS INTL CORP | 7.07% | 146 | -12.01% | 185 | -0.58% | 156 |
| MKC | MCCORMICK & CO INC | 22.74% | 67 | 8.58% | 69 | 8.23% | 69 |
| MCD | MCDONALDS CORP | 27.52% | 48 | 17.17% | 18 | 24.38% | 4 |
| MGRC | MCGRATH RENTCORP | 22.81% | 66 | -2.00% | 146 | 4.36% | 111 |
| MHP | MCGRAW HILL COS INC | 56.21% | 6 | 2.54% | 111 | -3.11% | 166 |
| MDU | MDU RES GROUP INC | 16.97% | 95 | -10.81% | 182 | -0.05% | 152 |
| MDT | MEDTRONIC INC | 14.32% | 109 | -11.74% | 184 | -3.98% | 169 |
| MCY | MERCURY GENL CORP NEW | 6.89% | 147 | -2.37% | 147 | 0.48% | 143 |
| MDP | MEREDITH CORP | -8.94% | 178 | 0.50% | 130 | -8.83% | 186 |

| Ticker | Name | Tot Ret. 1 Year | Rank 1 Year | Tot Ret. 3 Year | Rank 3 Year | Tot Ret. 5 Year | Rank 5 Year |
|---|---|---|---|---|---|---|---|
| VIVO | MERIDIAN BIOSCIENCE INC | 4.66% | 153 | -10.33% | 181 | 6.02% | 89 |
| MGEE | MGE ENERGY INC | 17.10% | 94 | 12.01% | 48 | 9.02% | 64 |
| MSEX | MIDDLESEX WATER CO | 15.74% | 103 | 5.33% | 98 | 1.69% | 135 |
| MSA | MINE SAFETY APPLIANCES CO | 39.93% | 24 | -1.66% | 144 | 0.30% | 146 |
| MUR | MURPHY OIL CORP | 1.80% | 165 | -10.31% | 180 | 3.44% | 123 |
| NC | NACCO INDS INC | 1.17% | 167 | -9.82% | 177 | -7.75% | 182 |
| NFG | NATIONAL FUEL GAS CO N J | 45.88% | 12 | 12.25% | 45 | 13.13% | 37 |
| NNN | NATIONAL RETAIL PROPERTIES I | 18.68% | 86 | 14.18% | 34 | 11.45% | 43 |
| NJR | NEW JERSEY RES | 30.99% | 39 | 13.12% | 40 | 11.00% | 47 |
| NEE | NEXTERA ENERGY INC | 9.80% | 133 | 1.92% | 116 | 8.60% | 66 |
| NDSN | NORDSON CORP | 38.10% | 29 | 19.56% | 10 | 18.75% | 8 |
| NU | NORTHEAST UTILS | 23.69% | 63 | 13.00% | 41 | 12.46% | 41 |
| NWN | NORTHWEST NAT GAS CO | 3.31% | 157 | 1.16% | 121 | 7.09% | 78 |
| NST | NSTAR | 24.94% | 58 | 15.45% | 28 | 11.33% | 44 |
| NUE | NUCOR CORP | 1.53% | 166 | -8.70% | 171 | -2.45% | 164 |
| ORI | OLD REP INTL CORP | -17.77% | 184 | 2.95% | 108 | -9.48% | 187 |
| OMI | OWENS & MINOR INC NEW | 13.30% | 111 | 0.94% | 124 | 8.88% | 65 |
| PH | PARKER HANNIFIN CORP | 26.22% | 51 | 6.69% | 85 | 10.06% | 55 |
| PNR | PENTAIR INC | 16.50% | 97 | 0.10% | 133 | 5.03% | 105 |
| PBCT | PEOPLES UNITED FINANCIAL INC | -2.89% | 173 | -9.43% | 175 | -3.87% | 168 |
| PEP | PEPSICO INC | 4.23% | 154 | 1.25% | 120 | 2.57% | 130 |
| PNY | PIEDMONT NAT GAS INC | 17.78% | 91 | 6.46% | 86 | 7.56% | 74 |
| PBI | PITNEY BOWES INC | 12.71% | 113 | -10.29% | 179 | -9.61% | 188 |
| PAA | PLAINS ALL AMERN PIPELINE L | 7.27% | 144 | 16.35% | 24 | 13.14% | 36 |
| PII | POLARIS INDS INC | 110.12% | 2 | 39.23% | 2 | 27.67% | 2 |
| PPG | PPG INDS INC | 19.55% | 80 | 10.79% | 56 | 7.45% | 75 |
| PPL | PPL CORP | 12.12% | 117 | -8.63% | 170 | 0.20% | 150 |
| PX | PRAXAIR INC | 16.79% | 96 | 5.38% | 96 | 13.63% | 32 |
| TROW | PRICE T ROWE GROUP INC | 24.60% | 60 | -1.22% | 142 | 5.98% | 90 |
| PG | PROCTER & GAMBLE CO | 10.11% | 131 | 0.03% | 134 | 3.32% | 124 |
| PRSP | PROSPERITY BANCSHARES INC | 35.27% | 34 | 7.71% | 77 | 3.04% | 127 |
| STR | QUESTAR CORP | 19.10% | 83 | 5.35% | 97 | 7.41% | 76 |
| RAVN | RAVEN INDS INC | 69.15% | 5 | 10.96% | 55 | 17.84% | 12 |
| O | REALTY INCOME CORP | 11.42% | 124 | 17.57% | 14 | 13.87% | 30 |
| RLI | RLI CORP | 39.94% | 23 | 10.98% | 54 | 10.04% | 56 |

| Ticker | Name | Tot Ret. 1 Year | Rank 1 Year | Tot Ret. 3 Year | Rank 3 Year | Tot Ret. 5 Year | Rank 5 Year |
|---|---|---|---|---|---|---|---|
| ROP | ROPER INDS INC NEW | 33.21% | 38 | 9.93% | 63 | 11.31% | 45 |
| ROST | ROSS STORES INC | 55.98% | 7 | 25.51% | 5 | 26.99% | 3 |
| RPM | RPM INTL INC | 28.02% | 45 | 3.41% | 104 | 6.34% | 85 |
| SCG | SCANA CORP NEW | 8.09% | 142 | 6.31% | 88 | 4.45% | 110 |
| SEIC | SEI INVESTMENTS CO | -2.39% | 172 | -9.32% | 174 | -6.97% | 181 |
| SHEN | TELECOMMUNICATIONS | -17.36% | 182 | -5.87% | 162 | 0.23% | 149 |
| SHW | SHERWIN WILLIAMS CO | 9.63% | 135 | 11.41% | 52 | 10.32% | 54 |
| SIAL | SIGMA ALDRICH CORP | 22.41% | 68 | 5.55% | 94 | 13.39% | 33 |
| SJW | SJW CORP | 3.87% | 156 | -3.04% | 152 | -2.73% | 165 |
| AOS | SMITH A O | 16.38% | 99 | 14.79% | 30 | 10.03% | 57 |
| SJM | SMUCKER J M CO | 26.49% | 50 | 16.57% | 22 | 13.10% | 38 |
| SON | SONOCO PRODS CO | 3.95% | 155 | 0.99% | 123 | 2.43% | 132 |
| SJI | SOUTH JERSEY INDS INC | 12.70% | 114 | 16.66% | 20 | 15.69% | 20 |
| SBSI | SOUTHSIDE BANCSHARES INC | 20.35% | 78 | 5.79% | 92 | 3.58% | 119 |
| SFG | STANCORP FINL GROUP INC | -12.50% | 180 | -12.65% | 186 | -6.33% | 179 |
| SWK | STANLEY BLACK & DECKER | 18.96% | 85 | 12.39% | 44 | 8.60% | 67 |
| SCL | STEPAN CO | 38.46% | 28 | 10.75% | 57 | 23.27% | 5 |
| SYK | STRYKER CORP | 14.48% | 107 | -9.09% | 172 | 1.17% | 140 |
| SPH | SUBURBAN PROPANE PART. | 2.49% | 162 | 15.53% | 27 | 14.46% | 27 |
| SYY | SYSCO CORP | 5.22% | 152 | -0.71% | 138 | 0.85% | 142 |
| SKT | TANGER FACT. OUTLET CTRS INC | 25.42% | 55 | 16.23% | 26 | 13.66% | 31 |
| TGT | TARGET CORP | 3.05% | 158 | 0.92% | 125 | 2.80% | 128 |
| TCLP | TC PIPELINES LP | 6.72% | 149 | 17.21% | 17 | 13.96% | 29 |
| TDS | TELEPHONE & DATA SYS INC | -10.00% | 179 | -11.38% | 183 | -8.55% | 185 |
| TNC | TENNANT CO | 43.21% | 17 | 14.69% | 32 | 12.31% | 42 |
| TJX | TJX COS INC NEW | 39.47% | 26 | 16.32% | 25 | 16.91% | 16 |
| TR | TOOTSIE ROLL INDS INC | 9.56% | 136 | 10.00% | 62 | 4.51% | 109 |
| TRH | TRANSATLANTIC HLDGS INC | 8.52% | 140 | -3.74% | 156 | -2.38% | 163 |
| UGI | UGI CORP NEW | 11.42% | 123 | 6.08% | 90 | 6.96% | 81 |
| UMBF | UMB FINL CORP | 24.10% | 61 | -7.65% | 168 | 3.89% | 115 |
| UNS | UNISOURCE ENERGY CORP | 21.70% | 71 | 10.37% | 59 | 5.95% | 91 |
| UBSI | UNITED BANKS. INC WEST VA | 2.35% | 164 | 0.55% | 128 | -5.46% | 177 |
| UTX | UNITED TECHNOLOGIES CORP | 16.50% | 98 | 6.94% | 82 | 5.76% | 92 |
| UVV | UNIVERSAL CORP VA | 19.62% | 79 | -3.36% | 154 | 5.37% | 101 |
| UFPI | UNIVERSAL FST PRODS INC | 19.44% | 82 | -1.44% | 143 | -8.28% | 183 |
| UHT | UNIVERSAL HEALTH RLTY INCM TR | 25.67% | 53 | 8.10% | 73 | 7.79% | 73 |

| Ticker | Name | Tot Ret. 1 Year | Rank 1 Year | Tot Ret. 3 Year | Rank 3 Year | Tot Ret. 5 Year | Rank 5 Year |
|---|---|---|---|---|---|---|---|
| UBA | URSTADT BIDDLE PPTYS INS | -3.51% | 174 | 5.62% | 93 | 5.38% | 100 |
| VFC | V F CORP | 70.69% | 4 | 17.79% | 13 | 14.45% | 28 |
| VAL | VALSPAR CORP | 9.35% | 137 | 13.57% | 37 | 6.36% | 84 |
| VGR | VECTOR GROUP LTD | 12.49% | 115 | 16.40% | 23 | 16.98% | 15 |
| VVC | VECTREN CORP | 17.46% | 93 | 5.21% | 100 | 5.12% | 102 |
| WPC | W P CAREY & CO LLC | 53.80% | 9 | 18.96% | 11 | 16.37% | 17 |
| WMT | WAL MART STORES INC | 8.94% | 139 | -1.16% | 140 | 5.73% | 94 |
| WAG | WALGREEN CO | 33.54% | 37 | 0.66% | 127 | -5.22% | 174 |
| WRE | WASHINGTON REAL ESTATE INVT | 6.88% | 148 | 1.93% | 115 | 0.30% | 145 |
| WST | WEST PHARMACE. SVSC INC | 21.31% | 73 | -4.77% | 158 | 1.60% | 136 |
| WABC | WESTAMERICA BANCORPORATION | -13.82% | 181 | -3.43% | 155 | 0.38% | 144 |
| WGL | WGL HLDGS INC | 22.05% | 69 | 13.55% | 38 | 10.54% | 51 |
| JW A | WILEY JOHN & SONS INC | 39.06% | 27 | 2.65% | 110 | 8.60% | 68 |

# Web Site And Dividend Reinvestment Plan Information

| Company | Ticker | Web Site | DRIP |
|---|---|---|---|
| 3M Co. | MMM | www.3m.com | Yes |
| Abbott Laboratories | ABT | www.abbott.com | Yes |
| ABM Industries, Inc. | ABM | www.abm.com | No |
| AFLAC Inc. | AFL | www.aflac.com | Yes |
| Air Products & Chemicals, Inc. | APD | www.airproducts.com | Yes |
| Albemarle Corp. | ALB | www.albemarle.com | Yes |
| Altria Group Inc. | MO | www.altriagroup.com | Yes |
| American States Water Co. | AWR | www.aswater.com | Yes |
| AptarGroup Inc. | ATR | www.aptargroup.com | No |
| Aqua America Inc. | WTR | www.aquaamerica.com | Yes |
| Archer Daniels Midland Co. | ADM | www.admworld.com | Yes |
| AT&T Inc. | T | www.att.com | Yes |
| Atlantic Tele Network Inc. | ATNI | www.atni.com | No |
| Atmos Energy Corp. | ATO | www.atmosenergy.com | Yes |
| Automatic Data Processing Inc. | ADP | www.adp.com | No |
| Avon Products, Inc. | AVP | www.avon.com | Yes |
| Badger Meter, Inc. | BMI | www.badgermeter.com | Yes |
| BancFirst Corp. | BANF | www.bancfirst.com | No |
| Bank of the Ozarks, Inc | OZRK | www.bankozarks.com | Yes |
| Bard (C.R.), Inc. | BCR | www.crbard.com | Yes |
| Becton, Dickinson and Co. | BDX | www.bd.com | Yes |
| Bemis Co Inc. | BMS | www.bemis.com | Yes |
| Black Hills Corporation | BKH | www.blackhillscorp.com | Yes |
| Brady Corp. | BRC | www.bradycorp.com | Yes |
| Brown & Brown, Inc. | BRO | www.bbinsurance.com | No |
| Brown-Forman Corp. | BF B | www.brown-forman.com | No |
| Buckeye Partners, L.P. | BPL | www.buckeye.com | No |
| California Water Service Group | CWT | www.calwatergroup.com | Yes |
| CARBO Ceramics Inc. | CRR | www.carboceramics.com | Yes |
| Cardinal Health, Inc. | CAH | www.cardinalhealth.com | No |
| Carlisle Companies Inc. | CSL | www.carlisle.com | Yes |
| Casey's General Stores Inc. | CASY | www.caseys.com | Yes |
| Caterpillar Inc. | CAT | www.cat.com | Yes |
| CenturyLink Inc. | CTL | www.centurylink.com | Yes |
| Chevron Corporation | CVX | www.chevron.com | Yes |
| Chubb Corp. | CB | www.chubb.com | Yes |

| Company | Ticker | Web Site | DRIP |
|---|---|---|---|
| Church & Dwight Co., Inc. | CHD | www.churchdwight.com | Yes |
| Cincinnati Financial Corp. | CINF | www.cinfin.com | Yes |
| Cintas Corporation | CTAS | www.cintas.com | No |
| Clarcor Inc. | CLC | www.clarcor.com | Yes |
| Clorox Co. | CLX | www.thecloroxcompany.com | Yes |
| Coca-Cola Co. | KO | www.coca-cola.com | Yes |
| Colgate-Palmolive Co. | CL | www.colgate.com | Yes |
| Commerce Bancshares, Inc. | CBSH | www.commercebank.com | Yes |
| Community Bank System, Inc. | CBU | www.communitybankna.com | Yes |
| Community Trust Bancorp, Inc. | CTBI | www.ctbi.com | No |
| Consolidated Edison Inc. | ED | www.conedison.com | Yes |
| ConocoPhillips | COP | www.conocophillips.com | Yes |
| Corporate Office Prop. Trust | OFC | www.copt.com | Yes |
| Cullen/Frost Bankers, Inc. | CFR | www.frostbank.com | No |
| Diebold, Inc. | DBD | www.diebold.com | Yes |
| Donaldson Co. Inc. | DCI | www.donaldson.com | Yes |
| Dover Corp. | DOV | www.dovercorporation.com | Yes |
| Eaton Vance Corp. | EV | www.eatonvance.com | No |
| Ecolab, Inc. | ECL | www.ecolab.com | Yes |
| Emerson Electric Co. | EMR | www.gotoemerson.com | Yes |
| Energen Corp. | EGN | www.energen.com | Yes |
| Enterprise Products Partners | EPD | www.epplp.com | Yes |
| EOG Research Inc. | EOG | www.eogresources.com | No |
| Erie Indemnity Co. | ERIE | www.erieinsurance.com | No |
| Essex Property Trust, Inc. | ESS | www.essexpropertytrust.com | Yes |
| Expeditors Int'l of Washington, Inc. | EXPD | www.expeditors.com | No |
| Exxon Mobil Corp. | XOM | www.exxonmobil.com | Yes |
| Factset Research Systems Inc. | FDS | www.factset.com | No |
| Family Dollar Stores, Inc. | FDO | www.familydollar.com | No |
| Fastenal Co. | FAST | www.fastenal.com | No |
| Federal Realty Investment Trust | FRT | www.federalrealty.com | Yes |
| First Financial Corp. | THFF | www.first-online.com | No |
| Franklin Electric Co., Inc. | FELE | www.franklin-electric.com | No |
| Franklin Resources, Inc. | BEN | www.franklintempleton.com | Yes |
| Fuller (H.B.) Company | FUL | www.hbfuller.com | Yes |

| Company | Ticker | Web Site | DRIP |
|---|---|---|---|
| General Dynamics Corp. | GD | www.generaldynamics.com | No |
| Genuine Parts Co. | GPC | www.genpt.com | Yes |
| Getty Realty Corp. (New) | GTY | www.gettyrealty.com | Yes |
| Gorman-Rupp Co. | GRC | www.gormanrupp.com | Yes |
| Graco Inc. | GGG | www.graco.com | No |
| Grainger (W.W.) Inc. | GWW | www.grainger.com | No |
| Harleysville Group, Inc. | HGIC | www.harleysvillegroup.com | Yes |
| Harsco Corp. | HSC | www.harsco.com | Yes |
| HCC Insurance Holdings, Inc. | HCC | www.hcc.com | No |
| HCP Inc. | HCP | www.hcpi.com | Yes |
| Helmerich & Payne Inc. | HP | www.hpinc.com | No |
| Henry (Jack) & Associates | JKHY | www.jackhenry.com | Yes |
| Hormel Foods Corp. | HRL | www.hormel.com | Yes |
| Hudson City Bancorp. | HCBK | www.hcsbonline.com | Yes |
| Illinois Tool Works, Inc. | ITW | www.itw.com | Yes |
| International Business Machines Corp. | IBM | www.ibm.com | Yes |
| Investors Real Estate Trust | IRET | www.iret.com | Yes |
| Johnson & Johnson | JNJ | www.jnj.com | Yes |
| Kimberly-Clark Corp. | KMB | www.kimberly-clark.com | Yes |
| Kinder Morgan Energy Partners | KMP | www.kindermorgan.com | No |
| Lancaster Colony Corp. | LANC | www.lancastercolony.com | Yes |
| Leggett & Platt, Inc. | LEG | www.leggett.com | No |
| Linear Technology Corp. | LLTC | www.linear.com | No |
| Lowe's Companies Inc. | LOW | www.lowes.com | Yes |
| Matthews International Corp | MATW | www.matw.com | No |
| McCormick & Co., Inc. | MKC | www.mccormick.com | No |
| McDonald's Corp. | MCD | www.mcdonalds.com | Yes |
| McGrath RentCorp | MGRC | www.mgrc.com | No |
| McGraw-Hill Cos., Inc. | MHP | www.mcgraw-hill.com | Yes |
| MDU Resources Group Inc. | MDU | www.mdu.com | Yes |
| Medtronic, Inc. | MDT | www.medtronic.com | Yes |

| Company | Ticker | Web Site | DRIP |
|---|---|---|---|
| Mercury General Corp. | MCY | www.mercuryinsurance.com | No |
| Meredith Corp. | MDP | www.meredith.com | No |
| Meridian Bioscience Inc | VIVO | www.meridianbioscience.com | Yes |
| MGE Energy Inc. | MGEE | www.mgeenergy.com | Yes |
| Middlesex Water Co. | MSEX | www.middlesexwater.com | Yes |
| Mine Safety Appliances Co. | MSA | www.msanet.com | No |
| Murphy Oil Corp. | MUR | www.murphyoilcorp.com | No |
| NACCO Industries Inc. | NC | www.nacco.com | No |
| National Fuel Gas Co. | NFG | www.nationalfuelgas.com | Yes |
| National Retail Properties Inc. | NNN | www.nnnreit.com | Yes |
| New Jersey Resources Corp. | NJR | www.njliving.com | Yes |
| Nextera Energy Inc. | NEE | www.nexteraenergy.com | Yes |
| Nordson Corp. | NDSN | www.nordson.com | Yes |
| Northeast Utility | NU | www.nu.com | Yes |
| Northwest Natural Gas | NWN | www.nwnatural.com | Yes |
| Nstar | NST | www.nstar.com | Yes |
| Nucor Corp. | NUE | www.nucor.com | Yes |
| Old Republic International Corp. | ORI | www.oldrepublic.com | Yes |
| Owens & Minor, Inc. | OMI | www.owens-minor.com | Yes |
| Parker Hannifin Corp. | PH | www.parker.com | Yes |
| Pentair, Inc. | PNR | www.pentair.com | Yes |
| Peoples United Financial Inc. | PBCT | www.peoples.com | Yes |
| PepsiCo Inc. | PEP | www.pepsico.com | Yes |
| Piedmont Natural Gas Co., Inc. | PNY | www.piedmontng.com | Yes |
| Pitney Bowes Inc. | PBI | www.pb.com | Yes |
| Plains All American Pipeline LTD | PAA | www.paalp.com | No |
| Polaris Industries Inc. | PII | www.polarisindustries.com | Yes |
| PPG Industries, Inc. | PPG | www.ppg.com | Yes |
| PPL Corp | PPL | www.pplweb.com | Yes |
| Praxair, Inc. | PX | www.praxair.com | Yes |
| Procter & Gamble Co. | PG | www.pg.com | Yes |
| Prosperity Bancshares Inc. | PRSP | www.prosperitybanktx.com | No |
| Questar Corp. | STR | www.questar.com | Yes |
| Raven Industries, Inc. | RAVN | www.ravenind.com | Yes |
| Realty Income Corp. | O | www.realtyincome.com | No |
| RLI Corp. | RLI | www.rlicorp.com | Yes |
| Robinson (C.H.) Worldwide, Inc. | CHRW | www.chrobinson.com | Yes |

| Company | Ticker | Web Site | DRIP |
|---|---|---|---|
| Roper Industries, Inc. | ROP | www.roperind.com | No |
| Ross Stores, Inc. | ROST | www.rossstores.com | No |
| RPM International Inc. | RPM | www.rpminc.com | Yes |
| Scana Energy Corp. | SCG | www.scana.com | Yes |
| SEI Investments Co. | SEIC | www.seic.com | No |
| Shenandoah Telecomm. Co. | SHEN | www.shentel.com | Yes |
| Sherwin-Williams Co. | SHW | www.sherwin.com | Yes |
| Sigma-Aldrich Corp. | SIAL | www.sigma-aldrich.com | No |
| SJW Corp. | SJW | www.sjwater.com | No |
| Smith (A.O.) Corp | AOS | www.aosmith.com | Yes |
| Smucker (J.M.) Co. | SJM | www.smuckers.com | Yes |
| Sonoco Products Co. | SON | www.sonoco.com | Yes |
| South Jersey Industries Inc. | SJI | www.sjindustries.com | Yes |
| Southside Bancshares, Inc. | SBSI | www.southside.com | Yes |
| Stancorp Financial Group Inc. | SFG | www.stancorpfinancial.com | No |
| Stanley Black & Decker Inc | SWK | www.stanleyblackanddecker.com | Yes |
| Stepan Co. | SCL | www.stepan.com | No |
| Stryker Corp. | SYK | www.stryker.com | No |
| Suburban Propane Partners L.P. | SPH | www.suburbanpropane.com | No |
| Sysco Corp. | SYY | www.sysco.com | Yes |
| T Rowe Price Group Inc. | TROW | www.troweprice.com | No |
| Tanger Factory Outlet Centers, Inc. | SKT | www.tangeroutlet.com | Yes |
| Target Corp. | TGT | www.target.com | Yes |
| TCPipelines LP | TCLP | www.tcpipelineslp.com | No |
| Telephone & Data Systems Inc. | TDS | www.teldta.com | Yes |
| Tennant Co. | TNC | www.tennantco.com | Yes |
| TJX Companies, Inc. | TJX | www.tjx.com | No |
| Tootsie Roll Industries Inc. | TR | www.tootsie.com | No |
| Transatlantic Holdings, Inc. | TRH | www.transre.com | No |
| UGI Corp. | UGI | www.ugicorp.com | Yes |
| UMB Financial Corp. | UMBF | www.umb.com | Yes |
| Unisource Energy Corp. | UNS | www.uns.com | Yes |
| United Bankshares, Inc. | UBSI | www.ubsi-wv.com | Yes |
| United Technologies Corp. | UTX | www.utc.com | Yes |
| Universal Corp. | UVV | www.universalcorp.com | Yes |

| Company | Ticker | Web Site | DRIP |
|---|---|---|---|
| Universal Forest Products Inc. | UFPI | www.ufpi.com | No |
| Universal Health Realty Income Trust | UHT | www.uhrit.com | Yes |
| Urstadt Biddle Properties Inc | UBA | www.ubproperties.com | Yes |
| Valspar Corp. | VAL | www.valspar.com | Yes |
| Vector Group Ltd | VGR | www.vectorgroupltd.com | Yes |
| Vectren Corp. | VVC | www.vectren.com | Yes |
| VF Corp. | VFC | www.vfc.com | Yes |
| W.P. Carey & Co. LLC | WPC | www.wpcarey.com | Yes |
| Walgreen Co. | WAG | www.walgreens.com | Yes |
| Wal-Mart Stores, Inc. | WMT | www.wal-mart.com | Yes |
| Washington Real Estate Invest Trust | WRE | www.writ.com | Yes |
| West Pharmaceutical Services, Inc. | WST | www.westpharma.com | Yes |
| WestAmerica Bancorporation | WABC | www.westamerica.com | Yes |
| WGL Holdings, Inc. | WGL | www.wglholdings.com | Yes |
| Wiley (John) & Sons Inc. | JW A | www.wiley.com | No |

# SIC Classification of Companies By Industry Sector

## Finance, Insurance & Real Estate

AFLAC Inc.
BancFirst Corp. (Oklahoma City, Okla)
Bank of the Ozarks, Inc.
Brown & Brown, Inc.
Chubb Corp.
Cincinnati Financial Corp.
Commerce Bancshares, Inc.
Community Bank System, Inc.
Community Trust Bancorp, Inc.
Corporate Office Properties Trust
Cullen/Frost Bankers, Inc.
Eaton Vance Corp
Erie Indemnity Co.
Essex Property Trust, Inc.
Federal Realty Investment Trust (MD)
First Financial Corp. (IN)
Franklin Resources, Inc.
Getty Realty Corp.
Harleysville Group, Inc. (PA)
HCC Insurance Holdings, Inc.
HCP, Inc.
Hudson City Bancorp, Inc.
Investors Real Estate Trust
Mercury General Corp.
National Retail Properties Inc
Old Republic International Corp.
People's United Financial, Inc.
Prosperity Bancshares Inc.
Realty Income Corp.
RLI Corp.
SEI Investments Co.
Southside Bancshares, Inc.
Stancorp Financial Group Inc
T Rowe Price Group Inc.
Tanger Factory Outlet Centers, Inc.
Transatlantic Holdings, Inc.
UMB Financial Corp
United Bankshares, Inc.
Universal Health Realty Income Trust
Urstadt Biddle Properties Inc
W.P. Carey & Co. LLC
Washington Real Estate Investment Trust
WestAmerica Bancorporation

## Manufacturing

3M Co
Abbott Laboratories
Air Products & Chemicals, Inc.
Albemarle Corp.
Altria Group Inc
AptarGroup Inc.
Archer Daniels Midland Co.
Avon Products, Inc.
Badger Meter, Inc.
Bard (C.R.), Inc.
Becton, Dickinson and Co.
Bemis Co Inc
Brady Corp.
Brown-Forman Corp.
Carbo Ceramics Inc.
Carlisle Companies Inc.
Caterpillar Inc.
Chevron Corporation
Church & Dwight Co., Inc.
Cintas Corporation
Clarcor Inc.
Clorox Co.
Coca-Cola Co (The)
Colgate-Palmolive Co.
ConocoPhillips
Diebold, Inc.
Donaldson Co. Inc.
Dover Corp
Lancaster Colony Corp.
Leggett & Platt, Inc.
Linear Technology Corp.
Matthews International Corp
McCormick & Co., Inc.
McGraw-Hill Cos., Inc. (The)
Medtronic, Inc.
Meredith Corp.
Meridian Bioscience Inc.
Mine Safety Appliances Co
NACCO Industries Inc.
Nordson Corp.
Nucor Corp.
Parker Hannifin Corp.
Pentair, Inc.
PepsiCo Inc.
Pitney Bowes Inc
Polaris Industries Inc.
PPG Industries, Inc.
Praxair, Inc.
Procter & Gamble Co.
Raven Industries, Inc.
Roper Industries, Inc
RPM International Inc (DE)
Smith (A.O.) Corp
Smucker (J.M.) Co.

## Manufacturing (Continued)

Ecolab, Inc.
Emerson Electric Co.
Exxon Mobil Corp.
Franklin Electric Co., Inc.
Fuller (H.B.) Company
General Dynamics Corp.
Gorman-Rupp Co.
Graco Inc.
Harsco Corp.
Hormel Foods Corp.
Illinois Tool Works, Inc.
International Business Machines Corp.
Johnson & Johnson
Kimberly-Clark Corp.
Sonoco Products Co.
Stanley Black & Decker, Inc.
Stepan Co.
Stryker Corp.
Tennant Co.
Tootsie Roll Industries Inc
United Technologies Corp.
Universal Forest Products Inc.
Valspar Corp.
Vector Group Ltd
VF Corp.
West Pharmaceutical Services, Inc.
Wiley (John) & Sons Inc.

## Mining

EOG Resources, Inc.
Helmerich & Payne, Inc.
MDU Resources Group Inc.
Murphy Oil Corp
Questar Corp.

## Retail Trade

Casey's General Stores, Inc.
Family Dollar Stores, Inc.
Fastenal Co.
Lowe's Companies Inc
McDonald's Corp
Ross Stores, Inc.
Sherwin-Williams Co.
Suburban Propane Partners L.P.
Target Corp
TJX Companies, Inc.
Walgreen Co.
Wal-Mart Stores, Inc.

## Services

ABM Industries, Inc.
Automatic Data Processing Inc.
FactSet Research Systems Inc.
Jack Henry & Associates, Inc.
McGrath RentCorp

## Transportation, Communications, & Utilities

American States Water Co.
Aqua America Inc
AT&T Inc
Atlantic Tele-Network, Inc.
Atmos Energy Corp.
Black Hills Corporation
Buckeye Partners, L.P.
California Water Service Group (DE)
CenturyLink Inc.
Consolidated Edison, Inc.
Energen Corp.
Enterprise Products Partners L.P.
Expeditors International of Washington, Inc.
Kinder Morgan Energy Partners, L.P.
MGE Energy Inc
Middlesex Water Co.
National Fuel Gas Co. (NJ)
New Jersey Resources Corp
Nextera Energy Inc.
Northeast Utilities
Northwest Natural Gas Co.
NSTAR
Piedmont Natural Gas Co., Inc.
Plains All American Pipeline, L.P.
PPL Corp
Robinson (C.H.) Worldwide, Inc.
Scana Corp.
Shenandoah Telecommunications Co.
SJW Corp.
South Jersey Industries, Inc.
TC PipeLines, LP
Telephone and Data Systems, Inc.
UGI Corp.
Unisource Energy Corp.
Vectren Corp
WGL Holdings, Inc.

## Wholesale

Cardinal Health, Inc.
Genuine Parts Co.
Grainger (W.W.) Inc.
Owens & Minor, Inc.
Sigma-Aldrich Corp.
Sysco Corp.
Universal Corp.

# Frequently Asked Questions

Topics Questions:

- How does a dividend-paying company become a Dividend Achiever?
- What percentage of dividend-paying companies classified as Dividend Achievers?
- How many economic sectors and industries are represented by Dividend Achievers?
- What distinguishes Dividend Achievers from other U.S. listed companies?
- How often is the Dividend Achievers Index reconstituted?
- How are corporate actions handled?

**Q: How does a dividend-paying company become a Dividend Achiever?**

*A: A publicly-traded company that has increased its dividends for the last ten or more consecutive years will be classified as a Dividend Achiever. Depending on the industry, companies must also meet certain capitalization requirements in order to be considered a Dividend Achiever.*

**Q: What percentage of dividend-paying companies** are **classified as Dividend Achievers?**

*A: Just over 6.19% of 3,700-plus North American-listed, dividend-paying common stocks are classified as Dividend Achievers.*

**Q: How many industry sectors and industries are represented by Dividend Achievers?**

*A: Dividend Achievers represent 7 industry sectors and more than 33 industries.*

**Q: What distinguishes Dividend Achievers from other U.S. listed companies?**

*A: Dividend Achievers have demonstrated the ability to consistently increase dividend payments over a substantial period of time, through volatile markets and challenging political climates.*

**Q: Does Mergent Inc. offer a Dividend Achiever Index?**

*A: Mergent currently offers an Index that tracks the daily performance of Dividend Achiever constituents. The inception date of the index was January 17, 2003. The real time price appreciation values are published by the American Stock Exchange under the Symbol* ***"DAA".***

**Q: How often is the index reconstituted?**

*A: The Dividend Index is reconstituted annually.*

**Q: How are corporate actions handled?**

*A: If an Index constituent is acquired and is no longer actively traded, the company will cease classification as a Dividend Achiever. If an Index constituent spins off a portion of its business or merges with another company, it will be handled on a case by case basis.*

# HOW TO USE THIS BOOK

***MERGENT'S Dividend Achievers*** is a compact, easy-to-use reference that provides basic financial and business information on companies that have increased their cash dividend payments for at least ten consecutive years, adjusting for splits. The presentation of background information plus current and historical data provides the answers to four basic questions for each company:

1. What does the company do? (See G.)
2. How has it done in the past? (See B, J.)
3. How is it doing now? (See C, D, H.)
4. How will it fare in the future? (See I.)

**A. CAPSULE STOCK INFORMATION** shows where the stock is traded and its symbol, a recent price and price/earnings ratio, plus the yield afforded by the indicated dividend based on a recent price. The indicated dividend is the current annualized dividend based on the most recent regular cash payment. Also shown is the 52-week range of the Company's stock price.

**B. LONG-TERM PRICE CHART** illustrates the pattern of monthly stock price movements, fully adjusted for stock dividends and splits. The chart points out the degree of volatility in the price movement of the company's stock and what its long-term trend has been. It also shows how it has performed long-term relative to an initial investment in the S&P 500 Index equal to the price of the company's stock at the beginning of the period shown in the price chart. It indicates areas of price support and resistance, plus other technical points to be considered by the investor. The bars at the base of the long-term price chart indicate the monthly trading volume. Monthly trading volume offers the individual an opportunity to recognize at what periods stock accumulation occurs and what percent of a company's outstanding shares are traded.

**PRICE SCORES** – Above each company's price/volume chart are its ***Mergent's Price Scores***. These are basic measures of the stock's performance. Each stock is measured against the New York Stock Exchange Composite Index. A score of 100 indicates that the stock did as well as the New York Stock Exchange Composite Index during the time period. A score of less than 100 means that the stock did not do as well; a score of more than 100 means that the stock outperformed the NYSE Composite Index. All stock prices are adjusted for splits and stock dividends. The time periods measured for each company conclude with the date of the recent price shown in the top line of each company's profile.

The ***7 YEAR PRICE SCORE*** mirrors the common stock's price growth over the previous seven years. The higher the price score, the better the relative performance. It is based on the ratio of the latest 12-month average price to the current seven-year average. This ratio is then indexed against the same ratio for the market as a whole (the New York Stock Exchange Composite Index), which is taken as 100.

The ***12 MONTH PRICE SCORE*** is a similar measurement but for a shorter period of time. It is based on the ratio of the latest two-month average price to the current 12-month average. As was done for the Long-Term Price Score, this ratio is also indexed to the same ratio for the market as a whole.

**C. INTERIM EARNINGS (Per Share)** – Figures are reported after the effect of extraordinary items, discontinued operations and cumulative effects of accounting changes. Each figure is for the quarterly period indicated. These figures are essentially as reported by the company, although all figures are adjusted for all stock dividends and splits.

**D. INTERIM DIVIDENDS (Per Share)** – The cash dividends are the actual dollar amounts declared by the company. No adjustments have been made for stock dividends and splits. **Ex-Dividend Date**: a stockholder must purchase the stock prior to this date in order to be entitled to the dividend. The **Record Date** indicates the date on which the shareholder had to have been a holder of record in order to qualify for the dividend. The **Payable Date** indicates the date the company paid or intends to pay the dividend. The cash amount shown in the first column is followed by a letter (example "Q" for quarterly) to indicate the frequency of the dividend. A notation of "Dividend

# ILLUSTRATIVE, INC.

| Exchange | A | Symbol | Price | 52Wk Range | Yield | P/E |
|---|---|---|---|---|---|---|
| NYS | | OOO | $28.48 (8/31/2011) | 31.86-27.03 | 6.04 | 8.30 |

***7 Year Price Score 98.02** *NYSE Composite Index=100 ***12 Month Price Score 101.69**

**Interim Earnings (Per Share)** C

| Qtr. | Mar | Jun | Sep | Dec |
|---|---|---|---|---|
| 2008 | 0.57 | 0.63 | 0.55 | 0.41 |
| 2009 | 0.53 | 0.54 | 0.54 | 0.51 |
| 2010 | 0.42 | 0.68 | 2.08 | 0.18 |
| 2011 | 0.57 | 0.60 | ... | ... |

**Interim Dividends (Per Share)** D

| Amt | Decl | Ex | Rec | Pay |
|---|---|---|---|---|
| 0.42Q | 09/24/2010 | 10/06/2010 | 10/08/2010 | 11/01/2010 |
| 0.43Q | 12/17/2010 | 01/06/2011 | 01/10/2011 | 02/01/2011 |
| 0.43Q | 03/25/2011 | 04/06/2011 | 04/08/2011 | 05/02/2011 |
| 0.43Q | 06/24/2011 | 07/06/2011 | 07/08/2011 | 08/01/2011 |

**Indicated Div: $1.72 (Div. Reinv. Plan)**

**Valuation Analysis** E

| | | | |
|---|---|---|---|
| Forecast EPS | $2.38 (09/05/2011) | | |
| Market Cap | $168.7 Billion | Book Value | $113.8 Billion |
| Price/Book | 1.48 | Price/Sales | 1.34 |

**Dividend Achiever Status** F

| | |
|---|---|
| **10 Year Growth Rate** | 5.09% |
| **Total Years of Dividend Growth** | 26 |

**Business Summary:** Services (MIC: 6.1.2 SIC: 4813 NAIC: 511140) G

ILLUS is a holding company. Through its subsidiaries and affiliates, Co. is a provider of telecommunications services. Co. has four segments: Wireless, which uses its nationwide network to provide wireless voice and data communications services; Wireline, which uses its regional, national and global network to provide landline voice and data communications services, ILLUS U-vEEsesm TV, broadband and voic services, and managed networking to business customers; Advertising Solutions, which publishes Yellow and White Pages directories and sells directory advertising, Internet-based advertising and local search; and Other, which includes customer information services such as operator services.

**Recent Developments:** For the quarter ended June 30 2011, income from continuing operations decreased 10.5% to US$3.66 billion from US$4.09 billion in the year-earlier quarter. Net income decreased 10.4% to US$3.66 billion from US$4.08 billion in the year-earlier quarter. Revenues were US$31.50 billion, up 2.2% from US$30.81 billion the year before. Operating income was US$6.17 billion versus US$6.08 billion in the prior-year quarter, an increase of 1.3%. Direct operating expenses rose 7.1% to US$13.33 billion from US$12.45 billion in the comparable period the year before. Indirect operating expenses decreased 2.2% to US$12.00 billion from US$12.27 billion in the equivalent prior-year period. H

**Prospects:** Our evaluation of ILLUS Inc. as of Sep. 6, 2011 is the result of our systematic analysis on three basic characteristics: earnings strength, relative valuation, and recent stock price movement. The company has managed to produce a neutral trend in earnings per share over the past 5 quarters. However, while recent estimates for the company have been mixed, I has posted better than expected results. Based on operating earnings yield, the company is undervalued when compared to all of the companies in our coverage universe. Share price changes over the past year indicates that ILLUS will perform poorly over the near term. I

**Financial Data**

| (US$ in Thousands) J | 6 Mos | 3 Mos | 12/31/2010 | 12/31/2009 | 12/31/2008 | 12/31/2007 | 12/31/2006 | 12/31/2005 |
|---|---|---|---|---|---|---|---|---|
| Earnings Per Share | 3.43 | 3.51 | 3.35 | 2.12 | 2.16 | 1.94 | 1.89 | 1.42 |
| Cash Flow Per Share | 6.06 | 5.99 | 5.92 | 5.84 | 5.66 | 5.56 | 4.02 | 3.85 |
| Tang Book Value Per Share | N.M. | N.M. | N.M. | N.M. | N.M. | N.M. | N.M. | 8.29 |
| Dividends Per Share | 1.700 | 1.690 | 1.680 | 1.640 | 1.600 | 1.420 | 1.330 | 1.290 |
| Dividend Payout % | 49.56 | 48.15 | 50.15 | 77.36 | 74.07 | 73.20 | 70.37 | 90.85 |
| **Income Statement** | | | | | | | | |
| Total Revenue | 62,742,000 | 31,247,000 | 124,280,000 | 123,018,000 | 124,028,000 | 118,928,000 | 63,055,000 | 43,862,000 |
| EBITDA | 21,245,000 | 10,451,000 | 36,872,000 | 37,603,000 | 37,787,000 | 36,644,000 | 19,178,000 | 13,554,000 |
| Depn & Amortn | 9,186,000 | 4,584,000 | 16,402,000 | 15,959,000 | 15,313,000 | 15,625,000 | 8,874,000 | 7,372,000 |
| Income Before Taxes | 10,365,000 | 5,021,000 | 17,476,000 | 18,265,000 | 19,084,000 | 17,512,000 | 8,838,000 | 5,109,000 |
| Income Taxes | 3,695,000 | 1,802,000 | (1,162,000) | 6,156,000 | 7,036,000 | 6,253,000 | 3,525,000 | 932,000 |
| Net Income | 6,999,000 | 3,408,000 | 19,864,000 | 12,535,000 | 12,867,000 | 11,951,000 | 7,356,000 | 4,786,000 |
| Average Shares | 5,952,999 | 5,944,999 | 5,937,999 | 5,923,999 | 5,957,999 | 6,169,999 | 3,902,000 | 3,379,000 |
| **Balance Sheet** | | | | | | | | |
| Current Assets | 22,239,000 | 19,737,000 | 19,951,000 | 24,334,000 | 22,556,000 | 24,686,000 | 25,553,000 | 14,654,000 |
| Total Assets | 272,014,000 | 268,085,000 | 268,488,000 | 268,752,000 | 265,245,000 | 275,644,000 | 270,634,000 | 145,632,000 |
| Current Liabilities | 33,537,000 | 33,254,000 | 33,951,000 | 36,705,000 | 42,290,000 | 39,274,000 | 40,482,000 | 25,418,000 |
| Long-Term Obligations | 58,663,000 | 58,126,000 | 58,971,000 | 64,720,000 | 60,872,000 | 57,255,000 | 50,063,000 | 26,115,000 |
| Total Liabilities | 158,211,000 | 155,541,000 | 156,841,000 | 166,852,000 | 168,898,000 | 160,277,000 | 155,094,000 | 90,942,000 |
| Stockholders' Equity | 113,803,000 | 112,544,000 | 111,647,000 | 101,900,000 | 96,347,000 | 115,367,000 | 115,540,000 | 54,690,000 |
| Shares Outstanding | 5,925,039 | 5,918,265 | 5,911,086 | 5,901,930 | 5,893,008 | 6,043,544 | 6,238,745 | 3,876,884 |
| **Statistical Record** | | | | | | | | |
| Return on Assets % | 7.55 | 7.79 | 7.39 | 4.69 | 4.74 | 4.38 | 3.53 | 3.76 |
| Return on Equity % | 18.78 | 19.39 | 18.60 | 12.65 | 12.12 | 10.35 | 8.64 | 10.06 |
| EBITDA Margin % | 33.86 | 33.45 | 29.67 | 30.57 | 30.47 | 30.81 | 30.41 | 30.90 |
| Net Margin % | 11.16 | 10.91 | 15.98 | 10.19 | 10.37 | 10.05 | 11.67 | 10.91 |
| Asset Turnover | 0.47 | 0.47 | 0.46 | 0.46 | 0.46 | 0.44 | 0.30 | 0.34 |
| Current Ratio | 0.66 | 0.59 | 0.59 | 0.66 | 0.53 | 0.63 | 0.63 | 0.58 |
| Debt to Equity | 0.52 | 0.52 | 0.53 | 0.64 | 0.63 | 0.50 | 0.43 | 0.48 |
| Price Range | 31.86-24.19 | 30.71-24.13 | 29.44-24.13 | 29.42-21.72 | 41.56-22.42 | 42.83-33.81 | 35.75-24.45 | 25.77-22.10 |
| P/E Ratio | 9.29-7.05 | 8.75-6.87 | 8.79-7.20 | 13.88-10.25 | 19.24-10.38 | 22.08-17.43 | 18.92-12.94 | 18.15-15.56 |
| Average Yield % | 5.94 | 6.19 | 6.30 | 6.40 | 4.81 | 3.62 | 4.54 | 5.38 |

| | | |
|---|---|---|
| **Address:** 000 Akard St., Dallas, TX 75202<br>**Telephone:** 200-888-44444<br>**Web Site:** www.ILLUS.com K | **Officers:** Thomas Tommas - Chairman, President, Chief Executive Officer William William - Senior Executive Vice President **Transfer Agents:** Illus Trust Company, N.A., Providence, RI | **Investor Contact:** 200-000-0000<br>**No of Institutions:** 1000<br>**Shares:** 3625,522,240 **% Held:** N/A |

payment suspended" indicates that dividend payments have been suspended within the most recent ten years.

**Indicated Dividend** This is the annualized amount (fully adjusted for splits) of the latest regular cash dividend. Companies with Dividend Reinvestment Plans are indicated here.

**E. VALUATION ANALYSIS** is a tool for evaluating a company's stock. Included are: Forecast Earnings Per Share (EPS), Market Capitalization, Book Value, Price/Book and Price/Sales.

**F. DIVIDEND ACHIEVER STATUS** – Presents the company's 10-year average annual compounded cash dividend growth rate, along with the total consecutive years of increases.

**G. BUSINESS SUMMARY** explains what a company does in terms of the products or services it sells, its markets, and the position the company occupies in its industry. For a quick reference, included are the Company's Standard Industrial Classification (SIC), North American Industry Classification (NAIC) and Mergent's Industry Classification (MIC).

**H. RECENT DEVELOPMENTS** – This section captures what has happened in the most recent quarter for which results are available. It includes recently released sales and earnings figures as well as expense trends.

**I. PROSPECTS** – This section focuses on what is anticipated for the immediate future, as well as the outlook for the next few years, based on analysis by Mergent.

**J. FINANCIAL DATA** (fully adjusted for stock dividends and splits) is provided for at least the past seven fiscal years preceded by the most recent three-, six- and nine-month results if available.

*Fiscal Years* are the annual financial reporting periods as determined by each company. Annual prices and dividends are displayed based on the Company's fiscal year.

**Per Share Data:**

*The Earnings Per Share* figure is based on a trailing 12-month period. Earnings per share, and all per share figures, are adjusted for subsequent stock dividends and splits. Earnings per share are presented on a diluted basis, as described by Financial Accounting Standards Board Statement 128.

*Cash Flow Per Share* represents the annualized cash flow from operating activities (or for quarters, TTM cash flow from operating activities) divided by the average shares outstanding.

*Tangible Book Value Per Share* is calculated as stockholders equity (the value of common shares, paid-in capital and retained earnings) minus preferred stock and intangibles such as goodwill, patents and excess acquisition costs, divided by shares outstanding. It demonstrates the underlying cash value of each common share if the company were to be liquidated as of that date.

*Dividends Per Share* is the total of cash payments made per share to shareholders for the trailing 12-month period.

*Dividend Payout %* is the proportion of earnings available for common stock that is paid to common shareholders in the form of cash dividends. It is significant because it indicates what percentage of earnings is being reinvested in the business for internal growth.

*EDITOR'S NOTE: TTM net income is net income for the last 365 days (normally four reported quarters) ended on the quarterly balance sheet date. Where that last 365 days does not exactly equate to the last four reported quarters the net income for any included partial quarter is adjusted on a pro-rata basis.*

**INCOME STATEMENT, BALANCE SHEET AND STATISTICAL RECORD**

Includes pertinent earnings and balance sheet information essential to analyzing a corporation's performance. The comparisons provide the necessary historical perspective to intelligently review the various operating and financial trends. Generic definitions follow.

**Income Statement:**

*Total Revenues* consists of all revenues from operations.

*EBITDA* represents earnings before, interest, taxes, depreciation and amortization, and special items.

# HOW TO USE THIS BOOK

*Depreciation and Amortization* includes all non-cash charges such as depletion and amortization as well as depreciation.

*Income Before Taxes* is the remaining income *after* deducting all costs, expenses, property charges, interest etc. but *before* deducting income taxes.

*Income Taxes* includes the amount charged against earnings to provide for current and deferred income taxes.

*Net Income* consists of all revenues less all expenses (operating and non-operating), and is presented before preference and common dividends.

*Average Shares Outstanding* is the weighted average number of shares including common equivalent shares outstanding during the year, as reported by the corporation and fully adjusted for all stock dividends and splits. The use of *average shares* minimizes the distortion in *earnings per share* which could result from issuance of a large amount of stock or the company's purchase of a large amount of its own stock during the year.

**Balance Sheet:**

*Current Assets* includes the short-term assets expected to be realized or consumed within one year. Normally includes cash and cash equivalents, short term investments, receivables, prepayments and inventories.

*Total Assets* represents all of the assets of the company, including tangible and intangible, and current and non-current.

*Current Liabilities* are all of the obligations of the company normally expected to be paid within one year. Includes bank overdrafts, short-term debt, payables and accruals.

*Long-Term Obligations* are the total long-term debts (due beyond one year) reported by the company, including bonds, capital lease obligations, notes, mortgages, debentures, etc.

*Total Liabilities* represents all liabilities of the company, whether current or non-current.

*Stockholders' Equity* is the sum of all capital stock accounts – paid in capital (including additional premium), retained earnings, and all other capital balances.

*Shares Outstanding* is the number of shares outstanding as of the date of the company's quarterly/annual report, exclusive of treasury stock and adjusted for subsequent stock dividends and splits.

**Statistical Record:**

*Return on Assets %* represents the ratio of annualized net income (or for Mos., TTM net income) to average total assets. This ratio represents how effectively assets are being used to produce a profit.

*Return on Equity %* is the ratio of annualized net income (or for Mos., TTM net income) to average stockholders' equity, expressed as a percentage. This ratio illustrates how effectively the investment of the stockholders is being utilized to earn a profit.

*EBITDA Margin %* represents earnings before interest, taxes, depreciation and amortization as a percentage of total revenue.

*Net Margin %* is net income expressed as a percentage of total revenues.

*Asset Turnover* is annualized total revenue (or for Mos., TTM total revenue) divided by average total assets. A measure of efficiency of the use of assets.

*Current Ratio* represents current assets divided by current liabilities. The higher the figure the better the company is able to meet its current liabilities out of its current assets. A key measure of liquidity for industrial companies.

*Debt to Equity* is the ratio of long-term obligations to stockholders' equity.

*Price Ranges* are based on each Company's fiscal year. Where actual stock sales did not take place, a range of lowest bid and highest asked prices is shown.

*Price/Earnings Ratio* is shown as a range. The figures are calculated by dividing the stock's highest price for the year and its lowest price by the year's earnings per share. Growth stocks tend to command higher P/Es than cyclical stocks.

*Average Yield %* is the ratio of annual dividends to the real average of the prices over the fiscal year.

EDITOR'S NOTE: In order to preserve the historical relationships between prices, earnings and dividends, figures are not restated to reflect subsequent events. Figures are presented in U.S. dollars unless otherwise indicated.

**K. ADDITIONAL INFORMATION** on each stock includes the officers of the company, address, telephone number, web site and transfer agent(s).

# HOW TO USE THIS BOOK

**L. INSTITUTIONAL HOLDINGS** indicates the number of investment companies, insurance companies, mutual funds, bank trust and college endowment funds holding the stock and the total number of shares held as last reported.

### OTHER DEFINITIONS

**Factors Pertaining Especially to Utilities**

*PPE Turnover* represents annualized total revenue (or for Mos., TTM total revenue) divided by average net property, plant and equipment.

**Factors Pertaining Especially to Banks**

*Interest Income* is all interest income, including income from loans and leases, securities and deposits.

*Interest Expense* is all interest expense, including from loans and leases, securities and deposits.

*Loans to Deposits* are net loans and leases divided by *total deposits*. A key measure of bank liquidity.

*Net Interest Income* is interest income less interest expense. This figure is presented before provision for losses.

*Provision for Losses* represents the amount charged against earnings to increase the provision made for losses on loans and leases.

*Non-Interest Income* is any income that is not interest-related. Such income could include trading revenue and gains on the sale of assets.

*Non-Interest Expense* is all expenses that are not interest-related, including employment costs, office costs, marketing costs, etc.

*Net Loans & Leases* includes all loans and leases net of provisions for losses. May include commercial, agricultural, real estate, consumer and foreign loans.

Total Deposits are all time and demand deposits entrusted to a bank.

*Net Interest Margin %* is net interest income before provisions expressed as a percentage of total interest income. A key measure of bank profitability.

*Efficiency Ratio %* is non-interest expense expressed as a percentage of total revenue.

**Factors Pertaining Especially to Insurance Companies**

*Premium Income* is the amount of insurance premiums received from policyholders. This is the primary revenue source for insurance companies.

*Benefits and Claims* represents the payments made to policyholders under the terms of insurance contracts.

*Loss Ratio %* is benefits and claims expressed as a percentage of premium income. A key ratio of insurance company profitability.

**Factors Pertaining Especially to Real Estate Investment Trusts**

*Property Income* is income from property rental and other associated activities.

*Non-Property Income* includes interest income and other income not from property activities.

# HOW TO USE THIS BOOK

## ABBREVIATIONS AND SYMBOLS

A.........................................Annual
ASE....................American Stock Exchange
()......................................Deficit
(Div. Reinv. Plan)....Dividend Reinvestment Plan offered
E...........................................Extra
M.........................................Monthly
N/A..............................Not Applicable
N.M..............................Not Meaningful
NMS................ National MarketSystem
NYS................New York Stock Exchange
Q......................................Quarterly
S..................................Semi-Annual
Sp..............................Special Dividend
U........................Frequency Unknown

# ABBOTT LABORATORIES

| Exchange | Symbol | Price | 52Wk Range | Yield | P/E |
|---|---|---|---|---|---|
| NYS | ABT | $52.51 (8/31/2011) | 54.00-45.16 | 3.66 | 16.06 |

***7 Year Price Score 99.41** *NYSE Composite Index=100 ***12 Month Price Score 103.29**

**Interim Earnings (Per Share)**

| Qtr. | Mar | Jun | Sep | Dec |
|---|---|---|---|---|
| 2008 | 0.60 | 0.85 | 0.69 | 0.98 |
| 2009 | 0.92 | 0.83 | 0.95 | 0.99 |
| 2010 | 0.64 | 0.83 | 0.57 | 0.92 |
| 2011 | 0.55 | 1.23 | ... | ... |

**Interim Dividends (Per Share)**

| Amt | Decl | Ex | Rec | Pay |
|---|---|---|---|---|
| 0.44Q | 09/16/2010 | 10/13/2010 | 10/15/2010 | 11/15/2010 |
| 0.44Q | 12/10/2010 | 01/12/2011 | 01/14/2011 | 02/15/2011 |
| 0.48Q | 02/18/2011 | 04/13/2011 | 04/15/2011 | 05/16/2011 |
| 0.48Q | 06/10/2011 | 07/13/2011 | 07/15/2011 | 08/15/2011 |

**Indicated Div: $1.92 (Div. Reinv. Plan)**

**Valuation Analysis**

| | | | |
|---|---|---|---|
| Forecast EPS | $4.64 (09/05/2011) | | |
| Market Cap | $81.7 Billion | Book Value | $26.4 Billion |
| Price/Book | 3.10 | Price/Sales | 2.19 |

**Dividend Achiever Status**

| | |
|---|---|
| **10 Year Growth Rate** | 7.69% |
| **Total Years of Dividend Growth** | 38 |

**Business Summary:** Pharmaceuticals (MIC: 4.1.1 SIC: 2834 NAIC: 325412)

Abbott Laboratories develops, manufactures and sells health care products. Co. has four segments: Pharmaceutical Products, which sells adult and pediatric pharmaceutical products; Nutritional Products, which sells pediatric and adult nutritional products; Diagnostic Products, which sells diagnostic systems and tests for blood banks, hospitals, commercial laboratories and alternate-care testing sites; and Vascular Products, which sells coronary, endovascular, and vessel closure devices. The principal products in Co.'s other businesses include blood glucose monitoring meters, test strips, data management software and accessories for people with diabetes, and medical devices for the eye.

**Recent Developments:** For the quarter ended June 30 2011, net income increased 50.4% to US$1.94 billion from US$1.29 billion in the year-earlier quarter. Revenues were US$9.62 billion, up 9.0% from US$8.83 billion the year before. Operating income was US$1.77 billion versus US$1.61 billion in the prior-year quarter, an increase of 10.4%. Direct operating expenses rose 9.2% to US$3.87 billion from US$3.54 billion in the comparable period the year before. Indirect operating expenses increased 8.1% to US$3.97 billion from US$3.68 billion in the equivalent prior-year period.

**Prospects:** Our evaluation of Abbott Laboratories as of Sep. 6, 2011 is the result of our systematic analysis on three basic characteristics: earnings strength, relative valuation, and recent stock price movement. The company has produced a positive trend in earnings per share over the past 5 quarters and while recent estimates for the company have remained steady, ABT has posted better than expected results. Based on operating earnings yield, the company is undervalued when compared to all of the companies in our coverage universe. Share price changes over the past year indicates that ABT will perform very poorly over the near term.

**Financial Data**

| (US$ in Thousands) | 6 Mos | 3 Mos | 12/31/2010 | 12/31/2009 | 12/31/2008 | 12/31/2007 | 12/31/2006 | 12/31/2005 |
|---|---|---|---|---|---|---|---|---|
| Earnings Per Share | 3.27 | 2.87 | 2.96 | 3.69 | 3.12 | 2.31 | 1.12 | 2.16 |
| Cash Flow Per Share | 6.02 | 5.94 | 5.65 | 4.70 | 4.51 | 3.36 | 3.44 | 3.25 |
| Tang Book Value Per Share | N.M. | N.M. | N.M. | 2.17 | 1.51 | 1.24 | N.M. | 2.89 |
| Dividends Per Share | 1.800 | 1.760 | 1.720 | 1.560 | 1.405 | 1.270 | 1.160 | 1.085 |
| Dividend Payout % | 55.05 | 61.32 | 58.11 | 42.28 | 45.03 | 54.98 | 103.57 | 50.23 |
| **Income Statement** | | | | | | | | |
| Total Revenue | 18,657,141 | 9,040,850 | 35,166,721 | 30,764,707 | 29,527,552 | 25,914,238 | 22,476,322 | 22,337,808 |
| EBITDA | 4,539,553 | 1,938,324 | 9,243,371 | 9,515,184 | 7,861,635 | 6,175,053 | 3,364,171 | 5,322,325 |
| Depn & Amortn | 1,557,079 | 745,667 | 3,082,855 | 1,939,533 | 1,797,101 | 1,747,031 | 1,271,265 | 990,131 |
| Income Before Taxes | 2,743,342 | 1,068,786 | 5,712,834 | 7,193,774 | 5,737,289 | 3,971,632 | 1,800,559 | 4,178,532 |
| Income Taxes | (63,258) | 204,968 | 1,086,662 | 1,447,936 | 1,122,070 | 863,334 | 559,615 | 1,247,855 |
| Net Income | 2,806,600 | 863,818 | 4,626,172 | 5,745,838 | 4,880,719 | 3,606,314 | 1,716,755 | 3,372,065 |
| Average Shares | 1,566,103 | 1,558,641 | 1,556,022 | 1,555,126 | 1,560,753 | 1,560,057 | 1,536,724 | 1,564,103 |
| **Balance Sheet** | | | | | | | | |
| Current Assets | 24,132,178 | 23,647,132 | 22,317,529 | 23,313,891 | 17,042,559 | 14,042,733 | 11,281,883 | 11,386,028 |
| Total Assets | 62,004,241 | 61,651,363 | 59,462,266 | 52,416,623 | 42,419,204 | 39,713,924 | 36,178,172 | 29,141,203 |
| Current Liabilities | 15,839,928 | 17,225,103 | 17,262,434 | 13,049,489 | 11,591,908 | 9,103,278 | 11,951,195 | 7,415,514 |
| Long-Term Obligations | 12,627,761 | 12,530,246 | 12,523,517 | 11,266,294 | 8,713,327 | 9,487,789 | 7,009,664 | 4,571,504 |
| Total Liabilities | 35,625,388 | 37,021,713 | 37,074,131 | 29,560,885 | 24,939,235 | 21,935,384 | 22,123,986 | 14,725,932 |
| Stockholders' Equity | 26,378,853 | 24,629,650 | 22,388,135 | 22,855,627 | 17,479,551 | 17,778,540 | 14,054,186 | 14,415,271 |
| Shares Outstanding | 1,556,576 | 1,623,287 | 1,546,983 | 1,551,167 | 1,552,432 | 1,549,910 | 1,537,243 | 1,539,234 |
| **Statistical Record** | | | | | | | | |
| Return on Assets % | 8.91 | 7.80 | 8.27 | 12.12 | 11.85 | 9.50 | 5.26 | 11.65 |
| Return on Equity % | 22.20 | 19.73 | 20.45 | 28.49 | 27.61 | 22.66 | 12.06 | 23.47 |
| EBITDA Margin % | 24.33 | 21.44 | 26.28 | 30.93 | 26.62 | 23.83 | 14.97 | 23.83 |
| Net Margin % | 15.04 | 9.55 | 13.15 | 18.68 | 16.53 | 13.92 | 7.64 | 15.10 |
| Asset Turnover | 0.65 | 0.63 | 0.63 | 0.65 | 0.72 | 0.68 | 0.69 | 0.77 |
| Current Ratio | 1.52 | 1.37 | 1.29 | 1.79 | 1.47 | 1.54 | 0.94 | 1.54 |
| Debt to Equity | 0.48 | 0.51 | 0.56 | 0.49 | 0.50 | 0.53 | 0.50 | 0.32 |
| Price Range | 54.00-45.16 | 53.67-45.16 | 56.24-45.86 | 57.25-41.52 | 60.50-49.45 | 59.43-48.97 | 49.48-39.55 | 49.99-37.63 |
| P/E Ratio | 16.51-13.81 | 18.70-15.74 | 19.00-15.49 | 15.51-11.25 | 19.39-15.85 | 25.73-21.20 | 44.18-35.31 | 23.14-17.42 |
| Average Yield % | 3.62 | 3.59 | 3.39 | 3.22 | 2.55 | 2.33 | 2.58 | 2.39 |

| | | |
|---|---|---|
| **Address:** 100 Abbott Park Road, Abbott Park, IL 60064-6400<br>**Telephone:** 847-937-6100<br>**Web Site:** www.abbott.com | **Officers:** Miles D. White - Chairman, Chief Executive Officer Thomas C. Freyman - Executive Vice President, Chief Financial Officer **Transfer Agents:** Computershare Trust Company, NA, Providence, RI | **No of Institutions:** 1699<br>**Shares:** 1,112,382,464 **% Held:** 62.54 |

# ABM INDUSTRIES, INC.

| Exchange | Symbol | Price | 52Wk Range | Yield | P/E |
|---|---|---|---|---|---|
| NYS | ABM | $20.44 (8/31/2011) | 27.00-17.29 | 2.74 | 16.35 |

*7 Year Price Score 111.68 *NYSE Composite Index=100 *12 Month Price Score 91.81

**Interim Earnings (Per Share)**

| Qtr. | Jan | Apr | Jul | Oct |
|---|---|---|---|---|
| 2007-08 | 0.13 | 0.22 | 0.32 | 0.22 |
| 2008-09 | 0.28 | 0.25 | 0.24 | 0.29 |
| 2009-10 | 0.24 | 0.16 | 0.40 | 0.43 |
| 2010-11 | 0.16 | 0.26 | ... | ... |

**Interim Dividends (Per Share)**

| Amt | Decl | Ex | Rec | Pay |
|---|---|---|---|---|
| 0.135Q | 08/31/2010 | 10/05/2010 | 10/07/2010 | 11/01/2010 |
| 0.14Q | 12/15/2010 | 01/04/2011 | 01/06/2011 | 02/07/2011 |
| 0.14Q | 03/07/2011 | 04/05/2011 | 04/07/2011 | 05/02/2011 |
| 0.14Q | 06/07/2011 | 07/05/2011 | 07/07/2011 | 08/01/2011 |

**Indicated Div: $0.56**

**Valuation Analysis**

| | | | |
|---|---|---|---|
| Forecast EPS | $1.45 (09/05/2011) | | |
| Market Cap | $1.1 Billion | Book Value | $760.3 Million |
| Price/Book | 1.43 | Price/Sales | 0.28 |

**Dividend Achiever Status**

| | |
|---|---|
| 10 Year Growth Rate | 5.05% |
| Total Years of Dividend Growth | 46 |

**Business Summary:** Sanitation Services (MIC: 7.5.3 SIC: 7349 NAIC: 561720)

ABM Industries operates through four segments: janitorial, parking, security and engineering. Co.'s janitorial services include floor cleaning and finishing, window washing, furniture polishing, carpet cleaning and dusting, and other building cleaning services. Co.'s Parking segment operates parking lots and garages. Security services include staffing of security officers, mobile patrol services, and investigative services; electronic monitoring of fire, life safety systems and access control devices; and security consulting services. Co.'s engineering segment provides on-site engineers to operate and maintain mechanical, electrical and plumbing systems.

**Recent Developments:** For the quarter ended Apr 30 2011, income from continuing operations increased 64.7% to US$14.2 million from US$8.6 million in the year-earlier quarter. Net income increased 65.5% to US$14.2 million from US$8.6 million in the year-earlier quarter. Revenues were US$1.06 billion, up 23.9% from US$855.5 million the year before. Operating income was US$26.5 million versus US$15.5 million in the prior-year quarter, an increase of 70.4%. Direct operating expenses rose 23.0% to US$949.6 million from US$772.0 million in the comparable period the year before. Indirect operating expenses increased 23.6% to US$84.0 million from US$67.9 million in the equivalent prior-year period.

**Prospects:** Our evaluation of ABM Industries Inc. as of Sep. 6, 2011 is the result of our systematic analysis on three basic characteristics: earnings strength, relative valuation, and recent stock price movement. The company has produced a positive trend in earnings per share over the past 5 quarters and while recent estimates for the company have remained steady, ABM has posted better than expected results. Based on operating earnings yield, the company is undervalued when compared to all of the companies in our coverage universe. Share price changes over the past year indicates that ABM will perform poorly over the near term.

**Financial Data**

| (US$ in Thousands) | 6 Mos | 3 Mos | 10/31/2010 | 10/31/2009 | 10/31/2008 | 10/31/2007 | 10/31/2006 | 10/31/2005 |
|---|---|---|---|---|---|---|---|---|
| Earnings Per Share | 1.25 | 1.15 | 1.23 | 1.05 | 0.88 | 1.04 | 1.88 | 1.15 |
| Cash Flow Per Share | 2.61 | 3.03 | 2.88 | 2.74 | 1.35 | 1.10 | 2.66 | 0.76 |
| Tang Book Value Per Share | N.M. | N.M. | 1.51 | 1.54 | 0.90 | 6.58 | 5.54 | 4.24 |
| Dividends Per Share | 0.550 | 0.545 | 0.540 | 0.520 | 0.500 | 0.480 | 0.440 | 0.420 |
| Dividend Payout % | 44.00 | 47.39 | 43.90 | 49.52 | 56.82 | 46.15 | 23.40 | 36.52 |
| **Income Statement** | | | | | | | | |
| Total Revenue | 2,089,252 | 1,029,169 | 3,495,747 | 3,481,823 | 3,623,590 | 2,842,811 | 2,792,668 | 2,587,761 |
| EBITDA | 54,374 | 22,209 | 144,976 | 123,825 | 127,544 | 99,019 | 179,000 | 70,943 |
| Depn & Amortn | 10,959 | 5,293 | 36,264 | 33,284 | 28,035 | 18,765 | 20,764 | 5,673 |
| Income Before Taxes | 35,052 | 12,870 | 104,073 | 84,660 | 84,316 | 79,787 | 157,741 | 64,386 |
| Income Taxes | 14,066 | 5,252 | 40,203 | 29,170 | 31,585 | 27,347 | 64,536 | 20,832 |
| Net Income | 22,581 | 8,390 | 64,121 | 54,293 | 45,434 | 52,440 | 93,205 | 57,941 |
| Average Shares | 54,159 | 53,893 | 52,908 | 51,845 | 51,386 | 50,629 | 49,678 | 50,367 |
| **Balance Sheet** | | | | | | | | |
| Current Assets | 715,965 | 736,752 | 608,756 | 620,997 | 635,069 | 642,890 | 631,741 | 521,453 |
| Total Assets | 1,916,991 | 1,955,839 | 1,548,670 | 1,521,153 | 1,549,913 | 1,120,673 | 1,016,274 | 903,710 |
| Current Liabilities | 402,359 | 420,580 | 333,851 | 342,694 | 361,089 | 289,744 | 319,285 | 275,074 |
| Long-Term Obligations | 396,000 | 430,000 | 140,500 | 172,500 | 230,000 | ... | ... | ... |
| Total Liabilities | 1,156,734 | 1,206,950 | 809,645 | 834,103 | 905,862 | 514,915 | 475,027 | 427,784 |
| Stockholders' Equity | 760,257 | 748,889 | 739,025 | 687,050 | 644,051 | 605,758 | 541,247 | 475,926 |
| Shares Outstanding | 53,119 | 52,989 | 52,635 | 51,688 | 50,963 | 50,019 | 48,634 | 49,051 |
| **Statistical Record** | | | | | | | | |
| Return on Assets % | 3.85 | 3.43 | 4.18 | 3.54 | 3.39 | 4.91 | 9.71 | 6.64 |
| Return on Equity % | 8.94 | 8.27 | 8.99 | 8.16 | 7.25 | 9.14 | 18.33 | 12.62 |
| EBITDA Margin % | 2.60 | 2.16 | 4.15 | 3.56 | 3.52 | 3.48 | 6.41 | 2.74 |
| Net Margin % | 1.08 | 0.82 | 1.83 | 1.56 | 1.25 | 1.84 | 3.34 | 2.24 |
| Asset Turnover | 2.27 | 2.10 | 2.28 | 2.27 | 2.71 | 2.66 | 2.91 | 2.96 |
| Current Ratio | 1.78 | 1.75 | 1.82 | 1.81 | 1.76 | 2.22 | 1.98 | 1.90 |
| Debt to Equity | 0.52 | 0.57 | 0.19 | 0.25 | 0.36 | ... | ... | ... |
| Price Range | 27.00-18.81 | 26.81-18.81 | 22.77-18.35 | 22.98-11.79 | 27.39-13.28 | 30.43-19.59 | 21.65-16.22 | 22.39-17.99 |
| P/E Ratio | 21.60-15.05 | 23.31-16.36 | 18.51-14.92 | 21.89-11.23 | 31.13-15.09 | 29.26-18.84 | 11.52-8.63 | 19.47-15.64 |
| Average Yield % | 2.36 | 2.47 | 2.59 | 2.93 | 2.37 | 1.96 | 2.38 | 2.15 |

**Address:** 551 Fifth Avenue, Suite 300, New York, NY 10176
**Telephone:** 212-297-0200
**Web Site:** www.abm.com

**Officers:** Maryellen C. Herringer - Chairman Henrik C. Slipsager - President, Chief Executive Officer
**Transfer Agents:**BNY Mellon Shareowner Services, Inc., Pittsburgh, PA

**Investor Contact:** 415-733-4000
**No of Institutions:** 162
**Shares:** 47,669,268 **% Held:** 85.89

# AFLAC INC.

| Exchange | Symbol | Price | 52Wk Range | Yield | P/E |
|---|---|---|---|---|---|
| NYS | AFL | $37.72 (8/31/2011) | 59.28-34.61 | 3.18 | 9.87 |

***7 Year Price Score 108.34** *NYSE Composite Index=100 ***12 Month Price Score 83.73**

**Interim Earnings (Per Share)**

| Qtr. | Mar | Jun | Sep | Dec |
|---|---|---|---|---|
| 2008 | 0.98 | 1.00 | 0.21 | 0.43 |
| 2009 | 1.22 | 0.67 | 0.77 | 0.53 |
| 2010 | 1.35 | 1.23 | 1.46 | 0.92 |
| 2011 | 0.84 | 0.60 | ... | ... |

**Interim Dividends (Per Share)**

| Amt | Decl | Ex | Rec | Pay |
|---|---|---|---|---|
| 0.30Q | 08/10/2010 | 11/15/2010 | 11/17/2010 | 12/01/2010 |
| 0.30Q | 02/01/2011 | 02/11/2011 | 02/15/2011 | 03/01/2011 |
| 0.30Q | 04/26/2011 | 05/16/2011 | 05/18/2011 | 06/01/2011 |
| 0.30Q | 07/27/2011 | 08/15/2011 | 08/17/2011 | 09/01/2011 |

**Indicated Div: $1.20 (Div. Reinv. Plan)**

**Valuation Analysis**

| | | | |
|---|---|---|---|
| Forecast EPS | $6.30 (09/02/2011) | | |
| Market Cap | $17.6 Billion | Book Value | $12.0 Billion |
| Price/Book | 1.47 | Price/Sales | 0.84 |

**Dividend Achiever Status**

| | |
|---|---|
| 10 Year Growth Rate | 19.47% |
| Total Years of Dividend Growth | 28 |

**Business Summary:** Life & Health (MIC: 5.2.2 SIC: 6321 NAIC: 524114)

AFLAC is a holding company. Through its subsidiaries, Co. sells health and life insurance in the U.S. and Japan. Co.'s insurance business is marketed and administered through American Family Life Assurance Company of Columbus, which operates in the U.S. (Aflac U.S.) and as a branch in Japan (Aflac Japan). Aflac Japan sells voluntary supplemental insurance products, including cancer plans, general medical indemnity plans, medical/sickness riders, care plans, living benefit life plans, ordinary life insurance plans and annuities. Aflac U.S. sells voluntary supplemental insurance products including loss-of-income products and products designed to protect individuals from depletion of assets.

**Recent Developments:** For the quarter ended June 30 2011, net income decreased 51.8% to US$280.0 million from US$581.0 million in the year-earlier quarter. Revenues were US$5.09 billion, up 2.2% from US$4.98 billion the year before. Net premiums earned were US$4.96 billion versus US$4.33 billion in the prior-year quarter, an increase of 14.4%. Net investment income rose 7.8% to US$784.0 million from US$727.0 million a year ago.

**Prospects:** Our evaluation of AFLAC Inc. as of Sep. 6, 2011 is the result of our systematic analysis on three basic characteristics: earnings strength, relative valuation, and recent stock price movement. The company has managed to produce a neutral trend in earnings per share over the past 5 quarters and while recent estimates for the company have been raised by analysts, AFL has posted better than expected results. Based on operating earnings yield, the company is undervalued when compared to all of the companies in our coverage universe. Share price changes over the past year indicates that AFL will perform well over the near term.

**Financial Data**

| (US$ in Thousands) | 6 Mos | 3 Mos | 12/31/2010 | 12/31/2009 | 12/31/2008 | 12/31/2007 | 12/31/2006 | 12/31/2005 |
|---|---|---|---|---|---|---|---|---|
| Earnings Per Share | 3.82 | 4.45 | 4.95 | 3.19 | 2.62 | 3.31 | 2.95 | 2.92 |
| Cash Flow Per Share | 17.89 | 16.83 | 14.90 | 13.21 | 10.46 | 9.54 | 8.87 | 8.85 |
| Tang Book Value Per Share | 25.65 | 23.58 | 23.54 | 17.96 | 14.23 | 18.08 | 16.93 | 15.89 |
| Dividends Per Share | 1.180 | 1.160 | 1.140 | 1.120 | 0.960 | 0.800 | 0.550 | 0.440 |
| Dividend Payout % | 30.89 | 26.07 | 23.03 | 35.11 | 36.64 | 24.17 | 18.64 | 15.07 |
| **Income Statement** | | | | | | | | |
| Premium Income | 9,828,000 | 4,872,000 | 18,073,000 | 16,621,000 | 14,947,000 | 12,973,000 | 12,314,000 | 11,990,000 |
| Total Revenue | 10,204,000 | 5,117,000 | 20,732,000 | 18,254,000 | 16,554,000 | 15,393,000 | 14,616,000 | 14,363,000 |
| Benefits & Claims | 6,532,000 | 3,222,000 | 12,106,000 | 11,308,000 | 10,499,000 | 9,285,000 | 9,016,000 | 8,890,000 |
| Income Before Taxes | 1,052,000 | 600,000 | 3,585,000 | 2,235,000 | 1,914,000 | 2,499,000 | 2,264,000 | 2,226,000 |
| Income Taxes | 378,000 | 205,000 | 1,241,000 | 738,000 | 660,000 | 865,000 | 781,000 | 743,000 |
| Net Income | 674,000 | 395,000 | 2,344,000 | 1,497,000 | 1,254,000 | 1,634,000 | 1,483,000 | 1,483,000 |
| Average Shares | 469,752 | 472,104 | 473,085 | 469,063 | 478,815 | 493,971 | 501,827 | 507,704 |
| **Balance Sheet** | | | | | | | | |
| Total Assets | 106,232,000 | 101,145,000 | 101,039,000 | 84,106,000 | 79,331,000 | 65,805,000 | 59,805,000 | 56,361,000 |
| Total Liabilities | 94,251,000 | 90,122,000 | 89,983,000 | 75,689,000 | 72,692,000 | 57,010,000 | 51,464,000 | 48,434,000 |
| Stockholders' Equity | 11,981,000 | 11,023,000 | 11,056,000 | 8,417,000 | 6,639,000 | 8,795,000 | 8,341,000 | 7,927,000 |
| Shares Outstanding | 467,067 | 467,564 | 469,661 | 468,568 | 466,615 | 486,530 | 492,550 | 498,894 |
| **Statistical Record** | | | | | | | | |
| Return on Assets % | 1.83 | 2.26 | 2.53 | 1.83 | 1.72 | 2.60 | 2.55 | 2.56 |
| Return on Equity % | 16.37 | 21.02 | 24.07 | 19.89 | 16.21 | 19.07 | 18.23 | 19.14 |
| Loss Ratio % | 66.46 | 66.13 | 66.98 | 68.03 | 70.24 | 71.57 | 73.22 | 74.15 |
| Net Margin % | 6.61 | 7.72 | 11.31 | 8.20 | 7.58 | 10.62 | 10.15 | 10.33 |
| Price Range | 59.28-42.67 | 59.28-40.48 | 57.85-40.48 | 47.14-11.49 | 68.22-30.38 | 62.90-45.64 | 49.30-42.46 | 49.60-35.70 |
| P/E Ratio | 15.52-11.17 | 13.32-9.10 | 11.69-8.18 | 14.78-3.60 | 26.04-11.60 | 19.00-13.79 | 16.71-14.39 | 16.99-12.23 |
| Average Yield % | 2.24 | 2.23 | 2.25 | 3.25 | 1.67 | 1.50 | 1.20 | 1.03 |

| | | |
|---|---|---|
| **Address:** 1932 Wynnton Road, Columbus, GA 31999<br>**Telephone:** 706-323-3431<br>**Web Site:** www.aflac.com | **Officers:** Daniel P. Amos - Chairman, Chief Executive Officer Kriss Cloninger - President, Chief Financial Officer, Treasurer **Transfer Agents:** AFLAC Incorporated, Columbus, GA | **Investor Contact:** 706-596-3264<br>**No of Institutions:** 941<br>**Shares:** 316,281,248 **% Held:** 58.79 |

# AIR PRODUCTS & CHEMICALS, INC.

| Exchange | Symbol | Price | 52Wk Range | Yield | P/E |
|---|---|---|---|---|---|
| NYS | APD | $81.87 (8/31/2011) | 97.79-74.03 | 2.83 | 15.25 |

***7 Year Price Score 118.04** *NYSE Composite Index=100 ***12 Month Price Score 100.23**

**Interim Earnings (Per Share)**

| Qtr. | Dec | Mar | Jun | Sep |
|---|---|---|---|---|
| 2007-08 | 1.19 | 1.43 | 0.32 | 1.20 |
| 2008-09 | 0.32 | 0.97 | 0.53 | 1.14 |
| 2009-10 | 1.16 | 1.16 | 1.17 | 1.25 |
| 2010-11 | 1.23 | 1.39 | 1.50 | ... |

**Interim Dividends (Per Share)**

| Amt | Decl | Ex | Rec | Pay |
|---|---|---|---|---|
| 0.49Q | 09/16/2010 | 09/29/2010 | 10/01/2010 | 11/08/2010 |
| 0.49Q | 11/18/2010 | 12/30/2010 | 01/03/2011 | 02/14/2011 |
| 0.58Q | 03/17/2011 | 03/30/2011 | 04/01/2011 | 05/09/2011 |
| 0.58Q | 05/18/2011 | 06/29/2011 | 07/01/2011 | 08/08/2011 |

**Indicated Div: $2.32 (Div. Reinv. Plan)**

**Valuation Analysis**

Forecast EPS $5.74 (09/05/2011)

| | | | |
|---|---|---|---|
| Market Cap | $17.4 Billion | Book Value | $6.2 Billion |
| Price/Book | 2.80 | Price/Sales | 1.78 |

**Dividend Achiever Status**

| | |
|---|---|
| **10 Year Growth Rate** | 9.43% |
| **Total Years of Dividend Growth** | 28 |

**Business Summary:** Specialty Chemicals (MIC: 8.3.2 SIC: 2813 NAIC: 325120)

Air Products & Chemicals serves technology, energy, industrial, and healthcare customers with a portfolio of products, services, and applications. Co. has four business segments: Merchant Gases, which sells atmospheric gases, process gases and medical gases, along with certain services and equipment; Tonnage Gases, which provides hydrogen, carbon monoxide, nitrogen, oxygen, and syngas; Electronics and Performance Materials, which provides gases, chemicals, services, and equipment for the electronics industry, as well as performance materials such as polyurethane catalysts; and Equipment and Energy, which designs and manufactures cryogenic equipment, and serves the energy markets.

**Recent Developments:** For the quarter ended June 30 2011, income from continuing operations increased 24.8% to US$326.1 million from US$261.3 million in the year-earlier quarter. Net income increased 28.2% to US$335.0 million from US$261.3 million in the year-earlier quarter. Revenues were US$2.58 billion, up 14.5% from US$2.25 billion the year before. Operating income was US$416.8 million versus US$336.4 million in the prior-year quarter, an increase of 23.9%. Direct operating expenses rose 16.8% to US$1.88 billion from US$1.61 billion in the comparable period the year before. Indirect operating expenses decreased 8.5% to US$278.9 million from US$304.9 million in the equivalent prior-year period.

**Prospects:** Our evaluation of Air Products & Chemicals Inc. as of Sep. 6, 2011 is the result of our systematic analysis on three basic characteristics: earnings strength, relative valuation, and recent stock price movement. The company has managed to produce a neutral trend in earnings per share over the past 5 quarters. However, while recent estimates for the company have been lowered by analysts, APD has posted better than expected results. Based on operating earnings yield, the company is undervalued when compared to all of the companies in our coverage universe. Share price changes over the past year indicates that APD will perform poorly over the near term.

**Financial Data**

| (US$ in Thousands) | 9 Mos | 6 Mos | 3 Mos | 09/30/2010 | 09/30/2009 | 09/30/2008 | 09/30/2007 | 09/30/2006 |
|---|---|---|---|---|---|---|---|---|
| Earnings Per Share | 5.37 | 5.04 | 4.81 | 4.74 | 2.96 | 4.15 | 4.64 | 3.18 |
| Cash Flow Per Share | 7.61 | 7.51 | 7.77 | 7.17 | 6.30 | 7.89 | 6.86 | 5.96 |
| Tang Book Value Per Share | 23.31 | 21.67 | 21.50 | 20.33 | 17.10 | 18.21 | 18.53 | 17.44 |
| Dividends Per Share | 2.140 | 2.050 | 1.960 | 1.920 | 1.790 | 1.700 | 1.480 | 1.340 |
| Dividend Payout % | 39.85 | 40.67 | 40.75 | 40.51 | 60.47 | 40.96 | 31.90 | 42.14 |
| **Income Statement** | | | | | | | | |
| Total Revenue | 7,470,800 | 4,893,000 | 2,391,700 | 9,026,000 | 8,256,200 | 10,414,500 | 10,037,800 | 8,850,400 |
| EBITDA | 1,854,200 | 1,215,200 | 578,200 | 2,231,700 | 1,664,900 | 2,345,400 | 2,230,300 | 1,813,600 |
| Depn & Amortn | 657,300 | 435,100 | 217,600 | 846,100 | 826,000 | 857,800 | 831,400 | 761,700 |
| Income Before Taxes | 1,110,000 | 719,700 | 329,600 | 1,267,100 | 724,400 | 1,333,800 | 1,244,500 | 941,600 |
| Income Taxes | 295,700 | 191,800 | 81,500 | 339,500 | 185,300 | 365,300 | 301,200 | 271,200 |
| Net Income | 899,400 | 572,900 | 268,600 | 1,029,100 | 631,300 | 909,700 | 1,035,600 | 723,400 |
| Average Shares | 217,300 | 218,800 | 219,200 | 217,100 | 213,500 | 219,200 | 223,200 | 227,500 |
| **Balance Sheet** | | | | | | | | |
| Current Assets | 3,276,500 | 2,976,500 | 2,870,200 | 3,033,800 | 2,997,800 | 2,848,100 | 2,858,400 | 2,612,600 |
| Total Assets | 14,451,500 | 13,820,700 | 13,459,700 | 13,505,900 | 13,029,100 | 12,571,300 | 12,659,500 | 11,180,700 |
| Current Liabilities | 2,103,800 | 2,211,300 | 1,937,100 | 2,244,100 | 2,503,600 | 2,212,000 | 2,422,700 | 2,323,400 |
| Long-Term Obligations | 4,054,300 | 3,711,800 | 3,617,400 | 3,659,800 | 3,715,600 | 3,515,400 | 2,976,500 | 2,280,200 |
| Total Liabilities | 8,219,300 | 7,995,500 | 7,649,700 | 7,959,000 | 8,237,200 | 7,540,600 | 7,163,900 | 6,256,700 |
| Stockholders' Equity | 6,232,200 | 5,825,200 | 5,810,000 | 5,546,900 | 4,791,900 | 5,030,700 | 5,495,600 | 4,924,000 |
| Shares Outstanding | 213,132 | 211,896 | 214,919 | 213,802 | 211,260 | 209,334 | 215,355 | 217,250 |
| **Statistical Record** | | | | | | | | |
| Return on Assets % | 8.54 | 8.14 | 7.93 | 7.76 | 4.93 | 7.19 | 8.69 | 6.70 |
| Return on Equity % | 20.44 | 19.80 | 19.29 | 19.91 | 12.85 | 17.24 | 19.88 | 15.23 |
| EBITDA Margin % | 24.82 | 24.84 | 24.18 | 24.73 | 20.17 | 22.52 | 22.22 | 20.49 |
| Net Margin % | 12.04 | 11.71 | 11.23 | 11.40 | 7.65 | 8.73 | 10.32 | 8.17 |
| Asset Turnover | 0.72 | 0.70 | 0.70 | 0.68 | 0.65 | 0.82 | 0.84 | 0.82 |
| Current Ratio | 1.56 | 1.35 | 1.48 | 1.35 | 1.20 | 1.29 | 1.18 | 1.12 |
| Debt to Equity | 0.65 | 0.64 | 0.62 | 0.66 | 0.78 | 0.70 | 0.54 | 0.46 |
| Price Range | 95.68-64.81 | 94.96-64.81 | 91.25-64.81 | 84.71-64.81 | 80.20-41.65 | 106.03-66.41 | 97.82-66.69 | 69.23-53.33 |
| P/E Ratio | 17.82-12.07 | 18.84-12.86 | 18.97-13.47 | 17.87-13.67 | 27.09-14.07 | 25.55-16.00 | 21.08-14.37 | 21.77-16.77 |
| Average Yield % | 2.50 | 2.55 | 2.54 | 2.53 | 2.95 | 1.79 | 1.91 | 2.14 |

**Address:** 7201 Hamilton Boulevard, Allentown, PA 18195-1501
**Telephone:** 610-481-4911
**Web Site:** www.airproducts.com

**Officers:** John E. McGlade - Chairman, President, Chief Executive Officer Paul E. Huck - Senior Vice President, Chief Financial Officer **Transfer Agents:** American Stock Transfer & Trust Company, New York, NY

**No of Institutions:** 839
**Shares:** 215,315,088 **% Held:** 82.43

# ALBEMARLE CORP.

| Exchange | Symbol | Price | 52Wk Range | Yield | P/E |
|---|---|---|---|---|---|
| NYS | ALB | $50.71 (8/31/2011) | 71.11-40.09 | 1.30 | 11.74 |

***7 Year Price Score 167.43** *NYSE Composite Index=100 ***12 Month Price Score 108.51**

**Interim Earnings (Per Share)**

| Qtr. | Mar | Jun | Sep | Dec |
|---|---|---|---|---|
| 2008 | 0.68 | 0.67 | 0.61 | 0.15 |
| 2009 | 0.28 | 0.42 | 0.57 | 0.68 |
| 2010 | 0.69 | 0.89 | 1.02 | 0.92 |
| 2011 | 1.15 | 1.23 | ... | ... |

**Interim Dividends (Per Share)**

| Amt | Decl | Ex | Rec | Pay |
|---|---|---|---|---|
| 0.14Q | 10/15/2010 | 12/13/2010 | 12/15/2010 | 01/01/2011 |
| 0.165Q | 02/16/2011 | 03/11/2011 | 03/15/2011 | 04/01/2011 |
| 0.165Q | 05/11/2011 | 06/13/2011 | 06/15/2011 | 07/01/2011 |
| 0.165Q | 07/12/2011 | 09/13/2011 | 09/15/2011 | 10/01/2011 |

**Indicated Div: $0.66 (Div. Reinv. Plan)**

**Valuation Analysis**

Forecast EPS $4.65 (09/03/2011)

Market Cap $4.7 Billion Book Value $1.7 Billion

Price/Book 2.70 Price/Sales 1.77

**Dividend Achiever Status**

**10 Year Growth Rate** 7.68%

**Total Years of Dividend Growth** 16

**Business Summary:** Specialty Chemicals (MIC: 8.3.2 SIC: 2821 NAIC: 325211)

Albemarle is a developer, manufacturer, and marketer of specialty chemicals for consumer electronics, petroleum refining, utilities, packaging, construction, automotive/transportation, pharmaceuticals, crop protection, food-safety and custom chemistry services. As of Dec 31 2010, Co. conducted its business through three reportable segments: Polymer Solutions, which is comprised of the flame retardants and stabilizers and curatives product areas; Catalysts, which is comprised of the refinery catalysts and polyolefin catalysts product areas; and Fine Chemistry, which is comprised of the performance chemicals and fine chemistry services and intermediates product areas.

**Recent Developments:** For the quarter ended June 30 2011, net income increased 43.7% to US$123.7 million from US$86.1 million in the year-earlier quarter. Revenues were US$742.1 million, up 25.3% from US$592.5 million the year before. Operating income was US$149.1 million versus US$106.6 million in the prior-year quarter, an increase of 39.8%. Direct operating expenses rose 21.2% to US$490.2 million from US$404.3 million in the comparable period the year before. Indirect operating expenses increased 26.2% to US$102.9 million from US$81.5 million in the equivalent prior-year period.

**Prospects:** Our evaluation of Albemarle Corp. as of Sep. 6, 2011 is the result of our systematic analysis on three basic characteristics: earnings strength, relative valuation, and recent stock price movement. The company has managed to produce a neutral trend in earnings per share over the past 5 quarters. However, while recent estimates for the company have been lowered by analysts, ALB has posted better than expected results. Based on operating earnings yield, the company is undervalued when compared to all of the companies in our coverage universe. Share price changes over the past year indicates that ALB will perform very well over the near term.

| **Financial Data** (US$ in Thousands) | 6 Mos | 3 Mos | 12/31/2010 | 12/31/2009 | 12/31/2008 | 12/31/2007 | 12/31/2006 | 12/31/2005 |
|---|---|---|---|---|---|---|---|---|
| Earnings Per Share | 4.32 | 3.98 | 3.51 | 1.94 | 2.10 | 2.36 | 1.47 | 1.21 |
| Cash Flow Per Share | 3.74 | 3.93 | 3.63 | 3.92 | 3.45 | 2.55 | 3.98 | 1.82 |
| Tang Book Value Per Share | 14.10 | 12.80 | 11.02 | 8.33 | 6.81 | 8.83 | 6.59 | 5.73 |
| Dividends Per Share | 0.610 | 0.585 | 0.560 | 0.500 | 0.480 | 0.420 | 0.345 | 0.310 |
| Dividend Payout % | 14.12 | 14.70 | 15.95 | 25.77 | 22.86 | 17.80 | 23.47 | 25.73 |
| **Income Statement** | | | | | | | | |
| Total Revenue | 1,438,638 | 696,530 | 2,362,764 | 2,005,394 | 2,467,115 | 2,336,187 | 2,368,506 | 2,107,499 |
| EBITDA | 338,345 | 165,704 | 500,136 | 272,157 | 318,918 | 409,151 | 276,250 | 179,334 |
| Depn & Amortn | 47,310 | 23,004 | 82,500 | 87,300 | 97,400 | 93,000 | 98,900 | 13,925 |
| Income Before Taxes | 272,169 | 133,108 | 392,103 | 160,273 | 183,343 | 277,819 | 133,386 | 123,438 |
| Income Taxes | 62,326 | 32,172 | 92,719 | (7,028) | (6,539) | 55,078 | 2,192 | 27,593 |
| Net Income | 220,739 | 106,580 | 323,720 | 178,368 | 194,202 | 229,690 | 142,969 | 114,867 |
| Average Shares | 92,795 | 92,517 | 92,184 | 92,046 | 92,530 | 97,216 | 97,136 | 95,496 |
| **Balance Sheet** | | | | | | | | |
| Current Assets | 1,455,696 | 1,346,374 | 1,348,198 | 1,032,087 | 1,178,923 | 1,053,438 | 960,854 | 873,663 |
| Total Assets | 3,292,347 | 3,139,881 | 3,068,081 | 2,771,557 | 2,872,717 | 2,830,450 | 2,530,368 | 2,547,243 |
| Current Liabilities | 394,413 | 381,611 | 364,177 | 353,264 | 438,367 | 402,917 | 482,949 | 421,917 |
| Long-Term Obligations | 758,867 | 758,597 | 851,927 | 776,403 | 906,062 | 707,311 | 681,859 | 775,889 |
| Total Liabilities | 1,566,319 | 1,543,772 | 1,652,007 | 1,565,861 | 1,806,946 | 1,552,145 | 1,502,270 | 1,616,968 |
| Stockholders' Equity | 1,726,028 | 1,596,109 | 1,416,074 | 1,205,696 | 1,065,771 | 1,278,305 | 1,028,098 | 930,275 |
| Shares Outstanding | 91,738 | 91,667 | 91,593 | 91,509 | 90,980 | 94,734 | 94,860 | 93,499 |
| **Statistical Record** | | | | | | | | |
| Return on Assets % | 13.26 | 12.45 | 11.09 | 6.32 | 6.79 | 8.57 | 5.63 | 4.60 |
| Return on Equity % | 27.32 | 26.25 | 24.69 | 15.71 | 16.52 | 19.92 | 14.60 | 13.99 |
| EBITDA Margin % | 23.52 | 23.79 | 21.17 | 13.57 | 12.93 | 17.51 | 11.66 | 8.51 |
| Net Margin % | 15.34 | 15.30 | 13.70 | 8.89 | 7.87 | 9.83 | 6.04 | 5.45 |
| Asset Turnover | 0.87 | 0.84 | 0.81 | 0.71 | 0.86 | 0.87 | 0.93 | 0.84 |
| Current Ratio | 3.69 | 3.53 | 3.70 | 2.92 | 2.69 | 2.61 | 1.99 | 2.07 |
| Debt to Equity | 0.44 | 0.48 | 0.60 | 0.64 | 0.85 | 0.55 | 0.66 | 0.83 |
| Price Range | 71.11-39.10 | 60.66-39.10 | 56.73-34.86 | 37.27-15.81 | 45.79-16.46 | 47.76-35.02 | 36.65-19.41 | 19.45-16.23 |
| P/E Ratio | 16.46-9.05 | 15.24-9.82 | 16.16-9.93 | 19.21-8.15 | 21.80-7.84 | 20.24-14.84 | 24.93-13.21 | 16.08-13.41 |
| Average Yield % | 1.12 | 1.21 | 1.27 | 1.77 | 1.40 | 1.02 | 1.34 | 1.70 |

**Address:** 451 Florida Street, Baton Rouge, LA 70801
**Telephone:** 225-388-8011
**Web Site:** www.albemarle.com

**Officers:** Mark C. Rohr - Chairman William M. Gottwald - Vice-Chairman **Transfer Agents:** Wells Fargo Bank, N.A., Shareowner Services, St. Paul, MN

**Investor Contact:** 804-788-6096
**No of Institutions:** 413
**Shares:** 75,764,336 **% Held:** 76.67

# ALTRIA GROUP INC

| Exchange | Symbol | Price | 52Wk Range | Yield | P/E |
|---|---|---|---|---|---|
| NYS | MO | $27.19 (8/31/2011) | 28.06-22.32 | 6.03 | 16.58 |

*7 Year Price Score 128.92 *NYSE Composite Index=100 *12 Month Price Score 104.13

**Interim Earnings (Per Share)**

| Qtr. | Mar | Jun | Sep | Dec |
|---|---|---|---|---|
| 2008 | 1.16 | 0.45 | 0.42 | 0.33 |
| 2009 | 0.28 | 0.49 | 0.42 | 0.35 |
| 2010 | 0.39 | 0.50 | 0.54 | 0.44 |
| 2011 | 0.45 | 0.21 | ... | ... |

**Interim Dividends (Per Share)**

| Amt | Decl | Ex | Rec | Pay |
|---|---|---|---|---|
| 0.38Q | 12/15/2010 | 12/23/2010 | 12/28/2010 | 01/10/2011 |
| 0.38Q | 02/24/2011 | 03/11/2011 | 03/15/2011 | 04/11/2011 |
| 0.38Q | 05/19/2011 | 06/13/2011 | 06/15/2011 | 07/11/2011 |
| 0.41Q | 08/26/2011 | 09/13/2011 | 09/15/2011 | 10/11/2011 |

**Indicated Div: $1.64 (Div. Reinv. Plan)**

**Valuation Analysis**

Forecast EPS $2.04 (09/05/2011)

Market Cap $56.3 Billion Book Value $4.6 Billion

Price/Book 12.16 Price/Sales 2.36

**Dividend Achiever Status**

**10 Year Growth Rate** 8.52%

**Total Years of Dividend Growth** 45

**Business Summary:** Tobacco Products (MIC: 1.3.1 SIC: 2111 NAIC: 312221)

Altria Group is a holding company. As of Dec 31 2010, Co.'s reportable segments were: cigarettes, smokeless products, cigars, wine and financial services. Co.'s wholly-owned subsidiaries as of Dec 31 2010 included Philip Morris USA Inc., which is engaged in the manufacture and sale of cigarettes and certain smokeless products in the U.S.; UST LLC, which is engaged in the manufacture and sale of smokeless products to customers; and John Middleton Co., which is engaged in the manufacture and sale of machine-made large cigars and pipe tobacco to customers. Philip Morris Capital Corporation, another wholly-owned subsidiary of Co., maintains a portfolio of direct finance leases.

**Recent Developments:** For the quarter ended June 30 2011, net income decreased 57.4% to US$444.0 million from US$1.04 billion in the year-earlier quarter. Revenues were US$5.92 billion, down 5.6% from US$6.27 billion the year before. Operating income was US$1.30 billion versus US$1.53 billion in the prior-year quarter, a decrease of 15.3%. Direct operating expenses rose 1.2% to US$3.95 billion from US$3.90 billion in the comparable period the year before. Indirect operating expenses decreased 19.9% to US$677.0 million from US$845.0 million in the equivalent prior-year period.

**Prospects:** Our evaluation of Altria Group Inc. as of Sep. 6, 2011 is the result of our systematic analysis on three basic characteristics: earnings strength, relative valuation, and recent stock price movement. The company has managed to produce a neutral trend in earnings per share over the past 5 quarters and while recent estimates for the company have remained steady, MO has posted results that were in line with analysts expectations. Based on operating earnings yield, the company is undervalued when compared to all of the companies in our coverage universe. Share price changes over the past year indicates that MO will perform very poorly over the near term.

**Financial Data**

| (US$ in Thousands) | 6 Mos | 3 Mos | 12/31/2010 | 12/31/2009 | 12/31/2008 | 12/31/2007 | 12/31/2006 | 12/31/2005 |
|---|---|---|---|---|---|---|---|---|
| Earnings Per Share | 1.64 | 1.93 | 1.87 | 1.54 | 2.36 | 4.62 | 5.71 | 4.99 |
| Cash Flow Per Share | 1.42 | 1.34 | 1.33 | 1.67 | 2.35 | 4.91 | 6.51 | 5.34 |
| Tang Book Value Per Share | N.M. | N.M. | N.M. | N.M. | N.M. | 2.66 | N.M. | N.M. |
| Dividends Per Share | 1.520 | 1.490 | 1.460 | 1.320 | 1.680 | 3.050 | 3.320 | 3.060 |
| Dividend Payout % | 92.68 | 77.20 | 78.07 | 85.71 | 71.19 | 66.02 | 58.14 | 61.32 |
| **Income Statement** | | | | | | | | |
| Total Revenue | 11,563,000 | 5,643,000 | 24,363,000 | 23,556,000 | 19,356,000 | 73,801,000 | 101,407,000 | 97,854,000 |
| EBITDA | 2,845,000 | 1,545,000 | 6,504,000 | 5,753,000 | 4,704,000 | 14,215,000 | 19,217,000 | 18,267,000 |
| Depn & Amortn | 11,000 | 6,000 | 276,000 | 291,000 | 215,000 | 980,000 | 1,804,000 | 1,675,000 |
| Income Before Taxes | 2,262,000 | 1,261,000 | 5,095,000 | 4,277,000 | 4,322,000 | 13,020,000 | 16,536,000 | 15,435,000 |
| Income Taxes | 1,224,000 | 512,000 | 1,816,000 | 1,669,000 | 1,699,000 | 4,096,000 | 4,351,000 | 4,618,000 |
| Net Income | 1,381,000 | 937,000 | 3,905,000 | 3,206,000 | 4,930,000 | 9,786,000 | 12,022,000 | 10,435,000 |
| Average Shares | 2,076,000 | 2,084,000 | 2,079,000 | 2,071,000 | 2,087,000 | 2,116,000 | 2,105,000 | 2,090,000 |
| **Balance Sheet** | | | | | | | | |
| Current Assets | 9,526,000 | 11,471,000 | 5,981,000 | 5,773,000 | 11,076,000 | 22,890,000 | 26,152,000 | 25,781,000 |
| Total Assets | 36,832,000 | 38,584,000 | 37,402,000 | 36,677,000 | 27,215,000 | 57,211,000 | 104,270,000 | 107,949,000 |
| Current Liabilities | 5,446,000 | 7,884,000 | 6,840,000 | 7,992,000 | 7,142,000 | 18,782,000 | 25,427,000 | 26,158,000 |
| Long-Term Obligations | 13,688,000 | 12,194,000 | 12,194,000 | 11,185,000 | 7,339,000 | 7,963,000 | 14,498,000 | 17,868,000 |
| Total Liabilities | 32,199,000 | 33,131,000 | 32,210,000 | 32,608,000 | 24,387,000 | 38,657,000 | 64,651,000 | 72,242,000 |
| Stockholders' Equity | 4,633,000 | 5,453,000 | 5,192,000 | 4,069,000 | 2,828,000 | 18,554,000 | 39,619,000 | 35,707,000 |
| Shares Outstanding | 2,071,249 | 2,093,319 | 2,088,739 | 2,076,028 | 2,061,371 | 2,107,676 | 2,097,080 | 2,084,264 |
| **Statistical Record** | | | | | | | | |
| Return on Assets % | 9.52 | 10.52 | 10.54 | 10.04 | 11.65 | 12.12 | 11.33 | 9.96 |
| Return on Equity % | 74.96 | 82.94 | 84.33 | 92.97 | 45.99 | 33.64 | 31.92 | 31.42 |
| EBITDA Margin % | 24.60 | 27.38 | 26.70 | 24.42 | 24.30 | 19.26 | 18.95 | 18.67 |
| Net Margin % | 11.94 | 16.60 | 16.03 | 13.61 | 25.47 | 13.26 | 11.86 | 10.66 |
| Asset Turnover | 0.66 | 0.63 | 0.66 | 0.74 | 0.46 | 0.91 | 0.96 | 0.93 |
| Current Ratio | 1.75 | 1.45 | 0.87 | 0.72 | 1.55 | 1.22 | 1.03 | 0.99 |
| Debt to Equity | 2.95 | 2.24 | 2.35 | 2.75 | 2.60 | 0.43 | 0.37 | 0.50 |
| Price Range | 28.06-20.04 | 26.15-19.57 | 26.15-19.37 | 20.37-14.62 | 24.43-14.45 | 24.12-19.03 | 19.96-15.90 | 17.90-14.01 |
| P/E Ratio | 17.11-12.22 | 13.55-10.14 | 13.98-10.36 | 13.23-9.49 | 10.35-6.12 | 5.22-4.12 | 3.50-2.78 | 3.59-2.81 |
| Average Yield % | 6.15 | 6.43 | 6.62 | 7.60 | 8.17 | 14.28 | 18.65 | 19.38 |

**Address:** 6601 West Broad Street, Richmond, VA 23230
**Telephone:** 804-274-2200
**Web Site:** www.altria.com

**Officers:** Michael E. Szymanczyk - Chairman, Chief Executive Officer David R. Beran - Vice-Chairman
**Transfer Agents:**Computershare Trust Company, N.A., Providence, RI

**No of Institutions:** 1235
**Shares:** 1,388,558,976 **% Held:** 58.38

# AMERICAN STATES WATER CO.

| Exchange | Symbol | Price | 52Wk Range | Yield | P/E |
|---|---|---|---|---|---|
| NYS | AWR | $35.50 (8/31/2011) | 38.13-31.27 | 3.15 | 16.99 |

***7 Year Price Score 99.94** *NYSE Composite Index=100 ***12 Month Price Score 98.86**

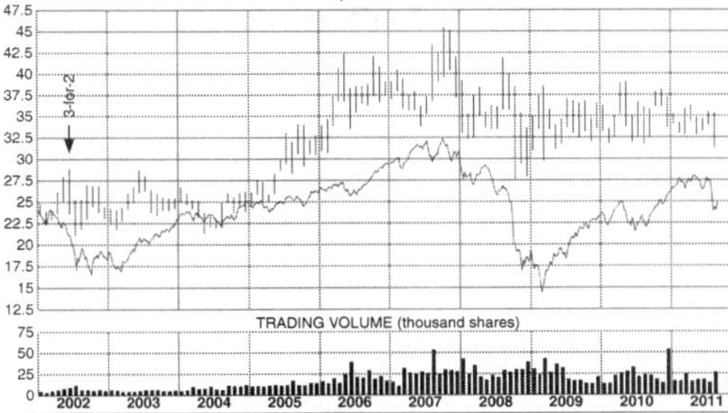


**Interim Earnings (Per Share)**

| Qtr. | Mar | Jun | Sep | Dec |
|---|---|---|---|---|
| 2008 | 0.30 | 0.53 | 0.26 | 0.16 |
| 2009 | 0.28 | 0.64 | 0.52 | 0.17 |
| 2010 | 0.45 | 0.48 | 0.35 | 0.49 |
| 2011 | 0.40 | 0.85 | ... | ... |

**Interim Dividends (Per Share)**

| Amt | Decl | Ex | Rec | Pay |
|---|---|---|---|---|
| 0.26Q | 10/25/2010 | 11/04/2010 | 11/08/2010 | 12/01/2010 |
| 0.26Q | 02/01/2011 | 02/10/2011 | 02/14/2011 | 03/01/2011 |
| 0.28Q | 04/26/2011 | 05/10/2011 | 05/12/2011 | 06/01/2011 |
| 0.28Q | 07/26/2011 | 08/09/2011 | 08/11/2011 | 09/01/2011 |

**Indicated Div: $1.12 (Div. Reinv. Plan)**

**Valuation Analysis**

| | | | |
|---|---|---|---|
| Forecast EPS | $2.13 (09/02/2011) | | |
| Market Cap | $663.3 Million | Book Value | $392.8 Million |
| Price/Book | 1.69 | Price/Sales | 1.58 |

**Dividend Achiever Status**

| | |
|---|---|
| **10 Year Growth Rate** | 1.84% |
| **Total Years of Dividend Growth** | 57 |

**Business Summary:** Water Utilities (MIC: 3.2.1 SIC: 4941 NAIC: 221310)

American States Water is a holding company. Co. is the parent company of Golden State Water Company (GSWC), Chaparral City Water Company (CCWC), and American States Utility Services, Inc. (ASUS) and its subsidiaries. Co. has three reportable segments: water, electric and contracted services. Within the segments, Co. has three principal business units: water and electric service utility operations conducted through GSWC; a water service utility operation conducted through CCWC; and contracted water and/or wastewater services conducted through ASUS and its subsidiaries. As of Dec 31 2010, GSWC served 255,562 water customers and 23,257 electric customers, while CCWC served 13,468 customers.

**Recent Developments:** For the quarter ended June 30 2011, income from continuing operations increased 43.5% to US$12.7 million from US$8.9 million in the year-earlier quarter. Net income increased 77.8% to US$16.0 million from US$9.0 million in the year-earlier quarter. Revenues were US$109.8 million, up 15.0% from US$95.5 million the year before. Operating income was US$29.1 million versus US$21.2 million in the prior-year quarter, an increase of 37.8%. Indirect operating expenses increased 8.6% to US$80.7 million from US$74.3 million in the equivalent prior-year period.

**Prospects:** Our evaluation of American States Water Co. as of Sep. 6, 2011 is the result of our systematic analysis on three basic characteristics: earnings strength, relative valuation, and recent stock price movement. The company has managed to produce a neutral trend in earnings per share over the past 5 quarters and while recent estimates for the company have been raised by analysts, AWR has posted better than expected results. Based on operating earnings yield, the company is about fairly valued when compared to all of the companies in our coverage universe. Share price changes over the past year indicates that AWR will perform very poorly over the near term.

**Financial Data**

| (US$ in Thousands) | 6 Mos | 3 Mos | 12/31/2010 | 12/31/2009 | 12/31/2008 | 12/31/2007 | 12/31/2006 | 12/31/2005 |
|---|---|---|---|---|---|---|---|---|
| Earnings Per Share | 2.09 | 1.72 | 1.77 | 1.62 | 1.26 | 1.61 | 1.33 | 1.57 |
| Cash Flow Per Share | 3.06 | 2.93 | 2.89 | 4.02 | 3.59 | 2.98 | 3.04 | 3.25 |
| Tang Book Value Per Share | 20.96 | 20.35 | 20.20 | 19.16 | 17.68 | 16.88 | 15.96 | 15.02 |
| Dividends Per Share | 1.060 | 1.040 | 1.040 | 1.010 | 1.000 | 0.955 | 0.910 | 0.900 |
| Dividend Payout % | 50.72 | 60.47 | 58.76 | 62.35 | 79.37 | 59.32 | 68.42 | 57.32 |
| **Income Statement** | | | | | | | | |
| Total Revenue | 204,136 | 94,307 | 398,942 | 360,973 | 318,718 | 301,370 | 268,629 | 236,197 |
| EBITDA | 66,200 | 27,793 | 111,523 | 103,272 | 86,439 | 96,972 | 83,337 | 82,094 |
| Depn & Amortn | 19,275 | 9,718 | 38,167 | 33,557 | 31,562 | 28,941 | 26,272 | 21,846 |
| Income Before Taxes | 34,610 | 12,468 | 54,126 | 48,356 | 35,384 | 48,820 | 38,762 | 46,649 |
| Income Taxes | 14,927 | 5,513 | 23,035 | 18,825 | 13,379 | 20,790 | 15,681 | 21,945 |
| Net Income | 23,551 | 7,589 | 33,197 | 29,531 | 22,005 | 28,030 | 23,081 | 26,766 |
| Average Shares | 18,738 | 18,778 | 18,736 | 18,188 | 17,394 | 17,177 | 17,101 | 16,809 |
| **Balance Sheet** | | | | | | | | |
| Current Assets | 172,173 | 204,179 | 204,984 | 96,015 | 90,614 | 63,015 | 64,436 | 68,866 |
| Total Assets | 1,197,879 | 1,204,548 | 1,192,035 | 1,113,293 | 1,061,287 | 963,898 | 936,955 | 876,777 |
| Current Liabilities | 124,630 | 195,990 | 178,842 | 99,706 | 137,397 | 94,251 | 85,903 | 77,585 |
| Long-Term Obligations | 340,395 | 299,763 | 299,839 | 305,866 | 266,536 | 267,226 | 267,833 | 268,405 |
| Total Liabilities | 805,070 | 823,651 | 814,494 | 753,863 | 750,784 | 661,769 | 653,221 | 612,683 |
| Stockholders' Equity | 392,809 | 380,897 | 377,541 | 359,430 | 310,503 | 302,129 | 283,734 | 264,094 |
| Shares Outstanding | 18,684 | 18,661 | 18,630 | 18,532 | 17,301 | 17,231 | 17,049 | 16,797 |
| **Statistical Record** | | | | | | | | |
| Return on Assets % | 3.33 | 2.76 | 2.88 | 2.72 | 2.17 | 2.95 | 2.55 | 3.17 |
| Return on Equity % | 10.31 | 8.67 | 9.01 | 8.82 | 7.16 | 9.57 | 8.43 | 10.38 |
| EBITDA Margin % | 32.43 | 29.47 | 27.95 | 28.61 | 27.12 | 32.18 | 31.02 | 34.76 |
| Net Margin % | 11.54 | 8.05 | 8.32 | 8.18 | 6.90 | 9.30 | 8.59 | 11.33 |
| Asset Turnover | 0.36 | 0.35 | 0.35 | 0.33 | 0.31 | 0.32 | 0.30 | 0.28 |
| Current Ratio | 1.38 | 1.04 | 1.15 | 0.96 | 0.66 | 0.67 | 0.75 | 0.89 |
| Debt to Equity | 0.87 | 0.79 | 0.79 | 0.85 | 0.86 | 0.88 | 0.94 | 1.02 |
| Price Range | 38.13-31.60 | 39.06-31.60 | 39.06-31.60 | 38.54-29.78 | 41.91-27.70 | 45.45-33.82 | 42.39-30.68 | 34.06-24.64 |
| P/E Ratio | 18.24-15.12 | 22.71-18.37 | 22.07-17.85 | 23.79-18.38 | 33.26-21.98 | 28.23-21.01 | 31.87-23.07 | 21.69-15.69 |
| Average Yield % | 3.06 | 2.97 | 2.98 | 2.94 | 2.86 | 2.46 | 2.47 | 3.12 |

**Address:** 630 East Foothill Boulevard, San Dimas, CA 91773-1212
**Telephone:** 909-394-3600
**Web Site:** www.aswater.com

**Officers:** Lloyd E. Ross - Chairman Floyd E. Wicks - Vice-Chairman **Transfer Agents:** BNY Mellon Shareowner Services, Pittsburgh, PA

**Investor Contact:** 909-394-3633
**No of Institutions:** 156
**Shares:** 12,081,399 **% Held:** 63.75

# APTARGROUP INC.

| Exchange | Symbol | Price | 52Wk Range | Yield | P/E |
|---|---|---|---|---|---|
| NYS | ATR | $50.48 (8/31/2011) | 54.34-41.65 | 1.74 | 19.12 |

*7 Year Price Score 138.04 *NYSE Composite Index=100 *12 Month Price Score 104.49

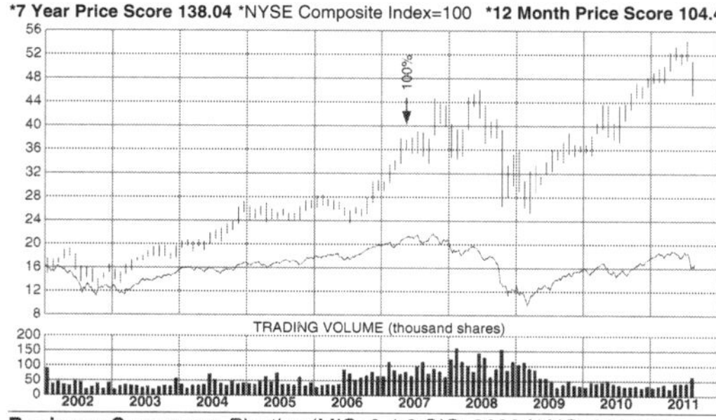


**Interim Earnings (Per Share)**

| Qtr. | Mar | Jun | Sep | Dec |
|---|---|---|---|---|
| 2008 | 0.52 | 0.64 | 0.57 | 0.46 |
| 2009 | 0.38 | 0.41 | 0.48 | 0.52 |
| 2010 | 0.56 | 0.67 | 0.68 | 0.58 |
| 2011 | 0.64 | 0.74 | ... | ... |

**Interim Dividends (Per Share)**

| Amt | Decl | Ex | Rec | Pay |
|---|---|---|---|---|
| 0.18Q | 10/20/2010 | 11/01/2010 | 11/03/2010 | 11/24/2010 |
| 0.18Q | 01/13/2011 | 01/31/2011 | 02/02/2011 | 02/23/2011 |
| 0.18Q | 04/15/2011 | 04/25/2011 | 04/27/2011 | 05/18/2011 |
| 0.22Q | 07/19/2011 | 07/29/2011 | 08/02/2011 | 08/23/2011 |

**Indicated Div: $0.88**

**Valuation Analysis**

| | | | |
|---|---|---|---|
| Forecast EPS | $2.78 (09/02/2011) | | |
| Market Cap | $3.4 Billion | Book Value | $1.4 Billion |
| Price/Book | 2.33 | Price/Sales | 1.50 |

**Dividend Achiever Status**

| | |
|---|---|
| 10 Year Growth Rate | 19.62% |
| Total Years of Dividend Growth | 17 |

**Business Summary:** Plastics (MIC: 8.4.2 SIC: 3089 NAIC: 326199)

AptarGroup is a supplier of a range of dispensing systems for the personal care, fragrance/cosmetic, pharmaceutical, household and food/beverage markets. Co.'s dispensing systems include: pumps, which are finger-actuated dispensing systems that dispense a spray or lotion from non-pressurized containers; closures, which include dispensing closures and non-dispensing closures; and aerosol valves, which dispense product from pressurized containers. Co. operates through three business segments: Beauty & Home, which sells pumps, aerosol valves, accessories and decorative components; Closures, which sells closures; and Pharma, which supplies pumps and metered dose inhaler valves.

**Recent Developments:** For the quarter ended June 30 2011, net income increased 9.7% to US$51.3 million from US$46.8 million in the year-earlier quarter. Revenues were US$614.9 million, up 17.6% from US$522.9 million the year before. Operating income was US$80.2 million versus US$74.1 million in the prior-year quarter, an increase of 8.4%. Direct operating expenses rose 18.6% to US$409.5 million from US$345.2 million in the comparable period the year before. Indirect operating expenses increased 20.7% to US$125.2 million from US$103.7 million in the equivalent prior-year period.

**Prospects:** Our evaluation of AptarGroup Inc. as of Sep. 6, 2011 is the result of our systematic analysis on three basic characteristics: earnings strength, relative valuation, and recent stock price movement. The company has managed to produce a neutral trend in earnings per share over the past 5 quarters. However, while recent estimates for the company have been mixed, ATR has posted results that fell short of analysts expectations. Based on operating earnings yield, the company is about fairly valued when compared to all of the companies in our coverage universe. Share price changes over the past year indicates that ATR will perform poorly over the near term.

**Financial Data**

| (US$ in Thousands) | 6 Mos | 3 Mos | 12/31/2010 | 12/31/2009 | 12/31/2008 | 12/31/2007 | 12/31/2006 | 12/31/2005 |
|---|---|---|---|---|---|---|---|---|
| Earnings Per Share | 2.64 | 2.57 | 2.48 | 1.79 | 2.18 | 1.98 | 1.44 | 1.39 |
| Cash Flow Per Share | 3.47 | 3.40 | 3.89 | 4.34 | 3.97 | 3.98 | 2.83 | 2.76 |
| Tang Book Value Per Share | 18.04 | 17.17 | 15.67 | 15.05 | 13.16 | 12.88 | 10.39 | 8.71 |
| Dividends Per Share | 0.720 | 0.690 | 0.660 | 0.600 | 0.560 | 0.500 | 0.420 | 0.350 |
| Dividend Payout % | 27.27 | 26.85 | 26.61 | 33.52 | 25.69 | 25.25 | 29.27 | 25.27 |
| **Income Statement** | | | | | | | | |
| Total Revenue | 1,191,447 | 576,518 | 2,076,719 | 1,841,616 | 2,071,685 | 1,892,167 | 1,601,385 | 1,380,009 |
| EBITDA | 217,821 | 102,948 | 394,832 | 324,755 | 351,115 | 328,999 | 269,688 | 245,798 |
| Depn & Amortn | 68,519 | 33,605 | 129,339 | 127,709 | 124,884 | 118,946 | 109,037 | 96,693 |
| Income Before Taxes | 143,171 | 66,275 | 254,370 | 183,894 | 220,664 | 199,479 | 147,880 | 139,965 |
| Income Taxes | 47,416 | 21,807 | 80,796 | 59,461 | 67,473 | 60,488 | 45,410 | 41,919 |
| Net Income | 95,766 | 44,477 | 173,481 | 124,623 | 153,495 | 141,739 | 102,896 | 100,034 |
| Average Shares | 69,438 | 69,914 | 69,815 | 69,785 | 70,518 | 71,523 | 71,744 | 72,354 |
| **Balance Sheet** | | | | | | | | |
| Current Assets | 1,205,010 | 1,201,631 | 1,063,983 | 943,491 | 859,749 | 1,003,445 | 762,820 | 605,291 |
| Total Assets | 2,245,682 | 2,201,048 | 2,032,718 | 1,956,193 | 1,831,822 | 1,911,950 | 1,592,012 | 1,357,319 |
| Current Liabilities | 478,612 | 481,110 | 423,322 | 417,315 | 375,027 | 565,189 | 400,185 | 320,762 |
| Long-Term Obligations | 257,036 | 259,572 | 258,773 | 209,616 | 226,888 | 146,711 | 168,877 | 144,541 |
| Total Liabilities | 801,063 | 815,029 | 753,795 | 703,348 | 700,792 | 792,932 | 645,612 | 547,931 |
| Stockholders' Equity | 1,444,619 | 1,386,019 | 1,278,923 | 1,252,845 | 1,131,030 | 1,119,018 | 946,400 | 809,388 |
| Shares Outstanding | 66,700 | 66,900 | 66,800 | 67,300 | 67,600 | 68,200 | 69,200 | 69,800 |
| **Statistical Record** | | | | | | | | |
| Return on Assets % | 9.03 | 8.59 | 8.70 | 6.58 | 8.18 | 8.09 | 6.98 | 7.32 |
| Return on Equity % | 14.13 | 13.66 | 13.70 | 10.46 | 13.61 | 13.72 | 11.72 | 11.89 |
| EBITDA Margin % | 18.28 | 17.86 | 19.01 | 17.63 | 16.95 | 17.39 | 16.84 | 17.81 |
| Net Margin % | 8.04 | 7.71 | 8.35 | 6.77 | 7.41 | 7.49 | 6.43 | 7.25 |
| Asset Turnover | 1.10 | 1.03 | 1.04 | 0.97 | 1.10 | 1.08 | 1.09 | 1.01 |
| Current Ratio | 2.52 | 2.50 | 2.51 | 2.26 | 2.29 | 1.78 | 1.91 | 1.89 |
| Debt to Equity | 0.18 | 0.19 | 0.20 | 0.17 | 0.20 | 0.13 | 0.18 | 0.18 |
| Price Range | 53.40-37.34 | 50.13-37.34 | 48.22-35.03 | 38.89-25.30 | 46.16-26.49 | 44.70-29.10 | 30.88-23.65 | 27.50-23.72 |
| P/E Ratio | 20.23-14.14 | 19.51-14.53 | 19.44-14.13 | 21.73-14.13 | 21.17-12.15 | 22.58-14.70 | 21.44-16.42 | 19.78-17.06 |
| Average Yield % | 1.53 | 1.55 | 1.58 | 1.80 | 1.47 | 1.36 | 1.56 | 1.38 |

**Address:** 475 West Terra Cotta Avenue, Suite E, Crystal Lake, IL 60014
**Telephone:** 815-477-0424
**Web Site:** www.aptar.com

**Officers:** King W. Harris - Chairman Peter H. Pfeiffer - President, Chief Executive Officer **Transfer Agents:** Wells Fargo Shareowner Services, South St. Paul, MN

**No of Institutions:** 323
**Shares:** 73,804,896 **% Held:** 82.07

# AQUA AMERICA INC

| Exchange | Symbol | Price | 52Wk Range | Yield | P/E |
|---|---|---|---|---|---|
| NYS | WTR | $22.08 (8/31/2011) | 23.65-19.28 | 2.99 | 21.65 |

***7 Year Price Score 103.91** *NYSE Composite Index=100 ***12 Month Price Score 98.46**

**Interim Earnings (Per Share)**

| Qtr. | Mar | Jun | Sep | Dec |
|---|---|---|---|---|
| 2008 | 0.11 | 0.17 | 0.26 | 0.19 |
| 2009 | 0.14 | 0.19 | 0.25 | 0.20 |
| 2010 | 0.16 | 0.22 | 0.32 | 0.21 |
| 2011 | 0.22 | 0.27 | ... | ... |

**Interim Dividends (Per Share)**

| Amt | Decl | Ex | Rec | Pay |
|---|---|---|---|---|
| 0.155Q | 02/01/2011 | 02/15/2011 | 02/17/2011 | 03/01/2011 |
| 0.155Q | 05/02/2011 | 05/13/2011 | 05/17/2011 | 06/01/2011 |
| 0.155Q | 08/02/2011 | 08/15/2011 | 08/17/2011 | 09/01/2011 |
| 0.165Q | 08/02/2011 | 11/15/2011 | 11/17/2011 | 12/01/2011 |

**Indicated Div: $0.66 (Div. Reinv. Plan)**

**Valuation Analysis**

| | | | |
|---|---|---|---|
| Forecast EPS | $1.06 (09/03/2011) | | |
| Market Cap | $3.1 Billion | Book Value | $1.2 Billion |
| Price/Book | 2.52 | Price/Sales | 4.09 |

**Dividend Achiever Status**

| | |
|---|---|
| 10 Year Growth Rate | 6.90% |
| Total Years of Dividend Growth | 19 |

**Business Summary:** Water Utilities (MIC: 3.2.1 SIC: 4941 NAIC: 221310)

Aqua America is the holding company for regulated utilities providing water or wastewater services in Pennsylvania, Texas, North Carolina, Ohio, Illinois, New Jersey, New York, Florida, Indiana, Virginia, Maine, Missouri, and Georgia. Co.'s subsidiary, Aqua Pennsylvania, Inc., provides water or wastewater services in the suburban areas in counties north and west of the City of Philadelphia and in 25 other counties in Pennsylvania. Co.'s other subsidiaries provide similar services in 12 other states. In addition, Co. provides water and wastewater services through operating and maintenance contracts with municipal authorities and other parties close to its utility companies' service areas.

**Recent Developments:** For the quarter ended June 30 2011, net income increased 25.9% to US$37.6 million from US$29.9 million in the year-earlier quarter. Revenues were US$188.2 million, up 5.5% from US$178.4 million the year before. Operating income was US$74.8 million versus US$66.1 million in the prior-year quarter, an increase of 13.3%. Direct operating expenses rose 1.6% to US$70.4 million from US$69.3 million in the comparable period the year before. Indirect operating expenses decreased 0.2% to US$43.0 million from US$43.1 million in the equivalent prior-year period.

**Prospects:** Our evaluation of Aqua America Inc. as of Sep. 6, 2011 is the result of our systematic analysis on three basic characteristics: earnings strength, relative valuation, and recent stock price movement. The company has managed to produce a neutral trend in earnings per share over the past 5 quarters and while recent estimates for the company have been raised by analysts, WTR has posted better than expected results. Based on operating earnings yield, the company is about fairly valued when compared to all of the companies in our coverage universe. Share price changes over the past year indicates that WTR will perform very poorly over the near term.

**Financial Data**

| (US$ in Thousands) | 6 Mos | 3 Mos | 12/31/2010 | 12/31/2009 | 12/31/2008 | 12/31/2007 | 12/31/2006 | 12/31/2005 |
|---|---|---|---|---|---|---|---|---|
| Earnings Per Share | 1.02 | 0.97 | 0.90 | 0.77 | 0.73 | 0.71 | 0.70 | 0.71 |
| Cash Flow Per Share | 2.17 | 1.98 | 1.93 | 1.90 | 1.64 | 1.46 | 1.31 | 1.57 |
| Tang Book Value Per Share | 8.46 | 8.33 | 8.23 | 7.81 | 7.52 | 7.04 | 6.79 | 6.14 |
| Dividends Per Share | 0.610 | 0.600 | 0.590 | 0.550 | 0.510 | 0.480 | 0.444 | 0.399 |
| Dividend Payout % | 59.80 | 61.86 | 65.56 | 71.43 | 69.86 | 67.61 | 63.40 | 56.25 |
| **Income Statement** | | | | | | | | |
| Total Revenue | 359,553 | 171,324 | 726,072 | 670,539 | 626,972 | 602,499 | 533,491 | 496,779 |
| EBITDA | 194,861 | 90,376 | 400,788 | 355,741 | 325,374 | 305,641 | 285,723 | 265,619 |
| Depn & Amortn | 54,871 | 27,293 | 121,067 | 114,939 | 94,300 | 83,178 | 75,041 | 65,488 |
| Income Before Taxes | 99,941 | 43,140 | 204,069 | 172,195 | 162,502 | 155,542 | 152,250 | 148,069 |
| Income Taxes | 32,000 | 12,789 | 80,094 | 67,842 | 64,584 | 60,528 | 60,246 | 56,913 |
| Net Income | 67,941 | 30,351 | 123,975 | 104,353 | 97,918 | 95,014 | 92,004 | 91,156 |
| Average Shares | 138,781 | 138,384 | 137,296 | 136,129 | 134,705 | 133,602 | 131,774 | 129,206 |
| **Balance Sheet** | | | | | | | | |
| Current Assets | 178,029 | 156,893 | 145,419 | 121,571 | 121,041 | 115,511 | 134,700 | 89,956 |
| Total Assets | 4,193,182 | 4,112,326 | 4,072,466 | 3,762,597 | 3,485,022 | 3,226,912 | 2,877,903 | 2,626,725 |
| Current Liabilities | 306,882 | 209,294 | 223,715 | 201,007 | 193,171 | 183,212 | 255,611 | 263,339 |
| Long-Term Obligations | 1,468,525 | 1,530,092 | 1,531,976 | 1,386,557 | 1,248,104 | 1,215,053 | 951,660 | 878,438 |
| Total Liabilities | 2,981,626 | 2,920,210 | 2,898,212 | 2,653,693 | 2,426,576 | 2,250,614 | 1,956,273 | 1,814,802 |
| Stockholders' Equity | 1,211,556 | 1,192,116 | 1,174,254 | 1,108,904 | 1,058,446 | 976,298 | 921,630 | 811,923 |
| Shares Outstanding | 138,402 | 138,208 | 137,775 | 136,486 | 135,369 | 133,400 | 132,325 | 128,970 |
| **Statistical Record** | | | | | | | | |
| Return on Assets % | 3.49 | 3.37 | 3.16 | 2.88 | 2.91 | 3.11 | 3.34 | 3.67 |
| Return on Equity % | 12.01 | 11.51 | 10.86 | 9.63 | 9.60 | 10.01 | 10.61 | 11.68 |
| EBITDA Margin % | 54.20 | 52.75 | 55.20 | 53.05 | 51.90 | 50.73 | 53.56 | 53.47 |
| Net Margin % | 18.90 | 17.72 | 17.07 | 15.56 | 15.62 | 15.77 | 17.25 | 18.35 |
| Asset Turnover | 0.19 | 0.19 | 0.19 | 0.19 | 0.19 | 0.20 | 0.19 | 0.20 |
| Current Ratio | 0.58 | 0.75 | 0.65 | 0.60 | 0.63 | 0.63 | 0.53 | 0.34 |
| Debt to Equity | 1.21 | 1.28 | 1.30 | 1.25 | 1.18 | 1.24 | 1.03 | 1.08 |
| Price Range | 23.65-17.48 | 23.65-16.73 | 22.89-16.59 | 21.19-15.45 | 21.93-14.66 | 26.44-21.20 | 29.59-20.61 | 28.97-17.61 |
| P/E Ratio | 23.19-17.14 | 24.38-17.25 | 25.43-18.43 | 27.52-20.06 | 30.04-20.08 | 37.24-29.86 | 42.27-29.44 | 40.80-24.80 |
| Average Yield % | 2.84 | 2.94 | 3.10 | 3.10 | 2.81 | 2.11 | 1.82 | 1.77 |

**Address:** 762 W. Lancaster Avenue, Bryn Mawr, PA 19010-3489
**Telephone:** 610-527-8000
**Web Site:** www.aquaamerica.com

**Officers:** Nicholas DeBenedictis - Chairman, President, Chief Executive Officer Christopher H. Franklin - Senior Vice President, Region Officer
**Transfer Agents:**Computershare Trust Company, N.A., Providence, RI

**No of Institutions:** 317
**Shares:** 54,860,916 **% Held:** 35.51

# ARCHER DANIELS MIDLAND CO.

| Exchange | Symbol | Price | 52Wk Range | Yield | P/E |
|---|---|---|---|---|---|
| NYS | ADM | $28.48 (8/31/2011) | 37.65-26.17 | 2.25 | 9.10 |

***7 Year Price Score 104.60** *NYSE Composite Index=100 ***12 Month Price Score 92.13**

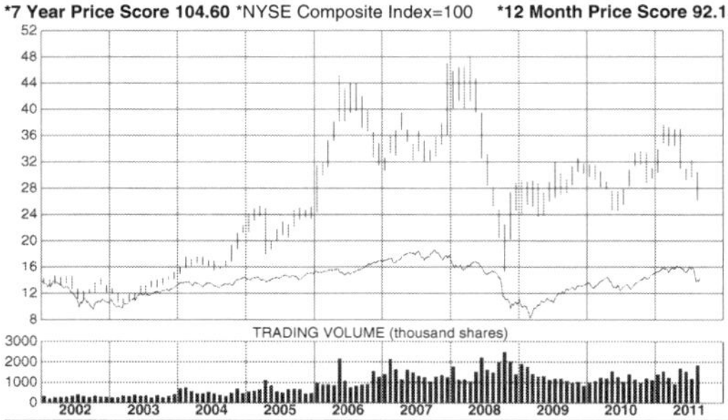

**Interim Earnings (Per Share)**

| Qtr. | Sep | Dec | Mar | Jun |
|---|---|---|---|---|
| 2006-07 | 0.61 | 0.67 | 0.56 | 1.47 |
| 2007-08 | 0.68 | 0.73 | 0.80 | 0.58 |
| 2008-09 | 1.63 | 0.91 | 0.01 | 0.10 |
| 2009-10 | 0.77 | 0.88 | 0.65 | 0.70 |
| 2010-11 | 0.54 | 1.14 | 0.86 | 0.58 |

**Interim Dividends (Per Share)**

| Amt | Decl | Ex | Rec | Pay |
|---|---|---|---|---|
| 0.15Q | 11/04/2010 | 11/16/2010 | 11/18/2010 | 12/09/2010 |
| 0.16Q | 02/02/2011 | 02/15/2011 | 02/17/2011 | 03/10/2011 |
| 0.16Q | 05/05/2011 | 05/17/2011 | 05/19/2011 | 06/09/2011 |
| 0.16Q | 08/04/2011 | 08/16/2011 | 08/18/2011 | 09/08/2011 |

**Indicated Div: $0.64 (Div. Reinv. Plan)**

**Valuation Analysis**

Forecast EPS $3.14 (09/02/2011)

| Market Cap | $19.3 Billion | Book Value | $18.8 Billion |
|---|---|---|---|
| Price/Book | 1.02 | Price/Sales | 0.24 |

**Dividend Achiever Status**

| | |
|---|---|
| **10 Year Growth Rate** | 12.02% |
| **Total Years of Dividend Growth** | 36 |

**Business Summary:** Food (MIC: 1.2.1 SIC: 2041 NAIC: 311211)

Archer Daniels Midland is a processor of oilseeds, corn, wheat, cocoa, and other agricultural commodities and is a manufacturer of vegetable oil, protein meal, corn sweeteners, flour, biodiesel, ethanol, and other food and feed ingredients. Co. has a grain elevator and transportation network to procure, store, clean, and transport agricultural commodities, such as oilseeds, corn, wheat, milo, and barley. Co. operates through three business segments: Oilseeds Processing, which is engaged in processing oilseeds; Corn Processing, which is engaged in corn wet milling and dry milling activities; and Agricultural Services, which buys, stores, cleans, and transports agricultural commodities.

**Recent Developments:** For the year ended June 30 2011, net income increased 5.2% to US$2.02 billion from US$1.92 billion in the prior year. Revenues were US$80.68 billion, up 30.8% from US$61.68 billion the year before. Direct operating expenses rose 32.0% to US$76.38 billion from US$57.84 billion in the comparable period the year before. Indirect operating expenses increased 15.2% to US$1.61 billion from US$1.40 billion in the equivalent prior-year period.

**Prospects:** Our evaluation of Archer Daniels Midland Co. as of Sep. 6, 2011 is the result of our systematic analysis on three basic characteristics: earnings strength, relative valuation, and recent stock price movement. The company has generated a negative trend in earnings per share over the past 5 quarters. However, while recent estimates for the company have been lowered by analysts, ADM has posted better than expected results. Based on operating earnings yield, the company is undervalued when compared to all of the companies in our coverage universe. Share price changes over the past year indicates that ADM will perform very poorly over the near term.

**Financial Data**

| (US$ in Thousands) | 06/30/2011 | 06/30/2010 | 06/30/2009 | 06/30/2008 | 06/30/2007 | 06/30/2006 | 06/30/2005 | 06/30/2004 |
|---|---|---|---|---|---|---|---|---|
| Earnings Per Share | 3.13 | 3.00 | 2.65 | 2.79 | 3.30 | 2.00 | 1.59 | 0.76 |
| Cash Flow Per Share | (3.64) | 4.17 | 8.31 | (4.96) | 0.47 | 2.11 | 3.25 | 0.05 |
| Tang Book Value Per Share | 26.93 | 22.04 | 20.20 | 20.16 | 17.80 | 14.47 | 12.47 | 11.31 |
| Dividends Per Share | 0.620 | 0.580 | 0.540 | 0.490 | 0.430 | 0.370 | 0.320 | 0.270 |
| Dividend Payout % | 19.81 | 19.33 | 20.38 | 17.56 | 13.03 | 18.50 | 20.13 | 35.53 |
| **Income Statement** | | | | | | | | |
| Total Revenue | 80,676,000 | 61,682,000 | 69,207,000 | 69,816,000 | 44,018,000 | 36,596,111 | 35,943,810 | 36,151,394 |
| EBITDA | 3,696,000 | 3,358,000 | 3,549,000 | 3,407,000 | 3,995,000 | 2,702,805 | 2,278,742 | 1,564,899 |
| Depn & Amortn | 877,000 | 912,000 | 730,000 | 721,000 | 701,000 | 656,714 | 664,652 | 685,613 |
| Income Before Taxes | 2,473,000 | 2,024,000 | 2,389,000 | 2,209,000 | 2,860,000 | 1,680,911 | 1,287,510 | 537,295 |
| Income Taxes | 997,000 | 666,000 | 827,000 | 822,000 | 992,000 | 543,180 | 471,990 | 223,301 |
| Net Income | 2,036,000 | 1,930,000 | 1,707,000 | 1,802,000 | 2,162,000 | 1,312,070 | 1,044,385 | 494,710 |
| Average Shares | 654,000 | 644,000 | 644,000 | 646,000 | 656,000 | 656,287 | 656,123 | 647,698 |
| **Balance Sheet** | | | | | | | | |
| Current Assets | 27,504,000 | 18,134,000 | 19,408,000 | 25,455,000 | 15,122,000 | 11,826,277 | 9,710,701 | 10,338,996 |
| Total Assets | 42,193,000 | 31,548,000 | 31,585,000 | 37,056,000 | 25,118,000 | 21,269,030 | 18,598,105 | 19,368,821 |
| Current Liabilities | 13,218,000 | 8,573,000 | 8,885,000 | 14,621,000 | 7,868,000 | 6,164,767 | 5,366,864 | 6,750,237 |
| Long-Term Obligations | 8,266,000 | 6,830,000 | 7,800,000 | 7,690,000 | 4,752,000 | 4,050,323 | 3,530,140 | 3,739,875 |
| Total Liabilities | 23,385,000 | 16,939,000 | 18,086,000 | 23,566,000 | 13,865,000 | 11,462,150 | 10,164,633 | 11,670,605 |
| Stockholders' Equity | 18,808,000 | 14,609,000 | 13,499,000 | 13,490,000 | 11,253,000 | 9,806,880 | 8,433,472 | 7,698,216 |
| Shares Outstanding | 676,000 | 639,000 | 642,000 | 644,000 | 614,400 | 655,685 | 650,399 | 650,748 |
| **Statistical Record** | | | | | | | | |
| Return on Assets % | 5.52 | 6.11 | 4.97 | 5.78 | 9.32 | 6.58 | 5.50 | 2.70 |
| Return on Equity % | 12.19 | 13.73 | 12.65 | 14.53 | 20.53 | 14.39 | 12.95 | 6.68 |
| EBITDA Margin % | 4.58 | 5.44 | 5.13 | 4.88 | 9.08 | 7.39 | 6.34 | 4.33 |
| Net Margin % | 2.52 | 3.13 | 2.47 | 2.58 | 4.91 | 3.59 | 2.91 | 1.37 |
| Asset Turnover | 2.19 | 1.95 | 2.02 | 2.24 | 1.90 | 1.84 | 1.89 | 1.97 |
| Current Ratio | 2.08 | 2.12 | 2.18 | 1.74 | 1.92 | 1.92 | 1.81 | 1.53 |
| Debt to Equity | 0.44 | 0.47 | 0.58 | 0.57 | 0.42 | 0.41 | 0.42 | 0.49 |
| Price Range | 37.65-25.50 | 32.61-24.51 | 33.75-15.29 | 48.18-32.09 | 44.00-30.70 | 45.25-20.56 | 25.32-15.43 | 17.59-12.08 |
| P/E Ratio | 12.03-8.15 | 10.87-8.17 | 12.74-5.77 | 17.27-11.50 | 13.33-9.30 | 22.63-10.28 | 15.92-9.70 | 23.14-15.89 |
| Average Yield % | 1.93 | 2.00 | 2.08 | 1.26 | 1.18 | 1.27 | 1.60 | 1.78 |

**Address:** 4666 Faries Parkway, P.O. Box 1470, Decatur, IL 62525
**Telephone:** 217-424-5200
**Web Site:** www.admworld.com

**Officers:** Patricia A. Woertz - Chairman, President, Chief Executive Officer John D. Rice - Vice-Chairman
**Transfer Agents:** Hickory Point Bank & Trust, fsb, Decatur, IL

**Investor Contact:** 217-424-4647
**No of Institutions:** 847
**Shares:** 570,960,320 **% Held:** 72.50

# AT&T INC

| Exchange | Symbol | Price | 52Wk Range | Yield | P/E |
|---|---|---|---|---|---|
| NYS | T | $28.48 (8/31/2011) | 31.86-27.03 | 6.04 | 8.30 |

*7 Year Price Score 98.02 *NYSE Composite Index=100 *12 Month Price Score 101.69

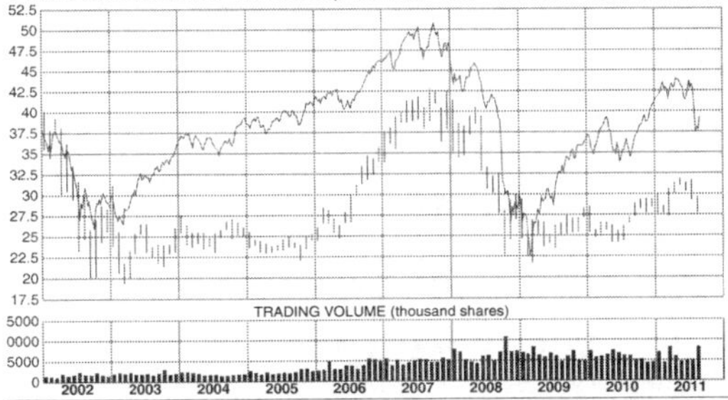


**Interim Earnings (Per Share)**

| Qtr. | Mar | Jun | Sep | Dec |
|---|---|---|---|---|
| 2008 | 0.57 | 0.63 | 0.55 | 0.41 |
| 2009 | 0.53 | 0.54 | 0.54 | 0.51 |
| 2010 | 0.42 | 0.68 | 2.08 | 0.18 |
| 2011 | 0.57 | 0.60 | ... | ... |

**Interim Dividends (Per Share)**

| Amt | Decl | Ex | Rec | Pay |
|---|---|---|---|---|
| 0.42Q | 09/24/2010 | 10/06/2010 | 10/08/2010 | 11/01/2010 |
| 0.43Q | 12/17/2010 | 01/06/2011 | 01/10/2011 | 02/01/2011 |
| 0.43Q | 03/25/2011 | 04/06/2011 | 04/08/2011 | 05/02/2011 |
| 0.43Q | 06/24/2011 | 07/06/2011 | 07/08/2011 | 08/01/2011 |

**Indicated Div: $1.72 (Div. Reinv. Plan)**

**Valuation Analysis**

Forecast EPS $2.38 (09/05/2011)

Market Cap $168.7 Billion Book Value $113.8 Billion

Price/Book 1.48 Price/Sales 1.34

**Dividend Achiever Status**

**10 Year Growth Rate** 5.09%

**Total Years of Dividend Growth** 26

**Business Summary:** Services (MIC: 6.1.2 SIC: 4813 NAIC: 511140)

AT&T is a holding company. Through its subsidiaries and affiliates, Co. is a provider of telecommunications services. Co. has four segments: Wireless, which uses its nationwide network to provide wireless voice and data communications services; Wireline, which uses its regional, national and global network to provide landline voice and data communications services, AT&T U-versesm TV, broadband and voice services, and managed networking to business customers; Advertising Solutions, which publishes Yellow and White Pages directories and sells directory advertising, Internet-based advertising and local search; and Other, which includes customer information services such as operator services.

**Recent Developments:** For the quarter ended June 30 2011, income from continuing operations decreased 10.5% to US$3.66 billion from US$4.09 billion in the year-earlier quarter. Net income decreased 10.4% to US$3.66 billion from US$4.08 billion in the year-earlier quarter. Revenues were US$31.50 billion, up 2.2% from US$30.81 billion the year before. Operating income was US$6.17 billion versus US$6.08 billion in the prior-year quarter, an increase of 1.3%. Direct operating expenses rose 7.1% to US$13.33 billion from US$12.45 billion in the comparable period the year before. Indirect operating expenses decreased 2.2% to US$12.00 billion from US$12.27 billion in the equivalent prior-year period.

**Prospects:** Our evaluation of AT&T Inc. as of Sep. 6, 2011 is the result of our systematic analysis on three basic characteristics: earnings strength, relative valuation, and recent stock price movement. The company has managed to produce a neutral trend in earnings per share over the past 5 quarters. However, while recent estimates for the company have been mixed, T has posted better than expected results. Based on operating earnings yield, the company is undervalued when compared to all of the companies in our coverage universe. Share price changes over the past year indicates that T will perform poorly over the near term.

**Financial Data**

| (US$ in Thousands) | 6 Mos | 3 Mos | 12/31/2010 | 12/31/2009 | 12/31/2008 | 12/31/2007 | 12/31/2006 | 12/31/2005 |
|---|---|---|---|---|---|---|---|---|
| Earnings Per Share | 3.43 | 3.51 | 3.35 | 2.12 | 2.16 | 1.94 | 1.89 | 1.42 |
| Cash Flow Per Share | 6.06 | 5.99 | 5.92 | 5.84 | 5.66 | 5.56 | 4.02 | 3.85 |
| Tang Book Value Per Share | N.M. | N.M. | N.M. | N.M. | N.M. | N.M. | N.M. | 8.29 |
| Dividends Per Share | 1.700 | 1.690 | 1.680 | 1.640 | 1.600 | 1.420 | 1.330 | 1.290 |
| Dividend Payout % | 49.56 | 48.15 | 50.15 | 77.36 | 74.07 | 73.20 | 70.37 | 90.85 |
| **Income Statement** | | | | | | | | |
| Total Revenue | 62,742,000 | 31,247,000 | 124,280,000 | 123,018,000 | 124,028,000 | 118,928,000 | 63,055,000 | 43,862,000 |
| EBITDA | 21,245,000 | 10,451,000 | 36,872,000 | 37,603,000 | 37,787,000 | 36,644,000 | 19,178,000 | 13,554,000 |
| Depn & Amortn | 9,186,000 | 4,584,000 | 16,402,000 | 15,959,000 | 15,313,000 | 15,625,000 | 8,874,000 | 7,372,000 |
| Income Before Taxes | 10,365,000 | 5,021,000 | 17,476,000 | 18,265,000 | 19,084,000 | 17,512,000 | 8,838,000 | 5,109,000 |
| Income Taxes | 3,695,000 | 1,802,000 | (1,162,000) | 6,156,000 | 7,036,000 | 6,253,000 | 3,525,000 | 932,000 |
| Net Income | 6,999,000 | 3,408,000 | 19,864,000 | 12,535,000 | 12,867,000 | 11,951,000 | 7,356,000 | 4,786,000 |
| Average Shares | 5,952,999 | 5,944,999 | 5,937,999 | 5,923,999 | 5,957,999 | 6,169,999 | 3,902,000 | 3,379,000 |
| **Balance Sheet** | | | | | | | | |
| Current Assets | 22,239,000 | 19,737,000 | 19,951,000 | 24,334,000 | 22,556,000 | 24,686,000 | 25,553,000 | 14,654,000 |
| Total Assets | 272,014,000 | 268,085,000 | 268,488,000 | 268,752,000 | 265,245,000 | 275,644,000 | 270,634,000 | 145,632,000 |
| Current Liabilities | 33,537,000 | 33,254,000 | 33,951,000 | 36,705,000 | 42,290,000 | 39,274,000 | 40,482,000 | 25,418,000 |
| Long-Term Obligations | 58,663,000 | 58,126,000 | 58,971,000 | 64,720,000 | 60,872,000 | 57,255,000 | 50,063,000 | 26,115,000 |
| Total Liabilities | 158,211,000 | 155,541,000 | 156,841,000 | 166,852,000 | 168,898,000 | 160,277,000 | 155,094,000 | 90,942,000 |
| Stockholders' Equity | 113,803,000 | 112,544,000 | 111,647,000 | 101,900,000 | 96,347,000 | 115,367,000 | 115,540,000 | 54,690,000 |
| Shares Outstanding | 5,925,039 | 5,918,265 | 5,911,086 | 5,901,930 | 5,893,008 | 6,043,544 | 6,238,745 | 3,876,884 |
| **Statistical Record** | | | | | | | | |
| Return on Assets % | 7.55 | 7.79 | 7.39 | 4.69 | 4.74 | 4.38 | 3.53 | 3.76 |
| Return on Equity % | 18.78 | 19.39 | 18.60 | 12.65 | 12.12 | 10.35 | 8.64 | 10.06 |
| EBITDA Margin % | 33.86 | 33.45 | 29.67 | 30.57 | 30.47 | 30.81 | 30.41 | 30.90 |
| Net Margin % | 11.16 | 10.91 | 15.98 | 10.19 | 10.37 | 10.05 | 11.67 | 10.91 |
| Asset Turnover | 0.47 | 0.47 | 0.46 | 0.46 | 0.46 | 0.44 | 0.30 | 0.34 |
| Current Ratio | 0.66 | 0.59 | 0.59 | 0.66 | 0.53 | 0.63 | 0.63 | 0.58 |
| Debt to Equity | 0.52 | 0.52 | 0.53 | 0.64 | 0.63 | 0.50 | 0.43 | 0.48 |
| Price Range | 31.86-24.19 | 30.71-24.13 | 29.44-24.13 | 29.42-21.72 | 41.56-22.42 | 42.83-33.81 | 35.75-24.45 | 25.77-22.10 |
| P/E Ratio | 9.29-7.05 | 8.75-6.87 | 8.79-7.20 | 13.88-10.25 | 19.24-10.38 | 22.08-17.43 | 18.92-12.94 | 18.15-15.56 |
| Average Yield % | 5.94 | 6.19 | 6.30 | 6.40 | 4.81 | 3.62 | 4.54 | 5.38 |


**Address:** 208 S. Akard St., Dallas, TX 75202
**Telephone:** 210-821-4105
**Web Site:** www.att.com


**Officers:** Randall L. Stephenson - Chairman, President, Chief Executive Officer William A. Blase - Senior Executive Vice President **Transfer Agents:** Computershare Trust Company, N.A., Providence, RI

**Investor Contact:** 210-351-3990
**No of Institutions:** 1751
**Shares:** 3,684,522,240 **% Held:** N/A

# ATLANTIC TELE-NETWORK, INC.

| Exchange | Symbol | Price | 52Wk Range | Yield | P/E |
|---|---|---|---|---|---|
| NMS | ATNI | $33.20 (8/31/2011) | 54.54-30.83 | 2.65 | 32.23 |

*7 Year Price Score 131.47 *NYSE Composite Index=100 *12 Month Price Score 95.02

**Interim Earnings (Per Share)**

| Qtr. | Mar | Jun | Sep | Dec |
|---|---|---|---|---|
| 2008 | 0.51 | 0.67 | 0.66 | 0.43 |
| 2009 | 0.58 | 0.63 | 0.78 | 0.34 |
| 2010 | 0.26 | 1.60 | 0.41 | 0.21 |
| 2011 | 0.29 | 0.12 | ... | ... |

**Interim Dividends (Per Share)**

| Amt | Decl | Ex | Rec | Pay |
|---|---|---|---|---|
| 0.22Q | 09/27/2010 | 10/04/2010 | 10/06/2010 | 10/12/2010 |
| 0.22Q | 12/10/2010 | 12/29/2010 | 12/31/2010 | 01/10/2011 |
| 0.22Q | 03/18/2011 | 03/29/2011 | 03/31/2011 | 04/11/2011 |
| 0.22Q | 06/16/2011 | 06/28/2011 | 06/30/2011 | 07/11/2011 |

**Indicated Div: $0.88**

**Valuation Analysis**

Forecast EPS $1.41 (09/02/2011)

| Market Cap | $511.3 Million | Book Value | $288.1 Million |
|---|---|---|---|
| Price/Book | 1.77 | Price/Sales | 0.65 |

**Dividend Achiever Status**

| | |
|---|---|
| **10 Year Growth Rate** | 10.22% |
| **Total Years of Dividend Growth** | 11 |

**Business Summary:** Services (MIC: 6.1.2 SIC: 4813 NAIC: 517110)

Atlantic Tele-Network is engaged in providing wireless and wireline in North America, Bermuda and the Caribbean. Through its operating subsidiaries, Co. provides the following services: wireless, including its wireless voice and data roaming services provided to national, regional and local wireless carriers in rural markets in the Southwest and Midwest U.S., Guyana, Bermuda and the Caribbean; and wireline, which includes local telephone and data services in Guyana and the mainland U.S. Co. also provides facilities-based integrated voice and data communications services to enterprise and residential customers in New England, and wholesale transport services in New York State.

**Recent Developments:** For the quarter ended June 30 2011, net income decreased 94.7% to US$1.3 million from US$25.0 million in the year-earlier quarter. Revenues were US$193.8 million, up 17.6% from US$164.7 million the year before. Operating income was US$6.3 million versus US$7.8 million in the prior-year quarter, a decrease of 19.3%. Direct operating expenses rose 22.7% to US$76.7 million from US$62.5 million in the comparable period the year before. Indirect operating expenses increased 17.4% to US$110.8 million from US$94.4 million in the equivalent prior-year period.

**Prospects:** Our evaluation of Atlantic Tele-Network Inc. as of Sep. 6, 2011 is the result of our systematic analysis on three basic characteristics: earnings strength, relative valuation, and recent stock price movement. The company has produced a positive trend in earnings per share over the past 5 quarters and while recent estimates for the company have been raised by analysts, ATNI has posted better than expected results. Based on operating earnings yield, the company is overvalued when compared to all of the companies in our coverage universe. Share price changes over the past year indicates that ATNI will perform poorly over the near term.

**Financial Data**

| (US$ in Thousands) | 6 Mos | 3 Mos | 12/31/2010 | 12/31/2009 | 12/31/2008 | 12/31/2007 | 12/31/2006 | 12/31/2005 |
|---|---|---|---|---|---|---|---|---|
| Earnings Per Share | 1.03 | 2.51 | 2.48 | 2.32 | 2.28 | 2.48 | 1.72 | 1.09 |
| Cash Flow Per Share | 5.53 | 7.39 | 6.71 | 6.08 | 4.48 | 4.56 | 3.78 | 2.46 |
| Tang Book Value Per Share | 6.09 | 6.60 | 6.24 | 11.73 | 10.02 | 10.02 | 7.85 | 6.05 |
| Dividends Per Share | 0.880 | 0.860 | 0.840 | 0.760 | 0.680 | 0.600 | 0.520 | 0.460 |
| Dividend Payout % | 85.44 | 34.26 | 33.87 | 32.76 | 29.82 | 24.19 | 30.23 | 42.20 |
| **Income Statement** | | | | | | | | |
| Total Revenue | 381,908 | 188,154 | 619,145 | 241,703 | 207,341 | 186,741 | 155,358 | 102,281 |
| EBITDA | 18,139 | 11,376 | 142,350 | 109,396 | 101,661 | 94,898 | 68,441 | 53,472 |
| Depn & Amortn | 873 | 391 | 76,500 | 39,100 | 31,700 | 25,500 | 14,730 | 17,110 |
| Income Before Taxes | 9,424 | 7,293 | 56,445 | 67,743 | 68,587 | 69,570 | 51,564 | 35,674 |
| Income Taxes | 4,882 | 3,830 | 19,606 | 31,160 | 29,551 | 28,929 | 25,538 | 20,801 |
| Net Income | 6,312 | 4,497 | 38,454 | 35,539 | 34,798 | 37,940 | 23,500 | 13,598 |
| Average Shares | 15,497 | 15,485 | 15,483 | 15,337 | 15,255 | 15,304 | 13,672 | 12,488 |
| **Balance Sheet** | | | | | | | | |
| Current Assets | 170,609 | 147,846 | 154,289 | 136,515 | 131,321 | 118,375 | 91,139 | 48,672 |
| Total Assets | 863,843 | 813,898 | 828,196 | 446,554 | 419,821 | 344,626 | 302,614 | 233,831 |
| Current Liabilities | 140,662 | 118,837 | 138,302 | 56,887 | 47,912 | 44,879 | 35,041 | 34,127 |
| Long-Term Obligations | 289,691 | 277,492 | 272,049 | 69,551 | 73,311 | 50,000 | 50,000 | 55,585 |
| Total Liabilities | 575,782 | 527,150 | 544,428 | 190,808 | 190,948 | 135,655 | 123,844 | 118,121 |
| Stockholders' Equity | 288,061 | 286,748 | 283,768 | 255,746 | 228,873 | 208,971 | 178,770 | 115,710 |
| Shares Outstanding | 15,400 | 15,392 | 15,383 | 15,233 | 15,228 | 15,220 | 15,170 | 12,463 |
| **Statistical Record** | | | | | | | | |
| Return on Assets % | 1.94 | 6.20 | 6.03 | 8.20 | 9.08 | 11.72 | 8.76 | 6.63 |
| Return on Equity % | 5.64 | 14.26 | 14.26 | 14.67 | 15.85 | 19.57 | 15.96 | 12.15 |
| EBITDA Margin % | 4.75 | 6.05 | 22.99 | 45.26 | 49.03 | 50.82 | 44.05 | 52.28 |
| Net Margin % | 1.65 | 2.39 | 6.21 | 14.70 | 16.78 | 20.32 | 15.13 | 13.29 |
| Asset Turnover | 0.95 | 1.20 | 0.97 | 0.56 | 0.54 | 0.58 | 0.58 | 0.50 |
| Current Ratio | 1.21 | 1.24 | 1.12 | 2.40 | 2.74 | 2.64 | 2.60 | 1.43 |
| Debt to Equity | 1.01 | 0.97 | 0.96 | 0.27 | 0.32 | 0.24 | 0.28 | 0.48 |
| Price Range | 54.54-30.83 | 58.22-30.83 | 58.22-32.51 | 57.28-13.95 | 34.93-18.46 | 38.43-23.73 | 29.96-15.30 | 17.40-11.14 |
| P/E Ratio | 52.95-29.93 | 23.20-12.28 | 23.48-13.11 | 24.69-6.01 | 15.32-8.10 | 15.50-9.57 | 17.42-8.90 | 15.96-10.22 |
| Average Yield % | 2.20 | 2.50 | 1.93 | 2.11 | 2.55 | 1.93 | 2.46 | 3.47 |

**Address:** 600 Cummings Center, Beverly, MA 01915
**Telephone:** 978-619-1300
**Web Site:** www.atni.com

**Officers:** Cornelius B. Prior - Chairman Michael T. Prior - President, Chief Executive Officer **Transfer Agents:** Bank of New York, New York, NY

**No of Institutions:** 114
**Shares:** 8,736,944 **% Held:** 56.64

# ATMOS ENERGY CORP.

| Exchange | Symbol | Price | 52Wk Range | Yield | P/E |
|---|---|---|---|---|---|
| NYS | ATO | $33.54 (8/31/2011) | 34.98-28.30 | 4.05 | 14.78 |

*7 Year Price Score 111.95 *NYSE Composite Index=100 *12 Month Price Score 102.60

**Interim Earnings (Per Share)**

| Qtr. | Dec | Mar | Jun | Sep |
|---|---|---|---|---|
| 2007-08 | 0.82 | 1.24 | (0.07) | 0.01 |
| 2008-09 | 0.83 | 1.41 | 0.02 | (0.18) |
| 2009-10 | 1.00 | 1.22 | (0.03) | 0.02 |
| 2010-11 | 0.81 | 1.45 | (0.01) | ... |

**Interim Dividends (Per Share)**

| Amt | Decl | Ex | Rec | Pay |
|---|---|---|---|---|
| 0.34Q | 11/03/2010 | 11/23/2010 | 11/26/2010 | 12/10/2010 |
| 0.34Q | 02/08/2011 | 02/23/2011 | 02/25/2011 | 03/10/2011 |
| 0.34Q | 05/04/2011 | 05/23/2011 | 05/25/2011 | 06/10/2011 |
| 0.34Q | 08/03/2011 | 08/23/2011 | 08/25/2011 | 09/12/2011 |

**Indicated Div: $1.36 (Div. Reinv. Plan)**

**Valuation Analysis**

| | | | |
|---|---|---|---|
| Forecast EPS | $2.27 (09/05/2011) | | |
| Market Cap | $3.0 Billion | Book Value | $2.3 Billion |
| Price/Book | 1.30 | Price/Sales | 0.69 |

**Dividend Achiever Status**

| | |
|---|---|
| **10 Year Growth Rate** | 1.45% |
| **Total Years of Dividend Growth** | 23 |

**Business Summary:** Gas Utilities (MIC: 3.3.1 SIC: 4924 NAIC: 486210)

Atmos Energy is engaged primarily in the regulated natural gas distribution and transmission and storage businesses as well as other nonregulated natural gas businesses. Co. operates through four segments: the natural gas distribution segment, which includes regulated natural gas distribution and related sales operations; the regulated transmission and storage segment, which includes the regulated pipeline and storage operations of Atmos Pipeline - Texas Division; the natural gas marketing segment, which includes nonregulated natural gas management services; and the pipeline, storage and other segment, which comprises of nonregulated natural gas gathering, transmission and storage services.

**Recent Developments:** For the quarter ended June 30 2011, loss from continuing operations was US$1.5 million compared with a loss of US$4.2 million in the year-earlier quarter. Net loss amounted to US$566,000 versus a net loss of US$3.2 million in the year-earlier quarter. Revenues were US$843.6 million, up 10.8% from US$761.3 million the year before. Operating income was US$34.1 million versus US$32.3 million in the prior-year quarter, an increase of 5.6%. Direct operating expenses rose 12.3% to US$576.8 million from US$513.6 million in the comparable period the year before. Indirect operating expenses increased 8.0% to US$232.7 million from US$215.4 million in the equivalent prior-year period.

**Prospects:** Our evaluation of Atmos Energy Corp. as of Sep. 6, 2011 is the result of our systematic analysis on three basic characteristics: earnings strength, relative valuation, and recent stock price movement. The company has enjoyed a very positive trend in earnings per share over the past 5 quarters. However, while recent estimates for the company have been mixed, ATO has posted results that fell short of analysts expectations. Based on operating earnings yield, the company is undervalued when compared to all of the companies in our coverage universe. Share price changes over the past year indicates that ATO will perform very poorly over the near term.

**Financial Data**

| (US$ in Thousands) | 9 Mos | 6 Mos | 3 Mos | 09/30/2010 | 09/30/2009 | 09/30/2008 | 09/30/2007 | 09/30/2006 |
|---|---|---|---|---|---|---|---|---|
| Earnings Per Share | 2.27 | 2.25 | 2.02 | 2.20 | 2.08 | 2.00 | 1.92 | 1.82 |
| Cash Flow Per Share | 7.23 | 7.55 | 7.52 | 7.91 | 10.09 | 4.14 | 6.29 | 3.86 |
| Tang Book Value Per Share | 17.68 | 18.09 | 16.93 | 15.95 | 15.52 | 14.46 | 13.75 | 11.13 |
| Dividends Per Share | 1.355 | 1.350 | 1.345 | 1.340 | 1.320 | 1.300 | 1.280 | 1.260 |
| Dividend Payout % | 59.69 | 60.00 | 66.58 | 60.91 | 63.46 | 65.00 | 66.67 | 69.23 |
| **Income Statement** | | | | | | | | |
| Total Revenue | 3,558,374 | 2,774,282 | 1,156,995 | 4,789,690 | 4,969,080 | 7,221,305 | 5,898,431 | 6,152,363 |
| EBITDA | 596,487 | 516,876 | 215,579 | 706,230 | 661,401 | 631,215 | 606,875 | 569,464 |
| Depn & Amortn | 171,875 | 113,395 | 56,207 | 217,133 | 217,302 | 200,589 | 199,055 | 185,967 |
| Income Before Taxes | 311,997 | 326,672 | 120,455 | 334,626 | 291,269 | 292,704 | 262,584 | 236,890 |
| Income Taxes | 114,211 | 120,466 | 46,458 | 128,787 | 100,291 | 112,373 | 94,092 | 89,153 |
| Net Income | 205,640 | 206,206 | 73,997 | 205,839 | 190,978 | 180,331 | 168,492 | 147,737 |
| Average Shares | 90,127 | 90,533 | 90,408 | 92,422 | 92,024 | 90,272 | 87,745 | 81,390 |
| **Balance Sheet** | | | | | | | | |
| Current Assets | 989,748 | 984,088 | 1,263,255 | 875,192 | 828,940 | 1,285,104 | 1,068,895 | 1,117,545 |
| Total Assets | 6,993,470 | 6,995,824 | 7,221,623 | 6,763,791 | 6,343,766 | 6,386,699 | 5,896,917 | 5,719,547 |
| Current Liabilities | 648,282 | 1,077,984 | 1,460,426 | 1,166,079 | 737,421 | 1,207,087 | 919,678 | 1,119,161 |
| Long-Term Obligations | 2,206,106 | 1,807,323 | 1,807,319 | 1,809,551 | 2,169,400 | 2,119,792 | 2,126,315 | 2,180,362 |
| Total Liabilities | 4,657,646 | 4,621,845 | 4,946,770 | 4,585,443 | 4,167,005 | 4,334,207 | 3,931,163 | 4,071,449 |
| Stockholders' Equity | 2,335,824 | 2,373,979 | 2,274,853 | 2,178,348 | 2,176,761 | 2,052,492 | 1,965,754 | 1,648,098 |
| Shares Outstanding | 90,284 | 90,329 | 90,638 | 90,164 | 92,551 | 90,814 | 89,326 | 81,739 |
| **Statistical Record** | | | | | | | | |
| Return on Assets % | 3.05 | 2.98 | 2.65 | 3.14 | 3.00 | 2.93 | 2.90 | 2.60 |
| Return on Equity % | 8.91 | 8.68 | 8.23 | 9.45 | 9.03 | 8.95 | 9.32 | 9.09 |
| EBITDA Margin % | 16.76 | 18.63 | 18.63 | 14.74 | 13.31 | 8.74 | 10.29 | 9.26 |
| Net Margin % | 5.78 | 7.43 | 6.40 | 4.30 | 3.84 | 2.50 | 2.86 | 2.40 |
| Asset Turnover | 0.65 | 0.63 | 0.66 | 0.73 | 0.78 | 1.17 | 1.02 | 1.08 |
| Current Ratio | 1.53 | 0.91 | 0.86 | 0.75 | 1.12 | 1.06 | 1.16 | 1.00 |
| Debt to Equity | 0.94 | 0.76 | 0.79 | 0.83 | 1.00 | 1.03 | 1.08 | 1.32 |
| Price Range | 34.98-26.82 | 34.98-26.41 | 31.72-26.41 | 30.06-26.41 | 28.80-20.20 | 29.46-25.09 | 33.11-26.47 | 29.11-25.79 |
| P/E Ratio | 15.41-11.81 | 15.55-11.74 | 15.70-13.07 | 13.66-12.00 | 13.85-9.71 | 14.73-12.55 | 17.24-13.79 | 15.99-14.17 |
| Average Yield % | 4.32 | 4.48 | 4.65 | 4.70 | 5.35 | 4.79 | 4.16 | 4.66 |

**Address:** Three Lincoln Centre, Suite 1800, 5430 LBJ Freeway, Dallas, TX 75240
**Telephone:** 972-934-9227
**Web Site:** www.atmosenergy.com

**Officers:** Robert W. Best - Executive Chairman, Chief Executive Officer Kim R. Cocklin - President, Chief Executive Officer **Transfer Agents:** American Stock Transfer & Trust Company, New York, NY

**No of Institutions:** 335
**Shares:** 55,750,328 **% Held:** 54.12

# AUTOMATIC DATA PROCESSING INC.

| Exchange | Symbol | Price | 52Wk Range | Yield | P/E |
|---|---|---|---|---|---|
| NMS | ADP | $50.03 (8/31/2011) | 55.11-38.61 | 2.88 | 19.85 |

***7 Year Price Score 109.15** *NYSE Composite Index=100 ***12 Month Price Score 104.70**

**Interim Earnings (Per Share)**

| Qtr. | Sep | Dec | Mar | Jun |
|---|---|---|---|---|
| 2006-07 | 0.46 | 0.54 | 0.70 | 0.35 |
| 2007-08 | 0.55 | 0.55 | 0.79 | 0.45 |
| 2008-09 | 0.54 | 0.59 | 0.80 | 0.70 |
| 2009-10 | 0.56 | 0.62 | 0.80 | 0.41 |
| 2010-11 | 0.56 | 0.62 | 0.85 | 0.49 |

**Interim Dividends (Per Share)**

| Amt | Decl | Ex | Rec | Pay |
|---|---|---|---|---|
| 0.36Q | 11/09/2010 | 12/08/2010 | 12/10/2010 | 01/01/2011 |
| 0.36Q | 02/08/2011 | 03/09/2011 | 03/11/2011 | 04/01/2011 |
| 0.36Q | 04/28/2011 | 06/08/2011 | 06/10/2011 | 07/01/2011 |
| 0.36Q | 08/09/2011 | 09/07/2011 | 09/09/2011 | 10/01/2011 |

**Indicated Div: $1.44**

**Valuation Analysis**

Forecast EPS $2.75 (09/02/2011)

| | | | |
|---|---|---|---|
| Market Cap | $24.6 Billion | Book Value | $6.0 Billion |
| Price/Book | 4.09 | Price/Sales | 2.49 |

**Dividend Achiever Status**

| | |
|---|---|
| **10 Year Growth Rate** | 12.74% |
| **Total Years of Dividend Growth** | 35 |

**Business Summary:** IT Services (MIC: 6.3.1 SIC: 7374 NAIC: 518210)

Automatic Data Processing provides business outsourcing services. Co. has three segments: Employer Services, which provides human resource (HR) information, payroll processing, time and labor management, and tax and benefits administration services; Professional Employer Organization Services, which provides employment administration outsourcing services, including payroll tax filing, benefits administration, compliance services, health and workers' compensation coverage; and Dealer Services, which provides dealer management systems, digital marketing applications, and other business management services to auto, truck, motorcycle, marine, recreational vehicle and heavy equipment retailers.

**Recent Developments:** For the year ended June 30 2011, income from continuing operations increased 3.9% to US$1.25 billion from US$1.21 billion a year earlier. Net income increased 3.5% to US$1.25 billion from US$1.21 billion in the prior year. Revenues were US$9.88 billion, up 10.7% from US$8.93 billion the year before. Direct operating expenses rose 14.0% to US$5.73 billion from US$5.03 billion in the comparable period the year before. Indirect operating expenses increased 9.2% to US$2.33 billion from US$2.14 billion in the equivalent prior-year period.

**Prospects:** Our evaluation of Automatic Data Processing Inc. as of Sep. 6, 2011 is the result of our systematic analysis on three basic characteristics: earnings strength, relative valuation, and recent stock price movement. The company has managed to produce a neutral trend in earnings per share over the past 5 quarters and while recent estimates for the company have been mixed, ADP has posted results that fell short of analysts expectations. Based on operating earnings yield, the company is about fairly valued when compared to all of the companies in our coverage universe. Share price changes over the past year indicates that ADP will perform in line with the market over the near term.

**Financial Data**

| (US$ in Thousands) | 06/30/2011 | 06/30/2010 | 06/30/2009 | 06/30/2008 | 06/30/2007 | 06/30/2006 | 06/30/2005 | 06/30/2004 |
|---|---|---|---|---|---|---|---|---|
| Earnings Per Share | 2.52 | 2.40 | 2.63 | 2.34 | 2.04 | 2.68 | 1.79 | 1.56 |
| Cash Flow Per Share | 3.46 | 3.36 | 3.11 | 3.39 | 2.36 | 3.15 | 2.46 | 2.35 |
| Tang Book Value Per Share | 4.53 | 5.19 | 4.72 | 3.97 | 3.93 | 5.21 | 4.55 | 4.23 |
| Dividends Per Share | 1.420 | 1.350 | 1.280 | 1.100 | 0.875 | 0.710 | 0.605 | 0.540 |
| Dividend Payout % | 56.35 | 56.25 | 48.67 | 47.01 | 42.89 | 26.49 | 33.80 | 34.62 |
| **Income Statement** | | | | | | | | |
| Total Revenue | 9,879,500 | 8,927,700 | 8,867,100 | 8,776,500 | 7,800,000 | 8,881,500 | 8,499,100 | 7,754,942 |
| EBITDA | 2,170,700 | 2,082,200 | 1,955,700 | 1,895,000 | 1,698,900 | 1,801,500 | 1,763,000 | 1,575,582 |
| Depn & Amortn | 318,200 | 309,200 | 151,900 | 152,000 | 145,500 | 127,600 | 147,500 | 145,000 |
| Income Before Taxes | 1,932,700 | 1,863,200 | 1,904,700 | 1,812,000 | 1,623,500 | 1,743,000 | 1,677,900 | 1,494,530 |
| Income Taxes | 678,500 | 655,900 | 576,500 | 650,300 | 602,300 | 670,600 | 622,500 | 558,960 |
| Net Income | 1,254,200 | 1,211,400 | 1,332,600 | 1,235,700 | 1,138,700 | 1,554,000 | 1,055,400 | 935,570 |
| Average Shares | 498,300 | 503,700 | 505,800 | 527,200 | 557,900 | 580,300 | 590,000 | 598,749 |
| **Balance Sheet** | | | | | | | | |
| Current Assets | 28,583,500 | 22,316,700 | 20,703,900 | 18,808,900 | 3,364,200 | 4,760,100 | 4,441,100 | 2,761,589 |
| Total Assets | 34,238,300 | 26,862,200 | 25,351,700 | 23,734,400 | 26,648,900 | 27,490,100 | 27,615,400 | 21,120,559 |
| Current Liabilities | 26,786,800 | 20,052,200 | 18,756,300 | 17,341,600 | 1,790,800 | 2,592,700 | 2,800,700 | 1,768,424 |
| Long-Term Obligations | 34,200 | 39,800 | 42,700 | 52,100 | 43,500 | 74,300 | 75,800 | 76,200 |
| Total Liabilities | 28,227,900 | 21,383,300 | 20,029,100 | 18,647,200 | 21,501,000 | 21,478,500 | 21,831,600 | 15,702,889 |
| Stockholders' Equity | 6,010,400 | 5,478,900 | 5,322,600 | 5,087,200 | 5,147,900 | 6,011,600 | 5,783,800 | 5,417,670 |
| Shares Outstanding | 490,800 | 492,000 | 501,700 | 510,300 | 535,800 | 561,400 | 580,200 | 587,115 |
| **Statistical Record** | | | | | | | | |
| Return on Assets % | 4.11 | 4.64 | 5.43 | 4.89 | 4.21 | 5.64 | 4.33 | 4.56 |
| Return on Equity % | 21.83 | 22.43 | 25.60 | 24.08 | 20.41 | 26.35 | 18.84 | 17.30 |
| EBITDA Margin % | 21.97 | 23.32 | 22.06 | 21.59 | 21.78 | 20.28 | 20.74 | 20.32 |
| Net Margin % | 12.69 | 13.57 | 15.03 | 14.08 | 14.60 | 17.50 | 12.42 | 12.06 |
| Asset Turnover | 0.32 | 0.34 | 0.36 | 0.35 | 0.29 | 0.32 | 0.35 | 0.38 |
| Current Ratio | 1.07 | 1.11 | 1.10 | 1.08 | 1.88 | 1.84 | 1.59 | 1.56 |
| Debt to Equity | 0.01 | 0.01 | 0.01 | 0.01 | 0.01 | 0.01 | 0.01 | 0.01 |
| Price Range | 55.11-38.61 | 45.48-33.33 | 45.84-31.03 | 49.56-37.90 | 51.26-42.63 | 47.95-41.62 | 46.23-38.88 | 46.84-33.86 |
| P/E Ratio | 21.87-15.32 | 18.95-13.89 | 17.43-11.80 | 21.18-16.20 | 25.13-20.90 | 17.89-15.53 | 25.83-21.72 | 30.03-21.71 |
| Average Yield % | 3.02 | 3.29 | 3.34 | 2.49 | 1.84 | 1.58 | 1.41 | 1.33 |

**Address:** One ADP Boulevard, Roseland, NJ 07068
**Telephone:** 973-974-5000
**Web Site:** www.adp.com

**Officers:** Carlos A. Rodriguez - President, Chief Operating Officer Benito Cachinero - Vice President
**Transfer Agents:** American Stock Transfer, New York, NY

**No of Institutions:** 1137
**Shares:** 407,899,168 **% Held:** 72.02

# AVON PRODUCTS, INC.

| Exchange | Symbol | Price | 52Wk Range | Yield | P/E |
|---|---|---|---|---|---|
| NYS | AVP | $22.56 (8/31/2011) | 35.49-20.48 | 4.08 | 13.27 |

***7 Year Price Score 86.40** *NYSE Composite Index=100 ***12 Month Price Score 89.30**

**Interim Earnings (Per Share)**

| Qtr. | Mar | Jun | Sep | Dec |
|---|---|---|---|---|
| 2008 | 0.43 | 0.55 | 0.52 | 0.55 |
| 2009 | 0.27 | 0.19 | 0.36 | 0.62 |
| 2010 | 0.10 | 0.39 | 0.38 | 0.52 |
| 2011 | 0.33 | 0.47 | ... | ... |

**Interim Dividends (Per Share)**

| Amt | Decl | Ex | Rec | Pay |
|---|---|---|---|---|
| 0.22Q | 11/02/2010 | 11/12/2010 | 11/16/2010 | 12/01/2010 |
| 0.23Q | 02/03/2011 | 02/15/2011 | 02/17/2011 | 03/01/2011 |
| 0.23Q | 05/05/2011 | 05/17/2011 | 05/19/2011 | 06/01/2011 |
| 0.23Q | 08/01/2011 | 08/11/2011 | 08/15/2011 | 09/01/2011 |

**Indicated Div: $0.92 (Div. Reinv. Plan)**

**Valuation Analysis**

| | | | |
|---|---|---|---|
| Forecast EPS | $2.05 (09/05/2011) | | |
| Market Cap | $9.7 Billion | Book Value | $2.0 Billion |
| Price/Book | 4.80 | Price/Sales | 0.87 |

**Dividend Achiever Status**

| | |
|---|---|
| **10 Year Growth Rate** | 8.76% |
| **Total Years of Dividend Growth** | 20 |

**Business Summary:** Household & Personal Products (MIC: 1.7.1 SIC: 2844 NAIC: 325620)

Avon Products manufactures and sells beauty and related products. Co.'s product categories are Beauty, which consists of color cosmetics, fragrances, skin care and personal care; Fashion, which consists of fashion jewelry, watches, apparel, footwear and accessories and children's products; and Home, which consists of gift and decorative products, housewares, entertainment and leisure products and nutritional products. Co. primarily sells its products through the direct-selling channel. Co.'s reportable segments are based on geographic operations in six regions: Latin America; North America; Central and Eastern Europe; Western Europe, Middle East and Africa; Asia Pacific; and China.

**Recent Developments:** For the quarter ended June 30 2011, income from continuing operations increased 26.5% to US$208.7 million from US$165.0 million in the year-earlier quarter. Net income increased 23.3% to US$208.7 million from US$169.2 million in the year-earlier quarter. Revenues were US$2.86 billion, up 8.7% from US$2.63 billion the year before. Operating income was US$316.6 million versus US$266.4 million in the prior-year quarter, an increase of 18.8%. Direct operating expenses rose 5.8% to US$1.02 billion from US$962.1 million in the comparable period the year before. Indirect operating expenses increased 8.7% to US$1.52 billion from US$1.40 billion in the equivalent prior-year period.

**Prospects:** Our evaluation of Avon Products Inc. as of Sep. 6, 2011 is the result of our systematic analysis on three basic characteristics: earnings strength, relative valuation, and recent stock price movement. The company has enjoyed a very positive trend in earnings per share over the past 5 quarters and while recent estimates for the company have remained steady, AVP has posted results that fell short of analysts expectations. Based on operating earnings yield, the company is undervalued when compared to all of the companies in our coverage universe. Share price changes over the past year indicates that AVP will perform in line with the market over the near term.

**Financial Data**

| (US$ in Thousands) | 6 Mos | 3 Mos | 12/31/2010 | 12/31/2009 | 12/31/2008 | 12/31/2007 | 12/31/2006 | 12/31/2005 |
|---|---|---|---|---|---|---|---|---|
| Earnings Per Share | 1.70 | 1.62 | 1.39 | 1.45 | 2.04 | 1.21 | 1.06 | 1.81 |
| Cash Flow Per Share | 1.25 | 1.49 | 1.61 | 1.83 | 1.75 | 1.36 | 1.78 | 1.92 |
| Tang Book Value Per Share | 2.27 | 1.81 | 1.10 | 2.16 | 0.76 | 1.66 | 1.79 | 1.76 |
| Dividends Per Share | 0.900 | 0.890 | 0.880 | 0.840 | 0.800 | 0.740 | 0.700 | 0.660 |
| Dividend Payout % | 52.94 | 54.94 | 63.31 | 57.93 | 39.22 | 61.16 | 66.04 | 36.46 |
| **Income Statement** | | | | | | | | |
| Total Revenue | 5,485,500 | 2,629,100 | 10,862,800 | 10,382,800 | 10,690,100 | 9,938,700 | 8,763,900 | 8,149,600 |
| EBITDA | 672,000 | 298,200 | 1,163,700 | 1,144,100 | 1,443,500 | 1,007,300 | 873,000 | 1,256,400 |
| Depn & Amortn | 115,500 | 55,400 | 145,200 | 133,000 | 141,900 | 128,900 | 115,600 | 106,500 |
| Income Before Taxes | 518,600 | 224,900 | 945,400 | 926,500 | 1,238,300 | 796,100 | 703,500 | 1,124,200 |
| Income Taxes | 157,700 | 72,700 | 350,200 | 298,300 | 362,700 | 262,800 | 223,400 | 269,700 |
| Net Income | 349,800 | 143,600 | 606,300 | 625,800 | 875,300 | 530,700 | 477,600 | 847,600 |
| Average Shares | 433,750 | 433,170 | 431,350 | 428,540 | 429,530 | 436,890 | 449,160 | 469,470 |
| **Balance Sheet** | | | | | | | | |
| Current Assets | 4,285,000 | 4,165,000 | 4,184,300 | 4,189,300 | 3,556,900 | 3,515,400 | 3,334,400 | 2,920,900 |
| Total Assets | 8,116,800 | 7,887,100 | 7,873,700 | 6,832,700 | 6,074,000 | 5,716,200 | 5,238,200 | 4,763,300 |
| Current Liabilities | 2,919,300 | 2,908,700 | 2,956,300 | 2,274,800 | 2,912,200 | 3,053,400 | 2,550,100 | 2,501,600 |
| Long-Term Obligations | 2,417,300 | 2,391,100 | 2,408,600 | 2,307,800 | 1,456,200 | 1,167,900 | 1,170,700 | 766,500 |
| Total Liabilities | 6,092,500 | 6,063,800 | 6,217,200 | 5,560,100 | 5,399,100 | 5,004,600 | 4,447,800 | 3,969,100 |
| Stockholders' Equity | 2,024,300 | 1,823,300 | 1,656,500 | 1,272,600 | 674,900 | 711,600 | 790,400 | 794,200 |
| Shares Outstanding | 430,706 | 430,188 | 429,500 | 427,480 | 426,300 | 427,700 | 441,300 | 451,480 |
| **Statistical Record** | | | | | | | | |
| Return on Assets % | 10.05 | 9.62 | 8.25 | 9.70 | 14.81 | 9.69 | 9.55 | 19.02 |
| Return on Equity % | 45.33 | 46.12 | 41.40 | 64.27 | 125.92 | 70.67 | 60.28 | 97.18 |
| EBITDA Margin % | 12.25 | 11.34 | 10.71 | 11.02 | 13.50 | 10.14 | 9.96 | 15.42 |
| Net Margin % | 6.38 | 5.46 | 5.58 | 6.03 | 8.19 | 5.34 | 5.45 | 10.40 |
| Asset Turnover | 1.51 | 1.50 | 1.48 | 1.61 | 1.81 | 1.81 | 1.75 | 1.83 |
| Current Ratio | 1.47 | 1.43 | 1.42 | 1.84 | 1.22 | 1.15 | 1.31 | 1.17 |
| Debt to Equity | 1.19 | 1.31 | 1.45 | 1.81 | 2.16 | 1.64 | 1.48 | 0.97 |
| Price Range | 35.49-26.16 | 35.49-25.73 | 35.49-25.73 | 36.12-15.20 | 45.25-18.38 | 41.66-31.97 | 33.88-27.01 | 45.07-24.71 |
| P/E Ratio | 20.88-15.39 | 21.91-15.88 | 25.53-18.51 | 24.91-10.48 | 22.18-9.01 | 34.43-26.42 | 31.96-25.48 | 24.90-13.65 |
| Average Yield % | 3.07 | 3.01 | 2.90 | 3.09 | 2.24 | 1.97 | 2.30 | 1.87 |

| | | |
|---|---|---|
| **Address:** 1345 Avenue of the Americas, New York, NY 10105-0196 | **Officers:** Andrea Jung - Chairman, Chief Executive Officer Kimberly Ross - Executive Vice President, Chief Financial Officer **Transfer Agents:** Computershare Trust Company, N.A., Providence, RI | **Investor Contact:** 212-282-5320 |
| **Telephone:** 212-282-5000 | | **No of Institutions:** 609 |
| **Web Site:** www.avon.com | | **Shares:** 398,018,208 **% Held:** 83.51 |

# BADGER METER, INC.

| Exchange | Symbol | Price | 52Wk Range | Yield | P/E |
|---|---|---|---|---|---|
| NYS | BMI | $35.03 (8/31/2011) | 45.19-31.83 | 1.83 | 19.90 |

***7 Year Price Score 121.58** *NYSE Composite Index=100 ***12 Month Price Score 92.86**

**Interim Earnings (Per Share)**

| Qtr. | Mar | Jun | Sep | Dec |
|---|---|---|---|---|
| 2008 | 0.41 | 0.48 | 0.39 | 0.42 |
| 2009 | 0.47 | 0.52 | 0.96 | 0.33 |
| 2010 | 0.36 | 0.53 | 0.60 | 0.42 |
| 2011 | 0.22 | 0.52 | ... | ... |

**Interim Dividends (Per Share)**

| Amt | Decl | Ex | Rec | Pay |
|---|---|---|---|---|
| 0.14Q | 11/12/2010 | 11/26/2010 | 11/30/2010 | 12/15/2010 |
| 0.14Q | 02/18/2011 | 02/24/2011 | 02/28/2011 | 03/15/2011 |
| 0.14Q | 04/29/2011 | 05/26/2011 | 05/31/2011 | 06/15/2011 |
| 0.16Q | 08/12/2011 | 08/29/2011 | 08/31/2011 | 09/15/2011 |

**Indicated Div: $0.64 (Div. Reinv. Plan)**

**Valuation Analysis**

| | | | |
|---|---|---|---|
| Forecast EPS | $1.72 (09/02/2011) | | |
| Market Cap | $529.4 Million | Book Value | $178.3 Million |
| Price/Book | 2.97 | Price/Sales | 1.94 |

**Dividend Achiever Status**

| | |
|---|---|
| **10 Year Growth Rate** | 7.60% |
| **Total Years of Dividend Growth** | 18 |

**Business Summary:** Industrial Machinery & Equipment (MIC: 7.2.1 SIC: 3824 NAIC: 334514)

Badger Meter manufactures and sells products incorporating liquid flow measurement and control technologies. Co.'s product lines fall into two categories: water applications and specialty applications. Water applications include the sale of water meters and related technologies and services used by water utilities. Co.'s products are also used for irrigation, water reclamation and industrial process applications. Specialty applications include the sale of meters and related technologies and services for measuring fluids in industries such as food and beverage, pharmaceutical production, petroleum, heating, ventilating and air conditioning, and measuring and dispensing automotive fluids.

**Recent Developments:** For the quarter ended June 30 2011, net income decreased 2.4% to US$7.8 million from US$8.0 million in the year-earlier quarter. Revenues were US$75.1 million, up 1.2% from US$74.3 million the year before. Operating income was US$12.3 million versus US$13.0 million in the prior-year quarter, a decrease of 5.4%. Direct operating expenses rose 1.4% to US$47.9 million from US$47.3 million in the comparable period the year before. Indirect operating expenses increased 6.4% to US$14.9 million from US$14.0 million in the equivalent prior-year period.

**Prospects:** Our evaluation of Badger Meter Inc. as of Sep. 6, 2011 is the result of our systematic analysis on three basic characteristics: earnings strength, relative valuation, and recent stock price movement. The company has generated a negative trend in earnings per share over the past 5 quarters. However, while recent estimates for the company have been mixed, BMI has posted better than expected results. Based on operating earnings yield, the company is about fairly valued when compared to all of the companies in our coverage universe. Share price changes over the past year indicates that BMI will perform very poorly over the near term.

**Financial Data**

| (US$ in Thousands) | 6 Mos | 3 Mos | 12/31/2010 | 12/31/2009 | 12/31/2008 | 12/31/2007 | 12/31/2006 | 12/31/2005 |
|---|---|---|---|---|---|---|---|---|
| Earnings Per Share | 1.76 | 1.77 | 1.91 | 2.28 | 1.69 | 1.13 | 0.52 | 0.94 |
| Cash Flow Per Share | 1.73 | 1.23 | 1.23 | 2.47 | 1.85 | 1.99 | 1.21 | 1.36 |
| Tang Book Value Per Share | 8.88 | 8.39 | 8.31 | 7.61 | 5.34 | 5.82 | 4.54 | 4.80 |
| Dividends Per Share | 0.560 | 0.540 | 0.520 | 0.460 | 0.400 | 0.340 | 0.310 | 0.290 |
| Dividend Payout % | 31.82 | 30.51 | 27.23 | 20.18 | 23.67 | 30.09 | 59.62 | 30.69 |
| **Income Statement** | | | | | | | | |
| Total Revenue | 132,507 | 57,359 | 276,634 | 250,337 | 279,552 | 234,816 | 229,754 | 216,654 |
| EBITDA | 22,480 | 7,722 | 51,527 | 48,974 | 46,856 | 36,924 | 35,377 | 30,570 |
| Depn & Amortn | 4,965 | 2,484 | 6,704 | 6,731 | 5,954 | 6,308 | 6,589 | 6,164 |
| Income Before Taxes | 17,307 | 5,126 | 44,438 | 42,333 | 39,555 | 29,325 | 27,489 | 22,798 |
| Income Taxes | 6,213 | 1,866 | 15,776 | 15,553 | 14,471 | 10,939 | 10,921 | 9,545 |
| Net Income | 11,094 | 3,260 | 28,662 | 34,170 | 25,084 | 16,457 | 7,548 | 13,253 |
| Average Shares | 15,052 | 15,058 | 15,006 | 14,948 | 14,837 | 14,617 | 14,389 | 14,022 |
| **Balance Sheet** | | | | | | | | |
| Current Assets | 104,272 | 100,152 | 97,337 | 86,680 | 86,529 | 79,934 | 79,359 | 72,564 |
| Total Assets | 223,105 | 220,279 | 215,864 | 191,016 | 195,358 | 150,301 | 139,383 | 145,867 |
| Current Liabilities | 30,763 | 34,860 | 32,679 | 26,261 | 50,789 | 41,209 | 45,711 | 39,586 |
| Long-Term Obligations | ... | ... | ... | ... | 5,504 | 3,129 | 5,928 | 15,360 |
| Total Liabilities | 44,855 | 49,380 | 47,481 | 46,555 | 84,335 | 58,332 | 67,564 | 72,451 |
| Stockholders' Equity | 178,250 | 170,899 | 168,383 | 144,461 | 111,023 | 91,969 | 71,819 | 73,416 |
| Shares Outstanding | 15,112 | 15,054 | 15,048 | 14,972 | 14,808 | 14,518 | 14,154 | 13,696 |
| **Statistical Record** | | | | | | | | |
| Return on Assets % | 12.21 | 12.69 | 14.09 | 17.69 | 14.47 | 11.36 | 5.29 | 9.18 |
| Return on Equity % | 15.83 | 16.65 | 18.32 | 26.75 | 24.65 | 20.10 | 10.39 | 19.28 |
| EBITDA Margin % | 16.97 | 13.46 | 18.63 | 19.56 | 16.76 | 15.72 | 15.40 | 14.11 |
| Net Margin % | 8.37 | 5.68 | 10.36 | 13.65 | 8.97 | 7.01 | 3.29 | 6.12 |
| Asset Turnover | 1.26 | 1.30 | 1.36 | 1.30 | 1.61 | 1.62 | 1.61 | 1.50 |
| Current Ratio | 3.39 | 2.87 | 2.98 | 3.30 | 1.70 | 1.94 | 1.74 | 1.83 |
| Debt to Equity | ... | ... | ... | ... | 0.05 | 0.03 | 0.08 | 0.21 |
| Price Range | 45.19-35.24 | 45.19-36.85 | 45.05-35.22 | 43.84-23.10 | 60.47-19.17 | 46.05-23.53 | 32.50-19.81 | 25.52-13.06 |
| P/E Ratio | 25.68-20.02 | 25.53-20.82 | 23.59-18.44 | 19.23-10.13 | 35.78-11.34 | 40.75-20.82 | 62.50-38.10 | 27.14-13.89 |
| Average Yield % | 1.41 | 1.33 | 1.30 | 1.30 | 0.95 | 1.09 | 1.21 | 1.57 |

**Address:** 4545 W. Brown Deer Road, Milwaukee, WI 53223
**Telephone:** 414-355-0400
**Web Site:** www.badgermeter.com

**Officers:** Richard A. Meeusen - Chairman, President, Chief Executive Officer Fred J. Begale - Vice President **Transfer Agents:** American Stock Transfer & Trust Company, LLC, New York, NY

**Investor Contact:** 414-371-5702
**No of Institutions:** 133
**Shares:** 10,966,585 **% Held:** 64.94

# BANCFIRST CORP. (OKLAHOMA CITY, OKLA)

| Exchange | Symbol | Price | 52Wk Range | Yield | P/E |
|---|---|---|---|---|---|
| NMS | BANF | $35.72 (8/31/2011) | 44.24-32.35 | 3.02 | 12.90 |

*7 Year Price Score 95.00 *NYSE Composite Index=100 *12 Month Price Score 93.29

**Interim Earnings (Per Share)**

| Qtr. | Mar | Jun | Sep | Dec |
|---|---|---|---|---|
| 2008 | 0.74 | 0.89 | 0.70 | 0.52 |
| 2009 | 0.46 | 0.40 | 0.60 | 0.63 |
| 2010 | 0.60 | 0.71 | 0.75 | 0.65 |
| 2011 | 0.72 | 0.65 | ... | ... |

**Interim Dividends (Per Share)**

| Amt | Decl | Ex | Rec | Pay |
|---|---|---|---|---|
| 0.25Q | 11/18/2010 | 12/29/2010 | 12/31/2010 | 01/18/2011 |
| 0.25Q | 02/24/2011 | 03/29/2011 | 03/31/2011 | 04/15/2011 |
| 0.25Q | 05/26/2011 | 06/28/2011 | 06/30/2011 | 07/15/2011 |
| 0.27Q | 08/25/2011 | 09/28/2011 | 09/30/2011 | 10/17/2011 |

**Indicated Div: $1.08**

**Valuation Analysis**

| | | | |
|---|---|---|---|
| Forecast EPS | $2.92 (09/02/2011) | | |
| Market Cap | $545.6 Million | Book Value | $470.4 Million |
| Price/Book | 1.16 | Price/Sales | N/A |

**Dividend Achiever Status**

| | |
|---|---|
| **10 Year Growth Rate** | 10.07% |
| **Total Years of Dividend Growth** | 17 |

**Business Summary:** Banking (MIC: 5.1.1 SIC: 6021 NAIC: 522110)

BancFirst is a financial holding company. Co. operates through its principal subsidiary, BancFirst. Co. has four business units: metropolitan banks, community banks, other financial services, and executive, operations and support. Metropolitan and community banks provide banking products such as commercial and retail lending, and a line of deposit accounts. Other financial services are specialty product business units including guaranteed small business lending, residential mortgage lending, trust services, securities brokerage, electronic banking and insurance. As of Dec 31 2010, Co. had total assets of $5.06 billion and total deposits of $4.50 billion.

**Recent Developments:** For the quarter ended June 30 2011, net income decreased 8.4% to US$10.1 million from US$11.0 million in the year-earlier quarter. Net interest income increased 6.6% to US$38.0 million from US$35.7 million in the year-earlier quarter. Provision for loan losses was US$2.0 million versus US$871,000 in the prior-year quarter, an increase of 131.1%. Non-interest income rose 15.6% to US$19.7 million from US$17.0 million, while non-interest expense advanced 14.8% to US$39.6 million.

**Prospects:** Our evaluation of BancFirst Corp. as of Sep. 6, 2011 is the result of our systematic analysis on three basic characteristics: earnings strength, relative valuation, and recent stock price movement. The company has generated a negative trend in earnings per share over the past 5 quarters and while recent estimates for the company have remained steady, BANF has posted results that fell short of analysts expectations. Based on operating earnings yield, the company is undervalued when compared to all of the companies in our coverage universe. Share price changes over the past year indicates that BANF will perform poorly over the near term.

**Financial Data**

| (US$ in Thousands) | 6 Mos | 3 Mos | 12/31/2010 | 12/31/2009 | 12/31/2008 | 12/31/2007 | 12/31/2006 | 12/31/2005 |
|---|---|---|---|---|---|---|---|---|
| Earnings Per Share | 2.77 | 2.83 | 2.70 | 2.09 | 2.85 | 3.33 | 3.07 | 2.68 |
| Cash Flow Per Share | 13.63 | 12.38 | 8.53 | 0.05 | 3.89 | 3.97 | 2.81 | 3.60 |
| Tang Book Value Per Share | 27.17 | 26.71 | 26.19 | 25.41 | 24.34 | 21.66 | 19.57 | 16.87 |
| Dividends Per Share | 1.000 | 0.980 | 0.960 | 0.900 | 0.840 | 0.760 | 0.680 | 0.600 |
| Dividend Payout % | 36.10 | 34.63 | 35.56 | 43.06 | 29.47 | 22.82 | 22.15 | 22.39 |
| **Income Statement** | | | | | | | | |
| Interest Income | 89,106 | 44,310 | 170,917 | 169,806 | 197,924 | 230,749 | 213,225 | 171,706 |
| Interest Expense | 13,789 | 7,020 | 28,141 | 38,485 | 58,817 | 82,463 | 69,537 | 40,255 |
| Net Interest Income | 75,317 | 37,290 | 142,776 | 131,321 | 139,107 | 148,286 | 143,688 | 131,451 |
| Provision for Losses | 2,801 | 788 | 2,954 | 10,389 | 10,676 | 3,329 | 1,790 | 4,607 |
| Non-Interest Income | 37,387 | 17,729 | 69,919 | 66,864 | 74,385 | 71,138 | 58,424 | 54,284 |
| Non-Interest Expense | 76,007 | 36,397 | 144,095 | 139,117 | 135,006 | 132,552 | 124,557 | 117,165 |
| Income Before Taxes | 33,896 | 17,834 | 65,646 | 48,679 | 67,810 | 81,649 | 75,765 | 63,963 |
| Income Taxes | 12,426 | 6,479 | 23,337 | 16,070 | 23,452 | 28,556 | 26,413 | 21,128 |
| Net Income | 21,470 | 11,355 | 42,309 | 32,609 | 44,358 | 53,093 | 49,352 | 42,835 |
| Average Shares | 15,651 | 15,679 | 15,651 | 15,593 | 15,578 | 15,944 | 16,094 | 16,000 |
| **Balance Sheet** | | | | | | | | |
| Net Loans & Leases | 2,824,752 | 2,760,254 | 2,776,219 | 2,702,271 | 2,723,564 | 2,457,972 | 2,297,848 | 2,289,909 |
| Total Assets | 5,267,445 | 5,239,658 | 5,060,249 | 4,416,115 | 3,867,204 | 3,743,006 | 3,418,574 | 3,223,030 |
| Total Deposits | 4,701,999 | 4,666,199 | 4,503,754 | 3,929,016 | 3,377,608 | 3,288,504 | 2,974,305 | 2,804,519 |
| Total Liabilities | 4,797,048 | 4,772,831 | 4,601,655 | 3,985,365 | 3,453,413 | 3,371,044 | 3,070,219 | 2,920,681 |
| Stockholders' Equity | 470,397 | 466,827 | 458,594 | 430,750 | 413,791 | 371,962 | 348,355 | 302,349 |
| Shares Outstanding | 15,273 | 15,390 | 15,368 | 15,308 | 15,281 | 15,217 | 15,764 | 15,637 |
| **Statistical Record** | | | | | | | | |
| Return on Assets % | 0.88 | 0.91 | 0.89 | 0.79 | 1.16 | 1.48 | 1.49 | 1.37 |
| Return on Equity % | 9.48 | 9.82 | 9.51 | 7.72 | 11.26 | 14.74 | 15.17 | 14.77 |
| Net Interest Margin % | 84.89 | 84.16 | 83.54 | 77.34 | 70.28 | 64.26 | 67.39 | 76.56 |
| Efficiency Ratio % | 61.45 | 58.67 | 59.83 | 58.78 | 49.58 | 43.91 | 45.85 | 51.85 |
| Loans to Deposits | 0.60 | 0.59 | 0.62 | 0.69 | 0.81 | 0.75 | 0.77 | 0.82 |
| Price Range | 44.24-35.10 | 47.11-35.10 | 47.11-35.10 | 53.23-29.42 | 73.10-39.10 | 54.02-39.30 | 55.18-39.76 | 45.22-31.80 |
| P/E Ratio | 15.97-12.67 | 16.65-12.40 | 17.45-13.00 | 25.47-14.08 | 25.65-13.72 | 16.22-11.80 | 17.97-12.95 | 16.87-11.86 |
| Average Yield % | 2.48 | 2.41 | 2.39 | 2.40 | 1.85 | 1.67 | 1.48 | 1.52 |

| | | |
|---|---|---|
| **Address:** 101 North Broadway, Oklahoma City, OK 73102-8405 | **Officers:** H. E. Rainbolt - Chairman James R. Daniel - Vice-Chairman **Transfer Agents:** | **Investor Contact:** 405-270-1044 |
| **Telephone:** 405-270-1086 | BancFirst Trust and Investment Management, | **No of Institutions:** 113 |
| **Web Site:** www.bancfirst.com | Oklahoma City, OK | **Shares:** 4,123,468 **% Held:** 24.47 |

# BANK OF THE OZARKS, INC.

| Exchange | Symbol | Price | 52Wk Range | Yield | P/E |
|---|---|---|---|---|---|
| NMS | OZRK | $22.72 (8/31/2011) | 26.94-17.73 | 1.67 | 7.68 |

***7 Year Price Score 136.13** *NYSE Composite Index=100 ***12 Month Price Score 115.27**

**Interim Earnings (Per Share)**

| Qtr. | Mar | Jun | Sep | Dec |
|---|---|---|---|---|
| 2008 | 0.23 | 0.26 | 0.27 | 0.27 |
| 2009 | 0.28 | 0.28 | 0.25 | 0.28 |
| 2010 | 0.47 | 0.32 | 0.59 | 0.49 |
| 2011 | 0.42 | 1.46 | ... | ... |

**Interim Dividends (Per Share)**

| Amt | Decl | Ex | Rec | Pay |
|---|---|---|---|---|
| 0.17Q | 01/03/2011 | 01/12/2011 | 01/14/2011 | 01/21/2011 |
| 0.18Q | 04/01/2011 | 04/13/2011 | 04/15/2011 | 04/22/2011 |
| 0.19Q | 07/01/2011 | 07/13/2011 | 07/15/2011 | 07/22/2011 |
| 100% | 07/19/2011 | 08/17/2011 | 08/05/2011 | 08/16/2011 |

**Indicated Div: $0.38 (Div. Reinv. Plan)**

**Valuation Analysis**

Forecast EPS $2.74 (09/02/2011)

| Market Cap | $777.9 Million | Book Value | $385.7 Million |
|---|---|---|---|
| Price/Book | 2.02 | Price/Sales | N/A |

**Dividend Achiever Status**

| | |
|---|---|
| **10 Year Growth Rate** | 17.96% |
| **Total Years of Dividend Growth** | 13 |

**Business Summary:** Banking (MIC: 5.1.1 SIC: 6022 NAIC: 522110)

Bank of the Ozarks is a bank holding company. Co. owns a wholly-owned state chartered bank subsidiary, Bank of the Ozarks. Co.'s market areas include the northern, western and central portions of Arkansas, the metropolitan Dallas, TX area, and the metropolitan Charlotte, NC area. Co.'s deposit products include checking accounts, transaction accounts, business sweep accounts, savings accounts, money market accounts, time deposits and individual retirement accounts. Co.'s loan portfolio includes real estate, consumer, commercial and industrial, agricultural, and other types of loans. At Dec 31 2010, Co. had total assets of $3.27 billion and total deposits of $2.54 billion.

**Recent Developments:** For the quarter ended June 30 2011, net income increased 362.4% to US$50.2 million from US$10.9 million in the year-earlier quarter. Net interest income increased 42.9% to US$42.5 million from US$29.7 million in the year-earlier quarter. Provision for loan losses was US$3.8 million versus US$3.4 million in the prior-year quarter, an increase of 10.3%. Non-interest income rose 722.4% to US$75.1 million from US$9.1 million, while non-interest expense advanced 66.7% to US$35.2 million.

**Prospects:** Our evaluation of Bank of the Ozarks Inc. as of Sep. 6, 2011 is the result of our systematic analysis on three basic characteristics: earnings strength, relative valuation, and recent stock price movement. The company has produced a positive trend in earnings per share over the past 5 quarters. However, while recent estimates for the company have been mixed, OZRK has posted better than expected results. Based on operating earnings yield, the company is undervalued when compared to all of the companies in our coverage universe. Share price changes over the past year indicates that OZRK will perform well over the near term.

**Financial Data**

| (US$ in Thousands) | 6 Mos | 3 Mos | 12/31/2010 | 12/31/2009 | 12/31/2008 | 12/31/2007 | 12/31/2006 | 12/31/2005 |
|---|---|---|---|---|---|---|---|---|
| Earnings Per Share | 2.96 | 1.83 | 1.88 | 1.09 | 1.02 | 0.94 | 0.94 | 0.94 |
| Cash Flow Per Share | 0.85 | 1.12 | 1.19 | 1.42 | 1.37 | 1.27 | 0.68 | 1.02 |
| Tang Book Value Per Share | 10.88 | 9.55 | 9.16 | 7.79 | 7.31 | 5.50 | 5.03 | 4.29 |
| Dividends Per Share | 0.660 | 0.630 | 0.600 | 0.520 | 0.500 | 0.430 | 0.400 | 0.370 |
| Dividend Payout % | 22.26 | 34.43 | 32.00 | 47.71 | 49.02 | 45.50 | 42.33 | 39.36 |
| **Income Statement** | | | | | | | | |
| Interest Income | 94,896 | 44,022 | 157,972 | 165,908 | 183,003 | 176,970 | 155,198 | 112,881 |
| Interest Expense | 16,337 | 7,939 | 34,337 | 47,585 | 84,302 | 99,352 | 84,478 | 44,305 |
| Net Interest Income | 78,559 | 36,083 | 123,635 | 118,323 | 98,701 | 77,618 | 70,720 | 68,576 |
| Provision for Losses | 6,000 | 2,250 | 16,000 | 44,800 | 19,025 | 6,150 | 2,450 | 2,300 |
| Non-Interest Income | 88,048 | 12,990 | 70,322 | 51,051 | 19,349 | 22,975 | 23,231 | 19,252 |
| Non-Interest Expense | 61,392 | 26,192 | 87,419 | 68,632 | 54,398 | 48,252 | 46,390 | 40,080 |
| Income Before Taxes | 99,215 | 20,631 | 90,538 | 55,942 | 44,627 | 46,191 | 45,111 | 45,448 |
| Income Taxes | 34,384 | 6,004 | 26,614 | 12,859 | 9,926 | 14,445 | 13,418 | 13,959 |
| Net Income | 64,831 | 14,627 | 63,924 | 43,083 | 34,701 | 31,746 | 31,693 | 31,489 |
| Average Shares | 34,464 | 34,366 | 34,090 | 33,800 | 33,748 | 33,668 | 33,606 | 33,532 |
| **Balance Sheet** | | | | | | | | |
| Net Loans & Leases | 1,763,003 | 1,768,669 | 1,816,199 | 1,864,485 | 1,991,687 | 1,851,578 | 1,659,690 | 1,353,716 |
| Total Assets | 4,026,841 | 3,326,878 | 3,273,659 | 2,770,811 | 3,233,303 | 2,710,875 | 2,529,400 | 2,134,882 |
| Total Deposits | 3,170,483 | 2,580,043 | 2,540,753 | 2,028,994 | 2,341,414 | 2,057,061 | 2,045,092 | 1,591,643 |
| Total Liabilities | 3,641,158 | 2,992,048 | 2,953,405 | 2,501,783 | 2,909,121 | 2,520,046 | 2,354,767 | 1,985,479 |
| Stockholders' Equity | 385,683 | 334,830 | 320,355 | 269,028 | 324,182 | 190,829 | 174,633 | 149,403 |
| Shares Outstanding | 34,236 | 34,195 | 34,107 | 33,809 | 33,728 | 33,636 | 33,493 | 33,329 |
| **Statistical Record** | | | | | | | | |
| Return on Assets % | 2.95 | 1.97 | 2.12 | 1.44 | 1.16 | 1.21 | 1.36 | 1.63 |
| Return on Equity % | 30.07 | 20.25 | 21.69 | 14.53 | 13.44 | 17.37 | 19.56 | 23.26 |
| Net Interest Margin % | 83.49 | 81.97 | 78.26 | 71.32 | 53.93 | 43.86 | 45.57 | 60.75 |
| Efficiency Ratio % | 27.95 | 45.94 | 38.29 | 31.63 | 26.88 | 24.13 | 26.00 | 30.33 |
| Loans to Deposits | 0.56 | 0.69 | 0.71 | 0.92 | 0.85 | 0.90 | 0.81 | 0.85 |
| Price Range | 26.03-17.20 | 22.29-16.83 | 22.29-14.33 | 14.89-8.53 | 16.18-7.07 | 16.75-13.10 | 18.84-15.00 | 19.21-15.42 |
| P/E Ratio | 8.79-5.81 | 12.18-9.20 | 11.86-7.62 | 13.66-7.82 | 15.86-6.93 | 17.82-13.93 | 20.05-15.96 | 20.44-16.40 |
| Average Yield % | 3.17 | 3.23 | 3.33 | 4.32 | 4.15 | 2.92 | 2.39 | 2.19 |

**Address:** 17901 Chenal Parkway, Little Rock, AR 72223
**Telephone:** 501-978-2265
**Web Site:** www.bankozarks.com

**Officers:** George Gleason - Chairman, Chief Executive Officer Mark Ross - Vice-Chairman, President, Chief Operating Officer **Transfer Agents:** Bank of the Ozarks, Little Rock, AR

**No of Institutions:** 170
**Shares:** 14,812,684 **% Held:** 84.26

# BARD (C.R.), INC.

| Exchange | Symbol | Price | 52Wk Range | Yield | P/E |
|---|---|---|---|---|---|
| NYS | BCR | $95.26 (8/31/2011) | 113.32-76.77 | 0.80 | 25.47 |

*7 Year Price Score 117.06 *NYSE Composite Index=100 *12 Month Price Score 104.40

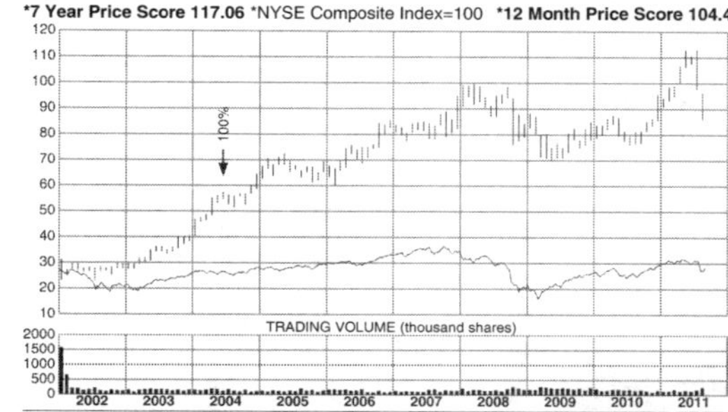

**Interim Earnings (Per Share)**

| Qtr. | Mar | Jun | Sep | Dec |
|---|---|---|---|---|
| 2008 | 0.76 | 0.76 | 1.09 | 1.46 |
| 2009 | 1.10 | 1.11 | 1.31 | 1.08 |
| 2010 | 1.24 | 1.29 | 1.34 | 1.46 |
| 2011 | 1.49 | (0.55) | ... | ... |

**Interim Dividends (Per Share)**

| Amt | Decl | Ex | Rec | Pay |
|---|---|---|---|---|
| 0.18Q | 10/13/2010 | 10/21/2010 | 10/25/2010 | 11/05/2010 |
| 0.18Q | 12/08/2010 | 01/20/2011 | 01/24/2011 | 02/04/2011 |
| 0.18Q | 04/20/2011 | 04/28/2011 | 05/02/2011 | 05/13/2011 |
| 0.19Q | 06/08/2011 | 07/21/2011 | 07/25/2011 | 08/05/2011 |

**Indicated Div: $0.76 (Div. Reinv. Plan)**

**Valuation Analysis**

| | | | |
|---|---|---|---|
| Forecast EPS | $6.38 (09/05/2011) | | |
| Market Cap | $8.3 Billion | Book Value | $1.9 Billion |
| Price/Book | 4.40 | Price/Sales | 2.93 |

**Dividend Achiever Status**

| | |
|---|---|
| 10 Year Growth Rate | 5.24% |
| Total Years of Dividend Growth | 39 |

**Business Summary:** Medical Instruments & Equipment (MIC: 4.3.1 SIC: 3841 NAIC: 339112)

C. R. Bard designs, manufactures, packages, distributes and sells medical, surgical, diagnostic and patient care devices. Co.'s products are intended to be used once and then discarded or implanted either temporarily or permanently. Co. has four major product group categories: vascular, for the treatment of peripheral vascular disease and heart arrhythmias; urology, which includes basic drainage products, continence products and urological specialty products; oncology, for the treatment and management of various cancers and other diseases and disorders; and surgical specialties, which include implanted patches and fixation systems, irrigation devices and products for topical hemostasis.

**Recent Developments:** For the quarter ended June 30 2011, net loss amounted to US$47.8 million versus net income of US$124.7 million in the year-earlier quarter. Revenues were US$725.0 million, up 7.6% from US$673.9 million the year before. Direct operating expenses rose 9.5% to US$275.5 million from US$251.7 million in the comparable period the year before. Indirect operating expenses increased 6.4% to US$252.7 million from US$237.4 million in the equivalent prior-year period.

**Prospects:** Our evaluation of Bard (C.R.) Inc. as of Sep. 6, 2011 is the result of our systematic analysis on three basic characteristics: earnings strength, relative valuation, and recent stock price movement. The company has managed to produce a neutral trend in earnings per share over the past 5 quarters. However, while recent estimates for the company have been mixed, BCR has posted results that fell short of analysts expectations. Based on operating earnings yield, the company is undervalued when compared to all of the companies in our coverage universe. Share price changes over the past year indicates that BCR will perform in line with the market over the near term.

**Financial Data**

| (US$ in Thousands) | 6 Mos | 3 Mos | 12/31/2010 | 12/31/2009 | 12/31/2008 | 12/31/2007 | 12/31/2006 | 12/31/2005 |
|---|---|---|---|---|---|---|---|---|
| Earnings Per Share | 3.74 | 5.58 | 5.32 | 4.60 | 4.06 | 3.84 | 2.55 | 3.12 |
| Cash Flow Per Share | 7.56 | 7.43 | 6.83 | 6.34 | 5.17 | 5.33 | 3.22 | 3.83 |
| Tang Book Value Per Share | 8.56 | 8.33 | 5.69 | 13.34 | 11.62 | 10.73 | 9.46 | 9.08 |
| Dividends Per Share | 0.720 | 0.710 | 0.700 | 0.660 | 0.620 | 0.580 | 0.540 | 0.500 |
| Dividend Payout % | 19.25 | 12.72 | 13.16 | 14.35 | 15.27 | 15.10 | 21.18 | 16.03 |
| **Income Statement** | | | | | | | | |
| Total Revenue | 1,425,300 | 700,300 | 2,720,200 | 2,534,900 | 2,452,100 | 2,202,000 | 1,985,500 | 1,771,300 |
| EBITDA | 259,700 | 220,600 | 778,500 | 730,700 | 596,800 | 607,100 | 381,200 | 482,300 |
| Depn & Amortn | 56,800 | 28,200 | 51,800 | 51,000 | 51,300 | 48,600 | 44,600 | 39,000 |
| Income Before Taxes | 186,700 | 184,000 | 717,700 | 671,500 | 549,900 | 577,300 | 347,600 | 449,600 |
| Income Taxes | 102,600 | 52,100 | 208,100 | 210,100 | 133,400 | 170,900 | 75,500 | 112,500 |
| Net Income | 84,100 | 131,900 | 509,200 | 460,100 | 416,500 | 406,400 | 272,100 | 337,100 |
| Average Shares | 86,200 | 87,000 | 94,600 | 99,000 | 102,500 | 105,900 | 106,900 | 108,000 |
| **Balance Sheet** | | | | | | | | |
| Current Assets | 1,873,400 | 1,642,400 | 1,529,300 | 1,491,800 | 1,354,200 | 1,242,000 | 1,133,900 | 1,264,100 |
| Total Assets | 3,503,200 | 3,288,300 | 3,171,500 | 2,906,900 | 2,665,700 | 2,475,500 | 2,277,200 | 2,265,600 |
| Current Liabilities | 452,300 | 286,300 | 397,700 | 281,700 | 273,100 | 281,700 | 295,900 | 640,600 |
| Long-Term Obligations | 901,100 | 895,300 | 896,900 | 149,800 | 149,800 | 149,800 | 150,600 | 800 |
| Total Liabilities | 1,628,700 | 1,436,600 | 1,540,000 | 713,300 | 688,500 | 627,500 | 579,200 | 729,500 |
| Stockholders' Equity | 1,874,500 | 1,851,700 | 1,631,500 | 2,193,600 | 1,977,200 | 1,848,000 | 1,698,000 | 1,536,100 |
| Shares Outstanding | 86,646 | 85,655 | 84,973 | 95,917 | 99,393 | 100,191 | 103,155 | 104,012 |
| **Statistical Record** | | | | | | | | |
| Return on Assets % | 10.94 | 16.75 | 16.75 | 16.51 | 16.16 | 17.10 | 11.98 | 15.77 |
| Return on Equity % | 17.33 | 25.58 | 26.62 | 22.06 | 21.72 | 22.92 | 16.83 | 23.28 |
| EBITDA Margin % | 18.22 | 31.50 | 28.62 | 28.83 | 24.34 | 27.57 | 19.20 | 27.23 |
| Net Margin % | 5.90 | 18.83 | 18.72 | 18.15 | 16.99 | 18.46 | 13.70 | 19.03 |
| Asset Turnover | 0.89 | 0.89 | 0.90 | 0.91 | 0.95 | 0.93 | 0.87 | 0.83 |
| Current Ratio | 4.14 | 5.74 | 3.85 | 5.30 | 4.96 | 4.41 | 3.83 | 1.97 |
| Debt to Equity | 0.48 | 0.48 | 0.55 | 0.07 | 0.08 | 0.08 | 0.09 | N.M. |
| Price Range | 112.91-76.18 | 99.36-76.18 | 95.72-76.18 | 88.41-70.39 | 99.66-75.99 | 95.05-77.25 | 85.43-60.25 | 72.79-61.36 |
| P/E Ratio | 30.19-20.37 | 17.81-13.65 | 17.99-14.32 | 19.22-15.30 | 24.55-18.72 | 24.75-20.12 | 33.50-23.63 | 23.33-19.67 |
| Average Yield % | 0.79 | 0.83 | 0.85 | 0.85 | 0.68 | 0.70 | 0.74 | 0.75 |

| | | |
|---|---|---|
| **Address:** 730 Central Avenue, Murray Hill, NJ 07974<br>**Telephone:** 908-277-8000<br>**Web Site:** www.crbard.com | **Officers:** Timothy M. Ring - Chairman, Chief Executive Officer John H. Weiland - President, Chief Operating Officer **Transfer Agents:** Computershare Trust Company, N.A., Canton, MA | **Investor Contact:** 908-277-8413<br>**No of Institutions:** 645<br>**Shares:** 89,614,192 **% Held:** 91.04 |

# BECTON, DICKINSON AND CO.

| Exchange | Symbol | Price | 52Wk Range | Yield | P/E |
|---|---|---|---|---|---|
| NYS | BDX | $81.38 (8/31/2011) | 89.74-68.19 | 2.02 | 13.68 |

***7 Year Price Score 112.54** *NYSE Composite Index=100 ***12 Month Price Score 103.06**

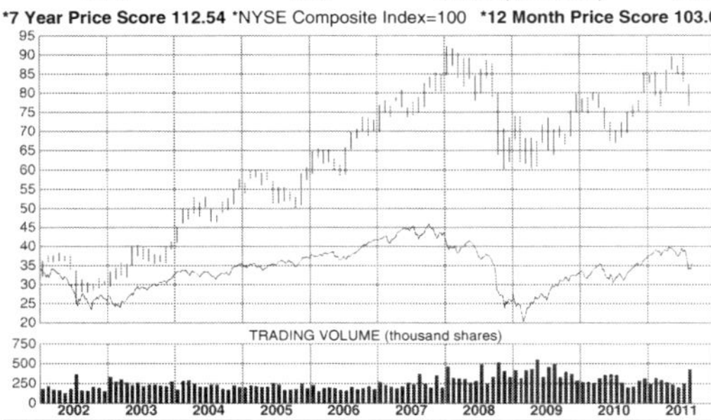


**Interim Earnings (Per Share)**

| Qtr. | Dec | Mar | Jun | Sep |
|---|---|---|---|---|
| 2007-08 | 1.07 | 1.09 | 1.18 | 1.12 |
| 2008-09 | 1.26 | 1.06 | 1.39 | 1.29 |
| 2009-10 | 1.30 | 1.24 | 1.29 | 1.68 |
| 2010-11 | 1.36 | 1.38 | 1.53 | ... |

**Interim Dividends (Per Share)**

| Amt | Decl | Ex | Rec | Pay |
|---|---|---|---|---|
| 0.41Q | 11/23/2010 | 12/08/2010 | 12/10/2010 | 12/31/2010 |
| 0.41Q | 02/01/2011 | 03/08/2011 | 03/10/2011 | 03/31/2011 |
| 0.41Q | 05/24/2011 | 06/07/2011 | 06/09/2011 | 06/30/2011 |
| 0.41Q | 07/26/2011 | 09/07/2011 | 09/09/2011 | 09/30/2011 |

**Indicated Div: $1.64 (Div. Reinv. Plan)**

**Valuation Analysis**

| | | | |
|---|---|---|---|
| Forecast EPS | $5.63 (09/02/2011) | | |
| Market Cap | $17.7 Billion | Book Value | $5.3 Billion |
| Price/Book | 3.34 | Price/Sales | 2.36 |

**Dividend Achiever Status**

| | |
|---|---|
| **10 Year Growth Rate** | 17.40% |
| **Total Years of Dividend Growth** | 38 |

**Business Summary:** Medical Instruments & Equipment (MIC: 4.3.1 SIC: 3841 NAIC: 339112)

Becton, Dickinson and Company is a medical application company engaged principally in the development, manufacture and sale of medical devices, instrument systems and reagents. Co.'s operations consist of three business segments: BD Medical, which produces an array of medical devices that are used in a range of healthcare settings; BD Diagnostics, which provides products for the collection and transport of diagnostics specimens, as well as instrument systems and reagents to detect a range of infectious diseases, healthcare-associated infections and cancers; and BD Biosciences, which produces research and clinical tools that facilitate the study of cells, and the components of cells.

**Recent Developments:** For the quarter ended June 30 2011, income from continuing operations increased 14.9% to US$338.1 million from US$294.2 million in the year-earlier quarter. Net income increased 11.8% to US$343.1 million from US$306.9 million in the year-earlier quarter. Revenues were US$2.01 billion, up 10.0% from US$1.83 billion the year before. Operating income was US$471.7 million versus US$423.0 million in the prior-year quarter, an increase of 11.5%. Direct operating expenses rose 7.8% to US$952.0 million from US$883.4 million in the comparable period the year before. Indirect operating expenses increased 12.6% to US$590.4 million from US$524.5 million in the equivalent prior-year period.

**Prospects:** Our evaluation of Becton, Dickinson and Co. as of Sep. 6, 2011 is the result of our systematic analysis on three basic characteristics: earnings strength, relative valuation, and recent stock price movement. The company has produced a positive trend in earnings per share over the past 5 quarters. However, while recent estimates for the company have been mixed, BDX has posted better than expected results. Based on operating earnings yield, the company is undervalued when compared to all of the companies in our coverage universe. Share price changes over the past year indicates that BDX will perform poorly over the near term.

**Financial Data**

| (US$ in Thousands) | 9 Mos | 6 Mos | 3 Mos | 09/30/2010 | 09/30/2009 | 09/30/2008 | 09/30/2007 | 09/30/2006 |
|---|---|---|---|---|---|---|---|---|
| Earnings Per Share | 5.95 | 5.71 | 5.57 | 5.49 | 4.99 | 4.46 | 3.49 | 2.93 |
| Cash Flow Per Share | 7.49 | 7.60 | 7.60 | 7.08 | 7.03 | 6.89 | 5.05 | 4.36 |
| Tang Book Value Per Share | 15.91 | 14.94 | 15.01 | 16.87 | 16.52 | 15.38 | 12.82 | 11.18 |
| Dividends Per Share | 1.600 | 1.560 | 1.520 | 1.480 | 1.320 | 1.140 | 0.980 | 0.860 |
| Dividend Payout % | 26.89 | 27.32 | 27.29 | 26.96 | 26.45 | 25.56 | 28.08 | 29.35 |
| **Income Statement** | | | | | | | | |
| Total Revenue | 5,778,109 | 3,764,028 | 1,842,005 | 7,372,333 | 7,160,874 | 7,155,910 | 6,359,708 | 5,834,827 |
| EBITDA | 1,689,854 | 1,091,697 | 531,674 | 2,179,407 | 2,116,696 | 1,856,092 | 1,484,501 | 1,306,169 |
| Depn & Amortn | 372,210 | 245,397 | 123,192 | 502,113 | 470,193 | 305,510 | 280,357 | 264,462 |
| Income Before Taxes | 1,297,253 | 836,612 | 408,151 | 1,661,160 | 1,639,262 | 1,553,607 | 1,203,945 | 1,034,957 |
| Income Taxes | 333,804 | 211,273 | 93,875 | 484,820 | 426,208 | 425,689 | 347,778 | 279,366 |
| Net Income | 971,015 | 627,956 | 315,937 | 1,317,610 | 1,231,603 | 1,126,996 | 890,033 | 752,280 |
| Average Shares | 223,567 | 225,467 | 232,915 | 240,136 | 246,798 | 252,681 | 254,810 | 256,554 |
| **Balance Sheet** | | | | | | | | |
| Current Assets | 5,073,133 | 4,856,630 | 4,950,841 | 4,505,250 | 4,646,954 | 3,614,675 | 3,130,566 | 3,185,253 |
| Total Assets | 10,620,819 | 10,344,223 | 10,071,270 | 9,650,694 | 9,304,624 | 7,912,943 | 7,329,365 | 6,824,525 |
| Current Liabilities | 1,657,926 | 1,578,911 | 1,612,353 | 1,671,673 | 1,777,093 | 1,416,579 | 1,478,809 | 1,576,329 |
| Long-Term Obligations | 2,484,953 | 2,484,168 | 2,485,019 | 1,495,357 | 1,488,460 | 953,226 | 955,713 | 956,971 |
| Total Liabilities | 5,322,419 | 5,245,162 | 5,193,337 | 4,216,114 | 4,161,912 | 2,977,375 | 2,967,408 | 2,988,321 |
| Stockholders' Equity | 5,298,400 | 5,099,061 | 4,877,933 | 5,434,580 | 5,142,712 | 4,935,568 | 4,361,957 | 3,836,204 |
| Shares Outstanding | 217,446 | 218,751 | 221,114 | 229,816 | 237,082 | 243,077 | 243,837 | 245,468 |
| **Statistical Record** | | | | | | | | |
| Return on Assets % | 13.92 | 13.81 | 13.75 | 13.90 | 14.31 | 14.75 | 12.58 | 11.67 |
| Return on Equity % | 26.17 | 25.98 | 25.98 | 24.91 | 24.44 | 24.18 | 21.71 | 21.13 |
| EBITDA Margin % | 29.25 | 29.00 | 28.86 | 29.56 | 29.56 | 25.94 | 23.34 | 22.39 |
| Net Margin % | 16.81 | 16.68 | 17.15 | 17.87 | 17.20 | 15.75 | 13.99 | 12.89 |
| Asset Turnover | 0.76 | 0.76 | 0.76 | 0.78 | 0.83 | 0.94 | 0.90 | 0.90 |
| Current Ratio | 3.06 | 3.08 | 3.07 | 2.70 | 2.61 | 2.55 | 2.12 | 2.02 |
| Debt to Equity | 0.47 | 0.49 | 0.51 | 0.28 | 0.29 | 0.19 | 0.22 | 0.25 |
| Price Range | 89.58-66.89 | 85.64-66.89 | 85.32-66.89 | 80.14-66.60 | 80.26-60.26 | 92.34-77.93 | 82.61-68.81 | 70.67-50.07 |
| P/E Ratio | 15.06-11.24 | 15.00-11.71 | 15.32-12.01 | 14.60-12.13 | 16.08-12.08 | 20.70-17.47 | 23.67-19.72 | 24.12-17.09 |
| Average Yield % | 2.03 | 2.05 | 2.02 | 2.01 | 1.94 | 1.34 | 1.30 | 1.40 |

| | | |
|---|---|---|
| **Address:** 1 Becton Drive, Franklin Lakes, NJ 07417-1880<br>**Telephone:** 201-847-6800<br>**Web Site:** www.bd.com | **Officers:** Edward J. Ludwig - Executive Chairman Vincent A. Forlenza - President, Chief Executive Officer, Chief Operating Officer **Transfer Agents:** Computershare Trust Company, N.A., Canton, MA | **Investor Contact:** 800-284-6845<br>**No of Institutions:** 998<br>**Shares:** 195,865,936 **% Held:** 77.02 |

# BEMIS CO INC

| Exchange | Symbol | Price | 52Wk Range | Yield | P/E |
|---|---|---|---|---|---|
| NYS | BMS | $31.06 (8/31/2011) | 34.25-28.60 | 3.09 | 15.45 |

***7 Year Price Score 109.70** *NYSE Composite Index=100 ***12 Month Price Score 99.29**

**Interim Earnings (Per Share)**

| Qtr. | Mar | Jun | Sep | Dec |
|---|---|---|---|---|
| 2008 | 0.42 | 0.46 | 0.44 | 0.33 |
| 2009 | 0.36 | 0.47 | 0.33 | 0.23 |
| 2010 | 0.28 | 0.54 | 0.55 | 0.48 |
| 2011 | 0.47 | 0.51 | ... | ... |

**Interim Dividends (Per Share)**

| Amt | Decl | Ex | Rec | Pay |
|---|---|---|---|---|
| 0.23Q | 11/04/2010 | 11/12/2010 | 11/16/2010 | 12/01/2010 |
| 0.24Q | 02/04/2011 | 02/11/2011 | 02/15/2011 | 03/01/2011 |
| 0.24Q | 05/05/2011 | 05/16/2011 | 05/18/2011 | 06/01/2011 |
| 0.24Q | 08/05/2011 | 08/15/2011 | 08/17/2011 | 09/01/2011 |

**Indicated Div: $0.96 (Div. Reinv. Plan)**

**Valuation Analysis**

| | | | |
|---|---|---|---|
| Forecast EPS | $2.13 (09/05/2011) | | |
| Market Cap | $3.2 Billion | Book Value | $1.9 Billion |
| Price/Book | 1.71 | Price/Sales | 0.62 |

**Dividend Achiever Status**

| | |
|---|---|
| **10 Year Growth Rate** | 6.29% |
| **Total Years of Dividend Growth** | 27 |

**Business Summary:** Containers & Packaging (MIC: 8.1.3 SIC: 2671 NAIC: 322221)

Bemis Company is a manufacturer of packaging products and pressure sensitive materials. Co.'s products are sold to customers primarily in the food industry. Other customers include companies in the following types of businesses: chemical, agribusiness, medical, pharmaceutical, personal care, electronics, automotive, construction, graphic industries, and other consumer goods. Co. operates in two business segments: flexible packaging, which manufactures a range of packaging for food, consumer goods, and industrial applications; and pressure sensitive materials, which manufactures pressure sensitive adhesive coated paper and film substrates sold into label, graphic, and technical markets.

**Recent Developments:** For the quarter ended June 30 2011, income from continuing operations decreased 6.8% to US$55.6 million from US$59.6 million in the year-earlier quarter. Net income decreased 9.8% to US$55.6 million from US$61.6 million in the year-earlier quarter. Revenues were US$1.37 billion, up 7.9% from US$1.27 billion the year before. Operating income was US$105.3 million versus US$112.5 million in the prior-year quarter, a decrease of 6.4%. Direct operating expenses rose 9.3% to US$1.13 billion from US$1.04 billion in the comparable period the year before. Indirect operating expenses increased 9.2% to US$132.7 million from US$121.5 million in the equivalent prior-year period.

**Prospects:** Our evaluation of Bemis Co Inc. as of Sep. 6, 2011 is the result of our systematic analysis on three basic characteristics: earnings strength, relative valuation, and recent stock price movement. The company has managed to produce a neutral trend in earnings per share over the past 5 quarters. However, while recent estimates for the company have been mixed, BMS has posted better than expected results. Based on operating earnings yield, the company is undervalued when compared to all of the companies in our coverage universe. Share price changes over the past year indicates that BMS will perform very poorly over the near term.

**Financial Data**

| (US$ in Thousands) | 6 Mos | 3 Mos | 12/31/2010 | 12/31/2009 | 12/31/2008 | 12/31/2007 | 12/31/2006 | 12/31/2005 |
|---|---|---|---|---|---|---|---|---|
| Earnings Per Share | 2.01 | 2.04 | 1.85 | 1.38 | 1.65 | 1.74 | 1.65 | 1.51 |
| Cash Flow Per Share | 3.10 | 3.37 | 3.39 | 4.60 | 2.93 | 3.94 | 3.33 | 2.63 |
| Tang Book Value Per Share | 6.32 | 6.30 | 6.18 | 9.90 | 6.72 | 8.12 | 7.31 | 6.29 |
| Dividends Per Share | 0.940 | 0.930 | 0.920 | 0.900 | 0.880 | 0.840 | 0.760 | 0.720 |
| Dividend Payout % | 46.77 | 45.59 | 49.73 | 65.22 | 53.33 | 48.28 | 46.06 | 47.68 |
| **Income Statement** | | | | | | | | |
| Total Revenue | 2,694,648 | 1,324,428 | 4,835,042 | 3,514,586 | 3,779,373 | 3,649,281 | 3,639,363 | 3,473,950 |
| EBITDA | 319,199 | 157,025 | 611,272 | 442,470 | 470,600 | 499,325 | 491,846 | 472,602 |
| Depn & Amortn | 112,097 | 55,593 | 210,500 | 160,108 | 162,662 | 159,452 | 153,258 | 151,499 |
| Income Before Taxes | 170,656 | 83,096 | 327,284 | 240,310 | 268,525 | 289,605 | 289,336 | 282,366 |
| Income Taxes | 62,300 | 30,300 | 117,600 | 87,800 | 96,300 | 104,300 | 109,500 | 113,900 |
| Net Income | 105,462 | 51,210 | 205,111 | 147,221 | 166,214 | 181,554 | 176,296 | 162,529 |
| Average Shares | 105,580 | 107,495 | 108,750 | 103,601 | 100,969 | 104,114 | 106,767 | 107,819 |
| **Balance Sheet** | | | | | | | | |
| Current Assets | 1,677,325 | 1,592,204 | 1,466,919 | 2,005,348 | 982,658 | 1,136,943 | 1,093,712 | 987,810 |
| Total Assets | 4,503,290 | 4,410,083 | 4,285,831 | 3,928,705 | 2,822,314 | 3,191,396 | 3,039,009 | 2,964,600 |
| Current Liabilities | 697,442 | 644,980 | 675,259 | 524,855 | 421,781 | 534,550 | 555,455 | 474,320 |
| Long-Term Obligations | 1,460,218 | 1,417,305 | 1,283,525 | 1,227,514 | 659,984 | 775,456 | 722,211 | 790,107 |
| Total Liabilities | 2,616,413 | 2,523,229 | 2,406,208 | 2,124,973 | 1,475,783 | 1,629,064 | 1,566,993 | 1,615,245 |
| Stockholders' Equity | 1,886,877 | 1,886,854 | 1,879,623 | 1,803,732 | 1,346,531 | 1,562,332 | 1,472,016 | 1,349,355 |
| Shares Outstanding | 104,095 | 106,201 | 107,673 | 108,223 | 99,708 | 100,518 | 104,841 | 105,305 |
| **Statistical Record** | | | | | | | | |
| Return on Assets % | 4.99 | 5.15 | 4.99 | 4.36 | 5.51 | 5.83 | 5.87 | 5.96 |
| Return on Equity % | 11.99 | 12.33 | 11.14 | 9.35 | 11.40 | 11.97 | 12.50 | 12.23 |
| EBITDA Margin % | 11.85 | 11.86 | 12.64 | 12.59 | 12.45 | 13.68 | 13.51 | 13.60 |
| Net Margin % | 3.91 | 3.87 | 4.24 | 4.19 | 4.40 | 4.98 | 4.84 | 4.68 |
| Asset Turnover | 1.19 | 1.17 | 1.18 | 1.04 | 1.25 | 1.17 | 1.21 | 1.27 |
| Current Ratio | 2.40 | 2.47 | 2.17 | 3.82 | 2.33 | 2.13 | 1.97 | 2.08 |
| Debt to Equity | 0.77 | 0.75 | 0.68 | 0.68 | 0.49 | 0.50 | 0.49 | 0.59 |
| Price Range | 33.90-26.72 | 33.90-26.72 | 33.90-26.72 | 30.90-17.09 | 29.31-21.57 | 36.23-25.85 | 34.82-28.49 | 31.36-23.44 |
| P/E Ratio | 16.87-13.29 | 16.62-13.10 | 18.32-14.44 | 22.39-12.38 | 17.76-13.07 | 20.82-14.86 | 21.10-17.27 | 20.77-15.52 |
| Average Yield % | 2.97 | 3.01 | 3.06 | 3.60 | 3.43 | 2.67 | 2.41 | 2.62 |

| | | |
|---|---|---|
| **Address:** One Neenah Center, 4th Floor, P.O. Box 669, Neenah, WI 54957-0669 **Telephone:** 920-727-4100 **Web Site:** www.bemis.com | **Officers:** Jeffrey H. Curler - Chairman, Chairman Emeritus Henry J. Theisen - President, Chief Executive Officer **Transfer Agents:** Wells Fargo Bank, N.A., South St. Paul, MN | **Investor Contact:** 920-727-4100 **No of Institutions:** 405 **Shares:** 91,785,072 **% Held:** 74.83 |

# BLACK HILLS CORPORATION

| Exchange | Symbol | Price | 52Wk Range | Yield | P/E |
|---|---|---|---|---|---|
| NYS | BKH | $30.60 (8/31/2011) | 34.80-26.61 | 4.77 | 14.93 |

*7 Year Price Score 93.77 *NYSE Composite Index=100 *12 Month Price Score 96.05

**Interim Earnings (Per Share)**

| Qtr. | Mar | Jun | Sep | Dec |
|---|---|---|---|---|
| 2008 | 0.44 | 0.58 | 4.29 | (2.56) |
| 2009 | 0.68 | 0.64 | (0.06) | 0.85 |
| 2010 | 0.81 | (0.22) | 0.32 | 0.86 |
| 2011 | 0.68 | 0.19 | ... | ... |

**Interim Dividends (Per Share)**

| Amt | Decl | Ex | Rec | Pay |
|---|---|---|---|---|
| 0.36Q | 10/28/2010 | 11/15/2010 | 11/17/2010 | 12/01/2010 |
| 0.365Q | 01/27/2011 | 02/11/2011 | 02/15/2011 | 03/01/2011 |
| 0.365Q | 04/26/2011 | 05/16/2011 | 05/18/2011 | 06/01/2011 |
| 0.365Q | 07/27/2011 | 08/16/2011 | 08/18/2011 | 09/01/2011 |

**Indicated Div: $1.46 (Div. Reinv. Plan)**

**Valuation Analysis**

| | | | |
|---|---|---|---|
| Forecast EPS | $1.75 (09/02/2011) | | |
| Market Cap | $1.2 Billion | Book Value | $1.1 Billion |
| Price/Book | 1.09 | Price/Sales | 0.95 |

**Dividend Achiever Status**

| | |
|---|---|
| 10 Year Growth Rate | 2.54% |
| Total Years of Dividend Growth | 39 |

**Business Summary:** Electric Utilities (MIC: 3.1.1 SIC: 4911 NAIC: 221121)

Black Hills is a holding company. Through its subsidiaries, Co. operates primarily in the U.S. with two business groups: Utilities, which comprised of its regulated Electric Utilities and regulated Gas Utilities segments; and Non-regulated Energy, which comprised of its Oil and Gas, Power Generation, Coal Mining, and Energy Marketing segments. As of Dec 31 2010, Co. generates, transmits and distributes electricity to approximately 201,000 customers in South Dakota, Wyoming, Colorado and Montana; and distributes natural gas to about 527,000 customers in Colorado, Iowa, Kansas and Nebraska. As of the same date, Co. had total oil and gas reserves of about 131.10 billion cubic feet equivalent.

**Recent Developments:** For the quarter ended June 30 2011, net income amounted to US$7.8 million versus a net loss of US$8.7 million in the year-earlier quarter. Revenues were US$273.1 million, up 6.5% from US$256.3 million the year before. Operating income was US$42.6 million versus US$30.8 million in the prior-year quarter, an increase of 38.2%. Direct operating expenses declined 0.6% to US$162.5 million from US$163.5 million in the comparable period the year before. Indirect operating expenses increased 9.7% to US$68.0 million from US$62.0 million in the equivalent prior-year period.

**Prospects:** Our evaluation of Black Hills Corp. as of Sep. 6, 2011 is the result of our systematic analysis on three basic characteristics: earnings strength, relative valuation, and recent stock price movement. The company has produced a positive trend in earnings per share over the past 5 quarters. However, while recent estimates for the company have been lowered by analysts, BKH has posted better than expected results. Based on operating earnings yield, the company is about fairly valued when compared to all of the companies in our coverage universe. Share price changes over the past year indicates that BKH will perform very poorly over the near term.

**Financial Data**

| (US$ in Thousands) | 6 Mos | 3 Mos | 12/31/2010 | 12/31/2009 | 12/31/2008 | 12/31/2007 | 12/31/2006 | 12/31/2005 |
|---|---|---|---|---|---|---|---|---|
| Earnings Per Share | 2.05 | 1.64 | 1.76 | 2.11 | 2.75 | 2.64 | 2.42 | 1.00 |
| Cash Flow Per Share | 4.75 | 4.36 | 3.80 | 7.01 | 3.80 | 6.81 | 7.83 | 5.34 |
| Tang Book Value Per Share | 19.00 | 19.14 | 18.88 | 18.65 | 17.76 | 24.32 | 22.03 | 20.49 |
| Dividends Per Share | 1.450 | 1.445 | 1.440 | 1.420 | 1.400 | 1.370 | 1.320 | 1.280 |
| Dividend Payout % | 70.73 | 88.11 | 81.82 | 67.30 | 50.91 | 51.89 | 54.55 | 128.00 |
| **Income Statement** | | | | | | | | |
| Total Revenue | 676,425 | 403,300 | 1,307,251 | 1,269,578 | 1,005,790 | 695,914 | 656,882 | 1,391,644 |
| EBITDA | 164,380 | 88,726 | 308,348 | 309,212 | 69,577 | 279,614 | 247,386 | 176,095 |
| Depn & Amortn | 64,321 | 31,987 | 126,894 | 121,297 | 107,263 | 99,700 | 94,083 | 89,306 |
| Income Before Taxes | 51,582 | 38,826 | 92,424 | 110,728 | (85,798) | 147,373 | 106,705 | 40,011 |
| Income Taxes | 17,953 | 12,909 | 25,298 | 33,315 | (29,395) | 45,641 | 33,802 | 18,299 |
| Net Income | 34,662 | 26,910 | 68,685 | 81,555 | 105,080 | 98,772 | 81,019 | 33,420 |
| Average Shares | 39,823 | 39,761 | 39,091 | 38,684 | 38,193 | 37,414 | 33,549 | 33,288 |
| **Balance Sheet** | | | | | | | | |
| Current Assets | 616,888 | 611,793 | 670,871 | 624,870 | 799,513 | 530,901 | 474,501 | 541,968 |
| Total Assets | 3,810,764 | 3,727,028 | 3,711,509 | 3,317,698 | 3,379,889 | 2,472,866 | 2,244,676 | 2,119,960 |
| Current Liabilities | 852,552 | 756,140 | 787,440 | 644,859 | 1,253,673 | 580,957 | 528,978 | 470,623 |
| Long-Term Obligations | 1,183,583 | 1,184,830 | 1,186,050 | 1,015,912 | 501,252 | 564,372 | 628,340 | 670,193 |
| Total Liabilities | 2,702,695 | 2,613,881 | 2,611,239 | 2,232,861 | 2,329,353 | 1,503,011 | 1,454,635 | 1,381,081 |
| Stockholders' Equity | 1,108,069 | 1,113,147 | 1,100,270 | 1,084,837 | 1,050,536 | 969,855 | 790,041 | 738,879 |
| Shares Outstanding | 39,438 | 39,408 | 39,269 | 38,968 | 38,635 | 37,796 | 33,369 | 33,155 |
| **Statistical Record** | | | | | | | | |
| Return on Assets % | 2.24 | 1.81 | 1.95 | 2.44 | 3.58 | 4.19 | 3.71 | 1.60 |
| Return on Equity % | 7.36 | 5.78 | 6.29 | 7.64 | 10.37 | 11.22 | 10.60 | 4.53 |
| EBITDA Margin % | 24.30 | 22.00 | 23.59 | 24.36 | 6.92 | 40.18 | 37.66 | 12.65 |
| Net Margin % | 5.12 | 6.67 | 5.25 | 6.42 | 10.45 | 14.19 | 12.33 | 2.40 |
| Asset Turnover | 0.35 | 0.36 | 0.37 | 0.38 | 0.34 | 0.30 | 0.30 | 0.67 |
| Current Ratio | 0.72 | 0.81 | 0.85 | 0.97 | 0.64 | 0.91 | 0.90 | 1.15 |
| Debt to Equity | 1.07 | 1.06 | 1.08 | 0.94 | 0.48 | 0.58 | 0.80 | 0.91 |
| Price Range | 34.80-28.17 | 34.11-27.62 | 34.11-25.86 | 27.82-14.59 | 44.10-21.99 | 44.90-35.76 | 37.93-32.75 | 43.54-29.42 |
| P/E Ratio | 16.98-13.74 | 20.80-16.84 | 19.38-14.69 | 13.18-6.91 | 16.04-8.00 | 17.01-13.55 | 15.67-13.53 | 43.54-29.42 |
| Average Yield % | 4.64 | 4.68 | 4.79 | 6.15 | 4.21 | 3.40 | 3.79 | 3.51 |

**Address:** 625 Ninth Street, Rapid City, SD 57701
**Telephone:** 605-721-1700
**Web Site:** www.blackhillscorp.com

**Officers:** David R. Emery - Chairman, President, Chief Executive Officer Anthony S. Cleberg - Executive Vice President, Chief Financial Officer
**Transfer Agents:** Wells Fargo Shareowner Services, St. Paul, MN

**Investor Contact:** 605-721-2765
**No of Institutions:** 217
**Shares:** 31,134,368 **% Held:** 75.17

# BRADY CORP.

| Exchange | Symbol | Price | 52Wk Range | Yield | P/E |
|---|---|---|---|---|---|
| NYS | BRC | $27.50 (8/31/2011) | 38.49-24.73 | 2.62 | 14.40 |

***7 Year Price Score 100.19** *NYSE Composite Index=100 ***12 Month Price Score 91.27**

**Interim Earnings (Per Share)**

| Qtr. | Oct | Jan | Apr | Jul |
|---|---|---|---|---|
| 2007-08 | 0.66 | 0.48 | 0.63 | 0.64 |
| 2008-09 | 0.69 | (0.08) | 0.34 | 0.37 |
| 2009-10 | 0.41 | 0.28 | 0.45 | 0.41 |
| 2010-11 | 0.50 | 0.46 | 0.54 | ... |

**Interim Dividends (Per Share)**

| Amt | Decl | Ex | Rec | Pay |
|---|---|---|---|---|
| 0.18Q | 09/09/2010 | 10/06/2010 | 10/08/2010 | 10/29/2010 |
| 0.18Q | 11/18/2010 | 01/06/2011 | 01/10/2011 | 01/31/2011 |
| 0.18Q | 02/17/2011 | 04/06/2011 | 04/08/2011 | 04/29/2011 |
| 0.18Q | 05/17/2011 | 07/06/2011 | 07/08/2011 | 07/29/2011 |

**Indicated Div: $0.72 (Div. Reinv. Plan)**

**Valuation Analysis**

| | | | |
|---|---|---|---|
| Forecast EPS | $2.20 (09/02/2011) | | |
| Market Cap | $1.5 Billion | Book Value | $1.1 Billion |
| Price/Book | 1.28 | Price/Sales | 1.10 |

**Dividend Achiever Status**

| | |
|---|---|
| **10 Year Growth Rate** | 6.80% |
| **Total Years of Dividend Growth** | 26 |

**Business Summary:** Electrical Equipment (MIC: 7.3.1 SIC: 3993 NAIC: 339950)

Brady provides identification applications and specialty products that identify and protect premises, products and people. Co.'s products include facility identification; safety and complementary products; wire and cable identification products; sorbent materials; people identification products; regulatory publishing; identification products for product identification and work-in-process identification; and bar-code labels and precision die-cut components for mobile telecommunications devices, hard disk drives, medical devices and supplies, and automotive and other electronics. Co. also provides poster printers, cutting systems, laminators and supplies to education and training markets.

**Recent Developments:** For the quarter ended Apr 30 2011, net income increased 20.7% to US$28.6 million from US$23.7 million in the year-earlier quarter. Revenues were US$337.9 million, up 5.0% from US$321.9 million the year before. Operating income was US$40.9 million versus US$35.9 million in the prior-year quarter, an increase of 13.8%. Direct operating expenses rose 5.3% to US$170.3 million from US$161.7 million in the comparable period the year before. Indirect operating expenses increased 2.0% to US$126.8 million from US$124.3 million in the equivalent prior-year period.

**Prospects:** Our evaluation of Brady Corp. as of Sep. 6, 2011 is the result of our systematic analysis on three basic characteristics: earnings strength, relative valuation, and recent stock price movement. The company has managed to produce a neutral trend in earnings per share over the past 5 quarters. However, while recent estimates for the company have been lowered by analysts, BRC has posted results that fell short of analysts expectations. Based on operating earnings yield, the company is undervalued when compared to all of the companies in our coverage universe. Share price changes over the past year indicates that BRC will perform in line with the market over the near term.

**Financial Data**

| (US$ in Thousands) | 9 Mos | 6 Mos | 3 Mos | 07/31/2010 | 07/31/2009 | 07/31/2008 | 07/31/2007 | 07/31/2006 |
|---|---|---|---|---|---|---|---|---|
| Earnings Per Share | 1.91 | 1.82 | 1.64 | 1.55 | 1.33 | 2.41 | 2.00 | 2.07 |
| Cash Flow Per Share | 2.99 | 2.94 | 2.81 | 3.15 | 2.41 | 4.15 | 2.52 | 2.32 |
| Tang Book Value Per Share | 4.48 | 3.74 | 3.24 | 2.53 | 1.60 | 1.64 | 0.07 | 0.45 |
| Dividends Per Share | 0.715 | 0.710 | 0.705 | 0.700 | 0.680 | 0.600 | 0.560 | 0.520 |
| Dividend Payout % | 37.43 | 39.01 | 42.99 | 45.16 | 51.13 | 24.90 | 28.00 | 25.12 |
| **Income Statement** | | | | | | | | |
| Total Revenue | 996,493 | 658,597 | 329,588 | 1,259,096 | 1,208,702 | 1,523,016 | 1,362,631 | 1,018,436 |
| EBITDA | 159,968 | 105,649 | 54,487 | 183,646 | 177,024 | 273,159 | 228,718 | 194,063 |
| Depn & Amortn | 37,522 | 25,502 | 12,594 | 53,022 | 54,851 | 60,587 | 53,856 | 35,144 |
| Income Before Taxes | 105,806 | 68,610 | 36,206 | 109,402 | 97,272 | 186,187 | 151,928 | 144,688 |
| Income Taxes | 26,737 | 18,130 | 9,925 | 27,446 | 27,150 | 53,999 | 42,540 | 40,513 |
| Net Income | 79,069 | 50,480 | 26,281 | 81,956 | 70,122 | 132,188 | 109,388 | 104,175 |
| Average Shares | 53,337 | 53,053 | 52,810 | 52,946 | 52,866 | 54,873 | 54,741 | 50,385 |
| **Balance Sheet** | | | | | | | | |
| Current Assets | 751,728 | 737,536 | 707,519 | 668,972 | 509,427 | 699,085 | 583,413 | 459,157 |
| Total Assets | 1,860,646 | 1,823,180 | 1,805,248 | 1,746,531 | 1,583,267 | 1,850,513 | 1,698,857 | 1,365,186 |
| Current Liabilities | 310,961 | 291,728 | 291,126 | 293,788 | 222,472 | 308,561 | 280,054 | 218,620 |
| Long-Term Obligations | 351,789 | 387,875 | 389,660 | 382,940 | 346,457 | 457,143 | 478,575 | 350,018 |
| Total Liabilities | 728,491 | 745,723 | 748,029 | 741,504 | 632,175 | 828,705 | 807,845 | 619,140 |
| Stockholders' Equity | 1,132,155 | 1,077,457 | 1,057,219 | 1,005,027 | 951,092 | 1,021,808 | 891,012 | 746,046 |
| Shares Outstanding | 52,765 | 52,644 | 52,519 | 52,624 | 52,529 | 53,753 | 54,125 | 53,727 |
| **Statistical Record** | | | | | | | | |
| Return on Assets % | 5.75 | 5.54 | 5.01 | 4.92 | 4.08 | 7.43 | 7.14 | 9.40 |
| Return on Equity % | 9.45 | 9.30 | 8.45 | 8.38 | 7.11 | 13.78 | 13.36 | 16.76 |
| EBITDA Margin % | 16.05 | 16.04 | 16.53 | 14.59 | 14.65 | 17.94 | 16.79 | 19.06 |
| Net Margin % | 7.93 | 7.66 | 7.97 | 6.51 | 5.80 | 8.68 | 8.03 | 10.23 |
| Asset Turnover | 0.75 | 0.75 | 0.73 | 0.76 | 0.70 | 0.86 | 0.89 | 0.92 |
| Current Ratio | 2.42 | 2.53 | 2.43 | 2.28 | 2.29 | 2.27 | 2.08 | 2.10 |
| Debt to Equity | 0.31 | 0.36 | 0.37 | 0.38 | 0.36 | 0.45 | 0.54 | 0.47 |
| Price Range | 37.71-24.37 | 35.28-24.37 | 35.28-24.37 | 35.28-24.37 | 39.68-14.61 | 43.78-28.58 | 40.52-30.91 | 41.83-27.01 |
| P/E Ratio | 19.74-12.76 | 19.38-13.39 | 21.51-14.86 | 22.76-15.72 | 29.83-10.98 | 18.17-11.86 | 20.26-15.46 | 20.21-13.05 |
| Average Yield % | 2.30 | 2.37 | 2.41 | 2.37 | 2.69 | 1.71 | 1.58 | 1.48 |

**Address:** 6555 West Good Hope Road, Milwaukee, WI 53223
**Telephone:** 414-358-6600
**Web Site:** www.bradycorp.com

**Officers:** Frank M. Jaehnert - President, Chief Executive Officer Thomas J. Felmer - Senior Vice President, Chief Financial Officer, Division Officer
**Transfer Agents:** Wells Fargo Bank Minnesota, N.A., St. Paul, MN

**Investor Contact:** 414-438-6940
**No of Institutions:** 216
**Shares:** 47,585,256 **% Held:** 80.46

# BROWN & BROWN, INC.

| Exchange | Symbol | Price | 52Wk Range | Yield | P/E |
|---|---|---|---|---|---|
| NYS | BRO | $21.01 (8/31/2011) | 26.91-18.38 | 1.52 | 18.93 |

***7 Year Price Score 100.52** *NYSE Composite Index=100 ***12 Month Price Score 93.75**

**Interim Earnings (Per Share)**

| Qtr. | Mar | Jun | Sep | Dec |
|---|---|---|---|---|
| 2008 | 0.37 | 0.29 | 0.29 | 0.23 |
| 2009 | 0.34 | 0.29 | 0.29 | 0.17 |
| 2010 | 0.31 | 0.29 | 0.31 | 0.22 |
| 2011 | 0.32 | 0.26 | ... | ... |

**Interim Dividends (Per Share)**

| Amt | Decl | Ex | Rec | Pay |
|---|---|---|---|---|
| 0.08Q | 10/20/2010 | 11/01/2010 | 11/03/2010 | 11/17/2010 |
| 0.08Q | 01/19/2011 | 01/31/2011 | 02/02/2011 | 02/16/2011 |
| 0.08Q | 04/20/2011 | 05/02/2011 | 05/04/2011 | 05/18/2011 |
| 0.08Q | 07/20/2011 | 08/08/2011 | 08/10/2011 | 08/17/2011 |

**Indicated Div: $0.32**

**Valuation Analysis**

| | | | |
|---|---|---|---|
| Forecast EPS | $1.11 (09/02/2011) | | |
| Market Cap | $3.0 Billion | Book Value | $1.6 Billion |
| Price/Book | 1.91 | Price/Sales | 3.04 |

**Dividend Achiever Status**

| | |
|---|---|
| **10 Year Growth Rate** | 14.60% |
| **Total Years of Dividend Growth** | 17 |

**Business Summary:** Brokers & Intermediaries (MIC: 5.2.3 SIC: 6411 NAIC: 524210)

Brown & Brown is an insurance agency, wholesale brokerage, insurance programs and service organization. Co. has four segments: Retail Division, which provides insurance products and services; National Programs Division including Professional Programs, which provides professional liability and related package products, and Special Programs, which markets targeted products and services for specific industries, trade groups, public entities, and market niches; Wholesale Brokerage Division, which markets and sells excess and surplus commercial insurance products and services and reinsurance products and services; and Services Division, which provides insurance-related services, among others.

**Recent Developments:** For the quarter ended June 30 2011, net income decreased 10.1% to US$37.0 million from US$41.2 million in the year-earlier quarter. Revenues were US$246.8 million, up 1.3% from US$243.7 million the year before.

**Prospects:** Our evaluation of Brown & Brown Inc. as of Sep. 6, 2011 is the result of our systematic analysis on three basic characteristics: earnings strength, relative valuation, and recent stock price movement. The company has generated a negative trend in earnings per share over the past 5 quarters and while recent estimates for the company have remained steady, BRO has posted results that fell short of analysts expectations. Based on operating earnings yield, the company is about fairly valued when compared to all of the companies in our coverage universe. Share price changes over the past year indicates that BRO will perform in line with the market over the near term.

| **Financial Data** (US$ in Thousands) | 6 Mos | 3 Mos | 12/31/2010 | 12/31/2009 | 12/31/2008 | 12/31/2007 | 12/31/2006 | 12/31/2005 |
|---|---|---|---|---|---|---|---|---|
| Earnings Per Share | 1.11 | 1.14 | 1.12 | 1.08 | 1.17 | 1.35 | 1.22 | 1.08 |
| Cash Flow Per Share | 1.83 | 1.98 | 2.15 | 1.62 | 2.42 | 1.53 | 1.61 | 1.55 |
| Dividends Per Share | 0.318 | 0.315 | 0.313 | 0.302 | 0.285 | 0.250 | 0.210 | 0.170 |
| Dividend Payout % | 28.60 | 27.63 | 27.90 | 28.01 | 24.36 | 18.52 | 17.21 | 15.74 |
| **Income Statement** | | | | | | | | |
| Total Revenue | 509,044 | 262,228 | 973,492 | 967,877 | 977,554 | 959,667 | 878,004 | 785,807 |
| EBITDA | 178,632 | 96,921 | 293,208 | 282,593 | 300,474 | 338,092 | 304,707 | 268,660 |
| Depn & Amortn | 33,279 | 16,644 | 12,639 | 13,240 | 13,286 | 12,763 | 11,309 | 10,061 |
| Income Before Taxes | 138,138 | 76,670 | 266,098 | 254,754 | 272,498 | 311,527 | 280,041 | 244,130 |
| Income Taxes | 54,810 | 30,377 | 104,346 | 101,460 | 106,374 | 120,568 | 107,691 | 93,579 |
| Net Income | 83,328 | 46,293 | 161,752 | 153,294 | 166,124 | 190,959 | 172,350 | 150,551 |
| Average Shares | 139,942 | 140,648 | 139,318 | 137,507 | 141,558 | 141,257 | 141,020 | 139,776 |
| **Balance Sheet** | | | | | | | | |
| Current Assets | 697,061 | 654,963 | 652,809 | 613,699 | 523,032 | 587,382 | 648,206 | 619,767 |
| Total Assets | 2,524,872 | 2,443,996 | 2,400,814 | 2,224,226 | 2,119,580 | 1,960,659 | 1,807,952 | 1,608,660 |
| Current Liabilities | 502,971 | 459,848 | 470,157 | 478,953 | 522,643 | 556,123 | 590,667 | 582,818 |
| Long-Term Obligations | 250,067 | 250,067 | 250,067 | 250,209 | 253,616 | 227,707 | 226,252 | 214,179 |
| Total Liabilities | 951,941 | 899,584 | 894,470 | 854,352 | 877,839 | 863,201 | 878,607 | 844,316 |
| Stockholders' Equity | 1,572,931 | 1,544,412 | 1,506,344 | 1,369,874 | 1,241,741 | 1,097,458 | 929,345 | 764,344 |
| Shares Outstanding | 142,924 | 142,548 | 142,795 | 142,076 | 141,544 | 140,673 | 140,016 | 139,383 |
| **Statistical Record** | | | | | | | | |
| Return on Assets % | 6.57 | 6.98 | 6.99 | 7.06 | 8.12 | 10.13 | 10.09 | 10.53 |
| Return on Equity % | 10.61 | 11.11 | 11.25 | 11.74 | 14.16 | 18.84 | 20.35 | 21.68 |
| EBITDA Margin % | 35.09 | 36.96 | 30.12 | 29.20 | 30.74 | 35.23 | 34.70 | 34.19 |
| Net Margin % | 16.37 | 17.65 | 16.62 | 15.84 | 16.99 | 19.90 | 19.63 | 19.16 |
| Asset Turnover | 0.41 | 0.42 | 0.42 | 0.45 | 0.48 | 0.51 | 0.51 | 0.55 |
| Current Ratio | 1.39 | 1.42 | 1.39 | 1.28 | 1.00 | 1.06 | 1.10 | 1.06 |
| Debt to Equity | 0.16 | 0.16 | 0.17 | 0.18 | 0.20 | 0.21 | 0.24 | 0.28 |
| Price Range | 26.91-18.90 | 26.51-17.73 | 24.20-16.50 | 21.39-15.65 | 23.96-16.59 | 28.96-23.10 | 35.23-27.42 | 31.24-21.30 |
| P/E Ratio | 24.24-17.03 | 23.25-15.55 | 21.61-14.73 | 19.81-14.49 | 20.48-14.18 | 21.45-17.11 | 28.88-22.48 | 28.93-19.72 |
| Average Yield % | 1.37 | 1.45 | 1.58 | 1.61 | 1.46 | 0.95 | 0.69 | 0.71 |

| | | |
|---|---|---|
| **Address:** 220 South Ridgewood Avenue, Daytona Beach, FL 32114<br>**Telephone:** 386-252-9601<br>**Web Site:** www.bbinsurance.com | **Officers:** J. Hyatt Brown - Chairman Jim W. Henderson - Vice-Chairman, Chief Operating Officer<br>**Transfer Agents:** American Stock Transfer & Trust Company, New York, NY | **No of Institutions:** 297<br>**Shares:** 111,452,448 **% Held:** 68.73 |

# BROWN-FORMAN CORP.

| Exchange | Symbol | Price | 52Wk Range | Yield | P/E |
|---|---|---|---|---|---|
| NYS | BFB | $71.75 (8/31/2011) | 76.51-58.27 | 1.78 | 18.40 |

*7 Year Price Score 123.63 *NYSE Composite Index=100 *12 Month Price Score 106.23

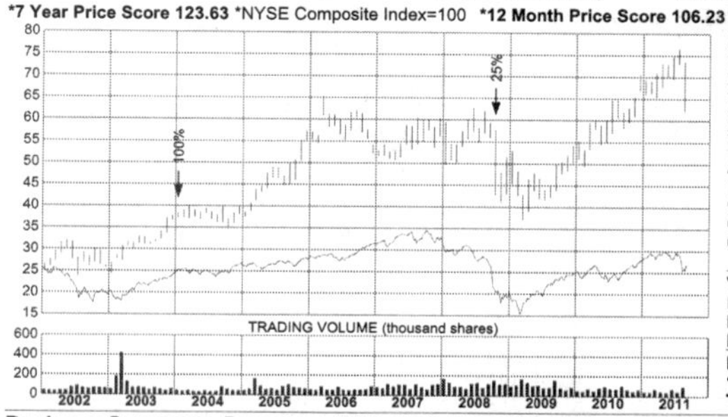


**Interim Earnings (Per Share)**

| Qtr. | Jul | Oct | Jan | Apr |
|---|---|---|---|---|
| 2006-07 | 0.61 | 0.80 | 0.68 | 0.43 |
| 2007-08 | 0.62 | 0.83 | 0.75 | 0.66 |
| 2008-09 | 0.58 | 0.94 | 0.81 | 0.53 |
| 2009-10 | 0.81 | 0.99 | 0.73 | 0.49 |
| 2010-11 | 0.76 | 1.05 | 0.96 | 1.13 |

**Interim Dividends (Per Share)**

| Amt | Decl | Ex | Rec | Pay |
|---|---|---|---|---|
| 1.00Sp | 12/01/2010 | 12/08/2010 | 12/10/2010 | 12/28/2010 |
| 0.32Q | 01/27/2011 | 03/07/2011 | 03/09/2011 | 04/01/2011 |
| 0.32Q | 05/26/2011 | 06/06/2011 | 06/08/2011 | 07/01/2011 |
| 0.32Q | 07/28/2011 | 09/01/2011 | 09/06/2011 | 10/03/2011 |

**Indicated Div: $1.28**

**Valuation Analysis**

| | | | |
|---|---|---|---|
| Forecast EPS | $3.70 (09/05/2011) | | |
| Market Cap | $10.4 Billion | Book Value | $2.1 Billion |
| Price/Book | 5.05 | Price/Sales | 4.02 |

**Dividend Achiever Status**

| | |
|---|---|
| **10 Year Growth Rate** | 11.15% |
| **Total Years of Dividend Growth** | 26 |

**Business Summary:** Beverages (MIC: 1.2.2 SIC: 2084 NAIC: 312130)

Brown-Forman is primarily engaged in the manufacturing, bottling, importing, exporting, and marketing of a variety of alcoholic beverage brands. Co.'s principal beverage brands are, but not limited to: Jack Daniel's Tennessee Whiskey, Jack Daniel's Single Barrel, Gentleman Jack, Southern Comfort, Southern Comfort Ready-to-Drinks, Finlandia Vodka, Antiguo Tequila, Canadian Mist Blended Canadian Whisky, Chambord Liqueur, Don Eduardo Tequila, Early Times Bourbon, Early Times Kentucky Whisky, El Jimador Tequila, Herradura Tequila, Korbel California Champagnes, New Mix Ready-to-Drinks, Old Forester Bourbon, Pepe Lopez Tequilas, Tuaca Liqueur, Chambord Vodka and Woodford Reserve Bourbon.

**Recent Developments:** For the year ended Apr 30 2011, net income increased 27.4% to US$572.0 million from US$449.0 million in the prior year. Revenues were US$2.59 billion, up 4.7% from US$2.47 billion the year before. Operating income was US$855.0 million versus US$710.0 million in the prior year, an increase of 20.4%. Direct operating expenses rose 0.5% to US$862.0 million from US$858.0 million in the comparable period the year before. Indirect operating expenses decreased 3.6% to US$869.0 million from US$901.0 million in the equivalent prior-year period.

**Prospects:** Our evaluation of Brown-Forman Corp. as of Sep. 6, 2011 is the result of our systematic analysis on three basic characteristics: earnings strength, relative valuation, and recent stock price movement. The company has managed to produce a neutral trend in earnings per share over the past 5 quarters. However, while recent estimates for the company have been mixed, BF.B has posted results that fell short of analysts expectations. Based on operating earnings yield, the company is about fairly valued when compared to all of the companies in our coverage universe. Share price changes over the past year indicates that BF.B will perform poorly over the near term.

**Financial Data**

| (US$ in Thousands) | 04/30/2011 | 04/30/2010 | 04/30/2009 | 04/30/2008 | 04/30/2007 | 04/30/2006 | 04/30/2005 | 04/30/2004 |
|---|---|---|---|---|---|---|---|---|
| Earnings Per Share | 3.90 | 3.02 | 2.87 | 2.85 | 2.51 | 2.08 | 2.02 | 1.69 |
| Cash Flow Per Share | 3.62 | 3.69 | 3.26 | 3.48 | 2.31 | 2.27 | 2.60 | 2.01 |
| Tang Book Value Per Share | 5.28 | 3.81 | 3.03 | 2.24 | 1.42 | 6.81 | 4.56 | 3.44 |
| Dividends Per Share | 2.240 | 1.175 | 1.119 | 1.028 | 2.255 | 0.840 | 0.732 | 0.640 |
| Dividend Payout % | 57.44 | 38.91 | 38.99 | 36.10 | 89.87 | 40.45 | 36.31 | 37.91 |
| **Income Statement** | | | | | | | | |
| Total Revenue | 2,586,000 | 2,469,000 | 2,481,000 | 2,582,000 | 2,218,000 | 1,976,000 | 2,312,000 | 2,213,000 |
| EBITDA | 911,000 | 769,000 | 716,000 | 737,000 | 646,000 | 607,000 | 548,000 | 463,000 |
| Depn & Amortn | 56,000 | 59,000 | 55,000 | 52,000 | 44,000 | 44,000 | 58,000 | 56,000 |
| Income Before Taxes | 829,000 | 682,000 | 630,000 | 644,000 | 586,000 | 559,000 | 476,000 | 388,000 |
| Income Taxes | 257,000 | 233,000 | 195,000 | 204,000 | 186,000 | 164,000 | 168,000 | 130,000 |
| Net Income | 572,000 | 449,000 | 435,000 | 440,000 | 389,000 | 320,000 | 308,000 | 258,000 |
| Average Shares | 146,513 | 148,575 | 151,522 | 154,511 | 155,251 | 152,482 | 153,133 | 152,482 |
| **Balance Sheet** | | | | | | | | |
| Current Assets | 1,976,000 | 1,527,000 | 1,574,000 | 1,456,000 | 1,635,000 | 1,610,000 | 1,317,000 | 1,083,000 |
| Total Assets | 3,712,000 | 3,383,000 | 3,475,000 | 3,405,000 | 3,551,000 | 2,728,000 | 2,624,000 | 2,376,000 |
| Current Liabilities | 707,000 | 546,000 | 836,000 | 984,000 | 1,347,000 | 569,000 | 638,000 | 369,000 |
| Long-Term Obligations | 504,000 | 508,000 | 509,000 | 417,000 | 422,000 | 351,000 | 352,000 | 630,000 |
| Total Liabilities | 1,652,000 | 1,488,000 | 1,659,000 | 1,680,000 | 1,978,000 | 1,165,000 | 1,314,000 | 1,291,000 |
| Stockholders' Equity | 2,060,000 | 1,895,000 | 1,816,000 | 1,725,000 | 1,573,000 | 1,563,000 | 1,310,000 | 1,085,000 |
| Shares Outstanding | 144,990 | 146,963 | 150,127 | 150,738 | 154,046 | 153,081 | 152,360 | 151,985 |
| **Statistical Record** | | | | | | | | |
| Return on Assets % | 16.12 | 13.09 | 12.65 | 12.62 | 12.39 | 11.96 | 12.32 | 11.09 |
| Return on Equity % | 28.93 | 24.20 | 24.57 | 26.61 | 24.81 | 22.28 | 25.72 | 26.73 |
| EBITDA Margin % | 35.23 | 31.15 | 28.86 | 28.54 | 29.13 | 30.72 | 23.70 | 20.92 |
| Net Margin % | 22.12 | 18.19 | 17.53 | 17.04 | 17.54 | 16.19 | 13.32 | 11.66 |
| Asset Turnover | 0.73 | 0.72 | 0.72 | 0.74 | 0.71 | 0.74 | 0.92 | 0.95 |
| Current Ratio | 2.79 | 2.80 | 1.88 | 1.48 | 1.21 | 2.83 | 2.06 | 2.93 |
| Debt to Equity | 0.24 | 0.27 | 0.28 | 0.24 | 0.27 | 0.22 | 0.27 | 0.58 |
| Price Range | 73.02-54.45 | 60.18-41.75 | 62.78-37.00 | 60.46-49.74 | 62.08-50.83 | 65.53-44.08 | 44.77-34.80 | 39.96-30.21 |
| P/E Ratio | 18.72-13.96 | 19.93-13.82 | 21.87-12.89 | 21.22-17.45 | 24.73-20.25 | 31.50-21.19 | 22.16-17.23 | 23.64-17.88 |
| Average Yield % | 3.51 | 2.36 | 2.19 | 1.84 | 4.01 | 1.62 | 1.89 | 1.85 |

| | | |
|---|---|---|
| **Address:** 850 Dixie Highway, Louisville, KY 40210<br>**Telephone:** 502-585-1100<br>**Web Site:** www.brown-forman.com | **Officers:** Paul C. Varga - Chairman, Chief Executive Officer Geo. Garvin Brown - Chairman **Transfer Agents:** National City Bank, Cleveland, OH | **No of Institutions:** 82<br>**Shares:** 39,782,012 **% Held:** 20.93 |

# BUCKEYE PARTNERS, L.P.

| Exchange | Symbol | Price | 52Wk Range | Yield | P/E |
|---|---|---|---|---|---|
| NYS | BPL | $62.98 (8/31/2011) | 69.80-57.61 | 6.31 | 32.80 |

*7 Year Price Score 128.46 *NYSE Composite Index=100 *12 Month Price Score 98.36

**Interim Earnings (Per Share)**

| Qtr. | Mar | Jun | Sep | Dec |
|---|---|---|---|---|
| 2008 | 0.76 | 0.70 | 0.79 | 0.90 |
| 2009 | 0.87 | (1.17) | 0.89 | 1.29 |
| 2010 | 0.73 | 0.78 | 0.93 | (0.80) |
| 2011 | 0.79 | 1.00 | ... | ... |

**Interim Dividends (Per Share)**

| Amt | Decl | Ex | Rec | Pay |
|---|---|---|---|---|
| 0.975Q | 11/08/2010 | 11/10/2010 | 11/15/2010 | 11/30/2010 |
| 0.988Q | 02/11/2011 | 02/16/2011 | 02/21/2011 | 02/28/2011 |
| 1.00Q | 05/06/2011 | 05/12/2011 | 05/16/2011 | 05/31/2011 |
| 1.013Q | 08/05/2011 | 08/11/2011 | 08/15/2011 | 08/31/2011 |

**Indicated Div: $3.98**

**Valuation Analysis**

| | | | |
|---|---|---|---|
| Forecast EPS | $3.52 (09/05/2011) | | |
| Market Cap | $5.9 Billion | Book Value | N/A |
| Price/Book | N/A | Price/Sales | 1.43 |

**Dividend Achiever Status**

| | |
|---|---|
| **10 Year Growth Rate** | 4.56% |
| **Total Years of Dividend Growth** | 15 |

**Business Summary:** Equipment & Services (MIC: 9.1.3 SIC: 4613 NAIC: 486910)

Buckeye Partners is a holding company. Through its subsidiaries, Co. is engaged primarily in the refined petroleum products transportation, storage and marketing businesses and natural gas storage business. As of Dec 31 2010, Co.'s refined petroleum products pipeline systems consisted of approximately 5,400 miles of pipeline and 69 active products terminals. In addition, Co. operates and maintains approximately 2,600 miles of other pipelines under agreements with oil and chemical companies. Co. also owns and operates a natural gas storage facility in northern California and is a wholesale distributor of refined petroleum products in areas also served by its pipelines and terminals.

**Recent Developments:** For the quarter ended June 30 2011, net income increased 68.9% to US$93.6 million from US$55.4 million in the year-earlier quarter. Revenues were US$1.08 billion, up 61.4% from US$667.3 million the year before. Operating income was US$85.9 million versus US$73.8 million in the prior-year quarter, an increase of 16.4%. Direct operating expenses rose 71.3% to US$854.3 million from US$498.6 million in the comparable period the year before. Indirect operating expenses increased 44.3% to US$136.8 million from US$94.8 million in the equivalent prior-year period.

**Prospects:** Our evaluation of Buckeye Partners, L.P. as of Sep. 6, 2011 is the result of our systematic analysis on three basic characteristics: earnings strength, relative valuation, and recent stock price movement. The company has produced a positive trend in earnings per share over the past 5 quarters. However, while recent estimates for the company have been mixed, BPL has posted better than expected results. Based on operating earnings yield, the company is about fairly valued when compared to all of the companies in our coverage universe. Share price changes over the past year indicates that BPL will perform very poorly over the near term.

**Financial Data**

| (US$ in Thousands) | 6 Mos | 3 Mos | 12/31/2010 | 12/31/2009 | 12/31/2008 | 12/31/2007 | 12/31/2006 | 12/31/2005 |
|---|---|---|---|---|---|---|---|---|
| Earnings Per Share | 1.92 | 1.70 | 1.65 | 1.84 | 3.15 | 3.03 | 2.64 | 2.69 |
| Cash Flow Per Share | 2.65 | 3.63 | 11.24 | 1.11 | 4.50 | 4.70 | 3.80 | 3.84 |
| Dividends Per Share | 3.925 | 3.875 | 3.825 | 3.625 | 3.425 | 3.225 | 3.025 | 2.825 |
| Dividend Payout % | 204.43 | 227.94 | 231.82 | 197.01 | 108.73 | 106.44 | 114.58 | 105.02 |
| **Income Statement** | | | | | | | | |
| Total Revenue | 2,329,628 | 1,252,536 | 3,151,268 | 1,770,372 | 1,896,652 | 519,347 | 461,760 | 408,446 |
| EBITDA | 265,170 | 117,365 | 333,514 | 259,920 | 304,746 | 245,134 | 201,053 | 175,137 |
| Depn & Amortn | 52,053 | 24,402 | 54,700 | 50,700 | 47,200 | 39,400 | 38,700 | 31,822 |
| Income Before Taxes | 156,024 | 64,466 | 189,645 | 134,369 | 183,159 | 155,356 | 110,240 | 99,958 |
| Net Income | 158,514 | 66,493 | 43,080 | 140,982 | 184,389 | 155,356 | 110,240 | 99,958 |
| Average Shares | 92,088 | 83,954 | 26,086 | 50,663 | 47,763 | 42,101 | 39,202 | 37,145 |
| **Balance Sheet** | | | | | | | | |
| Current Assets | 617,030 | 578,095 | 626,631 | 613,723 | 414,028 | 200,338 | 129,427 | 98,368 |
| Total Assets | 5,566,621 | 5,373,831 | 3,574,216 | 3,255,649 | 3,034,410 | 2,133,652 | 1,995,470 | 1,816,867 |
| Current Liabilities | 539,398 | 460,488 | 516,520 | 417,733 | 291,714 | 92,494 | 89,549 | 62,153 |
| Long-Term Obligations | 2,189,238 | 2,404,071 | 1,519,393 | 1,498,970 | 1,445,722 | 849,177 | 994,127 | 899,077 |
| Total Liabilities | 2,943,702 | 3,062,758 | 2,181,811 | 2,040,511 | 1,858,913 | 1,043,480 | 1,185,588 | 1,058,290 |
| Shares Outstanding | 92,922 | 87,270 | 71,436 | 51,682 | 48,616 | 45,962 | 39,697 | 38,162 |
| **Statistical Record** | | | | | | | | |
| Return on Assets % | 2.25 | 1.39 | 1.26 | 4.48 | 7.12 | 7.52 | 5.78 | 5.97 |
| EBITDA Margin % | 11.38 | 9.37 | 10.58 | 14.68 | 16.07 | 47.20 | 43.54 | 42.88 |
| Net Margin % | 6.80 | 5.31 | 1.37 | 7.96 | 9.72 | 29.91 | 23.87 | 24.47 |
| Asset Turnover | 0.94 | 0.86 | 0.92 | 0.56 | 0.73 | 0.25 | 0.24 | 0.24 |
| Current Ratio | 1.14 | 1.26 | 1.21 | 1.47 | 1.42 | 2.17 | 1.45 | 1.58 |
| Price Range | 69.80-57.92 | 69.80-52.33 | 69.80-52.33 | 55.59-32.25 | 50.29-25.69 | 55.49-46.00 | 46.78-40.71 | 50.21-41.92 |
| P/E Ratio | 36.35-30.17 | 41.06-30.78 | 42.30-31.72 | 30.21-17.53 | 15.97-8.16 | 18.31-15.18 | 17.72-15.42 | 18.67-15.58 |
| Average Yield % | 6.13 | 6.15 | 6.26 | 8.27 | 8.06 | 6.35 | 6.93 | 6.22 |

**Address:** One Greenway Plaza, Suite 600, Houston, TX 77046
**Telephone:** 832-615-8600
**Web Site:** www.buckeye.com

**Officers:** Forrest E. Wylie - Chairman, Chief Executive Officer, Associate/Affiliate Company Officer Clark C. Smith - President, Chief Operating Officer, Associate/Affiliate Company Officer
**Transfer Agents:** First Chicago Trust Company a Division of Equiserv, Jersey City, NJ

**Investor Contact:** 800-422-2825
**No of Institutions:** 326
**Shares:** 35,669,960 **% Held:** 65.56

# CALIFORNIA WATER SERVICE GROUP (DE)

| Exchange | Symbol | Price | 52Wk Range | Yield | P/E |
|---|---|---|---|---|---|
| NYS | CWT | $18.88 (8/31/2011) | 19.21-16.89 | 3.26 | 19.67 |

***7 Year Price Score 96.78** *NYSE Composite Index=100 ***12 Month Price Score 100.58**

**Interim Earnings (Per Share)**

| Qtr. | Mar | Jun | Sep | Dec |
|---|---|---|---|---|
| 2008 | 0.01 | 0.24 | 0.53 | 0.17 |
| 2009 | 0.06 | 0.29 | 0.47 | 0.16 |
| 2010 | 0.05 | 0.25 | 0.49 | 0.12 |
| 2011 | 0.07 | 0.29 | ... | ... |

**Interim Dividends (Per Share)**

| Amt | Decl | Ex | Rec | Pay |
|---|---|---|---|---|
| 0.154Q | 01/26/2011 | 02/03/2011 | 02/07/2011 | 02/18/2011 |
| 0.154Q | 04/27/2011 | 05/05/2011 | 05/09/2011 | 05/20/2011 |
| 100% | 05/24/2011 | 06/13/2011 | 06/03/2011 | 06/10/2011 |
| 0.154Q | 07/27/2011 | 08/04/2011 | 08/08/2011 | 08/19/2011 |

**Indicated Div: $0.61 (Div. Reinv. Plan)**

**Valuation Analysis**

| | | | |
|---|---|---|---|
| Forecast EPS | $1.09 (09/02/2011) | | |
| Market Cap | $788.3 Million | Book Value | $438.2 Million |
| Price/Book | 1.80 | Price/Sales | 1.64 |

**Dividend Achiever Status**

| | |
|---|---|
| **10 Year Growth Rate** | 0.65% |
| **Total Years of Dividend Growth** | 43 |

**Business Summary:** Water Utilities (MIC: 3.2.1 SIC: 4941 NAIC: 221310)

California Water Service Group is a holding company. Through its subsidiaries, Co. is engaged in the production, purchase, storage, treatment, testing, distribution and sale of water for domestic, industrial, public and irrigation uses, and for fire protection. In addition, Co. provides non-regulated water-related services under agreements with municipalities and other private companies including water system operation, billing and meter reading services. At Dec 31 2010, Co. provided its services to about 470,200 customers in 83 California communities; 15,700 customers in the Tacoma and Olympia areas; 7,800 customers in New Mexico; and 4,200 customers on the islands of Maui and Hawaii.

**Recent Developments:** For the quarter ended June 30 2011, net income increased 17.4% to US$12.2 million from US$10.4 million in the year-earlier quarter. Revenues were US$131.4 million, up 11.1% from US$118.3 million the year before. Operating income was US$19.6 million versus US$16.3 million in the prior-year quarter, an increase of 20.1%. Direct operating expenses rose 6.5% to US$65.8 million from US$61.7 million in the comparable period the year before. Indirect operating expenses increased 14.3% to US$46.1 million from US$40.3 million in the equivalent prior-year period.

**Prospects:** Our evaluation of California Water Service Group as of Sep. 6, 2011 is the result of our systematic analysis on three basic characteristics: earnings strength, relative valuation, and recent stock price movement. The company has enjoyed a very positive trend in earnings per share over the past 5 quarters and while recent estimates for the company have been raised by analysts, CWT has posted better than expected results. Based on operating earnings yield, the company is about fairly valued when compared to all of the companies in our coverage universe. Share price changes over the past year indicates that CWT will perform very poorly over the near term.

**Financial Data**

| (US$ in Thousands) | 6 Mos | 3 Mos | 12/31/2010 | 12/31/2009 | 12/31/2008 | 12/31/2007 | 12/31/2006 | 12/31/2005 |
|---|---|---|---|---|---|---|---|---|
| Earnings Per Share | 0.96 | 0.92 | 0.91 | 0.97 | 0.95 | 0.75 | 0.67 | 0.73 |
| Cash Flow Per Share | 2.16 | 1.87 | 1.81 | 1.75 | 2.30 | 1.21 | 1.61 | 2.35 |
| Tang Book Value Per Share | 10.43 | 10.29 | 10.39 | 10.07 | 9.63 | 9.33 | 9.16 | 7.99 |
| Dividends Per Share | 0.605 | 0.600 | 0.595 | 0.590 | 0.585 | 0.580 | 0.575 | 0.570 |
| Dividend Payout % | 63.02 | 65.22 | 65.75 | 60.51 | 61.58 | 77.33 | 85.82 | 77.55 |
| **Income Statement** | | | | | | | | |
| Total Revenue | 229,546 | 98,149 | 460,399 | 449,372 | 410,312 | 367,082 | 334,717 | 320,728 |
| EBITDA | 63,460 | 22,264 | 133,314 | 129,186 | 121,227 | 98,981 | 89,163 | 93,660 |
| Depn & Amortn | 25,837 | 13,014 | 46,244 | 42,613 | 40,158 | 34,236 | 31,317 | 28,731 |
| Income Before Taxes | 22,306 | 1,478 | 60,725 | 65,366 | 64,312 | 49,046 | 40,877 | 47,229 |
| Income Taxes | 7,397 | (1,241) | 23,069 | 24,812 | 24,507 | 17,887 | 15,297 | 20,006 |
| Net Income | 14,909 | 2,719 | 37,656 | 40,554 | 39,805 | 31,159 | 25,580 | 27,223 |
| Average Shares | 41,768 | 41,712 | 41,638 | 41,532 | 41,468 | 41,378 | 37,850 | 36,804 |
| **Balance Sheet** | | | | | | | | |
| Current Assets | 131,611 | 129,129 | 126,210 | 92,241 | 79,798 | 59,975 | 109,624 | 52,224 |
| Total Assets | 1,745,153 | 1,715,111 | 1,692,066 | 1,525,581 | 1,418,107 | 1,184,499 | 1,165,019 | 996,945 |
| Current Liabilities | 131,626 | 117,505 | 107,348 | 110,358 | 123,196 | 69,653 | 70,225 | 76,816 |
| Long-Term Obligations | 477,968 | 478,974 | 479,181 | 374,269 | 287,498 | 289,220 | 291,814 | 274,142 |
| Total Liabilities | 1,306,913 | 1,282,976 | 1,256,540 | 1,104,947 | 1,015,158 | 795,315 | 783,242 | 699,529 |
| Stockholders' Equity | 438,240 | 432,135 | 435,526 | 420,634 | 402,949 | 389,184 | 381,777 | 297,416 |
| Shares Outstanding | 41,752 | 41,752 | 41,666 | 41,530 | 41,446 | 41,332 | 41,314 | 36,780 |
| **Statistical Record** | | | | | | | | |
| Return on Assets % | 2.40 | 2.34 | 2.34 | 2.76 | 3.05 | 2.65 | 2.37 | 2.81 |
| Return on Equity % | 9.35 | 9.04 | 8.80 | 9.85 | 10.02 | 8.08 | 7.53 | 9.25 |
| EBITDA Margin % | 27.65 | 22.68 | 28.96 | 28.75 | 29.55 | 26.96 | 26.64 | 29.20 |
| Net Margin % | 6.49 | 2.77 | 8.18 | 9.02 | 9.70 | 8.49 | 7.64 | 8.49 |
| Asset Turnover | 0.29 | 0.29 | 0.29 | 0.31 | 0.31 | 0.31 | 0.31 | 0.33 |
| Current Ratio | 1.00 | 1.10 | 1.18 | 0.84 | 0.65 | 0.86 | 1.56 | 0.68 |
| Debt to Equity | 1.09 | 1.11 | 1.10 | 0.89 | 0.71 | 0.74 | 0.76 | 0.92 |
| Price Range | 19.20-17.04 | 19.77-16.98 | 19.77-16.98 | 23.22-16.77 | 23.22-14.87 | 22.27-17.23 | 22.68-16.86 | 20.95-16.06 |
| P/E Ratio | 19.99-17.74 | 21.49-18.46 | 21.73-18.66 | 23.93-17.29 | 24.44-15.65 | 29.69-22.97 | 33.85-25.16 | 28.70-22.00 |
| Average Yield % | 3.31 | 3.27 | 3.24 | 3.07 | 3.12 | 2.97 | 2.94 | 3.12 |

| | | |
|---|---|---|
| **Address:** 1720 North First Street, San Jose, CA 95112<br>**Telephone:** 408-367-8200<br>**Web Site:** www.calwatergroup.com | **Officers:** Robert W. Foy - Chairman Peter C. Nelson - President, Chief Executive Officer **Transfer Agents:** US Bank Trust, N.A., San Francisco, CA | **Investor Contact:** 408-367-8200<br>**No of Institutions:** 172<br>**Shares:** 21,082,664 **% Held:** 48.93 |

# CARBO CERAMICS INC.

| Exchange | Symbol | Price | 52Wk Range | Yield | P/E |
|---|---|---|---|---|---|
| NYS | CRR | $160.15 (8/31/2011) | 180.25-75.73 | 0.60 | 36.73 |

*7 Year Price Score 202.34 *NYSE Composite Index=100 *12 Month Price Score 127.52

**Interim Earnings (Per Share)**

| Qtr. | Mar | Jun | Sep | Dec |
|---|---|---|---|---|
| 2008 | 0.58 | 0.55 | 0.75 | 2.63 |
| 2009 | 0.70 | 0.41 | 0.62 | 0.54 |
| 2010 | 0.82 | 0.81 | 0.87 | 0.90 |
| 2011 | 1.30 | 1.29 | ... | ... |

**Interim Dividends (Per Share)**

| Amt | Decl | Ex | Rec | Pay |
|---|---|---|---|---|
| 0.20Q | 09/21/2010 | 10/28/2010 | 11/01/2010 | 11/15/2010 |
| 0.20Q | 01/18/2011 | 01/28/2011 | 02/01/2011 | 02/15/2011 |
| 0.20Q | 03/22/2011 | 04/28/2011 | 05/02/2011 | 05/16/2011 |
| 0.24Q | 07/19/2011 | 07/28/2011 | 08/01/2011 | 08/15/2011 |

**Indicated Div: $0.96**

**Valuation Analysis**

| | | | |
|---|---|---|---|
| Forecast EPS | $5.50 (09/02/2011) | | |
| Market Cap | $3.7 Billion | Book Value | $580.1 Million |
| Price/Book | 6.39 | Price/Sales | 6.89 |

**Dividend Achiever Status**

| | |
|---|---|
| **10 Year Growth Rate** | 12.70% |
| **Total Years of Dividend Growth** | 10 |

**Business Summary:** Equipment & Services (MIC: 9.1.3 SIC: 3299 NAIC: 327999)

CARBO Ceramics is a manufacturer of ceramic proppants. Co. sells its products and services to operators of oil and natural gas wells and to oilfield service companies. Co.'s products and services are primarily used in the hydraulic fracturing of natural gas and oil wells. Co. also sells fracture simulation software and provides fracture design, engineering and consulting services to oil and natural gas companies through its wholly-owned subsidiary, StrataGen, Inc. In addition, Co. provides a range of technologies for spill prevention, containment and countermeasures, along with geotechnical monitoring through its wholly owned subsidiary Applied Geomechanics, Inc.

**Recent Developments:** For the quarter ended June 30 2011, net income increased 59.8% to US$29.9 million from US$18.7 million in the year-earlier quarter. Revenues were US$149.7 million, up 34.2% from US$111.5 million the year before. Operating income was US$46.3 million versus US$28.8 million in the prior-year quarter, an increase of 60.8%. Direct operating expenses rose 24.6% to US$87.6 million from US$70.3 million in the comparable period the year before. Indirect operating expenses increased 27.1% to US$15.8 million from US$12.4 million in the equivalent prior-year period.

**Prospects:** Our evaluation of Carbo Ceramics Inc. as of Sep. 6, 2011 is the result of our systematic analysis on three basic characteristics: earnings strength, relative valuation, and recent stock price movement. The company has produced a positive trend in earnings per share over the past 5 quarters and while recent estimates for the company have been raised by analysts, CRR has posted better than expected results. Based on operating earnings yield, the company is overvalued when compared to all of the companies in our coverage universe. Share price changes over the past year indicates that CRR will perform well over the near term.

**Financial Data**

| (US$ in Thousands) | 6 Mos | 3 Mos | 12/31/2010 | 12/31/2009 | 12/31/2008 | 12/31/2007 | 12/31/2006 | 12/31/2005 |
|---|---|---|---|---|---|---|---|---|
| Earnings Per Share | 4.36 | 3.88 | 3.40 | 2.27 | 4.51 | 2.20 | 2.22 | 1.93 |
| Cash Flow Per Share | 3.91 | 4.16 | 4.00 | 0.95 | 3.11 | 2.45 | 2.09 | 2.20 |
| Tang Book Value Per Share | 24.52 | 23.14 | 22.02 | 19.22 | 18.52 | 14.94 | 13.16 | 11.18 |
| Dividends Per Share | 0.800 | 0.780 | 0.760 | 0.700 | 0.620 | 0.520 | 0.440 | 0.360 |
| Dividend Payout % | 18.35 | 20.10 | 22.35 | 30.84 | 13.75 | 23.64 | 19.82 | 18.65 |
| **Income Statement** | | | | | | | | |
| Total Revenue | 300,499 | 150,830 | 473,082 | 341,872 | 387,828 | 340,351 | 312,126 | 252,673 |
| EBITDA | 108,436 | 54,005 | 146,899 | 104,248 | 112,496 | 104,570 | 100,936 | 83,068 |
| Depn & Amortn | 16,487 | 8,180 | 27,728 | 24,905 | 24,638 | 23,589 | 18,712 | 12,949 |
| Income Before Taxes | 92,049 | 45,869 | 119,349 | 79,794 | 88,349 | 81,400 | 83,814 | 71,875 |
| Income Taxes | 31,941 | 15,705 | 40,633 | 26,984 | 27,944 | 27,530 | 29,561 | 25,463 |
| Net Income | 60,108 | 30,164 | 78,716 | 52,810 | 110,316 | 53,870 | 54,253 | 46,620 |
| Average Shares | 23,028 | 23,015 | 22,977 | 23,111 | 24,460 | 24,483 | 24,400 | 24,177 |
| **Balance Sheet** | | | | | | | | |
| Current Assets | 278,955 | 265,188 | 237,655 | 218,870 | 295,712 | 144,272 | 143,925 | 148,287 |
| Total Assets | 662,578 | 640,499 | 599,571 | 513,412 | 549,279 | 453,123 | 404,665 | 355,796 |
| Current Liabilities | 51,927 | 64,386 | 51,247 | 32,458 | 83,848 | 33,264 | 34,246 | 36,309 |
| Total Liabilities | 82,470 | 92,380 | 77,592 | 56,096 | 106,745 | 63,684 | 61,806 | 62,430 |
| Stockholders' Equity | 580,108 | 548,119 | 521,979 | 457,316 | 442,534 | 389,439 | 342,859 | 293,366 |
| Shares Outstanding | 23,162 | 23,162 | 23,108 | 23,077 | 23,637 | 24,516 | 24,391 | 24,286 |
| **Statistical Record** | | | | | | | | |
| Return on Assets % | 16.68 | 15.21 | 14.15 | 9.94 | 21.95 | 12.56 | 14.27 | 14.27 |
| Return on Equity % | 18.97 | 17.66 | 16.08 | 11.74 | 26.45 | 14.71 | 17.05 | 17.34 |
| EBITDA Margin % | 36.09 | 35.81 | 31.05 | 30.49 | 29.01 | 30.72 | 32.34 | 32.88 |
| Net Margin % | 20.00 | 20.00 | 16.64 | 15.45 | 28.44 | 15.83 | 17.38 | 18.45 |
| Asset Turnover | 0.89 | 0.85 | 0.85 | 0.64 | 0.77 | 0.79 | 0.82 | 0.77 |
| Current Ratio | 5.37 | 4.12 | 4.64 | 6.74 | 3.53 | 4.34 | 4.20 | 4.08 |
| Price Range | 162.95-72.10 | 141.12-62.09 | 103.81-59.27 | 70.77-27.43 | 61.83-31.50 | 51.94-34.34 | 67.37-32.90 | 67.57-41.77 |
| P/E Ratio | 37.37-16.54 | 36.37-16.00 | 30.53-17.43 | 31.18-12.08 | 13.71-6.98 | 23.61-15.61 | 30.35-14.82 | 35.01-21.64 |
| Average Yield % | 0.74 | 0.88 | 0.99 | 1.63 | 1.38 | 1.18 | 0.94 | 0.68 |

**Address:** 575 North Dairy Ashford, Suite 300, Houston, TX 77079
**Telephone:** 281-921-6400
**Web Site:** www.carboceramics.com

**Officers:** William C. Morris - Chairman Gary Kolstad - President, Chief Executive Officer **Transfer Agents:** BNY Mellon Shareholder Services, Jersey City, NJ

**Investor Contact:** 972-401-0090
**No of Institutions:** 317
**Shares:** 24,253,648 **% Held:** 82.83

# CARDINAL HEALTH, INC.

| Exchange | Symbol | Price | 52Wk Range | Yield | P/E |
|---|---|---|---|---|---|
| NYS | CAH | $42.50 (8/31/2011) | 46.83-29.96 | 2.02 | 15.62 |

*7 Year Price Score 99.66 *NYSE Composite Index=100 *12 Month Price Score 108.27

**Interim Earnings (Per Share)**

| Qtr. | Sep | Dec | Mar | Jun |
|---|---|---|---|---|
| 2006-07 | 0.66 | 1.80 | 0.05 | 2.26 |
| 2007-08 | 0.82 | 0.89 | 0.99 | 0.88 |
| 2008-09 | 0.69 | 0.88 | 0.87 | 0.75 |
| 2009-10 | (0.11) | 0.65 | 0.61 | 0.61 |
| 2010-11 | 0.84 | 0.61 | 0.70 | 0.57 |

**Interim Dividends (Per Share)**

| Amt | Decl | Ex | Rec | Pay |
|---|---|---|---|---|
| 0.195Q | 11/03/2010 | 12/29/2010 | 01/01/2011 | 01/15/2011 |
| 0.195Q | 02/01/2011 | 03/30/2011 | 04/01/2011 | 04/15/2011 |
| 0.215Q | 05/04/2011 | 06/29/2011 | 07/01/2011 | 07/15/2011 |
| 0.215Q | 08/03/2011 | 09/28/2011 | 10/01/2011 | 10/15/2011 |

**Indicated Div: $0.86**

**Valuation Analysis**

| | | | |
|---|---|---|---|
| Forecast EPS | $3.14 (09/05/2011) | | |
| Market Cap | $14.9 Billion | Book Value | $5.8 Billion |
| Price/Book | 2.55 | Price/Sales | 0.15 |

**Dividend Achiever Status**

| | |
|---|---|
| **10 Year Growth Rate** | 23.45% |
| **Total Years of Dividend Growth** | 14 |

**Business Summary:** Pharmaceuticals (MIC: 4.1.1 SIC: 5122 NAIC: 424210)

Cardinal Health is a healthcare services company. Co. operates in two segments: Pharmaceutical and Medical. The Pharmaceutical segment distributes branded and generic pharmaceutical, over-the-counter healthcare and consumer products; operates nuclear pharmacies and cyclotron facilities that prepare and deliver radiopharmaceuticals for use in nuclear imaging and other procedures in hospitals and clinics; and provides third-party logistics support services. The Medical segment distributes medical, surgical and laboratory products, including sterile and non-sterile procedure kits; single-use surgical drapes, gowns and apparel; exam and surgical gloves; and fluid suction and collection systems.

**Recent Developments:** For the year ended June 30 2011, income from continuing operations increased 64.6% to US$966.2 million from US$587.0 million a year earlier. Net income increased 49.3% to US$959.0 million from US$642.2 million in the prior year. Revenues were US$102.64 billion, up 4.2% from US$98.50 billion the year before. Operating income was US$1.51 billion versus US$1.31 billion in the prior year, an increase of 15.8%. Direct operating expenses rose 4.0% to US$98.48 billion from US$94.72 billion in the comparable period the year before. Indirect operating expenses increased 7.0% to US$2.65 billion from US$2.47 billion in the equivalent prior-year period.

**Prospects:** Our evaluation of Cardinal Health Inc. as of Sep. 6, 2011 is the result of our systematic analysis on three basic characteristics: earnings strength, relative valuation, and recent stock price movement. The company has managed to produce a neutral trend in earnings per share over the past 5 quarters and while recent estimates for the company have been raised by analysts, CAH has posted better than expected results. Based on operating earnings yield, the company is undervalued when compared to all of the companies in our coverage universe. Share price changes over the past year indicates that CAH will perform in line with the market over the near term.

**Financial Data**

| (US$ in Thousands) | 06/30/2011 | 06/30/2010 | 06/30/2009 | 06/30/2008 | 06/30/2007 | 06/30/2006 | 06/30/2005 | 06/30/2004 |
|---|---|---|---|---|---|---|---|---|
| Earnings Per Share | 2.72 | 1.77 | 3.18 | 3.57 | 4.77 | 2.33 | 2.41 | 3.35 |
| Cash Flow Per Share | 4.00 | 5.95 | 4.38 | 4.21 | 3.10 | 5.08 | 6.62 | 6.03 |
| Tang Book Value Per Share | 4.53 | 8.48 | 7.30 | 4.26 | 4.12 | 8.52 | 8.20 | 7.05 |
| Dividends Per Share | 0.800 | 0.720 | 0.595 | 0.500 | 0.390 | 0.270 | 0.150 | 0.120 |
| Dividend Payout % | 29.41 | 40.68 | 18.71 | 14.01 | 8.18 | 11.59 | 6.22 | 3.58 |
| **Income Statement** | | | | | | | | |
| Total Revenue | 102,644,200 | 98,502,800 | 99,512,400 | 91,091,400 | 86,852,000 | 81,363,600 | 74,910,700 | 65,053,500 |
| EBITDA | 1,854,100 | 1,558,500 | 2,192,000 | 2,410,900 | 1,625,900 | 2,298,900 | 2,100,600 | 2,615,300 |
| Depn & Amortn | 243,000 | 233,400 | 306,300 | 289,700 | 252,200 | 332,200 | 337,800 | 278,000 |
| Income Before Taxes | 1,518,300 | 1,211,600 | 1,667,000 | 1,949,800 | 1,252,300 | 1,835,000 | 1,629,300 | 2,238,400 |
| Income Taxes | 552,100 | 624,600 | 524,200 | 633,900 | 412,600 | 590,300 | 582,600 | 713,700 |
| Net Income | 959,000 | 642,200 | 1,151,600 | 1,300,600 | 1,931,100 | 1,000,100 | 1,050,700 | 1,474,500 |
| Average Shares | 352,500 | 361,400 | 361,500 | 364,000 | 404,700 | 428,500 | 435,700 | 440,000 |
| **Balance Sheet** | | | | | | | | |
| Current Assets | 16,315,900 | 14,918,900 | 15,799,000 | 14,184,200 | 14,544,500 | 14,776,700 | 13,442,700 | 13,057,900 |
| Total Assets | 22,845,900 | 19,990,200 | 25,118,800 | 23,448,200 | 23,153,800 | 23,374,100 | 22,059,200 | 21,369,100 |
| Current Liabilities | 13,369,500 | 11,537,600 | 11,399,800 | 10,375,900 | 11,459,700 | 11,372,800 | 10,105,000 | 9,369,400 |
| Long-Term Obligations | 2,175,300 | 1,896,100 | 3,280,000 | 3,687,400 | 3,457,300 | 2,599,700 | 2,319,900 | 2,834,700 |
| Total Liabilities | 16,997,300 | 14,714,100 | 16,394,100 | 15,700,700 | 15,776,900 | 14,883,400 | 13,466,200 | 13,392,800 |
| Stockholders' Equity | 5,848,600 | 5,276,100 | 8,724,700 | 7,747,500 | 7,376,900 | 8,490,700 | 8,593,000 | 7,976,300 |
| Shares Outstanding | 351,100 | 356,400 | 360,000 | 357,100 | 368,100 | 410,800 | 426,200 | 430,900 |
| **Statistical Record** | | | | | | | | |
| Return on Assets % | 4.48 | 2.85 | 4.74 | 5.57 | 8.30 | 4.40 | 4.84 | 7.37 |
| Return on Equity % | 17.24 | 9.17 | 13.98 | 17.15 | 24.34 | 11.71 | 12.68 | 18.69 |
| EBITDA Margin % | 1.81 | 1.58 | 2.20 | 2.65 | 1.87 | 2.83 | 2.80 | 4.02 |
| Net Margin % | 0.93 | 0.65 | 1.16 | 1.43 | 2.22 | 1.23 | 1.40 | 2.27 |
| Asset Turnover | 4.79 | 4.37 | 4.10 | 3.90 | 3.73 | 3.58 | 3.45 | 3.25 |
| Current Ratio | 1.22 | 1.29 | 1.39 | 1.37 | 1.27 | 1.30 | 1.33 | 1.39 |
| Debt to Equity | 0.37 | 0.36 | 0.38 | 0.48 | 0.47 | 0.31 | 0.27 | 0.36 |
| Price Range | 45.54-29.96 | 36.45-21.06 | 40.45-20.38 | 51.18-35.76 | 54.05-44.40 | 54.10-41.13 | 50.30-27.03 | 54.56-39.31 |
| P/E Ratio | 16.74-11.01 | 20.59-11.90 | 12.72-6.41 | 14.34-10.02 | 11.33-9.31 | 23.22-17.65 | 20.87-11.22 | 16.29-11.74 |
| Average Yield % | 2.10 | 2.34 | 2.10 | 1.16 | 0.80 | 0.57 | 0.40 | 0.26 |

**Address:** 7000 Cardinal Place, Dublin, OH 43017
**Telephone:** 614-757-5000
**Web Site:** www.cardinalhealth.com

**Officers:** George S. Barrett - Chairman, Chief Executive Officer Mark Blake - Executive Vice President **Transfer Agents:** Computershare, Providence, RI

**No of Institutions:** 660
**Shares:** 320,581,536 **% Held:** 82.66

# CARLISLE COMPANIES INC.

| Exchange | Symbol | Price | 52Wk Range | Yield | P/E |
|---|---|---|---|---|---|
| NYS | CSL | $39.21 (8/31/2011) | 50.55-28.05 | 1.84 | 14.47 |

***7 Year Price Score 112.60** *NYSE Composite Index=100 ***12 Month Price Score 105.07**

**Interim Earnings (Per Share)**

| Qtr. | Mar | Jun | Sep | Dec |
|---|---|---|---|---|
| 2008 | (1.03) | 0.88 | 0.82 | 0.22 |
| 2009 | 0.11 | 0.90 | 0.75 | 0.58 |
| 2010 | 0.39 | 0.62 | 0.81 | 0.51 |
| 2011 | 0.53 | 0.86 | ... | ... |

**Interim Dividends (Per Share)**

| Amt | Decl | Ex | Rec | Pay |
|---|---|---|---|---|
| 0.17Q | 11/03/2010 | 11/10/2010 | 11/15/2010 | 12/01/2010 |
| 0.17Q | 02/03/2011 | 02/16/2011 | 02/18/2011 | 03/01/2011 |
| 0.17Q | 05/13/2011 | 05/19/2011 | 05/23/2011 | 06/01/2011 |
| 0.18Q | 08/04/2011 | 08/15/2011 | 08/17/2011 | 09/01/2011 |

**Indicated Div: $0.72 (Div. Reinv. Plan)**

**Valuation Analysis**

| | | | |
|---|---|---|---|
| Forecast EPS | $2.95 (09/03/2011) | | |
| Market Cap | $2.4 Billion | Book Value | $1.4 Billion |
| Price/Book | 1.68 | Price/Sales | 0.85 |

**Dividend Achiever Status**

| | |
|---|---|
| **10 Year Growth Rate** | 4.88% |
| **Total Years of Dividend Growth** | 34 |

**Business Summary:** Rubber Products (MIC: 8.4.1 SIC: 3069 NAIC: 326299)

Carlisle Companies is a holding company. Through its subsidiaries, Co. is engaged as a manufacturing company. Co. has five segments: construction materials, which provide rubber and thermoplastic polyolefin roofing membranes, and related roofing accessories; transportation products, which comprise of the tire and wheel and power transmission belt product lines; brake and friction, which consists of off-highway braking systems and friction products.; interconnect technologies, which provide wire, cable, connectors and cable assemblies; and foodservice products, which include foodservice permanentware, table coverings, cookware, catering equipment, industrial brooms, brushes, and mops.

**Recent Developments:** For the quarter ended June 30 2011, income from continuing operations increased 42.5% to US$55.3 million from US$38.8 million in the year-earlier quarter. Net income increased 41.5% to US$54.6 million from US$38.6 million in the year-earlier quarter. Revenues were US$870.8 million, up 26.6% from US$687.6 million the year before. Operating income was nil versus US$64.0 million in the prior-year quarter, a decrease of 100.0%. Direct operating expenses rose 26.3% to US$687.1 million from US$544.0 million in the comparable period the year before. Indirect operating expenses increased 23.5% to US$98.3 million from US$79.6 million in the equivalent prior-year period.

**Prospects:** Our evaluation of Carlisle Companies Inc. as of Sep. 6, 2011 is the result of our systematic analysis on three basic characteristics: earnings strength, relative valuation, and recent stock price movement. The company has managed to produce a neutral trend in earnings per share over the past 5 quarters. However, while recent estimates for the company have been mixed, CSL has posted results that fell short of analysts expectations. Based on operating earnings yield, the company is undervalued when compared to all of the companies in our coverage universe. Share price changes over the past year indicates that CSL will perform well over the near term.

**Financial Data**

| (US$ in Thousands) | 6 Mos | 3 Mos | 12/31/2010 | 12/31/2009 | 12/31/2008 | 12/31/2007 | 12/31/2006 | 12/31/2005 |
|---|---|---|---|---|---|---|---|---|
| Earnings Per Share | 2.71 | 2.47 | 2.34 | 2.34 | 0.91 | 3.44 | 3.46 | 1.71 |
| Cash Flow Per Share | 1.64 | 2.03 | 1.76 | 7.38 | 4.52 | 4.20 | 0.32 | 3.47 |
| Tang Book Value Per Share | 7.76 | 6.72 | 6.16 | 9.79 | 8.46 | 11.79 | 9.98 | 6.57 |
| Dividends Per Share | 0.680 | 0.670 | 0.660 | 0.630 | 0.600 | 0.560 | 0.520 | 0.480 |
| Dividend Payout % | 25.09 | 27.13 | 28.21 | 26.92 | 65.93 | 16.28 | 15.01 | 28.07 |
| **Income Statement** | | | | | | | | |
| Total Revenue | 1,564,400 | 693,600 | 2,527,700 | 2,379,500 | 2,971,400 | 2,876,383 | 2,572,510 | 2,209,610 |
| EBITDA | 186,200 | 78,200 | 254,900 | 263,500 | 304,800 | 390,699 | 331,245 | 261,440 |
| Depn & Amortn | 45,600 | 23,000 | 58,800 | 56,600 | 59,400 | 61,313 | 55,614 | 51,974 |
| Income Before Taxes | 130,600 | 50,100 | 187,800 | 197,900 | 217,800 | 319,342 | 255,317 | 193,558 |
| Income Taxes | 42,000 | 16,800 | 57,200 | 46,100 | 68,300 | 106,321 | 78,031 | 60,224 |
| Net Income | 88,000 | 33,400 | 145,600 | 144,600 | 55,800 | 215,637 | 215,689 | 106,365 |
| Average Shares | 62,701 | 62,181 | 61,592 | 61,234 | 61,332 | 62,630 | 62,236 | 62,156 |
| **Balance Sheet** | | | | | | | | |
| Current Assets | 1,207,900 | 1,077,700 | 1,016,900 | 799,800 | 968,100 | 1,023,192 | 978,241 | 661,172 |
| Total Assets | 2,702,900 | 2,581,100 | 2,529,500 | 1,914,100 | 2,075,900 | 1,988,794 | 1,877,817 | 1,563,257 |
| Current Liabilities | 538,900 | 477,400 | 456,400 | 301,100 | 442,500 | 388,187 | 466,686 | 372,711 |
| Long-Term Obligations | 405,100 | 405,200 | 405,100 | 156,100 | 273,300 | 262,809 | 274,658 | 282,426 |
| Total Liabilities | 1,269,600 | 1,211,200 | 1,188,800 | 695,500 | 981,800 | 869,899 | 935,608 | 833,018 |
| Stockholders' Equity | 1,433,300 | 1,369,900 | 1,340,700 | 1,218,600 | 1,094,100 | 1,118,895 | 942,209 | 730,239 |
| Shares Outstanding | 61,578 | 61,133 | 61,024 | 60,645 | 60,532 | 60,603 | 61,450 | 60,714 |
| **Statistical Record** | | | | | | | | |
| Return on Assets % | 7.21 | 6.85 | 6.55 | 7.25 | 2.74 | 11.15 | 12.54 | 6.94 |
| Return on Equity % | 12.63 | 11.88 | 11.38 | 12.50 | 5.03 | 20.92 | 25.79 | 14.89 |
| EBITDA Margin % | 11.90 | 11.27 | 10.08 | 11.07 | 10.26 | 13.58 | 12.88 | 11.83 |
| Net Margin % | 5.63 | 4.82 | 5.76 | 6.08 | 1.88 | 7.50 | 8.38 | 4.81 |
| Asset Turnover | 1.21 | 1.19 | 1.14 | 1.19 | 1.46 | 1.49 | 1.50 | 1.44 |
| Current Ratio | 2.24 | 2.26 | 2.23 | 2.66 | 2.19 | 2.64 | 2.10 | 1.77 |
| Debt to Equity | 0.28 | 0.30 | 0.30 | 0.13 | 0.25 | 0.23 | 0.29 | 0.39 |
| Price Range | 50.55-28.05 | 45.56-28.05 | 41.63-28.05 | 36.28-18.11 | 39.67-17.26 | 50.00-36.80 | 45.04-33.84 | 37.31-29.78 |
| P/E Ratio | 18.65-10.35 | 18.45-11.36 | 17.79-11.99 | 15.50-7.74 | 43.59-18.97 | 14.53-10.70 | 13.02-9.78 | 21.82-17.42 |
| Average Yield % | 1.74 | 1.80 | 1.84 | 2.34 | 2.03 | 1.28 | 1.30 | 1.43 |

**Address:** 13925 Ballantyne Corporate Place, Suite 400, Charlotte, NC 28277
**Telephone:** 704-501-1100
**Web Site:** www.carlisle.com

**Officers:** David A. Roberts - Chairman, President, Chief Executive Officer Steven J. Ford - Vice President, Chief Financial Officer, Secretary, General Counsel **Transfer Agents:**
Computershare Investor Services LLC, Chicago, IL

**Investor Contact:** 704-501-1100
**No of Institutions:** 267
**Shares:** 54,210,156 **% Held:** 80.94

# CASEY'S GENERAL STORES, INC.

| Exchange | Symbol | Price | 52Wk Range | Yield | P/E |
|---|---|---|---|---|---|
| NMS | CASY | $45.00 (8/31/2011) | 46.97-35.83 | 1.33 | 20.27 |

***7 Year Price Score 147.94** *NYSE Composite Index=100 ***12 Month Price Score 107.43**

**Interim Earnings (Per Share)**

| Qtr. | Jul | Oct | Jan | Apr |
|---|---|---|---|---|
| 2006-07 | 0.33 | 0.34 | 0.22 | 0.33 |
| 2007-08 | 0.59 | 0.54 | 0.26 | 0.28 |
| 2008-09 | 0.57 | 0.54 | 0.28 | 0.30 |
| 2009-10 | 0.87 | 0.66 | 0.34 | 0.43 |
| 2010-11 | 0.73 | 0.51 | 0.34 | 0.59 |

**Interim Dividends (Per Share)**

| Amt | Decl | Ex | Rec | Pay |
|---|---|---|---|---|
| 0.135Q | 09/07/2010 | 10/28/2010 | 11/01/2010 | 11/15/2010 |
| 0.135Q | 12/07/2010 | 01/28/2011 | 02/01/2011 | 02/15/2011 |
| 0.135Q | 03/07/2011 | 04/28/2011 | 05/02/2011 | 05/16/2011 |
| 0.15Q | 06/13/2011 | 07/28/2011 | 08/01/2011 | 08/15/2011 |

**Indicated Div: $0.60 (Div. Reinv. Plan)**

**Valuation Analysis**

| | | | |
|---|---|---|---|
| Forecast EPS | $3.15 (09/05/2011) | | |
| Market Cap | $1.7 Billion | Book Value | $403.9 Million |
| Price/Book | 4.23 | Price/Sales | 0.30 |

**Dividend Achiever Status**

| | |
|---|---|
| 10 Year Growth Rate | 17.61% |
| Total Years of Dividend Growth | 11 |

**Business Summary:** Retail - Food & Beverage, Drug & Tobacco (MIC: 2.1.2 SIC: 5541 NAIC: 447110)

Casey's General Stores and its wholly owned subsidiaries operate convenience stores under the name Casey's General Store, HandiMart and Just Diesel in 11 Midwestern states, primarily Iowa, Missouri, and Illinois. The stores carry a selection of food, such as pizza, donuts, and sandwiches, beverages, tobacco products, health and beauty aids, automotive products, and other nonfood items. In addition, all of Casey's stores provide gasoline for sale on a self-service basis. At Apr 30 2011, there were a total of 1,637 Casey's General Stores in operation. Co. operates a central warehouse, Casey's Distribution Center, through which Co. supplies grocery and general merchandise items to its stores.

**Recent Developments:** For the year ended Apr 30 2011, net income decreased 19.1% to US$94.6 million from US$117.0 million in the prior year. Revenues were US$5.64 billion, up 21.5% from US$4.64 billion the year before. Direct operating expenses rose 23.7% to US$4.75 billion from US$3.84 billion in the comparable period the year before. Indirect operating expenses increased 17.6% to US$718.5 million from US$610.8 million in the equivalent prior-year period.

**Prospects:** Our evaluation of Casey's General Stores Inc. as of Sep. 6, 2011 is the result of our systematic analysis on three basic characteristics: earnings strength, relative valuation, and recent stock price movement. The company has produced a positive trend in earnings per share over the past 5 quarters and while recent estimates for the company have been mixed, CASY has posted better than expected results. Based on operating earnings yield, the company is about fairly valued when compared to all of the companies in our coverage universe. Share price changes over the past year indicates that CASY will perform very poorly over the near term.

**Financial Data**

| (US$ in Thousands) | 04/30/2011 | 04/30/2010 | 04/30/2009 | 04/30/2008 | 04/30/2007 | 04/30/2006 | 04/30/2005 | 04/30/2004 |
|---|---|---|---|---|---|---|---|---|
| Earnings Per Share | 2.22 | 2.29 | 1.68 | 1.67 | 1.22 | 1.19 | 0.73 | 0.73 |
| Cash Flow Per Share | 6.18 | 4.21 | 3.34 | 3.46 | 2.21 | 2.94 | 2.64 | 1.96 |
| Tang Book Value Per Share | 8.32 | 15.06 | 13.18 | 11.81 | 10.39 | 10.10 | 9.35 | 8.79 |
| Dividends Per Share | 0.505 | 0.340 | 0.300 | 0.260 | 0.200 | 0.180 | 0.160 | 0.140 |
| Dividend Payout % | 22.75 | 14.85 | 17.86 | 15.57 | 16.39 | 15.13 | 21.92 | 19.18 |
| **Income Statement** | | | | | | | | |
| Total Revenue | 5,635,240 | 4,637,087 | 4,687,895 | 4,827,087 | 4,024,010 | 3,515,145 | 2,810,485 | 2,369,142 |
| EBITDA | 263,077 | 266,264 | 219,009 | 211,725 | 173,308 | 166,068 | 129,668 | 114,821 |
| Depn & Amortn | 83,343 | 73,749 | 69,214 | 67,878 | 64,377 | 59,056 | 53,182 | 49,506 |
| Income Before Taxes | 151,237 | 181,582 | 139,169 | 134,055 | 97,747 | 98,116 | 65,747 | 52,917 |
| Income Taxes | 56,614 | 64,620 | 53,425 | 49,051 | 34,205 | 35,176 | 23,215 | 16,451 |
| Net Income | 94,623 | 116,962 | 85,690 | 84,891 | 61,891 | 60,468 | 36,753 | 36,466 |
| Average Shares | 42,566 | 51,053 | 50,917 | 50,858 | 50,667 | 50,610 | 50,284 | 50,041 |
| **Balance Sheet** | | | | | | | | |
| Current Assets | 293,887 | 310,263 | 284,727 | 313,256 | 240,825 | 191,406 | 142,430 | 146,807 |
| Total Assets | 1,610,955 | 1,388,775 | 1,262,695 | 1,219,200 | 1,129,271 | 987,539 | 870,909 | 834,586 |
| Current Liabilities | 294,500 | 240,886 | 221,243 | 259,099 | 234,267 | 243,696 | 170,127 | 145,840 |
| Long-Term Obligations | 678,680 | 154,754 | 167,887 | 181,443 | 199,504 | 106,512 | 123,064 | 144,158 |
| Total Liabilities | 1,207,059 | 564,456 | 541,665 | 571,728 | 557,007 | 464,349 | 401,772 | 394,792 |
| Stockholders' Equity | 403,896 | 824,319 | 721,030 | 647,472 | 572,264 | 523,190 | 469,137 | 439,794 |
| Shares Outstanding | 37,966 | 50,926 | 50,842 | 50,733 | 50,592 | 50,368 | 50,189 | 50,015 |
| **Statistical Record** | | | | | | | | |
| Return on Assets % | 6.31 | 8.82 | 6.91 | 7.21 | 5.85 | 6.51 | 4.31 | 4.52 |
| Return on Equity % | 15.41 | 15.14 | 12.52 | 13.88 | 11.30 | 12.19 | 8.09 | 8.62 |
| EBITDA Margin % | 4.67 | 5.74 | 4.67 | 4.39 | 4.31 | 4.72 | 4.61 | 4.85 |
| Net Margin % | 1.68 | 2.52 | 1.83 | 1.76 | 1.54 | 1.72 | 1.31 | 1.54 |
| Asset Turnover | 3.76 | 3.50 | 3.78 | 4.10 | 3.80 | 3.78 | 3.30 | 2.94 |
| Current Ratio | 1.00 | 1.29 | 1.29 | 1.21 | 1.03 | 0.79 | 0.84 | 1.01 |
| Debt to Equity | 1.68 | 0.19 | 0.23 | 0.28 | 0.35 | 0.20 | 0.26 | 0.33 |
| Price Range | 44.24-34.90 | 39.50-24.31 | 30.47-18.39 | 31.39-21.11 | 26.61-20.34 | 27.02-16.98 | 19.97-15.16 | 18.74-12.93 |
| P/E Ratio | 19.93-15.72 | 17.25-10.62 | 18.14-10.95 | 18.80-12.64 | 21.81-16.67 | 22.71-14.27 | 27.36-20.77 | 25.67-17.71 |
| Average Yield % | 1.28 | 1.14 | 1.20 | 0.98 | 0.83 | 0.81 | 0.91 | 0.89 |

| | | |
|---|---|---|
| **Address:** One Convenience Blvd., Ankeny, IA 50021<br>**Telephone:** 515-965-6100<br>**Web Site:** www.caseys.com | **Officers:** Ronald M. Lamb - Chairman Robert J. Myers - President, Chief Executive Officer **Transfer Agents:** UMB Bank, N.A., Kansas City , MO | **No of Institutions:** 254<br>**Shares:** 39,706,896 **% Held:** 81.96 |

# CATERPILLAR INC.

| Exchange | Symbol | Price | 52Wk Range | Yield | P/E |
|---|---|---|---|---|---|
| NYS | CAT | $91.00 (8/31/2011) | 115.41-65.16 | 2.02 | 15.04 |

*7 Year Price Score 145.92 *NYSE Composite Index=100 *12 Month Price Score 103.76

**Interim Earnings (Per Share)**

| Qtr. | Mar | Jun | Sep | Dec |
|---|---|---|---|---|
| 2008 | 1.45 | 1.74 | 1.39 | 1.09 |
| 2009 | (0.19) | 0.60 | 0.64 | 0.36 |
| 2010 | 0.36 | 1.09 | 1.22 | 1.47 |
| 2011 | 1.84 | 1.52 | ... | ... |

**Interim Dividends (Per Share)**

| Amt | Decl | Ex | Rec | Pay |
|---|---|---|---|---|
| 0.44Q | 10/13/2010 | 10/21/2010 | 10/25/2010 | 11/20/2010 |
| 0.44Q | 12/08/2010 | 01/18/2011 | 01/20/2011 | 02/19/2011 |
| 0.44Q | 04/12/2011 | 04/20/2011 | 04/25/2011 | 05/20/2011 |
| 0.46Q | 06/08/2011 | 07/18/2011 | 07/20/2011 | 08/20/2011 |

**Indicated Div: $1.84 (Div. Reinv. Plan)**

**Valuation Analysis**

| | | | |
|---|---|---|---|
| Forecast EPS | $6.75 (09/05/2011) | | |
| Market Cap | $58.8 Billion | Book Value | $13.4 Billion |
| Price/Book | 4.39 | Price/Sales | 1.15 |

**Dividend Achiever Status**

| | |
|---|---|
| 10 Year Growth Rate | 9.56% |
| Total Years of Dividend Growth | 17 |

**Business Summary:** Construction Services (MIC: 7.5.4 SIC: 3531 NAIC: 333120)

Caterpillar is engaged in three lines of business as of Dec 31 2010. Co.'s Machinery business designs, manufactures and sells construction, mining and forestry machinery, and designs, manufactures, remanufactures, maintains and services rail-related products. Co.'s Engines business designs, manufactures and sells engines for its machinery; electric power generation systems; locomotives; marine, petroleum, construction, industrial, agricultural and other applications; and related parts. Co.'s Financial Products business provides financing alternatives, loans and insurance services to customers and dealers for its machinery and engines, gas turbines and other equipment and marine vessels.

**Recent Developments:** For the quarter ended June 30 2011, net income increased 39.4% to US$1.02 billion from US$733.0 million in the year-earlier quarter. Revenues were US$14.23 billion, up 36.7% from US$10.41 billion the year before. Operating income was US$1.60 billion versus US$977.0 million in the prior-year quarter, an increase of 63.9%. Direct operating expenses rose 39.8% to US$10.30 billion from US$7.37 billion in the comparable period the year before. Indirect operating expenses increased 12.9% to US$2.33 billion from US$2.06 billion in the equivalent prior-year period.

**Prospects:** Our evaluation of Caterpillar Inc. as of Sep. 6, 2011 is the result of our systematic analysis on three basic characteristics: earnings strength, relative valuation, and recent stock price movement. The company has generated a negative trend in earnings per share over the past 5 quarters. However, while recent estimates for the company have been lowered by analysts, CAT has posted results that fell short of analysts expectations. Based on operating earnings yield, the company is undervalued when compared to all of the companies in our coverage universe. Share price changes over the past year indicates that CAT will perform well over the near term.

**Financial Data**

| (US$ in Thousands) | 6 Mos | 3 Mos | 12/31/2010 | 12/31/2009 | 12/31/2008 | 12/31/2007 | 12/31/2006 | 12/31/2005 |
|---|---|---|---|---|---|---|---|---|
| Earnings Per Share | 6.05 | 5.62 | 4.15 | 1.43 | 5.66 | 5.37 | 5.17 | 4.04 |
| Cash Flow Per Share | 10.16 | 8.14 | 7.93 | 10.31 | 7.82 | 12.43 | 8.80 | 4.59 |
| Tang Book Value Per Share | 15.49 | 14.32 | 11.59 | 9.61 | 5.51 | 10.33 | 7.07 | 9.77 |
| Dividends Per Share | 1.760 | 1.740 | 1.720 | 1.680 | 1.560 | 1.320 | 1.100 | 0.910 |
| Dividend Payout % | 29.09 | 30.96 | 41.45 | 117.48 | 27.56 | 24.58 | 21.28 | 22.52 |
| **Income Statement** | | | | | | | | |
| Total Revenue | 27,179,000 | 12,949,000 | 42,588,000 | 32,396,000 | 51,324,000 | 44,958,000 | 41,517,000 | 36,339,000 |
| EBITDA | 4,876,000 | 2,628,000 | 7,209,000 | 4,257,000 | 7,807,000 | 8,098,000 | 7,712,000 | 6,373,000 |
| Depn & Amortn | 1,174,000 | 575,000 | 2,202,000 | 2,254,000 | 1,907,000 | 1,725,000 | 1,554,000 | 1,444,000 |
| Income Before Taxes | 3,113,000 | 1,763,000 | 3,750,000 | 569,000 | 4,473,000 | 4,953,000 | 4,861,000 | 3,901,000 |
| Income Taxes | 830,000 | 512,000 | 968,000 | (270,000) | 953,000 | 1,485,000 | 1,405,000 | 1,120,000 |
| Net Income | 2,240,000 | 1,225,000 | 2,700,000 | 895,000 | 3,557,000 | 3,541,000 | 3,537,000 | 2,854,000 |
| Average Shares | 667,200 | 664,900 | 650,400 | 626,000 | 627,900 | 659,500 | 683,800 | 705,800 |
| **Balance Sheet** | | | | | | | | |
| Current Assets | 40,755,000 | 34,608,000 | 31,810,000 | 26,789,000 | 31,633,000 | 25,477,000 | 23,093,000 | 22,790,000 |
| Total Assets | 73,611,000 | 66,387,000 | 64,020,000 | 60,038,000 | 67,782,000 | 56,132,000 | 50,879,000 | 47,069,000 |
| Current Liabilities | 23,510,000 | 23,147,000 | 22,020,000 | 19,292,000 | 26,069,000 | 22,245,000 | 19,252,000 | 19,092,000 |
| Long-Term Obligations | 25,926,000 | 19,895,000 | 20,437,000 | 21,847,000 | 22,834,000 | 17,829,000 | 17,680,000 | 15,677,000 |
| Total Liabilities | 60,220,000 | 53,758,000 | 53,196,000 | 51,298,000 | 61,695,000 | 47,249,000 | 44,020,000 | 38,637,000 |
| Stockholders' Equity | 13,391,000 | 12,629,000 | 10,824,000 | 8,740,000 | 6,087,000 | 8,883,000 | 6,859,000 | 8,432,000 |
| Shares Outstanding | 646,066 | 644,452 | 638,822 | 624,722 | 601,526 | 623,986 | 645,808 | 670,867 |
| **Statistical Record** | | | | | | | | |
| Return on Assets % | 6.04 | 5.90 | 4.35 | 1.40 | 5.73 | 6.62 | 7.22 | 6.33 |
| Return on Equity % | 35.44 | 34.23 | 27.60 | 12.07 | 47.39 | 44.99 | 46.26 | 35.90 |
| EBITDA Margin % | 17.94 | 20.30 | 16.93 | 13.14 | 15.21 | 18.01 | 18.58 | 17.54 |
| Net Margin % | 8.24 | 9.46 | 6.34 | 2.76 | 6.93 | 7.88 | 8.52 | 7.85 |
| Asset Turnover | 0.77 | 0.76 | 0.69 | 0.51 | 0.83 | 0.84 | 0.85 | 0.81 |
| Current Ratio | 1.73 | 1.50 | 1.44 | 1.39 | 1.21 | 1.15 | 1.20 | 1.19 |
| Debt to Equity | 1.94 | 1.58 | 1.89 | 2.50 | 3.75 | 2.01 | 2.58 | 1.86 |
| Price Range | 115.41-59.18 | 111.53-55.83 | 94.63-50.78 | 60.40-22.17 | 85.28-32.78 | 86.98-58.17 | 81.14-57.80 | 59.64-41.73 |
| P/E Ratio | 19.08-9.78 | 19.85-9.93 | 22.80-12.24 | 42.24-15.50 | 15.07-5.79 | 16.20-10.83 | 15.69-11.18 | 14.76-10.33 |
| Average Yield % | 1.96 | 2.19 | 2.49 | 4.00 | 2.40 | 1.82 | 1.60 | 1.79 |

| | | |
|---|---|---|
| **Address:** 100 NE Adams Street, Peoria, IL 61629<br>**Telephone:** 309-675-1000<br>**Web Site:** www.caterpillar.com | **Officers:** James W. Owens - Chairman Douglas R. Oberhelman - Vice-Chairman, Chief Executive Officer<br>**Transfer Agents:**BNY Mellon Shareowner Services, Pittsburgh, PA | **Investor Contact:** 309-675-4549<br>**No of Institutions:** 1363<br>**Shares:** 473,066,656 **% Held:** 68.62 |

# CENTURYLINK, INC.

| Exchange | Symbol | Price | 52Wk Range | Yield | P/E |
|---|---|---|---|---|---|
| NYS | CTL | $36.15 (8/31/2011) | 46.80-31.82 | 8.02 | 15.32 |

***7 Year Price Score 109.82** *NYSE Composite Index=100 ***12 Month Price Score 90.88**

**Interim Earnings (Per Share)**

| Qtr. | Mar | Jun | Sep | Dec |
|---|---|---|---|---|
| 2008 | 0.83 | 0.88 | 0.84 | 1.01 |
| 2009 | 0.67 | 0.68 | 0.94 | 0.73 |
| 2010 | 0.84 | 0.79 | 0.76 | 0.74 |
| 2011 | 0.69 | 0.17 | ... | ... |

**Interim Dividends (Per Share)**

| Amt | Decl | Ex | Rec | Pay |
|---|---|---|---|---|
| 0.725Q | 11/09/2010 | 12/03/2010 | 12/07/2010 | 12/20/2010 |
| 0.725Q | 01/24/2011 | 02/16/2011 | 02/18/2011 | 02/25/2011 |
| 0.725Q | 05/18/2011 | 06/02/2011 | 06/06/2011 | 06/16/2011 |
| 0.725Q | 08/23/2011 | 09/01/2011 | 09/06/2011 | 09/16/2011 |

**Indicated Div: $2.90 (Div. Reinv. Plan)**

**Valuation Analysis**

| | | | |
|---|---|---|---|
| Forecast EPS | $1.59 (09/05/2011) | | |
| Market Cap | $21.7 Billion | Book Value | $21.6 Billion |
| Price/Book | 1.00 | Price/Sales | 2.27 |

**Dividend Achiever Status**

| | |
|---|---|
| **10 Year Growth Rate** | 30.66% |
| **Total Years of Dividend Growth** | 37 |

**Business Summary:** Services (MIC: 6.1.2 SIC: 4813 NAIC: 517110)

CenturyLink is a holding company. Through its subsidiaries, Co. is engaged in providing a range of communications services, including voice, Internet, data and video services. Co. also provides fiber transport, wholesale communications services, competitive local exchange carrier service, security monitoring and other communications, and business information services in certain local and regional markets. At Dec 31 2010, Co.'s incumbent local exchange telephone subsidiaries operated approximately 6.5 million telephone access lines in 33 states, with over 75.0% of these lines located in Florida, North Carolina, Missouri, Nevada, Ohio, Wisconsin, Virginia, Texas, Pennsylvania, and Alabama.

**Recent Developments:** For the quarter ended June 30 2011, net income decreased 57.1% to US$102.0 million from US$238.0 million in the year-earlier quarter. Revenues were US$4.41 billion, up 148.6% from US$1.77 billion the year before. Operating income was US$459.0 million versus US$523.0 million in the prior-year quarter, a decrease of 12.2%. Direct operating expenses rose 184.1% to US$1.78 billion from US$627.0 million in the comparable period the year before. Indirect operating expenses increased 248.2% to US$2.17 billion from US$622.0 million in the equivalent prior-year period.

**Prospects:** Our evaluation of CenturyLink, Inc. as of Sep. 6, 2011 is the result of our systematic analysis on three basic characteristics: earnings strength, relative valuation, and recent stock price movement. The company has generated a negative trend in earnings per share over the past 5 quarters. However, while recent estimates for the company have been lowered by analysts, CTL has posted results that fell short of analysts expectations. Based on operating earnings yield, the company is undervalued when compared to all of the companies in our coverage universe. Share price changes over the past year indicates that CTL will perform poorly over the near term.

**Financial Data**

| (US$ in Thousands) | 6 Mos | 3 Mos | 12/31/2010 | 12/31/2009 | 12/31/2008 | 12/31/2007 | 12/31/2006 | 12/31/2005 |
|---|---|---|---|---|---|---|---|---|
| Earnings Per Share | 2.36 | 2.98 | 3.13 | 3.23 | 3.56 | 3.72 | 3.07 | 2.49 |
| Cash Flow Per Share | 5.31 | 7.42 | 6.80 | 7.92 | 8.32 | 9.42 | 7.21 | 7.37 |
| Tang Book Value Per Share | N.M. | N.M. | N.M. | N.M. | N.M. | N.M. | N.M. | 0.90 |
| Dividends Per Share | 2.900 | 2.900 | 2.900 | 2.800 | 2.168 | 0.260 | 0.250 | 0.240 |
| Dividend Payout % | 122.88 | 97.32 | 92.65 | 86.69 | 60.88 | 6.99 | 8.14 | 9.64 |
| **Income Statement** | | | | | | | | |
| Total Revenue | 6,102,000 | 1,695,719 | 7,041,534 | 4,974,239 | 2,599,747 | 2,656,241 | 2,447,730 | 2,479,252 |
| EBITDA | 2,479,000 | 839,325 | 3,316,563 | 2,023,726 | 1,269,206 | 1,355,948 | 1,307,506 | 1,263,561 |
| Depn & Amortn | 1,567,000 | 368,547 | 1,227,000 | 838,800 | 506,900 | 524,100 | 520,400 | 528,900 |
| Income Before Taxes | 504,000 | 339,233 | 1,532,085 | 814,512 | 560,089 | 618,942 | 591,149 | 532,860 |
| Income Taxes | 191,000 | 127,742 | 582,951 | 301,881 | 194,357 | 200,572 | 221,122 | 203,291 |
| Net Income | 313,000 | 211,095 | 947,705 | 647,211 | 365,732 | 418,370 | 370,027 | 334,479 |
| Average Shares | 600,259 | 304,479 | 301,297 | 199,057 | 102,871 | 113,094 | 122,229 | 136,087 |
| **Balance Sheet** | | | | | | | | |
| Current Assets | 5,007,000 | 1,140,736 | 1,143,129 | 1,123,591 | 555,407 | 292,399 | 290,117 | 423,016 |
| Total Assets | 54,842,000 | 21,901,458 | 22,038,098 | 22,562,729 | 8,254,195 | 8,184,553 | 7,441,007 | 7,762,707 |
| Current Liabilities | 5,064,000 | 1,073,007 | 1,011,042 | 1,707,195 | 458,390 | 736,535 | 617,565 | 746,230 |
| Long-Term Obligations | 19,734,000 | 7,168,251 | 7,316,004 | 7,253,653 | 3,294,119 | 2,734,357 | 2,412,852 | 2,376,070 |
| Total Liabilities | 33,201,000 | 12,248,522 | 12,396,857 | 13,101,790 | 5,090,955 | 4,775,348 | 4,250,056 | 4,145,434 |
| Stockholders' Equity | 21,641,000 | 9,652,936 | 9,641,241 | 9,460,939 | 3,163,240 | 3,409,205 | 3,190,951 | 3,617,273 |
| Shares Outstanding | 601,570 | 305,778 | 304,947 | 299,189 | 100,277 | 108,491 | 113,253 | 131,074 |
| **Statistical Record** | | | | | | | | |
| Return on Assets % | 2.00 | 4.10 | 4.25 | 4.20 | 4.44 | 5.35 | 4.87 | 4.30 |
| Return on Equity % | 4.93 | 9.47 | 9.92 | 10.25 | 11.10 | 12.68 | 10.87 | 9.52 |
| EBITDA Margin % | 40.63 | 49.50 | 47.10 | 40.68 | 48.82 | 51.05 | 53.42 | 50.97 |
| Net Margin % | 5.13 | 12.45 | 13.46 | 13.01 | 14.07 | 15.75 | 15.12 | 13.49 |
| Asset Turnover | 0.25 | 0.31 | 0.32 | 0.32 | 0.32 | 0.34 | 0.32 | 0.32 |
| Current Ratio | 0.99 | 1.06 | 1.13 | 0.66 | 1.21 | 0.40 | 0.47 | 0.57 |
| Debt to Equity | 0.91 | 0.74 | 0.76 | 0.77 | 1.04 | 0.80 | 0.76 | 0.66 |
| Price Range | 46.80-33.15 | 46.80-32.93 | 46.80-32.93 | 36.82-23.56 | 41.58-21.81 | 49.52-40.30 | 43.79-32.84 | 36.28-30.26 |
| P/E Ratio | 19.83-14.05 | 15.70-11.05 | 14.95-10.52 | 11.40-7.29 | 11.68-6.13 | 13.31-10.83 | 14.26-10.70 | 14.57-12.15 |
| Average Yield % | 7.16 | 7.44 | 7.81 | 9.14 | 6.42 | 0.57 | 0.65 | 0.72 |

| | | |
|---|---|---|
| **Address:** 100 CenturyLink Drive, Monroe, LA 71203<br>**Telephone:** 318-388-9000<br>**Web Site:** www.centurylink.com | **Officers:** William Arthur Owens - Chairman Thomas A. Gerke - Executive Vice-Chairman **Transfer Agents:** ComputershareTrust Company, Providence, RI | **Investor Contact:** 800-833-1188<br>**No of Institutions:** 714<br>**Shares:** 448,426,528 **% Held:** 70.87 |

# CHEVRON CORPORATION

| Exchange | Symbol | Price | 52Wk Range | Yield | P/E |
|---|---|---|---|---|---|
| NYS | CVX | $98.84 (8/31/2011) | 109.66-74.08 | 3.16 | 8.63 |

***7 Year Price Score 126.28** *NYSE Composite Index=100 ***12 Month Price Score 108.24**

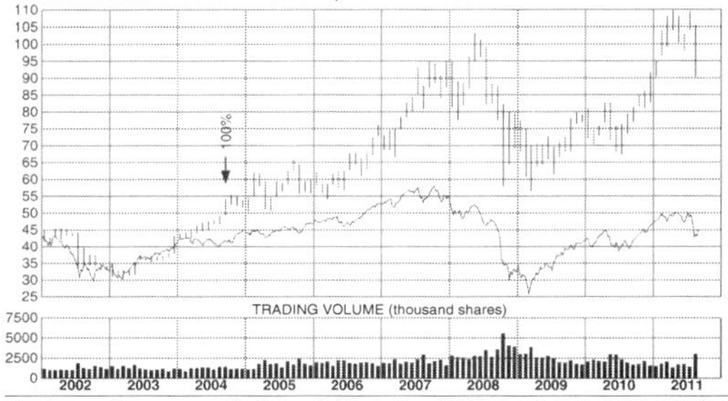


**Interim Earnings (Per Share)**

| Qtr. | Mar | Jun | Sep | Dec |
|---|---|---|---|---|
| 2008 | 2.48 | 2.90 | 3.85 | 2.44 |
| 2009 | 0.92 | 0.87 | 1.92 | 1.53 |
| 2010 | 2.27 | 2.70 | 1.87 | 2.64 |
| 2011 | 3.09 | 3.85 | ... | ... |

**Interim Dividends (Per Share)**

| Amt | Decl | Ex | Rec | Pay |
|---|---|---|---|---|
| 0.72Q | 10/27/2010 | 11/16/2010 | 11/18/2010 | 12/10/2010 |
| 0.72Q | 01/26/2011 | 02/14/2011 | 02/16/2011 | 03/10/2011 |
| 0.78Q | 04/26/2011 | 05/17/2011 | 05/19/2011 | 06/10/2011 |
| 0.78Q | 07/27/2011 | 08/17/2011 | 08/19/2011 | 09/12/2011 |

**Indicated Div: $3.12 (Div. Reinv. Plan)**

**Valuation Analysis**

| | | | |
|---|---|---|---|
| Forecast EPS | $13.62 (09/05/2011) | | |
| Market Cap | $198.0 Billion | Book Value | $115.7 Billion |
| Price/Book | 1.71 | Price/Sales | 0.85 |

**Dividend Achiever Status**

| | |
|---|---|
| **10 Year Growth Rate** | 7.92% |
| **Total Years of Dividend Growth** | 23 |

**Business Summary:** Refining & Marketing (MIC: 9.1.2 SIC: 2911 NAIC: 324110)

Chevron is engaged in petroleum and chemicals operations, mining operations, power generation and energy services. Co.'s operations consist of exploring for, developing and producing crude oil and natural gas; refining crude oil into finished petroleum products; marketing crude oil, natural gas and the products derived from petroleum; and transporting crude oil, natural gas and petroleum products. Co. also manufactures and markets commodity petrochemicals, plastics for industrial uses, and fuel and lubricant oil additives. At Dec 31 2010, Co. had net proved reserves of 6,503.0 million barrels of crude oil, condensate and natural gas liquids, and 24,251.00 billion cubic feet of natural gas.

**Recent Developments:** For the quarter ended June 30 2011, net income increased 42.5% to US$7.76 billion from US$5.44 billion in the year-earlier quarter. Revenues were US$68.95 billion, up 30.1% from US$53.00 billion the year before. Direct operating expenses rose 33.2% to US$40.76 billion from US$30.60 billion in the comparable period the year before. Indirect operating expenses increased 9.9% to US$14.98 billion from US$13.63 billion in the equivalent prior-year period.

**Prospects:** Our evaluation of ChevronTexaco Corp. as of Sep. 6, 2011 is the result of our systematic analysis on three basic characteristics: earnings strength, relative valuation, and recent stock price movement. The company has enjoyed a very positive trend in earnings per share over the past 5 quarters. However, while recent estimates for the company have been mixed, CVX has posted better than expected results. Based on operating earnings yield, the company is undervalued when compared to all of the companies in our coverage universe. Share price changes over the past year indicates that CVX will perform in line with the market over the near term.

**Financial Data**

| (US$ in Millions) | 6 Mos | 3 Mos | 12/31/2010 | 12/31/2009 | 12/31/2008 | 12/31/2007 | 12/31/2006 | 12/31/2005 |
|---|---|---|---|---|---|---|---|---|
| Earnings Per Share | 11.45 | 10.30 | 9.48 | 5.24 | 11.67 | 8.77 | 7.80 | 6.54 |
| Cash Flow Per Share | 18.43 | 16.87 | 15.70 | 9.73 | 14.51 | 11.79 | 11.13 | 9.38 |
| Tang Book Value Per Share | 55.42 | 52.45 | 50.04 | 43.48 | 40.93 | 34.66 | 29.71 | 26.00 |
| Dividends Per Share | 2.940 | 2.880 | 2.840 | 2.660 | 2.530 | 2.260 | 2.010 | 1.750 |
| Dividend Payout % | 25.68 | 27.96 | 29.96 | 50.76 | 21.68 | 25.77 | 25.77 | 26.76 |
| **Income Statement** | | | | | | | | |
| Total Revenue | 129,289 | 60,341 | 204,928 | 171,636 | 273,005 | 220,904 | 210,118 | 198,200 |
| EBITDA | 30,712 | 14,248 | 45,168 | 30,666 | 52,585 | 41,148 | 40,003 | 31,688 |
| Depn & Amortn | 6,383 | 3,126 | 13,063 | 12,110 | 9,528 | 8,708 | 7,506 | 5,913 |
| Income Before Taxes | 24,329 | 11,122 | 32,055 | 18,528 | 43,057 | 32,274 | 32,046 | 25,293 |
| Income Taxes | 10,330 | 4,883 | 12,919 | 7,965 | 19,026 | 13,479 | 14,838 | 11,098 |
| Net Income | 13,943 | 6,211 | 19,024 | 10,483 | 23,931 | 18,688 | 17,138 | 14,099 |
| Average Shares | 2,008 | 2,008 | 2,007 | 2,001 | 2,038 | 2,132 | 2,198 | 2,156 |
| **Balance Sheet** | | | | | | | | |
| Current Assets | 54,006 | 50,851 | 48,841 | 37,216 | 36,470 | 39,377 | 36,304 | 34,336 |
| Total Assets | 201,717 | 194,736 | 184,769 | 164,621 | 161,165 | 148,786 | 132,628 | 125,833 |
| Current Liabilities | 35,220 | 33,313 | 29,012 | 26,211 | 32,023 | 33,798 | 28,409 | 25,011 |
| Long-Term Obligations | 9,618 | 9,758 | 11,289 | 10,130 | 6,083 | 6,070 | 7,679 | 12,131 |
| Total Liabilities | 86,064 | 84,636 | 79,688 | 72,707 | 74,517 | 71,698 | 63,693 | 63,157 |
| Stockholders' Equity | 115,653 | 110,100 | 105,081 | 91,914 | 86,648 | 77,088 | 68,935 | 62,676 |
| Shares Outstanding | 2,002 | 2,010 | 2,007 | 2,007 | 2,004 | 2,090 | 2,165 | 2,233 |
| **Statistical Record** | | | | | | | | |
| Return on Assets % | 12.32 | 11.37 | 10.89 | 6.44 | 15.40 | 13.28 | 13.26 | 12.87 |
| Return on Equity % | 21.38 | 20.13 | 19.31 | 11.74 | 29.15 | 25.60 | 26.04 | 26.13 |
| EBITDA Margin % | 23.75 | 23.61 | 22.04 | 17.87 | 19.26 | 18.63 | 19.04 | 15.99 |
| Net Margin % | 10.78 | 10.29 | 9.28 | 6.11 | 8.77 | 8.46 | 8.16 | 7.11 |
| Asset Turnover | 1.25 | 1.19 | 1.17 | 1.05 | 1.76 | 1.57 | 1.63 | 1.81 |
| Current Ratio | 1.53 | 1.53 | 1.68 | 1.42 | 1.14 | 1.17 | 1.28 | 1.37 |
| Debt to Equity | 0.08 | 0.09 | 0.11 | 0.11 | 0.07 | 0.08 | 0.11 | 0.19 |
| Price Range | 109.66-67.31 | 108.01-67.31 | 91.60-67.31 | 79.64-56.46 | 103.09-57.83 | 94.86-66.43 | 75.97-54.08 | 65.77-50.51 |
| P/E Ratio | 9.58-5.88 | 10.49-6.53 | 9.66-7.10 | 15.20-10.77 | 8.83-4.96 | 10.82-7.57 | 9.74-6.93 | 10.06-7.72 |
| Average Yield % | 3.24 | 3.43 | 3.63 | 3.79 | 2.98 | 2.74 | 3.19 | 3.04 |

**Address:** 6001 Bollinger Canyon Road, San Ramon, CA 94583-2324
**Telephone:** 925-842-1000
**Web Site:** www.chevron.com

**Officers:** John S. Watson - Chairman, Chief Executive Officer George L. Kirkland - Vice-Chairman, Executive Vice President **Transfer Agents:** BNY Mellon Shareowner Services, Pittsburgh, PA

**Investor Contact:** 925-842-5690
**No of Institutions:** 1923
**Shares:** 1,400,440,320 **% Held:** 61.50

# CHUBB CORP.

| Exchange | Symbol | Price | 52Wk Range | Yield | P/E |
|---|---|---|---|---|---|
| NYS | CB | $61.89 (8/31/2011) | 65.87-55.13 | 2.52 | 8.94 |

***7 Year Price Score 119.76** *NYSE Composite Index=100 ***12 Month Price Score 101.98**

**Interim Earnings (Per Share)**

| Qtr. | Mar | Jun | Sep | Dec |
|---|---|---|---|---|
| 2008 | 1.77 | 1.27 | 0.73 | 1.14 |
| 2009 | 0.95 | 1.54 | 1.69 | 2.00 |
| 2010 | 1.39 | 1.59 | 1.80 | 2.00 |
| 2011 | 1.70 | 1.42 | ... | ... |

**Interim Dividends (Per Share)**

| Amt | Decl | Ex | Rec | Pay |
|---|---|---|---|---|
| 0.37Q | 09/02/2010 | 09/15/2010 | 09/17/2010 | 10/05/2010 |
| 0.37Q | 12/09/2010 | 12/21/2010 | 12/23/2010 | 01/11/2011 |
| 0.39Q | 02/24/2011 | 03/16/2011 | 03/18/2011 | 04/05/2011 |
| 0.39Q | 06/09/2011 | 06/22/2011 | 06/24/2011 | 07/12/2011 |

**Indicated Div: $1.56 (Div. Reinv. Plan)**

**Valuation Analysis**

| | | | |
|---|---|---|---|
| Forecast EPS | $5.75 (09/02/2011) | | |
| Market Cap | $18.4 Billion | Book Value | $15.8 Billion |
| Price/Book | 1.17 | Price/Sales | 1.36 |

**Dividend Achiever Status**

| | |
|---|---|
| **10 Year Growth Rate** | 8.02% |
| **Total Years of Dividend Growth** | 46 |

**Business Summary:** General Insurance (MIC: 5.2.1 SIC: 6331 NAIC: 524126)

Chubb is a holding company. Through its subsidiaries, Co. is principally engaged in the property and casualty insurance business. Co.'s Chubb Personal Insurance business unit provides coverage of homes, automobiles and other personal possessions. Co.'s Chubb Commercial Insurance business unit provides a range of commercial insurance products, including coverage for multiple peril, casualty, workers' compensation and property and marine. Co.'s Chubb Specialty Insurance business unit provides a variety of liability products for privately and publicly owned companies, financial institutions, firms and healthcare organizations. Chubb Specialty Insurance also includes Co.'s surety business.

**Recent Developments:** For the quarter ended June 30 2011, net income decreased 19.1% to US$419.0 million from US$518.0 million in the year-earlier quarter. Revenues were US$3.40 billion, up 2.5% from US$3.32 billion the year before. Net premiums earned were US$2.91 billion versus US$2.80 billion in the prior-year quarter, an increase of 4.1%.

**Prospects:** Our evaluation of Chubb Corp. as of Sep. 6, 2011 is the result of our systematic analysis on three basic characteristics: earnings strength, relative valuation, and recent stock price movement. The company has generated a negative trend in earnings per share over the past 5 quarters and while recent estimates for the company have been raised by analysts, CB has posted better than expected results. Based on operating earnings yield, the company is undervalued when compared to all of the companies in our coverage universe. Share price changes over the past year indicates that CB will perform poorly over the near term.

**Financial Data**

| (US$ in Thousands) | 6 Mos | 3 Mos | 12/31/2010 | 12/31/2009 | 12/31/2008 | 12/31/2007 | 12/31/2006 | 12/31/2005 |
|---|---|---|---|---|---|---|---|---|
| Earnings Per Share | 6.92 | 7.09 | 6.76 | 6.18 | 4.92 | 7.01 | 5.98 | 4.47 |
| Cash Flow Per Share | 7.50 | 7.45 | 7.37 | 6.96 | 7.03 | 8.11 | 8.10 | 9.47 |
| Tang Book Value Per Share | 51.55 | 51.66 | 50.67 | 45.68 | 36.81 | 37.31 | 32.57 | 28.56 |
| Dividends Per Share | 1.520 | 1.500 | 1.480 | 1.400 | 1.320 | 1.160 | 1.000 | 0.860 |
| Dividend Payout % | 21.97 | 21.16 | 21.89 | 22.65 | 26.83 | 16.55 | 16.72 | 19.24 |
| **Income Statement** | | | | | | | | |
| Premium Income | 5,767,000 | 2,854,000 | 11,215,000 | 11,331,000 | 11,828,000 | 11,946,000 | 11,958,000 | 12,176,000 |
| Total Revenue | 6,820,000 | 3,420,000 | 13,319,000 | 13,016,000 | 13,221,000 | 14,107,000 | 14,003,000 | 14,082,300 |
| Benefits & Claims | 3,612,000 | 1,765,000 | 6,499,000 | 6,268,000 | 6,898,000 | 6,299,000 | 6,574,000 | 7,813,500 |
| Income Before Taxes | 1,231,000 | 685,000 | 2,988,000 | 2,962,000 | 2,407,000 | 3,937,000 | 3,525,000 | 2,447,000 |
| Income Taxes | 303,000 | 176,000 | 814,000 | 779,000 | 603,000 | 1,130,000 | 997,000 | 621,100 |
| Net Income | 928,000 | 509,000 | 2,174,000 | 2,183,000 | 1,804,000 | 2,807,000 | 2,528,000 | 1,825,900 |
| Average Shares | 295,400 | 300,000 | 321,600 | 353,000 | 366,800 | 400,300 | 422,400 | 408,400 |
| **Balance Sheet** | | | | | | | | |
| Total Assets | 51,442,000 | 50,689,000 | 50,249,000 | 50,449,000 | 48,429,000 | 50,574,000 | 50,277,000 | 48,060,700 |
| Total Liabilities | 35,651,000 | 35,110,000 | 34,719,000 | 34,815,000 | 34,997,000 | 36,129,000 | 36,414,000 | 35,653,700 |
| Stockholders' Equity | 15,791,000 | 15,579,000 | 15,530,000 | 15,634,000 | 13,432,000 | 14,445,000 | 13,863,000 | 12,407,000 |
| Shares Outstanding | 297,272 | 292,545 | 297,272 | 332,007 | 352,254 | 374,649 | 411,276 | 418,076 |
| **Statistical Record** | | | | | | | | |
| Return on Assets % | 4.16 | 4.37 | 4.32 | 4.42 | 3.63 | 5.57 | 5.14 | 3.96 |
| Return on Equity % | 13.54 | 14.17 | 13.95 | 15.02 | 12.91 | 19.83 | 19.25 | 16.21 |
| Loss Ratio % | 62.63 | 61.84 | 57.95 | 55.32 | 58.32 | 52.73 | 54.98 | 64.17 |
| Net Margin % | 13.61 | 14.88 | 16.32 | 16.77 | 13.64 | 19.90 | 18.05 | 12.97 |
| Price Range | 65.87-49.20 | 61.31-49.10 | 60.23-47.66 | 53.79-35.00 | 64.50-38.75 | 55.91-47.36 | 54.65-46.80 | 49.06-36.67 |
| P/E Ratio | 9.52-7.11 | 8.65-6.93 | 8.91-7.05 | 8.70-5.66 | 13.11-7.88 | 7.98-6.76 | 9.14-7.83 | 10.98-8.20 |
| Average Yield % | 2.59 | 2.69 | 2.76 | 3.14 | 2.64 | 2.20 | 1.99 | 2.02 |

**Address:** 15 Mountain View Road, Warren, NJ 07059
**Telephone:** 908-903-2000
**Web Site:** www.chubb.com

**Officers:** John D. Finnegan - Chairman, President, Chief Executive Officer John J. Degnan - Vice-Chairman, Chief Operating Officer **Transfer Agents:** BNY Mellon Shareowner Services, Jersey City, NJ

**No of Institutions:** 924
**Shares:** 268,389,520 **% Held:** 82.99

# CHURCH & DWIGHT CO., INC.

| Exchange | Symbol | Price | 52Wk Range | Yield | P/E |
|---|---|---|---|---|---|
| NYS | CHD | $43.54 (8/31/2011) | 43.63-30.61 | 1.56 | 22.33 |

***7 Year Price Score 142.00** *NYSE Composite Index=100 ***12 Month Price Score 111.38**

**Interim Earnings (Per Share)**

| Qtr. | Mar | Jun | Sep | Dec |
|---|---|---|---|---|
| 2008 | 0.41 | 0.33 | 0.34 | 0.31 |
| 2009 | 0.44 | 0.41 | 0.49 | 0.37 |
| 2010 | 0.56 | 0.52 | 0.48 | 0.33 |
| 2011 | 0.57 | 0.57 | ... | ... |

**Interim Dividends (Per Share)**

| Amt | Decl | Ex | Rec | Pay |
|---|---|---|---|---|
| 0.17Q | 02/07/2011 | 02/16/2011 | 02/18/2011 | 03/01/2011 |
| 0.17Q | 05/05/2011 | 05/12/2011 | 05/16/2011 | 06/01/2011 |
| 100% | 05/05/2011 | 06/02/2011 | 05/16/2011 | 06/01/2011 |
| 0.17Q | 08/04/2011 | 08/11/2011 | 08/15/2011 | 09/01/2011 |

**Indicated Div: $0.68 (Div. Reinv. Plan)**

**Valuation Analysis**

| | | | |
|---|---|---|---|
| Forecast EPS | $2.19 (09/05/2011) | | |
| Market Cap | $6.2 Billion | Book Value | $2.0 Billion |
| Price/Book | 3.07 | Price/Sales | 2.37 |

**Dividend Achiever Status**

| | |
|---|---|
| **10 Year Growth Rate** | 12.36% |
| **Total Years of Dividend Growth** | 14 |

**Business Summary:** Household & Personal Products (MIC: 1.7.1 SIC: 2841 NAIC: 325611)

Church & Dwight develops, manufactures and markets a range of household, personal care and specialty products Co. operates three segments: Consumer Domestic segment, which sells ARM & HAMMER baking soda, carpet deodorization and laundry detergent, TROJAN Condoms, XTRA laundry detergent, OXICLEAN pre-wash laundry additive, NAIR depilatories, FIRST RESPONSE home pregnancy and ovulation test kits, ORAJEL oral analgesics, and SPINBRUSH battery-operated toothbrushes; Consumer International segment, which provides sales in international markets; and Specialty Products segment, which produces sodium bicarbonate, other inorganic chemicals, and a range of animal nutrition and cleaning products.

**Recent Developments:** For the quarter ended July 1 2011, net income increased 11.2% to US$82.6 million from US$74.3 million in the year-earlier quarter. Revenues were US$674.9 million, up 5.3% from US$640.9 million the year before. Operating income was US$117.8 million versus US$120.0 million in the prior-year quarter, a decrease of 1.8%. Direct operating expenses rose 7.1% to US$374.9 million from US$350.0 million in the comparable period the year before. Indirect operating expenses increased 6.6% to US$182.2 million from US$170.9 million in the equivalent prior-year period.

**Prospects:** Our evaluation of Church & Dwight Co. Inc. as of Sep. 6, 2011 is the result of our systematic analysis on three basic characteristics: earnings strength, relative valuation, and recent stock price movement. The company has enjoyed a very positive trend in earnings per share over the past 5 quarters. However, while recent estimates for the company have been mixed, CHD has posted better than expected results. Based on operating earnings yield, the company is about fairly valued when compared to all of the companies in our coverage universe. Share price changes over the past year indicates that CHD will perform very poorly over the near term.

**Financial Data**

| (US$ in Thousands) | 6 Mos | 3 Mos | 12/31/2010 | 12/31/2009 | 12/31/2008 | 12/31/2007 | 12/31/2006 | 12/31/2005 |
|---|---|---|---|---|---|---|---|---|
| Earnings Per Share | 1.95 | 1.90 | 1.88 | 1.71 | 1.39 | 1.23 | 1.03 | 0.92 |
| Cash Flow Per Share | 3.32 | 3.05 | 3.02 | 2.85 | 2.47 | 1.89 | 1.44 | 1.49 |
| Tang Book Value Per Share | 1.76 | 1.57 | 0.99 | N.M. | N.M. | N.M. | N.M. | N.M. |
| Dividends Per Share | 0.510 | 0.410 | 0.310 | 0.230 | 0.170 | 0.150 | 0.130 | 0.120 |
| Dividend Payout % | 26.15 | 21.64 | 16.53 | 13.49 | 12.23 | 12.20 | 12.56 | 13.11 |
| **Income Statement** | | | | | | | | |
| Total Revenue | 1,317,200 | 642,300 | 2,589,220 | 2,520,922 | 2,422,398 | 2,220,940 | 1,945,661 | 1,736,506 |
| EBITDA | 289,700 | 151,500 | 485,109 | 472,675 | 389,471 | 351,387 | 311,714 | 258,349 |
| Depn & Amortn | 39,200 | 19,400 | 44,113 | 56,921 | 45,600 | 35,800 | 51,727 | 44,158 |
| Income Before Taxes | 245,200 | 129,400 | 413,219 | 380,186 | 296,926 | 256,695 | 205,959 | 170,093 |
| Income Taxes | 84,400 | 48,000 | 147,562 | 148,715 | 113,078 | 95,900 | 74,171 | 52,068 |
| Net Income | 166,200 | 83,600 | 270,717 | 243,533 | 195,174 | 169,025 | 138,927 | 122,906 |
| Average Shares | 145,900 | 145,200 | 144,402 | 142,954 | 142,232 | 140,624 | 137,892 | 138,578 |
| **Balance Sheet** | | | | | | | | |
| Current Assets | 702,600 | 663,200 | 649,481 | 928,265 | 665,121 | 735,353 | 556,070 | 494,438 |
| Total Assets | 3,055,400 | 2,952,500 | 2,945,194 | 3,118,446 | 2,801,438 | 2,532,490 | 2,334,154 | 1,962,117 |
| Current Liabilities | 371,000 | 360,500 | 447,092 | 567,032 | 387,121 | 457,789 | 444,404 | 409,710 |
| Long-Term Obligations | 249,700 | 249,700 | 249,673 | 597,347 | 781,402 | 707,311 | 792,925 | 635,261 |
| Total Liabilities | 1,017,700 | 1,001,700 | 1,074,505 | 1,516,863 | 1,469,925 | 1,452,225 | 1,470,317 | 1,265,239 |
| Stockholders' Equity | 2,037,700 | 1,950,800 | 1,870,689 | 1,601,583 | 1,331,513 | 1,080,265 | 863,837 | 696,878 |
| Shares Outstanding | 143,510 | 142,866 | 142,409 | 141,098 | 140,145 | 132,487 | 130,722 | 128,777 |
| **Statistical Record** | | | | | | | | |
| Return on Assets % | 9.17 | 9.02 | 8.93 | 8.23 | 7.30 | 6.95 | 6.47 | 6.40 |
| Return on Equity % | 14.95 | 15.13 | 15.59 | 16.61 | 16.14 | 17.39 | 17.80 | 19.56 |
| EBITDA Margin % | 21.99 | 23.59 | 18.74 | 18.75 | 16.08 | 15.82 | 16.02 | 14.88 |
| Net Margin % | 12.62 | 13.02 | 10.46 | 9.66 | 8.06 | 7.61 | 7.14 | 7.08 |
| Asset Turnover | 0.85 | 0.85 | 0.85 | 0.85 | 0.91 | 0.91 | 0.91 | 0.90 |
| Current Ratio | 1.89 | 1.84 | 1.45 | 1.64 | 1.72 | 1.61 | 1.25 | 1.21 |
| Debt to Equity | 0.12 | 0.13 | 0.13 | 0.37 | 0.59 | 0.65 | 0.92 | 0.91 |
| Price Range | 42.05-30.16 | 40.24-30.16 | 35.33-29.86 | 30.97-23.14 | 32.19-24.85 | 28.47-21.63 | 21.69-16.48 | 19.52-16.15 |
| P/E Ratio | 21.56-15.46 | 21.18-15.87 | 18.79-15.89 | 18.11-13.53 | 23.15-17.88 | 23.14-17.58 | 21.06-16.00 | 21.22-17.55 |
| Average Yield % | 1.43 | 1.21 | 0.94 | 0.84 | 0.60 | 0.61 | 0.69 | 0.68 |

**Address:** 469 North Harrison Street, Princeton, NJ 08543
**Telephone:** 609-683-5900
**Web Site:** www.churchdwight.com

**Officers:** James R. Craigie - Chairman, Chief Executive Officer Susan E. Goldy - Executive Vice President, Secretary, General Counsel **Transfer Agents:** Computershare Investor Services LLC, Chicago, IL

**No of Institutions:** 514
**Shares:** 123,122,928 **% Held:** 77.91

# CINCINNATI FINANCIAL CORP.

| Exchange | Symbol | Price | 52Wk Range | Yield | P/E |
|---|---|---|---|---|---|
| NMS | CINF | $27.92 (8/31/2011) | 34.18-24.03 | 5.77 | 15.43 |

*7 Year Price Score 84.58 *NYSE Composite Index=100 *12 Month Price Score 90.33

**Interim Earnings (Per Share)**

| Qtr. | Mar | Jun | Sep | Dec |
|---|---|---|---|---|
| 2008 | (0.26) | 0.38 | 1.50 | 0.98 |
| 2009 | 0.22 | (0.12) | 1.05 | 1.50 |
| 2010 | 0.42 | 0.17 | 0.95 | 0.78 |
| 2011 | 0.38 | (0.30) | ... | ... |

**Interim Dividends (Per Share)**

| Amt | Decl | Ex | Rec | Pay |
|---|---|---|---|---|
| 0.40Q | 11/19/2010 | 12/20/2010 | 12/22/2010 | 01/17/2011 |
| 0.40Q | 01/28/2011 | 03/21/2011 | 03/23/2011 | 04/15/2011 |
| 0.40Q | 05/23/2011 | 06/20/2011 | 06/22/2011 | 07/15/2011 |
| 0.403Q | 08/15/2011 | 09/19/2011 | 09/21/2011 | 10/17/2011 |

**Indicated Div: $1.61 (Div. Reinv. Plan)**

**Valuation Analysis**

| | | | |
|---|---|---|---|
| Forecast EPS | $0.58 (09/02/2011) | | |
| Market Cap | $4.6 Billion | Book Value | $5.1 Billion |
| Price/Book | 0.90 | Price/Sales | 1.16 |

**Dividend Achiever Status**

| | |
|---|---|
| **10 Year Growth Rate** | 7.86% |
| **Total Years of Dividend Growth** | 50 |

**Business Summary:** General Insurance (MIC: 5.2.1 SIC: 6331 NAIC: 524126)

Cincinnati Financial is a holding company. Co.'s main business is property casualty insurance. Co.'s primary subsidiary, The Cincinnati Insurance Co., writes a range of business, homeowner and auto policies, and provides life insurance, disability income policies and annuities, as well as excess and surplus lines insurance products. Co. also has two non-insurance subsidiaries: CSU Producer Resources Inc., which provides insurance brokerage services to Co.'s independent agencies so their clients can access its excess and surplus lines insurance products; and CFC Investment Company, which provides commercial leasing and financing services to its agents, their clients and other customers.

**Recent Developments:** For the quarter ended June 30 2011, net loss amounted to US$49.0 million versus net income of US$27.0 million in the year-earlier quarter. Revenues were US$975.0 million, up 11.0% from US$878.0 million the year before. Net premiums earned were US$773.0 million versus US$768.0 million in the prior-year quarter, an increase of 0.7%. Net investment income rose 1.5% to US$132.0 million from US$130.0 million a year ago.

**Prospects:** Our evaluation of Cincinnati Financial Corp. as of Sep. 6, 2011 is the result of our systematic analysis on three basic characteristics: earnings strength, relative valuation, and recent stock price movement. The company has suffered a very negative trend in earnings per share over the past 5 quarters. However, while recent estimates for the company have been mixed, CINF has posted better than expected results. Based on operating earnings yield, the company is overvalued when compared to all of the companies in our coverage universe. Share price changes over the past year indicates that CINF will perform very poorly over the near term.

| **Financial Data** (US$ in Thousands) | 6 Mos | 3 Mos | 12/31/2010 | 12/31/2009 | 12/31/2008 | 12/31/2007 | 12/31/2006 | 12/31/2005 |
|---|---|---|---|---|---|---|---|---|
| Earnings Per Share | 1.81 | 2.28 | 2.31 | 2.65 | 2.62 | 4.97 | 5.30 | 3.40 |
| Cash Flow Per Share | 1.73 | 2.92 | 3.26 | 3.23 | 2.96 | 4.13 | 3.55 | 4.60 |
| Tang Book Value Per Share | 31.02 | 31.40 | 31.06 | 29.38 | 25.81 | 35.72 | 39.35 | 34.98 |
| Dividends Per Share | 1.600 | 1.595 | 1.590 | 1.570 | 1.560 | 1.420 | 1.340 | 1.205 |
| Dividend Payout % | 88.40 | 69.96 | 68.83 | 59.25 | 59.54 | 28.57 | 25.28 | 35.46 |
| **Income Statement** | | | | | | | | |
| Premium Income | 1,555,000 | 782,000 | 3,082,000 | 3,054,000 | 3,136,000 | 3,250,000 | 3,278,000 | 3,164,000 |
| Total Revenue | 1,904,000 | 929,000 | 3,772,000 | 3,903,000 | 3,824,000 | 4,259,000 | 4,550,000 | 3,767,000 |
| Benefits & Claims | 1,376,000 | 575,000 | 2,180,000 | 2,242,000 | 2,193,000 | 1,963,000 | 2,128,000 | 1,911,000 |
| Income Before Taxes | (21,000) | 76,000 | 501,000 | 582,000 | 540,000 | 1,192,000 | 1,329,000 | 823,000 |
| Income Taxes | (34,000) | 14,000 | 124,000 | 150,000 | 111,000 | 337,000 | 399,000 | 221,000 |
| Net Income | 13,000 | 62,000 | 377,000 | 432,000 | 429,000 | 855,000 | 930,000 | 602,000 |
| Average Shares | 163,068 | 163,669 | 163,274 | 162,866 | 163,362 | 172,167 | 175,451 | 177,116 |
| **Balance Sheet** | | | | | | | | |
| Total Assets | 15,702,000 | 15,369,000 | 15,095,000 | 14,440,000 | 13,369,000 | 16,637,000 | 17,222,000 | 16,003,000 |
| Total Liabilities | 10,645,000 | 10,251,000 | 10,063,000 | 9,680,000 | 9,187,000 | 10,708,000 | 10,414,000 | 9,917,000 |
| Stockholders' Equity | 5,057,000 | 5,118,000 | 5,032,000 | 4,760,000 | 4,182,000 | 5,929,000 | 6,808,000 | 6,086,000 |
| Shares Outstanding | 163,000 | 163,000 | 162,000 | 162,000 | 162,000 | 166,000 | 173,000 | 174,000 |
| **Statistical Record** | | | | | | | | |
| Return on Assets % | 1.95 | 2.47 | 2.55 | 3.11 | 2.85 | 5.05 | 5.60 | 3.75 |
| Return on Equity % | 6.02 | 7.43 | 7.70 | 9.66 | 8.46 | 13.43 | 14.43 | 9.76 |
| Loss Ratio % | 88.49 | 73.53 | 70.73 | 73.41 | 69.93 | 60.40 | 64.92 | 60.40 |
| Net Margin % | 0.68 | 6.67 | 9.99 | 11.07 | 11.22 | 20.08 | 20.44 | 15.98 |
| Price Range | 34.18-25.52 | 34.18-25.52 | 32.22-25.52 | 29.09-18.10 | 39.97-18.80 | 47.62-36.91 | 49.07-41.43 | 45.68-38.62 |
| P/E Ratio | 18.89-14.10 | 14.99-11.19 | 13.95-11.05 | 10.98-6.83 | 15.26-7.18 | 9.58-7.43 | 9.26-7.82 | 13.44-11.36 |
| Average Yield % | 5.27 | 5.37 | 5.61 | 6.49 | 4.95 | 3.30 | 2.94 | 2.88 |

**Address:** 6200 South Gilmore Road, Fairfield, OH 45014-5141
**Telephone:** 513-870-2000
**Web Site:** www.cinfin.com

**Officers:** Kenneth W. Stecher - Chairman James E. Benoski - Vice-Chairman **Transfer Agents:** Cincinnati Financial Corporation, Cincinnati, OH

**Investor Contact:** 513-870-2639
**No of Institutions:** 429
**Shares:** 112,092,912 **% Held:** 63.48

# CINTAS CORPORATION

| Exchange | Symbol | Price | 52Wk Range | Yield | P/E |
|---|---|---|---|---|---|
| NMS | CTAS | $31.98 (8/31/2011) | 34.37-25.49 | 1.53 | 19.04 |

*7 Year Price Score 86.62 *NYSE Composite Index=100 *12 Month Price Score 106.52

**Interim Earnings (Per Share)**

| Qtr. | Aug | Nov | Feb | May |
|---|---|---|---|---|
| 2006-07 | 0.53 | 0.51 | 0.48 | 0.57 |
| 2007-08 | 0.51 | 0.53 | 0.53 | 0.58 |
| 2008-09 | 0.51 | 0.47 | 0.47 | 0.03 |
| 2009-10 | 0.35 | 0.37 | 0.32 | 0.36 |
| 2010-11 | 0.40 | 0.38 | 0.41 | 0.49 |

**Interim Dividends (Per Share)**

| Amt | Decl | Ex | Rec | Pay |
|---|---|---|---|---|
| 0.46A | 01/15/2008 | 02/04/2008 | 02/06/2008 | 03/12/2008 |
| 0.47A | 01/13/2009 | 02/02/2009 | 02/04/2009 | 03/11/2009 |
| 0.48A | 01/26/2010 | 02/08/2010 | 02/10/2010 | 03/10/2010 |
| 0.49A | 10/26/2010 | 11/09/2010 | 11/12/2010 | 12/15/2010 |

**Indicated Div: $0.49**

**Valuation Analysis**

| | | | |
|---|---|---|---|
| Forecast EPS | $2.02 (09/02/2011) | | |
| Market Cap | $4.4 Billion | Book Value | $2.3 Billion |
| Price/Book | 1.91 | Price/Sales | 1.15 |

**Dividend Achiever Status**

| | |
|---|---|
| **10 Year Growth Rate** | 15.99% |
| **Total Years of Dividend Growth** | 28 |

**Business Summary:** Business Services (MIC: 7.5.2 SIC: 2326 NAIC: 315225)

Cintas is engaged in providing products and services to businesses primarily throughout North America, as well as Latin America, Europe and Asia. In North America, Co. is a provider of corporate identity uniforms through rental and sales programs, as well as a provider of related business services, including entrance mats, restroom cleaning services and supplies, carpet and tile cleaning services, first aid, safety and fire protection products and services, document management services and branded promotional products. Co. has four segments: Rental Uniforms and Ancillary Products, Uniform Direct Sales, First Aid, Safety and Fire Protection Services and Document Management Services.

**Recent Developments:** For the year ended May 31 2011, net income increased 14.5% to US$247.0 million from US$215.6 million in the prior year. Revenues were US$3.81 billion, up 7.4% from US$3.55 billion the year before. Operating income was US$440.3 million versus US$390.8 million in the prior year, an increase of 12.7%. Direct operating expenses rose 7.4% to US$2.20 billion from US$2.05 billion in the comparable period the year before. Indirect operating expenses increased 5.6% to US$1.17 billion from US$1.11 billion in the equivalent prior-year period.

**Prospects:** Our evaluation of Cintas Corp. as of Sep. 6, 2011 is the result of our systematic analysis on three basic characteristics: earnings strength, relative valuation, and recent stock price movement. The company has enjoyed a very positive trend in earnings per share over the past 5 quarters and while recent estimates for the company have remained steady, CTAS has posted better than expected results. Based on operating earnings yield, the company is about fairly valued when compared to all of the companies in our coverage universe. Share price changes over the past year indicates that CTAS will perform poorly over the near term.

**Financial Data**

| (US$ in Thousands) | 05/31/2011 | 05/31/2010 | 05/31/2009 | 05/31/2008 | 05/31/2007 | 05/31/2006 | 05/31/2005 | 05/31/2004 |
|---|---|---|---|---|---|---|---|---|
| Earnings Per Share | 1.68 | 1.40 | 1.48 | 2.15 | 2.09 | 1.94 | 1.74 | 1.58 |
| Cash Flow Per Share | 2.33 | 3.67 | 3.42 | 3.49 | 2.81 | 2.75 | 2.41 | 2.97 |
| Tang Book Value Per Share | 5.18 | 6.95 | 5.85 | 4.94 | 4.53 | 4.57 | 6.16 | 5.41 |
| Dividends Per Share | 0.490 | 0.480 | 0.470 | 0.460 | 0.390 | 0.350 | 0.320 | 0.290 |
| Dividend Payout % | 29.17 | 34.29 | 31.76 | 21.40 | 18.66 | 18.04 | 18.39 | 18.35 |
| **Income Statement** | | | | | | | | |
| Total Revenue | 3,810,384 | 3,547,339 | 3,774,685 | 3,937,900 | 3,706,900 | 3,403,608 | 3,067,283 | 2,814,059 |
| EBITDA | 591,229 | 542,868 | 566,637 | 726,021 | 712,578 | 673,955 | 614,340 | 571,816 |
| Depn & Amortn | 150,886 | 152,059 | 157,572 | 148,566 | 135,181 | 127,117 | 119,813 | 117,285 |
| Income Before Taxes | 392,669 | 343,892 | 361,593 | 530,704 | 533,553 | 521,815 | 476,993 | 432,080 |
| Income Taxes | 145,680 | 128,272 | 135,236 | 195,299 | 199,015 | 194,637 | 176,475 | 159,875 |
| Net Income | 246,989 | 215,620 | 226,357 | 335,405 | 334,538 | 327,178 | 300,518 | 272,205 |
| Average Shares | 146,586 | 152,858 | 153,366 | 155,930 | 160,187 | 168,545 | 172,649 | 172,372 |
| **Balance Sheet** | | | | | | | | |
| Current Assets | 1,700,777 | 1,524,944 | 1,270,273 | 1,282,336 | 1,156,736 | 1,178,008 | 1,166,544 | 1,034,243 |
| Total Assets | 4,351,940 | 3,969,736 | 3,720,951 | 3,808,601 | 3,570,480 | 3,425,237 | 3,059,744 | 2,810,297 |
| Current Liabilities | 434,139 | 383,682 | 317,465 | 367,242 | 403,038 | 411,828 | 356,481 | 325,686 |
| Long-Term Obligations | 1,284,790 | 785,444 | 786,058 | 942,736 | 877,074 | 794,454 | 465,291 | 473,685 |
| Total Liabilities | 2,049,291 | 1,435,707 | 1,353,542 | 1,554,470 | 1,402,742 | 1,337,274 | 955,609 | 922,328 |
| Stockholders' Equity | 2,302,649 | 2,534,029 | 2,367,409 | 2,254,131 | 2,167,738 | 2,087,963 | 2,104,135 | 1,887,969 |
| Shares Outstanding | 137,583 | 152,869 | 152,790 | 153,691 | 158,676 | 163,181 | 170,658 | 171,377 |
| **Statistical Record** | | | | | | | | |
| Return on Assets % | 5.94 | 5.61 | 6.01 | 9.07 | 9.56 | 10.09 | 10.24 | 10.07 |
| Return on Equity % | 10.21 | 8.80 | 9.80 | 15.13 | 15.72 | 15.61 | 15.06 | 15.36 |
| EBITDA Margin % | 15.52 | 15.30 | 15.01 | 18.44 | 19.22 | 19.80 | 20.03 | 20.32 |
| Net Margin % | 6.48 | 6.08 | 6.00 | 8.52 | 9.02 | 9.61 | 9.80 | 9.67 |
| Asset Turnover | 0.92 | 0.92 | 1.00 | 1.06 | 1.06 | 1.05 | 1.05 | 1.04 |
| Current Ratio | 3.92 | 3.97 | 4.00 | 3.49 | 2.87 | 2.86 | 3.27 | 3.18 |
| Debt to Equity | 0.56 | 0.31 | 0.33 | 0.42 | 0.40 | 0.38 | 0.22 | 0.25 |
| Price Range | 32.85-23.66 | 30.69-21.61 | 33.05-18.15 | 40.90-27.74 | 43.63-34.92 | 45.32-37.56 | 47.86-38.21 | 50.21-34.93 |
| P/E Ratio | 19.55-14.08 | 21.92-15.44 | 22.33-12.26 | 19.02-12.90 | 20.88-16.71 | 23.36-19.36 | 27.51-21.96 | 31.78-22.11 |
| Average Yield % | 1.75 | 1.80 | 1.86 | 1.36 | 0.99 | 0.84 | 0.74 | 0.68 |

**Address:** 6800 Cintas Boulevard, P.O. Box 625737, Cincinnati, OH 45262-5737
**Telephone:** 513-459-1200
**Web Site:** www.cintas.com

**Officers:** Robert J. Kohlhepp - Chairman James Phillip Holloman - President, Chief Operating Officer
**Transfer Agents:** Wells Fargo Bank, South St. Paul, MN

**No of Institutions:** 431
**Shares:** 106,153,976 **% Held:** 74.82

# CLARCOR INC.

| Exchange | Symbol | Price | 52Wk Range | Yield | P/E |
|---|---|---|---|---|---|
| NYS | CLC | $46.54 (8/31/2011) | 48.49-33.64 | 0.90 | 21.25 |

*7 Year Price Score 123.60 *NYSE Composite Index=100 *12 Month Price Score 106.17

**Interim Earnings (Per Share)**

| Qtr. | Feb | May | Aug | Nov |
|---|---|---|---|---|
| 2007-08 | 0.32 | 0.48 | 0.50 | 0.56 |
| 2008-09 | 0.17 | 0.33 | 0.42 | 0.48 |
| 2009-10 | 0.29 | 0.47 | 0.55 | 0.57 |
| 2010-11 | 0.43 | 0.64 | ... | ... |

**Interim Dividends (Per Share)**

| Amt | Decl | Ex | Rec | Pay |
|---|---|---|---|---|
| 0.105Q | 09/30/2010 | 10/06/2010 | 10/08/2010 | 10/22/2010 |
| 0.105Q | 12/16/2010 | 01/05/2011 | 01/07/2011 | 01/21/2011 |
| 0.105Q | 03/24/2011 | 04/06/2011 | 04/08/2011 | 04/22/2011 |
| 0.105Q | 06/23/2011 | 07/06/2011 | 07/08/2011 | 07/22/2011 |

**Indicated Div: $0.42 (Div. Reinv. Plan)**

**Valuation Analysis**

| | | | |
|---|---|---|---|
| Forecast EPS | $2.40 (09/02/2011) | | |
| Market Cap | $2.3 Billion | Book Value | $815.2 Million |
| Price/Book | 2.88 | Price/Sales | 2.19 |

**Dividend Achiever Status**

| | |
|---|---|
| 10 Year Growth Rate | 5.34% |
| Total Years of Dividend Growth | 30 |

**Business Summary:** Industrial Machinery & Equipment (MIC: 7.2.1 SIC: 3714 NAIC: 336399)

Clarcor is a global provider of filtration products, filtration systems and services, and consumer and industrial packaging products. Co. has three reportable segments: The Engine/Mobile Filtration, which manufactures and markets a line of filters used in the filtration of oils, air, fuel, coolant, hydraulic and transmission fluids; The Industrial/Environmental Filtration segment, which manufactures and markets a line of filters, cartridges, dust collectors, filtration systems, engineered filtration products and technologies used in the filtration of air and industrial fluid processes; and the Packaging segment, which manufactures and markets consumer and industrial packaging products.

**Recent Developments:** For the quarter ended May 28 2011, net income increased 37.4% to US$32.9 million from US$23.9 million in the year-earlier quarter. Revenues were US$288.5 million, up 11.9% from US$257.9 million the year before. Operating income was US$48.8 million versus US$36.2 million in the prior-year quarter, an increase of 34.7%. Direct operating expenses rose 9.3% to US$189.1 million from US$173.0 million in the comparable period the year before. Indirect operating expenses increased 4.2% to US$50.7 million from US$48.6 million in the equivalent prior-year period.

**Prospects:** Our evaluation of Clarcor Inc. as of Sep. 6, 2011 is the result of our systematic analysis on three basic characteristics: earnings strength, relative valuation, and recent stock price movement. The company has produced a positive trend in earnings per share over the past 5 quarters and while recent estimates for the company have been raised by analysts, CLC has posted better than expected results. Based on operating earnings yield, the company is about fairly valued when compared to all of the companies in our coverage universe. Share price changes over the past year indicates that CLC will perform very poorly over the near term.

| Financial Data (US$ in Thousands) | 6 Mos | 3 Mos | 11/27/2010 | 11/28/2009 | 11/29/2008 | 12/01/2007 | 12/02/2006 | 11/30/2005 |
|---|---|---|---|---|---|---|---|---|
| Earnings Per Share | 2.19 | 2.02 | 1.88 | 1.40 | 1.86 | 1.78 | 1.59 | 1.46 |
| Cash Flow Per Share | 2.20 | 2.29 | 2.82 | 2.24 | 2.12 | 2.74 | 1.23 | 1.73 |
| Tang Book Value Per Share | 9.45 | 8.83 | 8.69 | 7.19 | 6.55 | 7.68 | 7.21 | 6.10 |
| Dividends Per Share | 0.412 | 0.405 | 0.398 | 0.367 | 0.330 | 0.297 | 0.275 | 0.259 |
| Dividend Payout % | 18.84 | 20.05 | 21.14 | 26.25 | 17.74 | 16.71 | 17.30 | 17.72 |
| **Income Statement** | | | | | | | | |
| Total Revenue | 534,253 | 245,720 | 1,011,429 | 907,748 | 1,059,601 | 921,191 | 904,347 | 873,974 |
| EBITDA | 96,349 | 39,420 | 169,800 | 133,496 | 175,761 | 150,758 | 146,919 | 137,379 |
| Depn & Amortn | 16,706 | 8,329 | 26,119 | 26,005 | 25,231 | 20,858 | 20,891 | 19,749 |
| Income Before Taxes | 79,654 | 31,084 | 143,423 | 105,649 | 145,371 | 130,509 | 126,941 | 117,922 |
| Income Taxes | 24,852 | 9,163 | 47,072 | 33,819 | 49,310 | 39,675 | 43,795 | 40,968 |
| Net Income | 54,689 | 21,881 | 96,081 | 71,543 | 95,654 | 90,659 | 82,710 | 76,393 |
| Average Shares | 51,282 | 51,287 | 51,156 | 51,045 | 51,410 | 50,885 | 52,176 | 52,215 |
| **Balance Sheet** | | | | | | | | |
| Current Assets | 560,419 | 521,061 | 526,273 | 448,528 | 432,571 | 371,920 | 380,340 | 324,933 |
| Total Assets | 1,099,004 | 1,062,261 | 1,042,411 | 973,890 | 957,882 | 739,135 | 727,516 | 675,272 |
| Current Liabilities | 149,826 | 141,779 | 163,457 | 131,942 | 143,503 | 114,171 | 118,428 | 121,470 |
| Long-Term Obligations | 17,270 | 17,351 | 17,331 | 52,096 | 83,822 | 17,329 | 15,946 | 16,009 |
| Total Liabilities | 283,812 | 277,645 | 285,941 | 287,271 | 306,123 | 183,405 | 190,007 | 192,439 |
| Stockholders' Equity | 815,192 | 784,616 | 756,470 | 686,619 | 651,759 | 555,730 | 537,509 | 482,833 |
| Shares Outstanding | 50,410 | 50,414 | 50,334 | 50,392 | 50,794 | 49,218 | 51,082 | 51,594 |
| **Statistical Record** | | | | | | | | |
| Return on Assets % | 10.79 | 10.16 | 9.56 | 7.43 | 11.30 | 12.40 | 11.73 | 11.73 |
| Return on Equity % | 14.66 | 13.94 | 13.35 | 10.72 | 15.89 | 16.63 | 16.12 | 16.77 |
| EBITDA Margin % | 18.03 | 16.04 | 16.79 | 14.71 | 16.59 | 16.37 | 16.25 | 15.72 |
| Net Margin % | 10.24 | 8.90 | 9.50 | 7.88 | 9.03 | 9.84 | 9.15 | 8.74 |
| Asset Turnover | 1.03 | 1.03 | 1.01 | 0.94 | 1.25 | 1.26 | 1.28 | 1.34 |
| Current Ratio | 3.74 | 3.68 | 3.22 | 3.40 | 3.01 | 3.26 | 3.21 | 2.68 |
| Debt to Equity | 0.02 | 0.02 | 0.02 | 0.08 | 0.13 | 0.03 | 0.03 | 0.03 |
| Price Range | 45.42-33.58 | 44.59-32.75 | 42.01-30.72 | 34.19-23.41 | 44.25-25.62 | 41.88-30.07 | 36.27-26.97 | 31.51-24.88 |
| P/E Ratio | 20.74-15.33 | 22.07-16.21 | 22.35-16.34 | 24.42-16.72 | 23.79-13.77 | 23.53-16.89 | 22.81-16.96 | 21.58-17.04 |
| Average Yield % | 1.02 | 1.06 | 1.11 | 1.21 | 0.88 | 0.86 | 0.87 | 0.94 |

**Address:** 840 Crescent Centre Drive, Suite 600, Franklin, TN 37067
**Telephone:** 615-771-3100
**Web Site:** www.clarcor.com

**Officers:** Norman E. Johnson - Chairman, Chief Executive Officer David J. Lindsay - Vice President, Chief Administrative Officer **Transfer Agents:** Computershare Investor Services, Canton, MA

**No of Institutions:** 248
**Shares:** 51,159,632 **% Held:** 85.24

# CLOROX CO.

| Exchange | Symbol | Price | 52Wk Range | Yield | P/E |
|---|---|---|---|---|---|
| NYS | CLX | $69.70 (8/31/2011) | 74.55-61.57 | 3.44 | 17.34 |

***7 Year Price Score 109.16** *NYSE Composite Index=100 ***12 Month Price Score 104.43**

**Interim Earnings (Per Share)**

| Qtr. | Sep | Dec | Mar | Jun |
|---|---|---|---|---|
| 2006-07 | 0.73 | 0.62 | 0.84 | 1.07 |
| 2007-08 | 0.76 | 0.65 | 0.71 | 1.12 |
| 2008-09 | 0.91 | 0.62 | 1.08 | 1.21 |
| 2009-10 | 1.11 | 0.77 | 1.16 | 1.20 |
| 2010-11 | 1.52 | 0.15 | 1.09 | 1.25 |

**Interim Dividends (Per Share)**

| Amt | Decl | Ex | Rec | Pay |
|---|---|---|---|---|
| 0.55Q | 09/14/2010 | 10/25/2010 | 10/27/2010 | 11/12/2010 |
| 0.55Q | 11/16/2010 | 01/25/2011 | 01/27/2011 | 02/14/2011 |
| 0.55Q | 02/15/2011 | 04/25/2011 | 04/27/2011 | 05/13/2011 |
| 0.60Q | 05/18/2011 | 07/25/2011 | 07/27/2011 | 08/12/2011 |

**Indicated Div: $2.40 (Div. Reinv. Plan)**

**Valuation Analysis**

| | | | |
|---|---|---|---|
| Forecast EPS | $4.07 (09/05/2011) | | |
| Market Cap | $9.1 Billion | Book Value | N/A |
| Price/Book | N/A | Price/Sales | 1.75 |

**Dividend Achiever Status**

| | |
|---|---|
| **10 Year Growth Rate** | 9.60% |
| **Total Years of Dividend Growth** | 34 |

**Business Summary:** Household & Personal Products (MIC: 1.7.1 SIC: 2842 NAIC: 325612)

Clorox is a manufacturer and marketer of consumer and institutional products. Co. sells its products through mass merchandisers, grocery stores and other retail outlets. Within the U.S., Co. sells institutional, janitorial, healthcare and food-service versions of many of its products through distributors. Outside the U.S., Co. sells products to the retail trade through subsidiaries, licensees, distributors and joint-venture arrangements with local partners. Additionally, Co. sells many of its products through online retailers and sells its natural personal care products directly to consumers online. Co. operates four reportable segments: Cleaning, Lifestyle, Household and International.

**Recent Developments:** For the year ended June 30 2011, income from continuing operations decreased 45.4% to US$287.0 million from US$526.0 million a year earlier. Net income decreased 7.6% to US$557.0 million from US$603.0 million in the prior year. Revenues were US$5.23 billion, unchanged from the year before. Direct operating expenses rose 1.5% to US$2.96 billion from US$2.92 billion in the comparable period the year before. Indirect operating expenses increased 12.9% to US$1.71 billion from US$1.51 billion in the equivalent prior-year period.

**Prospects:** Our evaluation of Clorox Co. as of Sep. 6, 2011 is the result of our systematic analysis on three basic characteristics: earnings strength, relative valuation, and recent stock price movement. The company has managed to produce a neutral trend in earnings per share over the past 5 quarters. However, while recent estimates for the company have been mixed, CLX has posted better than expected results. Based on operating earnings yield, the company is about fairly valued when compared to all of the companies in our coverage universe. Share price changes over the past year indicates that CLX will perform very poorly over the near term.

**Financial Data**

| (US$ in Thousands) | 06/30/2011 | 06/30/2010 | 06/30/2009 | 06/30/2008 | 06/30/2007 | 06/30/2006 | 06/30/2005 | 06/30/2004 |
|---|---|---|---|---|---|---|---|---|
| Earnings Per Share | 4.02 | 4.24 | 3.81 | 3.24 | 3.26 | 2.90 | 6.11 | 2.56 |
| Cash Flow Per Share | 5.11 | 5.84 | 5.31 | 5.21 | 4.68 | 3.47 | 4.33 | 4.24 |
| Tang Book Value Per Share | ... | N.M. | ... | ... | N.M. | ... | ... | 0.77 |
| Dividends Per Share | 2.200 | 2.000 | 1.840 | 1.600 | 1.200 | 1.140 | 1.100 | 1.080 |
| Dividend Payout % | 54.73 | 47.17 | 48.29 | 49.38 | 36.81 | 39.31 | 18.00 | 42.19 |
| **Income Statement** | | | | | | | | |
| Total Revenue | 5,231,000 | 5,534,000 | 5,450,000 | 5,273,000 | 4,847,000 | 4,644,000 | 4,388,000 | 4,324,000 |
| EBITDA | 815,000 | 1,227,000 | 1,143,000 | 1,041,000 | 1,024,000 | 953,000 | 978,000 | 1,025,000 |
| Depn & Amortn | 162,000 | 174,000 | 180,000 | 193,000 | 180,000 | 175,000 | 174,000 | 176,000 |
| Income Before Taxes | 533,000 | 917,000 | 806,000 | 692,000 | 739,000 | 661,000 | 735,000 | 823,000 |
| Income Taxes | 276,000 | 322,000 | 274,000 | 232,000 | 247,000 | 210,000 | 214,000 | 294,000 |
| Net Income | 557,000 | 603,000 | 537,000 | 461,000 | 501,000 | 444,000 | 1,096,000 | 549,000 |
| Average Shares | 138,101 | 141,534 | 141,063 | 142,004 | 153,935 | 153,001 | 179,176 | 214,371 |
| **Balance Sheet** | | | | | | | | |
| Current Assets | 1,279,000 | 1,124,000 | 1,180,000 | 1,249,000 | 1,032,000 | 1,007,000 | 1,090,000 | 1,043,000 |
| Total Assets | 4,163,000 | 4,555,000 | 4,576,000 | 4,708,000 | 3,666,000 | 3,616,000 | 3,617,000 | 3,834,000 |
| Current Liabilities | 1,365,000 | 1,647,000 | 1,937,000 | 1,661,000 | 1,427,000 | 1,130,000 | 1,348,000 | 1,268,000 |
| Long-Term Obligations | 2,125,000 | 2,124,000 | 2,151,000 | 2,720,000 | 1,462,000 | 1,966,000 | 2,122,000 | 475,000 |
| Total Liabilities | 4,249,000 | 4,472,000 | 4,751,000 | 5,078,000 | 3,495,000 | 3,772,000 | 4,170,000 | 2,294,000 |
| Stockholders' Equity | (86,000) | 83,000 | (175,000) | (370,000) | 171,000 | (156,000) | (553,000) | 1,540,000 |
| Shares Outstanding | 131,066 | 138,764 | 139,157 | 138,038 | 151,256 | 151,298 | 151,683 | 212,988 |
| **Statistical Record** | | | | | | | | |
| Return on Assets % | 12.78 | 13.21 | 11.57 | 10.98 | 13.76 | 12.28 | 29.42 | 14.63 |
| Return on Equity % | ... | ... | ... | ... | 6,680.00 | ... | 222.09 | 39.75 |
| EBITDA Margin % | 15.58 | 22.17 | 20.97 | 19.74 | 21.13 | 20.52 | 22.29 | 23.70 |
| Net Margin % | 10.65 | 10.90 | 9.85 | 8.74 | 10.34 | 9.56 | 24.98 | 12.70 |
| Asset Turnover | 1.20 | 1.21 | 1.17 | 1.26 | 1.33 | 1.28 | 1.18 | 1.15 |
| Current Ratio | 0.94 | 0.68 | 0.61 | 0.75 | 0.72 | 0.89 | 0.81 | 0.82 |
| Debt to Equity | ... | 25.59 | ... | ... | 8.55 | ... | ... | 0.31 |
| Price Range | 71.26-61.57 | 65.32-55.83 | 63.95-45.90 | 66.74-51.82 | 68.50-58.35 | 64.76-53.32 | 65.27-49.56 | 53.95-42.00 |
| P/E Ratio | 17.73-15.32 | 15.41-13.17 | 16.78-12.05 | 20.60-15.99 | 21.01-17.90 | 22.33-18.39 | 10.68-8.11 | 21.07-16.41 |
| Average Yield % | 3.33 | 3.28 | 3.34 | 2.68 | 1.88 | 1.96 | 1.93 | 2.26 |

**Address:** 1221 Broadway, Oakland, CA 94612-1888
**Telephone:** 510-271-7000
**Web Site:** www.thecloroxcompany.com

**Officers:** Donald R. Knauss - Chairman, Chief Executive Officer Frank A. Tataseo - Executive Vice President **Transfer Agents:** Computershare, Providence, RI

**No of Institutions:** 705
**Shares:** 106,517,392 **% Held:** 67.95

# COCA-COLA CO (THE)

| Exchange | Symbol | Price | 52Wk Range | Yield | P/E |
|---|---|---|---|---|---|
| NYS | KO | $70.45 (8/31/2011) | 70.45-55.88 | 2.67 | 13.12 |

***7 Year Price Score 124.81** *NYSE Composite Index=100 ***12 Month Price Score 106.11**

**Interim Earnings (Per Share)**

| Qtr. | Mar | Jun | Sep | Dec |
|---|---|---|---|---|
| 2008 | 0.64 | 0.61 | 0.81 | 0.41 |
| 2009 | 0.58 | 0.88 | 0.81 | 0.66 |
| 2010 | 0.69 | 1.02 | 0.88 | 2.47 |
| 2011 | 0.82 | 1.20 | ... | ... |

**Interim Dividends (Per Share)**

| Amt | Decl | Ex | Rec | Pay |
|---|---|---|---|---|
| 0.44Q | 10/21/2010 | 11/29/2010 | 12/01/2010 | 12/15/2010 |
| 0.47Q | 02/17/2011 | 03/11/2011 | 03/15/2011 | 04/01/2011 |
| 0.47Q | 04/28/2011 | 06/13/2011 | 06/15/2011 | 07/01/2011 |
| 0.47Q | 07/21/2011 | 09/13/2011 | 09/15/2011 | 10/01/2011 |

**Indicated Div: $1.88 (Div. Reinv. Plan)**

**Valuation Analysis**

| | | | |
|---|---|---|---|
| Forecast EPS | $3.88 (09/05/2011) | | |
| Market Cap | $161.5 Billion | Book Value | $35.1 Billion |
| Price/Book | 4.60 | Price/Sales | 3.83 |

**Dividend Achiever Status**

| | |
|---|---|
| 10 Year Growth Rate | 9.35% |
| Total Years of Dividend Growth | 48 |

**Business Summary:** Beverages (MIC: 1.2.2 SIC: 2086 NAIC: 312111)

Coca-Cola is a nonalcoholic beverage company. Co. owns or licenses and markets more than 500 nonalcoholic beverage brands, primarily sparkling beverages, as well as a range of still beverages such as waters, juices and juice drinks, ready-to-drink teas and coffees, and energy and sports drinks. Along with Coca-Cola, Co. owns and markets other nonalcoholic sparkling beverage brands including Diet Coke, Fanta and Sprite. Finished beverage products bearing Co.'s trademarks are sold in the U.S. and in more than 200 other countries. As of Dec 31 2010, Co. had the following operating segments: Eurasia and Africa; Europe; Latin America; North America; Pacific; Bottling Investments; and Corporate.

**Recent Developments:** For the quarter ended July 1 2011, net income increased 17.7% to US$2.80 billion from US$2.38 billion in the year-earlier quarter. Revenues were US$12.74 billion, up 46.8% from US$8.67 billion the year before. Operating income was US$3.17 billion versus US$2.76 billion in the prior-year quarter, an increase of 14.9%. Direct operating expenses rose 68.8% to US$4.99 billion from US$2.96 billion in the comparable period the year before. Indirect operating expenses increased 54.7% to US$4.57 billion from US$2.96 billion in the equivalent prior-year period.

**Prospects:** Our evaluation of Coca-Cola Co as of Sep. 6, 2011 is the result of our systematic analysis on three basic characteristics: earnings strength, relative valuation, and recent stock price movement. The company has enjoyed a very positive trend in earnings per share over the past 5 quarters and while recent estimates for the company have remained steady, KO has posted better than expected results. Based on operating earnings yield, the company is about fairly valued when compared to all of the companies in our coverage universe. Share price changes over the past year indicates that KO will perform very poorly over the near term.

**Financial Data**

| (US$ in Thousands) | 6 Mos | 3 Mos | 12/31/2010 | 12/31/2009 | 12/31/2008 | 12/31/2007 | 12/31/2006 | 12/31/2005 |
|---|---|---|---|---|---|---|---|---|
| Earnings Per Share | 5.37 | 5.19 | 5.06 | 2.93 | 2.49 | 2.57 | 2.16 | 2.04 |
| Cash Flow Per Share | 3.87 | 3.78 | 4.13 | 3.54 | 3.26 | 3.09 | 2.54 | 2.69 |
| Tang Book Value Per Share | 3.35 | 2.15 | 1.79 | 5.20 | 3.45 | 4.11 | 5.08 | 5.29 |
| Dividends Per Share | 1.820 | 1.790 | 1.760 | 1.640 | 1.520 | 1.360 | 1.240 | 1.120 |
| Dividend Payout % | 33.89 | 34.49 | 34.78 | 55.97 | 61.04 | 52.92 | 57.41 | 54.90 |
| **Income Statement** | | | | | | | | |
| Total Revenue | 23,254,000 | 10,517,000 | 35,119,000 | 30,990,000 | 31,944,000 | 28,857,000 | 24,088,000 | 23,104,000 |
| EBITDA | 6,889,000 | 2,882,000 | 14,838,000 | 9,294,000 | 9,430,000 | 8,404,000 | 7,266,000 | 6,767,000 |
| Depn & Amortn | 957,000 | 486,000 | 1,204,000 | 1,023,000 | 1,012,000 | 979,000 | 763,000 | 752,000 |
| Income Before Taxes | 5,950,000 | 2,377,000 | 13,218,000 | 8,165,000 | 8,313,000 | 7,205,000 | 6,476,000 | 6,010,000 |
| Income Taxes | 1,588,000 | 598,000 | 2,384,000 | 2,040,000 | 1,632,000 | 1,892,000 | 1,498,000 | 1,818,000 |
| Net Income | 4,697,000 | 1,900,000 | 11,809,000 | 6,824,000 | 5,807,000 | 5,981,000 | 5,080,000 | 4,872,000 |
| Average Shares | 2,330,000 | 2,331,000 | 2,333,000 | 2,329,000 | 2,336,000 | 2,331,000 | 2,350,000 | 2,393,000 |
| **Balance Sheet** | | | | | | | | |
| Current Assets | 26,539,000 | 23,542,000 | 21,579,000 | 17,551,000 | 12,176,000 | 12,105,000 | 8,441,000 | 10,250,000 |
| Total Assets | 80,090,000 | 76,058,000 | 72,921,000 | 48,671,000 | 40,519,000 | 43,269,000 | 29,963,000 | 29,427,000 |
| Current Liabilities | 24,194,000 | 21,923,000 | 18,508,000 | 13,721,000 | 12,988,000 | 13,225,000 | 8,890,000 | 9,836,000 |
| Long-Term Obligations | 11,373,000 | 12,681,000 | 14,041,000 | 5,059,000 | 2,781,000 | 3,277,000 | 1,314,000 | 1,154,000 |
| Total Liabilities | 44,948,000 | 43,779,000 | 41,918,000 | 23,872,000 | 20,047,000 | 21,525,000 | 13,043,000 | 13,072,000 |
| Stockholders' Equity | 35,142,000 | 32,279,000 | 31,003,000 | 24,799,000 | 20,472,000 | 21,744,000 | 16,920,000 | 16,355,000 |
| Shares Outstanding | 2,293,000 | 2,287,000 | 2,292,000 | 2,303,000 | 2,312,000 | 2,318,000 | 2,318,000 | 2,369,000 |
| **Statistical Record** | | | | | | | | |
| Return on Assets % | 19.49 | 19.59 | 19.42 | 15.30 | 13.82 | 16.33 | 17.11 | 16.04 |
| Return on Equity % | 41.29 | 42.33 | 42.32 | 30.15 | 27.44 | 30.94 | 30.53 | 30.18 |
| EBITDA Margin % | 29.63 | 27.40 | 42.25 | 29.99 | 29.52 | 29.12 | 30.16 | 29.29 |
| Net Margin % | 20.20 | 18.07 | 33.63 | 22.02 | 18.18 | 20.73 | 21.09 | 21.09 |
| Asset Turnover | 0.66 | 0.62 | 0.58 | 0.69 | 0.76 | 0.79 | 0.81 | 0.76 |
| Current Ratio | 1.10 | 1.07 | 1.17 | 1.28 | 0.94 | 0.92 | 0.95 | 1.04 |
| Debt to Equity | 0.32 | 0.39 | 0.45 | 0.20 | 0.14 | 0.15 | 0.08 | 0.07 |
| Price Range | 68.46-50.03 | 67.22-50.03 | 65.77-50.03 | 59.11-37.85 | 65.56-41.01 | 64.09-45.89 | 49.00-40.09 | 45.25-40.31 |
| P/E Ratio | 12.75-9.32 | 12.95-9.64 | 13.00-9.89 | 20.17-12.92 | 26.33-16.47 | 24.94-17.86 | 22.69-18.56 | 22.18-19.76 |
| Average Yield % | 2.92 | 3.05 | 3.11 | 3.36 | 2.82 | 2.53 | 2.83 | 2.62 |

**Address:** One Coca-Cola Plaza, Atlanta, GA 30313
**Telephone:** 404-676-2121
**Web Site:** www.thecoca-colacompany.com

**Officers:** Ahmet Muhtar Kent - Chairman, President, Chief Executive Officer Alexander B. Cummings - Executive Vice President, Chief Administrative Officer
**Transfer Agents:**ComputerShare Investor Services, Providence, RI

**Investor Contact:** 404-676-5766
**No of Institutions:** 1728
**Shares:** 1,547,081,216 **% Held:** 60.18

# COLGATE-PALMOLIVE CO.

| Exchange | Symbol | Price | 52Wk Range | Yield | P/E |
|---|---|---|---|---|---|
| NYS | CL | $89.97 (8/31/2011) | 90.64-73.75 | 2.58 | 18.47 |

***7 Year Price Score 117.60** *NYSE Composite Index=100 ***12 Month Price Score 107.45**

**Interim Earnings (Per Share)**

| Qtr. | Mar | Jun | Sep | Dec |
|---|---|---|---|---|
| 2008 | 0.86 | 0.92 | 0.94 | 0.94 |
| 2009 | 0.97 | 1.07 | 1.12 | 1.21 |
| 2010 | 0.69 | 1.17 | 1.21 | 1.24 |
| 2011 | 1.16 | 1.26 | ... | ... |

**Interim Dividends (Per Share)**

| Amt | Decl | Ex | Rec | Pay |
|---|---|---|---|---|
| 0.53Q | 10/14/2010 | 10/21/2010 | 10/25/2010 | 11/15/2010 |
| 0.53Q | 01/13/2011 | 01/21/2011 | 01/25/2011 | 02/15/2011 |
| 0.58Q | 02/24/2011 | 04/21/2011 | 04/26/2011 | 05/16/2011 |
| 0.58Q | 07/14/2011 | 07/22/2011 | 07/26/2011 | 08/15/2011 |

**Indicated Div: $2.32 (Div. Reinv. Plan)**

**Valuation Analysis**

| | | | |
|---|---|---|---|
| Forecast EPS | $5.07 (09/05/2011) | | |
| Market Cap | $43.8 Billion | Book Value | $3.0 Billion |
| Price/Book | 14.74 | Price/Sales | 2.72 |

**Dividend Achiever Status**

| | |
|---|---|
| 10 Year Growth Rate | 11.64% |
| Total Years of Dividend Growth | 48 |

**Business Summary:** Household & Personal Products (MIC: 1.7.1 SIC: 2844 NAIC: 325611)

Colgate-Palmolive is a consumer products company. Co. manages its business in two product segments: Oral, Personal and Home Care, which includes toothpaste, toothbrushes, mouth rinses, bar and liquid hand soaps, shower gels, shampoos, conditioners, deodorants and antiperspirants, laundry and dishwashing detergents, fabric conditioners, household cleaners, bleaches and other similar items; and Pet Nutrition, which includes pet nutrition products manufactured and marketed by the segment. Co.'s Oral, Personal and Home Care products are sold primarily to wholesale and retail distributors worldwide, while the principal customers for its Pet Nutrition products are veterinarians and pet retailers.

**Recent Developments:** For the quarter ended June 30 2011, net income increased 2.5% to US$646.0 million from US$630.0 million in the year-earlier quarter. Revenues were US$4.19 billion, up 9.7% from US$3.81 billion the year before. Operating income was US$968.0 million versus US$948.0 million in the prior-year quarter, an increase of 2.1%. Direct operating expenses rose 13.3% to US$1.78 billion from US$1.57 billion in the comparable period the year before. Indirect operating expenses increased 11.0% to US$1.44 billion from US$1.29 billion in the equivalent prior-year period.

**Prospects:** Our evaluation of Colgate-Palmolive Co. as of Sep. 6, 2011 is the result of our systematic analysis on three basic characteristics: earnings strength, relative valuation, and recent stock price movement. The company has produced a positive trend in earnings per share over the past 5 quarters and while recent estimates for the company have been mixed, CL has posted better than expected results. Based on operating earnings yield, the company is about fairly valued when compared to all of the companies in our coverage universe. Share price changes over the past year indicates that CL will perform very poorly over the near term.

**Financial Data**

| (US$ in Thousands) | 6 Mos | 3 Mos | 12/31/2010 | 12/31/2009 | 12/31/2008 | 12/31/2007 | 12/31/2006 | 12/31/2005 |
|---|---|---|---|---|---|---|---|---|
| Earnings Per Share | 4.87 | 4.78 | 4.31 | 4.37 | 3.66 | 3.20 | 2.46 | 2.43 |
| Cash Flow Per Share | 6.26 | 6.40 | 6.58 | 6.56 | 4.41 | 4.31 | 3.54 | 3.43 |
| Dividends Per Share | 2.170 | 2.120 | 2.030 | 1.720 | 1.560 | 1.400 | 1.250 | 1.110 |
| Dividend Payout % | 44.56 | 44.35 | 47.10 | 39.36 | 42.62 | 43.75 | 50.81 | 45.68 |
| **Income Statement** | | | | | | | | |
| Total Revenue | 8,179,000 | 3,994,000 | 15,564,000 | 15,327,000 | 15,329,900 | 13,789,700 | 12,237,700 | 11,396,900 |
| EBITDA | 2,085,000 | 1,014,000 | 3,506,000 | 3,632,000 | 3,116,000 | 2,734,700 | 2,230,900 | 2,283,900 |
| Depn & Amortn | 202,000 | 99,000 | 22,000 | 22,000 | 18,800 | 18,200 | 16,300 | 15,600 |
| Income Before Taxes | 1,856,000 | 899,000 | 3,425,000 | 3,533,000 | 3,001,600 | 2,559,900 | 2,055,900 | 2,132,300 |
| Income Taxes | 603,000 | 292,000 | 1,117,000 | 1,141,000 | 967,900 | 759,100 | 648,400 | 727,600 |
| Net Income | 1,198,000 | 576,000 | 2,203,000 | 2,291,000 | 1,957,200 | 1,737,400 | 1,353,400 | 1,351,400 |
| Average Shares | 493,300 | 496,600 | 510,900 | 524,600 | 535,000 | 543,700 | 550,500 | 556,500 |
| **Balance Sheet** | | | | | | | | |
| Current Assets | 4,470,000 | 4,274,000 | 3,730,000 | 3,810,000 | 3,710,000 | 3,618,500 | 3,301,000 | 2,757,100 |
| Total Assets | 13,244,000 | 11,931,000 | 11,172,000 | 11,134,000 | 9,979,300 | 10,112,000 | 9,138,000 | 8,507,100 |
| Current Liabilities | 4,249,000 | 4,282,000 | 3,728,000 | 3,599,000 | 2,953,300 | 3,162,700 | 3,469,100 | 2,743,000 |
| Long-Term Obligations | 4,020,000 | 3,166,000 | 2,815,000 | 2,821,000 | 3,585,300 | 3,221,900 | 2,720,400 | 2,918,000 |
| Total Liabilities | 10,275,000 | 9,512,000 | 8,497,000 | 8,018,000 | 8,057,200 | 7,825,800 | 7,727,100 | 7,157,000 |
| Stockholders' Equity | 2,969,000 | 2,419,000 | 2,675,000 | 3,116,000 | 1,922,100 | 2,286,200 | 1,410,900 | 1,350,100 |
| Shares Outstanding | 486,495 | 488,893 | 494,850 | 494,165 | 501,412 | 509,034 | 512,658 | 516,170 |
| **Statistical Record** | | | | | | | | |
| Return on Assets % | 20.49 | 21.29 | 19.75 | 21.70 | 19.43 | 18.05 | 15.34 | 15.73 |
| Return on Equity % | 87.16 | 96.61 | 76.08 | 90.95 | 92.76 | 93.99 | 98.04 | 104.13 |
| EBITDA Margin % | 25.49 | 25.39 | 22.53 | 23.70 | 20.33 | 19.83 | 18.23 | 20.04 |
| Net Margin % | 14.65 | 14.42 | 14.15 | 14.95 | 12.77 | 12.60 | 11.06 | 11.86 |
| Asset Turnover | 1.35 | 1.38 | 1.40 | 1.45 | 1.52 | 1.43 | 1.39 | 1.33 |
| Current Ratio | 1.05 | 1.00 | 1.00 | 1.06 | 1.26 | 1.14 | 0.95 | 1.01 |
| Debt to Equity | 1.35 | 1.31 | 1.05 | 0.91 | 1.87 | 1.41 | 1.93 | 2.16 |
| Price Range | 89.11-73.75 | 85.81-73.75 | 85.81-73.75 | 86.32-55.05 | 80.98-54.77 | 80.64-64.44 | 66.83-53.70 | 56.39-48.55 |
| P/E Ratio | 18.30-15.14 | 17.95-15.43 | 19.91-17.11 | 19.75-12.60 | 22.13-14.96 | 25.20-20.14 | 27.17-21.83 | 23.21-19.98 |
| Average Yield % | 2.72 | 2.68 | 2.54 | 2.45 | 2.16 | 2.02 | 2.09 | 2.13 |

**Address:** 300 Park Avenue, New York, NY 10022
**Telephone:** 212-310-2000
**Web Site:** www.colgate.com

**Officers:** Ian M. Cook - Chairman, President, Chief Executive Officer Michael J. Tangney - Vice-Chairman **Transfer Agents:** BNY Mellon Shareowner Services, Pittsburgh, PA

**Investor Contact:** 212-310-3072
**No of Institutions:** 1265
**Shares:** 396,315,264 **% Held:** 69.00

# COMMERCE BANCSHARES, INC.

| Exchange | Symbol | Price | 52Wk Range | Yield | P/E |
|---|---|---|---|---|---|
| NMS | CBSH | $39.57 (8/31/2011) | 43.81-34.03 | 2.32 | 14.03 |

***7 Year Price Score 103.63** *NYSE Composite Index=100 ***12 Month Price Score 103.03**

**Interim Earnings (Per Share)**

| Qtr. | Mar | Jun | Sep | Dec |
|---|---|---|---|---|
| 2008 | 0.77 | 0.67 | 0.29 | 0.52 |
| 2009 | 0.36 | 0.44 | 0.54 | 0.57 |
| 2010 | 0.50 | 0.68 | 0.64 | 0.70 |
| 2011 | 0.69 | 0.79 | ... | ... |

**Interim Dividends (Per Share)**

| Amt | Decl | Ex | Rec | Pay |
|---|---|---|---|---|
| 5% | 10/23/2010 | 12/02/2010 | 12/06/2010 | 12/20/2010 |
| 0.23Q | 01/28/2011 | 03/09/2011 | 03/11/2011 | 03/28/2011 |
| 0.23Q | 04/20/2011 | 06/08/2011 | 06/10/2011 | 06/27/2011 |
| 0.23Q | 07/22/2011 | 09/07/2011 | 09/09/2011 | 09/26/2011 |

**Indicated Div: $0.92 (Div. Reinv. Plan)**

**Valuation Analysis**

| | | | |
|---|---|---|---|
| Forecast EPS | $2.99 (09/03/2011) | | |
| Market Cap | $3.4 Billion | Book Value | $2.1 Billion |
| Price/Book | 1.62 | Price/Sales | N/A |

**Dividend Achiever Status**

| | |
|---|---|
| **10 Year Growth Rate** | 8.58% |
| **Total Years of Dividend Growth** | 42 |

**Business Summary:** Banking (MIC: 5.1.1 SIC: 6022 NAIC: 522110)

Commerce Bancshares is a bank holding company. Through its subsidiary, Commerce Bank, N.A., Co. is engaged in banking business, providing a range of retail, corporate, investment, trust, and asset management products and services to individuals and businesses. Co. also owns various non-banking subsidiaries with activities that include underwriting credit life and credit accident and health insurance, selling property and casualty insurance, private equity investment, securities brokerage, mortgage banking, and leasing activities. Co. operates in three segments: consumer, commercial, and wealth. As of Dec 31 2010, Co. had total assets of $18.50 billion and total deposits of $15.09 billion.

**Recent Developments:** For the quarter ended June 30 2011, net income increased 16.4% to US$69.6 million from US$59.8 million in the year-earlier quarter. Net interest income increased 1.0% to US$164.7 million from US$163.1 million in the year-earlier quarter. Provision for loan losses was US$12.2 million versus US$22.2 million in the prior-year quarter, a decrease of 45.1%. Non-interest income rose 1.2% to US$103.3 million from US$102.1 million, while non-interest expense declined 1.5% to US$153.5 million.

**Prospects:** Our evaluation of Commerce Bancshares Inc. as of Sep. 6, 2011 is the result of our systematic analysis on three basic characteristics: earnings strength, relative valuation, and recent stock price movement. The company has managed to produce a neutral trend in earnings per share over the past 5 quarters. However, while recent estimates for the company have been lowered by analysts, CBSH has posted better than expected results. Based on operating earnings yield, the company is undervalued when compared to all of the companies in our coverage universe. Share price changes over the past year indicates that CBSH will perform in line with the market over the near term.

| Financial Data (US$ in Thousands) | 6 Mos | 3 Mos | 12/31/2010 | 12/31/2009 | 12/31/2008 | 12/31/2007 | 12/31/2006 | 12/31/2005 |
|---|---|---|---|---|---|---|---|---|
| Earnings Per Share | 2.82 | 2.71 | 2.52 | 1.97 | 2.25 | 2.44 | 2.54 | 2.48 |
| Cash Flow Per Share | 8.91 | 9.57 | 7.72 | 3.47 | 2.61 | 4.01 | 5.29 | 3.30 |
| Tang Book Value Per Share | 22.94 | 22.17 | 21.74 | 19.99 | 17.14 | 16.60 | 15.56 | 14.92 |
| Dividends Per Share | 0.908 | 0.901 | 0.895 | 0.871 | 0.864 | 0.823 | 0.768 | 0.716 |
| Dividend Payout % | 32.20 | 33.32 | 35.53 | 44.17 | 38.40 | 33.77 | 30.20 | 28.93 |
| **Income Statement** | | | | | | | | |
| Interest Income | 353,913 | 175,826 | 729,478 | 789,512 | 849,849 | 936,101 | 832,306 | 697,566 |
| Interest Expense | 28,230 | 14,853 | 83,546 | 154,010 | 257,110 | 398,029 | 319,107 | 195,864 |
| Net Interest Income | 325,683 | 160,973 | 645,932 | 635,502 | 592,739 | 538,072 | 513,199 | 501,702 |
| Provision for Losses | 27,977 | 15,789 | 100,000 | 160,697 | 108,900 | 42,732 | 25,649 | 28,785 |
| Non-Interest Income | 200,533 | 97,233 | 403,326 | 389,390 | 406,006 | 379,815 | 361,621 | 341,199 |
| Non-Interest Expense | 307,473 | 153,960 | 631,134 | 622,063 | 582,847 | 574,758 | 525,425 | 496,522 |
| Income Before Taxes | 190,766 | 88,457 | 318,124 | 242,132 | 273,732 | 300,397 | 323,746 | 317,594 |
| Income Taxes | 60,199 | 27,507 | 96,249 | 73,757 | 85,077 | 93,737 | 103,904 | 94,347 |
| Net Income | 129,487 | 60,453 | 221,710 | 169,075 | 188,655 | 206,660 | 219,842 | 223,247 |
| Average Shares | 86,927 | 86,836 | 87,382 | 85,550 | 83,939 | 84,725 | 86,449 | 90,055 |
| **Balance Sheet** | | | | | | | | |
| Net Loans & Leases | 9,087,899 | 9,233,796 | 9,277,195 | 10,295,847 | 11,471,925 | 10,707,678 | 9,828,388 | 8,770,736 |
| Total Assets | 19,570,860 | 19,017,296 | 18,502,339 | 18,120,189 | 17,532,447 | 16,204,831 | 15,230,349 | 13,885,545 |
| Total Deposits | 15,656,566 | 15,539,475 | 15,085,021 | 14,210,451 | 12,894,733 | 12,551,552 | 11,744,854 | 10,851,813 |
| Total Liabilities | 17,441,492 | 16,948,574 | 16,480,352 | 16,235,961 | 15,955,815 | 14,677,145 | 13,788,235 | 12,547,707 |
| Stockholders' Equity | 2,129,368 | 2,068,722 | 2,021,987 | 1,884,228 | 1,576,632 | 1,527,686 | 1,442,114 | 1,337,838 |
| Shares Outstanding | 86,941 | 87,190 | 86,726 | 87,260 | 83,660 | 83,217 | 85,127 | 86,395 |
| **Statistical Record** | | | | | | | | |
| Return on Assets % | 1.30 | 1.28 | 1.21 | 0.95 | 1.12 | 1.31 | 1.51 | 1.59 |
| Return on Equity % | 12.01 | 11.91 | 11.35 | 9.77 | 12.12 | 13.92 | 15.82 | 16.15 |
| Net Interest Margin % | 92.49 | 91.55 | 88.55 | 80.49 | 69.75 | 57.48 | 61.66 | 71.92 |
| Efficiency Ratio % | 54.56 | 56.38 | 55.71 | 52.77 | 46.41 | 43.68 | 44.01 | 47.80 |
| Loans to Deposits | 0.58 | 0.59 | 0.61 | 0.72 | 0.89 | 0.85 | 0.84 | 0.81 |
| Price Range | 43.26-33.70 | 42.59-33.70 | 40.96-33.70 | 39.86-25.43 | 46.62-32.65 | 41.73-35.78 | 41.61-37.77 | 41.75-34.76 |
| P/E Ratio | 15.34-11.95 | 15.72-12.43 | 16.25-13.37 | 20.24-12.91 | 20.72-14.51 | 17.10-14.66 | 16.38-14.87 | 16.84-14.02 |
| Average Yield % | 2.34 | 2.40 | 2.42 | 2.65 | 2.31 | 2.12 | 1.93 | 1.89 |

| | | |
|---|---|---|
| **Address:** 1000 Walnut, Kansas City, MO 64106<br>**Telephone:** 816-234-2000<br>**Web Site:** www.commercebank.com | **Officers:** David W. Kemper - Chairman, President, Chief Executive Officer Jonathan M. Kemper - Vice-Chairman **Transfer Agents:** Computershare Trust Company, N.A., Providence, RI | **Investor Contact:** 800-892-7100<br>**No of Institutions:** 283<br>**Shares:** 52,811,536 **% Held:** 55.11 |

# COMMUNITY BANK SYSTEM, INC.

| Exchange | Symbol | Price | 52Wk Range | Yield | P/E |
|---|---|---|---|---|---|
| NYS | CBU | $25.03 (8/31/2011) | 28.58-21.81 | 4.16 | 12.84 |

***7 Year Price Score 108.87** *NYSE Composite Index=100 ***12 Month Price Score 100.04**

**Interim Earnings (Per Share)**

| Qtr. | Mar | Jun | Sep | Dec |
|---|---|---|---|---|
| 2008 | 0.36 | 0.37 | 0.39 | 0.36 |
| 2009 | 0.32 | 0.28 | 0.38 | 0.29 |
| 2010 | 0.42 | 0.48 | 0.51 | 0.47 |
| 2011 | 0.48 | 0.49 | ... | ... |

**Interim Dividends (Per Share)**

| Amt | Decl | Ex | Rec | Pay |
|---|---|---|---|---|
| 0.24Q | 10/26/2010 | 12/13/2010 | 12/15/2010 | 01/10/2011 |
| 0.24Q | 01/24/2011 | 03/11/2011 | 03/15/2011 | 04/10/2011 |
| 0.24Q | 05/27/2011 | 06/13/2011 | 06/15/2011 | 07/11/2011 |
| 0.26Q | 07/26/2011 | 09/13/2011 | 09/15/2011 | 10/07/2011 |

**Indicated Div: $1.04 (Div. Reinv. Plan)**

**Valuation Analysis**

| | | | |
|---|---|---|---|
| Forecast EPS | $2.14 (09/02/2011) | | |
| Market Cap | $921.3 Million | Book Value | $730.1 Million |
| Price/Book | 1.26 | Price/Sales | N/A |

**Dividend Achiever Status**

| | |
|---|---|
| **10 Year Growth Rate** | 5.47% |
| **Total Years of Dividend Growth** | 19 |

**Business Summary:** Banking (MIC: 5.1.1 SIC: 6021 NAIC: 522110)

Community Bank System is a bank holding company. Through its Community Bank, N.A. (the Bank) subsidiary, Co. operates as a community bank providing an array of banking and financial services to retail, commercial, and municipal customers principally in non-metropolitan markets. The Bank's branches are located in its geographic market areas of Upstate New York and Northeastern Pennsylvania. Co.'s loan products include consumer mortgage, business lending, consumer installment, and home equity. Co.'s deposit products consist of noninterest checking, interest checking, savings, money market, and time. As of Dec 31 2010, Co. had total assets of $5.44 billion and total deposits of $3.93 billion.

**Recent Developments:** For the quarter ended June 30 2011, net income increased 11.3% to US$18.0 million from US$16.2 million in the year-earlier quarter. Net interest income increased 17.9% to US$54.2 million from US$45.9 million in the year-earlier quarter. Provision for loan losses was US$1.1 million versus US$2.1 million in the prior-year quarter, a decrease of 48.8%. Non-interest income rose 1.7% to US$22.8 million from US$22.4 million, while non-interest expense advanced 15.6% to US$51.1 million.

**Prospects:** Our evaluation of Community Bank System Inc. as of Sep. 6, 2011 is the result of our systematic analysis on three basic characteristics: earnings strength, relative valuation, and recent stock price movement. The company has managed to produce a neutral trend in earnings per share over the past 5 quarters and while recent estimates for the company have been raised by analysts, CBU has posted better than expected results. Based on operating earnings yield, the company is undervalued when compared to all of the companies in our coverage universe. Share price changes over the past year indicates that CBU will perform poorly over the near term.

**Financial Data**

| (US$ in Thousands) | 6 Mos | 3 Mos | 12/31/2010 | 12/31/2009 | 12/31/2008 | 12/31/2007 | 12/31/2006 | 12/31/2005 |
|---|---|---|---|---|---|---|---|---|
| Earnings Per Share | 1.95 | 1.94 | 1.89 | 1.26 | 1.49 | 1.42 | 1.26 | 1.65 |
| Cash Flow Per Share | 2.80 | 3.27 | 2.95 | 1.33 | 1.80 | 1.69 | 2.44 | 2.39 |
| Tang Book Value Per Share | 9.97 | 9.36 | 8.87 | 7.56 | 6.62 | 7.51 | 7.17 | 7.77 |
| Dividends Per Share | 0.960 | 0.960 | 0.940 | 0.880 | 0.860 | 0.820 | 0.780 | 0.740 |
| Dividend Payout % | 49.23 | 49.48 | 49.74 | 69.84 | 57.72 | 57.75 | 61.90 | 44.85 |
| **Income Statement** | | | | | | | | |
| Interest Income | 130,137 | 60,287 | 248,281 | 248,782 | 250,859 | 256,237 | 231,901 | 219,194 |
| Interest Expense | 30,427 | 14,764 | 66,597 | 83,282 | 102,352 | 120,263 | 97,092 | 75,572 |
| Net Interest Income | 99,710 | 45,523 | 181,684 | 165,500 | 148,507 | 135,974 | 134,809 | 143,622 |
| Provision for Losses | 2,100 | 1,050 | 7,205 | 9,790 | 6,730 | 2,004 | 6,585 | 8,534 |
| Non-Interest Income | 43,607 | 20,842 | 88,792 | 83,535 | 73,474 | 53,286 | 49,276 | 60,846 |
| Non-Interest Expense | 94,442 | 43,316 | 176,886 | 186,178 | 158,562 | 142,074 | 127,203 | 127,389 |
| Income Before Taxes | 46,775 | 21,999 | 86,385 | 53,067 | 56,689 | 45,182 | 50,297 | 68,545 |
| Income Taxes | 12,629 | 5,839 | 23,065 | 11,622 | 10,749 | 2,291 | 11,920 | 17,740 |
| Net Income | 34,146 | 16,160 | 63,320 | 41,445 | 45,940 | 42,891 | 38,377 | 50,805 |
| Average Shares | 36,784 | 33,717 | 33,269 | 32,821 | 30,826 | 30,232 | 30,392 | 30,838 |
| **Balance Sheet** | | | | | | | | |
| Net Loans & Leases | 3,436,488 | 2,958,579 | 2,987,805 | 3,059,354 | 3,096,565 | 2,784,628 | 2,665,245 | 2,379,236 |
| Total Assets | 6,390,485 | 5,549,372 | 5,444,506 | 5,402,813 | 5,174,552 | 4,697,502 | 4,497,797 | 4,152,734 |
| Total Deposits | 4,757,102 | 4,021,031 | 3,934,045 | 3,924,486 | 3,700,812 | 3,228,464 | 3,168,299 | 2,984,768 |
| Total Liabilities | 5,660,414 | 4,925,272 | 4,837,248 | 4,837,116 | 4,629,901 | 4,218,718 | 4,036,269 | 3,695,139 |
| Stockholders' Equity | 730,071 | 624,100 | 607,258 | 565,697 | 544,651 | 478,784 | 461,528 | 457,595 |
| Shares Outstanding | 36,807 | 33,428 | 33,318 | 32,800 | 32,633 | 29,634 | 30,020 | 29,956 |
| **Statistical Record** | | | | | | | | |
| Return on Assets % | 1.14 | 1.19 | 1.17 | 0.78 | 0.93 | 0.93 | 0.89 | 1.19 |
| Return on Equity % | 10.12 | 10.89 | 10.80 | 7.47 | 8.95 | 9.12 | 8.35 | 10.90 |
| Net Interest Margin % | 77.58 | 75.51 | 73.18 | 66.52 | 59.20 | 53.07 | 58.13 | 65.52 |
| Efficiency Ratio % | 55.20 | 53.39 | 52.48 | 56.02 | 48.89 | 45.90 | 45.24 | 45.49 |
| Loans to Deposits | 0.72 | 0.74 | 0.76 | 0.78 | 0.84 | 0.86 | 0.84 | 0.80 |
| Price Range | 28.58-22.02 | 28.58-21.47 | 28.58-17.87 | 24.39-13.74 | 29.80-18.09 | 23.61-17.09 | 24.85-18.90 | 28.25-21.42 |
| P/E Ratio | 14.66-11.29 | 14.73-11.07 | 15.12-9.46 | 19.36-10.90 | 20.00-12.14 | 16.63-12.04 | 19.72-15.00 | 17.12-12.98 |
| Average Yield % | 3.92 | 3.94 | 4.03 | 4.98 | 3.74 | 4.00 | 3.57 | 3.13 |

**Address:** 5790 Widewaters Parkway, DeWitt, NY 13214-1883
**Telephone:** 315-445-2282
**Web Site:** www.communitybankna.com

**Officers:** Mark E. Tryniski - President, Chief Executive Officer Brian D. Donahue - Executive Vice President, Chief Banking Officer **Transfer Agents:** American Stock Transfer & Trust Company, New York, NY

**Investor Contact:** 315-445-7300
**No of Institutions:** 177
**Shares:** 23,760,008 **% Held:** 67.84

# COMMUNITY TRUST BANCORP, INC.

| Exchange | Symbol | Price | 52Wk Range | Yield | P/E |
|---|---|---|---|---|---|
| NMS | CTBI | $25.25 (8/31/2011) | 30.20-24.50 | 4.91 | 10.79 |

*7 Year Price Score 90.04 *NYSE Composite Index=100 *12 Month Price Score 97.81

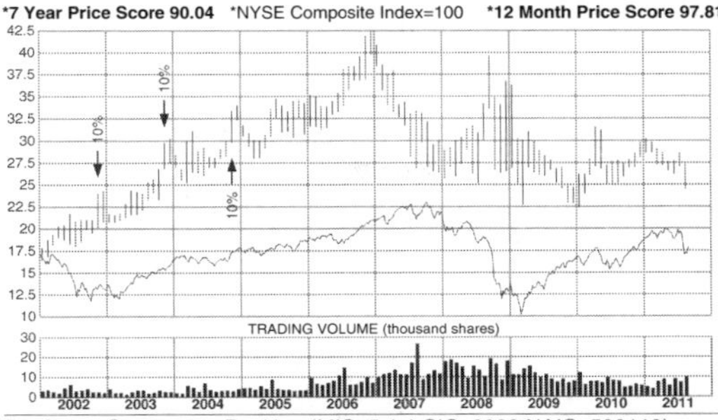

**Interim Earnings (Per Share)**

| Qtr. | Mar | Jun | Sep | Dec |
|---|---|---|---|---|
| 2008 | 0.57 | 0.57 | (0.04) | 0.43 |
| 2009 | 0.48 | 0.39 | 0.37 | 0.46 |
| 2010 | 0.45 | 0.56 | 0.55 | 0.60 |
| 2011 | 0.61 | 0.58 | ... | ... |

**Interim Dividends (Per Share)**

| Amt | Decl | Ex | Rec | Pay |
|---|---|---|---|---|
| 0.305Q | 10/26/2010 | 12/13/2010 | 12/15/2010 | 01/01/2011 |
| 0.305Q | 01/25/2011 | 03/11/2011 | 03/15/2011 | 04/01/2011 |
| 0.305Q | 04/26/2011 | 06/13/2011 | 06/15/2011 | 07/01/2011 |
| 0.31Q | 07/27/2011 | 09/13/2011 | 09/15/2011 | 10/01/2011 |

**Indicated Div: $1.24**

**Valuation Analysis**

| | | | |
|---|---|---|---|
| Forecast EPS | $2.37 (09/02/2011) | | |
| Market Cap | $389.0 Million | Book Value | $352.3 Million |
| Price/Book | 1.10 | Price/Sales | N/A |

**Dividend Achiever Status**

| | |
|---|---|
| **10 Year Growth Rate** | 7.20% |
| **Total Years of Dividend Growth** | 22 |

**Business Summary:** Banking (MIC: 5.1.1 SIC: 6022 NAIC: 522110)

Community Trust Bancorp is a bank holding company. Through its subsidiary, Community Trust Bank, Inc., Co. serves communities in eastern, northeastern, central, and south central Kentucky, southern West Virginia, and northeastern Tennessee, and is engaged in commercial and personal banking and trust activities, which include accepting time and demand deposits; making secured and unsecured loans to corporations, individuals and others; providing cash management services to corporate and individual customers; issuing letters of credit; renting safe deposit boxes; and providing funds transfer services. As of Dec 31 2010, Co. had total assets of $3.36 billion and deposits of $2.71 billion.

**Recent Developments:** For the quarter ended June 30 2011, net income increased 4.9% to US$9.0 million from US$8.6 million in the year-earlier quarter. Net interest income increased 12.3% to US$32.9 million from US$29.3 million in the year-earlier quarter. Provision for loan losses was US$3.3 million versus US$3.1 million in the prior-year quarter, an increase of 6.9%. Non-interest income rose 11.0% to US$10.6 million from US$9.5 million, while non-interest expense advanced 14.8% to US$27.1 million.

**Prospects:** Our evaluation of Community Trust Bancorp Inc. as of Sep. 6, 2011 is the result of our systematic analysis on three basic characteristics: earnings strength, relative valuation, and recent stock price movement. The company has managed to produce a neutral trend in earnings per share over the past 5 quarters and while recent estimates for the company have remained steady, CTBI has posted better than expected results. Based on operating earnings yield, the company is undervalued when compared to all of the companies in our coverage universe. Share price changes over the past year indicates that CTBI will perform poorly over the near term.

**Financial Data**

| (US$ in Thousands) | 6 Mos | 3 Mos | 12/31/2010 | 12/31/2009 | 12/31/2008 | 12/31/2007 | 12/31/2006 | 12/31/2005 |
|---|---|---|---|---|---|---|---|---|
| Earnings Per Share | 2.34 | 2.32 | 2.16 | 1.65 | 1.52 | 2.38 | 2.55 | 2.27 |
| Cash Flow Per Share | 4.08 | 3.72 | 4.02 | 2.49 | 3.64 | 3.37 | 3.68 | 3.06 |
| Tang Book Value Per Share | 18.34 | 17.83 | 17.58 | 16.62 | 15.91 | 15.36 | 14.17 | 12.48 |
| Dividends Per Share | 1.220 | 1.215 | 1.210 | 1.200 | 1.170 | 1.100 | 1.050 | 0.980 |
| Dividend Payout % | 52.14 | 52.37 | 56.02 | 72.73 | 76.97 | 46.22 | 41.18 | 43.17 |
| **Income Statement** | | | | | | | | |
| Interest Income | 79,701 | 39,860 | 154,511 | 153,050 | 167,611 | 196,864 | 189,145 | 160,162 |
| Interest Expense | 14,249 | 7,286 | 35,257 | 47,540 | 63,974 | 90,832 | 81,538 | 56,957 |
| Net Interest Income | 65,452 | 32,574 | 119,254 | 105,510 | 103,637 | 106,032 | 107,607 | 103,205 |
| Provision for Losses | 7,707 | 4,387 | 16,484 | 17,468 | 11,452 | 6,540 | 4,305 | 8,285 |
| Non-Interest Income | 21,331 | 10,738 | 40,926 | 41,420 | 21,767 | 36,608 | 32,719 | 33,467 |
| Non-Interest Expense | 53,693 | 26,547 | 96,050 | 93,801 | 82,532 | 83,055 | 80,407 | 78,569 |
| Income Before Taxes | 25,383 | 12,378 | 47,646 | 35,661 | 31,420 | 53,045 | 55,614 | 49,818 |
| Income Taxes | 7,109 | 3,074 | 14,612 | 10,602 | 8,347 | 16,418 | 16,550 | 15,406 |
| Net Income | 18,274 | 9,304 | 33,034 | 25,059 | 23,073 | 36,627 | 39,064 | 34,412 |
| Average Shares | 15,332 | 15,324 | 15,258 | 15,168 | 15,160 | 15,372 | 15,299 | 15,139 |
| **Balance Sheet** | | | | | | | | |
| Net Loans & Leases | 2,545,956 | 2,551,848 | 2,570,830 | 2,404,935 | 2,318,453 | 2,202,177 | 2,141,363 | 2,077,973 |
| Total Assets | 3,484,674 | 3,459,271 | 3,355,872 | 3,086,659 | 2,954,531 | 2,902,684 | 2,969,761 | 2,849,213 |
| Total Deposits | 2,781,121 | 2,792,235 | 2,706,117 | 2,462,209 | 2,331,834 | 2,293,164 | 2,341,167 | 2,246,551 |
| Total Liabilities | 3,132,408 | 3,114,759 | 3,017,234 | 2,765,202 | 2,646,325 | 2,601,329 | 2,687,386 | 2,595,268 |
| Stockholders' Equity | 352,266 | 344,512 | 338,638 | 321,457 | 308,206 | 301,355 | 282,375 | 253,945 |
| Shares Outstanding | 15,405 | 15,394 | 15,281 | 15,183 | 15,066 | 15,044 | 15,158 | 14,997 |
| **Statistical Record** | | | | | | | | |
| Return on Assets % | 1.07 | 1.07 | 1.03 | 0.83 | 0.79 | 1.25 | 1.34 | 1.24 |
| Return on Equity % | 10.54 | 10.62 | 10.01 | 7.96 | 7.55 | 12.55 | 14.57 | 14.04 |
| Net Interest Margin % | 82.52 | 81.72 | 77.18 | 68.94 | 61.83 | 53.86 | 56.89 | 64.44 |
| Efficiency Ratio % | 53.82 | 52.47 | 49.15 | 48.23 | 43.58 | 35.57 | 36.24 | 40.58 |
| Loans to Deposits | 0.92 | 0.91 | 0.95 | 0.98 | 0.99 | 0.96 | 0.91 | 0.92 |
| Price Range | 30.20-24.80 | 31.55-24.80 | 31.55-22.42 | 36.75-22.70 | 39.61-25.16 | 40.89-26.38 | 42.50-31.30 | 34.79-28.00 |
| P/E Ratio | 12.91-10.60 | 13.60-10.69 | 14.61-10.38 | 22.27-13.76 | 26.06-16.55 | 17.18-11.08 | 16.67-12.27 | 15.33-12.33 |
| Average Yield % | 4.41 | 4.36 | 4.47 | 4.45 | 3.89 | 3.36 | 2.94 | 3.11 |

**Address:** 346 North Mayo Trail, Pikeville, KY 41501
**Telephone:** 606-432-1414
**Web Site:** www.ctbi.com

**Officers:** Jean R. Hale - Chairman, President, Chief Executive Officer Mark A. Gooch - Executive Vice President, Secretary **Transfer Agents:** Community Trust Bank, Inc., Pikeville, KY

**Investor Contact:** 606-432-1414
**No of Institutions:** 99
**Shares:** 7,119,526 **% Held:** 45.90

# CONOCOPHILLIPS

| Exchange | Symbol | Price | 52Wk Range | Yield | P/E |
|---|---|---|---|---|---|
| NYS | COP | $68.07 (8/31/2011) | 81.21-52.43 | 3.88 | 8.55 |

***7 Year Price Score 109.15** *NYSE Composite Index=100 ***12 Month Price Score 103.19**

**Interim Earnings (Per Share)**

| Qtr. | Mar | Jun | Sep | Dec |
|---|---|---|---|---|
| 2008 | 2.62 | 3.50 | 3.39 | (20.66) |
| 2009 | 0.56 | 0.87 | 1.00 | 0.81 |
| 2010 | 1.40 | 2.77 | 2.05 | 1.41 |
| 2011 | 2.09 | 2.41 | ... | ... |

**Interim Dividends (Per Share)**

| Amt | Decl | Ex | Rec | Pay |
|---|---|---|---|---|
| 0.55Q | 10/06/2010 | 10/27/2010 | 10/29/2010 | 12/01/2010 |
| 0.66Q | 02/11/2011 | 02/17/2011 | 02/22/2011 | 03/01/2011 |
| 0.66Q | 05/11/2011 | 05/19/2011 | 05/23/2011 | 06/01/2011 |
| 0.66Q | 07/13/2011 | 07/21/2011 | 07/25/2011 | 09/01/2011 |

**Indicated Div: $2.64 (Div. Reinv. Plan)**

**Valuation Analysis**

| | | | |
|---|---|---|---|
| Forecast EPS | $8.29 (09/05/2011) | | |
| Market Cap | $95.9 Billion | Book Value | $70.1 Billion |
| Price/Book | 1.37 | Price/Sales | 0.42 |

**Dividend Achiever Status**

| | |
|---|---|
| **10 Year Growth Rate** | 11.88% |
| **Total Years of Dividend Growth** | 10 |

**Business Summary:** Refining & Marketing (MIC: 9.1.2 SIC: 2911 NAIC: 324110)

ConocoPhillips is an energy company. Co.'s Exploration and Production segment primarily explores for, produces, transports and markets crude oil, bitumen, natural gas, liquefied natural gas and natural gas liquids on a worldwide basis. The Midstream segment gathers and processes natural gas, and fractionates and markets natural gas liquids. The Refining and Marketing segment purchases, refines, markets and transports crude oil and petroleum products. The Chemicals segment produces and markets petrochemicals and plastics; and Emerging Businesses represents Co.'s investments in new technologies or businesses.

**Recent Developments:** For the quarter ended June 30 2011, net income decreased 18.3% to US$3.42 billion from US$4.18 billion in the year-earlier quarter. Revenues were US$66.96 billion, up 33.6% from US$50.13 billion the year before. Direct operating expenses rose 52.0% to US$52.74 billion from US$34.71 billion in the comparable period the year before. Indirect operating expenses decreased 13.0% to US$8.03 billion from US$9.23 billion in the equivalent prior-year period.

**Prospects:** Our evaluation of ConocoPhillips as of Sep. 6, 2011 is the result of our systematic analysis on three basic characteristics: earnings strength, relative valuation, and recent stock price movement. The company has enjoyed a very positive trend in earnings per share over the past 5 quarters and while recent estimates for the company have been raised by analysts, COP has posted better than expected results. Based on operating earnings yield, the company is undervalued when compared to all of the companies in our coverage universe. Share price changes over the past year indicates that COP will perform in line with the market over the near term.

**Financial Data**

| (US$ in Millions) | 6 Mos | 3 Mos | 12/31/2010 | 12/31/2009 | 12/31/2008 | 12/31/2007 | 12/31/2006 | 12/31/2005 |
|---|---|---|---|---|---|---|---|---|
| Earnings Per Share | 7.96 | 8.32 | 7.62 | 3.24 | (11.16) | 7.22 | 9.66 | 9.55 |
| Cash Flow Per Share | 13.40 | 11.14 | 11.52 | 8.39 | 14.83 | 15.12 | 13.57 | 12.65 |
| Tang Book Value Per Share | 46.59 | 45.19 | 43.69 | 38.04 | 33.23 | 36.40 | 30.50 | 26.34 |
| Dividends Per Share | 2.420 | 2.310 | 2.150 | 1.910 | 1.880 | 1.640 | 1.440 | 1.180 |
| Dividend Payout % | 30.40 | 27.76 | 28.22 | 58.95 | ... | 22.71 | 14.91 | 12.36 |
| **Income Statement** | | | | | | | | |
| Total Revenue | 125,208 | 58,247 | 198,655 | 152,840 | 246,182 | 194,495 | 188,523 | 183,364 |
| EBITDA | 16,642 | 8,128 | 29,997 | 20,616 | 6,424 | 32,910 | 36,780 | 28,330 |
| Depn & Amortn | 4,145 | 2,070 | 9,060 | 9,295 | 9,012 | 8,298 | 7,284 | 4,253 |
| Income Before Taxes | 11,988 | 5,796 | 19,750 | 10,032 | (3,523) | 23,359 | 28,409 | 23,580 |
| Income Taxes | 5,527 | 2,754 | 8,333 | 5,096 | 13,405 | 11,381 | 12,783 | 9,907 |
| Net Income | 6,430 | 3,028 | 11,358 | 4,858 | (16,998) | 11,891 | 15,550 | 13,529 |
| Average Shares | 1,412 | 1,445 | 1,491 | 1,497 | 1,523 | 1,645 | 1,609 | 1,417 |
| **Balance Sheet** | | | | | | | | |
| Current Assets | 34,678 | 35,613 | 34,660 | 21,167 | 20,843 | 24,735 | 25,066 | 19,612 |
| Total Assets | 160,068 | 159,643 | 156,314 | 152,588 | 142,865 | 177,757 | 164,781 | 106,999 |
| Current Liabilities | 29,344 | 29,218 | 27,419 | 23,695 | 21,780 | 26,882 | 26,431 | 21,359 |
| Long-Term Obligations | 22,590 | 22,604 | 22,656 | 26,925 | 27,085 | 20,289 | 23,091 | 10,758 |
| Total Liabilities | 90,009 | 89,671 | 87,752 | 90,121 | 87,700 | 88,774 | 82,135 | 54,268 |
| Stockholders' Equity | 70,059 | 69,972 | 68,562 | 62,467 | 55,165 | 88,983 | 82,646 | 52,731 |
| Shares Outstanding | 1,409 | 1,450 | 1,467 | 1,524 | 1,520 | 1,613 | 1,646 | 1,377 |
| **Statistical Record** | | | | | | | | |
| Return on Assets % | 7.40 | 7.82 | 7.35 | 3.29 | N.M. | 6.94 | 11.44 | 13.54 |
| Return on Equity % | 17.02 | 18.50 | 17.34 | 8.26 | N.M. | 13.86 | 22.97 | 28.35 |
| EBITDA Margin % | 13.29 | 13.95 | 15.10 | 13.49 | 2.61 | 16.92 | 19.51 | 15.45 |
| Net Margin % | 5.14 | 5.20 | 5.72 | 3.18 | N.M. | 6.11 | 8.25 | 7.38 |
| Asset Turnover | 1.46 | 1.34 | 1.29 | 1.03 | 1.53 | 1.14 | 1.39 | 1.83 |
| Current Ratio | 1.18 | 1.22 | 1.26 | 0.89 | 0.96 | 0.92 | 0.95 | 0.92 |
| Debt to Equity | 0.32 | 0.32 | 0.33 | 0.43 | 0.49 | 0.23 | 0.28 | 0.20 |
| Price Range | 81.21-48.82 | 80.69-48.82 | 68.10-47.37 | 55.68-35.13 | 95.78-41.80 | 90.17-61.82 | 73.07-56.03 | 70.91-41.78 |
| P/E Ratio | 10.20-6.13 | 9.70-5.87 | 8.94-6.22 | 17.19-10.84 | ... | 12.49-8.56 | 7.56-5.80 | 7.43-4.37 |
| Average Yield % | 3.66 | 3.78 | 3.88 | 4.19 | 2.50 | 2.14 | 2.25 | 2.05 |

| | | |
|---|---|---|
| **Address:** 600 North Dairy Ashford, Houston, TX 77079<br>**Telephone:** 281-293-1000<br>**Web Site:** www.conocophillips.com | **Officers:** James J. Mulva - Chairman, Chief Executive Officer John A. Carrig - President, Chief Operating Officer **Transfer Agents:**<br>BNY Mellon Shareowner Services, Jersey City, NJ | **No of Institutions:** 1720<br>**Shares:** 1,090,390,528 **% Held:** 67.86 |

# CONSOLIDATED EDISON, INC.

| Exchange | Symbol | Price | 52Wk Range | Yield | P/E |
|---|---|---|---|---|---|
| NYS | ED | $56.21 (8/31/2011) | 56.90-47.53 | 4.27 | 15.44 |

***7 Year Price Score 111.31** *NYSE Composite Index=100 ***12 Month Price Score 106.45**

**Interim Earnings (Per Share)**

| Qtr. | Mar | Jun | Sep | Dec |
|---|---|---|---|---|
| 2008 | 1.11 | 2.02 | 0.66 | 0.58 |
| 2009 | 0.66 | 0.55 | 1.22 | 0.72 |
| 2010 | 0.80 | 0.64 | 1.23 | 0.79 |
| 2011 | 1.06 | 0.56 | ... | ... |

**Interim Dividends (Per Share)**

| Amt | Decl | Ex | Rec | Pay |
|---|---|---|---|---|
| 0.595Q | 10/20/2010 | 11/15/2010 | 11/17/2010 | 12/15/2010 |
| 0.60Q | 01/20/2011 | 02/14/2011 | 02/16/2011 | 03/15/2011 |
| 0.60Q | 04/21/2011 | 05/16/2011 | 05/18/2011 | 06/15/2011 |
| 0.60Q | 07/21/2011 | 08/15/2011 | 08/17/2011 | 09/15/2011 |

**Indicated Div: $2.40 (Div. Reinv. Plan)**

**Valuation Analysis**

| | | | |
|---|---|---|---|
| Forecast EPS | $3.55 (09/05/2011) | | |
| Market Cap | $16.5 Billion | Book Value | $11.5 Billion |
| Price/Book | 1.44 | Price/Sales | 1.25 |

**Dividend Achiever Status**

| | |
|---|---|
| **10 Year Growth Rate** | 0.79% |
| **Total Years of Dividend Growth** | 36 |

**Business Summary:** Electric Utilities (MIC: 3.1.1 SIC: 4931 NAIC: 221121)

Consolidated Edison is a holding company. Co. owns Consolidated Edison Company of New York, Inc., which delivers electricity, natural gas and steam to customers in New York City and Westchester County; and Orange and Rockland Utilities, Inc., which delivers electricity and natural gas to customers in southeastern New York, northern New Jersey and northeastern Pennsylvania. Co. also has the following competitive energy businesses: Consolidated Edison Solutions, Inc., a retail energy services company; Consolidated Edison Energy, Inc., a wholesale energy supply and services company; and Consolidated Edison Development, Inc., a company that develops and participates in infrastructure projects.

**Recent Developments:** For the quarter ended June 30 2011, net income decreased 9.7% to US$168.0 million from US$186.0 million in the year-earlier quarter. Revenues were US$2.99 billion, down 0.8% from US$3.02 billion the year before. Operating income was US$398.0 million versus US$429.0 million in the prior-year quarter, a decrease of 7.2%. Direct operating expenses declined 2.1% to US$1.93 billion from US$1.97 billion in the comparable period the year before. Indirect operating expenses increased 7.8% to US$664.0 million from US$616.0 million in the equivalent prior-year period.

**Prospects:** Our evaluation of Consolidated Edison Inc. as of Sep. 6, 2011 is the result of our systematic analysis on three basic characteristics: earnings strength, relative valuation, and recent stock price movement. The company has produced a positive trend in earnings per share over the past 5 quarters and while recent estimates for the company have been raised by analysts, ED has posted better than expected results. Based on operating earnings yield, the company is about fairly valued when compared to all of the companies in our coverage universe. Share price changes over the past year indicates that ED will perform very poorly over the near term.

**Financial Data**

| (US$ in Thousands) | 6 Mos | 3 Mos | 12/31/2010 | 12/31/2009 | 12/31/2008 | 12/31/2007 | 12/31/2006 | 12/31/2005 |
|---|---|---|---|---|---|---|---|---|
| Earnings Per Share | 3.64 | 3.72 | 3.47 | 3.14 | 4.37 | 3.47 | 2.95 | 2.94 |
| Cash Flow Per Share | 10.85 | 9.39 | 8.37 | 8.96 | 2.30 | 5.84 | 5.43 | 3.25 |
| Tang Book Value Per Share | 36.94 | 36.95 | 37.18 | 35.72 | 34.69 | 32.64 | 30.03 | 28.65 |
| Dividends Per Share | 2.390 | 2.385 | 2.380 | 2.360 | 2.340 | 2.320 | 2.300 | 2.280 |
| Dividend Payout % | 65.66 | 64.11 | 68.59 | 75.16 | 53.55 | 66.86 | 77.97 | 77.55 |
| **Income Statement** | | | | | | | | |
| Total Revenue | 6,342,000 | 3,349,000 | 13,325,000 | 13,032,000 | 13,583,000 | 13,120,000 | 12,137,000 | 11,690,000 |
| EBITDA | 1,470,000 | 849,000 | 3,013,000 | 2,658,000 | 3,005,000 | 1,903,000 | 1,705,000 | 1,570,000 |
| Depn & Amortn | 437,000 | 218,000 | 853,000 | 728,000 | 541,000 | 9,000 | 10,000 | 10,000 |
| Income Before Taxes | 735,000 | 483,000 | 1,551,000 | 1,319,000 | 1,920,000 | 1,377,000 | 1,145,000 | 1,096,000 |
| Income Taxes | 252,000 | 169,000 | 548,000 | 440,000 | 524,000 | 437,000 | 390,000 | 341,000 |
| Net Income | 483,000 | 314,000 | 1,003,000 | 879,000 | 1,196,000 | 929,000 | 737,000 | 719,000 |
| Average Shares | 294,300 | 293,600 | 285,900 | 276,300 | 273,600 | 267,300 | 250,300 | 244,700 |
| **Balance Sheet** | | | | | | | | |
| Current Assets | 3,209,000 | 3,590,000 | 3,507,000 | 3,243,000 | 3,319,000 | 2,605,000 | 2,937,000 | 3,153,000 |
| Total Assets | 36,019,000 | 36,186,000 | 36,146,000 | 33,873,000 | 33,498,000 | 28,343,000 | 26,699,000 | 24,850,000 |
| Current Liabilities | 2,473,000 | 2,676,000 | 2,366,000 | 2,952,000 | 3,205,000 | 3,895,000 | 2,917,000 | 3,323,000 |
| Long-Term Obligations | 10,673,000 | 10,675,000 | 10,678,000 | 9,868,000 | 9,249,000 | 7,633,000 | 8,324,000 | 7,428,000 |
| Total Liabilities | 24,555,000 | 24,742,000 | 24,872,000 | 23,411,000 | 23,587,000 | 19,054,000 | 18,482,000 | 17,327,000 |
| Stockholders' Equity | 11,464,000 | 11,444,000 | 11,274,000 | 10,462,000 | 9,911,000 | 9,289,000 | 8,217,000 | 7,523,000 |
| Shares Outstanding | 292,875 | 292,272 | 291,616 | 281,123 | 273,721 | 272,024 | 257,456 | 245,286 |
| **Statistical Record** | | | | | | | | |
| Return on Assets % | 3.04 | 3.08 | 2.86 | 2.61 | 3.86 | 3.38 | 2.86 | 3.03 |
| Return on Equity % | 9.70 | 9.89 | 9.23 | 8.63 | 12.42 | 10.61 | 9.36 | 9.72 |
| EBITDA Margin % | 23.18 | 25.35 | 22.61 | 20.40 | 22.12 | 14.50 | 14.05 | 13.43 |
| Net Margin % | 7.62 | 9.38 | 7.53 | 6.74 | 8.81 | 7.08 | 6.07 | 6.15 |
| Asset Turnover | 0.37 | 0.37 | 0.38 | 0.39 | 0.44 | 0.48 | 0.47 | 0.49 |
| Current Ratio | 1.30 | 1.34 | 1.48 | 1.10 | 1.04 | 0.67 | 1.01 | 0.95 |
| Debt to Equity | 0.93 | 0.93 | 0.95 | 0.94 | 0.93 | 0.82 | 1.01 | 0.99 |
| Price Range | 54.24-42.90 | 51.00-41.66 | 51.00-41.66 | 46.13-32.70 | 48.85-37.53 | 52.63-43.65 | 49.13-41.40 | 49.24-41.41 |
| P/E Ratio | 14.90-11.79 | 13.71-11.20 | 14.70-12.01 | 14.69-10.41 | 11.18-8.59 | 15.17-12.58 | 16.65-14.03 | 16.75-14.09 |
| Average Yield % | 4.83 | 5.02 | 5.16 | 5.99 | 5.67 | 4.84 | 5.04 | 5.04 |

| | | |
|---|---|---|
| **Address:** 4 Irving Place, New York, NY 10003<br>**Telephone:** 212-460-4600<br>**Web Site:** www.conedison.com | **Officers:** Kevin Burke - Chairman, President, Chief Executive Officer John D. McMahon - Executive Vice President **Transfer Agents:**<br>The Bank of New York Mellon, Pittsburgh, PA | **Investor Contact:** 212-460-6611<br>**No of Institutions:** 664<br>**Shares:** 137,622,864 **% Held:** 45.25 |

# CORPORATE OFFICE PROPERTIES TRUST

| Exchange | Symbol | Price | 52Wk Range | Yield | P/E |
|---|---|---|---|---|---|
| NYS | OFC | $26.79 (8/31/2011) | 38.64-23.08 | 6.16 | N/A |

***7 Year Price Score 93.90** *NYSE Composite Index=100 ***12 Month Price Score 85.09**

**Interim Earnings (Per Share)**

| Qtr. | Mar | Jun | Sep | Dec |
|---|---|---|---|---|
| 2008 | 0.15 | 0.18 | 0.19 | 0.35 |
| 2009 | 0.23 | 0.22 | 0.18 | 0.08 |
| 2010 | 0.10 | 0.07 | 0.08 | 0.19 |
| 2011 | (0.33) | (0.42) | ... | ... |

**Interim Dividends (Per Share)**

| Amt | Decl | Ex | Rec | Pay |
|---|---|---|---|---|
| 0.412Q | 09/16/2010 | 09/28/2010 | 09/30/2010 | 10/15/2010 |
| 0.412Q | 12/02/2010 | 12/29/2010 | 12/31/2010 | 01/18/2011 |
| 0.412Q | 03/03/2011 | 03/29/2011 | 03/31/2011 | 04/15/2011 |
| 0.412Q | 05/12/2011 | 06/28/2011 | 06/30/2011 | 07/15/2011 |

**Indicated Div: $1.65**

**Valuation Analysis**

Forecast EPS $-0.01 (09/03/2011)

Market Cap $1.9 Billion Book Value $1.3 Billion

Price/Book 1.53 Price/Sales 3.38

**Dividend Achiever Status**

**10 Year Growth Rate** 6.98%

**Total Years of Dividend Growth** 13

**Business Summary:** REITs (MIC: 5.3.1 SIC: 6798 NAIC: 525930)

Corporate Office Properties Trust is an office real estate investment trust that focuses on customer relationships and tenant requirements in the U.S. Government and defense information technology sectors and data centers serving such sectors. As of Dec 31 2010, Co. had: 252 wholly owned operating office properties; 21 wholly owned office properties under construction, development or redevelopment; wholly owned land parcels totaling 1,497 acres; and partial ownership interests through real estate joint ventures in the following: 20 operating office properties; two office properties under development; and land parcels totaling 755 acres (including 563 acres under contract).

**Recent Developments:** For the quarter ended June 30 2011, loss from continuing operations was US$20.6 million compared with income of US$7.6 million in the year-earlier quarter. Net loss amounted to US$26.0 million versus net income of US$9.2 million in the year-earlier quarter. Revenues were US$146.6 million, up 10.4% from US$132.8 million the year before. Revenues from property income rose 11.1% to US$118.5 million from US$106.7 million in the corresponding quarter a year earlier.

**Prospects:** Our evaluation of Corporate Office Properties Trust as of Sep. 6, 2011 is the result of our systematic analysis on three basic characteristics: earnings strength, relative valuation, and recent stock price movement. The company has produced a positive trend in earnings per share over the past 5 quarters. Because the company lacks sufficient analyst estimate data, we place greater weight on the historical EPS trend as the measure of earnings strength. Based on operating earnings yield, the company is overvalued when compared to all of the companies in our coverage universe. Share price changes over the past year indicates that OFC will perform poorly over the near term.

| **Financial Data** (US$ in Thousands) | 6 Mos | 3 Mos | 12/31/2010 | 12/31/2009 | 12/31/2008 | 12/31/2007 | 12/31/2006 | 12/31/2005 |
|---|---|---|---|---|---|---|---|---|
| Earnings Per Share | (0.48) | 0.01 | 0.43 | 0.70 | 0.87 | 0.39 | 0.69 | 0.63 |
| Cash Flow Per Share | 2.49 | 2.32 | 2.62 | 3.48 | 3.77 | 2.96 | 2.73 | 2.57 |
| Tang Book Value Per Share | 15.99 | 15.84 | 16.63 | 15.88 | 16.25 | 15.07 | 13.68 | 12.31 |
| Dividends Per Share | 1.650 | 1.630 | 1.610 | 1.530 | 1.425 | 1.300 | 1.180 | 1.070 |
| Dividend Payout % | ... | 16,300.00 | 374.42 | 218.57 | 163.79 | 333.33 | 171.01 | 169.84 |
| **Income Statement** | | | | | | | | |
| Total Revenue | 287,826 | 143,395 | 564,475 | 767,519 | 588,018 | 410,174 | 361,403 | 329,145 |
| EBITDA | 58,699 | 32,776 | 357,687 | 333,434 | 323,270 | 315,493 | 269,374 | 224,355 |
| Depn & Amortn | 6,480 | 3,201 | 135,453 | 117,311 | 106,859 | 109,316 | 81,151 | 65,369 |
| Income Before Taxes | 2,897 | 3,815 | 129,937 | 139,079 | 134,835 | 120,469 | 113,998 | 100,091 |
| Income Taxes | (5,586) | (544) | 108 | 196 | 201 | 569 | 887 | 668 |
| Net Income | (42,014) | (17,790) | 42,760 | 56,329 | 58,668 | 34,784 | 49,227 | 39,031 |
| Average Shares | 72,828 | 66,340 | 59,944 | 56,407 | 48,865 | 47,630 | 43,262 | 38,997 |
| **Balance Sheet** | | | | | | | | |
| Current Assets | 56,453 | 71,288 | 60,994 | 74,599 | 85,518 | 84,015 | 105,470 | 47,866 |
| Total Assets | 3,868,230 | 3,865,809 | 3,844,517 | 3,380,022 | 3,112,867 | 2,931,853 | 2,419,601 | 2,130,376 |
| Current Liabilities | 176,954 | 165,518 | 164,288 | 177,072 | 149,883 | 128,782 | 107,591 | 73,170 |
| Long-Term Obligations | 2,299,416 | 2,396,795 | 2,323,681 | 2,053,841 | 1,866,623 | 1,825,842 | 1,498,537 | 1,348,351 |
| Total Liabilities | 2,608,713 | 2,687,929 | 2,617,880 | 2,352,502 | 2,179,553 | 2,109,211 | 1,745,298 | 1,547,863 |
| Stockholders' Equity | 1,259,517 | 1,177,880 | 1,226,637 | 1,027,520 | 933,314 | 822,642 | 674,303 | 582,513 |
| Shares Outstanding | 71,891 | 67,103 | 66,931 | 58,342 | 51,790 | 47,366 | 42,897 | 39,927 |
| **Statistical Record** | | | | | | | | |
| Return on Assets % | N.M. | 0.41 | 1.18 | 1.74 | 1.94 | 1.30 | 2.16 | 2.02 |
| Return on Equity % | N.M. | 1.37 | 3.79 | 5.75 | 6.66 | 4.65 | 7.83 | 7.07 |
| EBITDA Margin % | 20.39 | 22.86 | 63.37 | 43.44 | 54.98 | 76.92 | 74.54 | 68.16 |
| Net Margin % | N.M. | N.M. | 7.58 | 7.34 | 9.98 | 8.48 | 13.62 | 11.86 |
| Asset Turnover | 0.16 | 0.15 | 0.16 | 0.24 | 0.19 | 0.15 | 0.16 | 0.17 |
| Current Ratio | 0.32 | 0.43 | 0.37 | 0.42 | 0.57 | 0.65 | 0.98 | 0.65 |
| Debt to Equity | 1.83 | 2.03 | 1.89 | 2.00 | 2.00 | 2.22 | 2.22 | 2.31 |
| Price Range | 39.27-30.79 | 43.19-33.40 | 43.19-33.16 | 39.34-21.36 | 42.60-21.39 | 56.00-30.97 | 51.20-36.24 | 36.90-25.35 |
| P/E Ratio | ... | N.M. | 100.44-77.12 | 56.20-30.51 | 48.97-24.59 | 143.59-79.41 | 74.20-52.52 | 58.57-40.24 |
| Average Yield % | 4.63 | 4.40 | 4.28 | 4.88 | 4.25 | 3.00 | 2.69 | 3.50 |

**Address:** 6711 Columbia Gateway Drive, Suite 300, Columbia, MD 21046
**Telephone:** 443-285-5400
**Web Site:** www.copt.com

**Officers:** Jay H. Shidler - Chairman Clay W. Hamlin - Vice-Chairman **Transfer Agents:** Wells Fargo Bank, N.A., South St. Paul, MN

**Investor Contact:** 443-285-5450
**No of Institutions:** 272
**Shares:** 73,670,768 **% Held:** 103.07

# CULLEN/FROST BANKERS, INC.

| Exchange | Symbol | Price | 52Wk Range | Yield | P/E |
|---|---|---|---|---|---|
| NYS | CFR | $50.99 (8/31/2011) | 62.57-46.21 | 3.61 | 14.44 |

*7 Year Price Score 106.39 *NYSE Composite Index=100 *12 Month Price Score 94.87

**Interim Earnings (Per Share)**

| Qtr. | Mar | Jun | Sep | Dec |
|---|---|---|---|---|
| 2008 | 0.89 | 0.89 | 0.82 | 0.89 |
| 2009 | 0.76 | 0.63 | 0.75 | 0.86 |
| 2010 | 0.79 | 0.87 | 0.90 | 0.87 |
| 2011 | 0.85 | 0.91 | ... | ... |

**Interim Dividends (Per Share)**

| Amt | Decl | Ex | Rec | Pay |
|---|---|---|---|---|
| 0.45Q | 10/28/2010 | 11/29/2010 | 12/01/2010 | 12/15/2010 |
| 0.45Q | 01/27/2011 | 02/25/2011 | 03/01/2011 | 03/15/2011 |
| 0.46Q | 04/28/2011 | 05/27/2011 | 06/01/2011 | 06/15/2011 |
| 0.46Q | 07/28/2011 | 08/30/2011 | 09/01/2011 | 09/15/2011 |

**Indicated Div: $1.84**

**Valuation Analysis**

| | | | |
|---|---|---|---|
| Forecast EPS | $3.49 (09/03/2011) | | |
| Market Cap | $3.1 Billion | Book Value | $2.2 Billion |
| Price/Book | 1.43 | Price/Sales | N/A |

**Dividend Achiever Status**

| | |
|---|---|
| **10 Year Growth Rate** | 7.80% |
| **Total Years of Dividend Growth** | 17 |

**Business Summary:** Banking (MIC: 5.1.1 SIC: 6021 NAIC: 522110)

Cullen/Frost Bankers is a financial holding company and a bank holding company. Through its subsidiaries, Co. provides an array of products and services throughout the Texas markets. Co. provides commercial and consumer banking services, as well as trust and investment management, mutual funds, property exchange services, investment banking, insurance, brokerage, leasing, asset-based lending, treasury management and item processing services. Co.'s operations are managed along two reportable operating segments consisting of Banking and the Financial Management Group. As of Dec 31 2010, Co. had total assets of $17.62 billion and total deposits of $14.48 billion.

**Recent Developments:** For the quarter ended June 30 2011, net income increased 5.3% to US$55.7 million from US$52.9 million in the year-earlier quarter. Net interest income increased 1.7% to US$144.3 million from US$141.9 million in the year-earlier quarter. Provision for loan losses was US$9.0 million versus US$8.7 million in the prior-year quarter, an increase of 3.9%. Non-interest income rose 1.2% to US$70.8 million from US$69.9 million, while non-interest expense advanced 1.6% to US$136.8 million.

**Prospects:** Our evaluation of Cullen/Frost Bankers Inc. as of Sep. 6, 2011 is the result of our systematic analysis on three basic characteristics: earnings strength, relative valuation, and recent stock price movement. The company has managed to produce a neutral trend in earnings per share over the past 5 quarters. However, while recent estimates for the company have been mixed, CFR has posted better than expected results. Based on operating earnings yield, the company is undervalued when compared to all of the companies in our coverage universe. Share price changes over the past year indicates that CFR will perform poorly over the near term.

**Financial Data**

| (US$ in Thousands) | 6 Mos | 3 Mos | 12/31/2010 | 12/31/2009 | 12/31/2008 | 12/31/2007 | 12/31/2006 | 12/31/2005 |
|---|---|---|---|---|---|---|---|---|
| Earnings Per Share | 3.53 | 3.49 | 3.44 | 3.00 | 3.50 | 3.55 | 3.42 | 3.07 |
| Cash Flow Per Share | 7.08 | 6.73 | 7.03 | 4.61 | 3.97 | 3.41 | (0.96) | 2.52 |
| Tang Book Value Per Share | 26.71 | 25.41 | 24.95 | 22.44 | 20.41 | 15.66 | 13.61 | 14.65 |
| Dividends Per Share | 1.810 | 1.800 | 1.780 | 1.710 | 1.660 | 1.540 | 1.320 | 1.165 |
| Dividend Payout % | 51.27 | 51.58 | 51.74 | 57.00 | 47.43 | 43.38 | 38.60 | 37.95 |
| **Income Statement** | | | | | | | | |
| Interest Income | 309,726 | 153,593 | 617,339 | 623,036 | 675,651 | 768,847 | 683,959 | 509,827 |
| Interest Expense | 23,634 | 11,834 | 53,880 | 86,357 | 141,626 | 250,110 | 214,796 | 118,561 |
| Net Interest Income | 286,092 | 141,759 | 563,459 | 536,679 | 534,025 | 518,737 | 469,163 | 391,266 |
| Provision for Losses | 18,435 | 9,450 | 43,611 | 65,392 | 37,823 | 14,660 | 14,150 | 10,250 |
| Non-Interest Income | 143,125 | 72,333 | 282,033 | 293,706 | 287,322 | 268,231 | 240,747 | 230,379 |
| Non-Interest Expense | 276,858 | 140,061 | 535,541 | 532,238 | 486,645 | 462,446 | 410,353 | 367,007 |
| Income Before Taxes | 133,924 | 64,581 | 266,340 | 232,755 | 296,879 | 309,862 | 285,407 | 244,388 |
| Income Taxes | 26,310 | 12,653 | 57,576 | 53,721 | 89,624 | 97,791 | 91,816 | 78,965 |
| Net Income | 107,614 | 51,928 | 208,764 | 179,034 | 207,255 | 212,071 | 193,591 | 165,423 |
| Average Shares | 61,390 | 61,334 | 60,585 | 59,513 | 59,285 | 59,713 | 56,642 | 53,803 |
| **Balance Sheet** | | | | | | | | |
| Net Loans & Leases | 7,945,471 | 7,900,759 | 7,990,704 | 8,242,471 | 8,733,838 | 7,677,023 | 7,277,299 | 6,004,730 |
| Total Assets | 18,478,386 | 17,941,644 | 17,617,092 | 16,288,038 | 15,034,142 | 13,485,014 | 13,224,189 | 11,741,437 |
| Total Deposits | 15,104,131 | 14,709,559 | 14,479,342 | 13,313,310 | 11,508,937 | 10,529,673 | 10,387,909 | 9,146,394 |
| Total Liabilities | 16,301,741 | 15,844,293 | 15,555,412 | 14,393,614 | 13,270,615 | 12,007,926 | 11,847,306 | 10,759,201 |
| Stockholders' Equity | 2,176,645 | 2,097,351 | 2,061,680 | 1,894,424 | 1,763,527 | 1,477,088 | 1,376,883 | 982,236 |
| Shares Outstanding | 61,245 | 61,241 | 60,909 | 60,038 | 59,416 | 58,662 | 59,839 | 54,482 |
| **Statistical Record** | | | | | | | | |
| Return on Assets % | 1.21 | 1.23 | 1.23 | 1.14 | 1.45 | 1.59 | 1.55 | 1.53 |
| Return on Equity % | 10.23 | 10.52 | 10.55 | 9.79 | 12.76 | 14.86 | 16.41 | 18.33 |
| Net Interest Margin % | 92.44 | 92.30 | 91.27 | 86.14 | 79.04 | 67.47 | 68.60 | 76.74 |
| Efficiency Ratio % | 60.28 | 61.99 | 59.55 | 58.06 | 50.54 | 44.59 | 44.38 | 49.58 |
| Loans to Deposits | 0.53 | 0.54 | 0.55 | 0.62 | 0.76 | 0.73 | 0.70 | 0.66 |
| Price Range | 62.57-50.61 | 62.57-50.61 | 62.01-50.00 | 53.19-36.61 | 62.75-45.38 | 56.84-48.10 | 59.44-52.26 | 56.05-42.45 |
| P/E Ratio | 17.73-14.34 | 17.93-14.50 | 18.03-14.53 | 17.73-12.20 | 17.93-12.97 | 16.01-13.55 | 17.38-15.28 | 18.26-13.83 |
| Average Yield % | 3.21 | 3.22 | 3.27 | 3.61 | 3.13 | 2.94 | 2.36 | 2.40 |

**Address:** 100 W. Houston Street, San Antonio, TX 78205
**Telephone:** 210-220-4011
**Web Site:** www.frostbank.com

**Officers:** Richard W. Evans - Chairman, President, Chief Executive Officer Phillip D. Green - Group Executive Vice President, Chief Financial Officer
**Transfer Agents:** Bank of New York Mellon Corporation, Pittsburgh, PA

**Investor Contact:** 210-220-5632
**No of Institutions:** 321
**Shares:** 50,251,376 **% Held:** 74.52

# DIEBOLD, INC.

| Exchange | Symbol | Price | 52Wk Range | Yield | P/E |
|---|---|---|---|---|---|
| NYS | DBD | $28.64 (8/31/2011) | 36.94-24.76 | 3.91 | N/A |

***7 Year Price Score 83.57** *NYSE Composite Index=100 ***12 Month Price Score 93.47**

**Interim Earnings (Per Share)**

| Qtr. | Mar | Jun | Sep | Dec |
|---|---|---|---|---|
| 2008 | 0.21 | 0.41 | 0.70 | 0.01 |
| 2009 | 0.02 | 0.46 | (0.11) | 0.02 |
| 2010 | 0.36 | 0.45 | 0.69 | (1.81) |
| 2011 | 0.04 | 0.32 | ... | ... |

**Interim Dividends (Per Share)**

| Amt | Decl | Ex | Rec | Pay |
|---|---|---|---|---|
| 0.27Q | 10/07/2010 | 11/17/2010 | 11/19/2010 | 12/10/2010 |
| 0.28Q | 02/09/2011 | 02/16/2011 | 02/21/2011 | 03/07/2011 |
| 0.28Q | 04/28/2011 | 05/11/2011 | 05/13/2011 | 06/03/2011 |
| 0.28Q | 08/04/2011 | 08/17/2011 | 08/19/2011 | 09/09/2011 |

**Indicated Div: $1.12 (Div. Reinv. Plan)**

**Valuation Analysis**

| | | | |
|---|---|---|---|
| Forecast EPS | $2.07 (09/02/2011) | | |
| Market Cap | $1.8 Billion | Book Value | $951.3 Million |
| Price/Book | 1.94 | Price/Sales | 0.66 |

**Dividend Achiever Status**

| | |
|---|---|
| **10 Year Growth Rate** | 5.37% |
| **Total Years of Dividend Growth** | 57 |

**Business Summary:** Computer Hardware & Equipment (MIC: 6.2.1 SIC: 3578 NAIC: 333313)

Diebold provides self-service delivery and security systems and services. Co. has two lines of business: Self-Service Solutions, which provide hardware, software, and support and maintenance services; and Security Solutions, which provide physical security and facility products, electronic security products, and monitoring and services. Co.'s segments are comprised of two sales channels: Diebold North America, which sells and services financial and retail systems in the U.S. and Canada; and Diebold International, which sells and services financial and retail systems over the remainder of the globe through wholly-owned subsidiaries, majority-owned joint ventures and independent distributors.

**Recent Developments:** For the quarter ended June 30 2011, income from continuing operations decreased 30.5% to US$21.6 million from US$31.1 million in the year-earlier quarter. Net income decreased 27.2% to US$22.1 million from US$30.4 million in the year-earlier quarter. Revenues were US$662.4 million, down 0.4% from US$665.2 million the year before. Operating income was US$25.1 million versus US$46.9 million in the prior-year quarter, a decrease of 46.4%. Direct operating expenses rose 1.2% to US$492.9 million from US$487.0 million in the comparable period the year before. Indirect operating expenses increased 10.0% to US$144.4 million from US$131.3 million in the equivalent prior-year period.

**Prospects:** Our evaluation of Diebold Inc. as of Sep. 6, 2011 is the result of our systematic analysis on three basic characteristics: earnings strength, relative valuation, and recent stock price movement. The company has generated a negative trend in earnings per share over the past 5 quarters. However, while recent estimates for the company have been mixed, DBD has posted better than expected results. Based on operating earnings yield, the company is undervalued when compared to all of the companies in our coverage universe. Share price changes over the past year indicates that DBD will perform poorly over the near term.

**Financial Data**

| (US$ in Thousands) | 6 Mos | 3 Mos | 12/31/2010 | 12/31/2009 | 12/31/2008 | 12/31/2007 | 12/31/2006 | 12/31/2005 |
|---|---|---|---|---|---|---|---|---|
| Earnings Per Share | (0.76) | (0.63) | (0.31) | 0.39 | 1.33 | 0.59 | 1.29 | 1.36 |
| Cash Flow Per Share | 2.91 | 3.63 | 4.15 | 4.52 | 4.30 | 2.28 | 3.76 | 1.66 |
| Tang Book Value Per Share | 10.44 | 10.30 | 10.53 | 8.98 | 8.14 | 9.84 | 9.62 | 11.11 |
| Dividends Per Share | 1.100 | 1.090 | 1.080 | 1.040 | 1.000 | 0.940 | 0.860 | 0.820 |
| Dividend Payout % | ... | ... | ... | 266.67 | 75.19 | 159.32 | 66.67 | 60.29 |
| **Income Statement** | | | | | | | | |
| Total Revenue | 1,276,539 | 614,157 | 2,823,793 | 2,718,292 | 3,170,080 | 2,964,837 | 2,906,232 | 2,587,049 |
| EBITDA | 90,419 | 30,727 | 86,915 | 209,344 | 247,917 | 171,489 | 207,455 | 211,468 |
| Depn & Amortn | 33,978 | 11,983 | 51,425 | 50,085 | 55,295 | 45,549 | 40,385 | 49,877 |
| Income Before Taxes | 38,253 | 10,071 | (2,397) | 123,807 | 147,375 | 83,703 | 131,046 | 145,080 |
| Income Taxes | 12,505 | 5,925 | 14,561 | 44,477 | 37,425 | 35,797 | 37,902 | 55,347 |
| Net Income | 23,305 | 2,501 | (20,252) | 26,026 | 88,583 | 39,541 | 86,547 | 96,746 |
| Average Shares | 65,482 | 66,230 | 65,907 | 66,867 | 66,492 | 66,673 | 66,885 | 70,966 |
| **Balance Sheet** | | | | | | | | |
| Current Assets | 1,790,431 | 1,721,231 | 1,714,036 | 1,588,085 | 1,614,118 | 1,630,532 | 1,595,681 | 1,427,880 |
| Total Assets | 2,596,598 | 2,531,537 | 2,519,790 | 2,554,865 | 2,537,936 | 2,631,126 | 2,514,279 | 2,353,193 |
| Current Liabilities | 808,385 | 788,077 | 809,765 | 743,091 | 735,397 | 750,638 | 598,736 | 580,031 |
| Long-Term Obligations | 644,661 | 615,010 | 550,368 | 540,000 | 594,588 | 609,264 | 665,481 | 454,722 |
| Total Liabilities | 1,645,290 | 1,584,507 | 1,558,635 | 1,508,486 | 1,591,335 | 1,516,292 | 1,422,878 | 1,200,344 |
| Stockholders' Equity | 951,308 | 947,030 | 961,155 | 1,046,379 | 946,601 | 1,114,834 | 1,091,401 | 1,152,849 |
| Shares Outstanding | 64,460 | 65,528 | 65,717 | 66,327 | 66,114 | 65,965 | 65,595 | 68,721 |
| **Statistical Record** | | | | | | | | |
| Return on Assets % | N.M. | N.M. | N.M. | 1.02 | 3.42 | 1.54 | 3.56 | 4.31 |
| Return on Equity % | N.M. | N.M. | N.M. | 2.61 | 8.57 | 3.58 | 7.71 | 8.02 |
| EBITDA Margin % | 7.08 | 5.00 | 3.08 | 7.70 | 7.82 | 5.78 | 7.14 | 8.17 |
| Net Margin % | 1.83 | 0.41 | N.M. | 0.96 | 2.79 | 1.33 | 2.98 | 3.74 |
| Asset Turnover | 1.12 | 1.12 | 1.11 | 1.07 | 1.22 | 1.15 | 1.19 | 1.15 |
| Current Ratio | 2.21 | 2.18 | 2.12 | 2.14 | 2.19 | 2.17 | 2.67 | 2.46 |
| Debt to Equity | 0.68 | 0.65 | 0.57 | 0.52 | 0.63 | 0.55 | 0.61 | 0.39 |
| Price Range | 36.94-25.94 | 35.73-25.94 | 34.87-25.94 | 32.93-19.05 | 40.30-23.37 | 54.25-28.89 | 46.93-37.01 | 57.58-33.37 |
| P/E Ratio | ... | ... | ... | 84.44-48.85 | 30.30-17.57 | 91.95-48.97 | 36.38-28.69 | 42.34-24.54 |
| Average Yield % | 3.48 | 3.51 | 3.58 | 3.85 | 3.02 | 2.08 | 2.05 | 1.74 |

**Address:** 5995 Mayfair Road, P.O. Box 3077, North Canton, OH 44720-8077
**Telephone:** 330-490-4000
**Web Site:** www.diebold.com

**Officers:** Thomas W. Swidarski - President, Chief Executive Officer George S. Mayes - Executive Vice President **Transfer Agents:**
BNY Mellon Shareowner Services, Pittsburgh, PA

**Investor Contact:** 330-490-5900
**No of Institutions:** 305
**Shares:** 70,703,168 **% Held:** 79.59

# DONALDSON CO. INC.

| Exchange | Symbol | Price | 52Wk Range | Yield | P/E |
|---|---|---|---|---|---|
| NYS | DCI | $58.98 (8/31/2011) | 62.58-41.90 | 1.02 | 22.01 |

***7 Year Price Score 140.13** *NYSE Composite Index=100 ***12 Month Price Score 101.50**

**Interim Earnings (Per Share)**

| Qtr. | Oct | Jan | Apr | Jul |
|---|---|---|---|---|
| 2007-08 | 0.53 | 0.42 | 0.57 | 0.60 |
| 2008-09 | 0.60 | 0.43 | 0.34 | 0.30 |
| 2009-10 | 0.44 | 0.39 | 0.62 | 0.65 |
| 2010-11 | 0.68 | 0.56 | 0.79 | ... |

**Interim Dividends (Per Share)**

| Amt | Decl | Ex | Rec | Pay |
|---|---|---|---|---|
| 0.13Q | 11/19/2010 | 12/02/2010 | 12/06/2010 | 12/17/2010 |
| 0.13Q | 01/28/2011 | 02/23/2011 | 02/25/2011 | 03/18/2011 |
| 0.15Q | 05/24/2011 | 06/08/2011 | 06/10/2011 | 06/24/2011 |
| 0.15Q | 07/29/2011 | 08/22/2011 | 08/24/2011 | 09/16/2011 |

**Indicated Div: $0.60 (Div. Reinv. Plan)**

**Valuation Analysis**

| | | | |
|---|---|---|---|
| Forecast EPS | $3.30 (09/02/2011) | | |
| Market Cap | $4.5 Billion | Book Value | $955.2 Million |
| Price/Book | 4.72 | Price/Sales | 2.06 |

**Dividend Achiever Status**

| | |
|---|---|
| **10 Year Growth Rate** | 12.68% |
| **Total Years of Dividend Growth** | 15 |

**Business Summary:** Industrial Machinery & Equipment (MIC: 7.2.1 SIC: 3564 NAIC: 333411)

Donaldson Company is a manufacturer of filtration systems and replacement parts. Co. has two segments: Engine Products, which sells products that include air filtration systems, exhaust and emissions systems, liquid filtration systems, and replacement filters; and Industrial Products, which sells products that include dust, fume and mist collectors, compressed air purification systems, liquid filtration systems, air filtration systems for gas turbines, polytetrafluoroethylene membranes and laminates, and air filtration systems for a range of applications including computer hard disk drives. Co.'s products are sold to original equipment manufacturers, distributors and dealers, and end users.

**Recent Developments:** For the quarter ended Apr 30 2011, net income increased 25.0% to US$61.8 million from US$49.5 million in the year-earlier quarter. Revenues were US$594.6 million, up 19.5% from US$497.6 million the year before. Operating income was US$83.3 million versus US$72.1 million in the prior-year quarter, an increase of 15.6%. Direct operating expenses rose 20.3% to US$385.4 million from US$320.2 million in the comparable period the year before. Indirect operating expenses increased 19.5% to US$125.8 million from US$105.3 million in the equivalent prior-year period.

**Prospects:** Our evaluation of Donaldson Co. Inc. as of Sep. 6, 2011 is the result of our systematic analysis on three basic characteristics: earnings strength, relative valuation, and recent stock price movement. The company has managed to produce a neutral trend in earnings per share over the past 5 quarters and while recent estimates for the company have been raised by analysts, DCI has posted better than expected results. Based on operating earnings yield, the company is about fairly valued when compared to all of the companies in our coverage universe. Share price changes over the past year indicates that DCI will perform poorly over the near term.

**Financial Data**

| (US$ in Thousands) | 9 Mos | 6 Mos | 3 Mos | 07/31/2010 | 07/31/2009 | 07/31/2008 | 07/31/2007 | 07/31/2006 |
|---|---|---|---|---|---|---|---|---|
| Earnings Per Share | 2.68 | 2.51 | 2.34 | 2.10 | 1.67 | 2.12 | 1.83 | 1.55 |
| Cash Flow Per Share | 2.88 | 2.72 | 2.54 | 2.61 | 3.56 | 2.18 | 1.45 | 1.89 |
| Tang Book Value Per Share | 9.51 | 8.47 | 7.97 | 6.84 | 5.87 | 7.21 | 5.73 | 5.14 |
| Dividends Per Share | 0.505 | 0.495 | 0.480 | 0.470 | 0.455 | 0.420 | 0.360 | 0.320 |
| Dividend Payout % | 18.84 | 19.72 | 20.51 | 22.38 | 27.25 | 19.81 | 19.67 | 20.65 |
| **Income Statement** | | | | | | | | |
| Total Revenue | 1,668,579 | 1,074,014 | 536,909 | 1,877,064 | 1,868,629 | 2,232,521 | 1,918,828 | 1,694,327 |
| EBITDA | 276,542 | 177,031 | 90,528 | 295,351 | 231,343 | 305,113 | 266,020 | 241,642 |
| Depn & Amortn | 45,276 | 30,478 | 14,918 | 53,200 | 52,900 | 52,400 | 46,600 | 42,600 |
| Income Before Taxes | 221,780 | 139,964 | 71,957 | 230,176 | 161,425 | 236,163 | 204,861 | 189,167 |
| Income Taxes | 62,256 | 42,251 | 18,823 | 64,013 | 29,518 | 64,210 | 54,144 | 56,860 |
| Net Income | 159,524 | 97,713 | 53,134 | 166,163 | 131,907 | 171,953 | 150,717 | 132,307 |
| Average Shares | 78,704 | 78,977 | 78,484 | 79,177 | 79,172 | 81,211 | 82,435 | 85,139 |
| **Balance Sheet** | | | | | | | | |
| Current Assets | 1,082,296 | 958,370 | 937,450 | 860,215 | 676,767 | 853,757 | 673,644 | 561,405 |
| Total Assets | 1,741,807 | 1,595,107 | 1,590,486 | 1,499,506 | 1,333,996 | 1,548,622 | 1,319,017 | 1,124,067 |
| Current Liabilities | 494,148 | 417,877 | 387,805 | 389,256 | 300,084 | 516,707 | 458,944 | 359,869 |
| Long-Term Obligations | 204,689 | 211,965 | 257,183 | 256,192 | 253,674 | 176,475 | 129,004 | 100,495 |
| Total Liabilities | 786,590 | 718,504 | 753,865 | 752,873 | 645,378 | 808,587 | 694,319 | 577,265 |
| Stockholders' Equity | 955,217 | 876,603 | 836,621 | 746,633 | 688,618 | 740,035 | 624,698 | 546,802 |
| Shares Outstanding | 76,425 | 77,001 | 76,563 | 76,420 | 77,347 | 77,621 | 79,142 | 80,540 |
| **Statistical Record** | | | | | | | | |
| Return on Assets % | 13.31 | 13.36 | 12.41 | 11.73 | 9.15 | 11.96 | 12.34 | 11.84 |
| Return on Equity % | 24.41 | 24.49 | 23.52 | 23.15 | 18.47 | 25.13 | 25.73 | 24.70 |
| EBITDA Margin % | 16.57 | 16.48 | 16.86 | 15.73 | 12.38 | 13.67 | 13.86 | 14.26 |
| Net Margin % | 9.56 | 9.10 | 9.90 | 8.85 | 7.06 | 7.70 | 7.85 | 7.81 |
| Asset Turnover | 1.38 | 1.41 | 1.33 | 1.32 | 1.30 | 1.55 | 1.57 | 1.52 |
| Current Ratio | 2.19 | 2.29 | 2.42 | 2.21 | 2.26 | 1.65 | 1.47 | 1.56 |
| Debt to Equity | 0.21 | 0.24 | 0.31 | 0.34 | 0.37 | 0.24 | 0.21 | 0.18 |
| Price Range | 62.53-41.05 | 60.02-38.17 | 49.84-35.71 | 47.67-32.88 | 47.94-22.00 | 51.55-35.92 | 38.55-32.00 | 35.93-28.70 |
| P/E Ratio | 23.33-15.32 | 23.91-15.21 | 21.30-15.26 | 22.70-15.66 | 28.71-13.17 | 24.32-16.94 | 21.07-17.49 | 23.18-18.52 |
| Average Yield % | 0.99 | 1.04 | 1.10 | 1.13 | 1.34 | 0.99 | 1.01 | 0.99 |

| | | |
|---|---|---|
| **Address:** 1400 West 94th Street, Minneapolis, MN 55431<br>**Telephone:** 952-887-3131<br>**Web Site:** www.donaldson.com | **Officers:** William M. Cook - Chairman, President, Chief Executive Officer Charles J. McMurray - Senior Vice President, Chief Administrative Officer<br>**Transfer Agents:** Wells Fargo Bank, N.A., South St. Paul, MN | **Investor Contact:** 952-887-3753<br>**No of Institutions:** 318<br>**Shares:** 66,572,912 **% Held:** 68.86 |

# DOVER CORP

| Exchange | Symbol | Price | 52Wk Range | Yield | P/E |
|---|---|---|---|---|---|
| NYS | DOV | $57.52 (8/31/2011) | 69.84-44.76 | 2.19 | 12.56 |

*7 Year Price Score 131.49 *NYSE Composite Index=100 *12 Month Price Score 101.09

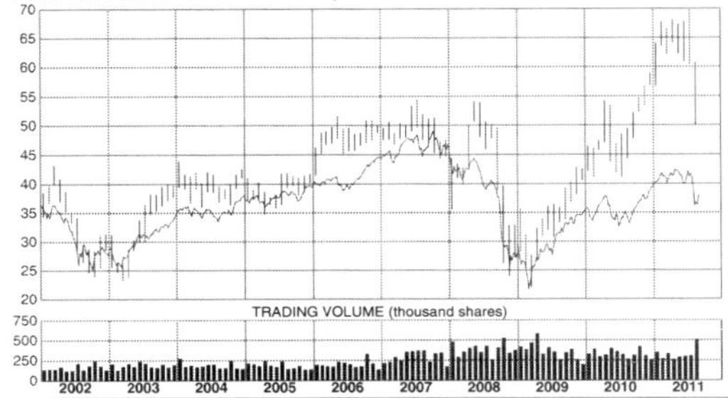


**Interim Earnings (Per Share)**

| Qtr. | Mar | Jun | Sep | Dec |
|---|---|---|---|---|
| 2008 | 0.76 | 0.71 | 1.00 | 0.65 |
| 2009 | 0.29 | 0.52 | 0.57 | 0.53 |
| 2010 | 0.58 | 0.90 | 1.19 | 1.04 |
| 2011 | 1.03 | 1.32 | ... | ... |

**Interim Dividends (Per Share)**

| Amt | Decl | Ex | Rec | Pay |
|---|---|---|---|---|
| 0.275Q | 11/04/2010 | 11/26/2010 | 11/30/2010 | 12/15/2010 |
| 0.275Q | 02/10/2011 | 02/24/2011 | 02/28/2011 | 03/15/2011 |
| 0.275Q | 05/06/2011 | 05/26/2011 | 05/31/2011 | 06/15/2011 |
| 0.315Q | 08/04/2011 | 08/29/2011 | 08/31/2011 | 09/15/2011 |

**Indicated Div: $1.26 (Div. Reinv. Plan)**

**Valuation Analysis**

| | | | |
|---|---|---|---|
| Forecast EPS | $4.58 (09/05/2011) | | |
| Market Cap | $10.7 Billion | Book Value | $4.9 Billion |
| Price/Book | 2.18 | Price/Sales | 1.36 |

**Dividend Achiever Status**

| | |
|---|---|
| 10 Year Growth Rate | 7.48% |
| Total Years of Dividend Growth | 55 |

**Business Summary:** Industrial Machinery & Equipment (MIC: 7.2.1 SIC: 3559 NAIC: 333220)

Dover owns and operates manufacturing companies providing components and equipment, systems and support services for a range of applications. Co. designs, manufactures, assembles and/or services industrial products, which include material handling equipment and mobile equipment related products; engineered systems, which include engineered products such as refrigeration display cases, and identification related products such as industrial marking and coding systems; fluid management, which include energy market production and distribution products, as well as fluid application products; and electronic technologies, which include electronic technology equipment and devices/components.

**Recent Developments:** For the quarter ended June 30 2011, income from continuing operations increased 44.9% to US$249.1 million from US$171.9 million in the year-earlier quarter. Net income increased 47.0% to US$249.8 million from US$169.9 million in the year-earlier quarter. Revenues were US$2.16 billion, up 20.7% from US$1.79 billion the year before. Operating income was US$341.7 million versus US$264.9 million in the prior-year quarter, an increase of 29.0%. Direct operating expenses rose 22.1% to US$1.34 billion from US$1.10 billion in the comparable period the year before. Indirect operating expenses increased 11.9% to US$474.1 million from US$423.8 million in the equivalent prior-year period.

**Prospects:** Our evaluation of Dover Corp. as of Sep. 6, 2011 is the result of our systematic analysis on three basic characteristics: earnings strength, relative valuation, and recent stock price movement. The company has managed to produce a neutral trend in earnings per share over the past 5 quarters. However, while recent estimates for the company have been lowered by analysts, DOV has posted better than expected results. Based on operating earnings yield, the company is undervalued when compared to all of the companies in our coverage universe. Share price changes over the past year indicates that DOV will perform in line with the market over the near term.

**Financial Data**

| (US$ in Thousands) | 6 Mos | 3 Mos | 12/31/2010 | 12/31/2009 | 12/31/2008 | 12/31/2007 | 12/31/2006 | 12/31/2005 |
|---|---|---|---|---|---|---|---|---|
| Earnings Per Share | 4.58 | 4.16 | 3.70 | 1.91 | 3.12 | 3.26 | 2.73 | 2.50 |
| Cash Flow Per Share | 5.23 | 5.34 | 5.09 | 4.31 | 5.35 | 4.48 | 4.31 | 3.25 |
| Tang Book Value Per Share | 1.38 | 0.32 | 1.35 | N.M. | N.M. | N.M. | N.M. | N.M. |
| Dividends Per Share | 1.100 | 1.085 | 1.070 | 1.020 | 0.900 | 0.770 | 0.710 | 0.660 |
| Dividend Payout % | 24.02 | 26.08 | 28.92 | 53.40 | 28.85 | 23.62 | 26.01 | 26.40 |
| **Income Statement** | | | | | | | | |
| Total Revenue | 4,115,892 | 1,959,021 | 7,132,648 | 5,775,689 | 7,568,888 | 7,226,089 | 6,511,623 | 6,078,380 |
| EBITDA | 757,644 | 342,773 | 1,195,340 | 751,593 | 1,201,356 | 1,127,012 | 1,032,453 | 847,194 |
| Depn & Amortn | 148,205 | 73,687 | 163,915 | 159,600 | 159,300 | 150,400 | 132,600 | 131,400 |
| Income Before Taxes | 553,019 | 240,800 | 925,084 | 491,618 | 946,019 | 887,604 | 822,869 | 643,588 |
| Income Taxes | 120,619 | 57,494 | 217,176 | 119,724 | 251,261 | 234,331 | 219,541 | 169,135 |
| Net Income | 444,674 | 194,905 | 700,104 | 356,438 | 590,831 | 661,080 | 561,782 | 510,142 |
| Average Shares | 189,705 | 190,090 | 189,170 | 186,736 | 189,269 | 202,918 | 205,497 | 204,177 |
| **Balance Sheet** | | | | | | | | |
| Current Assets | 3,753,415 | 3,591,317 | 3,261,871 | 2,522,707 | 2,614,185 | 2,544,238 | 2,271,506 | 1,975,925 |
| Total Assets | 9,482,038 | 9,360,143 | 8,562,894 | 7,882,403 | 7,867,304 | 8,069,770 | 7,626,658 | 6,573,032 |
| Current Liabilities | 1,263,966 | 1,273,850 | 1,194,386 | 969,176 | 1,237,580 | 1,681,192 | 1,433,980 | 1,207,454 |
| Long-Term Obligations | 2,186,238 | 2,185,991 | 1,790,886 | 1,825,260 | 1,860,729 | 1,452,003 | 1,480,491 | 1,344,173 |
| Total Liabilities | 4,569,081 | 4,616,099 | 4,036,332 | 3,798,795 | 4,074,438 | 4,123,597 | 3,815,636 | 3,243,509 |
| Stockholders' Equity | 4,912,957 | 4,744,044 | 4,526,562 | 4,083,608 | 3,792,866 | 3,946,173 | 3,811,022 | 3,329,523 |
| Shares Outstanding | 186,023 | 186,579 | 186,488 | 186,876 | 185,996 | 194,038 | 204,316 | 202,850 |
| **Statistical Record** | | | | | | | | |
| Return on Assets % | 9.87 | 9.05 | 8.51 | 4.53 | 7.39 | 8.42 | 7.91 | 8.25 |
| Return on Equity % | 19.27 | 17.88 | 16.26 | 9.05 | 15.23 | 17.04 | 15.73 | 15.82 |
| EBITDA Margin % | 18.41 | 17.50 | 16.76 | 13.01 | 15.87 | 15.60 | 15.86 | 13.94 |
| Net Margin % | 10.80 | 9.95 | 9.82 | 6.17 | 7.81 | 9.15 | 8.63 | 8.39 |
| Asset Turnover | 0.90 | 0.86 | 0.87 | 0.73 | 0.95 | 0.92 | 0.92 | 0.98 |
| Current Ratio | 2.97 | 2.82 | 2.73 | 2.60 | 2.11 | 1.51 | 1.58 | 1.64 |
| Debt to Equity | 0.44 | 0.46 | 0.40 | 0.45 | 0.49 | 0.37 | 0.39 | 0.40 |
| Price Range | 68.04-41.11 | 67.75-41.11 | 58.96-41.05 | 42.87-22.06 | 54.18-23.97 | 54.44-44.34 | 51.58-41.49 | 41.94-34.70 |
| P/E Ratio | 14.86-8.98 | 16.29-9.88 | 15.94-11.09 | 22.45-11.55 | 17.37-7.68 | 16.70-13.60 | 18.89-15.20 | 16.78-13.88 |
| Average Yield % | 1.91 | 2.04 | 2.20 | 2.99 | 2.14 | 1.57 | 1.49 | 1.69 |

**Address:** 3005 Highland Parkway, Suite 200, Downers Grove, IL 60515
**Telephone:** 630-541-1540
**Web Site:** www.dovercorporation.com

**Officers:** Robert W. Cremin - Chairman Robert A. Livingston - President, Chief Executive Officer
**Transfer Agents:** BNY Mellon Shareowner Services, Inc., Pittsburgh, PA

**Investor Contact:** 212-922-1640
**No of Institutions:** 718
**Shares:** 177,643,904 **% Held:** 85.31

# EATON VANCE CORP

| Exchange | Symbol | Price | 52Wk Range | Yield | P/E |
|---|---|---|---|---|---|
| NYS | EV | $24.41 (8/31/2011) | 33.92-21.14 | 2.95 | 15.75 |

*7 Year Price Score 98.97 *NYSE Composite Index=100 *12 Month Price Score 88.22

**Interim Earnings (Per Share)**

| Qtr. | Jan | Apr | Jul | Oct |
|---|---|---|---|---|
| 2007-08 | 0.46 | 0.43 | 0.40 | 0.29 |
| 2008-09 | 0.21 | 0.22 | 0.26 | 0.40 |
| 2009-10 | 0.37 | 0.29 | 0.34 | 0.41 |
| 2010-11 | 0.30 | 0.50 | ... | ... |

**Interim Dividends (Per Share)**

| Amt | Decl | Ex | Rec | Pay |
|---|---|---|---|---|
| 0.18Q | 10/20/2010 | 10/27/2010 | 10/29/2010 | 11/10/2010 |
| 0.18Q | 01/12/2011 | 01/27/2011 | 01/31/2011 | 02/11/2011 |
| 0.18Q | 04/13/2011 | 04/27/2011 | 04/29/2011 | 05/09/2011 |
| 0.18Q | 07/13/2011 | 07/27/2011 | 07/29/2011 | 08/12/2011 |

**Indicated Div: $0.72**

**Valuation Analysis**

Forecast EPS $1.82 (09/03/2011)

| Market Cap | $2.9 Billion | Book Value | $476.3 Million |
|---|---|---|---|
| Price/Book | 6.08 | Price/Sales | 2.38 |

**Dividend Achiever Status**

| | |
|---|---|
| 10 Year Growth Rate | 17.99% |
| Total Years of Dividend Growth | 29 |

**Business Summary:** Wealth Management (MIC: 5.5.2 SIC: 6282 NAIC: 523930)

Eaton Vance is engaged in the management of investment funds and provision of investment management and counseling services to individuals and institutions. Co.'s product line provides fund shareholders, retail managed account investors, institutional investors and clients a range of products and services. Co. provides investment advisory services to funds, high-net-worth separate accounts, institutional separate accounts and retail managed accounts across a range of equity and fixed and floating-rate income asset classes. As of Oct 31 2010, Co. had $185.24 billion in assets under management.

**Recent Developments:** For the quarter ended Apr 30 2011, net income increased 16.9% to US$53.8 million from US$46.0 million in the year-earlier quarter. Revenues were US$325.8 million, up 19.4% from US$273.0 million the year before. Operating income was US$117.0 million versus US$81.1 million in the prior-year quarter, an increase of 44.3%. Indirect operating expenses increased 8.8% to US$208.8 million from US$191.9 million in the equivalent prior-year period.

**Prospects:** Our evaluation of Eaton Vance Corp. as of Sep. 6, 2011 is the result of our systematic analysis on three basic characteristics: earnings strength, relative valuation, and recent stock price movement. The company has managed to produce a neutral trend in earnings per share over the past 5 quarters. However, while recent estimates for the company have been mixed, EV has posted better than expected results. Based on operating earnings yield, the company is undervalued when compared to all of the companies in our coverage universe. Share price changes over the past year indicates that EV will perform in line with the market over the near term.

**Financial Data**

| (US$ in Thousands) | 6 Mos | 3 Mos | 10/31/2010 | 10/31/2009 | 10/31/2008 | 10/31/2007 | 10/31/2006 | 10/31/2005 |
|---|---|---|---|---|---|---|---|---|
| Earnings Per Share | 1.55 | 1.34 | 1.40 | 1.08 | 1.57 | 1.06 | 1.17 | 1.13 |
| Cash Flow Per Share | 0.53 | 0.84 | 0.82 | 1.41 | 1.31 | 2.14 | 2.06 | 0.82 |
| Tang Book Value Per Share | 2.22 | 2.14 | 1.70 | 1.11 | 0.67 | 0.76 | 2.89 | 2.51 |
| Dividends Per Share | 0.700 | 0.680 | 0.660 | 0.625 | 0.605 | 0.630 | 0.400 | 0.240 |
| Dividend Payout % | 45.16 | 50.75 | 47.14 | 57.87 | 38.54 | 59.43 | 34.19 | 21.24 |
| **Income Statement** | | | | | | | | |
| Total Revenue | 638,125 | 312,287 | 1,121,661 | 890,371 | 1,095,800 | 1,084,100 | 862,194 | 753,175 |
| EBITDA | 215,957 | 106,829 | 373,163 | 251,700 | 355,765 | 238,632 | 271,819 | 261,300 |
| Depn & Amortn | 19,258 | 10,270 | 15,400 | 14,100 | 10,400 | 7,900 | 4,000 | 3,000 |
| Income Before Taxes | 186,448 | 92,573 | 326,961 | 207,663 | 322,847 | 238,349 | 263,002 | 261,190 |
| Income Taxes | 75,859 | 34,522 | 126,263 | 71,044 | 125,154 | 93,200 | 102,245 | 97,500 |
| Net Income | 100,014 | 37,535 | 174,298 | 130,107 | 195,663 | 142,811 | 159,377 | 159,884 |
| Average Shares | 122,292 | 122,175 | 122,632 | 120,728 | 124,483 | 135,252 | 137,004 | 141,632 |
| **Balance Sheet** | | | | | | | | |
| Current Assets | 588,080 | 614,544 | 499,274 | 488,162 | 484,801 | 610,152 | 329,367 | 368,588 |
| Total Assets | 1,806,487 | 1,780,191 | 1,280,607 | 1,075,067 | 968,355 | 966,831 | 668,195 | 702,544 |
| Current Liabilities | 154,712 | 142,698 | 258,001 | 188,323 | 191,431 | 217,699 | 139,645 | 116,357 |
| Long-Term Obligations | 979,277 | 956,963 | 500,000 | 500,000 | 500,000 | 500,000 | ... | 75,467 |
| Total Liabilities | 1,330,231 | 1,317,031 | 870,322 | 727,959 | 728,228 | 737,663 | 171,710 | 247,591 |
| Stockholders' Equity | 476,256 | 463,160 | 410,285 | 347,108 | 240,127 | 229,168 | 496,485 | 454,953 |
| Shares Outstanding | 118,580 | 119,126 | 118,326 | 117,519 | 115,811 | 118,169 | 126,435 | 129,552 |
| **Statistical Record** | | | | | | | | |
| Return on Assets % | 13.08 | 11.46 | 14.80 | 12.73 | 20.17 | 17.47 | 23.25 | 22.11 |
| Return on Equity % | 45.66 | 41.14 | 46.03 | 44.31 | 83.16 | 39.36 | 33.50 | 35.35 |
| EBITDA Margin % | 33.84 | 34.21 | 33.27 | 28.27 | 32.47 | 22.01 | 31.53 | 34.69 |
| Net Margin % | 15.67 | 12.02 | 15.54 | 14.61 | 17.86 | 13.17 | 18.49 | 21.23 |
| Asset Turnover | 0.83 | 0.80 | 0.95 | 0.87 | 1.13 | 1.33 | 1.26 | 1.04 |
| Current Ratio | 3.80 | 4.31 | 1.94 | 2.59 | 2.53 | 2.80 | 2.36 | 3.17 |
| Debt to Equity | 2.06 | 2.07 | 1.22 | 1.44 | 2.08 | 2.18 | ... | 0.17 |
| Price Range | 35.72-25.90 | 35.72-25.90 | 35.72-25.90 | 30.67-12.36 | 50.03-16.70 | 50.03-29.87 | 31.10-24.14 | 27.30-21.80 |
| P/E Ratio | 23.05-16.71 | 26.66-19.33 | 25.51-18.50 | 28.40-11.44 | 31.87-10.64 | 47.20-28.18 | 26.58-20.63 | 24.16-19.29 |
| Average Yield % | 2.30 | 2.23 | 2.17 | 2.60 | 1.65 | 1.65 | 1.47 | 0.98 |

**Address:** Two International Place, Boston, MA 02110
**Telephone:** 617-482-8260
**Web Site:** www.eatonvance.com

**Officers:** Thomas E. Faust - Chairman, President, Chief Executive Officer Duncan W. Richardson - Executive Vice President, Chief Equity Investment Officer **Transfer Agents:**
ComputerShare Investor Services, Providence, RI

**Investor Contact:** 617-482-8260
**No of Institutions:** 358
**Shares:** 93,867,232 **% Held:** 73.80

# ECOLAB, INC.

| | Symbol | Price | 52Wk Range | Yield | P/E |
|---|---|---|---|---|---|
| ,e 3 | ECL | $53.60 (8/31/2011) | 56.76-44.53 | 1.31 | 24.14 |

,ce Score 119.04 *NYSE Composite Index=100 *12 Month Price Score 102.11

**Interim Earnings (Per Share)**

| Qtr. | Mar | Jun | Sep | Dec |
|---|---|---|---|---|
| 2008 | 0.41 | 0.55 | 0.50 | 0.34 |
| 2009 | 0.24 | 0.41 | 0.60 | 0.48 |
| 2010 | 0.40 | 0.54 | 0.74 | 0.55 |
| 2011 | 0.40 | 0.53 | ... | ... |

**Interim Dividends (Per Share)**

| Amt | Decl | Ex | Rec | Pay |
|---|---|---|---|---|
| 0.175Q | 12/02/2010 | 12/17/2010 | 12/21/2010 | 01/18/2011 |
| 0.175Q | 02/25/2011 | 03/04/2011 | 03/08/2011 | 04/15/2011 |
| 0.175Q | 05/05/2011 | 06/17/2011 | 06/21/2011 | 07/15/2011 |
| 0.175Q | 08/04/2011 | 09/16/2011 | 09/20/2011 | 10/17/2011 |

**Indicated Div: $0.70 (Div. Reinv. Plan)**

**Valuation Analysis**

| | | | |
|---|---|---|---|
| Forecast EPS | $2.55 (09/03/2011) | | |
| Market Cap | $12.4 Billion | Book Value | $2.3 Billion |
| Price/Book | 5.32 | Price/Sales | 1.96 |

**Dividend Achiever Status**

| | |
|---|---|
| 10 Year Growth Rate | 9.08% |
| Total Years of Dividend Growth | 18 |

**Business Summary:** Specialty Chemicals (MIC: 8.3.2 SIC: 2842 NAIC: 325612)

Ecolab develops and markets products and services for the hospitality, foodservice, healthcare and industrial markets. Co.'s 12 operating segments have been aggregated into three reportable segments: U.S. Cleaning and Sanitizing provides cleaning and sanitizing products to U.S. markets through its Institutional, Food and Beverage, Kay, Textile Care, Healthcare and Vehicle Care divisions; U.S. Co.'s Other Services segment provides pest elimination and kitchen equipment repair and maintenance through its Pest Elimination and GCS Service operating segments; and its International segment includes its operations across Europe, Asia Pacific, Latin America, Canada, Africa and the Middle East.

**Recent Developments:** For the quarter ended June 30 2011, net income decreased 2.5% to US$126.2 million from US$129.5 million in the year-earlier quarter. Revenues were US$1.70 billion, up 11.7% from US$1.52 billion the year before. Operating income was US$198.3 million versus US$204.3 million in the prior-year quarter, a decrease of 2.9%. Direct operating expenses rose 14.8% to US$860.8 million from US$750.0 million in the comparable period the year before. Indirect operating expenses increased 13.0% to US$639.7 million from US$565.9 million in the equivalent prior-year period.

**Prospects:** Our evaluation of Ecolab Inc. as of Sep. 6, 2011 is the result of our systematic analysis on three basic characteristics: earnings strength, relative valuation, and recent stock price movement. The company has managed to produce a neutral trend in earnings per share over the past 5 quarters. However, while recent estimates for the company have been mixed, ECL has posted better than expected results. Based on operating earnings yield, the company is about fairly valued when compared to all of the companies in our coverage universe. Share price changes over the past year indicates that ECL will perform very poorly over the near term.

**Financial Data**

| (US$ in Thousands) | 6 Mos | 3 Mos | 12/31/2010 | 12/31/2009 | 12/31/2008 | 12/31/2007 | 12/31/2006 | 12/31/2005 |
|---|---|---|---|---|---|---|---|---|
| Earnings Per Share | 2.22 | 2.23 | 2.23 | 1.74 | 1.80 | 1.70 | 1.43 | 1.23 |
| Cash Flow Per Share | 3.83 | 3.75 | 4.07 | 2.94 | 3.06 | 3.23 | 2.49 | 2.31 |
| Tang Book Value Per Share | 1.75 | 1.32 | 2.23 | 1.16 | N.M. | 1.33 | 1.67 | 2.00 |
| Dividends Per Share | 0.680 | 0.660 | 0.640 | 0.575 | 0.530 | 0.475 | 0.415 | 0.362 |
| Dividend Payout % | 30.63 | 29.60 | 28.70 | 33.05 | 29.44 | 27.94 | 29.02 | 29.47 |
| **Income Statement** | | | | | | | | |
| Total Revenue | 3,217,100 | 1,518,300 | 6,089,700 | 5,900,600 | 6,137,500 | 5,469,600 | 4,895,814 | 4,534,832 |
| EBITDA | 537,900 | 242,900 | 1,112,800 | 971,300 | 998,500 | 928,200 | 847,442 | 765,132 |
| Depn & Amortn | 187,900 | 91,200 | 306,000 | 290,000 | 286,000 | 260,900 | 235,800 | 222,712 |
| Income Before Taxes | 323,400 | 138,200 | 747,700 | 620,100 | 650,900 | 616,300 | 567,224 | 498,182 |
| Income Taxes | 103,400 | 44,400 | 216,600 | 201,400 | 202,800 | 189,100 | 198,609 | 178,701 |
| Net Income | 219,500 | 93,600 | 530,300 | 417,300 | 448,100 | 427,200 | 368,615 | 319,481 |
| Average Shares | 236,100 | 235,900 | 237,600 | 239,900 | 249,300 | 251,800 | 257,144 | 260,098 |
| **Balance Sheet** | | | | | | | | |
| Current Assets | 1,994,200 | 1,888,900 | 1,869,900 | 1,814,200 | 1,691,100 | 1,717,300 | 1,853,557 | 1,421,666 |
| Total Assets | 5,407,400 | 5,262,300 | 4,872,200 | 5,020,900 | 4,756,900 | 4,722,800 | 4,419,365 | 3,796,628 |
| Current Liabilities | 1,639,600 | 1,650,200 | 1,324,800 | 1,250,200 | 1,441,900 | 1,518,300 | 1,502,730 | 1,119,357 |
| Long-Term Obligations | 703,300 | 683,700 | 656,400 | 868,800 | 799,300 | 599,900 | 557,058 | 519,374 |
| Total Liabilities | 3,069,200 | 3,051,700 | 2,743,000 | 3,020,000 | 3,185,300 | 2,787,100 | 2,739,135 | 2,147,418 |
| Stockholders' Equity | 2,338,200 | 2,210,600 | 2,129,200 | 2,000,900 | 1,571,600 | 1,935,700 | 1,680,230 | 1,649,210 |
| Shares Outstanding | 231,900 | 231,994 | 232,512 | 236,594 | 236,179 | 246,825 | 251,336 | 254,143 |
| **Statistical Record** | | | | | | | | |
| Return on Assets % | 10.43 | 10.53 | 10.72 | 8.54 | 9.43 | 9.35 | 8.97 | 8.50 |
| Return on Equity % | 25.02 | 25.96 | 25.68 | 23.36 | 25.48 | 23.63 | 22.14 | 19.89 |
| EBITDA Margin % | 16.72 | 16.00 | 18.27 | 16.46 | 16.27 | 16.97 | 17.31 | 16.87 |
| Net Margin % | 6.82 | 6.16 | 8.71 | 7.07 | 7.30 | 7.81 | 7.53 | 7.05 |
| Asset Turnover | 1.26 | 1.23 | 1.23 | 1.21 | 1.29 | 1.20 | 1.19 | 1.21 |
| Current Ratio | 1.22 | 1.14 | 1.41 | 1.45 | 1.17 | 1.13 | 1.23 | 1.27 |
| Debt to Equity | 0.30 | 0.31 | 0.31 | 0.43 | 0.51 | 0.31 | 0.33 | 0.31 |
| Price Range | 56.38-44.91 | 52.30-43.95 | 52.30-41.33 | 47.48-29.85 | 51.24-30.62 | 52.30-40.16 | 46.19-33.85 | 36.76-31.06 |
| P/E Ratio | 25.40-20.23 | 23.45-19.71 | 23.45-18.53 | 27.29-17.16 | 28.47-17.01 | 30.76-23.62 | 32.30-23.67 | 29.89-25.25 |
| Average Yield % | 1.36 | 1.36 | 1.36 | 1.45 | 1.21 | 1.07 | 1.02 | 1.10 |

**Address:** 370 Wabasha Street North, St. Paul, MN 55102
**Telephone:** 651-293-2233
**Web Site:** www.ecolab.com

**Officers:** Douglas M. Baker - Chairman, President, Chief Executive Officer Larry L. Berger - Senior Vice President, Chief Technical Officer **Transfer Agents:** Computershare Trust Company, N.A., Canton, MA

**Investor Contact:** 612-293-2809
**No of Institutions:** 682
**Shares:** 207,745,936 **% Held:** 77.01

# EMERSON ELECTRIC CO.

| Exchange | Symbol | Price | 52Wk Range | Yield | P/E |
|---|---|---|---|---|---|
| NYS | EMR | $46.55 (8/31/2011) | 61.85-41.89 | 2.96 | 14.37 |

***7 Year Price Score 125.82** *NYSE Composite Index=100 ***12 Month Price Score 90.55**

**Interim Earnings (Per Share)**

| Qtr. | Dec | Mar | Jun | Sep |
|---|---|---|---|---|
| 2007-08 | 0.71 | 0.69 | 0.78 | 0.88 |
| 2008-09 | 0.60 | 0.49 | 0.51 | 0.67 |
| 2009-10 | 0.56 | 0.53 | 0.77 | 0.98 |
| 2010-11 | 0.63 | 0.73 | 0.90 | ... |

**Interim Dividends (Per Share)**

| Amt | Decl | Ex | Rec | Pay |
|---|---|---|---|---|
| 0.345Q | 11/02/2010 | 11/09/2010 | 11/12/2010 | 12/10/2010 |
| 0.345Q | 02/01/2011 | 02/09/2011 | 02/11/2011 | 03/10/2011 |
| 0.345Q | 05/03/2011 | 05/11/2011 | 05/13/2011 | 06/10/2011 |
| 0.345Q | 08/02/2011 | 08/10/2011 | 08/12/2011 | 09/09/2011 |

**Indicated Div: $1.38 (Div. Reinv. Plan)**

**Valuation Analysis**

| | | | |
|---|---|---|---|
| Forecast EPS | $3.23 (09/05/2011) | | |
| Market Cap | $34.8 Billion | Book Value | $10.8 Billion |
| Price/Book | 3.21 | Price/Sales | 1.52 |

**Dividend Achiever Status**

| | |
|---|---|
| **10 Year Growth Rate** | 5.81% |
| **Total Years of Dividend Growth** | 54 |

**Business Summary:** Electrical Equipment (MIC: 7.3.1 SIC: 3679 NAIC: 334419)

Emerson Electric is a global technology company. Co. has five business segments: Process Management, which provides product technology as well as engineering and project management services; Industrial Automation, which provides motors, power transmission applications, alternators, fluid controls and materials joining equipment; Network Power, which designs, manufactures, installs and maintains power systems; Climate Technologies, which supplies compressors, temperature sensors and controls, thermostats, flow controls and remote monitoring services; and Tools and Storage, which provides tools for professionals and homeowners, home and commercial storage systems, and appliance applications.

**Recent Developments:** For the quarter ended June 30 2011, income from continuing operations increased 16.9% to US$698.0 million from US$597.0 million in the year-earlier quarter. Net income increased 16.1% to US$698.0 million from US$601.0 million in the year-earlier quarter. Revenues were US$6.29 billion, up 16.1% from US$5.42 billion the year before. Direct operating expenses rose 16.5% to US$3.79 billion from US$3.25 billion in the comparable period the year before. Indirect operating expenses increased 16.7% to US$1.36 billion from US$1.17 billion in the equivalent prior-year period.

**Prospects:** Our evaluation of Emerson Electric Co. as of Sep. 6, 2011 is the result of our systematic analysis on three basic characteristics: earnings strength, relative valuation, and recent stock price movement. The company has produced a positive trend in earnings per share over the past 5 quarters. However, while recent estimates for the company have been lowered by analysts, EMR has posted results that fell short of analysts expectations. Based on operating earnings yield, the company is undervalued when compared to all of the companies in our coverage universe. Share price changes over the past year indicates that EMR will perform poorly over the near term.

**Financial Data**

| (US$ in Thousands) | 9 Mos | 6 Mos | 3 Mos | 09/30/2010 | 09/30/2009 | 09/30/2008 | 09/30/2007 | 09/30/2006 |
|---|---|---|---|---|---|---|---|---|
| Earnings Per Share | 3.24 | 3.11 | 2.91 | 2.84 | 2.27 | 3.06 | 2.66 | 2.24 |
| Cash Flow Per Share | 4.34 | 4.05 | 3.89 | 4.39 | 4.09 | 4.21 | 3.80 | 3.08 |
| Tang Book Value Per Share | N.M. | N.M. | N.M. | N.M. | 0.73 | 2.49 | 2.30 | 2.08 |
| Dividends Per Share | 1.370 | 1.360 | 1.350 | 1.340 | 1.320 | 1.200 | 1.050 | 0.890 |
| Dividend Payout % | 42.28 | 43.73 | 46.39 | 47.18 | 58.15 | 39.22 | 39.47 | 39.73 |
| **Income Statement** | | | | | | | | |
| Total Revenue | 17,677,000 | 11,389,000 | 5,535,000 | 21,039,000 | 20,915,000 | 24,807,000 | 22,572,000 | 20,133,000 |
| EBITDA | 2,517,000 | 1,533,000 | 707,000 | 3,878,000 | 3,288,000 | 4,417,000 | 3,923,000 | 3,438,000 |
| Depn & Amortn | (195,000) | (131,000) | (67,000) | 738,000 | 651,000 | 638,000 | 588,000 | 547,000 |
| Income Before Taxes | 2,538,000 | 1,546,000 | 713,000 | 2,879,000 | 2,417,000 | 3,591,000 | 3,107,000 | 2,684,000 |
| Income Taxes | 782,000 | 488,000 | 222,000 | 848,000 | 693,000 | 1,137,000 | 971,000 | 839,000 |
| Net Income | 1,719,000 | 1,036,000 | 480,000 | 2,164,000 | 1,724,000 | 2,412,000 | 2,136,000 | 1,845,000 |
| Average Shares | 753,300 | 757,300 | 758,100 | 757,000 | 758,700 | 789,400 | 803,900 | 824,400 |
| **Balance Sheet** | | | | | | | | |
| Current Assets | 9,283,000 | 8,798,000 | 8,305,000 | 8,363,000 | 7,653,000 | 9,331,000 | 8,065,000 | 7,330,000 |
| Total Assets | 24,104,000 | 23,535,000 | 22,703,000 | 22,843,000 | 19,763,000 | 21,040,000 | 19,680,000 | 18,672,000 |
| Current Liabilities | 6,308,000 | 5,934,000 | 5,600,000 | 5,849,000 | 4,956,000 | 6,573,000 | 5,546,000 | 5,374,000 |
| Long-Term Obligations | 4,353,000 | 4,353,000 | 4,352,000 | 4,586,000 | 3,998,000 | 3,297,000 | 3,372,000 | 3,128,000 |
| Total Liabilities | 13,260,000 | 12,890,000 | 12,533,000 | 13,051,000 | 11,208,000 | 11,927,000 | 10,908,000 | 10,518,000 |
| Stockholders' Equity | 10,844,000 | 10,645,000 | 10,170,000 | 9,792,000 | 8,555,000 | 9,113,000 | 8,772,000 | 8,154,000 |
| Shares Outstanding | 746,860 | 752,690 | 754,113 | 752,690 | 751,872 | 771,216 | 788,434 | 804,693 |
| **Statistical Record** | | | | | | | | |
| Return on Assets % | 10.49 | 10.47 | 10.04 | 10.16 | 8.45 | 11.81 | 11.14 | 10.28 |
| Return on Equity % | 24.97 | 24.31 | 23.41 | 23.59 | 19.52 | 26.90 | 25.24 | 23.72 |
| EBITDA Margin % | 14.24 | 13.46 | 12.77 | 18.43 | 15.72 | 17.81 | 17.38 | 17.08 |
| Net Margin % | 9.72 | 9.10 | 8.67 | 10.29 | 8.24 | 9.72 | 9.46 | 9.16 |
| Asset Turnover | 0.97 | 0.98 | 0.98 | 0.99 | 1.03 | 1.22 | 1.18 | 1.12 |
| Current Ratio | 1.47 | 1.48 | 1.48 | 1.43 | 1.54 | 1.42 | 1.45 | 1.36 |
| Debt to Equity | 0.40 | 0.41 | 0.43 | 0.47 | 0.47 | 0.36 | 0.38 | 0.38 |
| Price Range | 61.85-43.40 | 61.85-43.29 | 58.68-41.54 | 53.62-37.75 | 41.24-24.87 | 58.32-38.46 | 53.37-41.10 | 43.73-33.97 |
| P/E Ratio | 19.09-13.40 | 19.89-13.92 | 20.16-14.27 | 18.88-13.29 | 18.17-10.96 | 19.06-12.57 | 20.06-15.45 | 19.52-15.16 |
| Average Yield % | 2.51 | 2.57 | 2.71 | 2.91 | 3.93 | 2.32 | 2.31 | 2.24 |

**Address:** 8000 W. Florissant Avenue, St. Louis, MO 63136
**Telephone:** 314-553-2000
**Web Site:** www.emerson.com

**Officers:** David N. Farr - Chairman, Chief Executive Officer Walter J. Galvin - Vice-Chairman, Chief Financial Officer **Transfer Agents:** BNY Mellon Shareowner Services LLC, Pittsburgh, PA

**Investor Contact:** 314-553-2197
**No of Institutions:** 1385
**Shares:** 602,209,856 **% Held:** 69.93

# ENERGEN CORP.

| Exchange | Symbol | Price | 52Wk Range | Yield | P/E |
|---|---|---|---|---|---|
| NYS | EGN | $49.10 (8/31/2011) | 65.01-42.68 | 1.10 | 12.85 |

***7 Year Price Score 117.63** *NYSE Composite Index=100 ***12 Month Price Score 103.95**

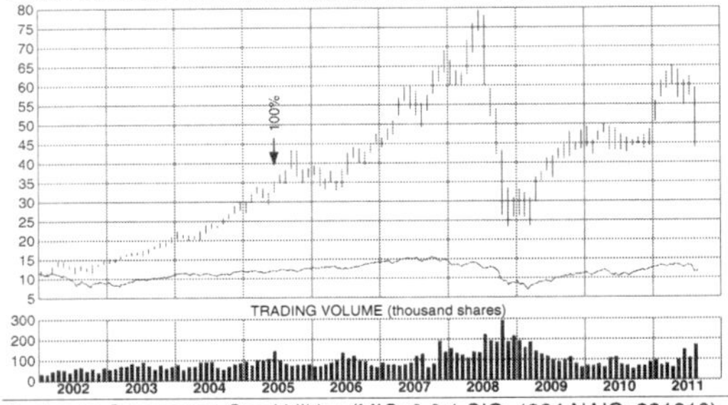


**Interim Earnings (Per Share)**

| Qtr. | Mar | Jun | Sep | Dec |
|---|---|---|---|---|
| 2008 | 1.62 | 0.93 | 1.01 | 0.91 |
| 2009 | 1.33 | 0.76 | 0.65 | 0.82 |
| 2010 | 1.62 | 0.77 | 0.53 | 1.12 |
| 2011 | 1.30 | 0.87 | ... | ... |

**Interim Dividends (Per Share)**

| Amt | Decl | Ex | Rec | Pay |
|---|---|---|---|---|
| 0.13Q | 10/27/2010 | 11/10/2010 | 11/15/2010 | 12/01/2010 |
| 0.135Q | 01/26/2011 | 02/11/2011 | 02/15/2011 | 03/01/2011 |
| 0.135Q | 04/27/2011 | 05/11/2011 | 05/13/2011 | 06/01/2011 |
| 0.135Q | 07/27/2011 | 08/11/2011 | 08/15/2011 | 09/01/2011 |

**Indicated Div: $0.54 (Div. Reinv. Plan)**

**Valuation Analysis**

| | | | |
|---|---|---|---|
| Forecast EPS | $3.95 (09/05/2011) | | |
| Market Cap | $3.5 Billion | Book Value | $2.3 Billion |
| Price/Book | 1.56 | Price/Sales | 2.38 |

**Dividend Achiever Status**

| | |
|---|---|
| **10 Year Growth Rate** | 4.19% |
| **Total Years of Dividend Growth** | 28 |

**Business Summary:** Gas Utilities (MIC: 3.3.1 SIC: 4924 NAIC: 221210)

Energen is an energy holding company. Through its principal subsidiaries, Energen Resources Corporation (Energen Resources) and Alabama Gas Corporation (Alagasco), Co. is engaged in the development, acquisition, exploration and production of oil, natural gas and natural gas liquids in the U.S. and in the purchase, distribution and sale of natural gas in central and north Alabama. As of Dec 31 2010, Energen Resources' proved oil and gas reserves totaled 1.82 trillion cubic feet equivalent, most of which were located in the San Juan Basin, the Permian Basin, and the Black Warrior Basin, and Alagasco served customers in 180 cities and communities in 28 counties.

**Recent Developments:** For the quarter ended June 30 2011, net income increased 14.0% to US$63.3 million from US$55.5 million in the year-earlier quarter. Revenues were US$330.4 million, down 1.0% from US$333.7 million the year before. Operating income was US$106.3 million versus US$98.3 million in the prior-year quarter, an increase of 8.2%. Direct operating expenses declined 11.4% to US$135.7 million from US$153.2 million in the comparable period the year before. Indirect operating expenses increased 7.5% to US$88.4 million from US$82.3 million in the equivalent prior-year period.

**Prospects:** Our evaluation of Energen Corp. as of Sep. 6, 2011 is the result of our systematic analysis on three basic characteristics: earnings strength, relative valuation, and recent stock price movement. The company has generated a negative trend in earnings per share over the past 5 quarters and while recent estimates for the company have been raised by analysts, EGN has posted better than expected results. Based on operating earnings yield, the company is undervalued when compared to all of the companies in our coverage universe. Share price changes over the past year indicates that EGN will perform well over the near term.

| **Financial Data** (US$ in Thousands) | 6 Mos | 3 Mos | 12/31/2010 | 12/31/2009 | 12/31/2008 | 12/31/2007 | 12/31/2006 | 12/31/2005 |
|---|---|---|---|---|---|---|---|---|
| Earnings Per Share | 3.82 | 3.72 | 4.04 | 3.57 | 4.47 | 4.28 | 3.73 | 2.35 |
| Cash Flow Per Share | 9.87 | 9.23 | 9.34 | 9.48 | 7.93 | 6.76 | 6.66 | 4.59 |
| Tang Book Value Per Share | 31.37 | 29.86 | 30.02 | 27.77 | 26.74 | 19.47 | 17.06 | 12.15 |
| Dividends Per Share | 0.530 | 0.525 | 0.520 | 0.500 | 0.480 | 0.460 | 0.440 | 0.400 |
| Dividend Payout % | 13.87 | 14.11 | 12.87 | 14.01 | 10.74 | 10.75 | 11.80 | 17.02 |
| **Income Statement** | | | | | | | | |
| Total Revenue | 816,763 | 486,364 | 1,578,534 | 1,440,420 | 1,568,910 | 1,435,060 | 1,393,986 | 1,128,394 |
| EBITDA | 375,839 | 222,076 | 744,884 | 674,759 | 745,352 | 685,118 | 619,291 | 448,896 |
| Depn & Amortn | 126,757 | 61,128 | 247,865 | 235,084 | 188,413 | 161,377 | 142,086 | 131,719 |
| Income Before Taxes | 249,082 | 151,544 | 457,797 | 400,296 | 514,958 | 476,641 | 428,553 | 270,377 |
| Income Taxes | 91,489 | 57,276 | 166,990 | 143,971 | 193,043 | 167,429 | 155,030 | 97,491 |
| Net Income | 157,593 | 94,268 | 290,807 | 256,325 | 321,915 | 309,233 | 273,570 | 173,012 |
| Average Shares | 72,420 | 72,240 | 72,050 | 71,885 | 72,030 | 72,180 | 73,278 | 73,714 |
| **Balance Sheet** | | | | | | | | |
| Current Assets | 342,936 | 429,928 | 486,283 | 515,606 | 643,041 | 449,030 | 489,579 | 478,491 |
| Total Assets | 4,511,394 | 4,389,465 | 4,363,560 | 3,803,118 | 3,775,404 | 3,079,653 | 2,836,887 | 2,618,226 |
| Current Liabilities | 784,315 | 785,494 | 818,611 | 520,761 | 510,101 | 606,230 | 570,642 | 688,309 |
| Long-Term Obligations | 404,980 | 405,232 | 405,254 | 410,786 | 561,631 | 562,365 | 582,490 | 683,236 |
| Total Liabilities | 2,253,956 | 2,240,948 | 2,209,517 | 1,814,875 | 1,862,114 | 1,700,995 | 1,634,818 | 1,725,548 |
| Stockholders' Equity | 2,257,438 | 2,148,517 | 2,154,043 | 1,988,243 | 1,913,290 | 1,378,658 | 1,202,069 | 892,678 |
| Shares Outstanding | 71,952 | 71,946 | 71,761 | 71,602 | 71,544 | 70,816 | 70,445 | 73,493 |
| **Statistical Record** | | | | | | | | |
| Return on Assets % | 6.48 | 6.37 | 7.12 | 6.76 | 9.37 | 10.45 | 10.03 | 7.21 |
| Return on Equity % | 12.43 | 12.55 | 14.04 | 13.14 | 19.50 | 23.96 | 26.12 | 20.40 |
| EBITDA Margin % | 46.02 | 45.66 | 47.19 | 46.84 | 47.51 | 47.74 | 44.43 | 39.78 |
| Net Margin % | 19.29 | 19.38 | 18.42 | 17.80 | 20.52 | 21.55 | 19.63 | 15.33 |
| Asset Turnover | 0.35 | 0.35 | 0.39 | 0.38 | 0.46 | 0.49 | 0.51 | 0.47 |
| Current Ratio | 0.44 | 0.55 | 0.59 | 0.99 | 1.26 | 0.74 | 0.86 | 0.70 |
| Debt to Equity | 0.18 | 0.19 | 0.19 | 0.21 | 0.29 | 0.41 | 0.48 | 0.77 |
| Price Range | 65.01-42.59 | 63.36-42.59 | 49.76-42.08 | 48.26-23.57 | 79.40-23.30 | 69.18-43.99 | 47.38-32.77 | 43.40-27.14 |
| P/E Ratio | 17.02-11.15 | 17.03-11.45 | 12.32-10.42 | 13.52-6.60 | 17.76-5.21 | 16.16-10.28 | 12.70-8.79 | 18.47-11.55 |
| Average Yield % | 1.02 | 1.08 | 1.13 | 1.32 | 0.86 | 0.83 | 1.13 | 1.15 |

**Address:** 605 Richard Arrington Jr. Boulevard North, Birmingham, AL 35203-2707
**Telephone:** 205-326-2700
**Web Site:** www.energen.com

**Officers:** James T. McManus - Chairman, President, Chief Executive Officer, Chief Operating Officer Charles W. Porter - Vice President, Chief Financial Officer, Treasurer **Transfer Agents:** BNY Mellon Shareowner Services, Jersey City, NJ

**Investor Contact:** 205-326-8421
**No of Institutions:** 377
**Shares:** 60,699,068 **% Held:** 71.47

# ENTERPRISE PRODUCTS PARTNERS L.P.

| Exchange | Symbol | Price | 52Wk Range | Yield | P/E |
|---|---|---|---|---|---|
| NYS | EPD | $42.15 (8/31/2011) | 44.30-36.97 | 5.63 | 35.72 |

***7 Year Price Score 137.79** *NYSE Composite Index=100 ***12 Month Price Score 100.30**

**Interim Earnings (Per Share)**

| Qtr. | Mar | Jun | Sep | Dec |
|---|---|---|---|---|
| 2008 | 0.51 | 0.52 | 0.38 | 0.43 |
| 2009 | 0.41 | 0.32 | 0.36 | 0.64 |
| 2010 | 0.50 | 0.46 | 0.47 | (0.29) |
| 2011 | 0.49 | 0.51 | ... | ... |

**Interim Dividends (Per Share)**

| Amt | Decl | Ex | Rec | Pay |
|---|---|---|---|---|
| 0.583Q | 10/14/2010 | 10/27/2010 | 10/29/2010 | 11/08/2010 |
| 0.59Q | 01/14/2011 | 01/27/2011 | 01/31/2011 | 02/07/2011 |
| 0.598Q | 04/14/2011 | 04/27/2011 | 04/29/2011 | 05/06/2011 |
| 0.605Q | 07/15/2011 | 07/27/2011 | 07/29/2011 | 08/10/2011 |

**Indicated Div: $2.38 (Div. Reinv. Plan)**

**Valuation Analysis**

| | | | |
|---|---|---|---|
| Forecast EPS | $1.97 (09/05/2011) | | |
| Market Cap | $35.8 Billion | Book Value | N/A |
| Price/Book | N/A | Price/Sales | 0.92 |

**Dividend Achiever Status**

| | |
|---|---|
| 10 Year Growth Rate | 7.05% |
| Total Years of Dividend Growth | 12 |

**Business Summary:** Equipment & Services (MIC: 9.1.3 SIC: 4922 NAIC: 486210)

Enterprise Products Partners is a North American midstream energy company providing a range of services to producers and consumers of natural gas, natural gas liquids (NGLs), crude oil and certain petrochemicals. Co.'s midstream energy operations include: natural gas gathering, treating, processing, transportation and storage; NGL transportation, fractionation, storage, and import and export terminaling; crude oil and refined products transportation, storage, and terminaling; offshore production platforms; petrochemical transportation and services; and a marine transportation business that operates primarily on the U.S. inland and Intracoastal Waterway systems and in the Gulf of Mexico.

**Recent Developments:** For the quarter ended June 30 2011, net income increased 26.6% to US$448.5 million from US$354.4 million in the year-earlier quarter. Revenues were US$11.22 billion, up 48.7% from US$7.54 billion the year before. Operating income was US$643.9 million versus US$539.7 million in the prior-year quarter, an increase of 19.3%. Direct operating expenses rose 51.0% to US$10.53 billion from US$6.97 billion in the comparable period the year before. Indirect operating expenses increased 33.2% to US$39.3 million from US$29.5 million in the equivalent prior-year period.

**Prospects:** Our evaluation of Enterprise Products Partners L.P. as of Sep. 6, 2011 is the result of our systematic analysis on three basic characteristics: earnings strength, relative valuation, and recent stock price movement. The company has enjoyed a very positive trend in earnings per share over the past 5 quarters and while recent estimates for the company have been raised by analysts, EPD has posted better than expected results. Based on operating earnings yield, the company is about fairly valued when compared to all of the companies in our coverage universe. Share price changes over the past year indicates that EPD will perform very poorly over the near term.

**Financial Data**

| (US$ in Thousands) | 6 Mos | 3 Mos | 12/31/2010 | 12/31/2009 | 12/31/2008 | 12/31/2007 | 12/31/2006 | 12/31/2005 |
|---|---|---|---|---|---|---|---|---|
| Earnings Per Share | 1.18 | 1.13 | 1.15 | 1.73 | 1.85 | 0.96 | 1.22 | 0.91 |
| Cash Flow Per Share | 3.87 | 2.97 | 8.38 | 4.88 | 2.82 | 3.67 | 2.84 | 1.65 |
| Dividends Per Share | 2.345 | 2.315 | 2.285 | 2.165 | 2.045 | 1.915 | 1.795 | 1.660 |
| Dividend Payout % | 198.73 | 204.87 | 198.70 | 125.14 | 110.54 | 199.48 | 147.13 | 182.42 |
| **Income Statement** | | | | | | | | |
| Total Revenue | 21,400,200 | 10,183,700 | 33,739,300 | 25,510,900 | 21,905,656 | 16,950,125 | 13,990,969 | 12,256,959 |
| EBITDA | 1,618,000 | 795,400 | 2,833,600 | 2,446,800 | 1,823,911 | 1,267,980 | 1,189,754 | 982,539 |
| Depn & Amortn | 376,300 | 186,500 | 745,700 | 678,100 | 466,054 | 414,901 | 350,800 | 328,700 |
| Income Before Taxes | 870,200 | 425,400 | 1,347,800 | 1,129,200 | 962,694 | 549,916 | 608,520 | 423,290 |
| Income Taxes | 14,500 | 7,100 | 26,100 | 25,300 | 26,401 | 15,257 | 21,323 | 8,362 |
| Net Income | 854,400 | 420,700 | 320,800 | 1,030,900 | 954,021 | 533,674 | 601,155 | 419,508 |
| Average Shares | 851,400 | 850,300 | 278,500 | 487,800 | 437,582 | 434,427 | 414,759 | 382,963 |
| **Balance Sheet** | | | | | | | | |
| Current Assets | 5,938,500 | 5,446,800 | 5,507,100 | 4,246,900 | 2,163,720 | 2,537,885 | 1,922,158 | 1,971,447 |
| Total Assets | 32,978,400 | 31,821,200 | 31,360,800 | 26,151,600 | 17,957,535 | 16,608,007 | 13,989,718 | 12,591,016 |
| Current Liabilities | 7,358,800 | 6,458,100 | 5,880,200 | 4,536,000 | 2,223,149 | 3,044,683 | 1,984,921 | 1,890,271 |
| Long-Term Obligations | 13,544,700 | 13,273,600 | 13,281,200 | 11,346,400 | 9,108,410 | 6,906,145 | 5,295,590 | 4,833,781 |
| Total Liabilities | 21,724,200 | 20,544,300 | 19,986,600 | 16,639,500 | 11,872,547 | 10,476,358 | 7,509,485 | 6,911,707 |
| Shares Outstanding | 850,356 | 849,951 | 848,202 | 610,444 | 441,435 | 435,297 | 432,408 | 389,109 |
| **Statistical Record** | | | | | | | | |
| Return on Assets % | 1.44 | 1.25 | 1.12 | 4.67 | 5.50 | 3.49 | 4.52 | 3.51 |
| EBITDA Margin % | 7.56 | 7.81 | 8.40 | 9.59 | 8.33 | 7.48 | 8.50 | 8.02 |
| Net Margin % | 3.99 | 4.13 | 0.95 | 4.04 | 4.36 | 3.15 | 4.30 | 3.42 |
| Asset Turnover | 1.27 | 1.21 | 1.17 | 1.16 | 1.26 | 1.11 | 1.05 | 1.03 |
| Current Ratio | 0.81 | 0.84 | 0.94 | 0.94 | 0.97 | 0.83 | 0.97 | 1.04 |
| Price Range | 44.30-34.76 | 44.30-31.68 | 44.30-30.34 | 32.15-17.95 | 32.48-17.26 | 33.33-28.00 | 29.80-23.90 | 27.70-23.47 |
| P/E Ratio | 37.54-29.46 | 39.20-28.04 | 38.52-26.38 | 18.58-10.38 | 17.56-9.33 | 34.72-29.17 | 24.43-19.59 | 30.44-25.79 |
| Average Yield % | 5.73 | 5.91 | 6.23 | 8.38 | 7.36 | 6.16 | 6.90 | 6.41 |

| | | |
|---|---|---|
| **Address:** 1100 Louisiana Street, 10th Floor, Houston, TX 77002<br>**Telephone:** 713-381-6500<br>**Web Site:** www.epplp.com | **Officers:** Ralph S. Cunningham - Chairman Michael A. Creel - President, Chief Executive Officer<br>**Transfer Agents:**Mellon Investor Services LLC, Jersey City, NJ | **No of Institutions:** 608<br>**Shares:** 192,429,872 **% Held:** 20.84 |

# EOG RESOURCES, INC.

| Exchange | Symbol | Price | 52Wk Range | Yield | P/E |
|---|---|---|---|---|---|
| NYS | EOG | $92.59 (8/31/2011) | 119.67-86.35 | 0.69 | 59.74 |

***7 Year Price Score 125.78** *NYSE Composite Index=100 ***12 Month Price Score 97.55**

**Interim Earnings (Per Share)**

| Qtr. | Mar | Jun | Sep | Dec |
|---|---|---|---|---|
| 2008 | 0.96 | 0.71 | 6.20 | 1.84 |
| 2009 | 0.63 | (0.07) | 0.02 | 1.59 |
| 2010 | 0.46 | 0.24 | (0.28) | 0.21 |
| 2011 | 0.52 | 1.10 | ... | ... |

**Interim Dividends (Per Share)**

| Amt | Decl | Ex | Rec | Pay |
|---|---|---|---|---|
| 0.155Q | 09/09/2010 | 10/13/2010 | 10/15/2010 | 10/29/2010 |
| 0.155Q | 12/14/2010 | 01/12/2011 | 01/14/2011 | 01/31/2011 |
| 0.16Q | 02/17/2011 | 04/13/2011 | 04/15/2011 | 04/29/2011 |
| 0.16Q | 05/04/2011 | 07/13/2011 | 07/15/2011 | 07/29/2011 |

**Indicated Div: $0.64**

**Valuation Analysis**

| | | | |
|---|---|---|---|
| Forecast EPS | $3.64 (09/05/2011) | | |
| Market Cap | $24.9 Billion | Book Value | $12.1 Billion |
| Price/Book | 2.06 | Price/Sales | 3.17 |

**Dividend Achiever Status**

| | |
|---|---|
| **10 Year Growth Rate** | 22.91% |
| **Total Years of Dividend Growth** | 11 |

**Business Summary:** Production & Extraction (MIC: 9.1.1 SIC: 1311 NAIC: 211111)

EOG Resources, together with its subsidiaries, explores for, develops, produces and markets crude oil and natural gas mainly in major producing basins in the U.S., Canada, Trinidad and Tobago, the U.K., China and other international areas. At Dec 31 2010, Co.'s total estimated net proved reserves were 1,950.0 million barrels of oil equivalent (MMBoe), of which 386.0 million barrels (MMBbl) were crude oil and condensate reserves, 152.0 MMBbl were natural gas liquids reserves and 8,470.00 billion cubic feet, or 1,412.0 MMBoe, were natural gas reserves. At such date, about 82.0% of Co.'s reserves (on a crude oil equivalent basis) were located in the U.S., 11.0% in Canada and 7.0% in Trinidad.

**Recent Developments:** For the quarter ended June 30 2011, net income increased 393.7% to US$295.6 million from US$59.9 million in the year-earlier quarter. Revenues were US$2.57 billion, up 89.3% from US$1.36 billion the year before. Operating income was US$588.3 million versus US$140.5 million in the prior-year quarter, an increase of 318.7%. Direct operating expenses rose 25.4% to US$336.4 million from US$268.3 million in the comparable period the year before. Indirect operating expenses increased 73.4% to US$1.65 billion from US$949.2 million in the equivalent prior-year period.

**Prospects:** Our evaluation of EOG Resources Inc. as of Sep. 6, 2011 is the result of our systematic analysis on three basic characteristics: earnings strength, relative valuation, and recent stock price movement. The company has enjoyed a very positive trend in earnings per share over the past 5 quarters. However, while recent estimates for the company have been lowered by analysts, EOG has posted better than expected results. Based on operating earnings yield, the company is overvalued when compared to all of the companies in our coverage universe. Share price changes over the past year indicates that EOG will perform in line with the market over the near term.

**Financial Data**

| (US$ in Thousands) | 6 Mos | 3 Mos | 12/31/2010 | 12/31/2009 | 12/31/2008 | 12/31/2007 | 12/31/2006 | 12/31/2005 |
|---|---|---|---|---|---|---|---|---|
| Earnings Per Share | 1.55 | 0.69 | 0.63 | 2.17 | 9.72 | 4.37 | 5.24 | 5.13 |
| Cash Flow Per Share | 13.08 | 11.93 | 10.80 | 11.74 | 18.73 | 11.88 | 10.66 | 9.92 |
| Tang Book Value Per Share | 44.97 | 43.92 | 40.27 | 39.59 | 36.11 | 28.33 | 22.76 | 17.42 |
| Dividends Per Share | 0.625 | 0.620 | 0.610 | 0.570 | 0.465 | 0.330 | 0.220 | 0.150 |
| Dividend Payout % | 40.32 | 89.86 | 96.83 | 26.27 | 4.78 | 7.55 | 4.20 | 2.92 |
| **Income Statement** | | | | | | | | |
| Total Revenue | 4,467,356 | 1,897,106 | 6,099,896 | 4,786,959 | 7,127,143 | 4,190,791 | 3,904,415 | 3,620,213 |
| EBITDA | 2,041,702 | 844,281 | 2,479,488 | 2,522,100 | 5,125,072 | 2,743,191 | 2,772,888 | 2,681,901 |
| Depn & Amortn | 1,171,170 | 568,226 | 1,941,926 | 1,549,188 | 1,326,875 | 1,065,545 | 817,089 | 654,258 |
| Income Before Taxes | 768,946 | 225,722 | 407,976 | 872,011 | 3,746,539 | 1,630,868 | 1,912,641 | 1,965,137 |
| Income Taxes | 339,399 | 91,749 | 247,322 | 325,384 | 1,309,620 | 540,950 | 612,756 | 705,561 |
| Net Income | 429,547 | 133,973 | 160,654 | 546,627 | 2,436,919 | 1,089,918 | 1,299,885 | 1,259,576 |
| Average Shares | 269,332 | 258,819 | 254,500 | 251,884 | 250,542 | 247,637 | 246,100 | 243,975 |
| **Balance Sheet** | | | | | | | | |
| Current Assets | 3,637,950 | 3,597,603 | 2,527,446 | 1,839,541 | 2,108,451 | 1,292,039 | 1,350,080 | 1,563,238 |
| Total Assets | 23,959,379 | 23,545,522 | 21,624,233 | 18,118,667 | 15,951,226 | 12,088,907 | 9,402,160 | 7,753,320 |
| Current Liabilities | 2,476,238 | 2,500,191 | 2,220,099 | 1,345,560 | 1,764,916 | 1,474,170 | 1,255,012 | 1,172,041 |
| Long-Term Obligations | 5,006,251 | 5,004,725 | 5,003,341 | 2,760,000 | 1,860,000 | 1,185,000 | 733,442 | 858,992 |
| Total Liabilities | 11,882,194 | 11,757,143 | 11,392,601 | 8,120,625 | 6,936,729 | 5,098,813 | 3,802,489 | 3,437,028 |
| Stockholders' Equity | 12,077,185 | 11,788,379 | 10,231,632 | 9,998,042 | 9,014,497 | 6,990,094 | 5,599,671 | 4,316,292 |
| Shares Outstanding | 268,555 | 268,419 | 254,077 | 252,508 | 249,631 | 246,524 | 243,735 | 242,074 |
| **Statistical Record** | | | | | | | | |
| Return on Assets % | 1.90 | 0.84 | 0.81 | 3.21 | 17.33 | 10.14 | 15.15 | 18.59 |
| Return on Equity % | 3.71 | 1.61 | 1.59 | 5.75 | 30.37 | 17.31 | 26.22 | 34.69 |
| EBITDA Margin % | 45.70 | 44.50 | 40.65 | 52.69 | 71.91 | 65.46 | 71.02 | 74.08 |
| Net Margin % | 9.62 | 7.06 | 2.63 | 11.42 | 34.19 | 26.01 | 33.29 | 34.79 |
| Asset Turnover | 0.36 | 0.32 | 0.31 | 0.28 | 0.51 | 0.39 | 0.46 | 0.53 |
| Current Ratio | 1.47 | 1.44 | 1.14 | 1.37 | 1.19 | 0.88 | 1.08 | 1.33 |
| Debt to Equity | 0.41 | 0.42 | 0.49 | 0.28 | 0.21 | 0.17 | 0.13 | 0.20 |
| Price Range | 119.67-86.62 | 119.67-86.62 | 113.72-86.62 | 100.58-45.59 | 143.41-59.59 | 91.02-59.96 | 84.81-57.36 | 80.84-32.48 |
| P/E Ratio | 77.21-55.88 | 173.43-125.54 | 180.51-137.49 | 46.35-21.01 | 14.75-6.13 | 20.83-13.72 | 16.19-10.95 | 15.76-6.33 |
| Average Yield % | 0.62 | 0.62 | 0.63 | 0.78 | 0.46 | 0.44 | 0.32 | 0.26 |

**Address:** 1111 Bagby, Sky Lobby 2, Houston, TX 77002
**Telephone:** 713-651-7000
**Web Site:** www.eogresources.com

**Officers:** Mark G. Papa - Chairman, Chief Executive Officer Gary L. Thomas - Senior Executive Vice President **Transfer Agents:** Computershare Trust Company, N.A., Providence, RI

**Investor Contact:** 713-651-7000
**No of Institutions:** 674
**Shares:** 281,919,456 **% Held:** 95.24

# ERIE INDEMNITY CO.

| Exchange | Symbol | Price | 52Wk Range | Yield | P/E |
|---|---|---|---|---|---|
| NMS | ERIE | $73.53 (8/31/2011) | 74.73-52.50 | 2.80 | 25.44 |

***7 Year Price Score 129.09** *NYSE Composite Index=100 ***12 Month Price Score 107.63**

**Interim Earnings (Per Share)**

| Qtr. | Mar | Jun | Sep | Dec |
|---|---|---|---|---|
| 2008 | 0.51 | 0.71 | 0.07 | (0.11) |
| 2009 | 0.19 | 0.57 | 0.69 | 0.43 |
| 2010 | 0.82 | 0.86 | 0.94 | 0.23 |
| 2011 | 0.78 | 0.94 | ... | ... |

**Interim Dividends (Per Share)**

| Amt | Decl | Ex | Rec | Pay |
|---|---|---|---|---|
| 0.515Q | 12/07/2010 | 01/03/2011 | 01/05/2011 | 01/20/2011 |
| 0.515Q | 02/24/2011 | 04/04/2011 | 04/06/2011 | 04/20/2011 |
| 0.515Q | 04/19/2011 | 07/01/2011 | 07/06/2011 | 07/20/2011 |
| 0.515Q | 08/02/2011 | 10/04/2011 | 10/06/2011 | 10/20/2011 |

**Indicated Div: $2.06**

**Valuation Analysis**

| | | | |
|---|---|---|---|
| Forecast EPS | $3.10 (09/02/2011) | | |
| Market Cap | $3.6 Billion | Book Value | $866.0 Million |
| Price/Book | 4.14 | Price/Sales | 0.67 |

**Dividend Achiever Status**

| | |
|---|---|
| **10 Year Growth Rate** | 12.15% |
| **Total Years of Dividend Growth** | 15 |

**Business Summary:** General Insurance (MIC: 5.2.1 SIC: 6411 NAIC: 524126)

Erie Indemnity is the managing attorney-in-fact for the subscribers at Erie Insurance Exchange (Exchange). The Exchange is a subscriber (policyholder) owned Pennsylvania-domiciled reciprocal insurer that writes property/casualty insurance. Co.'s primary function is to perform certain services for the Exchange relating to sales, underwriting and issuance of policies on behalf of the Exchange.

**Recent Developments:** For the quarter ended June 30 2011, net loss amounted to US$107.0 million versus a net loss of US$31.0 million in the year-earlier quarter. Revenues were US$1.25 billion, up 35.9% from US$916.0 million the year before. Net premiums earned were US$1.05 billion versus US$989.0 million in the prior-year quarter, an increase of 5.9%. Net investment income rose 4.6% to US$113.0 million from US$108.0 million a year ago.

**Prospects:** Our evaluation of Erie Indemnity Co. as of Sep. 6, 2011 is the result of our systematic analysis on three basic characteristics: earnings strength, relative valuation, and recent stock price movement. The company has managed to produce a neutral trend in earnings per share over the past 5 quarters. Because the company lacks sufficient analyst estimate data, we place greater weight on the historical EPS trend as the measure of earnings strength. Based on operating earnings yield, the company is overvalued when compared to all of the companies in our coverage universe. Share price changes over the past year indicates that ERIE will perform poorly over the near term.

**Financial Data**

| (US$ in Thousands) | 6 Mos | 3 Mos | 12/31/2010 | 12/31/2009 | 12/31/2008 | 12/31/2007 | 12/31/2006 | 12/31/2005 |
|---|---|---|---|---|---|---|---|---|
| Earnings Per Share | 2.89 | 2.81 | 2.85 | 1.89 | 1.19 | 3.43 | 3.31 | 3.34 |
| Cash Flow Per Share | 14.40 | 15.79 | 14.22 | 3.52 | 2.90 | 4.44 | 4.60 | 4.83 |
| Tang Book Value Per Share | 17.76 | 18.03 | 18.22 | 17.61 | 15.44 | 19.71 | 20.11 | 20.90 |
| Dividends Per Share | 1.990 | 1.955 | 1.920 | 1.830 | 1.760 | 1.600 | 1.440 | 1.300 |
| Dividend Payout % | 68.86 | 69.57 | 67.37 | 96.83 | 147.90 | 46.65 | 43.50 | 38.92 |
| **Income Statement** | | | | | | | | |
| Premium Income | 2,077,000 | 1,030,000 | 3,987,000 | 209,457 | 207,407 | 207,562 | 213,665 | 215,824 |
| Total Revenue | 2,610,000 | 1,365,000 | 4,890,000 | 1,120,220 | 1,074,103 | 1,239,622 | 1,233,003 | 1,240,187 |
| Benefits & Claims | 1,876,000 | 706,000 | 2,900,000 | 145,452 | 137,167 | 125,903 | 139,630 | 140,385 |
| Income Before Taxes | 238,000 | 412,000 | 999,000 | 152,075 | 122,706 | 309,168 | 298,799 | 339,456 |
| Income Taxes | 71,000 | 138,000 | 339,000 | 48,787 | 39,865 | 99,137 | 99,055 | 111,733 |
| Net Income | 96,000 | 44,000 | 162,000 | 108,490 | 69,238 | 212,945 | 204,025 | 231,104 |
| Average Shares | 55,436 | 55,968 | 56,884 | 57,385 | 57,967 | 62,096 | 65,256 | 69,293 |
| **Balance Sheet** | | | | | | | | |
| Total Assets | 14,723,000 | 14,553,000 | 14,344,000 | 2,666,517 | 2,613,386 | 2,878,623 | 3,039,361 | 3,101,261 |
| Total Liabilities | 13,857,000 | 13,660,000 | 13,432,000 | 1,764,540 | 1,821,511 | 1,827,344 | 1,877,513 | 1,822,659 |
| Stockholders' Equity | 866,000 | 893,000 | 912,000 | 901,977 | 791,875 | 1,051,279 | 1,161,848 | 1,278,602 |
| Shares Outstanding | 48,756 | 49,525 | 50,057 | 51,206 | 51,285 | 53,341 | 57,778 | 61,165 |
| **Statistical Record** | | | | | | | | |
| Return on Assets % | 1.15 | 1.14 | 1.90 | 4.11 | 2.51 | 7.20 | 6.65 | 7.60 |
| Return on Equity % | 17.94 | 17.46 | 17.86 | 12.81 | 7.49 | 19.24 | 16.72 | 18.16 |
| Loss Ratio % | 90.32 | 68.54 | 72.74 | 69.44 | 66.13 | 60.66 | 65.35 | 65.05 |
| Net Margin % | 3.68 | 3.22 | 3.31 | 9.68 | 6.45 | 17.18 | 16.55 | 18.63 |
| Price Range | 72.44-44.38 | 71.11-42.59 | 65.47-38.03 | 40.18-28.57 | 56.04-31.52 | 61.31-50.94 | 58.19-48.58 | 54.83-50.15 |
| P/E Ratio | 25.07-15.36 | 25.31-15.16 | 22.97-13.34 | 21.26-15.12 | 47.09-26.49 | 17.87-14.85 | 17.58-14.68 | 16.42-15.01 |
| Average Yield % | 3.19 | 3.48 | 3.71 | 5.09 | 4.02 | 2.91 | 2.76 | 2.47 |

| | | |
|---|---|---|
| **Address:** 100 Erie Insurance Place, Erie, PA 16530<br>**Telephone:** 814-870-2000<br>**Web Site:** www.erieinsurance.com | **Officers:** Thomas B. Hagen - Chairman Terrence W. Cavanaugh - President, Chief Executive Officer<br>**Transfer Agents:** American Stock Transfer & Trust Company, New York, NY | **No of Institutions:** 154<br>**Shares:** 26,020,388 **% Held:** 26.63 |

# ESSEX PROPERTY TRUST, INC.

| Exchange | Symbol | Price | 52Wk Range | Yield | P/E |
|---|---|---|---|---|---|
| NYS | ESS | $143.55 (8/31/2011) | 143.55-105.77 | 2.90 | 151.11 |

*7 Year Price Score 120.08 *NYSE Composite Index=100 *12 Month Price Score 112.16

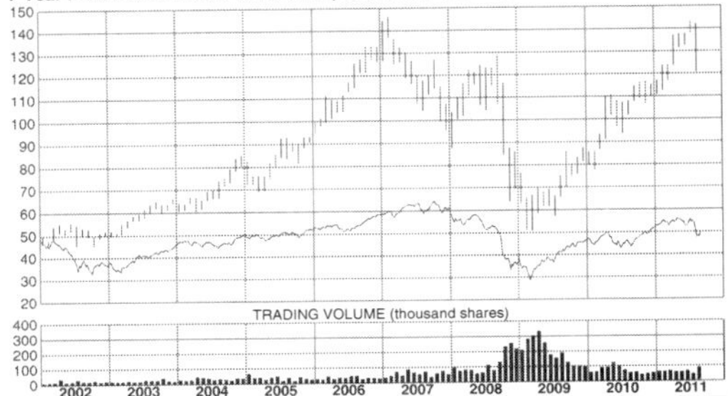

**Interim Earnings (Per Share)**

| Qtr. | Mar | Jun | Sep | Dec |
|---|---|---|---|---|
| 2008 | 0.63 | 0.38 | 0.49 | 0.71 |
| 2009 | 1.53 | 0.43 | 0.74 | 0.22 |
| 2010 | 0.45 | 0.32 | 0.21 | 0.15 |
| 2011 | 0.27 | 0.32 | ... | ... |

**Interim Dividends (Per Share)**

| Amt | Decl | Ex | Rec | Pay |
|---|---|---|---|---|
| 1.033Q | 09/15/2010 | 09/28/2010 | 09/30/2010 | 10/15/2010 |
| 1.033Q | 12/15/2010 | 12/30/2010 | 01/03/2011 | 01/14/2011 |
| 1.04Q | 02/23/2011 | 03/29/2011 | 03/31/2011 | 04/15/2011 |
| 1.04Q | 05/31/2011 | 06/28/2011 | 06/30/2011 | 07/15/2011 |

**Indicated Div: $4.16 (Div. Reinv. Plan)**

**Valuation Analysis**

| | | | |
|---|---|---|---|
| Forecast EPS | $1.16 (09/05/2011) | | |
| Market Cap | $4.7 Billion | Book Value | $1.3 Billion |
| Price/Book | 3.53 | Price/Sales | 10.56 |

**Dividend Achiever Status**

| | |
|---|---|
| 10 Year Growth Rate | 4.30% |
| Total Years of Dividend Growth | 16 |

**Business Summary:** REITs (MIC: 5.3.1 SIC: 6798 NAIC: 525930)

Essex Property Trust is a real estate investment trust. Co. is primarily engaged in the ownership, operation, management, acquisition, development and redevelopment of apartment communities directly or indirectly through Essex Portfolio, L.P. (the Operating Partnership). As of Dec 31 2010, Co. was the sole general partner of the Operating Partnership and owned a 93.4% general partnership interest. As of the same date, Co. owned or held an interest in 147 apartment communities, aggregating 30,072 units, located along the West Coast, as well as five commercial buildings (totaling approximately 215,840 square feet), and two development projects with 436 units under development.

**Recent Developments:** For the quarter ended June 30 2011, income from continuing operations decreased 21.9% to US$10.7 million from US$13.7 million in the year-earlier quarter. Net income increased 15.7% to US$16.1 million from US$13.9 million in the year-earlier quarter. Revenues were US$117.2 million, up 17.0% from US$100.2 million the year before. Revenues from property income rose 16.8% to US$115.8 million from US$99.2 million in the corresponding quarter a year earlier.

**Prospects:** Our evaluation of Essex Property Trust Inc. as of Sep. 6, 2011 is the result of our systematic analysis on three basic characteristics: earnings strength, relative valuation, and recent stock price movement. The company has enjoyed a very positive trend in earnings per share over the past 5 quarters. Because the company lacks sufficient analyst estimate data, we place greater weight on the historical EPS trend as the measure of earnings strength. Based on operating earnings yield, the company is overvalued when compared to all of the companies in our coverage universe. Share price changes over the past year indicates that ESS will perform poorly over the near term.

| Financial Data (US$ in Thousands) | 6 Mos | 3 Mos | 12/31/2010 | 12/31/2009 | 12/31/2008 | 12/31/2007 | 12/31/2006 | 12/31/2005 |
|---|---|---|---|---|---|---|---|---|
| Earnings Per Share | 0.95 | 0.95 | 1.14 | 2.91 | 2.21 | 4.24 | 2.45 | 3.32 |
| Cash Flow Per Share | 5.94 | 5.72 | 5.92 | 6.37 | 7.17 | 7.78 | 6.93 | 5.41 |
| Tang Book Value Per Share | 38.43 | 36.10 | 36.05 | 35.79 | 36.59 | 36.63 | 31.31 | 24.14 |
| Dividends Per Share | 4.145 | 4.138 | 4.130 | 4.120 | 4.080 | 3.720 | 3.360 | 3.240 |
| Dividend Payout % | 436.32 | 435.53 | 362.28 | 141.58 | 184.62 | 87.74 | 137.14 | 97.59 |
| **Income Statement** | | | | | | | | |
| Total Revenue | 230,511 | 113,773 | 415,732 | 411,389 | 412,895 | 388,523 | 348,074 | 327,291 |
| EBITDA | 182,732 | 87,634 | 327,455 | 228,737 | 267,155 | 240,265 | 212,608 | 210,104 |
| Depn & Amortn | 77,158 | 37,031 | 125,904 | 116,902 | 110,860 | 100,389 | 83,036 | 80,075 |
| Income Before Taxes | 70,672 | 32,928 | 113,966 | 25,819 | 78,092 | 58,881 | 56,674 | 56,415 |
| Income Taxes | ... | ... | ... | ... | ... | 400 | 525 | 2,538 |
| Net Income | 22,709 | 8,961 | 35,934 | 37,108 | 65,354 | 115,638 | 62,748 | 79,716 |
| Average Shares | 32,135 | 31,546 | 29,734 | 29,746 | 25,346 | 25,100 | 23,551 | 23,388 |
| **Balance Sheet** | | | | | | | | |
| Current Assets | 158,476 | 244,640 | 177,448 | 209,083 | 147,666 | 75,036 | 43,014 | 36,651 |
| Total Assets | 3,825,855 | 3,866,686 | 3,732,887 | 3,254,637 | 3,164,823 | 2,980,323 | 2,485,840 | 2,239,290 |
| Current Liabilities | 98,616 | 101,607 | 90,178 | 82,591 | 88,952 | 86,669 | 63,524 | 55,478 |
| Long-Term Obligations | 2,254,461 | 2,370,220 | 2,258,745 | 1,847,442 | 1,760,647 | 1,657,691 | 1,411,554 | 1,354,918 |
| Total Liabilities | 2,494,642 | 2,697,976 | 2,578,592 | 2,197,192 | 2,173,993 | 2,044,093 | 1,727,719 | 1,658,323 |
| Stockholders' Equity | 1,331,213 | 1,168,710 | 1,154,295 | 1,057,445 | 990,830 | 936,230 | 758,121 | 580,967 |
| Shares Outstanding | 32,724 | 31,679 | 31,324 | 28,849 | 26,395 | 24,876 | 23,416 | 23,033 |
| **Statistical Record** | | | | | | | | |
| Return on Assets % | 0.98 | 0.87 | 1.03 | 1.16 | 2.12 | 4.23 | 2.66 | 3.58 |
| Return on Equity % | 2.97 | 2.82 | 3.25 | 3.62 | 6.76 | 13.65 | 9.37 | 13.60 |
| EBITDA Margin % | 79.27 | 77.03 | 78.77 | 55.60 | 64.70 | 61.84 | 61.08 | 64.19 |
| Net Margin % | 9.85 | 7.88 | 8.64 | 9.02 | 15.83 | 29.76 | 18.03 | 24.36 |
| Asset Turnover | 0.12 | 0.12 | 0.12 | 0.13 | 0.13 | 0.14 | 0.15 | 0.15 |
| Current Ratio | 1.61 | 2.41 | 1.97 | 2.53 | 1.66 | 0.87 | 0.68 | 0.66 |
| Debt to Equity | 1.69 | 2.03 | 1.96 | 1.75 | 1.78 | 1.77 | 1.86 | 2.33 |
| Price Range | 137.71-93.47 | 124.00-89.95 | 116.94-77.66 | 87.34-50.76 | 129.00-63.95 | 146.40-95.34 | 133.47-94.42 | 93.15-69.10 |
| P/E Ratio | 144.96-98.39 | 130.53-94.68 | 102.58-68.12 | 30.01-17.44 | 58.37-28.94 | 34.53-22.49 | 54.48-38.54 | 28.06-20.81 |
| Average Yield % | 3.55 | 3.78 | 4.06 | 5.93 | 3.87 | 3.08 | 2.95 | 3.92 |

**Address:** 925 East Meadow Drive, Palo Alto, CA 94303
**Telephone:** 650-494-3700
**Web Site:** www.essexpropertytrust.com

**Officers:** George M. Marcus - Chairman Michael J. Schall - President, Chief Executive Officer, Senior Executive Vice President, Chief Operating Officer
**Transfer Agents:** Computershare Investor Services, LLC, Chicago, IL

**Investor Contact:** 650-849-1600
**No of Institutions:** 278
**Shares:** 36,469,500 **% Held:** 104.42

# EXPEDITORS INTERNATIONAL OF WASHINGTON, INC.

| Exchange | Symbol | Price | 52Wk Range | Yield | P/E |
|---|---|---|---|---|---|
| NMS | EXPD | $45.50 (8/31/2011) | 56.96-39.60 | 1.10 | 26.00 |

*7 Year Price Score 126.27 *NYSE Composite Index=100 *12 Month Price Score 94.92

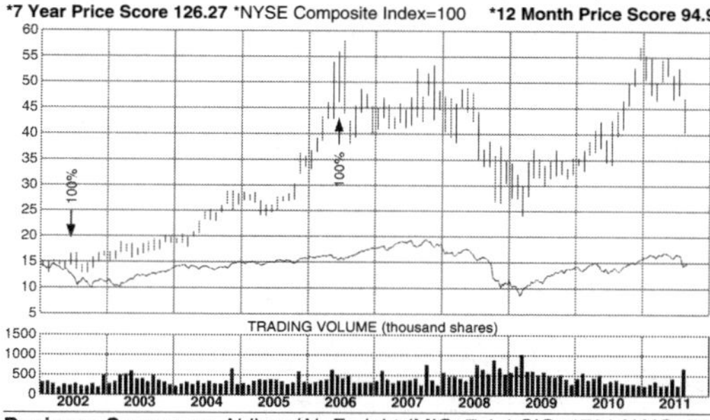


**Interim Earnings (Per Share)**

| Qtr. | Mar | Jun | Sep | Dec |
|---|---|---|---|---|
| 2008 | 0.30 | 0.32 | 0.39 | 0.35 |
| 2009 | 0.27 | 0.25 | 0.27 | 0.32 |
| 2010 | 0.28 | 0.42 | 0.44 | 0.45 |
| 2011 | 0.42 | 0.44 | ... | ... |

**Interim Dividends (Per Share)**

| Amt | Decl | Ex | Rec | Pay |
|---|---|---|---|---|
| 0.19S | 11/03/2009 | 11/27/2009 | 12/01/2009 | 12/15/2009 |
| 0.20S | 05/06/2010 | 05/27/2010 | 06/01/2010 | 06/15/2010 |
| 0.20S | 11/02/2010 | 11/29/2010 | 12/01/2010 | 12/15/2010 |
| 0.25S | 05/05/2011 | 05/27/2011 | 06/01/2011 | 06/15/2011 |

**Indicated Div: $0.50**

**Valuation Analysis**

Forecast EPS $1.85 (09/05/2011)

| | | | |
|---|---|---|---|
| Market Cap | $9.6 Billion | Book Value | $1.9 Billion |
| Price/Book | 5.15 | Price/Sales | 1.53 |

**Dividend Achiever Status**

| | |
|---|---|
| **10 Year Growth Rate** | 23.11% |
| **Total Years of Dividend Growth** | 16 |

**Business Summary:** Airlines/Air Freight (MIC: 7.4.4 SIC: 4731 NAIC: 541614)

Expeditors International of Washington is engaged in the business of providing global logistics services. Co. provides its customers with an international network supporting the movement and positioning of goods. Co.'s services include the consolidation or forwarding of air and ocean freight. In each U.S. office, and in various overseas offices, Co. acts as a customs broker. In addition, Co. provides additional services including distribution management, vendor consolidation, cargo insurance, purchase order management and customized logistics information. Co.'s customers include retailing and wholesaling, electronics, and manufacturing companies around the world.

**Recent Developments:** For the quarter ended June 30 2011, net income increased 5.1% to US$95.0 million from US$90.4 million in the year-earlier quarter. Revenues were US$1.58 billion, up 4.3% from US$1.52 billion the year before. Operating income was US$152.3 million versus US$138.5 million in the prior-year quarter, an increase of 9.9%. Direct operating expenses rose 1.0% to US$1.11 billion from US$1.10 billion in the comparable period the year before. Indirect operating expenses increased 14.2% to US$320.3 million from US$280.4 million in the equivalent prior-year period.

**Prospects:** Our evaluation of Expeditors International of Washington Inc. as of Sep. 6, 2011 is the result of our systematic analysis on three basic characteristics: earnings strength, relative valuation, and recent stock price movement. The company has generated a negative trend in earnings per share over the past 5 quarters. However, while recent estimates for the company have been lowered by analysts, EXPD has posted results that fell short of analysts expectations. Based on operating earnings yield, the company is about fairly valued when compared to all of the companies in our coverage universe. Share price changes over the past year indicates that EXPD will perform poorly over the near term.

**Financial Data**

| (US$ in Thousands) | 6 Mos | 3 Mos | 12/31/2010 | 12/31/2009 | 12/31/2008 | 12/31/2007 | 12/31/2006 | 12/31/2005 |
|---|---|---|---|---|---|---|---|---|
| Earnings Per Share | 1.75 | 1.73 | 1.59 | 1.11 | 1.37 | 1.21 | 1.06 | 0.98 |
| Cash Flow Per Share | 2.37 | 2.10 | 1.86 | 1.56 | 1.92 | 1.47 | 1.56 | 1.31 |
| Tang Book Value Per Share | 8.78 | 8.63 | 8.16 | 7.26 | 6.38 | 5.68 | 4.95 | 4.21 |
| Dividends Per Share | 0.450 | 0.400 | 0.400 | 0.380 | 0.320 | 0.280 | 0.220 | 0.150 |
| Dividend Payout % | 25.71 | 23.12 | 25.16 | 34.23 | 23.36 | 23.14 | 20.75 | 15.31 |
| **Income Statement** | | | | | | | | |
| Total Revenue | 3,042,216 | 1,460,848 | 5,967,573 | 4,092,283 | 5,633,878 | 5,235,171 | 4,625,966 | 3,901,781 |
| EBITDA | 319,910 | 157,521 | 559,055 | 394,714 | 480,296 | 428,770 | 379,211 | 310,474 |
| Depn & Amortn | 18,431 | 9,174 | 1,413 | 1,520 | 1,618 | 1,483 | 1,369 | 1,422 |
| Income Before Taxes | 305,668 | 150,453 | 564,068 | 402,872 | 499,572 | 449,673 | 395,664 | 320,154 |
| Income Taxes | 119,441 | 59,246 | 219,863 | 162,475 | 196,593 | 179,815 | 160,661 | 94,624 |
| Net Income | 186,232 | 91,232 | 344,172 | 240,217 | 301,014 | 269,154 | 235,094 | 218,634 |
| Average Shares | 215,659 | 215,863 | 216,446 | 216,533 | 219,170 | 221,799 | 222,223 | 223,267 |
| **Balance Sheet** | | | | | | | | |
| Current Assets | 2,313,042 | 2,280,825 | 2,140,355 | 1,787,830 | 1,573,359 | 1,534,697 | 1,341,837 | 1,201,961 |
| Total Assets | 2,878,004 | 2,836,732 | 2,679,179 | 2,323,722 | 2,100,839 | 2,069,065 | 1,822,338 | 1,566,044 |
| Current Liabilities | 921,525 | 914,985 | 861,978 | 708,386 | 670,349 | 769,753 | 709,145 | 612,501 |
| Total Liabilities | 1,005,956 | 994,823 | 938,273 | 770,715 | 734,421 | 842,494 | 752,403 | 652,323 |
| Stockholders' Equity | 1,872,048 | 1,841,909 | 1,740,906 | 1,553,007 | 1,366,418 | 1,226,571 | 1,069,935 | 913,721 |
| Shares Outstanding | 211,992 | 212,034 | 212,047 | 212,025 | 211,973 | 212,996 | 213,080 | 213,227 |
| **Statistical Record** | | | | | | | | |
| Return on Assets % | 13.97 | 14.23 | 13.76 | 10.86 | 14.40 | 13.83 | 13.88 | 14.92 |
| Return on Equity % | 21.66 | 21.61 | 20.90 | 16.46 | 23.15 | 23.44 | 23.70 | 25.41 |
| EBITDA Margin % | 10.52 | 10.78 | 9.37 | 9.65 | 8.53 | 8.19 | 8.20 | 7.96 |
| Net Margin % | 6.12 | 6.25 | 5.77 | 5.87 | 5.34 | 5.14 | 5.08 | 5.60 |
| Asset Turnover | 2.32 | 2.37 | 2.39 | 1.85 | 2.69 | 2.69 | 2.73 | 2.66 |
| Current Ratio | 2.51 | 2.49 | 2.48 | 2.52 | 2.35 | 1.99 | 1.89 | 1.96 |
| Price Range | 56.96-33.97 | 56.96-33.97 | 56.96-32.87 | 37.15-24.02 | 48.98-26.56 | 53.34-40.91 | 58.28-33.11 | 36.26-23.86 |
| P/E Ratio | 32.55-19.41 | 32.92-19.64 | 35.82-20.67 | 33.47-21.64 | 35.75-19.39 | 44.08-33.81 | 54.98-31.24 | 36.99-24.35 |
| Average Yield % | 0.92 | 0.88 | 0.95 | 1.18 | 0.81 | 0.63 | 0.50 | 0.53 |

| | | |
|---|---|---|
| **Address:** 1015 Third Avenue, 12th Floor, Seattle, WA 98104<br>**Telephone:** 206-674-3400<br>**Web Site:** www.expeditors.com | **Officers:** Peter J. Rose - Chairman, Chief Executive Officer R. Jordan Gates - President, Chief Operating Officer **Transfer Agents:**<br>Computershare Trust Company, N.A., Canton, MA | **No of Institutions:** 599<br>**Shares:** 208,467,920 **% Held:** 86.20 |

# EXXON MOBIL CORP.

| Exchange | Symbol | Price | 52Wk Range | Yield | P/E |
|---|---|---|---|---|---|
| NYS | XOM | $74.02 (8/31/2011) | 87.98-59.11 | 2.54 | 9.73 |

***7 Year Price Score 106.31** *NYSE Composite Index=100 ***12 Month Price Score 103.26**

**Interim Earnings (Per Share)**

| Qtr. | Mar | Jun | Sep | Dec |
|---|---|---|---|---|
| 2008 | 2.03 | 2.22 | 2.86 | 1.58 |
| 2009 | 0.92 | 0.81 | 0.98 | 1.27 |
| 2010 | 1.33 | 1.60 | 1.44 | 1.85 |
| 2011 | 2.14 | 2.18 | ... | ... |

**Interim Dividends (Per Share)**

| Amt | Decl | Ex | Rec | Pay |
|---|---|---|---|---|
| 0.44Q | 10/27/2010 | 11/09/2010 | 11/12/2010 | 12/10/2010 |
| 0.44Q | 01/26/2011 | 02/08/2011 | 02/10/2011 | 03/10/2011 |
| 0.47Q | 04/27/2011 | 05/11/2011 | 05/13/2011 | 06/10/2011 |
| 0.47Q | 07/27/2011 | 08/10/2011 | 08/12/2011 | 09/09/2011 |

**Indicated Div: $1.88 (Div. Reinv. Plan)**

**Valuation Analysis**

Forecast EPS $8.59 (09/05/2011)

Market Cap $359.9 Billion Book Value $155.6 Billion

Price/Book 2.31 Price/Sales 0.82

**Dividend Achiever Status**

**10 Year Growth Rate** 6.81%

**Total Years of Dividend Growth** 28

**Business Summary:** Refining & Marketing (MIC: 9.1.2 SIC: 2911 NAIC: 324110)

Exxon Mobil's principal business is energy, involving the exploration for, and production of, crude oil and natural gas, the manufacture of petroleum products, and the transportation and sale of crude oil, natural gas and petroleum products. Co. is a manufacturer and marketer of commodity petrochemicals, including olefins, aromatics, polyethylene and polypropylene plastics and a variety of specialty products. Co. also has interests in electric power generation facilities. Co. has a number of divisions and affiliates, with names that include ExxonMobil, Exxon, Esso or Mobil. As of Dec 31 2010, Co. had 24.81 billion barrels of oil-equivalent proved reserves.

**Recent Developments:** For the quarter ended June 30 2011, net income increased 40.7% to US$10.90 billion from US$7.75 billion in the year-earlier quarter. Revenues were US$125.49 billion, up 35.7% from US$92.49 billion the year before. Direct operating expenses rose 38.5% to US$88.38 billion from US$63.79 billion in the comparable period the year before. Indirect operating expenses increased 15.6% to US$18.49 billion from US$15.99 billion in the equivalent prior-year period.

**Prospects:** Our evaluation of Exxon Mobil Corp. as of Sep. 6, 2011 is the result of our systematic analysis on three basic characteristics: earnings strength, relative valuation, and recent stock price movement. The company has managed to produce a neutral trend in earnings per share over the past 5 quarters. However, while recent estimates for the company have been mixed, XOM has posted results that fell short of analysts expectations. Based on operating earnings yield, the company is undervalued when compared to all of the companies in our coverage universe. Share price changes over the past year indicates that XOM will perform in line with the market over the near term.

**Financial Data**

| (US$ in Thousands) | 6 Mos | 3 Mos | 12/31/2010 | 12/31/2009 | 12/31/2008 | 12/31/2007 | 12/31/2006 | 12/31/2005 |
|---|---|---|---|---|---|---|---|---|
| Earnings Per Share | 7.61 | 7.03 | 6.22 | 3.98 | 8.69 | 7.28 | 6.62 | 5.71 |
| Cash Flow Per Share | 11.39 | 10.52 | 9.91 | 5.89 | 11.57 | 9.43 | 8.34 | 7.68 |
| Tang Book Value Per Share | 31.99 | 30.75 | 29.49 | 23.39 | 22.70 | 22.62 | 19.87 | 18.13 |
| Dividends Per Share | 1.790 | 1.760 | 1.740 | 1.660 | 1.550 | 1.370 | 1.280 | 1.140 |
| Dividend Payout % | 23.52 | 25.04 | 27.97 | 41.71 | 17.84 | 18.82 | 19.34 | 19.96 |
| **Income Statement** | | | | | | | | |
| Total Revenue | 239,490,000 | 114,004,000 | 383,221,000 | 310,586,000 | 477,359,000 | 404,552,000 | 377,635,000 | 370,680,000 |
| EBITDA | 45,252,000 | 22,707,000 | 67,978,000 | 47,242,000 | 96,449,000 | 83,124,000 | 79,472,000 | 70,181,000 |
| Depn & Amortn | 7,642,000 | 3,761,000 | 14,760,000 | 11,917,000 | 12,379,000 | 12,250,000 | 11,416,000 | 10,253,000 |
| Income Before Taxes | 37,536,000 | 18,917,000 | 52,959,000 | 34,777,000 | 83,397,000 | 70,474,000 | 67,402,000 | 59,432,000 |
| Income Taxes | 15,725,000 | 8,004,000 | 21,561,000 | 15,119,000 | 36,530,000 | 29,864,000 | 27,902,000 | 23,302,000 |
| Net Income | 21,330,000 | 10,650,000 | 30,460,000 | 19,280,000 | 45,220,000 | 40,610,000 | 39,500,000 | 36,130,000 |
| Average Shares | 4,911,999 | 4,970,999 | 4,884,999 | 4,847,999 | 5,202,999 | 5,576,999 | 5,969,999 | 6,321,999 |
| **Balance Sheet** | | | | | | | | |
| Current Assets | 72,305,000 | 72,022,000 | 58,984,000 | 55,235,000 | 72,266,000 | 85,963,000 | 75,777,000 | 73,342,000 |
| Total Assets | 326,204,000 | 319,533,000 | 302,510,000 | 233,323,000 | 228,052,000 | 242,082,000 | 219,015,000 | 208,335,000 |
| Current Liabilities | 74,533,000 | 73,576,000 | 62,633,000 | 52,061,000 | 49,100,000 | 58,312,000 | 48,817,000 | 46,307,000 |
| Long-Term Obligations | 12,123,000 | 12,316,000 | 12,227,000 | 7,129,000 | 7,025,000 | 7,183,000 | 6,645,000 | 6,220,000 |
| Total Liabilities | 170,653,000 | 168,053,000 | 155,671,000 | 122,754,000 | 115,087,000 | 120,320,000 | 105,171,000 | 97,149,000 |
| Stockholders' Equity | 155,551,000 | 151,480,000 | 146,839,000 | 110,569,000 | 112,965,000 | 121,762,000 | 113,844,000 | 111,186,000 |
| Shares Outstanding | 4,861,999 | 4,925,999 | 4,978,999 | 4,726,999 | 4,975,999 | 5,381,999 | 5,728,999 | 6,132,999 |
| **Statistical Record** | | | | | | | | |
| Return on Assets % | 12.29 | 12.38 | 11.37 | 8.36 | 19.18 | 17.61 | 18.49 | 17.90 |
| Return on Equity % | 25.65 | 26.37 | 23.67 | 17.25 | 38.42 | 34.47 | 35.11 | 33.93 |
| EBITDA Margin % | 18.90 | 19.92 | 17.74 | 15.21 | 20.20 | 20.55 | 21.04 | 18.93 |
| Net Margin % | 8.91 | 9.34 | 7.95 | 6.21 | 9.47 | 10.04 | 10.46 | 9.75 |
| Asset Turnover | 1.43 | 1.45 | 1.43 | 1.35 | 2.03 | 1.75 | 1.77 | 1.84 |
| Current Ratio | 0.97 | 0.98 | 0.94 | 1.06 | 1.47 | 1.47 | 1.55 | 1.58 |
| Debt to Equity | 0.08 | 0.08 | 0.08 | 0.06 | 0.06 | 0.06 | 0.06 | 0.06 |
| Price Range | 87.98-56.57 | 87.07-56.57 | 73.42-56.57 | 81.64-62.22 | 94.56-62.35 | 95.05-69.86 | 78.73-56.65 | 64.98-49.49 |
| P/E Ratio | 11.56-7.43 | 12.39-8.05 | 11.80-9.09 | 20.51-15.63 | 10.88-7.17 | 13.06-9.60 | 11.89-8.56 | 11.38-8.67 |
| Average Yield % | 2.45 | 2.56 | 2.68 | 2.34 | 1.87 | 1.64 | 1.96 | 1.96 |

**Address:** 5959 Las Colinas Boulevard, Irving, TX 75039-2298
**Telephone:** 972-444-1000
**Web Site:** www.exxonmobil.com

**Officers:** Rex W. Tillerson - Chairman, Chief Executive Officer Donald D. Humphreys - Senior Vice President, Treasurer **Transfer Agents:** Computershare Trust Company, N.A., Providence, RI

**No of Institutions:** 2144
**Shares:** 2,678,496,256 **% Held:** 46.50

# FACTSET RESEARCH SYSTEMS INC.

| Exchange | Symbol | Price | 52Wk Range | Yield | P/E |
|---|---|---|---|---|---|
| NYS | FDS | $87.90 (8/31/2011) | 111.76-73.55 | 1.23 | 24.55 |

***7 Year Price Score 163.25** *NYSE Composite Index=100 ***12 Month Price Score 96.22**

**Interim Earnings (Per Share)**

| Qtr. | Nov | Feb | May | Aug |
|---|---|---|---|---|
| 2007-08 | 0.58 | 0.59 | 0.65 | 0.68 |
| 2008-09 | 0.73 | 0.71 | 0.79 | 0.74 |
| 2009-10 | 0.74 | 0.75 | 0.81 | 0.83 |
| 2010-11 | 0.88 | 0.95 | 0.92 | ... |

**Interim Dividends (Per Share)**

| Amt | Decl | Ex | Rec | Pay |
|---|---|---|---|---|
| 0.23Q | 11/10/2010 | 11/26/2010 | 11/30/2010 | 12/21/2010 |
| 0.23Q | 02/09/2011 | 02/24/2011 | 02/28/2011 | 03/15/2011 |
| 0.27Q | 05/09/2011 | 05/26/2011 | 05/31/2011 | 06/21/2011 |
| 0.27Q | 08/11/2011 | 08/29/2011 | 08/31/2011 | 09/20/2011 |

**Indicated Div: $1.08**

**Valuation Analysis**

| | | | |
|---|---|---|---|
| Forecast EPS | $3.69 (09/02/2011) | | |
| Market Cap | $4.0 Billion | Book Value | $554.4 Million |
| Price/Book | 7.27 | Price/Sales | 5.73 |

**Dividend Achiever Status**

| | |
|---|---|
| **10 Year Growth Rate** | 24.43% |
| **Total Years of Dividend Growth** | 11 |

**Business Summary:** Internet & Software (MIC: 6.3.2 SIC: 7371 NAIC: 541511)

FactSet Research Systems is a provider of global financial and economic information. Co. supports the investment process from initial research to published results for buy and sell-side professionals, such as portfolio managers, research and performance analysts, risk managers, marketing professionals, sell-side equity research professionals, investment bankers and fixed income professionals. Co.'s applications provide users access to multicompany comparisons, company, industry and portfolio analysis, company screening, predictive risk measurements, alphatesting, portfolio optimization and simulation as well as news and quotes and tools to analyze fixed income securities and portfolios.

**Recent Developments:** For the quarter ended May 31 2011, net income increased 12.0% to US$43.3 million from US$38.7 million in the year-earlier quarter. Revenues were US$183.6 million, up 14.6% from US$160.3 million the year before. Operating income was US$61.8 million versus US$55.7 million in the prior-year quarter, an increase of 11.0%. Direct operating expenses rose 21.2% to US$62.2 million from US$51.4 million in the comparable period the year before. Indirect operating expenses increased 11.9% to US$59.6 million from US$53.3 million in the equivalent prior-year period.

**Prospects:** Our evaluation of FactSet Research Systems Inc. as of Sep. 6, 2011 is the result of our systematic analysis on three basic characteristics: earnings strength, relative valuation, and recent stock price movement. The company has produced a positive trend in earnings per share over the past 5 quarters and while recent estimates for the company have been mixed, FDS has posted better than expected results. Based on operating earnings yield, the company is about fairly valued when compared to all of the companies in our coverage universe. Share price changes over the past year indicates that FDS will perform in line with the market over the near term.

**Financial Data**

| (US$ in Thousands) | 9 Mos | 6 Mos | 3 Mos | 08/31/2010 | 08/31/2009 | 08/31/2008 | 08/31/2007 | 08/31/2006 |
|---|---|---|---|---|---|---|---|---|
| Earnings Per Share | 3.58 | 3.47 | 3.27 | 3.13 | 2.97 | 2.50 | 2.14 | 1.64 |
| Cash Flow Per Share | 4.51 | 4.62 | 4.49 | 4.52 | 4.41 | 2.97 | 3.19 | 2.48 |
| Tang Book Value Per Share | 6.05 | 6.10 | 5.80 | 4.96 | 5.84 | 4.57 | 4.68 | 3.56 |
| Dividends Per Share | 0.960 | 0.920 | 0.890 | 0.860 | 0.760 | 0.600 | 0.360 | 0.220 |
| Dividend Payout % | 26.82 | 26.51 | 27.22 | 27.48 | 25.59 | 24.00 | 16.82 | 13.41 |
| **Income Statement** | | | | | | | | |
| Total Revenue | 534,571 | 350,924 | 173,289 | 641,059 | 622,023 | 575,519 | 475,801 | 387,350 |
| EBITDA | 207,724 | 136,537 | 68,946 | 250,981 | 238,222 | 211,947 | 183,576 | 142,132 |
| Depn & Amortn | 27,950 | 18,758 | 9,392 | 28,800 | 26,100 | 22,900 | 20,700 | 16,100 |
| Income Before Taxes | 179,774 | 117,779 | 59,554 | 222,181 | 212,122 | 189,047 | 162,876 | 126,032 |
| Income Taxes | 49,608 | 30,924 | 17,953 | 71,970 | 67,172 | 64,030 | 53,309 | 43,116 |
| Net Income | 130,166 | 86,855 | 41,601 | 150,211 | 144,950 | 125,017 | 109,567 | 82,916 |
| Average Shares | 47,154 | 47,427 | 47,487 | 48,004 | 48,789 | 50,080 | 51,284 | 50,592 |
| **Balance Sheet** | | | | | | | | |
| Current Assets | 298,490 | 298,452 | 278,894 | 265,145 | 299,410 | 234,523 | 252,332 | 206,980 |
| Total Assets | 684,631 | 683,070 | 659,407 | 644,608 | 633,137 | 587,274 | 523,750 | 457,228 |
| Current Liabilities | 97,277 | 91,327 | 85,512 | 109,276 | 99,363 | 92,626 | 90,650 | 79,301 |
| Total Liabilities | 130,194 | 124,883 | 116,849 | 142,202 | 132,308 | 121,803 | 114,439 | 98,540 |
| Stockholders' Equity | 554,437 | 558,187 | 542,558 | 502,406 | 500,829 | 465,471 | 409,311 | 358,688 |
| Shares Outstanding | 45,830 | 46,139 | 46,346 | 46,024 | 46,739 | 47,968 | 48,348 | 48,889 |
| **Statistical Record** | | | | | | | | |
| Return on Assets % | 26.29 | 25.42 | 24.14 | 23.51 | 23.75 | 22.44 | 22.34 | 20.61 |
| Return on Equity % | 32.53 | 31.10 | 29.14 | 29.95 | 30.00 | 28.50 | 28.53 | 26.46 |
| EBITDA Margin % | 38.86 | 38.91 | 39.79 | 39.15 | 38.30 | 36.83 | 38.58 | 36.69 |
| Net Margin % | 24.35 | 24.75 | 24.01 | 23.43 | 23.30 | 21.72 | 23.03 | 21.41 |
| Asset Turnover | 1.09 | 1.05 | 1.02 | 1.00 | 1.02 | 1.03 | 0.97 | 0.96 |
| Current Ratio | 3.07 | 3.27 | 3.26 | 2.43 | 3.01 | 2.53 | 2.78 | 2.61 |
| Price Range | 111.76-65.77 | 107.88-65.77 | 90.80-62.19 | 78.69-54.95 | 63.59-33.18 | 73.53-44.53 | 69.36-43.32 | 47.30-32.00 |
| P/E Ratio | 31.22-18.37 | 31.09-18.95 | 27.77-19.02 | 25.14-17.56 | 21.41-11.17 | 29.41-17.81 | 32.41-20.24 | 28.84-19.51 |
| Average Yield % | 1.07 | 1.13 | 1.20 | 1.24 | 1.62 | 1.00 | 0.61 | 0.54 |

| | | |
|---|---|---|
| **Address:** 601 Merritt 7, Norwalk, CT 06851<br>**Telephone:** 203-810-1000<br>**Web Site:** www.factset.com | **Officers:** Philip A. Hadley - Chairman, Chief Executive Officer Charles J. Snyder - Vice-Chairman<br>**Transfer Agents:** BNY Mellon Shareowner Services | **No of Institutions:** 372<br>**Shares:** 48,726,668 **% Held:** 86.83 |

# FAMILY DOLLAR STORES, INC.

| Exchange | Symbol | Price | 52Wk Range | Yield | P/E |
|---|---|---|---|---|---|
| NYS | FDO | $53.39 (8/31/2011) | 55.74-41.38 | 1.35 | 17.62 |

*7 Year Price Score 157.68 *NYSE Composite Index=100 *12 Month Price Score 104.92

**Interim Earnings (Per Share)**

| Qtr. | Nov | Feb | May | Aug |
|---|---|---|---|---|
| 2007-08 | 0.37 | 0.45 | 0.46 | 0.38 |
| 2008-09 | 0.42 | 0.60 | 0.62 | 0.43 |
| 2009-10 | 0.49 | 0.81 | 0.77 | 0.56 |
| 2010-11 | 0.58 | 0.98 | 0.91 | ... |

**Interim Dividends (Per Share)**

| Amt | Decl | Ex | Rec | Pay |
|---|---|---|---|---|
| 0.155Q | 10/25/2010 | 12/13/2010 | 12/15/2010 | 01/14/2011 |
| 0.18Q | 01/20/2011 | 03/11/2011 | 03/15/2011 | 04/15/2011 |
| 0.18Q | 05/11/2011 | 06/13/2011 | 06/15/2011 | 07/15/2011 |
| 0.18Q | 08/12/2011 | 09/13/2011 | 09/15/2011 | 10/14/2011 |

**Indicated Div: $0.72**

**Valuation Analysis**

| | | | |
|---|---|---|---|
| Forecast EPS | $3.10 (09/05/2011) | | |
| Market Cap | $6.4 Billion | Book Value | $1.2 Billion |
| Price/Book | 5.44 | Price/Sales | 0.77 |

**Dividend Achiever Status**

| | |
|---|---|
| 10 Year Growth Rate | 9.83% |
| Total Years of Dividend Growth | 34 |

**Business Summary:** Retail - General Merchandise/Department Stores (MIC: 2.1.1 SIC: 5331 NAIC: 452990)

Family Dollar Stores operates general merchandise retail discount stores that provide primarily low- and middle-income consumers with a range of merchandise in a number of categories, such as health and beauty aids, packaged food and refrigerated products, home cleaning supplies, housewares, stationery, seasonal goods, apparel and home fashions. Co. sells merchandise at prices that generally range from less than $1 to $10. At Oct 1 2010, Co. had 6,817 stores in 44 states and the District of Columbia. Co.'s stores are located in urban, suburban, small town and rural markets, and are freestanding or located in shopping centers. All of Co.'s stores operate under the Family Dollar name.

**Recent Developments:** For the quarter ended May 28 2011, net income increased 6.5% to US$111.1 million from US$104.4 million in the year-earlier quarter. Revenues were US$2.15 billion, up 7.8% from US$2.00 billion the year before. Operating income was US$184.4 million versus US$170.1 million in the prior-year quarter, an increase of 8.4%. Direct operating expenses rose 8.4% to US$1.37 billion from US$1.27 billion in the comparable period the year before. Indirect operating expenses increased 6.3% to US$595.4 million from US$560.2 million in the equivalent prior-year period.

**Prospects:** Our evaluation of Family Dollar Stores Inc. as of Sep. 6, 2011 is the result of our systematic analysis on three basic characteristics: earnings strength, relative valuation, and recent stock price movement. The company has managed to produce a neutral trend in earnings per share over the past 5 quarters and while recent estimates for the company have been mixed, FDO has posted results that fell short of analysts expectations. Based on operating earnings yield, the company is about fairly valued when compared to all of the companies in our coverage universe. Share price changes over the past year indicates that FDO will perform poorly over the near term.

**Financial Data**

| (US$ in Thousands) | 9 Mos | 6 Mos | 3 Mos | 08/28/2010 | 08/29/2009 | 08/30/2008 | 09/01/2007 | 08/26/2006 |
|---|---|---|---|---|---|---|---|---|
| Earnings Per Share | 3.03 | 2.89 | 2.72 | 2.62 | 2.07 | 1.66 | 1.62 | 1.26 |
| Cash Flow Per Share | 4.32 | 4.01 | 4.31 | 4.37 | 3.80 | 3.69 | 2.74 | 2.92 |
| Tang Book Value Per Share | 9.82 | 9.68 | 9.73 | 10.90 | 10.38 | 8.98 | 8.19 | 8.04 |
| Dividends Per Share | 0.645 | 0.620 | 0.600 | 0.580 | 0.520 | 0.480 | 0.440 | 0.400 |
| Dividend Payout % | 21.29 | 21.45 | 22.06 | 22.14 | 25.12 | 28.92 | 27.16 | 31.75 |
| **Income Statement** | | | | | | | | |
| Total Revenue | 6,413,505 | 4,260,110 | 1,996,941 | 7,866,971 | 7,400,606 | 6,983,628 | 6,834,305 | 6,394,772 |
| EBITDA | 641,326 | 410,884 | 165,574 | 747,635 | 617,077 | 514,904 | 532,693 | 451,942 |
| Depn & Amortn | 135,026 | 88,937 | 43,992 | 172,037 | 159,808 | 149,598 | 144,060 | 134,637 |
| Income Before Taxes | 492,320 | 314,656 | 118,451 | 563,858 | 450,925 | 361,762 | 381,896 | 311,144 |
| Income Taxes | 183,724 | 117,161 | 44,136 | 205,723 | 159,659 | 128,689 | 139,042 | 116,033 |
| Net Income | 308,596 | 197,495 | 74,315 | 358,135 | 291,266 | 233,073 | 242,854 | 195,111 |
| Average Shares | 122,656 | 125,701 | 129,141 | 136,596 | 140,522 | 140,494 | 149,599 | 155,124 |
| **Balance Sheet** | | | | | | | | |
| Current Assets | 1,633,886 | 1,640,743 | 1,414,745 | 1,660,208 | 1,599,438 | 1,344,091 | 1,537,280 | 1,418,848 |
| Total Assets | 3,002,752 | 3,003,244 | 2,741,119 | 2,982,057 | 2,842,722 | 2,661,782 | 2,624,156 | 2,523,029 |
| Current Liabilities | 1,003,917 | 1,011,909 | 1,017,019 | 1,054,487 | 1,059,707 | 1,068,985 | 1,130,303 | 986,111 |
| Long-Term Obligations | 532,332 | 532,294 | 233,800 | 250,000 | 250,000 | 250,000 | 250,000 | 250,000 |
| Total Liabilities | 1,820,505 | 1,813,440 | 1,511,851 | 1,560,503 | 1,402,662 | 1,407,699 | 1,449,515 | 1,314,636 |
| Stockholders' Equity | 1,182,247 | 1,189,804 | 1,229,268 | 1,421,554 | 1,440,060 | 1,254,083 | 1,174,641 | 1,208,393 |
| Shares Outstanding | 120,358 | 122,928 | 126,384 | 130,452 | 138,795 | 139,704 | 143,344 | 150,210 |
| **Statistical Record** | | | | | | | | |
| Return on Assets % | 13.18 | 12.84 | 13.26 | 12.33 | 10.61 | 8.84 | 9.28 | 7.93 |
| Return on Equity % | 29.38 | 28.70 | 26.99 | 25.10 | 21.68 | 19.25 | 20.05 | 14.84 |
| EBITDA Margin % | 10.00 | 9.64 | 8.29 | 9.50 | 8.34 | 7.37 | 7.79 | 7.07 |
| Net Margin % | 4.81 | 4.64 | 3.72 | 4.55 | 3.94 | 3.34 | 3.55 | 3.05 |
| Asset Turnover | 2.88 | 2.81 | 2.92 | 2.71 | 2.70 | 2.65 | 2.61 | 2.60 |
| Current Ratio | 1.63 | 1.62 | 1.39 | 1.57 | 1.51 | 1.26 | 1.36 | 1.44 |
| Debt to Equity | 0.45 | 0.45 | 0.19 | 0.18 | 0.17 | 0.20 | 0.21 | 0.21 |
| Price Range | 55.56-36.00 | 53.25-32.61 | 50.68-27.39 | 43.56-25.95 | 34.63-21.96 | 29.31-15.85 | 35.23-23.81 | 27.22-19.67 |
| P/E Ratio | 18.34-11.88 | 18.43-11.28 | 18.63-10.07 | 16.63-9.90 | 16.73-10.61 | 17.66-9.55 | 21.75-14.70 | 21.60-15.61 |
| Average Yield % | 1.40 | 1.46 | 1.56 | 1.70 | 1.82 | 2.18 | 1.45 | 1.69 |

**Address:** P.O. Box 1017, 10401 Monroe Road, Charlotte, NC 28201-1017
**Telephone:** 704-847-6961
**Web Site:** www.familydollar.com

**Officers:** Howard R. Levine - Chairman, Chief Executive Officer R. James Kelly - President, Chief Operating Officer **Transfer Agents:** American Stock Transfer & Trust Company, LLC, Brooklyn, NY

**No of Institutions:** 503
**Shares:** 126,414,784 **% Held:** 79.98

# FASTENAL CO.

| Exchange | Symbol | Price | 52Wk Range | Yield | P/E |
|---|---|---|---|---|---|
| NMS | FAST | $33.47 (8/31/2011) | 36.65-22.64 | 1.55 | 31.58 |

*7 Year Price Score 141.92 *NYSE Composite Index=100 *12 Month Price Score 110.53

**Interim Earnings (Per Share)**

| Qtr. | Mar | Jun | Sep | Dec |
|---|---|---|---|---|
| 2008 | 0.23 | 0.26 | 0.25 | 0.21 |
| 2009 | 0.17 | 0.14 | 0.16 | 0.15 |
| 2010 | 0.19 | 0.23 | 0.26 | 0.22 |
| 2011 | 0.27 | 0.32 | ... | ... |

**Interim Dividends (Per Share)**

| Amt | Decl | Ex | Rec | Pay |
|---|---|---|---|---|
| 0.25Q | 01/17/2011 | 02/11/2011 | 02/15/2011 | 02/25/2011 |
| 0.13Q | 04/11/2011 | 04/13/2011 | 04/12/2011 | 04/28/2011 |
| 2-for-1 | 04/19/2011 | 05/23/2011 | 05/02/2011 | 05/20/2011 |
| 0.13Q | 07/11/2011 | 07/21/2011 | 07/25/2011 | 08/22/2011 |

**Indicated Div: $0.52**

**Valuation Analysis**

| | | | |
|---|---|---|---|
| Forecast EPS | $1.20 (09/05/2011) | | |
| Market Cap | $9.9 Billion | Book Value | $1.4 Billion |
| Price/Book | 7.29 | Price/Sales | 3.92 |

**Dividend Achiever Status**

| | |
|---|---|
| **10 Year Growth Rate** | 43.27% |
| **Total Years of Dividend Growth** | 12 |

**Business Summary:** Retail - Hardware & Home Improvement (MIC: 2.1.8 SIC: 5251 NAIC: 444130)

Fastenal is engaged in the distribution of industrial and construction supplies operating stores primarily located in North America. Co.'s product line consists of two categories: threaded fasteners, such as bolts, nuts, screws, studs, and related washers; and miscellaneous supplies, such as paints, various pins and machinery keys, concrete anchors, batteries, sealants, metal framing systems, wire rope, strut, private-label stud anchors, rivets, and related accessories. As of Dec 31 2010, Co. operated 2,490 store locations in the U.S., Puerto Rico, Dominican Republic, Canada, Mexico, Panama, China, Singapore, Malaysia, the Netherlands, Hungary and the U.K.

**Recent Developments:** For the quarter ended June 30 2011, net income increased 36.1% to US$94.1 million from US$69.2 million in the year-earlier quarter. Revenues were US$701.7 million, up 22.9% from US$571.2 million the year before. Operating income was US$150.1 million versus US$111.8 million in the prior-year quarter, an increase of 34.2%. Direct operating expenses rose 22.7% to US$335.5 million from US$273.5 million in the comparable period the year before. Indirect operating expenses increased 16.3% to US$216.1 million from US$185.8 million in the equivalent prior-year period.

**Prospects:** Our evaluation of Fastenal Co. as of Sep. 6, 2011 is the result of our systematic analysis on three basic characteristics: earnings strength, relative valuation, and recent stock price movement. The company has produced a positive trend in earnings per share over the past 5 quarters and while recent estimates for the company have remained steady, FAST has posted better than expected results. Based on operating earnings yield, the company is overvalued when compared to all of the companies in our coverage universe. Share price changes over the past year indicates that FAST will perform poorly over the near term.

**Financial Data**

| (US$ in Thousands) | 6 Mos | 3 Mos | 12/31/2010 | 12/31/2009 | 12/31/2008 | 12/31/2007 | 12/31/2006 | 12/31/2005 |
|---|---|---|---|---|---|---|---|---|
| Earnings Per Share | 1.06 | 0.98 | 0.90 | 0.62 | 0.94 | 0.78 | 0.66 | 0.55 |
| Cash Flow Per Share | 0.75 | 0.80 | 0.82 | 1.03 | 0.87 | 0.76 | 0.32 | 0.40 |
| Tang Book Value Per Share | 4.59 | 4.38 | 4.35 | 4.04 | 3.85 | 3.39 | 3.05 | 2.59 |
| Dividends Per Share | 0.800 | 0.670 | 0.620 | 0.360 | 0.395 | 0.220 | 0.200 | 0.155 |
| Dividend Payout % | 75.12 | 68.37 | 68.89 | 58.06 | 42.02 | 28.39 | 30.30 | 28.18 |
| **Income Statement** | | | | | | | | |
| Total Revenue | 1,342,313 | 640,583 | 2,269,471 | 1,930,330 | 2,340,425 | 2,061,819 | 1,809,337 | 1,523,333 |
| EBITDA | 300,429 | 139,292 | 470,444 | 335,880 | 489,505 | 413,824 | 353,439 | 296,937 |
| Depn & Amortn | 21,660 | 10,629 | 40,755 | 40,087 | 39,268 | 37,399 | 33,597 | 29,073 |
| Income Before Taxes | 278,993 | 128,811 | 430,640 | 297,490 | 451,167 | 377,899 | 321,029 | 269,056 |
| Income Taxes | 105,334 | 49,264 | 165,284 | 113,133 | 171,462 | 145,277 | 121,991 | 102,242 |
| Net Income | 173,659 | 79,547 | 265,356 | 184,357 | 279,705 | 232,622 | 199,038 | 166,814 |
| Average Shares | 295,916 | 295,428 | 294,861 | 296,715 | 297,662 | 301,110 | 302,330 | 303,016 |
| **Balance Sheet** | | | | | | | | |
| Current Assets | 1,171,815 | 1,132,921 | 1,085,698 | 982,364 | 975,403 | 880,771 | 767,776 | 649,008 |
| Total Assets | 1,581,871 | 1,524,613 | 1,468,283 | 1,327,358 | 1,304,149 | 1,163,061 | 1,039,016 | 890,035 |
| Current Liabilities | 204,394 | 209,516 | 162,185 | 119,509 | 147,993 | 137,791 | 103,896 | 91,538 |
| Total Liabilities | 227,700 | 233,096 | 185,771 | 136,515 | 161,890 | 152,900 | 116,923 | 106,486 |
| Stockholders' Equity | 1,354,171 | 1,291,517 | 1,282,512 | 1,190,843 | 1,142,259 | 1,010,161 | 922,093 | 783,549 |
| Shares Outstanding | 295,099 | 294,861 | 294,861 | 294,861 | 297,061 | 298,242 | 302,414 | 302,110 |
| **Statistical Record** | | | | | | | | |
| Return on Assets % | 20.76 | 19.96 | 18.98 | 14.01 | 22.61 | 21.13 | 20.64 | 20.09 |
| Return on Equity % | 24.02 | 23.27 | 21.46 | 15.80 | 25.92 | 24.08 | 23.34 | 22.73 |
| EBITDA Margin % | 22.38 | 21.74 | 20.73 | 17.40 | 20.92 | 20.07 | 19.53 | 19.49 |
| Net Margin % | 12.94 | 12.42 | 11.69 | 9.55 | 11.95 | 11.28 | 11.00 | 10.95 |
| Asset Turnover | 1.67 | 1.65 | 1.62 | 1.47 | 1.89 | 1.87 | 1.88 | 1.84 |
| Current Ratio | 5.73 | 5.41 | 6.69 | 8.22 | 6.59 | 6.39 | 7.39 | 7.09 |
| Price Range | 36.01-22.55 | 32.41-22.55 | 30.06-20.61 | 21.09-13.08 | 27.73-15.94 | 25.54-17.02 | 24.42-16.61 | 20.82-12.78 |
| P/E Ratio | 33.97-21.27 | 33.08-23.01 | 33.39-22.89 | 34.02-21.10 | 29.49-16.95 | 32.74-21.81 | 37.00-25.17 | 37.86-23.24 |
| Average Yield % | 2.77 | 2.46 | 2.46 | 2.03 | 1.81 | 1.07 | 0.99 | 0.98 |

| | | |
|---|---|---|
| **Address:** 2001 Theurer Boulevard, Winona, MN 55987-1500<br>**Telephone:** 507-454-5374<br>**Web Site:** www.fastenal.com | **Officers:** Robert A. Kierlin - Chairman Willard D. Oberton - President, Chief Executive Officer **Transfer Agents:** Wells Fargo Bank, National Association, Minneapolis, MN | **No of Institutions:** 509<br>**Shares:** 265,109,616 **% Held:** 84.51 |

# FEDERAL REALTY INVESTMENT TRUST (MD)

| Exchange | Symbol | Price | 52Wk Range | Yield | P/E |
|---|---|---|---|---|---|
| NYS | FRT | $90.55 (8/31/2011) | 90.55-74.87 | 3.05 | 43.96 |

***7 Year Price Score 116.15** *NYSE Composite Index=100 ***12 Month Price Score 105.03**

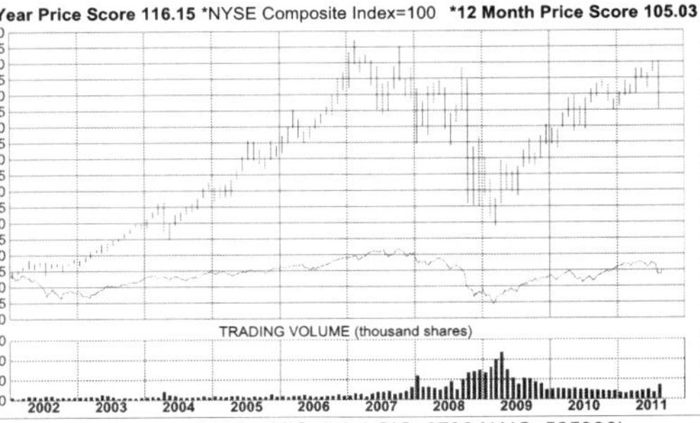


**Interim Earnings (Per Share)**

| Qtr. | Mar | Jun | Sep | Dec |
|---|---|---|---|---|
| 2008 | 0.51 | 0.49 | 0.63 | 0.57 |
| 2009 | 0.17 | 0.48 | 0.45 | 0.53 |
| 2010 | 0.47 | 0.50 | 0.48 | 0.53 |
| 2011 | 0.50 | 0.55 | ... | ... |

**Interim Dividends (Per Share)**

| Amt | Decl | Ex | Rec | Pay |
|---|---|---|---|---|
| 0.67Q | 11/03/2010 | 12/30/2010 | 01/03/2011 | 01/18/2011 |
| 0.67Q | 02/15/2011 | 03/15/2011 | 03/17/2011 | 04/15/2011 |
| 0.67Q | 05/05/2011 | 06/21/2011 | 06/23/2011 | 07/15/2011 |
| 0.69Q | 08/03/2011 | 09/20/2011 | 09/22/2011 | 10/14/2011 |

**Indicated Div: $2.76 (Div. Reinv. Plan)**

**Valuation Analysis**

| | | | |
|---|---|---|---|
| Forecast EPS | $2.08 (09/05/2011) | | |
| Market Cap | $5.7 Billion | Book Value | $1.2 Billion |
| Price/Book | 4.61 | Price/Sales | 10.39 |

**Dividend Achiever Status**

| | |
|---|---|
| **10 Year Growth Rate** | 3.44% |
| **Total Years of Dividend Growth** | 43 |

**Business Summary:** REITs (MIC: 5.3.1 SIC: 6798 NAIC: 525930)

Federal Realty Investment Trust is an equity real estate investment trust engaged in the ownership, management, and redevelopment of retail and mixed-use properties located in selected metropolitan markets in the Northeast and Mid-Atlantic regions of the U.S., as well as in California. As of Dec 31 2010, Co. owned or had a majority interest in community and neighborhood shopping centers and mixed-use properties which were operated as 85 predominantly retail real estate projects comprising approximately 18.3 million square feet. Also, as of that date, a joint venture, in which Co. owned a 30.0% interest, owned seven retail real estate projects totaling approximately 1.0 million square feet.

**Recent Developments:** For the quarter ended Mar 31 2011, income from continuing operations increased 5.7% to US$32.3 million from US$30.6 million in the year-earlier quarter. Net income increased 6.0% to US$32.4 million from US$30.6 million in the year-earlier quarter. Revenues were US$138.5 million, up 0.1% from US$138.3 million the year before. Revenues from property income rose 3.0% to US$135.3 million from US$131.3 million in the corresponding quarter a year earlier.

**Prospects:** Our evaluation of Federal Realty Investment Trust as of Sep. 6, 2011 is the result of our systematic analysis on three basic characteristics: earnings strength, relative valuation, and recent stock price movement. The company has managed to produce a neutral trend in earnings per share over the past 5 quarters. Because the company lacks sufficient analyst estimate data, we place greater weight on the historical EPS trend as the measure of earnings strength. Based on operating earnings yield, the company is overvalued when compared to all of the companies in our coverage universe. Share price changes over the past year indicates that FRT will perform very poorly over the near term.

| **Financial Data** (US$ in Thousands) | 6 Mos | 3 Mos | 12/31/2010 | 12/31/2009 | 12/31/2008 | 12/31/2007 | 12/31/2006 | 12/31/2005 |
|---|---|---|---|---|---|---|---|---|
| Earnings Per Share | 2.06 | 2.01 | 1.98 | 1.63 | 2.19 | 3.45 | 1.92 | 1.94 |
| Cash Flow Per Share | 3.96 | 3.98 | 4.20 | 4.30 | 3.88 | 3.82 | 3.45 | 3.32 |
| Tang Book Value Per Share | 19.47 | 18.97 | 18.53 | 19.06 | 18.73 | 18.84 | 14.17 | 12.10 |
| Dividends Per Share | 2.680 | 2.670 | 2.660 | 2.620 | 2.520 | 2.370 | 2.460 | 2.365 |
| Dividend Payout % | 130.10 | 132.84 | 134.34 | 160.74 | 115.07 | 68.70 | 128.13 | 121.91 |
| **Income Statement** | | | | | | | | |
| Total Revenue | 273,929 | 138,481 | 544,674 | 531,019 | 520,525 | 485,892 | 451,022 | 410,330 |
| EBITDA | 224,486 | 112,029 | 348,550 | 324,336 | 330,020 | 318,380 | 297,571 | 268,310 |
| Depn & Amortn | 62,632 | 30,569 | 119,817 | 115,093 | 111,069 | 105,966 | 97,879 | 91,503 |
| Income Before Taxes | 112,940 | 56,431 | 127,107 | 102,356 | 120,704 | 101,970 | 99,429 | 90,456 |
| Net Income | 65,943 | 31,186 | 122,790 | 98,304 | 129,787 | 195,537 | 118,712 | 114,612 |
| Average Shares | 62,391 | 61,629 | 61,324 | 59,830 | 58,914 | 56,543 | 53,962 | 53,050 |
| **Balance Sheet** | | | | | | | | |
| Current Assets | 93,765 | 81,409 | 129,607 | 255,916 | 134,691 | 152,437 | 99,744 | 87,331 |
| Total Assets | 3,220,668 | 3,217,461 | 3,159,553 | 3,222,309 | 3,092,776 | 2,989,297 | 2,688,606 | 2,350,852 |
| Current Liabilities | 140,869 | 134,319 | 155,926 | 161,571 | 136,978 | 146,205 | 139,662 | 128,164 |
| Long-Term Obligations | 1,760,292 | 1,804,055 | 1,767,149 | 1,793,848 | 1,745,785 | 1,638,460 | 1,696,930 | 1,390,143 |
| Total Liabilities | 1,988,103 | 2,027,045 | 2,009,720 | 2,044,972 | 1,978,174 | 1,874,665 | 1,904,528 | 1,576,005 |
| Stockholders' Equity | 1,232,565 | 1,190,416 | 1,149,833 | 1,177,337 | 1,114,602 | 1,114,632 | 784,078 | 774,847 |
| Shares Outstanding | 62,798 | 62,231 | 61,526 | 61,242 | 58,985 | 58,645 | 55,320 | 52,890 |
| **Statistical Record** | | | | | | | | |
| Return on Assets % | 4.06 | 3.95 | 3.85 | 3.11 | 4.26 | 6.89 | 4.71 | 4.96 |
| Return on Equity % | 10.72 | 10.57 | 10.55 | 8.58 | 11.61 | 20.60 | 15.23 | 14.64 |
| EBITDA Margin % | 81.95 | 80.90 | 63.99 | 61.08 | 63.40 | 65.52 | 65.98 | 65.39 |
| Net Margin % | 24.07 | 22.52 | 22.54 | 18.51 | 24.93 | 40.24 | 26.32 | 27.93 |
| Asset Turnover | 0.17 | 0.17 | 0.17 | 0.17 | 0.17 | 0.17 | 0.18 | 0.18 |
| Current Ratio | 0.67 | 0.61 | 0.83 | 1.58 | 0.98 | 1.04 | 0.71 | 0.68 |
| Debt to Equity | 1.43 | 1.52 | 1.54 | 1.52 | 1.57 | 1.47 | 2.16 | 1.79 |
| Price Range | 88.12-68.91 | 84.32-68.35 | 84.32-63.07 | 70.49-38.82 | 88.37-44.87 | 97.12-73.82 | 87.15-61.63 | 65.73-46.50 |
| P/E Ratio | 42.78-33.45 | 41.95-34.00 | 42.59-31.85 | 43.25-23.82 | 40.35-20.49 | 28.15-21.40 | 45.39-32.10 | 33.88-23.97 |
| Average Yield % | 3.32 | 3.42 | 3.53 | 4.70 | 3.52 | 2.76 | 3.40 | 4.17 |

**Address:** 1626 East Jefferson Street, Rockville, MD 20852
**Telephone:** 301-998-8100
**Web Site:** www.federalrealty.com

**Officers:** Donald C. Wood - President, Chief Executive Officer Dawn M. Becker - Executive Vice President, Chief Operating Officer, Secretary, General Counsel **Transfer Agents:**
American Stock Transfer & Trust Company, New York, NY

**No of Institutions:** 344
**Shares:** 64,638,564 **% Held:** 95.78

# FIRST FINANCIAL CORP. (IN)

| Exchange | Symbol | Price | 52Wk Range | Yield | P/E |
|---|---|---|---|---|---|
| NMS | THFF | $30.90 (8/31/2011) | 36.46-28.04 | 3.04 | 12.72 |

*7 Year Price Score 99.78 *NYSE Composite Index=100 *12 Month Price Score 101.81

**Interim Earnings (Per Share)**

| Qtr. | Mar | Jun | Sep | Dec |
|---|---|---|---|---|
| 2008 | 0.53 | 0.55 | 0.27 | 0.55 |
| 2009 | 0.35 | 0.35 | 0.59 | 0.44 |
| 2010 | 0.43 | 0.59 | 0.48 | 0.64 |
| 2011 | 0.67 | 0.64 | ... | ... |

**Interim Dividends (Per Share)**

| Amt | Decl | Ex | Rec | Pay |
|---|---|---|---|---|
| 0.45S | 12/16/2009 | 12/23/2009 | 12/28/2009 | 01/04/2010 |
| 0.46S | 05/18/2010 | 06/11/2010 | 06/15/2010 | 07/01/2010 |
| 0.46S | 11/17/2010 | 12/13/2010 | 12/15/2010 | 01/03/2011 |
| 0.47S | 05/18/2011 | 06/13/2011 | 06/15/2011 | 07/01/2011 |

**Indicated Div: $0.94**

**Valuation Analysis**

| | | | |
|---|---|---|---|
| Forecast EPS | $2.56 (09/02/2011) | | |
| Market Cap | $406.4 Million | Book Value | $342.7 Million |
| Price/Book | 1.19 | Price/Sales | N/A |

**Dividend Achiever Status**

| | |
|---|---|
| 10 Year Growth Rate | 4.97% |
| Total Years of Dividend Growth | 20 |

**Business Summary:** Banking (MIC: 5.1.1 SIC: 6022 NAIC: 522110)

First Financial is a financial holding company. Through its wholly-owned subsidiaries, First Financial Bank, N.A. of Vigo County, Indiana, The Morris Plan Company of Terre Haute, and Forrest Sherer Inc., an insurance agency, Co. provides a range of financial services including commercial, mortgage and consumer lending, lease financing, trust account services and depositor services in west-central Indiana and east-central Illinois. In addition, Co. provides loans to customers, primarily middle-income individuals, and investment activities. As of Dec 31 2010, Co. had total assets of $2.45 billion and total deposits of $1.90 billion.

**Recent Developments:** For the quarter ended June 30 2011, net income increased 9.1% to US$8.4 million from US$7.7 million in the year-earlier quarter. Net interest income increased 4.5% to US$25.2 million from US$24.1 million in the year-earlier quarter. Provision for loan losses was US$1.4 million versus US$2.2 million in the prior-year quarter, a decrease of 38.3%. Non-interest income was unchanged at US$7.9 million, while non-interest expense advanced 3.8% to US$19.4 million.

**Prospects:** Our evaluation of First Financial Corp. (IN) as of Sep. 6, 2011 is the result of our systematic analysis on three basic characteristics: earnings strength, relative valuation, and recent stock price movement. The company has generated a negative trend in earnings per share over the past 5 quarters. Because the company lacks sufficient analyst estimate data, we place greater weight on the historical EPS trend as the measure of earnings strength. Based on operating earnings yield, the company is undervalued when compared to all of the companies in our coverage universe. Share price changes over the past year indicates that THFF will perform in line with the market over the near term.

| **Financial Data** (US$ in Thousands) | 6 Mos | 3 Mos | 12/31/2010 | 12/31/2009 | 12/31/2008 | 12/31/2007 | 12/31/2006 | 12/31/2005 |
|---|---|---|---|---|---|---|---|---|
| Earnings Per Share | 2.43 | 2.38 | 2.14 | 1.73 | 1.89 | 1.94 | 1.77 | 1.72 |
| Cash Flow Per Share | 3.13 | 3.87 | 3.70 | 2.24 | 2.78 | 2.69 | 3.19 | 2.90 |
| Tang Book Value Per Share | 25.25 | 24.61 | 23.61 | 22.43 | 21.21 | 20.76 | 19.73 | 19.39 |
| Dividends Per Share | 0.930 | 0.920 | 0.920 | 0.900 | 0.890 | 0.870 | 0.850 | 0.820 |
| Dividend Payout % | 38.27 | 38.66 | 42.99 | 52.02 | 47.09 | 44.85 | 48.02 | 47.67 |
| **Income Statement** | | | | | | | | |
| Interest Income | 58,786 | 29,291 | 123,582 | 126,255 | 133,954 | 137,734 | 130,832 | 121,647 |
| Interest Expense | 8,872 | 4,536 | 26,966 | 39,261 | 52,490 | 62,961 | 57,129 | 47,469 |
| Net Interest Income | 49,914 | 24,755 | 96,616 | 86,994 | 81,464 | 74,773 | 73,703 | 74,178 |
| Provision for Losses | 2,534 | 1,182 | 9,200 | 11,870 | 7,855 | 6,580 | 6,983 | 11,698 |
| Non-Interest Income | 16,188 | 8,302 | 29,797 | 28,532 | 25,410 | 31,497 | 28,826 | 32,025 |
| Non-Interest Expense | 38,362 | 18,950 | 77,202 | 73,381 | 66,447 | 64,726 | 64,656 | 63,538 |
| Income Before Taxes | 25,206 | 12,925 | 40,011 | 30,275 | 32,572 | 34,964 | 30,890 | 30,967 |
| Income Taxes | 7,986 | 4,122 | 11,967 | 7,555 | 7,803 | 9,384 | 7,351 | 7,913 |
| Net Income | 17,220 | 8,803 | 28,044 | 22,720 | 24,769 | 25,580 | 23,539 | 23,054 |
| Average Shares | 13,152 | 13,152 | 13,120 | 13,119 | 13,110 | 13,178 | 13,295 | 13,433 |
| **Balance Sheet** | | | | | | | | |
| Net Loans & Leases | 1,623,449 | 1,588,712 | 1,617,810 | 1,612,327 | 1,455,047 | 1,427,716 | 1,376,586 | 1,379,699 |
| Total Assets | 2,501,952 | 2,496,164 | 2,451,095 | 2,518,722 | 2,302,675 | 2,231,562 | 2,175,998 | 2,136,918 |
| Total Deposits | 1,893,328 | 1,943,524 | 1,903,043 | 1,789,701 | 1,563,498 | 1,529,721 | 1,502,682 | 1,464,918 |
| Total Liabilities | 2,159,287 | 2,161,532 | 2,129,378 | 2,212,239 | 2,015,831 | 1,949,870 | 1,904,738 | 1,867,595 |
| Stockholders' Equity | 342,665 | 334,632 | 321,717 | 306,483 | 286,844 | 281,692 | 271,260 | 269,323 |
| Shares Outstanding | 13,151 | 13,151 | 13,151 | 13,129 | 13,116 | 13,136 | 13,270 | 13,373 |
| **Statistical Record** | | | | | | | | |
| Return on Assets % | 1.27 | 1.25 | 1.13 | 0.94 | 1.09 | 1.16 | 1.09 | 1.07 |
| Return on Equity % | 9.63 | 9.58 | 8.93 | 7.66 | 8.69 | 9.25 | 8.71 | 8.58 |
| Net Interest Margin % | 85.30 | 84.51 | 78.18 | 68.90 | 60.81 | 54.29 | 56.33 | 60.98 |
| Efficiency Ratio % | 51.93 | 50.41 | 50.33 | 47.41 | 41.70 | 38.25 | 40.50 | 41.35 |
| Loans to Deposits | 0.86 | 0.82 | 0.85 | 0.90 | 0.93 | 0.93 | 0.92 | 0.94 |
| Price Range | 36.46-25.31 | 36.46-25.31 | 36.46-25.31 | 42.67-26.90 | 49.30-25.30 | 35.74-23.48 | 35.92-27.00 | 35.03-25.39 |
| P/E Ratio | 15.00-10.42 | 15.32-10.63 | 17.04-11.83 | 24.66-15.55 | 26.08-13.39 | 18.42-12.10 | 20.29-15.25 | 20.37-14.76 |
| Average Yield % | 3.01 | 3.06 | 3.16 | 2.74 | 2.56 | 2.90 | 2.76 | 2.85 |

**Address:** One First Financial Plaza, Terre Haute, IN 47807
**Telephone:** 812-238-6000
**Web Site:** www.first-online.com

**Officers:** Donald E. Smith - Chairman, President Norman L. Lowery - Vice-Chairman, Chief Executive Officer **Transfer Agents:**
American Stock Transfer & Trust Company, New York, NY

**Investor Contact:** 812-238-6264
**No of Institutions:** 82
**Shares:** 8,085,720 **% Held:** 41.50

# FRANKLIN ELECTRIC CO., INC.

| Exchange | Symbol | Price | 52Wk Range | Yield | P/E |
|---|---|---|---|---|---|
| NMS | FELE | $42.91 (8/31/2011) | 50.33-31.67 | 1.26 | 19.16 |

***7 Year Price Score 103.19** *NYSE Composite Index=100 ***12 Month Price Score 108.35**

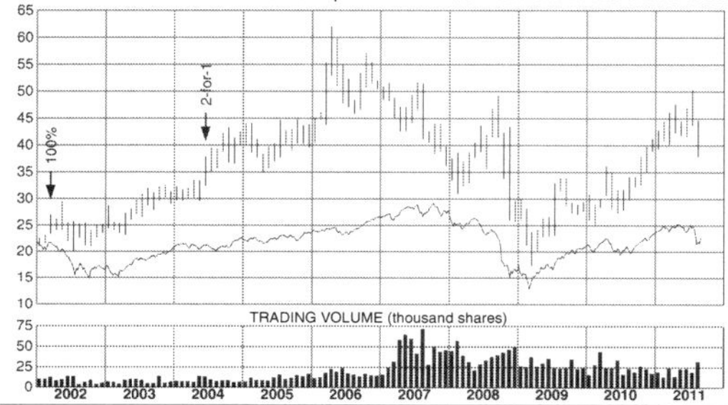


**Interim Earnings (Per Share)**

| Qtr. | Mar | Jun | Sep | Dec |
|---|---|---|---|---|
| 2008 | 0.35 | 0.66 | 0.74 | 0.15 |
| 2009 | 0.17 | 0.25 | 0.37 | 0.33 |
| 2010 | 0.31 | 0.47 | 0.52 | 0.36 |
| 2011 | 0.45 | 0.91 | ... | ... |

**Interim Dividends (Per Share)**

| Amt | Decl | Ex | Rec | Pay |
|---|---|---|---|---|
| 0.13Q | 10/27/2010 | 11/08/2010 | 11/11/2010 | 11/24/2010 |
| 0.13Q | 01/27/2011 | 02/08/2011 | 02/10/2011 | 02/24/2011 |
| 0.135Q | 05/06/2011 | 05/10/2011 | 05/12/2011 | 05/26/2011 |
| 0.135Q | 07/29/2011 | 08/09/2011 | 08/11/2011 | 08/25/2011 |

**Indicated Div: $0.54**

**Valuation Analysis**

| | | | |
|---|---|---|---|
| Forecast EPS | $2.68 (09/02/2011) | | |
| Market Cap | $994.6 Million | Book Value | $462.2 Million |
| Price/Book | 2.15 | Price/Sales | 1.29 |

**Dividend Achiever Status**

| | |
|---|---|
| **10 Year Growth Rate** | 8.16% |
| **Total Years of Dividend Growth** | 17 |

**Business Summary:** Electrical Equipment (MIC: 7.3.1 SIC: 3621 NAIC: 335312)

Franklin Electric designs, manufactures and distributes groundwater and fuel pumping systems, including submersible motors, pumps, electronic controls and related parts and equipment. Co.'s business consists of two segments. The Water Systems segment designs, manufactures and sells motors, pumps, electronic controls and related parts and equipment for use in groundwater and wastewater applications and, through the Fueling Segment, for fuel transfer applications. Fueling Systems designs, manufactures and sells pumps, pipe, sumps, fittings, vapor recovery components, electronic controls, monitoring devices and related parts and equipment for use in submersible fueling system applications.

**Recent Developments:** For the quarter ended July 2 2011, net income increased 92.2% to US$22.0 million from US$11.5 million in the year-earlier quarter. Revenues were US$224.1 million, up 17.7% from US$190.4 million the year before. Operating income was US$32.8 million versus US$18.6 million in the prior-year quarter, an increase of 76.4%. Direct operating expenses rose 16.8% to US$146.9 million from US$125.8 million in the comparable period the year before. Indirect operating expenses decreased 3.5% to US$44.4 million from US$46.1 million in the equivalent prior-year period.

**Prospects:** Our evaluation of Franklin Electric Co. Inc. as of Sep. 6, 2011 is the result of our systematic analysis on three basic characteristics: earnings strength, relative valuation, and recent stock price movement. The company has enjoyed a very positive trend in earnings per share over the past 5 quarters. Because the company lacks sufficient analyst estimate data, we place greater weight on the historical EPS trend as the measure of earnings strength. Based on operating earnings yield, the company is about fairly valued when compared to all of the companies in our coverage universe. Share price changes over the past year indicates that FELE will perform in line with the market over the near ter

**Financial Data**

| (US$ in Thousands) | 6 Mos | 3 Mos | 01/01/2011 | 01/02/2010 | 01/03/2009 | 12/29/2007 | 12/30/2006 | 12/31/2005 |
|---|---|---|---|---|---|---|---|---|
| Earnings Per Share | 2.24 | 1.80 | 1.66 | 1.12 | 1.90 | 1.22 | 2.44 | 1.98 |
| Cash Flow Per Share | 3.38 | 3.28 | 4.09 | 4.89 | 1.90 | 0.18 | 2.44 | 3.35 |
| Tang Book Value Per Share | 7.92 | 8.00 | 7.04 | 5.95 | 5.44 | 7.43 | 7.26 | 9.32 |
| Dividends Per Share | 0.525 | 0.520 | 0.515 | 0.500 | 0.495 | 0.470 | 0.430 | 0.380 |
| Dividend Payout % | 23.44 | 28.89 | 31.02 | 44.64 | 26.05 | 38.52 | 17.62 | 19.19 |
| **Income Statement** | | | | | | | | |
| Total Revenue | 409,449 | 185,331 | 713,792 | 625,991 | 745,627 | 602,025 | 557,948 | 439,559 |
| EBITDA | 62,684 | 23,001 | 84,270 | 68,640 | 97,504 | 68,764 | 106,606 | 86,830 |
| Depn & Amortn | 12,729 | 5,840 | 19,500 | 20,200 | 19,500 | 16,500 | 15,800 | 14,971 |
| Income Before Taxes | 45,343 | 14,955 | 55,078 | 38,892 | 67,036 | 44,117 | 87,433 | 71,093 |
| Income Taxes | 12,433 | 4,053 | 15,106 | 12,168 | 22,925 | 15,434 | 30,671 | 25,084 |
| Net Income | 32,330 | 10,679 | 38,968 | 25,986 | 44,111 | 28,683 | 56,998 | 46,009 |
| Average Shares | 23,700 | 23,700 | 23,500 | 23,300 | 23,200 | 23,500 | 23,300 | 23,200 |
| **Balance Sheet** | | | | | | | | |
| Current Assets | 410,336 | 385,364 | 370,455 | 311,593 | 317,660 | 309,479 | 217,790 | 203,020 |
| Total Assets | 863,761 | 799,857 | 779,914 | 718,298 | 694,057 | 662,237 | 526,925 | 379,762 |
| Current Liabilities | 135,131 | 109,844 | 109,307 | 83,143 | 81,412 | 90,649 | 93,957 | 64,022 |
| Long-Term Obligations | 154,384 | 151,207 | 151,245 | 151,242 | 185,528 | 151,287 | 51,043 | 12,324 |
| Total Liabilities | 401,513 | 357,306 | 362,065 | 330,125 | 345,120 | 283,693 | 181,094 | 112,200 |
| Stockholders' Equity | 462,248 | 442,551 | 417,849 | 388,173 | 348,937 | 378,544 | 345,831 | 267,562 |
| Shares Outstanding | 23,178 | 23,264 | 23,257 | 23,127 | 23,018 | 23,091 | 23,009 | 22,485 |
| **Statistical Record** | | | | | | | | |
| Return on Assets % | 6.64 | 5.55 | 5.22 | 3.69 | 6.40 | 4.84 | 12.61 | 12.94 |
| Return on Equity % | 12.48 | 10.19 | 9.70 | 7.07 | 11.93 | 7.94 | 18.64 | 18.38 |
| EBITDA Margin % | 15.31 | 12.41 | 11.81 | 10.97 | 13.08 | 11.42 | 19.11 | 19.75 |
| Net Margin % | 7.90 | 5.76 | 5.46 | 4.15 | 5.92 | 4.76 | 10.22 | 10.47 |
| Asset Turnover | 0.97 | 0.97 | 0.96 | 0.89 | 1.08 | 1.02 | 1.23 | 1.24 |
| Current Ratio | 3.04 | 3.51 | 3.39 | 3.75 | 3.90 | 3.41 | 2.32 | 3.17 |
| Debt to Equity | 0.33 | 0.34 | 0.36 | 0.39 | 0.53 | 0.40 | 0.15 | 0.05 |
| Price Range | 47.94-27.90 | 46.56-27.26 | 41.23-25.10 | 34.06-17.34 | 49.18-25.56 | 51.78-36.19 | 62.08-40.47 | 44.70-34.93 |
| P/E Ratio | 21.40-12.46 | 25.87-15.14 | 24.84-15.12 | 30.41-15.48 | 25.88-13.45 | 42.44-29.66 | 25.44-16.59 | 22.58-17.64 |
| Average Yield % | 1.35 | 1.45 | 1.59 | 1.87 | 1.33 | 1.05 | 0.85 | 0.94 |

**Address:** 400 East Spring Street, Bluffton, IN 46714
**Telephone:** 260-824-2900
**Web Site:** www.franklin-electric.com

**Officers:** R. Scott Trumbull - Chairman, Chief Executive Officer Gregg C. Sengstack - Senior Vice President, Division Officer **Transfer Agents:** LaSalle Bank National Association, Chicago, IL

**Investor Contact:** 260-824-2900
**No of Institutions:** 167
**Shares:** 18,356,464 **% Held:** 71.73

# FRANKLIN RESOURCES, INC.

| Exchange | Symbol | Price | 52Wk Range | Yield | P/E |
|---|---|---|---|---|---|
| NYS | BEN | $119.92 (8/31/2011) | 137.26-96.51 | 0.83 | 14.29 |

***7 Year Price Score 121.87** *NYSE Composite Index=100 ***12 Month Price Score 104.69**

**Interim Earnings (Per Share)**

| Qtr. | Dec | Mar | Jun | Sep |
|---|---|---|---|---|
| 2007-08 | 2.12 | 1.54 | 1.71 | 1.29 |
| 2008-09 | 0.52 | 0.48 | 1.29 | 1.59 |
| 2009-10 | 1.54 | 1.55 | 1.58 | 1.65 |
| 2010-11 | 2.23 | 2.25 | 2.26 | ... |

**Interim Dividends (Per Share)**

| Amt | Decl | Ex | Rec | Pay |
|---|---|---|---|---|
| 0.22Q | 09/16/2010 | 09/28/2010 | 09/30/2010 | 10/08/2010 |
| 0.25Q | 12/16/2010 | 12/29/2010 | 12/31/2010 | 01/07/2011 |
| 0.25Q | 03/15/2011 | 03/29/2011 | 03/31/2011 | 04/15/2011 |
| 0.25Q | 06/14/2011 | 06/28/2011 | 06/30/2011 | 07/15/2011 |

**Indicated Div: $1.00 (Div. Reinv. Plan)**

**Valuation Analysis**

Forecast EPS $9.01 (09/02/2011)

| Market Cap | $26.4 Billion | Book Value | $8.7 Billion |
|---|---|---|---|
| Price/Book | 3.04 | Price/Sales | 3.87 |

**Dividend Achiever Status**

| | |
|---|---|
| **10 Year Growth Rate** | 12.97% |
| **Total Years of Dividend Growth** | 21 |

**Business Summary:** Wealth Management (MIC: 5.5.2 SIC: 6282 NAIC: 523930)

Franklin Resources is a holding company. Through its subsidiaries, Co. provides fund administration, shareholder services, transfer agency, underwriting, distribution, custodial, trustee and other fiduciary services to its retail and institutional mutual funds, unregistered funds, and to institutional, high net-worth and separately-managed accounts and other investment products. Co.'s services are provided under the Franklin®, Templeton®, Mutual Series®, Bissett®, Fiduciary™ and Darby® brand names. Co. also provides retail banking, private banking and consumer lending services through its banking/finance segment. At Sep 30 2010, Co.'s total assets under management were $644.90 billion.

**Recent Developments:** For the quarter ended June 30 2011, net income increased 33.0% to US$478.2 million from US$359.7 million in the year-earlier quarter. Revenues were US$1.85 billion, up 20.8% from US$1.53 billion the year before. Operating income was US$682.7 million versus US$521.6 million in the prior-year quarter, an increase of 30.9%. Indirect operating expenses increased 15.6% to US$1.17 billion from US$1.01 billion in the equivalent prior-year period.

**Prospects:** Our evaluation of Franklin Resources Inc. as of Sep. 6, 2011 is the result of our systematic analysis on three basic characteristics: earnings strength, relative valuation, and recent stock price movement. The company has managed to produce a neutral trend in earnings per share over the past 5 quarters and while recent estimates for the company have been raised by analysts, BEN has posted better than expected results. Based on operating earnings yield, the company is undervalued when compared to all of the companies in our coverage universe. Share price changes over the past year indicates that BEN will perform in line with the market over the near term.

| **Financial Data** (US$ in Thousands) | 9 Mos | 6 Mos | 3 Mos | 09/30/2010 | 09/30/2009 | 09/30/2008 | 09/30/2007 | 09/30/2006 |
|---|---|---|---|---|---|---|---|---|
| Earnings Per Share | 8.39 | 7.71 | 7.01 | 6.33 | 3.87 | 6.67 | 7.03 | 4.86 |
| Cash Flow Per Share | 5.99 | 6.51 | 7.08 | 7.30 | 2.78 | 5.95 | 6.72 | 5.01 |
| Tang Book Value Per Share | 29.91 | 28.55 | 27.42 | 25.54 | 24.54 | 21.72 | 21.49 | 18.57 |
| Dividends Per Share | 0.970 | 0.940 | 0.910 | 3.880 | 0.840 | 0.800 | 0.600 | 0.480 |
| Dividend Payout % | 11.56 | 12.19 | 12.98 | 61.30 | 21.70 | 11.99 | 8.53 | 9.88 |
| **Income Statement** | | | | | | | | |
| Total Revenue | 5,302,909 | 3,449,876 | 1,700,313 | 5,852,999 | 4,194,087 | 6,032,386 | 6,205,769 | 5,050,726 |
| EBITDA | 2,203,995 | 1,467,134 | 741,288 | 2,121,149 | 1,296,718 | 2,181,766 | 2,687,140 | 1,878,809 |
| Depn & Amortn | 181,765 | 123,627 | 62,478 | 67,700 | 61,500 | 58,200 | 198,619 | 14,022 |
| Income Before Taxes | 2,004,137 | 1,332,810 | 673,775 | 2,049,860 | 1,263,365 | 2,208,236 | 2,465,301 | 1,835,566 |
| Income Taxes | 599,498 | 390,554 | 207,550 | 618,312 | 384,314 | 648,376 | 692,363 | 567,998 |
| Net Income | 1,507,604 | 1,004,257 | 501,157 | 1,445,689 | 896,778 | 1,588,213 | 1,772,938 | 1,267,568 |
| Average Shares | 221,284 | 222,696 | 224,253 | 227,353 | 231,454 | 238,281 | 252,118 | 261,745 |
| **Balance Sheet** | | | | | | | | |
| Current Assets | 7,746,798 | 7,418,674 | 6,954,569 | 6,932,798 | 5,948,987 | 5,494,883 | 5,896,637 | 5,443,823 |
| Total Assets | 13,150,999 | 12,827,382 | 12,391,955 | 10,708,088 | 9,468,463 | 9,176,520 | 9,943,250 | 9,499,859 |
| Current Liabilities | 1,969,954 | 1,956,738 | 1,785,687 | 1,662,390 | 1,390,120 | 1,534,720 | 2,129,405 | 1,825,762 |
| Long-Term Obligations | 2,029,302 | 2,081,041 | 2,123,093 | 949,903 | 57,000 | 227,433 | 162,125 | 627,919 |
| Total Liabilities | 4,464,500 | 4,413,874 | 4,262,227 | 2,981,094 | 1,836,290 | 2,102,156 | 2,610,975 | 2,815,131 |
| Stockholders' Equity | 8,686,499 | 8,413,508 | 8,129,728 | 7,726,994 | 7,632,173 | 7,074,364 | 7,332,275 | 6,684,728 |
| Shares Outstanding | 220,425 | 221,843 | 223,293 | 224,007 | 229,324 | 232,777 | 245,469 | 253,249 |
| **Statistical Record** | | | | | | | | |
| Return on Assets % | 15.96 | 15.55 | 14.72 | 14.33 | 9.62 | 16.57 | 18.24 | 13.78 |
| Return on Equity % | 23.34 | 22.00 | 20.85 | 18.83 | 12.20 | 21.99 | 25.30 | 20.50 |
| EBITDA Margin % | 41.56 | 42.53 | 43.60 | 36.24 | 30.92 | 36.17 | 43.30 | 37.20 |
| Net Margin % | 28.43 | 29.11 | 29.47 | 24.70 | 21.38 | 26.33 | 28.57 | 25.10 |
| Asset Turnover | 0.58 | 0.58 | 0.57 | 0.58 | 0.45 | 0.63 | 0.64 | 0.55 |
| Current Ratio | 3.93 | 3.79 | 3.89 | 4.17 | 4.28 | 3.58 | 2.77 | 2.98 |
| Debt to Equity | 0.23 | 0.25 | 0.26 | 0.12 | 0.01 | 0.03 | 0.02 | 0.09 |
| Price Range | 131.29-84.97 | 130.40-84.97 | 124.59-84.97 | 121.31-84.97 | 103.46-38.66 | 142.21-83.01 | 143.95-103.87 | 105.79-78.24 |
| P/E Ratio | 15.65-10.13 | 16.91-11.02 | 17.77-12.12 | 19.16-13.42 | 26.73-9.99 | 21.32-12.45 | 20.48-14.78 | 21.77-16.10 |
| Average Yield % | 0.84 | 0.85 | 0.86 | 3.76 | 1.23 | 0.71 | 0.48 | 0.52 |

| | | |
|---|---|---|
| **Address:** One Franklin Parkway, San Mateo, CA 94403<br>**Telephone:** 650-312-2000<br>**Web Site:** www.franklintempleton.com | **Officers:** Charles B. Johnson - Chairman Rupert H. Johnson - Vice-Chairman **Transfer Agents:** BNY Mellon Shareowner Services, Pittsburgh, PA | **No of Institutions:** 704<br>**Shares:** 120,164,752 **% Held:** 46.15 |

# FULLER (H.B.) COMPANY

| Exchange | Symbol | Price | 52Wk Range | Yield | P/E |
|---|---|---|---|---|---|
| NYS | FUL | $22.17 (8/31/2011) | 25.19-18.99 | 1.35 | 13.77 |

***7 Year Price Score 102.68** *NYSE Composite Index=100 ***12 Month Price Score 106.25**

**Interim Earnings (Per Share)**

| Qtr. | Feb | May | Aug | Nov |
|---|---|---|---|---|
| 2007-08 | 0.32 | 0.41 | 0.44 | (0.80) |
| 2008-09 | 0.13 | 0.36 | 0.72 | 0.49 |
| 2009-10 | 0.38 | 0.22 | 0.38 | 0.44 |
| 2010-11 | 0.29 | 0.50 | ... | ... |

**Interim Dividends (Per Share)**

| Amt | Decl | Ex | Rec | Pay |
|---|---|---|---|---|
| 0.07Q | 09/30/2010 | 10/12/2010 | 10/14/2010 | 10/28/2010 |
| 0.07Q | 01/20/2011 | 02/01/2011 | 02/03/2011 | 02/17/2011 |
| 0.075Q | 04/14/2011 | 04/26/2011 | 04/28/2011 | 05/12/2011 |
| 0.075Q | 07/07/2011 | 07/19/2011 | 07/21/2011 | 08/04/2011 |

**Indicated Div: $0.30 (Div. Reinv. Plan)**

**Valuation Analysis**

| | | | |
|---|---|---|---|
| Forecast EPS | $1.87 (09/03/2011) | | |
| Market Cap | $1.1 Billion | Book Value | $722.1 Million |
| Price/Book | 1.52 | Price/Sales | 0.76 |

**Dividend Achiever Status**

| | |
|---|---|
| 10 Year Growth Rate | 2.66% |
| Total Years of Dividend Growth | 43 |

**Business Summary:** Specialty Chemicals (MIC: 8.3.2 SIC: 2891 NAIC: 325520)

H.B. Fuller formulates, manufactures and markets adhesives, sealants, paints and other specialty chemical products. Co.'s adhesives products are used in manufacturing consumer goods such as food and beverage containers, disposable diapers, windows, doors, flooring, appliances, sportswear and footwear. Co. also provides adhesives for industrial applications such as water filtration products and multi-wall bags. In addition, Co. provides tile-setting adhesives, grout, sealants and related products for residential construction markets. Co.'s business is reported in four regional operating segments: North America, EIMEA (Europe, India, Middle East and Africa), Latin America and Asia Pacific.

**Recent Developments:** For the quarter ended May 28 2011, net income increased 125.5% to US$24.9 million from US$11.0 million in the year-earlier quarter. Revenues were US$393.7 million, up 13.2% from US$347.9 million the year before. Direct operating expenses rose 13.9% to US$281.1 million from US$246.8 million in the comparable period the year before. Indirect operating expenses decreased 7.7% to US$77.6 million from US$84.1 million in the equivalent prior-year period.

**Prospects:** Our evaluation of Fuller (H.B.) Company as of Sep. 6, 2011 is the result of our systematic analysis on three basic characteristics: earnings strength, relative valuation, and recent stock price movement. The company has enjoyed a very positive trend in earnings per share over the past 5 quarters. However, while recent estimates for the company have been lowered by analysts, FUL has posted better than expected results. Based on operating earnings yield, the company is undervalued when compared to all of the companies in our coverage universe. Share price changes over the past year indicates that FUL will perform poorly over the near term.

**Financial Data**

| (US$ in Thousands) | 6 Mos | 3 Mos | 11/27/2010 | 11/28/2009 | 11/29/2008 | 12/01/2007 | 12/02/2006 | 12/03/2005 |
|---|---|---|---|---|---|---|---|---|
| Earnings Per Share | 1.61 | 1.33 | 1.43 | 1.70 | 0.36 | 1.68 | 2.23 | 1.05 |
| Cash Flow Per Share | 1.87 | 1.52 | 1.53 | 1.48 | 0.85 | 2.35 | 3.20 | 2.15 |
| Tang Book Value Per Share | 9.56 | 8.56 | 7.96 | 7.12 | 6.17 | 7.92 | 6.84 | 8.33 |
| Dividends Per Share | 0.285 | 0.280 | 0.278 | 0.270 | 0.263 | 0.256 | 0.249 | 0.241 |
| Dividend Payout % | 17.70 | 21.05 | 19.44 | 15.88 | 72.92 | 15.24 | 11.15 | 22.87 |
| **Income Statement** | | | | | | | | |
| Total Revenue | 733,270 | 339,548 | 1,356,161 | 1,234,659 | 1,391,554 | 1,400,258 | 1,472,391 | 1,512,193 |
| EBITDA | 76,109 | 31,279 | 127,847 | 155,964 | 53,151 | 179,346 | 152,927 | 145,233 |
| Depn & Amortn | 19,963 | 10,066 | 30,361 | 34,709 | 34,369 | 36,349 | 39,460 | 52,712 |
| Income Before Taxes | 50,993 | 18,632 | 87,718 | 114,620 | 10,208 | 136,887 | 100,031 | 82,401 |
| Income Taxes | 16,269 | 6,285 | 25,307 | 36,728 | (5,693) | 37,712 | 23,682 | 24,990 |
| Net Income | 39,477 | 14,351 | 70,877 | 83,654 | 18,889 | 102,173 | 134,213 | 61,576 |
| Average Shares | 49,850 | 49,877 | 49,608 | 49,117 | 51,835 | 60,991 | 60,065 | 58,476 |
| **Balance Sheet** | | | | | | | | |
| Current Assets | 588,860 | 551,025 | 533,617 | 473,656 | 479,057 | 635,950 | 669,094 | 582,434 |
| Total Assets | 1,249,859 | 1,173,721 | 1,153,457 | 1,100,445 | 1,081,328 | 1,364,602 | 1,478,471 | 1,107,557 |
| Current Liabilities | 252,194 | 229,704 | 231,333 | 236,008 | 229,954 | 297,835 | 342,442 | 261,858 |
| Long-Term Obligations | 189,521 | 193,096 | 200,978 | 162,713 | 204,000 | 137,000 | 224,000 | 112,001 |
| Total Liabilities | 527,768 | 508,841 | 521,523 | 509,091 | 545,717 | 565,609 | 700,679 | 523,114 |
| Stockholders' Equity | 722,091 | 664,880 | 631,934 | 591,354 | 535,611 | 798,993 | 777,792 | 584,443 |
| Shares Outstanding | 49,348 | 49,419 | 49,194 | 48,657 | 48,447 | 57,436 | 59,931 | 58,369 |
| **Statistical Record** | | | | | | | | |
| Return on Assets % | 6.75 | 5.75 | 6.31 | 7.69 | 1.55 | 7.21 | 10.41 | 5.40 |
| Return on Equity % | 12.49 | 10.62 | 11.62 | 14.89 | 2.84 | 13.00 | 19.76 | 10.65 |
| EBITDA Margin % | 10.38 | 9.21 | 9.43 | 12.63 | 3.82 | 12.81 | 10.39 | 9.60 |
| Net Margin % | 5.38 | 4.23 | 5.23 | 6.78 | 1.36 | 7.30 | 9.12 | 4.07 |
| Asset Turnover | 1.20 | 1.20 | 1.21 | 1.13 | 1.14 | 0.99 | 1.14 | 1.33 |
| Current Ratio | 2.33 | 2.40 | 2.31 | 2.01 | 2.08 | 2.14 | 1.95 | 2.22 |
| Debt to Equity | 0.26 | 0.29 | 0.32 | 0.28 | 0.38 | 0.17 | 0.29 | 0.19 |
| Price Range | 23.58-18.69 | 24.56-18.69 | 24.56-18.69 | 22.88-9.76 | 27.41-12.94 | 31.35-24.11 | 27.54-15.65 | 17.93-12.73 |
| P/E Ratio | 14.65-11.61 | 18.47-14.05 | 17.17-13.07 | 13.46-5.74 | 76.14-35.94 | 18.66-14.35 | 12.35-7.02 | 17.08-12.12 |
| Average Yield % | 1.36 | 1.31 | 1.30 | 1.55 | 1.20 | 0.94 | 1.14 | 1.59 |

**Address:** 1200 Willow Lake Boulevard, St. Paul, MN 55110-5101
**Telephone:** 651-236-5900
**Web Site:** www.hbfuller.com

**Officers:** Lee R. Mitau - Chairman James J. Owens - President, Chief Executive Officer **Transfer Agents:** Wells Fargo Shareowner Services, Minnesota, MN

**Investor Contact:** 651-236-5150
**No of Institutions:** 193
**Shares:** 48,278,284 **% Held:** 86.81

# GENERAL DYNAMICS CORP.

| Exchange | Symbol | Price | 52Wk Range | Yield | P/E |
|---|---|---|---|---|---|
| NYS | GD | $64.08 (8/31/2011) | 78.11-55.87 | 2.93 | 9.14 |

*7 Year Price Score 102.37 *NYSE Composite Index=100 *12 Month Price Score 96.75

**Interim Earnings (Per Share)**

| Qtr. | Mar | Jun | Sep | Dec |
|---|---|---|---|---|
| 2008 | 1.42 | 1.60 | 1.59 | 1.57 |
| 2009 | 1.53 | 1.60 | 1.47 | 1.57 |
| 2010 | 1.53 | 1.67 | 1.70 | 1.91 |
| 2011 | 1.64 | 1.76 | ... | ... |

**Interim Dividends (Per Share)**

| Amt | Decl | Ex | Rec | Pay |
|---|---|---|---|---|
| 0.42Q | 12/01/2010 | 01/12/2011 | 01/14/2011 | 02/04/2011 |
| 0.47Q | 03/02/2011 | 04/06/2011 | 04/08/2011 | 05/06/2011 |
| 0.47Q | 06/01/2011 | 06/29/2011 | 07/01/2011 | 08/05/2011 |
| 0.47Q | 08/03/2011 | 10/05/2011 | 10/07/2011 | 11/10/2011 |

**Indicated Div: $1.88**

**Valuation Analysis**

Forecast EPS $7.20 (09/05/2011)

| | | | |
|---|---|---|---|
| Market Cap | $23.2 Billion | Book Value | $13.9 Billion |
| Price/Book | 1.66 | Price/Sales | 0.72 |

**Dividend Achiever Status**

| | |
|---|---|
| **10 Year Growth Rate** | 11.54% |
| **Total Years of Dividend Growth** | 19 |

**Business Summary:** Aerospace (MIC: 7.1.1 SIC: 3721 NAIC: 336411)

General Dynamics operates through four business groups: Aerospace, which produces Gulfstream aircraft, performs aircraft outfitting and refurbishments for other manufacturers, and provides aircraft services; Combat Systems, which designs and manufactures combat vehicles, weapons systems and munitions; Marine Systems, which designs and constructs surface ships and submarines; and Information Systems and Technology, which provides communications and information technology products and services. Co.'s primary customers are the U.S. military, other U.S. government organizations, the armed forces of other nations, and corporate and individual buyers of business aircraft.

**Recent Developments:** For the quarter ended July 3 2011, income from continuing operations increased 2.3% to US$666.0 million from US$651.0 million in the year-earlier quarter. Net income increased 0.8% to US$653.0 million from US$648.0 million in the year-earlier quarter. Revenues were US$7.88 billion, down 2.8% from US$8.10 billion the year before. Operating income was US$949.0 million versus US$985.0 million in the prior-year quarter, a decrease of 3.7%. Direct operating expenses declined 3.3% to US$6.43 billion from US$6.64 billion in the comparable period the year before. Indirect operating expenses increased 5.6% to US$505.0 million from US$478.0 million in the equivalent prior-year period.

**Prospects:** Our evaluation of General Dynamics Corp. as of Sep. 6, 2011 is the result of our systematic analysis on three basic characteristics: earnings strength, relative valuation, and recent stock price movement. The company has managed to produce a neutral trend in earnings per share over the past 5 quarters. However, while recent estimates for the company have been lowered by analysts, GD has posted better than expected results. Based on operating earnings yield, the company is undervalued when compared to all of the companies in our coverage universe. Share price changes over the past year indicates that GD will perform in line with the market over the near term.

**Financial Data**

| (US$ in Millions) | 6 Mos | 3 Mos | 12/31/2010 | 12/31/2009 | 12/31/2008 | 12/31/2007 | 12/31/2006 | 12/31/2005 |
|---|---|---|---|---|---|---|---|---|
| Earnings Per Share | 7.01 | 6.92 | 6.81 | 6.17 | 6.17 | 5.08 | 4.56 | 3.61 |
| Cash Flow Per Share | 9.17 | 8.33 | 7.83 | 7.41 | 7.83 | 7.23 | 5.27 | 5.12 |
| Tang Book Value Per Share | N.M. | N.M. | N.M. | N.M. | N.M. | 4.59 | 0.25 | 1.40 |
| Dividends Per Share | 1.780 | 1.680 | 1.640 | 1.490 | 1.340 | 1.100 | 0.890 | 0.780 |
| Dividend Payout % | 25.39 | 24.28 | 24.08 | 24.15 | 21.72 | 21.65 | 19.52 | 21.61 |
| **Income Statement** | | | | | | | | |
| Total Revenue | 15,677 | 7,798 | 32,466 | 31,981 | 29,300 | 27,240 | 24,063 | 21,244 |
| EBITDA | 2,208 | 1,073 | 4,516 | 4,235 | 4,263 | 3,685 | 3,145 | 2,319 |
| Depn & Amortn | 288 | 143 | 569 | 562 | 593 | 568 | 517 | 101 |
| Income Before Taxes | 1,855 | 896 | 3,790 | 3,513 | 3,604 | 3,047 | 2,527 | 2,100 |
| Income Taxes | 571 | 278 | 1,162 | 1,106 | 1,126 | 967 | 817 | 632 |
| Net Income | 1,271 | 618 | 2,624 | 2,394 | 2,459 | 2,072 | 1,856 | 1,461 |
| Average Shares | 371 | 376 | 385 | 387 | 398 | 408 | 406 | 404 |
| **Balance Sheet** | | | | | | | | |
| Current Assets | 14,673 | 14,795 | 14,186 | 13,249 | 11,950 | 12,298 | 9,880 | 9,173 |
| Total Assets | 33,361 | 33,104 | 32,545 | 31,077 | 28,373 | 25,733 | 22,376 | 19,591 |
| Current Liabilities | 11,493 | 11,252 | 11,177 | 10,371 | 10,360 | 9,164 | 7,824 | 6,907 |
| Long-Term Obligations | 2,409 | 2,411 | 2,430 | 3,159 | 3,113 | 2,118 | 2,774 | 2,781 |
| Total Liabilities | 19,436 | 19,227 | 19,229 | 18,654 | 18,320 | 13,965 | 12,549 | 11,446 |
| Stockholders' Equity | 13,925 | 13,877 | 13,316 | 12,423 | 10,053 | 11,768 | 9,827 | 8,145 |
| Shares Outstanding | 361 | 372 | 372 | 385 | 386 | 403 | 405 | 400 |
| **Statistical Record** | | | | | | | | |
| Return on Assets % | 8.25 | 8.24 | 8.25 | 8.05 | 9.06 | 8.61 | 8.85 | 7.87 |
| Return on Equity % | 19.80 | 19.85 | 20.39 | 21.30 | 22.48 | 19.19 | 20.65 | 19.06 |
| EBITDA Margin % | 14.08 | 13.76 | 13.91 | 13.24 | 14.55 | 13.53 | 13.07 | 10.92 |
| Net Margin % | 8.11 | 7.93 | 8.08 | 7.49 | 8.39 | 7.61 | 7.71 | 6.88 |
| Asset Turnover | 1.01 | 1.01 | 1.02 | 1.08 | 1.08 | 1.13 | 1.15 | 1.14 |
| Current Ratio | 1.28 | 1.31 | 1.27 | 1.28 | 1.15 | 1.34 | 1.26 | 1.33 |
| Debt to Equity | 0.17 | 0.17 | 0.18 | 0.25 | 0.31 | 0.18 | 0.28 | 0.34 |
| Price Range | 78.11-55.87 | 78.67-55.87 | 78.67-55.87 | 70.66-36.31 | 94.60-48.54 | 94.00-73.95 | 77.69-56.80 | 60.53-49.38 |
| P/E Ratio | 11.14-7.97 | 11.37-8.07 | 11.55-8.20 | 11.45-5.88 | 15.33-7.87 | 18.50-14.56 | 17.04-12.46 | 16.77-13.68 |
| Average Yield % | 2.58 | 2.46 | 2.43 | 2.62 | 1.70 | 1.35 | 1.33 | 1.41 |

**Address:** 2941 Fairview Park Drive, Suite 100, Falls Church, VA 22042-4513
**Telephone:** 703-876-3000
**Web Site:** www.generaldynamics.com

**Officers:** Jay L. Johnson - Chairman, Chief Executive Officer Gerard J. DeMuro - Executive Vice President
**Transfer Agents:** Computershare Trust Company N.A., Providence, RI

**Investor Contact:** 703-876-3195
**No of Institutions:** 943
**Shares:** 304,139,712 **% Held:** 73.74

# GENUINE PARTS CO.

| Exchange | Symbol | Price | 52Wk Range | Yield | P/E |
|---|---|---|---|---|---|
| NYS | GPC | $55.02 (8/31/2011) | 57.37-41.93 | 3.27 | 16.47 |

*7 Year Price Score 115.86 *NYSE Composite Index=100 *12 Month Price Score 105.28

**Interim Earnings (Per Share)**

| Qtr. | Mar | Jun | Sep | Dec |
|---|---|---|---|---|
| 2008 | 0.75 | 0.81 | 0.81 | 0.56 |
| 2009 | 0.56 | 0.65 | 0.67 | 0.62 |
| 2010 | 0.63 | 0.78 | 0.83 | 0.75 |
| 2011 | 0.80 | 0.96 | ... | ... |

**Interim Dividends (Per Share)**

| Amt | Decl | Ex | Rec | Pay |
|---|---|---|---|---|
| 0.41Q | 11/15/2010 | 12/08/2010 | 12/10/2010 | 01/03/2011 |
| 0.45Q | 02/21/2011 | 03/09/2011 | 03/11/2011 | 04/01/2011 |
| 0.45Q | 04/18/2011 | 06/08/2011 | 06/10/2011 | 07/01/2011 |
| 0.45Q | 08/15/2011 | 09/07/2011 | 09/09/2011 | 10/03/2011 |

**Indicated Div: $1.80 (Div. Reinv. Plan)**

**Valuation Analysis**

| | | | |
|---|---|---|---|
| Forecast EPS | $3.50 (09/03/2011) | | |
| Market Cap | $8.6 Billion | Book Value | $2.9 Billion |
| Price/Book | 2.95 | Price/Sales | 0.72 |

**Dividend Achiever Status**

| | |
|---|---|
| 10 Year Growth Rate | 3.73% |
| Total Years of Dividend Growth | 54 |

**Business Summary:** Retail - General Merchandise/Department Stores (MIC: 2.1.1 SIC: 5013 NAIC: 423120)

Genuine Parts is a service organization that distributes automotive replacement parts, industrial replacement parts, office products and electrical/electronic materials. Co. has four segments: Automotive Parts, which distributes automotive replacement parts and accessory items; Industrial Parts, which distributes maintenance, repair, and operation industrial replacement parts and related supplies; Office Products, which engages in the wholesale distribution of office and business related products that are used in the daily operation of businesses, schools, offices and institutions; and Electrical/Electronic Materials, which distributes materials to electrical and electronic manufacturers.

**Recent Developments:** For the quarter ended June 30 2011, net income increased 22.0% to US$151.8 million from US$124.5 million in the year-earlier quarter. Revenues were US$3.18 billion, up 11.9% from US$2.85 billion the year before. Direct operating expenses rose 12.0% to US$2.27 billion from US$2.02 billion in the comparable period the year before. Indirect operating expenses increased 8.5% to US$674.6 million from US$621.5 million in the equivalent prior-year period.

**Prospects:** Our evaluation of Genuine Parts Co. as of Sep. 6, 2011 is the result of our systematic analysis on three basic characteristics: earnings strength, relative valuation, and recent stock price movement. The company has managed to produce a neutral trend in earnings per share over the past 5 quarters. However, while recent estimates for the company have been mixed, GPC has posted better than expected results. Based on operating earnings yield, the company is about fairly valued when compared to all of the companies in our coverage universe. Share price changes over the past year indicates that GPC will perform very poorly over the near term.

**Financial Data**

| (US$ in Thousands) | 6 Mos | 3 Mos | 12/31/2010 | 12/31/2009 | 12/31/2008 | 12/31/2007 | 12/31/2006 | 12/31/2005 |
|---|---|---|---|---|---|---|---|---|
| Earnings Per Share | 3.34 | 3.16 | 3.00 | 2.50 | 2.92 | 2.98 | 2.76 | 2.50 |
| Cash Flow Per Share | 3.65 | 3.76 | 4.29 | 5.30 | 3.26 | 3.79 | 2.53 | 2.53 |
| Tang Book Value Per Share | 17.19 | 16.79 | 16.39 | 15.42 | 13.58 | 15.86 | 14.59 | 15.21 |
| Dividends Per Share | 1.720 | 1.680 | 1.640 | 1.600 | 1.560 | 1.460 | 1.350 | 1.250 |
| Dividend Payout % | 51.50 | 53.16 | 54.67 | 64.00 | 53.42 | 48.99 | 48.91 | 50.00 |
| **Income Statement** | | | | | | | | |
| Total Revenue | 6,159,182 | 2,974,198 | 11,207,589 | 10,057,512 | 11,015,263 | 10,843,195 | 10,457,942 | 9,783,050 |
| EBITDA | 479,004 | 214,525 | 794,581 | 675,694 | 803,050 | 935,774 | 875,915 | 774,593 |
| Depn & Amortn | 45,473 | 22,545 | 4,737 | 3,644 | 2,861 | 87,702 | 73,423 | 65,529 |
| Income Before Taxes | 433,531 | 191,980 | 761,783 | 644,165 | 768,468 | 816,745 | 770,916 | 709,064 |
| Income Taxes | 155,204 | 65,465 | 286,272 | 244,590 | 293,051 | 310,406 | 295,511 | 271,630 |
| Net Income | 278,327 | 126,515 | 475,511 | 399,575 | 475,417 | 506,339 | 475,405 | 437,434 |
| Average Shares | 158,243 | 158,656 | 158,461 | 159,707 | 162,986 | 170,135 | 172,486 | 175,007 |
| **Balance Sheet** | | | | | | | | |
| Current Assets | 4,633,291 | 4,495,229 | 4,414,887 | 4,032,828 | 3,871,420 | 4,053,012 | 3,835,127 | 3,806,882 |
| Total Assets | 5,717,001 | 5,569,520 | 5,465,044 | 5,004,689 | 4,786,350 | 4,774,069 | 4,496,984 | 4,771,538 |
| Current Liabilities | 2,107,415 | 2,003,636 | 1,971,814 | 1,408,284 | 1,287,103 | 1,547,976 | 1,198,768 | 1,249,104 |
| Long-Term Obligations | 250,000 | 250,000 | 262,622 | 513,504 | 512,708 | 263,707 | 512,248 | 500,000 |
| Total Liabilities | 2,794,977 | 2,699,258 | 2,671,225 | 2,383,359 | 2,462,018 | 2,057,353 | 1,946,993 | 2,077,581 |
| Stockholders' Equity | 2,922,024 | 2,870,262 | 2,793,819 | 2,621,330 | 2,324,332 | 2,716,716 | 2,549,991 | 2,693,957 |
| Shares Outstanding | 156,766 | 157,321 | 157,636 | 158,917 | 159,442 | 166,065 | 170,530 | 173,032 |
| **Statistical Record** | | | | | | | | |
| Return on Assets % | 9.67 | 9.34 | 9.08 | 8.16 | 9.92 | 10.92 | 10.26 | 9.48 |
| Return on Equity % | 18.93 | 18.08 | 17.56 | 16.16 | 18.81 | 19.23 | 18.13 | 16.70 |
| EBITDA Margin % | 7.78 | 7.21 | 7.09 | 6.72 | 7.29 | 8.63 | 8.38 | 7.92 |
| Net Margin % | 4.52 | 4.25 | 4.24 | 3.97 | 4.32 | 4.67 | 4.55 | 4.47 |
| Asset Turnover | 2.18 | 2.16 | 2.14 | 2.05 | 2.30 | 2.34 | 2.26 | 2.12 |
| Current Ratio | 2.20 | 2.24 | 2.24 | 2.86 | 3.01 | 2.62 | 3.20 | 3.05 |
| Debt to Equity | 0.09 | 0.09 | 0.09 | 0.20 | 0.22 | 0.10 | 0.20 | 0.19 |
| Price Range | 55.90-39.44 | 55.25-38.98 | 51.50-36.96 | 39.38-25.06 | 46.30-31.21 | 51.43-46.30 | 48.02-40.26 | 46.50-40.98 |
| P/E Ratio | 16.74-11.81 | 17.48-12.34 | 17.17-12.32 | 15.75-10.02 | 15.86-10.69 | 17.26-15.54 | 17.40-14.59 | 18.60-16.39 |
| Average Yield % | 3.50 | 3.63 | 3.80 | 4.63 | 3.84 | 2.98 | 3.09 | 2.87 |

**Address:** 2999 Circle 75 Parkway, Atlanta, GA 30339
**Telephone:** 770-953-1700
**Web Site:** www.genpt.com

**Officers:** Thomas C. Gallagher - Chairman, President, Chief Executive Officer Jerry W. Nix - Vice-Chairman, Executive Vice President, Chief Financial Officer **Transfer Agents:** Computershare, Providence, RI

**Investor Contact:** 770-953-1700
**No of Institutions:** 624
**Shares:** 125,129,528 **% Held:** 70.14

# GETTY REALTY CORP.

| Exchange | Symbol | Price | 52Wk Range | Yield | P/E |
|---|---|---|---|---|---|
| NYS | GTY | $19.01 (8/31/2011) | 32.15-16.52 | 10.10 | 11.45 |

*7 Year Price Score 103.53 *NYSE Composite Index=100 *12 Month Price Score 84.90

**Interim Earnings (Per Share)**

| Qtr. | Mar | Jun | Sep | Dec |
|---|---|---|---|---|
| 2008 | 0.46 | 0.43 | 0.42 | 0.38 |
| 2009 | 0.40 | 0.55 | 0.49 | 0.46 |
| 2010 | 0.48 | 0.51 | 0.45 | 0.41 |
| 2011 | 0.35 | 0.45 | ... | ... |

**Interim Dividends (Per Share)**

| Amt | Decl | Ex | Rec | Pay |
|---|---|---|---|---|
| 0.48Q | 08/19/2010 | 09/28/2010 | 09/30/2010 | 10/14/2010 |
| 0.48Q | 11/18/2010 | 12/30/2010 | 01/03/2011 | 01/13/2011 |
| 0.48Q | 03/07/2011 | 03/29/2011 | 03/31/2011 | 04/14/2011 |
| 0.48Q | 05/19/2011 | 06/28/2011 | 06/30/2011 | 07/14/2011 |

**Indicated Div: $1.92 (Div. Reinv. Plan)**

**Valuation Analysis**

| | | | |
|---|---|---|---|
| Forecast EPS | N/A | | |
| Market Cap | $634.8 Million | Book Value | $402.8 Million |
| Price/Book | 1.58 | Price/Sales | 6.54 |

**Dividend Achiever Status**

| | |
|---|---|
| 10 Year Growth Rate | 8.25% |
| Total Years of Dividend Growth | 13 |

**Business Summary:** REITs (MIC: 5.3.1 SIC: 6798 NAIC: 525930)

Getty Realty is a real estate investment trust. Co. owns, leases and finances retail motor fuel and convenience store properties and petroleum distribution terminals. The operators of Co.'s properties are primarily distributors and retailers engaged in the sale of gasoline and other motor fuel products, convenience store products, and automotive repair services. Co.'s properties are located in the Northeast and Mid-Atlantic regions of the U.S., primarily in New York, Massachusetts, New Jersey, Pennsylvania, Connecticut, Maryland, Virginia, New Hampshire, Maine, Rhode Island, Texas, North Carolina, Delaware, Hawaii, California, Florida, Ohio, Arkansas, Illinois, North Dakota and Vermont.

**Recent Developments:** For the quarter ended June 30 2011, net income increased 8.9% to US$15.2 million from US$14.0 million in the year-earlier quarter. Revenues were US$27.9 million, up 28.0% from US$21.8 million the year before. Revenues from property income rose 24 8% to US$27.1 million from US$21.7 million in the corresponding quarter a year earlier.

**Prospects:** Our evaluation of Getty Realty Corp. as of Sep. 6, 2011 is the result of our systematic analysis on three basic characteristics: earnings strength, relative valuation, and recent stock price movement. The company has enjoyed a very positive trend in earnings per share over the past 5 quarters. Because the company lacks sufficient analyst estimate data, we place greater weight on the historical EPS trend as the measure of earnings strength. Based on operating earnings yield, the company is undervalued when compared to all of the companies in our coverage universe. Share price changes over the past year indicates that GTY will perform well over the near term.

| **Financial Data** (US$ in Thousands) | 6 Mos | 3 Mos | 12/31/2010 | 12/31/2009 | 12/31/2008 | 12/31/2007 | 12/31/2006 | 12/31/2005 |
|---|---|---|---|---|---|---|---|---|
| Earnings Per Share | 1.66 | 1.72 | 1.85 | 1.90 | 1.69 | 1.37 | 1.73 | 1.84 |
| Cash Flow Per Share | 1.84 | 1.79 | 2.04 | 2.12 | 1.92 | 1.80 | 1.85 | 1.84 |
| Tang Book Value Per Share | 12.06 | 12.07 | 10.52 | 8.39 | 8.31 | 8.57 | 9.11 | 9.22 |
| Dividends Per Share | 1.920 | 1.915 | 1.910 | 1.890 | 1.870 | 1.850 | 1.810 | 1.760 |
| Dividend Payout % | 115.66 | 111.34 | 103.24 | 99.47 | 110.65 | 135.04 | 104.62 | 95.65 |
| **Income Statement** | | | | | | | | |
| Total Revenue | 53,297 | 25,025 | 88,332 | 84,539 | 81,163 | 78,462 | 72,405 | 71,377 |
| EBITDA | 28,691 | 12,573 | 63,312 | 56,240 | 57,281 | 44,610 | 53,435 | 53,832 |
| Depn & Amortn | (262) | (46) | 8,155 | 9,725 | 11,085 | 8,747 | 7,883 | 8,255 |
| Income Before Taxes | 26,288 | 11,300 | 50,107 | 41,424 | 39,162 | 28,103 | 42,025 | 43,954 |
| Income Taxes | ... | ... | ... | ... | ... | ... | (700) | (1,494) |
| Net Income | 26,588 | 11,386 | 51,700 | 47,049 | 41,810 | 33,894 | 42,725 | 45,448 |
| Average Shares | 33,395 | 32,504 | 27,953 | 24,767 | 24,774 | 24,787 | 24,759 | 24,729 |
| **Balance Sheet** | | | | | | | | |
| Current Assets | 78,716 | 86,917 | 46,234 | 46,511 | 43,568 | 45,122 | 41,814 | 39,286 |
| Total Assets | 636,842 | 650,552 | 427,144 | 432,872 | 387,813 | 396,911 | 309,283 | 299,981 |
| Current Liabilities | 219,091 | 232,929 | 47,319 | 49,633 | 51,666 | 52,233 | 38,514 | 37,874 |
| Long-Term Obligations | ... | ... | 64,890 | 175,570 | 130,250 | 132,500 | 45,194 | 34,224 |
| Total Liabilities | 234,091 | 247,641 | 112,209 | 225,203 | 181,916 | 184,733 | 83,708 | 72,098 |
| Stockholders' Equity | 402,751 | 402,911 | 314,935 | 207,669 | 205,897 | 212,178 | 225,575 | 227,883 |
| Shares Outstanding | 33,394 | 33,394 | 29,944 | 24,766 | 24,766 | 24,765 | 24,764 | 24,716 |
| **Statistical Record** | | | | | | | | |
| Return on Assets % | 9.76 | 9.46 | 12.02 | 11.47 | 10.63 | 9.60 | 14.03 | 15.39 |
| Return on Equity % | 14.57 | 16.75 | 19.79 | 22.75 | 19.95 | 15.49 | 18.84 | 20.05 |
| EBITDA Margin % | 53.83 | 50.24 | 71.68 | 66.53 | 70.58 | 56.86 | 73.80 | 75.42 |
| Net Margin % | 49.89 | 45.50 | 58.53 | 55.65 | 51.51 | 43.20 | 59.01 | 63.67 |
| Asset Turnover | 0.18 | 0.17 | 0.21 | 0.21 | 0.21 | 0.22 | 0.24 | 0.24 |
| Current Ratio | 0.36 | 0.37 | 0.98 | 0.94 | 0.84 | 0.86 | 1.09 | 1.04 |
| Debt to Equity | ... | ... | 0.21 | 0.85 | 0.63 | 0.62 | 0.20 | 0.15 |
| Price Range | 32.15-21.51 | 32.15-20.72 | 32.15-20.72 | 25.98-13.69 | 28.55-13.67 | 31.96-24.69 | 33.53-25.75 | 30.69-25.03 |
| P/E Ratio | 19.37-12.96 | 18.69-12.05 | 17.38-11.20 | 13.67-7.21 | 16.89-8.09 | 23.33-18.02 | 19.38-14.88 | 16.68-13.60 |
| Average Yield % | 7.27 | 7.38 | 7.63 | 9.06 | 9.34 | 6.57 | 6.27 | 6.44 |

| | | |
|---|---|---|
| **Address:** 125 Jericho Turnpike, Suite 103, Jericho, NY 11753<br>**Telephone:** 516-478-5400<br>**Web Site:** www.gettyrealty.com | **Officers:** Leo Liebowitz - Chairman David B. Driscoll - President, Chief Executive Officer **Transfer Agents:** Registrar and Transfer Company, Cranford, NJ | **No of Institutions:** 181<br>**Shares:** 17,579,542 **% Held:** 53.98 |

# GORMAN-RUPP CO.

| Exchange | Symbol | Price | 52Wk Range | Yield | P/E |
|---|---|---|---|---|---|
| ASE | GRC | $29.20 (8/31/2011) | 35.49-20.56 | 1.23 | 19.34 |

***7 Year Price Score 138.57** *NYSE Composite Index=100 ***12 Month Price Score 113.10**

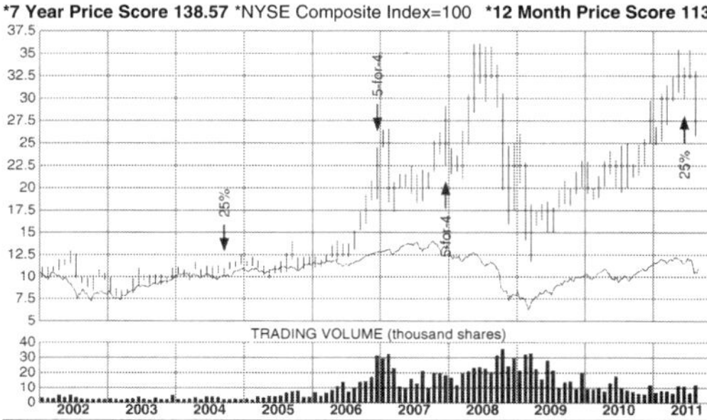


**Interim Earnings (Per Share)**

| Qtr. | Mar | Jun | Sep | Dec |
|---|---|---|---|---|
| 2008 | 0.34 | 0.38 | 0.35 | 0.23 |
| 2009 | 0.22 | 0.23 | 0.25 | 0.18 |
| 2010 | 0.22 | 0.27 | 0.30 | 0.46 |
| 2011 | 0.34 | 0.42 | ... | ... |

**Interim Dividends (Per Share)**

| Amt | Decl | Ex | Rec | Pay |
|---|---|---|---|---|
| 0.084Q | 01/27/2011 | 02/11/2011 | 02/15/2011 | 03/10/2011 |
| 0.09Q | 04/28/2011 | 05/11/2011 | 05/13/2011 | 06/10/2011 |
| 25% | 04/28/2011 | 06/13/2011 | 05/13/2011 | 06/10/2011 |
| 0.09Q | 07/28/2011 | 08/11/2011 | 08/15/2011 | 09/09/2011 |

**Indicated Div: $0.36 (Div. Reinv. Plan)**

**Valuation Analysis**

| | | | |
|---|---|---|---|
| Forecast EPS | $1.58 (09/02/2011) | | |
| Market Cap | $612.8 Million | Book Value | $214.1 Million |
| Price/Book | 2.86 | Price/Sales | 1.83 |

**Dividend Achiever Status**

| | |
|---|---|
| **10 Year Growth Rate** | 2.51% |
| **Total Years of Dividend Growth** | 38 |

**Business Summary:** Industrial Machinery & Equipment (MIC: 7.2.1 SIC: 3561 NAIC: 333911)

Gorman-Rupp designs, manufactures and sells pumps and related equipment (pump and motor controls) for use in water, wastewater, construction, industrial, petroleum, original equipment, agriculture, fire protection, heating, ventilating and air conditioning, military and other liquid-handling applications. Co.'s product line consists of pump models ranging in size from 0.25 inch to 144 inches and ranging in rated capacity from less than one gallon per minute to in excess of 750,000 gallons per minute. Co. produces types of pumps which include self priming centrifugal, standard centrifugal, magnetic drive centrifugal, axial and mixed flow, rotary gear, diaphragm, bellows and oscillating.

**Recent Developments:** For the quarter ended June 30 2011, net income increased 57.8% to US$8.9 million from US$5.7 million in the year-earlier quarter. Revenues were US$92.2 million, up 27.3% from US$72.4 million the year before. Operating income was US$13.5 million versus US$8.9 million in the prior-year quarter, an increase of 51.3%. Direct operating expenses rose 23.3% to US$67.9 million from US$55.1 million in the comparable period the year before. Indirect operating expenses increased 28.6% to US$10.8 million from US$8.4 million in the equivalent prior-year period.

**Prospects:** Our evaluation of Gorman-Rupp Co. as of Sep. 6, 2011 is the result of our systematic analysis on three basic characteristics: earnings strength, relative valuation, and recent stock price movement. The company has generated a negative trend in earnings per share over the past 5 quarters. However, while recent estimates for the company have been mixed, GRC has posted better than expected results. Based on operating earnings yield, the company is about fairly valued when compared to all of the companies in our coverage universe. Share price changes over the past year indicates that GRC will perform well over the near term.

**Financial Data**

| (US$ in Thousands) | 6 Mos | 3 Mos | 12/31/2010 | 12/31/2009 | 12/31/2008 | 12/31/2007 | 12/31/2006 | 12/31/2005 |
|---|---|---|---|---|---|---|---|---|
| Earnings Per Share | 1.51 | 1.36 | 1.24 | 0.87 | 1.30 | 1.10 | 0.92 | 0.52 |
| Cash Flow Per Share | 0.93 | 1.19 | 1.37 | 2.38 | 1.40 | 1.67 | 0.90 | 0.15 |
| Tang Book Value Per Share | 8.96 | 8.57 | 8.26 | 8.01 | 7.14 | 6.70 | 5.79 | 5.74 |
| Dividends Per Share | 0.342 | 0.336 | 0.336 | 0.324 | 0.320 | 0.310 | 0.292 | 0.287 |
| Dividend Payout % | 22.68 | 24.71 | 27.10 | 37.16 | 24.54 | 28.32 | 31.89 | 54.91 |
| **Income Statement** | | | | | | | | |
| Total Revenue | 176,233 | 84,074 | 296,808 | 266,242 | 330,646 | 305,562 | 270,910 | 231,249 |
| EBITDA | 29,672 | 13,433 | 38,754 | 36,210 | 48,342 | 42,980 | 34,414 | 23,946 |
| Depn & Amortn | 5,629 | 2,805 | 421 | 8,955 | 7,848 | 7,597 | 6,688 | 6,808 |
| Income Before Taxes | 24,043 | 10,628 | 38,333 | 27,255 | 40,494 | 35,383 | 27,726 | 17,138 |
| Income Taxes | 7,999 | 3,509 | 12,370 | 8,986 | 13,297 | 12,524 | 8,654 | 6,235 |
| Net Income | 16,044 | 7,119 | 25,963 | 18,269 | 27,197 | 22,859 | 19,072 | 10,903 |
| Average Shares | 20,984 | 20,985 | 20,905 | 20,886 | 20,881 | 20,876 | 20,872 | 20,867 |
| **Balance Sheet** | | | | | | | | |
| Current Assets | 158,158 | 148,567 | 143,194 | 131,400 | 134,266 | 135,288 | 120,118 | 110,501 |
| Total Assets | 305,109 | 293,601 | 286,707 | 249,424 | 231,538 | 211,534 | 187,540 | 179,541 |
| Current Liabilities | 63,542 | 60,241 | 59,678 | 43,175 | 35,569 | 33,481 | 27,646 | 28,219 |
| Total Liabilities | 91,050 | 87,625 | 86,873 | 72,519 | 72,950 | 62,094 | 59,398 | 52,493 |
| Stockholders' Equity | 214,059 | 205,976 | 199,834 | 176,905 | 158,588 | 149,440 | 128,142 | 127,048 |
| Shares Outstanding | 20,984 | 20,985 | 20,985 | 20,888 | 20,884 | 20,878 | 20,874 | 20,870 |
| **Statistical Record** | | | | | | | | |
| Return on Assets % | 11.51 | 10.51 | 9.69 | 7.60 | 12.24 | 11.46 | 10.39 | 6.32 |
| Return on Equity % | 16.09 | 14.82 | 13.78 | 10.89 | 17.61 | 16.47 | 14.95 | 8.76 |
| EBITDA Margin % | 16.84 | 15.98 | 13.06 | 13.60 | 14.62 | 14.07 | 12.70 | 10.36 |
| Net Margin % | 9.10 | 8.47 | 8.75 | 6.86 | 8.23 | 7.48 | 7.04 | 4.71 |
| Asset Turnover | 1.21 | 1.16 | 1.11 | 1.11 | 1.49 | 1.53 | 1.48 | 1.34 |
| Current Ratio | 2.49 | 2.47 | 2.40 | 3.04 | 3.77 | 4.04 | 4.34 | 3.92 |
| Price Range | 35.49-19.52 | 31.51-19.52 | 29.80-18.68 | 26.08-11.72 | 36.12-15.92 | 29.20-17.34 | 24.54-11.06 | 14.00-9.80 |
| P/E Ratio | 23.50-12.93 | 23.17-14.35 | 24.03-15.06 | 29.98-13.47 | 27.78-12.25 | 26.55-15.77 | 26.68-12.02 | 26.93-18.85 |
| Average Yield % | 1.28 | 1.39 | 1.50 | 1.74 | 1.19 | 1.41 | 2.00 | 2.52 |

| | | |
|---|---|---|
| **Address:** 600 South Airport Road, Mansfield, OH 44903<br>**Telephone:** 419-755-1011<br>**Web Site:** www.gormanrupp.com | **Officers:** James C. Gorman - Chairman Jeffrey S. Gorman - President, Chief Executive Officer **Transfer Agents:** Computershare Investor Services, LLC, Canton, MA | **Investor Contact:** 419-755-1294<br>**No of Institutions:** 106<br>**Shares:** 11,189,808 **% Held:** 50.49 |

# GRACO INC.

| Exchange | Symbol | Price | 52Wk Range | Yield | P/E |
|---|---|---|---|---|---|
| NYS | GGG | $39.48 (8/31/2011) | 53.84-27.91 | 2.13 | 18.28 |

***7 Year Price Score 114.55** *NYSE Composite Index=100 ***12 Month Price Score 107.15**

**Interim Earnings (Per Share)**

| Qtr. | Mar | Jun | Sep | Dec |
|---|---|---|---|---|
| 2008 | 0.57 | 0.69 | 0.54 | 0.18 |
| 2009 | 0.05 | 0.19 | 0.29 | 0.28 |
| 2010 | 0.34 | 0.41 | 0.50 | 0.44 |
| 2011 | 0.61 | 0.61 | ... | ... |

**Interim Dividends (Per Share)**

| Amt | Decl | Ex | Rec | Pay |
|---|---|---|---|---|
| 0.20Q | 09/17/2010 | 10/14/2010 | 10/18/2010 | 11/03/2010 |
| 0.21Q | 12/03/2010 | 01/13/2011 | 01/18/2011 | 02/02/2011 |
| 0.21Q | 02/18/2011 | 04/14/2011 | 04/18/2011 | 05/04/2011 |
| 0.21Q | 06/10/2011 | 07/14/2011 | 07/18/2011 | 08/03/2011 |

**Indicated Div: $0.84**

**Valuation Analysis**

| | | | |
|---|---|---|---|
| Forecast EPS | $2.25 (09/02/2011) | | |
| Market Cap | $2.4 Billion | Book Value | $342.7 Million |
| Price/Book | 7.01 | Price/Sales | 2.86 |

**Dividend Achiever Status**

| | |
|---|---|
| **10 Year Growth Rate** | 16.23% |
| **Total Years of Dividend Growth** | 11 |

**Business Summary:** Industrial Machinery & Equipment (MIC: 7.2.1 SIC: 3561 NAIC: 333911)
Graco designs, manufactures and sells equipment that pumps, meters, mixes, dispenses and sprays a variety of fluids and semi-solids. Co. operates its business in three reportable segments: Industrial, which markets equipment and pre-engineered packages for moving and applying paints, coatings, sealants, adhesives and other fluids; Contractor, which markets sprayers for architectural coatings for painting, corrosion control, texture, and line striping; and Lubrication, which markets products to move and dispense lubricants for oil change facilities, service garages, fleet service centers, automobile dealerships, the mining industry and industrial lubrication applications.

**Recent Developments:** For the quarter ended July 1 2011, net income increased 53.4% to US$38.1 million from US$24.8 million in the year-earlier quarter. Revenues were US$234.7 million, up 22.2% from US$192.1 million the year before. Operating income was US$58.3 million versus US$39.2 million in the prior-year quarter, an increase of 48.6%. Direct operating expenses rose 13.4% to US$102.2 million from US$90.2 million in the comparable period the year before. Indirect operating expenses increased 18.3% to US$74.2 million from US$62.7 million in the equivalent prior-year period.

**Prospects:** Our evaluation of Graco Inc. as of Sep. 6, 2011 is the result of our systematic analysis on three basic characteristics: earnings strength, relative valuation, and recent stock price movement. The company has generated a negative trend in earnings per share over the past 5 quarters. However, while recent estimates for the company have been lowered by analysts, GGG has posted results that fell short of analysts expectations. Based on operating earnings yield, the company is about fairly valued when compared to all of the companies in our coverage universe. Share price changes over the past year indicates that GGG will perform well over the near term.

| **Financial Data** (US$ in Thousands) | 6 Mos | 3 Mos | 12/31/2010 | 12/25/2009 | 12/26/2008 | 12/28/2007 | 12/29/2006 | 12/30/2005 |
|---|---|---|---|---|---|---|---|---|
| Earnings Per Share | 2.16 | 1.96 | 1.69 | 0.81 | 1.99 | 2.32 | 2.17 | 1.80 |
| Cash Flow Per Share | 1.93 | 1.65 | 1.65 | 2.45 | 2.70 | 2.73 | 2.30 | 2.23 |
| Tang Book Value Per Share | 3.72 | 3.12 | 2.38 | 1.28 | 0.37 | 2.19 | 3.20 | 2.87 |
| Dividends Per Share | 0.820 | 0.810 | 0.800 | 0.760 | 0.740 | 0.660 | 0.580 | 0.520 |
| Dividend Payout % | 37.96 | 41.33 | 47.34 | 93.83 | 37.19 | 28.45 | 26.73 | 28.89 |
| **Income Statement** | | | | | | | | |
| Total Revenue | 452,342 | 217,679 | 744,065 | 579,212 | 817,270 | 841,339 | 816,468 | 731,702 |
| EBITDA | 132,542 | 65,496 | 173,924 | 95,221 | 207,112 | 251,769 | 243,512 | 209,028 |
| Depn & Amortn | 17,542 | 8,427 | 21,200 | 21,700 | 20,900 | 19,500 | 18,200 | 18,300 |
| Income Before Taxes | 112,652 | 56,453 | 148,540 | 68,667 | 178,579 | 228,836 | 224,366 | 189,354 |
| Income Taxes | 37,300 | 19,200 | 45,700 | 19,700 | 57,700 | 76,000 | 74,600 | 63,500 |
| Net Income | 75,352 | 37,253 | 102,840 | 48,967 | 120,879 | 152,836 | 149,766 | 125,854 |
| Average Shares | 62,070 | 61,360 | 60,803 | 60,229 | 60,835 | 65,984 | 68,977 | 69,862 |
| **Balance Sheet** | | | | | | | | |
| Current Assets | 417,136 | 380,525 | 252,408 | 188,993 | 260,595 | 248,832 | 238,983 | 213,898 |
| Total Assets | 692,269 | 655,422 | 530,474 | 476,434 | 579,850 | 536,724 | 511,603 | 445,630 |
| Current Liabilities | 121,286 | 121,763 | 119,754 | 103,815 | 121,160 | 125,877 | 128,929 | 111,581 |
| Long-Term Obligations | 150,000 | 150,000 | 70,255 | 86,260 | 180,000 | 107,060 | ... | ... |
| Total Liabilities | 349,532 | 349,200 | 266,360 | 266,780 | 412,216 | 292,050 | 180,599 | 157,946 |
| Stockholders' Equity | 342,737 | 306,222 | 264,114 | 209,654 | 167,634 | 244,674 | 331,004 | 287,684 |
| Shares Outstanding | 60,850 | 60,649 | 60,047 | 59,999 | 59,516 | 61,963 | 66,804 | 68,387 |
| **Statistical Record** | | | | | | | | |
| Return on Assets % | 21.85 | 20.60 | 20.10 | 9.30 | 21.71 | 29.24 | 31.38 | 30.88 |
| Return on Equity % | 45.65 | 44.54 | 42.71 | 26.03 | 58.80 | 53.24 | 48.55 | 48.68 |
| EBITDA Margin % | 29.30 | 30.09 | 23.37 | 16.44 | 25.34 | 29.92 | 29.83 | 28.57 |
| Net Margin % | 16.66 | 17.11 | 13.82 | 8.45 | 14.79 | 18.17 | 18.34 | 17.20 |
| Asset Turnover | 1.38 | 1.37 | 1.45 | 1.10 | 1.47 | 1.61 | 1.71 | 1.80 |
| Current Ratio | 3.44 | 3.13 | 2.11 | 1.82 | 2.15 | 1.98 | 1.85 | 1.92 |
| Debt to Equity | 0.44 | 0.49 | 0.27 | 0.41 | 1.07 | 0.44 | ... | ... |
| Price Range | 51.53-27.57 | 45.49-27.57 | 40.29-26.38 | 30.70-14.48 | 41.84-17.67 | 46.07-36.25 | 48.95-36.48 | 40.68-31.83 |
| P/E Ratio | 23.86-12.76 | 23.21-14.07 | 23.84-15.61 | 37.90-17.88 | 21.03-8.88 | 19.86-15.63 | 22.56-16.81 | 22.60-17.68 |
| Average Yield % | 2.11 | 2.31 | 2.51 | 3.18 | 2.17 | 1.66 | 1.39 | 1.44 |

**Address:** 88 - 11th Avenue N.E., Minneapolis, MN 55413
**Telephone:** 612-623-6000
**Web Site:** www.graco.com

**Officers:** Lee R. Mitau - Chairman Patrick J. McHale - President, Chief Executive Officer **Transfer Agents:** Wells Fargo Bank, N.A., St. Paul, MN

**Investor Contact:** 612-623-6659
**No of Institutions:** 298
**Shares:** 56,655,360 **% Held:** 81.35

# GRAINGER (W.W.) INC.

| Exchange | Symbol | Price | 52Wk Range | Yield | P/E |
|---|---|---|---|---|---|
| NYS | GWW | $154.10 (8/31/2011) | 160.78-105.79 | 1.71 | 18.32 |

***7 Year Price Score 154.46** *NYSE Composite Index=100 ***12 Month Price Score 109.08**

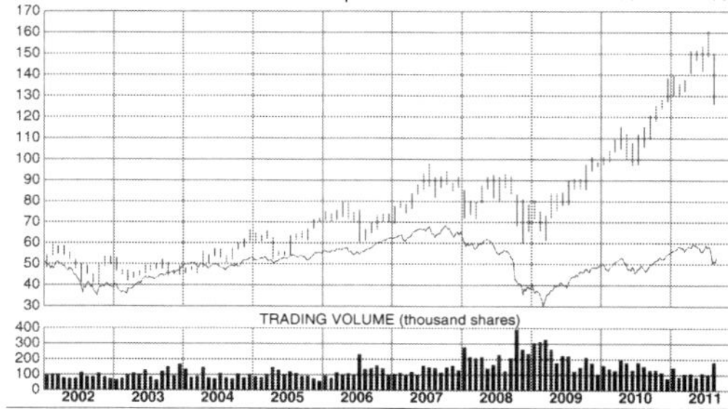


**Interim Earnings (Per Share)**

| Qtr. | Mar | Jun | Sep | Dec |
|---|---|---|---|---|
| 2008 | 1.43 | 1.43 | 1.79 | 1.39 |
| 2009 | 1.25 | 1.21 | 1.88 | 1.28 |
| 2010 | 1.31 | 1.73 | 2.06 | 1.83 |
| 2011 | 2.18 | 2.34 | ... | ... |

**Interim Dividends (Per Share)**

| Amt | Decl | Ex | Rec | Pay |
|---|---|---|---|---|
| 0.54Q | 10/26/2010 | 11/04/2010 | 11/08/2010 | 12/01/2010 |
| 0.54Q | 01/26/2011 | 02/10/2011 | 02/14/2011 | 03/01/2011 |
| 0.66Q | 04/27/2011 | 05/05/2011 | 05/09/2011 | 06/01/2011 |
| 0.66Q | 07/27/2011 | 08/04/2011 | 08/08/2011 | 09/01/2011 |

**Indicated Div: $2.64**

**Valuation Analysis**

| | | | |
|---|---|---|---|
| Forecast EPS | $8.70 (09/05/2011) | | |
| Market Cap | $10.8 Billion | Book Value | $2.5 Billion |
| Price/Book | 4.33 | Price/Sales | 1.41 |

**Dividend Achiever Status**

| | |
|---|---|
| **10 Year Growth Rate** | 11.59% |
| **Total Years of Dividend Growth** | 39 |

**Business Summary:** Electrical Equipment (MIC: 7.3.1 SIC: 5099 NAIC: 423990)

W.W. Grainger is a distributor of maintenance, repair and operating supplies and other related products and services used by businesses and institutions primarily in the U.S., Canada, and also in Asia and Latin America. Co. has two segments: The U.S., which provides material handling equipment, safety and security supplies, lighting and electrical products, power and hand tools, pumps and plumbing supplies, cleaning and maintenance supplies, forestry and agriculture equipment, vehicle and fleet components and other items focused on the facilities maintenance market; and Canada, which distributes tools, fasteners, safety supplies, instruments, welding and shop equipment, and other items.

**Recent Developments:** For the quarter ended June 30 2011, net income increased 32.3% to US$171.6 million from US$129.7 million in the year-earlier quarter. Revenues were US$2.00 billion, up 12.3% from US$1.78 billion the year before. Operating income was US$265.3 million versus US$214.9 million in the prior-year quarter, an increase of 23.4%. Direct operating expenses rose 10.0% to US$1.14 billion from US$1.04 billion in the comparable period the year before. Indirect operating expenses increased 12.2% to US$597.1 million from US$532.2 million in the equivalent prior-year period.

**Prospects:** Our evaluation of Grainger (W.W.) Inc. as of Sep. 6, 2011 is the result of our systematic analysis on three basic characteristics: earnings strength, relative valuation, and recent stock price movement. The company has managed to produce a neutral trend in earnings per share over the past 5 quarters. However, while recent estimates for the company have been lowered by analysts, GWW has posted better than expected results. Based on operating earnings yield, the company is about fairly valued when compared to all of the companies in our coverage universe. Share price changes over the past year indicates that GWW will perform very poorly over the near term.

**Financial Data**

| (US$ in Thousands) | 6 Mos | 3 Mos | 12/31/2010 | 12/31/2009 | 12/31/2008 | 12/31/2007 | 12/31/2006 | 12/31/2005 |
|---|---|---|---|---|---|---|---|---|
| Earnings Per Share | 8.41 | 7.80 | 6.93 | 5.62 | 6.04 | 4.94 | 4.24 | 3.78 |
| Cash Flow Per Share | 8.90 | 8.67 | 8.42 | 9.93 | 6.90 | 5.69 | 4.97 | 4.83 |
| Tang Book Value Per Share | 29.96 | 27.81 | 26.20 | 25.08 | 24.35 | 23.47 | 23.40 | 23.48 |
| Dividends Per Share | 2.280 | 2.160 | 2.080 | 1.780 | 1.550 | 1.340 | 1.110 | 0.920 |
| Dividend Payout % | 27.11 | 27.69 | 30.01 | 31.67 | 25.66 | 27.13 | 26.18 | 24.34 |
| **Income Statement** | | | | | | | | |
| Total Revenue | 3,886,634 | 1,883,612 | 7,182,158 | 6,221,991 | 6,850,032 | 6,418,014 | 5,883,654 | 5,526,636 |
| EBITDA | 593,753 | 295,033 | 1,010,610 | 860,779 | 918,562 | 802,693 | 699,061 | 627,628 |
| Depn & Amortn | 66,044 | 32,571 | 149,678 | 147,531 | 139,570 | 131,999 | 118,568 | 108,782 |
| Income Before Taxes | 524,858 | 261,064 | 853,960 | 705,840 | 769,576 | 679,845 | 600,063 | 529,865 |
| Income Taxes | 194,333 | 102,076 | 340,196 | 276,565 | 297,863 | 261,741 | 219,624 | 186,350 |
| Net Income | 327,818 | 157,933 | 510,865 | 430,466 | 475,355 | 420,120 | 383,399 | 346,324 |
| Average Shares | 71,122 | 70,906 | 72,138 | 74,891 | 78,750 | 85,044 | 90,523 | 91,588 |
| **Balance Sheet** | | | | | | | | |
| Current Assets | 2,506,258 | 2,261,702 | 2,238,071 | 2,131,515 | 2,144,109 | 1,800,817 | 1,862,086 | 1,997,868 |
| Total Assets | 4,200,435 | 3,933,424 | 3,904,377 | 3,726,332 | 3,515,417 | 3,094,028 | 3,046,088 | 3,107,921 |
| Current Liabilities | 1,078,773 | 781,967 | 869,303 | 776,799 | 761,734 | 826,403 | 706,323 | 726,964 |
| Long-Term Obligations | 200,469 | 413,339 | 420,446 | 437,500 | 488,228 | 4,895 | 4,895 | 4,895 |
| Total Liabilities | 1,712,137 | 1,616,798 | 1,699,161 | 1,562,612 | 1,481,612 | 995,920 | 868,473 | 818,945 |
| Stockholders' Equity | 2,488,298 | 2,316,626 | 2,205,216 | 2,163,720 | 2,033,805 | 2,098,108 | 2,177,615 | 2,288,976 |
| Shares Outstanding | 69,893 | 69,270 | 69,377 | 72,276 | 74,781 | 79,459 | 84,067 | 89,715 |
| **Statistical Record** | | | | | | | | |
| Return on Assets % | 15.39 | 14.71 | 13.39 | 11.89 | 14.34 | 13.68 | 12.46 | 11.71 |
| Return on Equity % | 26.35 | 24.70 | 23.39 | 20.51 | 22.95 | 19.65 | 17.17 | 15.90 |
| EBITDA Margin % | 15.28 | 15.66 | 14.07 | 13.83 | 13.41 | 12.51 | 11.88 | 11.36 |
| Net Margin % | 8.43 | 8.38 | 7.11 | 6.92 | 6.94 | 6.55 | 6.52 | 6.27 |
| Asset Turnover | 1.92 | 1.91 | 1.88 | 1.72 | 2.07 | 2.09 | 1.91 | 1.87 |
| Current Ratio | 2.32 | 2.89 | 2.57 | 2.74 | 2.81 | 2.18 | 2.64 | 2.75 |
| Debt to Equity | 0.08 | 0.18 | 0.19 | 0.20 | 0.24 | N.M. | N.M. | N.M. |
| Price Range | 153.65-97.54 | 139.54-97.29 | 138.65-96.83 | 101.43-61.37 | 93.10-59.92 | 98.45-69.34 | 79.73-60.62 | 71.97-52.29 |
| P/E Ratio | 18.27-11.60 | 17.89-12.47 | 20.01-13.97 | 18.05-10.92 | 15.41-9.92 | 19.93-14.04 | 18.80-14.30 | 19.04-13.83 |
| Average Yield % | 1.76 | 1.80 | 1.86 | 2.13 | 1.91 | 1.57 | 1.56 | 1.48 |

**Address:** 100 Grainger Parkway, Lake Forest, IL 60045-5201
**Telephone:** 847-535-1000
**Web Site:** www.grainger.com

**Officers:** James T. Ryan - Chairman, President, Chief Executive Officer Court D. Carruthers - Senior Vice President, Division Officer **Transfer Agents:** ComputerShare Investor Services, Providence, RI

**Investor Contact:** 847-535-1000
**No of Institutions:** 611
**Shares:** 55,687,444 **% Held:** 70.58

# HARLEYSVILLE GROUP, INC. (PA)

| Exchange | Symbol | Price | 52Wk Range | Yield | P/E |
|---|---|---|---|---|---|
| NMS | HGIC | $28.67 (8/31/2011) | 37.51-27.05 | 5.30 | 16.29 |

*7 Year Price Score 106.65 *NYSE Composite Index=100 *12 Month Price Score 90.72

**Interim Earnings (Per Share)**

| Qtr. | Mar | Jun | Sep | Dec |
|---|---|---|---|---|
| 2008 | 0.79 | 0.31 | 0.15 | 0.17 |
| 2009 | 0.61 | 0.72 | 0.88 | 0.87 |
| 2010 | 0.29 | 0.61 | 0.76 | 0.77 |
| 2011 | 0.66 | (0.43) | ... | ... |

**Interim Dividends (Per Share)**

| Amt | Decl | Ex | Rec | Pay |
|---|---|---|---|---|
| 1.44Sp | 11/01/2010 | 11/10/2010 | 11/15/2010 | 11/30/2010 |
| 0.36Q | 02/17/2011 | 03/11/2011 | 03/15/2011 | 03/30/2011 |
| 0.36Q | 05/03/2011 | 06/13/2011 | 06/15/2011 | 06/30/2011 |
| 0.38Q | 08/05/2011 | 09/13/2011 | 09/15/2011 | 09/30/2011 |

**Indicated Div: $1.52 (Div. Reinv. Plan)**

**Valuation Analysis**

| | | | |
|---|---|---|---|
| Forecast EPS | $1.27 (09/02/2011) | | |
| Market Cap | $777.8 Million | Book Value | $781.7 Million |
| Price/Book | 1.00 | Price/Sales | 0.79 |

**Dividend Achiever Status**

| | |
|---|---|
| **10 Year Growth Rate** | 8.98% |
| **Total Years of Dividend Growth** | 24 |

**Business Summary:** General Insurance (MIC: 5.2.1 SIC: 6331 NAIC: 524126)

Harleysville Group is an insurance holding company. Through its subsidiaries, Co. is engaged in underwriting property and casualty insurance in both the personal and commercial lines of insurance. The personal lines of insurance include both auto and homeowners, and the commercial lines include auto, commercial multi-peril and workers compensation. Using independent agents, Co. markets personal lines of insurance to individuals, and commercial lines of insurance to small and medium-sized businesses in the eastern and midwestern U.S. Co. has three reportable segments, which consist of the personal lines of insurance, the commercial lines of insurance and the investment function.

**Recent Developments:** For the quarter ended June 30 2011, net loss amounted to US$11.3 million versus net income of US$17.1 million in the year-earlier quarter. Revenues were US$230.7 million, down 5.3% from US$243.5 million the year before. Net premiums earned were US$201.0 million versus US$213.5 million in the prior-year quarter, a decrease of 5.9%. Net investment income fell 3.8% to US$24.8 million from US$25.8 million a year ago.

**Prospects:** Our evaluation of Harleysville Group Inc. (PA) as of Sep. 6, 2011 is the result of our systematic analysis on three basic characteristics: earnings strength, relative valuation, and recent stock price movement. The company has suffered a very negative trend in earnings per share over the past 5 quarters. However, while recent estimates for the company have been lowered by analysts, HGIC has posted results that fell short of analysts expectations. Based on operating earnings yield, the company is about fairly valued when compared to all of the companies in our coverage universe. Share price changes over the past year indicates that HGIC will perform poorly over the near term.

| **Financial Data** (US$ in Thousands) | 6 Mos | 3 Mos | 12/31/2010 | 12/31/2009 | 12/31/2008 | 12/31/2007 | 12/31/2006 | 12/31/2005 |
|---|---|---|---|---|---|---|---|---|
| Earnings Per Share | 1.76 | 2.80 | 2.42 | 3.07 | 1.44 | 3.19 | 3.52 | 2.01 |
| Cash Flow Per Share | (0.11) | 2.02 | 3.57 | 3.77 | 6.79 | 5.55 | 5.35 | 5.44 |
| Tang Book Value Per Share | 28.81 | 28.58 | 28.42 | 27.98 | 23.18 | 25.03 | 22.49 | 20.07 |
| Dividends Per Share | 2.880 | 2.845 | 2.810 | 1.250 | 1.100 | 0.880 | 0.730 | 0.690 |
| Dividend Payout % | 163.64 | 101.61 | 116.12 | 40.72 | 76.39 | 27.59 | 20.74 | 34.33 |
| **Income Statement** | | | | | | | | |
| Premium Income | 400,729 | 199,753 | 866,350 | 858,500 | 918,515 | 833,024 | 838,821 | 841,567 |
| Total Revenue | 476,189 | 245,522 | 986,272 | 980,620 | 985,316 | 962,012 | 999,171 | 948,340 |
| Benefits & Claims | 327,281 | 144,195 | 589,105 | 552,491 | 610,768 | 523,030 | 539,823 | 567,396 |
| Income Before Taxes | 96 | 25,494 | 82,712 | 115,998 | 50,962 | 142,995 | 156,368 | 78,921 |
| Income Taxes | (6,803) | 7,267 | 15,814 | 29,702 | 8,643 | 42,941 | 46,241 | 17,490 |
| Net Income | 6,899 | 18,227 | 66,898 | 86,296 | 42,319 | 100,054 | 111,069 | 61,431 |
| Average Shares | 27,090 | 27,612 | 27,727 | 28,127 | 29,320 | 31,354 | 31,525 | 30,585 |
| **Balance Sheet** | | | | | | | | |
| Total Assets | 3,239,465 | 3,228,913 | 3,278,232 | 3,301,986 | 3,155,318 | 3,072,445 | 2,990,984 | 2,905,266 |
| Total Liabilities | 2,457,801 | 2,454,122 | 2,509,599 | 2,529,358 | 2,502,684 | 2,313,604 | 2,278,822 | 2,290,883 |
| Stockholders' Equity | 781,664 | 774,791 | 768,633 | 772,628 | 652,634 | 758,841 | 712,162 | 614,383 |
| Shares Outstanding | 27,128 | 27,106 | 27,044 | 27,615 | 28,156 | 30,322 | 31,662 | 30,610 |
| **Statistical Record** | | | | | | | | |
| Return on Assets % | 1.49 | 2.36 | 2.03 | 2.67 | 1.36 | 3.30 | 3.77 | 2.18 |
| Return on Equity % | 6.20 | 9.92 | 8.68 | 12.11 | 5.98 | 13.60 | 16.75 | 10.22 |
| Loss Ratio % | 81.67 | 72.19 | 68.00 | 64.36 | 66.50 | 62.79 | 64.35 | 67.42 |
| Net Margin % | 1.45 | 7.42 | 6.78 | 8.80 | 4.29 | 10.40 | 11.12 | 6.48 |
| Price Range | 37.51-29.85 | 37.51-30.56 | 37.51-30.76 | 34.73-26.51 | 40.37-27.22 | 37.55-28.01 | 38.64-26.11 | 27.80-18.90 |
| P/E Ratio | 21.31-16.96 | 13.40-10.91 | 15.50-12.71 | 11.31-8.64 | 28.03-18.90 | 11.77-8.78 | 10.98-7.42 | 13.83-9.40 |
| Average Yield % | 8.60 | 8.44 | 8.47 | 4.07 | 3.12 | 2.70 | 2.32 | 3.08 |

**Address:** 355 Maple Avenue, Harleysville, PA 19438-2297
**Telephone:** 215-256-5000
**Web Site:** www.harleysvillegroup.com

**Officers:** Michael L. Browne - President, Chief Executive Officer Mark R. Cummins - Executive Vice President, Chief Investment Officer, Treasurer, Affiliate Officer **Transfer Agents:** Mellon Investor Services, South Hackensack, NJ

**Investor Contact:** 215-256-5151
**No of Institutions:** 111
**Shares:** 11,088,116 **% Held:** 34.97

# HARSCO CORP.

| Exchange | Symbol | Price | 52Wk Range | Yield | P/E |
|---|---|---|---|---|---|
| NYS | HSC | $22.86 (8/31/2011) | 36.49-19.94 | 3.59 | 103.91 |

*7 Year Price Score 79.54 *NYSE Composite Index=100 *12 Month Price Score 93.42

**Interim Earnings (Per Share)**

| Qtr. | Mar | Jun | Sep | Dec |
|---|---|---|---|---|
| 2008 | 0.67 | 1.06 | 0.95 | 0.19 |
| 2009 | 0.23 | 0.50 | 0.25 | 0.48 |
| 2010 | 0.10 | 0.37 | 0.25 | (0.64) |
| 2011 | 0.14 | 0.47 | ... | ... |

**Interim Dividends (Per Share)**

| Amt | Decl | Ex | Rec | Pay |
|---|---|---|---|---|
| 0.205Q | 09/21/2010 | 10/13/2010 | 10/15/2010 | 11/15/2010 |
| 0.205Q | 11/18/2010 | 01/12/2011 | 01/14/2011 | 02/15/2011 |
| 0.205Q | 02/22/2011 | 04/12/2011 | 04/14/2011 | 05/16/2011 |
| 0.205Q | 06/14/2011 | 07/13/2011 | 07/15/2011 | 08/15/2011 |

**Indicated Div: $0.82 (Div. Reinv. Plan)**

**Valuation Analysis**

| | | | |
|---|---|---|---|
| Forecast EPS | $1.42 (09/02/2011) | | |
| Market Cap | $1.8 Billion | Book Value | $1.5 Billion |
| Price/Book | 1.22 | Price/Sales | 0.58 |

**Dividend Achiever Status**

| | |
|---|---|
| 10 Year Growth Rate | 5.50% |
| Total Years of Dividend Growth | 16 |

**Business Summary:** Industrial Machinery & Equipment (MIC: 7.2.1 SIC: 3441 NAIC: 332312)

Harsco is a provider of industrial services and engineered products. Co.'s operations fall into four segments: Harsco Infrastructure, which provides the rental of scaffolding, shoring, concrete forming and other access-related applications; Harsco Metals & Minerals, which provide on-site, outsourced services; Harsco Rail, which provides equipment and services to maintain, repair and construct railway track; and Harsco Industrial, which includes: Harsco Industrial IKG, which manufactures a line of industrial grating products; Harsco Industrial Air-X-Changers, which supplies air-cooled heat exchangers; and Harsco Industrial Patterson-Kelley, which manufactures heat transfer products.

**Recent Developments:** For the quarter ended June 30 2011, income from continuing operations increased 14.3% to US$39.2 million from US$34.3 million in the year-earlier quarter. Net income increased 23.1% to US$38.7 million from US$31.5 million in the year-earlier quarter. Revenues were US$875.1 million, up 11.3% from US$786.5 million the year before. Operating income was US$64.4 million versus US$61.9 million in the prior-year quarter, an increase of 4.1%. Direct operating expenses rose 13.0% to US$667.2 million from US$590.5 million in the comparable period the year before. Indirect operating expenses increased 6.9% to US$143.4 million from US$134.1 million in the equivalent prior-year period.

**Prospects:** Our evaluation of Harsco Corp. as of Sep. 6, 2011 is the result of our systematic analysis on three basic characteristics: earnings strength, relative valuation, and recent stock price movement. The company has enjoyed a very positive trend in earnings per share over the past 5 quarters. However, while recent estimates for the company have been mixed, HSC has posted better than expected results. Based on operating earnings yield, the company is about fairly valued when compared to all of the companies in our coverage universe. Share price changes over the past year indicates that HSC will perform well over the near term.

**Financial Data**

| (US$ in Thousands) | 6 Mos | 3 Mos | 12/31/2010 | 12/31/2009 | 12/31/2008 | 12/31/2007 | 12/31/2006 | 12/31/2005 |
|---|---|---|---|---|---|---|---|---|
| Earnings Per Share | 0.22 | 0.12 | 0.08 | 1.47 | 2.87 | 3.53 | 2.33 | 1.86 |
| Cash Flow Per Share | 4.24 | 4.77 | 4.98 | 5.41 | 6.85 | 5.60 | 4.88 | 3.79 |
| Tang Book Value Per Share | 8.54 | 7.93 | 7.70 | 7.76 | 7.99 | 7.78 | 5.30 | 4.25 |
| Dividends Per Share | 0.820 | 0.820 | 0.820 | 0.795 | 0.780 | 0.710 | 0.650 | 0.600 |
| Dividend Payout % | 372.73 | 683.33 | 1,025.00 | 54.08 | 27.18 | 20.11 | 27.96 | 32.26 |
| **Income Statement** | | | | | | | | |
| Total Revenue | 1,654,146 | 779,055 | 3,038,678 | 2,990,577 | 3,967,822 | 3,688,160 | 3,423,293 | 2,766,210 |
| EBITDA | 248,395 | 105,558 | 357,665 | 501,632 | 719,835 | 735,202 | 603,866 | 464,087 |
| Depn & Amortn | 154,926 | 76,522 | 279,234 | 282,976 | 307,847 | 277,397 | 245,397 | 195,139 |
| Income Before Taxes | 70,229 | 17,821 | 20,476 | 158,838 | 342,436 | 381,390 | 301,700 | 230,195 |
| Income Taxes | 17,735 | 4,400 | 4,276 | 18,509 | 91,820 | 117,598 | 97,523 | 64,771 |
| Net Income | 49,158 | 11,431 | 6,754 | 118,777 | 240,945 | 299,492 | 196,398 | 156,657 |
| Average Shares | 81,010 | 80,944 | 80,761 | 80,586 | 84,029 | 84,724 | 84,430 | 84,160 |
| **Balance Sheet** | | | | | | | | |
| Current Assets | 1,232,154 | 1,197,058 | 1,154,946 | 1,169,338 | 1,205,488 | 1,345,337 | 1,231,622 | 1,101,023 |
| Total Assets | 3,620,046 | 3,550,510 | 3,469,220 | 3,639,240 | 3,562,970 | 3,905,430 | 3,326,423 | 2,975,804 |
| Current Liabilities | 828,044 | 809,337 | 767,864 | 751,102 | 888,426 | 873,970 | 910,775 | 748,403 |
| Long-Term Obligations | 855,490 | 854,495 | 849,724 | 901,734 | 891,817 | 1,012,087 | 864,817 | 905,859 |
| Total Liabilities | 2,110,950 | 2,087,384 | 2,037,526 | 2,165,663 | 2,149,294 | 2,339,311 | 2,180,059 | 1,981,910 |
| Stockholders' Equity | 1,509,096 | 1,463,126 | 1,431,694 | 1,473,577 | 1,413,676 | 1,566,119 | 1,146,364 | 993,894 |
| Shares Outstanding | 80,712 | 80,670 | 80,514 | 80,353 | 80,174 | 84,459 | 84,037 | 83,566 |
| **Statistical Record** | | | | | | | | |
| Return on Assets % | 0.51 | 0.29 | 0.19 | 3.30 | 6.43 | 8.28 | 6.23 | 5.84 |
| Return on Equity % | 1.25 | 0.70 | 0.46 | 8.23 | 16.13 | 22.08 | 18.35 | 16.42 |
| EBITDA Margin % | 15.02 | 13.55 | 11.77 | 16.77 | 18.14 | 19.93 | 17.64 | 16.78 |
| Net Margin % | 2.97 | 1.47 | 0.22 | 3.97 | 6.07 | 8.12 | 5.74 | 5.66 |
| Asset Turnover | 0.89 | 0.86 | 0.85 | 0.83 | 1.06 | 1.02 | 1.09 | 1.03 |
| Current Ratio | 1.49 | 1.48 | 1.50 | 1.56 | 1.36 | 1.54 | 1.35 | 1.47 |
| Debt to Equity | 0.57 | 0.58 | 0.59 | 0.61 | 0.63 | 0.65 | 0.75 | 0.91 |
| Price Range | 36.49-19.94 | 36.21-19.94 | 35.23-19.94 | 37.37-17.34 | 64.07-18.04 | 65.75-37.21 | 44.01-34.28 | 34.70-24.97 |
| P/E Ratio | 165.86-90.64 | 301.75-166.17 | 440.37-249.25 | 25.42-11.80 | 22.32-6.29 | 18.63-10.54 | 18.89-14.71 | 18.66-13.42 |
| Average Yield % | 2.86 | 2.97 | 3.02 | 2.73 | 1.65 | 1.37 | 1.65 | 2.02 |

**Address:** 350 Poplar Church Road, Camp Hill, PA 17011
**Telephone:** 717-763-7064
**Web Site:** www.harsco.com

**Officers:** Salvatore D. Fazzolari - Chairman, President, Chief Executive Officer Richard C. Neuffer - Vice-Chairman **Transfer Agents:** BNY Mellon Shareowner Services, Pittsburgh, PA

**Investor Contact:** 717-975-5677
**No of Institutions:** 348
**Shares:** 61,348,980 **% Held:** 72.40

# HCC INSURANCE HOLDINGS, INC.

| Exchange | Symbol | Price | 52Wk Range | Yield | P/E |
|---|---|---|---|---|---|
| NYS | HCC | $29.24 (8/31/2011) | 33.09-24.89 | 2.12 | 10.95 |

***7 Year Price Score 106.21** *NYSE Composite Index=100 ***12 Month Price Score 99.52**

**Interim Earnings (Per Share)**

| Qtr. | Mar | Jun | Sep | Dec |
|---|---|---|---|---|
| 2008 | 0.70 | 0.80 | 0.51 | 0.63 |
| 2009 | 0.73 | 0.81 | 0.83 | 0.74 |
| 2010 | 0.62 | 0.72 | 0.81 | 0.84 |
| 2011 | 0.41 | 0.61 | ... | ... |

**Interim Dividends (Per Share)**

| Amt | Decl | Ex | Rec | Pay |
|---|---|---|---|---|
| 0.145Q | 12/08/2010 | 12/30/2010 | 01/03/2011 | 01/14/2011 |
| 0.145Q | 03/14/2011 | 03/30/2011 | 04/01/2011 | 04/15/2011 |
| 0.145Q | 05/27/2011 | 06/29/2011 | 07/01/2011 | 07/15/2011 |
| 0.155Q | 08/26/2011 | 09/29/2011 | 10/03/2011 | 10/17/2011 |

**Indicated Div: $0.62**

**Valuation Analysis**

Forecast EPS $2.60 (09/02/2011)

| Market Cap | $3.2 Billion | Book Value | $3.3 Billion |
|---|---|---|---|
| Price/Book | 0.99 | Price/Sales | 1.40 |

**Dividend Achiever Status**

**10 Year Growth Rate** 13.02%

**Total Years of Dividend Growth** 14

**Business Summary:** General Insurance (MIC: 5.2.1 SIC: 6331 NAIC: 524126)

HCC Insurance Holdings is an insurance holding company. Through its subsidiaries, Co. underwrites a variety of relatively non-correlated specialty lines of business. Co.'s agencies underwrite insurance products and provide claims management services, primarily for its insurance companies. Insurance products are marketed through a network of independent agents and brokers, managing general agents and directly to consumers. As of Dec 31 2010, Co.'s businesses were managed through five underwriting segments and its Investing segment. Co.'s underwriting segments are U.S. Property & Casualty, Professional Liability, Accident & Health, U.S. Surety & Credit and International.

**Recent Developments:** For the quarter ended June 30 2011, net income decreased 16.7% to US$69.5 million from US$83.4 million in the year-earlier quarter. Revenues were US$584.9 million, up 2.9% from US$568.1 million the year before. Net premiums earned were US$524.3 million versus US$506.4 million in the prior-year quarter, an increase of 3.5%. Net investment income rose 4.4% to US$52.4 million from US$50.2 million a year ago.

**Prospects:** Our evaluation of HCC Insurance Holdings Inc. as of Sep. 6, 2011 is the result of our systematic analysis on three basic characteristics: earnings strength, relative valuation, and recent stock price movement. The company has produced a positive trend in earnings per share over the past 5 quarters. However, while recent estimates for the company have been lowered by analysts, HCC has posted results that were in line with analysts expectations. Based on operating earnings yield, the company is undervalued when compared to all of the companies in our coverage universe. Share price changes over the past year indicates that HCC will perform poorly over the near term.

**Financial Data**

| (US$ in Thousands) | 6 Mos | 3 Mos | 12/31/2010 | 12/31/2009 | 12/31/2008 | 12/31/2007 | 12/31/2006 | 12/31/2005 |
|---|---|---|---|---|---|---|---|---|
| Earnings Per Share | 2.67 | 2.78 | 2.99 | 3.11 | 2.64 | 3.38 | 2.93 | 1.79 |
| Cash Flow Per Share | 3.57 | 4.00 | 3.65 | 5.19 | 4.39 | 6.44 | 5.87 | 5.92 |
| Tang Book Value Per Share | 22.01 | 21.52 | 21.53 | 19.37 | 15.69 | 14.46 | 11.64 | 10.48 |
| Dividends Per Share | 0.580 | 0.570 | 0.560 | 0.520 | 0.470 | 0.420 | 0.375 | 0.282 |
| Dividend Payout % | 21.72 | 20.50 | 18.73 | 16.72 | 17.80 | 12.43 | 12.80 | 15.74 |
| **Income Statement** | | | | | | | | |
| Premium Income | 1,032,731 | 508,480 | 2,041,924 | 2,037,235 | 2,007,774 | 1,985,086 | 1,709,189 | 1,369,988 |
| Total Revenue | 1,148,560 | 563,708 | 2,302,254 | 2,373,928 | 2,279,423 | 2,388,373 | 2,075,295 | 1,644,342 |
| Benefits & Claims | 681,868 | 347,586 | 1,213,029 | 1,215,759 | 1,211,873 | 1,183,947 | 1,011,856 | 921,197 |
| Income Before Taxes | 159,784 | 62,879 | 489,827 | 518,551 | 436,312 | 585,870 | 509,834 | 278,747 |
| Income Taxes | 43,316 | 15,889 | 144,731 | 164,683 | 131,544 | 190,441 | 167,549 | 85,647 |
| Net Income | 116,468 | 46,990 | 345,096 | 353,868 | 304,768 | 395,429 | 342,285 | 195,860 |
| Average Shares | 111,757 | 114,106 | 114,077 | 113,058 | 115,474 | 116,997 | 116,736 | 109,437 |
| **Balance Sheet** | | | | | | | | |
| Total Assets | 9,475,126 | 9,256,301 | 9,064,082 | 8,834,391 | 8,332,383 | 8,074,645 | 7,630,132 | 7,026,066 |
| Total Liabilities | 6,205,432 | 5,948,141 | 5,767,650 | 5,803,208 | 5,693,042 | 5,634,280 | 5,587,329 | 5,332,370 |
| Stockholders' Equity | 3,269,694 | 3,308,160 | 3,296,432 | 3,031,183 | 2,639,341 | 2,440,365 | 2,042,803 | 1,693,696 |
| Shares Outstanding | 110,274 | 114,586 | 114,968 | 114,051 | 113,444 | 115,069 | 111,731 | 110,803 |
| **Statistical Record** | | | | | | | | |
| Return on Assets % | 3.31 | 3.54 | 3.86 | 4.12 | 3.70 | 5.04 | 4.67 | 3.02 |
| Return on Equity % | 9.49 | 10.02 | 10.91 | 12.48 | 11.97 | 17.64 | 18.32 | 12.98 |
| Loss Ratio % | 66.03 | 68.36 | 59.41 | 59.68 | 60.36 | 59.64 | 59.20 | 67.24 |
| Net Margin % | 10.14 | 8.34 | 14.99 | 14.91 | 13.37 | 16.56 | 16.49 | 11.91 |
| Price Range | 33.09-24.18 | 31.90-24.18 | 29.09-24.18 | 28.95-20.39 | 28.75-16.75 | 34.24-26.57 | 35.09-28.58 | 32.86-21.34 |
| P/E Ratio | 12.39-9.06 | 11.47-8.70 | 9.73-8.09 | 9.31-6.56 | 10.89-6.34 | 10.13-7.86 | 11.98-9.75 | 18.36-11.92 |
| Average Yield % | 2.00 | 2.08 | 2.09 | 2.05 | 1.97 | 1.37 | 1.18 | 1.07 |

| | | |
|---|---|---|
| **Address:** 13403 Northwest Freeway, Houston, TX 77040-6094<br>**Telephone:** 713-690-7300<br>**Web Site:** www.hcc.com | **Officers:** Robert A. Rosholt - Chairman Christopher J.B. Williams - President **Transfer Agents:** American Stock Transfer & Trust Company, New York, NY | **No of Institutions:** 365<br>**Shares:** 116,384,776 **% Held:** 87.51 |

# HCP, INC.

| Exchange | Symbol | Price | 52Wk Range | Yield | P/E |
|---|---|---|---|---|---|
| NYS | HCP | $37.28 (8/31/2011) | 40.60-28.77 | 5.15 | 31.07 |

*7 Year Price Score 118.60 *NYSE Composite Index=100 *12 Month Price Score 97.61

**Interim Earnings (Per Share)**

| Qtr. | Mar | Jun | Sep | Dec |
|---|---|---|---|---|
| 2008 | 0.21 | 0.96 | 0.49 | 0.11 |
| 2009 | 0.17 | 0.35 | (0.18) | 0.09 |
| 2010 | 0.25 | 0.27 | 0.05 | 0.43 |
| 2011 | 0.17 | 0.55 | ... | ... |

**Interim Dividends (Per Share)**

| Amt | Decl | Ex | Rec | Pay |
|---|---|---|---|---|
| 0.465Q | 10/28/2010 | 11/04/2010 | 11/08/2010 | 11/23/2010 |
| 0.48Q | 01/27/2011 | 02/08/2011 | 02/10/2011 | 02/23/2011 |
| 0.48Q | 04/28/2011 | 05/05/2011 | 05/09/2011 | 05/24/2011 |
| 0.48Q | 07/28/2011 | 08/04/2011 | 08/08/2011 | 08/23/2011 |

**Indicated Div: $1.92 (Div. Reinv. Plan)**

**Valuation Analysis**

| | | | |
|---|---|---|---|
| Forecast EPS | $1.61 (09/05/2011) | | |
| Market Cap | $15.2 Billion | Book Value | $9.1 Billion |
| Price/Book | 1.66 | Price/Sales | 10.26 |

**Dividend Achiever Status**

| | |
|---|---|
| **10 Year Growth Rate** | 1.84% |
| **Total Years of Dividend Growth** | 25 |

**Business Summary:** REITs (MIC: 5.3.1 SIC: 6798 NAIC: 525930)

HCP is a real estate investment trust which, together with its consolidated entities, invests primarily in real estate serving the healthcare industry in the U.S. Co. acquires, develops, leases, manages and disposes of healthcare real estate and provides financing to healthcare providers. Co.'s portfolio is comprised of investments in five healthcare segments: senior housing, life science, medical office, post-acute/skilled nursing and hospital. At Dec 31 2010, Co.'s properties under lease and debt investments in its owned portfolio consisted of 226 senior housing facilities, 98 life science properties, 187 medical office buildings, 45 post-acute/skilled nursing facilities, and 17 hospitals.

**Recent Developments:** For the quarter ended June 30 2011, income from continuing operations increased 167.5% to US$234.3 million from US$87.6 million in the year-earlier quarter. Net income increased 164.4% to US$234.3 million from US$88.6 million in the year-earlier quarter. Revenues were US$488.7 million, up 61.9% from US$301.9 million the year before. Revenues from property income rose 12.5% to US$284.0 million from US$252.4 million in the corresponding quarter a year earlier.

**Prospects:** Our evaluation of HCP Inc. as of Sep. 6, 2011 is the result of our systematic analysis on three basic characteristics: earnings strength, relative valuation, and recent stock price movement. The company has enjoyed a very positive trend in earnings per share over the past 5 quarters. Because the company lacks sufficient analyst estimate data, we place greater weight on the historical EPS trend as the measure of earnings strength. Based on operating earnings yield, the company is about fairly valued when compared to all of the companies in our coverage universe. Share price changes over the past year indicates that HCP will perform very poorly over the near term.

**Financial Data**

| (US$ in Thousands) | 6 Mos | 3 Mos | 12/31/2010 | 12/31/2009 | 12/31/2008 | 12/31/2007 | 12/31/2006 | 12/31/2005 |
|---|---|---|---|---|---|---|---|---|
| Earnings Per Share | 1.20 | 0.92 | 1.00 | 0.40 | 1.79 | 2.71 | 2.66 | 1.12 |
| Cash Flow Per Share | 1.81 | 1.67 | 1.90 | 1.88 | 2.39 | 2.18 | 2.25 | 2.09 |
| Tang Book Value Per Share | 20.66 | 20.57 | 19.70 | 17.22 | 17.18 | 14.50 | 12.74 | 7.90 |
| Dividends Per Share | 1.890 | 1.875 | 1.860 | 1.840 | 1.820 | 1.780 | 1.700 | 1.680 |
| Dividend Payout % | 157.50 | 203.80 | 186.00 | 460.00 | 101.68 | 65.68 | 63.91 | 150.00 |
| **Income Statement** | | | | | | | | |
| Total Revenue | 820,411 | 331,705 | 1,255,134 | 1,157,030 | 1,025,818 | 982,509 | 619,087 | 477,276 |
| EBITDA | 522,787 | 195,841 | 655,380 | 388,871 | 409,768 | 363,304 | 333,942 | 277,380 |
| Depn & Amortn | 16,309 | 14,042 | (6,378) | (14,780) | (8,440) | (6,056) | (797) | (1,912) |
| Income Before Taxes | 292,773 | 73,223 | 373,108 | 104,754 | 226,558 | 88,012 | 121,435 | 172,091 |
| Income Taxes | 285 | 37 | 412 | 1,924 | 4,292 | ... | ... | ... |
| Net Income | 298,852 | 70,093 | 330,709 | 146,151 | 448,495 | 589,015 | 417,547 | 173,057 |
| Average Shares | 411,710 | 373,960 | 306,900 | 274,631 | 239,296 | 209,254 | 149,226 | 135,560 |
| **Balance Sheet** | | | | | | | | |
| Current Assets | 344,648 | 4,060,951 | 1,107,524 | 188,985 | 126,851 | 177,588 | 91,713 | 36,925 |
| Total Assets | 17,693,058 | 17,499,652 | 13,331,923 | 12,209,735 | 11,849,826 | 12,521,772 | 10,012,749 | 3,597,265 |
| Current Liabilities | 589,818 | 321,558 | 461,878 | 509,856 | 444,345 | 511,895 | 334,138 | 68,718 |
| Long-Term Obligations | 7,577,129 | 7,697,302 | 4,646,345 | 5,656,143 | 5,937,456 | 7,510,907 | 6,202,015 | 1,956,946 |
| Total Liabilities | 8,547,530 | 8,422,119 | 5,374,556 | 6,429,198 | 6,648,555 | 8,418,063 | 6,718,713 | 2,197,499 |
| Stockholders' Equity | 9,145,528 | 9,077,533 | 7,957,367 | 5,780,537 | 5,201,271 | 4,103,709 | 3,294,036 | 1,399,766 |
| Shares Outstanding | 407,120 | 406,008 | 370,924 | 293,548 | 253,601 | 216,818 | 198,599 | 136,193 |
| **Statistical Record** | | | | | | | | |
| Return on Assets % | 3.10 | 2.16 | 2.59 | 1.21 | 3.67 | 5.23 | 6.14 | 5.17 |
| Return on Equity % | 6.07 | 4.32 | 4.81 | 2.66 | 9.61 | 15.92 | 17.79 | 12.28 |
| EBITDA Margin % | 63.72 | 59.04 | 52.22 | 33.61 | 39.95 | 36.98 | 53.94 | 58.12 |
| Net Margin % | 36.43 | 21.13 | 26.35 | 12.63 | 43.72 | 59.95 | 67.45 | 36.26 |
| Asset Turnover | 0.10 | 0.09 | 0.10 | 0.10 | 0.08 | 0.09 | 0.09 | 0.14 |
| Current Ratio | 0.58 | 12.63 | 2.40 | 0.37 | 0.29 | 0.35 | 0.27 | 0.54 |
| Debt to Equity | 0.83 | 0.85 | 0.58 | 0.98 | 1.14 | 1.83 | 1.88 | 1.40 |
| Price Range | 40.60-31.42 | 38.02-30.01 | 37.97-27.06 | 32.84-16.08 | 41.25-15.80 | 41.88-25.76 | 36.88-25.37 | 28.68-23.45 |
| P/E Ratio | 33.83-26.18 | 41.33-32.62 | 37.97-27.06 | 82.10-40.20 | 23.04-8.83 | 15.45-9.51 | 13.86-9.54 | 25.61-20.94 |
| Average Yield % | 5.23 | 5.38 | 5.60 | 7.44 | 5.76 | 5.33 | 5.85 | 6.43 |

**Address:** 3760 Kilroy Airport Way, Suite 300, Long Beach, CA 90806
**Telephone:** 562-733-5100
**Web Site:** www.hcpi.com

**Officers:** James F. Flaherty - Chairman, President, Chief Executive Officer Paul F. Gallagher - Executive Vice President, Chief Investment Officer **Transfer Agents:** Wells Fargo Bank, N.A., South St. Paul, MN

**Investor Contact:** 949-221-0600
**No of Institutions:** 601
**Shares:** 391,273,472 **% Held:** N/A

# HELMERICH & PAYNE, INC.

| Exchange | Symbol | Price | 52Wk Range | Yield | P/E |
|---|---|---|---|---|---|
| NYS | HP | $57.02 (8/31/2011) | 72.60-37.04 | 0.49 | 15.62 |

***7 Year Price Score 153.78** *NYSE Composite Index=100 ***12 Month Price Score 115.34**

**Interim Earnings (Per Share)**

| Qtr. | Dec | Mar | Jun | Sep |
|---|---|---|---|---|
| 2007-08 | 1.02 | 0.96 | 1.18 | 1.18 |
| 2008-09 | 1.36 | 0.98 | 0.50 | 0.48 |
| 2009-10 | 0.59 | 0.43 | (0.34) | 0.77 |
| 2010-11 | 0.96 | 0.91 | 1.01 | ... |

**Interim Dividends (Per Share)**

| Amt | Decl | Ex | Rec | Pay |
|---|---|---|---|---|
| 0.06Q | 09/01/2010 | 11/10/2010 | 11/15/2010 | 12/01/2010 |
| 0.06Q | 12/07/2010 | 02/11/2011 | 02/15/2011 | 03/01/2011 |
| 0.06Q | 03/02/2011 | 05/11/2011 | 05/13/2011 | 06/01/2011 |
| 0.07Q | 06/01/2011 | 08/11/2011 | 08/15/2011 | 09/01/2011 |

**Indicated Div: $0.28**

**Valuation Analysis**

| | | | |
|---|---|---|---|
| Forecast EPS | $3.92 (09/05/2011) | | |
| Market Cap | $6.1 Billion | Book Value | $3.2 Billion |
| Price/Book | 1.89 | Price/Sales | 2.54 |

**Dividend Achiever Status**

| | |
|---|---|
| **10 Year Growth Rate** | 3.90% |
| **Total Years of Dividend Growth** | 34 |

**Business Summary:** Production & Extraction (MIC: 9.1.1 SIC: 1381 NAIC: 213111)

Helmerich & Payne is a holding company that operated 248 drilling rigs at Sep 30 2010. Co.'s drilling business consists of three segments: U.S. land drilling, which operates in Oklahoma, California, Texas, Wyoming, Colorado, Louisiana, Mississippi, Pennsylvania, Utah, Arkansas, New Mexico, Alabama, Montana, North Dakota and West Virginia; offshore drilling, which operates in the Gulf of Mexico, offshore of California, Trinidad and Equatorial Guinea; and international land drilling, which operates in Ecuador, Colombia, Argentina, Mexico, Tunisia, Bahrain and Venezuela. Co. also owns, develops and operates commercial real estate, as well as researches and develops rotary steerable technology.

**Recent Developments:** For the quarter ended June 30 2011, income from continuing operations increased 69.3% to US$109.8 million from US$64.9 million in the year-earlier quarter. Net income amounted to US$109.8 million versus a net loss of US$36.7 million in the year-earlier quarter. Revenues were US$644.1 million, up 33.2% from US$483.4 million the year before. Operating income was US$174.4 million versus US$111.5 million in the prior-year quarter, an increase of 56.5%. Direct operating expenses rose 28.0% to US$365.6 million from US$285.6 million in the comparable period the year before. Indirect operating expenses increased 20.6% to US$104.1 million from US$86.3 million in the equivalent prior-year period.

**Prospects:** Our evaluation of Helmerich & Payne Inc. as of Sep. 6, 2011 is the result of our systematic analysis on three basic characteristics: earnings strength, relative valuation, and recent stock price movement. The company has managed to produce a neutral trend in earnings per share over the past 5 quarters and while recent estimates for the company have been mixed, HP has posted better than expected results. Based on operating earnings yield, the company is undervalued when compared to all of the companies in our coverage universe. Share price changes over the past year indicates that HP will perform very well over the near term.

**Financial Data**

| (US$ in Thousands) | 9 Mos | 6 Mos | 3 Mos | 09/30/2010 | 09/30/2009 | 09/30/2008 | 09/30/2007 | 09/30/2006 |
|---|---|---|---|---|---|---|---|---|
| Earnings Per Share | 3.65 | 2.30 | 1.82 | 1.45 | 3.32 | 4.34 | 4.27 | 2.77 |
| Cash Flow Per Share | 7.72 | 6.65 | 5.48 | 4.37 | 8.52 | 5.84 | 5.43 | 2.83 |
| Tang Book Value Per Share | 30.10 | 29.26 | 27.89 | 26.53 | 25.43 | 21.53 | 17.54 | 13.30 |
| Dividends Per Share | 0.240 | 0.230 | 0.220 | 0.210 | 0.200 | 0.185 | 0.180 | 0.169 |
| Dividend Payout % | 6.58 | 10.00 | 12.09 | 14.48 | 6.02 | 4.26 | 4.22 | 6.09 |
| **Income Statement** | | | | | | | | |
| Total Revenue | 1,843,143 | 1,199,048 | 594,642 | 1,875,162 | 1,894,038 | 2,036,543 | 1,629,658 | 1,224,813 |
| EBITDA | 738,980 | 484,730 | 244,072 | 716,241 | 820,777 | 924,346 | 842,287 | 539,374 |
| Depn & Amortn | 228,450 | 149,341 | 73,180 | 262,658 | 236,437 | 210,766 | 146,042 | 101,583 |
| Income Before Taxes | 498,918 | 326,095 | 166,755 | 438,236 | 575,815 | 699,929 | 690,353 | 440,981 |
| Income Taxes | 185,764 | 122,769 | 62,390 | 152,155 | 232,381 | 255,557 | 250,984 | 154,391 |
| Net Income | 312,766 | 202,940 | 104,150 | 156,312 | 353,545 | 461,738 | 449,261 | 293,858 |
| Average Shares | 108,784 | 108,595 | 107,852 | 107,404 | 106,650 | 106,424 | 105,128 | 106,091 |
| **Balance Sheet** | | | | | | | | |
| Current Assets | 882,609 | 803,587 | 710,424 | 652,804 | 522,932 | 690,647 | 498,964 | 428,691 |
| Total Assets | 4,911,036 | 4,725,712 | 4,465,619 | 4,265,370 | 4,161,024 | 3,588,045 | 2,885,369 | 2,134,712 |
| Current Liabilities | 261,909 | 215,748 | 211,820 | 232,638 | 301,906 | 308,957 | 226,612 | 264,548 |
| Long-Term Obligations | 350,000 | 350,000 | 350,000 | 360,000 | 420,000 | 475,000 | 445,000 | 175,000 |
| Total Liabilities | 1,690,798 | 1,598,718 | 1,502,277 | 1,457,905 | 1,478,015 | 1,322,571 | 1,069,853 | 752,820 |
| Stockholders' Equity | 3,220,238 | 3,126,994 | 2,963,342 | 2,807,465 | 2,683,009 | 2,265,474 | 1,815,516 | 1,381,892 |
| Shares Outstanding | 106,986 | 106,860 | 106,251 | 105,819 | 105,486 | 105,222 | 103,484 | 103,869 |
| **Statistical Record** | | | | | | | | |
| Return on Assets % | 8.81 | 5.58 | 4.53 | 3.71 | 9.12 | 14.23 | 17.90 | 15.47 |
| Return on Equity % | 13.36 | 8.42 | 6.90 | 5.69 | 14.29 | 22.57 | 28.10 | 23.88 |
| EBITDA Margin % | 40.09 | 40.43 | 41.05 | 38.20 | 43.33 | 45.39 | 51.68 | 44.04 |
| Net Margin % | 16.97 | 16.93 | 17.51 | 8.34 | 18.67 | 22.67 | 27.57 | 23.99 |
| Asset Turnover | 0.53 | 0.50 | 0.48 | 0.45 | 0.49 | 0.63 | 0.65 | 0.64 |
| Current Ratio | 3.37 | 3.72 | 3.35 | 2.81 | 1.73 | 2.24 | 2.20 | 1.62 |
| Debt to Equity | 0.11 | 0.11 | 0.12 | 0.13 | 0.16 | 0.21 | 0.25 | 0.13 |
| Price Range | 70.34-36.33 | 68.69-33.42 | 49.06-33.42 | 48.58-33.42 | 43.19-18.10 | 76.99-30.40 | 36.43-21.75 | 39.95-22.02 |
| P/E Ratio | 19.27-9.95 | 29.87-14.53 | 26.96-18.36 | 33.50-23.05 | 13.01-5.45 | 17.74-7.00 | 8.53-5.09 | 14.42-7.95 |
| Average Yield % | 0.47 | 0.51 | 0.53 | 0.52 | 0.69 | 0.39 | 0.61 | 0.56 |

**Address:** 1437 South Boulder Avenue, Suite 1400, Tulsa, OK 74119-3623
**Telephone:** 918-742-5531
**Web Site:** www.hpinc.com

**Officers:** W. H. Helmerich - Chairman Hans Helmerich - President, Chief Executive Officer
**Transfer Agents:** Computershare Trust Company, N.A., Providence, RI

**Investor Contact:** 918-742-5531
**No of Institutions:** 564
**Shares:** 111,426,480 **% Held:** 89.00

# HORMEL FOODS CORP.

| Exchange | Symbol | Price | 52Wk Range | Yield | P/E |
|---|---|---|---|---|---|
| NYS | HRL | $27.61 (8/31/2011) | 30.37-21.57 | 1.85 | 16.15 |

***7 Year Price Score 137.86** *NYSE Composite Index=100 ***12 Month Price Score 109.40**

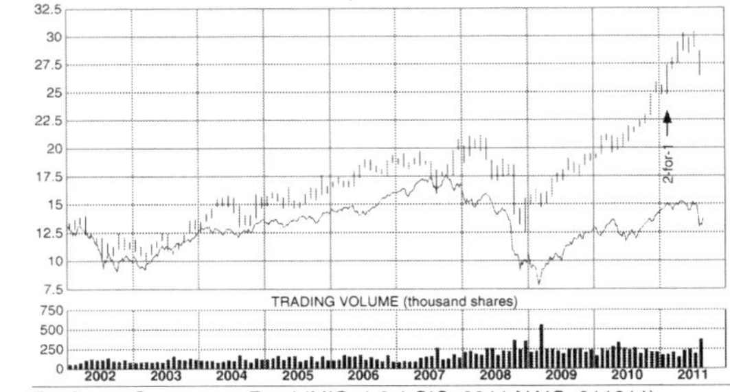


**Interim Earnings (Per Share)**

| Qtr. | Jan | Apr | Jul | Oct |
|---|---|---|---|---|
| 2007-08 | 0.32 | 0.28 | 0.19 | 0.25 |
| 2008-09 | 0.30 | 0.29 | 0.28 | 0.39 |
| 2009-10 | 0.41 | 0.28 | 0.32 | 0.45 |
| 2010-11 | 0.55 | 0.40 | ... | ... |

**Interim Dividends (Per Share)**

| Amt | Decl | Ex | Rec | Pay |
|---|---|---|---|---|
| 0.128Q | 11/22/2010 | 01/19/2011 | 01/23/2011 | 02/15/2011 |
| 2-for-1 | 01/31/2011 | 02/15/2011 | 01/31/2011 | 02/14/2011 |
| 0.128Q | 03/28/2011 | 04/19/2011 | 04/23/2011 | 05/15/2011 |
| 0.128Q | 05/23/2011 | 07/20/2011 | 07/23/2011 | 08/15/2011 |

**Indicated Div: $0.51 (Div. Reinv. Plan)**

**Valuation Analysis**

| | | | |
|---|---|---|---|
| Forecast EPS | $1.73 (09/02/2011) | | |
| Market Cap | $7.4 Billion | Book Value | $2.6 Billion |
| Price/Book | 2.80 | Price/Sales | 0.96 |

**Dividend Achiever Status**

| | |
|---|---|
| **10 Year Growth Rate** | 8.54% |
| **Total Years of Dividend Growth** | 44 |

**Business Summary:** Food (MIC: 1.2.1 SIC: 2011 NAIC: 311611)

Hormel Foods processes food products for retail, foodservice, and fresh product customers. Co. has five segments: Grocery Products, which processes, markets, and sells shelf-stable food products; Refrigerated Foods, which processes, markets and sells pork and beef products; Jennie-O Turkey Store, which consists of the processing, marketing, and sale of turkey products; Specialty Foods, which consists of the packaging and sale of sugar and sugar substitute products, salt and pepper products, liquid portion products, dessert mixes, sports nutrition products, gelatin products, and private label canned meats; and All Other, which manufactures, markets, and sells Co.'s products internationally.

**Recent Developments:** For the quarter ended May 1 2011, net income increased 41.0% to US$110.7 million from US$78.5 million in the year-earlier quarter. Revenues were US$1.96 billion, up 15.3% from US$1.70 billion the year before. Operating income was US$172.8 million versus US$137.6 million in the prior-year quarter, an increase of 25.5%. Direct operating expenses rose 15.0% to US$1.63 billion from US$1.42 billion in the comparable period the year before. Indirect operating expenses increased 7.4% to US$153.5 million from US$142.8 million in the equivalent prior-year period.

**Prospects:** Our evaluation of Hormel Foods Corp. as of Sep. 6, 2011 is the result of our systematic analysis on three basic characteristics: earnings strength, relative valuation, and recent stock price movement. The company has managed to produce a neutral trend in earnings per share over the past 5 quarters. However, while recent estimates for the company have been mixed, HRL has posted better than expected results. Based on operating earnings yield, the company is about fairly valued when compared to all of the companies in our coverage universe. Share price changes over the past year indicates that HRL will perform in line with the market over the near term.

**Financial Data**

| (US$ in Thousands) | 6 Mos | 3 Mos | 10/31/2010 | 10/25/2009 | 10/26/2008 | 10/28/2007 | 10/29/2006 | 10/30/2005 |
|---|---|---|---|---|---|---|---|---|
| Earnings Per Share | 1.71 | 1.60 | 1.46 | 1.26 | 1.04 | 1.09 | 1.02 | 0.91 |
| Cash Flow Per Share | 2.18 | 2.01 | 1.79 | 2.06 | 1.01 | 1.23 | 1.19 | 1.55 |
| Tang Book Value Per Share | 6.99 | 6.66 | 6.13 | 5.10 | 4.60 | 4.15 | 4.02 | 3.38 |
| Dividends Per Share | 0.465 | 0.443 | 0.420 | 0.380 | 0.370 | 0.300 | 0.280 | 0.260 |
| Dividend Payout % | 27.19 | 27.74 | 28.77 | 30.04 | 35.58 | 27.65 | 27.32 | 28.57 |
| **Income Statement** | | | | | | | | |
| Total Revenue | 3,880,599 | 1,921,558 | 7,220,719 | 6,533,671 | 6,754,903 | 6,193,032 | 5,745,481 | 5,413,997 |
| EBITDA | 457,216 | 260,041 | 774,137 | 688,851 | 619,066 | 632,932 | 584,468 | 551,709 |
| Depn & Amortn | 62,281 | 31,197 | 136,123 | 137,502 | 137,742 | 138,858 | 132,842 | 124,604 |
| Income Before Taxes | 383,582 | 222,706 | 611,425 | 523,354 | 453,301 | 466,367 | 425,990 | 399,361 |
| Income Taxes | 136,422 | 79,576 | 224,775 | 182,169 | 172,036 | 167,945 | 144,404 | 151,427 |
| Net Income | 258,405 | 148,826 | 395,587 | 342,813 | 285,500 | 301,892 | 286,139 | 253,459 |
| Average Shares | 272,847 | 271,740 | 270,698 | 270,978 | 274,256 | 278,302 | 279,122 | 279,154 |
| **Balance Sheet** | | | | | | | | |
| Current Assets | 2,287,204 | 1,949,230 | 1,858,166 | 1,574,733 | 1,438,178 | 1,231,725 | 1,141,671 | 1,041,084 |
| Total Assets | 4,451,417 | 4,122,948 | 4,053,918 | 3,692,055 | 3,616,471 | 3,393,650 | 3,060,306 | 2,822,406 |
| Current Liabilities | 1,005,936 | 1,020,203 | 1,101,213 | 685,029 | 781,233 | 664,777 | 585,014 | 583,172 |
| Long-Term Obligations | 250,000 | ... | ... | 350,000 | 350,000 | 350,005 | 350,054 | 350,430 |
| Total Liabilities | 1,813,602 | 1,575,235 | 1,653,261 | 1,568,603 | 1,608,899 | 1,508,867 | 1,257,394 | 1,247,830 |
| Stockholders' Equity | 2,637,815 | 2,547,713 | 2,400,657 | 2,123,452 | 2,007,572 | 1,884,783 | 1,802,912 | 1,574,576 |
| Shares Outstanding | 267,418 | 266,918 | 265,963 | 267,187 | 269,041 | 271,354 | 274,679 | 275,686 |
| **Statistical Record** | | | | | | | | |
| Return on Assets % | 11.29 | 11.03 | 10.05 | 9.41 | 8.17 | 9.38 | 9.75 | 9.46 |
| Return on Equity % | 18.98 | 18.21 | 17.21 | 16.64 | 14.71 | 16.42 | 16.99 | 17.05 |
| EBITDA Margin % | 11.78 | 13.53 | 10.72 | 10.54 | 9.16 | 10.22 | 10.17 | 10.19 |
| Net Margin % | 6.66 | 7.75 | 5.48 | 5.25 | 4.23 | 4.87 | 4.98 | 4.68 |
| Asset Turnover | 1.86 | 1.89 | 1.83 | 1.79 | 1.93 | 1.92 | 1.96 | 2.02 |
| Current Ratio | 2.27 | 1.91 | 1.69 | 2.30 | 1.84 | 1.85 | 1.95 | 1.79 |
| Debt to Equity | 0.09 | ... | ... | 0.16 | 0.17 | 0.19 | 0.19 | 0.22 |
| Price Range | 29.41-19.77 | 25.91-19.41 | 22.96-18.15 | 19.11-12.51 | 21.23-14.24 | 19.75-15.88 | 19.01-15.85 | 16.54-13.79 |
| P/E Ratio | 17.20-11.56 | 16.19-12.13 | 15.73-12.43 | 15.16-9.92 | 20.42-13.69 | 18.11-14.57 | 18.64-15.54 | 18.18-15.15 |
| Average Yield % | 1.96 | 2.01 | 2.04 | 2.32 | 1.95 | 1.62 | 1.61 | 1.69 |

**Address:** 1 Hormel Place, Austin, MN 55912-3680
**Telephone:** 507-437-5611
**Web Site:** www.hormel.com

**Officers:** Jeffrey M. Ettinger - Chairman, President, Chief Executive Officer Ronald W. Fielding - Executive Vice President **Transfer Agents:** Wells Fargo Bank N.A., South St. Paul, MN

**Investor Contact:** 507-437-5944
**No of Institutions:** 393
**Shares:** 90,986,912 **% Held:** 32.03

# HUDSON CITY BANCORP, INC.

| Exchange | Symbol | Price | 52Wk Range | Yield | P/E |
|---|---|---|---|---|---|
| NMS | HCBK | $6.21 (8/31/2011) | 13.25-5.50 | 5.15 | N/A |

***7 Year Price Score 77.92** *NYSE Composite Index=100 ***12 Month Price Score 73.86**

**Interim Earnings (Per Share)**

| Qtr. | Mar | Jun | Sep | Dec |
|---|---|---|---|---|
| 2008 | 0.18 | 0.22 | 0.25 | 0.25 |
| 2009 | 0.26 | 0.26 | 0.27 | 0.27 |
| 2010 | 0.30 | 0.29 | 0.25 | 0.25 |
| 2011 | (1.13) | 0.19 | ... | ... |

**Interim Dividends (Per Share)**

| Amt | Decl | Ex | Rec | Pay |
|---|---|---|---|---|
| 0.15Q | 10/20/2010 | 11/03/2010 | 11/05/2010 | 11/30/2010 |
| 0.15Q | 01/18/2011 | 02/02/2011 | 02/04/2011 | 02/25/2011 |
| 0.08Q | 04/20/2011 | 05/03/2011 | 05/05/2011 | 05/27/2011 |
| 0.08Q | 07/20/2011 | 08/03/2011 | 08/05/2011 | 08/30/2011 |

**Indicated Div: $0.32 (Div. Reinv. Plan)**

**Valuation Analysis**

| | | | |
|---|---|---|---|
| Forecast EPS | $-0.56 (09/02/2011) | | |
| Market Cap | $3.3 Billion | Book Value | $4.9 Billion |
| Price/Book | 0.67 | Price/Sales | N/A |

**Dividend Achiever Status**

| | |
|---|---|
| **10 Year Growth Rate** | 23.40% |
| **Total Years of Dividend Growth** | 11 |

**Business Summary:** Credit & Lending (MIC: 5.4.1 SIC: 6036 NAIC: 522120)

Hudson City Bancorp is a bank holding company. Through its Hudson City Savings Bank subsidiary, Co. is engaged as a retail savings bank that provides deposit products, residential real estate mortgage loans and consumer loans. In addition, Co. purchases mortgages and mortgage-backed securities and other securities issued by U.S. government-sponsored enterprises as well as other investments permitted by applicable laws and regulations. Co.'s loan portfolio primarily consists of one- to four-family residential first mortgage loans. As of Dec 31 2010, Co. had total assets of $61.17 billion and total deposits of $25.17 billion.

**Recent Developments:** For the quarter ended June 30 2011, net income decreased 32.7% to US$96.0 million from US$142.6 million in the year-earlier quarter. Net interest income decreased 14.0% to US$272.9 million from US$317.5 million in the year-earlier quarter. Provision for loan losses was US$30.0 million versus US$50.0 million in the prior-year quarter, a decrease of 40.0%. Non-interest income fell 91.8% to US$2.7 million from US$33.2 million, while non-interest expense advanced 32.9% to US$85.8 million.

**Prospects:** Our evaluation of Hudson City Bancorp Inc. as of Sep. 6, 2011 is the result of our systematic analysis on three basic characteristics: earnings strength, relative valuation, and recent stock price movement. The company has enjoyed a very positive trend in earnings per share over the past 5 quarters. Because the company lacks sufficient analyst estimate data, we place greater weight on the historical EPS trend as the measure of earnings strength. Based on operating earnings yield, the company is undervalued when compared to all of the companies in our coverage universe. Share price changes over the past year indicates that HCBK will perform well over the near term.

**Financial Data**

| (US$ in Thousands) | 6 Mos | 3 Mos | 12/31/2010 | 12/31/2009 | 12/31/2008 | 12/31/2007 | 12/31/2006 | 12/31/2005 |
|---|---|---|---|---|---|---|---|---|
| Earnings Per Share | (0.44) | (0.34) | 1.09 | 1.07 | 0.90 | 0.58 | 0.53 | 0.48 |
| Cash Flow Per Share | 1.70 | 1.40 | 1.53 | 1.07 | 0.93 | 0.70 | 0.60 | 0.50 |
| Tang Book Value Per Share | 8.99 | 8.69 | 10.17 | 9.85 | 9.14 | 8.60 | 8.54 | 8.83 |
| Dividends Per Share | 0.530 | 0.600 | 0.600 | 0.590 | 0.450 | 0.330 | 0.300 | 0.268 |
| Dividend Payout % | ... | ... | 55.05 | 55.14 | 50.00 | 56.90 | 56.60 | 55.81 |
| **Income Statement** | | | | | | | | |
| Interest Income | 1,170,255 | 617,523 | 2,784,496 | 2,941,786 | 2,653,225 | 2,127,505 | 1,614,843 | 1,178,908 |
| Interest Expense | 640,945 | 361,122 | 1,593,669 | 1,698,308 | 1,711,248 | 1,480,322 | 1,001,610 | 616,774 |
| Net Interest Income | 529,310 | 256,401 | 1,190,827 | 1,243,478 | 941,977 | 647,183 | 613,233 | 562,134 |
| Provision for Losses | 70,000 | 40,000 | 195,000 | 137,500 | 19,500 | 4,800 | ... | 65 |
| Non-Interest Income | 107,939 | 105,207 | 162,994 | 33,584 | 8,485 | 7,273 | 6,291 | 8,007 |
| Non-Interest Expense | 154,313 | 68,476 | 266,388 | 265,596 | 198,076 | 167,913 | 158,955 | 127,703 |
| Income Before Taxes | (759,156) | (918,960) | 892,433 | 873,966 | 732,886 | 481,743 | 460,569 | 442,373 |
| Income Taxes | (299,500) | (363,296) | 355,227 | 346,722 | 287,328 | 185,885 | 171,990 | 166,318 |
| Net Income | (459,656) | (555,664) | 537,206 | 527,244 | 445,558 | 295,858 | 288,579 | 276,055 |
| Average Shares | 494,751 | 493,843 | 494,314 | 491,296 | 495,856 | 509,927 | 546,790 | 581,063 |
| **Balance Sheet** | | | | | | | | |
| Net Loans & Leases | 30,203,196 | 30,182,380 | 30,773,956 | 31,721,154 | 29,440,761 | 24,198,138 | 19,069,151 | 15,036,709 |
| Total Assets | 51,778,639 | 52,429,066 | 61,166,033 | 60,267,760 | 54,145,328 | 44,423,971 | 35,506,581 | 28,075,353 |
| Total Deposits | 25,554,601 | 25,461,079 | 25,173,126 | 24,578,048 | 18,464,042 | 15,153,382 | 13,415,587 | 11,383,300 |
| Total Liabilities | 46,890,680 | 47,700,219 | 55,655,795 | 54,928,608 | 49,206,532 | 39,812,664 | 30,576,325 | 22,873,877 |
| Stockholders' Equity | 4,887,959 | 4,728,847 | 5,510,238 | 5,339,152 | 4,938,796 | 4,611,307 | 4,930,256 | 5,201,476 |
| Shares Outstanding | 526,707 | 526,718 | 526,718 | 526,493 | 523,770 | 518,569 | 557,787 | 588,905 |
| **Statistical Record** | | | | | | | | |
| Return on Assets % | N.M. | N.M. | 0.88 | 0.92 | 0.90 | 0.74 | 0.91 | 1.14 |
| Return on Equity % | N.M. | N.M. | 9.90 | 10.26 | 9.31 | 6.20 | 5.70 | 8.36 |
| Net Interest Margin % | 49.37 | 41.52 | 42.77 | 42.27 | 35.50 | 30.42 | 37.97 | 47.68 |
| Efficiency Ratio % | ·15.45 | 9.47 | 9.04 | 8.93 | 7.44 | 7.87 | 9.81 | 10.76 |
| Loans to Deposits | 1.18 | 1.19 | 1.22 | 1.29 | 1.59 | 1.60 | 1.42 | 1.32 |
| Price Range | 13.25-7.94 | 14.72-9.61 | 14.72-11.35 | 15.96-8.53 | 20.42-13.90 | 15.94-11.58 | 14.03-12.10 | 12.55-10.17 |
| P/E Ratio | ... | ... | 13.51-10.41 | 14.92-7.97 | 22.69-15.44 | 27.48-19.97 | 26.47-22.83 | 26.15-21.18 |
| Average Yield % | 4.79 | 4.95 | 4.72 | 4.60 | 2.63 | 2.38 | 2.27 | 2.34 |


**Address:** West 80 Century Road, Paramus, NJ 07652
**Telephone:** 201-967-1900
**Web Site:** www.hcsbonline.com


**Officers:** Ronald E. Hermance - Chairman, Chief Executive Officer Denis J. Salamone - President, Chief Operating Officer **Transfer Agents:** Mellon Investor Services LLC, Jersey City, NJ

**Investor Contact:** 201-967-8290
**No of Institutions:** 477
**Shares:** 331,337,408 **% Held:** 61.25

# ILLINOIS TOOL WORKS, INC.

| Exchange | Symbol | Price | 52Wk Range | Yield | P/E |
|---|---|---|---|---|---|
| NYS | ITW | $46.54 (8/31/2011) | 59.02-41.26 | 3.09 | 12.12 |

***7 Year Price Score 110.14** *NYSE Composite Index=100 ***12 Month Price Score 97.30**

**Interim Earnings (Per Share)**

| Qtr. | Mar | Jun | Sep | Dec |
|---|---|---|---|---|
| 2008 | 0.57 | 1.01 | 0.87 | 0.46 |
| 2009 | (0.08) | 0.35 | 0.60 | 1.01 |
| 2010 | 0.58 | 0.83 | 0.83 | 0.78 |
| 2011 | 1.24 | 0.99 | ... | ... |

**Interim Dividends (Per Share)**

| Amt | Decl | Ex | Rec | Pay |
|---|---|---|---|---|
| 0.34Q | 10/29/2010 | 12/29/2010 | 12/31/2010 | 01/11/2011 |
| 0.34Q | 02/11/2011 | 03/29/2011 | 03/31/2011 | 04/12/2011 |
| 0.34Q | 05/06/2011 | 06/28/2011 | 06/30/2011 | 07/12/2011 |
| 0.36Q | 08/05/2011 | 09/28/2011 | 09/30/2011 | 10/12/2011 |

**Indicated Div: $1.44 (Div. Reinv. Plan)**

**Valuation Analysis**

| | | | |
|---|---|---|---|
| Forecast EPS | $3.80 (09/11/2011) | | |
| Market Cap | $22.9 Billion | Book Value | $10.4 Billion |
| Price/Book | 2.20 | Price/Sales | N/A |

**Dividend Achiever Status**

| | |
|---|---|
| **10 Year Growth Rate** | 11.97% |
| **Total Years of Dividend Growth** | 48 |

**Business Summary:** Industrial Machinery & Equipment (MIC: 7.2.1 SIC: 3569 NAIC: 333999)

Illinois Tool Works manufactures industrial products and equipment. Co.'s reportable segments include: Transportation, which produce polymers, as well as truck remanufacturing and related parts and service; Industrial Packaging, which produce equipment used for bundling, and shipping; Power Systems and Electronics, which produce equipment associated with power conversion, electronics; Food Equipment, which produce commercial food equipment; Construction Products, which produce tools, fasteners and other products; Polymers and Fluids, which produce lubrication and cutting fluids and hygiene products; Decorative Surfaces, which produce decorative surfacing materials; and Other.

**Recent Developments:** For the quarter ended June 30 2011, income from continuing operations increased 20.9% to US$483.5 million from US$399.8 million in the year-earlier quarter. Net income increased 21.1% to US$498.4 million from US$411.5 million in the year-earlier quarter. Revenues were US$4.61 billion, up 17.5% from US$3.93 billion the year before. Operating income was US$711.1 million versus US$626.0 million in the prior-year quarter, an increase of 13.6%. Direct operating expenses rose 19.2% to US$3.00 billion from US$2.51 billion in the comparable period the year before. Indirect operating expenses increased 15.2% to US$907.9 million from US$787.8 million in the equivalent prior-year period.

**Prospects:** Our evaluation of Illinois Tool Works Inc. as of Sep. 11, 2011 is the result of our systematic analysis on three basic characteristics: earnings strength, relative valuation, and recent stock price movement. The company has managed to produce a neutral trend in earnings per share over the past 5 quarters. However, while recent estimates for the company have been mixed, ITW has posted results that fell short of analysts expectations. Based on operating earnings yield, the company is undervalued when compared to all of the companies in our coverage universe. Share price changes over the past year indicates that ITW will perform in line with the market over the near term.

**Financial Data**

| (US$ in Thousands) | 6 Mos | 3 Mos | 12/31/2010 | 12/31/2009 | 12/31/2008 | 12/31/2007 | 12/31/2006 | 12/31/2005 |
|---|---|---|---|---|---|---|---|---|
| Earnings Per Share | 3.84 | 3.68 | 3.03 | 1.89 | 2.91 | 3.36 | 3.01 | 2.60 |
| Cash Flow Per Share | ... | ... | 3.12 | 4.29 | 4.27 | 4.50 | 3.65 | 3.23 |
| Tang Book Value Per Share | 6.52 | 6.26 | 5.62 | 4.43 | 2.78 | 6.92 | 6.94 | 6.89 |
| Dividends Per Share | 1.360 | 1.330 | 1.300 | 1.240 | 1.180 | 0.980 | 0.750 | 0.610 |
| Dividend Payout % | 35.42 | 36.14 | 42.90 | 65.61 | 40.55 | 29.17 | 24.92 | 23.46 |
| **Income Statement** | | | | | | | | |
| Total Revenue | 8,886,759 | 4,387,579 | 15,870,376 | 13,877,068 | 15,869,354 | 16,170,611 | 14,055,049 | 12,921,792 |
| EBITDA | 1,677,929 | 827,413 | 2,913,307 | 2,035,248 | 2,990,379 | 3,184,402 | 2,943,859 | 2,623,780 |
| Depn & Amortn | 287,035 | 139,248 | 548,278 | 674,170 | 675,630 | 521,495 | 443,906 | 383,074 |
| Income Before Taxes | 1,301,516 | 644,140 | 2,211,993 | 1,213,790 | 2,191,366 | 2,580,979 | 2,445,246 | 2,181,569 |
| Income Taxes | 211,750 | 21,000 | 684,800 | 244,300 | 608,100 | 754,900 | 727,500 | 686,700 |
| Net Income | 1,121,570 | 623,140 | 1,527,193 | 947,009 | 1,519,003 | 1,869,862 | 1,717,746 | 1,494,869 |
| Average Shares | 501,861 | 502,710 | 503,350 | 501,921 | 521,213 | 556,030 | 569,892 | 575,434 |
| **Balance Sheet** | | | | | | | | |
| Current Assets | 7,557,079 | 6,596,423 | 5,968,401 | 5,674,595 | 5,923,718 | 6,165,655 | 5,206,405 | 4,111,605 |
| Total Assets | 18,526,175 | 17,641,206 | 16,250,273 | 16,081,984 | 15,213,083 | 15,525,862 | 13,880,439 | 11,445,643 |
| Current Liabilities | 4,062,155 | 3,249,556 | 3,093,592 | 2,835,638 | 4,875,581 | 2,960,285 | 2,636,584 | 2,000,731 |
| Long-Term Obligations | 2,622,796 | 2,597,310 | 2,511,959 | 2,914,874 | 1,243,693 | 1,888,839 | 955,610 | 958,321 |
| Total Liabilities | 8,117,688 | 7,274,332 | 6,879,997 | 7,273,777 | 7,549,608 | 6,174,537 | 4,862,931 | 3,898,748 |
| Stockholders' Equity | 10,408,487 | 10,366,874 | 9,370,276 | 8,808,207 | 7,663,475 | 9,351,325 | 9,017,508 | 7,546,895 |
| Shares Outstanding | 491,414 | 500,049 | 497,744 | 502,336 | 499,114 | 530,096 | 558,749 | 561,627 |
| **Statistical Record** | | | | | | | | |
| Return on Assets % | ... | ... | 9.45 | 6.05 | 9.86 | 12.72 | 13.57 | 13.11 |
| Return on Equity % | ... | ... | 16.80 | 11.50 | 17.81 | 20.36 | 20.74 | 19.70 |
| EBITDA Margin % | 18.88 | 18.86 | 18.36 | 14.67 | 18.84 | 19.69 | 20.95 | 20.31 |
| Net Margin % | 12.62 | 14.20 | 9.62 | 6.82 | 9.57 | 11.56 | 12.22 | 11.57 |
| Asset Turnover | ... | ... | 0.98 | 0.89 | 1.03 | 1.10 | 1.11 | 1.13 |
| Current Ratio | 1.86 | 2.03 | 1.93 | 2.00 | 1.21 | 2.08 | 1.97 | 2.06 |
| Debt to Equity | 0.25 | 0.25 | 0.27 | 0.33 | 0.16 | 0.20 | 0.11 | 0.13 |
| Price Range | 58.41-40.77 | 56.15-40.77 | 53.73-40.77 | 51.02-26.19 | 55.23-28.75 | 60.00-45.89 | 53.29-42.00 | 47.15-39.43 |
| P/E Ratio | 15.21-10.62 | 15.26-11.08 | 17.73-13.46 | 26.99-13.86 | 18.98-9.88 | 17.86-13.66 | 17.70-13.95 | 18.13-15.17 |
| Average Yield % | 2.68 | 2.73 | 2.79 | 3.20 | 2.61 | 1.82 | 1.61 | 1.42 |

**Address:** 3600 West Lake Avenue, Glenview, IL 60026-1215
**Telephone:** 847-724-7500
**Web Site:** www.itw.com

**Officers:** David B. Speer - Chairman, Chief Executive Officer Thomas J. Hansen - Vice-Chairman **Transfer Agents:** Computershare Investor Services LLC, Canton, MA

**Investor Contact:** 847-657-4104
**No of Institutions:** 1011
**Shares:** 462,598,784 **% Held:** 77.11

# INTERNATIONAL BUSINESS MACHINES CORP.

| Exchange | Symbol | Price | 52Wk Range | Yield | P/E |
|---|---|---|---|---|---|
| NYS | IBM | $171.91 (8/31/2011) | 185.21-123.13 | 1.75 | 14.01 |

***7 Year Price Score 142.17** *NYSE Composite Index=100 ***12 Month Price Score 111.87**

**Interim Earnings (Per Share)**

| Qtr. | Mar | Jun | Sep | Dec |
|---|---|---|---|---|
| 2008 | 1.65 | 1.98 | 2.05 | 3.25 |
| 2009 | 1.70 | 2.32 | 2.40 | 3.59 |
| 2010 | 1.97 | 2.61 | 2.82 | 4.14 |
| 2011 | 2.31 | 3.00 | ... | ... |

**Interim Dividends (Per Share)**

| Amt | Decl | Ex | Rec | Pay |
|---|---|---|---|---|
| 0.65Q | 10/26/2010 | 11/08/2010 | 11/10/2010 | 12/10/2010 |
| 0.65Q | 01/25/2011 | 02/08/2011 | 02/10/2011 | 03/10/2011 |
| 0.75Q | 04/26/2011 | 05/06/2011 | 05/10/2011 | 06/10/2011 |
| 0.75Q | 07/26/2011 | 08/08/2011 | 08/10/2011 | 09/10/2011 |

**Indicated Div: $3.00 (Div. Reinv. Plan)**

**Valuation Analysis**

| | | | |
|---|---|---|---|
| Forecast EPS | $13.30 (09/10/2011) | | |
| Market Cap | $205.3 Billion | Book Value | N/A |
| Price/Book | N/A | Price/Sales | 1.96 |

**Dividend Achiever Status**

| | |
|---|---|
| **10 Year Growth Rate** | 16.35% |
| **Total Years of Dividend Growth** | 15 |

**Business Summary:** IT Services (MIC: 6.3.1 SIC: 7379 NAIC: 541519)

International Business Machines operates in five principal business segments: Global Technology Services, which primarily provides information technology infrastructure services and business process services; Global Business Services, which primarily provides professional services and application outsourcing services; Software, which consists primarily of middleware and operating systems software; Systems and Technology, which provides business applications requiring enhanced computing power and storage capabilities; and Global Financing, which facilitates clients' acquisition of its systems, software and services.

**Recent Developments:** For the quarter ended June 30 2011, net income increased 8.2% to US$3.66 billion from US$3.39 billion in the year-earlier quarter. Revenues were US$26.67 billion, up 12.4% from US$23.72 billion the year before. Direct operating expenses rose 10.6% to US$14.28 billion from US$12.91 billion in the comparable period the year before. Indirect operating expenses increased 17.1% to US$7.31 billion from US$6.24 billion in the equivalent prior-year period.

**Prospects:** Our evaluation of International Business Machines Corp. as of Sep. 11, 2011 is the result of our systematic analysis on three basic characteristics: earnings strength, relative valuation, and recent stock price movement. The company has managed to produce a neutral trend in earnings per share over the past 5 quarters. However, while recent estimates for the company have been lowered by analysts, IBM has posted better than expected results. Based on operating earnings yield, the company is undervalued when compared to all of the companies in our coverage universe. Share price changes over the past year indicates that IBM will perform well over the near term.

**Financial Data**

| (US$ in Thousands) | 6 Mos | 3 Mos | 12/31/2010 | 12/31/2009 | 12/31/2008 | 12/31/2007 | 12/31/2006 | 12/31/2005 |
|---|---|---|---|---|---|---|---|---|
| Earnings Per Share | 12.27 | 11.88 | 11.52 | 10.01 | 8.93 | 7.18 | 6.11 | 4.87 |
| Cash Flow Per Share | 16.12 | 15.47 | 15.41 | 15.65 | 13.80 | 11.31 | 9.81 | 9.32 |
| Tang Book Value Per Share | N.M. | N.M. | N.M. | N.M. | N.M. | 8.72 | 8.93 | 13.97 |
| Dividends Per Share | 2.700 | 2.600 | 2.500 | 2.150 | 1.900 | 1.500 | 1.100 | 0.780 |
| Dividend Payout % | 22.00 | 21.89 | 21.70 | 21.48 | 21.28 | 20.89 | 18.00 | 16.02 |
| **Income Statement** | | | | | | | | |
| Total Revenue | ... | 24,607,000 | 99,870,000 | 95,758,000 | 103,630,000 | 98,786,000 | 91,424,000 | 91,134,000 |
| EBITDA | 11,261,000 | 5,102,000 | 24,830,000 | 23,440,000 | 22,495,000 | 19,736,000 | 18,042,000 | 17,327,000 |
| Depn & Amortn | 2,435,000 | 1,228,000 | 4,831,000 | 4,994,000 | 5,450,000 | 5,201,000 | 4,983,000 | 5,188,000 |
| Income Before Taxes | 8,702,000 | 3,817,000 | 19,723,000 | 18,138,000 | 16,715,000 | 14,489,000 | 13,317,000 | 12,226,000 |
| Income Taxes | ... | 954,000 | 4,890,000 | 4,713,000 | 4,381,000 | 4,071,000 | 3,901,000 | 4,232,000 |
| Net Income | 6,526,000 | 2,863,000 | 14,833,000 | 13,425,000 | 12,334,000 | 10,418,000 | 9,492,000 | 7,934,000 |
| Average Shares | 1,221,400 | 1,240,000 | 1,287,355 | 1,341,352 | 1,381,773 | 1,450,570 | 1,553,535 | 1,627,632 |
| **Balance Sheet** | | | | | | | | |
| Current Assets | ... | 47,524,000 | 48,116,000 | 48,935,000 | 49,004,000 | 53,177,000 | 44,660,000 | 45,661,000 |
| Total Assets | 113,474,000 | 112,960,000 | 113,452,000 | 109,022,000 | 109,524,000 | 120,431,000 | 103,234,000 | 105,748,000 |
| Current Liabilities | ... | 40,387,000 | 40,562,000 | 36,002,000 | 42,435,000 | 44,310,000 | 40,091,000 | 35,152,000 |
| Long-Term Obligations | ... | 21,749,000 | 21,846,000 | 21,932,000 | 22,689,000 | 23,039,000 | 13,780,000 | 15,425,000 |
| Total Liabilities | ... | 90,289,000 | 90,405,000 | 86,385,000 | 96,058,000 | 91,962,000 | 74,728,000 | 72,650,000 |
| Stockholders' Equity | 23,127,000 | 22,671,000 | 23,046,000 | 22,637,000 | 13,465,000 | 28,470,000 | 28,506,000 | 33,098,000 |
| Shares Outstanding | 1,194,278 | 1,211,200 | 1,227,993 | 1,305,337 | 1,339,095 | 1,385,234 | 1,506,482 | 1,573,979 |
| **Statistical Record** | | | | | | | | |
| Return on Assets % | 14.18 | 13.84 | 13.33 | 12.29 | 10.70 | 9.32 | 9.08 | 7.38 |
| Return on Equity % | ... | 67.53 | 64.94 | 74.37 | 58.66 | 36.57 | 30.82 | 25.25 |
| EBITDA Margin % | ... | 20.73 | 24.86 | 24.48 | 21.71 | 19.98 | 19.73 | 19.01 |
| Net Margin % | 12.73 | 11.63 | 14.85 | 14.02 | 11.90 | 10.55 | 10.38 | 8.71 |
| Asset Turnover | ... | 0.93 | 0.90 | 0.88 | 0.90 | 0.88 | 0.87 | 0.85 |
| Current Ratio | ... | 1.18 | 1.19 | 1.36 | 1.15 | 1.20 | 1.11 | 1.30 |
| Debt to Equity | ... | 0.96 | 0.95 | 0.97 | 1.69 | 0.81 | 0.48 | 0.47 |
| Price Range | 172.87-121.86 | 166.05-121.86 | 146.92-121.86 | 132.57-81.98 | 130.00-71.74 | 119.60-90.90 | 97.20-73.57 | 98.58-72.01 |
| P/E Ratio | 14.09-9.93 | 13.98-10.26 | 12.75-10.58 | 13.24-8.19 | 14.56-8.03 | 16.66-12.66 | 15.91-12.04 | 20.24-14.79 |
| Average Yield % | 1.81 | 1.86 | 1.90 | 1.97 | 1.73 | 1.42 | 1.32 | 0.93 |

**Address:** One New Orchard Road, Armonk, NY 10504
**Telephone:** 914-499-1900
**Web Site:** www.ibm.com

**Officers:** Samuel J. Palmisano - Chairman, President, Chief Executive Officer Mark Loughridge - Senior Vice President, Chief Financial Officer **Transfer Agents:**Computershare Trust Company, N.A., Providence, RI

**No of Institutions:** 1974
**Shares:** 806,201,728 **% Held:** 55.14

# INVESTORS REAL ESTATE TRUST

| Exchange | Symbol | Price | 52Wk Range | Yield | P/E |
|---|---|---|---|---|---|
| NMS | IRET | $7.78 (8/31/2011) | 9.69-7.09 | 8.28 | 35.36 |

***7 Year Price Score 91.43** *NYSE Composite Index=100 ***12 Month Price Score 90.52**

**Interim Earnings (Per Share)**

| Qtr. | Jul | Oct | Jan | Apr |
|---|---|---|---|---|
| 2006-07 | 0.05 | 0.06 | 0.06 | 0.07 |
| 2007-08 | 0.05 | 0.04 | 0.04 | 0.04 |
| 2008-09 | 0.03 | 0.03 | 0.02 | 0.03 |
| 2009-10 | 0.02 | 0.00 | 0.00 | 0.01 |
| 2010-11 | 0.02 | 0.07 | 0.14 | (0.01) |

**Interim Dividends (Per Share)**

| Amt | Decl | Ex | Rec | Pay |
|---|---|---|---|---|
| 0.172Q | 12/08/2010 | 12/30/2010 | 01/03/2011 | 01/14/2011 |
| 0.172Q | 03/09/2011 | 03/17/2011 | 03/21/2011 | 04/01/2011 |
| 0.172Q | 06/03/2011 | 06/13/2011 | 06/15/2011 | 07/01/2011 |
| 0.13Q | 09/02/2011 | 09/08/2011 | 09/12/2011 | 10/03/2011 |

**Indicated Div: $0.64 (Div. Reinv. Plan)**

**Valuation Analysis**

| | | | |
|---|---|---|---|
| Forecast EPS | $0.02 (09/02/2011) | | |
| Market Cap | $626.5 Million | Book Value | $411.7 Million |
| Price/Book | 1.52 | Price/Sales | 2.64 |

**Dividend Achiever Status**

| | |
|---|---|
| 10 Year Growth Rate | 1.78% |
| Total Years of Dividend Growth | 12 |

**Business Summary:** REITs (MIC: 5.3.1 SIC: 6798 NAIC: 525930)

Investors Real Estate Trust is a real estate investment trust. Co. conducts its business operations through its operating partnership, IRET Properties. Co.'s investments consist of multi-family residential properties and commercial office, commercial medical, commercial industrial and commercial retail properties. These properties are located primarily in the upper Midwest states of Minnesota and North Dakota. At Apr 30 2011, Co.'s real estate portfolio consisted of 78 multi-family residential properties and 176 commercial properties, consisting of commercial office, commercial medical, commercial industrial and commercial retail properties.

**Recent Developments:** For the year ended Apr 30 2011, income from continuing operations decreased 14.1% to US$4.5 million from US$5.2 million a year earlier. Net income increased 431.1% to US$24.4 million from US$4.6 million in the prior year. Revenues were US$237.4 million, up 2.5% from US$231.5 million the year before.

**Prospects:** Our evaluation of Investors Real Estate Trust as of Sep. 6, 2011 is the result of our systematic analysis on three basic characteristics: earnings strength, relative valuation, and recent stock price movement. The company has managed to produce a neutral trend in earnings per share over the past 5 quarters and while recent estimates for the company have remained steady, IRET has posted results that fell short of analysts expectations. Based on operating earnings yield, the company is overvalued when compared to all of the companies in our coverage universe. Share price changes over the past year indicates that IRET will perform poorly over the near term.

**Financial Data**

| (US$ in Thousands) | 04/30/2011 | 04/30/2010 | 04/30/2009 | 04/30/2008 | 04/30/2007 | 04/30/2006 | 04/30/2005 | 04/30/2004 |
|---|---|---|---|---|---|---|---|---|
| Earnings Per Share | 0.22 | 0.03 | 0.11 | 0.18 | 0.24 | 0.20 | 0.30 | 0.24 |
| Cash Flow Per Share | 0.75 | 0.89 | 1.03 | 1.16 | 1.23 | 1.06 | 1.12 | 0.73 |
| Tang Book Value Per Share | 4.14 | 4.35 | 4.20 | 4.41 | 4.59 | 5.00 | 5.90 | 5.99 |
| Dividends Per Share | 0.686 | 0.685 | 0.677 | 0.669 | 0.661 | 0.653 | 0.644 | 0.637 |
| Dividend Payout % | 311.82 | 2,281.67 | 615.45 | 371.67 | 275.42 | 326.50 | 214.83 | 265.42 |
| **Income Statement** | | | | | | | | |
| Total Revenue | 237,407 | 242,775 | 240,005 | 221,170 | 197,817 | 172,799 | 156,447 | 140,505 |
| EBITDA | 69,442 | 134,329 | 89,072 | 83,605 | 114,836 | 100,363 | 92,520 | 81,031 |
| Depn & Amortn | 1,200 | 61,184 | 11,200 | 10,000 | 46,695 | 39,219 | 35,803 | 26,034 |
| Income Before Taxes | 4,480 | 4,585 | 9,737 | 12,261 | 11,635 | 9,754 | 9,723 | 11,880 |
| Net Income | 20,082 | 4,001 | 8,526 | 12,088 | 14,110 | 11,567 | 15,076 | 9,440 |
| Average Shares | 98,782 | 89,918 | 79,820 | 73,477 | 64,689 | 59,046 | 55,835 | 50,433 |
| **Balance Sheet** | | | | | | | | |
| Current Assets | 66,395 | 77,447 | 52,414 | 72,177 | 62,293 | 31,725 | 34,600 | 42,171 |
| Total Assets | 1,615,363 | 1,660,930 | 1,605,091 | 1,618,026 | 1,435,389 | 1,207,315 | 1,151,158 | 1,076,317 |
| Current Liabilities | 37,879 | 38,514 | 32,773 | 33,757 | 28,995 | 27,723 | 22,914 | 47,896 |
| Long-Term Obligations | 1,023,803 | 1,064,169 | 1,075,658 | 1,063,858 | 951,139 | 765,890 | 708,558 | 633,124 |
| Total Liabilities | 1,203,673 | 1,251,407 | 1,271,156 | 1,273,020 | 1,150,420 | 917,755 | 855,986 | 797,688 |
| Stockholders' Equity | 411,690 | 409,523 | 333,935 | 345,006 | 284,969 | 289,560 | 295,172 | 278,629 |
| Shares Outstanding | 80,523 | 75,805 | 60,304 | 57,731 | 48,570 | 46,915 | 45,187 | 41,693 |
| **Statistical Record** | | | | | | | | |
| Return on Assets % | 1.23 | 0.25 | 0.53 | 0.79 | 1.07 | 0.98 | 1.35 | 0.96 |
| Return on Equity % | 4.89 | 1.08 | 2.51 | 3.83 | 4.91 | 3.96 | 5.25 | 3.82 |
| EBITDA Margin % | 29.25 | 55.33 | 37.11 | 37.80 | 58.05 | 58.08 | 59.14 | 57.67 |
| Net Margin % | 8.46 | 1.65 | 3.55 | 5.47 | 7.13 | 6.69 | 9.64 | 6.72 |
| Asset Turnover | 0.14 | 0.15 | 0.15 | 0.14 | 0.15 | 0.15 | 0.14 | 0.14 |
| Current Ratio | 1.75 | 2.01 | 1.60 | 2.14 | 2.15 | 1.14 | 1.51 | 0.88 |
| Debt to Equity | 2.49 | 2.60 | 3.22 | 3.08 | 3.34 | 2.65 | 2.40 | 2.27 |
| Price Range | 9.54-8.10 | 9.75-8.19 | 11.19-7.43 | 11.59-8.84 | 11.00-8.85 | 10.24-8.85 | 10.72-8.90 | 10.55-9.40 |
| P/E Ratio | 43.36-36.82 | 325.00-273.00 | 101.73-67.55 | 64.39-49.11 | 45.83-36.88 | 51.20-44.25 | 35.73-29.67 | 43.96-39.17 |
| Average Yield % | 7.76 | 7.71 | 6.87 | 6.59 | 6.69 | 6.87 | 6.49 | 6.32 |

**Address:** 3015 16th Street SW, Suite 100, Minot, ND 58701
**Telephone:** 701-837-4738
**Web Site:** www.iret.com

**Officers:** Jeffrey L. Miller - Chairman Timothy P. Mihalick - President, Chief Executive Officer
**Transfer Agents:** Investors Real Estate Trust, Minot, ND

**No of Institutions:** 132
**Shares:** 30,965,776 **% Held:** 40.45

# JACK HENRY & ASSOCIATES, INC.

| Exchange | Symbol | Price | 52Wk Range | Yield | P/E |
|---|---|---|---|---|---|
| NMS | JKHY | $29.24 (8/31/2011) | 33.99-23.53 | 1.44 | 19.24 |

***7 Year Price Score 127.87** *NYSE Composite Index=100 ***12 Month Price Score 97.57**

**Interim Earnings (Per Share)**

| Qtr. | Sep | Dec | Mar | Jun |
|---|---|---|---|---|
| 2007-08 | 0.26 | 0.32 | 0.30 | 0.28 |
| 2008-09 | 0.26 | 0.33 | 0.30 | 0.33 |
| 2009-10 | 0.31 | 0.35 | 0.37 | 0.35 |
| 2010-11 | 0.37 | 0.42 | 0.38 | ... |

**Interim Dividends (Per Share)**

| Amt | Decl | Ex | Rec | Pay |
|---|---|---|---|---|
| 0.095Q | 11/10/2010 | 11/30/2010 | 12/02/2010 | 12/17/2010 |
| 0.105Q | 02/04/2011 | 02/17/2011 | 02/22/2011 | 03/10/2011 |
| 0.105Q | 05/09/2011 | 05/18/2011 | 05/20/2011 | 06/02/2011 |
| 0.105Q | 08/22/2011 | 09/06/2011 | 09/08/2011 | 09/28/2011 |

**Indicated Div: $0.42 (Div. Reinv. Plan)**

**Valuation Analysis**

| | | | |
|---|---|---|---|
| Forecast EPS | $1.73 (09/03/2011) | | |
| Market Cap | $2.5 Billion | Book Value | $849.5 Million |
| Price/Book | 2.97 | Price/Sales | 2.67 |

**Dividend Achiever Status**

| | |
|---|---|
| **10 Year Growth Rate** | 12.22% |
| **Total Years of Dividend Growth** | 19 |

**Business Summary:** Internet & Software (MIC: 6.3.2 SIC: 7373 NAIC: 541512)

Jack Henry & Associates provides integrated computer systems for in-house and outsourced data processing to commercial banks, credit unions and other financial institutions. Co.'s products and services include processing transactions, automating business processes, and managing information for financial institutions and corporate entities. Co. provides its products and services through four marketed brands: Jack Henry Banking, a provider of data processing systems to banks; Symitar, a provider of data processing applications for credit unions; ProfitStars, a provider of products and services to financial institutions; and iPay Technologies, a provider of electronic bill pay services.

**Recent Developments:** For the quarter ended Mar 31 2011, net income increased 4.6% to US$33.1 million from US$31.6 million in the year-earlier quarter. Revenues were US$240.2 million, up 11.4% from US$215.5 million the year before. Operating income was US$50.5 million versus US$43.7 million in the prior-year quarter, an increase of 15.7%. Direct operating expenses rose 12.3% to US$144.9 million from US$129.0 million in the comparable period the year before. Indirect operating expenses increased 4.5% to US$44.8 million from US$42.9 million in the equivalent prior-year period.

**Prospects:** Our evaluation of Jack Henry & Associates Inc. as of Sep. 6, 2011 is the result of our systematic analysis on three basic characteristics: earnings strength, relative valuation, and recent stock price movement. The company has managed to produce a neutral trend in earnings per share over the past 5 quarters. However, while recent estimates for the company have been mixed, JKHY has posted better than expected results. Based on operating earnings yield, the company is about fairly valued when compared to all of the companies in our coverage universe. Share price changes over the past year indicates that JKHY will perform very poorly over the near term.

**Financial Data**

| (US$ in Thousands) | 9 Mos | 6 Mos | 3 Mos | 06/30/2010 | 06/30/2009 | 06/30/2008 | 06/30/2007 | 06/30/2006 |
|---|---|---|---|---|---|---|---|---|
| Earnings Per Share | 1.52 | 1.51 | 1.44 | 1.38 | 1.22 | 1.16 | 1.14 | 0.96 |
| Cash Flow Per Share | 2.81 | 2.67 | 2.67 | 2.59 | 2.46 | 2.04 | 1.93 | 1.85 |
| Tang Book Value Per Share | 0.12 | N.M. | N.M. | N.M. | 2.30 | 1.96 | 2.53 | 2.76 |
| Dividends Per Share | 0.390 | 0.380 | 0.370 | 0.360 | 0.320 | 0.280 | 0.240 | 0.200 |
| Dividend Payout % | 25.66 | 25.17 | 25.69 | 26.09 | 26.23 | 24.14 | 21.05 | 20.83 |
| **Income Statement** | | | | | | | | |
| Total Revenue | 717,642 | 477,457 | 234,822 | 836,586 | 745,593 | 742,926 | 668,062 | 592,205 |
| EBITDA | 225,884 | 152,806 | 74,946 | 218,842 | 196,745 | 204,404 | 194,981 | 172,799 |
| Depn & Amortn | 67,617 | 45,042 | 22,171 | 36,589 | 38,859 | 40,195 | 36,427 | 33,442 |
| Income Before Taxes | 151,288 | 102,434 | 49,900 | 180,796 | 157,310 | 164,426 | 160,203 | 140,068 |
| Income Taxes | 50,391 | 34,618 | 18,129 | 62,926 | 54,208 | 59,139 | 55,522 | 50,145 |
| Net Income | 100,897 | 67,816 | 31,771 | 117,870 | 103,102 | 104,222 | 104,681 | 89,923 |
| Average Shares | 86,972 | 86,523 | 86,147 | 85,381 | 84,830 | 89,702 | 92,032 | 93,787 |
| **Balance Sheet** | | | | | | | | |
| Current Assets | 231,754 | 239,063 | 248,754 | 393,102 | 359,646 | 329,757 | 350,385 | 306,410 |
| Total Assets | 1,384,786 | 1,397,646 | 1,415,505 | 1,564,146 | 1,050,700 | 1,021,044 | 999,340 | 906,067 |
| Current Liabilities | 207,152 | 249,258 | 305,040 | 446,985 | 344,407 | 341,175 | 330,477 | 263,492 |
| Long-Term Obligations | 224,587 | 229,889 | 235,422 | 272,732 | ... | ... | ... | ... |
| Total Liabilities | 535,264 | 578,499 | 638,341 | 813,774 | 424,194 | 419,593 | 400,975 | 330,855 |
| Stockholders' Equity | 849,522 | 819,147 | 777,164 | 750,372 | 626,506 | 601,451 | 598,365 | 575,212 |
| Shares Outstanding | 86,309 | 86,090 | 85,560 | 85,401 | 83,614 | 86,401 | 89,102 | 91,189 |
| **Statistical Record** | | | | | | | | |
| Return on Assets % | 10.76 | 10.63 | 10.30 | 9.02 | 9.95 | 10.29 | 10.99 | 10.45 |
| Return on Equity % | 16.64 | 17.21 | 17.21 | 17.12 | 16.79 | 17.33 | 17.84 | 16.46 |
| EBITDA Margin % | 31.48 | 32.00 | 31.92 | 26.16 | 26.39 | 27.51 | 29.19 | 29.18 |
| Net Margin % | 14.06 | 14.20 | 13.53 | 14.09 | 13.83 | 14.03 | 15.67 | 15.18 |
| Asset Turnover | 0.78 | 0.76 | 0.74 | 0.64 | 0.72 | 0.73 | 0.70 | 0.69 |
| Current Ratio | 1.12 | 0.96 | 0.82 | 0.88 | 1.04 | 0.97 | 1.06 | 1.16 |
| Debt to Equity | 0.26 | 0.28 | 0.30 | 0.36 | ... | ... | ... | ... |
| Price Range | 33.89-22.94 | 29.81-21.31 | 26.05-21.31 | 26.03-19.66 | 24.15-14.35 | 29.22-21.64 | 26.52-17.63 | 23.67-17.29 |
| P/E Ratio | 22.30-15.09 | 19.74-14.11 | 18.09-14.80 | 18.86-14.25 | 19.80-11.76 | 25.19-18.66 | 23.26-15.46 | 24.66-18.01 |
| Average Yield % | 1.44 | 1.51 | 1.54 | 1.54 | 1.72 | 1.11 | 1.08 | 1.00 |

**Address:** 663 Highway 60, P.O. Box 807, Monett, MO 65708
**Telephone:** 417-235-6652
**Web Site:** www.jackhenry.com

**Officers:** Michael E. Henry - Chairman Jerry D. Hall - Vice-Chairman, Executive Vice President **Transfer Agents:** Boston Equiserve, Boston, MA

**Investor Contact:** 417-235-6652
**No of Institutions:** 288
**Shares:** 79,141,144 **% Held:** 84.12

# JOHNSON & JOHNSON

| Exchange | Symbol | Price | 52Wk Range | Yield | P/E |
|---|---|---|---|---|---|
| NYS | JNJ | $65.80 (8/31/2011) | 67.92-57.02 | 3.47 | 15.74 |

*7 Year Price Score 99.35 *NYSE Composite Index=100 *12 Month Price Score 103.93

**Interim Earnings (Per Share)**

| Qtr. | Mar | Jun | Sep | Dec |
|---|---|---|---|---|
| 2008 | 1.26 | 1.17 | 1.17 | 0.97 |
| 2009 | 1.26 | 1.15 | 1.20 | 0.79 |
| 2010 | 1.62 | 1.23 | 1.23 | 0.70 |
| 2011 | 1.25 | 1.00 | ... | ... |

**Interim Dividends (Per Share)**

| Amt | Decl | Ex | Rec | Pay |
|---|---|---|---|---|
| 0.54Q | 10/21/2010 | 11/26/2010 | 11/30/2010 | 12/14/2010 |
| 0.54Q | 01/03/2011 | 02/25/2011 | 03/01/2011 | 03/15/2011 |
| 0.57Q | 04/28/2011 | 05/26/2011 | 05/31/2011 | 06/14/2011 |
| 0.57Q | 07/18/2011 | 08/26/2011 | 08/30/2011 | 09/13/2011 |

**Indicated Div: $2.28 (Div. Reinv. Plan)**

**Valuation Analysis**

| | | | |
|---|---|---|---|
| Forecast EPS | $4.96 (09/05/2011) | | |
| Market Cap | $180.3 Billion | Book Value | $62.1 Billion |
| Price/Book | 2.90 | Price/Sales | 2.84 |

**Dividend Achiever Status**

| | |
|---|---|
| 10 Year Growth Rate | 11.67% |
| Total Years of Dividend Growth | 48 |

**Business Summary:** Pharmaceuticals (MIC: 4.1.1 SIC: 2834 NAIC: 325412)

Johnson & Johnson is a holding company. Through its subsidiaries, Co. is engaged in the research and development, manufacture and sale of a range of products in the health care field. Co. has three segments: Consumer, which includes products used in the baby care, skin care, wound care, and women's health care fields, as well as nutritional and over-the-counter pharmaceutical products; Pharmaceutical, which includes products in areas such as anti-infective, antipsychotic, contraceptive, dermatology, gastrointestinal, hematology and immunology; and Medical Devices and Diagnostics, which includes products used by physicians, nurses, therapists, hospitals, diagnostic laboratories and clinics.

**Recent Developments:** For the quarter ended July 3 2011, net income decreased 19.5% to US$2.78 billion from US$3.45 billion in the year-earlier quarter. Revenues were US$16.60 billion, up 8.3% from US$15.33 billion the year before. Direct operating expenses rose 11.7% to US$5.17 billion from US$4.63 billion in the comparable period the year before. Indirect operating expenses increased 23.5% to US$8.00 billion from US$6.48 billion in the equivalent prior-year period.

**Prospects:** Our evaluation of Johnson & Johnson as of Sep. 6, 2011 is the result of our systematic analysis on three basic characteristics: earnings strength, relative valuation, and recent stock price movement. The company has managed to produce a neutral trend in earnings per share over the past 5 quarters and while recent estimates for the company have remained steady, JNJ has posted better than expected results. Based on operating earnings yield, the company is undervalued when compared to all of the companies in our coverage universe. Share price changes over the past year indicates that JNJ will perform very poorly over the near term.

**Financial Data**

| (US$ in Millions) | 6 Mos | 3 Mos | 01/02/2011 | 01/03/2010 | 12/28/2008 | 12/30/2007 | 12/31/2006 | 01/01/2006 |
|---|---|---|---|---|---|---|---|---|
| Earnings Per Share | 4.18 | 4.41 | 4.78 | 4.40 | 4.57 | 3.63 | 3.73 | 3.46 |
| Cash Flow Per Share | 5.50 | 5.48 | 5.97 | 5.91 | 5.36 | 5.30 | 4.87 | 4.00 |
| Tang Book Value Per Share | 10.04 | 9.15 | 8.97 | 7.04 | 5.35 | 5.12 | 3.67 | 8.64 |
| Dividends Per Share | 2.190 | 2.160 | 2.110 | 1.930 | 1.795 | 1.620 | 1.455 | 1.275 |
| Dividend Payout % | 52.39 | 48.98 | 44.14 | 43.86 | 39.28 | 44.63 | 39.01 | 36.85 |
| **Income Statement** | | | | | | | | |
| Total Revenue | 32,770 | 16,173 | 61,587 | 61,897 | 63,747 | 61,095 | 53,324 | 50,514 |
| EBITDA | 9,679 | 5,369 | 20,243 | 18,891 | 19,791 | 15,871 | 16,015 | 15,244 |
| Depn & Amortn | 1,532 | 755 | 2,948 | 2,775 | 2,788 | 2,744 | 2,194 | 2,021 |
| Income Before Taxes | 7,932 | 4,510 | 16,947 | 15,755 | 16,929 | 13,283 | 14,587 | 13,656 |
| Income Taxes | 1,680 | 1,034 | 3,613 | 3,489 | 3,980 | 2,707 | 3,534 | 3,245 |
| Net Income | 6,252 | 3,476 | 13,334 | 12,266 | 12,949 | 10,576 | 11,053 | 10,411 |
| Average Shares | 2,782 | 2,773 | 2,789 | 2,790 | 2,836 | 2,911 | 2,962 | 3,013 |
| **Balance Sheet** | | | | | | | | |
| Current Assets | 52,673 | 49,221 | 47,307 | 39,541 | 34,377 | 29,945 | 22,975 | 31,394 |
| Total Assets | 112,114 | 108,150 | 102,908 | 94,682 | 84,912 | 80,954 | 70,556 | 58,025 |
| Current Liabilities | 20,985 | 24,011 | 23,072 | 21,731 | 20,852 | 19,837 | 19,161 | 12,635 |
| Long-Term Obligations | 13,680 | 9,255 | 9,156 | 8,223 | 8,120 | 7,074 | 2,014 | 2,017 |
| Total Liabilities | 49,982 | 48,287 | 46,329 | 44,094 | 42,401 | 37,635 | 31,238 | 20,154 |
| Stockholders' Equity | 62,132 | 59,863 | 56,579 | 50,588 | 42,511 | 43,319 | 39,318 | 37,871 |
| Shares Outstanding | 2,741 | 2,739 | 2,739 | 2,755 | 2,770 | 2,841 | 2,894 | 2,975 |
| **Statistical Record** | | | | | | | | |
| Return on Assets % | 11.36 | 12.19 | 13.53 | 13.44 | 15.66 | 14.00 | 17.24 | 18.75 |
| Return on Equity % | 20.20 | 21.78 | 24.95 | 25.92 | 30.26 | 25.67 | 28.72 | 29.96 |
| EBITDA Margin % | 29.54 | 33.20 | 32.87 | 30.52 | 31.05 | 25.98 | 30.03 | 30.18 |
| Net Margin % | 19.08 | 21.49 | 21.65 | 19.82 | 20.31 | 17.31 | 20.73 | 20.61 |
| Asset Turnover | 0.62 | 0.62 | 0.63 | 0.68 | 0.77 | 0.81 | 0.83 | 0.91 |
| Current Ratio | 2.51 | 2.05 | 2.05 | 1.82 | 1.65 | 1.51 | 1.20 | 2.48 |
| Debt to Equity | 0.22 | 0.15 | 0.16 | 0.16 | 0.19 | 0.16 | 0.05 | 0.05 |
| Price Range | 67.30-57.02 | 66.03-57.02 | 66.03-57.02 | 64.96-46.60 | 72.22-55.33 | 68.40-59.77 | 69.10-56.80 | 69.40-60.04 |
| P/E Ratio | 16.10-13.64 | 14.97-12.93 | 13.81-11.93 | 14.76-10.59 | 15.80-12.11 | 18.84-16.47 | 18.53-15.23 | 20.06-17.35 |
| Average Yield % | 3.53 | 3.52 | 3.39 | 3.34 | 2.76 | 2.53 | 2.34 | 1.97 |

| | | |
|---|---|---|
| **Address:** One Johnson & Johnson Plaza, New Brunswick, NJ 08933<br>**Telephone:** 732-524-0400<br>**Web Site:** www.jnj.com | **Officers:** William C. Weldon - Chairman, Chief Executive Officer Dominic J. Caruso - Vice President, Chief Financial Officer **Transfer Agents:** Computershare Trust Company, Canton, MA | **Investor Contact:** 735-524-2455<br>**No of Institutions:** 2118<br>**Shares:** 1,957,585,536 **% Held:** 60.89 |

# KIMBERLY-CLARK CORP.

| Exchange | Symbol | Price | 52Wk Range | Yield | P/E |
|---|---|---|---|---|---|
| NYS | KMB | $69.16 (8/31/2011) | 69.16-61.29 | 4.05 | 16.35 |

***7 Year Price Score 102.54** *NYSE Composite Index=100 ***12 Month Price Score 102.95**

**Interim Earnings (Per Share)**

| Qtr. | Mar | Jun | Sep | Dec |
|---|---|---|---|---|
| 2008 | 1.04 | 0.99 | 0.99 | 1.01 |
| 2009 | 0.98 | 0.97 | 1.40 | 1.17 |
| 2010 | 0.92 | 1.20 | 1.14 | 1.20 |
| 2011 | 0.86 | 1.03 | ... | ... |

**Interim Dividends (Per Share)**

| Amt | Decl | Ex | Rec | Pay |
|---|---|---|---|---|
| 0.66Q | 11/18/2010 | 12/08/2010 | 12/10/2010 | 01/04/2011 |
| 0.70Q | 01/25/2011 | 03/02/2011 | 03/04/2011 | 04/04/2011 |
| 0.70Q | 04/20/2011 | 06/08/2011 | 06/10/2011 | 07/05/2011 |
| 0.70Q | 08/01/2011 | 09/07/2011 | 09/09/2011 | 10/04/2011 |

**Indicated Div: $2.80 (Div. Reinv. Plan)**

**Valuation Analysis**

| | | | |
|---|---|---|---|
| Forecast EPS | $4.85 (09/05/2011) | | |
| Market Cap | $27.1 Billion | Book Value | $5.6 Billion |
| Price/Book | 4.88 | Price/Sales | 1.33 |

**Dividend Achiever Status**

| | |
|---|---|
| **10 Year Growth Rate** | 8.80% |
| **Total Years of Dividend Growth** | 36 |

**Business Summary:** Household & Personal Products (MIC: 1.7.1 SIC: 2679 NAIC: 322299)

Kimberly-Clark manufactures and sells products made from natural or synthetic fibers. Co. has four segments: Personal Care, which provides disposable diapers, training and youth pants, swimpants, baby wipes, and feminine and incontinence care products; Consumer Tissue, which provides facial and bathroom tissue, paper towels, napkins and related products; K-C Professional and Other, which provides facial and bathroom tissue, paper towels, napkins, wipers and a range of safety products for the away-from-home marketplace; and Health Care, which provides disposable health care products such as surgical drapes and gowns, infection control products and other disposable medical products.

**Recent Developments:** For the quarter ended June 30 2011, net income decreased 17.4% to US$432.0 million from US$523.0 million in the year-earlier quarter. Revenues were US$5.26 billion, up 8.3% from US$4.86 billion the year before. Operating income was US$625.0 million versus US$711.0 million in the prior-year quarter, a decrease of 12.1%. Direct operating expenses rose 15.2% to US$3.70 billion from US$3.21 billion in the comparable period the year before. Indirect operating expenses decreased 0.1% to US$932.0 million from US$933.0 million in the equivalent prior-year period.

**Prospects:** Our evaluation of Kimberly-Clark Corp. as of Sep. 6, 2011 is the result of our systematic analysis on three basic characteristics: earnings strength, relative valuation, and recent stock price movement. The company has produced a positive trend in earnings per share over the past 5 quarters and while recent estimates for the company have remained steady, KMB has posted better than expected results. Based on operating earnings yield, the company is undervalued when compared to all of the companies in our coverage universe. Share price changes over the past year indicates that KMB will perform very poorly over the near term.

**Financial Data**

| (US$ in Thousands) | 6 Mos | 3 Mos | 12/31/2010 | 12/31/2009 | 12/31/2008 | 12/31/2007 | 12/31/2006 | 12/31/2005 |
|---|---|---|---|---|---|---|---|---|
| Earnings Per Share | 4.23 | 4.40 | 4.45 | 4.52 | 4.04 | 4.09 | 3.25 | 3.28 |
| Cash Flow Per Share | 6.90 | 6.27 | 6.65 | 8.37 | 6.02 | 5.50 | 5.63 | 4.88 |
| Tang Book Value Per Share | 5.28 | 5.11 | 6.80 | 7.63 | 5.19 | 7.81 | 8.85 | 7.87 |
| Dividends Per Share | 2.720 | 2.680 | 2.640 | 2.400 | 2.320 | 2.120 | 1.960 | 1.800 |
| Dividend Payout % | 64.30 | 60.91 | 59.33 | 53.10 | 57.43 | 51.83 | 60.31 | 54.88 |
| **Income Statement** | | | | | | | | |
| Total Revenue | 10,288,000 | 5,029,000 | 19,746,000 | 19,115,000 | 19,415,000 | 18,266,000 | 16,746,900 | 15,902,600 |
| EBITDA | 1,699,000 | 787,000 | 2,798,000 | 2,843,000 | 2,559,000 | 2,563,500 | 2,075,000 | 2,157,600 |
| Depn & Amortn | 530,000 | 243,000 | 25,000 | 18,000 | 12,000 | 14,000 | 39,000 | 26,000 |
| Income Before Taxes | 1,042,000 | 484,000 | 2,550,000 | 2,576,000 | 2,289,000 | 2,317,500 | 1,844,900 | 1,968,900 |
| Income Taxes | 325,000 | 152,000 | 788,000 | 746,000 | 618,000 | 536,500 | 469,200 | 438,400 |
| Net Income | 758,000 | 350,000 | 1,843,000 | 1,884,000 | 1,690,000 | 1,822,900 | 1,499,500 | 1,568,300 |
| Average Shares | 396,000 | 405,900 | 414,400 | 416,800 | 418,600 | 445,600 | 461,600 | 477,400 |
| **Balance Sheet** | | | | | | | | |
| Current Assets | 6,722,000 | 6,300,000 | 6,328,000 | 5,864,000 | 5,813,000 | 6,096,600 | 5,269,700 | 4,783,100 |
| Total Assets | 20,480,000 | 19,992,000 | 19,864,000 | 19,209,000 | 18,089,000 | 18,439,700 | 17,067,000 | 16,303,200 |
| Current Liabilities | 6,188,000 | 5,792,000 | 5,338,000 | 4,923,000 | 4,752,000 | 4,928,600 | 5,015,800 | 4,642,900 |
| Long-Term Obligations | 5,424,000 | 5,406,000 | 5,120,000 | 4,792,000 | 4,882,000 | 4,393,900 | 2,276,000 | 2,594,700 |
| Total Liabilities | 14,924,000 | 14,558,000 | 13,406,000 | 12,751,000 | 13,200,000 | 12,211,400 | 10,176,200 | 9,987,600 |
| Stockholders' Equity | 5,556,000 | 5,434,000 | 6,458,000 | 6,458,000 | 4,889,000 | 6,228,300 | 6,890,800 | 6,315,600 |
| Shares Outstanding | 392,200 | 392,878 | 406,856 | 417,000 | 413,600 | 420,921 | 455,619 | 461,489 |
| **Statistical Record** | | | | | | | | |
| Return on Assets % | 8.77 | 9.28 | 9.43 | 10.10 | 9.23 | 10.27 | 8.99 | 9.41 |
| Return on Equity % | 32.52 | 33.41 | 28.54 | 33.21 | 30.32 | 27.79 | 22.71 | 22.95 |
| EBITDA Margin % | 16.51 | 15.65 | 14.17 | 14.87 | 13.18 | 14.03 | 12.39 | 13.57 |
| Net Margin % | 7.37 | 6.96 | 9.33 | 9.86 | 8.70 | 9.98 | 8.95 | 9.86 |
| Asset Turnover | 1.04 | 1.02 | 1.01 | 1.02 | 1.06 | 1.03 | 1.00 | 0.95 |
| Current Ratio | 1.09 | 1.09 | 1.19 | 1.19 | 1.22 | 1.24 | 1.05 | 1.03 |
| Debt to Equity | 0.98 | 0.99 | 0.79 | 0.74 | 1.00 | 0.71 | 0.33 | 0.41 |
| Price Range | 68.43-60.19 | 66.91-60.18 | 66.91-58.86 | 66.82-43.41 | 69.50-50.74 | 71.98-65.76 | 68.13-56.66 | 68.15-55.97 |
| P/E Ratio | 16.18-14.23 | 15.21-13.68 | 15.04-13.23 | 14.78-9.60 | 17.20-12.56 | 17.60-16.08 | 20.96-17.43 | 20.78-17.06 |
| Average Yield % | 4.20 | 4.22 | 4.21 | 4.36 | 3.77 | 3.06 | 3.17 | 2.88 |

| | | |
|---|---|---|
| **Address:** P.O. Box 619100, Dallas, TX 75261-9100<br>**Telephone:** 972-281-1200<br>**Web Site:** www.kimberly-clark.com | **Officers:** Thomas Falk - Chairman, President, Chief Executive Officer Christian A. Brickman - Senior Vice President, Chief Strategy Officer **Transfer Agents:** ComputerShare Investor Services, Providence, RI | **Investor Contact:** 972-281-1478<br>**No of Institutions:** 1154<br>**Shares:** 298,661,920 **% Held:** 62.78 |

# KINDER MORGAN ENERGY PARTNERS, L.P.

| Exchange | Symbol | Price | 52Wk Range | Yield | P/E |
|---|---|---|---|---|---|
| NYS | KMP | $70.16 (8/31/2011) | 77.83-64.58 | 6.46 | 120.97 |

*7 Year Price Score 128.44 *NYSE Composite Index=100 *12 Month Price Score 98.99

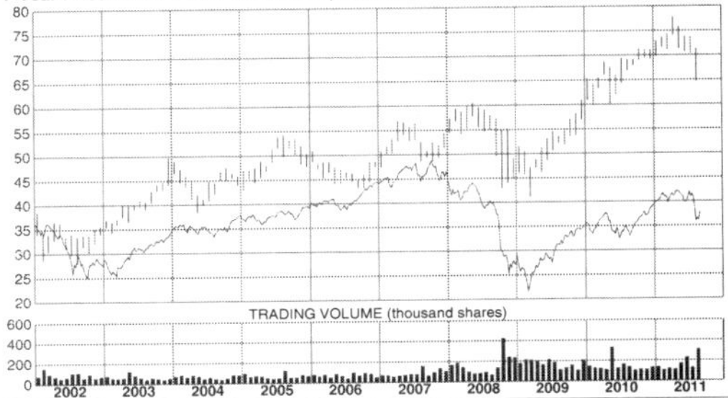

**Interim Earnings (Per Share)**

| Qtr. | Mar | Jun | Sep | Dec |
|---|---|---|---|---|
| 2008 | 0.63 | 0.65 | 0.48 | 0.18 |
| 2009 | 0.15 | 0.33 | 0.43 | 0.26 |
| 2010 | (0.08) | 0.88 | 0.17 | 0.42 |
| 2011 | 0.18 | (0.19) | ... | ... |

**Interim Dividends (Per Share)**

| Amt | Decl | Ex | Rec | Pay |
|---|---|---|---|---|
| 1.11Q | 10/20/2010 | 10/27/2010 | 10/29/2010 | 11/12/2010 |
| 1.13Q | 01/19/2011 | 01/27/2011 | 01/31/2011 | 02/14/2011 |
| 1.14Q | 04/20/2011 | 04/27/2011 | 04/29/2011 | 05/13/2011 |
| 1.15Q | 07/20/2011 | 07/28/2011 | 08/01/2011 | 08/12/2011 |

**Indicated Div: $4.53**

**Valuation Analysis**

| | | | |
|---|---|---|---|
| Forecast EPS | $1.89 (09/05/2011) | | |
| Market Cap | $16.1 Billion | Book Value | N/A |
| Price/Book | N/A | Price/Sales | 2.01 |

**Dividend Achiever Status**

| | |
|---|---|
| 10 Year Growth Rate | 7.61% |
| Total Years of Dividend Growth | 14 |

**Business Summary:** Equipment & Services (MIC: 9.1.3 SIC: 4922 NAIC: 486210)

Kinder Morgan Energy Partners is a pipeline transportation and energy storage company. Co.'s pipelines transport natural gas, refined petroleum products, crude oil, carbon dioxide and other products, and its terminals store petroleum products and chemicals and handle bulk materials like coal and petroleum coke. Co. is also a provider of carbon dioxide, for oil recovery projects in North America. As of Dec 31 2010, Co. owned an interest in or operated about 28,000 miles of pipelines and 180 terminals. At Dec 31 2010, Co. had proved reserves of 84.2 million barrels of crude oil and 4.9 million barrels of natural gas liquids. Co. conducts its business through five reportable business segments.

**Recent Developments:** For the quarter ended June 30 2011, net income decreased 36.5% to US$231.9 million from US$365.1 million in the year-earlier quarter. Revenues were US$2.02 billion, up 2.9% from US$1.96 billion the year before. Operating income was US$290.2 million versus US$443.6 million in the prior-year quarter, a decrease of 34.6%. Direct operating expenses rose 16.9% to US$1.36 billion from US$1.17 billion in the comparable period the year before. Indirect operating expenses increased 3.9% to US$366.3 million from US$352.4 million in the equivalent prior-year period.

**Prospects:** Our evaluation of Kinder Morgan Energy Partners, L.P. as of Sep. 6, 2011 is the result of our systematic analysis on three basic characteristics: earnings strength, relative valuation, and recent stock price movement. The company has suffered a very negative trend in earnings per share over the past 5 quarters. However, while recent estimates for the company have been lowered by analysts, KMP has posted results that fell short of analysts expectations. Based on operating earnings yield, the company is overvalued when compared to all of the companies in our coverage universe. Share price changes over the past year indicates that KMP will perform very poorly over the near term.

| Financial Data (US$ in Thousands) | 6 Mos | 3 Mos | 12/31/2010 | 12/31/2009 | 12/31/2008 | 12/31/2007 | 12/31/2006 | 12/31/2005 |
|---|---|---|---|---|---|---|---|---|
| Earnings Per Share | 0.58 | 1.65 | 1.40 | 1.18 | 1.94 | (0.09) | 2.04 | 1.58 |
| Cash Flow Per Share | 8.52 | 7.63 | 7.88 | 7.52 | 8.67 | 7.35 | 5.60 | 6.08 |
| Dividends Per Share | 4.470 | 4.400 | 4.320 | 4.200 | 3.890 | 3.390 | 3.230 | 3.070 |
| Dividend Payout % | 770.69 | 266.67 | 308.57 | 355.93 | 200.52 | ... | 158.33 | 194.30 |
| **Income Statement** | | | | | | | | |
| Total Revenue | 4,012,100 | 1,992,800 | 8,077,700 | 7,003,400 | 11,740,300 | 9,217,700 | 8,954,583 | 9,787,128 |
| EBITDA | 707,300 | 410,700 | 2,476,300 | 2,388,400 | 2,249,200 | 1,345,400 | 1,659,060 | 1,350,731 |
| Depn & Amortn | 3,100 | 1,500 | 852,800 | 829,600 | 684,200 | 529,300 | 397,525 | 339,580 |
| Income Before Taxes | 453,100 | 282,500 | 1,138,600 | 1,149,800 | 1,176,800 | 424,700 | 930,036 | 752,290 |
| Income Taxes | 21,600 | 6,500 | 34,600 | 55,700 | 20,400 | 71,000 | 19,048 | 24,461 |
| Net Income | 568,300 | 337,800 | 1,316,300 | 1,267,500 | 1,304,800 | 590,300 | 972,143 | 812,227 |
| Average Shares | 321,400 | 317,200 | 307,100 | 281,500 | 257,200 | 236,900 | 224,914 | 212,429 |
| **Balance Sheet** | | | | | | | | |
| Current Assets | 1,490,500 | 1,187,700 | 1,286,700 | 1,244,700 | 1,244,400 | 1,209,700 | 1,036,745 | 1,215,224 |
| Total Assets | 22,341,700 | 21,793,300 | 21,861,100 | 20,262,200 | 17,885,800 | 15,177,800 | 12,246,394 | 11,923,462 |
| Current Liabilities | 2,482,400 | 2,776,200 | 2,764,200 | 2,017,600 | 1,782,100 | 2,558,300 | 2,885,699 | 1,808,885 |
| Long-Term Obligations | 11,063,600 | 10,946,000 | 10,882,300 | 10,330,200 | 9,226,200 | 6,608,100 | 4,426,962 | 5,319,356 |
| Total Liabilities | 14,725,500 | 14,774,900 | 14,650,400 | 13,617,700 | 11,840,200 | 10,742,100 | 8,224,741 | 8,309,722 |
| Shares Outstanding | 229,289 | 318,832 | 316,101 | 296,872 | 266,280 | 247,966 | 230,431 | 220,237 |
| **Statistical Record** | | | | | | | | |
| Return on Assets % | 5.88 | 6.73 | 6.25 | 6.65 | 7.87 | 4.30 | 8.04 | 7.23 |
| EBITDA Margin % | 17.63 | 20.61 | 30.66 | 34.10 | 19.16 | 14.60 | 18.53 | 13.80 |
| Net Margin % | 14.16 | 16.95 | 16.30 | 18.10 | 11.11 | 6.40 | 10.86 | 8.30 |
| Asset Turnover | 0.36 | 0.37 | 0.38 | 0.37 | 0.71 | 0.67 | 0.74 | 0.87 |
| Current Ratio | 0.60 | 0.43 | 0.47 | 0.62 | 0.70 | 0.47 | 0.36 | 0.67 |
| Price Range | 77.83-64.24 | 74.29-60.05 | 71.39-59.69 | 60.99-41.15 | 60.54-42.90 | 56.96-47.46 | 50.88-43.15 | 54.18-42.95 |
| P/E Ratio | 134.19-110.76 | 45.02-36.39 | 50.99-42.64 | 51.69-34.87 | 31.21-22.11 | ... | 24.94-21.15 | 34.29-27.18 |
| Average Yield % | 6.30 | 6.39 | 6.48 | 8.15 | 7.08 | 6.48 | 6.96 | 6.25 |

**Address:** 500 Dallas Street, Suite 1000, Houston, TX 77002
**Telephone:** 713-369-9000
**Web Site:** www.kindermorgan.com

**Officers:** Richard D. Kinder - Chairman, Chief Executive Officer, Holding/Parent Company Officer C. Park Sharper - President, Holding/Parent Company Officer **Transfer Agents:** Computershare Trust Company, N.A., Providence, RI

**Investor Contact:** 713-369-9490
**No of Institutions:** 623
**Shares:** 44,953,336 **% Held:** 12.22

# LANCASTER COLONY CORP.

| Exchange | Symbol | Price | 52Wk Range | Yield | P/E |
|---|---|---|---|---|---|
| NMS | LANC | $60.62 (8/31/2011) | 64.62-45.47 | 2.18 | 15.79 |

***7 Year Price Score 124.49** *NYSE Composite Index=100 ***12 Month Price Score 107.06**

**Interim Earnings (Per Share)**

| Qtr. | Sep | Dec | Mar | Jun |
|---|---|---|---|---|
| 2006-07 | 0.43 | 0.56 | 0.43 | 0.03 |
| 2007-08 | 0.51 | 0.54 | 0.30 | (0.07) |
| 2008-09 | 0.39 | 1.02 | 0.76 | 1.02 |
| 2009-10 | 1.01 | 1.40 | 0.86 | 0.80 |
| 2010-11 | 0.81 | 1.25 | 0.71 | 1.07 |

**Interim Dividends (Per Share)**

| Amt | Decl | Ex | Rec | Pay |
|---|---|---|---|---|
| 0.33Q | 11/15/2010 | 12/08/2010 | 12/10/2010 | 12/31/2010 |
| 0.33Q | 02/22/2011 | 03/08/2011 | 03/10/2011 | 03/31/2011 |
| 0.33Q | 05/25/2011 | 06/08/2011 | 06/10/2011 | 06/30/2011 |
| 0.33Q | 08/17/2011 | 09/07/2011 | 09/09/2011 | 09/30/2011 |

**Indicated Div: $1.32 (Div. Reinv. Plan)**

**Valuation Analysis**

| | | | |
|---|---|---|---|
| Forecast EPS | $3.85 (09/02/2011) | | |
| Market Cap | $1.7 Billion | Book Value | $517.5 Million |
| Price/Book | 3.21 | Price/Sales | 1.52 |

**Dividend Achiever Status**

| | |
|---|---|
| **10 Year Growth Rate** | 5.95% |
| **Total Years of Dividend Growth** | 41 |

**Business Summary:** Food (MIC: 1.2.1 SIC: 2038 NAIC: 311412)

Lancaster Colony is a manufacturer and marketer of consumer products for foods for the retail and foodservice markets. Co. has two segments: Specialty Foods, and Glassware and Candles. Specialty Foods manufactures and sells food products that include salad dressings and sauces; fruit glazes, vegetable dips and fruit dips; frozen breads; frozen yeast dinner rolls and sweet rolls, as well as biscuits; dry egg noodles; frozen specialty noodles and pastas; croutons; and caviar. Glassware and Candles sells candles, candle accessories, and other home fragrance products in a variety of sizes, forms and fragrance in retail markets to mass merchants, supermarkets, drug stores and specialty shops.

**Recent Developments:** For the year ended June 30 2011, net income decreased 7.5% to US$106.4 million from US$115.0 million in the prior year. Revenues were US$1.09 billion, up 3.2% from US$1.06 billion the year before. Operating income was US$147.0 million versus US$174.2 million in the prior year, a decrease of 15.6%. Direct operating expenses rose 7.8% to US$847.5 million from US$786.3 million in the comparable period the year before. Indirect operating expenses decreased 0.7% to US$95.4 million from US$96.1 million in the equivalent prior-year period.

**Prospects:** Our evaluation of Lancaster Colony Corp. as of Sep. 6, 2011 is the result of our systematic analysis on three basic characteristics: earnings strength, relative valuation, and recent stock price movement. The company has enjoyed a very positive trend in earnings per share over the past 5 quarters. However, while recent estimates for the company have been lowered by analysts, LANC has posted better than expected results. Based on operating earnings yield, the company is about fairly valued when compared to all of the companies in our coverage universe. Share price changes over the past year indicates that LANC will perform poorly over the near term.

**Financial Data**

| (US$ in Thousands) | 06/30/2011 | 06/30/2010 | 06/30/2009 | 06/30/2008 | 06/30/2007 | 06/30/2006 | 06/30/2005 | 06/30/2004 |
|---|---|---|---|---|---|---|---|---|
| Earnings Per Share | 3.84 | 4.07 | 3.18 | 1.28 | 1.45 | 2.48 | 2.67 | 2.24 |
| Cash Flow Per Share | 5.33 | 3.83 | 4.75 | 2.40 | 2.82 | 2.90 | 3.35 | 3.34 |
| Tang Book Value Per Share | 15.31 | 13.69 | 10.75 | 9.05 | 11.11 | 12.74 | 14.71 | 14.16 |
| Dividends Per Share | 1.290 | 1.185 | 1.135 | 1.110 | 1.070 | 3.030 | 0.980 | 0.890 |
| Dividend Payout % | 33.59 | 29.12 | 35.69 | 86.72 | 73.79 | 122.18 | 36.70 | 39.73 |
| **Income Statement** | | | | | | | | |
| Total Revenue | 1,089,946 | 1,056,608 | 1,051,491 | 980,915 | 1,091,162 | 1,175,260 | 1,131,466 | 1,096,953 |
| EBITDA | 177,353 | 192,092 | 156,444 | 102,008 | 129,920 | 157,172 | 177,401 | 157,997 |
| Depn & Amortn | 15,961 | 17,000 | 18,100 | 24,138 | 28,766 | 32,341 | 33,262 | 31,267 |
| Income Before Taxes | 161,506 | 175,138 | 137,006 | 75,668 | 102,003 | 128,801 | 148,021 | 128,464 |
| Income Taxes | 55,142 | 60,169 | 47,920 | 27,229 | 37,322 | 45,847 | 54,933 | 48,462 |
| Net Income | 106,364 | 114,969 | 89,086 | 37,620 | 45,684 | 82,954 | 93,088 | 80,002 |
| Average Shares | 27,689 | 28,174 | 28,051 | 29,499 | 31,603 | 33,502 | 34,925 | 35,778 |
| **Balance Sheet** | | | | | | | | |
| Current Assets | 333,196 | 317,399 | 222,812 | 233,674 | 278,911 | 338,783 | 474,405 | 451,005 |
| Total Assets | 622,089 | 586,453 | 498,481 | 520,178 | 598,497 | 628,021 | 731,278 | 712,887 |
| Current Liabilities | 76,156 | 77,953 | 74,579 | 88,749 | 141,790 | 103,500 | 103,846 | 92,731 |
| Long-Term Obligations | ... | ... | ... | 55,000 | ... | ... | ... | ... |
| Total Liabilities | 104,550 | 101,545 | 95,925 | 160,960 | 154,188 | 133,600 | 143,552 | 126,102 |
| Stockholders' Equity | 517,539 | 484,908 | 402,556 | 359,218 | 444,309 | 494,421 | 587,726 | 586,785 |
| Shares Outstanding | 27,385 | 28,167 | 28,101 | 28,452 | 30,748 | 32,245 | 34,235 | 35,472 |
| **Statistical Record** | | | | | | | | |
| Return on Assets % | 17.60 | 21.19 | 17.49 | 6.71 | 7.45 | 12.21 | 12.89 | 11.56 |
| Return on Equity % | 21.22 | 25.91 | 23.39 | 9.34 | 9.73 | 15.33 | 15.85 | 14.07 |
| EBITDA Margin % | 16.27 | 18.18 | 14.88 | 10.40 | 11.91 | 13.37 | 15.68 | 14.40 |
| Net Margin % | 9.76 | 10.88 | 8.47 | 3.84 | 4.19 | 7.06 | 8.23 | 7.29 |
| Asset Turnover | 1.80 | 1.95 | 2.06 | 1.75 | 1.78 | 1.73 | 1.57 | 1.58 |
| Current Ratio | 4.38 | 4.07 | 2.99 | 2.63 | 1.97 | 3.27 | 4.57 | 4.86 |
| Debt to Equity | ... | ... | ... | 0.15 | ... | ... | ... | ... |
| Price Range | 64.62-45.47 | 61.14-42.03 | 48.35-26.35 | 43.13-30.28 | 47.32-37.62 | 45.75-37.05 | 44.63-38.26 | 46.11-38.20 |
| P/E Ratio | 16.83-11.84 | 15.02-10.33 | 15.20-8.29 | 33.70-23.66 | 32.63-25.94 | 18.45-14.94 | 16.72-14.33 | 20.58-17.05 |
| Average Yield % | 2.36 | 2.27 | 3.04 | 2.94 | 2.49 | 7.40 | 2.32 | 2.15 |

**Address:** 37 West Broad Street, Columbus, OH 43215
**Telephone:** 614-224-7141
**Web Site:** www.lancastercolony.com

**Officers:** John B. Gerlach - Chairman, President, Chief Executive Officer John L. Boylan - Vice President, Chief Financial Officer, Treasurer, Assistant Secretary **Transfer Agents:** American Stock Transfer and Trust Company, New York, NY

**No of Institutions:** 167
**Shares:** 17,556,458 **% Held:** 55.02

# LEGGETT & PLATT, INC.

| Exchange | Symbol | Price | 52Wk Range | Yield | P/E |
|---|---|---|---|---|---|
| NYS | LEG | $22.19 (8/31/2011) | 26.37-17.87 | 5.05 | 18.65 |

*7 Year Price Score 103.71 *NYSE Composite Index=100 *12 Month Price Score 96.05

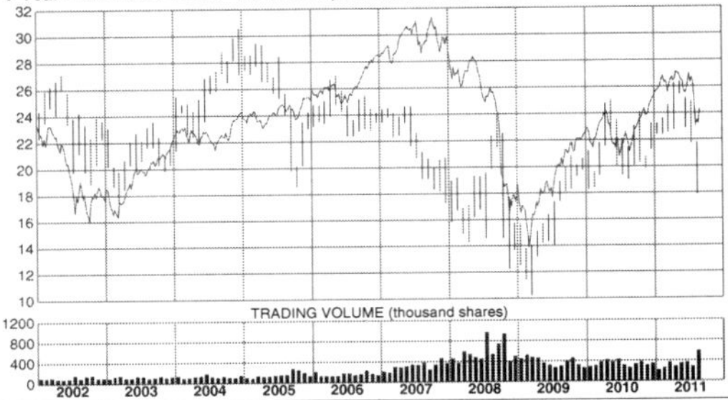

**Interim Earnings (Per Share)**

| Qtr. | Mar | Jun | Sep | Dec |
|---|---|---|---|---|
| 2008 | 0.25 | 0.27 | 0.20 | (0.10) |
| 2009 | 0.02 | 0.12 | 0.34 | 0.22 |
| 2010 | 0.29 | 0.34 | 0.31 | 0.21 |
| 2011 | 0.30 | 0.37 | ... | ... |

**Interim Dividends (Per Share)**

| Amt | Decl | Ex | Rec | Pay |
|---|---|---|---|---|
| 0.27Q | 11/11/2010 | 12/13/2010 | 12/15/2010 | 01/14/2011 |
| 0.27Q | 02/24/2011 | 03/11/2011 | 03/15/2011 | 04/15/2011 |
| 0.27Q | 05/12/2011 | 06/13/2011 | 06/15/2011 | 07/15/2011 |
| 0.28Q | 08/02/2011 | 09/13/2011 | 09/15/2011 | 10/14/2011 |

**Indicated Div: $1.12**

**Valuation Analysis**

| | | | |
|---|---|---|---|
| Forecast EPS | $1.34 (09/02/2011) | | |
| Market Cap | $3.1 Billion | Book Value | $1.4 Billion |
| Price/Book | 2.19 | Price/Sales | 0.90 |

**Dividend Achiever Status**

| | |
|---|---|
| **10 Year Growth Rate** | 8.37% |
| **Total Years of Dividend Growth** | 39 |

**Business Summary:** Furniture (MIC: 1.6.2 SIC: 2519 NAIC: 337121)

Leggett & Platt designs and produces a range of components and products found in most homes, offices, and automobiles, and many retail stores. Co. has four operating segments: Residential Furnishings provides components for bedding, furniture and other furnishings, as well as related consumer products; Commercial Fixturing & Components provides retail store fixtures, displays and components for office and institutional furnishings; Industrial Materials provides drawn steel wire, specialty wire products and welded steel tubing; and Specialized Products provides automotive seating components, specialized machinery and equipment, and commercial vehicle interiors.

**Recent Developments:** For the quarter ended June 30 2011, income from continuing operations increased 3.5% to US$55.5 million from US$53.6 million in the year-earlier quarter. Net income increased 2.6% to US$55.5 million from US$54.1 million in the year-earlier quarter. Revenues were US$945.2 million, up 8.1% from US$874.3 million the year before. Operating income was US$79.1 million versus US$85.1 million in the prior-year quarter, a decrease of 7.1%. Direct operating expenses rose 9.9% to US$763.3 million from US$694.6 million in the comparable period the year before. Indirect operating expenses increased 8.7% to US$102.8 million from US$94.6 million in the equivalent prior-year period.

**Prospects:** Our evaluation of Leggett & Platt Inc. as of Sep. 6, 2011 is the result of our systematic analysis on three basic characteristics: earnings strength, relative valuation, and recent stock price movement. The company has enjoyed a very positive trend in earnings per share over the past 5 quarters. However, while recent estimates for the company have been mixed, LEG has posted results that fell short of analysts expectations. Based on operating earnings yield, the company is about fairly valued when compared to all of the companies in our coverage universe. Share price changes over the past year indicates that LEG will perform very poorly over the near term.

**Financial Data**

| (US$ in Thousands) | 6 Mos | 3 Mos | 12/31/2010 | 12/31/2009 | 12/31/2008 | 12/31/2007 | 12/31/2006 | 12/31/2005 |
|---|---|---|---|---|---|---|---|---|
| Earnings Per Share | 1.19 | 1.16 | 1.15 | 0.70 | 0.62 | (0.06) | 1.61 | 1.30 |
| Cash Flow Per Share | 2.37 | 2.40 | 2.40 | 3.55 | 2.59 | 3.42 | 2.57 | 2.33 |
| Tang Book Value Per Share | 2.44 | 2.46 | 2.90 | 3.06 | 3.72 | 5.74 | 5.72 | 5.55 |
| Dividends Per Share | 1.080 | 1.070 | 1.060 | 1.020 | 1.000 | 0.780 | 0.670 | 0.630 |
| Dividend Payout % | 90.76 | 92.24 | 92.17 | 145.71 | 161.29 | ... | 41.61 | 48.46 |
| **Income Statement** | | | | | | | | |
| Total Revenue | 1,841,000 | 895,800 | 3,359,100 | 3,055,100 | 4,076,100 | 4,306,400 | 5,505,400 | 5,299,300 |
| EBITDA | 213,600 | 104,300 | 410,800 | 360,600 | 368,100 | 357,700 | 657,400 | 567,300 |
| Depn & Amortn | 60,300 | 30,100 | 122,800 | 130,300 | 140,400 | 180,200 | 175,400 | 171,100 |
| Income Before Taxes | 138,200 | 66,200 | 255,500 | 198,400 | 188,000 | 128,400 | 434,800 | 356,200 |
| Income Taxes | 36,400 | 19,900 | 71,900 | 77,300 | 65,100 | 77,400 | 134,500 | 104,900 |
| Net Income | 99,700 | 45,000 | 176,600 | 111,800 | 104,400 | (11,200) | 300,300 | 251,300 |
| Average Shares | 147,400 | 150,800 | 153,268 | 159,964 | 168,186 | 179,827 | 186,832 | 193,574 |
| **Balance Sheet** | | | | | | | | |
| Current Assets | 1,317,900 | 1,290,400 | 1,219,100 | 1,213,600 | 1,306,800 | 1,834,400 | 1,894,100 | 1,763,300 |
| Total Assets | 3,094,700 | 3,066,900 | 3,001,000 | 3,061,200 | 3,161,900 | 4,072,500 | 4,265,300 | 4,052,600 |
| Current Liabilities | 577,800 | 585,700 | 523,000 | 535,100 | 524,200 | 799,600 | 691,200 | 738,000 |
| Long-Term Obligations | 856,600 | 821,900 | 762,200 | 789,300 | 851,200 | 1,000,600 | 1,060,000 | 921,600 |
| Total Liabilities | 1,659,600 | 1,627,700 | 1,493,700 | 1,507,200 | 1,508,900 | 1,939,800 | 1,914,200 | 1,803,600 |
| Stockholders' Equity | 1,435,100 | 1,439,200 | 1,507,300 | 1,554,000 | 1,653,000 | 2,132,700 | 2,351,100 | 2,249,000 |
| Shares Outstanding | 141,582 | 142,895 | 146,200 | 148,793 | 155,813 | 168,725 | 178,000 | 182,576 |
| **Statistical Record** | | | | | | | | |
| Return on Assets % | 5.78 | 5.73 | 5.83 | 3.59 | 2.88 | N.M. | 7.22 | 6.09 |
| Return on Equity % | 12.31 | 11.94 | 11.54 | 6.97 | 5.50 | N.M. | 13.06 | 11.02 |
| EBITDA Margin % | 11.60 | 11.64 | 12.23 | 11.80 | 9.03 | 8.31 | 11.94 | 10.71 |
| Net Margin % | 5.42 | 5.02 | 5.26 | 3.66 | 2.56 | N.M. | 5.45 | 4.74 |
| Asset Turnover | 1.14 | 1.12 | 1.11 | 0.98 | 1.12 | 1.03 | 1.32 | 1.28 |
| Current Ratio | 2.28 | 2.20 | 2.33 | 2.27 | 2.49 | 2.29 | 2.74 | 2.39 |
| Debt to Equity | 0.60 | 0.57 | 0.51 | 0.51 | 0.51 | 0.47 | 0.45 | 0.41 |
| Price Range | 26.37-19.01 | 25.02-19.01 | 25.02-18.26 | 20.82-10.21 | 23.98-12.24 | 24.62-17.27 | 26.96-22.39 | 29.44-18.55 |
| P/E Ratio | 22.16-15.97 | 21.57-16.39 | 21.76-15.88 | 29.74-14.59 | 38.68-19.74 | ... | 16.75-13.91 | 22.65-14.27 |
| Average Yield % | 4.80 | 4.84 | 4.95 | 6.28 | 5.71 | 3.59 | 2.76 | 2.47 |

**Address:** No. 1 Leggett Road, Carthage, MO 64836
**Telephone:** 417-358-8131
**Web Site:** www.leggett.com

**Officers:** David S. Haffner - President, Chief Executive Officer Karl G. Glassman - Executive Vice President, Chief Operating Officer **Transfer Agents:** Wells Fargo Shareowner Services, St. Paul, MN

**Investor Contact:** 417-358-8131
**No of Institutions:** 390
**Shares:** 108,948,264 **% Held:** 62.05

# LINEAR TECHNOLOGY CORP.

| Exchange | Symbol | Price | 52Wk Range | Yield | P/E |
|---|---|---|---|---|---|
| NMS | LLTC | $28.63 (8/31/2011) | 36.13-26.08 | 3.35 | 11.45 |

***7 Year Price Score 100.34** *NYSE Composite Index=100 ***12 Month Price Score 91.53**

**Interim Earnings (Per Share)**

| Qtr. | Sep | Dec | Mar | Jun |
|---|---|---|---|---|
| 2006-07 | 0.37 | 0.34 | 0.32 | 0.36 |
| 2007-08 | 0.40 | 0.41 | 0.44 | 0.45 |
| 2008-09 | 0.48 | 0.43 | 0.25 | 0.26 |
| 2009-10 | 0.27 | 0.33 | 0.44 | 0.54 |
| 2010-11 | 0.59 | 0.62 | 0.61 | 0.68 |

**Interim Dividends (Per Share)**

| Amt | Decl | Ex | Rec | Pay |
|---|---|---|---|---|
| 0.23Q | 10/12/2010 | 11/09/2010 | 11/12/2010 | 11/24/2010 |
| 0.24Q | 01/18/2011 | 02/16/2011 | 02/18/2011 | 03/02/2011 |
| 0.24Q | 04/19/2011 | 05/18/2011 | 05/20/2011 | 06/01/2011 |
| 0.24Q | 07/26/2011 | 08/17/2011 | 08/19/2011 | 08/31/2011 |

**Indicated Div: $0.96**

**Valuation Analysis**

| | | | |
|---|---|---|---|
| Forecast EPS | $2.11 (09/05/2011) | | |
| Market Cap | $6.5 Billion | Book Value | $505.6 Million |
| Price/Book | 12.89 | Price/Sales | 4.39 |

**Dividend Achiever Status**

| | |
|---|---|
| **10 Year Growth Rate** | 19.89% |
| **Total Years of Dividend Growth** | 18 |

**Business Summary:** Semiconductors (MIC: 6.2.4 SIC: 3674 NAIC: 334413)

Linear Technology designs, manufactures and markets linear integrated circuits. Co.'s products include amplifiers, comparators, voltage references, monolithic filters, linear regulators, direct current (DC)-DC converters, battery chargers, data converters, communications interface circuits, radio frequency signal conditioning circuits, μModule products, and other analog functions. Applications for Co.'s circuits include telecommunications, cellular telephones, networking products such as optical switches; notebook, tablet and desktop computers; computer peripherals, video/multimedia, industrial instrumentation, security monitoring devices, and consumer products such as digital cameras.

**Recent Developments:** For the year ended July 3 2011, net income increased 60.7% to US$580.8 million from US$361.3 million in the prior year. Revenues were US$1.48 billion, up 26.8% from US$1.17 billion the year before. Operating income was US$767.3 million versus US$563.4 million in the prior year, an increase of 36.2%. Direct operating expenses rose 20.6% to US$324.4 million from US$269.1 million in the comparable period the year before. Indirect operating expenses increased 16.2% to US$392.2 million from US$337.5 million in the equivalent prior-year period.

**Prospects:** Our evaluation of Linear Technology Corp. as of Sep. 6, 2011 is the result of our systematic analysis on three basic characteristics: earnings strength, relative valuation, and recent stock price movement. The company has generated a negative trend in earnings per share over the past 5 quarters. However, while recent estimates for the company have been mixed, LLTC has posted better than expected results. Based on operating earnings yield, the company is undervalued when compared to all of the companies in our coverage universe. Share price changes over the past year indicates that LLTC will perform poorly over the near term.

| **Financial Data** (US$ in Thousands) | 07/03/2011 | 06/27/2010 | 06/28/2009 | 06/29/2008 | 07/01/2007 | 07/02/2006 | 07/03/2005 | 06/27/2004 |
|---|---|---|---|---|---|---|---|---|
| Earnings Per Share | 2.50 | 1.58 | 1.41 | 1.71 | 1.39 | 1.37 | 1.38 | 1.02 |
| Cash Flow Per Share | 2.86 | 2.17 | 1.88 | 2.39 | 1.65 | 1.68 | 1.58 | 1.47 |
| Tang Book Value Per Share | 2.22 | 0.18 | ... | ... | ... | 6.94 | 6.55 | 5.87 |
| Dividends Per Share | 0.940 | 0.900 | 0.860 | 0.780 | 0.660 | 0.500 | 0.360 | 0.280 |
| Dividend Payout % | 37.60 | 56.96 | 60.99 | 45.61 | 47.48 | 36.50 | 26.09 | 27.45 |
| **Income Statement** | | | | | | | | |
| Total Revenue | 1,483,962 | 1,169,988 | 968,498 | 1,175,153 | 1,083,078 | 1,092,977 | 1,049,694 | 807,281 |
| EBITDA | 839,122 | 627,445 | 484,310 | 609,464 | 567,718 | 606,350 | 631,829 | 479,830 |
| Depn & Amortn | 71,812 | 74,492 | 47,982 | 40,800 | 43,400 | 42,400 | 42,200 | 43,100 |
| Income Before Taxes | 723,838 | 490,411 | 407,009 | 540,954 | 569,924 | 616,808 | 619,964 | 462,213 |
| Income Taxes | 143,056 | 129,070 | 93,499 | 153,341 | 158,249 | 188,128 | 185,990 | 134,042 |
| Net Income | 580,782 | 361,341 | 313,510 | 387,613 | 411,675 | 428,680 | 433,974 | 328,171 |
| Average Shares | 232,772 | 228,860 | 222,461 | 226,257 | 296,616 | 313,285 | 315,067 | 321,456 |
| **Balance Sheet** | | | | | | | | |
| Current Assets | 1,246,290 | 1,264,301 | 1,089,251 | 1,245,540 | 861,104 | 2,077,136 | 2,007,309 | 1,832,095 |
| Total Assets | 1,631,166 | 1,590,718 | 1,421,529 | 1,583,889 | 1,218,857 | 2,390,895 | 2,286,234 | 2,087,703 |
| Current Liabilities | 182,806 | 582,510 | 125,341 | 175,158 | 179,869 | 236,826 | 207,739 | 202,614 |
| Long-Term Obligations | 785,732 | 766,960 | 1,405,644 | 1,700,000 | 1,700,000 | ... | ... | ... |
| Total Liabilities | 1,125,555 | 1,552,346 | 1,688,131 | 2,017,807 | 1,926,822 | 286,397 | 279,200 | 277,098 |
| Stockholders' Equity | 505,611 | 39,785 | (266,602) | (433,918) | (707,965) | 2,104,498 | 2,007,034 | 1,810,605 |
| Shares Outstanding | 227,607 | 224,231 | 222,276 | 221,508 | 229,655 | 303,092 | 306,587 | 308,548 |
| **Statistical Record** | | | | | | | | |
| Return on Assets % | 35.47 | 24.06 | 20.92 | 27.74 | 22.87 | 18.38 | 19.52 | 15.88 |
| Return on Equity % | 209.53 | ... | ... | ... | 59.12 | 20.91 | 22.37 | 18.15 |
| EBITDA Margin % | 56.55 | 53.63 | 50.01 | 51.86 | 52.42 | 55.48 | 60.19 | 59.44 |
| Net Margin % | 39.14 | 30.88 | 32.37 | 32.98 | 38.01 | 39.22 | 41.34 | 40.65 |
| Asset Turnover | 0.91 | 0.78 | 0.65 | 0.84 | 0.60 | 0.47 | 0.47 | 0.39 |
| Current Ratio | 6.82 | 2.17 | 8.69 | 7.11 | 4.79 | 8.77 | 9.66 | 9.04 |
| Debt to Equity | 1.55 | 19.28 | ... | ... | ... | ... | ... | ... |
| Price Range | 36.13-27.81 | 31.37-22.55 | 34.12-18.56 | 38.22-26.54 | 38.74-29.87 | 41.54-32.90 | 40.31-34.42 | 44.95-32.17 |
| P/E Ratio | 14.45-11.12 | 19.85-14.27 | 24.20-13.16 | 22.35-15.52 | 27.87-21.49 | 30.32-24.01 | 29.21-24.94 | 44.07-31.54 |
| Average Yield % | 2.88 | 3.25 | 3.45 | 2.38 | 2.00 | 1.37 | 0.96 | 0.71 |

| | | |
|---|---|---|
| **Address:** 1630 McCarthy Boulevard, Milpitas, CA 95035<br>**Telephone:** 408-432-1900<br>**Web Site:** www.linear.com | **Officers:** Robert H. Swanson - Executive Chairman<br>Lothar Maier - Chief Executive Officer **Transfer Agents:** Computershare Trust Company N.A., Providence, RI | **Investor Contact:** 408-432-1900<br>**No of Institutions:** 537<br>**Shares:** 250,610,464 **% Held:** 92.30 |

# LOWE'S COMPANIES INC

| Exchange | Symbol | Price | 52Wk Range | Yield | P/E |
|---|---|---|---|---|---|
| NYS | LOW | $19.93 (8/31/2011) | 27.28-18.11 | 2.81 | 13.47 |

***7 Year Price Score 89.94** *NYSE Composite Index=100 ***12 Month Price Score 90.35**

**Interim Earnings (Per Share)**

| Qtr. | Apr | Jul | Oct | Jan |
|---|---|---|---|---|
| 2008-09 | 0.41 | 0.64 | 0.33 | 0.11 |
| 2009-10 | 0.32 | 0.51 | 0.23 | 0.14 |
| 2010-11 | 0.34 | 0.58 | 0.29 | 0.21 |
| 2011-12 | 0.34 | 0.64 | ... | ... |

**Interim Dividends (Per Share)**

| Amt | Decl | Ex | Rec | Pay |
|---|---|---|---|---|
| 0.11Q | 11/12/2010 | 01/14/2011 | 01/19/2011 | 02/02/2011 |
| 0.11Q | 03/21/2011 | 04/18/2011 | 04/20/2011 | 05/04/2011 |
| 0.14Q | 05/27/2011 | 07/18/2011 | 07/20/2011 | 08/03/2011 |
| 0.14Q | 08/22/2011 | 10/17/2011 | 10/19/2011 | 11/02/2011 |

**Indicated Div: $0.56 (Div. Reinv. Plan)**

**Valuation Analysis**

| | | | |
|---|---|---|---|
| Forecast EPS | $1.60 (09/05/2011) | | |
| Market Cap | $25.1 Billion | Book Value | $16.8 Billion |
| Price/Book | 1.50 | Price/Sales | 0.51 |

**Dividend Achiever Status**

| | |
|---|---|
| **10 Year Growth Rate** | 26.71% |
| **Total Years of Dividend Growth** | 49 |

**Business Summary:** Retail - Hardware & Home Improvement (MIC: 2.1.8 SIC: 5211 NAIC: 444110)

Lowe's Companies is a home improvement retailer providing products in the following categories: appliances, lumber, paint, millwork, building materials, lawn & landscape products, flooring, rough plumbing, seasonal living, tools, hardware, fashion plumbing, lighting, nursery, outdoor power equipment, cabinets & countertops, home organization, rough electrical and home fashion. As of Jan 28 2011, Co. operated 1,749 stores, comprised of 1,723 stores across the U.S., 24 stores in Canada and two stores in Mexico. Co. provides national brand name merchandise such as Whirlpool® appliances and water heaters and Stainmaster® carpets, as well as private brands such as Aquasource® faucets and sinks.

**Recent Developments:** For the quarter ended July 29 2011, net income decreased 0.2% to US$830.0 million from US$832.0 million in the year-earlier quarter. Revenues were US$14.54 billion, up 1.3% from US$14.36 billion the year before. Direct operating expenses rose 1.8% to US$9.53 billion from US$9.36 billion in the comparable period the year before. Indirect operating expenses increased 0.3% to US$3.60 billion from US$3.59 billion in the equivalent prior-year period.

**Prospects:** Our evaluation of Lowe's Companies Inc. as of Sep. 6, 2011 is the result of our systematic analysis on three basic characteristics: earnings strength, relative valuation, and recent stock price movement. The company has managed to produce a neutral trend in earnings per share over the past 5 quarters. However, while recent estimates for the company have been lowered by analysts, LOW has posted better than expected results. Based on operating earnings yield, the company is undervalued when compared to all of the companies in our coverage universe. Share price changes over the past year indicates that LOW will perform poorly over the near term.

**Financial Data**

| (US$ in Thousands) | 6 Mos | 3 Mos | 01/28/2011 | 01/29/2010 | 01/30/2009 | 02/01/2008 | 02/02/2007 | 02/03/2006 |
|---|---|---|---|---|---|---|---|---|
| Earnings Per Share | 1.48 | 1.42 | 1.42 | 1.21 | 1.49 | 1.86 | 1.99 | 1.73 |
| Cash Flow Per Share | 3.42 | 2.67 | 2.76 | 2.78 | 2.84 | 2.94 | 2.94 | 2.43 |
| Tang Book Value Per Share | 13.32 | 13.25 | 13.38 | 13.07 | 12.28 | 11.04 | 10.31 | 9.14 |
| Dividends Per Share | 0.470 | 0.440 | 0.420 | 0.355 | 0.335 | 0.290 | 0.180 | 0.110 |
| Dividend Payout % | 31.76 | 30.99 | 29.58 | 29.34 | 22.48 | 15.59 | 9.05 | 6.36 |
| **Income Statement** | | | | | | | | |
| Total Revenue | 26,728,000 | 12,185,000 | 48,815,000 | 47,220,000 | 48,230,000 | 48,283,000 | 46,927,000 | 43,243,000 |
| EBITDA | 2,984,000 | 1,199,000 | 5,146,000 | 4,726,000 | 5,325,000 | 6,071,000 | 6,314,000 | 5,644,000 |
| Depn & Amortn | 737,000 | 371,000 | 1,586,000 | 1,614,000 | 1,539,000 | 1,366,000 | 1,162,000 | 980,000 |
| Income Before Taxes | 2,069,000 | 740,000 | 3,228,000 | 2,825,000 | 3,506,000 | 4,511,000 | 4,998,000 | 4,506,000 |
| Income Taxes | 777,000 | 279,000 | 1,218,000 | 1,042,000 | 1,311,000 | 1,702,000 | 1,893,000 | 1,735,000 |
| Net Income | 1,292,000 | 461,000 | 2,010,000 | 1,783,000 | 2,195,000 | 2,809,000 | 3,105,000 | 2,771,000 |
| Average Shares | 1,278,000 | 1,328,000 | 1,403,000 | 1,464,000 | 1,472,000 | 1,510,000 | 1,566,000 | 1,606,000 |
| **Balance Sheet** | | | | | | | | |
| Current Assets | 10,168,000 | 11,973,000 | 9,967,000 | 9,732,000 | 9,251,000 | 8,686,000 | 8,314,000 | 7,831,000 |
| Total Assets | 34,045,000 | 35,884,000 | 33,699,000 | 33,005,000 | 32,686,000 | 30,869,000 | 27,767,000 | 24,682,000 |
| Current Liabilities | 8,677,000 | 9,921,000 | 7,119,000 | 7,355,000 | 8,022,000 | 7,751,000 | 6,539,000 | 5,832,000 |
| Long-Term Obligations | 6,581,000 | 6,538,000 | 6,537,000 | 4,528,000 | 5,039,000 | 5,576,000 | 4,325,000 | 3,499,000 |
| Total Liabilities | 17,266,000 | 18,425,000 | 15,587,000 | 13,936,000 | 14,631,000 | 14,771,000 | 12,042,000 | 10,343,000 |
| Stockholders' Equity | 16,779,000 | 17,459,000 | 18,112,000 | 19,069,000 | 18,055,000 | 16,098,000 | 15,725,000 | 14,339,000 |
| Shares Outstanding | 1,260,000 | 1,318,000 | 1,354,000 | 1,459,000 | 1,470,000 | 1,458,000 | 1,524,500 | 1,568,200 |
| **Statistical Record** | | | | | | | | |
| Return on Assets % | 5.77 | 5.41 | 6.04 | 5.44 | 6.93 | 9.61 | 11.87 | 11.88 |
| Return on Equity % | 11.00 | 10.87 | 10.84 | 9.63 | 12.89 | 17.70 | 20.71 | 21.07 |
| EBITDA Margin % | 11.16 | 9.84 | 10.54 | 10.01 | 11.04 | 12.57 | 13.45 | 13.05 |
| Net Margin % | 4.83 | 3.78 | 4.12 | 3.78 | 4.55 | 5.82 | 6.62 | 6.41 |
| Asset Turnover | 1.42 | 1.33 | 1.47 | 1.44 | 1.52 | 1.65 | 1.79 | 1.85 |
| Current Ratio | 1.17 | 1.21 | 1.40 | 1.32 | 1.15 | 1.12 | 1.27 | 1.34 |
| Debt to Equity | 0.39 | 0.37 | 0.36 | 0.24 | 0.28 | 0.35 | 0.28 | 0.24 |
| Price Range | 27.28-19.59 | 27.74-19.59 | 28.22-19.59 | 24.17-13.39 | 27.36-16.82 | 34.93-20.31 | 34.65-26.37 | 34.70-25.75 |
| P/E Ratio | 18.43-13.24 | 19.54-13.80 | 19.87-13.80 | 19.98-11.07 | 18.36-11.29 | 18.78-10.92 | 17.41-13.25 | 20.06-14.88 |
| Average Yield % | 1.98 | 1.86 | 1.81 | 1.74 | 1.50 | 1.01 | 0.59 | 0.36 |

**Address:** 1000 Lowe's Boulevard, Mooresville, NC 28117
**Telephone:** 704-758-1000
**Web Site:** www.lowes.com

**Officers:** Robert A. Niblock - Chairman, Chief Executive Officer Larry D. Stone - President, Chief Operating Officer **Transfer Agents:** Computershare Trust Company, N.A., Providence, RI

**No of Institutions:** 1104
**Shares:** 989,094,272 **% Held:** 66.76

# MATTHEWS INTERNATIONAL CORP

| Exchange | Symbol | Price | 52Wk Range | Yield | P/E |
|---|---|---|---|---|---|
| NMS | MATW | $33.41 (8/31/2011) | 40.83-29.85 | 0.96 | 13.81 |

***7 Year Price Score 92.88** *NYSE Composite Index=100 ***12 Month Price Score 100.56**

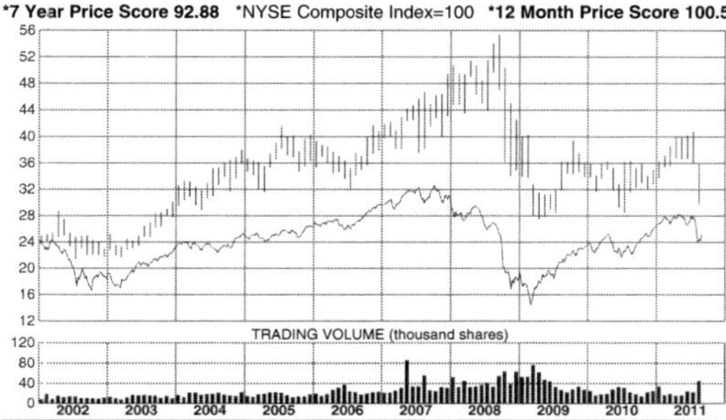


**Interim Earnings (Per Share)**

| Qtr. | Dec | Mar | Jun | Sep |
|---|---|---|---|---|
| 2007-08 | 0.56 | 0.65 | 0.69 | 0.65 |
| 2008-09 | 0.37 | 0.42 | 0.60 | 0.52 |
| 2009-10 | 0.43 | 0.53 | 0.68 | 0.67 |
| 2010-11 | 0.45 | 0.56 | 0.74 | ... |

**Interim Dividends (Per Share)**

| Amt | Decl | Ex | Rec | Pay |
|---|---|---|---|---|
| 0.08Q | 10/14/2010 | 10/21/2010 | 10/25/2010 | 11/08/2010 |
| 0.08Q | 01/20/2011 | 01/27/2011 | 01/31/2011 | 02/14/2011 |
| 0.08Q | 04/21/2011 | 04/28/2011 | 05/02/2011 | 05/16/2011 |
| 0.08Q | 07/21/2011 | 07/28/2011 | 08/01/2011 | 08/15/2011 |

**Indicated Div: $0.32**

**Valuation Analysis**

Forecast EPS $2.45 (09/02/2011)

| Market Cap | $976.7 Million | Book Value | $513.1 Million |
|---|---|---|---|
| Price/Book | 1.90 | Price/Sales | 1.12 |

**Dividend Achiever Status**

| | |
|---|---|
| **10 Year Growth Rate** | 11.10% |
| **Total Years of Dividend Growth** | 16 |

**Business Summary:** Miscellaneous Consumer Services (MIC: 2.2.3 SIC: 3995 NAIC: 339995)

Matthews International is a designer, manufacturer and marketer primarily of memorialization products, which consist mainly of bronze and granite memorials and other memorialization products, caskets and cremation equipment for the cemetery and funeral home industries; and brand products, which include graphics imaging products and services, marking products, and merchandising products. Co.'s products and operations are comprised of six business segments: Bronze, Casket, Cremation, Graphics Imaging, Marking Products and Merchandising Solutions. Co. has manufacturing and marketing facilities in the U.S., Mexico, Canada, Europe, Australia and Asia.

**Recent Developments:** For the quarter ended June 30 2011, net income increased 4.5% to US$22.2 million from US$21.2 million in the year-earlier quarter. Revenues were US$231.5 million, up 8.5% from US$213.3 million the year before. Operating income was US$35.1 million versus US$34.5 million in the prior-year quarter, an increase of 1.6%. Direct operating expenses rose 8.7% to US$139.6 million from US$128.4 million in the comparable period the year before. Indirect operating expenses increased 12.7% to US$56.9 million from US$50.5 million in the equivalent prior-year period.

**Prospects:** Our evaluation of Matthews International Corp. as of Sep. 6, 2011 is the result of our systematic analysis on three basic characteristics: earnings strength, relative valuation, and recent stock price movement. The company has enjoyed a very positive trend in earnings per share over the past 5 quarters and while recent estimates for the company have remained steady, MATW has posted better than expected results. Based on operating earnings yield, the company is undervalued when compared to all of the companies in our coverage universe. Share price changes over the past year indicates that MATW will perform in line with the market over the near term.

**Financial Data**

| (US$ in Thousands) | 9 Mos | 6 Mos | 3 Mos | 09/30/2010 | 09/30/2009 | 09/30/2008 | 09/30/2007 | 09/30/2006 |
|---|---|---|---|---|---|---|---|---|
| Earnings Per Share | 2.42 | 2.36 | 2.33 | 2.31 | 1.90 | 2.55 | 2.04 | 2.06 |
| Cash Flow Per Share | 2.94 | 2.92 | 3.54 | 3.59 | 3.00 | 3.37 | 2.36 | 2.07 |
| Tang Book Value Per Share | 0.26 | N.M. | N.M. | N.M. | N.M. | 0.47 | 1.84 | 1.56 |
| Dividends Per Share | 0.310 | 0.300 | 0.290 | 0.280 | 0.260 | 0.240 | 0.220 | 0.200 |
| Dividend Payout % | 12.81 | 12.71 | 12.45 | 12.12 | 13.68 | 9.41 | 10.78 | 9.71 |
| **Income Statement** | | | | | | | | |
| Total Revenue | 659,006 | 427,495 | 207,344 | 821,829 | 780,908 | 818,623 | 749,352 | 715,891 |
| EBITDA | 106,698 | 64,761 | 29,609 | 121,552 | 107,357 | 138,806 | 116,697 | 117,590 |
| Depn & Amortn | 20,447 | 13,627 | 6,761 | 3,720 | 4,310 | 3,536 | 2,129 | 2,216 |
| Income Before Taxes | 80,246 | 47,295 | 21,096 | 110,413 | 90,994 | 124,865 | 106,449 | 108,379 |
| Income Taxes | 27,433 | 16,653 | 7,573 | 38,639 | 30,811 | 42,088 | 38,990 | 38,964 |
| Net Income | 51,676 | 29,801 | 13,214 | 69,057 | 57,732 | 79,484 | 64,726 | 66,444 |
| Average Shares | 28,881 | 29,005 | 29,228 | 29,898 | 30,435 | 31,158 | 31,679 | 32,251 |
| **Balance Sheet** | | | | | | | | |
| Current Assets | 368,156 | 351,314 | 326,808 | 335,655 | 305,422 | 303,115 | 266,514 | 242,843 |
| Total Assets | 1,071,462 | 1,052,370 | 1,010,719 | 993,825 | 949,653 | 914,282 | 771,069 | 716,090 |
| Current Liabilities | 156,034 | 139,675 | 138,354 | 148,113 | 132,340 | 161,710 | 123,456 | 137,209 |
| Long-Term Obligations | 259,991 | 248,445 | 236,626 | 225,256 | 237,530 | 219,124 | 142,273 | 120,289 |
| Total Liabilities | 558,351 | 559,637 | 539,907 | 531,880 | 515,435 | 480,327 | 344,291 | 323,665 |
| Stockholders' Equity | 513,111 | 492,733 | 470,812 | 461,945 | 434,218 | 433,955 | 426,778 | 392,425 |
| Shares Outstanding | 29,234 | 29,513 | 29,587 | 29,478 | 30,302 | 30,859 | 31,057 | 31,634 |
| **Statistical Record** | | | | | | | | |
| Return on Assets % | 7.07 | 7.00 | 7.07 | 7.11 | 6.19 | 9.41 | 8.70 | 9.64 |
| Return on Equity % | 15.09 | 14.98 | 15.22 | 15.41 | 13.30 | 18.42 | 15.80 | 18.28 |
| EBITDA Margin % | 16.19 | 15.15 | 14.28 | 14.79 | 13.75 | 16.96 | 15.57 | 16.43 |
| Net Margin % | 7.84 | 6.97 | 6.37 | 8.40 | 7.39 | 9.71 | 8.64 | 9.28 |
| Asset Turnover | 0.87 | 0.86 | 0.85 | 0.85 | 0.84 | 0.97 | 1.01 | 1.04 |
| Current Ratio | 2.36 | 2.52 | 2.36 | 2.27 | 2.31 | 1.87 | 2.16 | 1.77 |
| Debt to Equity | 0.51 | 0.50 | 0.50 | 0.49 | 0.55 | 0.50 | 0.33 | 0.31 |
| Price Range | 40.17-28.44 | 38.55-28.44 | 36.40-28.44 | 39.44-28.44 | 50.74-27.49 | 55.35-39.99 | 46.76-35.66 | 40.23-31.87 |
| P/E Ratio | 16.60-11.75 | 16.33-12.05 | 15.62-12.21 | 17.07-12.31 | 26.71-14.47 | 21.71-15.68 | 22.92-17.48 | 19.53-15.47 |
| Average Yield % | 0.88 | 0.88 | 0.86 | 0.82 | 0.75 | 0.50 | 0.53 | 0.55 |

| | | |
|---|---|---|
| **Address:** Two Northshore Center, Pittsburgh, PA 15212-5851<br>**Telephone:** 412-442-8200<br>**Web Site:** www.matw.com | **Officers:** John D. Turner - Chairman Joseph C. Bartolacci - President, Chief Executive Officer<br>**Transfer Agents:** Computershare Investor Services LLC, Chicago Illinois | **Investor Contact:** 412-442-8200<br>**No of Institutions:** 170<br>**Shares:** 29,800,156 **% Held:** 75.62 |

# MCCORMICK & CO., INC.

| Exchange | Symbol | Price | 52Wk Range | Yield | P/E |
|---|---|---|---|---|---|
| NYS | MKC V | $47.79 (8/31/2011) | 51.00-39.87 | 2.34 | 16.65 |

***7 Year Price Score 123.85** *NYSE Composite Index=100 ***12 Month Price Score 104.14**

**Interim Earnings (Per Share)**

| Qtr. | Feb | May | Aug | Nov |
|---|---|---|---|---|
| 2007-08 | 0.39 | 0.41 | 0.52 | 0.62 |
| 2008-09 | 0.44 | 0.38 | 0.57 | 0.88 |
| 2009-10 | 0.51 | 0.49 | 0.76 | 0.99 |
| 2010-11 | 0.57 | 0.55 | ... | ... |

**Interim Dividends (Per Share)**

| Amt | Decl | Ex | Rec | Pay |
|---|---|---|---|---|
| 0.26Q | 09/28/2010 | 10/06/2010 | 10/11/2010 | 10/25/2010 |
| 0.28Q | 11/23/2010 | 12/29/2010 | 12/31/2010 | 01/14/2011 |
| 0.28Q | 03/30/2011 | 04/07/2011 | 04/11/2011 | 04/25/2011 |
| 0.28Q | 06/28/2011 | 07/07/2011 | 07/11/2011 | 07/25/2011 |

**Indicated Div: $1.12**

**Valuation Analysis**

| | | | |
|---|---|---|---|
| Forecast EPS | $2.78 (09/02/2011) | | |
| Market Cap | $6.3 Billion | Book Value | $1.6 Billion |
| Price/Book | 3.87 | Price/Sales | 1.84 |

**Dividend Achiever Status**

| | |
|---|---|
| **10 Year Growth Rate** | 10.03% |
| **Total Years of Dividend Growth** | 24 |

**Business Summary:** Food (MIC: 1.2.1 SIC: 2099 NAIC: 311942)

McCormick & Company is engaged in the manufacture, marketing and distribution of spices, herbs, seasonings, specialty foods and flavors to the food industry. As of Nov 30 2010, Co. operated in two business segments: consumer and industrial. Co.'s consumer segment sells spices, herbs, extracts, seasoning blends, sauces, marinades, and specialty foods to the consumer food market under a range of brands worldwide, including McCormick®, Lawry's®, Zatarain's®, Old Bay®, Thai Kitchen®, Simply Asia®, Ducros®, and Billy Bee®. The industrial segment sells seasoning blends and wet flavors, among others, to food manufacturers and foodservice customers, both directly and indirectly via distributors.

**Recent Developments:** For the quarter ended May 31 2011, net income increased 11.2% to US$73.6 million from US$66.2 million in the year-earlier quarter. Revenues were US$883.7 million, up 10.7% from US$798.3 million the year before. Operating income was US$109.3 million versus US$97.5 million in the prior-year quarter, an increase of 12.1%. Direct operating expenses rose 13.0% to US$533.0 million from US$471.6 million in the comparable period the year before. Indirect operating expenses increased 5.3% to US$241.4 million from US$229.2 million in the equivalent prior-year period.

**Prospects:** Our evaluation of McCormick & Co. Inc. as of Sep. 6, 2011 is the result of our systematic analysis on three basic characteristics: earnings strength, relative valuation, and recent stock price movement. The company has managed to produce a neutral trend in earnings per share over the past 5 quarters and while recent estimates for the company have remained steady, MKC has posted better than expected results. Based on operating earnings yield, the company is about fairly valued when compared to all of the companies in our coverage universe. Share price changes over the past year indicates that MKC will perform poorly over the near term.

**Financial Data**

| (US$ in Thousands) | 6 Mos | 3 Mos | 11/30/2010 | 11/30/2009 | 11/30/2008 | 11/30/2007 | 11/30/2006 | 11/30/2005 |
|---|---|---|---|---|---|---|---|---|
| Earnings Per Share | 2.87 | 2.81 | 2.75 | 2.27 | 1.94 | 1.73 | 1.50 | 1.56 |
| Cash Flow Per Share | 2.71 | 2.78 | 2.92 | 3.18 | 2.43 | 1.74 | 2.36 | 2.52 |
| Dividends Per Share | 1.080 | 1.060 | 1.040 | 0.960 | 0.880 | 0.800 | 0.720 | 0.640 |
| Dividend Payout % | 37.63 | 37.72 | 37.82 | 42.29 | 45.36 | 46.24 | 48.00 | 41.03 |
| **Income Statement** | | | | | | | | |
| Total Revenue | 1,666,500 | 782,800 | 3,336,800 | 3,192,100 | 3,176,600 | 2,916,200 | 2,716,400 | 2,592,000 |
| EBITDA | 269,800 | 134,800 | 591,000 | 550,100 | 462,100 | 432,700 | 350,400 | 418,000 |
| Depn & Amortn | 48,500 | 23,700 | 79,000 | 80,800 | 67,600 | 69,700 | 73,700 | 74,100 |
| Income Before Taxes | 196,800 | 98,900 | 462,700 | 416,500 | 337,800 | 302,400 | 223,000 | 295,700 |
| Income Taxes | 60,400 | 30,000 | 118,000 | 133,000 | 100,600 | 92,200 | 64,700 | 96,700 |
| Net Income | 150,400 | 76,800 | 370,200 | 299,800 | 255,800 | 230,100 | 202,200 | 214,900 |
| Average Shares | 134,100 | 134,600 | 134,700 | 132,300 | 131,800 | 132,700 | 135,000 | 138,100 |
| **Balance Sheet** | | | | | | | | |
| Current Assets | 1,079,600 | 1,015,600 | 1,015,900 | 970,500 | 968,300 | 983,100 | 899,400 | 800,200 |
| Total Assets | 3,589,400 | 3,477,600 | 3,419,700 | 3,387,800 | 3,220,300 | 2,787,500 | 2,568,000 | 2,272,700 |
| Current Liabilities | 846,500 | 806,700 | 834,800 | 818,200 | 1,034,100 | 861,300 | 780,500 | 699,000 |
| Long-Term Obligations | 781,200 | 775,700 | 779,900 | 875,000 | 885,200 | 573,500 | 569,600 | 463,900 |
| Total Liabilities | 1,956,500 | 1,910,200 | 1,966,000 | 2,053,200 | 2,165,000 | 1,702,400 | 1,634,700 | 1,472,800 |
| Stockholders' Equity | 1,632,900 | 1,567,400 | 1,453,700 | 1,334,600 | 1,055,300 | 1,085,100 | 933,300 | 799,900 |
| Shares Outstanding | 132,275 | 132,496 | 133,100 | 131,800 | 130,100 | 127,800 | 116,900 | 132,600 |
| **Statistical Record** | | | | | | | | |
| Return on Assets % | 11.40 | 11.28 | 10.88 | 9.07 | 8.49 | 8.59 | 8.35 | 9.26 |
| Return on Equity % | 26.55 | 26.24 | 26.55 | 25.09 | 23.84 | 22.80 | 23.33 | 25.44 |
| EBITDA Margin % | 16.19 | 17.22 | 17.71 | 17.23 | 14.55 | 14.84 | 12.90 | 16.13 |
| Net Margin % | 9.02 | 9.81 | 11.09 | 9.39 | 8.05 | 7.89 | 7.44 | 8.29 |
| Asset Turnover | 1.01 | 1.00 | 0.98 | 0.97 | 1.05 | 1.09 | 1.12 | 1.12 |
| Current Ratio | 1.28 | 1.26 | 1.22 | 1.19 | 0.94 | 1.14 | 1.15 | 1.14 |
| Debt to Equity | 0.48 | 0.49 | 0.54 | 0.66 | 0.84 | 0.53 | 0.61 | 0.58 |
| Price Range | 50.50-37.53 | 47.71-37.33 | 44.81-35.56 | 36.45-28.53 | 41.97-28.79 | 39.58-34.16 | 38.92-29.82 | 39.06-29.24 |
| P/E Ratio | 17.60-13.08 | 16.98-13.28 | 16.29-12.93 | 16.06-12.57 | 21.63-14.84 | 22.88-19.75 | 25.95-19.88 | 25.04-18.74 |
| Average Yield % | 2.45 | 2.55 | 2.65 | 3.00 | 2.39 | 2.15 | 2.10 | 1.86 |

**Address:** 18 Loveton Circle, P.O. Box 6000, Sparks, MD 21152-6000
**Telephone:** 410-771-7301
**Web Site:** www.mccormickcorporation.com

**Officers:** Alan D. Wilson - Chairman, President, Chief Executive Officer Gordon M. Stetz - Executive Vice President, Chief Financial Officer **Transfer Agents:** Wells Fargo Bank, N.A., South St. Paul, MN

**Investor Contact:** 410-771-7244
**No of Institutions:** 600
**Shares:** 112,479,264 **% Held:** 69.58

# MCDONALD'S CORP

| Exchange | Symbol | Price | 52Wk Range | Yield | P/E |
|---|---|---|---|---|---|
| NYS | MCD | $90.41 (8/31/2011) | 90.79-72.67 | 2.70 | 18.26 |

***7 Year Price Score 147.71** *NYSE Composite Index=100 ***12 Month Price Score 110.87**

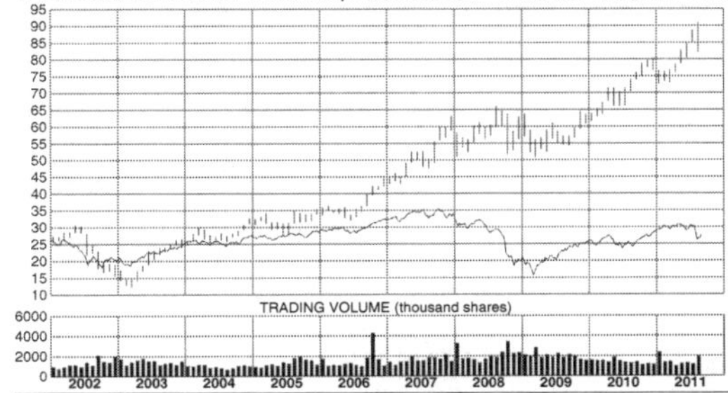


**Interim Earnings (Per Share)**

| Qtr. | Mar | Jun | Sep | Dec |
|---|---|---|---|---|
| 2008 | 0.81 | 1.04 | 1.05 | 0.87 |
| 2009 | 0.87 | 0.98 | 1.15 | 1.11 |
| 2010 | 1.00 | 1.13 | 1.29 | 1.16 |
| 2011 | 1.15 | 1.35 | ... | ... |

**Interim Dividends (Per Share)**

| Amt | Decl | Ex | Rec | Pay |
|---|---|---|---|---|
| 0.61Q | 09/22/2010 | 11/29/2010 | 12/01/2010 | 12/15/2010 |
| 0.61Q | 01/27/2011 | 02/25/2011 | 03/01/2011 | 03/15/2011 |
| 0.61Q | 05/18/2011 | 05/27/2011 | 06/01/2011 | 06/15/2011 |
| 0.61Q | 07/21/2011 | 08/30/2011 | 09/01/2011 | 09/16/2011 |

**Indicated Div: $2.44 (Div. Reinv. Plan)**

**Valuation Analysis**

| | | | |
|---|---|---|---|
| Forecast EPS | $5.23 (09/05/2011) | | |
| Market Cap | $93.3 Billion | Book Value | $15.0 Billion |
| Price/Book | 6.24 | Price/Sales | 3.65 |

**Dividend Achiever Status**

| | |
|---|---|
| **10 Year Growth Rate** | 25.95% |
| **Total Years of Dividend Growth** | 34 |

**Business Summary:** Hotels, Restaurants & Travel (MIC: 2.2.1 SIC: 5812 NAIC: 722211)

McDonald's franchises and operates McDonald's restaurants. Co.'s reportable segments include: the U.S.; Europe; Asia/Pacific, Middle East and Africa; and Other Countries & Corporate. Co.'s menu includes hamburgers and cheeseburgers, Big Mac, Quarter Pounder with Cheese, Filet-O-Fish, several chicken sandwiches, Chicken McNuggets, Chicken Selects, Snack Wraps, french fries, salads, shakes, McFlurry desserts, sundaes, soft serve cones, pies, cookies, soft drinks, coffee, McCafé beverages and other beverages. At Dec 31 2010, Co. had a total of 32,737 restaurants in 117 countries, including 26,338 that were franchised or licensed, and 6,399 operated by Co.

**Recent Developments:** For the quarter ended June 30 2011, net income increased 15.0% to US$1.41 billion from US$1.23 billion in the year-earlier quarter. Revenues were US$6.91 billion, up 16.1% from US$5.95 billion the year before. Operating income was US$2.19 billion versus US$1.85 billion in the prior-year quarter, an increase of 18.6%. Direct operating expenses rose 18.4% to US$3.81 billion from US$3.21 billion in the comparable period the year before. Indirect operating expenses increased 2.7% to US$909.5 million from US$885.4 million in the equivalent prior-year period.

**Prospects:** Our evaluation of McDonald's Corp. as of Sep. 6, 2011 is the result of our systematic analysis on three basic characteristics: earnings strength, relative valuation, and recent stock price movement. The company has produced a positive trend in earnings per share over the past 5 quarters and while recent estimates for the company have been raised by analysts, MCD has posted better than expected results. Based on operating earnings yield, the company is about fairly valued when compared to all of the companies in our coverage universe. Share price changes over the past year indicates that MCD will perform very poorly over the near term.

**Financial Data**

| (US$ in Thousands) | 6 Mos | 3 Mos | 12/31/2010 | 12/31/2009 | 12/31/2008 | 12/31/2007 | 12/31/2006 | 12/31/2005 |
|---|---|---|---|---|---|---|---|---|
| Earnings Per Share | 4.95 | 4.73 | 4.58 | 4.11 | 3.76 | 1.98 | 2.83 | 2.04 |
| Cash Flow Per Share | 6.63 | 6.21 | 5.95 | 5.27 | 5.24 | 4.10 | 3.52 | 3.44 |
| Tang Book Value Per Share | 11.85 | 11.36 | 11.44 | 10.78 | 9.99 | 11.14 | 11.01 | 10.45 |
| Dividends Per Share | 2.380 | 2.320 | 2.260 | 2.050 | 1.625 | 1.500 | 1.000 | 0.670 |
| Dividend Payout % | 48.08 | 49.05 | 49.34 | 49.88 | 43.22 | 75.76 | 35.34 | 32.84 |
| **Income Statement** | | | | | | | | |
| Total Revenue | 13,017,000 | 6,111,600 | 24,074,600 | 22,744,700 | 23,522,400 | 22,786,600 | 21,586,400 | 20,460,200 |
| EBITDA | 4,599,300 | 2,113,100 | 8,487,300 | 7,953,200 | 7,731,500 | 5,011,600 | 5,671,800 | 5,191,600 |
| Depn & Amortn | 689,200 | 339,100 | 1,200,400 | 1,160,800 | 1,161,600 | 1,145,000 | 1,180,200 | 1,186,700 |
| Income Before Taxes | 3,685,500 | 1,661,700 | 6,836,000 | 6,319,200 | 6,047,300 | 3,456,500 | 4,089,600 | 3,648,800 |
| Income Taxes | 1,146,100 | 489,900 | 2,054,000 | 1,936,000 | 1,844,800 | 1,237,100 | 1,293,400 | 1,099,400 |
| Net Income | 2,619,200 | 1,209,000 | 4,946,300 | 4,551,000 | 4,313,200 | 2,395,100 | 3,544,200 | 2,602,200 |
| Average Shares | 1,047,700 | 1,054,600 | 1,080,300 | 1,107,400 | 1,146,000 | 1,211,800 | 1,251,700 | 1,274,200 |
| **Balance Sheet** | | | | | | | | |
| Current Assets | 4,025,400 | 3,824,200 | 4,368,500 | 3,416,300 | 3,517,600 | 3,581,900 | 3,625,300 | 5,849,700 |
| Total Assets | 32,833,000 | 32,080,200 | 31,975,200 | 30,224,900 | 28,461,500 | 29,391,700 | 29,023,800 | 29,988,800 |
| Current Liabilities | 3,948,800 | 4,254,100 | 2,924,700 | 2,988,700 | 2,537,900 | 4,498,500 | 3,008,100 | 4,036,300 |
| Long-Term Obligations | 11,062,800 | 10,524,300 | 11,497,000 | 10,560,300 | 10,186,000 | 7,310,000 | 8,416,500 | 8,937,400 |
| Total Liabilities | 17,880,200 | 17,626,600 | 17,341,000 | 16,191,000 | 15,078,900 | 14,111,900 | 13,565,500 | 14,842,700 |
| Stockholders' Equity | 14,952,800 | 14,453,600 | 14,634,200 | 14,033,900 | 13,382,600 | 15,279,800 | 15,458,300 | 15,146,100 |
| Shares Outstanding | 1,031,700 | 1,037,600 | 1,053,600 | 1,076,700 | 1,115,300 | 1,165,300 | 1,203,700 | 1,263,200 |
| **Statistical Record** | | | | | | | | |
| Return on Assets % | 17.07 | 16.37 | 15.90 | 15.51 | 14.87 | 8.20 | 12.01 | 9.00 |
| Return on Equity % | 37.39 | 35.46 | 34.51 | 33.20 | 30.01 | 15.58 | 23.16 | 17.73 |
| EBITDA Margin % | 35.33 | 34.58 | 35.25 | 34.97 | 32.87 | 21.99 | 26.27 | 25.37 |
| Net Margin % | 20.12 | 19.78 | 20.55 | 20.01 | 18.34 | 10.51 | 16.42 | 12.72 |
| Asset Turnover | 0.83 | 0.79 | 0.77 | 0.78 | 0.81 | 0.78 | 0.73 | 0.71 |
| Current Ratio | 1.02 | 0.90 | 1.49 | 1.14 | 1.39 | 0.80 | 1.21 | 1.45 |
| Debt to Equity | 0.74 | 0.73 | 0.79 | 0.75 | 0.76 | 0.48 | 0.54 | 0.59 |
| Price Range | 84.57-65.87 | 80.34-65.87 | 80.34-61.45 | 64.53-50.86 | 65.95-50.75 | 63.13-42.91 | 44.36-31.94 | 35.50-27.70 |
| P/E Ratio | 17.08-13.31 | 16.99-13.93 | 17.54-13.42 | 15.70-12.37 | 17.54-13.50 | 31.88-21.67 | 15.67-11.29 | 17.40-13.58 |
| Average Yield % | 3.12 | 3.16 | 3.19 | 3.57 | 2.80 | 2.94 | 2.72 | 2.10 |

**Address:** One McDonald's Plaza, Oak Brook, IL 60523
**Telephone:** 630-623-3000
**Web Site:** www.mcdonalds.com

**Officers:** James A. Skinner - Vice-Chairman, Chief Executive Officer Donald Thompson - President, Chief Operating Officer **Transfer Agents:** Computershare Trust Company, N.A., Canton, MA

**Investor Contact:** 630-623-7428
**No of Institutions:** 1594
**Shares:** 771,232,704 **% Held:** 62.08

# MCGRATH RENTCORP

| Exchange | Symbol | Price | 52Wk Range | Yield | P/E |
|---|---|---|---|---|---|
| NMS | MGRC | $23.84 (8/31/2011) | 28.89-20.09 | 3.86 | 13.47 |

*7 Year Price Score 103.05 *NYSE Composite Index=100 *12 Month Price Score 100.60

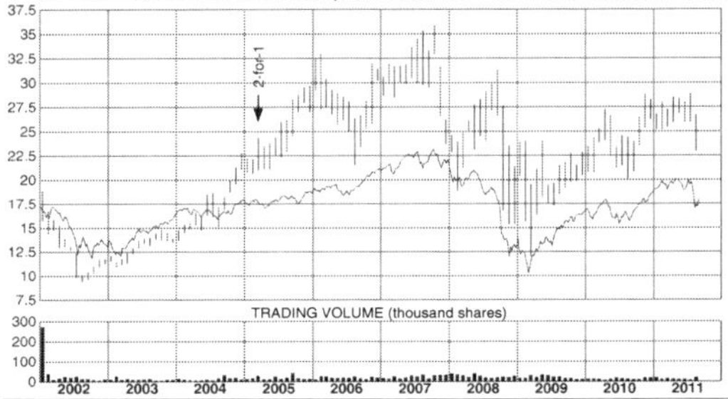


**Interim Earnings (Per Share)**

| Qtr. | Mar | Jun | Sep | Dec |
|---|---|---|---|---|
| 2008 | 0.43 | 0.42 | 0.48 | 0.39 |
| 2009 | 0.33 | 0.30 | 0.40 | 0.38 |
| 2010 | 0.28 | 0.31 | 0.40 | 0.52 |
| 2011 | 0.39 | 0.46 | ... | ... |

**Interim Dividends (Per Share)**

| Amt | Decl | Ex | Rec | Pay |
|---|---|---|---|---|
| 0.225Q | 10/04/2010 | 10/13/2010 | 10/15/2010 | 10/29/2010 |
| 0.225Q | 12/09/2010 | 01/12/2011 | 01/17/2011 | 01/31/2011 |
| 0.23Q | 02/23/2011 | 04/13/2011 | 04/15/2011 | 04/29/2011 |
| 0.23Q | 06/08/2011 | 07/13/2011 | 07/15/2011 | 07/29/2011 |

**Indicated Div: $0.92**

**Valuation Analysis**

| | | | |
|---|---|---|---|
| Forecast EPS | $1.75 (09/02/2011) | | |
| Market Cap | $580.8 Million | Book Value | $309.3 Million |
| Price/Book | 1.88 | Price/Sales | 1.84 |

**Dividend Achiever Status**

| | |
|---|---|
| 10 Year Growth Rate | 11.18% |
| Total Years of Dividend Growth | 20 |

**Business Summary:** Business Services (MIC: 7.5.2 SIC: 6514 NAIC: 531110)

McGrath RentCorp is a business-to-business rental company with three rental divisions: relocatable modular buildings, electronic test equipment, and liquid and solid containment tanks and boxes. Co. operates through four business segments: Mobile Modular Management Corporation, its modular building rental division; TRS-RenTelco, its electronic test equipment rental division; Adler Tank Rentals, LLC, its wholly-owned subsidiary providing containment applications for the storage of hazardous and non-hazardous liquids and solids; and Enviroplex, Inc., its wholly-owned subsidiary classroom manufacturing business selling modular buildings used primarily as classrooms in California.

**Recent Developments:** For the quarter ended June 30 2011, net income increased 54.4% to US$11.4 million from US$7.4 million in the year-earlier quarter. Revenues were US$79.5 million, up 19.6% from US$66.5 million the year before. Revenues from property income rose 19.4% to US$57.1 million from US$47.9 million in the corresponding quarter a year earlier.

**Prospects:** Our evaluation of McGrath RentCorp as of Sep. 6, 2011 is the result of our systematic analysis on three basic characteristics: earnings strength, relative valuation, and recent stock price movement. The company has managed to produce a neutral trend in earnings per share over the past 5 quarters and while recent estimates for the company have been raised by analysts, MGRC has posted better than expected results. Based on operating earnings yield, the company is undervalued when compared to all of the companies in our coverage universe. Share price changes over the past year indicates that MGRC will perform in line with the market over the near term.

**Financial Data**

| (US$ in Thousands) | 6 Mos | 3 Mos | 12/31/2010 | 12/31/2009 | 12/31/2008 | 12/31/2007 | 12/31/2006 | 12/31/2005 |
|---|---|---|---|---|---|---|---|---|
| Earnings Per Share | 1.77 | 1.62 | 1.50 | 1.40 | 1.72 | 1.67 | 1.63 | 1.61 |
| Cash Flow Per Share | 5.30 | 4.43 | 4.20 | 5.15 | 4.15 | 3.76 | 3.97 | 3.32 |
| Tang Book Value Per Share | 11.05 | 10.72 | 10.50 | 9.50 | 8.78 | 9.93 | 9.20 | 7.99 |
| Dividends Per Share | 0.905 | 0.900 | 0.895 | 0.860 | 0.780 | 0.700 | 0.620 | 0.530 |
| Dividend Payout % | 51.13 | 55.56 | 59.67 | 61.43 | 45.35 | 41.92 | 38.04 | 32.92 |
| **Income Statement** | | | | | | | | |
| Total Revenue | 152,503 | 72,973 | 291,374 | 275,643 | 304,159 | 280,409 | 267,066 | 272,180 |
| EBITDA | 67,445 | 31,889 | 121,635 | 118,294 | 138,095 | 134,532 | 123,788 | 120,053 |
| Depn & Amortn | 29,437 | 14,595 | 56,399 | 57,215 | 60,416 | 54,002 | 47,461 | 46,433 |
| Income Before Taxes | 34,572 | 15,812 | 59,050 | 53,974 | 67,702 | 69,811 | 65,567 | 65,730 |
| Income Taxes | 13,552 | 6,198 | 22,571 | 20,649 | 26,498 | 27,337 | 24,209 | 24,649 |
| Net Income | 21,020 | 9,614 | 36,479 | 33,325 | 41,204 | 42,410 | 41,078 | 40,819 |
| Average Shares | 24,742 | 24,660 | 24,289 | 23,869 | 23,944 | 25,443 | 25,231 | 25,331 |
| **Balance Sheet** | | | | | | | | |
| Current Assets | 79,267 | 77,173 | 83,609 | 78,035 | 95,263 | 72,151 | 60,183 | 63,978 |
| Total Assets | 866,700 | 832,032 | 813,562 | 757,936 | 784,497 | 642,236 | 585,542 | 542,438 |
| Current Liabilities | 557,378 | 318,460 | 49,612 | 50,975 | 55,471 | 55,642 | 55,509 | 51,690 |
| Long-Term Obligations | ... | ... | 265,640 | 247,334 | 305,500 | 197,729 | 165,557 | 163,232 |
| Total Liabilities | 557,378 | 531,056 | 518,585 | 490,523 | 534,616 | 398,205 | 354,750 | 343,969 |
| Stockholders' Equity | 309,322 | 300,976 | 294,977 | 267,413 | 249,881 | 244,031 | 230,792 | 198,469 |
| Shares Outstanding | 24,361 | 24,301 | 24,235 | 23,795 | 23,709 | 24,578 | 25,090 | 24,832 |
| **Statistical Record** | | | | | | | | |
| Return on Assets % | 5.29 | 4.97 | 4.64 | 4.32 | 5.76 | 6.91 | 7.28 | 8.03 |
| Return on Equity % | 14.87 | 13.77 | 12.97 | 12.88 | 16.64 | 17.86 | 19.14 | 22.34 |
| EBITDA Margin % | 44.23 | 43.70 | 41.75 | 42.92 | 45.40 | 47.98 | 46.35 | 44.11 |
| Net Margin % | 13.78 | 13.17 | 12.52 | 12.09 | 13.55 | 15.12 | 15.38 | 15.00 |
| Asset Turnover | 0.38 | 0.38 | 0.37 | 0.36 | 0.43 | 0.46 | 0.47 | 0.54 |
| Current Ratio | 0.14 | 0.24 | 1.69 | 1.53 | 1.72 | 1.30 | 1.08 | 1.24 |
| Debt to Equity | ... | ... | 0.90 | 0.92 | 1.22 | 0.81 | 0.72 | 0.82 |
| Price Range | 28.79-20.09 | 28.79-20.09 | 28.79-20.09 | 24.05-12.04 | 31.28-15.33 | 35.88-23.66 | 33.05-21.53 | 29.69-20.65 |
| P/E Ratio | 16.27-11.35 | 17.77-12.40 | 19.19-13.39 | 17.18-8.60 | 18.19-8.91 | 21.49-14.17 | 20.28-13.21 | 18.44-12.82 |
| Average Yield % | 3.54 | 3.62 | 3.71 | 4.31 | 3.23 | 2.27 | 2.22 | 2.16 |

**Address:** 5700 Las Positas Road, Livermore, CA 94551-7800
**Telephone:** 925-606-9200
**Web Site:** www.mgrc.com

**Officers:** Robert P. McGrath - Chairman Dennis C. Kakures - President, Chief Executive Officer
**Transfer Agents:** U.S. Stock Transfer, Glendale, CA

**Investor Contact:** 206-652-9704
**No of Institutions:** 117
**Shares:** 21,767,384 **% Held:** 83.03

# MCGRAW-HILL COS., INC. (THE)

| Exchange | Symbol | Price | 52Wk Range | Yield | P/E |
|---|---|---|---|---|---|
| NYS | MHP | $42.11 (8/31/2011) | 44.65-27.65 | 2.37 | 15.04 |

*7 Year Price Score 87.48 *NYSE Composite Index=100 *12 Month Price Score 109.82

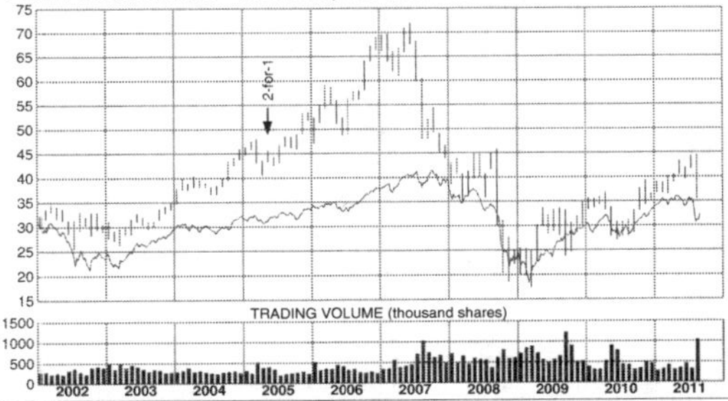


**Interim Earnings (Per Share)**

| Qtr. | Mar | Jun | Sep | Dec |
|---|---|---|---|---|
| 2008 | 0.25 | 0.66 | 1.23 | 0.38 |
| 2009 | 0.20 | 0.52 | 1.07 | 0.53 |
| 2010 | 0.33 | 0.61 | 1.23 | 0.50 |
| 2011 | 0.39 | 0.68 | ... | ... |

**Interim Dividends (Per Share)**

| Amt | Decl | Ex | Rec | Pay |
|---|---|---|---|---|
| 0.235Q | 10/29/2010 | 11/23/2010 | 11/26/2010 | 12/10/2010 |
| 0.25Q | 01/19/2011 | 02/22/2011 | 02/24/2011 | 03/10/2011 |
| 0.25Q | 04/27/2011 | 05/24/2011 | 05/26/2011 | 06/10/2011 |
| 0.25Q | 07/29/2011 | 08/24/2011 | 08/26/2011 | 09/12/2011 |

**Indicated Div: $1.00 (Div. Reinv. Plan)**

**Valuation Analysis**

| | | | |
|---|---|---|---|
| Forecast EPS | $2.89 (09/03/2011) | | |
| Market Cap | $12.7 Billion | Book Value | $2.3 Billion |
| Price/Book | 5.63 | Price/Sales | 1.99 |

**Dividend Achiever Status**

| | |
|---|---|
| 10 Year Growth Rate | 6.73% |
| Total Years of Dividend Growth | 37 |

**Business Summary:** Publishing (MIC: 2.3.3 SIC: 2731 NAIC: 511130)

McGraw-Hill Companies is an information services provider serving the education, financial services, and business information markets. Co.'s operations consist of four business segments: S&P, which is a provider of credit ratings; MH Financial, which is a global provider of research and analytical tools for investment advisors, wealth managers and institutional investors; McGraw-Hill Education, which is an educational publisher and consists of two operating groups: the School Education Group and the Higher Education, Professional and International Group; and McGraw-Hill Information and Media, which consists of two operating groups: the Business-to- Business Group and the Broadcasting Group.

**Recent Developments:** For the quarter ended June 30 2011, net income increased 11.1% to US$215.8 million from US$194.2 million in the year-earlier quarter. Revenues were US$1.58 billion, up 7.2% from US$1.47 billion the year before. Operating income was US$358.8 million versus US$326.3 million in the prior-year quarter, an increase of 10.0%. Direct operating expenses rose 8.2% to US$606.9 million from US$560.9 million in the comparable period the year before. Indirect operating expenses increased 4.8% to US$615.1 million from US$586.9 million in the equivalent prior-year period.

**Prospects:** Our evaluation of McGraw-Hill Cos. Inc. as of Sep. 6, 2011 is the result of our systematic analysis on three basic characteristics: earnings strength, relative valuation, and recent stock price movement. The company has managed to produce a neutral trend in earnings per share over the past 5 quarters. However, while recent estimates for the company have been mixed, MHP has posted better than expected results. Based on operating earnings yield, the company is undervalued when compared to all of the companies in our coverage universe. Share price changes over the past year indicates that MHP will perform well over the near term.

**Financial Data**
(US$ in Thousands)

| | 6 Mos | 3 Mos | 12/31/2010 | 12/31/2009 | 12/31/2008 | 12/31/2007 | 12/31/2006 | 12/31/2005 |
|---|---|---|---|---|---|---|---|---|
| Earnings Per Share | 2.80 | 2.73 | 2.65 | 2.33 | 2.51 | 2.94 | 2.40 | 2.21 |
| Cash Flow Per Share | 4.73 | 4.60 | 4.71 | 4.23 | 3.69 | 5.11 | 4.23 | 4.16 |
| Tang Book Value Per Share | N.M. | N.M. | N.M. | N.M. | N.M. | N.M. | 1.00 | 2.04 |
| Dividends Per Share | 0.970 | 0.955 | 0.940 | 0.900 | 0.880 | 0.820 | 0.726 | 0.660 |
| Dividend Payout % | 34.64 | 34.98 | 35.47 | 38.63 | 35.06 | 27.89 | 30.25 | 29.86 |
| **Income Statement** | | | | | | | | |
| Total Revenue | 2,862,700 | 1,281,900 | 6,168,331 | 5,951,782 | 6,355,055 | 6,772,281 | 6,255,138 | 6,003,642 |
| EBITDA | 742,800 | 279,000 | 1,592,146 | 1,421,220 | 1,533,156 | 1,824,102 | 1,580,041 | 1,516,149 |
| Depn & Amortn | 169,600 | 64,600 | 171,087 | 165,484 | 178,346 | 160,989 | 161,587 | 150,985 |
| Income Before Taxes | 534,600 | 195,300 | 1,339,416 | 1,178,869 | 1,279,186 | 1,622,532 | 1,404,823 | 1,359,962 |
| Income Taxes | 194,600 | 71,100 | 487,547 | 429,108 | 479,695 | 608,973 | 522,592 | 515,656 |
| Net Income | 331,100 | 120,000 | 828,063 | 730,502 | 799,491 | 1,013,559 | 882,231 | 844,306 |
| Average Shares | 309,200 | 309,600 | 312,220 | 313,296 | 318,687 | 344,785 | 366,878 | 382,570 |
| **Balance Sheet** | | | | | | | | |
| Current Assets | 3,126,400 | 2,924,000 | 3,294,611 | 2,936,396 | 2,302,723 | 2,333,035 | 2,257,938 | 2,590,939 |
| Total Assets | 6,944,000 | 6,789,700 | 7,046,561 | 6,475,250 | 6,080,142 | 6,357,336 | 6,042,890 | 6,395,808 |
| Current Liabilities | 2,523,200 | 2,380,000 | 2,680,874 | 2,451,954 | 2,530,703 | 2,656,860 | 2,468,016 | 2,224,826 |
| Long-Term Obligations | 1,198,000 | 1,198,000 | 1,197,965 | 1,197,791 | 1,197,611 | 1,197,425 | 314 | 339 |
| Total Liabilities | 4,689,000 | 4,560,500 | 4,836,265 | 4,627,963 | 4,797,806 | 4,750,686 | 3,363,272 | 3,282,660 |
| Stockholders' Equity | 2,255,000 | 2,229,200 | 2,210,296 | 1,847,287 | 1,282,336 | 1,606,650 | 2,679,618 | 3,113,148 |
| Shares Outstanding | 301,300 | 304,700 | 307,621 | 315,340 | 314,405 | 322,367 | 353,958 | 372,698 |
| **Statistical Record** | | | | | | | | |
| Return on Assets % | 13.00 | 12.92 | 12.25 | 11.64 | 12.82 | 16.35 | 14.19 | 13.77 |
| Return on Equity % | 42.21 | 40.91 | 40.82 | 46.68 | 55.20 | 47.29 | 30.46 | 27.69 |
| EBITDA Margin % | 25.95 | 21.76 | 25.81 | 23.88 | 24.12 | 26.93 | 25.26 | 25.25 |
| Net Margin % | 11.57 | 9.36 | 13.42 | 12.27 | 12.58 | 14.97 | 14.10 | 14.06 |
| Asset Turnover | 0.96 | 0.96 | 0.91 | 0.95 | 1.02 | 1.09 | 1.01 | 0.98 |
| Current Ratio | 1.24 | 1.23 | 1.23 | 1.20 | 0.91 | 0.88 | 0.91 | 1.16 |
| Debt to Equity | 0.53 | 0.54 | 0.54 | 0.65 | 0.93 | 0.75 | N.M. | N.M. |
| Price Range | 43.26-27.64 | 40.11-27.02 | 39.31-27.02 | 34.82-17.39 | 45.86-18.59 | 71.96-43.81 | 69.10-47.06 | 53.52-40.56 |
| P/E Ratio | 15.45-9.87 | 14.69-9.90 | 14.83-10.20 | 14.94-7.46 | 18.27-7.41 | 24.48-14.90 | 28.79-19.61 | 24.22-18.35 |
| Average Yield % | 2.69 | 2.83 | 2.86 | 3.22 | 2.41 | 1.38 | 1.28 | 1.42 |

**Address:** 1221 Avenue Of The Americas, New York, NY 10020
**Telephone:** 212-512-2000
**Web Site:** www.mcgraw-hill.com

**Officers:** Harold McGraw - Chairman, President, Chief Executive Officer Jack F. Callahan - Executive Vice President, Chief Financial Officer **Transfer Agents:**BNY Mellon Shareowner Services, New York, NY

**No of Institutions:** 670
**Shares:** 284,701,792 **% Held:** 78.52

# MDU RESOURCES GROUP INC.

| Exchange | Symbol | Price | 52Wk Range | Yield | P/E |
|---|---|---|---|---|---|
| NYS | MDU | $21.34 (8/31/2011) | 23.95-18.66 | 3.05 | 16.94 |

***7 Year Price Score 92.75** *NYSE Composite Index=100 ***12 Month Price Score 100.40**

**Interim Earnings (Per Share)**

| Qtr. | Mar | Jun | Sep | Dec |
|---|---|---|---|---|
| 2008 | 0.39 | 0.63 | 0.64 | (0.07) |
| 2009 | (1.87) | 0.30 | 0.50 | 0.40 |
| 2010 | 0.22 | 0.26 | 0.32 | 0.47 |
| 2011 | 0.23 | 0.24 | ... | ... |

**Interim Dividends (Per Share)**

| Amt | Decl | Ex | Rec | Pay |
|---|---|---|---|---|
| 0.163Q | 11/11/2010 | 12/07/2010 | 12/09/2010 | 01/01/2011 |
| 0.163Q | 02/17/2011 | 03/08/2011 | 03/10/2011 | 04/01/2011 |
| 0.163Q | 05/12/2011 | 06/07/2011 | 06/09/2011 | 07/01/2011 |
| 0.163Q | 08/11/2011 | 09/06/2011 | 09/08/2011 | 10/01/2011 |

**Indicated Div: $0.65 (Div. Reinv. Plan)**

**Valuation Analysis**

| | | | |
|---|---|---|---|
| Forecast EPS | $1.28 (09/05/2011) | | |
| Market Cap | $4.0 Billion | Book Value | $2.7 Billion |
| Price/Book | 1.48 | Price/Sales | 1.01 |

**Dividend Achiever Status**

| | |
|---|---|
| **10 Year Growth Rate** | 4.76% |
| **Total Years of Dividend Growth** | 20 |

**Business Summary:** Mining (MIC: 8.2.4 SIC: 1429 NAIC: 212319)

MDU Resources Group, through its subsidiaries, operates in the following segments: electric; natural gas distribution; construction services; pipeline and energy services; natural gas and oil production; construction materials and contracting; and others. As of Dec 31 2010, Co. provided electric service to over 124,000 customers, and sold natural gas to over 839,000 customers. Co.'s electric segment operates in Montana, North Dakota, South Dakota and Wyoming. The natural gas distribution segment operates in those states as well as in Idaho, Minnesota, Oregon and Washington. Also, as of such date, Co. had proved reserves of 645.60 billion cubic feet of natural gas equivalent.

**Recent Developments:** For the quarter ended June 30 2011, income from continuing operations decreased 7.6% to US$45.2 million from US$48.9 million in the year-earlier quarter. Net income decreased 7.9% to US$45.1 million from US$48.9 million in the year-earlier quarter. Revenues were US$930.8 million, up 2.7% from US$906.4 million the year before. Operating income was US$82.3 million versus US$88.7 million in the prior-year quarter, a decrease of 7.2%. Direct operating expenses rose 3.9% to US$722.6 million from US$695.8 million in the comparable period the year before. Indirect operating expenses increased 3.2% to US$125.8 million from US$121.9 million in the equivalent prior-year period.

**Prospects:** Our evaluation of MDU Resources Group Inc. as of Sep. 6, 2011 is the result of our systematic analysis on three basic characteristics: earnings strength, relative valuation, and recent stock price movement. The company has managed to produce a neutral trend in earnings per share over the past 5 quarters. However, while recent estimates for the company have been lowered by analysts, MDU has posted better than expected results. Based on operating earnings yield, the company is about fairly valued when compared to all of the companies in our coverage universe. Share price changes over the past year indicates that MDU will perform poorly over the near term.

**Financial Data**

| (US$ in Thousands) | 6 Mos | 3 Mos | 12/31/2010 | 12/31/2009 | 12/31/2008 | 12/31/2007 | 12/31/2006 | 12/31/2005 |
|---|---|---|---|---|---|---|---|---|
| Earnings Per Share | 1.26 | 1.28 | 1.27 | (0.67) | 1.59 | 2.36 | 1.74 | 1.53 |
| Cash Flow Per Share | 3.19 | 3.11 | 2.93 | 4.57 | 4.28 | 3.10 | 3.66 | 2.71 |
| Tang Book Value Per Share | 10.87 | 10.67 | 10.71 | 10.10 | 11.44 | 11.31 | 10.49 | 9.04 |
| Dividends Per Share | 0.645 | 0.640 | 0.635 | 0.623 | 0.600 | 0.560 | 0.523 | 0.493 |
| Dividend Payout % | 51.19 | 50.00 | 50.00 | ... | 37.74 | 23.73 | 30.08 | 32.31 |
| **Income Statement** | | | | | | | | |
| Total Revenue | 1,832,562 | 901,805 | 3,909,695 | 4,176,501 | 5,003,278 | 4,247,896 | 4,070,684 | 3,455,414 |
| EBITDA | 332,141 | 164,640 | 747,588 | 186,776 | 882,069 | 867,370 | 816,005 | 684,077 |
| Depn & Amortn | 167,964 | 84,674 | 328,843 | 330,542 | 366,020 | 301,932 | 271,583 | 228,657 |
| Income Before Taxes | 122,124 | 57,949 | 335,734 | (227,865) | 434,522 | 493,201 | 472,327 | 400,670 |
| Income Taxes | 35,793 | 15,904 | 122,530 | (96,092) | 147,476 | 190,024 | 165,248 | 145,779 |
| Net Income | 88,044 | 42,977 | 240,659 | (123,274) | 293,673 | 432,120 | 315,757 | 275,083 |
| Average Shares | 188,968 | 188,815 | 188,229 | 185,175 | 183,807 | 182,902 | 181,392 | 179,490 |
| **Balance Sheet** | | | | | | | | |
| Current Assets | 1,071,031 | 1,064,003 | 1,167,168 | 1,061,658 | 1,272,292 | 1,214,332 | 993,735 | 933,196 |
| Total Assets | 6,257,381 | 6,191,291 | 6,303,549 | 5,990,952 | 6,587,845 | 5,592,434 | 4,903,474 | 4,423,562 |
| Current Liabilities | 723,419 | 654,770 | 768,076 | 667,185 | 967,475 | 849,888 | 653,962 | 628,928 |
| Long-Term Obligations | 1,369,534 | 1,414,077 | 1,433,955 | 1,486,677 | 1,568,636 | 1,146,781 | 1,170,548 | 1,104,752 |
| Total Liabilities | 3,532,031 | 3,502,208 | 3,610,747 | 3,419,305 | 3,826,769 | 3,061,115 | 2,738,561 | 2,531,940 |
| Stockholders' Equity | 2,725,350 | 2,689,083 | 2,692,802 | 2,571,647 | 2,761,076 | 2,531,319 | 2,164,913 | 1,891,622 |
| Shares Outstanding | 188,793 | 188,793 | 188,362 | 187,850 | 183,669 | 182,407 | 181,018 | 179,856 |
| **Statistical Record** | | | | | | | | |
| Return on Assets % | 3.85 | 3.97 | 3.91 | N.M. | 4.81 | 8.23 | 6.77 | 6.74 |
| Return on Equity % | 8.89 | 9.13 | 9.14 | N.M. | 11.07 | 18.40 | 15.57 | 15.40 |
| EBITDA Margin % | 18.12 | 18.26 | 19.12 | 4.47 | 17.63 | 20.42 | 20.05 | 19.80 |
| Net Margin % | 4.80 | 4.77 | 6.16 | N.M. | 5.87 | 10.17 | 7.76 | 7.96 |
| Asset Turnover | 0.65 | 0.65 | 0.64 | 0.66 | 0.82 | 0.81 | 0.87 | 0.85 |
| Current Ratio | 1.48 | 1.63 | 1.52 | 1.59 | 1.32 | 1.43 | 1.52 | 1.48 |
| Debt to Equity | 0.50 | 0.53 | 0.53 | 0.58 | 0.57 | 0.45 | 0.54 | 0.58 |
| Price Range | 23.95-17.76 | 22.97-17.56 | 23.91-17.56 | 24.13-13.04 | 34.90-15.59 | 31.27-24.80 | 26.90-21.99 | 24.47-17.07 |
| P/E Ratio | 19.01-14.10 | 17.95-13.72 | 18.83-13.83 | ... | 21.95-9.81 | 13.25-10.51 | 15.46-12.64 | 15.99-11.15 |
| Average Yield % | 3.07 | 3.16 | 3.12 | 3.22 | 2.22 | 2.02 | 2.18 | 2.48 |

**Address:** 1200 West Century Avenue, P.O. Box 5650, Bismarck, ND 58506-5650
**Telephone:** 701-530-1000
**Web Site:** www.mdu.com

**Officers:** Harry J. Pearce - Chairman Terry D. Hildestad - President, Chief Executive Officer
**Transfer Agents:** Wells Fargo Bank, N.A., St. Paul, MN

**No of Institutions:** 362
**Shares:** 104,091,984 **% Held:** 50.96

# MEDTRONIC, INC.

| Exchange | Symbol | Price | 52Wk Range | Yield | P/E |
|---|---|---|---|---|---|
| NYS | MDT | $35.07 (8/31/2011) | 43.20-30.41 | 2.77 | 12.26 |

*7 Year Price Score 80.11 *NYSE Composite Index=100 *12 Month Price Score 95.65

**Interim Earnings (Per Share)**

| Qtr. | Jul | Oct | Jan | Apr |
|---|---|---|---|---|
| 2006-07 | 0.51 | 0.59 | 0.61 | 0.70 |
| 2007-08 | 0.59 | 0.58 | 0.07 | 0.71 |
| 2008-09 | 0.66 | 0.51 | 0.65 | 0.12 |
| 2009-10 | 0.40 | 0.78 | 0.75 | 0.86 |
| 2010-11 | 0.76 | 0.52 | 0.86 | 0.72 |

**Interim Dividends (Per Share)**

| Amt | Decl | Ex | Rec | Pay |
|---|---|---|---|---|
| 0.225Q | 12/09/2010 | 01/05/2011 | 01/07/2011 | 01/28/2011 |
| 0.225Q | 02/17/2011 | 04/06/2011 | 04/08/2011 | 04/29/2011 |
| 0.242Q | 06/23/2011 | 07/06/2011 | 07/08/2011 | 07/29/2011 |
| 0.242Q | 08/25/2011 | 10/05/2011 | 10/07/2011 | 10/28/2011 |

**Indicated Div: $0.97 (Div. Reinv. Plan)**

**Valuation Analysis**

| | | | |
|---|---|---|---|
| Forecast EPS | $3.45 (09/05/2011) | | |
| Market Cap | $37.5 Billion | Book Value | $16.0 Billion |
| Price/Book | 2.35 | Price/Sales | 2.36 |

**Dividend Achiever Status**

| | |
|---|---|
| **10 Year Growth Rate** | 14.87% |
| **Total Years of Dividend Growth** | 33 |

**Business Summary:** Medical Instruments & Equipment (MIC: 4.3.1 SIC: 3845 NAIC: 334510)

Medtronic is a medical technology company. Co.'s primary products include those for cardiac rhythm disorders, cardiovascular disease, neurological disorders, spinal conditions and musculoskeletal trauma, urological and digestive disorders, diabetes, and ear, nose, and throat conditions. As of Apr 29 2011, Co. conductted its businesses through two operating groups that manufacture and sell device-based medical therapies. Co.'s Cardiac and Vascular group is composed of its Cardiac Rhythm Disease Management, CardioVascular, and Physio-Control businesses. Co.'s Restorative Therapies group is consisted of its Spinal, Neuromodulation, Diabetes, and Surgical Technologies businesses.

**Recent Developments:** For the year ended Apr 29 2011, net income was unchanged at US$3.10 billion versus US$3.10 billion the prior year. Revenues were US$15.93 billion, up 0.7% from US$15.82 billion the year before. Direct operating expenses rose 2.6% to US$3.91 billion from US$3.81 billion in the comparable period the year before. Indirect operating expenses increased 3.3% to US$7.56 billion from US$7.32 billion in the equivalent prior-year period.

**Prospects:** Our evaluation of Medtronic Inc. as of Sep. 6, 2011 is the result of our systematic analysis on three basic characteristics: earnings strength, relative valuation, and recent stock price movement. The company has produced a positive trend in earnings per share over the past 5 quarters. However, while recent estimates for the company have been lowered by analysts, MDT has posted results that fell short of analysts expectations. Based on operating earnings yield, the company is undervalued when compared to all of the companies in our coverage universe. Share price changes over the past year indicates that MDT will perform very poorly over the near term.

| **Financial Data** (US$ in Thousands) | 04/29/2011 | 04/30/2010 | 04/24/2009 | 04/25/2008 | 04/27/2007 | 04/28/2006 | 04/29/2005 | 04/30/2004 |
|---|---|---|---|---|---|---|---|---|
| Earnings Per Share | 2.86 | 2.79 | 1.93 | 1.95 | 2.41 | 2.09 | 1.48 | 1.60 |
| Cash Flow Per Share | 3.48 | 3.67 | 3.48 | 3.09 | 2.60 | 1.84 | 2.34 | 2.31 |
| Tang Book Value Per Share | 3.41 | 3.35 | 1.95 | 1.62 | 4.56 | 2.98 | 4.26 | 3.18 |
| Dividends Per Share | 0.900 | 0.820 | 0.750 | 0.500 | 0.440 | 0.385 | 0.335 | 0.290 |
| Dividend Payout % | 31.47 | 29.39 | 38.86 | 25.64 | 18.26 | 18.42 | 22.64 | 18.13 |
| **Income Statement** | | | | | | | | |
| Total Revenue | 15,933,000 | 15,817,000 | 14,599,000 | 13,515,000 | 12,299,000 | 11,292,000 | 10,054,600 | 9,087,200 |
| EBITDA | 4,465,000 | 4,669,000 | 3,041,000 | 3,193,000 | 3,762,000 | 3,443,100 | 2,961,700 | 3,236,700 |
| Depn & Amortn | 464,000 | 454,000 | 418,000 | 417,000 | 401,000 | 369,200 | 463,300 | 442,600 |
| Income Before Taxes | 3,723,000 | 3,969,000 | 2,594,000 | 2,885,000 | 3,515,000 | 3,161,300 | 2,543,500 | 2,796,900 |
| Income Taxes | 627,000 | 870,000 | 425,000 | 654,000 | 713,000 | 614,600 | 739,600 | 837,600 |
| Net Income | 3,096,000 | 3,099,000 | 2,169,000 | 2,231,000 | 2,802,000 | 2,546,700 | 1,803,900 | 1,959,300 |
| Average Shares | 1,081,700 | 1,109,400 | 1,124,000 | 1,142,100 | 1,161,800 | 1,217,300 | 1,220,800 | 1,225,200 |
| **Balance Sheet** | | | | | | | | |
| Current Assets | 9,117,000 | 9,839,000 | 7,460,000 | 7,322,000 | 7,918,000 | 10,376,600 | 7,421,500 | 5,312,700 |
| Total Assets | 30,424,000 | 28,090,000 | 23,661,000 | 22,198,000 | 19,512,000 | 19,664,800 | 16,617,400 | 14,110,800 |
| Current Liabilities | 4,714,000 | 5,121,000 | 3,147,000 | 3,535,000 | 2,563,000 | 4,405,800 | 3,380,000 | 4,240,600 |
| Long-Term Obligations | 8,112,000 | 6,944,000 | 6,772,000 | 5,802,000 | 5,578,000 | 5,486,300 | 1,973,200 | 1,100 |
| Total Liabilities | 14,456,000 | 13,461,000 | 10,810,000 | 10,662,000 | 8,535,000 | 10,282,300 | 6,167,900 | 5,033,800 |
| Stockholders' Equity | 15,968,000 | 14,629,000 | 12,851,000 | 11,536,000 | 10,977,000 | 9,382,500 | 10,449,500 | 9,077,000 |
| Shares Outstanding | 1,070,162 | 1,097,342 | 1,119,140 | 1,124,926 | 1,143,407 | 1,155,237 | 1,210,186 | 1,209,459 |
| **Statistical Record** | | | | | | | | |
| Return on Assets % | 10.61 | 11.78 | 9.49 | 10.73 | 14.34 | 14.08 | 11.77 | 14.59 |
| Return on Equity % | 20.29 | 22.19 | 17.84 | 19.87 | 27.60 | 25.75 | 18.53 | 22.70 |
| EBITDA Margin % | 28.02 | 29.52 | 20.83 | 23.63 | 30.59 | 30.49 | 29.46 | 35.62 |
| Net Margin % | 19.43 | 19.59 | 14.86 | 16.51 | 22.78 | 22.55 | 17.94 | 21.56 |
| Asset Turnover | 0.55 | 0.60 | 0.64 | 0.65 | 0.63 | 0.62 | 0.66 | 0.68 |
| Current Ratio | 1.93 | 1.92 | 2.37 | 2.07 | 3.09 | 2.36 | 2.20 | 1.25 |
| Debt to Equity | 0.51 | 0.47 | 0.53 | 0.50 | 0.51 | 0.58 | 0.19 | N.M. |
| Price Range | 44.13-31.21 | 46.03-29.58 | 56.55-24.38 | 57.86-45.25 | 54.58-42.47 | 59.54-49.05 | 54.92-46.40 | 52.65-43.36 |
| P/E Ratio | 15.43-10.91 | 16.50-10.60 | 29.30-12.63 | 29.67-23.21 | 22.65-17.62 | 28.49-23.47 | 37.11-31.35 | 32.91-27.10 |
| Average Yield % | 2.42 | 2.09 | 1.81 | 0.98 | 0.88 | 0.71 | 0.66 | 0.60 |

**Address:** 710 Medtronic Parkway, Minneapolis, MN 55432
**Telephone:** 763-514-4000
**Web Site:** www.medtronic.com

**Officers:** Omar Ishrak - Chairman, Chief Executive Officer Jean-Luc Butel - Executive Vice President, Region Officer **Transfer Agents:**
Wells Fargo Bank, N.A., South St. Paul, MN

**Investor Contact:** 763-505-2692
**No of Institutions:** 1301
**Shares:** 894,046,400 **% Held:** 70.40

# MERCURY GENERAL CORP.

| Exchange | Symbol | Price | 52Wk Range | Yield | P/E |
|---|---|---|---|---|---|
| NYS | MCY | $39.51 (8/31/2011) | 44.79-33.86 | 6.07 | 11.49 |

*7 Year Price Score 84.11 *NYSE Composite Index=100 *12 Month Price Score 93.57

**Interim Earnings (Per Share)**

| Qtr. | Mar | Jun | Sep | Dec |
|---|---|---|---|---|
| 2008 | (0.07) | 1.29 | (2.57) | (3.07) |
| 2009 | 1.75 | 2.07 | 2.85 | 0.62 |
| 2010 | 1.12 | 0.32 | 1.77 | (0.43) |
| 2011 | 1.06 | 1.04 | ... | ... |

**Interim Dividends (Per Share)**

| Amt | Decl | Ex | Rec | Pay |
|---|---|---|---|---|
| 0.60Q | 11/01/2010 | 12/14/2010 | 12/16/2010 | 12/30/2010 |
| 0.60Q | 02/07/2011 | 03/14/2011 | 03/16/2011 | 03/31/2011 |
| 0.60Q | 05/02/2011 | 06/14/2011 | 06/16/2011 | 06/30/2011 |
| 0.60Q | 08/01/2011 | 09/14/2011 | 09/16/2011 | 09/30/2011 |

**Indicated Div: $2.40**

**Valuation Analysis**

Forecast EPS $2.80 (09/02/2011)

Market Cap $2.2 Billion Book Value $1.8 Billion

Price/Book 1.17 Price/Sales 0.76

**Dividend Achiever Status**

**10 Year Growth Rate** 8.38%

**Total Years of Dividend Growth** 24

**Business Summary:** General Insurance (MIC: 5.2.1 SIC: 6331 NAIC: 524126)

Mercury General is an insurance holding company. Co. and its subsidiaries are primarily engaged in writing automobile insurance. Co. provides automobile policyholders the following coverages: bodily injury liability, underinsured and uninsured motorist, personal injury protection, property damage liability, comprehensive, collision and other hazards. Co. also writes homeowners, mechanical breakdown, fire, umbrella, and commercial automobile and property insurance. As of Dec 31 2010, Co. sold its policies through about 5,700 independent agents and brokers in California, Florida, Georgia, Illinois, Texas, Oklahoma, New York, New Jersey, Virginia, Pennsylvania, Arizona, Nevada, and Michigan.

**Recent Developments:** For the quarter ended June 30 2011, net income increased 221.3% to US$57.3 million from US$17.8 million in the year-earlier quarter. Revenues were US$706.5 million, up 8.1% from US$653.7 million the year before. Net premiums earned were US$642.3 million versus US$642.7 million in the prior-year quarter, a decrease of 0.1%. Net investment income fell 1.3% to US$36.0 million from US$36.5 million a year ago.

**Prospects:** Our evaluation of Mercury General Corp. as of Sep. 6, 2011 is the result of our systematic analysis on three basic characteristics: earnings strength, relative valuation, and recent stock price movement. The company has enjoyed a very positive trend in earnings per share over the past 5 quarters and while recent estimates for the company have been raised by analysts, MCY has posted better than expected results. Based on operating earnings yield, the company is about fairly valued when compared to all of the companies in our coverage universe. Share price changes over the past year indicates that MCY will perform very poorly over the near term.

**Financial Data**

| (US$ in Thousands) | 6 Mos | 3 Mos | 12/31/2010 | 12/31/2009 | 12/31/2008 | 12/31/2007 | 12/31/2006 | 12/31/2005 |
|---|---|---|---|---|---|---|---|---|
| Earnings Per Share | 3.44 | 2.72 | 2.78 | 7.32 | (4.42) | 4.34 | 3.92 | 4.63 |
| Cash Flow Per Share | 2.42 | 1.72 | 1.68 | 3.45 | 1.18 | 3.95 | 6.62 | 8.98 |
| Tang Book Value Per Share | 31.85 | 31.37 | 30.87 | 30.33 | 27.28 | 34.02 | 31.54 | 29.44 |
| Dividends Per Share | 2.390 | 2.380 | 2.370 | 2.330 | 2.320 | 2.080 | 1.920 | 1.720 |
| Dividend Payout % | 69.48 | 87.50 | 85.25 | 31.83 | ... | 47.93 | 48.98 | 37.15 |
| **Income Statement** | | | | | | | | |
| Premium Income | 1,280,818 | 638,487 | 2,566,685 | 2,625,133 | 2,808,839 | 2,993,877 | 2,997,023 | 2,847,733 |
| Total Revenue | 1,412,090 | 705,543 | 2,775,885 | 3,121,493 | 2,414,196 | 3,178,750 | 3,168,743 | 2,991,913 |
| Benefits & Claims | 897,799 | 446,461 | 1,825,766 | 1,782,233 | 2,060,409 | 2,036,644 | 2,021,646 | 1,862,936 |
| Income Before Taxes | 152,524 | 76,911 | 182,390 | 571,541 | (450,861) | 315,036 | 312,409 | 352,639 |
| Income Taxes | 37,047 | 18,685 | 30,192 | 168,469 | (208,742) | 77,204 | 97,592 | 99,380 |
| Net Income | 115,477 | 58,226 | 152,198 | 403,072 | (242,119) | 237,832 | 214,817 | 253,259 |
| Average Shares | 54,837 | 54,831 | 54,826 | 55,092 | 54,917 | 54,829 | 54,786 | 54,717 |
| **Balance Sheet** | | | | | | | | |
| Total Assets | 4,246,515 | 4,208,575 | 4,203,364 | 4,232,633 | 3,950,195 | 4,414,496 | 4,301,062 | 4,041,551 |
| Total Liabilities | 2,400,913 | 2,387,698 | 2,408,549 | 2,461,687 | 2,456,144 | 2,552,498 | 2,576,932 | 2,433,714 |
| Stockholders' Equity | 1,845,602 | 1,820,877 | 1,794,815 | 1,770,946 | 1,494,051 | 1,861,998 | 1,724,130 | 1,607,837 |
| Shares Outstanding | 54,822 | 54,818 | 54,803 | 54,776 | 54,763 | 54,729 | 54,669 | 54,605 |
| **Statistical Record** | | | | | | | | |
| Return on Assets % | 4.48 | 3.53 | 3.61 | 9.85 | N.M. | 5.46 | 5.15 | 6.62 |
| Return on Equity % | 10.39 | 8.24 | 8.54 | 24.69 | N.M. | 13.26 | 12.89 | 16.51 |
| Loss Ratio % | 70.10 | 69.92 | 71.13 | 67.89 | 73.35 | 68.03 | 67.46 | 65.42 |
| Net Margin % | 8.18 | 8.25 | 5.48 | 12.91 | (10.03) | 7.48 | 6.78 | 8.46 |
| Price Range | 44.79-37.54 | 46.26-37.54 | 46.26-37.49 | 45.99-22.68 | 61.90-36.93 | 57.57-49.17 | 59.52-49.02 | 60.45-51.62 |
| P/E Ratio | 13.02-10.91 | 17.01-13.80 | 16.64-13.49 | 6.28-3.10 | ... | 13.26-11.33 | 15.18-12.51 | 13.06-11.15 |
| Average Yield % | 5.82 | 5.66 | 5.64 | 6.66 | 4.85 | 3.90 | 3.54 | 3.04 |

**Address:** 4484 Wilshire Boulevard, Los Angeles, CA 90010
**Telephone:** 323-937-1060
**Web Site:** www.mercuryinsurance.com

**Officers:** George Joseph - Chairman Gabriel Tirador - President, Chief Executive Officer **Transfer Agents:** BNY Mellon Shareowner Services, Pittsburgh, PA

**No of Institutions:** 224
**Shares:** 25,079,504 **% Held:** 37.94

# MEREDITH CORP.

| Exchange | Symbol | Price | 52Wk Range | Yield | P/E |
|---|---|---|---|---|---|
| NYS | MDP | $25.80 (8/31/2011) | 36.81-23.45 | 3.95 | 9.28 |

***7 Year Price Score 79.03** *NYSE Composite Index=100 ***12 Month Price Score 87.44**

**Interim Earnings (Per Share)**

| Qtr. | Sep | Dec | Mar | Jun |
|---|---|---|---|---|
| 2006-07 | 0.62 | 0.72 | 0.92 | 1.05 |
| 2007-08 | 0.68 | 0.75 | 0.97 | 0.43 |
| 2008-09 | 0.41 | 0.28 | 0.56 | (3.63) |
| 2009-10 | 0.40 | 0.42 | 0.73 | 0.73 |
| 2010-11 | 0.56 | 0.88 | 0.67 | 0.66 |

**Interim Dividends (Per Share)**

| Amt | Decl | Ex | Rec | Pay |
|---|---|---|---|---|
| 0.23Q | 11/04/2010 | 11/26/2010 | 11/30/2010 | 12/15/2010 |
| 0.255Q | 01/31/2011 | 02/24/2011 | 02/28/2011 | 03/15/2011 |
| 0.255Q | 05/11/2011 | 05/26/2011 | 05/31/2011 | 06/15/2011 |
| 0.255Q | 08/11/2011 | 08/29/2011 | 08/31/2011 | 09/15/2011 |

**Indicated Div: $1.02**

**Valuation Analysis**

| | | | |
|---|---|---|---|
| Forecast EPS | $2.65 (09/02/2011) | | |
| Market Cap | $1.2 Billion | Book Value | $775.0 Million |
| Price/Book | 1.50 | Price/Sales | 0.83 |

**Dividend Achiever Status**

| | |
|---|---|
| **10 Year Growth Rate** | 10.47% |
| **Total Years of Dividend Growth** | 17 |

**Business Summary:** Publishing (MIC: 2.3.3 SIC: 2721 NAIC: 511120)

Meredith is a media and marketing company focused primarily on the home and family marketplace. Co. operates two business segments: national media and local media. The national media segment includes magazine publishing, brand licensing, integrated marketing, interactive media, database-related activities, and other related operations. The local media segment consists primarily of the operations of network-affiliated television stations, related interactive media operations, and video production related operations. As of June 30 2011, the local media segment had 12 network-affiliated television stations located across the U.S. and one AM radio station.

**Recent Developments:** For the year ended June 30 2011, income from continuing operations increased 24.6% to US$131.6 million from US$105.6 million a year earlier. Net income increased 22.6% to US$127.4 million from US$104.0 million in the prior year. Revenues were US$1.40 billion, up 1.3% from US$1.38 billion the year before. Operating income was US$225.3 million versus US$185.1 million in the prior year, an increase of 21.7%. Direct operating expenses declined 3.2% to US$554.1 million from US$572.3 million in the comparable period the year before. Indirect operating expenses decreased 0.7% to US$621.1 million from US$625.4 million in the equivalent prior-year period.

**Prospects:** Our evaluation of Meredith Corp. as of Sep. 6, 2011 is the result of our systematic analysis on three basic characteristics: earnings strength, relative valuation, and recent stock price movement. The company has generated a negative trend in earnings per share over the past 5 quarters. However, while recent estimates for the company have been mixed, MDP has posted better than expected results. Based on operating earnings yield, the company is undervalued when compared to all of the companies in our coverage universe. Share price changes over the past year indicates that MDP will perform in line with the market over the near term.

| **Financial Data** (US$ in Thousands) | 06/30/2011 | 06/30/2010 | 06/30/2009 | 06/30/2008 | 06/30/2007 | 06/30/2006 | 06/30/2005 | 06/30/2004 |
|---|---|---|---|---|---|---|---|---|
| Earnings Per Share | 2.78 | 2.28 | (2.38) | 2.83 | 3.31 | 2.86 | 2.52 | 2.14 |
| Cash Flow Per Share | 4.72 | 4.23 | 4.02 | 5.44 | 4.38 | 3.93 | 3.43 | 3.40 |
| Dividends Per Share | 0.970 | 0.910 | 0.880 | 0.800 | 0.690 | 0.600 | 0.520 | 0.430 |
| Dividend Payout % | 34.89 | 39.91 | ... | 28.27 | 20.85 | 20.98 | 20.63 | 20.09 |
| **Income Statement** | | | | | | | | |
| Total Revenue | 1,400,480 | 1,387,730 | 1,408,797 | 1,586,531 | 1,615,985 | 1,597,564 | 1,221,289 | 1,161,652 |
| EBITDA | 272,073 | 236,472 | (77,066) | 303,386 | 348,079 | 326,769 | 288,371 | 263,900 |
| Depn & Amortn | 46,782 | 54,088 | 58,062 | 61,881 | 59,830 | 60,178 | 60,317 | 60,786 |
| Income Before Taxes | 212,353 | 163,851 | (155,249) | 220,205 | 262,653 | 237,364 | 209,052 | 180,613 |
| Income Taxes | 80,743 | 59,888 | (52,742) | 86,100 | 93,823 | 92,572 | 80,903 | 69,897 |
| Net Income | 127,432 | 103,963 | (107,084) | 134,672 | 162,346 | 144,792 | 129,042 | 110,716 |
| Average Shares | 45,832 | 45,544 | 45,042 | 47,585 | 49,108 | 50,610 | 51,220 | 51,689 |
| **Balance Sheet** | | | | | | | | |
| Current Assets | 333,738 | 381,427 | 340,140 | 403,090 | 452,640 | 431,520 | 304,495 | 314,014 |
| Total Assets | 1,712,829 | 1,727,316 | 1,669,303 | 2,059,620 | 2,089,951 | 2,040,675 | 1,491,308 | 1,465,927 |
| Current Liabilities | 408,992 | 438,306 | 349,216 | 443,137 | 487,029 | 463,946 | 439,080 | 370,961 |
| Long-Term Obligations | 145,000 | 250,000 | 380,000 | 410,000 | 375,000 | 515,000 | 125,000 | 225,000 |
| Total Liabilities | 937,844 | 1,038,971 | 1,059,920 | 1,271,765 | 1,256,750 | 1,342,571 | 839,481 | 877,197 |
| Stockholders' Equity | 774,985 | 688,345 | 609,383 | 787,855 | 833,201 | 698,104 | 651,827 | 588,730 |
| Shares Outstanding | 45,058 | 45,415 | 45,067 | 45,476 | 48,232 | 48,191 | 49,296 | 50,484 |
| **Statistical Record** | | | | | | | | |
| Return on Assets % | 7.41 | 6.12 | N.M. | 6.47 | 7.86 | 8.20 | 8.73 | 7.61 |
| Return on Equity % | 17.42 | 16.02 | N.M. | 16.57 | 21.20 | 21.45 | 20.80 | 20.27 |
| EBITDA Margin % | 19.43 | 17.04 | N.M. | 19.12 | 21.54 | 20.45 | 23.61 | 22.72 |
| Net Margin % | 9.10 | 7.49 | N.M. | 8.49 | 10.05 | 9.06 | 10.57 | 9.53 |
| Asset Turnover | 0.81 | 0.82 | 0.76 | 0.76 | 0.78 | 0.90 | 0.83 | 0.80 |
| Current Ratio | 0.82 | 0.87 | 0.97 | 0.91 | 0.93 | 0.93 | 0.69 | 0.85 |
| Debt to Equity | 0.19 | 0.36 | 0.62 | 0.52 | 0.45 | 0.74 | 0.19 | 0.38 |
| Price Range | 36.81-29.26 | 37.81-23.93 | 30.08-10.88 | 62.42-28.29 | 63.25-46.18 | 56.48-47.65 | 55.13-44.81 | 55.75-44.00 |
| P/E Ratio | 13.24-10.53 | 16.58-10.50 | ... | 22.06-10.00 | 19.11-13.95 | 19.75-16.66 | 21.88-17.78 | 26.05-20.56 |
| Average Yield % | 2.92 | 2.94 | 4.08 | 1.65 | 1.26 | 1.17 | 1.04 | 0.87 |

**Address:** 1716 Locust Street, Des Moines, IA 50309-3023
**Telephone:** 515-284-3000
**Web Site:** www.meredith.com

**Officers:** Stephen M. Lacy - President, Chief Executive Officer, Principal Accounting Officer, Principal Financial Officer, Acting Vice President Joseph H. Ceryanec - Vice President, Chief Financial Officer **Transfer Agents:**
Wells Fargo Bank, N.A., South St. Paul, MN

**No of Institutions:** 252
**Shares:** 46,627,996 **% Held:** 96.65

# MERIDIAN BIOSCIENCE INC.

| Exchange | Symbol | Price | 52Wk Range | Yield | P/E |
|---|---|---|---|---|---|
| NMS | VIVO | $18.50 (8/31/2011) | 27.32-17.01 | 4.11 | 29.37 |

*7 Year Price Score 113.62 *NYSE Composite Index=100 *12 Month Price Score 96.67

**Interim Earnings (Per Share)**

| Qtr. | Dec | Mar | Jun | Sep |
|---|---|---|---|---|
| 2007-08 | 0.18 | 0.18 | 0.19 | 0.19 |
| 2008-09 | 0.20 | 0.18 | 0.21 | 0.21 |
| 2009-10 | 0.22 | 0.15 | 0.16 | 0.13 |
| 2010-11 | 0.15 | 0.18 | 0.17 | ... |

**Interim Dividends (Per Share)**

| Amt | Decl | Ex | Rec | Pay |
|---|---|---|---|---|
| 0.19Q | 11/11/2010 | 11/18/2010 | 11/22/2010 | 12/03/2010 |
| 0.19Q | 01/20/2011 | 01/27/2011 | 01/31/2011 | 02/10/2011 |
| 0.19Q | 04/21/2011 | 04/28/2011 | 05/02/2011 | 05/12/2011 |
| 0.19Q | 07/21/2011 | 07/28/2011 | 08/01/2011 | 08/11/2011 |

**Indicated Div: $0.76 (Div. Reinv. Plan)**

**Valuation Analysis**

Forecast EPS $0.70 (09/02/2011)

| | | | |
|---|---|---|---|
| Market Cap | $759.4 Million | Book Value | $138.1 Million |
| Price/Book | 5.50 | Price/Sales | 4.93 |

**Dividend Achiever Status**

| | |
|---|---|
| 10 Year Growth Rate | 20.73% |
| Total Years of Dividend Growth | 18 |

**Business Summary:** Medical Instruments & Equipment (MIC: 4.3.1 SIC: 2835 NAIC: 325413)

Meridian Bioscience is a life science company. Co.'s businesses include: the development, manufacture, sale and distribution of diagnostic test kits for certain gastrointestinal, viral, respiratory and parasitic infectious diseases; the manufacture and distribution of bulk antigens, antibodies, PCR/qPCR reagents, nucleotides, competent cells and bioresearch reagents used by researchers and other diagnostic manufacturers; and the contract development and manufacture of proteins and other biologicals for use by biopharmaceutical and biotechnology companies engaged in research for new drugs and vaccines. Co. has three operating segments: U.S. Diagnostics, European Diagnostics, and Life Science.

**Recent Developments:** For the quarter ended June 30 2011, net income increased 6.4% to US$6.8 million from US$6.4 million in the year-earlier quarter. Revenues were US$40.1 million, up 18.3% from US$33.9 million the year before. Operating income was US$10.1 million versus US$9.8 million in the prior-year quarter, an increase of 3.6%. Direct operating expenses rose 20.7% to US$14.6 million from US$12.1 million in the comparable period the year before. Indirect operating expenses increased 27.9% to US$15.3 million from US$12.0 million in the equivalent prior-year period.

**Prospects:** Our evaluation of Meridian Bioscience Inc. as of Sep. 6, 2011 is the result of our systematic analysis on three basic characteristics: earnings strength, relative valuation, and recent stock price movement. The company has produced a positive trend in earnings per share over the past 5 quarters. However, while recent estimates for the company have been mixed, VIVO has posted results that fell short of analysts expectations. Based on operating earnings yield, the company is about fairly valued when compared to all of the companies in our coverage universe. Share price changes over the past year indicates that VIVO will perform in line with the market over the near term.

**Financial Data**

| (US$ in Thousands) | 9 Mos | 6 Mos | 3 Mos | 09/30/2010 | 09/30/2009 | 09/30/2008 | 09/30/2007 | 09/30/2006 |
|---|---|---|---|---|---|---|---|---|
| Earnings Per Share | 0.63 | 0.62 | 0.59 | 0.65 | 0.80 | 0.74 | 0.66 | 0.45 |
| Cash Flow Per Share | 0.59 | 0.61 | 0.78 | 0.77 | 0.80 | 0.74 | 0.67 | 0.57 |
| Tang Book Value Per Share | 2.51 | 2.49 | 2.47 | 2.47 | 2.98 | 2.72 | 2.35 | 1.89 |
| Dividends Per Share | 0.760 | 0.760 | 0.760 | 0.740 | 0.650 | 0.530 | 0.400 | 0.283 |
| Dividend Payout % | 120.63 | 122.58 | 128.81 | 113.85 | 81.25 | 71.62 | 60.61 | 62.50 |
| **Income Statement** | | | | | | | | |
| Total Revenue | 118,374 | 78,322 | 37,263 | 143,000 | 148,274 | 139,639 | 122,963 | 108,413 |
| EBITDA | 34,942 | 23,310 | 10,733 | 45,961 | 53,227 | 47,316 | 37,842 | 29,775 |
| Depn & Amortn | 4,402 | 2,937 | 1,440 | 4,685 | 4,360 | 2,857 | 2,764 | 2,717 |
| Income Before Taxes | 30,610 | 20,417 | 9,310 | 41,400 | 49,323 | 45,992 | 36,682 | 28,053 |
| Income Taxes | 10,489 | 7,132 | 3,285 | 14,753 | 16,564 | 15,790 | 9,961 | 9,728 |
| Net Income | 20,121 | 13,285 | 6,025 | 26,647 | 32,759 | 30,202 | 26,721 | 18,325 |
| Average Shares | 41,394 | 41,348 | 41,294 | 41,149 | 41,110 | 41,029 | 40,738 | 40,164 |
| **Balance Sheet** | | | | | | | | |
| Current Assets | 92,522 | 93,823 | 95,188 | 94,020 | 117,147 | 99,458 | 93,745 | 81,169 |
| Total Assets | 157,951 | 157,171 | 156,168 | 154,785 | 155,997 | 146,431 | 132,698 | 120,955 |
| Current Liabilities | 17,182 | 16,967 | 17,485 | 14,147 | 16,752 | 16,061 | 17,067 | 20,617 |
| Long-Term Obligations | ... | ... | ... | ... | ... | ... | ... | 1,803 |
| Total Liabilities | 19,831 | 19,581 | 19,616 | 17,424 | 18,092 | 17,942 | 19,750 | 26,178 |
| Stockholders' Equity | 138,120 | 137,590 | 136,552 | 137,361 | 137,905 | 128,489 | 112,948 | 94,777 |
| Shares Outstanding | 41,048 | 40,953 | 40,960 | 40,654 | 40,493 | 40,313 | 39,847 | 39,235 |
| **Statistical Record** | | | | | | | | |
| Return on Assets % | 16.56 | 16.19 | 15.28 | 17.15 | 21.66 | 21.58 | 21.07 | 15.83 |
| Return on Equity % | 18.47 | 18.11 | 17.15 | 19.36 | 24.59 | 24.95 | 25.73 | 20.53 |
| EBITDA Margin % | 29.52 | 29.76 | 28.80 | 32.14 | 35.90 | 33.88 | 30.78 | 27.46 |
| Net Margin % | 17.00 | 16.96 | 16.17 | 18.63 | 22.09 | 21.63 | 21.73 | 16.90 |
| Asset Turnover | 1.00 | 0.96 | 0.89 | 0.92 | 0.98 | 1.00 | 0.97 | 0.94 |
| Current Ratio | 5.38 | 5.53 | 5.44 | 6.65 | 6.99 | 6.19 | 5.49 | 3.94 |
| Debt to Equity | ... | ... | ... | ... | ... | ... | ... | 0.02 |
| Price Range | 24.71-16.79 | 24.20-16.31 | 24.20-16.31 | 25.01-16.31 | 29.55-15.43 | 35.90-23.96 | 30.67-14.03 | 18.37-12.07 |
| P/E Ratio | 39.22-26.65 | 39.03-26.31 | 41.02-27.64 | 38.48-25.09 | 36.94-19.29 | 48.51-32.38 | 46.47-21.25 | 40.81-26.81 |
| Average Yield % | 3.45 | 3.67 | 3.71 | 3.64 | 2.98 | 1.76 | 1.99 | 1.86 |

**Address:** 3471 River Hills Drive, Cincinnati, OH 45244
**Telephone:** 513-271-3700
**Web Site:** www.meridianbioscience.com

**Officers:** William J. Motto - Executive Chairman John A. Kraeutler - Chief Executive Officer **Transfer Agents:**Computershare Investor Services LLC, Providence, RI

**Investor Contact:** 513-271-3700
**No of Institutions:** 189
**Shares:** 40,434,052 **% Held:** 90.36

# MGE ENERGY INC

| Exchange | Symbol | Price | 52Wk Range | Yield | P/E |
|---|---|---|---|---|---|
| NMS | MGEE | $42.15 (8/31/2011) | 43.44-37.26 | 3.63 | 15.61 |

*7 Year Price Score 115.29 *NYSE Composite Index=100 *12 Month Price Score 101.12

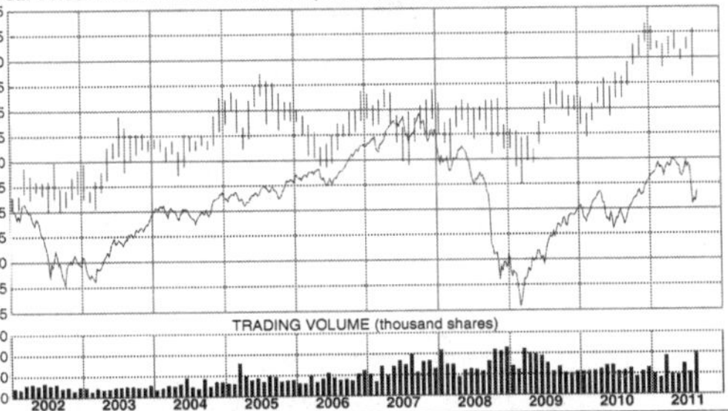


**Interim Earnings (Per Share)**

| Qtr. | Mar | Jun | Sep | Dec |
|---|---|---|---|---|
| 2008 | 0.63 | 0.48 | 0.78 | 0.49 |
| 2009 | 0.65 | 0.43 | 0.55 | 0.58 |
| 2010 | 0.62 | 0.50 | 0.86 | 0.52 |
| 2011 | 0.77 | 0.55 | ... | ... |

**Interim Dividends (Per Share)**

| Amt | Decl | Ex | Rec | Pay |
|---|---|---|---|---|
| 0.375Q | 11/19/2010 | 11/29/2010 | 12/01/2010 | 12/15/2010 |
| 0.375Q | 01/21/2011 | 02/25/2011 | 03/01/2011 | 03/15/2011 |
| 0.375Q | 05/17/2011 | 05/27/2011 | 06/01/2011 | 06/15/2011 |
| 0.383Q | 08/19/2011 | 08/30/2011 | 09/01/2011 | 09/15/2011 |

**Indicated Div: $1.53 (Div. Reinv. Plan)**

**Valuation Analysis**

| | | | |
|---|---|---|---|
| Forecast EPS | $2.82 (09/02/2011) | | |
| Market Cap | $974.3 Million | Book Value | $538.3 Million |
| Price/Book | 1.81 | Price/Sales | 1.79 |

**Dividend Achiever Status**

| | |
|---|---|
| **10 Year Growth Rate** | 1.14% |
| **Total Years of Dividend Growth** | 35 |

**Business Summary:** Electric Utilities (MIC: 3.1.1 SIC: 4911 NAIC: 221122)

MGE Energy is a public utility holding company. Through its subsidiaries, Co. operates in five business segments: electric utility operations, providing electricity in Dane County, WI; gas utility operations, distributing natural gas in seven south-central Wisconsin counties; nonregulated energy operations, which engage in constructing, owning, and leasing new electric generating capacity; transmission investments, including the American Transmission Company LLC, a provider of electric transmission services; and all other. At Dec 31 2010, Co., through its subsidiary, Madison Gas and Electric Company, supplied electricity and natural gas to about 139,000 and 143,000 customers, respectively.

**Recent Developments:** For the quarter ended June 30 2011, net income increased 10.1% to US$12.7 million from US$11.6 million in the year-earlier quarter. Revenues were US$117.3 million, up 7.5% from US$109.1 million the year before. Operating income was US$23.2 million versus US$20.1 million in the prior-year quarter, an increase of 15.3%. Direct operating expenses rose 6.4% to US$90.1 million from US$84.7 million in the comparable period the year before. Indirect operating expenses decreased 6.5% to US$4.0 million from US$4.3 million in the equivalent prior-year period.

**Prospects:** Our evaluation of MGE Energy Inc. as of Sep. 6, 2011 is the result of our systematic analysis on three basic characteristics: earnings strength, relative valuation, and recent stock price movement. The company has produced a positive trend in earnings per share over the past 5 quarters and while recent estimates for the company have been mixed, MGEE has posted results that fell short of analysts expectations. Based on operating earnings yield, the company is undervalued when compared to all of the companies in our coverage universe. Share price changes over the past year indicates that MGEE will perform very poorly over the near term.

| **Financial Data** (US$ in Thousands) | 6 Mos | 3 Mos | 12/31/2010 | 12/31/2009 | 12/31/2008 | 12/31/2007 | 12/31/2006 | 12/31/2005 |
|---|---|---|---|---|---|---|---|---|
| Earnings Per Share | 2.70 | 2.65 | 2.50 | 2.21 | 2.38 | 2.27 | 2.06 | 1.57 |
| Cash Flow Per Share | 5.50 | 5.71 | 5.37 | 5.11 | 3.36 | 3.56 | 4.91 | 2.44 |
| Tang Book Value Per Share | 23.29 | 23.11 | 22.72 | 21.71 | 20.88 | 19.49 | 17.89 | 16.81 |
| Dividends Per Share | 1.500 | 1.494 | 1.487 | 1.460 | 1.433 | 1.407 | 1.387 | 1.373 |
| Dividend Payout % | 55.57 | 56.37 | 59.48 | 66.07 | 60.23 | 61.97 | 67.31 | 87.47 |
| **Income Statement** | | | | | | | | |
| Total Revenue | 281,864 | 164,605 | 532,591 | 533,819 | 595,993 | 537,594 | 507,546 | 513,370 |
| EBITDA | 79,007 | 43,300 | 145,655 | 133,841 | 135,293 | 122,068 | 114,828 | 94,718 |
| Depn & Amortn | 20,373 | 10,016 | 37,960 | 41,080 | 39,467 | 32,332 | 31,505 | 29,308 |
| Income Before Taxes | 48,729 | 28,434 | 91,538 | 79,167 | 81,824 | 76,680 | 68,322 | 51,962 |
| Income Taxes | 18,223 | 10,651 | 33,820 | 28,170 | 29,056 | 27,855 | 25,899 | 19,871 |
| Net Income | 30,506 | 17,783 | 57,718 | 50,997 | 52,768 | 48,825 | 42,423 | 32,091 |
| Average Shares | 23,114 | 23,114 | 23,114 | 23,070 | 22,197 | 21,520 | 20,564 | 20,436 |
| **Balance Sheet** | | | | | | | | |
| Current Assets | 157,764 | 155,455 | 162,302 | 165,081 | 193,878 | 155,675 | 149,413 | 160,905 |
| Total Assets | 1,330,414 | 1,317,131 | 1,317,893 | 1,281,885 | 1,268,275 | 1,111,587 | 982,232 | 916,907 |
| Current Liabilities | 52,254 | 51,489 | 81,212 | 127,138 | 205,241 | 220,112 | 143,861 | 152,980 |
| Long-Term Obligations | 362,210 | 362,864 | 334,351 | 320,942 | 272,408 | 232,346 | 237,284 | 222,312 |
| Total Liabilities | 792,102 | 782,866 | 792,813 | 780,090 | 790,073 | 683,861 | 606,884 | 573,024 |
| Stockholders' Equity | 538,312 | 534,265 | 525,080 | 501,795 | 478,202 | 427,726 | 375,348 | 343,883 |
| Shares Outstanding | 23,114 | 23,114 | 23,114 | 23,113 | 22,904 | 21,950 | 20,975 | 20,451 |
| **Statistical Record** | | | | | | | | |
| Return on Assets % | 4.79 | 4.71 | 4.44 | 4.00 | 4.42 | 4.66 | 4.47 | 3.68 |
| Return on Equity % | 11.90 | 11.76 | 11.24 | 10.41 | 11.62 | 12.16 | 11.80 | 9.41 |
| EBITDA Margin % | 28.03 | 26.31 | 27.35 | 25.07 | 22.70 | 22.71 | 22.62 | 18.45 |
| Net Margin % | 10.82 | 10.80 | 10.84 | 9.55 | 8.85 | 9.08 | 8.36 | 6.25 |
| Asset Turnover | 0.42 | 0.41 | 0.41 | 0.42 | 0.50 | 0.51 | 0.53 | 0.59 |
| Current Ratio | 3.02 | 3.02 | 2.00 | 1.30 | 0.94 | 0.71 | 1.04 | 1.05 |
| Debt to Equity | 0.67 | 0.68 | 0.64 | 0.64 | 0.57 | 0.54 | 0.63 | 0.65 |
| Price Range | 43.44-35.97 | 43.44-34.25 | 43.44-32.17 | 37.70-27.59 | 36.02-29.86 | 37.00-29.48 | 36.97-29.28 | 38.63-31.18 |
| P/E Ratio | 16.09-13.32 | 16.39-12.92 | 17.38-12.87 | 17.06-12.48 | 15.13-12.55 | 16.30-12.99 | 17.95-14.21 | 24.61-19.86 |
| Average Yield % | 3.72 | 3.82 | 3.97 | 4.36 | 4.24 | 4.12 | 4.25 | 3.90 |

| | | |
|---|---|---|
| **Address:** 133 South Blair Street, Madison, WI 53703<br>**Telephone:** 608-252-7000<br>**Web Site:** www.mgeenergy.com | **Officers:** Gary J. Wolter - Chairman, President, Chief Executive Officer Jeffrey C. Newman - Vice President, Chief Financial Officer, Treasurer, Secretary **Transfer Agents:**Continental Stock Transfer & Trust Co., New York, NY | **No of Institutions:** 136<br>**Shares:** 8,306,947 **% Held:** 31.91 |

# MIDDLESEX WATER CO.

| Exchange | Symbol | Price | 52Wk Range | Yield | P/E |
|---|---|---|---|---|---|
| NMS | MSEX | $18.19 (8/31/2011) | 19.29-16.07 | 4.01 | 19.77 |

*7 Year Price Score 99.53 *NYSE Composite Index=100 *12 Month Price Score 102.11

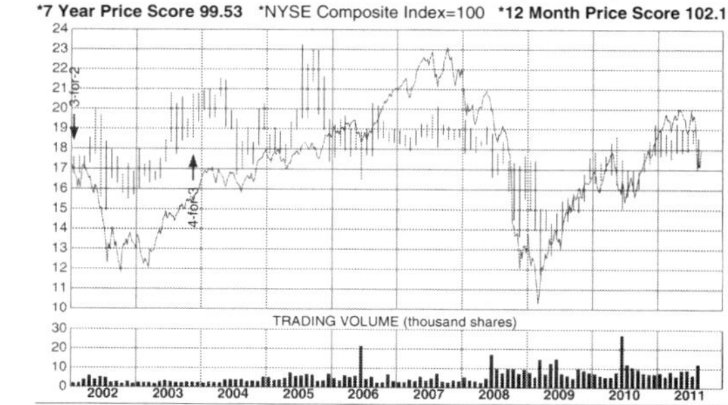


**Interim Earnings (Per Share)**

| Qtr. | Mar | Jun | Sep | Dec |
|---|---|---|---|---|
| 2008 | 0.15 | 0.26 | 0.35 | 0.14 |
| 2009 | 0.10 | 0.21 | 0.29 | 0.12 |
| 2010 | 0.11 | 0.31 | 0.36 | 0.16 |
| 2011 | 0.17 | 0.23 | ... | ... |

**Interim Dividends (Per Share)**

| Amt | Decl | Ex | Rec | Pay |
|---|---|---|---|---|
| 0.183Q | 10/26/2010 | 11/10/2010 | 11/15/2010 | 12/01/2010 |
| 0.183Q | 01/25/2011 | 02/11/2011 | 02/15/2011 | 03/01/2011 |
| 0.183Q | 04/26/2011 | 05/12/2011 | 05/16/2011 | 06/01/2011 |
| 0.183Q | 07/25/2011 | 08/11/2011 | 08/15/2011 | 09/01/2011 |

**Indicated Div: $0.73 (Div. Reinv. Plan)**

**Valuation Analysis**

| | | | |
|---|---|---|---|
| Forecast EPS | $0.92 (09/02/2011) | | |
| Market Cap | $284.0 Million | Book Value | $178.1 Million |
| Price/Book | 1.59 | Price/Sales | 2.71 |

**Dividend Achiever Status**

| | |
|---|---|
| 10 Year Growth Rate | 1.50% |
| Total Years of Dividend Growth | 38 |

**Business Summary:** Water Utilities (MIC: 3.2.1 SIC: 4941 NAIC: 221310)

Middlesex Water is a water utility company. Co. is in the business of collecting, treating, distributing and selling water for domestic, commercial, municipal, industrial and fire protection purposes. Co. owns and operates regulated water utility and wastewater systems in New Jersey, Delaware and Pennsylvania. Co. also operates a New Jersey municipal water and wastewater system under contract and provides wastewater services in New Jersey and Delaware through its subsidiaries. As of Dec. 31, 2010, Co.'s Middlesex System in New Jersey provided water services to approximately 60,000 retail customers, primarily in eastern Middlesex County, NJ.

**Recent Developments:** For the quarter ended June 30 2011, net income decreased 18.1% to US$3.6 million from US$4.4 million in the year-earlier quarter. Revenues were US$26.1 million, down 1.6% from US$26.5 million the year before. Operating income was US$6.7 million versus US$7.9 million in the prior-year quarter, a decrease of 14.6%. Indirect operating expenses increased 3.9% to US$19.4 million from US$18.6 million in the equivalent prior-year period.

**Prospects:** Our evaluation of Middlesex Water Co. as of Sep. 6, 2011 is the result of our systematic analysis on three basic characteristics: earnings strength, relative valuation, and recent stock price movement. The company has generated a negative trend in earnings per share over the past 5 quarters. However, while recent estimates for the company have been lowered by analysts, MSEX has posted results that fell short of analysts expectations. Based on operating earnings yield, the company is about fairly valued when compared to all of the companies in our coverage universe. Share price changes over the past year indicates that MSEX will perform poorly over the near term.

**Financial Data**

| (US$ in Thousands) | 6 Mos | 3 Mos | 12/31/2010 | 12/31/2009 | 12/31/2008 | 12/31/2007 | 12/31/2006 | 12/31/2005 |
|---|---|---|---|---|---|---|---|---|
| Earnings Per Share | 0.92 | 1.00 | 0.96 | 0.72 | 0.89 | 0.87 | 0.82 | 0.71 |
| Cash Flow Per Share | 1.66 | 1.78 | 1.74 | 1.38 | 1.43 | 1.43 | 1.34 | 1.18 |
| Tang Book Value Per Share | 11.19 | 11.13 | 11.13 | 10.33 | 10.28 | 10.05 | 9.82 | 8.60 |
| Dividends Per Share | 0.728 | 0.725 | 0.723 | 0.713 | 0.703 | 0.693 | 0.683 | 0.672 |
| Dividend Payout % | 79.08 | 72.50 | 75.26 | 98.96 | 78.93 | 79.60 | 83.23 | 94.72 |
| **Income Statement** | | | | | | | | |
| Total Revenue | 50,098 | 23,996 | 102,735 | 91,243 | 91,038 | 86,114 | 81,061 | 74,613 |
| EBITDA | 16,925 | 7,482 | 37,285 | 30,446 | 33,243 | 31,737 | 29,152 | 24,418 |
| Depn & Amortn | 4,829 | 2,412 | 9,244 | 8,559 | 7,922 | 7,539 | 7,060 | 6,460 |
| Income Before Taxes | 9,168 | 3,856 | 21,116 | 15,137 | 18,264 | 17,579 | 15,079 | 11,713 |
| Income Taxes | 2,913 | 1,226 | 6,786 | 5,160 | 6,056 | 5,736 | 5,041 | 3,237 |
| Net Income | 6,255 | 2,630 | 14,330 | 9,977 | 12,208 | 11,843 | 10,039 | 8,476 |
| Average Shares | 15,861 | 15,839 | 14,916 | 13,716 | 13,615 | 13,534 | 12,174 | 11,783 |
| **Balance Sheet** | | | | | | | | |
| Current Assets | 25,451 | 21,439 | 22,765 | 22,045 | 20,576 | 17,433 | 20,912 | 16,984 |
| Total Assets | 502,133 | 490,030 | 489,185 | 458,086 | 440,000 | 392,675 | 370,267 | 324,383 |
| Current Liabilities | 43,660 | 41,668 | 40,740 | 60,668 | 61,470 | 27,009 | 18,139 | 21,485 |
| Long-Term Obligations | 134,709 | 133,012 | 133,844 | 124,910 | 118,217 | 131,615 | 130,706 | 128,175 |
| Total Liabilities | 324,028 | 313,194 | 312,544 | 315,082 | 298,822 | 255,539 | 236,965 | 220,833 |
| Stockholders' Equity | 178,105 | 176,836 | 176,641 | 143,004 | 141,178 | 137,136 | 133,302 | 103,550 |
| Shares Outstanding | 15,611 | 15,592 | 15,566 | 13,519 | 13,404 | 13,246 | 13,168 | 11,584 |
| **Statistical Record** | | | | | | | | |
| Return on Assets % | 2.99 | 3.23 | 3.03 | 2.22 | 2.92 | 3.10 | 2.89 | 2.72 |
| Return on Equity % | 8.31 | 9.64 | 8.97 | 7.02 | 8.75 | 8.76 | 8.48 | 8.36 |
| EBITDA Margin % | 33.78 | 31.18 | 36.29 | 33.37 | 36.52 | 36.85 | 35.96 | 32.73 |
| Net Margin % | 12.49 | 10.96 | 13.95 | 10.93 | 13.41 | 13.75 | 12.38 | 11.36 |
| Asset Turnover | 0.21 | 0.22 | 0.22 | 0.20 | 0.22 | 0.23 | 0.23 | 0.24 |
| Current Ratio | 0.58 | 0.51 | 0.56 | 0.36 | 0.33 | 0.65 | 1.15 | 0.79 |
| Debt to Equity | 0.76 | 0.75 | 0.76 | 0.87 | 0.84 | 0.96 | 0.98 | 1.24 |
| Price Range | 19.29-15.67 | 19.25-15.06 | 19.25-15.06 | 17.62-11.76 | 19.49-13.65 | 20.16-17.91 | 20.32-16.50 | 23.26-17.34 |
| P/E Ratio | 20.97-17.03 | 19.25-15.06 | 20.05-15.69 | 24.47-16.33 | 21.90-15.34 | 23.17-20.59 | 24.78-20.12 | 32.76-24.42 |
| Average Yield % | 4.11 | 4.17 | 4.22 | 4.71 | 4.00 | 3.69 | 3.67 | 3.45 |

**Address:** 1500 Ronson Road, Iselin, NJ 08830
**Telephone:** 732-634-1500
**Web Site:** www.middlesexwater.com

**Officers:** Dennis W. Doll - President, Chief Executive Officer James P. Garrett - Vice President **Transfer Agents:**Registrar and Transfer Company, Cranford, NJ

**Investor Contact:** 732-634-1500
**No of Institutions:** 91
**Shares:** 6,458,163 **% Held:** 40.38

# MINE SAFETY APPLIANCES CO

| Exchange | Symbol | Price | 52Wk Range | Yield | P/E |
|---|---|---|---|---|---|
| NYS | MSA | $30.90 (8/31/2011) | 40.22-22.80 | 3.37 | 20.88 |

***7 Year Price Score 89.13** *NYSE Composite Index=100 ***12 Month Price Score 102.04**

**Interim Earnings (Per Share)**

| Qtr. | Mar | Jun | Sep | Dec |
|---|---|---|---|---|
| 2008 | 0.44 | 0.55 | 0.50 | 0.46 |
| 2009 | 0.20 | 0.35 | 0.30 | 0.36 |
| 2010 | 0.14 | 0.32 | 0.26 | 0.33 |
| 2011 | 0.36 | 0.53 | ... | ... |

**Interim Dividends (Per Share)**

| Amt | Decl | Ex | Rec | Pay |
|---|---|---|---|---|
| 0.25Q | 11/04/2010 | 11/16/2010 | 11/18/2010 | 12/10/2010 |
| 0.25Q | 01/14/2011 | 02/11/2011 | 02/15/2011 | 03/10/2011 |
| 0.26Q | 05/11/2011 | 05/19/2011 | 05/23/2011 | 06/10/2011 |
| 0.26Q | 08/04/2011 | 08/16/2011 | 08/18/2011 | 09/10/2011 |

**Indicated Div: $1.04**

**Valuation Analysis**

| | | | |
|---|---|---|---|
| Forecast EPS | $1.89 (09/02/2011) | | |
| Market Cap | $1.1 Billion | Book Value | $483.2 Million |
| Price/Book | 2.34 | Price/Sales | 1.02 |

**Dividend Achiever Status**

| | |
|---|---|
| **10 Year Growth Rate** | 18.59% |
| **Total Years of Dividend Growth** | 40 |

**Business Summary:** Office Equipment & Furniture (MIC: 7.5.1 SIC: 3842 NAIC: 922160)

Mine Safety Appliances is engaged in the development, manufacture and supply of products for people's health and safety. Co.'s line of safety products is used by workers in the fire service, homeland security, construction, and other industries, as well as the military. Co.'s products includes self-contained breathing apparatus, gas masks, gas detection instruments, head protection, respirators, thermal imaging cameras, fall protection, and ballistic helmets and body armor. Co. also provides a range of consumer and contractor safety products through retail channels. As of Dec 31 2010, Co. organized its business into three geographic segments: North America, Europe and International.

**Recent Developments:** For the quarter ended June 30 2011, net income increased 63.2% to US$19.5 million from US$11.9 million in the year-earlier quarter. Revenues were US$295.9 million, up 24.7% from US$237.2 million the year before. Direct operating expenses rose 19.6% to US$175.7 million from US$146.9 million in the comparable period the year before. Indirect operating expenses increased 26.2% to US$90.9 million from US$72.0 million in the equivalent prior-year period.

**Prospects:** Our evaluation of Mine Safety Appliances Co as of Sep. 6, 2011 is the result of our systematic analysis on three basic characteristics: earnings strength, relative valuation, and recent stock price movement. The company has produced a positive trend in earnings per share over the past 5 quarters. However, while recent estimates for the company have been lowered by analysts, MSA has posted better than expected results. Based on operating earnings yield, the company is undervalued when compared to all of the companies in our coverage universe. Share price changes over the past year indicates that MSA will perform well over the near term.

| **Financial Data** (US$ in Thousands) | 6 Mos | 3 Mos | 12/31/2010 | 12/31/2009 | 12/31/2008 | 12/31/2007 | 12/31/2006 | 12/31/2005 |
|---|---|---|---|---|---|---|---|---|
| Earnings Per Share | 1.48 | 1.27 | 1.05 | 1.21 | 1.96 | 1.86 | 1.73 | 2.19 |
| Cash Flow Per Share | 1.72 | 1.35 | 0.88 | 3.39 | 1.68 | 1.16 | 1.73 | 2.35 |
| Tang Book Value Per Share | 5.78 | 5.36 | 5.06 | 9.68 | 8.58 | 10.40 | 9.85 | 8.84 |
| Dividends Per Share | 1.010 | 1.000 | 0.990 | 0.960 | 0.940 | 0.840 | 0.680 | 0.520 |
| Dividend Payout % | 68.24 | 78.74 | 94.29 | 79.34 | 47.96 | 45.16 | 39.31 | 23.74 |
| **Income Statement** | | | | | | | | |
| Total Revenue | 573,187 | 277,295 | 982,668 | 915,851 | 1,139,543 | 1,007,648 | 919,098 | 911,970 |
| EBITDA | 73,676 | 32,277 | 95,248 | 99,782 | 149,028 | 140,464 | 121,015 | 153,625 |
| Depn & Amortn | 16,728 | 8,425 | 29,192 | 27,362 | 27,647 | 24,363 | 22,147 | 24,345 |
| Income Before Taxes | 49,723 | 20,415 | 57,349 | 65,340 | 112,458 | 106,188 | 92,640 | 123,796 |
| Income Taxes | 16,746 | 6,919 | 18,290 | 22,003 | 42,036 | 38,600 | 28,722 | 42,013 |
| Net Income | 32,901 | 13,309 | 38,104 | 43,295 | 70,422 | 67,588 | 63,918 | 81,783 |
| Average Shares | 36,854 | 36,795 | 36,422 | 35,879 | 35,949 | 36,240 | 36,928 | 37,301 |
| **Balance Sheet** | | | | | | | | |
| Current Assets | 507,224 | 496,813 | 477,389 | 434,025 | 477,775 | 497,050 | 416,859 | 377,226 |
| Total Assets | 1,251,795 | 1,230,963 | 1,197,188 | 875,228 | 875,810 | 1,016,306 | 898,620 | 725,357 |
| Current Liabilities | 182,286 | 183,740 | 181,741 | 168,450 | 219,687 | 209,189 | 127,435 | 130,859 |
| Long-Term Obligations | 382,076 | 379,585 | 367,094 | 82,114 | 94,082 | 103,726 | 112,541 | 45,834 |
| Total Liabilities | 768,573 | 764,812 | 745,820 | 438,612 | 482,044 | 554,775 | 460,767 | 342,960 |
| Stockholders' Equity | 483,222 | 466,151 | 451,368 | 436,616 | 393,766 | 461,531 | 437,853 | 382,397 |
| Shares Outstanding | 36,626 | 36,600 | 36,519 | 35,972 | 35,786 | 35,661 | 36,015 | 36,545 |
| **Statistical Record** | | | | | | | | |
| Return on Assets % | 5.07 | 4.41 | 3.68 | 4.95 | 7.42 | 7.06 | 7.87 | 11.21 |
| Return on Equity % | 12.02 | 10.39 | 8.58 | 10.43 | 16.42 | 15.03 | 15.59 | 21.52 |
| EBITDA Margin % | 12.85 | 11.64 | 9.69 | 10.90 | 13.08 | 13.94 | 13.17 | 16.85 |
| Net Margin % | 5.74 | 4.80 | 3.88 | 4.73 | 6.18 | 6.71 | 6.95 | 8.97 |
| Asset Turnover | 1.03 | 0.99 | 0.95 | 1.05 | 1.20 | 1.05 | 1.13 | 1.25 |
| Current Ratio | 2.78 | 2.70 | 2.63 | 2.58 | 2.17 | 2.38 | 3.27 | 2.88 |
| Debt to Equity | 0.79 | 0.81 | 0.81 | 0.19 | 0.24 | 0.22 | 0.26 | 0.12 |
| Price Range | 40.22-22.73 | 36.67-22.73 | 32.37-22.73 | 29.54-15.97 | 51.87-20.04 | 56.00-37.39 | 43.50-34.45 | 51.00-34.45 |
| P/E Ratio | 27.18-15.36 | 28.87-17.90 | 30.83-21.65 | 24.41-13.20 | 26.46-10.22 | 30.11-20.10 | 25.14-19.91 | 23.29-15.73 |
| Average Yield % | 3.30 | 3.50 | 3.71 | 4.01 | 2.57 | 1.88 | 1.76 | 1.24 |

**Address:** 1000 Cranberry Woods Drive, Cranberry Township, Pittsburgh, PA 16066-5296
**Telephone:** 724-776-8600
**Web Site:** www.msanet.com

**Officers:** John T. Ryan - Chairman William M. Lambert - President, Chief Executive Officer
**Transfer Agents:** Wells Fargo Bank, N.A., South St. Paul, MN

**No of Institutions:** 168
**Shares:** 23,366,420 **% Held:** 61.97

# MURPHY OIL CORP

| Exchange | Symbol | Price | 52Wk Range | Yield | P/E |
|---|---|---|---|---|---|
| NYS | MUR | $53.58 (8/31/2011) | 77.48-47.86 | 2.05 | 10.89 |

***7 Year Price Score 114.58** *NYSE Composite Index=100 ***12 Month Price Score 91.76**

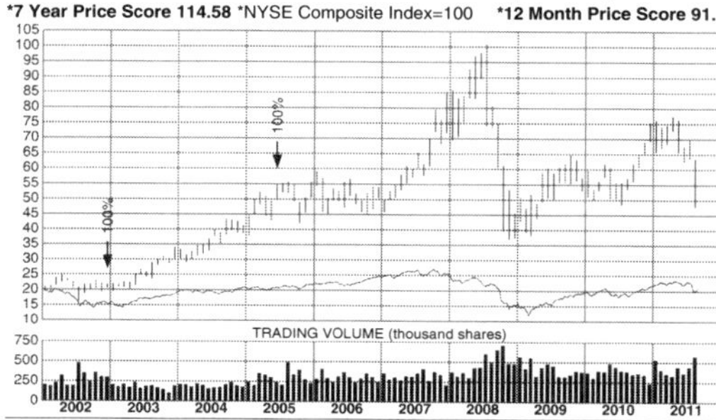


**Interim Earnings (Per Share)**

| Qtr. | Mar | Jun | Sep | Dec |
|---|---|---|---|---|
| 2008 | 2.14 | 3.22 | 3.04 | 0.67 |
| 2009 | 0.89 | 0.83 | 0.98 | 1.65 |
| 2010 | 0.77 | 1.41 | 1.05 | 0.89 |
| 2011 | 1.38 | 1.60 | ... | ... |

**Interim Dividends (Per Share)**

| Amt | Decl | Ex | Rec | Pay |
|---|---|---|---|---|
| 0.275Q | 10/06/2010 | 11/09/2010 | 11/12/2010 | 12/01/2010 |
| 0.275Q | 02/02/2011 | 02/11/2011 | 02/15/2011 | 03/01/2011 |
| 0.275Q | 04/06/2011 | 05/11/2011 | 05/13/2011 | 06/01/2011 |
| 0.275Q | 08/03/2011 | 08/11/2011 | 08/15/2011 | 09/01/2011 |

**Indicated Div: $1.10**

**Valuation Analysis**

| | | | |
|---|---|---|---|
| Forecast EPS | $5.86 (09/03/2011) | | |
| Market Cap | $10.4 Billion | Book Value | $8.8 Billion |
| Price/Book | 1.17 | Price/Sales | 0.36 |

**Dividend Achiever Status**

| | |
|---|---|
| **10 Year Growth Rate** | 10.84% |
| **Total Years of Dividend Growth** | 11 |

**Business Summary:** Refining & Marketing (MIC: 9.1.2 SIC: 2911 NAIC: 324110)

Murphy Oil is a holding company. Through its operating subsidiaries, Co. produces oil and/or natural gas in the U.S., Canada, the U.K., Malaysia and Republic of the Congo and conducts oil and natural gas exploration activities worldwide. Co. has an interest in a Canadian synthetic oil operation, owns two petroleum refineries and two ethanol production facilities in the U.S. and one refinery in the U.K. Co. markets petroleum products under various brand names and to unbranded wholesale customers in the U.S. and the U.K. As of Dec 31 2010 Co.'s total proved reserves for synthetic oil and natural gas were 129.2 million barrels and 883.10 billion cubic feet, respectively.

**Recent Developments:** For the quarter ended June 30 2011, net income increased 14.4% to US$311.6 million from US$272.3 million in the year-earlier quarter. Revenues were US$8.72 billion, up 56.0% from US$5.59 billion the year before. Direct operating expenses rose 62.7% to US$7.67 billion from US$4.71 billion in the comparable period the year before. Indirect operating expenses increased 15.1% to US$499.0 million from US$433.5 million in the equivalent prior-year period.

**Prospects:** Our evaluation of Murphy Oil Corp. as of Sep. 6, 2011 is the result of our systematic analysis on three basic characteristics: earnings strength, relative valuation, and recent stock price movement. The company has generated a negative trend in earnings per share over the past 5 quarters. However, while recent estimates for the company have been lowered by analysts, MUR has posted results that fell short of analysts expectations. Based on operating earnings yield, the company is undervalued when compared to all of the companies in our coverage universe. Share price changes over the past year indicates that MUR will perform well over the near term.

**Financial Data**

| (US$ in Thousands) | 6 Mos | 3 Mos | 12/31/2010 | 12/31/2009 | 12/31/2008 | 12/31/2007 | 12/31/2006 | 12/31/2005 |
|---|---|---|---|---|---|---|---|---|
| Earnings Per Share | 4.92 | 4.73 | 4.13 | 4.35 | 9.06 | 4.01 | 3.37 | 4.51 |
| Cash Flow Per Share | 13.43 | 14.62 | 16.31 | 9.77 | 15.99 | 9.26 | 5.17 | 6.65 |
| Tang Book Value Per Share | 45.40 | 43.88 | 42.30 | 38.22 | 32.73 | 26.43 | 21.37 | 18.38 |
| Dividends Per Share | 1.100 | 1.075 | 1.050 | 1.000 | 0.875 | 0.675 | 0.525 | 0.450 |
| Dividend Payout % | 22.36 | 22.73 | 25.42 | 22.99 | 9.66 | 16.83 | 15.58 | 9.98 |
| **Income Statement** | | | | | | | | |
| Total Revenue | 16,073,158 | 7,351,667 | 23,345,071 | 19,012,392 | 27,512,540 | 18,439,098 | 14,307,387 | 11,877,151 |
| EBITDA | 1,112,322 | 741,622 | 2,760,877 | 2,329,935 | 3,714,876 | 1,807,455 | 1,444,486 | 1,800,518 |
| Depn & Amortn | 84,050 | 275,972 | 1,311,918 | 1,028,371 | 852,348 | 545,159 | 406,529 | 419,694 |
| Income Before Taxes | 1,013,025 | 460,364 | 1,414,231 | 1,277,173 | 2,818,849 | 1,236,684 | 1,028,481 | 1,372,059 |
| Income Taxes | 432,509 | 191,461 | 616,150 | 536,656 | 1,078,565 | 470,703 | 390,146 | 534,156 |
| Net Income | 580,516 | 268,903 | 798,081 | 837,621 | 1,739,986 | 766,529 | 638,279 | 846,452 |
| Average Shares | 194,916 | 194,597 | 193,157 | 192,468 | 192,133 | 191,140 | 189,158 | 187,889 |
| **Balance Sheet** | | | | | | | | |
| Current Assets | 4,213,517 | 3,921,489 | 3,550,693 | 3,375,695 | 2,846,964 | 2,886,792 | 2,107,091 | 1,838,946 |
| Total Assets | 15,567,036 | 14,884,121 | 14,233,243 | 12,756,359 | 11,149,098 | 10,535,849 | 7,445,727 | 6,368,511 |
| Current Liabilities | 3,343,068 | 3,180,961 | 2,930,910 | 2,181,608 | 1,888,146 | 2,109,262 | 1,311,105 | 1,287,008 |
| Long-Term Obligations | 1,184,529 | 974,392 | 939,350 | 1,353,183 | 1,026,222 | 1,516,156 | 840,275 | 609,574 |
| Total Liabilities | 6,737,870 | 6,352,884 | 6,033,693 | 5,410,333 | 4,870,153 | 5,469,675 | 3,393,051 | 2,907,521 |
| Stockholders' Equity | 8,829,166 | 8,531,237 | 8,199,550 | 7,346,026 | 6,278,945 | 5,066,174 | 4,052,676 | 3,460,990 |
| Shares Outstanding | 193,512 | 193,426 | 192,836 | 191,115 | 190,713 | 189,714 | 187,572 | 185,946 |
| **Statistical Record** | | | | | | | | |
| Return on Assets % | 6.58 | 6.55 | 5.91 | 7.01 | 16.00 | 8.53 | 9.24 | 14.31 |
| Return on Equity % | 11.61 | 11.42 | 10.27 | 12.30 | 30.59 | 16.81 | 16.99 | 27.71 |
| EBITDA Margin % | 6.92 | 10.09 | 11.83 | 12.25 | 13.50 | 9.80 | 10.10 | 15.16 |
| Net Margin % | 3.61 | 3.66 | 3.42 | 4.41 | 6.32 | 4.16 | 4.46 | 7.13 |
| Asset Turnover | 1.97 | 1.82 | 1.73 | 1.59 | 2.53 | 2.05 | 2.07 | 2.01 |
| Current Ratio | 1.26 | 1.23 | 1.21 | 1.55 | 1.51 | 1.37 | 1.61 | 1.43 |
| Debt to Equity | 0.13 | 0.11 | 0.11 | 0.18 | 0.16 | 0.30 | 0.21 | 0.18 |
| Price Range | 77.48-48.44 | 76.11-48.44 | 75.37-48.44 | 64.66-38.18 | 100.93-37.00 | 85.38-45.93 | 59.15-45.12 | 55.98-38.05 |
| P/E Ratio | 15.75-9.85 | 16.09-10.24 | 18.25-11.73 | 14.86-8.78 | 11.14-4.08 | 21.29-11.45 | 17.55-13.39 | 12.41-8.44 |
| Average Yield % | 1.67 | 1.72 | 1.80 | 1.87 | 1.21 | 1.09 | 1.03 | 0.92 |

**Address:** 200 Peach Street, P.O. Box 7000, El Dorado, AR 71731-7000
**Telephone:** 870-862-6411
**Web Site:** www.murphyoilcorp.com

**Officers:** William C. Nolan - Chairman David M. Wood - President, Chief Executive Officer **Transfer Agents:**Computershare Investor Services, L.L.C., Chicago, IL

**Investor Contact:** 870-864-6496
**No of Institutions:** 607
**Shares:** 162,361,056 % **Held:** 78.48

# NACCO INDUSTRIES INC.

| Exchange | Symbol | Price | 52Wk Range | Yield | P/E |
|---|---|---|---|---|---|
| NYS | NC | $76.71 (8/31/2011) | 125.57-68.97 | 2.78 | 4.80 |

***7 Year Price Score 100.43** *NYSE Composite Index=100 ***12 Month Price Score 89.32**

**Interim Earnings (Per Share)**

| Qtr. | Mar | Jun | Sep | Dec |
|---|---|---|---|---|
| 2008 | 0.33 | 0.29 | (2.10) | (51.35) |
| 2009 | (1.10) | 0.19 | (0.47) | 7.85 |
| 2010 | 1.40 | 1.91 | 1.62 | 4.60 |
| 2011 | 7.48 | 2.29 | ... | ... |

**Interim Dividends (Per Share)**

| Amt | Decl | Ex | Rec | Pay |
|---|---|---|---|---|
| 0.522Q | 11/10/2010 | 11/29/2010 | 12/01/2010 | 12/15/2010 |
| 0.522Q | 02/09/2011 | 02/25/2011 | 03/01/2011 | 03/15/2011 |
| 0.532Q | 05/11/2011 | 05/27/2011 | 06/01/2011 | 06/15/2011 |
| 0.532Q | 08/10/2011 | 08/30/2011 | 09/01/2011 | 09/15/2011 |

**Indicated Div: $2.13**

**Valuation Analysis**

| | | | |
|---|---|---|---|
| Forecast EPS | $12.50 (09/02/2011) | | |
| Market Cap | $643.9 Million | Book Value | $540.5 Million |
| Price/Book | 1.19 | Price/Sales | 0.21 |

**Dividend Achiever Status**

| | |
|---|---|
| **10 Year Growth Rate** | 8.41% |
| **Total Years of Dividend Growth** | 27 |

**Business Summary:** Construction Services (MIC: 7.5.4 SIC: 3537 NAIC: 333924)

NACCO Industries is a holding company. Co. operates through the following subsidiaries: NMHG Holding Co., which designs, engineers, manufactures, sells, services and leases a line of lift trucks and aftermarket parts under the Hyster® and Yale® brand names; Hamilton Beach Brands, Inc., which designs, markets and distributes small electric household appliances, as well as commercial products for restaurants, bars and hotels; Kitchen Collection, Inc., a retailer of kitchenware and gourmet foods under the Kitchen Collection® and Le Gourmet Chef® store names; and The North American Coal Corp., which mines and markets coal primarily as fuel for power generation and provides mining services.

**Recent Developments:** For the quarter ended June 30 2011, net income increased 19.4% to US$19.1 million from US$16.0 million in the year-earlier quarter. Revenues were US$811.0 million, up 35.4% from US$598.8 million the year before. Operating income was US$31.1 million versus US$27.3 million in the prior-year quarter, an increase of 13.9%. Direct operating expenses rose 41.5% to US$673.1 million from US$475.7 million in the comparable period the year before. Indirect operating expenses increased 11.5% to US$106.8 million from US$95.8 million in the equivalent prior-year period.

**Prospects:** Our evaluation of NACCO Industries Inc. as of Sep. 6, 2011 is the result of our systematic analysis on three basic characteristics: earnings strength, relative valuation, and recent stock price movement. The company has generated a negative trend in earnings per share over the past 5 quarters. However, while recent estimates for the company have been mixed, NC has posted results that fell short of analysts expectations. Based on operating earnings yield, the company is undervalued when compared to all of the companies in our coverage universe. Share price changes over the past year indicates that NC will perform well over the near term.

| **Financial Data** (US$ in Thousands) | 6 Mos | 3 Mos | 12/31/2010 | 12/31/2009 | 12/31/2008 | 12/31/2007 | 12/31/2006 | 12/31/2005 |
|---|---|---|---|---|---|---|---|---|
| Earnings Per Share | 15.99 | 15.61 | 9.53 | 6.47 | (52.84) | 10.80 | 12.89 | 7.60 |
| Cash Flow Per Share | 9.48 | 8.35 | 7.58 | 18.94 | 0.59 | 9.88 | 21.07 | 9.15 |
| Tang Book Value Per Share | 57.35 | 54.37 | 46.49 | 40.16 | 35.00 | 45.86 | 34.12 | 23.49 |
| Dividends Per Share | 2.100 | 2.090 | 2.085 | 2.067 | 2.045 | 1.980 | 1.905 | 1.847 |
| Dividend Payout % | 13.13 | 13.39 | 21.88 | 31.96 | ... | 18.33 | 14.78 | 24.31 |
| **Income Statement** | | | | | | | | |
| Total Revenue | 1,556,500 | 745,500 | 2,687,500 | 2,310,600 | 3,680,300 | 3,602,700 | 3,349,000 | 3,157,400 |
| EBITDA | 105,400 | 81,800 | 124,600 | 71,700 | (372,200) | 152,800 | 179,600 | 137,600 |
| Depn & Amortn | 1,400 | 700 | 48,700 | 50,700 | 57,600 | 57,600 | 59,500 | 60,400 |
| Income Before Taxes | 91,700 | 74,900 | 51,100 | (8,000) | (462,800) | 66,500 | 78,300 | 29,700 |
| Income Taxes | 31,400 | 24,200 | 17,400 | 20,500 | 18,600 | 23,100 | 27,800 | 13,100 |
| Net Income | 82,000 | 62,800 | 79,500 | 31,100 | (437,600) | 89,300 | 106,200 | 62,500 |
| Average Shares | 8,407 | 8,399 | 8,344 | 8,290 | 8,281 | 8,272 | 8,242 | 8,226 |
| **Balance Sheet** | | | | | | | | |
| Current Assets | 1,311,400 | 1,283,400 | 1,214,200 | 967,600 | 1,141,200 | 1,434,800 | 1,153,800 | 1,073,700 |
| Total Assets | 1,754,400 | 1,727,200 | 1,658,300 | 1,488,700 | 1,687,900 | 2,428,200 | 2,156,300 | 2,094,000 |
| Current Liabilities | 719,500 | 661,900 | 663,500 | 479,300 | 675,300 | 856,500 | 751,000 | 704,700 |
| Long-Term Obligations | 300,800 | 354,000 | 355,300 | 377,600 | 400,500 | 439,500 | 359,900 | 406,200 |
| Total Liabilities | 1,213,900 | 1,211,300 | 1,210,900 | 1,092,100 | 1,331,200 | 1,536,100 | 1,363,200 | 1,390,700 |
| Stockholders' Equity | 540,500 | 515,900 | 447,400 | 396,600 | 356,700 | 892,100 | 793,100 | 703,300 |
| Shares Outstanding | 8,394 | 8,393 | 8,333 | 8,293 | 8,285 | 8,268 | 8,237 | 8,226 |
| **Statistical Record** | | | | | | | | |
| Return on Assets % | 8.27 | 8.22 | 5.05 | 1.96 | N.M. | 3.90 | 5.00 | 3.02 |
| Return on Equity % | 28.88 | 28.89 | 18.84 | 8.26 | N.M. | 10.60 | 14.19 | 8.98 |
| EBITDA Margin % | 6.77 | 10.97 | 4.64 | 3.10 | N.M. | 4.24 | 5.36 | 4.36 |
| Net Margin % | 5.27 | 8.42 | 2.96 | 1.35 | N.M. | 2.48 | 3.17 | 1.98 |
| Asset Turnover | 1.91 | 1.81 | 1.71 | 1.45 | 1.78 | 1.57 | 1.58 | 1.53 |
| Current Ratio | 1.82 | 1.94 | 1.83 | 2.02 | 1.69 | 1.68 | 1.54 | 1.52 |
| Debt to Equity | 0.56 | 0.69 | 0.79 | 0.95 | 1.12 | 0.49 | 0.45 | 0.58 |
| Price Range | 125.57-77.13 | 125.57-71.10 | 119.26-45.18 | 70.90-13.85 | 120.76-27.92 | 174.03-90.57 | 170.70-119.85 | 122.44-94.95 |
| P/E Ratio | 7.85-4.82 | 8.04-4.55 | 12.51-4.74 | 10.96-2.14 | ... | 16.11-8.39 | 13.24-9.30 | 16.11-12.49 |
| Average Yield % | 2.11 | 2.15 | 2.45 | 4.81 | 2.54 | 1.51 | 1.35 | 1.70 |

| | | |
|---|---|---|
| **Address:** 5875 Landerbrook Drive, Cleveland, OH 44124-4069<br>**Telephone:** 440-449-9600<br>**Web Site:** www.nacco.com | **Officers:** Alfred M. Rankin - Chairman, President, Chief Executive Officer Charles A. Bittenbender - Vice President, Secretary, General Counsel **Transfer Agents:** Computershare, Cleveland, OH | **No of Institutions:** 150<br>**Shares:** 4,834,550 **% Held:** 55.08 |

# NATIONAL FUEL GAS CO. (NJ)

| Exchange | Symbol | Price | 52Wk Range | Yield | P/E |
|---|---|---|---|---|---|
| NYS | NFG | $61.35 (8/31/2011) | 75.40-42.98 | 2.31 | 19.79 |

*7 Year Price Score 150.07 *NYSE Composite Index=100 *12 Month Price Score 104.45

**Interim Earnings (Per Share)**

| Qtr. | Dec | Mar | Jun | Sep |
|---|---|---|---|---|
| 2007-08 | 0.82 | 1.11 | 0.72 | 0.53 |
| 2008-09 | (0.53) | 0.92 | 0.53 | 0.33 |
| 2009-10 | 0.78 | 0.97 | 0.51 | 0.46 |
| 2010-11 | 0.70 | 1.38 | 0.56 | ... |

**Interim Dividends (Per Share)**

| Amt | Decl | Ex | Rec | Pay |
|---|---|---|---|---|
| 0.345Q | 09/14/2010 | 09/28/2010 | 09/30/2010 | 10/15/2010 |
| 0.345Q | 12/09/2010 | 12/29/2010 | 12/31/2010 | 01/14/2011 |
| 0.345Q | 03/10/2011 | 03/29/2011 | 03/31/2011 | 04/15/2011 |
| 0.355Q | 06/09/2011 | 06/28/2011 | 06/30/2011 | 07/15/2011 |

**Indicated Div: $1.42 (Div. Reinv. Plan)**

**Valuation Analysis**

| | | | |
|---|---|---|---|
| Forecast EPS | $2.69 (09/05/2011) | | |
| Market Cap | $5.1 Billion | Book Value | $1.9 Billion |
| Price/Book | 2.74 | Price/Sales | 2.87 |

**Dividend Achiever Status**

| | |
|---|---|
| **10 Year Growth Rate** | 3.28% |
| **Total Years of Dividend Growth** | 39 |

**Business Summary:** Gas Utilities (MIC: 3.3.1 SIC: 4924 NAIC: 221210)

National Fuel Gas is a holding company. Co. has four business segments: Utility, which sells natural gas or provides natural gas transportation services; Pipeline and Storage, which provides interstate natural gas transportation and storage services and owns two pipelines in New York; Exploration and Production, which engages in the exploration for, and development and purchase of, natural gas and oil reserves; and Energy Marketing, which markets natural gas to industrial, wholesale, commercial, public authority and residential customers. At Sep 30 2010, Co. had U.S. proved developed and undeveloped reserves of 45,239.0 million barrels of oil and 428.41 billion cubic feet of natural gas.

**Recent Developments:** For the quarter ended June 30 2011, income from continuing operations increased 10.0% to US$46.9 million from US$42.6 million in the year-earlier quarter. Net income increased 10.1% to US$46.9 million from US$42.6 million in the year-earlier quarter. Revenues were US$381.0 million, up 8.2% from US$352.0 million the year before. Operating income was US$94.8 million versus US$89.2 million in the prior-year quarter, an increase of 6.3%. Direct operating expenses rose 7.7% to US$208.7 million from US$193.8 million in the comparable period the year before. Indirect operating expenses increased 12.3% to US$77.5 million from US$69.0 million in the equivalent prior-year period.

**Prospects:** Our evaluation of National Fuel Gas Co. as of Sep. 6, 2011 is the result of our systematic analysis on three basic characteristics: earnings strength, relative valuation, and recent stock price movement. The company has enjoyed a very positive trend in earnings per share over the past 5 quarters. However, while recent estimates for the company have been mixed, NFG has posted better than expected results. Based on operating earnings yield, the company is about fairly valued when compared to all of the companies in our coverage universe. Share price changes over the past year indicates that NFG will perform very well over the near term.

**Financial Data**

| (US$ in Thousands) | 9 Mos | 6 Mos | 3 Mos | 09/30/2010 | 09/30/2009 | 09/30/2008 | 09/30/2007 | 09/30/2006 |
|---|---|---|---|---|---|---|---|---|
| Earnings Per Share | 3.10 | 3.05 | 2.64 | 2.73 | 1.25 | 3.18 | 3.96 | 1.61 |
| Cash Flow Per Share | 6.97 | 6.35 | 5.82 | 5.65 | 7.65 | 5.85 | 4.74 | 5.61 |
| Tang Book Value Per Share | 22.31 | 21.94 | 21.25 | 21.19 | 19.41 | 19.87 | 19.12 | 16.87 |
| Dividends Per Share | 1.390 | 1.380 | 1.370 | 1.360 | 1.320 | 1.270 | 1.220 | 1.180 |
| Dividend Payout % | 44.84 | 45.25 | 51.89 | 49.82 | 105.60 | 39.94 | 30.81 | 73.29 |
| **Income Statement** | | | | | | | | |
| Total Revenue | 1,492,808 | 1,111,829 | 450,948 | 1,760,503 | 2,057,852 | 2,400,361 | 2,039,566 | 2,311,659 |
| EBITDA | 592,295 | 438,308 | 171,717 | 635,898 | 403,012 | 664,124 | 572,237 | 458,515 |
| Depn & Amortn | 170,617 | 113,324 | 53,313 | 191,809 | 173,410 | 170,623 | 170,803 | 179,615 |
| Income Before Taxes | 362,947 | 284,962 | 97,695 | 353,872 | 148,462 | 430,347 | 328,509 | 210,594 |
| Income Taxes | 141,204 | 110,187 | 38,052 | 137,227 | 51,120 | 167,922 | 131,813 | 76,086 |
| Net Income | 221,045 | 174,154 | 58,543 | 225,913 | 100,708 | 268,728 | 337,455 | 138,091 |
| Average Shares | 83,782 | 83,673 | 83,420 | 82,660 | 80,628 | 84,474 | 85,301 | 86,028 |
| **Balance Sheet** | | | | | | | | |
| Current Assets | 520,788 | 620,115 | 525,609 | 775,377 | 776,970 | 499,478 | 554,138 | 519,453 |
| Total Assets | 5,133,265 | 5,183,317 | 4,981,981 | 5,105,625 | 4,769,129 | 4,130,187 | 3,888,412 | 3,734,331 |
| Current Liabilities | 513,310 | 603,618 | 531,817 | 524,324 | 318,507 | 374,571 | 439,346 | 290,345 |
| Long-Term Obligations | 899,000 | 899,000 | 899,000 | 1,049,000 | 1,249,000 | 999,000 | 799,000 | 1,095,675 |
| Total Liabilities | 3,282,654 | 3,366,802 | 3,227,039 | 3,359,654 | 3,179,893 | 2,526,588 | 2,258,293 | 2,290,769 |
| Stockholders' Equity | 1,850,611 | 1,816,515 | 1,754,942 | 1,745,971 | 1,589,236 | 1,603,599 | 1,630,119 | 1,443,562 |
| Shares Outstanding | 82,700 | 82,544 | 82,338 | 82,075 | 80,499 | 79,120 | 83,461 | 83,402 |
| **Statistical Record** | | | | | | | | |
| Return on Assets % | 5.15 | 5.02 | 4.49 | 4.58 | 2.26 | 6.68 | 8.85 | 3.70 |
| Return on Equity % | 14.44 | 14.47 | 12.98 | 13.55 | 6.31 | 16.57 | 21.96 | 10.33 |
| EBITDA Margin % | 39.68 | 39.42 | 38.08 | 36.12 | 19.58 | 27.67 | 28.06 | 19.83 |
| Net Margin % | 14.81 | 15.66 | 12.98 | 12.83 | 4.89 | 11.20 | 16.55 | 5.97 |
| Asset Turnover | 0.35 | 0.34 | 0.36 | 0.36 | 0.46 | 0.60 | 0.54 | 0.62 |
| Current Ratio | 1.01 | 1.03 | 0.99 | 1.48 | 2.44 | 1.33 | 1.26 | 1.79 |
| Debt to Equity | 0.49 | 0.49 | 0.51 | 0.60 | 0.79 | 0.62 | 0.49 | 0.76 |
| Price Range | 75.40-42.98 | 74.00-42.98 | 66.38-42.98 | 54.32-42.98 | 47.83-27.06 | 61.93-39.55 | 47.76-35.59 | 38.78-29.53 |
| P/E Ratio | 24.32-13.86 | 24.26-14.09 | 25.14-16.28 | 19.90-15.74 | 38.26-21.65 | 19.47-12.44 | 12.06-8.99 | 24.09-18.34 |
| Average Yield % | 2.25 | 2.43 | 2.64 | 2.78 | 3.79 | 2.57 | 2.89 | 3.49 |

**Address:** 6363 Main Street, Williamsville, NY 14221
**Telephone:** 716-857-7000
**Web Site:** www.nationalfuelgas.com

**Officers:** David F. Smith - Chairman, Chief Executive Officer Ronald J. Tanski - President, Chief Operating Officer **Transfer Agents:** BNY Mellon Shareowner Services, Pittsburgh, PA

**Investor Contact:** 716-857-6987
**No of Institutions:** 400
**Shares:** 50,179,156 **% Held:** 53.59

# NATIONAL RETAIL PROPERTIES INC

| Exchange | Symbol | Price | 52Wk Range | Yield | P/E |
|---|---|---|---|---|---|
| NYS | NNN | $27.26 (8/31/2011) | 27.73-22.92 | 5.59 | 32.45 |

***7 Year Price Score 117.45** *NYSE Composite Index=100 ***12 Month Price Score 99.64**

**Interim Earnings (Per Share)**

| Qtr. | Mar | Jun | Sep | Dec |
|---|---|---|---|---|
| 2008 | 0.43 | 0.40 | 0.39 | 0.34 |
| 2009 | 0.32 | 0.32 | 0.26 | (0.29) |
| 2010 | 0.18 | 0.23 | 0.23 | 0.15 |
| 2011 | 0.23 | 0.23 | ... | ... |

**Interim Dividends (Per Share)**

| Amt | Decl | Ex | Rec | Pay |
|---|---|---|---|---|
| 0.38Q | 10/15/2010 | 10/27/2010 | 10/29/2010 | 11/15/2010 |
| 0.38Q | 01/14/2011 | 01/27/2011 | 01/31/2011 | 02/15/2011 |
| 0.38Q | 04/15/2011 | 04/27/2011 | 04/29/2011 | 05/16/2011 |
| 0.385Q | 07/15/2011 | 07/27/2011 | 07/29/2011 | 08/15/2011 |

**Indicated Div: $1.52 (Div. Reinv. Plan)**

**Valuation Analysis**

| | | | |
|---|---|---|---|
| Forecast EPS | $0.92 (09/05/2011) | | |
| Market Cap | $2.3 Billion | Book Value | $1.6 Billion |
| Price/Book | 1.51 | Price/Sales | 9.54 |

**Dividend Achiever Status**

| | |
|---|---|
| **10 Year Growth Rate** | 1.83% |
| **Total Years of Dividend Growth** | 21 |

**Business Summary:** REITs (MIC: 5.3.1 SIC: 6798 NAIC: 525930)

National Retail Properties is a real estate investment trust. Co.'s operations are divided into two primary business segments: investment assets, including real estate assets, mortgages and notes receivable, and commercial mortgage residual interests; and inventory real estate assets. As of Dec 31 2010, Co. owned 1,195 properties that were leased to retail tenants and held for investment (including 11 properties with retail operations that Co. operated), with an aggregate leasable area of 13.0 million square feet, located in 46 states. Also, as of such date, Co. owned 17 investment interests in real estate assets acquired or developed for the purpose of selling the real estate.

**Recent Developments:** For the quarter ended June 30 2011, net income decreased 1.8% to US$21.3 million from US$21.7 million in the year-earlier quarter. Revenues were US$75.0 million, up 14.0% from US$65.7 million the year before. Revenues from property income rose 12.1% to US$61.2 million from US$54.6 million in the corresponding quarter a year earlier.

**Prospects:** Our evaluation of National Retail Properties Inc. as of Sep. 6, 2011 is the result of our systematic analysis on three basic characteristics: earnings strength, relative valuation, and recent stock price movement. The company has enjoyed a very positive trend in earnings per share over the past 5 quarters. Because the company lacks sufficient analyst estimate data, we place greater weight on the historical EPS trend as the measure of earnings strength. Based on operating earnings yield, the company is overvalued when compared to all of the companies in our coverage universe. Share price changes over the past year indicates that NNN will perform very poorly over the near term.

| **Financial Data** (US$ in Thousands) | 6 Mos | 3 Mos | 12/31/2010 | 12/31/2009 | 12/31/2008 | 12/31/2007 | 12/31/2006 | 12/31/2005 |
|---|---|---|---|---|---|---|---|---|
| Earnings Per Share | 0.84 | 0.84 | 0.80 | 0.60 | 1.56 | 2.26 | 3.05 | 1.56 |
| Cash Flow Per Share | 1.84 | 2.29 | 2.27 | 1.87 | 3.18 | 1.96 | 0.32 | 0.58 |
| Tang Book Value Per Share | 17.01 | 17.07 | 17.17 | 17.86 | 18.49 | 18.13 | 16.05 | 13.76 |
| Dividends Per Share | 1.520 | 1.515 | 1.510 | 1.500 | 1.480 | 1.400 | 1.320 | 1.300 |
| Dividend Payout % | 180.95 | 180.36 | 188.75 | 250.00 | 94.87 | 61.95 | 43.28 | 83.33 |
| **Income Statement** | | | | | | | | |
| Total Revenue | 145,769 | 70,802 | 229,056 | 231,799 | 226,516 | 186,411 | 150,788 | 145,177 |
| EBITDA | 79,642 | 39,528 | 190,193 | 175,015 | 190,261 | 153,738 | 118,674 | 106,030 |
| Depn & Amortn | 3,250 | 1,611 | 55,278 | 54,332 | 45,429 | 32,831 | 24,316 | 22,129 |
| Income Before Taxes | 41,843 | 20,597 | 71,249 | 59,907 | 90,097 | 76,374 | 52,299 | 50,014 |
| Income Taxes | 191 | (19) | 475 | (1,126) | (7,501) | (8,537) | (11,143) | (2,776) |
| Net Income | 42,123 | 20,820 | 72,997 | 54,810 | 123,082 | 157,110 | 182,505 | 89,400 |
| Average Shares | 84,725 | 83,570 | 82,849 | 79,953 | 74,521 | 66,407 | 58,079 | 54,640 |
| **Balance Sheet** | | | | | | | | |
| Current Assets | 6,012 | 5,388 | 61,317 | 84,892 | 90,682 | 121,933 | 103,535 | 126,057 |
| Total Assets | 2,798,807 | 2,753,697 | 2,713,575 | 2,590,962 | 2,649,362 | 2,539,605 | 1,916,785 | 1,733,416 |
| Current Liabilities | 226,485 | 203,215 | 168,342 | 7,471 | 34,108 | 142,714 | 40,329 | 181,587 |
| Long-Term Obligations | 975,479 | 974,067 | 972,685 | 987,346 | 1,026,304 | 930,270 | 748,737 | 698,745 |
| Total Liabilities | 1,243,646 | 1,218,158 | 1,186,092 | 1,026,722 | 1,107,153 | 1,132,320 | 820,280 | 905,329 |
| Stockholders' Equity | 1,555,161 | 1,535,539 | 1,527,483 | 1,564,240 | 1,542,209 | 1,407,285 | 1,096,505 | 828,087 |
| Shares Outstanding | 86,034 | 84,570 | 83,613 | 82,427 | 78,415 | 72,527 | 59,823 | 55,130 |
| **Statistical Record** | | | | | | | | |
| Return on Assets % | 2.88 | 2.89 | 2.75 | 2.09 | 4.73 | 7.05 | 10.00 | 5.89 |
| Return on Equity % | 5.00 | 5.01 | 4.72 | 3.53 | 8.32 | 12.55 | 18.97 | 11.28 |
| EBITDA Margin % | 54.64 | 55.83 | 83.03 | 75.50 | 83.99 | 82.47 | 78.70 | 73.03 |
| Net Margin % | 28.90 | 29.41 | 31.87 | 23.65 | 54.34 | 84.28 | 121.03 | 61.58 |
| Asset Turnover | 0.09 | 0.09 | 0.09 | 0.09 | 0.09 | 0.08 | 0.08 | 0.10 |
| Current Ratio | 0.03 | 0.03 | 0.36 | 11.36 | 2.66 | 0.85 | 2.57 | 0.69 |
| Debt to Equity | 0.63 | 0.63 | 0.64 | 0.63 | 0.67 | 0.66 | 0.68 | 0.84 |
| Price Range | 27.73-21.05 | 27.73-20.86 | 27.73-19.45 | 22.29-12.96 | 24.57-10.53 | 26.11-20.77 | 23.97-18.90 | 21.53-18.16 |
| P/E Ratio | 33.01-25.06 | 33.01-24.83 | 34.66-24.31 | 37.15-21.60 | 15.75-6.75 | 11.55-9.19 | 7.86-6.20 | 13.80-11.64 |
| Average Yield % | 6.03 | 6.18 | 6.38 | 8.28 | 7.18 | 5.88 | 6.10 | 6.61 |

| | | |
|---|---|---|
| **Address:** 450 South Orange Avenue, Suite 900, Orlando, FL 32801<br>**Telephone:** 407-265-7348<br>**Web Site:** www.nnnreit.com | **Officers:** Craig Macnab - Chairman, Chief Executive Officer Julian E. Whitehurst - President, Chief Operating Officer **Transfer Agents:**<br>American Stock Transfer & Trust Company, New York, NY | **No of Institutions:** 256<br>**Shares:** 85,968,944 **% Held:** N/A |

# NEW JERSEY RESOURCES CORP

| Exchange | Symbol | Price | 52Wk Range | Yield | P/E |
|---|---|---|---|---|---|
| NYS | NJR | $47.11 (8/31/2011) | 47.14-37.21 | 3.06 | 17.71 |

***7 Year Price Score 121.78** *NYSE Composite Index=100 ***12 Month Price Score 105.27**

**Interim Earnings (Per Share)**

| Qtr. | Dec | Mar | Jun | Sep |
|---|---|---|---|---|
| 2007-08 | 0.72 | 0.30 | (0.18) | 1.86 |
| 2008-09 | 0.28 | 0.83 | (0.34) | (0.13) |
| 2009-10 | 1.24 | 1.78 | (0.25) | 0.04 |
| 2010-11 | 0.59 | 1.54 | 0.49 | ... |

**Interim Dividends (Per Share)**

| Amt | Decl | Ex | Rec | Pay |
|---|---|---|---|---|
| 0.36Q | 11/17/2010 | 12/13/2010 | 12/15/2010 | 01/03/2011 |
| 0.36Q | 01/27/2011 | 03/11/2011 | 03/15/2011 | 04/01/2011 |
| 0.36Q | 05/12/2011 | 06/13/2011 | 06/15/2011 | 07/01/2011 |
| 0.36Q | 07/13/2011 | 09/13/2011 | 09/15/2011 | 10/03/2011 |

**Indicated Div: $1.44 (Div. Reinv. Plan)**

**Valuation Analysis**

| | | | |
|---|---|---|---|
| Forecast EPS | $2.60 (09/03/2011) | | |
| Market Cap | $2.0 Billion | Book Value | $796.3 Million |
| Price/Book | 2.45 | Price/Sales | 0.66 |

**Dividend Achiever Status**

| | |
|---|---|
| **10 Year Growth Rate** | 5.69% |
| **Total Years of Dividend Growth** | 15 |

**Business Summary:** Gas Utilities (MIC: 3.3.1 SIC: 4924 NAIC: 221210)

New Jersey Resources is an energy services holding company providing retail and wholesale energy services to customers in states from the Gulf Coast and Mid-Continent regions to the Appalachian and Northeast regions, the West Coast and Canada. Co. operates within three reportable business segments: Natural Gas Distribution, which consists of regulated energy and off-system, capacity and storage management operations; Energy Services, which consists of unregulated wholesale energy operations; and Midstream Asset, which consists of investments in the midstream natural gas market, such as natural gas transportation and storage facilities.

**Recent Developments:** For the quarter ended June 30 2011, net income amounted to US$20.4 million versus a net loss of US$10.2 million in the year-earlier quarter. Revenues were US$648.2 million, up 35.1% from US$479.9 million the year before. Operating income was US$27.2 million versus a loss of US$18.8 million in the prior-year quarter. Direct operating expenses rose 24.7% to US$595.9 million from US$477.9 million in the comparable period the year before. Indirect operating expenses increased 20.4% to US$25.1 million from US$20.8 million in the equivalent prior-year period.

**Prospects:** Our evaluation of New Jersey Resources Corp. as of Sep. 6, 2011 is the result of our systematic analysis on three basic characteristics: earnings strength, relative valuation, and recent stock price movement. The company has produced a positive trend in earnings per share over the past 5 quarters and while recent estimates for the company have been raised by analysts, NJR has posted better than expected results. Based on operating earnings yield, the company is about fairly valued when compared to all of the companies in our coverage universe. Share price changes over the past year indicates that NJR will perform very poorly over the near term.

**Financial Data**

| (US$ in Thousands) | 9 Mos | 6 Mos | 3 Mos | 09/30/2010 | 09/30/2009 | 09/30/2008 | 09/30/2007 | 09/30/2006 |
|---|---|---|---|---|---|---|---|---|
| Earnings Per Share | 2.66 | 1.92 | 2.16 | 2.82 | 0.64 | 2.70 | 1.55 | 1.87 |
| Cash Flow Per Share | 5.09 | 1.82 | 1.45 | 3.37 | 6.34 | 3.15 | 2.92 | (0.55) |
| Tang Book Value Per Share | 19.22 | 18.98 | 17.81 | 17.62 | 16.59 | 17.28 | 15.50 | 14.24 |
| Dividends Per Share | 1.420 | 1.400 | 1.380 | 1.360 | 1.240 | 1.107 | 1.013 | 0.960 |
| Dividend Payout % | 53.38 | 72.92 | 63.89 | 48.23 | 193.75 | 40.99 | 65.24 | 51.43 |
| **Income Statement** | | | | | | | | |
| Total Revenue | 2,338,308 | 1,690,139 | 713,152 | 2,639,304 | 2,592,460 | 3,816,210 | 3,021,765 | 3,299,608 |
| EBITDA | 188,518 | 152,084 | 49,162 | 226,575 | 83,621 | 245,185 | 168,080 | 188,963 |
| Depn & Amortn | 25,445 | 17,369 | 8,454 | 33,192 | 31,142 | 39,367 | 36,536 | 34,753 |
| Income Before Taxes | 147,988 | 124,374 | 35,445 | 172,132 | 31,465 | 180,007 | 103,931 | 128,541 |
| Income Taxes | 48,662 | 42,465 | 13,853 | 64,692 | 8,488 | 68,085 | 40,312 | 50,022 |
| Net Income | 108,810 | 88,436 | 24,509 | 117,457 | 27,242 | 113,910 | 65,281 | 78,519 |
| Average Shares | 41,597 | 41,553 | 41,510 | 41,630 | 42,465 | 42,176 | 42,112 | 42,121 |
| **Balance Sheet** | | | | | | | | |
| Current Assets | 741,667 | 709,555 | 917,611 | 785,008 | 684,189 | 1,109,666 | 799,866 | 965,516 |
| Total Assets | 2,573,956 | 2,501,691 | 2,710,692 | 2,563,133 | 2,321,030 | 2,625,392 | 2,230,745 | 2,398,928 |
| Current Liabilities | 631,083 | 585,230 | 841,629 | 705,798 | 556,165 | 893,969 | 703,266 | 897,155 |
| Long-Term Obligations | 428,200 | 429,990 | 432,450 | 428,925 | 455,492 | 455,117 | 383,184 | 332,332 |
| Total Liabilities | 1,777,676 | 1,716,617 | 1,973,178 | 1,837,650 | 1,631,304 | 1,898,434 | 1,585,948 | 1,777,266 |
| Stockholders' Equity | 796,280 | 785,074 | 737,514 | 725,483 | 689,726 | 726,958 | 644,797 | 621,662 |
| Shares Outstanding | 41,436 | 41,370 | 41,417 | 41,173 | 41,585 | 42,057 | 41,611 | 43,647 |
| **Statistical Record** | | | | | | | | |
| Return on Assets % | 4.40 | 3.19 | 3.50 | 4.81 | 1.10 | 4.68 | 2.82 | 3.41 |
| Return on Equity % | 14.35 | 10.27 | 12.33 | 16.60 | 3.85 | 16.56 | 10.31 | 14.82 |
| EBITDA Margin % | 8.06 | 9.00 | 6.89 | 8.58 | 3.23 | 6.42 | 5.56 | 5.73 |
| Net Margin % | 4.65 | 5.23 | 3.44 | 4.45 | 1.05 | 2.98 | 2.16 | 2.38 |
| Asset Turnover | 1.18 | 1.12 | 1.07 | 1.08 | 1.05 | 1.57 | 1.31 | 1.43 |
| Current Ratio | 1.18 | 1.21 | 1.09 | 1.11 | 1.23 | 1.24 | 1.14 | 1.08 |
| Debt to Equity | 0.54 | 0.55 | 0.59 | 0.59 | 0.66 | 0.63 | 0.59 | 0.53 |
| Price Range | 46.08-34.87 | 43.95-34.23 | 43.92-34.03 | 39.22-34.03 | 41.47-29.38 | 38.90-29.81 | 37.00-30.83 | 34.01-27.69 |
| P/E Ratio | 17.32-13.11 | 22.89-17.83 | 20.33-15.75 | 13.91-12.07 | 64.80-45.91 | 14.41-11.04 | 23.87-19.89 | 18.19-14.81 |
| Average Yield % | 3.44 | 3.54 | 3.61 | 3.70 | 3.46 | 3.34 | 3.01 | 3.19 |

**Address:** 1415 Wyckoff Road, Wall, NJ 07719
**Telephone:** 732-938-1480
**Web Site:** www.njresources.com

**Officers:** Laurence M. Downes - Chairman, President, Chief Executive Officer Glenn C. Lockwood - Senior Vice President, Chief Financial Officer **Transfer Agents:** Wells Fargo Shareowner Services, St. Paul, MN

**Investor Contact:** 732-938-1229
**No of Institutions:** 202
**Shares:** 27,915,174 **% Held:** 55.54

# NEXTERA ENERGY INC

| Exchange | Symbol | Price | 52Wk Range | Yield | P/E |
|---|---|---|---|---|---|
| NYS | NEE | $56.72 (8/31/2011) | 58.88-50.17 | 3.88 | 12.92 |

*7 Year Price Score 105.08 *NYSE Composite Index=100 *12 Month Price Score 101.68

**Interim Earnings (Per Share)**

| Qtr. | Mar | Jun | Sep | Dec |
|---|---|---|---|---|
| 2008 | 0.62 | 0.52 | 1.92 | 1.01 |
| 2009 | 0.90 | 0.91 | 1.31 | 0.85 |
| 2010 | 1.36 | 1.01 | 1.74 | 0.63 |
| 2011 | 0.64 | 1.38 | ... | ... |

**Interim Dividends (Per Share)**

| Amt | Decl | Ex | Rec | Pay |
|---|---|---|---|---|
| 0.50Q | 10/15/2010 | 11/23/2010 | 11/26/2010 | 12/15/2010 |
| 0.55Q | 02/18/2011 | 03/02/2011 | 03/04/2011 | 03/15/2011 |
| 0.55Q | 05/20/2011 | 06/01/2011 | 06/03/2011 | 06/15/2011 |
| 0.55Q | 07/29/2011 | 08/24/2011 | 08/26/2011 | 09/15/2011 |

**Indicated Div: $2.20 (Div. Reinv. Plan)**

**Valuation Analysis**

| | | | |
|---|---|---|---|
| Forecast EPS | $4.50 (09/03/2011) | | |
| Market Cap | $24.0 Billion | Book Value | $14.9 Billion |
| Price/Book | 1.61 | Price/Sales | 1.58 |

**Dividend Achiever Status**

| | |
|---|---|
| **10 Year Growth Rate** | 5.97% |
| **Total Years of Dividend Growth** | 15 |

**Business Summary:** Electric Utilities (MIC: 3.1.1 SIC: 4911 NAIC: 221121)

NextEra Energy is a holding company. Co. has two principal operating subsidiaries: Florida Power & Light Co. (FPL) and NextEra Energy Resources, LLC. FPL is a rate-regulated utility engaged in the generation, transmission, distribution and sale of electric energy throughout most of the east and lower west coasts of Florida, serving more than 8.7 million people. NextEra Energy Resources owns, develops, constructs, manages and operates electric-generating facilities in wholesale energy markets. NextEra Energy Resources also provides energy and capacity requirement services to distribution utilities in certain markets and owns a retail electric provider based in Texas.

**Recent Developments:** For the quarter ended June 30 2011, net income increased 39.1% to US$580.0 million from US$417.0 million in the year-earlier quarter. Revenues were US$3.96 billion, up 10.3% from US$3.59 billion the year before. Operating income was US$907.0 million versus US$709.0 million in the prior-year quarter, an increase of 27.9%. Direct operating expenses rose 5.5% to US$2.33 billion from US$2.21 billion in the comparable period the year before. Indirect operating expenses increased 7.6% to US$726.0 million from US$675.0 million in the equivalent prior-year period.

**Prospects:** Our evaluation of NextEra Energy Inc. as of Sep. 6, 2011 is the result of our systematic analysis on three basic characteristics: earnings strength, relative valuation, and recent stock price movement. The company has enjoyed a very positive trend in earnings per share over the past 5 quarters and while recent estimates for the company have remained steady, NEE has posted better than expected results. Based on operating earnings yield, the company is undervalued when compared to all of the companies in our coverage universe. Share price changes over the past year indicates that NEE will perform very poorly over the near term.

| **Financial Data** (US$ in Thousands) | 6 Mos | 3 Mos | 12/31/2010 | 12/31/2009 | 12/31/2008 | 12/31/2007 | 12/31/2006 | 12/31/2005 |
|---|---|---|---|---|---|---|---|---|
| Earnings Per Share | 4.39 | 4.02 | 4.74 | 3.97 | 4.07 | 3.27 | 3.23 | 2.29 |
| Cash Flow Per Share | 9.78 | 9.43 | 9.34 | 11.04 | 8.48 | 9.03 | 6.35 | 4.07 |
| Tang Book Value Per Share | 35.29 | 34.60 | 34.36 | 31.35 | 28.57 | 26.35 | 24.49 | 21.52 |
| Dividends Per Share | 2.100 | 2.050 | 2.000 | 1.890 | 1.780 | 1.640 | 1.500 | 1.420 |
| Dividend Payout % | 47.84 | 51.00 | 42.19 | 47.61 | 43.73 | 50.15 | 46.44 | 62.01 |
| **Income Statement** | | | | | | | | |
| Total Revenue | 7,094,000 | 3,134,000 | 15,317,000 | 15,643,000 | 16,410,000 | 15,263,000 | 15,710,000 | 11,846,000 |
| EBITDA | 1,538,000 | 530,000 | 5,374,000 | 4,612,000 | 4,345,000 | 3,741,000 | 3,550,000 | 3,035,000 |
| Depn & Amortn | 131,000 | 71,000 | 2,092,000 | 2,004,000 | 1,643,000 | 1,479,000 | 1,421,000 | 1,496,000 |
| Income Before Taxes | 934,000 | 226,000 | 2,431,000 | 1,890,000 | 1,996,000 | 1,612,000 | 1,497,000 | 1,033,000 |
| Income Taxes | 115,000 | (32,000) | 532,000 | 327,000 | 450,000 | 368,000 | 397,000 | 272,000 |
| Net Income | 848,000 | 268,000 | 1,957,000 | 1,615,000 | 1,639,000 | 1,312,000 | 1,281,000 | 885,000 |
| Average Shares | 419,300 | 418,400 | 413,000 | 407,200 | 402,700 | 400,600 | 396,500 | 385,700 |
| **Balance Sheet** | | | | | | | | |
| Current Assets | 4,813,000 | 4,519,000 | 5,258,000 | 4,337,000 | 5,392,000 | 3,779,000 | 4,999,000 | 4,987,000 |
| Total Assets | 54,557,000 | 53,257,000 | 52,994,000 | 48,458,000 | 44,821,000 | 40,123,000 | 35,991,000 | 33,004,000 |
| Current Liabilities | 6,389,000 | 6,739,000 | 6,904,000 | 6,449,000 | 7,689,000 | 5,758,000 | 6,493,000 | 7,267,000 |
| Long-Term Obligations | 19,235,000 | 18,288,000 | 18,013,000 | 16,300,000 | 13,833,000 | 11,280,000 | 9,591,000 | 8,039,000 |
| Total Liabilities | 39,651,000 | 38,658,000 | 38,533,000 | 35,491,000 | 33,140,000 | 29,388,000 | 26,061,000 | 24,505,000 |
| Stockholders' Equity | 14,906,000 | 14,599,000 | 14,461,000 | 12,967,000 | 11,681,000 | 10,735,000 | 9,930,000 | 8,499,000 |
| Shares Outstanding | 422,340 | 421,960 | 420,861 | 413,622 | 408,915 | 407,344 | 405,404 | 394,854 |
| **Statistical Record** | | | | | | | | |
| Return on Assets % | 3.46 | 3.20 | 3.86 | 3.46 | 3.85 | 3.45 | 3.71 | 2.89 |
| Return on Equity % | 12.88 | 11.94 | 14.27 | 13.10 | 14.58 | 12.70 | 13.90 | 11.04 |
| EBITDA Margin % | 21.68 | 16.91 | 35.09 | 29.48 | 26.48 | 24.51 | 22.60 | 25.62 |
| Net Margin % | 11.95 | 8.55 | 12.78 | 10.32 | 9.99 | 8.60 | 8.15 | 7.47 |
| Asset Turnover | 0.29 | 0.28 | 0.30 | 0.34 | 0.39 | 0.40 | 0.46 | 0.39 |
| Current Ratio | 0.75 | 0.67 | 0.76 | 0.67 | 0.70 | 0.66 | 0.77 | 0.69 |
| Debt to Equity | 1.29 | 1.25 | 1.25 | 1.26 | 1.18 | 1.05 | 0.97 | 0.95 |
| Price Range | 58.88-48.76 | 56.03-48.33 | 56.03-45.57 | 60.05-41.78 | 72.03-37.08 | 72.56-53.85 | 55.10-38.03 | 47.84-36.03 |
| P/E Ratio | 13.41-11.11 | 13.94-12.02 | 11.82-9.61 | 15.13-10.52 | 17.70-9.11 | 22.19-16.47 | 17.06-11.77 | 20.89-15.73 |
| Average Yield % | 3.87 | 3.89 | 3.90 | 3.56 | 3.02 | 2.66 | 3.41 | 3.42 |

**Address:** 700 Universe Boulevard, Juno Beach, FL 33408
**Telephone:** 561-694-4000
**Web Site:** www.nexteraenergy.com

**Officers:** Lewis Hay - Chairman, Chief Executive Officer Moray P. Dewhurst - Vice-Chairman, Chief of Staff **Transfer Agents:** Computershare Investor Services, LLC, Canton, MA

**No of Institutions:** 966
**Shares:** 298,310,112 **% Held:** N/A

# NORDSON CORP.

| Exchange | Symbol | Price | 52Wk Range | Yield | P/E |
|---|---|---|---|---|---|
| NMS | NDSN | $43.90 (8/31/2011) | 59.01-32.09 | 1.14 | 13.72 |

*7 Year Price Score 172.63 *NYSE Composite Index=100 *12 Month Price Score 105.86

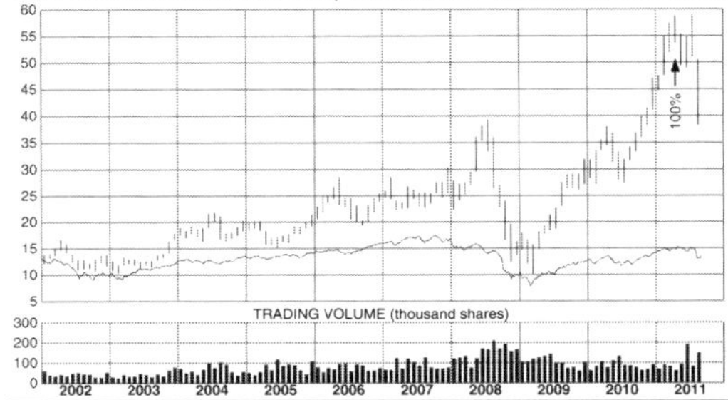


**Interim Earnings (Per Share)**

| Qtr. | Jan | Apr | Jul | Oct |
|---|---|---|---|---|
| 2007-08 | 0.31 | 0.48 | 0.47 | 0.45 |
| 2008-09 | 0.17 | 0.20 | 0.35 | (3.12) |
| 2009-10 | 0.39 | 0.47 | 0.81 | 0.78 |
| 2010-11 | 0.67 | 0.95 | ... | ... |

**Interim Dividends (Per Share)**

| Amt | Decl | Ex | Rec | Pay |
|---|---|---|---|---|
| 0.105Q | 02/15/2011 | 02/25/2011 | 03/01/2011 | 03/15/2011 |
| 100% | 03/01/2011 | 04/13/2011 | 03/25/2011 | 04/12/2011 |
| 0.105Q | 05/17/2011 | 05/27/2011 | 06/01/2011 | 06/14/2011 |
| 0.125Q | 08/16/2011 | 08/26/2011 | 08/30/2011 | 09/13/2011 |

**Indicated Div: $0.50 (Div. Reinv. Plan)**

**Valuation Analysis**

| | | | |
|---|---|---|---|
| Forecast EPS | $3.23 (09/03/2011) | | |
| Market Cap | $3.0 Billion | Book Value | $621.5 Million |
| Price/Book | 4.82 | Price/Sales | 2.58 |

**Dividend Achiever Status**

| | |
|---|---|
| 10 Year Growth Rate | 3.37% |
| Total Years of Dividend Growth | 30 |

**Business Summary:** Industrial Machinery & Equipment (MIC: 7.2.1 SIC: 3569 NAIC: 333999)

Nordson manufactures equipment used for precision material dispensing, testing and inspection, surface preparation and curing. Co.'s equipment ranges from manual, stand-alone units for low-volume operations to microprocessor-based automated systems for high-volume production lines. Co. serves several markets, including the the appliance, automotive, bookbinding, container, converting, electronics, food and beverage, furniture, life sciences and medical, light emitting diodes, metal finishing, nonwoven, packaging, semiconductor and solar energy industries. Co. operates through three segments: Adhesive Dispensing Systems, Advanced Technology Systems, and Industrial Coating Systems.

**Recent Developments:** For the quarter ended Apr 30 2011, net income increased 101.2% to US$65.2 million from US$32.4 million in the year-earlier quarter. Revenues were US$318.9 million, up 26.7% from US$251.7 million the year before. Operating income was US$92.4 million versus US$57.6 million in the prior-year quarter, an increase of 60.5%. Direct operating expenses rose 23.9% to US$121.2 million from US$97.8 million in the comparable period the year before. Indirect operating expenses increased 9.4% to US$105.3 million from US$96.3 million in the equivalent prior-year period.

**Prospects:** Our evaluation of Nordson Corp. as of Sep. 6, 2011 is the result of our systematic analysis on three basic characteristics: earnings strength, relative valuation, and recent stock price movement. The company has generated a negative trend in earnings per share over the past 5 quarters. However, while recent estimates for the company have been lowered by analysts, NDSN has posted results that fell short of analysts expectations. Based on operating earnings yield, the company is undervalued when compared to all of the companies in our coverage universe. Share price changes over the past year indicates that NDSN will perform well over the near term.

**Financial Data**

| (US$ in Thousands) | 6 Mos | 3 Mos | 10/31/2010 | 10/31/2009 | 10/31/2008 | 10/31/2007 | 10/31/2006 | 10/30/2005 |
|---|---|---|---|---|---|---|---|---|
| Earnings Per Share | 3.20 | 2.72 | 2.46 | (2.38) | 1.72 | 1.33 | 1.33 | 1.07 |
| Cash Flow Per Share | 3.43 | 2.16 | 2.07 | 2.51 | 1.69 | 1.85 | 1.79 | 1.67 |
| Tang Book Value Per Share | 3.11 | 1.97 | 1.69 | N.M. | N.M. | N.M. | 1.34 | N.M. |
| Dividends Per Share | 0.410 | 0.400 | 0.390 | 0.369 | 0.365 | 0.350 | 0.335 | 0.323 |
| Dividend Payout % | 12.81 | 14.71 | 15.89 | ... | 21.28 | 26.42 | 25.28 | 30.14 |
| **Income Statement** | | | | | | | | |
| Total Revenue | 589,886 | 270,962 | 1,041,551 | 819,165 | 1,124,829 | 993,649 | 892,221 | 839,162 |
| EBITDA | 174,925 | 73,775 | 259,388 | (93,602) | 221,692 | 179,543 | 168,868 | 145,869 |
| Depn & Amortn | 14,246 | 7,315 | 22,625 | 26,310 | 26,440 | 23,784 | 22,284 | 22,632 |
| Income Before Taxes | 158,186 | 65,190 | 231,319 | (127,191) | 179,788 | 135,722 | 136,434 | 111,276 |
| Income Taxes | 47,047 | 19,293 | 63,271 | 32,864 | 62,284 | 45,030 | 38,767 | 32,938 |
| Net Income | 111,139 | 45,897 | 168,048 | (160,055) | 117,504 | 90,692 | 90,598 | 78,338 |
| Average Shares | 69,002 | 68,878 | 68,442 | 67,130 | 68,614 | 68,364 | 68,360 | 73,054 |
| **Balance Sheet** | | | | | | | | |
| Current Assets | 497,379 | 441,425 | 451,031 | 346,671 | 384,313 | 409,924 | 347,304 | 311,716 |
| Total Assets | 1,058,906 | 997,434 | 986,354 | 890,674 | 1,166,669 | 1,211,840 | 822,890 | 788,526 |
| Current Liabilities | 182,252 | 167,790 | 191,914 | 156,422 | 373,996 | 509,914 | 241,325 | 250,074 |
| Long-Term Obligations | 51,865 | 87,915 | 99,316 | 155,242 | 74,648 | 29,878 | 52,201 | 106,351 |
| Total Liabilities | 437,402 | 454,659 | 481,282 | 520,698 | 592,557 | 680,723 | 392,362 | 457,614 |
| Stockholders' Equity | 621,504 | 542,775 | 505,072 | 369,976 | 574,112 | 531,117 | 430,528 | 330,912 |
| Shares Outstanding | 68,248 | 68,220 | 67,870 | 67,356 | 67,414 | 67,420 | 66,822 | 65,822 |
| **Statistical Record** | | | | | | | | |
| Return on Assets % | 22.27 | 19.77 | 17.91 | N.M. | 9.85 | 8.91 | 11.21 | 9.65 |
| Return on Equity % | 42.58 | 40.40 | 38.41 | N.M. | 21.21 | 18.86 | 23.73 | 21.40 |
| EBITDA Margin % | 29.65 | 27.23 | 24.90 | N.M. | 19.71 | 18.07 | 18.93 | 17.38 |
| Net Margin % | 18.84 | 16.94 | 16.13 | N.M. | 10.45 | 9.13 | 10.15 | 9.34 |
| Asset Turnover | 1.17 | 1.15 | 1.11 | 0.80 | 0.94 | 0.98 | 1.10 | 1.03 |
| Current Ratio | 2.73 | 2.63 | 2.35 | 2.22 | 1.03 | 0.80 | 1.44 | 1.25 |
| Debt to Equity | 0.08 | 0.16 | 0.20 | 0.42 | 0.13 | 0.06 | 0.12 | 0.32 |
| Price Range | 58.74-27.39 | 47.58-27.11 | 39.88-26.05 | 29.29-10.20 | 39.31-16.48 | 28.57-21.86 | 28.59-18.59 | 20.23-14.98 |
| P/E Ratio | 18.36-8.56 | 17.49-9.97 | 16.21-10.59 | ... | 22.85-9.58 | 21.48-16.43 | 21.49-13.97 | 18.91-14.00 |
| Average Yield % | 1.00 | 1.11 | 1.20 | 1.90 | 1.29 | 1.42 | 1.48 | 1.80 |

| | | |
|---|---|---|
| **Address:** 28601 Clemens Road, Westlake, OH 44145<br>**Telephone:** 440-892-1580<br>**Web Site:** www.nordson.com | **Officers:** Michael F. Hilton - President, Chief Executive Officer John J. Keane - Senior Vice President **Transfer Agents:** National City Bank, Cleveland, OH | **Investor Contact:** 440-414-5344<br>**No of Institutions:** 300<br>**Shares:** 57,738,768 **% Held:** 77.38 |

# NORTHEAST UTILITIES

| Exchange | Symbol | Price | 52Wk Range | Yield | P/E |
|---|---|---|---|---|---|
| NYS | NU | $34.70 (8/31/2011) | 36.31-28.97 | 3.17 | 14.58 |

***7 Year Price Score 128.56** *NYSE Composite Index=100 ***12 Month Price Score 103.38**

**Interim Earnings (Per Share)**

| Qtr. | Mar | Jun | Sep | Dec |
|---|---|---|---|---|
| 2008 | 0.38 | 0.37 | 0.47 | 0.46 |
| 2009 | 0.60 | 0.47 | 0.37 | 0.48 |
| 2010 | 0.49 | 0.41 | 0.57 | 0.73 |
| 2011 | 0.64 | 0.44 | ... | ... |

**Interim Dividends (Per Share)**

| Amt | Decl | Ex | Rec | Pay |
|---|---|---|---|---|
| 0.256Q | 10/12/2010 | 11/29/2010 | 12/01/2010 | 12/31/2010 |
| 0.275Q | 02/08/2011 | 02/25/2011 | 03/01/2011 | 03/31/2011 |
| 0.275Q | 04/12/2011 | 05/27/2011 | 06/01/2011 | 06/30/2011 |
| 0.275Q | 07/12/2011 | 08/30/2011 | 09/01/2011 | 09/30/2011 |

**Indicated Div: $1.10 (Div. Reinv. Plan)**

**Valuation Analysis**

| | | | |
|---|---|---|---|
| Forecast EPS | $2.35 (09/05/2011) | | |
| Market Cap | $6.1 Billion | Book Value | $3.9 Billion |
| Price/Book | 1.57 | Price/Sales | 1.30 |

**Dividend Achiever Status**

| | |
|---|---|
| **10 Year Growth Rate** | 8.58% |
| **Total Years of Dividend Growth** | 11 |

**Business Summary:** Electric Utilities (MIC: 3.1.1 SIC: 4911 NAIC: 221122)

Northeast Utilities is a public utility holding company, engaged in the energy delivery business through its utility subsidiaries: The Connecticut Light and Power Company, which serves residential, commercial and industrial customers in Connecticut; Public Service Company of New Hampshire, which serves residential, commercial and industrial customers in New Hampshire; Western Massachusetts Electric Company, which serves residential, commercial and industrial customers in western Massachusetts; and Yankee Gas Services Company, which serves residential, commercial and industrial customers in Connecticut. Co.'s segments include: the electricity distribution; and the electricity transmission.

**Recent Developments:** For the quarter ended June 30 2011, net income increased 7.3% to US$78.7 million from US$73.3 million in the year-earlier quarter. Revenues were US$1.05 billion, down 5.8% from US$1.11 billion the year before. Operating income was US$178.1 million versus US$178.3 million in the prior-year quarter, a decrease of 0.1%. Direct operating expenses declined 17.7% to US$419.1 million from US$509.0 million in the comparable period the year before. Indirect operating expenses increased 6.2% to US$450.2 million from US$424.0 million in the equivalent prior-year period.

**Prospects:** Our evaluation of Northeast Utilities as of Sep. 6, 2011 is the result of our systematic analysis on three basic characteristics: earnings strength, relative valuation, and recent stock price movement. The company has generated a negative trend in earnings per share over the past 5 quarters. However, while recent estimates for the company have been mixed, NU has posted results that fell short of analysts expectations. Based on operating earnings yield, the company is undervalued when compared to all of the companies in our coverage universe. Share price changes over the past year indicates that NU will perform very poorly over the near term.

**Financial Data**

| (US$ in Thousands) | 6 Mos | 3 Mos | 12/31/2010 | 12/31/2009 | 12/31/2008 | 12/31/2007 | 12/31/2006 | 12/31/2005 |
|---|---|---|---|---|---|---|---|---|
| Earnings Per Share | 2.38 | 2.35 | 2.19 | 1.91 | 1.67 | 1.59 | 3.05 | (1.93) |
| Cash Flow Per Share | 7.03 | 7.00 | 6.19 | 5.73 | 4.16 | 1.61 | 2.65 | 3.35 |
| Tang Book Value Per Share | 20.51 | 20.36 | 20.63 | 19.40 | 18.28 | 17.68 | 17.03 | 14.74 |
| Dividends Per Share | 1.063 | 1.044 | 1.025 | 0.950 | 0.825 | 0.775 | 0.725 | 0.675 |
| Dividend Payout % | 44.64 | 44.41 | 46.80 | 49.74 | 49.40 | 48.74 | 23.77 | ... |
| **Income Statement** | | | | | | | | |
| Total Revenue | 2,282,732 | 1,235,251 | 4,898,167 | 5,439,430 | 5,800,095 | 5,822,226 | 6,884,388 | 7,397,390 |
| EBITDA | 656,762 | 356,510 | 1,142,544 | 1,098,794 | 919,781 | 866,417 | 532,140 | 120,293 |
| Depn & Amortn | 233,624 | 125,640 | 300,737 | 309,618 | 278,588 | 265,297 | 243,822 | 236,921 |
| Income Before Taxes | 302,355 | 173,621 | 604,516 | 515,539 | 372,048 | 360,875 | 50,280 | (386,429) |
| Income Taxes | 108,052 | 63,537 | 210,409 | 179,947 | 105,661 | 109,420 | (81,429) | (162,765) |
| Net Income | 191,433 | 114,155 | 387,949 | 330,033 | 260,828 | 246,483 | 470,578 | (253,488) |
| Average Shares | 177,626 | 177,480 | 176,885 | 172,717 | 155,999 | 155,304 | 154,146 | 131,638 |
| **Balance Sheet** | | | | | | | | |
| Current Assets | 1,337,862 | 1,406,965 | 1,317,742 | 1,267,854 | 1,505,564 | 1,286,256 | 1,731,051 | 2,376,843 |
| Total Assets | 14,442,346 | 14,418,532 | 14,522,042 | 14,057,679 | 13,988,480 | 11,581,822 | 11,303,236 | 12,569,075 |
| Current Liabilities | 1,476,027 | 1,207,187 | 1,238,075 | 979,412 | 1,703,462 | 1,206,150 | 1,363,835 | 1,975,230 |
| Long-Term Obligations | 4,356,052 | 4,630,724 | 4,632,866 | 4,492,935 | 4,103,162 | 3,483,599 | 2,960,435 | 3,027,288 |
| Total Liabilities | 10,527,240 | 10,533,197 | 10,594,666 | 10,363,577 | 10,851,968 | 8,551,787 | 8,388,857 | 10,023,631 |
| Stockholders' Equity | 3,915,106 | 3,885,335 | 3,927,376 | 3,694,102 | 3,136,512 | 3,030,035 | 2,914,379 | 2,545,444 |
| Shares Outstanding | 176,825 | 176,747 | 176,448 | 175,620 | 155,834 | 155,079 | 154,233 | 153,225 |
| **Statistical Record** | | | | | | | | |
| Return on Assets % | 2.94 | 2.92 | 2.71 | 2.35 | 2.03 | 2.15 | 3.94 | N.M. |
| Return on Equity % | 11.12 | 11.07 | 10.18 | 9.66 | 8.44 | 8.29 | 17.24 | N.M. |
| EBITDA Margin % | 28.77 | 28.86 | 23.33 | 20.20 | 15.86 | 14.88 | 7.73 | 1.63 |
| Net Margin % | 8.39 | 9.24 | 7.92 | 6.07 | 4.50 | 4.23 | 6.84 | N.M. |
| Asset Turnover | 0.33 | 0.34 | 0.34 | 0.39 | 0.45 | 0.51 | 0.58 | 0.61 |
| Current Ratio | 0.91 | 1.17 | 1.06 | 1.29 | 0.88 | 1.07 | 1.27 | 1.20 |
| Debt to Equity | 1.11 | 1.19 | 1.18 | 1.22 | 1.31 | 1.15 | 1.02 | 1.19 |
| Price Range | 36.31-25.48 | 35.07-25.28 | 32.05-24.78 | 26.33-19.45 | 31.31-19.15 | 33.53-26.93 | 28.81-19.24 | 21.79-17.61 |
| P/E Ratio | 15.26-10.71 | 14.92-10.76 | 14.63-11.32 | 13.79-10.18 | 18.75-11.47 | 21.09-16.94 | 9.45-6.31 | ... |
| Average Yield % | 3.32 | 3.49 | 3.64 | 4.16 | 3.24 | 2.60 | 3.28 | 3.48 |

**Address:** One Federal Street, Building 111-4, Springfield, MA 01105
**Telephone:** 413-785-5871
**Web Site:** www.nu.com

**Officers:** Charles W. Shivery - Chairman, President, Chief Executive Officer David R. McHale - Executive Vice President, Chief Financial Officer **Transfer Agents:**BNY Mellon Shareowner Services, Jersey City, NJ

**Investor Contact:** 800-286-5000
**No of Institutions:** 412
**Shares:** 149,661,728 **% Held:** 77.21

# NORTHWEST NATURAL GAS CO.

| Exchange | Symbol | Price | 52Wk Range | Yield | P/E |
|---|---|---|---|---|---|
| NYS | NWN | $45.22 (8/31/2011) | 50.64-40.09 | 3.85 | 18.53 |

***7 Year Price Score 107.53** *NYSE Composite Index=100 ***12 Month Price Score 96.74**

**Interim Earnings (Per Share)**

| Qtr. | Mar | Jun | Sep | Dec |
|---|---|---|---|---|
| 2008 | 1.63 | 0.12 | (0.38) | 1.24 |
| 2009 | 1.78 | 0.12 | (0.25) | 1.19 |
| 2010 | 1.64 | 0.26 | (0.28) | 1.11 |
| 2011 | 1.53 | 0.08 | ... | ... |

**Interim Dividends (Per Share)**

| Amt | Decl | Ex | Rec | Pay |
|---|---|---|---|---|
| 0.435Q | 10/04/2010 | 10/27/2010 | 10/29/2010 | 11/15/2010 |
| 0.435Q | 01/13/2011 | 01/27/2011 | 01/31/2011 | 02/15/2011 |
| 0.435Q | 04/06/2011 | 04/27/2011 | 04/29/2011 | 05/13/2011 |
| 0.435Q | 07/01/2011 | 07/27/2011 | 07/29/2011 | 08/15/2011 |

**Indicated Div: $1.74 (Div. Reinv. Plan)**

**Valuation Analysis**

Forecast EPS $2.52 (09/05/2011)

| Market Cap | $1.2 Billion | Book Value | $714.6 Million |
|---|---|---|---|
| Price/Book | 1.69 | Price/Sales | 1.42 |

**Dividend Achiever Status**

**10 Year Growth Rate** 3.04%

**Total Years of Dividend Growth** 55

**Business Summary:** Gas Utilities (MIC: 3.3.1 SIC: 4924 NAIC: 221210)

Northwest Natural Gas is engaged in the distribution of natural gas business. Co. operates in two primary segments: Local Gas Distribution, which involves building and maintaining a pipeline distribution system, purchasing gas from producers and marketers, contracting for the transportation of gas over pipelines and reselling the gas to customers; and Gas Storage, which includes natural gas storage services provided to customers from its Gill Ranch Storage, LLC gas storage facility and the non-utility portion of the Mist gas storage facility near Mist, OR. In addition, Co.'s Other segment includes other investments and business activities not related to one of these two reporting segments.

**Recent Developments:** For the quarter ended June 30 2011, net income decreased 68.2% to US$2.2 million from US$6.9 million in the year-earlier quarter. Revenues were US$161.2 million, down 0.7% from US$162.4 million the year before. Operating income was US$12.7 million versus US$20.2 million in the prior-year quarter, a decrease of 37.4%. Direct operating expenses rose 4.2% to US$94.0 million from US$90.2 million in the comparable period the year before. Indirect operating expenses increased 5.0% to US$54.6 million from US$52.0 million in the equivalent prior-year period.

**Prospects:** Our evaluation of Northwest Natural Gas Co. as of Sep. 6, 2011 is the result of our systematic analysis on three basic characteristics: earnings strength, relative valuation, and recent stock price movement. The company has managed to produce a neutral trend in earnings per share over the past 5 quarters. However, while recent estimates for the company have been mixed, NWN has posted better than expected results. Based on operating earnings yield, the company is about fairly valued when compared to all of the companies in our coverage universe. Share price changes over the past year indicates that NWN will perform very poorly over the near term.

**Financial Data**

| (US$ in Thousands) | 6 Mos | 3 Mos | 12/31/2010 | 12/31/2009 | 12/31/2008 | 12/31/2007 | 12/31/2006 | 12/31/2005 |
|---|---|---|---|---|---|---|---|---|
| Earnings Per Share | 2.44 | 2.62 | 2.73 | 2.83 | 2.61 | 2.76 | 2.29 | 2.11 |
| Cash Flow Per Share | 7.16 | 6.01 | 4.76 | 9.07 | 1.31 | 6.85 | 5.39 | 2.87 |
| Tang Book Value Per Share | 26.79 | 27.11 | 25.99 | 24.88 | 23.71 | 22.52 | 21.97 | 21.28 |
| Dividends Per Share | 1.720 | 1.700 | 1.680 | 1.600 | 1.520 | 1.440 | 1.390 | 1.320 |
| Dividend Payout % | 70.49 | 64.89 | 61.54 | 56.54 | 58.24 | 52.17 | 60.70 | 62.56 |
| **Income Statement** | | | | | | | | |
| Total Revenue | 484,285 | 323,088 | 812,106 | 1,012,711 | 1,037,855 | 1,033,193 | 1,013,172 | 910,486 |
| EBITDA | 139,838 | 103,029 | 227,807 | 225,033 | 219,691 | 224,174 | 203,331 | 189,797 |
| Depn & Amortn | 34,855 | 17,309 | 65,124 | 62,814 | 72,159 | 68,343 | 64,435 | 61,645 |
| Income Before Taxes | 87,313 | 76,792 | 122,129 | 121,793 | 110,203 | 118,557 | 99,649 | 90,869 |
| Income Taxes | 43,994 | 36,019 | 49,462 | 46,671 | 40,678 | 44,060 | 36,234 | 32,720 |
| Net Income | 42,966 | 40,773 | 72,667 | 75,122 | 69,525 | 74,497 | 63,415 | 58,149 |
| Average Shares | 26,727 | 26,724 | 26,657 | 26,576 | 26,594 | 26,995 | 27,657 | 27,621 |
| **Balance Sheet** | | | | | | | | |
| Current Assets | 227,894 | 280,705 | 330,265 | 328,235 | 480,970 | 276,799 | 308,793 | 323,710 |
| Total Assets | 2,521,994 | 2,571,553 | 2,616,616 | 2,399,252 | 2,378,152 | 2,014,183 | 1,956,856 | 2,042,031 |
| Current Liabilities | 380,824 | 422,911 | 468,161 | 392,569 | 551,320 | 389,866 | 339,479 | 326,565 |
| Long-Term Obligations | 551,700 | 551,700 | 591,700 | 601,700 | 512,000 | 512,000 | 517,000 | 521,500 |
| Total Liabilities | 1,807,366 | 1,848,325 | 1,923,515 | 1,739,147 | 1,749,779 | 1,419,432 | 1,357,311 | 1,455,100 |
| Stockholders' Equity | 714,628 | 723,228 | 693,101 | 660,105 | 628,373 | 594,751 | 599,545 | 586,931 |
| Shares Outstanding | 26,673 | 26,673 | 26,668 | 26,533 | 26,501 | 26,407 | 27,283 | 27,579 |
| **Statistical Record** | | | | | | | | |
| Return on Assets % | 2.65 | 2.79 | 2.90 | 3.14 | 3.16 | 3.75 | 3.17 | 3.08 |
| Return on Equity % | 9.27 | 9.86 | 10.74 | 11.66 | 11.34 | 12.48 | 10.69 | 10.07 |
| EBITDA Margin % | 28.88 | 31.89 | 28.05 | 22.22 | 21.17 | 21.70 | 20.07 | 20.85 |
| Net Margin % | 8.87 | 12.62 | 8.95 | 7.42 | 6.70 | 7.21 | 6.26 | 6.39 |
| Asset Turnover | 0.34 | 0.34 | 0.32 | 0.42 | 0.47 | 0.52 | 0.51 | 0.48 |
| Current Ratio | 0.60 | 0.66 | 0.71 | 0.84 | 0.87 | 0.71 | 0.91 | 0.99 |
| Debt to Equity | 0.77 | 0.76 | 0.85 | 0.91 | 0.81 | 0.86 | 0.86 | 0.89 |
| Price Range | 50.64-43.17 | 50.64-42.96 | 50.64-41.62 | 46.19-38.50 | 54.07-41.38 | 52.62-40.21 | 43.00-33.27 | 39.50-32.61 |
| P/E Ratio | 20.75-17.69 | 19.33-16.40 | 18.55-15.25 | 16.32-13.60 | 20.72-15.85 | 19.07-14.57 | 18.78-14.53 | 18.72-15.45 |
| Average Yield % | 3.71 | 3.65 | 3.63 | 3.73 | 3.28 | 3.12 | 3.74 | 3.68 |

**Address:** 220 N.W. Second Avenue, Portland, OR 97209
**Telephone:** 503-226-4211
**Web Site:** www.nwnatural.com

**Officers:** Russell F. Tromley - Chairman Gregg S. Kantor - President, Chief Executive Officer **Transfer Agents:** American Stock Transfer & Trust Company, New York, NY

**Investor Contact:** 503-226-4211
**No of Institutions:** 180
**Shares:** 18,343,574 **% Held:** 60.70

# NSTAR

| Exchange | Symbol | Price | 52Wk Range | Yield | P/E |
|---|---|---|---|---|---|
| NYS | NST | $45.72 (8/31/2011) | 47.27-38.03 | 3.72 | 19.79 |

***7 Year Price Score 127.76** *NYSE Composite Index=100 ***12 Month Price Score 102.60**

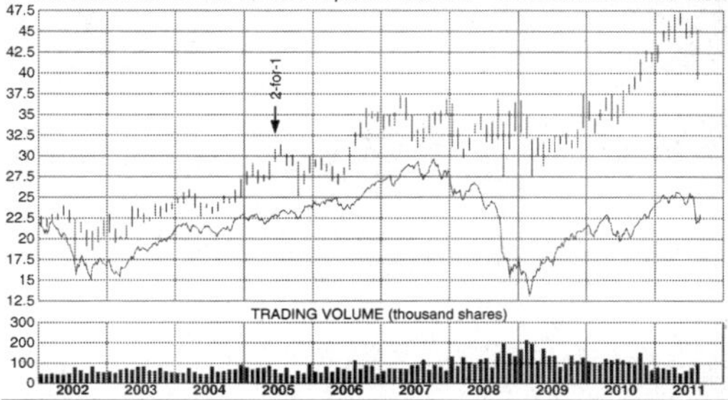


**Interim Earnings (Per Share)**

| Qtr. | Mar | Jun | Sep | Dec |
|---|---|---|---|---|
| 2008 | 0.55 | 0.47 | 0.80 | 0.39 |
| 2009 | 0.57 | 0.53 | 0.82 | 0.45 |
| 2010 | 0.56 | 1.61 | 0.73 | 0.45 |
| 2011 | 0.54 | 0.59 | ... | ... |

**Interim Dividends (Per Share)**

| Amt | Decl | Ex | Rec | Pay |
|---|---|---|---|---|
| 0.40Q | 09/23/2010 | 10/06/2010 | 10/08/2010 | 11/01/2010 |
| 0.425Q | 11/18/2010 | 01/05/2011 | 01/07/2011 | 02/01/2011 |
| 0.425Q | 03/24/2011 | 04/06/2011 | 04/08/2011 | 05/02/2011 |
| 0.425Q | 06/23/2011 | 07/06/2011 | 07/08/2011 | 08/01/2011 |

**Indicated Div: $1.70 (Div. Reinv. Plan)**

**Valuation Analysis**

| | | | |
|---|---|---|---|
| Forecast EPS | $2.65 (09/02/2011) | | |
| Market Cap | $4.7 Billion | Book Value | $2.0 Billion |
| Price/Book | 2.42 | Price/Sales | 1.61 |

**Dividend Achiever Status**

| | |
|---|---|
| 10 Year Growth Rate | 4.50% |
| Total Years of Dividend Growth | 11 |

**Business Summary:** Electric Utilities (MIC: 3.1.1 SIC: 4911 NAIC: 221210)

NSTAR is a holding company. Through its subsidiaries, Co. is engaged in the energy delivery business. As of Dec 31 2010, Co. served about 1.4 million customers in Massachusetts, including approximately 1.1 million electric distribution customers in 81 communities and approximately 300,000 natural gas distribution customers in 51 communities. Co.'s primary business is electric and natural gas distribution operations that provide energy transmission and delivery services. Co.'s unregulated operations include telecommunications, which are provided through its subsidiary, NSTAR Communications, Inc.; and liquefied natural gas service, which is provided through its subsidiary, Hopkinton LNG Corp.

**Recent Developments:** For the quarter ended June 30 2011, income from continuing operations increased 1.7% to US$61.6 million from US$60.6 million in the year-earlier quarter. Net income decreased 64.1% to US$61.6 million from US$171.5 million in the year-earlier quarter. Revenues were US$651.4 million, down 0.8% from US$656.6 million the year before. Operating income was US$122.5 million versus US$122.6 million in the prior-year quarter, a decrease of 0.1%. Direct operating expenses declined 5.3% to US$387.9 million from US$409.7 million in the comparable period the year before. Indirect operating expenses increased 13.5% to US$141.1 million from US$124.3 million in the equivalent prior-year period.

**Prospects:** Our evaluation of Nstar as of Sep. 6, 2011 is the result of our systematic analysis on three basic characteristics: earnings strength, relative valuation, and recent stock price movement. The company has produced a positive trend in earnings per share over the past 5 quarters and while recent estimates for the company have been raised by analysts, NST has posted better than expected results. Based on operating earnings yield, the company is about fairly valued when compared to all of the companies in our coverage universe. Share price changes over the past year indicates that NST will perform very poorly over the near term.

**Financial Data**

| (US$ in Thousands) | 6 Mos | 3 Mos | 12/31/2010 | 12/31/2009 | 12/31/2008 | 12/31/2007 | 12/31/2006 | 12/31/2005 |
|---|---|---|---|---|---|---|---|---|
| Earnings Per Share | 2.31 | 3.33 | 3.35 | 2.37 | 2.22 | 2.07 | 1.93 | 1.83 |
| Cash Flow Per Share | 7.69 | 5.27 | 5.24 | 5.97 | 5.07 | 4.60 | 4.99 | (0.25) |
| Tang Book Value Per Share | 18.93 | 18.74 | 18.68 | 17.53 | 17.14 | 16.35 | 15.22 | 14.77 |
| Dividends Per Share | 1.650 | 1.625 | 1.600 | 1.500 | 1.400 | 1.300 | 1.210 | 1.160 |
| Dividend Payout % | 71.43 | 48.80 | 47.76 | 63.29 | 63.06 | 62.80 | 62.69 | 63.39 |
| **Income Statement** | | | | | | | | |
| Total Revenue | 1,444,109 | 792,698 | 2,916,921 | 3,050,044 | 3,345,387 | 3,261,784 | 3,577,702 | 3,243,120 |
| EBITDA | 241,225 | 120,155 | 529,200 | 518,769 | 539,060 | 521,615 | 508,281 | 476,779 |
| Depn & Amortn | 2,769 | 1,385 | 2,500 | 2,500 | 12,300 | 11,500 | 12,800 | 8,900 |
| Income Before Taxes | 191,690 | 93,323 | 417,716 | 392,891 | 381,431 | 351,939 | 326,116 | 306,825 |
| Income Taxes | 73,166 | 36,422 | 179,762 | 146,916 | 143,884 | 130,424 | 119,342 | 110,690 |
| Net Income | 118,524 | 56,901 | 354,909 | 255,208 | 237,547 | 221,515 | 206,774 | 196,135 |
| Average Shares | 104,004 | 103,975 | 105,218 | 106,996 | 107,045 | 107,122 | 107,125 | 107,100 |
| **Balance Sheet** | | | | | | | | |
| Current Assets | 715,552 | 891,147 | 996,673 | 1,191,227 | 1,121,361 | 1,088,571 | 959,754 | 1,036,283 |
| Total Assets | 7,672,419 | 7,839,428 | 7,933,925 | 8,144,786 | 8,269,489 | 7,759,545 | 7,769,395 | 7,645,564 |
| Current Liabilities | 836,599 | 1,015,080 | 1,077,441 | 1,729,149 | 1,394,982 | 1,190,312 | 1,239,933 | 1,169,445 |
| Long-Term Obligations | 2,241,408 | 2,257,896 | 2,301,283 | 1,966,441 | 2,343,676 | 2,501,400 | 2,360,775 | 2,402,377 |
| Total Liabilities | 5,711,786 | 5,898,675 | 5,999,362 | 6,272,180 | 6,438,334 | 6,012,730 | 6,143,832 | 6,067,549 |
| Stockholders' Equity | 1,960,633 | 1,940,753 | 1,934,563 | 1,872,606 | 1,831,155 | 1,746,815 | 1,625,563 | 1,578,015 |
| Shares Outstanding | 103,586 | 103,586 | 103,586 | 106,808 | 106,808 | 106,808 | 106,808 | 106,808 |
| **Statistical Record** | | | | | | | | |
| Return on Assets % | 3.12 | 4.44 | 4.41 | 3.11 | 2.96 | 2.85 | 2.68 | 2.66 |
| Return on Equity % | 12.54 | 18.36 | 18.64 | 13.78 | 13.24 | 13.14 | 12.91 | 12.81 |
| EBITDA Margin % | 16.70 | 15.16 | 18.14 | 17.01 | 16.11 | 15.99 | 14.21 | 14.70 |
| Net Margin % | 8.21 | 7.18 | 12.17 | 8.37 | 7.10 | 6.79 | 5.78 | 6.05 |
| Asset Turnover | 0.38 | 0.37 | 0.36 | 0.37 | 0.42 | 0.42 | 0.46 | 0.44 |
| Current Ratio | 0.86 | 0.88 | 0.93 | 0.69 | 0.80 | 0.91 | 0.77 | 0.89 |
| Debt to Equity | 1.14 | 1.16 | 1.19 | 1.05 | 1.28 | 1.43 | 1.45 | 1.52 |
| Price Range | 47.27-34.78 | 46.28-33.91 | 42.71-32.78 | 37.57-27.62 | 36.88-27.50 | 37.27-31.02 | 35.79-26.55 | 31.40-25.05 |
| P/E Ratio | 20.46-15.06 | 13.90-10.18 | 12.75-9.79 | 15.85-11.65 | 16.61-12.39 | 18.00-14.99 | 18.54-13.76 | 17.16-13.69 |
| Average Yield % | 3.91 | 4.09 | 4.27 | 4.67 | 4.26 | 3.78 | 3.95 | 4.08 |

**Address:** 800 Boylston Street, Boston, MA 02199
**Telephone:** 617-424-2000
**Web Site:** www.nstar.com

**Officers:** Thomas J. May - Chairman, President, Chief Executive Officer James J. Judge - Senior Vice President, Chief Financial Officer, Treasurer **Transfer Agents:** Boston EquiServe, Boston, MA

**Investor Contact:** 617-424-2562
**No of Institutions:** 324
**Shares:** 52,688,848 **% Held:** 40.25

# NUCOR CORP.

| Exchange | Symbol | Price | 52Wk Range | Yield | P/E |
|---|---|---|---|---|---|
| NYS | NUE | $36.08 (8/31/2011) | 48.88-31.48 | 4.02 | 24.54 |

*7 Year Price Score 91.43 *NYSE Composite Index=100 *12 Month Price Score 90.48

**Interim Earnings (Per Share)**

| Qtr. | Mar | Jun | Sep | Dec |
|---|---|---|---|---|
| 2008 | 1.41 | 1.94 | 2.31 | 0.28 |
| 2009 | (0.60) | (0.43) | (0.10) | 0.18 |
| 2010 | 0.10 | 0.29 | 0.07 | (0.04) |
| 2011 | 0.50 | 0.94 | ... | ... |

**Interim Dividends (Per Share)**

| Amt | Decl | Ex | Rec | Pay |
|---|---|---|---|---|
| 0.36Q | 09/08/2010 | 09/28/2010 | 09/30/2010 | 11/11/2010 |
| 0.362Q | 12/08/2010 | 12/29/2010 | 12/31/2010 | 02/11/2011 |
| 0.362Q | 02/16/2011 | 03/29/2011 | 03/31/2011 | 05/11/2011 |
| 0.362Q | 06/07/2011 | 06/28/2011 | 06/30/2011 | 08/11/2011 |

**Indicated Div: $1.45 (Div. Reinv. Plan)**

**Valuation Analysis**

| | | | |
|---|---|---|---|
| Forecast EPS | $2.73 (09/05/2011) | | |
| Market Cap | $11.4 Billion | Book Value | $7.5 Billion |
| Price/Book | 1.53 | Price/Sales | 0.64 |

**Dividend Achiever Status**

| | |
|---|---|
| 10 Year Growth Rate | 24.19% |
| Total Years of Dividend Growth | 38 |

**Business Summary:** Non-Precious Metals (MIC: 8.2.2 SIC: 3312 NAIC: 331111)

Nucor is a manufacturer of steel and steel products, as well as a scrap processor. Co. also produces direct reduced iron (DRI) for use in its steel mills. Through The David J. Joseph Company and its affiliates, Co. also processes ferrous and nonferrous metals and brokers ferrous and nonferrous metals, pig iron, hot briquetted iron and DRI. Co. reports its results in three segments: steel mills, steel products and raw materials. Most of Co.'s operating facilities and customers are located in North America. Co.'s operations include a number of international trading companies that buy and sell steel and steel products manufactured by Co. and others.

**Recent Developments:** For the quarter ended July 2 2011, net income increased 202.8% to US$321.6 million from US$106.2 million in the year-earlier quarter. Revenues were US$5.11 billion, up 21.7% from US$4.20 billion the year before. Direct operating expenses rose 14.2% to US$4.44 billion from US$3.89 billion in the comparable period the year before. Indirect operating expenses increased 23.9% to US$188.9 million from US$152.5 million in the equivalent prior-year period.

**Prospects:** Our evaluation of Nucor Corp. as of Sep. 6, 2011 is the result of our systematic analysis on three basic characteristics: earnings strength, relative valuation, and recent stock price movement. The company has enjoyed a very positive trend in earnings per share over the past 5 quarters. However, while recent estimates for the company have been lowered by analysts, NUE has posted better than expected results. Based on operating earnings yield, the company is about fairly valued when compared to all of the companies in our coverage universe. Share price changes over the past year indicates that NUE will perform poorly over the near term.

**Financial Data**

| (US$ in Thousands) | 6 Mos | 3 Mos | 12/31/2010 | 12/31/2009 | 12/31/2008 | 12/31/2007 | 12/31/2006 | 12/31/2005 |
|---|---|---|---|---|---|---|---|---|
| Earnings Per Share | 1.47 | 0.82 | 0.42 | (0.94) | 5.98 | 4.94 | 5.68 | 4.13 |
| Cash Flow Per Share | 4.61 | 2.92 | 2.76 | 3.75 | 8.18 | 6.54 | 7.34 | 6.80 |
| Tang Book Value Per Share | 15.14 | 14.42 | 14.02 | 14.88 | 16.72 | 13.18 | 16.04 | 13.80 |
| Dividends Per Share | 1.448 | 1.445 | 1.442 | 1.410 | 1.910 | 2.440 | 2.150 | 0.925 |
| Dividend Payout % | 98.47 | 176.22 | 343.45 | ... | 31.94 | 49.39 | 37.85 | 22.40 |
| **Income Statement** | | | | | | | | |
| Total Revenue | 9,941,743 | 4,833,934 | 15,844,627 | 11,190,296 | 23,663,324 | 16,592,976 | 14,751,270 | 12,700,999 |
| EBITDA | 1,122,974 | 457,697 | 964,437 | 297,150 | 3,674,358 | 2,955,457 | 3,239,610 | 2,506,297 |
| Depn & Amortn | 290,739 | 144,666 | 512,147 | 494,035 | 479,484 | 403,172 | 363,936 | 375,054 |
| Income Before Taxes | 746,485 | 270,465 | 299,197 | (331,637) | 3,104,391 | 2,546,816 | 2,913,039 | 2,127,042 |
| Income Taxes | 240,842 | 85,133 | 60,792 | (176,800) | 959,480 | 781,368 | 936,137 | 706,084 |
| Net Income | 459,614 | 159,841 | 134,092 | (293,613) | 1,830,990 | 1,471,947 | 1,757,681 | 1,310,284 |
| Average Shares | 317,022 | 316,874 | 316,510 | 314,873 | 306,092 | 297,878 | 309,381 | 317,130 |
| **Balance Sheet** | | | | | | | | |
| Current Assets | 6,716,495 | 6,295,610 | 5,861,175 | 5,182,248 | 6,397,486 | 5,073,249 | 4,675,036 | 4,071,553 |
| Total Assets | 14,733,549 | 14,344,446 | 13,921,910 | 12,571,904 | 13,874,443 | 9,826,122 | 7,884,989 | 7,138,787 |
| Current Liabilities | 2,002,685 | 1,787,626 | 1,504,438 | 1,227,057 | 1,854,192 | 1,582,036 | 1,450,028 | 1,255,699 |
| Long-Term Obligations | 4,280,200 | 4,280,200 | 4,280,200 | 3,080,200 | 3,086,200 | 2,250,300 | 922,300 | 922,300 |
| Total Liabilities | 7,268,601 | 7,093,072 | 6,801,840 | 5,181,378 | 5,945,239 | 4,713,205 | 3,059,000 | 2,858,999 |
| Stockholders' Equity | 7,464,948 | 7,251,374 | 7,120,070 | 7,390,526 | 7,929,204 | 5,112,917 | 4,825,989 | 4,279,788 |
| Shares Outstanding | 316,503 | 316,061 | 315,791 | 314,856 | 313,977 | 287,993 | 300,949 | 310,220 |
| **Statistical Record** | | | | | | | | |
| Return on Assets % | 3.44 | 1.94 | 1.01 | N.M. | 15.41 | 16.62 | 23.40 | 19.75 |
| Return on Equity % | 6.41 | 3.61 | 1.85 | N.M. | 28.00 | 29.62 | 38.61 | 33.88 |
| EBITDA Margin % | 11.30 | 9.47 | 6.09 | 2.66 | 15.53 | 17.81 | 21.96 | 19.73 |
| Net Margin % | 4.62 | 3.31 | 0.85 | N.M. | 7.74 | 8.87 | 11.92 | 10.32 |
| Asset Turnover | 1.31 | 1.25 | 1.20 | 0.85 | 1.99 | 1.87 | 1.96 | 1.91 |
| Current Ratio | 3.35 | 3.52 | 3.90 | 4.22 | 3.45 | 3.21 | 3.22 | 3.24 |
| Debt to Equity | 0.57 | 0.59 | 0.60 | 0.42 | 0.39 | 0.44 | 0.19 | 0.22 |
| Price Range | 48.88-36.38 | 48.88-36.38 | 49.93-36.38 | 49.84-30.74 | 82.07-25.52 | 69.25-45.86 | 65.84-34.23 | 34.62-22.81 |
| P/E Ratio | 33.25-24.75 | 59.61-44.37 | 118.88-86.62 | ... | 13.72-4.27 | 14.02-9.28 | 11.59-6.03 | 8.38-5.52 |
| Average Yield % | 3.44 | 3.42 | 3.45 | 3.28 | 3.37 | 4.07 | 4.21 | 3.26 |

| | | |
|---|---|---|
| **Address:** 1915 Rexford Road, Charlotte, NC 28211<br>**Telephone:** 704-366-7000<br>**Web Site:** www.nucor.com | **Officers:** Daniel R. DiMicco - Chairman, Chief Executive Officer John J. Ferriola - President, Chief Operating Officer **Transfer Agents:** American Stock Transfer & Trust Company, New York, NY | **No of Institutions:** 745<br>**Shares:** 296,801,120 **% Held:** 74.86 |

# OLD REPUBLIC INTERNATIONAL CORP.

| Exchange | Symbol | Price | 52Wk Range | Yield | P/E |
|---|---|---|---|---|---|
| NYS | ORI | $9.94 (8/31/2011) | 14.11-9.13 | 7.04 | N/A |

***7 Year Price Score 76.79** *NYSE Composite Index=100 ***12 Month Price Score 85.48**

**Interim Earnings (Per Share)**

| Qtr. | Mar | Jun | Sep | Dec |
|---|---|---|---|---|
| 2008 | (0.08) | (1.58) | (0.21) | (0.54) |
| 2009 | (0.23) | (0.07) | (0.20) | 0.07 |
| 2010 | 0.11 | 0.23 | (0.16) | (0.05) |
| 2011 | (0.05) | (0.26) | ... | ... |

**Interim Dividends (Per Share)**

| Amt | Decl | Ex | Rec | Pay |
|---|---|---|---|---|
| 0.172Q | 11/26/2010 | 12/02/2010 | 12/06/2010 | 12/15/2010 |
| 0.175Q | 02/24/2011 | 03/02/2011 | 03/04/2011 | 03/15/2011 |
| 0.175Q | 05/11/2011 | 06/01/2011 | 06/03/2011 | 06/15/2011 |
| 0.175Q | 08/25/2011 | 09/01/2011 | 09/06/2011 | 09/15/2011 |

**Indicated Div: $0.70 (Div. Reinv. Plan)**

**Valuation Analysis**

| | | | |
|---|---|---|---|
| Forecast EPS | $-0.51 (09/02/2011) | | |
| Market Cap | $2.6 Billion | Book Value | $4.0 Billion |
| Price/Book | 0.65 | Price/Sales | 0.59 |

**Dividend Achiever Status**

| | |
|---|---|
| **10 Year Growth Rate** | 8.17% |
| **Total Years of Dividend Growth** | 29 |

**Business Summary:** General Insurance (MIC: 5.2.1 SIC: 6351 NAIC: 524127)

Old Republic International is a holding company engaged in the business of insurance underwriting. Co. has three key segments: General Insurance, which is characterized as a commercial lines insurance business with a focus on liability insurance coverages; Mortgage Guaranty, which protects mortgage lenders and investors from default related losses on residential mortgage loans made primarily to homebuyers who make down payments of less than 20.0% of the home's purchase price; and Title Insurance, which consists mainly of the issuance of policies to real estate purchasers and investors based upon searches of the public records, which contain information concerning interests in real property.

**Recent Developments:** For the quarter ended June 30 2011, net loss amounted to US$66.3 million versus net income of US$57.4 million in the year-earlier quarter. Revenues were US$1.09 billion, up 8.6% from US$1.01 billion the year before. Net premiums earned were US$890.5 million versus US$746.2 million in the prior-year quarter, an increase of 19.3%. Net investment income fell 2.0% to US$93.1 million from US$95.0 million a year ago.

**Prospects:** Our evaluation of Old Republic International Corp. as of Sep. 6, 2011 is the result of our systematic analysis on three basic characteristics: earnings strength, relative valuation, and recent stock price movement. The company has managed to produce a neutral trend in earnings per share over the past 5 quarters. Because the company lacks sufficient analyst estimate data, we place greater weight on the historical EPS trend as the measure of earnings strength. Based on operating earnings yield, the company is overvalued when compared to all of the companies in our coverage universe. Share price changes over the past year indicates that ORI will perform poorly over the near term.

**Financial Data**

| (US$ in Thousands) | 6 Mos | 3 Mos | 12/31/2010 | 12/31/2009 | 12/31/2008 | 12/31/2007 | 12/31/2006 | 12/31/2005 |
|---|---|---|---|---|---|---|---|---|
| Earnings Per Share | (0.52) | (0.03) | 0.13 | (0.42) | (2.41) | 1.17 | 1.99 | 2.37 |
| Cash Flow Per Share | (0.88) | (1.24) | (1.17) | 2.26 | 2.44 | 3.73 | 4.35 | 3.83 |
| Tang Book Value Per Share | 15.32 | 15.62 | 15.90 | 16.17 | 15.55 | 19.71 | 18.91 | 17.53 |
| Dividends Per Share | 0.695 | 0.693 | 0.690 | 0.680 | 0.670 | 0.630 | 0.590 | 1.312 |
| Dividend Payout % | ... | ... | 530.77 | ... | ... | 53.85 | 29.65 | 55.36 |
| **Income Statement** | | | | | | | | |
| Premium Income | 1,813,300 | 922,800 | 3,225,500 | 3,111,500 | 3,125,100 | 3,389,000 | 3,154,100 | 3,062,300 |
| Total Revenue | 2,224,500 | 1,129,500 | 4,102,700 | 3,803,600 | 3,237,700 | 4,091,000 | 3,794,200 | 3,805,900 |
| Benefits & Claims | 1,320,700 | 636,600 | 2,253,200 | 2,591,000 | 2,700,400 | 2,156,900 | 1,532,300 | 1,460,100 |
| Income Before Taxes | (133,300) | (24,900) | 27,600 | ... | ... | ... | ... | ... |
| Income Taxes | (54,000) | (11,900) | (2,500) | (174,400) | (260,800) | 105,900 | 215,200 | 195,900 |
| Net Income | (79,200) | (12,900) | 30,100 | (99,100) | (558,300) | 272,400 | 464,800 | 551,400 |
| Average Shares | 254,972 | 254,769 | 241,327 | 235,657 | 231,484 | 232,912 | 233,034 | 232,108 |
| **Balance Sheet** | | | | | | | | |
| Total Assets | 16,086,900 | 16,303,600 | 15,882,700 | 14,190,000 | 13,266,000 | 13,290,600 | 12,612,200 | 11,543,200 |
| Total Liabilities | 12,114,500 | 12,253,500 | 11,761,300 | 10,298,600 | 9,525,700 | 8,749,000 | 8,243,000 | 7,519,100 |
| Stockholders' Equity | 3,972,400 | 4,050,100 | 4,121,400 | 3,891,400 | 3,740,300 | 4,541,600 | 4,369,200 | 4,024,000 |
| Shares Outstanding | 259,281 | 259,268 | 259,222 | 240,685 | 240,520 | 230,472 | 231,047 | 229,575 |
| **Statistical Record** | | | | | | | | |
| Return on Assets % | N.M. | N.M. | 0.20 | N.M. | N.M. | 2.10 | 3.85 | 4.99 |
| Return on Equity % | N.M. | N.M. | 0.75 | N.M. | N.M. | 6.11 | 11.08 | 13.98 |
| Loss Ratio % | 72.83 | 68.99 | 69.86 | 83.27 | 86.41 | 63.64 | 48.58 | 47.68 |
| Net Margin % | (3.56) | (1.14) | 0.73 | (2.61) | (17.24) | 6.66 | 12.25 | 14.49 |
| Price Range | 14.11-11.62 | 15.29-11.73 | 15.29-10.04 | 12.71-7.40 | 16.50-7.39 | 23.51-13.73 | 23.50-20.20 | 22.44-17.85 |
| P/E Ratio | ... | ... | 117.62-77.23 | ... | ... | 20.09-11.74 | 11.81-10.15 | 9.47-7.53 |
| Average Yield % | 5.43 | 5.29 | 5.42 | 6.36 | 5.49 | 3.19 | 2.71 | 6.55 |

| | | |
|---|---|---|
| **Address:** 307 North Michigan Avenue, Chicago, IL 60601<br>**Telephone:** 312-346-8100<br>**Web Site:** www.oldrepublic.com | **Officers:** Aldo C. Zucaro - Chairman, Chief Executive Officer James A. Kellogg - Executive Vice-Chairman<br>**Transfer Agents:** Wells Fargo Shareowner Services, St. Paul, MN | **No of Institutions:** 355<br>**Shares:** 229,987,424 **% Held:** 75.71 |

# OWENS & MINOR, INC.

| Exchange | Symbol | Price | 52Wk Range | Yield | P/E |
|---|---|---|---|---|---|
| NYS | OMI | $29.44 (8/31/2011) | 35.48-26.02 | 2.72 | 16.73 |

***7 Year Price Score 119.90** *NYSE Composite Index=100 ***12 Month Price Score 101.07**

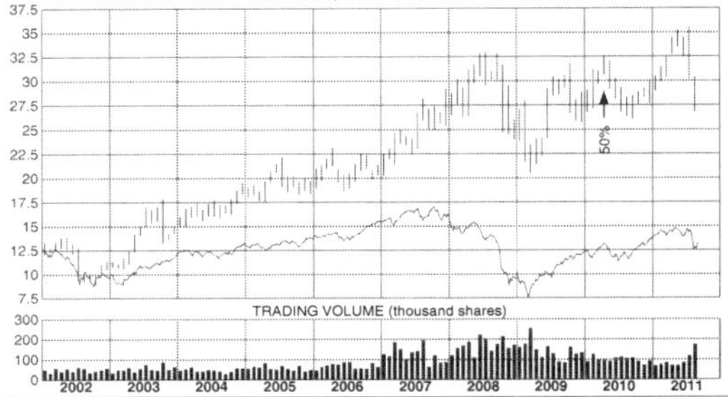


**Interim Earnings (Per Share)**

| Qtr. | Mar | Jun | Sep | Dec |
|---|---|---|---|---|
| 2008 | 0.39 | 0.38 | 0.41 | 0.33 |
| 2009 | 0.23 | 0.38 | 0.55 | 0.51 |
| 2010 | 0.44 | 0.46 | 0.50 | 0.35 |
| 2011 | 0.45 | 0.46 | ... | ... |

**Interim Dividends (Per Share)**

| Amt | Decl | Ex | Rec | Pay |
|---|---|---|---|---|
| 0.177Q | 10/21/2010 | 12/13/2010 | 12/15/2010 | 12/31/2010 |
| 0.20Q | 02/07/2011 | 03/11/2011 | 03/15/2011 | 03/31/2011 |
| 0.20Q | 04/28/2011 | 06/13/2011 | 06/15/2011 | 06/30/2011 |
| 0.20Q | 07/21/2011 | 09/13/2011 | 09/15/2011 | 09/30/2011 |

**Indicated Div: $0.80 (Div. Reinv. Plan)**

**Valuation Analysis**

| | | | |
|---|---|---|---|
| Forecast EPS | $1.97 (09/05/2011) | | |
| Market Cap | $1.9 Billion | Book Value | $895.8 Million |
| Price/Book | 2.10 | Price/Sales | 0.22 |

**Dividend Achiever Status**

| | |
|---|---|
| **10 Year Growth Rate** | 14.57% |
| **Total Years of Dividend Growth** | 13 |

**Business Summary:** Pharmaceuticals (MIC: 4.1.1 SIC: 5047 NAIC: 423450)

Owens & Minor is engaged in providing distribution, third-party logistics, and other supply-chain management services to healthcare providers and suppliers of medical and surgical products, and is a distributor of medical and surgical supplies to the acute-care market. Co.'s service consists of the distribution of finished medical and surgical products procured from suppliers to healthcare providers from distribution and service centers nationwide. Co. also performs distribution and inventory management services from facilities that are owned by customers. Co. also provides third-party logistics services for the manufacturers and suppliers of healthcare and life-science products.

**Recent Developments:** For the quarter ended June 30 2011, net income decreased 1.0% to US$29.2 million from US$29.5 million in the year-earlier quarter. Revenues were US$2.13 billion, up 5.5% from US$2.02 billion the year before. Operating income was US$51.0 million versus US$52.2 million in the prior-year quarter, a decrease of 2.2%. Direct operating expenses rose 5.2% to US$1.92 billion from US$1.82 billion in the comparable period the year before. Indirect operating expenses increased 12.4% to US$165.0 million from US$146.8 million in the equivalent prior-year period.

**Prospects:** Our evaluation of Owens & Minor Inc. as of Sep. 6, 2011 is the result of our systematic analysis on three basic characteristics: earnings strength, relative valuation, and recent stock price movement. The company has managed to produce a neutral trend in earnings per share over the past 5 quarters and while recent estimates for the company have remained steady, OMI has posted results that fell short of analysts expectations. Based on operating earnings yield, the company is undervalued when compared to all of the companies in our coverage universe. Share price changes over the past year indicates that OMI will perform poorly over the near term.

**Financial Data**

| (US$ in Thousands) | 6 Mos | 3 Mos | 12/31/2010 | 12/31/2009 | 12/31/2008 | 12/31/2007 | 12/31/2006 | 12/31/2005 |
|---|---|---|---|---|---|---|---|---|
| Earnings Per Share | 1.76 | 1.76 | 1.75 | 1.67 | 1.50 | 1.19 | 0.80 | 1.07 |
| Cash Flow Per Share | 0.43 | 2.50 | 3.92 | 2.68 | 1.02 | 3.64 | (1.23) | 2.28 |
| Tang Book Value Per Share | 9.80 | 9.56 | 9.23 | 7.86 | 6.58 | 5.06 | 3.89 | 4.19 |
| Dividends Per Share | 0.754 | 0.731 | 0.708 | 0.613 | 0.533 | 0.453 | 0.400 | 0.347 |
| Dividend Payout % | 42.84 | 41.53 | 40.44 | 36.80 | 35.56 | 37.99 | 50.00 | 32.30 |
| **Income Statement** | | | | | | | | |
| Total Revenue | 4,255,263 | 2,123,815 | 8,123,608 | 8,037,624 | 7,243,237 | 6,800,466 | 5,533,736 | 4,822,414 |
| EBITDA | 119,052 | 59,764 | 216,936 | 219,875 | 196,725 | 168,913 | 111,153 | 128,932 |
| Depn & Amortn | 17,016 | 8,767 | 21,000 | 18,600 | 16,000 | 25,700 | 19,800 | 11,500 |
| Income Before Taxes | 95,299 | 47,280 | 181,613 | 188,247 | 164,726 | 120,230 | 78,080 | 105,574 |
| Income Taxes | 37,395 | 18,540 | 71,034 | 71,388 | 63,469 | 47,520 | 29,328 | 41,154 |
| Net Income | 57,904 | 28,740 | 110,579 | 104,658 | 93,327 | 72,710 | 48,752 | 64,420 |
| Average Shares | 63,198 | 62,861 | 62,563 | 62,083 | 62,244 | 60,984 | 60,700 | 60,084 |
| **Balance Sheet** | | | | | | | | |
| Current Assets | 1,485,916 | 1,493,234 | 1,403,789 | 1,342,067 | 1,311,794 | 1,089,857 | 1,266,770 | 894,552 |
| Total Assets | 1,905,870 | 1,911,180 | 1,822,039 | 1,747,088 | 1,776,190 | 1,515,080 | 1,685,750 | 1,239,850 |
| Current Liabilities | 733,033 | 760,836 | 694,481 | 700,116 | 667,511 | 568,464 | 670,503 | 488,868 |
| Long-Term Obligations | 212,137 | 209,007 | 209,096 | 208,418 | 359,237 | 283,845 | 433,133 | 204,418 |
| Total Liabilities | 1,010,091 | 1,030,494 | 964,521 | 977,909 | 1,087,139 | 900,721 | 1,138,296 | 727,852 |
| Stockholders' Equity | 895,779 | 880,686 | 857,518 | 769,179 | 689,051 | 614,359 | 547,454 | 511,998 |
| Shares Outstanding | 63,769 | 63,713 | 63,433 | 62,869 | 62,161 | 61,311 | 60,385 | 59,835 |
| **Statistical Record** | | | | | | | | |
| Return on Assets % | 5.99 | 6.09 | 6.20 | 5.94 | 5.66 | 4.54 | 3.33 | 5.43 |
| Return on Equity % | 13.00 | 13.33 | 13.60 | 14.35 | 14.28 | 12.52 | 9.20 | 13.25 |
| EBITDA Margin % | 2.80 | 2.81 | 2.67 | 2.74 | 2.72 | 2.48 | 2.01 | 2.67 |
| Net Margin % | 1.36 | 1.35 | 1.36 | 1.30 | 1.29 | 1.07 | 0.88 | 1.34 |
| Asset Turnover | 4.52 | 4.52 | 4.55 | 4.56 | 4.39 | 4.25 | 3.78 | 4.07 |
| Current Ratio | 2.03 | 1.96 | 2.02 | 1.92 | 1.97 | 1.92 | 1.89 | 1.83 |
| Debt to Equity | 0.24 | 0.24 | 0.24 | 0.27 | 0.52 | 0.46 | 0.79 | 0.40 |
| Price Range | 35.20-26.02 | 32.60-26.02 | 32.60-26.02 | 31.85-20.52 | 32.97-23.97 | 29.18-20.27 | 23.15-18.64 | 22.19-17.57 |
| P/E Ratio | 20.00-14.78 | 18.52-14.78 | 18.63-14.87 | 19.07-12.29 | 21.98-15.98 | 24.52-17.03 | 28.93-23.30 | 20.74-16.42 |
| Average Yield % | 2.51 | 2.50 | 2.45 | 2.31 | 1.84 | 1.84 | 1.93 | 1.79 |

**Address:** 9120 Lockwood Boulevard, Mechanicsville, VA 23116
**Telephone:** 804-723-7000
**Web Site:** www.owens-minor.com

**Officers:** G. Gilmer Minor - Chairman Craig R. Smith - President, Chief Executive Officer **Transfer Agents:** BNY Mellon Shareowner Services, Pittsburgh, PA

**Investor Contact:** 804-747-9794
**No of Institutions:** 290
**Shares:** 64,463,328 **% Held:** 95.14

# PARKER HANNIFIN CORP.

| Exchange | Symbol | Price | 52Wk Range | Yield | P/E |
|---|---|---|---|---|---|
| NYS | PH | $73.43 (8/31/2011) | 98.49-59.16 | 2.02 | 11.53 |

*7 Year Price Score 140.68 *NYSE Composite Index=100 *12 Month Price Score 93.96

**Interim Earnings (Per Share)**

| Qtr. | Sep | Dec | Mar | Jun |
|---|---|---|---|---|
| 2006-07 | 1.17 | 1.09 | 1.19 | 1.23 |
| 2007-08 | 1.33 | 1.23 | 1.49 | 1.48 |
| 2008-09 | 1.50 | 0.96 | 0.33 | 0.32 |
| 2009-10 | 0.45 | 0.64 | 0.94 | 1.36 |
| 2010-11 | 1.51 | 1.39 | 1.68 | 1.79 |

**Interim Dividends (Per Share)**

| Amt | Decl | Ex | Rec | Pay |
|---|---|---|---|---|
| 0.29Q | 10/28/2010 | 11/08/2010 | 11/10/2010 | 12/03/2010 |
| 0.32Q | 01/27/2011 | 02/08/2011 | 02/10/2011 | 03/04/2011 |
| 0.37Q | 04/27/2011 | 05/06/2011 | 05/10/2011 | 06/03/2011 |
| 0.37Q | 08/18/2011 | 08/25/2011 | 08/29/2011 | 09/09/2011 |

**Indicated Div: $1.48 (Div. Reinv. Plan)**

**Valuation Analysis**

| | | | |
|---|---|---|---|
| Forecast EPS | $7.25 (09/05/2011) | | |
| Market Cap | $11.4 Billion | Book Value | $5.4 Billion |
| Price/Book | 2.12 | Price/Sales | 0.92 |

**Dividend Achiever Status**

| | |
|---|---|
| **10 Year Growth Rate** | 8.35% |
| **Total Years of Dividend Growth** | 54 |

**Business Summary:** Industrial Machinery & Equipment (MIC: 7.2.1 SIC: 3491 NAIC: 332911)

Parker-Hannifin is a manufacturer of motion and control technologies and systems, including fluid power systems, electromechanical controls and related components. Co. is also a producer of fluid purification, fluid and fuel control, process instrumentation, air conditioning, refrigeration, electromagnetic shielding as well as thermal management products and systems. Co.'s motion control technology is used in the products of its three key business segments: Industrial; Aerospace; and Climate & Industrial Controls. The products are sold as original and replacement equipment, and are marketed through direct-sales employees, independent distributors, sales representatives and builder/dealers.

**Recent Developments:** For the year ended June 30 2011, net income increased 90.0% to US$1.06 billion from US$556.4 million in the prior year. Revenues were US$12.35 billion, up 23.5% from US$9.99 billion the year before. Direct operating expenses rose 19.6% to US$9.39 billion from US$7.85 billion in the comparable period the year before. Indirect operating expenses increased 14.9% to US$1.47 billion from US$1.28 billion in the equivalent prior-year period.

**Prospects:** Our evaluation of Parker Hannifin Corp. as of Sep. 6, 2011 is the result of our systematic analysis on three basic characteristics: earnings strength, relative valuation, and recent stock price movement. The company has generated a negative trend in earnings per share over the past 5 quarters. However, while recent estimates for the company have been lowered by analysts, PH has posted results that fell short of analysts expectations. Based on operating earnings yield, the company is undervalued when compared to all of the companies in our coverage universe. Share price changes over the past year indicates that PH will perform poorly over the near term.

**Financial Data**

| (US$ in Thousands) | 06/30/2011 | 06/30/2010 | 06/30/2009 | 06/30/2008 | 06/30/2007 | 06/30/2006 | 06/30/2005 | 06/30/2004 |
|---|---|---|---|---|---|---|---|---|
| Earnings Per Share | 6.37 | 3.40 | 3.13 | 5.53 | 4.67 | 3.71 | 3.35 | 1.94 |
| Cash Flow Per Share | 7.24 | 7.57 | 6.99 | 7.80 | 5.47 | 5.34 | 4.89 | 3.74 |
| Tang Book Value Per Share | 7.72 | 2.68 | 0.64 | 8.59 | 10.69 | 9.75 | 9.23 | 9.38 |
| Dividends Per Share | 1.250 | 1.010 | 1.000 | 0.840 | 0.693 | 0.613 | 0.520 | 0.507 |
| Dividend Payout % | 19.62 | 29.71 | 31.95 | 15.19 | 14.84 | 16.52 | 15.54 | 26.12 |
| **Income Statement** | | | | | | | | |
| Total Revenue | 12,345,870 | 9,993,166 | 10,309,015 | 12,145,605 | 10,718,059 | 9,385,888 | 8,215,095 | 7,106,907 |
| EBITDA | 1,742,663 | 1,103,711 | 1,046,124 | 1,683,090 | 1,487,754 | 1,221,402 | 1,070,718 | 807,885 |
| Depn & Amortn | 229,238 | 245,295 | 252,599 | 257,570 | 245,058 | 245,681 | 247,215 | 242,191 |
| Income Before Taxes | 1,413,721 | 754,817 | 681,454 | 1,326,524 | 1,159,282 | 899,958 | 756,473 | 494,068 |
| Income Taxes | 356,571 | 198,452 | 172,939 | 377,058 | 329,236 | 261,682 | 208,500 | 148,285 |
| Net Income | 1,057,150 | 556,365 | 508,515 | 949,466 | 830,046 | 673,167 | 604,692 | 345,783 |
| Average Shares | 164,798 | 162,901 | 162,719 | 171,643 | 177,494 | 181,326 | 180,673 | 178,509 |
| **Balance Sheet** | | | | | | | | |
| Current Assets | 4,305,256 | 3,588,796 | 3,123,781 | 4,095,625 | 3,386,175 | 3,138,978 | 2,785,872 | 2,536,933 |
| Total Assets | 10,886,805 | 9,910,382 | 9,855,902 | 10,386,854 | 8,441,413 | 8,173,432 | 6,898,961 | 6,256,904 |
| Current Liabilities | 2,391,043 | 2,204,891 | 2,005,754 | 2,183,256 | 1,925,245 | 1,681,105 | 1,335,927 | 1,259,741 |
| Long-Term Obligations | 1,691,086 | 1,413,634 | 1,839,705 | 1,952,452 | 1,089,916 | 1,059,461 | 938,424 | 953,804 |
| Total Liabilities | 5,502,951 | 5,542,417 | 5,576,277 | 5,127,883 | 3,729,748 | 3,932,229 | 3,558,814 | 3,274,450 |
| Stockholders' Equity | 5,383,854 | 4,367,965 | 4,279,625 | 5,258,971 | 4,711,665 | 4,241,203 | 3,340,147 | 2,982,454 |
| Shares Outstanding | 155,090 | 161,256 | 160,488 | 167,715 | 174,238 | 180,472 | 179,540 | 179,225 |
| **Statistical Record** | | | | | | | | |
| Return on Assets % | 10.17 | 5.63 | 5.02 | 10.06 | 9.99 | 8.93 | 9.19 | 5.63 |
| Return on Equity % | 21.68 | 12.87 | 10.66 | 18.99 | 18.54 | 17.76 | 19.13 | 12.53 |
| EBITDA Margin % | 14.12 | 11.04 | 10.15 | 13.86 | 13.88 | 13.01 | 13.03 | 11.37 |
| Net Margin % | 8.56 | 5.57 | 4.93 | 7.82 | 7.74 | 7.17 | 7.36 | 4.87 |
| Asset Turnover | 1.19 | 1.01 | 1.02 | 1.29 | 1.29 | 1.25 | 1.25 | 1.16 |
| Current Ratio | 1.80 | 1.63 | 1.56 | 1.88 | 1.76 | 1.87 | 2.09 | 2.01 |
| Debt to Equity | 0.31 | 0.32 | 0.43 | 0.37 | 0.23 | 0.25 | 0.28 | 0.32 |
| Price Range | 98.49-54.80 | 71.23-39.98 | 72.33-27.86 | 86.15-60.32 | 68.39-46.50 | 57.34-40.53 | 51.87-35.71 | 40.61-27.81 |
| P/E Ratio | 15.46-8.60 | 20.95-11.76 | 23.11-8.90 | 15.58-10.91 | 14.65-9.96 | 15.46-10.93 | 15.48-10.66 | 20.93-14.33 |
| Average Yield % | 1.56 | 1.79 | 2.19 | 1.15 | 1.25 | 1.28 | 1.22 | 1.43 |

**Address:** 6035 Parkland Boulevard, Cleveland, OH 44124-4141
**Telephone:** 216-896-3000
**Web Site:** www.parker.com

**Officers:** Donald E. Washkewicz - Chairman, President, Chief Executive Officer Jon P. Marten - Executive Vice President, Chief Financial Officer, Controller, Principal Accounting Officer, Principal Financial Officer **Transfer Agents:**
Wells Fargo Shareowner Services, St. Paul, MN

**Investor Contact:** 216-896-2240
**No of Institutions:** 681
**Shares:** 131,346,944 % **Held:** 76.47

# PENTAIR, INC.

| Exchange | Symbol | Price | 52Wk Range | Yield | P/E |
|---|---|---|---|---|---|
| NYS | PNR | $34.32 (8/31/2011) | 42.25-30.08 | 2.33 | 15.60 |

*7 Year Price Score 105.10 *NYSE Composite Index=100 *12 Month Price Score 101.53

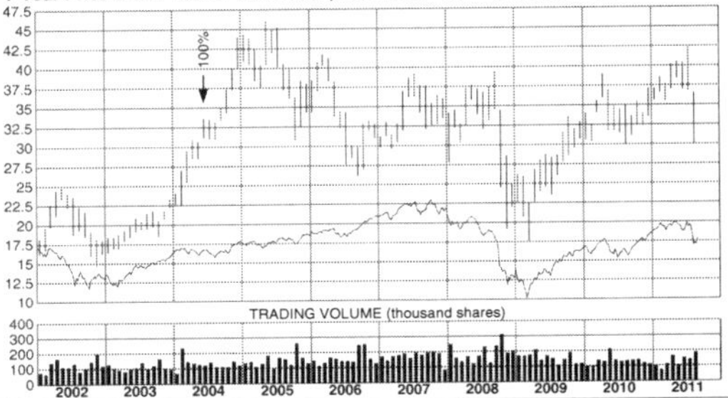


**Interim Earnings (Per Share)**

| Qtr. | Mar | Jun | Sep | Dec |
|---|---|---|---|---|
| 2008 | 0.45 | 1.39 | 0.42 | 0.05 |
| 2009 | 0.18 | 0.33 | 0.38 | 0.29 |
| 2010 | 0.36 | 0.61 | 0.55 | 0.47 |
| 2011 | 0.51 | 0.67 | ... | ... |

**Interim Dividends (Per Share)**

| Amt | Decl | Ex | Rec | Pay |
|---|---|---|---|---|
| 0.19Q | 10/14/2010 | 10/27/2010 | 10/29/2010 | 11/12/2010 |
| 0.20Q | 01/13/2011 | 01/26/2011 | 01/28/2011 | 02/11/2011 |
| 0.20Q | 04/14/2011 | 04/27/2011 | 04/29/2011 | 05/13/2011 |
| 0.20Q | 07/14/2011 | 07/27/2011 | 07/29/2011 | 08/12/2011 |

**Indicated Div: $0.80 (Div. Reinv. Plan)**

**Valuation Analysis**

| | | | |
|---|---|---|---|
| Forecast EPS | $2.46 (09/05/2011) | | |
| Market Cap | $3.4 Billion | Book Value | $2.2 Billion |
| Price/Book | 1.51 | Price/Sales | 1.05 |

**Dividend Achiever Status**

| | |
|---|---|
| **10 Year Growth Rate** | 8.06% |
| **Total Years of Dividend Growth** | 34 |

**Business Summary:** Industrial Machinery & Equipment (MIC: 7.2.1 SIC: 3559 NAIC: 333298)

Pentair is an industrial manufacturing company. Co. is comprised of two operating segments: Water, and Technical Products. Co.'s Water segment manufactures and markets products and systems used in the movement, storage, treatment and enjoyment of water, with products including water and wastewater pumps, filtration and purification components and systems, storage tanks and pressure vessels; and pool and spa equipment and accessories. Co.'s Technical Products segment designs, manufactures and markets standard, modified and custom enclosures that include metallic and composite enclosures, cabinets, cases, subracks, backplanes and associated thermal management systems.

**Recent Developments:** For the quarter ended July 2 2011, income from continuing operations increased 10.6% to US$68.1 million from US$61.6 million in the year-earlier quarter. Net income increased 9.5% to US$68.1 million from US$62.2 million in the year-earlier quarter. Revenues were US$910.2 million, up 14.3% from US$796.2 million the year before. Operating income was US$109.4 million versus US$100.1 million in the prior-year quarter, an increase of 9.3%. Direct operating expenses rose 13.6% to US$622.4 million from US$548.0 million in the comparable period the year before. Indirect operating expenses increased 20.4% to US$178.3 million from US$148.0 million in the equivalent prior-year period.

**Prospects:** Our evaluation of Pentair Inc. as of Sep. 6, 2011 is the result of our systematic analysis on three basic characteristics: earnings strength, relative valuation, and recent stock price movement. The company has managed to produce a neutral trend in earnings per share over the past 5 quarters. However, while recent estimates for the company have been mixed, PNR has posted better than expected results. Based on operating earnings yield, the company is undervalued when compared to all of the companies in our coverage universe. Share price changes over the past year indicates that PNR will perform in line with the market over the near term.

| **Financial Data** (US$ in Thousands) | 6 Mos | 3 Mos | 12/31/2010 | 12/31/2009 | 12/31/2008 | 12/31/2007 | 12/31/2006 | 12/31/2005 |
|---|---|---|---|---|---|---|---|---|
| Earnings Per Share | 2.20 | 2.14 | 1.99 | 1.17 | 2.31 | 2.10 | 1.81 | 1.80 |
| Cash Flow Per Share | 2.71 | 2.37 | 2.76 | 2.65 | 2.08 | 3.46 | 2.32 | 2.46 |
| Dividends Per Share | 0.780 | 0.770 | 0.760 | 0.720 | 0.680 | 0.600 | 0.560 | 0.522 |
| Dividend Payout % | 35.45 | 35.98 | 38.19 | 61.54 | 29.44 | 28.57 | 30.94 | 29.03 |
| **Income Statement** | | | | | | | | |
| Total Revenue | 1,700,448 | 790,273 | 3,030,773 | 2,692,468 | 3,351,976 | 3,398,698 | 3,154,469 | 2,946,579 |
| EBITDA | 245,464 | 107,802 | 392,150 | 279,967 | 489,289 | 435,693 | 364,249 | 385,072 |
| Depn & Amortn | 49,865 | 21,625 | 57,995 | 64,823 | 59,673 | 58,948 | 56,899 | 56,565 |
| Income Before Taxes | 171,661 | 76,852 | 298,039 | 174,026 | 370,181 | 306,508 | 255,469 | 283,518 |
| Income Taxes | 52,397 | 25,053 | 97,200 | 56,428 | 108,344 | 93,154 | 71,702 | 98,469 |
| Net Income | 117,253 | 50,541 | 197,828 | 115,493 | 228,734 | 210,927 | 183,731 | 185,049 |
| Average Shares | 100,065 | 99,670 | 99,294 | 98,522 | 99,068 | 100,205 | 101,371 | 102,618 |
| **Balance Sheet** | | | | | | | | |
| Current Assets | 1,334,639 | 1,209,077 | 1,069,297 | 946,298 | 1,032,179 | 1,038,021 | 957,628 | 895,024 |
| Total Assets | 5,052,312 | 4,162,687 | 3,973,533 | 3,911,334 | 4,053,213 | 4,000,614 | 3,364,979 | 3,253,755 |
| Current Liabilities | 711,402 | 546,361 | 546,796 | 446,279 | 498,504 | 560,906 | 521,282 | 524,670 |
| Long-Term Obligations | 1,384,167 | 802,321 | 702,521 | 803,351 | 953,468 | 1,042,223 | 721,873 | 748,477 |
| Total Liabilities | 2,802,958 | 1,995,527 | 1,880,380 | 1,899,246 | 2,154,532 | 2,089,743 | 1,694,980 | 1,698,145 |
| Stockholders' Equity | 2,249,354 | 2,167,160 | 2,093,153 | 2,012,088 | 1,898,681 | 1,910,871 | 1,669,999 | 1,555,610 |
| Shares Outstanding | 98,766 | 98,419 | 98,409 | 98,655 | 98,276 | 99,221 | 99,777 | 101,202 |
| **Statistical Record** | | | | | | | | |
| Return on Assets % | 4.91 | 5.23 | 5.02 | 2.90 | 5.66 | 5.73 | 5.55 | 5.81 |
| Return on Equity % | 10.34 | 10.23 | 9.64 | 5.91 | 11.98 | 11.78 | 11.39 | 12.32 |
| EBITDA Margin % | 14.44 | 13.64 | 12.94 | 10.40 | 14.60 | 12.82 | 11.55 | 13.07 |
| Net Margin % | 6.90 | 6.40 | 6.53 | 4.29 | 6.82 | 6.21 | 5.82 | 6.28 |
| Asset Turnover | 0.72 | 0.76 | 0.77 | 0.68 | 0.83 | 0.92 | 0.95 | 0.92 |
| Current Ratio | 1.88 | 2.21 | 1.96 | 2.12 | 2.07 | 1.85 | 1.84 | 1.71 |
| Debt to Equity | 0.62 | 0.37 | 0.34 | 0.40 | 0.50 | 0.55 | 0.43 | 0.48 |
| Price Range | 41.27-29.96 | 38.98-29.96 | 38.98-29.96 | 33.63-17.60 | 39.47-19.14 | 39.21-29.50 | 41.69-26.13 | 46.03-30.80 |
| P/E Ratio | 18.76-13.62 | 18.21-14.00 | 19.59-15.06 | 28.74-15.04 | 17.09-8.29 | 18.67-14.05 | 23.03-14.44 | 25.57-17.11 |
| Average Yield % | 2.19 | 2.22 | 2.26 | 2.68 | 2.11 | 1.77 | 1.65 | 1.32 |

**Address:** 5500 Wayzata Boulevard, Suite 800, Golden Valley, MN 55416-1261
**Telephone:** 763-545-1730
**Web Site:** www.pentair.com

**Officers:** Randall J. Hogan - Chairman, Chief Executive Officer Michael V. Schrock - President, Chief Operating Officer **Transfer Agents:** Wells Fargo Bank, N.A., St. Paul, MN

**Investor Contact:** 651-639-5278
**No of Institutions:** 328
**Shares:** 84,413,040 **% Held:** 82.35

# PEOPLE'S UNITED FINANCIAL, INC.

| Exchange | Symbol | Price | 52Wk Range | Yield | P/E |
|---|---|---|---|---|---|
| NMS | PBCT | $11.75 (8/31/2011) | 14.42-10.56 | 5.36 | 25.54 |

***7 Year Price Score N/A** *NYSE Composite Index=100 ***12 Month Price Score 96.48**

**Interim Earnings (Per Share)**

| Qtr. | Mar | Jun | Sep | Dec |
|---|---|---|---|---|
| 2008 | 0.05 | 0.13 | 0.14 | 0.10 |
| 2009 | 0.08 | 0.08 | 0.08 | 0.07 |
| 2010 | 0.04 | 0.04 | 0.07 | 0.09 |
| 2011 | 0.15 | 0.15 | ... | ... |

**Interim Dividends (Per Share)**

| Amt | Decl | Ex | Rec | Pay |
|---|---|---|---|---|
| 0.155Q | 10/21/2010 | 10/28/2010 | 11/01/2010 | 11/15/2010 |
| 0.155Q | 01/20/2011 | 01/28/2011 | 02/01/2011 | 02/15/2011 |
| 0.158Q | 04/20/2011 | 04/27/2011 | 05/01/2011 | 05/15/2011 |
| 0.158Q | 07/21/2011 | 07/28/2011 | 08/01/2011 | 08/15/2011 |

**Indicated Div: $0.63 (Div. Reinv. Plan)**

**Valuation Analysis**

| | | | |
|---|---|---|---|
| Forecast EPS | $0.66 (09/02/2011) | | |
| Market Cap | $4.2 Billion | Book Value | $5.2 Billion |
| Price/Book | 0.80 | Price/Sales | N/A |

**Dividend Achiever Status**

| | |
|---|---|
| **10 Year Growth Rate** | 0.36% |
| **Total Years of Dividend Growth** | 17 |

**Business Summary:** Credit & Lending (MIC: 5.4.1 SIC: 6035 NAIC: 522120)

People's United Financial is a savings and loan holding company. Through People's United Bank and subsidiaries, Co. provides commercial banking, retail and small business banking, and wealth management services to individual, corporate and municipal customers. Co.'s banking activities include originating commercial and consumer loans, mortgage loans, and accepting consumer, commercial and municipal deposits. Through its non-banking subsidiaries, Co. provides brokerage, financial advisory services, investment management services and life insurance; equipment financing; and other insurance services. At Dec 31 2010, Co. had total assets of $25.04 billion and total deposits of $17.93 billion.

**Recent Developments:** For the quarter ended June 30 2011, net income increased 220.0% to US$51.2 million from US$16.0 million in the year-earlier quarter. Net interest income increased 27.3% to US$221.2 million from US$173.8 million in the year-earlier quarter. Provision for loan losses was US$14.0 million versus US$17.8 million in the prior-year quarter, a decrease of 21.3%. Non-interest income rose 9.9% to US$76.6 million from US$69.7 million, while non-interest expense advanced 2.1% to US$207.0 million.

**Prospects:** Our evaluation of People's United Financial Inc. as of Sep. 6, 2011 is the result of our systematic analysis on three basic characteristics: earnings strength, relative valuation, and recent stock price movement. The company has enjoyed a very positive trend in earnings per share over the past 5 quarters and while recent estimates for the company have been mixed, PBCT has posted better than expected results. Based on operating earnings yield, the company is about fairly valued when compared to all of the companies in our coverage universe. Share price changes over the past year indicates that PBCT will perform poorly over the near term.

**Financial Data**

| (US$ in Thousands) | 6 Mos | 3 Mos | 12/31/2010 | 12/31/2009 | 12/31/2008 | 12/31/2007 | 12/31/2006 | 12/31/2005 |
|---|---|---|---|---|---|---|---|---|
| Earnings Per Share | 0.46 | 0.35 | 0.24 | 0.30 | 0.42 | 0.52 | 0.87 | 0.97 |
| Cash Flow Per Share | 0.36 | 0.42 | 0.65 | 0.31 | 0.72 | 0.62 | 0.42 | 0.66 |
| Tang Book Value Per Share | 9.15 | 9.04 | 9.07 | 10.39 | 10.56 | 14.55 | 8.68 | 8.35 |
| Dividends Per Share | 0.623 | 0.620 | 0.618 | 0.608 | 0.583 | 0.397 | 0.970 | 0.850 |
| Dividend Payout % | 135.33 | 177.14 | 257.29 | 202.50 | 138.88 | 76.27 | 111.49 | 87.63 |
| **Income Statement** | | | | | | | | |
| Interest Income | 505,600 | 252,800 | 828,800 | 766,800 | 917,200 | 707,000 | 582,100 | 507,900 |
| Interest Expense | 64,100 | 32,500 | 129,800 | 190,000 | 280,800 | 220,400 | 199,700 | 138,200 |
| Net Interest Income | 441,500 | 220,300 | 699,000 | 576,800 | 636,400 | 486,600 | 382,400 | 369,700 |
| Provision for Losses | 28,600 | 14,600 | 60,000 | 57,000 | 26,200 | 8,000 | 3,400 | 8,600 |
| Non-Interest Income | 151,200 | 74,600 | 299,200 | 309,100 | 303,600 | 185,400 | 147,400 | 171,800 |
| Non-Interest Expense | 409,800 | 202,800 | 811,200 | 684,600 | 706,300 | 439,300 | 346,900 | 342,900 |
| Income Before Taxes | 154,300 | 77,500 | 127,000 | 144,300 | 207,500 | 224,700 | 179,500 | 190,000 |
| Income Taxes | 51,400 | 25,800 | 41,300 | 43,100 | 68,000 | 75,500 | 57,800 | 64,100 |
| Net Income | 102,900 | 51,700 | 85,700 | 101,200 | 139,500 | 150,700 | 124,000 | 137,100 |
| Average Shares | 343,900 | 346,000 | 352,600 | 332,300 | 330,700 | 292,300 | 142,200 | 141,700 |
| **Balance Sheet** | | | | | | | | |
| Net Loans & Leases | 17,511,000 | 17,345,600 | 17,345,700 | 14,061,300 | 14,408,200 | 8,877,000 | 9,297,700 | 8,497,900 |
| Total Assets | 25,322,500 | 24,962,300 | 25,037,100 | 21,257,200 | 20,167,700 | 13,554,800 | 10,686,900 | 10,932,500 |
| Total Deposits | 18,278,300 | 18,110,100 | 17,933,100 | 15,445,600 | 14,269,400 | 8,880,600 | 9,082,600 | 9,082,600 |
| Total Liabilities | 20,128,600 | 19,802,000 | 19,817,800 | 16,156,500 | 14,992,200 | 9,109,400 | 9,347,400 | 9,643,900 |
| Stockholders' Equity | 5,193,900 | 5,160,300 | 5,219,300 | 5,100,700 | 5,175,500 | 4,445,400 | 1,339,500 | 1,288,600 |
| Shares Outstanding | 355,000 | 355,000 | 359,100 | 345,000 | 344,700 | 298,300 | 142,200 | 141,600 |
| **Statistical Record** | | | | | | | | |
| Return on Assets % | 0.67 | 0.53 | 0.37 | 0.49 | 0.83 | 1.24 | 1.15 | 1.27 |
| Return on Equity % | 3.00 | 2.33 | 1.66 | 1.97 | 2.89 | 5.21 | 9.44 | 11.02 |
| Net Interest Margin % | 87.50 | 87.14 | 84.34 | 75.22 | 69.39 | 68.83 | 65.69 | 72.79 |
| Efficiency Ratio % | 62.84 | 61.94 | 71.91 | 63.63 | 57.86 | 49.23 | 47.55 | 50.45 |
| Loans to Deposits | 0.96 | 0.96 | 0.97 | 0.91 | 1.01 | 1.00 | 1.02 | 0.94 |
| Price Range | 14.42-12.20 | 16.65-12.20 | 17.00-12.23 | 18.29-14.94 | 21.75-14.58 | 20.85-14.99 | ... | ... |
| P/E Ratio | 31.35-26.52 | 47.57-34.86 | 70.83-50.96 | 60.97-49.80 | 51.79-34.71 | 40.10-28.83 | ... | ... |
| Average Yield % | 4.73 | 4.55 | 4.32 | 3.72 | 3.41 | 2.21 | ... | ... |

**Address:** 850 Main Street, Bridgeport, CT 06604
**Telephone:** 203-338-7171
**Web Site:** www.peoples.com

**Officers:** George P. Carter - Chairman John P. Barnes - President, Chief Executive Officer **Transfer Agents:** BNY Mellon Share Owner Services, Jersey City, NJ

**Investor Contact:** 203-338-4114
**No of Institutions:** 472
**Shares:** 261,615,232 **% Held:** 64.90

# PEPSICO INC.

| Exchange | Symbol | Price | 52Wk Range | Yield | P/E |
|---|---|---|---|---|---|
| NYS | PEP | $64.43 (8/31/2011) | 71.78-60.32 | 3.20 | 16.44 |

*7 Year Price Score 105.61 *NYSE Composite Index=100 *12 Month Price Score 99.18

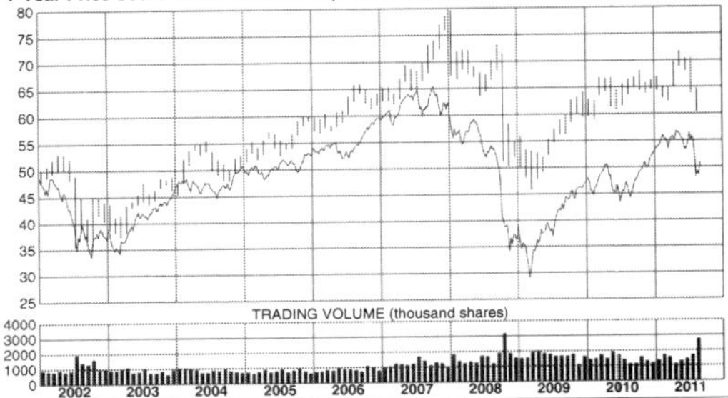


**Interim Earnings (Per Share)**

| Qtr. | Mar | Jun | Aug | Dec |
|---|---|---|---|---|
| 2008 | 0.70 | 1.05 | 0.99 | 0.47 |
| 2009 | 0.72 | 1.06 | 1.09 | 0.90 |
| 2010 | 0.89 | 0.98 | 1.19 | 0.85 |
| 2011 | 0.71 | 1.17 | ... | ... |

**Interim Dividends (Per Share)**

| Amt | Decl | Ex | Rec | Pay |
|---|---|---|---|---|
| 0.48Q | 11/12/2010 | 12/01/2010 | 12/03/2010 | 01/03/2011 |
| 0.48Q | 02/04/2011 | 03/02/2011 | 03/04/2011 | 03/31/2011 |
| 0.515Q | 05/04/2011 | 06/01/2011 | 06/03/2011 | 06/30/2011 |
| 0.515Q | 07/15/2011 | 08/31/2011 | 09/02/2011 | 09/30/2011 |

**Indicated Div: $2.06 (Div. Reinv. Plan)**

**Valuation Analysis**

| | | | |
|---|---|---|---|
| Forecast EPS | $4.45 (09/05/2011) | | |
| Market Cap | $102.1 Billion | Book Value | $24.0 Billion |
| Price/Book | 4.26 | Price/Sales | 1.63 |

**Dividend Achiever Status**

| | |
|---|---|
| 10 Year Growth Rate | 12.55% |
| Total Years of Dividend Growth | 39 |

**Business Summary:** Beverages (MIC: 1.2.2 SIC: 2086 NAIC: 312111)

PepsiCo is a food, snack, and beverage company. Co. is organized into four business units: PepsiCo Americas Foods, which includes Frito-Lay North America, Quaker Foods North America, Quaker Foods North America, and all of its Latin American food and snack businesses, including its Sabritas and Gamesa businesses in Mexico; PepsiCo Americas Beverages, which includes PepsiCo Beverages Americas and Pepsi Beverages Company; PepsiCo Europe, which includes all beverage, food and snack businesses in Europe; as well as PepsiCo Asia, Middle East and Africa, which includes all beverage, food and snack businesses in Asia, Middle East and Africa.

**Recent Developments:** For the quarter ended June 11 2011, net income increased 18.1% to US$1.91 billion from US$1.61 billion in the year-earlier quarter. Revenues were US$16.83 billion, up 13.7% from US$14.80 billion the year before. Operating income was US$2.75 billion versus US$2.46 billion in the prior-year quarter, an increase of 11.9%. Direct operating expenses rose 18.1% to US$7.96 billion from US$6.75 billion in the comparable period the year before. Indirect operating expenses increased 9.2% to US$6.11 billion from US$5.60 billion in the equivalent prior-year period.

**Prospects:** Our evaluation of PepsiCo Inc. as of Sep. 6, 2011 is the result of our systematic analysis on three basic characteristics: earnings strength, relative valuation, and recent stock price movement. The company has produced a positive trend in earnings per share over the past 5 quarters. However, while recent estimates for the company have been mixed, PEP has posted better than expected results. Based on operating earnings yield, the company is undervalued when compared to all of the companies in our coverage universe. Share price changes over the past year indicates that PEP will perform very poorly over the near term.

| Financial Data (US$ in Thousands) | 6 Mos | 3 Mos | 12/25/2010 | 12/26/2009 | 12/27/2008 | 12/29/2007 | 12/30/2006 | 12/31/2005 |
|---|---|---|---|---|---|---|---|---|
| Earnings Per Share | 3.92 | 3.73 | 3.91 | 3.77 | 3.21 | 3.41 | 3.34 | 2.39 |
| Cash Flow Per Share | 5.28 | 5.42 | 5.33 | 4.37 | 4.46 | 4.29 | 3.70 | 3.45 |
| Tang Book Value Per Share | N.M. | N.M. | N.M. | 4.86 | 3.30 | 6.24 | 5.45 | 5.16 |
| Dividends Per Share | 1.955 | 1.920 | 1.890 | 1.775 | 1.650 | 1.425 | 1.160 | 1.010 |
| Dividend Payout % | 49.87 | 51.47 | 48.34 | 47.08 | 51.40 | 41.79 | 34.73 | 42.26 |
| **Income Statement** | | | | | | | | |
| Total Revenue | 28,764,000 | 11,937,000 | 57,838,000 | 43,232,000 | 43,251,000 | 39,474,000 | 35,137,000 | 32,562,000 |
| EBITDA | 4,545,000 | 1,751,000 | 10,573,000 | 9,607,000 | 8,421,000 | 8,532,000 | 7,783,000 | 7,175,000 |
| Depn & Amortn | 65,000 | 25,000 | 2,241,000 | 1,563,000 | 1,486,000 | 1,362,000 | 1,344,000 | 1,253,000 |
| Income Before Taxes | 4,138,000 | 1,563,000 | 7,497,000 | 7,714,000 | 6,647,000 | 7,071,000 | 6,373,000 | 5,825,000 |
| Income Taxes | 1,089,000 | 419,000 | 1,894,000 | 2,100,000 | 1,879,000 | 1,973,000 | 1,347,000 | 2,304,000 |
| Net Income | 3,028,000 | 1,143,000 | 6,320,000 | 5,946,000 | 5,142,000 | 5,658,000 | 5,642,000 | 4,078,000 |
| Average Shares | 1,605,000 | 1,605,000 | 1,614,000 | 1,577,000 | 1,602,000 | 1,658,000 | 1,687,000 | 1,706,000 |
| **Balance Sheet** | | | | | | | | |
| Current Assets | 17,917,000 | 16,512,000 | 17,569,000 | 12,571,000 | 10,806,000 | 10,151,000 | 9,130,000 | 10,454,000 |
| Total Assets | 75,680,000 | 73,085,000 | 68,153,000 | 39,848,000 | 35,994,000 | 34,628,000 | 29,930,000 | 31,727,000 |
| Current Liabilities | 18,057,000 | 16,840,000 | 15,892,000 | 8,756,000 | 8,787,000 | 7,753,000 | 6,860,000 | 9,406,000 |
| Long-Term Obligations | 21,607,000 | 20,942,000 | 19,999,000 | 7,400,000 | 7,858,000 | 4,203,000 | 2,550,000 | 2,313,000 |
| Total Liabilities | 51,728,000 | 51,100,000 | 46,989,000 | 23,044,000 | 23,888,000 | 17,394,000 | 14,562,000 | 17,476,000 |
| Stockholders' Equity | 23,952,000 | 21,985,000 | 21,164,000 | 16,804,000 | 12,106,000 | 17,234,000 | 15,368,000 | 14,251,000 |
| Shares Outstanding | 1,584,000 | 1,581,000 | 1,581,000 | 1,565,000 | 1,553,000 | 1,605,000 | 1,638,000 | 1,656,000 |
| **Statistical Record** | | | | | | | | |
| Return on Assets % | 8.97 | 8.79 | 11.74 | 15.72 | 14.60 | 17.58 | 18.35 | 13.44 |
| Return on Equity % | 28.98 | 27.70 | 33.38 | 41.25 | 35.15 | 34.80 | 38.20 | 28.89 |
| EBITDA Margin % | 15.80 | 14.67 | 18.28 | 22.22 | 19.47 | 21.61 | 22.15 | 22.03 |
| Net Margin % | 10.53 | 9.58 | 10.93 | 13.75 | 11.89 | 14.33 | 16.06 | 12.52 |
| Asset Turnover | 0.89 | 0.88 | 1.07 | 1.14 | 1.23 | 1.23 | 1.14 | 1.07 |
| Current Ratio | 0.99 | 0.98 | 1.11 | 1.44 | 1.23 | 1.31 | 1.33 | 1.11 |
| Debt to Equity | 0.90 | 0.95 | 0.94 | 0.44 | 0.65 | 0.24 | 0.17 | 0.16 |
| Price Range | 71.78-60.77 | 68.11-60.77 | 68.11-58.96 | 64.23-45.81 | 79.57-50.29 | 78.69-62.16 | 65.91-56.77 | 59.90-51.57 |
| P/E Ratio | 18.31-15.50 | 18.26-16.29 | 17.42-15.08 | 17.04-12.15 | 24.79-15.67 | 23.08-18.23 | 19.73-17.00 | 25.06-21.58 |
| Average Yield % | 2.98 | 2.96 | 2.94 | 3.21 | 2.50 | 2.09 | 1.90 | 1.82 |

**Address:** 700 Anderson Hill Road, Purchase, NY 10577
**Telephone:** 914-253-2000
**Web Site:** www.pepsico.com

**Officers:** Indra K. Nooyi - Chairman, President, Chief Executive Officer Hugh F. Johnston - Executive Vice President, Chief Financial Officer **Transfer Agents:** BNY Mellon Shareowner Services, Pittsburgh, PA

**No of Institutions:** 1835
**Shares:** 1,194,440,960 **% Held:** 67.13

# PIEDMONT NATURAL GAS CO., INC.

| Exchange | Symbol | Price | 52Wk Range | Yield | P/E |
|---|---|---|---|---|---|
| NYS | PNY | $30.90 (8/31/2011) | 31.97-25.99 | 3.75 | 19.68 |

***7 Year Price Score 111.59** *NYSE Composite Index=100 ***12 Month Price Score 100.73**

**Interim Earnings (Per Share)**

| Qtr. | Jan | Apr | Jul | Oct |
|---|---|---|---|---|
| 2007-08 | 1.12 | 0.66 | (0.10) | (0.18) |
| 2008-09 | 1.10 | 0.73 | (0.10) | (0.06) |
| 2009-10 | 1.55 | 0.65 | (0.13) | (0.12) |
| 2010-11 | 1.16 | 0.66 | ... | ... |

**Interim Dividends (Per Share)**

| Amt | Decl | Ex | Rec | Pay |
|---|---|---|---|---|
| 0.28Q | 09/02/2010 | 09/20/2010 | 09/22/2010 | 10/15/2010 |
| 0.28Q | 12/16/2010 | 12/22/2010 | 12/27/2010 | 01/18/2011 |
| 0.29Q | 03/04/2011 | 03/23/2011 | 03/25/2011 | 04/15/2011 |
| 0.29Q | 06/03/2011 | 06/22/2011 | 06/24/2011 | 07/15/2011 |

**Indicated Div: $1.16 (Div. Reinv. Plan)**

**Valuation Analysis**

| | | | |
|---|---|---|---|
| Forecast EPS | $1.58 (09/02/2011) | | |
| Market Cap | $2.2 Billion | Book Value | $1.0 Billion |
| Price/Book | 2.12 | Price/Sales | 1.53 |

**Dividend Achiever Status**

| | |
|---|---|
| **10 Year Growth Rate** | 3.86% |
| **Total Years of Dividend Growth** | 31 |

**Business Summary:** Gas Utilities (MIC: 3.3.1 SIC: 4924 NAIC: 221210)

Piedmont Natural Gas Company has two business segments: regulated utility and non-utility activities. Through its regulated utility segment, Co. is engaged in the distribution of natural gas to residential, commercial, industrial and power generation customers in portions of North Carolina, South Carolina and Tennessee, including customers served by municipalities who are Co.'s wholesale customers. The non-utility activities segment consists of Co.'s equity method investments in joint venture, energy-related businesses that are involved in unregulated retail natural gas marketing, and regulated interstate natural gas storage and intrastate natural gas transportation.

**Recent Developments:** For the quarter ended Apr 30 2011, net income increased 1.2% to US$47.4 million from US$46.8 million in the year-earlier quarter. Revenues were US$392.6 million, down 17.0% from US$472.8 million the year before. Operating income was US$52.9 million versus US$52.2 million in the prior-year quarter, an increase of 1.3%. Direct operating expenses declined 27.8% to US$219.6 million from US$304.2 million in the comparable period the year before. Indirect operating expenses increased 3.0% to US$120.0 million from US$116.5 million in the equivalent prior-year period.

**Prospects:** Our evaluation of Piedmont Natural Gas Co. Inc. as of Sep. 6, 2011 is the result of our systematic analysis on three basic characteristics: earnings strength, relative valuation, and recent stock price movement. The company has produced a positive trend in earnings per share over the past 5 quarters. However, while recent estimates for the company have been mixed, PNY has posted results that fell short of analysts expectations. Based on operating earnings yield, the company is about fairly valued when compared to all of the companies in our coverage universe. Share price changes over the past year indicates that PNY will perform very poorly over the near term.

**Financial Data**

| (US$ in Thousands) | 6 Mos | 3 Mos | 10/31/2010 | 10/31/2009 | 10/31/2008 | 10/31/2007 | 10/31/2006 | 10/31/2005 |
|---|---|---|---|---|---|---|---|---|
| Earnings Per Share | 1.57 | 1.56 | 1.96 | 1.67 | 1.49 | 1.40 | 1.28 | 1.32 |
| Cash Flow Per Share | 3.96 | 4.58 | 4.99 | 4.71 | 0.94 | 3.14 | 1.37 | 2.39 |
| Tang Book Value Per Share | 13.87 | 13.47 | 12.67 | 12.00 | 11.45 | 11.18 | 11.07 | 10.91 |
| Dividends Per Share | 1.130 | 1.120 | 1.110 | 1.070 | 1.030 | 0.990 | 0.950 | 0.905 |
| Dividend Payout % | 71.97 | 71.79 | 56.63 | 64.07 | 69.13 | 70.71 | 74.22 | 68.56 |
| **Income Statement** | | | | | | | | |
| Total Revenue | 1,044,623 | 652,056 | 1,552,295 | 1,638,116 | 2,089,108 | 1,711,292 | 1,924,628 | 1,761,091 |
| EBITDA | 275,937 | 171,019 | 313,711 | 332,090 | 340,601 | 297,432 | 293,381 | 279,543 |
| Depn & Amortn | 50,287 | 24,954 | 98,494 | 97,425 | 93,121 | 88,654 | 89,696 | 85,169 |
| Income Before Taxes | 201,770 | 135,048 | 171,506 | 187,990 | 188,207 | 151,506 | 151,375 | 150,118 |
| Income Taxes | 85,781 | 54,887 | 91,876 | 81,882 | 73,492 | 65,626 | 62,430 | 62,326 |
| Net Income | 131,848 | 84,440 | 141,954 | 122,824 | 110,007 | 104,387 | 97,189 | 101,270 |
| Average Shares | 72,061 | 72,514 | 72,525 | 73,461 | 73,612 | 74,472 | 76,156 | 76,992 |
| **Balance Sheet** | | | | | | | | |
| Current Assets | 250,894 | 510,385 | 327,840 | 513,148 | 600,752 | 435,344 | 475,964 | 504,911 |
| Total Assets | 3,057,800 | 3,289,610 | 3,053,275 | 3,118,819 | 3,093,580 | 2,820,318 | 2,733,939 | 2,602,490 |
| Current Liabilities | 555,560 | 653,922 | 498,560 | 600,211 | 681,533 | 424,511 | 400,389 | 528,564 |
| Long-Term Obligations | 475,000 | 671,904 | 671,922 | 732,512 | 794,261 | 824,887 | 825,000 | 625,000 |
| Total Liabilities | 2,010,856 | 2,274,096 | 2,088,334 | 2,190,871 | 2,206,336 | 1,941,944 | 1,851,014 | 1,718,298 |
| Stockholders' Equity | 1,046,944 | 1,015,514 | 964,941 | 927,948 | 887,244 | 878,374 | 882,925 | 884,192 |
| Shares Outstanding | 71,961 | 71,766 | 72,282 | 73,266 | 73,246 | 74,208 | 75,464 | 76,698 |
| **Statistical Record** | | | | | | | | |
| Return on Assets % | 3.76 | 3.43 | 4.60 | 3.95 | 3.71 | 3.76 | 3.64 | 4.10 |
| Return on Equity % | 10.99 | 11.22 | 15.00 | 13.53 | 12.43 | 11.85 | 11.00 | 11.65 |
| EBITDA Margin % | 26.41 | 26.23 | 20.21 | 20.27 | 16.30 | 17.38 | 15.24 | 15.87 |
| Net Margin % | 12.62 | 12.95 | 9.14 | 7.50 | 5.27 | 6.10 | 5.05 | 5.75 |
| Asset Turnover | 0.48 | 0.47 | 0.50 | 0.53 | 0.70 | 0.62 | 0.72 | 0.71 |
| Current Ratio | 0.45 | 0.78 | 0.66 | 0.85 | 0.88 | 1.03 | 1.19 | 0.96 |
| Debt to Equity | 0.45 | 0.66 | 0.70 | 0.79 | 0.90 | 0.94 | 0.93 | 0.71 |
| Price Range | 31.75-24.77 | 30.00-24.20 | 29.70-22.74 | 33.76-21.25 | 33.24-24.32 | 28.28-23.19 | 27.27-22.09 | 25.47-21.93 |
| P/E Ratio | 20.22-15.78 | 19.23-15.51 | 15.15-11.60 | 20.22-12.72 | 22.31-16.32 | 20.20-16.56 | 21.30-17.26 | 19.30-16.61 |
| Average Yield % | 4.00 | 4.07 | 4.18 | 4.15 | 3.81 | 3.78 | 3.86 | 3.83 |

**Address:** 4720 Piedmont Row Drive, Charlotte, NC 28210
**Telephone:** 704-364-3120
**Web Site:** www.piedmontng.com

**Officers:** Thomas E. Skains - Chairman, President, Chief Executive Officer David J. Dzuricky - Senior Vice President, Chief Financial Officer **Transfer Agents:** American Stock Transfer & Trust Company, New York, NY

**No of Institutions:** 255
**Shares:** 37,334,592 **% Held:** 41.87

# PITNEY BOWES INC

| Exchange | Symbol | Price | 52Wk Range | Yield | P/E |
|---|---|---|---|---|---|
| NYS | PBI | $20.31 (8/31/2011) | 26.18-18.15 | 7.29 | 12.31 |

***7 Year Price Score 66.08** *NYSE Composite Index=100 ***12 Month Price Score 92.06**

**Interim Earnings (Per Share)**

| Qtr. | Mar | Jun | Sep | Dec |
|---|---|---|---|---|
| 2008 | 0.56 | 0.61 | 0.47 | 0.36 |
| 2009 | 0.50 | 0.57 | 0.50 | 0.47 |
| 2010 | 0.38 | 0.30 | 0.43 | 0.30 |
| 2011 | 0.42 | 0.50 | ... | ... |

**Interim Dividends (Per Share)**

| Amt | Decl | Ex | Rec | Pay |
|---|---|---|---|---|
| 0.365Q | 11/05/2010 | 11/17/2010 | 11/19/2010 | 12/12/2010 |
| 0.37Q | 02/08/2011 | 02/16/2011 | 02/18/2011 | 03/12/2011 |
| 0.37Q | 04/11/2011 | 05/11/2011 | 05/13/2011 | 06/12/2011 |
| 0.37Q | 07/11/2011 | 08/10/2011 | 08/12/2011 | 09/12/2011 |

**Indicated Div: $1.48 (Div. Reinv. Plan)**

**Valuation Analysis**

| | | | |
|---|---|---|---|
| Forecast EPS | $2.23 (09/02/2011) | | |
| Market Cap | $4.1 Billion | Book Value | N/A |
| Price/Book | N/A | Price/Sales | 0.76 |

**Dividend Achiever Status**

| | |
|---|---|
| **10 Year Growth Rate** | 2.33% |
| **Total Years of Dividend Growth** | 27 |

**Business Summary:** Office Equipment & Furniture (MIC: 7.5.1 SIC: 3579 NAIC: 333313)

Pitney Bowes is a provider of mail processing equipment and integrated mail applications. Co. provides a range of equipment, supplies, software, services and end-to-end applications, which enable its customers to manage and integrate physical and digital communication channels. Co. conducts its business activities in seven segments within two business groups, Small and Medium Business Solutions and Enterprise Business Solutions, based on the customers they primarily serve. Small and Medium Business Solutions include U.S. Mailing and International Mailing while Enterprise Business Solutions include Production Mail, Software, Management Services, Mail Services and Marketing Services.

**Recent Developments:** For the quarter ended June 30 2011, income from continuing operations increased 54.8% to US$106.2 million from US$68.6 million in the year-earlier quarter. Net income increased 60.1% to US$105.5 million from US$65.9 million in the year-earlier quarter. Revenues were US$1.31 billion, up 1.3% from US$1.30 billion the year before. Direct operating expenses declined 0.2% to US$650.5 million from US$651.9 million in the comparable period the year before. Indirect operating expenses decreased 6.8% to US$504.8 million from US$541.5 million in the equivalent prior-year period.

**Prospects:** Our evaluation of Pitney Bowes Inc. as of Sep. 6, 2011 is the result of our systematic analysis on three basic characteristics: earnings strength, relative valuation, and recent stock price movement. The company has managed to produce a neutral trend in earnings per share over the past 5 quarters. However, while recent estimates for the company have been lowered by analysts, PBI has posted better than expected results. Based on operating earnings yield, the company is undervalued when compared to all of the companies in our coverage universe. Share price changes over the past year indicates that PBI will perform poorly over the near term.

**Financial Data**

| (US$ in Thousands) | 6 Mos | 3 Mos | 12/31/2010 | 12/31/2009 | 12/31/2008 | 12/31/2007 | 12/31/2006 | 12/31/2005 |
|---|---|---|---|---|---|---|---|---|
| Earnings Per Share | 1.65 | 1.45 | 1.41 | 2.04 | 2.00 | 1.66 | 0.47 | 2.27 |
| Cash Flow Per Share | 4.81 | 4.63 | 4.62 | 3.99 | 4.74 | 4.85 | (1.29) | 2.36 |
| Dividends Per Share | 1.470 | 1.465 | 1.460 | 1.440 | 1.400 | 1.320 | 1.280 | 1.240 |
| Dividend Payout % | 89.09 | 101.03 | 103.55 | 70.59 | 70.00 | 79.52 | 272.34 | 54.63 |
| **Income Statement** | | | | | | | | |
| Total Revenue | 2,637,543 | 1,323,069 | 5,425,254 | 5,569,171 | 6,262,305 | 6,129,795 | 5,730,018 | 5,492,183 |
| EBITDA | 484,622 | 230,794 | 978,801 | 1,166,882 | 1,236,427 | 1,220,682 | 1,438,286 | 1,367,582 |
| Depn & Amortn | 137,635 | 69,318 | 242,900 | 269,800 | 306,800 | 318,100 | 311,200 | 292,200 |
| Income Before Taxes | 293,350 | 134,174 | 534,577 | 693,176 | 713,177 | 660,711 | 914,490 | 867,124 |
| Income Taxes | 94,406 | 41,394 | 205,770 | 240,154 | 244,929 | 280,222 | 335,004 | 340,546 |
| Net Income | 187,239 | 86,304 | 310,703 | 444,913 | 419,793 | 366,781 | 105,347 | 526,578 |
| Average Shares | 204,085 | 204,195 | 206,753 | 207,322 | 209,699 | 221,219 | 225,443 | 231,771 |
| **Balance Sheet** | | | | | | | | |
| Current Assets | 2,990,969 | 3,082,013 | 3,008,241 | 2,971,236 | 3,032,613 | 3,319,613 | 2,918,670 | 2,742,315 |
| Total Assets | 8,368,954 | 8,496,854 | 8,444,023 | 8,533,911 | 8,736,431 | 9,549,943 | 8,480,420 | 10,621,382 |
| Current Liabilities | 2,464,326 | 2,517,116 | 2,553,579 | 2,566,447 | 3,243,118 | 3,556,439 | 2,746,833 | 2,910,897 |
| Long-Term Obligations | 4,239,965 | 4,236,437 | 4,239,248 | 4,213,640 | 3,934,865 | 3,802,075 | 3,847,617 | 3,849,623 |
| Total Liabilities | 8,370,123 | 8,521,944 | 8,540,604 | 8,520,248 | 8,550,145 | 8,522,475 | 7,397,066 | 9,009,441 |
| Stockholders' Equity | (1,169) | (25,090) | (96,581) | 13,663 | 186,286 | 1,027,468 | 1,083,354 | 1,611,941 |
| Shares Outstanding | 202,141 | 203,848 | 203,431 | 207,197 | 206,181 | 214,514 | 220,613 | 226,707 |
| **Statistical Record** | | | | | | | | |
| Return on Assets % | 4.19 | 3.66 | 3.66 | 5.15 | 4.58 | 4.07 | 1.10 | 5.15 |
| Return on Equity % | ... | ... | ... | 445.03 | 68.98 | 34.75 | 7.82 | 32.79 |
| EBITDA Margin % | 18.37 | 17.44 | 18.04 | 20.95 | 19.74 | 19.91 | 25.10 | 24.90 |
| Net Margin % | 7.10 | 6.52 | 5.73 | 7.99 | 6.70 | 5.98 | 1.84 | 9.59 |
| Asset Turnover | 0.65 | 0.64 | 0.64 | 0.64 | 0.68 | 0.68 | 0.60 | 0.54 |
| Current Ratio | 1.21 | 1.22 | 1.18 | 1.16 | 0.94 | 0.93 | 1.06 | 0.94 |
| Debt to Equity | ... | ... | ... | 308.40 | 21.12 | 3.70 | 3.55 | 2.39 |
| Price Range | 26.18-19.24 | 26.07-19.24 | 25.88-19.24 | 27.11-17.77 | 38.55-21.52 | 48.66-36.94 | 47.68-40.34 | 47.30-40.49 |
| P/E Ratio | 15.87-11.66 | 17.98-13.27 | 18.35-13.65 | 13.29-8.71 | 19.27-10.76 | 29.31-22.25 | 101.45-85.83 | 20.84-17.84 |
| Average Yield % | 6.32 | 6.33 | 6.44 | 6.25 | 4.29 | 2.92 | 2.94 | 2.84 |

| | | |
|---|---|---|
| **Address:** 1 Elmcroft Road, Stamford, CT 06926-0700<br>**Telephone:** 203-356-5000<br>**Web Site:** www.pb.com | **Officers:** Murray D. Martin - Chairman, President, Chief Executive Officer Vicki A. O'Meara - President, Executive Vice President, Division Officer **Transfer Agents:** Computershare Trust Company, N.A. Providence, RI | **No of Institutions:** 576<br>**Shares:** 189,539,104 **% Held:** 81.03 |

# PLAINS ALL AMERICAN PIPELINE, L.P.

| Exchange | Symbol | Price | 52Wk Range | Yield | P/E |
|---|---|---|---|---|---|
| NYS | PAA | $60.63 (8/31/2011) | 65.57-57.04 | 6.37 | 20.28 |

*7 Year Price Score 125.80 *NYSE Composite Index=100 *12 Month Price Score 99.33

**Interim Earnings (Per Share)**

| Qtr. | Mar | Jun | Sep | Dec |
|---|---|---|---|---|
| 2008 | 0.57 | 0.13 | 1.14 | 0.55 |
| 2009 | 1.41 | 0.78 | 0.65 | 0.50 |
| 2010 | 0.80 | 0.65 | 0.28 | 0.68 |
| 2011 | 0.90 | 1.13 | ... | ... |

**Interim Dividends (Per Share)**

| Amt | Decl | Ex | Rec | Pay |
|---|---|---|---|---|
| 0.95Q | 10/12/2010 | 10/29/2010 | 11/02/2010 | 11/12/2010 |
| 0.958Q | 01/12/2011 | 02/02/2011 | 02/04/2011 | 02/14/2011 |
| 0.97Q | 04/11/2011 | 04/29/2011 | 05/03/2011 | 05/13/2011 |
| 0.983Q | 07/11/2011 | 07/29/2011 | 08/02/2011 | 08/12/2011 |

**Indicated Div: $3.86**

**Valuation Analysis**

| | | | |
|---|---|---|---|
| Forecast EPS | $3.95 (09/05/2011) | | |
| Market Cap | $9.1 Billion | Book Value | N/A |
| Price/Book | N/A | Price/Sales | 0.30 |

**Dividend Achiever Status**

| | |
|---|---|
| 10 Year Growth Rate | 6.77% |
| Total Years of Dividend Growth | 11 |

**Business Summary:** Equipment & Services (MIC: 9.1.3 SIC: 4612 NAIC: 486110)

Plains All American Pipeline is a holding company. Co. is engaged in the transportation, storage, terminalling and marketing of crude oil, refined products and liquefied petroleum gas and other natural gas-related petroleum products (LPG). Co. is also engaged in the acquisition, development and operation of natural gas storage facilities. Co. has three segments: transportation, which transports crude oil and refined products on pipelines, gathering systems, trucks and barges; facilities, which provides storage, terminalling and throughput services; and supply and logistics, which consists of the sale of gathered and bulk-purchased crude oil, refined products and LPG volumes.

**Recent Developments:** For the quarter ended June 30 2011, net income increased 75.2% to US$233.0 million from US$133.0 million in the year-earlier quarter. Revenues were US$8.86 billion, up 44.7% from US$6.12 billion the year before. Operating income was US$298.0 million versus US$192.0 million in the prior-year quarter, an increase of 55.2%. Direct operating expenses rose 45.4% to US$8.20 billion from US$5.64 billion in the comparable period the year before. Indirect operating expenses increased 23.4% to US$359.0 million from US$291.0 million in the equivalent prior-year period.

**Prospects:** Our evaluation of Plains All American Pipeline, L.P. as of Sep. 6, 2011 is the result of our systematic analysis on three basic characteristics: earnings strength, relative valuation, and recent stock price movement. The company has produced a positive trend in earnings per share over the past 5 quarters and while recent estimates for the company have been raised by analysts, PAA has posted better than expected results. Based on operating earnings yield, the company is about fairly valued when compared to all of the companies in our coverage universe. Share price changes over the past year indicates that PAA will perform very poorly over the near term.

**Financial Data**

| (US$ in Thousands) | 6 Mos | 3 Mos | 12/31/2010 | 12/31/2009 | 12/31/2008 | 12/31/2007 | 12/31/2006 | 12/31/2005 |
|---|---|---|---|---|---|---|---|---|
| Earnings Per Share | 2.99 | 2.51 | 2.40 | 3.32 | 2.67 | 2.52 | 2.88 | 2.72 |
| Cash Flow Per Share | 6.36 | 3.65 | 1.89 | 2.81 | 7.12 | 7.04 | (3.39) | 0.35 |
| Dividends Per Share | 3.820 | 3.785 | 3.755 | 3.623 | 3.495 | 3.283 | 2.870 | 2.575 |
| Dividend Payout % | 127.76 | 150.80 | 156.46 | 109.11 | 130.90 | 130.26 | 99.65 | 94.67 |
| **Income Statement** | | | | | | | | |
| Total Revenue | 16,553,000 | 7,694,000 | 25,893,000 | 18,520,000 | 30,061,000 | 20,394,000 | 22,444,400 | 31,177,300 |
| EBITDA | 689,000 | 326,000 | 993,000 | 995,000 | 790,000 | 699,000 | 521,600 | 412,600 |
| Depn & Amortn | 126,000 | 63,000 | 235,000 | 216,000 | 196,000 | 181,000 | 91,300 | 79,200 |
| Income Before Taxes | 435,000 | 198,000 | 510,000 | 571,000 | 431,000 | 366,000 | 347,000 | 274,600 |
| Income Taxes | 22,000 | 13,000 | (1,000) | 6,000 | 8,000 | 16,000 | 300 | ... |
| Net Income | 408,000 | 182,000 | 505,000 | 579,000 | 437,000 | 365,000 | 285,100 | 217,800 |
| Average Shares | 150,000 | 144,000 | 138,000 | 131,000 | 121,000 | 114,000 | 81,900 | 70,500 |
| **Balance Sheet** | | | | | | | | |
| Current Assets | 4,633,000 | 4,607,000 | 4,381,000 | 3,658,000 | 2,596,000 | 3,673,000 | 3,157,600 | 1,805,200 |
| Total Assets | 14,913,000 | 14,745,000 | 13,703,000 | 12,358,000 | 10,032,000 | 9,906,000 | 8,714,900 | 4,120,300 |
| Current Liabilities | 3,983,000 | 4,051,000 | 4,215,000 | 3,782,000 | 2,960,000 | 3,729,000 | 3,024,700 | 1,793,300 |
| Long-Term Obligations | 4,995,000 | 4,976,000 | 4,631,000 | 4,142,000 | 3,259,000 | 2,624,000 | 2,626,300 | 951,700 |
| Total Liabilities | 9,763,000 | 9,863,000 | 9,361,000 | 8,262,000 | 6,480,000 | 6,482,000 | 5,738,100 | 2,789,600 |
| Shares Outstanding | 149,357 | 149,138 | 141,199 | 136,135 | 122,911 | 115,981 | 109,405 | 73,768 |
| **Statistical Record** | | | | | | | | |
| Return on Assets % | 4.62 | 3.99 | 3.88 | 5.17 | 4.37 | 3.92 | 4.44 | 5.98 |
| EBITDA Margin % | 4.16 | 4.24 | 3.84 | 5.37 | 2.63 | 3.43 | 2.32 | 1.32 |
| Net Margin % | 2.46 | 2.37 | 1.95 | 3.13 | 1.45 | 1.79 | 1.27 | 0.70 |
| Asset Turnover | 2.21 | 2.05 | 1.99 | 1.65 | 3.01 | 2.19 | 3.50 | 8.56 |
| Current Ratio | 1.16 | 1.14 | 1.04 | 0.97 | 0.88 | 0.98 | 1.04 | 1.01 |
| Price Range | 65.57-57.96 | 65.57-52.33 | 64.81-51.67 | 53.03-34.69 | 52.00-26.01 | 65.05-49.16 | 52.45-40.42 | 47.52-36.70 |
| P/E Ratio | 21.93-19.38 | 26.12-20.85 | 27.00-21.53 | 15.97-10.45 | 19.48-9.74 | 25.81-19.51 | 18.21-14.03 | 17.47-13.49 |
| Average Yield % | 6.10 | 6.16 | 6.34 | 8.21 | 7.96 | 5.80 | 6.28 | 6.18 |

**Address:** 333 Clay Street, Suite 1600, Houston, TX 77002
**Telephone:** 713-646-4100
**Web Site:** www.paalp.com

**Officers:** Greg L. Armstrong - Chairman, Chief Executive Officer Harry N. Pefanis - President, Chief Operating Officer **Transfer Agents:** American Stock Tranfer & Trust Company, New York,NY

**Investor Contact:** 713-646-4491
**No of Institutions:** 364
**Shares:** 70,161,376 **% Held:** 37.44

# POLARIS INDUSTRIES INC.

| Exchange | Symbol | Price | 52Wk Range | Yield | P/E |
|---|---|---|---|---|---|
| NYS | PII | $109.87 (8/31/2011) | 122.25-53.33 | 1.64 | 19.45 |

***7 Year Price Score 162.89** *NYSE Composite Index=100 ***12 Month Price Score 129.40**

**Interim Earnings (Per Share)**

| Qtr. | Mar | Jun | Sep | Dec |
|---|---|---|---|---|
| 2008 | 0.55 | 0.72 | 1.13 | 1.10 |
| 2009 | 0.26 | 0.53 | 0.94 | 1.32 |
| 2010 | 0.59 | 0.75 | 1.37 | 1.57 |
| 2011 | 1.34 | 1.37 | ... | ... |

**Interim Dividends (Per Share)**

| Amt | Decl | Ex | Rec | Pay |
|---|---|---|---|---|
| 0.45Q | 01/20/2011 | 01/28/2011 | 02/01/2011 | 02/15/2011 |
| 0.45Q | 04/21/2011 | 04/28/2011 | 05/02/2011 | 05/16/2011 |
| 0.45Q | 07/20/2011 | 07/28/2011 | 08/01/2011 | 08/15/2011 |
| 100% | 07/20/2011 | 09/13/2011 | 09/02/2011 | 09/12/2011 |

**Indicated Div: $1.80 (Div. Reinv. Plan)**

**Valuation Analysis**

| | | | |
|---|---|---|---|
| Forecast EPS | $6.17 (09/05/2011) | | |
| Market Cap | $3.8 Billion | Book Value | $451.4 Million |
| Price/Book | 8.39 | Price/Sales | 1.62 |

**Dividend Achiever Status**

| | |
|---|---|
| **10 Year Growth Rate** | 12.33% |
| **Total Years of Dividend Growth** | 15 |

**Business Summary:** Leisure Equipment (MIC: 1.6.1 SIC: 3799 NAIC: 336999)

Polaris Industries designs, engineers and manufactures off-road vehicles (ORV), including all-terrain vehicles and side-by-side vehicles for recreational and utility use, snowmobiles, and on-road vehicles, including motorcycles and low emission vehicles, together with the related replacement parts, garments and accessories. Co.'s line of ORVs consists of 32 models, including two-, four- and six-wheel drive general purpose, sport and side-by-side models. Co.'s line of snowmobiles consists of 26 models, ranging from youth models to utility and economy models to performance and competition models. Co.'s On-Road vehicles include V-twin cruiser motorcycles under the Victory brand name.

**Recent Developments:** For the quarter ended June 30 2011, net income increased 90.2% to US$48.7 million from US$25.6 million in the year-earlier quarter. Revenues were US$607.9 million, up 41.1% from US$430.9 million the year before. Operating income was US$76.9 million versus US$42.9 million in the prior-year quarter, an increase of 79.1%. Direct operating expenses rose 35.4% to US$430.3 million from US$317.8 million in the comparable period the year before. Indirect operating expenses increased 43.5% to US$100.7 million from US$70.1 million in the equivalent prior-year period.

**Prospects:** Our evaluation of Polaris Industries Inc. as of Sep. 6, 2011 is the result of our systematic analysis on three basic characteristics: earnings strength, relative valuation, and recent stock price movement. The company has managed to produce a neutral trend in earnings per share over the past 5 quarters and while recent estimates for the company have been mixed, PII has posted better than expected results. Based on operating earnings yield, the company is about fairly valued when compared to all of the companies in our coverage universe. Share price changes over the past year indicates that PII will perform very well over the near term.

**Financial Data**

| (US$ in Thousands) | 6 Mos | 3 Mos | 12/31/2010 | 12/31/2009 | 12/31/2008 | 12/31/2007 | 12/31/2006 | 12/31/2005 |
|---|---|---|---|---|---|---|---|---|
| Earnings Per Share | 5.65 | 5.03 | 4.28 | 3.05 | 3.50 | 3.07 | 2.58 | 3.27 |
| Cash Flow Per Share | 8.79 | 8.71 | 8.90 | 5.96 | 5.35 | 5.96 | 3.61 | 3.83 |
| Tang Book Value Per Share | 13.09 | 11.41 | 9.92 | 5.47 | 3.46 | 4.28 | 4.01 | 8.27 |
| Dividends Per Share | 1.700 | 1.650 | 1.600 | 1.560 | 1.520 | 1.360 | 1.240 | 1.120 |
| Dividend Payout % | 30.09 | 32.80 | 37.38 | 51.15 | 43.43 | 44.30 | 48.06 | 34.25 |
| **Income Statement** | | | | | | | | |
| Total Revenue | 1,145,119 | 537,198 | 1,991,139 | 1,565,887 | 1,948,254 | 1,780,009 | 1,656,518 | 1,869,819 |
| EBITDA | 183,058 | 91,566 | 287,740 | 219,878 | 252,948 | 247,530 | 241,074 | 278,974 |
| Depn & Amortn | 34,995 | 18,782 | 66,519 | 64,593 | 66,112 | 62,093 | 71,164 | 67,936 |
| Income Before Taxes | 146,567 | 72,273 | 218,541 | 151,174 | 177,218 | 170,336 | 160,137 | 206,325 |
| Income Taxes | 50,528 | 24,963 | 71,403 | 50,157 | 59,667 | 57,738 | 50,988 | 64,348 |
| Net Income | 96,039 | 47,310 | 147,138 | 101,017 | 117,395 | 111,650 | 106,985 | 143,278 |
| Average Shares | 35,607 | 35,331 | 34,382 | 33,074 | 33,564 | 36,324 | 41,451 | 43,881 |
| **Balance Sheet** | | | | | | | | |
| Current Assets | 797,296 | 801,472 | 808,145 | 491,500 | 443,612 | 447,556 | 392,961 | 373,988 |
| Total Assets | 1,091,262 | 1,057,083 | 1,061,647 | 763,653 | 751,148 | 769,881 | 778,791 | 768,956 |
| Current Liabilities | 533,637 | 561,261 | 584,210 | 343,074 | 404,833 | 388,246 | 361,420 | 375,614 |
| Long-Term Obligations | 100,000 | 100,000 | 100,000 | 200,000 | 200,000 | 200,000 | 250,000 | 18,000 |
| Total Liabilities | 639,821 | 667,907 | 690,656 | 559,112 | 614,121 | 596,899 | 611,420 | 399,299 |
| Stockholders' Equity | 451,441 | 389,176 | 370,991 | 204,541 | 137,027 | 172,982 | 167,371 | 369,657 |
| Shares Outstanding | 34,479 | 34,109 | 34,234 | 32,648 | 32,492 | 34,212 | 35,455 | 41,687 |
| **Statistical Record** | | | | | | | | |
| Return on Assets % | 20.68 | 19.43 | 16.12 | 13.34 | 15.39 | 14.42 | 13.82 | 18.35 |
| Return on Equity % | 57.23 | 58.08 | 51.13 | 59.15 | 75.53 | 65.61 | 39.84 | 39.18 |
| EBITDA Margin % | 15.99 | 17.05 | 14.45 | 14.04 | 12.98 | 13.91 | 14.55 | 14.92 |
| Net Margin % | 8.39 | 8.81 | 7.39 | 6.45 | 6.03 | 6.27 | 6.46 | 7.66 |
| Asset Turnover | 2.45 | 2.41 | 2.18 | 2.07 | 2.55 | 2.30 | 2.14 | 2.39 |
| Current Ratio | 1.49 | 1.43 | 1.38 | 1.43 | 1.10 | 1.15 | 1.09 | 1.00 |
| Debt to Equity | 0.22 | 0.26 | 0.27 | 0.98 | 1.46 | 1.16 | 1.49 | 0.05 |
| Price Range | 111.25-52.64 | 87.12-51.16 | 80.70-42.58 | 48.74-14.59 | 52.49-20.20 | 57.74-42.70 | 54.56-36.20 | 73.85-44.43 |
| P/E Ratio | 19.69-9.32 | 17.32-10.17 | 18.86-9.95 | 15.98-4.78 | 15.00-5.77 | 18.81-13.91 | 21.15-14.03 | 22.58-13.59 |
| Average Yield % | 2.19 | 2.47 | 2.70 | 4.67 | 3.79 | 2.76 | 2.74 | 1.97 |

| | | |
|---|---|---|
| **Address:** 2100 Highway 55, Medina, MN 55340<br>**Telephone:** 763-542-0500<br>**Web Site:** www.polarisindustries.com | **Officers:** Bennett J. Morgan - President, Chief Operating Officer Scott W. Wine - Chief Executive Officer **Transfer Agents:** Wells Fargo Bank, N.A., Shareowner Services, South St. Paul, MN | **Investor Contact:** 763-513-3477<br>**No of Institutions:** 358<br>**Shares:** 25,415,280 **% Held:** 69.07 |

# PPG INDUSTRIES, INC.

| Exchange | Symbol | Price | 52Wk Range | Yield | P/E |
|---|---|---|---|---|---|
| NYS | PPG | $76.59 (8/31/2011) | 96.49-65.83 | 2.98 | 12.08 |

***7 Year Price Score 126.66** *NYSE Composite Index=100 ***12 Month Price Score 99.78**

**Interim Earnings (Per Share)**

| Qtr. | Mar | Jun | Sep | Dec |
|---|---|---|---|---|
| 2008 | 0.61 | 1.51 | 0.70 | 0.43 |
| 2009 | (0.68) | 0.89 | 0.96 | 0.86 |
| 2010 | 0.18 | 1.63 | 1.58 | 1.24 |
| 2011 | 1.40 | 2.12 | ... | ... |

**Interim Dividends (Per Share)**

| Amt | Decl | Ex | Rec | Pay |
|---|---|---|---|---|
| 0.55Q | 10/21/2010 | 11/08/2010 | 11/10/2010 | 12/10/2010 |
| 0.55Q | 01/20/2011 | 02/16/2011 | 02/18/2011 | 03/11/2011 |
| 0.57Q | 04/21/2011 | 05/06/2011 | 05/10/2011 | 06/10/2011 |
| 0.57Q | 07/21/2011 | 08/08/2011 | 08/10/2011 | 09/12/2011 |

**Indicated Div: $2.28 (Div. Reinv. Plan)**

**Valuation Analysis**

| | | | |
|---|---|---|---|
| Forecast EPS | $6.90 (09/02/2011) | | |
| Market Cap | $12.1 Billion | Book Value | $4.1 Billion |
| Price/Book | 2.98 | Price/Sales | 0.84 |

**Dividend Achiever Status**

| | |
|---|---|
| **10 Year Growth Rate** | 2.64% |
| **Total Years of Dividend Growth** | 39 |

**Business Summary:** Construction Materials (MIC: 8.5.1 SIC: 2851 NAIC: 325510)

PPG Industries operates in six segments. The Performance Coatings, Industrial Coatings and Architectural Coatings - Europe, Middle East and Africa segments supply protective and decorative finishes; factory-finished aluminum extrusions and steel and aluminum coils; marine and aircraft equipment; automotive original equipment, and other industrial and consumer products. The Optical and Specialty Materials segment is comprised of Co.'s optical products and silicas businesses. The Commodity Chemicals segment produces chlor-alkali and derivative products including caustic soda and chlorinated solvents. The Glass business segment is comprised of Co.'s flat glass and fiber glass businesses.

**Recent Developments:** For the quarter ended June 30 2011, net income increased 23.6% to US$372.0 million from US$301.0 million in the year-earlier quarter. Revenues were US$3.99 billion, up 15.3% from US$3.46 billion the year before. Direct operating expenses rose 16.4% to US$2.42 billion from US$2.08 billion in the comparable period the year before. Indirect operating expenses increased 10.2% to US$1.07 billion from US$970.0 million in the equivalent prior-year period.

**Prospects:** Our evaluation of PPG Industries Inc. as of Sep. 6, 2011 is the result of our systematic analysis on three basic characteristics: earnings strength, relative valuation, and recent stock price movement. The company has generated a negative trend in earnings per share over the past 5 quarters. However, while recent estimates for the company have been lowered by analysts, PPG has posted better than expected results. Based on operating earnings yield, the company is undervalued when compared to all of the companies in our coverage universe. Share price changes over the past year indicates that PPG will perform in line with the market over the near term.

**Financial Data**

| (US$ in Thousands) | 6 Mos | 3 Mos | 12/31/2010 | 12/31/2009 | 12/31/2008 | 12/31/2007 | 12/31/2006 | 12/31/2005 |
|---|---|---|---|---|---|---|---|---|
| Earnings Per Share | 6.34 | 5.85 | 4.63 | 2.03 | 3.25 | 5.03 | 4.27 | 3.49 |
| Cash Flow Per Share | 7.55 | 7.53 | 7.96 | 8.16 | 8.23 | 6.05 | 6.82 | 6.28 |
| Tang Book Value Per Share | N.M. | N.M. | N.M. | N.M. | N.M. | 12.59 | 7.63 | 8.46 |
| Dividends Per Share | 2.220 | 2.190 | 2.180 | 2.130 | 2.090 | 2.040 | 1.910 | 1.860 |
| Dividend Payout % | 35.02 | 37.44 | 47.08 | 104.93 | 64.31 | 40.56 | 44.73 | 53.30 |
| **Income Statement** | | | | | | | | |
| Total Revenue | 7,519,000 | 3,533,000 | 13,423,000 | 12,239,000 | 15,849,000 | 11,206,000 | 11,037,000 | 10,201,000 |
| EBITDA | 1,133,000 | 490,000 | 1,751,000 | 1,141,000 | 1,561,000 | 1,608,000 | 1,432,000 | 1,341,000 |
| Depn & Amortn | 174,000 | 86,000 | 346,000 | 354,000 | 428,000 | 322,000 | 337,000 | 340,000 |
| Income Before Taxes | 851,000 | 351,000 | 1,250,000 | 622,000 | 905,000 | 1,213,000 | 1,026,000 | 933,000 |
| Income Taxes | 220,000 | 92,000 | 415,000 | 191,000 | 284,000 | 355,000 | 278,000 | 282,000 |
| Net Income | 568,000 | 228,000 | 769,000 | 336,000 | 538,000 | 834,000 | 711,000 | 596,000 |
| Average Shares | 160,300 | 162,500 | 165,900 | 165,500 | 165,400 | 165,900 | 166,500 | 170,900 |
| **Balance Sheet** | | | | | | | | |
| Current Assets | 7,239,000 | 7,084,000 | 7,058,000 | 5,981,000 | 6,348,000 | 7,136,000 | 4,592,000 | 4,019,000 |
| Total Assets | 15,267,000 | 15,103,000 | 14,975,000 | 14,240,000 | 14,698,000 | 12,629,000 | 10,021,000 | 8,681,000 |
| Current Liabilities | 3,922,000 | 3,749,000 | 3,625,000 | 3,577,000 | 4,210,000 | 4,661,000 | 2,787,000 | 2,349,000 |
| Long-Term Obligations | 3,613,000 | 3,993,000 | 4,043,000 | 3,074,000 | 3,009,000 | 1,201,000 | 1,155,000 | 1,169,000 |
| Total Liabilities | 11,213,000 | 11,337,000 | 11,337,000 | 10,487,000 | 11,365,000 | 8,478,000 | 6,787,000 | 5,628,000 |
| Stockholders' Equity | 4,054,000 | 3,766,000 | 3,638,000 | 3,753,000 | 3,333,000 | 4,151,000 | 3,234,000 | 3,053,000 |
| Shares Outstanding | 157,518 | 158,152 | 160,381 | 165,667 | 164,198 | 163,800 | 164,081 | 165,277 |
| **Statistical Record** | | | | | | | | |
| Return on Assets % | 7.23 | 6.70 | 5.26 | 2.32 | 3.93 | 7.36 | 7.60 | 6.77 |
| Return on Equity % | 27.59 | 26.28 | 20.81 | 9.48 | 14.34 | 22.59 | 22.62 | 17.99 |
| EBITDA Margin % | 15.07 | 13.87 | 13.04 | 9.32 | 9.85 | 14.35 | 12.97 | 13.15 |
| Net Margin % | 7.55 | 6.45 | 5.73 | 2.75 | 3.39 | 7.44 | 6.44 | 5.84 |
| Asset Turnover | 1.00 | 0.96 | 0.92 | 0.85 | 1.16 | 0.99 | 1.18 | 1.16 |
| Current Ratio | 1.85 | 1.89 | 1.95 | 1.67 | 1.51 | 1.53 | 1.65 | 1.71 |
| Debt to Equity | 0.89 | 1.06 | 1.11 | 0.82 | 0.90 | 0.29 | 0.36 | 0.38 |
| Price Range | 96.49-60.41 | 95.93-60.41 | 84.21-57.68 | 62.08-28.48 | 70.23-36.98 | 82.20-64.30 | 69.28-56.92 | 73.80-55.95 |
| P/E Ratio | 15.22-9.53 | 16.40-10.33 | 18.19-12.46 | 30.58-14.03 | 21.61-11.38 | 16.34-12.78 | 16.22-13.33 | 21.15-16.03 |
| Average Yield % | 2.76 | 2.94 | 3.17 | 4.39 | 3.59 | 2.82 | 2.98 | 2.88 |

**Address:** One PPG Place, Pittsburgh, PA 15272
**Telephone:** 412-434-3131
**Web Site:** www.ppg.com

**Officers:** Charles E. Bunch - Chairman, Chief Executive Officer J. Rich Alexander - Senior Vice President **Transfer Agents:** BNY Mellon Shareowner Services, Jersey City, NJ

**Investor Contact:** 412-434-3318
**No of Institutions:** 685
**Shares:** 133,163,792 **% Held:** 70.72

# PPL CORP

| Exchange | Symbol | Price | 52Wk Range | Yield | P/E |
|---|---|---|---|---|---|
| NYS | PPL | $28.88 (8/31/2011) | 28.88-24.35 | 4.85 | 11.79 |

*7 Year Price Score 78.48 *NYSE Composite Index=100 *12 Month Price Score 104.54

**Interim Earnings (Per Share)**

| Qtr. | Mar | Jun | Sep | Dec |
|---|---|---|---|---|
| 2008 | 0.69 | 0.50 | 0.54 | 0.74 |
| 2009 | 0.64 | (0.02) | 0.05 | 0.41 |
| 2010 | 0.66 | 0.22 | 0.51 | 0.77 |
| 2011 | 0.82 | 0.35 | ... | ... |

**Interim Dividends (Per Share)**

| Amt | Decl | Ex | Rec | Pay |
|---|---|---|---|---|
| 0.35Q | 11/19/2010 | 12/08/2010 | 12/10/2010 | 01/03/2011 |
| 0.35Q | 02/25/2011 | 03/08/2011 | 03/10/2011 | 04/01/2011 |
| 0.35Q | 05/18/2011 | 06/08/2011 | 06/10/2011 | 07/01/2011 |
| 0.35Q | 08/26/2011 | 09/07/2011 | 09/09/2011 | 10/03/2011 |

**Indicated Div: $1.40 (Div. Reinv. Plan)**

**Valuation Analysis**

| | | | |
|---|---|---|---|
| Forecast EPS | $2.60 (09/05/2011) | | |
| Market Cap | $16.7 Billion | Book Value | $10.7 Billion |
| Price/Book | 1.57 | Price/Sales | 1.77 |

**Dividend Achiever Status**

| | |
|---|---|
| 10 Year Growth Rate | 10.16% |
| Total Years of Dividend Growth | 11 |

**Business Summary:** Electric Utilities (MIC: 3.1.1 SIC: 4911 NAIC: 221122)

PPL is an energy and utility holding company. Co. generates electricity, markets wholesale or retail energy as well as delivers electricity and natural gas to customers. Co. has four segments: Kentucky Regulated, which consists of the operations of LG&E and KU Energy LLC; International Regulated, which includes the operations of WPDH Limited; Pennsylvania Regulated, which includes the regulated electric delivery operations of PPL Electric Utilities Corp.; and Supply, which owns and operates domestic power plants to generate electricity; markets and trades this electricity and other purchased power to wholesale and retail markets; and acquires and develops domestic generation projects.

**Recent Developments:** For the quarter ended June 30 2011, net income increased 117.4% to US$200.0 million from US$92.0 million in the year-earlier quarter. Revenues were US$2.49 billion, up 69.0% from US$1.47 billion the year before. Operating income was US$595.0 million versus US$226.0 million in the prior-year quarter, an increase of 163.3%. Direct operating expenses rose 50.9% to US$1.46 billion from US$969.0 million in the comparable period the year before. Indirect operating expenses increased 55.4% to US$432.0 million from US$278.0 million in the equivalent prior-year period.

**Prospects:** Our evaluation of PPL Corp. as of Sep. 6, 2011 is the result of our systematic analysis on three basic characteristics: earnings strength, relative valuation, and recent stock price movement. The company has generated a negative trend in earnings per share over the past 5 quarters and while recent estimates for the company have been mixed, PPL has posted better than expected results. Based on operating earnings yield, the company is undervalued when compared to all of the companies in our coverage universe. Share price changes over the past year indicates that PPL will perform very poorly over the near term.

**Financial Data**

| (US$ in Thousands) | 6 Mos | 3 Mos | 12/31/2010 | 12/31/2009 | 12/31/2008 | 12/31/2007 | 12/31/2006 | 12/31/2005 |
|---|---|---|---|---|---|---|---|---|
| Earnings Per Share | 2.45 | 2.32 | 2.17 | 1.08 | 2.47 | 3.35 | 2.24 | 1.77 |
| Cash Flow Per Share | 4.05 | 2.96 | 4.71 | 4.92 | 4.24 | 4.13 | 4.62 | 3.66 |
| Tang Book Value Per Share | 9.33 | 11.92 | 11.34 | 10.80 | 9.91 | 11.33 | 9.35 | 7.72 |
| Dividends Per Share | 1.400 | 1.400 | 1.400 | 1.380 | 1.340 | 1.220 | 1.100 | 0.960 |
| Dividend Payout % | 57.14 | 60.34 | 64.52 | 127.78 | 54.25 | 36.42 | 49.11 | 54.24 |
| **Income Statement** | | | | | | | | |
| Total Revenue | 5,399,000 | 2,910,000 | 8,521,000 | 7,556,000 | 8,044,000 | 6,498,000 | 6,899,000 | 6,219,000 |
| EBITDA | 1,910,000 | 1,037,000 | 2,391,000 | 1,449,000 | 2,265,000 | 2,171,000 | 2,068,000 | 1,772,000 |
| Depn & Amortn | 572,000 | 255,000 | 567,000 | 471,000 | 461,000 | 458,000 | 446,000 | 423,000 |
| Income Before Taxes | 904,000 | 610,000 | 1,239,000 | 596,000 | 1,378,000 | 1,300,000 | 1,181,000 | 864,000 |
| Income Taxes | 319,000 | 223,000 | 263,000 | 130,000 | 440,000 | 270,000 | 275,000 | 121,000 |
| Net Income | 597,000 | 401,000 | 938,000 | 407,000 | 930,000 | 1,288,000 | 865,000 | 678,000 |
| Average Shares | 562,019 | 484,345 | 431,569 | 376,406 | 376,526 | 385,111 | 386,769 | 383,737 |
| **Balance Sheet** | | | | | | | | |
| Current Assets | 5,364,000 | 5,747,000 | 6,188,000 | 4,752,000 | 4,383,000 | 3,168,000 | 3,630,000 | 2,910,000 |
| Total Assets | 40,537,000 | 32,741,000 | 32,837,000 | 22,165,000 | 21,405,000 | 19,972,000 | 19,747,000 | 17,926,000 |
| Current Liabilities | 4,593,000 | 4,902,000 | 5,214,000 | 4,182,000 | 4,293,000 | 2,882,000 | 3,348,000 | 3,340,000 |
| Long-Term Obligations | 17,532,000 | 12,247,000 | 12,161,000 | 7,143,000 | 7,151,000 | 6,890,000 | 6,728,000 | 6,044,000 |
| Total Liabilities | 29,886,000 | 24,211,000 | 24,627,000 | 16,669,000 | 16,027,000 | 14,115,000 | 14,324,000 | 13,457,000 |
| Stockholders' Equity | 10,651,000 | 8,530,000 | 8,210,000 | 5,496,000 | 5,378,000 | 5,857,000 | 5,423,000 | 4,469,000 |
| Shares Outstanding | 577,265 | 484,618 | 483,391 | 377,183 | 375,000 | 373,271 | 385,039 | 380,145 |
| **Statistical Record** | | | | | | | | |
| Return on Assets % | 3.61 | 3.78 | 3.41 | 1.87 | 4.48 | 6.49 | 4.59 | 3.80 |
| Return on Equity % | 12.91 | 15.10 | 13.69 | 7.49 | 16.51 | 22.84 | 17.49 | 15.48 |
| EBITDA Margin % | 35.38 | 35.64 | 28.06 | 19.18 | 28.16 | 33.41 | 29.98 | 28.49 |
| Net Margin % | 11.06 | 13.78 | 11.01 | 5.39 | 11.56 | 19.82 | 12.54 | 10.90 |
| Asset Turnover | 0.28 | 0.29 | 0.31 | 0.35 | 0.39 | 0.33 | 0.37 | 0.35 |
| Current Ratio | 1.17 | 1.17 | 1.19 | 1.14 | 1.02 | 1.10 | 1.08 | 0.87 |
| Debt to Equity | 1.65 | 1.44 | 1.48 | 1.30 | 1.33 | 1.18 | 1.24 | 1.35 |
| Price Range | 28.28-24.35 | 28.64-24.24 | 32.61-24.24 | 34.34-24.46 | 55.16-28.69 | 53.96-34.62 | 37.30-28.47 | 33.31-25.57 |
| P/E Ratio | 11.54-9.94 | 12.34-10.45 | 15.03-11.17 | 31.80-22.65 | 22.33-11.62 | 16.11-10.33 | 16.65-12.71 | 18.82-14.45 |
| Average Yield % | 5.29 | 5.34 | 5.14 | 4.50 | 3.10 | 2.69 | 3.41 | 3.30 |

**Address:** Two North Ninth Street, Allentown, PA 18101-1179
**Telephone:** 610-774-5151
**Web Site:** www.pplweb.com

**Officers:** James H. Miller - Chairman, Chief Executive Officer William H. Spence - President, Chief Operating Officer **Transfer Agents:** Wells Fargo Bank, N.A., Shareowner Services, South St. Paul, MN

**Investor Contact:** 800-345-3085
**No of Institutions:** 611
**Shares:** 426,107,712 **% Held:** N/A

# PRAXAIR, INC.

| Exchange | Symbol | Price | 52Wk Range | Yield | P/E |
|---|---|---|---|---|---|
| NYS | PX | $98.49 (8/31/2011) | 111.30-86.03 | 2.03 | 22.85 |

*7 Year Price Score 135.66 *NYSE Composite Index=100 *12 Month Price Score 104.80

**Interim Earnings (Per Share)**

| Qtr. | Mar | Jun | Sep | Dec |
|---|---|---|---|---|
| 2008 | 0.96 | 1.08 | 1.11 | 0.65 |
| 2009 | 0.93 | 0.96 | 1.04 | 1.08 |
| 2010 | 1.01 | 1.19 | 1.21 | 0.43 |
| 2011 | 1.29 | 1.38 | ... | ... |

**Interim Dividends (Per Share)**

| Amt | Decl | Ex | Rec | Pay |
|---|---|---|---|---|
| 0.45Q | 10/27/2010 | 12/03/2010 | 12/07/2010 | 12/15/2010 |
| 0.50Q | 01/26/2011 | 03/03/2011 | 03/07/2011 | 03/15/2011 |
| 0.50Q | 04/27/2011 | 06/03/2011 | 06/07/2011 | 06/15/2011 |
| 0.50Q | 07/27/2011 | 09/02/2011 | 09/07/2011 | 09/15/2011 |

**Indicated Div: $2.00 (Div. Reinv. Plan)**

**Valuation Analysis**

| | | | |
|---|---|---|---|
| Forecast EPS | $5.47 (09/02/2011) | | |
| Market Cap | $29.8 Billion | Book Value | $6.4 Billion |
| Price/Book | 4.65 | Price/Sales | 2.78 |

**Dividend Achiever Status**

| | |
|---|---|
| 10 Year Growth Rate | 18.14% |
| Total Years of Dividend Growth | 18 |

**Business Summary:** Specialty Chemicals (MIC: 8.3.2 SIC: 2819 NAIC: 325188)

Praxair is an industrial gases supplier. Co.'s primary products for its industrial gases business are atmospheric gases (oxygen, nitrogen, argon, rare gases) and process gases (carbon dioxide, helium, hydrogen, electronic gases, specialty gases, acetylene). Co. also designs, engineers, and builds equipment that produces industrial gases for internal use and external sale. Co. operates five segments: North America; Europe; South America; Asia; and surface technologies. The surface technologies segment is operated through Co.'s Praxair Surface Technologies, Inc. subsidiary, which supplies wear-resistant and high-temperature corrosion-resistant metallic and ceramic coatings and powders.

**Recent Developments:** For the quarter ended June 30 2011, net income increased 15.2% to US$439.0 million from US$381.0 million in the year-earlier quarter. Revenues were US$2.86 billion, up 13.1% from US$2.53 billion the year before. Operating income was US$627.0 million versus US$547.0 million in the prior-year quarter, an increase of 14.6%. Direct operating expenses rose 14.1% to US$1.64 billion from US$1.44 billion in the comparable period the year before. Indirect operating expenses increased 8.8% to US$591.0 million from US$543.0 million in the equivalent prior-year period.

**Prospects:** Our evaluation of Praxair Inc. as of Sep. 6, 2011 is the result of our systematic analysis on three basic characteristics: earnings strength, relative valuation, and recent stock price movement. The company has produced a positive trend in earnings per share over the past 5 quarters. However, while recent estimates for the company have been lowered by analysts, PX has posted better than expected results. Based on operating earnings yield, the company is about fairly valued when compared to all of the companies in our coverage universe. Share price changes over the past year indicates that PX will perform poorly over the near term.

| **Financial Data** (US$ in Thousands) | 6 Mos | 3 Mos | 12/31/2010 | 12/31/2009 | 12/31/2008 | 12/31/2007 | 12/31/2006 | 12/31/2005 |
|---|---|---|---|---|---|---|---|---|
| Earnings Per Share | 4.31 | 4.12 | 3.84 | 4.01 | 3.80 | 3.62 | 3.00 | 2.20 |
| Cash Flow Per Share | 5.99 | 5.86 | 6.21 | 7.05 | 6.50 | 6.14 | 5.42 | 4.56 |
| Tang Book Value Per Share | 13.71 | 12.95 | 11.82 | 10.12 | 6.45 | 9.64 | 8.94 | 7.06 |
| Dividends Per Share | 1.900 | 1.850 | 1.800 | 1.600 | 1.500 | 1.200 | 1.000 | 0.720 |
| Dividend Payout % | 44.08 | 44.90 | 46.88 | 39.90 | 39.47 | 33.15 | 33.33 | 32.73 |
| **Income Statement** | | | | | | | | |
| Total Revenue | 5,560,000 | 2,702,000 | 10,116,000 | 8,956,000 | 10,796,000 | 9,402,000 | 8,324,000 | 7,656,000 |
| EBITDA | 1,716,000 | 835,000 | 3,007,000 | 2,421,000 | 2,733,000 | 2,560,000 | 2,215,000 | 1,958,000 |
| Depn & Amortn | 498,000 | 244,000 | 925,000 | 846,000 | 850,000 | 774,000 | 696,000 | 665,000 |
| Income Before Taxes | 1,147,000 | 556,000 | 1,964,000 | 1,442,000 | 1,685,000 | 1,613,000 | 1,364,000 | 1,130,000 |
| Income Taxes | 319,000 | 156,000 | 768,000 | 169,000 | 465,000 | 419,000 | 355,000 | 376,000 |
| Net Income | 823,000 | 398,000 | 1,195,000 | 1,254,000 | 1,211,000 | 1,177,000 | 988,000 | 726,000 |
| Average Shares | 308,253 | 308,595 | 311,395 | 312,382 | 318,302 | 324,842 | 329,293 | 329,685 |
| **Balance Sheet** | | | | | | | | |
| Current Assets | 2,758,000 | 2,598,000 | 2,378,000 | 2,223,000 | 2,301,000 | 2,408,000 | 2,059,000 | 2,133,000 |
| Total Assets | 16,410,000 | 15,834,000 | 15,274,000 | 14,317,000 | 13,054,000 | 13,382,000 | 11,102,000 | 10,491,000 |
| Current Liabilities | 1,996,000 | 1,921,000 | 2,110,000 | 1,813,000 | 2,979,000 | 2,650,000 | 1,758,000 | 2,001,000 |
| Long-Term Obligations | 5,685,000 | 5,481,000 | 5,155,000 | 4,757,000 | 3,709,000 | 3,364,000 | 2,981,000 | 2,926,000 |
| Total Liabilities | 10,010,000 | 9,669,000 | 9,482,000 | 9,002,000 | 9,045,000 | 8,240,000 | 6,548,000 | 6,589,000 |
| Stockholders' Equity | 6,400,000 | 6,165,000 | 5,792,000 | 5,315,000 | 4,009,000 | 5,142,000 | 4,554,000 | 3,902,000 |
| Shares Outstanding | 302,158 | 303,381 | 303,996 | 306,477 | 306,861 | 315,488 | 320,860 | 322,338 |
| **Statistical Record** | | | | | | | | |
| Return on Assets % | 8.68 | 8.37 | 8.08 | 9.16 | 9.14 | 9.61 | 9.15 | 7.13 |
| Return on Equity % | 22.49 | 22.12 | 21.52 | 26.90 | 26.39 | 24.28 | 23.37 | 19.33 |
| EBITDA Margin % | 30.86 | 30.90 | 29.73 | 27.03 | 25.31 | 27.23 | 26.61 | 25.57 |
| Net Margin % | 14.80 | 14.73 | 11.81 | 14.00 | 11.22 | 12.52 | 11.87 | 9.48 |
| Asset Turnover | 0.70 | 0.68 | 0.68 | 0.65 | 0.81 | 0.77 | 0.77 | 0.75 |
| Current Ratio | 1.38 | 1.35 | 1.13 | 1.23 | 0.77 | 0.91 | 1.17 | 1.07 |
| Debt to Equity | 0.89 | 0.89 | 0.89 | 0.90 | 0.93 | 0.65 | 0.65 | 0.75 |
| Price Range | 108.39-75.99 | 101.60-74.12 | 95.97-74.01 | 84.89-53.93 | 99.50-47.80 | 91.75-58.85 | 63.54-50.95 | 54.08-41.07 |
| P/E Ratio | 25.15-17.63 | 24.66-17.99 | 24.99-19.27 | 21.17-13.45 | 26.18-12.58 | 25.35-16.26 | 21.18-16.98 | 24.58-18.67 |
| Average Yield % | 2.01 | 2.08 | 2.13 | 2.19 | 1.85 | 1.65 | 1.78 | 1.51 |

**Address:** 39 Old Ridgebury Road, Danbury, CT 06810-5113
**Telephone:** 203-837-2000
**Web Site:** www.praxair.com

**Officers:** Stephen F. Angel - Chairman, Chief Executive Officer James S. Sawyer - Executive Vice President, Chief Financial Officer **Transfer Agents:** Registrar and Transfer Company, Cranford, NJ

**Investor Contact:** 203-837-2210
**No of Institutions:** 979
**Shares:** 294,530,176 **% Held:** 84.94

# PROCTER & GAMBLE CO.

| Exchange | Symbol | Price | 52Wk Range | Yield | P/E |
|---|---|---|---|---|---|
| NYS | PG | $63.68 (8/31/2011) | 67.46-58.51 | 3.30 | 16.20 |

***7 Year Price Score 102.92** *NYSE Composite Index=100 ***12 Month Price Score 99.44**

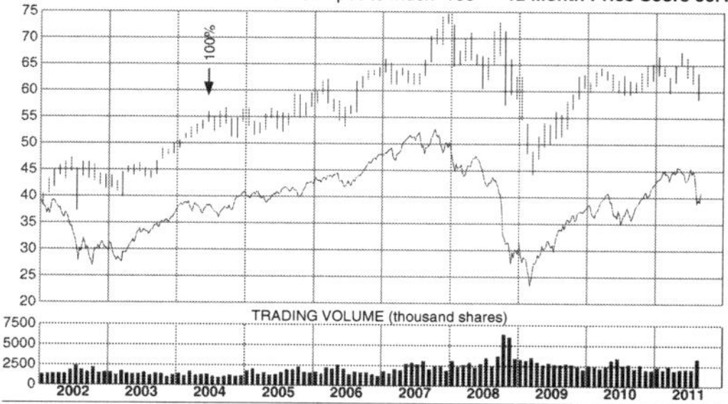


**Interim Earnings (Per Share)**

| Qtr. | Sep | Dec | Mar | Jun |
|---|---|---|---|---|
| 2006-07 | 0.79 | 0.84 | 0.74 | 0.67 |
| 2007-08 | 0.92 | 0.98 | 0.82 | 0.92 |
| 2008-09 | 1.03 | 1.58 | 0.84 | 0.80 |
| 2009-10 | 1.06 | 1.49 | 0.83 | 0.72 |
| 2010-11 | 1.02 | 1.11 | 0.96 | 0.84 |

**Interim Dividends (Per Share)**

| Amt | Decl | Ex | Rec | Pay |
|---|---|---|---|---|
| 0.482Q | 10/12/2010 | 10/20/2010 | 10/22/2010 | 11/15/2010 |
| 0.482Q | 01/11/2011 | 01/19/2011 | 01/21/2011 | 02/15/2011 |
| 0.525Q | 04/11/2011 | 04/27/2011 | 04/29/2011 | 05/16/2011 |
| 0.525Q | 07/12/2011 | 07/20/2011 | 07/22/2011 | 08/15/2011 |

**Indicated Div: $2.10 (Div. Reinv. Plan)**

**Valuation Analysis**

| | | | |
|---|---|---|---|
| Forecast EPS | $4.23 (09/05/2011) | | |
| Market Cap | $176.1 Billion | Book Value | $67.6 Billion |
| Price/Book | 2.60 | Price/Sales | 2.13 |

**Dividend Achiever Status**

| | |
|---|---|
| **10 Year Growth Rate** | 9.95% |
| **Total Years of Dividend Growth** | 57 |

**Business Summary:** Household & Personal Products (MIC: 1.7.1 SIC: 2841 NAIC: 325611)

Procter & Gamble is engaged in providing branded consumer goods products. Co.'s products are sold in more than 180 countries primarily through mass merchandisers, grocery stores, membership club stores, drug stores and high-frequency stores, the neighborhood stores which serve many consumers in developing markets. Co. has on-the-ground operations in approximately 80 countries. As of June 30 2011, Co. was organized into two Global Business Units (GBU's): Beauty and Grooming and Household Care. The business units comprising the GBUs are aggregated into six reportable segments: Beauty; Grooming; Health Care; Snacks and Pet Care; Fabric Care and Home Care; and Baby Care and Family Care.

**Recent Developments:** For the year ended June 30 2011, income from continuing operations increased 7.8% to US$11.80 billion from US$10.95 billion a year earlier. Net income decreased 7.4% to US$11.80 billion from US$12.74 billion in the prior year. Revenues were US$82.56 billion, up 4.6% from US$78.94 billion the year before. Operating income was US$15.82 billion versus US$16.02 billion in the prior year, a decrease of 1.3%. Direct operating expenses rose 7.5% to US$40.77 billion from US$37.92 billion in the comparable period the year before. Indirect operating expenses increased 3.9% to US$25.97 billion from US$25.00 billion in the equivalent prior-year period.

**Prospects:** Our evaluation of Procter & Gamble Co. as of Sep. 6, 2011 is the result of our systematic analysis on three basic characteristics: earnings strength, relative valuation, and recent stock price movement. The company has managed to produce a neutral trend in earnings per share over the past 5 quarters. However, while recent estimates for the company have been lowered by analysts, PG has posted better than expected results. Based on operating earnings yield, the company is about fairly valued when compared to all of the companies in our coverage universe. Share price changes over the past year indicates that PG will perform very poorly over the near term.

**Financial Data**

| (US$ in Millions) | 06/30/2011 | 06/30/2010 | 06/30/2009 | 06/30/2008 | 06/30/2007 | 06/30/2006 | 06/30/2005 | 06/30/2004 |
|---|---|---|---|---|---|---|---|---|
| Earnings Per Share | 3.93 | 4.11 | 4.26 | 3.64 | 3.04 | 2.64 | 2.66 | 2.32 |
| Cash Flow Per Share | 4.72 | 5.54 | 5.05 | 5.12 | 4.25 | 3.72 | 3.47 | 3.62 |
| Dividends Per Share | 1.970 | 1.802 | 1.640 | 1.450 | 1.280 | 1.150 | 1.030 | 0.933 |
| Dividend Payout % | 50.14 | 43.84 | 38.50 | 39.84 | 42.11 | 43.56 | 38.72 | 40.19 |
| **Income Statement** | | | | | | | | |
| Total Revenue | 82,559 | 78,938 | 79,029 | 83,503 | 76,476 | 68,222 | 56,741 | 51,407 |
| EBITDA | 18,858 | 19,101 | 19,765 | 20,711 | 19,144 | 16,159 | 13,157 | 11,712 |
| Depn & Amortn | 2,838 | 3,108 | 3,082 | 3,166 | 3,130 | 2,627 | 1,884 | 1,733 |
| Income Before Taxes | 15,189 | 15,047 | 15,325 | 16,078 | 14,710 | 12,413 | 10,439 | 9,350 |
| Income Taxes | 3,392 | 4,101 | 4,032 | 4,003 | 4,370 | 3,729 | 3,182 | 2,869 |
| Net Income | 11,797 | 12,736 | 13,436 | 12,075 | 10,340 | 8,684 | 7,257 | 6,481 |
| Average Shares | 3,002 | 3,100 | 3,155 | 3,317 | 3,399 | 3,286 | 2,727 | 2,791 |
| **Balance Sheet** | | | | | | | | |
| Current Assets | 21,970 | 18,782 | 21,905 | 24,515 | 24,031 | 24,329 | 20,329 | 17,115 |
| Total Assets | 138,354 | 128,172 | 134,833 | 143,992 | 138,014 | 135,695 | 61,527 | 57,048 |
| Current Liabilities | 27,293 | 24,282 | 30,901 | 30,958 | 30,717 | 19,985 | 25,039 | 22,147 |
| Long-Term Obligations | 22,033 | 21,360 | 20,652 | 23,581 | 23,375 | 35,976 | 12,887 | 12,554 |
| Total Liabilities | 70,714 | 67,057 | 71,734 | 74,498 | 71,254 | 72,787 | 44,050 | 39,770 |
| Stockholders' Equity | 67,640 | 61,115 | 63,099 | 69,494 | 66,760 | 62,908 | 17,477 | 17,278 |
| Shares Outstanding | 2,766 | 2,844 | 2,918 | 3,033 | 3,132 | 3,179 | 2,473 | 2,544 |
| **Statistical Record** | | | | | | | | |
| Return on Assets % | 8.85 | 9.68 | 9.64 | 8.54 | 7.56 | 8.81 | 12.24 | 12.83 |
| Return on Equity % | 18.32 | 20.51 | 20.27 | 17.68 | 15.95 | 21.61 | 41.76 | 38.63 |
| EBITDA Margin % | 22.84 | 24.20 | 25.01 | 24.80 | 25.03 | 23.69 | 23.19 | 22.78 |
| Net Margin % | 14.29 | 16.13 | 17.00 | 14.46 | 13.52 | 12.73 | 12.79 | 12.61 |
| Asset Turnover | 0.62 | 0.60 | 0.57 | 0.59 | 0.56 | 0.69 | 0.96 | 1.02 |
| Current Ratio | 0.80 | 0.77 | 0.71 | 0.79 | 0.78 | 1.22 | 0.81 | 0.77 |
| Debt to Equity | 0.33 | 0.35 | 0.33 | 0.34 | 0.35 | 0.57 | 0.74 | 0.73 |
| Price Range | 67.46-59.34 | 64.53-51.10 | 73.15-44.18 | 74.67-60.49 | 66.09-55.60 | 62.25-52.16 | 56.73-50.97 | 55.96-43.35 |
| P/E Ratio | 17.17-15.10 | 15.70-12.43 | 17.17-10.37 | 20.51-16.62 | 21.74-18.29 | 23.58-19.76 | 21.33-19.16 | 24.12-18.69 |
| Average Yield % | 3.13 | 3.02 | 2.80 | 2.14 | 2.05 | 2.03 | 1.90 | 1.89 |

| | | |
|---|---|---|
| **Address:** One Procter & Gamble Plaza, Cincinnati, OH 45202<br>**Telephone:** 513-983-1100<br>**Web Site:** www.pg.com | **Officers:** Robert A. McDonald - Chairman, President, Chief Executive Officer Werner Geissler - Vice-Chairman **Transfer Agents:**<br>The Procter & Gamble Company, Cincinnati, OH | **Investor Contact:** 800-742-6253<br>**No of Institutions:** 1953<br>**Shares:** 1,772,251,520 **% Held:** 52.65 |

# PROSPERITY BANCSHARES INC.

| Exchange | Symbol | Price | 52Wk Range | Yield | P/E |
|---|---|---|---|---|---|
| NMS | PRSP | $37.85 (8/31/2011) | 46.50-28.49 | 1.85 | 13.23 |

*7 Year Price Score 117.50 *NYSE Composite Index=100 *12 Month Price Score 105.46

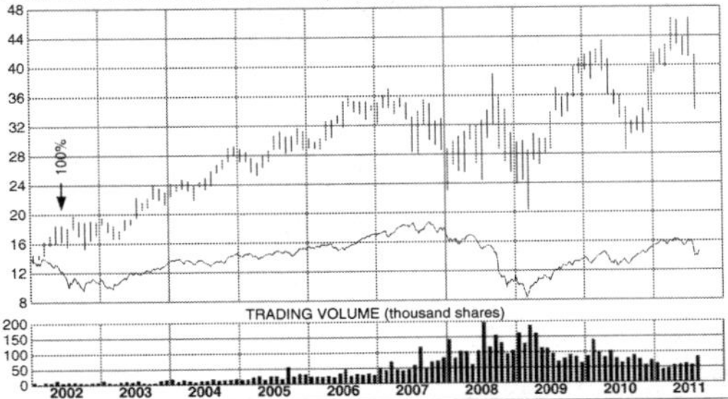


**Interim Earnings (Per Share)**

| Qtr. | Mar | Jun | Sep | Dec |
|---|---|---|---|---|
| 2008 | 0.52 | 0.52 | 0.33 | 0.49 |
| 2009 | 0.55 | 0.57 | 0.63 | 0.65 |
| 2010 | 0.66 | 0.68 | 0.69 | 0.70 |
| 2011 | 0.72 | 0.75 | ... | ... |

**Interim Dividends (Per Share)**

| Amt | Decl | Ex | Rec | Pay |
|---|---|---|---|---|
| 0.155Q | 09/03/2010 | 09/15/2010 | 09/17/2010 | 10/01/2010 |
| 0.175Q | 10/22/2010 | 12/15/2010 | 12/17/2010 | 12/31/2010 |
| 0.175Q | 03/04/2011 | 03/16/2011 | 03/18/2011 | 04/01/2011 |
| 0.175Q | 06/06/2011 | 06/15/2011 | 06/17/2011 | 07/01/2011 |

**Indicated Div: $0.70**

**Valuation Analysis**

| | | | |
|---|---|---|---|
| Forecast EPS | $3.00 (09/03/2011) | | |
| Market Cap | $1.8 Billion | Book Value | $1.5 Billion |
| Price/Book | 1.17 | Price/Sales | N/A |

**Dividend Achiever Status**

| | |
|---|---|
| **10 Year Growth Rate** | 15.39% |
| **Total Years of Dividend Growth** | 11 |

**Business Summary:** Banking (MIC: 5.1.1 SIC: 6022 NAIC: 522110)

Prosperity Bancshares is a financial holding company. Through its bank subsidiary, Prosperity Bank® (the Bank), Co. provides a range of loan and deposit products to its customers, which consist primarily of consumers and small and medium-sized businesses. As of Dec 31 2010, the Bank operated 175 banking locations; with 60 in the Houston area, 20 in the South Texas area including Corpus Christi and Victoria, 33 in the Central Texas area, 10 in the Bryan/College Station area, 21 in East Texas and 31 in the Dallas/Fort Worth, TX area. As of Dec 31 2010, Co. had total assets of $9.48 billion and total deposits of $7.46 billion.

**Recent Developments:** For the quarter ended June 30 2011, net income increased 10.5% to US$35.1 million from US$31.7 million in the year-earlier quarter. Net interest income increased 3.8% to US$83.6 million from US$80.6 million in the year-earlier quarter. Provision for loan losses was US$1.4 million versus US$3.3 million in the prior-year quarter, a decrease of 57.3%. Non-interest income rose 1.8% to US$13.5 million from US$13.3 million, while non-interest expense declined 1.2% to US$42.5 million.

**Prospects:** Our evaluation of Prosperity Bancshares Inc. as of Sep. 6, 2011 is the result of our systematic analysis on three basic characteristics: earnings strength, relative valuation, and recent stock price movement. The company has enjoyed a very positive trend in earnings per share over the past 5 quarters. However, while recent estimates for the company have been lowered by analysts, PRSP has posted better than expected results. Based on operating earnings yield, the company is undervalued when compared to all of the companies in our coverage universe. Share price changes over the past year indicates that PRSP will perform well over the near term.

| **Financial Data** (US$ in Thousands) | 6 Mos | 3 Mos | 12/31/2010 | 12/31/2009 | 12/31/2008 | 12/31/2007 | 12/31/2006 | 12/31/2005 |
|---|---|---|---|---|---|---|---|---|
| Earnings Per Share | 2.86 | 2.79 | 2.73 | 2.41 | 1.86 | 1.94 | 1.94 | 1.77 |
| Cash Flow Per Share | 4.21 | 4.05 | 3.81 | 1.59 | 2.72 | 5.50 | 2.39 | 2.46 |
| Tang Book Value Per Share | 11.99 | 11.31 | 10.70 | 9.43 | 7.43 | 7.41 | 6.62 | 6.48 |
| Dividends Per Share | 0.680 | 0.660 | 0.640 | 0.568 | 0.512 | 0.463 | 0.412 | 0.347 |
| Dividend Payout % | 23.78 | 23.66 | 23.44 | 23.55 | 27.55 | 23.84 | 21.26 | 19.63 |
| **Income Statement** | | | | | | | | |
| Interest Income | 189,061 | 93,409 | 384,537 | 409,614 | 347,878 | 340,608 | 231,739 | 162,123 |
| Interest Expense | 25,018 | 12,996 | 66,389 | 102,513 | 120,149 | 140,173 | 93,594 | 51,226 |
| Net Interest Income | 164,043 | 80,413 | 318,148 | 307,101 | 227,729 | 200,435 | 138,145 | 110,897 |
| Provision for Losses | 3,100 | 1,700 | 13,585 | 28,775 | 9,867 | 760 | 504 | 480 |
| Non-Interest Income | 27,397 | 13,867 | 53,833 | 60,097 | 52,370 | 52,923 | 33,982 | 30,021 |
| Non-Interest Expense | 84,209 | 41,695 | 166,594 | 169,700 | 143,796 | 126,843 | 77,669 | 68,957 |
| Income Before Taxes | 104,131 | 50,885 | 191,802 | 168,723 | 126,436 | 125,755 | 93,954 | 71,481 |
| Income Taxes | 35,161 | 17,007 | 64,094 | 56,844 | 41,929 | 41,604 | 32,229 | 23,621 |
| Net Income | 68,970 | 33,878 | 127,708 | 111,879 | 84,507 | 84,151 | 61,725 | 47,860 |
| Average Shares | 47,057 | 46,942 | 46,832 | 46,354 | 45,479 | 43,310 | 31,893 | 27,024 |
| **Balance Sheet** | | | | | | | | |
| Net Loans & Leases | 3,613,316 | 3,521,160 | 3,433,439 | 3,324,840 | 3,530,087 | 3,110,428 | 2,152,517 | 1,524,922 |
| Total Assets | 9,657,147 | 9,722,947 | 9,476,572 | 8,850,400 | 9,072,364 | 6,372,343 | 4,586,769 | 3,585,982 |
| Total Deposits | 7,667,692 | 7,816,384 | 7,454,920 | 7,258,550 | 7,303,297 | 4,966,407 | 3,725,678 | 2,920,318 |
| Total Liabilities | 8,145,499 | 8,242,449 | 8,024,233 | 7,499,155 | 7,817,258 | 5,244,912 | 3,922,358 | 3,121,265 |
| Stockholders' Equity | 1,511,648 | 1,480,498 | 1,452,339 | 1,351,245 | 1,255,106 | 1,127,431 | 664,411 | 464,717 |
| Shares Outstanding | 46,888 | 46,781 | 46,684 | 46,540 | 46,079 | 44,188 | 32,792 | 27,820 |
| **Statistical Record** | | | | | | | | |
| Return on Assets % | 1.39 | 1.38 | 1.39 | 1.25 | 1.09 | 1.54 | 1.51 | 1.52 |
| Return on Equity % | 9.19 | 9.14 | 9.11 | 8.59 | 7.07 | 9.39 | 10.93 | 12.93 |
| Net Interest Margin % | 87.43 | 86.09 | 82.74 | 74.97 | 65.46 | 58.85 | 59.61 | 68.40 |
| Efficiency Ratio % | 38.94 | 38.87 | 38.00 | 36.13 | 35.93 | 32.23 | 29.23 | 35.89 |
| Loans to Deposits | 0.47 | 0.45 | 0.46 | 0.46 | 0.48 | 0.63 | 0.58 | 0.52 |
| Price Range | 46.50-28.49 | 43.53-28.49 | 43.53-28.49 | 40.98-20.33 | 39.00-23.04 | 37.09-28.18 | 36.07-28.81 | 31.70-25.19 |
| P/E Ratio | 16.26-9.96 | 15.60-10.21 | 15.95-10.44 | 17.00-8.44 | 20.97-12.39 | 19.12-14.53 | 18.59-14.85 | 17.91-14.23 |
| Average Yield % | 1.80 | 1.81 | 1.76 | 1.80 | 1.73 | 1.39 | 1.27 | 1.21 |

**Address:** Prosperity Bank Plaza, 4295 San Felipe, Houston, TX 77027
**Telephone:** 281-269-7199
**Web Site:** www.prosperitybanktx.com

**Officers:** David Zalman - Chairman, Chief Executive Officer H. E. Timanus - Vice-Chairman **Transfer Agents:** Computershare Investor Services, Golden, CO

**Investor Contact:** 713-693-9300
**No of Institutions:** 229
**Shares:** 40,091,008 **% Held:** 81.53

# QUESTAR CORP.

| Exchange | Symbol | Price | 52Wk Range | Yield | P/E |
|---|---|---|---|---|---|
| NYS | STR | $18.74 (8/31/2011) | 18.90-16.28 | 3.26 | 16.73 |

*7 Year Price Score 124.12 *NYSE Composite Index=100 *12 Month Price Score 103.90

**Interim Earnings (Per Share)**

| Qtr. | Mar | Jun | Sep | Dec |
|---|---|---|---|---|
| 2008 | 1.05 | 0.98 | 1.16 | 0.69 |
| 2009 | 0.38 | 0.44 | 0.56 | 0.85 |
| 2010 | 0.85 | 0.55 | 0.15 | 0.36 |
| 2011 | 0.39 | 0.22 | ... | ... |

**Interim Dividends (Per Share)**

| Amt | Decl | Ex | Rec | Pay |
|---|---|---|---|---|
| 0.14Q | 10/26/2010 | 11/17/2010 | 11/19/2010 | 12/13/2010 |
| 0.153Q | 02/18/2011 | 03/02/2011 | 03/04/2011 | 03/21/2011 |
| 0.153Q | 05/10/2011 | 05/18/2011 | 05/20/2011 | 06/13/2011 |
| 0.153Q | 08/09/2011 | 08/17/2011 | 08/19/2011 | 09/12/2011 |

**Indicated Div: $0.61 (Div. Reinv. Plan)**

**Valuation Analysis**

| | | | |
|---|---|---|---|
| Forecast EPS | $1.12 (09/05/2011) | | |
| Market Cap | $3.3 Billion | Book Value | $1.1 Billion |
| Price/Book | 3.01 | Price/Sales | 2.77 |

**Dividend Achiever Status**

| | |
|---|---|
| **10 Year Growth Rate** | 4.36% |
| **Total Years of Dividend Growth** | 31 |

**Business Summary:** Gas Utilities (MIC: 3.3.1 SIC: 1311 NAIC: 211111)

Questar is a holding company. Co. is a Rockies-based integrated natural gas company with three complementary lines of business operated through its Wexpro Company (Wexpro), Questar Pipeline Company (Questar Pipeline), and Questar Gas Company (Questar Gas) wholly owned subsidiaries. Wexpro is engaged in developing and producing natural gas on behalf of Questar Gas. Questar Pipeline operates interstate natural gas pipelines and storage facilities in the western U.S. and provides other energy services. Questar Gas provides retail natural gas distribution in Utah, Wyoming and Idaho.

**Recent Developments:** For the quarter ended June 30 2011, income from continuing operations increased 40.4% to US$40.3 million from US$28.7 million in the year-earlier quarter. Net income decreased 58.7% to US$40.3 million from US$97.5 million in the year-earlier quarter. Revenues were US$222.9 million, up 10.8% from US$201.1 million the year before. Operating income was US$73.7 million versus US$56.3 million in the prior-year quarter, an increase of 30.9%. Direct operating expenses rose 23.1% to US$71.0 million from US$57.7 million in the comparable period the year before. Indirect operating expenses decreased 10.2% to US$78.2 million from US$87.1 million in the equivalent prior-year period.

**Prospects:** Our evaluation of Questar Corp. as of Sep. 6, 2011 is the result of our systematic analysis on three basic characteristics: earnings strength, relative valuation, and recent stock price movement. The company has produced a positive trend in earnings per share over the past 5 quarters and while recent estimates for the company have been mixed, STR has posted better than expected results. Based on operating earnings yield, the company is about fairly valued when compared to all of the companies in our coverage universe. Share price changes over the past year indicates that STR will perform very poorly over the near term.

**Financial Data**

| (US$ in Thousands) | 6 Mos | 3 Mos | 12/31/2010 | 12/31/2009 | 12/31/2008 | 12/31/2007 | 12/31/2006 | 12/31/2005 |
|---|---|---|---|---|---|---|---|---|
| Earnings Per Share | 1.12 | 1.45 | 1.91 | 2.23 | 3.88 | 2.88 | 2.54 | 1.87 |
| Cash Flow Per Share | 2.62 | 1.21 | 2.00 | 9.06 | 8.63 | 6.63 | 5.65 | 4.12 |
| Tang Book Value Per Share | 6.23 | 6.14 | 5.81 | 19.66 | 19.29 | 14.51 | 12.43 | 8.60 |
| Dividends Per Share | 0.585 | 0.563 | 0.540 | 0.505 | 0.492 | 0.485 | 0.465 | 0.445 |
| Dividend Payout % | 52.23 | 38.79 | 28.27 | 22.65 | 12.69 | 16.84 | 18.34 | 23.80 |
| **Income Statement** | | | | | | | | |
| Total Revenue | 692,900 | 470,000 | 1,123,600 | 3,038,000 | 3,465,100 | 2,726,600 | 2,835,600 | 2,724,888 |
| EBITDA | 279,600 | 164,600 | 505,100 | 1,438,700 | 1,663,400 | 1,222,800 | 1,068,900 | 821,463 |
| Depn & Amortn | 83,100 | 41,800 | 161,800 | 714,600 | 502,100 | 375,800 | 316,100 | 259,734 |
| Income Before Taxes | 170,900 | 109,700 | 297,900 | 611,400 | 1,068,500 | 789,100 | 692,100 | 506,136 |
| Income Taxes | 62,600 | 40,700 | 109,400 | 222,000 | 378,000 | 290,600 | 255,500 | 187,923 |
| Net Income | 110,200 | 69,900 | 339,200 | 393,300 | 683,800 | 507,400 | 444,100 | 325,681 |
| Average Shares | 178,800 | 178,500 | 178,000 | 176,300 | 176,100 | 175,900 | 175,200 | 174,268 |
| **Balance Sheet** | | | | | | | | |
| Current Assets | 197,300 | 282,000 | 399,600 | 831,100 | 1,185,000 | 658,900 | 753,400 | 755,840 |
| Total Assets | 3,221,400 | 3,267,500 | 3,373,600 | 8,897,700 | 8,630,700 | 5,944,200 | 5,064,700 | 4,357,073 |
| Current Liabilities | 384,300 | 473,200 | 655,100 | 948,100 | 1,131,600 | 998,700 | 678,900 | 873,574 |
| Long-Term Obligations | 901,800 | 898,500 | 898,500 | 2,179,900 | 2,078,900 | 1,021,200 | 1,022,400 | 983,200 |
| Total Liabilities | 2,115,300 | 2,177,800 | 2,337,500 | 5,395,500 | 5,212,700 | 3,366,300 | 2,859,200 | 2,807,270 |
| Stockholders' Equity | 1,106,100 | 1,089,700 | 1,036,100 | 3,502,200 | 3,418,000 | 2,577,900 | 2,205,500 | 1,549,803 |
| Shares Outstanding | 177,507 | 177,482 | 176,500 | 174,600 | 173,600 | 172,800 | 171,800 | 170,639 |
| **Statistical Record** | | | | | | | | |
| Return on Assets % | 6.40 | 4.15 | 5.53 | 4.49 | 9.36 | 9.22 | 9.43 | 8.14 |
| Return on Equity % | 19.41 | 10.53 | 14.95 | 11.37 | 22.75 | 21.22 | 23.65 | 21.79 |
| EBITDA Margin % | 40.35 | 35.02 | 44.95 | 47.36 | 48.00 | 44.85 | 37.70 | 30.15 |
| Net Margin % | 15.90 | 14.87 | 30.19 | 12.95 | 19.73 | 18.61 | 15.66 | 11.95 |
| Asset Turnover | 0.38 | 0.19 | 0.18 | 0.35 | 0.47 | 0.50 | 0.60 | 0.68 |
| Current Ratio | 0.51 | 0.60 | 0.61 | 0.88 | 1.05 | 0.66 | 1.11 | 0.87 |
| Debt to Equity | 0.82 | 0.82 | 0.87 | 0.62 | 0.61 | 0.40 | 0.46 | 0.63 |
| Price Range | 18.26-14.66 | 18.26-13.92 | 18.08-12.83 | 13.87-8.14 | 23.65-7.13 | 18.66-12.40 | 14.51-10.97 | 14.38-7.55 |
| P/E Ratio | 16.30-13.09 | 12.59-9.60 | 9.47-6.72 | 6.22-3.65 | 6.09-1.84 | 6.48-4.30 | 5.71-4.32 | 7.69-4.04 |
| Average Yield % | 3.40 | 3.38 | 3.43 | 4.51 | 3.03 | 3.05 | 3.64 | 4.14 |

**Address:** 180 East 100 South Street, P.O. Box 45433, Salt Lake City, UT 84145-0433
**Telephone:** 801-324-5000
**Web Site:** www.questar.com

**Officers:** Keith O. Rattie - Chairman Ronald W. Jibson - President, Chief Executive Officer **Transfer Agents:** Wells Fargo Shareowner Services, South St. Paul, MN

**No of Institutions:** 457
**Shares:** 142,792,720 **% Held:** 75.77

# RAVEN INDUSTRIES, INC.

| Exchange | Symbol | Price | 52Wk Range | Yield | P/E |
|---|---|---|---|---|---|
| NMS | RAVN | $54.33 (8/31/2011) | 61.42-33.71 | 1.33 | 22.83 |

*7 Year Price Score 149.62 *NYSE Composite Index=100 *12 Month Price Score 108.42

**Interim Earnings (Per Share)**

| Qtr. | Apr | Jul | Oct | Jan |
|---|---|---|---|---|
| 2008-09 | 0.60 | 0.38 | 0.46 | 0.26 |
| 2009-10 | 0.51 | 0.34 | 0.40 | 0.32 |
| 2010-11 | 0.72 | 0.46 | 0.65 | 0.41 |
| 2011-12 | 0.86 | ... | ... | ... |

**Interim Dividends (Per Share)**

| Amt | Decl | Ex | Rec | Pay |
|---|---|---|---|---|
| 0.16Q | 11/30/2010 | 12/29/2010 | 12/31/2010 | 01/14/2011 |
| 0.18Q | 03/21/2011 | 03/29/2011 | 03/31/2011 | 04/15/2011 |
| 0.18Q | 05/24/2011 | 06/28/2011 | 06/30/2011 | 07/15/2011 |
| 0.18Q | 08/31/2011 | 09/28/2011 | 09/30/2011 | 10/14/2011 |

**Indicated Div: $0.72 (Div. Reinv. Plan)**

**Valuation Analysis**

| | | | |
|---|---|---|---|
| Forecast EPS | $2.65 (09/02/2011) | | |
| Market Cap | $982.2 Million | Book Value | $154.3 Million |
| Price/Book | 6.36 | Price/Sales | 2.97 |

**Dividend Achiever Status**

| | |
|---|---|
| 10 Year Growth Rate | 17.37% |
| Total Years of Dividend Growth | 23 |

**Business Summary:** Electrical Equipment (MIC: 7.3.1 SIC: 3081 NAIC: 326113)

Raven Industries is an industrial manufacturer providing a variety of products. Co. has four business segments: Applied Technology Division, which includes electronic and Global Positioning System devices; Engineered Films Division, which produces rugged reinforced plastic sheeting for industrial, construction and agricultural applications; Aerostar Division, which sells high-altitude and tethered aerostats for government and commercial research; and Electronic Systems Division, which includes manufactured assemblies for avionics, secure communication, environmental controls and other products.

**Recent Developments:** For the quarter ended Apr 30 2011, net income increased 21.4% to US$15.7 million from US$12.9 million in the year-earlier quarter. Revenues were US$101.5 million, up 19.4% from US$85.0 million the year before. Operating income was US$23.5 million versus US$19.5 million in the prior-year quarter, an increase of 20.7%. Direct operating expenses rose 18.6% to US$68.6 million from US$57.9 million in the comparable period the year before. Indirect operating expenses increased 22.7% to US$9.4 million from US$7.7 million in the equivalent prior-year period.

**Prospects:** Our evaluation of Raven Industries Inc. as of Sep. 6, 2011 is the result of our systematic analysis on three basic characteristics: earnings strength, relative valuation, and recent stock price movement. The company has managed to produce a neutral trend in earnings per share over the past 5 quarters. Because the company lacks sufficient analyst estimate data, we place greater weight on the historical EPS trend as the measure of earnings strength. Based on operating earnings yield, the company is about fairly valued when compared to all of the companies in our coverage universe. Share price changes over the past year indicates that RAVN will perform well over the near term.

| Financial Data (US$ in Thousands) | 3 Mos | 01/31/2011 | 01/31/2010 | 01/31/2009 | 01/31/2008 | 01/31/2007 | 01/31/2006 | 01/31/2005 |
|---|---|---|---|---|---|---|---|---|
| Earnings Per Share | 2.38 | 2.24 | 1.58 | 1.70 | 1.53 | 1.39 | 1.32 | 0.97 |
| Cash Flow Per Share | 2.36 | 2.33 | 2.64 | 2.16 | 1.50 | 1.46 | 1.17 | 1.04 |
| Tang Book Value Per Share | 7.85 | 7.13 | 6.68 | 5.81 | 6.05 | 4.97 | 4.19 | 3.33 |
| Dividends Per Share | 1.910 | 1.890 | 0.550 | 1.770 | 0.440 | 0.360 | 0.280 | 0.845 |
| Dividend Payout % | 80.25 | 84.38 | 34.81 | 104.12 | 28.76 | 25.90 | 21.21 | 87.11 |
| **Income Statement** | | | | | | | | |
| Total Revenue | 101,541 | 314,708 | 237,782 | 279,913 | 233,957 | 217,529 | 204,528 | 168,086 |
| EBITDA | 25,505 | 67,834 | 50,328 | 54,152 | 48,489 | 44,187 | 42,435 | 31,703 |
| Depn & Amortn | 1,985 | 7,631 | 7,108 | 7,758 | 7,344 | 5,885 | 5,151 | 3,841 |
| Income Before Taxes | 23,520 | 60,282 | 43,322 | 46,901 | 42,224 | 38,835 | 37,494 | 27,955 |
| Income Taxes | 7,804 | 19,745 | 14,748 | 16,131 | 14,422 | 13,394 | 13,232 | 10,064 |
| Net Income | 15,716 | 40,537 | 28,574 | 30,770 | 27,802 | 25,441 | 24,262 | 17,891 |
| Average Shares | 18,212 | 18,110 | 18,043 | 18,080 | 18,204 | 18,272 | 18,314 | 18,410 |
| **Balance Sheet** | | | | | | | | |
| Current Assets | 144,696 | 128,181 | 117,747 | 98,073 | 100,869 | 73,219 | 71,345 | 61,592 |
| Total Assets | 204,235 | 187,760 | 170,309 | 144,415 | 147,861 | 119,764 | 106,157 | 88,509 |
| Current Liabilities | 37,262 | 34,335 | 25,960 | 23,322 | 22,108 | 16,464 | 20,050 | 20,950 |
| Long-Term Obligations | ... | ... | ... | ... | ... | ... | 9 | ... |
| Total Liabilities | 49,899 | 46,546 | 37,058 | 30,859 | 29,586 | 21,496 | 21,768 | 22,427 |
| Stockholders' Equity | 154,336 | 141,214 | 133,251 | 113,556 | 118,275 | 98,268 | 84,389 | 66,082 |
| Shares Outstanding | 18,079 | 18,062 | 18,029 | 18,012 | 18,120 | 18,039 | 18,072 | 17,999 |
| **Statistical Record** | | | | | | | | |
| Return on Assets % | 21.96 | 22.64 | 18.16 | 21.00 | 20.78 | 22.52 | 24.93 | 21.24 |
| Return on Equity % | 29.07 | 29.54 | 23.15 | 26.47 | 25.68 | 27.86 | 32.25 | 26.92 |
| EBITDA Margin % | 25.12 | 21.55 | 21.17 | 19.35 | 20.73 | 20.31 | 20.75 | 18.86 |
| Net Margin % | 15.48 | 12.88 | 12.02 | 10.99 | 11.88 | 11.70 | 11.86 | 10.64 |
| Asset Turnover | 1.68 | 1.76 | 1.51 | 1.91 | 1.75 | 1.93 | 2.10 | 2.00 |
| Current Ratio | 3.88 | 3.73 | 4.54 | 4.21 | 4.56 | 4.45 | 3.56 | 2.94 |
| Price Range | 61.42-29.35 | 49.32-26.67 | 32.93-15.42 | 46.14-21.46 | 43.21-26.59 | 41.73-25.89 | 32.75-17.08 | 26.56-13.34 |
| P/E Ratio | 25.81-12.33 | 22.02-11.91 | 20.84-9.76 | 27.14-12.62 | 28.24-17.38 | 30.02-18.63 | 24.81-12.94 | 27.38-13.75 |
| Average Yield % | 4.47 | 5.16 | 2.10 | 5.51 | 1.26 | 1.14 | 1.11 | 4.60 |

**Address:** 205 East 6th Street, P.O. Box 5107, Sioux Falls, SD 57117-5107
**Telephone:** 605-336-2750
**Web Site:** www.ravenind.com

**Officers:** Thomas S. Everist - Chairman Daniel A. Rykhus - President, Chief Executive Officer **Transfer Agents:** Wells Fargo Bank, N.A., South St. Paul, MN

**Investor Contact:** 605-336-2750
**No of Institutions:** 133
**Shares:** 15,027,382 **% Held:** 68.53

# REALTY INCOME CORP.

| Exchange | Symbol | Price | 52Wk Range | Yield | P/E |
|---|---|---|---|---|---|
| NYS | O | $34.68 (8/31/2011) | 36.07-28.04 | 5.01 | 33.03 |

***7 Year Price Score 128.25** *NYSE Composite Index=100 ***12 Month Price Score 96.24**

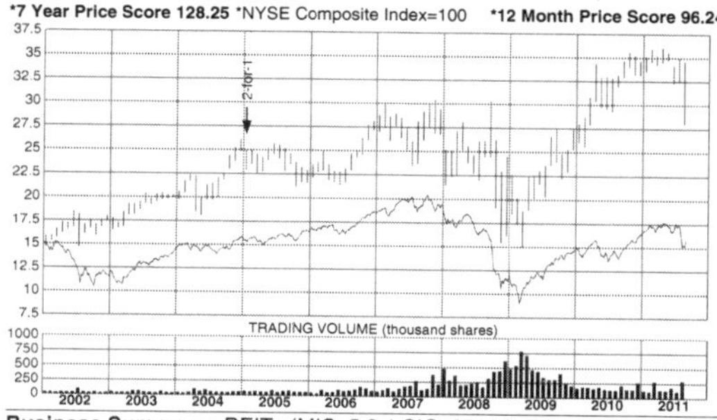


**Interim Earnings (Per Share)**

| Qtr. | Mar | Jun | Sep | Dec |
|---|---|---|---|---|
| 2008 | 0.24 | 0.27 | 0.29 | 0.27 |
| 2009 | 0.23 | 0.26 | 0.26 | 0.28 |
| 2010 | 0.23 | 0.24 | 0.25 | 0.29 |
| 2011 | 0.25 | 0.26 | ... | ... |

**Interim Dividends (Per Share)**

| Amt | Decl | Ex | Rec | Pay |
|---|---|---|---|---|
| 0.145M | 05/03/2011 | 05/27/2011 | 06/01/2011 | 06/15/2011 |
| 0.145M | 06/21/2011 | 06/29/2011 | 07/01/2011 | 07/15/2011 |
| 0.145M | 07/19/2011 | 07/28/2011 | 08/01/2011 | 08/15/2011 |
| 0.145M | 08/25/2011 | 09/01/2011 | 09/06/2011 | 09/15/2011 |

**Indicated Div: $1.74**

**Valuation Analysis**

| | | | |
|---|---|---|---|
| Forecast EPS | $1.09 (09/05/2011) | | |
| Market Cap | $4.4 Billion | Book Value | $2.1 Billion |
| Price/Book | 2.10 | Price/Sales | 11.60 |

**Dividend Achiever Status**

| | |
|---|---|
| 10 Year Growth Rate | 4.38% |
| Total Years of Dividend Growth | 16 |

**Business Summary:** REITs (MIC: 5.3.1 SIC: 6798 NAIC: 525930)

Realty Income is an equity real estate investment trust engaged in leasing retail properties to regional and national commercial enterprises. At Dec 31 2010, Co. owned a portfolio of 2,496 retail properties located in 49 states, with over 21.2 million square feet of leasable space. Of the 2,496 retail properties, 2,402 were leased under net-lease agreements. A net lease typically requires the tenant to be responsible for minimum monthly rent and property operating expenses including property taxes, insurance and maintenance. Co. has a subsidiary, Crest Net Lease, Inc., which was created to buy and sell properties, primarily to individual investors who are involved in tax-deferred exchanges.

**Recent Developments:** For the quarter ended June 30 2011, income from continuing operations increased 31.1% to US$38.0 million from US$29.0 million in the year-earlier quarter. Net income increased 26.4% to US$39.2 million from US$31.0 million in the year-earlier quarter. Revenues were US$102.6 million, up 24.6% from US$82.4 million the year before. Revenues from property income rose 24.5% to US$102.4 million from US$82.2 million in the corresponding quarter a year earlier.

**Prospects:** Our evaluation of Realty Income Corp. as of Sep. 6, 2011 is the result of our systematic analysis on three basic characteristics: earnings strength, relative valuation, and recent stock price movement. The company has produced a positive trend in earnings per share over the past 5 quarters. Because the company lacks sufficient analyst estimate data, we place greater weight on the historical EPS trend as the measure of earnings strength. Based on operating earnings yield, the company is overvalued when compared to all of the companies in our coverage universe. Share price changes over the past year indicates that O will perform very poorly over the near term.

**Financial Data**

| (US$ in Thousands) | 6 Mos | 3 Mos | 12/31/2010 | 12/31/2009 | 12/31/2008 | 12/31/2007 | 12/31/2006 | 12/31/2005 |
|---|---|---|---|---|---|---|---|---|
| Earnings Per Share | 1.05 | 1.03 | 1.01 | 1.03 | 1.06 | 1.16 | 1.11 | 1.12 |
| Cash Flow Per Share | 2.14 | 2.09 | 2.30 | 2.19 | 2.43 | 3.18 | 0.97 | 1.37 |
| Tang Book Value Per Share | 16.35 | 16.50 | 15.50 | 14.10 | 14.75 | 15.05 | 15.47 | 11.61 |
| Dividends Per Share | 1.730 | 1.727 | 1.723 | 1.708 | 1.667 | 1.571 | 1.448 | 1.353 |
| Dividend Payout % | 164.80 | 167.63 | 170.58 | 165.81 | 157.29 | 135.39 | 130.41 | 120.76 |
| **Income Statement** | | | | | | | | |
| Total Revenue | 200,354 | 97,756 | 345,009 | 327,581 | 330,200 | 296,513 | 240,100 | 196,676 |
| EBITDA | 78,128 | 37,783 | 316,332 | 303,770 | 306,583 | 272,763 | 219,871 | 178,771 |
| Depn & Amortn | 4,347 | 2,180 | 101,679 | 96,109 | 95,781 | 81,049 | 62,443 | 48,605 |
| Income Before Taxes | 23,012 | 10,481 | 121,416 | 122,133 | 116,846 | 127,383 | 106,065 | 89,217 |
| Net Income | 75,247 | 35,999 | 130,784 | 131,127 | 131,841 | 140,409 | 110,781 | 99,119 |
| Average Shares | 126,202 | 119,109 | 105,942 | 103,581 | 101,209 | 100,333 | 89,917 | 80,208 |
| **Balance Sheet** | | | | | | | | |
| Current Assets | 175,496 | 155,332 | 28,908 | 20,422 | 57,439 | 200,243 | 16,526 | 70,748 |
| Total Assets | 3,991,053 | 3,770,556 | 3,535,590 | 2,914,787 | 2,994,179 | 3,077,352 | 2,546,508 | 1,920,988 |
| Current Liabilities | 72,364 | 44,160 | 85,173 | 70,046 | 54,820 | 67,400 | 42,100 | 30,512 |
| Long-Term Obligations | 1,809,606 | 1,600,000 | 1,600,000 | 1,354,600 | 1,370,000 | 1,470,000 | 920,000 | 891,700 |
| Total Liabilities | 1,900,060 | 1,660,408 | 1,688,625 | 1,426,778 | 1,439,518 | 1,539,260 | 970,516 | 931,774 |
| Stockholders' Equity | 2,090,993 | 2,110,148 | 1,846,965 | 1,488,009 | 1,554,661 | 1,538,092 | 1,575,992 | 989,214 |
| Shares Outstanding | 126,865 | 126,828 | 118,058 | 104,286 | 104,211 | 101,082 | 100,746 | 83,696 |
| **Statistical Record** | | | | | | | | |
| Return on Assets % | 4.06 | 4.09 | 4.06 | 4.44 | 4.33 | 4.99 | 4.96 | 5.89 |
| Return on Equity % | 8.18 | 7.64 | 7.84 | 8.62 | 8.50 | 9.02 | 8.64 | 10.42 |
| EBITDA Margin % | 38.99 | 38.65 | 91.69 | 92.73 | 92.85 | 91.99 | 91.57 | 90.90 |
| Net Margin % | 37.56 | 36.83 | 37.91 | 40.03 | 39.93 | 47.35 | 46.14 | 50.40 |
| Asset Turnover | 0.11 | 0.11 | 0.11 | 0.11 | 0.11 | 0.11 | 0.11 | 0.12 |
| Current Ratio | 2.43 | 3.52 | 0.34 | 0.29 | 1.05 | 2.97 | 0.39 | 2.32 |
| Debt to Equity | 0.87 | 0.76 | 0.87 | 0.91 | 0.88 | 0.96 | 0.58 | 0.90 |
| Price Range | 36.07-29.33 | 35.97-29.33 | 35.65-25.52 | 27.54-15.03 | 30.32-15.47 | 30.45-23.47 | 28.17-21.30 | 25.68-21.20 |
| P/E Ratio | 34.35-27.93 | 34.92-28.48 | 35.30-25.27 | 26.74-14.59 | 28.60-14.59 | 26.25-20.23 | 25.38-19.19 | 22.93-18.93 |
| Average Yield % | 5.09 | 5.19 | 5.44 | 7.63 | 6.98 | 5.70 | 6.03 | 5.72 |

**Address:** 600 La Terraza Boulevard, Escondido, CA 92025-3873
**Telephone:** 760-741-2111
**Web Site:** www.realtyincome.com

**Officers:** Thomas A. Lewis - Vice-Chairman, Chief Executive Officer Gary M. Malino - President, Chief Operating Officer **Transfer Agents:** Wells Fargo Shareowner Services, St. Paul, MN

**Investor Contact:** 760-741-2111
**No of Institutions:** 319
**Shares:** 64,772,752 **% Held:** 57.89

# RLI CORP.

| Exchange | Symbol | Price | 52Wk Range | Yield | P/E |
|---|---|---|---|---|---|
| NYS | RLI | $63.22 (8/31/2011) | 66.28-50.98 | 1.90 | 9.46 |

***7 Year Price Score 109.19** *NYSE Composite Index=100 ***12 Month Price Score 107.95**

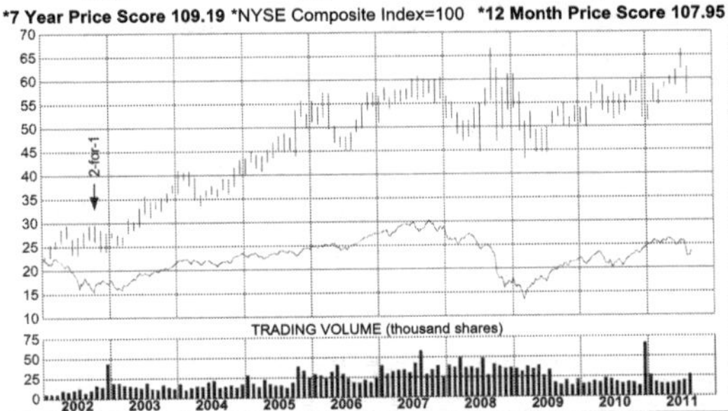


**Interim Earnings (Per Share)**

| Qtr. | Mar | Jun | Sep | Dec |
|---|---|---|---|---|
| 2008 | 1.14 | 1.77 | 0.40 | 0.28 |
| 2009 | (0.08) | 1.57 | 1.42 | 1.41 |
| 2010 | 1.13 | 1.65 | 1.33 | 1.89 |
| 2011 | 1.24 | 2.22 | ... | ... |

**Interim Dividends (Per Share)**

| Amt | Decl | Ex | Rec | Pay |
|---|---|---|---|---|
| 7.00Sp | 12/01/2010 | 12/14/2010 | 12/16/2010 | 12/29/2010 |
| 0.29Q | 02/10/2011 | 02/24/2011 | 02/28/2011 | 03/18/2011 |
| 0.30Q | 05/05/2011 | 05/26/2011 | 05/31/2011 | 06/20/2011 |
| 0.30Q | 08/18/2011 | 08/29/2011 | 08/31/2011 | 09/20/2011 |

**Indicated Div: $1.20 (Div. Reinv. Plan)**

**Valuation Analysis**

| | | | |
|---|---|---|---|
| Forecast EPS | $5.20 (09/02/2011) | | |
| Market Cap | $1.3 Billion | Book Value | $864.4 Million |
| Price/Book | 1.54 | Price/Sales | 2.24 |

**Dividend Achiever Status**

| | |
|---|---|
| **10 Year Growth Rate** | 16.52% |
| **Total Years of Dividend Growth** | 34 |

**Business Summary:** General Insurance (MIC: 5.2.1 SIC: 6331 NAIC: 524126)

RLI is an insurance holding company. Through its subsidiaries, Co. underwrites selected property and casualty insurance. Co. has three main business segments: casualty, which includes general liability, personal umbrella, transportation, executive products, commercial umbrella, multi-peril program business and other coverages; property, which includes commercial fire, earthquake, wind, flood and collapse coverages as well as cargo, hull and protection and indemnity, marine liability, and inland marine; and surety, which engages in writing small-to-large commercial and small contract surety coverages, as well as those for the energy, petrochemical and refining industries.

**Recent Developments:** For the quarter ended June 30 2011, net income increased 35.4% to US$47.4 million from US$35.0 million in the year-earlier quarter. Revenues were US$156.1 million, up 9.3% from US$142.8 million the year before. Net premiums earned were US$130.8 million versus US$121.8 million in the prior-year quarter, an increase of 7.4%. Net investment income fell 9.5% to US$15.2 million from US$16.8 million a year ago.

**Prospects:** Our evaluation of RLI Corp. as of Sep. 6, 2011 is the result of our systematic analysis on three basic characteristics: earnings strength, relative valuation, and recent stock price movement. The company has generated a negative trend in earnings per share over the past 5 quarters and while recent estimates for the company have remained steady, RLI has posted better than expected results. Based on operating earnings yield, the company is undervalued when compared to all of the companies in our coverage universe. Share price changes over the past year indicates that RLI will perform poorly over the near term.

| **Financial Data** (US$ in Thousands) | 6 Mos | 3 Mos | 12/31/2010 | 12/31/2009 | 12/31/2008 | 12/31/2007 | 12/31/2006 | 12/31/2005 |
|---|---|---|---|---|---|---|---|---|
| Earnings Per Share | 6.68 | 6.11 | 6.00 | 4.32 | 3.60 | 7.30 | 5.27 | 4.07 |
| Cash Flow Per Share | 7.05 | 5.74 | 4.77 | 5.93 | 7.47 | 5.39 | 6.89 | 7.78 |
| Tang Book Value Per Share | 38.34 | 37.69 | 36.50 | 37.90 | 31.76 | 33.77 | 30.09 | 26.09 |
| Dividends Per Share | 8.170 | 8.160 | 8.150 | 1.080 | 0.990 | 0.870 | 0.750 | 0.630 |
| Dividend Payout % | 122.31 | 133.55 | 135.83 | 25.00 | 27.50 | 11.92 | 14.23 | 15.48 |
| **Income Statement** | | | | | | | | |
| Premium Income | 246,877 | 116,051 | 493,382 | 491,961 | 528,764 | 544,478 | 530,338 | 491,307 |
| Total Revenue | 292,882 | 136,826 | 583,424 | 546,552 | 561,012 | 652,345 | 632,708 | 569,302 |
| Benefits & Claims | 77,234 | 46,871 | 201,332 | 203,388 | 247,174 | 190,868 | 256,889 | 251,170 |
| Income Before Taxes | 103,809 | 36,290 | 171,389 | 127,385 | 101,754 | 247,161 | 171,776 | 132,980 |
| Income Taxes | 36,469 | 12,445 | 51,058 | 38,592 | 27,922 | 78,609 | 52,254 | 36,742 |
| Net Income | 73,842 | 26,461 | 127,432 | 93,845 | 78,676 | 175,867 | 134,639 | 107,134 |
| Average Shares | 21,332 | 21,285 | 21,241 | 21,731 | 21,848 | 24,085 | 25,571 | 26,324 |
| **Balance Sheet** | | | | | | | | |
| Total Assets | 2,730,264 | 2,522,930 | 2,514,592 | 2,538,653 | 2,419,401 | 2,626,523 | 2,771,296 | 2,735,870 |
| Total Liabilities | 1,865,843 | 1,703,070 | 1,723,216 | 1,706,403 | 1,711,247 | 1,852,101 | 2,014,776 | 2,042,929 |
| Stockholders' Equity | 864,421 | 819,860 | 791,376 | 832,250 | 708,154 | 774,422 | 756,520 | 692,941 |
| Shares Outstanding | 21,072 | 21,055 | 20,964 | 21,264 | 21,474 | 22,155 | 24,272 | 25,551 |
| **Statistical Record** | | | | | | | | |
| Return on Assets % | 5.32 | 5.09 | 5.04 | 3.79 | 3.11 | 6.52 | 4.89 | 4.12 |
| Return on Equity % | 16.49 | 15.53 | 15.70 | 12.18 | 10.58 | 22.98 | 18.58 | 16.27 |
| Loss Ratio % | 31.28 | 40.39 | 40.81 | 41.34 | 46.75 | 35.06 | 48.44 | 51.12 |
| Net Margin % | 25.21 | 19.34 | 21.84 | 17.17 | 14.02 | 26.96 | 21.28 | 18.82 |
| Price Range | 61.92-50.98 | 61.09-50.98 | 61.09-49.91 | 61.17-43.13 | 66.61-44.64 | 60.82-51.00 | 57.41-45.16 | 55.68-40.28 |
| P/E Ratio | 9.27-7.63 | 10.00-8.34 | 10.18-8.32 | 14.16-9.98 | 18.50-12.40 | 8.33-6.99 | 10.89-8.57 | 13.68-9.90 |
| Average Yield % | 14.46 | 14.64 | 14.72 | 2.12 | 1.85 | 1.52 | 1.46 | 1.37 |

| | | |
|---|---|---|
| **Address:** 9025 North Lindbergh Drive, Peoria, IL 61615<br>**Telephone:** 309-692-1000<br>**Web Site:** www.rlicorp.com | **Officers:** Gerald D. Stephens - Chairman Jonathan E. Michael - President, Chief Executive Officer **Transfer Agents:** Wells Fargo Shareholder Services, St. Paul, MN | **Investor Contact:** 309-693-5846<br>**No of Institutions:** 187<br>**Shares:** 21,235,516 **% Held:** 85.23 |

# ROBINSON (C.H.) WORLDWIDE, INC.

| Exchange | Symbol | Price | 52Wk Range | Yield | P/E |
|---|---|---|---|---|---|
| NMS | CHRW | $70.50 (8/31/2011) | 82.10-62.95 | 1.65 | 28.20 |

*7 Year Price Score 145.10 *NYSE Composite Index=100 *12 Month Price Score 97.92

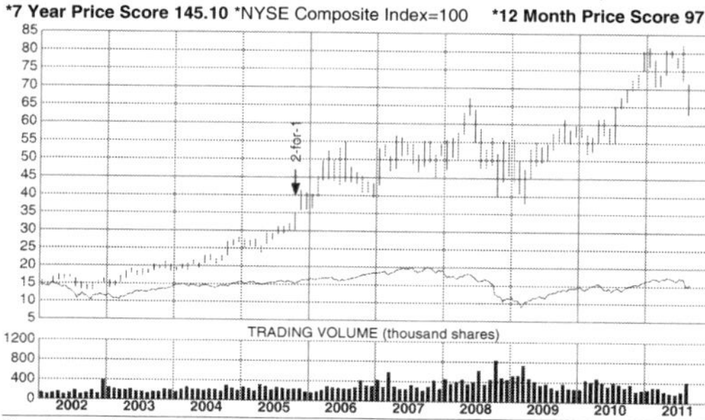


**Interim Earnings (Per Share)**

| Qtr. | Mar | Jun | Sep | Dec |
|---|---|---|---|---|
| 2008 | 0.50 | 0.52 | 0.54 | 0.52 |
| 2009 | 0.50 | 0.54 | 0.57 | 0.52 |
| 2010 | 0.50 | 0.59 | 0.62 | 0.62 |
| 2011 | 0.59 | 0.67 | ... | ... |

**Interim Dividends (Per Share)**

| Amt | Decl | Ex | Rec | Pay |
|---|---|---|---|---|
| 0.29Q | 12/09/2010 | 12/16/2010 | 12/20/2010 | 01/03/2011 |
| 0.29Q | 02/10/2011 | 03/02/2011 | 03/04/2011 | 04/01/2011 |
| 0.29Q | 05/12/2011 | 06/01/2011 | 06/03/2011 | 07/01/2011 |
| 0.29Q | 08/11/2011 | 08/31/2011 | 09/02/2011 | 10/03/2011 |

**Indicated Div: $1.16 (Div. Reinv. Plan)**

**Valuation Analysis**

| | | | |
|---|---|---|---|
| Forecast EPS | $2.69 (09/05/2011) | | |
| Market Cap | $11.7 Billion | Book Value | $1.3 Billion |
| Price/Book | 9.06 | Price/Sales | 1.19 |

**Dividend Achiever Status**

| | |
|---|---|
| 10 Year Growth Rate | 25.89% |
| Total Years of Dividend Growth | 13 |

**Business Summary:** Airlines/Air Freight (MIC: 7.4.4 SIC: 4731 NAIC: 488510)

Robinson (C.H.) Worldwide is a logistics company. Co. has contractual relationships with a range of transportation companies to transport its customers' freight. Co. provides a range of logistics services such as supply chain analysis, freight consolidation, core carrier program management, and information reporting. Co.'s transportation and logistics services include truckload, less than truckload, intermodal, ocean, air and other logistics services. Co. also has sourcing services, which buy, sell and market fresh produce, as well as information services, which include its T-Chek Systems, Inc. subsidiary, a business-to-business provider of spend management and payment processing services.

**Recent Developments:** For the quarter ended June 30 2011, net income increased 14.2% to US$111.0 million from US$97.2 million in the year-earlier quarter. Revenues were US$2.71 billion, up 10.3% from US$2.45 billion the year before. Operating income was US$180.1 million versus US$156.5 million in the prior-year quarter, an increase of 15.1%. Direct operating expenses rose 9.6% to US$2.29 billion from US$2.09 billion in the comparable period the year before. Indirect operating expenses increased 14.2% to US$237.8 million from US$208.2 million in the equivalent prior-year period.

**Prospects:** Our evaluation of Robinson (C.H.) Worldwide Inc. as of Sep. 6, 2011 is the result of our systematic analysis on three basic characteristics: earnings strength, relative valuation, and recent stock price movement. The company has managed to produce a neutral trend in earnings per share over the past 5 quarters. However, while recent estimates for the company have been mixed, CHRW has posted results that fell short of analysts expectations. Based on operating earnings yield, the company is overvalued when compared to all of the companies in our coverage universe. Share price changes over the past year indicates that CHRW will perform poorly over the near term.

**Financial Data**

| (US$ in Thousands) | 6 Mos | 3 Mos | 12/31/2010 | 12/31/2009 | 12/31/2008 | 12/31/2007 | 12/31/2006 | 12/31/2005 |
|---|---|---|---|---|---|---|---|---|
| Earnings Per Share | 2.50 | 2.42 | 2.33 | 2.13 | 2.08 | 1.86 | 1.53 | 1.16 |
| Cash Flow Per Share | 2.51 | 2.38 | 2.09 | 2.22 | 2.64 | 1.81 | 2.01 | 1.35 |
| Tang Book Value Per Share | 5.61 | 5.24 | 5.01 | 4.19 | 4.50 | 4.38 | 3.86 | 3.11 |
| Dividends Per Share | 1.120 | 1.080 | 1.040 | 0.970 | 0.900 | 0.760 | 0.570 | 0.355 |
| Dividend Payout % | 44.80 | 44.63 | 44.64 | 45.54 | 43.27 | 40.86 | 37.25 | 30.60 |
| **Income Statement** | | | | | | | | |
| Total Revenue | 5,073,134 | 2,365,472 | 9,274,305 | 7,577,189 | 8,578,614 | 7,316,223 | 6,556,194 | 5,688,948 |
| EBITDA | 352,660 | 164,079 | 644,495 | 606,361 | 599,087 | 541,914 | 446,188 | 339,145 |
| Depn & Amortn | 15,299 | 7,139 | 20,393 | 19,300 | 20,700 | 18,400 | 16,500 | 12,700 |
| Income Before Taxes | 337,361 | 156,940 | 624,102 | 587,061 | 578,387 | 523,514 | 429,688 | 332,753 |
| Income Taxes | 129,310 | 59,912 | 237,076 | 226,231 | 219,210 | 199,253 | 162,763 | 129,395 |
| Net Income | 208,051 | 97,028 | 387,026 | 360,830 | 359,177 | 324,261 | 266,925 | 203,358 |
| Average Shares | 165,194 | 165,764 | 165,972 | 169,194 | 172,733 | 174,040 | 174,787 | 174,698 |
| **Balance Sheet** | | | | | | | | |
| Current Assets | 1,676,081 | 1,582,071 | 1,481,768 | 1,307,269 | 1,347,871 | 1,389,156 | 1,256,148 | 1,084,781 |
| Total Assets | 2,193,797 | 2,096,334 | 1,995,699 | 1,834,248 | 1,815,721 | 1,811,307 | 1,631,693 | 1,395,068 |
| Current Liabilities | 889,887 | 851,759 | 771,607 | 731,807 | 697,653 | 757,619 | 686,949 | 612,483 |
| Total Liabilities | 905,371 | 868,808 | 791,631 | 754,348 | 708,500 | 769,058 | 687,971 | 615,031 |
| Stockholders' Equity | 1,288,426 | 1,227,526 | 1,204,068 | 1,079,900 | 1,107,221 | 1,042,249 | 943,722 | 780,037 |
| Shares Outstanding | 165,620 | 165,750 | 166,048 | 167,098 | 170,437 | 170,822 | 172,656 | 173,029 |
| **Statistical Record** | | | | | | | | |
| Return on Assets % | 20.11 | 20.31 | 20.21 | 19.77 | 19.75 | 18.84 | 17.64 | 16.43 |
| Return on Equity % | 34.58 | 34.93 | 33.89 | 33.00 | 33.33 | 32.66 | 30.97 | 29.03 |
| EBITDA Margin % | 6.95 | 6.94 | 6.95 | 8.00 | 6.98 | 7.41 | 6.81 | 5.96 |
| Net Margin % | 4.10 | 4.10 | 4.17 | 4.76 | 4.19 | 4.43 | 4.07 | 3.57 |
| Asset Turnover | 4.77 | 4.86 | 4.84 | 4.15 | 4.72 | 4.25 | 4.33 | 4.60 |
| Current Ratio | 1.88 | 1.86 | 1.92 | 1.79 | 1.93 | 1.83 | 1.83 | 1.77 |
| Price Range | 81.51-55.05 | 81.51-54.74 | 80.50-51.84 | 61.47-38.05 | 67.27-39.88 | 56.76-42.89 | 54.79-36.33 | 41.48-23.65 |
| P/E Ratio | 32.60-22.02 | 33.68-22.62 | 34.55-22.25 | 28.86-17.86 | 32.34-19.17 | 30.52-23.06 | 35.81-23.75 | 35.76-20.39 |
| Average Yield % | 1.54 | 1.59 | 1.65 | 1.85 | 1.68 | 1.50 | 1.27 | 1.18 |

**Address:** 14701 Charlson Road, Eden Prairie, MN 55347-5088
**Telephone:** 952-937-8500
**Web Site:** www.chrobinson.com

**Officers:** John P. Wiehoff - Chairman, President, Chief Executive Officer Chad M. Lindbloom - Senior Vice President, Chief Financial Officer **Transfer Agents:** Wells Fargo Bank Minnesota, N.A., South St. Paul, MN

**Investor Contact:** 952-937-7847
**No of Institutions:** 501
**Shares:** 145,825,408 **% Held:** N/A

# ROPER INDUSTRIES, INC

| Exchange | Symbol | Price | 52Wk Range | Yield | P/E |
|---|---|---|---|---|---|
| NYS | ROP | $76.95 (8/31/2011) | 88.45-58.08 | 0.57 | 19.38 |

***7 Year Price Score 144.84** *NYSE Composite Index=100 ***12 Month Price Score 102.62**

**Interim Earnings (Per Share)**

| Qtr. | Mar | Jun | Sep | Dec |
|---|---|---|---|---|
| 2008 | 0.68 | 0.80 | 0.80 | 0.78 |
| 2009 | 0.56 | 0.64 | 0.61 | 0.77 |
| 2010 | 0.62 | 0.74 | 0.87 | 1.11 |
| 2011 | 0.91 | 1.08 | ... | ... |

**Interim Dividends (Per Share)**

| Amt | Decl | Ex | Rec | Pay |
|---|---|---|---|---|
| 0.11Q | 12/08/2010 | 01/05/2011 | 01/07/2011 | 01/28/2011 |
| 0.11Q | 03/21/2011 | 04/06/2011 | 04/08/2011 | 04/22/2011 |
| 0.11Q | 06/20/2011 | 07/06/2011 | 07/08/2011 | 07/29/2011 |
| 0.11Q | 08/12/2011 | 10/05/2011 | 10/07/2011 | 10/28/2011 |

**Indicated Div: $0.44**

**Valuation Analysis**

| | | | |
|---|---|---|---|
| Forecast EPS | $4.25 (09/03/2011) | | |
| Market Cap | $7.4 Billion | Book Value | $3.0 Billion |
| Price/Book | 2.48 | Price/Sales | 2.81 |

**Dividend Achiever Status**

| | |
|---|---|
| **10 Year Growth Rate** | 9.74% |
| **Total Years of Dividend Growth** | 18 |

**Business Summary:** Electrical Equipment (MIC: 7.3.1 SIC: 3823 NAIC: 334513)

Roper Industries is engaged in the design, manufacturing and distribution of medical and scientific imaging products and software, energy systems and controls, industrial technology products and radio frequency (RF) products and services. Co. markets these products and services to selected segments of a range of markets including RF applications, medical, water, energy, research, education, food and food services, security and other niche markets. As of Dec 31 2010, Co. conducted its operations through four reportable segments: Medical and Scientific Imaging, Energy Systems and Controls, Industrial Technology and RF Technology.

**Recent Developments:** For the quarter ended June 30 2011, net income increased 49.1% to US$106.3 million from US$71.3 million in the year-earlier quarter. Revenues were US$699.9 million, up 23.4% from US$567.1 million the year before. Operating income was US$164.0 million versus US$119.2 million in the prior-year quarter, an increase of 37.6%. Direct operating expenses rose 21.7% to US$322.8 million from US$265.2 million in the comparable period the year before. Indirect operating expenses increased 16.6% to US$213.1 million from US$182.8 million in the equivalent prior-year period.

**Prospects:** Our evaluation of Roper Industries Inc. as of Sep. 6, 2011 is the result of our systematic analysis on three basic characteristics: earnings strength, relative valuation, and recent stock price movement. The company has managed to produce a neutral trend in earnings per share over the past 5 quarters. However, while recent estimates for the company have been lowered by analysts, ROP has posted better than expected results. Based on operating earnings yield, the company is about fairly valued when compared to all of the companies in our coverage universe. Share price changes over the past year indicates that ROP will perform in line with the market over the near term.

| **Financial Data** (US$ in Thousands) | 6 Mos | 3 Mos | 12/31/2010 | 12/31/2009 | 12/31/2008 | 12/31/2007 | 12/31/2006 | 12/31/2005 |
|---|---|---|---|---|---|---|---|---|
| Earnings Per Share | 3.97 | 3.63 | 3.34 | 2.58 | 3.06 | 2.68 | 2.13 | 1.74 |
| Cash Flow Per Share | 5.60 | 5.15 | 5.30 | 4.05 | 4.84 | 3.89 | 3.02 | 3.29 |
| Dividends Per Share | 0.410 | 0.395 | 0.380 | 0.330 | 0.290 | 0.260 | 0.235 | 0.212 |
| Dividend Payout % | 10.33 | 10.88 | 11.38 | 12.79 | 9.48 | 9.70 | 11.03 | 12.21 |
| **Income Statement** | | | | | | | | |
| Total Revenue | 1,345,180 | 645,309 | 2,386,112 | 2,049,668 | 2,306,371 | 2,102,049 | 1,700,734 | 1,453,731 |
| EBITDA | 365,371 | 168,356 | 637,948 | 501,760 | 523,535 | 467,657 | 367,612 | 292,374 |
| Depn & Amortn | 51,447 | 25,645 | 123,021 | 103,448 | 33,900 | 31,805 | 29,939 | 28,413 |
| Income Before Taxes | 281,032 | 126,015 | 448,394 | 339,768 | 435,955 | 383,657 | 292,872 | 220,567 |
| Income Taxes | 85,742 | 37,036 | 125,814 | 100,287 | 149,440 | 133,624 | 99,548 | 67,392 |
| Net Income | 195,290 | 88,979 | 322,580 | 239,481 | 286,515 | 250,033 | 193,324 | 153,175 |
| Average Shares | 98,412 | 98,153 | 96,653 | 92,820 | 93,699 | 93,229 | 90,880 | 87,884 |
| **Balance Sheet** | | | | | | | | |
| Current Assets | 1,002,059 | 1,029,640 | 998,091 | 870,745 | 858,307 | 951,137 | 627,495 | 498,207 |
| Total Assets | 5,263,992 | 5,096,894 | 5,069,524 | 4,327,736 | 3,971,538 | 3,453,184 | 2,995,359 | 2,522,306 |
| Current Liabilities | 541,623 | 507,541 | 539,645 | 478,011 | 619,208 | 667,530 | 587,649 | 505,625 |
| Long-Term Obligations | 1,173,694 | 1,159,961 | 1,247,703 | 1,040,962 | 1,033,689 | 727,489 | 726,881 | 620,958 |
| Total Liabilities | 2,280,438 | 2,214,765 | 2,318,617 | 1,906,246 | 1,967,800 | 1,663,378 | 1,508,520 | 1,272,518 |
| Stockholders' Equity | 2,983,554 | 2,882,129 | 2,750,907 | 2,421,490 | 2,003,738 | 1,789,806 | 1,486,839 | 1,249,788 |
| Shares Outstanding | 96,072 | 95,897 | 95,088 | 93,618 | 89,721 | 88,773 | 87,779 | 85,960 |
| **Statistical Record** | | | | | | | | |
| Return on Assets % | 8.02 | 7.50 | 6.87 | 5.77 | 7.70 | 7.75 | 7.01 | 6.27 |
| Return on Equity % | 14.09 | 13.20 | 12.47 | 10.82 | 15.06 | 15.26 | 14.13 | 12.96 |
| EBITDA Margin % | 27.16 | 26.09 | 26.74 | 24.48 | 22.70 | 22.25 | 21.61 | 20.11 |
| Net Margin % | 14.52 | 13.79 | 13.52 | 11.68 | 12.42 | 11.89 | 11.37 | 10.54 |
| Asset Turnover | 0.54 | 0.53 | 0.51 | 0.49 | 0.62 | 0.65 | 0.62 | 0.59 |
| Current Ratio | 1.85 | 2.03 | 1.85 | 1.82 | 1.39 | 1.42 | 1.07 | 0.99 |
| Debt to Equity | 0.39 | 0.40 | 0.45 | 0.43 | 0.52 | 0.41 | 0.49 | 0.50 |
| Price Range | 88.45-54.78 | 87.49-54.78 | 78.43-50.08 | 55.04-36.96 | 67.70-35.19 | 70.81-48.61 | 51.31-38.46 | 40.71-28.39 |
| P/E Ratio | 22.28-13.80 | 24.10-15.09 | 23.48-14.99 | 21.33-14.33 | 22.12-11.50 | 26.42-18.14 | 24.09-18.06 | 23.40-16.31 |
| Average Yield % | 0.55 | 0.58 | 0.62 | 0.71 | 0.52 | 0.44 | 0.51 | 0.60 |

**Address:** 6901 Professional Parkway East, Suite 200, Sarasota, FL 34240
**Telephone:** 941-556-2601
**Web Site:** www.roperind.com

**Officers:** Brian D. Jellison - Chairman, President, Chief Executive Officer John M. Humphrey - Vice President, Chief Financial Officer **Transfer Agents:** American Stock Transfer & Trust Company, New York, NY

**No of Institutions:** 505
**Shares:** 98,982,800 **% Held:** 92.55

# ROSS STORES, INC.

| Exchange | Symbol | Price | 52Wk Range | Yield | P/E |
|---|---|---|---|---|---|
| NMS | ROST | $76.55 (8/31/2011) | 82.64-49.63 | 1.15 | 14.86 |

*7 Year Price Score 175.28 *NYSE Composite Index=100 *12 Month Price Score 111.55

**Interim Earnings (Per Share)**

| Qtr. | Apr | Jul | Oct | Jan |
|---|---|---|---|---|
| 2008-09 | 0.60 | 0.54 | 0.44 | 0.76 |
| 2009-10 | 0.72 | 0.82 | 0.84 | 1.15 |
| 2010-11 | 1.16 | 1.07 | 1.02 | 1.37 |
| 2011-12 | 1.48 | 1.28 | ... | ... |

**Interim Dividends (Per Share)**

| Amt | Decl | Ex | Rec | Pay |
|---|---|---|---|---|
| 0.16Q | 11/17/2010 | 12/03/2010 | 12/07/2010 | 12/31/2010 |
| 0.22Q | 02/03/2011 | 02/16/2011 | 02/18/2011 | 03/31/2011 |
| 0.22Q | 05/18/2011 | 06/03/2011 | 06/07/2011 | 06/30/2011 |
| 0.22Q | 08/17/2011 | 08/31/2011 | 09/02/2011 | 09/30/2011 |

**Indicated Div: $0.88**

**Valuation Analysis**

| | | | |
|---|---|---|---|
| Forecast EPS | $5.40 (09/03/2011) | | |
| Market Cap | $8.8 Billion | Book Value | $1.4 Billion |
| Price/Book | 6.21 | Price/Sales | 1.08 |

**Dividend Achiever Status**

| | |
|---|---|
| 10 Year Growth Rate | 21.74% |
| Total Years of Dividend Growth | 16 |

**Business Summary:** Retail - Apparel and Accessories (MIC: 2.1.5 SIC: 5651 NAIC: 448140)

Ross Stores is a retailer of apparel, accessories, footwear, and home fashions. As of Jan 29 2011, Co. operated a total of 1,055 stores, of which 988 were Ross Dress for Less® (Ross) locations in 27 states and Guam and 67 were dd's DISCOUNTS® stores in six states. Co.'s stores are located in predominantly community and neighborhood shopping centers in urban and suburban areas. Both brands target women and men between the ages of 18 and 54. Ross target customers are primarily from middle income households, while the dd's DISCOUNTS target customer is from moderate income households. Co.'s registered trademarks are Ross Dress For Less® and dd's DISCOUNTS®.

**Recent Developments:** For the quarter ended July 30 2011, net income increased 14.7% to US$148.3 million from US$129.3 million in the year-earlier quarter. Revenues were US$2.09 billion, up 9.3% from US$1.91 billion the year before. Direct operating expenses rose 9.2% to US$1.52 billion from US$1.40 billion in the comparable period the year before. Indirect operating expenses increased 5.8% to US$323.5 million from US$305.8 million in the equivalent prior-year period.

**Prospects:** Our evaluation of Ross Stores Inc. as of Sep. 6, 2011 is the result of our systematic analysis on three basic characteristics: earnings strength, relative valuation, and recent stock price movement. The company has managed to produce a neutral trend in earnings per share over the past 5 quarters and while recent estimates for the company have been raised by analysts, ROST has posted results that were in line with analysts expectations. Based on operating earnings yield, the company is undervalued when compared to all of the companies in our coverage universe. Share price changes over the past year indicates that ROST will perform in line with the market over the near term.

**Financial Data**

| (US$ in Thousands) | 6 Mos | 3 Mos | 01/29/2011 | 01/30/2010 | 01/31/2009 | 02/02/2008 | 02/03/2007 | 01/28/2006 |
|---|---|---|---|---|---|---|---|---|
| Earnings Per Share | 5.15 | 4.94 | 4.63 | 3.54 | 2.33 | 1.90 | 1.70 | 1.36 |
| Cash Flow Per Share | 4.66 | 4.57 | 5.73 | 7.25 | 4.53 | 2.62 | 3.58 | 2.61 |
| Tang Book Value Per Share | 12.34 | 12.02 | 11.26 | 9.39 | 7.80 | 7.22 | 6.51 | 5.80 |
| Dividends Per Share | 0.760 | 0.700 | 0.640 | 0.440 | 0.380 | 0.300 | 0.240 | 0.210 |
| Dividend Payout % | 14.76 | 14.17 | 13.82 | 12.43 | 16.31 | 15.79 | 14.12 | 15.44 |
| **Income Statement** | | | | | | | | |
| Total Revenue | 4,163,986 | 2,074,576 | 7,866,100 | 7,184,213 | 6,486,139 | 5,975,212 | 5,570,210 | 4,944,179 |
| EBITDA | 605,844 | 324,144 | 1,067,290 | 879,222 | 629,206 | 541,791 | 497,450 | 419,144 |
| Depn & Amortn | 77,416 | 39,934 | 160,700 | 153,100 | 134,000 | 120,700 | 107,800 | 93,700 |
| Income Before Taxes | 523,364 | 281,715 | 897,021 | 718,529 | 495,363 | 425,120 | 398,277 | 328,342 |
| Income Taxes | 202,115 | 108,742 | 342,224 | 275,772 | 189,922 | 164,069 | 156,643 | 128,710 |
| Net Income | 321,249 | 172,973 | 554,797 | 442,757 | 305,441 | 261,051 | 241,634 | 199,632 |
| Average Shares | 115,588 | 116,773 | 119,902 | 125,014 | 131,315 | 137,142 | 141,883 | 146,532 |
| **Balance Sheet** | | | | | | | | |
| Current Assets | 1,869,862 | 1,997,241 | 2,043,239 | 1,745,447 | 1,313,715 | 1,398,001 | 1,514,956 | 1,228,847 |
| Total Assets | 3,055,275 | 3,101,994 | 3,116,204 | 2,768,633 | 2,355,511 | 2,371,322 | 2,358,591 | 1,938,738 |
| Current Liabilities | 1,164,731 | 1,238,794 | 1,352,320 | 1,190,514 | 955,259 | 1,010,605 | 1,083,257 | 878,983 |
| Long-Term Obligations | 150,000 | 150,000 | 150,000 | 150,000 | 150,000 | 150,000 | 150,000 | |
| Total Liabilities | 1,629,346 | 1,695,888 | 1,783,512 | 1,611,340 | 1,359,142 | 1,400,673 | 1,448,761 | ... |
| Stockholders' Equity | 1,425,929 | 1,406,106 | 1,332,692 | 1,157,293 | 996,369 | 970,649 | 909,830 | 1,102,566 |
| Shares Outstanding | 115,598 | 116,956 | 118,063 | 122,929 | 127,346 | 134,096 | 139,356 | 836,172 |
| **Statistical Record** | | | | | | | | 144,112 |
| Return on Assets % | 20.47 | 19.56 | 18.91 | 17.33 | 12.96 | 11.07 | 11.06 | 10.89 |
| Return on Equity % | 45.06 | 44.43 | 44.68 | 41.23 | 31.14 | 27.84 | 27.23 | 25.00 |
| EBITDA Margin % | 14.55 | 15.62 | 13.57 | 12.24 | 9.70 | 9.07 | 8.93 | 8.48 |
| Net Margin % | 7.71 | 8.34 | 7.05 | 6.16 | 4.71 | 4.37 | 4.34 | 4.04 |
| Asset Turnover | 2.77 | 2.68 | 2.68 | 2.81 | 2.75 | 2.53 | 2.55 | 2.70 |
| Current Ratio | 1.61 | 1.61 | 1.51 | 1.47 | 1.38 | 1.38 | 1.40 | 1.40 |
| Debt to Equity | 0.11 | 0.11 | 0.11 | 0.13 | 0.15 | 0.15 | 0.16 | ... |
| Price Range | 82.64-49.03 | 74.02-49.03 | 66.99-45.19 | 48.46-28.25 | 41.31-22.10 | 34.86-21.48 | 33.37-22.80 | 30.50-22.71 |
| P/E Ratio | 16.05-9.52 | 14.98-9.93 | 14.47-9.76 | 13.69-7.98 | 17.73-9.48 | 18.35-11.31 | 19.63-13.41 | 22.43-16.70 |
| Average Yield % | 1.14 | 1.16 | 1.14 | 1.07 | 1.16 | 1.02 | 0.85 | 0.77 |

**Address:** 4440 Rosewood Drive, Pleasanton, CA 94588-3050
**Telephone:** 925-965-4400
**Web Site:** www.rossstores.com

**Officers:** Norman A. Ferber - Chairman Michael Balmuth - Vice-Chairman, Chief Executive Officer
**Transfer Agents:** Bank of New York

**No of Institutions:** 566
**Shares:** 121,251,168 **% Held:** 89.32

# RPM INTERNATIONAL INC (DE)

| Exchange | Symbol | Price | 52Wk Range | Yield | P/E |
|---|---|---|---|---|---|
| NYS | RPM | $20.84 (8/31/2011) | 25.22-16.90 | 4.03 | 14.37 |

*7 Year Price Score 111.45 *NYSE Composite Index=100 *12 Month Price Score 96.27

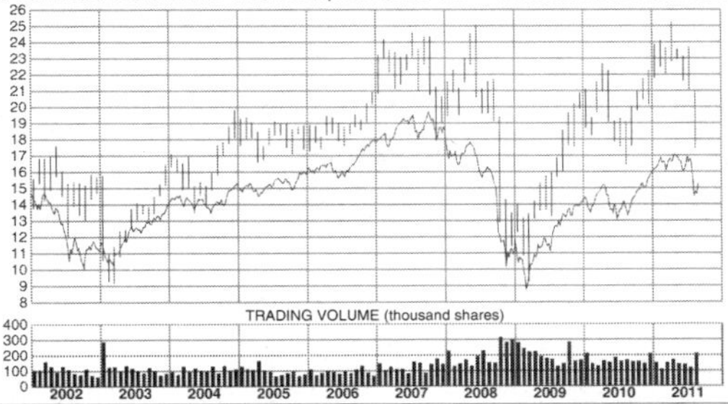


**Interim Earnings (Per Share)**

| Qtr. | Aug | Nov | Feb | May |
|---|---|---|---|---|
| 2006-07 | 0.49 | 0.42 | 0.08 | 0.65 |
| 2007-08 | 0.53 | 0.43 | 0.10 | (0.67) |
| 2008-09 | 0.54 | 0.33 | (0.24) | 0.30 |
| 2009-10 | 0.57 | 0.43 | (0.07) | 0.46 |
| 2010-11 | 0.53 | 0.38 | 0.01 | 0.54 |

**Interim Dividends (Per Share)**

| Amt | Decl | Ex | Rec | Pay |
|---|---|---|---|---|
| 0.21Q | 10/07/2010 | 10/14/2010 | 10/18/2010 | 10/29/2010 |
| 0.21Q | 01/04/2011 | 01/12/2011 | 01/14/2011 | 01/31/2011 |
| 0.21Q | 04/05/2011 | 04/11/2011 | 04/13/2011 | 04/29/2011 |
| 0.21Q | 07/05/2011 | 07/13/2011 | 07/15/2011 | 07/29/2011 |

**Indicated Div: $0.84 (Div. Reinv. Plan)**

**Valuation Analysis**

| | | | |
|---|---|---|---|
| Forecast EPS | $1.65 (09/02/2011) | | |
| Market Cap | $2.7 Billion | Book Value | $1.3 Billion |
| Price/Book | 2.15 | Price/Sales | 0.80 |

**Dividend Achiever Status**

| | |
|---|---|
| 10 Year Growth Rate | 5.14% |
| Total Years of Dividend Growth | 37 |

**Business Summary:** Specialty Chemicals (MIC: 8.3.2 SIC: 2851 NAIC: 325510)

RPM International manufactures, markets and sells specialty chemical product lines, including specialty paints, protective coatings, roofing systems, sealants and adhesives. Co.'s family of products includes those marketed under brand names such as Carboline, DAP, EUCO, Fibergrate, Flecto, Flowcrete, Hummervoll, Universal Sealants, illbruck, Rust-Oleum, Stonhard, Tremco, Watco and Zinsser. Co. has two segments: industrial, which includes maintenance and protection products for roofing and waterproofing systems, flooring, corrosion control and other specialty applications, and consumer, which manufactures and markets professional use and do-it-yourself products for consumer applications.

**Recent Developments:** For the year ended May 31 2011, net income increased 12.2% to US$203.2 million from US$181.1 million in the prior year. Revenues were US$3.38 billion, down 0.9% from US$3.41 billion the year before. Direct operating expenses was unchanged at US$1.98 billion versus the comparable period the year before. Indirect operating expenses decreased 4.6% to US$1.06 billion from US$1.11 billion in the equivalent prior-year period.

**Prospects:** Our evaluation of RPM Inc. as of Sep. 6, 2011 is the result of our systematic analysis on three basic characteristics: earnings strength, relative valuation, and recent stock price movement. The company has produced a positive trend in earnings per share over the past 5 quarters. However, while recent estimates for the company have been lowered by analysts, RPM has posted better than expected results. Based on operating earnings yield, the company is undervalued when compared to all of the companies in our coverage universe. Share price changes over the past year indicates that RPM will perform in line with the market over the near term.

**Financial Data**

| (US$ in Thousands) | 05/31/2011 | 05/31/2010 | 05/31/2009 | 05/31/2008 | 05/31/2007 | 05/31/2006 | 05/31/2005 | 05/31/2004 |
|---|---|---|---|---|---|---|---|---|
| Earnings Per Share | 1.45 | 1.39 | 0.93 | 0.39 | 1.64 | (0.65) | 0.86 | 1.22 |
| Cash Flow Per Share | 1.87 | 1.61 | 2.11 | 1.95 | 1.71 | 1.59 | 1.35 | 1.32 |
| Tang Book Value Per Share | 0.91 | 0.06 | N.M. | N.M. | N.M. | N.M. | 0.91 | 0.38 |
| Dividends Per Share | 0.835 | 0.815 | 0.790 | 0.745 | 0.685 | 0.630 | 0.590 | 0.550 |
| Dividend Payout % | 57.59 | 58.63 | 84.95 | 191.03 | 41.77 | ... | 68.60 | 45.08 |
| **Income Statement** | | | | | | | | |
| Total Revenue | 3,381,841 | 3,412,716 | 3,368,167 | 3,643,791 | 3,338,764 | 3,008,338 | 2,555,735 | 2,341,572 |
| EBITDA | 427,807 | 407,715 | 314,272 | 168,856 | 431,324 | (9,369) | 261,947 | 322,638 |
| Depn & Amortn | 72,385 | 84,023 | 84,879 | 82,838 | 76,756 | 71,763 | 62,841 | 76,077 |
| Income Before Taxes | 295,053 | 268,454 | 180,868 | 39,054 | 307,535 | (122,475) | 163,728 | 217,616 |
| Income Taxes | 91,885 | 87,327 | 61,252 | (8,655) | 99,246 | (46,270) | 58,696 | 75,730 |
| Net Income | 189,058 | 180,037 | 119,616 | 47,709 | 208,289 | (76,205) | 105,032 | 141,886 |
| Average Shares | 128,066 | 127,731 | 128,255 | 130,539 | 128,711 | 116,837 | 126,364 | 116,710 |
| **Balance Sheet** | | | | | | | | |
| Current Assets | 1,867,970 | 1,448,736 | 1,552,916 | 1,783,975 | 1,570,249 | 1,369,218 | 1,271,495 | 994,617 |
| Total Assets | 3,515,029 | 3,004,024 | 3,409,921 | 3,763,567 | 3,333,149 | 2,980,218 | 2,656,245 | 2,353,119 |
| Current Liabilities | 735,289 | 631,494 | 849,162 | 846,361 | 864,740 | 713,500 | 575,339 | 477,493 |
| Long-Term Obligations | 1,106,304 | 924,308 | 762,295 | 1,066,687 | 886,416 | 870,415 | 837,948 | 718,929 |
| Total Liabilities | 2,251,865 | 1,924,551 | 2,266,250 | 2,627,011 | 2,246,279 | 2,054,277 | 1,609,736 | 1,377,827 |
| Stockholders' Equity | 1,263,164 | 1,079,473 | 1,143,671 | 1,136,556 | 1,086,870 | 925,941 | 1,046,509 | 975,292 |
| Shares Outstanding | 130,580 | 129,918 | 128,501 | 122,189 | 120,906 | 118,743 | 117,554 | 116,122 |
| **Statistical Record** | | | | | | | | |
| Return on Assets % | 5.80 | 5.61 | 3.33 | 1.34 | 6.60 | N.M. | 4.19 | 6.15 |
| Return on Equity % | 16.14 | 16.20 | 10.49 | 4.28 | 20.70 | N.M. | 10.39 | 15.28 |
| EBITDA Margin % | 12.65 | 11.95 | 9.33 | 4.63 | 12.92 | N.M. | 10.25 | 13.78 |
| Net Margin % | 5.59 | 5.28 | 3.55 | 1.31 | 6.24 | N.M. | 4.11 | 6.06 |
| Asset Turnover | 1.04 | 1.06 | 0.94 | 1.02 | 1.06 | 1.07 | 1.02 | 1.02 |
| Current Ratio | 2.54 | 2.29 | 1.83 | 2.11 | 1.82 | 1.92 | 2.21 | 2.08 |
| Debt to Equity | 0.88 | 0.86 | 0.67 | 0.94 | 0.82 | 0.94 | 0.80 | 0.74 |
| Price Range | 25.22-16.37 | 22.69-13.28 | 25.07-9.24 | 24.63-17.92 | 24.18-17.64 | 19.46-17.11 | 19.83-14.02 | 17.10-12.55 |
| P/E Ratio | 17.39-11.29 | 16.32-9.55 | 26.96-9.94 | 63.15-45.95 | 14.74-10.76 | ... | 23.06-16.30 | 14.02-10.29 |
| Average Yield % | 3.98 | 4.38 | 4.94 | 3.41 | 3.35 | 3.43 | 3.43 | 3.73 |

| | | |
|---|---|---|
| **Address:** 2628 Pearl Road, P.O. Box 777, Medina, OH 44258<br>**Telephone:** 330-273-5090<br>**Web Site:** www.rpminc.com | **Officers:** Frank C. Sullivan - Chairman, Chief Executive Officer Ronald A. Rice - President, Chief Operating Officer **Transfer Agents:** Wells Fargo Shareowner Services, St. Paul, MN | **No of Institutions:** 326<br>**Shares:** 96,627,104 **% Held:** 64.28 |

# SCANA CORP

| Exchange | Symbol | Price | 52Wk Range | Yield | P/E |
|---|---|---|---|---|---|
| NYS | SCG | $40.22 (8/31/2011) | 42.80-35.12 | 4.82 | 13.59 |

***7 Year Price Score 103.14** *NYSE Composite Index=100 ***12 Month Price Score 97.32**

**Interim Earnings (Per Share)**

| Qtr. | Mar | Jun | Sep | Dec |
|---|---|---|---|---|
| 2008 | 0.94 | 0.48 | 0.80 | 0.73 |
| 2009 | 0.94 | 0.45 | 0.84 | 0.62 |
| 2010 | 1.02 | 0.43 | 0.79 | 0.74 |
| 2011 | 1.00 | 0.43 | ... | ... |

**Interim Dividends (Per Share)**

| Amt | Decl | Ex | Rec | Pay |
|---|---|---|---|---|
| 0.475Q | 10/27/2010 | 12/08/2010 | 12/10/2010 | 01/01/2011 |
| 0.485Q | 02/11/2011 | 03/08/2011 | 03/10/2011 | 04/01/2011 |
| 0.485Q | 04/21/2011 | 06/08/2011 | 06/10/2011 | 07/01/2011 |
| 0.485Q | 08/11/2011 | 09/07/2011 | 09/09/2011 | 10/01/2011 |

**Indicated Div: $1.94 (Div. Reinv. Plan)**

**Valuation Analysis**

| | | | |
|---|---|---|---|
| Forecast EPS | $3.05 (09/05/2011) | | |
| Market Cap | $5.2 Billion | Book Value | $3.8 Billion |
| Price/Book | 1.36 | Price/Sales | 1.15 |

**Dividend Achiever Status**

| | |
|---|---|
| **10 Year Growth Rate** | 4.78% |
| **Total Years of Dividend Growth** | 10 |

**Business Summary:** Electric Utilities (MIC: 3.1.1 SIC: 4931 NAIC: 221122)

SCANA is a holding company. Through its wholly-owned regulated subsidiaries, Co. is primarily engaged in the generation, transmission, distribution and sale of electricity in parts of South Carolina and in the purchase, transmission and sale of natural gas in portions of North Carolina and South Carolina. Through a wholly-owned nonregulated subsidiary, Co. markets natural gas to retail customers in Georgia and to wholesale customers primarily in the southeast. Other wholly-owned nonregulated subsidiaries provide fiber optic and other telecommunications services and provide service contracts to homeowners on certain home appliances and heating and air conditioning units.

**Recent Developments:** For the quarter ended June 30 2011, net income increased 3.7% to US$56.0 million from US$54.0 million in the year-earlier quarter. Revenues were US$1.00 billion, up 6.5% from US$939.0 million the year before. Operating income was US$142.0 million versus US$137.0 million in the prior-year quarter, an increase of 3.6%. Direct operating expenses rose 7.8% to US$721.0 million from US$669.0 million in the comparable period the year before. Indirect operating expenses increased 3.0% to US$137.0 million from US$133.0 million in the equivalent prior-year period.

**Prospects:** Our evaluation of SCANA Corp. as of Sep. 6, 2011 is the result of our systematic analysis on three basic characteristics: earnings strength, relative valuation, and recent stock price movement. The company has managed to produce a neutral trend in earnings per share over the past 5 quarters. However, while recent estimates for the company have been mixed, SCG has posted results that fell short of analysts expectations. Based on operating earnings yield, the company is undervalued when compared to all of the companies in our coverage universe. Share price changes over the past year indicates that SCG will perform very poorly over the near term.

**Financial Data**

| (US$ in Thousands) | 6 Mos | 3 Mos | 12/31/2010 | 12/31/2009 | 12/31/2008 | 12/31/2007 | 12/31/2006 | 12/31/2005 |
|---|---|---|---|---|---|---|---|---|
| Earnings Per Share | 2.96 | 2.96 | 2.98 | 2.85 | 2.95 | 2.74 | 2.68 | 2.81 |
| Cash Flow Per Share | 6.82 | 6.87 | 6.45 | 5.56 | 3.87 | 6.26 | 6.50 | 4.10 |
| Tang Book Value Per Share | 29.49 | 29.59 | 27.34 | 25.84 | 23.92 | 23.39 | 22.43 | 21.41 |
| Dividends Per Share | 1.920 | 1.910 | 1.900 | 1.880 | 1.840 | 1.760 | 1.680 | 1.560 |
| Dividend Payout % | 64.86 | 64.53 | 63.76 | 65.96 | 62.37 | 64.23 | 62.69 | 55.52 |
| **Income Statement** | | | | | | | | |
| Total Revenue | 2,281,000 | 1,281,000 | 4,601,000 | 4,237,000 | 5,319,000 | 4,621,000 | 4,563,000 | 4,777,000 |
| EBITDA | 417,000 | 264,000 | 1,177,000 | 1,102,000 | 1,098,000 | 1,020,000 | 981,000 | 996,000 |
| Depn & Amortn | 14,000 | 9,000 | 377,000 | 347,000 | 344,000 | 341,000 | 333,000 | 510,000 |
| Income Before Taxes | 264,000 | 185,000 | 534,000 | 522,000 | 527,000 | 473,000 | 439,000 | 274,000 |
| Income Taxes | 80,000 | 57,000 | 159,000 | 167,000 | 189,000 | 140,000 | 119,000 | (118,000) |
| Net Income | 184,000 | 128,000 | 376,000 | 357,000 | 346,000 | 320,000 | 310,000 | 320,000 |
| Average Shares | 129,700 | 129,000 | 126,300 | 122,100 | 117,000 | 116,700 | 115,800 | 113,800 |
| **Balance Sheet** | | | | | | | | |
| Current Assets | 1,435,000 | 1,395,000 | 1,631,000 | 1,521,000 | 1,836,000 | 1,301,000 | 1,376,000 | 1,464,000 |
| Total Assets | 13,144,000 | 12,873,000 | 12,968,000 | 12,094,000 | 11,502,000 | 10,165,000 | 9,817,000 | 9,519,000 |
| Current Liabilities | 1,653,000 | 1,825,000 | 1,867,000 | 1,256,000 | 1,155,000 | 1,721,000 | 1,405,000 | 1,500,000 |
| Long-Term Obligations | 4,379,000 | 3,989,000 | 4,152,000 | 4,483,000 | 4,361,000 | 2,879,000 | 3,067,000 | 2,948,000 |
| Total Liabilities | 9,339,000 | 9,073,000 | 9,266,000 | 8,686,000 | 8,344,000 | 7,092,000 | 6,857,000 | 6,728,000 |
| Stockholders' Equity | 3,805,000 | 3,800,000 | 3,702,000 | 3,408,000 | 3,158,000 | 3,073,000 | 2,960,000 | 2,791,000 |
| Shares Outstanding | 129,019 | 128,428 | 127,000 | 123,000 | 118,000 | 117,000 | 117,000 | 114,671 |
| **Statistical Record** | | | | | | | | |
| Return on Assets % | 2.99 | 3.02 | 3.00 | 3.03 | 3.19 | 3.20 | 3.21 | 3.46 |
| Return on Equity % | 10.34 | 10.36 | 10.58 | 10.87 | 11.08 | 10.61 | 10.78 | 11.95 |
| EBITDA Margin % | 18.28 | 20.61 | 25.58 | 26.01 | 20.64 | 22.07 | 21.50 | 20.85 |
| Net Margin % | 8.07 | 9.99 | 8.17 | 8.43 | 6.50 | 6.92 | 6.79 | 6.70 |
| Asset Turnover | 0.36 | 0.36 | 0.37 | 0.36 | 0.49 | 0.46 | 0.47 | 0.52 |
| Current Ratio | 0.87 | 0.76 | 0.87 | 1.21 | 1.59 | 0.76 | 0.98 | 0.98 |
| Debt to Equity | 1.15 | 1.05 | 1.12 | 1.32 | 1.38 | 0.94 | 1.04 | 1.06 |
| Price Range | 42.80-35.43 | 42.80-34.93 | 41.69-34.55 | 38.44-26.37 | 42.51-30.03 | 45.26-36.70 | 41.99-37.16 | 43.40-37.10 |
| P/E Ratio | 14.46-11.97 | 14.46-11.80 | 13.99-11.59 | 13.49-9.25 | 14.41-10.18 | 16.52-13.39 | 15.67-13.87 | 15.44-13.20 |
| Average Yield % | 4.78 | 4.84 | 4.93 | 5.67 | 4.92 | 4.30 | 4.20 | 3.88 |

**Address:** 100 SCANA Parkway, Cayce, SC 29033
**Telephone:** 803-217-9000
**Web Site:** www.scana.com

**Officers:** William B. Timmerman - Chairman, Chief Executive Officer Kevin B. Marsh - President, Chief Operating Officer **Transfer Agents:** SCANA Corporation, Columbia, SC

**Investor Contact:** 803-217-9240
**No of Institutions:** 443
**Shares:** 63,942,184 **% Held:** 47.39

# SEI INVESTMENTS CO.

| Exchange | Symbol | Price | 52Wk Range | Yield | P/E |
|---|---|---|---|---|---|
| NMS | SEIC | $17.11 (8/31/2011) | 24.74-15.71 | 1.40 | 13.91 |

*7 Year Price Score 99.42 *NYSE Composite Index=100 *12 Month Price Score 89.49

**Interim Earnings (Per Share)**

| Qtr. | Mar | Jun | Sep | Dec |
|---|---|---|---|---|
| 2008 | 0.25 | 0.24 | 0.18 | 0.05 |
| 2009 | 0.18 | 0.22 | 0.27 | 0.24 |
| 2010 | 0.31 | 0.28 | 0.30 | 0.33 |
| 2011 | 0.31 | 0.29 | ... | ... |

**Interim Dividends (Per Share)**

| Amt | Decl | Ex | Rec | Pay |
|---|---|---|---|---|
| 0.09S | 12/15/2009 | 12/31/2009 | 01/05/2010 | 01/21/2010 |
| 0.10S | 05/25/2010 | 06/21/2010 | 06/23/2010 | 06/28/2010 |
| 0.10S | 12/14/2010 | 12/21/2010 | 12/23/2010 | 12/30/2010 |
| 0.12S | 05/25/2011 | 06/16/2011 | 06/20/2011 | 06/28/2011 |

**Indicated Div: $0.24**

**Valuation Analysis**

| | | | |
|---|---|---|---|
| Forecast EPS | $1.19 (09/02/2011) | | |
| Market Cap | $3.1 Billion | Book Value | $1.1 Billion |
| Price/Book | 2.93 | Price/Sales | 3.40 |

**Dividend Achiever Status**

| | |
|---|---|
| 10 Year Growth Rate | 15.49% |
| Total Years of Dividend Growth | 19 |

**Business Summary:** Finance Intermediaries & Services (MIC: 5.5.1 SIC: 6211 NAIC: 523120)

SEI Investments is a provider of investment processing, fund processing, and investment management business outsourcing applications. Co.'s reportable business segments consists of: Private Banks, which provides investment processing and investment management programs; Investment Advisors, which provides investment management programs; Institutional Investors, which provides investment management programs and administrative outsourcing applications; Investment Managers, which provides investment processing, fund processing, and operational outsourcing applications; and Investments in New Businesses, which provides investment management programs through the SEI Wealth Network®.

**Recent Developments:** For the quarter ended June 30 2011, net income increased 0.5% to US$54.1 million from US$53.8 million in the year-earlier quarter. Revenues were US$237.8 million, up 4.1% from US$228.4 million the year before. Operating income was US$54.0 million versus US$57.2 million in the prior-year quarter, a decrease of 5.6%. Indirect operating expenses increased 7.4% to US$183.8 million from US$171.2 million in the equivalent prior-year period.

**Prospects:** Our evaluation of SEI Investments Co. as of Sep. 6, 2011 is the result of our systematic analysis on three basic characteristics: earnings strength, relative valuation, and recent stock price movement. The company has managed to produce a neutral trend in earnings per share over the past 5 quarters and while recent estimates for the company have remained steady, SEIC has posted results that fell short of analysts expectations. Based on operating earnings yield, the company is undervalued when compared to all of the companies in our coverage universe. Share price changes over the past year indicates that SEIC will perform in line with the market over the near term.

| Financial Data (US$ in Thousands) | 6 Mos | 3 Mos | 12/31/2010 | 12/31/2009 | 12/31/2008 | 12/31/2007 | 12/31/2006 | 12/31/2005 |
|---|---|---|---|---|---|---|---|---|
| Earnings Per Share | 1.23 | 1.22 | 1.22 | 0.91 | 0.71 | 1.28 | 1.17 | 0.92 |
| Cash Flow Per Share | 1.39 | 1.45 | 1.22 | 1.81 | 1.48 | 1.84 | 1.75 | 1.07 |
| Tang Book Value Per Share | 4.19 | 4.20 | 4.01 | 2.96 | 2.20 | 2.27 | 1.82 | 1.55 |
| Dividends Per Share | 0.220 | 0.200 | 0.200 | 0.170 | 0.160 | 0.140 | 0.120 | 0.110 |
| Dividend Payout % | 17.89 | 16.39 | 16.39 | 18.68 | 22.54 | 10.38 | 10.30 | 12.02 |
| **Income Statement** | | | | | | | | |
| Total Revenue | 470,253 | 232,493 | 900,835 | 1,060,548 | 1,247,919 | 1,369,028 | 1,175,749 | 773,007 |
| EBITDA | 137,909 | 73,717 | 293,704 | 387,593 | 379,628 | 609,675 | 528,214 | 236,539 |
| Depn & Amortn | 24,025 | 11,842 | 21,902 | 21,531 | 21,980 | 19,547 | 17,032 | 14,624 |
| Income Before Taxes | 116,505 | 63,215 | 270,324 | 362,318 | 354,230 | 585,419 | 505,718 | 220,391 |
| Income Taxes | 62,831 | 34,124 | 136,461 | 89,886 | 85,720 | 149,731 | 121,766 | 106,865 |
| Net Income | 111,331 | 57,728 | 231,687 | 174,335 | 139,254 | 259,809 | 236,990 | 188,344 |
| Average Shares | 187,020 | 188,495 | 190,321 | 191,783 | 195,233 | 202,231 | 203,266 | 206,276 |
| **Balance Sheet** | | | | | | | | |
| Current Assets | 665,133 | 702,747 | 683,719 | 841,403 | 739,671 | 694,934 | 586,473 | 305,976 |
| Total Assets | 1,330,805 | 1,378,035 | 1,377,223 | 1,533,808 | 1,341,715 | 1,252,365 | 1,079,705 | 657,147 |
| Current Liabilities | 104,551 | 125,066 | 127,600 | 163,055 | 329,894 | 230,367 | 196,127 | 167,470 |
| Long-Term Obligations | 40,000 | 60,000 | 95,000 | 247,152 | 24,332 | 43,971 | 67,538 | 9,000 |
| Total Liabilities | 260,645 | 300,966 | 335,653 | 624,085 | 575,711 | 495,982 | 449,193 | 235,459 |
| Stockholders' Equity | 1,070,160 | 1,077,069 | 1,041,570 | 909,723 | 766,004 | 756,383 | 630,512 | 421,688 |
| Shares Outstanding | 183,175 | 185,059 | 186,141 | 190,208 | 191,195 | 194,375 | 197,906 | 197,160 |
| **Statistical Record** | | | | | | | | |
| Return on Assets % | 17.17 | 16.57 | 15.92 | 12.13 | 10.71 | 22.28 | 27.29 | 29.60 |
| Return on Equity % | 22.46 | 22.55 | 23.75 | 20.81 | 18.24 | 37.47 | 45.05 | 45.62 |
| EBITDA Margin % | 29.33 | 31.71 | 32.60 | 36.55 | 30.42 | 44.53 | 44.93 | 30.60 |
| Net Margin % | 23.67 | 24.83 | 25.72 | 16.44 | 11.16 | 18.98 | 20.16 | 24.37 |
| Asset Turnover | 0.69 | 0.66 | 0.62 | 0.74 | 0.96 | 1.17 | 1.35 | 1.21 |
| Current Ratio | 6.36 | 5.62 | 5.36 | 5.16 | 2.24 | 3.02 | 2.99 | 1.83 |
| Debt to Equity | 0.04 | 0.06 | 0.09 | 0.27 | 0.03 | 0.06 | 0.11 | 0.02 |
| Price Range | 24.74-17.57 | 24.74-17.57 | 24.34-16.94 | 20.26-9.45 | 32.17-12.25 | 33.12-23.34 | 30.26-18.68 | 21.05-16.07 |
| P/E Ratio | 20.11-14.28 | 20.28-14.40 | 19.95-13.89 | 22.26-10.38 | 45.31-17.25 | 25.87-18.23 | 25.86-15.96 | 22.88-17.47 |
| Average Yield % | 1.00 | 0.91 | 0.96 | 1.14 | 0.67 | 0.50 | 0.50 | 0.59 |

**Address:** 1 Freedom Valley Drive, Oaks, PA 19456-1100
**Telephone:** 610-676-1000
**Web Site:** www.seic.com

**Officers:** Alfred P. West - Chairman, Chief Executive Officer Kathy Heilig - Chief Accounting Officer, Controller **Transfer Agents:** American Stock Transfer & Trust Co., New York, NY

**Investor Contact:** 610-676-1000
**No of Institutions:** 353
**Shares:** 126,270,304 **% Held:** 62.11

# SHENANDOAH TELECOMMUNICATIONS CO.

| Exchange | Symbol | Price | 52Wk Range | Yield | P/E |
|---|---|---|---|---|---|
| NMS | SHEN | $13.73 (8/31/2011) | 19.96-12.47 | 2.40 | 25.43 |

***7 Year Price Score 103.40** *NYSE Composite Index=100 ***12 Month Price Score 89.24**

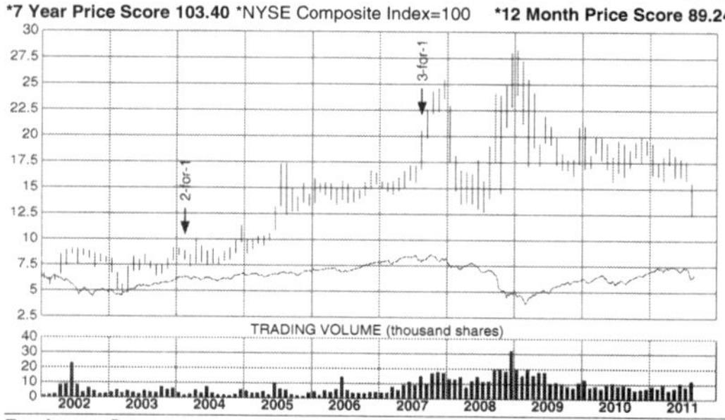


**Interim Earnings (Per Share)**

| Qtr. | Mar | Jun | Sep | Dec |
|---|---|---|---|---|
| 2008 | 0.20 | 0.31 | 0.29 | 0.24 |
| 2009 | (0.18) | 0.29 | 0.27 | 0.27 |
| 2010 | 0.29 | 0.19 | 0.17 | 0.11 |
| 2011 | 0.13 | 0.13 | ... | ... |

**Interim Dividends (Per Share)**

| Amt | Decl | Ex | Rec | Pay |
|---|---|---|---|---|
| 0.27A | 10/23/2007 | 11/09/2007 | 11/14/2007 | 11/30/2007 |
| 0.30A | 10/22/2008 | 11/07/2008 | 11/12/2008 | 12/01/2008 |
| 0.32A | 10/20/2009 | 11/06/2009 | 11/10/2009 | 12/01/2009 |
| 0.33A | 10/19/2010 | 11/05/2010 | 11/09/2010 | 12/01/2010 |

**Indicated Div: $0.33 (Div. Reinv. Plan)**

**Valuation Analysis**

| | | | |
|---|---|---|---|
| Forecast EPS | $0.62 (09/02/2011) | | |
| Market Cap | $326.5 Million | Book Value | $197.1 Million |
| Price/Book | 1.66 | Price/Sales | 1.40 |

**Dividend Achiever Status**

| | |
|---|---|
| **10 Year Growth Rate** | 10.96% |
| **Total Years of Dividend Growth** | 14 |

**Business Summary:** Services (MIC: 6.1.2 SIC: 4813 NAIC: 517110)

Shenandoah Telecommunications is a telecommunications holding company. Through its operating subsidiaries, Co. provides both regulated and unregulated telecommunications services to end-user customers and other communications providers in the southeastern U.S. Co. provides wireless personal communications service under the Sprint brand name, telephone service, cable television, unregulated communications equipment sales and services, and Internet access. In addition, Co. leases towers and operates and maintains an interstate fiber optic network. Co. provides its services over its own fiber optic network of approximately 2,656 total miles as of Dec 31 2010.

**Recent Developments:** For the quarter ended June 30 2011, income from continuing operations decreased 32.7% to US$3.0 million from US$4.5 million in the year-earlier quarter. Net income decreased 34.6% to US$3.0 million from US$4.6 million in the year-earlier quarter. Revenues were US$61.6 million, up 45.3% from US$42.4 million the year before. Operating income was US$8.0 million versus US$7.8 million in the prior-year quarter, an increase of 2.6%. Direct operating expenses rose 65.0% to US$25.2 million from US$15.3 million in the comparable period the year before. Indirect operating expenses increased 46.9% to US$28.3 million from US$19.3 million in the equivalent prior-year period.

**Prospects:** Our evaluation of Shenandoah Telecommunications Co. as of Sep. 6, 2011 is the result of our systematic analysis on three basic characteristics: earnings strength, relative valuation, and recent stock price movement. The company has enjoyed a very positive trend in earnings per share over the past 5 quarters. However, while recent estimates for the company have been lowered by analysts, SHEN has posted results that fell short of analysts expectations. Based on operating earnings yield, the company is about fairly valued when compared to all of the companies in our coverage universe. Share price changes over the past year indicates that SHEN will perform poorly over the near term.

**Financial Data**

| (US$ in Thousands) | 6 Mos | 3 Mos | 12/31/2010 | 12/31/2009 | 12/31/2008 | 12/31/2007 | 12/31/2006 | 12/31/2005 |
|---|---|---|---|---|---|---|---|---|
| Earnings Per Share | 0.54 | 0.60 | 0.76 | 0.64 | 1.04 | 0.80 | 0.77 | 0.46 |
| Cash Flow Per Share | 3.13 | 3.25 | 3.17 | 3.13 | 2.12 | 1.87 | 1.48 | 1.40 |
| Tang Book Value Per Share | 4.23 | 4.01 | 3.74 | 7.13 | 6.77 | 5.91 | 5.26 | 4.69 |
| Dividends Per Share | 0.330 | 0.330 | 0.330 | 0.320 | 0.300 | 0.270 | 0.250 | 0.153 |
| Dividend Payout % | 61.11 | 55.00 | 43.42 | 50.00 | 28.85 | 33.75 | 32.61 | 33.09 |
| **Income Statement** | | | | | | | | |
| Total Revenue | 121,983 | 60,428 | 194,889 | 160,616 | 144,424 | 141,183 | 169,195 | 146,391 |
| EBITDA | 43,726 | 21,122 | 73,342 | 75,928 | 74,418 | 62,250 | 59,190 | 42,447 |
| Depn & Amortn | 28,382 | 13,938 | 36,553 | 32,018 | 29,411 | 28,603 | 26,459 | 21,920 |
| Income Before Taxes | 10,679 | 5,365 | 32,073 | 42,549 | 43,998 | 31,774 | 30,369 | 17,451 |
| Income Taxes | 4,581 | 2,305 | 13,355 | 17,465 | 17,669 | 12,971 | 12,370 | 6,716 |
| Net Income | 6,019 | 3,027 | 18,075 | 15,092 | 24,405 | 18,803 | 17,922 | 10,735 |
| Average Shares | 23,797 | 23,849 | 23,823 | 23,701 | 23,609 | 23,497 | 23,331 | 23,109 |
| **Balance Sheet** | | | | | | | | |
| Current Assets | 68,340 | 65,063 | 70,800 | 52,635 | 72,421 | 41,136 | 30,863 | 20,801 |
| Total Assets | 467,299 | 463,165 | 466,437 | 271,725 | 265,981 | 221,524 | 207,720 | 204,921 |
| Current Liabilities | 48,550 | 44,605 | 44,898 | 24,628 | 24,385 | 24,056 | 21,280 | 22,741 |
| Long-Term Obligations | 169,500 | 174,901 | 180,289 | 28,399 | 36,960 | 17,659 | 21,907 | 31,392 |
| Total Liabilities | 270,157 | 269,519 | 276,132 | 96,053 | 98,373 | 70,400 | 72,531 | 83,321 |
| Stockholders' Equity | 197,142 | 193,646 | 190,305 | 175,672 | 167,608 | 151,124 | 135,189 | 121,600 |
| Shares Outstanding | 23,781 | 23,767 | 23,766 | 23,680 | 23,605 | 23,509 | 23,283 | 23,061 |
| **Statistical Record** | | | | | | | | |
| Return on Assets % | 3.40 | 3.89 | 4.90 | 5.61 | 9.98 | 8.76 | 8.69 | 5.16 |
| Return on Equity % | 6.59 | 7.61 | 9.88 | 8.79 | 15.27 | 13.13 | 13.96 | 9.12 |
| EBITDA Margin % | 35.85 | 34.95 | 37.63 | 47.27 | 51.53 | 44.09 | 34.98 | 29.00 |
| Net Margin % | 4.93 | 5.01 | 9.27 | 9.40 | 16.90 | 13.32 | 10.59 | 7.33 |
| Asset Turnover | 0.62 | 0.58 | 0.53 | 0.60 | 0.59 | 0.66 | 0.82 | 0.70 |
| Current Ratio | 1.41 | 1.46 | 1.58 | 2.14 | 2.97 | 1.71 | 1.45 | 0.91 |
| Debt to Equity | 0.86 | 0.90 | 0.95 | 0.16 | 0.22 | 0.12 | 0.16 | 0.26 |
| Price Range | 19.96-15.77 | 19.96-15.68 | 20.99-15.68 | 28.32-16.25 | 28.05-12.72 | 25.53-14.41 | 16.66-13.42 | 17.32-8.63 |
| P/E Ratio | 36.96-29.20 | 33.27-26.13 | 27.62-20.63 | 44.25-25.39 | 26.97-12.23 | 31.91-18.01 | 21.64-17.42 | 37.65-18.75 |
| Average Yield % | 1.85 | 1.84 | 1.82 | 1.60 | 1.66 | 1.46 | 1.69 | 1.26 |

**Address:** 500 Shentel Way, Edinburg, VA 22824
**Telephone:** 540-984-4141
**Web Site:** www.shentel.com

**Officers:** Christopher E. French - President, Chief Executive Officer Earle A. MacKenzie - Executive Vice President, Chief Operating Officer **Transfer Agents:** Shenandoah Telecommunications Company, Edinburg, VA

**Investor Contact:** 540-984-5200
**No of Institutions:** 69
**Shares:** 8,832,811 **% Held:** 32.16

# SHERWIN-WILLIAMS CO.

| Exchange | Symbol | Price | 52Wk Range | Yield | P/E |
|---|---|---|---|---|---|
| NYS | SHW | $75.74 (8/31/2011) | 87.84-69.57 | 1.93 | 16.57 |

***7 Year Price Score 133.23** *NYSE Composite Index=100 ***12 Month Price Score 97.85**

**Interim Earnings (Per Share)**

| Qtr. | Mar | Jun | Sep | Dec |
|---|---|---|---|---|
| 2008 | 0.64 | 1.45 | 1.50 | 0.43 |
| 2009 | 0.32 | 1.35 | 1.51 | 0.61 |
| 2010 | 0.30 | 1.64 | 1.60 | 0.68 |
| 2011 | 0.63 | 1.66 | ... | ... |

**Interim Dividends (Per Share)**

| Amt | Decl | Ex | Rec | Pay |
|---|---|---|---|---|
| 0.36Q | 10/20/2010 | 11/17/2010 | 11/19/2010 | 12/03/2010 |
| 0.365Q | 02/16/2011 | 02/23/2011 | 02/25/2011 | 03/11/2011 |
| 0.365Q | 04/20/2011 | 05/18/2011 | 05/20/2011 | 06/03/2011 |
| 0.365Q | 07/20/2011 | 08/17/2011 | 08/19/2011 | 09/09/2011 |

**Indicated Div: $1.46 (Div. Reinv. Plan)**

**Valuation Analysis**

| | | | |
|---|---|---|---|
| Forecast EPS | $4.80 (09/02/2011) | | |
| Market Cap | $8.0 Billion | Book Value | $1.7 Billion |
| Price/Book | 4.61 | Price/Sales | 0.97 |

**Dividend Achiever Status**

| | |
|---|---|
| **10 Year Growth Rate** | 9.52% |
| **Total Years of Dividend Growth** | 31 |

**Business Summary:** Specialty Chemicals (MIC: 8.3.2 SIC: 5231 NAIC: 444120)

Sherwin-Williams is a provider of paint, coatings and related products. Co. has three segments: Paint Stores Group, which sells Sherwin-Williams® architectural paint and coatings, industrial and marine products, original equipment manufacturer (OEM) product finishes and related items; Consumer Group, which provides paint, coatings and related products to customers in the U.S. and Canada and the Paint Stores Group; and Global Finishes Group, which develops, licenses, manufactures, distributes and sells architectural paint and coatings, industrial and marine products, automotive finishes and refinish products, OEM coatings and related products in North and South America, Europe and Asia.

**Recent Developments:** For the quarter ended June 30 2011, net income decreased 1.4% to US$179.1 million from US$181.7 million in the year-earlier quarter. Revenues were US$2.35 billion, up 9.9% from US$2.14 billion the year before. Direct operating expenses rose 13.7% to US$1.33 billion from US$1.17 billion in the comparable period the year before. Indirect operating expenses increased 9.3% to US$755.6 million from US$691.2 million in the equivalent prior-year period.

**Prospects:** Our evaluation of Sherwin-Williams Co. as of Sep. 6, 2011 is the result of our systematic analysis on three basic characteristics: earnings strength, relative valuation, and recent stock price movement. The company has managed to produce a neutral trend in earnings per share over the past 5 quarters. However, while recent estimates for the company have been lowered by analysts, SHW has posted results that fell short of analysts expectations. Based on operating earnings yield, the company is about fairly valued when compared to all of the companies in our coverage universe. Share price changes over the past year indicates that SHW will perform poorly over the near term.

| **Financial Data** (US$ in Thousands) | 6 Mos | 3 Mos | 12/31/2010 | 12/31/2009 | 12/31/2008 | 12/31/2007 | 12/31/2006 | 12/31/2005 |
|---|---|---|---|---|---|---|---|---|
| Earnings Per Share | 4.57 | 4.55 | 4.21 | 3.78 | 4.00 | 4.70 | 4.19 | 3.28 |
| Cash Flow Per Share | 5.52 | 6.37 | 6.60 | 7.57 | 7.48 | 6.87 | 6.11 | 5.24 |
| Tang Book Value Per Share | 1.12 | N.M. | N.M. | N.M. | 0.70 | 0.92 | 2.67 | 3.83 |
| Dividends Per Share | 1.450 | 1.445 | 1.440 | 1.420 | 1.400 | 1.260 | 1.000 | 0.820 |
| Dividend Payout % | 31.73 | 31.76 | 34.20 | 37.57 | 35.00 | 26.81 | 23.87 | 25.00 |
| **Income Statement** | | | | | | | | |
| Total Revenue | 4,210,337 | 1,855,586 | 7,776,424 | 7,094,249 | 7,979,727 | 8,005,292 | 7,809,759 | 7,190,661 |
| EBITDA | 460,954 | 148,791 | 920,761 | 831,354 | 941,740 | 1,133,953 | 1,022,780 | 844,723 |
| Depn & Amortn | 87,934 | 43,726 | 175,311 | 170,904 | 165,511 | 163,479 | 145,917 | 143,517 |
| Income Before Taxes | 351,729 | 94,713 | 677,784 | 622,817 | 714,475 | 912,943 | 834,312 | 656,215 |
| Income Taxes | 104,298 | 26,397 | 215,299 | 186,969 | 237,599 | 297,365 | 258,254 | 191,601 |
| Net Income | 247,431 | 68,316 | 462,485 | 435,848 | 476,876 | 615,578 | 576,058 | 463,258 |
| Average Shares | 106,876 | 107,362 | 108,785 | 113,514 | 119,343 | 130,924 | 137,342 | 141,078 |
| **Balance Sheet** | | | | | | | | |
| Current Assets | 2,638,182 | 2,466,400 | 2,213,722 | 1,770,019 | 1,909,205 | 2,069,580 | 2,450,281 | 1,894,385 |
| Total Assets | 5,633,769 | 5,443,653 | 5,169,235 | 4,323,855 | 4,415,759 | 4,855,340 | 4,995,087 | 4,369,195 |
| Current Liabilities | 2,389,812 | 2,327,162 | 2,063,940 | 1,393,668 | 1,936,736 | 2,141,385 | 2,074,815 | 1,554,371 |
| Long-Term Obligations | 644,255 | 650,881 | 648,326 | 782,670 | 303,727 | 293,454 | 291,876 | 486,996 |
| Total Liabilities | 3,886,957 | 3,835,761 | 3,559,795 | 2,832,905 | 2,810,111 | 3,069,613 | 3,002,727 | 2,638,583 |
| Stockholders' Equity | 1,746,812 | 1,607,892 | 1,609,440 | 1,490,950 | 1,605,648 | 1,785,727 | 1,992,360 | 1,730,612 |
| Shares Outstanding | 106,278 | 106,463 | 107,020 | 109,436 | 117,035 | 122,814 | 133,565 | 135,139 |
| **Statistical Record** | | | | | | | | |
| Return on Assets % | 9.55 | 10.01 | 9.74 | 9.97 | 10.26 | 12.50 | 12.30 | 10.72 |
| Return on Equity % | 30.24 | 32.11 | 29.83 | 28.15 | 28.05 | 32.59 | 30.95 | 27.43 |
| EBITDA Margin % | 10.95 | 8.02 | 11.84 | 11.72 | 11.80 | 14.17 | 13.10 | 11.75 |
| Net Margin % | 5.88 | 3.68 | 5.95 | 6.14 | 5.98 | 7.69 | 7.38 | 6.44 |
| Asset Turnover | 1.60 | 1.62 | 1.64 | 1.62 | 1.72 | 1.63 | 1.67 | 1.66 |
| Current Ratio | 1.10 | 1.06 | 1.07 | 1.27 | 0.99 | 0.97 | 1.18 | 1.22 |
| Debt to Equity | 0.37 | 0.40 | 0.40 | 0.52 | 0.19 | 0.16 | 0.15 | 0.28 |
| Price Range | 87.84-66.88 | 86.09-66.88 | 84.50-58.00 | 63.75-42.98 | 63.36-45.06 | 72.99-57.65 | 64.61-41.29 | 48.63-40.75 |
| P/E Ratio | 19.22-14.63 | 18.92-14.70 | 20.07-13.78 | 16.87-11.37 | 15.84-11.27 | 15.53-12.27 | 15.42-9.85 | 14.83-12.42 |
| Average Yield % | 1.85 | 1.89 | 2.01 | 2.54 | 2.55 | 1.92 | 1.91 | 1.84 |

**Address:** 101 West Prospect Avenue, Cleveland, OH 44115-1075
**Telephone:** 216-566-2000
**Web Site:** www.sherwin.com

**Officers:** Christopher M. Connor - Chairman, Chief Executive Officer John G. Morikis - President, Chief Operating Officer **Transfer Agents:** BNY Mellon Shareowner Services, Jersey City, NJ

**Investor Contact:** 216-566-2000
**No of Institutions:** 527
**Shares:** 91,747,736 **% Held:** 70.88

# SIGMA-ALDRICH CORP.

| Exchange | Symbol | Price | 52Wk Range | Yield | P/E |
|---|---|---|---|---|---|
| NMS | SIAL | $64.39 (8/31/2011) | 75.81-53.17 | 1.12 | 18.94 |

*7 Year Price Score 140.14 *NYSE Composite Index=100 *12 Month Price Score 103.32

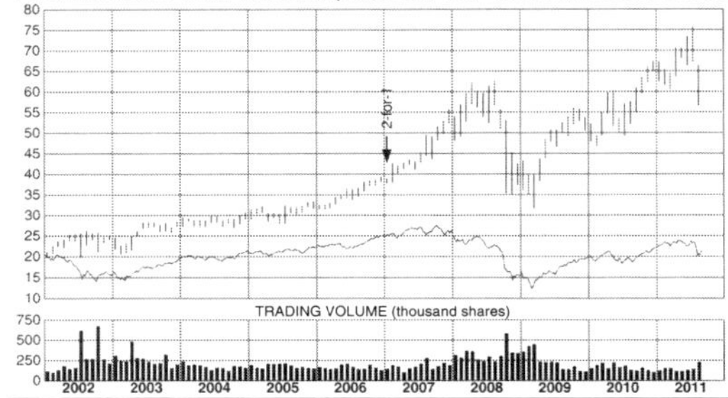


**Interim Earnings (Per Share)**

| Qtr. | Mar | Jun | Sep | Dec |
|---|---|---|---|---|
| 2008 | 0.64 | 0.70 | 0.64 | 0.67 |
| 2009 | 0.68 | 0.68 | 0.70 | 0.74 |
| 2010 | 0.81 | 0.79 | 0.76 | 0.76 |
| 2011 | 0.97 | 0.91 | ... | ... |

**Interim Dividends (Per Share)**

| Amt | Decl | Ex | Rec | Pay |
|---|---|---|---|---|
| 0.16Q | 11/09/2010 | 11/29/2010 | 12/01/2010 | 12/15/2010 |
| 0.18Q | 02/08/2011 | 02/25/2011 | 03/01/2011 | 03/15/2011 |
| 0.18Q | 05/03/2011 | 05/27/2011 | 06/01/2011 | 06/15/2011 |
| 0.18Q | 08/10/2011 | 08/30/2011 | 09/01/2011 | 09/15/2011 |

**Indicated Div: $0.72**

**Valuation Analysis**

| | | | |
|---|---|---|---|
| Forecast EPS | $3.71 (09/05/2011) | | |
| Market Cap | $7.9 Billion | Book Value | $2.3 Billion |
| Price/Book | 3.46 | Price/Sales | 3.25 |

**Dividend Achiever Status**

| | |
|---|---|
| **10 Year Growth Rate** | 14.52% |
| **Total Years of Dividend Growth** | 29 |

**Business Summary:** Specialty Chemicals (MIC: 8.3.2 SIC: 5169 NAIC: 424690)

Sigma-Aldrich develops, manufactures, purchases and distributes a range of chemicals, biochemicals and equipment used in scientific research. Co. has four business units: Research Essentials sells biological buffers, cell culture reagents, biochemicals, chemicals, solvents, and other reagents and kits; Research Specialties sells organic chemicals, biochemicals, analytical reagents, chromatography and other laboratory consumables, reference materials and high-purity products; Research Biotech supplies immunochemical, molecular biology, cell biology, proteomic, genomic, transgenic and other life science products; and SAFC (Fine Chemicals) supplies organic chemicals and biochemicals.

**Recent Developments:** For the quarter ended June 30 2011, net income increased 16.5% to US$113.0 million from US$97.0 million in the year-earlier quarter. Revenues were US$637.0 million, up 15.0% from US$554.0 million the year before. Operating income was US$160.0 million versus US$142.0 million in the prior-year quarter, an increase of 12.7%. Direct operating expenses rose 17.7% to US$306.0 million from US$260.0 million in the comparable period the year before. Indirect operating expenses increased 12.5% to US$171.0 million from US$152.0 million in the equivalent prior-year period.

**Prospects:** Our evaluation of Sigma-Aldrich Corp. as of Sep. 6, 2011 is the result of our systematic analysis on three basic characteristics: earnings strength, relative valuation, and recent stock price movement. The company has produced a positive trend in earnings per share over the past 5 quarters and while recent estimates for the company have remained steady, SIAL has posted better than expected results. Based on operating earnings yield, the company is about fairly valued when compared to all of the companies in our coverage universe. Share price changes over the past year indicates that SIAL will perform poorly over the near term.

**Financial Data**

| (US$ in Thousands) | 6 Mos | 3 Mos | 12/31/2010 | 12/31/2009 | 12/31/2008 | 12/31/2007 | 12/31/2006 | 12/31/2005 |
|---|---|---|---|---|---|---|---|---|
| Earnings Per Share | 3.40 | 3.28 | 3.12 | 2.80 | 2.65 | 2.34 | 2.05 | 1.88 |
| Cash Flow Per Share | 4.34 | 4.29 | 4.32 | 4.23 | 3.19 | 3.21 | 2.49 | 2.07 |
| Tang Book Value Per Share | 13.30 | 12.39 | 11.43 | 9.50 | 7.13 | 8.19 | 7.00 | 5.71 |
| Dividends Per Share | 0.680 | 0.660 | 0.640 | 0.580 | 0.520 | 0.460 | 0.420 | 0.380 |
| Dividend Payout % | 20.00 | 20.12 | 20.51 | 20.71 | 19.62 | 19.66 | 20.49 | 20.21 |
| **Income Statement** | | | | | | | | |
| Total Revenue | 1,269,000 | 632,000 | 2,271,000 | 2,147,600 | 2,200,700 | 2,038,700 | 1,797,500 | 1,666,500 |
| EBITDA | 379,000 | 193,000 | 631,000 | 580,700 | 590,900 | 545,700 | 482,700 | 439,800 |
| Depn & Amortn | 52,000 | 26,000 | 80,000 | 81,100 | 87,100 | 86,100 | 80,000 | 78,400 |
| Income Before Taxes | 323,000 | 165,000 | 544,000 | 489,600 | 489,500 | 437,600 | 378,700 | 343,300 |
| Income Taxes | 91,000 | 46,000 | 160,000 | 142,900 | 148,000 | 126,500 | 101,900 | 85,000 |
| Net Income | 232,000 | 119,000 | 384,000 | 346,700 | 341,500 | 311,100 | 276,800 | 258,300 |
| Average Shares | 124,000 | 123,000 | 123,000 | 123,700 | 128,800 | 133,100 | 134,900 | 137,400 |
| **Balance Sheet** | | | | | | | | |
| Current Assets | 1,833,000 | 1,726,000 | 1,602,000 | 1,383,500 | 1,309,200 | 1,282,500 | 1,112,900 | 950,200 |
| Total Assets | 3,339,000 | 3,174,000 | 3,014,000 | 2,713,800 | 2,556,500 | 2,629,100 | 2,334,300 | 2,131,300 |
| Current Liabilities | 546,000 | 537,000 | 530,000 | 741,900 | 793,900 | 635,000 | 442,600 | 460,700 |
| Long-Term Obligations | 300,000 | 300,000 | 300,000 | 100,000 | 200,100 | 207,000 | 337,900 | 283,200 |
| Total Liabilities | 1,068,000 | 1,054,000 | 1,038,000 | 1,027,800 | 1,177,300 | 1,012,500 | 923,400 | 897,900 |
| Stockholders' Equity | 2,271,000 | 2,120,000 | 1,976,000 | 1,686,000 | 1,379,200 | 1,616,600 | 1,410,900 | 1,233,400 |
| Shares Outstanding | 122,000 | 122,000 | 122,000 | 121,700 | 122,100 | 129,400 | 132,000 | 134,400 |
| **Statistical Record** | | | | | | | | |
| Return on Assets % | 13.83 | 13.56 | 13.41 | 13.16 | 13.14 | 12.54 | 12.40 | 13.33 |
| Return on Equity % | 21.09 | 21.10 | 20.97 | 22.62 | 22.74 | 20.55 | 20.94 | 21.13 |
| EBITDA Margin % | 29.87 | 30.54 | 27.79 | 27.04 | 26.85 | 26.77 | 26.85 | 26.39 |
| Net Margin % | 18.28 | 18.83 | 16.91 | 16.14 | 15.52 | 15.26 | 15.40 | 15.50 |
| Asset Turnover | 0.80 | 0.78 | 0.79 | 0.81 | 0.85 | 0.82 | 0.81 | 0.86 |
| Current Ratio | 3.36 | 3.21 | 3.02 | 1.86 | 1.65 | 2.02 | 2.51 | 2.06 |
| Debt to Equity | 0.13 | 0.14 | 0.15 | 0.06 | 0.15 | 0.13 | 0.24 | 0.23 |
| Price Range | 73.38-49.30 | 67.40-49.30 | 67.40-46.79 | 56.16-31.63 | 62.56-34.98 | 55.87-37.77 | 39.41-31.54 | 33.34-27.86 |
| P/E Ratio | 21.58-14.50 | 20.55-15.03 | 21.60-15.00 | 20.06-11.30 | 23.61-13.20 | 23.88-16.14 | 19.22-15.38 | 17.73-14.82 |
| Average Yield % | 1.08 | 1.11 | 1.14 | 1.24 | 0.99 | 1.02 | 1.19 | 1.24 |

**Address:** 3050 Spruce Street, St. Louis, MO 63103
**Telephone:** 314-771-5765
**Web Site:** www.sigma-aldrich.com

**Officers:** Barrett A. Toan - Chairman Rakesh Sachdev - President, Chief Executive Officer, Senior Vice President, Chief Administrative Officer **Transfer Agents:** Computershare Investor Services, Chicago, IL

**Investor Contact:** 314-286-8004
**No of Institutions:** 588
**Shares:** 119,084,888 **% Held:** 77.18

# SJW CORP.

| Exchange | Symbol | Price | 52Wk Range | Yield | P/E |
|---|---|---|---|---|---|
| NYS | SJW | $23.32 (8/31/2011) | 27.88-21.52 | 2.96 | 17.53 |

***7 Year Price Score 91.03** *NYSE Composite Index=100 ***12 Month Price Score 97.73**

**Interim Earnings (Per Share)**

| Qtr. | Mar | Jun | Sep | Dec |
|---|---|---|---|---|
| 2008 | 0.15 | 0.34 | 0.44 | 0.22 |
| 2009 | 0.01 | 0.23 | 0.43 | 0.14 |
| 2010 | 0.05 | 0.24 | 0.58 | 0.43 |
| 2011 | 0.03 | 0.29 | ... | ... |

**Interim Dividends (Per Share)**

| Amt | Decl | Ex | Rec | Pay |
|---|---|---|---|---|
| 0.17Q | 10/27/2010 | 11/04/2010 | 11/08/2010 | 12/01/2010 |
| 0.172Q | 01/26/2011 | 02/03/2011 | 02/07/2011 | 03/01/2011 |
| 0.172Q | 04/27/2011 | 05/05/2011 | 05/09/2011 | 06/01/2011 |
| 0.172Q | 07/27/2011 | 08/04/2011 | 08/08/2011 | 09/01/2011 |

**Indicated Div: $0.69**

**Valuation Analysis**

| | | | |
|---|---|---|---|
| Forecast EPS | $0.99 (09/02/2011) | | |
| Market Cap | $433.2 Million | Book Value | $255.1 Million |
| Price/Book | 1.70 | Price/Sales | 1.94 |

**Dividend Achiever Status**

| | |
|---|---|
| **10 Year Growth Rate** | 4.72% |
| **Total Years of Dividend Growth** | 43 |

**Business Summary:** Water Utilities (MIC: 3.2.1 SIC: 4941 NAIC: 221310)

SJW is a holding company. Through its subsidiaries, Co. produces, purchases, stores, purifies, distributes, wholesales, and sells water. Co.'s subsidiaries include: San Jose Water Company, a public utility providing regulated and non-regulated water service; SJW Land Company, which owns undeveloped land in California and Tennessee, owns and operates commercial buildings in California, Florida, Connecticut, Texas, Arizona and Tennessee, and has a 70.0% interest in 444 West Santa Clara Street, L.P.; SJWTX, Inc., a public utility providing water service in western Comal County and southern Blanco County; and Texas Water Alliance Limited, which is developing a water supply project in Texas.

**Recent Developments:** For the quarter ended June 30 2011, net income increased 20.7% to US$5.5 million from US$4.5 million in the year-earlier quarter. Revenues were US$59.0 million, up 9.0% from US$54.1 million the year before. Operating income was US$13.8 million versus US$11.3 million in the prior-year quarter, an increase of 21.5%. Indirect operating expenses increased 5.7% to US$45.2 million from US$42.8 million in the equivalent prior-year period.

**Prospects:** Our evaluation of SJW Corp. as of Sep. 6, 2011 is the result of our systematic analysis on three basic characteristics: earnings strength, relative valuation, and recent stock price movement. The company has produced a positive trend in earnings per share over the past 5 quarters. However, while recent estimates for the company have been mixed, SJW has posted better than expected results. Based on operating earnings yield, the company is about fairly valued when compared to all of the companies in our coverage universe. Share price changes over the past year indicates that SJW will perform very poorly over the near term.

**Financial Data**

| (US$ in Thousands) | 6 Mos | 3 Mos | 12/31/2010 | 12/31/2009 | 12/31/2008 | 12/31/2007 | 12/31/2006 | 12/31/2005 |
|---|---|---|---|---|---|---|---|---|
| Earnings Per Share | 1.33 | 1.28 | 1.30 | 0.81 | 1.15 | 1.04 | 2.08 | 1.18 |
| Cash Flow Per Share | 2.41 | 2.03 | 2.01 | 2.95 | 2.81 | 2.29 | 2.44 | 2.33 |
| Tang Book Value Per Share | 13.73 | 13.61 | 13.75 | 13.66 | 13.78 | 12.90 | 12.48 | 10.51 |
| Dividends Per Share | 0.685 | 0.683 | 0.680 | 0.660 | 0.645 | 0.605 | 0.565 | 0.535 |
| Dividend Payout % | 51.50 | 53.32 | 52.31 | 81.48 | 56.09 | 58.17 | 27.16 | 45.34 |
| **Income Statement** | | | | | | | | |
| Total Revenue | 102,703 | 43,696 | 215,638 | 216,097 | 220,347 | 206,601 | 189,238 | 180,105 |
| EBITDA | 35,310 | 13,568 | 68,420 | 54,796 | 58,255 | 53,288 | 69,801 | 50,687 |
| Depn & Amortn | 15,586 | 7,794 | 26,331 | 23,655 | 22,067 | 20,956 | 20,095 | 18,654 |
| Income Before Taxes | 10,311 | 1,043 | 24,406 | 15,171 | 21,461 | 19,323 | 38,581 | 21,840 |
| Income Taxes | 4,250 | 433 | ... | 10,280 | ... | 12,549 | ... | ... |
| Net Income | 6,061 | 610 | 24,406 | 15,171 | 21,461 | 19,323 | 38,581 | 21,840 |
| Average Shares | 18,784 | 18,775 | 18,742 | 18,680 | 18,609 | 18,552 | 18,528 | 18,480 |
| **Balance Sheet** | | | | | | | | |
| Current Assets | 83,814 | 39,061 | 38,027 | 28,010 | 31,961 | 31,591 | 59,475 | 31,692 |
| Total Assets | 1,000,314 | 947,678 | 935,362 | 878,474 | 850,877 | 767,326 | 705,864 | 587,709 |
| Current Liabilities | 39,364 | 41,071 | 29,155 | 31,958 | 43,323 | 32,954 | 37,246 | 20,944 |
| Long-Term Obligations | 344,811 | 295,059 | 295,704 | 246,879 | 216,613 | 216,312 | 163,648 | 145,281 |
| Total Liabilities | 745,166 | 694,905 | 680,330 | 625,718 | 596,551 | 530,392 | 477,682 | 391,801 |
| Stockholders' Equity | 255,148 | 252,773 | 255,032 | 252,756 | 254,326 | 236,934 | 228,182 | 195,908 |
| Shares Outstanding | 18,577 | 18,577 | 18,551 | 18,499 | 18,452 | 18,361 | 18,281 | 18,270 |
| **Statistical Record** | | | | | | | | |
| Return on Assets % | 2.56 | 2.61 | 2.69 | 1.75 | 2.65 | 2.62 | 5.97 | 3.83 |
| Return on Equity % | 9.85 | 9.53 | 9.61 | 5.98 | 8.71 | 8.31 | 18.19 | 11.48 |
| EBITDA Margin % | 34.38 | 31.05 | 31.73 | 25.36 | 26.44 | 25.79 | 36.89 | 28.14 |
| Net Margin % | 5.90 | 1.40 | 11.32 | 7.02 | 9.74 | 9.35 | 20.39 | 12.13 |
| Asset Turnover | 0.23 | 0.24 | 0.24 | 0.25 | 0.27 | 0.28 | 0.29 | 0.32 |
| Current Ratio | 2.13 | 0.95 | 1.30 | 0.88 | 0.74 | 0.96 | 1.60 | 1.51 |
| Debt to Equity | 1.35 | 1.17 | 1.16 | 0.98 | 0.85 | 0.91 | 0.72 | 0.74 |
| Price Range | 27.88-21.99 | 28.23-22.48 | 28.23-21.76 | 29.94-18.72 | 34.67-21.71 | 43.00-28.19 | 39.50-21.56 | 27.69-16.15 |
| P/E Ratio | 20.96-16.53 | 22.05-17.56 | 21.72-16.74 | 36.96-23.11 | 30.15-18.88 | 41.35-27.11 | 18.99-10.37 | 23.47-13.68 |
| Average Yield % | 2.85 | 2.76 | 2.78 | 2.83 | 2.27 | 1.74 | 2.03 | 2.43 |

**Address:** 110 West Taylor Street, San Jose, CA 95110
**Telephone:** 408-279-7800
**Web Site:** www.sjwater.com

**Officers:** W. Richard Roth - President, Chief Executive Officer George J. Belhumeur - Senior Vice President **Transfer Agents:** American Stock Transfer & Trust Company, Brooklyn, NY

**No of Institutions:** 87
**Shares:** 9,189,119 **% Held:** 48.19

# SMITH (A.O.) CORP

| Exchange | Symbol | Price | 52Wk Range | Yield | P/E |
|---|---|---|---|---|---|
| NYS | AOS | $39.29 (8/31/2011) | 44.65-34.23 | 1.63 | 11.73 |

*7 Year Price Score 147.29 *NYSE Composite Index=100 *12 Month Price Score 100.74

**Interim Earnings (Per Share)**

| Qtr. | Mar | Jun | Sep | Dec |
|---|---|---|---|---|
| 2008 | 0.48 | 0.71 | 0.47 | 0.15 |
| 2009 | 0.19 | 0.56 | 0.76 | 0.47 |
| 2010 | 0.67 | 0.36 | 0.69 | 0.69 |
| 2011 | 0.88 | 1.08 | ... | ... |

**Interim Dividends (Per Share)**

| Amt | Decl | Ex | Rec | Pay |
|---|---|---|---|---|
| 50% | 10/14/2010 | 11/16/2010 | 10/29/2010 | 11/15/2010 |
| 0.14Q | 01/14/2011 | 01/27/2011 | 01/31/2011 | 02/15/2011 |
| 0.14Q | 04/12/2011 | 04/27/2011 | 04/29/2011 | 05/16/2011 |
| 0.16Q | 07/11/2011 | 07/27/2011 | 07/29/2011 | 08/15/2011 |

**Indicated Div: $0.64 (Div. Reinv. Plan)**

**Valuation Analysis**

| | | | |
|---|---|---|---|
| Forecast EPS | $2.15 (09/02/2011) | | |
| Market Cap | $1.8 Billion | Book Value | $969.8 Million |
| Price/Book | 1.87 | Price/Sales | 1.49 |

**Dividend Achiever Status**

| | |
|---|---|
| **10 Year Growth Rate** | 4.53% |
| **Total Years of Dividend Growth** | 18 |

**Business Summary:** Metal Products (MIC: 8.2.3 SIC: 3621 NAIC: 335312)

A.O. Smith is a manufacturer of water heating equipment, serving a mix of residential and commercial end markets. Co. is comprised of one reporting segment: Water Products, which manufacture and market a line of residential gas, gas tankless and electric water heaters, commercial water heating equipment, copper-tube boilers, water treatment products and water systems tanks. Co.'s products are manufactured and marketed primarily in North America and China. Water heaters are sold through both wholesale and retail channels to plumbing wholesalers and retail outlets.

**Recent Developments:** For the quarter ended June 30 2011, income from continuing operations was US$28.6 million compared with a loss of US$900,000 in the year-earlier quarter. Net income increased 203.0% to US$50.3 million from US$16.6 million in the year-earlier quarter. Revenues were US$405.3 million, up 8.1% from US$375.0 million the year before. Direct operating expenses rose 12.5% to US$293.4 million from US$260.8 million in the comparable period the year before. Indirect operating expenses decreased 37.4% to US$73.9 million from US$118.0 million in the equivalent prior-year period.

**Prospects:** Our evaluation of Smith (A.O.) Corp. as of Sep. 6, 2011 is the result of our systematic analysis on three basic characteristics: earnings strength, relative valuation, and recent stock price movement. The company has enjoyed a very positive trend in earnings per share over the past 5 quarters. However, while recent estimates for the company have been mixed, AOS has posted better than expected results. Based on operating earnings yield, the company is about fairly valued when compared to all of the companies in our coverage universe. Share price changes over the past year indicates that AOS will perform in line with the market over the near term.

**Financial Data**

| (US$ in Thousands) | 6 Mos | 3 Mos | 12/31/2010 | 12/31/2009 | 12/31/2008 | 12/31/2007 | 12/31/2006 | 12/31/2005 |
|---|---|---|---|---|---|---|---|---|
| Earnings Per Share | 3.35 | 2.63 | 2.42 | 2.26 | 1.80 | 1.90 | 1.65 | 1.03 |
| Cash Flow Per Share | (0.27) | 1.85 | 2.73 | 7.49 | 2.36 | 4.16 | 2.82 | 4.19 |
| Tang Book Value Per Share | 11.69 | 10.30 | 9.84 | 1.83 | 1.27 | 3.51 | 2.11 | 6.34 |
| Dividends Per Share | 0.560 | 0.550 | 0.540 | 0.513 | 0.493 | 0.467 | 0.440 | 0.427 |
| Dividend Payout % | 16.73 | 20.94 | 22.31 | 22.71 | 27.41 | 24.56 | 26.72 | 41.56 |
| **Income Statement** | | | | | | | | |
| Total Revenue | 822,700 | 417,400 | 1,489,300 | 1,991,500 | 2,304,900 | 2,312,100 | 2,161,300 | 1,689,200 |
| EBITDA | 100,400 | 46,300 | 122,100 | 198,900 | 195,600 | 194,100 | 190,600 | 134,500 |
| Depn & Amortn | 21,800 | 10,800 | 40,800 | 67,500 | 66,300 | 67,500 | 60,900 | 52,800 |
| Income Before Taxes | 74,700 | 33,700 | 74,400 | 119,600 | 110,100 | 99,900 | 104,800 | 68,700 |
| Income Taxes | 21,900 | 9,500 | 17,300 | 29,600 | 27,900 | 11,700 | 28,600 | 22,200 |
| Net Income | 91,300 | 41,000 | 111,700 | 81,300 | 81,900 | 88,200 | 76,500 | 46,500 |
| Average Shares | 46,646 | 46,540 | 46,162 | 35,931 | 45,434 | 46,459 | 46,505 | 45,422 |
| **Balance Sheet** | | | | | | | | |
| Current Assets | 991,200 | 987,000 | 896,000 | 740,000 | 781,300 | 767,600 | 760,000 | 576,000 |
| Total Assets | 2,143,100 | 2,205,300 | 2,112,000 | 1,901,300 | 1,883,900 | 1,854,400 | 1,839,900 | 1,292,700 |
| Current Liabilities | 535,900 | 555,400 | 536,800 | 491,300 | 505,000 | 472,600 | 437,300 | 307,600 |
| Long-Term Obligations | 356,900 | 321,200 | 242,400 | 232,100 | 317,300 | 379,600 | 432,100 | 162,400 |
| Total Liabilities | 1,173,300 | 1,283,400 | 1,230,600 | 1,130,600 | 1,242,800 | 1,096,600 | 1,155,300 | 679,800 |
| Stockholders' Equity | 969,800 | 921,900 | 881,400 | 770,700 | 641,100 | 757,800 | 684,600 | 612,900 |
| Shares Outstanding | 46,209 | 47,676 | 45,833 | 45,520 | 45,266 | 45,079 | 46,026 | 45,620 |
| **Statistical Record** | | | | | | | | |
| Return on Assets % | 7.57 | 5.85 | 5.57 | 4.30 | 4.37 | 4.77 | 4.88 | 3.57 |
| Return on Equity % | 17.52 | 14.13 | 13.52 | 11.52 | 11.68 | 12.23 | 11.79 | 7.73 |
| EBITDA Margin % | 12.20 | 11.09 | 8.20 | 9.99 | 8.49 | 8.39 | 8.82 | 7.96 |
| Net Margin % | 11.10 | 9.82 | 7.50 | 4.08 | 3.55 | 3.81 | 3.54 | 2.75 |
| Asset Turnover | 0.59 | 0.66 | 0.74 | 1.05 | 1.23 | 1.25 | 1.38 | 1.30 |
| Current Ratio | 1.85 | 1.78 | 1.67 | 1.51 | 1.55 | 1.62 | 1.74 | 1.87 |
| Debt to Equity | 0.37 | 0.35 | 0.28 | 0.30 | 0.49 | 0.50 | 0.63 | 0.26 |
| Price Range | 44.35-32.11 | 44.34-30.09 | 43.07-27.64 | 29.96-14.19 | 31.33-16.29 | 34.10-21.86 | 37.77-22.70 | 24.75-16.75 |
| P/E Ratio | 13.24-9.59 | 16.86-11.44 | 17.80-11.42 | 13.26-6.28 | 17.41-9.05 | 17.95-11.51 | 22.89-13.76 | 24.03-16.27 |
| Average Yield % | 1.42 | 1.47 | 1.56 | 2.24 | 2.15 | 1.73 | 1.55 | 2.16 |

**Address:** 11270 West Park Place, Milwaukee, WI 53224-9508
**Telephone:** 414-359-4000
**Web Site:** www.aosmith.com

**Officers:** Paul W. Jones - Chairman, President, Chief Executive Officer Ajita G. Rajendra - President, Chief Operating Officer, Executive Vice President, Division Officer **Transfer Agents:**
Wells Fargo Bank, N.A., South St. Paul, MN

**Investor Contact:** 414-359-4009
**No of Institutions:** 233
**Shares:** 36,338,056 **% Held:** 72.12

# SMUCKER (J.M.) CO.

| Exchange | Symbol | Price | 52Wk Range | Yield | P/E |
|---|---|---|---|---|---|
| NYS | SJM | $72.09 (8/31/2011) | 80.00-58.48 | 2.66 | 17.80 |

*7 Year Price Score 130.24 *NYSE Composite Index=100 *12 Month Price Score 110.15

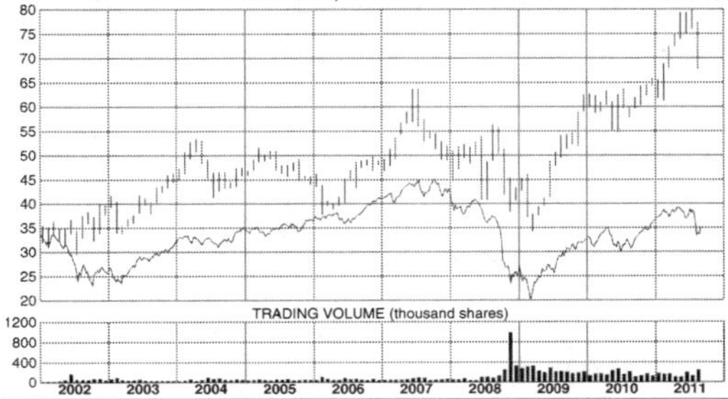


**Interim Earnings (Per Share)**

| Qtr. | Jul | Oct | Jan | Apr |
|---|---|---|---|---|
| 2006-07 | 0.50 | 0.80 | 0.71 | 0.75 |
| 2007-08 | 0.71 | 0.87 | 0.75 | 0.67 |
| 2008-09 | 0.77 | 0.94 | 0.68 | 0.82 |
| 2009-10 | 0.83 | 1.18 | 1.14 | 1.01 |
| 2010-11 | 0.86 | 1.25 | 1.11 | 0.82 |

**Interim Dividends (Per Share)**

| Amt | Decl | Ex | Rec | Pay |
|---|---|---|---|---|
| 0.40Q | 10/26/2010 | 11/09/2010 | 11/12/2010 | 12/01/2010 |
| 0.44Q | 01/27/2011 | 02/09/2011 | 02/11/2011 | 03/01/2011 |
| 0.44Q | 04/21/2011 | 05/11/2011 | 05/13/2011 | 06/01/2011 |
| 0.48Q | 07/22/2011 | 08/10/2011 | 08/12/2011 | 09/01/2011 |

**Indicated Div: $1.92 (Div. Reinv. Plan)**

**Valuation Analysis**

| | | | |
|---|---|---|---|
| Forecast EPS | $5.13 (09/02/2011) | | |
| Market Cap | $8.2 Billion | Book Value | $5.3 Billion |
| Price/Book | 1.56 | Price/Sales | 1.71 |

**Dividend Achiever Status**

| | |
|---|---|
| **10 Year Growth Rate** | 9.25% |
| **Total Years of Dividend Growth** | 13 |

**Business Summary:** Food (MIC: 1.2.1 SIC: 2033 NAIC: 311421)

Smucker (J.M.) markets and manufactures fruit spreads, retail packaged coffee, peanut butter, shortening and oils, ice cream toppings, sweetened condensed milk, and health and natural foods beverages in North America. Co.'s family of brands includes Smucker's, Folgers, Dunkin' Donuts, Jif, Crisco, Pillsbury, Eagle Brand, R.W. Knudsen Family, Hungry Jack, Cafe Bustelo, Cafe Pilon, White Lily, and Martha White in the U.S., along with Robin Hood, Five Roses, Carnation, Europe's Best, and Bick's in Canada. In addition to these brands, Co. markets products under numerous other brands, including Millstone, Dickinson's, Laura Scudder's, Adams, Double Fruit (Canada), and Santa Cruz Organic.

**Recent Developments:** For the year ended Apr 30 2011, net income decreased 3.0% to US$479.5 million from US$494.1 million in the prior year. Revenues were US$4.83 billion, up 4.8% from US$4.61 billion the year before. Operating income was US$784.3 million versus US$790.9 million in the prior year, a decrease of 0.8%. Direct operating expenses rose 7.4% to US$3.03 billion from US$2.82 billion in the comparable period the year before. Indirect operating expenses increased 1.9% to US$1.01 billion from US$995.8 million in the equivalent prior-year period.

**Prospects:** Our evaluation of Smucker (J.M.) Co. as of Sep. 6, 2011 is the result of our systematic analysis on three basic characteristics: earnings strength, relative valuation, and recent stock price movement. The company has managed to produce a neutral trend in earnings per share over the past 5 quarters. However, while recent estimates for the company have been lowered by analysts, SJM has posted better than expected results. Based on operating earnings yield, the company is undervalued when compared to all of the companies in our coverage universe. Share price changes over the past year indicates that SJM will perform in line with the market over the near term.

| **Financial Data** (US$ in Thousands) | 04/30/2011 | 04/30/2010 | 04/30/2009 | 04/30/2008 | 04/30/2007 | 04/30/2006 | 04/30/2005 | 04/30/2004 |
|---|---|---|---|---|---|---|---|---|
| Earnings Per Share | 4.05 | 4.15 | 3.12 | 3.00 | 2.76 | 2.45 | 2.24 | 2.21 |
| Cash Flow Per Share | 3.35 | 6.00 | 5.24 | 3.40 | 4.85 | 3.43 | 3.41 | 2.52 |
| Tang Book Value Per Share | N.M. | N.M. | N.M. | 0.98 | 5.75 | 5.52 | 4.61 | 7.10 |
| Dividends Per Share | 1.640 | 1.400 | 6.280 | 1.200 | 1.120 | 1.080 | 1.000 | 0.920 |
| Dividend Payout % | 40.49 | 33.73 | 201.28 | 40.00 | 40.58 | 44.08 | 44.64 | 41.63 |
| **Income Statement** | | | | | | | | |
| Total Revenue | 4,825,743 | 4,605,289 | 3,757,933 | 2,524,774 | 2,148,017 | 2,154,726 | 2,043,877 | 1,417,011 |
| EBITDA | 950,041 | 901,372 | 531,000 | 342,171 | 312,488 | 296,604 | 276,563 | 221,672 |
| Depn & Amortn | 165,795 | 108,225 | 79,450 | 58,497 | 57,346 | 63,638 | 54,077 | 39,858 |
| Income Before Taxes | 717,164 | 730,753 | 396,065 | 254,788 | 241,004 | 215,570 | 204,614 | 178,819 |
| Income Taxes | 237,682 | 236,615 | 130,112 | 84,409 | 83,785 | 72,216 | 74,154 | 67,469 |
| Net Income | 479,482 | 494,138 | 265,953 | 170,379 | 157,219 | 143,354 | 129,073 | 111,350 |
| Average Shares | 117,119 | 119,081 | 85,285 | 56,720 | 57,056 | 58,425 | 57,748 | 50,395 |
| **Balance Sheet** | | | | | | | | |
| Current Assets | 1,636,999 | 1,223,630 | 1,398,891 | 776,207 | 639,366 | 571,495 | 555,851 | 425,258 |
| Total Assets | 8,324,585 | 7,974,853 | 8,192,161 | 3,129,881 | 2,693,823 | 2,649,744 | 2,635,894 | 1,684,125 |
| Current Liabilities | 482,676 | 478,897 | 1,061,236 | 239,397 | 236,468 | 235,440 | 308,292 | 174,883 |
| Long-Term Obligations | 1,304,039 | 900,000 | 910,000 | 789,684 | 392,643 | 428,602 | 431,560 | 135,000 |
| Total Liabilities | 3,032,222 | 2,648,533 | 3,252,230 | 1,330,028 | 898,166 | 921,685 | 945,094 | 473,432 |
| Stockholders' Equity | 5,292,363 | 5,326,320 | 4,939,931 | 1,799,853 | 1,795,657 | 1,728,059 | 1,690,800 | 1,210,693 |
| Shares Outstanding | 114,172 | 119,119 | 118,422 | 54,622 | 56,779 | 56,949 | 58,540 | 50,174 |
| **Statistical Record** | | | | | | | | |
| Return on Assets % | 5.88 | 6.11 | 4.70 | 5.84 | 5.88 | 5.42 | 5.98 | 6.73 |
| Return on Equity % | 9.03 | 9.63 | 7.89 | 9.45 | 8.92 | 8.39 | 8.90 | 9.51 |
| EBITDA Margin % | 19.69 | 19.57 | 14.13 | 13.55 | 14.55 | 13.77 | 13.53 | 15.64 |
| Net Margin % | 9.94 | 10.73 | 7.08 | 6.75 | 7.32 | 6.65 | 6.32 | 7.86 |
| Asset Turnover | 0.59 | 0.57 | 0.66 | 0.86 | 0.80 | 0.82 | 0.95 | 0.86 |
| Current Ratio | 3.39 | 2.56 | 1.32 | 3.24 | 2.70 | 2.43 | 1.80 | 2.43 |
| Debt to Equity | 0.25 | 0.17 | 0.18 | 0.44 | 0.22 | 0.25 | 0.26 | 0.11 |
| Price Range | 75.07-54.75 | 63.26-39.40 | 56.36-34.22 | 63.66-44.66 | 56.88-39.53 | 50.87-37.78 | 53.09-41.28 | 53.38-35.95 |
| P/E Ratio | 18.54-13.52 | 15.24-9.49 | 18.06-10.97 | 21.22-14.89 | 20.61-14.32 | 20.76-15.42 | 23.70-18.43 | 24.15-16.27 |
| Average Yield % | 2.59 | 2.58 | 13.91 | 2.25 | 2.36 | 2.38 | 2.13 | 2.09 |

**Address:** One Strawberry Lane, Orrville, OH 44667-0280
**Telephone:** 330-682-3000
**Web Site:** www.smuckers.com

**Officers:** Timothy P. Smucker - Chairman, Co-Chief Executive Officer Richard K. Smucker - Executive Chairman, President, Co-Chief Executive Officer
**Transfer Agents:** Computershare Investor Services, LLC, Canton, MA

**No of Institutions:** 615
**Shares:** 88,335,840 **% Held:** 69.33

# SONOCO PRODUCTS CO.

| Exchange | Symbol | Price | 52Wk Range | Yield | P/E |
|---|---|---|---|---|---|
| NYS | SON | $31.59 (8/31/2011) | 36.80-27.92 | 3.67 | 15.95 |

*7 Year Price Score 108.78 *NYSE Composite Index=100 *12 Month Price Score 94.75

**Interim Earnings (Per Share)**

| Qtr. | Mar | Jun | Sep | Dec |
|---|---|---|---|---|
| 2008 | 0.13 | 0.57 | 0.57 | 0.36 |
| 2009 | 0.23 | 0.33 | 0.47 | 0.47 |
| 2010 | 0.48 | 0.58 | 0.57 | 0.33 |
| 2011 | 0.56 | 0.52 | ... | ... |

**Interim Dividends (Per Share)**

| Amt | Decl | Ex | Rec | Pay |
|---|---|---|---|---|
| 0.28Q | 10/18/2010 | 11/17/2010 | 11/19/2010 | 12/10/2010 |
| 0.28Q | 02/08/2011 | 02/16/2011 | 02/18/2011 | 03/10/2011 |
| 0.29Q | 04/20/2011 | 05/11/2011 | 05/13/2011 | 06/10/2011 |
| 0.29Q | 07/20/2011 | 08/17/2011 | 08/19/2011 | 09/09/2011 |

**Indicated Div: $1.16 (Div. Reinv. Plan)**

**Valuation Analysis**

| | | | |
|---|---|---|---|
| Forecast EPS | $2.47 (09/05/2011) | | |
| Market Cap | $3.2 Billion | Book Value | $1.6 Billion |
| Price/Book | 1.99 | Price/Sales | 0.71 |

**Dividend Achiever Status**

| | |
|---|---|
| **10 Year Growth Rate** | 3.33% |
| **Total Years of Dividend Growth** | 27 |

**Business Summary:** Containers & Packaging (MIC: 8.1.3 SIC: 2671 NAIC: 322221)

Sonoco Products is a manufacturer of industrial and consumer packaging products and a provider of packaging services. Co.'s Consumer Packaging segment provides paper packaging, blow molded plastics packaging, thermoformed plastic packaging, ends and closures, and printed flexible packaging. Co.'s Tubes and Cores/Paper segment provides tubes and cores, paper, and recycling items. Through its Packaging Services segment, Co. provides packaging supply chain management and point-of-purchase displays, as well as contract packing, co-packing and fulfillment services. Co.'s All Other Sonoco segment provides wire and cable reels, molded and extruded plastics, paperboard, and protective packaging.

**Recent Developments:** For the quarter ended July 3 2011, net income decreased 8.9% to US$53.7 million from US$59.0 million in the year-earlier quarter. Revenues were US$1.13 billion, up 11.7% from US$1.01 billion the year before. Operating income was US$82.2 million versus US$90.4 million in the prior-year quarter, a decrease of 9.0%. Direct operating expenses rose 14.6% to US$936.8 million from US$817.6 million in the comparable period the year before. Indirect operating expenses increased 6.6% to US$108.9 million from US$102.2 million in the equivalent prior-year period.

**Prospects:** Our evaluation of Sonoco Products Co. as of Sep. 6, 2011 is the result of our systematic analysis on three basic characteristics: earnings strength, relative valuation, and recent stock price movement. The company has managed to produce a neutral trend in earnings per share over the past 5 quarters. However, while recent estimates for the company have been lowered by analysts, SON has posted results that fell short of analysts expectations. Based on operating earnings yield, the company is undervalued when compared to all of the companies in our coverage universe. Share price changes over the past year indicates that SON will perform very poorly over the near term.

**Financial Data**

| (US$ in Thousands) | 6 Mos | 3 Mos | 12/31/2010 | 12/31/2009 | 12/31/2008 | 12/31/2007 | 12/31/2006 | 12/31/2005 |
|---|---|---|---|---|---|---|---|---|
| Earnings Per Share | 1.98 | 2.04 | 1.96 | 1.50 | 1.63 | 2.10 | 1.92 | 1.61 |
| Cash Flow Per Share | 2.89 | 2.84 | 3.69 | 3.88 | 3.77 | 4.42 | 4.82 | 2.29 |
| Tang Book Value Per Share | 6.06 | 5.60 | 5.19 | 4.37 | 2.60 | 4.76 | 4.53 | 6.16 |
| Dividends Per Share | 1.130 | 1.120 | 1.110 | 1.080 | 1.070 | 1.020 | 0.950 | 0.910 |
| Dividend Payout % | 57.07 | 54.90 | 56.63 | 72.00 | 65.64 | 48.57 | 49.48 | 56.52 |
| **Income Statement** | | | | | | | | |
| Total Revenue | 2,245,188 | 1,117,323 | 4,124,121 | 3,597,331 | 4,122,385 | 4,039,992 | 3,656,839 | 3,528,574 |
| EBITDA | 259,512 | 133,935 | 446,089 | 413,966 | 419,605 | 477,897 | 477,118 | 430,159 |
| Depn & Amortn | 87,679 | 44,341 | 156,529 | 161,180 | 170,032 | 170,013 | 157,000 | 155,412 |
| Income Before Taxes | 154,922 | 80,857 | 254,454 | 214,221 | 202,376 | 255,626 | 274,808 | 231,126 |
| Income Taxes | 48,959 | 25,184 | 64,485 | 66,818 | 54,797 | 55,186 | 93,329 | 84,174 |
| Net Income | 110,799 | 57,391 | 201,053 | 151,482 | 164,608 | 214,156 | 195,081 | 161,877 |
| Average Shares | 101,982 | 102,754 | 102,543 | 101,029 | 100,986 | 101,875 | 101,534 | 100,418 |
| **Balance Sheet** | | | | | | | | |
| Current Assets | 1,245,401 | 1,264,556 | 1,157,516 | 996,573 | 929,990 | 1,027,679 | 942,798 | 885,500 |
| Total Assets | 3,393,589 | 3,397,236 | 3,281,014 | 3,062,580 | 3,086,466 | 3,340,243 | 2,916,678 | 2,981,740 |
| Current Liabilities | 786,592 | 803,572 | 780,649 | 805,639 | 698,196 | 758,081 | 659,824 | 620,486 |
| Long-Term Obligations | 716,807 | 745,188 | 603,941 | 462,743 | 656,847 | 804,339 | 712,089 | 657,075 |
| Total Liabilities | 1,805,401 | 1,861,577 | 1,789,223 | 1,696,199 | 1,923,491 | 1,898,706 | 1,697,610 | 1,718,426 |
| Stockholders' Equity | 1,588,188 | 1,535,659 | 1,491,791 | 1,366,381 | 1,162,975 | 1,441,537 | 1,219,068 | 1,263,314 |
| Shares Outstanding | 99,883 | 99,649 | 100,510 | 100,149 | 99,732 | 99,431 | 100,550 | 99,988 |
| **Statistical Record** | | | | | | | | |
| Return on Assets % | 6.27 | 6.44 | 6.34 | 4.93 | 5.11 | 6.85 | 6.61 | 5.38 |
| Return on Equity % | 13.65 | 14.37 | 14.07 | 11.98 | 12.61 | 16.10 | 15.72 | 13.40 |
| EBITDA Margin % | 11.56 | 11.99 | 10.82 | 11.51 | 10.18 | 11.83 | 13.05 | 12.19 |
| Net Margin % | 4.93 | 5.14 | 4.88 | 4.21 | 3.99 | 5.30 | 5.33 | 4.59 |
| Asset Turnover | 1.36 | 1.32 | 1.30 | 1.17 | 1.28 | 1.29 | 1.24 | 1.17 |
| Current Ratio | 1.58 | 1.57 | 1.48 | 1.24 | 1.33 | 1.36 | 1.43 | 1.43 |
| Debt to Equity | 0.45 | 0.49 | 0.40 | 0.34 | 0.56 | 0.56 | 0.58 | 0.52 |
| Price Range | 36.80-30.58 | 36.80-29.18 | 34.83-26.95 | 30.31-16.95 | 35.61-21.22 | 44.89-28.51 | 38.64-29.25 | 30.48-25.68 |
| P/E Ratio | 18.59-15.44 | 18.04-14.30 | 17.77-13.75 | 20.21-11.30 | 21.85-13.02 | 21.38-13.58 | 20.13-15.23 | 18.93-15.95 |
| Average Yield % | 3.31 | 3.35 | 3.48 | 4.33 | 3.62 | 2.77 | 2.86 | 3.27 |

**Address:** 1 North Second Street, Hartsville, SC 29550
**Telephone:** 843-383-7000
**Web Site:** www.sonoco.com

**Officers:** Harris E. DeLoach - Chairman, Chief Executive Officer Mancil Jack Sanders - President, Chief Operating Officer **Transfer Agents:** BNY Mellon Shareowner Services, Pittsburg, PA

**Investor Contact:** 843-383-7524
**No of Institutions:** 363
**Shares:** 68,227,296 **% Held:** 60.16

# SOUTH JERSEY INDUSTRIES, INC.

| Exchange | Symbol | Price | 52Wk Range | Yield | P/E |
|---|---|---|---|---|---|
| NYS | SJI | $51.53 (8/31/2011) | 57.49-43.44 | 2.83 | 18.40 |

***7 Year Price Score 142.30** *NYSE Composite Index=100 ***12 Month Price Score 96.79**

**Interim Earnings (Per Share)**

| Qtr. | Mar | Jun | Sep | Dec |
|---|---|---|---|---|
| 2008 | 0.83 | (0.45) | 1.47 | 0.73 |
| 2009 | 1.06 | 0.17 | (0.06) | 0.78 |
| 2010 | 1.05 | 0.28 | 0.04 | 0.84 |
| 2011 | 1.72 | 0.20 | ... | ... |

**Interim Dividends (Per Share)**

| Amt | Decl | Ex | Rec | Pay |
|---|---|---|---|---|
| 0.365Q | 11/22/2010 | 12/08/2010 | 12/10/2010 | 12/29/2010 |
| 0.365Q | 01/24/2011 | 03/08/2011 | 03/10/2011 | 04/05/2011 |
| 0.365Q | 05/02/2011 | 06/08/2011 | 06/10/2011 | 07/05/2011 |
| 0.365Q | 07/05/2011 | 09/07/2011 | 09/09/2011 | 10/04/2011 |

**Indicated Div: $1.46 (Div. Reinv. Plan)**

**Valuation Analysis**

| | | | |
|---|---|---|---|
| Forecast EPS | $3.00 (09/02/2011) | | |
| Market Cap | $1.5 Billion | Book Value | $606.3 Million |
| Price/Book | 2.55 | Price/Sales | 1.65 |

**Dividend Achiever Status**

| | |
|---|---|
| 10 Year Growth Rate | 6.27% |
| Total Years of Dividend Growth | 11 |

**Business Summary:** Gas Utilities (MIC: 3.3.1 SIC: 4924 NAIC: 221210)

South Jersey Industries provides energy related products and services primarily through the following subsidiaries: South Jersey Gas Company, which distributes natural gas in the seven southernmost counties of New Jersey; South Jersey Resources Group, LLC, which markets wholesale natural gas storage, commodity and transportation in the mid-Atlantic, Appalachian and southern states; Marina Energy, LLC, which develops and operates on-site energy-related projects; South Jersey Energy Company, which acquires and markets natural gas and electricity; and South Jersey Energy Service Plus, LLC, which installs residential and small commercial heating, ventilating, and air conditioning systems.

**Recent Developments:** For the quarter ended June 30 2011, income from continuing operations decreased 26.9% to US$6.2 million from US$8.5 million in the year-earlier quarter. Net income decreased 28.0% to US$6.1 million from US$8.4 million in the year-earlier quarter. Revenues were US$160.5 million, up 5.8% from US$151.6 million the year before. Operating income was US$12.4 million versus US$15.4 million in the prior-year quarter, a decrease of 19.3%. Direct operating expenses rose 9.0% to US$137.1 million from US$125.8 million in the comparable period the year before. Indirect operating expenses increased 5.1% to US$11.0 million from US$10.4 million in the equivalent prior-year period.

**Prospects:** Our evaluation of South Jersey Industries Inc. as of Sep. 6, 2011 is the result of our systematic analysis on three basic characteristics: earnings strength, relative valuation, and recent stock price movement. The company has generated a negative trend in earnings per share over the past 5 quarters. However, while recent estimates for the company have been mixed, SJI has posted results that fell short of analysts expectations. Based on operating earnings yield, the company is about fairly valued when compared to all of the companies in our coverage universe. Share price changes over the past year indicates that SJI will perform very poorly over the near term.

**Financial Data**

| (US$ in Thousands) | 6 Mos | 3 Mos | 12/31/2010 | 12/31/2009 | 12/31/2008 | 12/31/2007 | 12/31/2006 | 12/31/2005 |
|---|---|---|---|---|---|---|---|---|
| Earnings Per Share | 2.80 | 2.88 | 2.22 | 1.94 | 2.58 | 2.10 | 2.44 | 1.69 |
| Cash Flow Per Share | 5.92 | 5.59 | 5.33 | 5.88 | 0.89 | 5.02 | 1.00 | 1.40 |
| Tang Book Value Per Share | 20.24 | 20.37 | 19.08 | 18.24 | 17.33 | 16.25 | 15.11 | 13.50 |
| Dividends Per Share | 1.425 | 1.390 | 1.355 | 1.222 | 1.107 | 1.005 | 0.920 | 0.863 |
| Dividend Payout % | 50.84 | 48.21 | 61.04 | 63.02 | 42.93 | 47.86 | 37.70 | 51.04 |
| **Income Statement** | | | | | | | | |
| Total Revenue | 492,399 | 331,922 | 925,067 | 845,444 | 961,977 | 956,371 | 931,428 | 920,982 |
| EBITDA | 113,368 | 88,271 | 155,061 | 143,801 | 183,863 | 159,987 | 174,723 | 126,434 |
| Depn & Amortn | 17,505 | 8,652 | 34,018 | 31,280 | 29,237 | 27,942 | 26,249 | 24,031 |
| Income Before Taxes | 83,648 | 73,638 | 99,147 | 93,529 | 128,950 | 104,830 | 120,803 | 81,453 |
| Income Taxes | 25,514 | 22,510 | 28,811 | 34,302 | 51,948 | 43,056 | 49,683 | 33,767 |
| Net Income | 57,527 | 51,448 | 66,652 | 58,105 | 76,931 | 62,268 | 71,432 | 47,919 |
| Average Shares | 30,037 | 29,991 | 29,974 | 29,893 | 29,843 | 29,593 | 29,261 | 28,399 |
| **Balance Sheet** | | | | | | | | |
| Current Assets | 360,024 | 348,749 | 423,837 | 368,355 | 435,084 | 328,330 | 371,724 | 357,463 |
| Total Assets | 2,061,579 | 2,019,133 | 2,076,615 | 1,782,008 | 1,793,427 | 1,529,441 | 1,573,032 | 1,436,146 |
| Current Liabilities | 472,743 | 456,809 | 640,524 | 478,784 | 499,907 | 328,311 | 422,794 | 403,106 |
| Long-Term Obligations | 426,400 | 401,400 | 340,000 | 312,793 | 332,784 | 357,896 | 358,022 | 319,066 |
| Total Liabilities | 1,455,309 | 1,409,052 | 1,506,518 | 1,238,407 | 1,278,173 | 1,048,361 | 1,129,996 | 1,044,961 |
| Stockholders' Equity | 606,270 | 610,081 | 570,097 | 543,601 | 515,254 | 481,080 | 443,036 | 391,185 |
| Shares Outstanding | 29,954 | 29,953 | 29,872 | 29,796 | 29,728 | 29,607 | 29,325 | 28,982 |
| **Statistical Record** | | | | | | | | |
| Return on Assets % | 4.32 | 4.49 | 3.45 | 3.25 | 4.62 | 4.01 | 4.75 | 3.58 |
| Return on Equity % | 14.51 | 14.72 | 11.97 | 10.98 | 15.40 | 13.48 | 17.13 | 13.00 |
| EBITDA Margin % | 23.02 | 26.59 | 16.76 | 17.01 | 19.11 | 16.73 | 18.76 | 13.73 |
| Net Margin % | 11.68 | 15.50 | 7.21 | 6.87 | 8.00 | 6.51 | 7.67 | 5.20 |
| Asset Turnover | 0.48 | 0.48 | 0.48 | 0.47 | 0.58 | 0.62 | 0.62 | 0.69 |
| Current Ratio | 0.76 | 0.76 | 0.66 | 0.77 | 0.87 | 1.00 | 0.88 | 0.89 |
| Debt to Equity | 0.70 | 0.66 | 0.60 | 0.58 | 0.65 | 0.74 | 0.81 | 0.82 |
| Price Range | 57.49-42.48 | 57.02-41.75 | 54.01-37.53 | 39.94-32.66 | 39.85-28.01 | 40.43-31.96 | 33.90-26.00 | 32.00-25.18 |
| P/E Ratio | 20.53-15.17 | 19.80-14.50 | 24.33-16.91 | 20.59-16.84 | 15.45-10.86 | 19.25-15.22 | 13.89-10.66 | 18.93-14.90 |
| Average Yield % | 2.76 | 2.84 | 2.98 | 3.43 | 3.08 | 2.80 | 3.16 | 3.04 |

**Address:** 1 South Jersey Plaza, Folsom, NJ 08037
**Telephone:** 609-561-9000
**Web Site:** www.sjindustries.com

**Officers:** Edward J. Graham - Chairman, President, Chief Executive Officer Jeffrey E. DuBois - Vice President **Transfer Agents:** American Stock Tranfer & Trust Company, New York, NY

**No of Institutions:** 192
**Shares:** 18,691,004 **% Held:** 57.90

# SOUTHSIDE BANCSHARES, INC.

| Exchange | Symbol | Price | 52Wk Range | Yield | P/E |
|---|---|---|---|---|---|
| NMS | SBSI | $19.88 (8/31/2011) | 22.04-17.22 | 3.62 | 8.84 |

***7 Year Price Score 108.38** *NYSE Composite Index=100 ***12 Month Price Score 102.30**

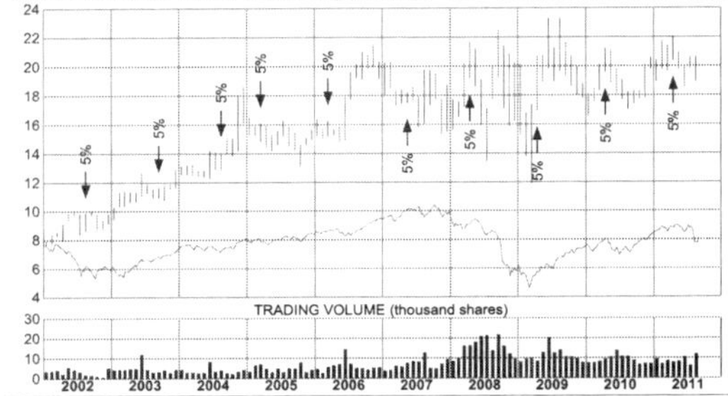


**Interim Earnings (Per Share)**

| Qtr. | Mar | Jun | Sep | Dec |
|---|---|---|---|---|
| 2008 | 0.34 | 0.52 | 0.38 | 0.72 |
| 2009 | 0.86 | 0.56 | 0.64 | 0.63 |
| 2010 | 0.70 | 0.55 | 0.67 | 0.47 |
| 2011 | 0.45 | 0.67 | ... | ... |

**Interim Dividends (Per Share)**

| Amt | Decl | Ex | Rec | Pay |
|---|---|---|---|---|
| 0.162Q | 02/17/2011 | 03/01/2011 | 03/03/2011 | 03/17/2011 |
| 5% | 03/31/2011 | 04/18/2011 | 04/20/2011 | 05/11/2011 |
| 0.17Q | 05/11/2011 | 05/24/2011 | 05/26/2011 | 06/09/2011 |
| 0.18Q | 08/15/2011 | 08/23/2011 | 08/25/2011 | 09/08/2011 |

**Indicated Div: $0.72 (Div. Reinv. Plan)**

**Valuation Analysis**

| | | | |
|---|---|---|---|
| Forecast EPS | $2.33 (09/02/2011) | | |
| Market Cap | $327.0 Million | Book Value | $242.5 Million |
| Price/Book | 1.35 | Price/Sales | N/A |

**Dividend Achiever Status**

| | |
|---|---|
| **10 Year Growth Rate** | 15.75% |
| **Total Years of Dividend Growth** | 12 |

**Business Summary:** Banking (MIC: 5.1.1 SIC: 6022 NAIC: 522110)

Southside Bancshares is a bank holding company. Through Southside Bancshares, Inc. and its wholly-owned subsidiary, Southside Delaware Financial Corporation, Co. offers a range of financial services to individuals, businesses, municipal entities, and non-profit organizations. These services include consumer and commercial loans, deposit accounts, trust services, safe deposit services and brokerage services. Co.'s primary market areas include Smith, Gregg, Tarrant, Travis, Cherokee, Anderson, Kaufman, Henderson and Wood Counties in Texas, and to a lesser extent, portions of adjoining counties. At Dec 31 2010, Co. had total assets of $3.00 billion and deposits of $2.13 billion.

**Recent Developments:** For the quarter ended June 30 2011, net income increased 18.0% to US$11.5 million from US$9.8 million in the year-earlier quarter. Net interest income increased 26.8% to US$24.6 million from US$19.4 million in the year-earlier quarter. Provision for loan losses was US$1.9 million versus US$2.3 million in the prior-year quarter, a decrease of 17.7%. Non-interest income fell 22.7% to US$10.2 million from US$13.2 million, while non-interest expense advanced 0.8% to US$18.1 million.

**Prospects:** Our evaluation of Southside Bancshares Inc. as of Sep. 6, 2011 is the result of our systematic analysis on three basic characteristics: earnings strength, relative valuation, and recent stock price movement. The company has produced a positive trend in earnings per share over the past 5 quarters. Because the company lacks sufficient analyst estimate data, we place greater weight on the historical EPS trend as the measure of earnings strength. Based on operating earnings yield, the company is undervalued when compared to all of the companies in our coverage universe. Share price changes over the past year indicates that SBSI will perform poorly over the near term.

**Financial Data**

| (US$ in Thousands) | 6 Mos | 3 Mos | 12/31/2010 | 12/31/2009 | 12/31/2008 | 12/31/2007 | 12/31/2006 | 12/31/2005 |
|---|---|---|---|---|---|---|---|---|
| Earnings Per Share | 2.25 | 2.14 | 2.39 | 2.68 | 1.96 | 1.07 | 0.97 | 1.00 |
| Cash Flow Per Share | 3.46 | 3.13 | 3.18 | 1.52 | 1.88 | 1.50 | 0.78 | 1.77 |
| Tang Book Value Per Share | 13.36 | 12.03 | 11.66 | 10.82 | 8.87 | 7.15 | 7.36 | 7.76 |
| Dividends Per Share | 0.818 | 0.810 | 0.802 | 0.675 | 0.513 | 0.407 | 0.364 | 0.339 |
| Dividend Payout % | 36.28 | 37.90 | 33.54 | 25.13 | 26.20 | 38.00 | 37.51 | 34.09 |
| **Income Statement** | | | | | | | | |
| Interest Income | 65,629 | 31,905 | 131,374 | 145,193 | 136,176 | 105,741 | 96,952 | 79,681 |
| Interest Expense | 18,803 | 9,646 | 45,307 | 52,672 | 60,363 | 61,863 | 55,284 | 38,422 |
| Net Interest Income | 46,826 | 22,259 | 86,067 | 92,521 | 75,813 | 43,878 | 41,668 | 41,259 |
| Provision for Losses | 3,998 | 2,138 | 13,737 | 15,093 | 13,675 | 2,351 | 1,080 | 1,463 |
| Non-Interest Income | 18,188 | 8,009 | 51,396 | 56,674 | 40,302 | 26,418 | 23,481 | 21,248 |
| Non-Interest Expense | 36,848 | 18,732 | 71,314 | 71,630 | 60,494 | 47,285 | 44,967 | 43,159 |
| Income Before Taxes | 24,168 | 9,398 | 52,412 | 62,472 | 41,946 | 20,660 | 19,102 | 17,885 |
| Income Taxes | 4,457 | 1,216 | 11,966 | 16,609 | 11,250 | 3,976 | 4,100 | 3,293 |
| Net Income | 18,353 | 7,317 | 39,491 | 44,396 | 30,696 | 16,684 | 15,002 | 14,592 |
| Average Shares | 16,445 | 16,434 | 16,548 | 16,541 | 15,655 | 15,564 | 15,475 | 14,628 |
| **Balance Sheet** | | | | | | | | |
| Net Loans & Leases | 1,022,137 | 1,046,529 | 1,063,792 | 1,016,537 | 1,006,948 | 954,838 | 755,863 | 677,555 |
| Total Assets | 3,115,208 | 3,098,716 | 2,999,621 | 3,024,288 | 2,700,238 | 2,196,322 | 1,890,976 | 1,783,462 |
| Total Deposits | 2,239,537 | 2,200,823 | 2,134,428 | 1,870,421 | 1,556,131 | 1,530,491 | 1,282,475 | 1,110,813 |
| Total Liabilities | 2,872,729 | 2,878,196 | 2,785,298 | 2,822,507 | 2,539,621 | 2,063,994 | 1,780,372 | 1,674,172 |
| Stockholders' Equity | 242,479 | 220,520 | 214,323 | 201,781 | 160,617 | 132,328 | 110,604 | 109,290 |
| Shares Outstanding | 16,450 | 16,441 | 16,418 | 16,516 | 15,462 | 15,211 | 15,019 | 14,084 |
| **Statistical Record** | | | | | | | | |
| Return on Assets % | 1.21 | 1.14 | 1.31 | 1.55 | 1.25 | 0.82 | 0.82 | 0.86 |
| Return on Equity % | 16.03 | 16.46 | 18.98 | 24.50 | 20.90 | 13.74 | 13.64 | 13.64 |
| Net Interest Margin % | 72.85 | 69.77 | 65.51 | 63.72 | 55.67 | 41.50 | 42.98 | 51.78 |
| Efficiency Ratio % | 41.26 | 46.93 | 39.02 | 35.48 | 34.28 | 35.78 | 37.34 | 42.76 |
| Loans to Deposits | 0.46 | 0.48 | 0.50 | 0.54 | 0.65 | 0.62 | 0.59 | 0.61 |
| Price Range | 22.04-17.01 | 21.72-17.01 | 21.24-16.58 | 23.32-11.89 | 22.45-13.39 | 20.30-15.35 | 21.51-14.77 | 16.54-13.14 |
| P/E Ratio | 9.80-7.56 | 10.15-7.95 | 8.89-6.94 | 8.70-4.44 | 11.45-6.83 | 18.97-14.35 | 22.17-15.23 | 16.54-13.14 |
| Average Yield % | 4.22 | 4.20 | 4.26 | 3.57 | 2.79 | 2.27 | 2.05 | 2.24 |

**Address:** 1201 S. Beckham, Tyler, TX 75701
**Telephone:** 903-531-7111
**Web Site:** www.southside.com

**Officers:** B. G. Hartley - Chairman, Chief Executive Officer Robbie N. Edmonson - Vice-Chairman

**No of Institutions:** 108
**Shares:** 6,525,128 **% Held:** 39.18

# STANCORP FINANCIAL GROUP INC

| Exchange | Symbol | Price | 52Wk Range | Yield | P/E |
|---|---|---|---|---|---|
| NYS | SFG | $30.55 (8/31/2011) | 48.64-26.77 | 2.82 | 9.37 |

*7 Year Price Score 95.81 *NYSE Composite Index=100 *12 Month Price Score 82.30

**Interim Earnings (Per Share)**

| Qtr. | Mar | Jun | Sep | Dec |
|---|---|---|---|---|
| 2008 | 1.02 | 0.98 | 0.82 | 0.49 |
| 2009 | 0.67 | 1.15 | 1.21 | 1.23 |
| 2010 | 1.04 | 0.87 | 0.99 | 1.12 |
| 2011 | 0.73 | 0.42 | ... | ... |

**Interim Dividends (Per Share)**

| Amt | Decl | Ex | Rec | Pay |
|---|---|---|---|---|
| 0.72A | 11/05/2007 | 11/14/2007 | 11/16/2007 | 12/07/2007 |
| 0.75A | 11/03/2008 | 11/12/2008 | 11/14/2008 | 12/05/2008 |
| 0.80A | 11/09/2009 | 11/18/2009 | 11/20/2009 | 12/04/2009 |
| 0.86A | 11/08/2010 | 11/17/2010 | 11/19/2010 | 12/03/2010 |

**Indicated Div: $0.86**

**Valuation Analysis**

| | | | |
|---|---|---|---|
| Forecast EPS | $2.80 (09/02/2011) | | |
| Market Cap | $1.4 Billion | Book Value | $1.9 Billion |
| Price/Book | 0.71 | Price/Sales | 0.48 |

**Dividend Achiever Status**

| | |
|---|---|
| 10 Year Growth Rate | 19.08% |
| Total Years of Dividend Growth | 11 |

**Business Summary:** Life & Health (MIC: 5.2.2 SIC: 6321 NAIC: 524114)

StanCorp Financial Group is a holding company. Through its subsidiaries, Co. underwrites insurance products in all 50 states as well as the District of Columbia and the U.S. territories of Guam and the Virgin Islands. Co. operates through two segments: Insurance Services, which provides group and individual disability insurance, group life and accidental death and dismemberment insurance, group dental and group vision insurance, and absence management services; and Asset Management, which provides 401(k) plans, 403(b) plans, 457 plans, defined benefit plans, money purchase pension plans, profit sharing plans and non-qualified deferred compensation products and services.

**Recent Developments:** For the quarter ended June 30 2011, net income decreased 54.3% to US$18.8 million from US$41.1 million in the year-earlier quarter. Revenues were US$706.0 million, up 2.1% from US$691.2 million the year before. Net premiums earned were US$537.0 million versus US$532.9 million in the prior-year quarter, an increase of 0.8%. Net investment income rose 7.5% to US$152.6 million from US$141.9 million a year ago.

**Prospects:** Our evaluation of Stancorp Financial Group Inc. as of Sep. 6, 2011 is the result of our systematic analysis on three basic characteristics: earnings strength, relative valuation, and recent stock price movement. The company has generated a negative trend in earnings per share over the past 5 quarters. However, while recent estimates for the company have been lowered by analysts, SFG has posted results that fell short of analysts expectations. Based on operating earnings yield, the company is undervalued when compared to all of the companies in our coverage universe. Share price changes over the past year indicates that SFG will perform in line with the market over the near term.

| **Financial Data** (US$ in Thousands) | 6 Mos | 3 Mos | 12/31/2010 | 12/31/2009 | 12/31/2008 | 12/31/2007 | 12/31/2006 | 12/31/2005 |
|---|---|---|---|---|---|---|---|---|
| Earnings Per Share | 3.26 | 3.71 | 4.02 | 4.26 | 3.30 | 4.35 | 3.73 | 3.76 |
| Cash Flow Per Share | 7.89 | 7.87 | 7.59 | 9.02 | 7.38 | 9.37 | 7.21 | 7.34 |
| Tang Book Value Per Share | 42.26 | 41.11 | 40.64 | 35.59 | 27.44 | 29.07 | 27.33 | 25.84 |
| Dividends Per Share | 0.860 | 0.860 | 0.860 | 0.800 | 0.750 | 0.720 | 0.650 | 0.625 |
| Dividend Payout % | 26.38 | 23.18 | 21.39 | 18.78 | 22.73 | 16.55 | 17.43 | 16.62 |
| **Income Statement** | | | | | | | | |
| Premium Income | 1,070,800 | 533,800 | 2,097,700 | 2,101,900 | 2,140,200 | 2,078,300 | 1,935,000 | 1,826,500 |
| Total Revenue | 1,423,700 | 717,700 | 2,765,100 | 2,770,000 | 2,667,000 | 2,709,200 | 2,492,900 | 2,337,200 |
| Benefits & Claims | 892,500 | 440,100 | 1,619,800 | 1,575,700 | 1,589,400 | 1,591,800 | 1,513,100 | 1,392,300 |
| Income Before Taxes | 76,000 | 50,100 | 282,800 | 315,700 | 241,100 | 341,700 | 309,700 | 325,600 |
| Income Taxes | 23,500 | 16,400 | 93,800 | 106,800 | 78,200 | 114,200 | 105,900 | 114,500 |
| Net Income | 52,500 | 33,700 | 189,000 | 208,900 | 162,900 | 227,500 | 203,800 | 211,100 |
| Average Shares | 45,056 | 46,190 | 47,006 | 49,044 | 49,292 | 52,344 | 54,688 | 56,076 |
| **Balance Sheet** | | | | | | | | |
| Total Assets | 18,454,400 | 18,181,200 | 17,843,300 | 16,569,500 | 14,555,200 | 14,982,900 | 13,638,600 | 12,450,700 |
| Total Liabilities | 16,536,100 | 16,279,500 | 15,931,200 | 14,834,100 | 13,174,900 | 13,553,900 | 12,174,100 | 11,036,900 |
| Stockholders' Equity | 1,918,300 | 1,901,700 | 1,912,100 | 1,735,400 | 1,380,300 | 1,429,000 | 1,464,500 | 1,413,800 |
| Shares Outstanding | 44,540 | 45,384 | 46,159 | 47,744 | 48,989 | 49,155 | 53,592 | 54,712 |
| **Statistical Record** | | | | | | | | |
| Return on Assets % | 0.86 | 0.99 | 1.10 | 1.34 | 1.10 | 1.59 | 1.56 | 1.78 |
| Return on Equity % | 7.87 | 9.34 | 10.36 | 13.41 | 11.57 | 15.72 | 14.16 | 15.00 |
| Loss Ratio % | 83.35 | 82.45 | 77.22 | 74.97 | 74.26 | 76.59 | 78.20 | 76.23 |
| Net Margin % | 3.69 | 4.70 | 6.84 | 7.54 | 6.11 | 8.40 | 8.18 | 9.03 |
| Price Range | 48.64-35.47 | 50.19-35.47 | 50.19-35.47 | 42.10-13.96 | 55.28-23.92 | 55.13-41.44 | 55.75-42.07 | 52.95-36.05 |
| P/E Ratio | 14.92-10.88 | 13.53-9.56 | 12.49-8.82 | 9.88-3.28 | 16.75-7.25 | 12.67-9.53 | 14.95-11.28 | 14.08-9.59 |
| Average Yield % | 2.03 | 2.00 | 2.03 | 2.50 | 1.63 | 1.46 | 1.34 | 1.48 |

**Address:** 1100 SW Sixth Avenue, Portland, OR 97204
**Telephone:** 971-321-7000
**Web Site:** www.stancorpfinancial.com

**Officers:** Eric E. Parsons - Non-Executive Chairman
J. Gregory Ness - President, Chief Executive Officer
**Transfer Agents:** Mellon Investor Services, LLC, South Hackensack, NJ

**Investor Contact:** 503-321-7529
**No of Institutions:** 235
**Shares:** 36,909,884 **% Held:** 72.70

# STANLEY BLACK & DECKER, INC.

| Exchange | Symbol | Price | 52Wk Range | Yield | P/E |
|---|---|---|---|---|---|
| NYS | SWK | $61.98 (8/31/2011) | 77.29-53.64 | 2.65 | 16.80 |

*7 Year Price Score 131.96 *NYSE Composite Index=100 *12 Month Price Score 97.53

**Interim Earnings (Per Share)**

| Qtr. | Mar | Jun | Sep | Dec |
|---|---|---|---|---|
| 2008 | 0.85 | 1.00 | 2.06 | 0.02 |
| 2009 | 0.47 | 0.87 | 0.75 | 0.69 |
| 2010 | (1.11) | 0.28 | 0.73 | 0.90 |
| 2011 | 0.92 | 1.14 | ... | ... |

**Interim Dividends (Per Share)**

| Amt | Decl | Ex | Rec | Pay |
|---|---|---|---|---|
| 0.34Q | 10/15/2010 | 12/01/2010 | 12/03/2010 | 12/14/2010 |
| 0.41Q | 02/15/2011 | 02/28/2011 | 03/02/2011 | 03/22/2011 |
| 0.41Q | 04/19/2011 | 05/27/2011 | 06/01/2011 | 06/21/2011 |
| 0.41Q | 07/15/2011 | 08/31/2011 | 09/02/2011 | 09/20/2011 |

**Indicated Div: $1.64 (Div. Reinv. Plan)**

**Valuation Analysis**

| | | | |
|---|---|---|---|
| Forecast EPS | $5.29 (09/05/2011) | | |
| Market Cap | $10.4 Billion | Book Value | $7.5 Billion |
| Price/Book | 1.39 | Price/Sales | 1.07 |

**Dividend Achiever Status**

| | |
|---|---|
| **10 Year Growth Rate** | 3.61% |
| **Total Years of Dividend Growth** | 43 |

**Business Summary:** Industrial Machinery & Equipment (MIC: 7.2.1 SIC: 3423 NAIC: 332212)

Stanley Black & Decker is a manufacturer of hand and power tools. Co. operates in three business segments: Security, which provides access and security products mainly for consumers, retailers, educational, financial and healthcare institutions, and industrial customers; Industrial, which manufactures and markets industrial and automotive mechanics tools and storage systems, metal and plastic fasteners and fastening systems, hydraulic tools and accessories, and specialty tools; and Construction & Do-It-Yourself, which manufactures and markets hand tools, electric power tools and equipment, lawn and garden products, consumer portable power products, home products as well as plumbing products.

**Recent Developments:** For the quarter ended July 2 2011, net income increased 326.1% to US$197.3 million from US$46.3 million in the year-earlier quarter. Revenues were US$2.62 billion, up 10.9% from US$2.37 billion the year before. Direct operating expenses rose 3.7% to US$1.66 billion from US$1.60 billion in the comparable period the year before. Indirect operating expenses decreased 2.3% to US$742.2 million from US$759.7 million in the equivalent prior-year period.

**Prospects:** Our evaluation of Stanley Black & Decker, Inc. as of Sep. 6, 2011 is the result of our systematic analysis on three basic characteristics: earnings strength, relative valuation, and recent stock price movement. The company has managed to produce a neutral trend in earnings per share over the past 5 quarters and while recent estimates for the company have been raised by analysts, SWK has posted better than expected results. Based on operating earnings yield, the company is undervalued when compared to all of the companies in our coverage universe. Share price changes over the past year indicates that SWK will perform in line with the market over the near term.

**Financial Data**

| (US$ in Thousands) | 6 Mos | 3 Mos | 01/01/2011 | 01/02/2010 | 01/03/2009 | 12/29/2007 | 12/30/2006 | 12/31/2005 |
|---|---|---|---|---|---|---|---|---|
| Earnings Per Share | 3.69 | 2.83 | 1.32 | 2.79 | 3.92 | 4.00 | 3.46 | 3.16 |
| Cash Flow Per Share | 5.05 | 5.34 | 5.04 | 6.78 | 6.44 | 6.63 | 5.38 | 4.36 |
| Tang Book Value Per Share | N.M. | N.M. | N.M. | N.M. | N.M. | N.M. | N.M. | 4.59 |
| Dividends Per Share | 1.500 | 1.420 | 1.340 | 1.300 | 1.260 | 1.220 | 1.180 | 1.140 |
| Dividend Payout % | 40.65 | 50.18 | 101.52 | 46.59 | 32.14 | 30.50 | 34.10 | 36.08 |
| **Income Statement** | | | | | | | | |
| Total Revenue | 5,003,900 | 2,380,700 | 8,409,600 | 3,737,100 | 4,426,200 | 4,483,800 | 4,018,600 | 3,285,300 |
| EBITDA | 660,700 | 314,900 | 744,500 | 491,100 | 559,100 | 697,900 | 501,400 | 445,500 |
| Depn & Amortn | 197,700 | 103,900 | 406,800 | 191,000 | 185,000 | 166,600 | 69,400 | 53,500 |
| Income Before Taxes | 406,700 | 181,500 | 237,100 | 283,300 | 301,300 | 451,100 | 367,100 | 358,200 |
| Income Taxes | 51,000 | 23,100 | 38,900 | 54,500 | 75,900 | 114,500 | 76,400 | 86,500 |
| Net Income | 356,000 | 158,700 | 198,200 | 224,300 | 313,300 | 336,600 | 289,500 | 269,600 |
| Average Shares | 173,075 | 171,945 | 150,167 | 80,396 | 79,874 | 84,045 | 83,704 | 85,405 |
| **Balance Sheet** | | | | | | | | |
| Current Assets | 5,339,000 | 5,174,500 | 4,815,600 | 1,411,900 | 1,499,300 | 1,768,400 | 1,638,500 | 1,825,600 |
| Total Assets | 16,033,500 | 15,756,000 | 15,139,400 | 4,769,100 | 4,879,200 | 4,779,900 | 3,935,400 | 3,545,100 |
| Current Liabilities | 3,404,700 | 2,992,100 | 2,742,200 | 1,192,000 | 1,197,200 | 1,277,500 | 1,251,100 | 875,300 |
| Long-Term Obligations | 2,729,000 | 3,008,500 | 3,018,100 | 1,084,700 | 1,419,500 | 1,212,100 | 679,200 | 895,300 |
| Total Liabilities | 8,502,100 | 8,422,600 | 8,122,400 | 2,783,000 | 3,191,200 | 3,051,400 | 2,383,400 | 2,100,200 |
| Stockholders' Equity | 7,531,400 | 7,333,400 | 7,017,000 | 1,986,100 | 1,688,000 | 1,728,500 | 1,552,000 | 1,444,900 |
| Shares Outstanding | 168,359 | 168,112 | 166,347 | 80,478 | 78,876 | 80,378 | 81,841 | 83,791 |
| **Statistical Record** | | | | | | | | |
| Return on Assets % | 4.11 | 3.06 | 2.00 | 4.66 | 6.38 | 7.75 | 7.76 | 8.45 |
| Return on Equity % | 8.73 | 6.72 | 4.42 | 12.24 | 18.04 | 20.58 | 19.37 | 20.28 |
| EBITDA Margin % | 13.20 | 13.23 | 8.85 | 13.14 | 12.63 | 15.56 | 12.48 | 13.56 |
| Net Margin % | 7.11 | 6.67 | 2.36 | 6.00 | 7.08 | 7.51 | 7.20 | 8.21 |
| Asset Turnover | 0.65 | 0.63 | 0.85 | 0.78 | 0.90 | 1.03 | 1.08 | 1.03 |
| Current Ratio | 1.57 | 1.73 | 1.76 | 1.18 | 1.25 | 1.38 | 1.31 | 2.09 |
| Debt to Equity | 0.36 | 0.41 | 0.43 | 0.55 | 0.84 | 0.70 | 0.44 | 0.62 |
| Price Range | 77.29-49.58 | 77.22-49.58 | 67.29-49.58 | 53.13-22.75 | 51.42-25.38 | 63.92-47.46 | 54.33-41.95 | 51.17-42.20 |
| P/E Ratio | 20.95-13.44 | 27.29-17.52 | 50.98-37.56 | 19.04-8.15 | 13.12-6.47 | 15.98-11.87 | 15.70-12.12 | 16.19-13.35 |
| Average Yield % | 2.27 | 2.28 | 2.30 | 3.38 | 2.88 | 2.17 | 2.40 | 2.46 |

**Address:** 1000 Stanley Drive, New Britain, CT 06053
**Telephone:** 860-225-5111
**Web Site:** www.stanleyworks.com

**Officers:** Nolan D. Archibald - Chairman John F. Lundgren - President, Chief Executive Officer
**Transfer Agents:**Computershare Investor Services LLC, Chicago, IL

**Investor Contact:** 860-827-3833
**No of Institutions:** 567
**Shares:** 148,235,232 **% Held:** N/A

# STEPAN CO.

| Exchange | Symbol | Price | 52Wk Range | Yield | P/E |
|---|---|---|---|---|---|
| NYS | SCL | $75.65 (8/31/2011) | 79.89-55.45 | 1.37 | 12.52 |

*7 Year Price Score 165.43 *NYSE Composite Index=100 *12 Month Price Score 107.55

**Interim Earnings (Per Share)**

| Qtr. | Mar | Jun | Sep | Dec |
|---|---|---|---|---|
| 2008 | 0.85 | 0.93 | 1.59 | 0.13 |
| 2009 | 1.43 | 1.83 | 1.80 | 0.78 |
| 2010 | 1.88 | 1.53 | 1.73 | 0.76 |
| 2011 | 1.68 | 1.87 | ... | ... |

**Interim Dividends (Per Share)**

| Amt | Decl | Ex | Rec | Pay |
|---|---|---|---|---|
| 0.26Q | 10/19/2010 | 11/26/2010 | 11/30/2010 | 12/15/2010 |
| 0.26Q | 02/08/2011 | 02/24/2011 | 02/28/2011 | 03/15/2011 |
| 0.26Q | 05/03/2011 | 05/25/2011 | 05/27/2011 | 06/15/2011 |
| 0.26Q | 07/27/2011 | 08/29/2011 | 08/31/2011 | 09/15/2011 |

**Indicated Div: $1.04**

**Valuation Analysis**

| | | | |
|---|---|---|---|
| Forecast EPS | $6.58 (09/02/2011) | | |
| Market Cap | $768.3 Million | Book Value | $397.2 Million |
| Price/Book | 1.93 | Price/Sales | 0.47 |

**Dividend Achiever Status**

| | |
|---|---|
| 10 Year Growth Rate | 3.31% |
| Total Years of Dividend Growth | 43 |

**Business Summary:** Specialty Chemicals (MIC: 8.3.2 SIC: 2843 NAIC: 325613)

Stepan produces and sells intermediate chemicals that are used in a range of applications worldwide. Co.'s business comprises three reportable segments: surfactants, which are principal ingredients in consumer and industrial cleaning products such as detergents for washing clothes, dishes, carpets, floors and walls, as well as shampoos, body washes, toothpastes and fabric softeners; polymers, which provides polymers used in construction, refrigeration, automotive, boating and other consumer product industries, consisting of polyols and phthalic anhydride product lines; and specialty products, which includes flavors, emulsifiers and solubilizers used in the food and pharmaceutical industries.

**Recent Developments:** For the quarter ended June 30 2011, net income increased 23.1% to US$21.0 million from US$17.1 million in the year-earlier quarter. Revenues were US$477.0 million, up 30.1% from US$366.5 million the year before. Operating income was US$34.1 million versus US$29.8 million in the prior-year quarter, an increase of 14.5%. Direct operating expenses rose 34.4% to US$407.4 million from US$303.0 million in the comparable period the year before. Indirect operating expenses increased 5.3% to US$35.5 million from US$33.7 million in the equivalent prior-year period.

**Prospects:** Our evaluation of Stepan Co. as of Sep. 6, 2011 is the result of our systematic analysis on three basic characteristics: earnings strength, relative valuation, and recent stock price movement. The company has produced a positive trend in earnings per share over the past 5 quarters and while recent estimates for the company have been raised by analysts, SCL has posted better than expected results. Based on operating earnings yield, the company is undervalued when compared to all of the companies in our coverage universe. Share price changes over the past year indicates that SCL will perform in line with the market over the near term.

**Financial Data**

| (US$ in Thousands) | 6 Mos | 3 Mos | 12/31/2010 | 12/31/2009 | 12/31/2008 | 12/31/2007 | 12/31/2006 | 12/31/2005 |
|---|---|---|---|---|---|---|---|---|
| Earnings Per Share | 6.04 | 5.70 | 5.90 | 5.84 | 3.52 | 1.50 | 0.63 | 1.35 |
| Cash Flow Per Share | 3.08 | 4.26 | 6.51 | 16.86 | 3.04 | 5.05 | 4.25 | 4.67 |
| Tang Book Value Per Share | 35.86 | 34.36 | 32.11 | 26.76 | 19.07 | 19.40 | 16.43 | 15.07 |
| Dividends Per Share | 1.020 | 1.000 | 0.980 | 0.900 | 0.850 | 0.825 | 0.805 | 0.785 |
| Dividend Payout % | 16.89 | 17.54 | 16.61 | 15.41 | 24.15 | 55.00 | 127.78 | 58.15 |
| **Income Statement** | | | | | | | | |
| Total Revenue | 899,587 | 422,598 | 1,431,122 | 1,276,382 | 1,600,130 | 1,329,901 | 1,172,583 | 1,078,377 |
| EBITDA | 87,501 | 41,257 | 149,834 | 144,282 | 104,017 | 71,037 | 55,470 | 62,935 |
| Depn & Amortn | 23,007 | 11,094 | 40,351 | 37,171 | 36,928 | 37,176 | 38,384 | 36,759 |
| Income Before Taxes | 60,237 | 28,100 | 103,142 | 100,840 | 57,575 | 24,131 | 8,201 | 18,375 |
| Income Taxes | 18,645 | 8,319 | 35,888 | 34,028 | 17,615 | 8,687 | 900 | 4,170 |
| Net Income | 39,628 | 18,761 | 65,427 | 63,049 | 37,172 | 15,118 | 6,670 | 13,159 |
| Average Shares | 11,178 | 11,169 | 11,090 | 10,796 | 10,549 | 10,113 | 9,284 | 9,725 |
| **Balance Sheet** | | | | | | | | |
| Current Assets | 504,592 | 462,085 | 427,826 | 349,592 | 328,423 | 293,932 | 268,469 | 259,248 |
| Total Assets | 910,925 | 858,118 | 811,431 | 634,203 | 611,897 | 573,185 | 546,055 | 516,159 |
| Current Liabilities | 262,534 | 239,999 | 205,627 | 163,295 | 212,135 | 200,978 | 180,495 | 162,904 |
| Long-Term Obligations | 154,956 | 149,102 | 159,963 | 93,911 | 104,725 | 96,939 | 107,403 | 108,945 |
| Total Liabilities | 513,754 | 484,252 | 461,940 | 344,918 | 403,753 | 367,134 | 365,269 | 349,325 |
| Stockholders' Equity | 397,171 | 373,866 | 349,491 | 289,285 | 208,144 | 206,051 | 180,786 | 166,834 |
| Shares Outstanding | 10,156 | 10,162 | 10,105 | 9,948 | 9,632 | 9,309 | 9,207 | 9,040 |
| **Statistical Record** | | | | | | | | |
| Return on Assets % | 8.22 | 8.39 | 9.05 | 10.12 | 6.26 | 2.70 | 1.26 | 2.61 |
| Return on Equity % | 18.88 | 18.74 | 20.49 | 25.35 | 17.90 | 7.82 | 3.84 | 7.85 |
| EBITDA Margin % | 9.73 | 9.76 | 10.47 | 11.30 | 6.50 | 5.34 | 4.73 | 5.84 |
| Net Margin % | 4.41 | 4.44 | 4.57 | 4.94 | 2.32 | 1.14 | 0.57 | 1.22 |
| Asset Turnover | 1.99 | 2.00 | 1.98 | 2.05 | 2.69 | 2.38 | 2.21 | 2.14 |
| Current Ratio | 1.92 | 1.93 | 2.08 | 2.14 | 1.55 | 1.46 | 1.49 | 1.59 |
| Debt to Equity | 0.39 | 0.40 | 0.46 | 0.32 | 0.50 | 0.47 | 0.59 | 0.65 |
| Price Range | 77.25-54.39 | 79.27-54.39 | 79.27-47.16 | 67.46-23.09 | 60.23-28.63 | 34.90-25.40 | 33.00-25.05 | 27.48-20.80 |
| P/E Ratio | 12.79-9.00 | 13.91-9.54 | 13.44-7.99 | 11.55-3.95 | 17.11-8.13 | 23.27-16.93 | 52.38-39.76 | 20.36-15.41 |
| Average Yield % | 1.50 | 1.46 | 1.52 | 1.93 | 2.02 | 2.73 | 2.74 | 3.26 |

**Address:** Edens & Winnetka Road, Northfield, IL 60093
**Telephone:** 847-446-7500
**Web Site:** www.stepan.com

**Officers:** F. Quinn Stepan - Chairman F. Quinn Stepan - President, Chief Executive Officer **Transfer Agents:** ComputerShare Investor Services, Chicago, IL

**Investor Contact:** 847-446-7500
**No of Institutions:** 131
**Shares:** 6,404,232 **% Held:** 61.88

# STRYKER CORP.

| Exchange | Symbol | Price | 52Wk Range | Yield | P/E |
|---|---|---|---|---|---|
| NYS | SYK | $48.84 (8/31/2011) | 65.07-43.19 | 1.47 | 15.46 |

***7 Year Price Score 103.54** *NYSE Composite Index=100 ***12 Month Price Score 96.01**

**Interim Earnings (Per Share)**

| Qtr. | Mar | Jun | Sep | Dec |
|---|---|---|---|---|
| 2008 | 0.70 | 0.73 | 0.66 | 0.69 |
| 2009 | 0.71 | 0.73 | 0.57 | 0.76 |
| 2010 | 0.80 | 0.80 | 0.85 | 0.74 |
| 2011 | 0.78 | 0.79 | ... | ... |

**Interim Dividends (Per Share)**

| Amt | Decl | Ex | Rec | Pay |
|---|---|---|---|---|
| 0.18Q | 12/08/2010 | 12/29/2010 | 12/31/2010 | 01/31/2011 |
| 0.18Q | 02/09/2011 | 03/29/2011 | 03/31/2011 | 04/29/2011 |
| 0.18Q | 06/09/2011 | 06/28/2011 | 06/30/2011 | 07/29/2011 |
| 0.18Q | 08/19/2011 | 09/28/2011 | 09/30/2011 | 10/31/2011 |

**Indicated Div: $0.72**

**Valuation Analysis**

| | | | |
|---|---|---|---|
| Forecast EPS | $3.71 (09/05/2011) | | |
| Market Cap | $19.0 Billion | Book Value | $7.8 Billion |
| Price/Book | 2.44 | Price/Sales | 2.42 |

**Dividend Achiever Status**

| | |
|---|---|
| **10 Year Growth Rate** | 31.10% |
| **Total Years of Dividend Growth** | 18 |

**Business Summary:** Medical Instruments & Equipment (MIC: 4.3.1 SIC: 3841 NAIC: 339112)

Stryker is a medical technology company. Co.'s products include implants used in joint replacement, trauma and spinal surgeries; surgical equipment and surgical navigation systems; endoscopic and communications systems; patient handling and emergency medical equipment as well as other medical device products used in a variety of medical specialties. Co. has two segments: Orthopaedic Implants, which includes orthopaedic reconstructive (hip and knee), trauma and spinal implant systems and other related products; and MedSurg Equipment, which includes surgical equipment and surgical navigation systems; endoscopic and communications systems; patient handling and emergency medical equipment.

**Recent Developments:** For the quarter ended June 30 2011, net income decreased 3.1% to US$309.1 million from US$319.0 million in the year-earlier quarter. Revenues were US$2.05 billion, up 16.3% from US$1.76 billion the year before. Operating income was US$400.3 million versus US$448.1 million in the prior-year quarter, a decrease of 10.7%. Direct operating expenses rose 32.2% to US$712.8 million from US$539.3 million in the comparable period the year before. Indirect operating expenses increased 21.0% to US$932.4 million from US$770.8 million in the equivalent prior-year period.

**Prospects:** Our evaluation of Stryker Corp. as of Sep. 6, 2011 is the result of our systematic analysis on three basic characteristics: earnings strength, relative valuation, and recent stock price movement. The company has managed to produce a neutral trend in earnings per share over the past 5 quarters and while recent estimates for the company have remained steady, SYK has posted better than expected results. Based on operating earnings yield, the company is undervalued when compared to all of the companies in our coverage universe. Share price changes over the past year indicates that SYK will perform in line with the market over the near term.

**Financial Data**

| (US$ in Thousands) | 6 Mos | 3 Mos | 12/31/2010 | 12/31/2009 | 12/31/2008 | 12/31/2007 | 12/31/2006 | 12/31/2005 |
|---|---|---|---|---|---|---|---|---|
| Earnings Per Share | 3.16 | 3.17 | 3.19 | 2.77 | 2.78 | 2.44 | 1.89 | 1.64 |
| Cash Flow Per Share | 3.37 | 3.79 | 3.90 | 3.68 | 2.87 | 2.51 | 2.13 | 2.14 |
| Tang Book Value Per Share | 10.39 | 10.25 | 13.80 | 12.58 | 11.28 | 10.83 | 7.98 | 5.75 |
| Dividends Per Share | 0.690 | 0.660 | 0.630 | 0.250 | 0.400 | 0.330 | 0.220 | 0.110 |
| Dividend Payout % | 21.84 | 20.82 | 19.75 | 9.03 | 14.39 | 13.52 | 11.64 | 6.71 |
| **Income Statement** | | | | | | | | |
| Total Revenue | 4,060,700 | 2,015,200 | 7,320,000 | 6,723,100 | 6,718,200 | 6,000,500 | 5,405,600 | 4,871,500 |
| EBITDA | 1,057,400 | 526,700 | 1,952,400 | 1,824,600 | 1,775,600 | 1,548,600 | 1,270,900 | 1,158,200 |
| Depn & Amortn | 235,600 | 114,900 | 222,800 | 200,700 | 195,400 | 178,500 | 167,100 | 154,900 |
| Income Before Taxes | 821,800 | 411,800 | 1,729,600 | 1,623,900 | 1,580,200 | 1,370,100 | 1,103,800 | 1,003,300 |
| Income Taxes | 205,300 | 104,400 | 456,200 | 516,500 | 432,400 | 383,400 | 326,100 | 328,100 |
| Net Income | 616,500 | 307,400 | 1,273,400 | 1,107,400 | 1,147,800 | 1,017,400 | 777,700 | 675,200 |
| Average Shares | 392,000 | 394,200 | 399,500 | 399,400 | 413,600 | 417,200 | 411,800 | 411,600 |
| **Balance Sheet** | | | | | | | | |
| Current Assets | 6,502,700 | 6,501,200 | 7,631,400 | 5,851,200 | 4,979,300 | 4,904,900 | 3,534,300 | 2,870,100 |
| Total Assets | 11,596,400 | 11,231,000 | 10,895,100 | 9,071,300 | 7,603,300 | 7,354,000 | 5,873,800 | 4,944,100 |
| Current Liabilities | 1,603,500 | 1,586,800 | 1,605,000 | 1,441,000 | 1,462,100 | 1,333,000 | 1,351,500 | 1,248,800 |
| Long-Term Obligations | 996,700 | 996,600 | 996,500 | ... | ... | ... | ... | 184,200 |
| Total Liabilities | 3,818,400 | 3,778,600 | 3,721,500 | 2,476,200 | 2,196,600 | 1,975,500 | 1,682,800 | 1,692,300 |
| Stockholders' Equity | 7,778,000 | 7,452,400 | 7,173,600 | 6,595,100 | 5,406,700 | 5,378,500 | 4,191,000 | 3,251,800 |
| Shares Outstanding | 388,300 | 388,000 | 391,100 | 397,900 | 396,400 | 411,000 | 407,900 | 405,200 |
| **Statistical Record** | | | | | | | | |
| Return on Assets % | 11.54 | 11.81 | 12.76 | 13.28 | 15.31 | 15.38 | 14.38 | 14.96 |
| Return on Equity % | 17.20 | 17.83 | 18.50 | 18.45 | 21.23 | 21.26 | 20.90 | 22.49 |
| EBITDA Margin % | 26.04 | 26.14 | 26.67 | 27.14 | 26.43 | 25.81 | 23.51 | 23.78 |
| Net Margin % | 15.18 | 15.25 | 17.40 | 16.47 | 17.08 | 16.96 | 14.39 | 13.86 |
| Asset Turnover | 0.72 | 0.71 | 0.73 | 0.81 | 0.90 | 0.91 | 1.00 | 1.08 |
| Current Ratio | 4.06 | 4.10 | 4.75 | 4.06 | 3.41 | 3.68 | 2.62 | 2.30 |
| Debt to Equity | 0.13 | 0.13 | 0.14 | ... | ... | ... | ... | 0.06 |
| Price Range | 65.07-42.88 | 65.07-42.88 | 58.89-42.88 | 52.20-31.19 | 74.72-36.48 | 76.48-55.12 | 55.45-40.88 | 56.10-39.80 |
| P/E Ratio | 20.59-13.57 | 20.53-13.53 | 18.46-13.44 | 18.84-11.26 | 26.88-13.12 | 31.34-22.59 | 29.34-21.63 | 34.21-24.27 |
| Average Yield % | 1.26 | 1.23 | 1.21 | 0.60 | 0.66 | 0.49 | 0.46 | 0.23 |

**Address:** 2825 Airview Boulevard, Kalamazoo, MI 49002
**Telephone:** 269-385-2600
**Web Site:** www.stryker.com

**Officers:** John W. Brown - Chairman Stephen P. MacMillan - President, Chief Executive Officer
**Transfer Agents:** American Stock Transfer & Trust Company, LLC, New York, NY

**Investor Contact:** 616-385-2600
**No of Institutions:** 993
**Shares:** 272,187,904 **% Held:** 60.92

## SUBURBAN PROPANE PARTNERS L.P.

| Exchange | Symbol | Price | 52Wk Range | Yield | P/E |
|---|---|---|---|---|---|
| NYS | SPH | $47.49 (8/31/2011) | 58.75-41.04 | 7.18 | 15.17 |

*7 Year Price Score 130.50 *NYSE Composite Index=100 *12 Month Price Score 88.00

**Interim Earnings (Per Share)**

| Qtr. | Dec | Mar | Jun | Sep |
|---|---|---|---|---|
| 2007-08 | 2.60 | 2.87 | (0.42) | (0.35) |
| 2008-09 | 2.45 | 3.48 | (0.23) | (0.77) |
| 2009-10 | 1.36 | 2.78 | (0.19) | (0.70) |
| 2010-11 | 1.21 | 2.81 | (0.19) | ... |

**Interim Dividends (Per Share)**

| Amt | Decl | Ex | Rec | Pay |
|---|---|---|---|---|
| 0.85Q | 10/21/2010 | 10/29/2010 | 11/02/2010 | 11/09/2010 |
| 0.853Q | 01/19/2011 | 01/28/2011 | 02/01/2011 | 02/08/2011 |
| 0.853Q | 04/20/2011 | 04/29/2011 | 05/03/2011 | 05/10/2011 |
| 0.853Q | 07/20/2011 | 07/29/2011 | 08/02/2011 | 08/09/2011 |

**Indicated Div: $3.41**

**Valuation Analysis**

| | | | |
|---|---|---|---|
| Forecast EPS | $3.23 (09/05/2011) | | |
| Market Cap | $1.7 Billion | Book Value | N/A |
| Price/Book | N/A | Price/Sales | 1.43 |

**Dividend Achiever Status**

| | |
|---|---|
| **10 Year Growth Rate** | 4.36% |
| **Total Years of Dividend Growth** | 12 |

**Business Summary:** Gas Utilities (MIC: 3.3.1 SIC: 5999 NAIC: 453998)

Suburban Propane Partners is a nationwide marketer and distributor of a range of products meeting the energy needs of its customers. Co. is engaged in the distribution of propane, fuel oil and refined fuels, as well as the marketing of natural gas and electricity in deregulated markets. In support of its marketing and distribution operations, Co. installs and services a variety of home comfort equipment in the areas of heating and ventilation. At Sep 25 2010, Co. operated about 300 locations in 30 states located primarily in the east and west coast regions of the U.S., including Alaska. Co. has three reportable segments: Propane; Fuel Oil and Refined Fuels; and Natural Gas and Electricity.

**Recent Developments:** For the quarter ended June 25 2011, net loss amounted to US$6.8 million versus a net loss of US$6.6 million in the year-earlier quarter. Revenues were US$216.6 million, up 9.3% from US$198.1 million the year before. Operating income was US$353,000 versus US$555,000 in the prior-year quarter, a decrease of 36.4%. Direct operating expenses rose 17.4% to US$125.2 million from US$106.6 million in the comparable period the year before. Indirect operating expenses increased 0.2% to US$91.0 million from US$90.9 million in the equivalent prior-year period.

**Prospects:** Our evaluation of Suburban Propane Partners L.P. as of Sep. 6, 2011 is the result of our systematic analysis on three basic characteristics: earnings strength, relative valuation, and recent stock price movement. The company has enjoyed a very positive trend in earnings per share over the past 5 quarters. However, while recent estimates for the company have been lowered by analysts, SPH has posted results that fell short of analysts expectations. Based on operating earnings yield, the company is undervalued when compared to all of the companies in our coverage universe. Share price changes over the past year indicates that SPH will perform very poorly over the near term.

**Financial Data**

| (US$ in Thousands) | 9 Mos | 6 Mos | 3 Mos | 09/25/2010 | 09/26/2009 | 09/27/2008 | 09/29/2007 | 09/30/2006 |
|---|---|---|---|---|---|---|---|---|
| Earnings Per Share | 3.13 | 3.13 | 3.10 | 3.24 | 4.96 | 4.70 | 3.89 | 2.83 |
| Cash Flow Per Share | 3.82 | 4.18 | 4.67 | 4.42 | 7.46 | 3.69 | 4.50 | 5.53 |
| Dividends Per Share | 3.400 | 3.388 | 3.370 | 3.350 | 3.255 | 3.087 | 2.763 | 2.475 |
| Dividend Payout % | 108.63 | 108.23 | 108.71 | 103.40 | 65.63 | 65.69 | 71.02 | 87.46 |
| **Income Statement** | | | | | | | | |
| Total Revenue | 1,008,972 | 792,409 | 328,307 | 1,136,694 | 1,143,154 | 1,574,163 | 1,439,563 | 1,661,640 |
| EBITDA | 184,231 | 174,208 | 58,521 | 172,306 | 234,114 | 178,522 | 193,838 | 165,335 |
| Depn & Amortn | 26,304 | 16,634 | 8,180 | 28,411 | 28,123 | 28,394 | 29,242 | 33,151 |
| Income Before Taxes | 137,395 | 143,909 | 43,495 | 116,498 | 167,724 | 113,076 | 129,000 | 91,504 |
| Income Taxes | 737 | 464 | 366 | 1,182 | 2,486 | 1,903 | 5,653 | 764 |
| Net Income | 136,658 | 143,445 | 43,129 | 115,316 | 165,238 | 154,880 | 127,287 | 90,740 |
| Average Shares | 35,540 | 35,757 | 35,682 | 35,613 | 33,315 | 32,950 | 32,730 | 30,453 |
| **Balance Sheet** | | | | | | | | |
| Current Assets | 313,002 | 355,720 | 324,880 | 296,427 | 307,556 | 359,551 | 282,211 | 235,351 |
| Total Assets | 976,123 | 1,022,532 | 997,127 | 970,260 | 977,514 | 1,035,713 | 975,218 | 953,886 |
| Current Liabilities | 123,079 | 136,240 | 177,382 | 164,514 | 180,059 | 223,615 | 196,410 | 192,616 |
| Long-Term Obligations | 348,115 | 348,061 | 348,007 | 347,953 | 349,415 | 531,772 | 548,538 | 548,304 |
| Total Liabilities | 557,483 | 568,339 | 615,542 | 605,423 | 617,797 | 815,637 | 808,941 | 853,185 |
| Shares Outstanding | 35,423 | 35,398 | 35,395 | 35,318 | 35,227 | 32,725 | 32,674 | 30,314 |
| **Statistical Record** | | | | | | | | |
| Return on Assets % | 11.40 | 10.91 | 11.05 | 11.87 | 16.46 | 15.45 | 13.23 | 9.30 |
| EBITDA Margin % | 18.26 | 21.98 | 17.83 | 15.16 | 20.48 | 11.34 | 13.47 | 9.95 |
| Net Margin % | 13.54 | 18.10 | 13.14 | 10.14 | 14.45 | 9.84 | 8.84 | 5.46 |
| Asset Turnover | 1.20 | 1.13 | 1.17 | 1.17 | 1.14 | 1.57 | 1.50 | 1.70 |
| Current Ratio | 2.54 | 2.61 | 1.83 | 1.80 | 1.71 | 1.61 | 1.44 | 1.22 |
| Price Range | 58.75-46.43 | 58.75-43.82 | 56.49-43.82 | 54.10-41.24 | 45.88-22.64 | 48.15-33.99 | 49.16-33.61 | 35.43-24.04 |
| P/E Ratio | 18.77-14.83 | 18.77-14.00 | 18.22-14.14 | 16.70-12.73 | 9.25-4.56 | 10.24-7.23 | 12.64-8.64 | 12.52-8.49 |
| Average Yield % | 6.34 | 6.52 | 6.79 | 7.14 | 8.71 | 7.67 | 6.48 | 8.40 |

| | | |
|---|---|---|
| **Address:** 240 Route 10 West, Whippany, NJ 07981<br>**Telephone:** 973-887-5300<br>**Web Site:** www.suburbanpropane.com | **Officers:** Harold R. Logan - Chairman Michael J. Dunn - President, Chief Executive Officer, Holding/Parent Company Officer **Transfer Agents:** Computershare Trust Company, N.A, Providence, RI | **No of Institutions:** 161<br>**Shares:** 7,192,826 **% Held:** 19.24 |

# SYSCO CORP.

| Exchange | Symbol | Price | 52Wk Range | Yield | P/E |
|---|---|---|---|---|---|
| NYS | SYY | $27.93 (8/31/2011) | 32.65-26.83 | 3.72 | 14.25 |

*7 Year Price Score 95.57 *NYSE Composite Index=100 *12 Month Price Score 102.29

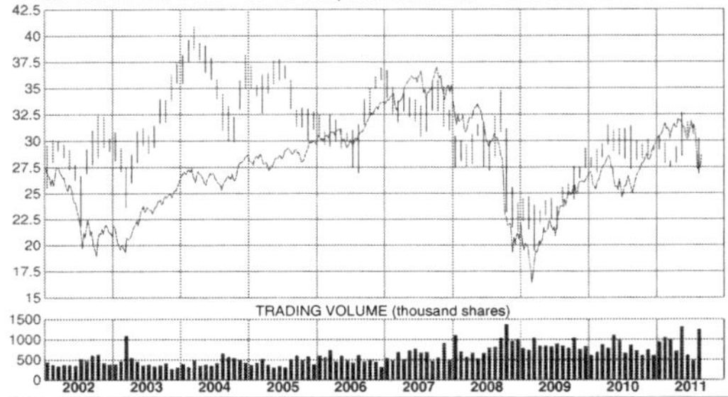


**Interim Earnings (Per Share)**

| Qtr. | Sep | Dec | Mar | Jun |
|---|---|---|---|---|
| 2006-07 | 0.30 | 0.38 | 0.35 | 0.49 |
| 2007-08 | 0.43 | 0.43 | 0.40 | 0.55 |
| 2008-09 | 0.46 | 0.40 | 0.38 | 0.53 |
| 2009-10 | 0.55 | 0.45 | 0.42 | 0.57 |
| 2010-11 | 0.51 | 0.44 | 0.44 | 0.57 |

**Interim Dividends (Per Share)**

| Amt | Decl | Ex | Rec | Pay |
|---|---|---|---|---|
| 0.26Q | 11/12/2010 | 01/05/2011 | 01/07/2011 | 01/28/2011 |
| 0.26Q | 02/25/2011 | 03/30/2011 | 04/01/2011 | 04/21/2011 |
| 0.26Q | 05/20/2011 | 06/29/2011 | 07/01/2011 | 07/22/2011 |
| 0.26Q | 08/26/2011 | 10/05/2011 | 10/07/2011 | 10/28/2011 |

**Indicated Div: $1.04 (Div. Reinv. Plan)**

**Valuation Analysis**

| | | | |
|---|---|---|---|
| Forecast EPS | $2.04 (09/02/2011) | | |
| Market Cap | $16.5 Billion | Book Value | $4.7 Billion |
| Price/Book | 3.51 | Price/Sales | 0.42 |

**Dividend Achiever Status**

| | |
|---|---|
| **10 Year Growth Rate** | 13.58% |
| **Total Years of Dividend Growth** | 34 |

**Business Summary:** Retail - Food & Beverage, Drug & Tobacco (MIC: 2.1.2 SIC: 5141 NAIC: 424410)

Sysco is a distributor of food and related products primarily to the foodservice or food-away-from-home industry. Co. provides products and related services to approximately 400,000 customers, including restaurants, healthcare and educational facilities, lodging establishments and other foodservice customers. The products Co. distributes includes frozen foods, canned and dry foods, meats, dairy products, beverage products, imported specialties, and fresh produce. Co. also supplies non-food items, including paper products such as disposable napkins, plates and cups; tableware; cookware such as pots, pans and utensils; restaurant and kitchen equipment and supplies; and cleaning supplies.

**Recent Developments:** For the year ended July 2 2011, net income decreased 2.4% to US$1.15 billion from US$1.18 billion in the prior year. Revenues were US$39.32 billion, up 5.6% from US$37.24 billion the year before. Operating income was US$1.93 billion versus US$1.98 billion in the prior year, a decrease of 2.2%. Direct operating expenses rose 6.2% to US$32.00 billion from US$30.14 billion in the comparable period the year before. Indirect operating expenses increased 5.0% to US$5.39 billion from US$5.13 billion in the equivalent prior-year period.

**Prospects:** Our evaluation of Sysco Corp. as of Sep. 6, 2011 is the result of our systematic analysis on three basic characteristics: earnings strength, relative valuation, and recent stock price movement. The company has managed to produce a neutral trend in earnings per share over the past 5 quarters. However, while recent estimates for the company have been lowered by analysts, SYY has posted results that were in line with analysts expectations. Based on operating earnings yield, the company is undervalued when compared to all of the companies in our coverage universe. Share price changes over the past year indicates that SYY will perform poorly over the near term.

**Financial Data**

| (US$ in Thousands) | 07/02/2011 | 07/03/2010 | 06/27/2009 | 06/28/2008 | 06/30/2007 | 07/01/2006 | 07/02/2005 | 07/03/2004 |
|---|---|---|---|---|---|---|---|---|
| Earnings Per Share | 1.96 | 1.99 | 1.77 | 1.81 | 1.60 | 1.36 | 1.47 | 1.37 |
| Cash Flow Per Share | 1.87 | 1.47 | 2.67 | 2.64 | 2.28 | 1.81 | 1.88 | 1.82 |
| Tang Book Value Per Share | 5.01 | 3.69 | 3.08 | 3.17 | 2.99 | 2.67 | 2.35 | 2.11 |
| Dividends Per Share | 1.030 | 0.990 | 0.920 | 0.820 | 0.720 | 0.490 | 0.580 | 0.610 |
| Dividend Payout % | 52.55 | 49.75 | 51.98 | 45.30 | 45.00 | 36.03 | 39.46 | 44.53 |
| **Income Statement** | | | | | | | | |
| Total Revenue | 39,323,489 | 37,243,495 | 36,853,330 | 37,522,111 | 35,042,075 | 32,628,438 | 30,281,914 | 29,335,403 |
| EBITDA | 2,319,721 | 2,336,766 | 2,248,218 | 2,255,448 | 2,067,931 | 1,824,715 | 1,906,116 | 1,818,054 |
| Depn & Amortn | 374,000 | 361,700 | 361,062 | 352,569 | 341,714 | 320,669 | 305,680 | 273,030 |
| Income Before Taxes | 1,827,454 | 1,849,589 | 1,770,834 | 1,791,338 | 1,621,215 | 1,394,946 | 1,525,436 | 1,475,144 |
| Income Taxes | 675,424 | 669,606 | 714,886 | 685,187 | 620,139 | 548,906 | 563,979 | 567,930 |
| Net Income | 1,152,030 | 1,179,983 | 1,055,948 | 1,106,151 | 1,001,076 | 855,325 | 961,457 | 907,214 |
| Average Shares | 588,691 | 593,590 | 596,069 | 610,970 | 626,366 | 628,800 | 653,157 | 661,919 |
| **Balance Sheet** | | | | | | | | |
| Current Assets | 5,732,882 | 5,076,258 | 5,270,679 | 5,175,033 | 4,675,546 | 4,399,694 | 4,001,786 | 3,851,411 |
| Total Assets | 11,385,555 | 10,313,701 | 10,216,619 | 10,082,293 | 9,518,931 | 8,992,025 | 8,267,902 | 7,847,632 |
| Current Liabilities | 3,575,075 | 3,009,198 | 3,150,154 | 3,499,343 | 3,415,089 | 3,226,403 | 3,457,570 | 3,126,634 |
| Long-Term Obligations | 2,279,517 | 2,472,662 | 2,467,486 | 1,975,435 | 1,758,227 | 1,627,127 | 956,177 | 1,231,493 |
| Total Liabilities | 6,680,313 | 6,486,175 | 6,766,917 | 6,673,307 | 6,240,531 | 5,939,741 | 5,509,063 | 5,283,126 |
| Stockholders' Equity | 4,705,242 | 3,827,526 | 3,449,702 | 3,408,986 | 3,278,400 | 3,052,284 | 2,758,839 | 2,564,506 |
| Shares Outstanding | 591,577 | 588,406 | 590,026 | 601,232 | 611,840 | 618,895 | 628,567 | 636,535 |
| **Statistical Record** | | | | | | | | |
| Return on Assets % | 10.65 | 11.31 | 10.43 | 11.32 | 10.85 | 9.94 | 11.96 | 12.07 |
| Return on Equity % | 27.08 | 31.90 | 30.88 | 33.17 | 31.71 | 29.52 | 36.22 | 37.49 |
| EBITDA Margin % | 5.90 | 6.27 | 6.10 | 6.01 | 5.90 | 5.59 | 6.29 | 6.20 |
| Net Margin % | 2.93 | 3.17 | 2.87 | 2.95 | 2.86 | 2.62 | 3.18 | 3.09 |
| Asset Turnover | 3.63 | 3.57 | 3.64 | 3.84 | 3.80 | 3.79 | 3.77 | 3.90 |
| Current Ratio | 1.60 | 1.69 | 1.67 | 1.48 | 1.37 | 1.36 | 1.16 | 1.23 |
| Debt to Equity | 0.48 | 0.65 | 0.72 | 0.58 | 0.54 | 0.53 | 0.35 | 0.48 |
| Price Range | 32.65-27.29 | 31.54-21.51 | 34.80-19.45 | 35.84-27.48 | 36.95-26.91 | 37.20-29.25 | 38.20-29.89 | 40.90-28.75 |
| P/E Ratio | 16.66-13.92 | 15.85-10.81 | 19.66-10.99 | 19.80-15.18 | 23.09-16.82 | 27.35-21.51 | 25.99-20.33 | 29.85-20.99 |
| Average Yield % | 3.50 | 3.60 | 3.63 | 2.63 | 2.17 | 1.54 | 1.67 | 1.72 |

| | | |
|---|---|---|
| **Address:** 1390 Enclave Parkway, Houston, TX 77077-2099<br>**Telephone:** 281-584-1390<br>**Web Site:** www.sysco.com | **Officers:** Richard J. Schnieders - Chairman William J. DeLaney - President, Chief Executive Officer<br>**Transfer Agents:** American Stock Transfer & Trust Company, New York, NY | **Investor Contact:** 281-584-1308<br>**No of Institutions:** 1057<br>**Shares:** 519,143,040 **% Held:** 72.15 |

# T ROWE PRICE GROUP INC.

| Exchange | Symbol | Price | 52Wk Range | Yield | P/E |
|---|---|---|---|---|---|
| NMS | TROW | $53.48 (8/31/2011) | 71.10-43.79 | 2.32 | 18.83 |

***7 Year Price Score 129.22** *NYSE Composite Index=100 ***12 Month Price Score 93.26**

**Interim Earnings (Per Share)**

| Qtr. | Mar | Jun | Sep | Dec |
|---|---|---|---|---|
| 2008 | 0.55 | 0.60 | 0.56 | 0.11 |
| 2009 | 0.19 | 0.38 | 0.50 | 0.58 |
| 2010 | 0.57 | 0.59 | 0.64 | 0.72 |
| 2011 | 0.72 | 0.76 | ... | ... |

**Interim Dividends (Per Share)**

| Amt | Decl | Ex | Rec | Pay |
|---|---|---|---|---|
| 0.27Q | 10/18/2010 | 12/10/2010 | 12/14/2010 | 12/28/2010 |
| 0.31Q | 02/17/2011 | 03/11/2011 | 03/15/2011 | 03/29/2011 |
| 0.31Q | 06/03/2011 | 06/10/2011 | 06/14/2011 | 06/28/2011 |
| 0.31Q | 09/02/2011 | 09/12/2011 | 09/14/2011 | 09/28/2011 |

**Indicated Div: $1.24**

**Valuation Analysis**

| | | | |
|---|---|---|---|
| Forecast EPS | $3.11 (09/02/2011) | | |
| Market Cap | $13.7 Billion | Book Value | $3.4 Billion |
| Price/Book | 4.02 | Price/Sales | 5.21 |

**Dividend Achiever Status**

| | |
|---|---|
| **10 Year Growth Rate** | 13.67% |
| **Total Years of Dividend Growth** | 24 |

**Business Summary:** Wealth Management (MIC: 5.5.2 SIC: 6282 NAIC: 523930)

T Rowe Price Group is a financial services holding company. Through its subsidiaries, Co. provides investment advisory services to investors in the sponsored T. Rowe Price mutual funds and other investment portfolios. Co. also provides its investment advisory clients with administrative services. As of Dec 31 2010, Co.'s total assets under management were $482.00 billion, which included $360.60 billion in equity and blended asset investment portfolios and $121.40 billion in fixed income investment portfolios. As of that date, Co.'s investment portfolios consisted of $282.60 billion in the T. Rowe Price mutual funds distributed in the U.S. and $199.40 billion in other investment portfolios.

**Recent Developments:** For the quarter ended June 30 2011, net income increased 29.1% to US$204.7 million from US$158.5 million in the year-earlier quarter. Revenues were US$713.7 million, up 23.6% from US$577.4 million the year before. Operating income was US$326.6 million versus US$253.1 million in the prior-year quarter, an increase of 29.0%. Indirect operating expenses increased 19.4% to US$387.1 million from US$324.3 million in the equivalent prior-year period.

**Prospects:** Our evaluation of T Rowe Price Group Inc. as of Sep. 6, 2011 is the result of our systematic analysis on three basic characteristics: earnings strength, relative valuation, and recent stock price movement. The company has produced a positive trend in earnings per share over the past 5 quarters. However, while recent estimates for the company have been lowered by analysts, TROW has posted results that fell short of analysts expectations. Based on operating earnings yield, the company is about fairly valued when compared to all of the companies in our coverage universe. Share price changes over the past year indicates that TROW will perform in line with the market over the near term.

| **Financial Data** (US$ in Thousands) | 6 Mos | 3 Mos | 12/31/2010 | 12/31/2009 | 12/31/2008 | 12/31/2007 | 12/31/2006 | 12/31/2005 |
|---|---|---|---|---|---|---|---|---|
| Earnings Per Share | 2.84 | 2.67 | 2.53 | 1.65 | 1.82 | 2.40 | 1.90 | 1.58 |
| Cash Flow Per Share | 3.45 | 3.14 | 2.85 | 2.09 | 2.85 | 2.86 | 2.25 | 2.07 |
| Tang Book Value Per Share | 10.71 | 10.78 | 10.17 | 8.57 | 7.10 | 7.97 | 6.63 | 5.20 |
| Dividends Per Share | 1.160 | 1.120 | 1.080 | 1.000 | 0.960 | 0.750 | 0.590 | 0.485 |
| Dividend Payout % | 40.85 | 41.95 | 42.69 | 60.61 | 52.75 | 31.25 | 31.05 | 30.79 |
| **Income Statement** | | | | | | | | |
| Total Revenue | 1,396,100 | 682,400 | 2,370,700 | 1,871,900 | 2,121,300 | 2,233,100 | 1,819,300 | 1,515,815 |
| EBITDA | 647,800 | 315,500 | 1,070,400 | 689,400 | 796,800 | 1,077,400 | 858,700 | 721,663 |
| Depn & Amortn | 200 | 100 | 400 | 500 | 600 | 600 | 400 | 42,272 |
| Income Before Taxes | 647,600 | 315,400 | 1,070,000 | 688,900 | 796,200 | 1,076,800 | 858,300 | 679,391 |
| Income Taxes | 248,300 | 120,800 | 397,800 | 255,300 | 305,400 | 406,200 | 328,700 | 248,462 |
| Net Income | 399,300 | 194,600 | 672,200 | 433,600 | 490,800 | 670,600 | 529,600 | 430,929 |
| Average Shares | 266,700 | 268,500 | 265,100 | 262,300 | 270,100 | 279,200 | 278,700 | 273,196 |
| **Balance Sheet** | | | | | | | | |
| Current Assets | 1,346,700 | 1,386,300 | 1,121,000 | 989,500 | 796,400 | 1,050,400 | 996,500 | 978,619 |
| Total Assets | 3,882,400 | 3,886,000 | 3,642,000 | 3,210,300 | 2,819,400 | 3,177,300 | 2,765,300 | 2,310,546 |
| Current Liabilities | 469,600 | 430,100 | 185,100 | 166,800 | 172,800 | 285,900 | 223,700 | 170,615 |
| Total Liabilities | 469,600 | 430,100 | 345,500 | 328,100 | 330,600 | 400,200 | 338,400 | 274,444 |
| Stockholders' Equity | 3,412,800 | 3,455,900 | 3,296,500 | 2,882,200 | 2,488,800 | 2,777,100 | 2,426,900 | 2,036,102 |
| Shares Outstanding | 256,518 | 258,760 | 258,760 | 258,534 | 256,856 | 264,605 | 264,959 | 263,356 |
| **Statistical Record** | | | | | | | | |
| Return on Assets % | 20.86 | 19.61 | 19.62 | 14.38 | 16.32 | 22.57 | 20.87 | 20.33 |
| Return on Equity % | 23.85 | 22.09 | 21.76 | 16.15 | 18.59 | 25.77 | 23.73 | 23.09 |
| EBITDA Margin % | 46.40 | 46.23 | 45.15 | 36.83 | 37.56 | 48.25 | 47.20 | 47.61 |
| Net Margin % | 28.60 | 28.52 | 28.35 | 23.16 | 23.14 | 30.03 | 29.11 | 28.43 |
| Asset Turnover | 0.72 | 0.69 | 0.69 | 0.62 | 0.71 | 0.75 | 0.72 | 0.72 |
| Current Ratio | 2.87 | 3.22 | 6.06 | 5.93 | 4.61 | 3.67 | 4.45 | 5.74 |
| Price Range | 71.10-43.60 | 71.10-43.60 | 65.37-43.60 | 54.27-21.01 | 65.01-25.13 | 64.70-44.60 | 48.31-35.24 | 37.37-27.41 |
| P/E Ratio | 25.04-15.35 | 26.63-16.33 | 25.84-17.23 | 32.89-12.73 | 35.72-13.81 | 26.96-18.58 | 25.43-18.55 | 23.65-17.35 |
| Average Yield % | 1.99 | 2.00 | 2.05 | 2.49 | 1.91 | 1.42 | 1.43 | 1.54 |

| | | |
|---|---|---|
| **Address:** 100 East Pratt Street, Baltimore, MD 21202<br>**Telephone:** 410-345-2000<br>**Web Site:** www.troweprice.com | **Officers:** Brian C. Rogers - Chairman, Vice President, Chief Investment Officer Edward C. Bernard - Vice-Chairman **Transfer Agents:** T. Rowe Price Services, Inc. | **Investor Contact:** 410-345-2124<br>**No of Institutions:** 756<br>**Shares:** 189,698,048 **% Held:** 64.15 |

# TANGER FACTORY OUTLET CENTERS, INC.

| Exchange | Symbol | Price | 52Wk Range | Yield | P/E |
|---|---|---|---|---|---|
| NYS | SKT | $28.13 (8/31/2011) | 28.92-22.39 | 2.84 | 58.60 |

***7 Year Price Score 137.38** *NYSE Composite Index=100 ***12 Month Price Score 104.76**

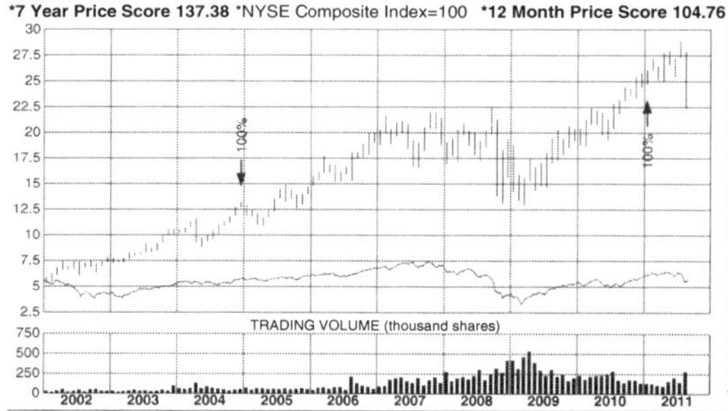


**Interim Earnings (Per Share)**

| Qtr. | Mar | Jun | Sep | Dec |
|---|---|---|---|---|
| 2008 | 0.09 | 0.00 | 0.14 | 0.13 |
| 2009 | 0.46 | 0.15 | 0.03 | 0.12 |
| 2010 | 0.01 | 0.04 | 0.14 | 0.12 |
| 2011 | 0.11 | 0.11 | ... | ... |

**Interim Dividends (Per Share)**

| Amt | Decl | Ex | Rec | Pay |
|---|---|---|---|---|
| 100% | 01/05/2011 | 01/25/2011 | 01/13/2011 | 01/24/2011 |
| 0.194Q | 01/05/2011 | 01/27/2011 | 01/31/2011 | 02/15/2011 |
| 0.20Q | 04/07/2011 | 04/27/2011 | 04/29/2011 | 05/13/2011 |
| 0.20Q | 07/07/2011 | 07/27/2011 | 07/29/2011 | 08/15/2011 |

**Indicated Div: $0.80 (Div. Reinv. Plan)**

**Valuation Analysis**

| | | | |
|---|---|---|---|
| Forecast EPS | $0.59 (09/05/2011) | | |
| Market Cap | $2.3 Billion | Book Value | $357.0 Million |
| Price/Book | 6.41 | Price/Sales | 7.95 |

**Dividend Achiever Status**

| | |
|---|---|
| **10 Year Growth Rate** | 2.40% |
| **Total Years of Dividend Growth** | 17 |

**Business Summary:** REITs (MIC: 5.3.1 SIC: 6798 NAIC: 525930)

Tanger Factory Outlet Centers is a real estate investment trust, which develops, acquires, owns, operates and manages outlet shopping centers. Co.'s outlet centers and other assets are held by, and all of its operations are conducted by, Tanger Properties Limited Partnership and subsidiaries (Operating Partnership). Co. owns the majority of the units of partnership interest issued by the Operating Partnership, through its two wholly-owned subsidiaries, the Tanger GP Trust and the Tanger LP Trust. At Dec 31 2010, Co. owned and operated 31 outlet centers, with a total gross leasable area of about 9.2 million square feet, and operated and had partial ownership interests in two outlet centers.

**Recent Developments:** For the quarter ended June 30 2011, income from continuing operations increased 101.0% to US$10.8 million from US$5.4 million in the year-earlier quarter. Net income increased 101.1% to US$10.8 million from US$5.4 million in the year-earlier quarter. Revenues were US$72.1 million, up 10.4% from US$65.3 million the year before. Revenues from property income rose 10.6% to US$70.1 million from US$63.4 million in the corresponding quarter a year earlier.

**Prospects:** Our evaluation of Tanger Factory Outlet Centers Inc. as of Sep. 6, 2011 is the result of our systematic analysis on three basic characteristics: earnings strength, relative valuation, and recent stock price movement. The company has generated a negative trend in earnings per share over the past 5 quarters. Because the company lacks sufficient analyst estimate data, we place greater weight on the historical EPS trend as the measure of earnings strength. Based on operating earnings yield, the company is overvalued when compared to all of the companies in our coverage universe. Share price changes over the past year indicates that SKT will perform very poorly over the near term.

**Financial Data**

| (US$ in Thousands) | 6 Mos | 3 Mos | 12/31/2010 | 12/31/2009 | 12/31/2008 | 12/31/2007 | 12/31/2006 | 12/31/2005 |
|---|---|---|---|---|---|---|---|---|
| Earnings Per Share | 0.48 | 0.41 | 0.32 | 0.72 | 0.35 | 0.36 | 0.52 | 0.08 |
| Cash Flow Per Share | 1.54 | 1.50 | 1.48 | 1.77 | 1.56 | 1.60 | 1.44 | 1.48 |
| Tang Book Value Per Share | 4.39 | 4.46 | 3.61 | 3.81 | 1.32 | 1.60 | 1.97 | 1.92 |
| Dividends Per Share | 0.781 | 0.775 | 0.772 | 0.764 | 0.750 | 0.710 | 0.671 | 0.640 |
| Dividend Payout % | 161.08 | 186.75 | 241.41 | 106.08 | 211.27 | 197.22 | 130.34 | 800.00 |
| **Income Statement** | | | | | | | | |
| Total Revenue | 142,840 | 70,739 | 276,303 | 271,685 | 245,391 | 228,765 | 211,711 | 202,799 |
| EBITDA | 44,486 | 21,664 | 137,426 | 171,590 | 119,794 | 121,965 | 109,435 | 114,352 |
| Depn & Amortn | 993 | 490 | 64,500 | 64,900 | 49,800 | 50,400 | 40,336 | 38,137 |
| Income Before Taxes | 22,455 | 10,849 | 38,806 | 69,007 | 31,551 | 31,499 | 28,324 | 33,288 |
| Net Income | 18,820 | 9,398 | 34,249 | 58,019 | 28,032 | 28,576 | 37,309 | 5,089 |
| Average Shares | 81,104 | 80,552 | 80,390 | 72,024 | 62,724 | 63,336 | 62,162 | 57,292 |
| **Balance Sheet** | | | | | | | | |
| Current Assets | 18,438 | 731 | 6,481 | 3,267 | 4,977 | 2,412 | 8,453 | 5,567 |
| Total Assets | 1,367,589 | 1,218,244 | 1,216,934 | 1,178,861 | 1,121,855 | 1,060,280 | 1,040,877 | 1,000,605 |
| Current Liabilities | 54,462 | 64,487 | 63,425 | 46,110 | 69,159 | 70,998 | 48,598 | 37,418 |
| Long-Term Obligations | 886,644 | 720,970 | 714,616 | 584,611 | 795,319 | 706,345 | 678,579 | 663,607 |
| Total Liabilities | 1,010,550 | 855,928 | 850,005 | 716,190 | 893,799 | 811,076 | 766,201 | 750,391 |
| Stockholders' Equity | 357,039 | 362,316 | 366,929 | 462,671 | 228,056 | 249,204 | 274,676 | 250,214 |
| Shares Outstanding | 81,316 | 81,315 | 80,996 | 80,554 | 63,335 | 62,658 | 62,082 | 61,497 |
| **Statistical Record** | | | | | | | | |
| Return on Assets % | 3.57 | 3.42 | 2.86 | 5.04 | 2.56 | 2.72 | 3.66 | 0.53 |
| Return on Equity % | 11.29 | 10.04 | 8.26 | 16.80 | 11.71 | 10.91 | 14.22 | 2.47 |
| EBITDA Margin % | 31.14 | 30.63 | 49.74 | 63.16 | 48.82 | 53.31 | 51.69 | 56.39 |
| Net Margin % | 13.18 | 13.29 | 12.40 | 21.36 | 11.42 | 12.49 | 17.62 | 2.51 |
| Asset Turnover | 0.23 | 0.24 | 0.23 | 0.24 | 0.22 | 0.22 | 0.21 | 0.21 |
| Current Ratio | 0.34 | 0.01 | 0.10 | 0.07 | 0.07 | 0.03 | 0.17 | 0.15 |
| Debt to Equity | 2.48 | 1.99 | 1.95 | 1.26 | 3.49 | 2.83 | 2.47 | 2.65 |
| Price Range | 27.96-20.43 | 27.20-19.30 | 25.85-18.68 | 20.68-12.96 | 22.39-13.10 | 22.02-16.61 | 20.05-14.74 | 14.93-10.82 |
| P/E Ratio | 58.25-42.55 | 66.34-47.06 | 80.78-58.36 | 28.72-18.00 | 63.96-37.43 | 61.17-46.13 | 38.55-28.35 | 186.63-135.25 |
| Average Yield % | 3.14 | 3.30 | 3.49 | 4.46 | 4.01 | 3.57 | 3.95 | 4.94 |

**Address:** 3200 Northline Avenue, Suite 360, Greensboro, NC 27408
**Telephone:** 336-292-3010
**Web Site:** www.tangeroutlet.com

**Officers:** Steven B. Tanger - President, Chief Executive Officer Frank C. Marchisello - Executive Vice President, Chief Financial Officer, Secretary
**Transfer Agents:** Computershare Trust Company, N.A, Providence, RI

**Investor Contact:** 336-292-3010
**No of Institutions:** 250
**Shares:** 81,212,216 **% Held:** 96.70

# TARGET CORP

| Exchange | Symbol | Price | 52Wk Range | Yield | P/E |
|---|---|---|---|---|---|
| NYS | TGT | $51.67 (8/31/2011) | 60.77-46.33 | 2.32 | 12.33 |

***7 Year Price Score 100.75** *NYSE Composite Index=100 ***12 Month Price Score 95.08**

**Interim Earnings (Per Share)**

| Qtr. | Apr | Jul | Oct | Jan |
|---|---|---|---|---|
| 2008-09 | 0.74 | 0.82 | 0.49 | 0.80 |
| 2009-10 | 0.69 | 0.79 | 0.58 | 1.24 |
| 2010-11 | 0.90 | 0.92 | 0.74 | 1.43 |
| 2011-12 | 0.99 | 1.03 | ... | ... |

**Interim Dividends (Per Share)**

| Amt | Decl | Ex | Rec | Pay |
|---|---|---|---|---|
| 0.25Q | 09/09/2010 | 11/17/2010 | 11/20/2010 | 12/10/2010 |
| 0.25Q | 01/13/2011 | 02/14/2011 | 02/16/2011 | 03/10/2011 |
| 0.25Q | 03/10/2011 | 05/16/2011 | 05/18/2011 | 06/10/2011 |
| 0.30Q | 06/08/2011 | 08/16/2011 | 08/18/2011 | 09/10/2011 |

**Indicated Div: $1.20 (Div. Reinv. Plan)**

**Valuation Analysis**

| | | | |
|---|---|---|---|
| Forecast EPS | $4.22 (09/03/2011) | | |
| Market Cap | $34.9 Billion | Book Value | $15.1 Billion |
| Price/Book | 2.31 | Price/Sales | 0.51 |

**Dividend Achiever Status**

| | |
|---|---|
| **10 Year Growth Rate** | 14.34% |
| **Total Years of Dividend Growth** | 39 |

**Business Summary:** Retail - General Merchandise/Department Stores (MIC: 2.1.1 SIC: 5331 NAIC: 452990)

Target operates as two reportable segments. Co.'s Retail Segment includes its merchandising operations, including its online business, Target.com. Co.'s Credit Card Segment provides the Target Visa and the Target Card credit cards, as well as the Target Debit Card. Co. operates Target general merchandise stores and SuperTarget® stores, providing a range of general merchandise and food. Co.'s merchandise includes household products, hardlines, apparel and accessories, home furnishings and décor, and food and pet supplies. Co.'s food product includes some perishables and some additional dry, dairy and frozen items. At Jan 29 2011, Co. had 1,750 stores in 49 states and the District of Columbia.

**Recent Developments:** For the quarter ended July 30 2011, net income increased 3.7% to US$704.0 million from US$679.0 million in the year-earlier quarter. Revenues were US$16.24 billion, up 4.6% from US$15.53 billion the year before. Operating income was US$1.30 billion versus US$1.27 billion in the prior-year quarter, an increase of 2.7%. Direct operating expenses rose 4.3% to US$10.96 billion from US$10.51 billion in the comparable period the year before. Indirect operating expenses increased 5.9% to US$3.98 billion from US$3.76 billion in the equivalent prior-year period.

**Prospects:** Our evaluation of Target Corp. as of Sep. 6, 2011 is the result of our systematic analysis on three basic characteristics: earnings strength, relative valuation, and recent stock price movement. The company has managed to produce a neutral trend in earnings per share over the past 5 quarters. However, while recent estimates for the company have been mixed, TGT has posted better than expected results. Based on operating earnings yield, the company is undervalued when compared to all of the companies in our coverage universe. Share price changes over the past year indicates that TGT will perform very poorly over the near term.

**Financial Data**

| (US$ in Millions) | 6 Mos | 3 Mos | 01/29/2011 | 01/30/2010 | 01/31/2009 | 02/02/2008 | 02/03/2007 | 01/28/2006 |
|---|---|---|---|---|---|---|---|---|
| Earnings Per Share | 4.19 | 4.08 | 4.00 | 3.30 | 2.86 | 3.33 | 3.21 | 2.71 |
| Cash Flow Per Share | 8.49 | 7.46 | 7.30 | 7.84 | 5.77 | 4.89 | 5.55 | 5.06 |
| Tang Book Value Per Share | 22.37 | 22.10 | 21.68 | 20.29 | 17.91 | 18.44 | 17.94 | 16.04 |
| Dividends Per Share | 1.000 | 0.920 | 0.840 | 0.660 | 0.600 | 0.520 | 0.440 | 0.360 |
| Dividend Payout % | 23.87 | 22.55 | 21.00 | 20.00 | 20.98 | 15.62 | 13.71 | 13.28 |
| **Income Statement** | | | | | | | | |
| Total Revenue | 32,175 | 15,935 | 67,390 | 65,357 | 64,948 | 63,367 | 59,490 | 52,620 |
| EBITDA | 3,586 | 1,776 | 7,312 | 6,672 | 6,206 | 6,916 | 6,578 | 5,707 |
| Depn & Amortn | 1,022 | 512 | 2,060 | 1,999 | 1,804 | 1,644 | 1,509 | 1,384 |
| Income Before Taxes | 2,190 | 1,081 | 4,495 | 3,872 | 3,536 | 4,625 | 4,497 | 3,860 |
| Income Taxes | 797 | 392 | 1,575 | 1,384 | 1,322 | 1,776 | 1,710 | 1,452 |
| Net Income | 1,393 | 689 | 2,920 | 2,488 | 2,214 | 2,849 | 2,787 | 2,408 |
| Average Shares | 685 | 697 | 729 | 754 | 773 | 850 | 868 | 889 |
| **Balance Sheet** | | | | | | | | |
| Current Assets | 16,059 | 16,368 | 17,213 | 18,424 | 17,488 | 18,906 | 14,706 | 14,405 |
| Total Assets | 45,499 | 42,996 | 43,705 | 44,533 | 44,106 | 44,560 | 37,349 | 34,995 |
| Current Liabilities | 11,620 | 10,838 | 10,070 | 11,327 | 10,512 | 11,782 | 11,117 | 9,588 |
| Long-Term Obligations | 16,160 | 14,416 | 15,607 | 15,118 | 17,490 | 15,126 | 8,675 | 9,119 |
| Total Liabilities | 30,393 | 27,766 | 28,218 | 29,186 | 30,394 | 29,253 | 21,716 | 20,790 |
| Stockholders' Equity | 15,106 | 15,230 | 15,487 | 15,347 | 13,712 | 15,307 | 15,633 | 14,205 |
| Shares Outstanding | 675 | 689 | 704 | 744 | 752 | 818 | 859 | 874 |
| **Statistical Record** | | | | | | | | |
| Return on Assets % | 6.65 | 6.81 | 6.64 | 5.63 | 5.01 | 6.98 | 7.58 | 7.18 |
| Return on Equity % | 19.51 | 19.06 | 18.99 | 17.17 | 15.30 | 18.47 | 18.38 | 17.73 |
| EBITDA Margin % | 11.15 | 11.15 | 10.85 | 10.21 | 9.56 | 10.91 | 11.06 | 10.85 |
| Net Margin % | 4.33 | 4.32 | 4.33 | 3.81 | 3.41 | 4.50 | 4.68 | 4.58 |
| Asset Turnover | 1.54 | 1.57 | 1.53 | 1.48 | 1.47 | 1.55 | 1.62 | 1.57 |
| Current Ratio | 1.38 | 1.51 | 1.71 | 1.63 | 1.66 | 1.60 | 1.32 | 1.50 |
| Debt to Equity | 1.07 | 0.95 | 1.01 | 0.99 | 1.28 | 0.99 | 0.55 | 0.64 |
| Price Range | 60.77-46.33 | 60.77-49.00 | 60.77-48.64 | 52.02-25.37 | 57.89-26.96 | 70.14-48.08 | 62.35-45.28 | 59.98-46.28 |
| P/E Ratio | 14.50-11.06 | 14.89-12.01 | 15.19-12.16 | 15.76-7.69 | 20.24-9.43 | 21.06-14.44 | 19.42-14.11 | 22.13-17.08 |
| Average Yield % | 1.90 | 1.72 | 1.56 | 1.56 | 1.30 | 0.86 | 0.82 | 0.68 |

**Address:** 1000 Nicollet Mall, Minneapolis, MN 55403
**Telephone:** 612-304-6073
**Web Site:** www.target.com

**Officers:** Gregg W. Steinhafel - Chairman, President, Chief Executive Officer Douglas A. Scovanner - Executive Vice President, Chief Financial Officer
**Transfer Agents:** BNY Mellon Shareowner Services, Pittsburgh, PA

**Investor Contact:** 612-370-6736
**No of Institutions:** 1224
**Shares:** 602,010,816 **% Held:** 78.61

# TC PIPELINES, LP

| Exchange | Symbol | Price | 52Wk Range | Yield | P/E |
|---|---|---|---|---|---|
| NMS | TCLP | $43.60 (8/31/2011) | 54.45-40.17 | 6.93 | 13.63 |

*7 Year Price Score 129.57 *NYSE Composite Index=100 *12 Month Price Score 93.19

**Interim Earnings (Per Share)**

| Qtr. | Mar | Jun | Sep | Dec |
|---|---|---|---|---|
| 2008 | 0.87 | 0.47 | 0.72 | 0.67 |
| 2009 | 0.82 | 0.31 | 0.65 | 0.56 |
| 2010 | 0.71 | 0.59 | 0.82 | 0.79 |
| 2011 | 0.90 | 0.69 | ... | ... |

**Interim Dividends (Per Share)**

| Amt | Decl | Ex | Rec | Pay |
|---|---|---|---|---|
| 0.75Q | 10/20/2010 | 10/27/2010 | 10/31/2010 | 11/12/2010 |
| 0.75Q | 01/18/2011 | 01/27/2011 | 01/31/2011 | 02/14/2011 |
| 0.75Q | 04/18/2011 | 04/27/2011 | 04/30/2011 | 05/13/2011 |
| 0.77Q | 07/19/2011 | 07/27/2011 | 07/31/2011 | 08/12/2011 |

**Indicated Div: $3.02**

**Valuation Analysis**

| | | | |
|---|---|---|---|
| Forecast EPS | $3.22 (09/05/2011) | | |
| Market Cap | $2.3 Billion | Book Value | N/A |
| Price/Book | N/A | Price/Sales | 10.82 |

**Dividend Achiever Status**

| | |
|---|---|
| **10 Year Growth Rate** | 4.19% |
| **Total Years of Dividend Growth** | 11 |

**Business Summary:** Equipment & Services (MIC: 9.1.3 SIC: 4922 NAIC: 486210)

TC PipeLines acquires, owns and participates in the management of energy infrastructure businesses. As of Dec 31 2010, Co. owned a 46.5% general partner interest in Great Lakes Gas Transmission Limited Partnership, which transports natural gas in Minnesota, Wisconsin, Michigan and Eastern Canada; a 50.0% general partner interest in Northern Border Pipeline Co., which transports natural gas from the Montana-Saskatchewan border to the Midwestern U.S.; 100.0% of North Baja Pipeline, LLC, which transports natural gas between an interconnection near Ehrenberg, AZ and an interconnection near Ogilby, CA; and 100.0% of Tuscarora Gas Transmission Co., which transports natural gas from Oregon.

**Recent Developments:** For the quarter ended June 30 2011, net income increased 30.3% to US$36.1 million from US$27.7 million in the year-earlier quarter. Revenues were US$55.1 million, up 30.3% from US$42.3 million the year before. Indirect operating expenses increased 86.4% to US$8.2 million from US$4.4 million in the equivalent prior-year period.

**Prospects:** Our evaluation of TC PipeLines L.P. as of Sep. 6, 2011 is the result of our systematic analysis on three basic characteristics: earnings strength, relative valuation, and recent stock price movement. The company has managed to produce a neutral trend in earnings per share over the past 5 quarters. However, while recent estimates for the company have been mixed, TCLP has posted results that fell short of analysts expectations. Based on operating earnings yield, the company is undervalued when compared to all of the companies in our coverage universe. Share price changes over the past year indicates that TCLP will perform very poorly over the near term.

**Financial Data**
(US$ in Thousands)

| | 6 Mos | 3 Mos | 12/31/2010 | 12/31/2009 | 12/31/2008 | 12/31/2007 | 12/31/2006 | 12/31/2005 |
|---|---|---|---|---|---|---|---|---|
| Earnings Per Share | 3.20 | 3.10 | 2.91 | 2.34 | 2.75 | 2.51 | 2.39 | 2.70 |
| Cash Flow Per Share | 3.28 | 3.53 | 3.38 | 3.19 | 3.25 | 2.83 | ... | 2.86 |
| Dividends Per Share | 2.980 | 2.960 | 2.940 | 2.870 | 2.775 | 2.565 | 2.325 | 2.300 |
| Dividend Payout % | 93.13 | 95.48 | 101.03 | 122.65 | 100.91 | 102.19 | 97.28 | 85.19 |
| **Income Statement** | | | | | | | | |
| Total Revenue | 111,000 | 55,900 | 195,100 | 167,300 | 154,200 | 137,400 | 63,400 | 53,200 |
| EBITDA | 114,900 | 58,500 | 160,700 | 134,600 | 137,300 | 128,700 | 59,800 | 51,200 |
| Depn & Amortn | 9,300 | 3,800 | 15,000 | 14,700 | 6,900 | 6,300 | 200 | ... |
| Income Before Taxes | 105,600 | 54,700 | 137,100 | 106,100 | 107,700 | 89,000 | 44,700 | 50,200 |
| Net Income | 78,400 | 42,300 | 137,100 | 106,100 | 107,700 | 89,000 | 44,700 | 50,200 |
| Average Shares | 50,900 | 46,200 | 46,200 | 38,700 | 34,900 | 34,900 | 17,500 | 17,500 |
| **Balance Sheet** | | | | | | | | |
| Current Assets | 10,300 | 11,500 | 12,300 | 11,700 | 11,800 | 11,000 | 6,500 | 2,300 |
| Total Assets | 2,040,200 | 1,646,100 | 1,650,500 | 1,675,100 | 1,448,500 | 1,492,600 | 777,800 | 315,700 |
| Current Liabilities | 314,400 | 494,100 | 506,600 | 72,100 | 20,500 | 13,800 | 9,300 | 14,100 |
| Long-Term Obligations | 393,100 | 30,100 | 30,100 | 487,900 | 532,400 | 568,800 | 463,400 | ... |
| Total Liabilities | 708,800 | 525,100 | 538,000 | 571,600 | 572,900 | 592,500 | 473,900 | 14,100 |
| Shares Outstanding | 53,500 | 46,200 | 46,227 | 46,227 | 34,856 | 34,856 | 17,500 | 17,500 |
| **Statistical Record** | | | | | | | | |
| Return on Assets % | 8.32 | 8.76 | 8.25 | 6.79 | 7.30 | 7.84 | ... | 15.50 |
| EBITDA Margin % | 103.51 | 104.65 | 82.37 | 80.45 | 89.04 | 93.67 | 94.32 | 96.24 |
| Net Margin % | 70.63 | 75.67 | 70.27 | 63.42 | 69.84 | 64.77 | 70.50 | 94.36 |
| Asset Turnover | 0.12 | 0.12 | 0.12 | 0.11 | 0.10 | 0.12 | ... | 0.16 |
| Current Ratio | 0.03 | 0.02 | 0.02 | 0.16 | 0.58 | 0.80 | 0.70 | 0.16 |
| Price Range | 54.45-40.35 | 54.45-34.72 | 52.00-34.40 | 41.10-23.25 | 37.30-18.82 | 42.83-32.98 | 36.00-30.00 | 40.60-31.20 |
| P/E Ratio | 17.02-12.61 | 17.56-11.20 | 17.87-11.82 | 17.56-9.94 | 13.56-6.84 | 17.06-13.14 | 15.06-12.55 | 15.04-11.56 |
| Average Yield % | 6.24 | 6.52 | 7.05 | 8.61 | 8.71 | 6.80 | 7.08 | 6.61 |

**Address:** 13710 FNB Parkway, Suite 300, Omaha, NE 68154-5200
**Telephone:**
**Web Site:** www.tcpipelineslp.com

**Officers:** Gregory A. Lohnes - Chairman Steven D. Becker - President **Transfer Agents:**
BNY Mellon Shareowner Services, Pittsburg, PA

**Investor Contact:** 187-729-02772
**No of Institutions:** 133
**Shares:** 21,584,796 **% Held:** 44.99

# TELEPHONE & DATA SYSTEMS, INC.

| Exchange | Symbol | Price | 52Wk Range | Yield | P/E |
|---|---|---|---|---|---|
| NYS | TDS | $25.63 (8/31/2011) | 37.72-21.35 | 1.83 | 14.32 |

*7 Year Price Score 80.15 *NYSE Composite Index=100 *12 Month Price Score 84.36

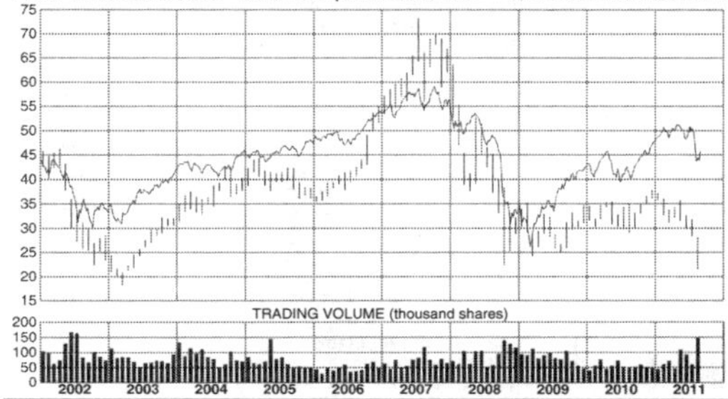


**Interim Earnings (Per Share)**

| Qtr. | Mar | Jun | Sep | Dec |
|---|---|---|---|---|
| 2008 | 0.62 | 0.75 | 0.87 | (1.44) |
| 2009 | 0.64 | 0.63 | 0.33 | 0.17 |
| 2010 | 0.46 | 0.38 | 0.38 | 0.14 |
| 2011 | 0.40 | 0.87 | ... | ... |

**Interim Dividends (Per Share)**

| Amt | Decl | Ex | Rec | Pay |
|---|---|---|---|---|
| 0.113Q | 11/18/2010 | 12/15/2010 | 12/17/2010 | 12/30/2010 |
| 0.117Q | 03/01/2011 | 03/15/2011 | 03/17/2011 | 03/31/2011 |
| 0.117Q | 05/19/2011 | 06/15/2011 | 06/17/2011 | 06/30/2011 |
| 0.117Q | 08/25/2011 | 09/14/2011 | 09/16/2011 | 09/30/2011 |

**Indicated Div: $0.47 (Div. Reinv. Plan)**

**Valuation Analysis**

| | | | |
|---|---|---|---|
| Forecast EPS | $1.89 (09/03/2011) | | |
| Market Cap | $2.6 Billion | Book Value | $3.9 Billion |
| Price/Book | 0.68 | Price/Sales | 0.52 |

**Dividend Achiever Status**

| | |
|---|---|
| **10 Year Growth Rate** | 6.05% |
| **Total Years of Dividend Growth** | 36 |

**Business Summary:** Services (MIC: 6.1.2 SIC: 4813 NAIC: 517110)

Telephone and Data Systems is a telecommunications company. Co. conducts substantially all of its wireless operations through its 83.0%-owned subsidiary, United States Cellular Corporation, and provides wireline services through its incumbent local exchange carrier and competitive local exchange carrier operations under its wholly owned subsidiary, TDS Telecommunications Corporation. Co. also conducts printing and distribution services through its majority-owned subsidiary, Suttle-Straus, Inc. As of Dec 31 2010, Co. served approximately 7.2 million customers in 36 states, including 6.1 million wireless customers and 1.1 million wireline equivalent access lines.

**Recent Developments:** For the quarter ended June 30 2011, net income increased 107.4% to US$108.7 million from US$52.4 million in the year-earlier quarter. Revenues were US$1.28 billion, up 3.8% from US$1.23 billion the year before. Operating income was US$125.6 million versus US$86.4 million in the prior-year quarter, an increase of 45.5%. Direct operating expenses rose 4.6% to US$473.9 million from US$453.0 million in the comparable period the year before. Indirect operating expenses decreased 1.8% to US$680.1 million from US$692.8 million in the equivalent prior-year period.

**Prospects:** Our evaluation of Telephone and Data Systems Inc. as of Sep. 6, 2011 is the result of our systematic analysis on three basic characteristics: earnings strength, relative valuation, and recent stock price movement. The company has produced a positive trend in earnings per share over the past 5 quarters and while recent estimates for the company have been raised by analysts, TDS has posted better than expected results. Based on operating earnings yield, the company is undervalued when compared to all of the companies in our coverage universe. Share price changes over the past year indicates that TDS will perform poorly over the near term.

**Financial Data**

| (US$ in Thousands) | 6 Mos | 3 Mos | 12/31/2010 | 12/31/2009 | 12/31/2008 | 12/31/2007 | 12/31/2006 | 12/31/2005 |
|---|---|---|---|---|---|---|---|---|
| Earnings Per Share | 1.79 | 1.30 | 1.36 | 1.77 | 0.80 | 3.22 | 1.37 | 1.91 |
| Cash Flow Per Share | 11.18 | 11.28 | 10.67 | 10.08 | 7.31 | 8.00 | 7.65 | 7.63 |
| Tang Book Value Per Share | 16.33 | 15.66 | 15.35 | 15.10 | 14.13 | 14.48 | 11.81 | 9.26 |
| Dividends Per Share | 0.460 | 0.455 | 0.450 | 0.430 | 0.410 | 0.390 | 0.370 | 0.438 |
| Dividend Payout % | 25.70 | 35.00 | 33.09 | 24.29 | 51.25 | 12.11 | 27.01 | 22.91 |
| **Income Statement** | | | | | | | | |
| Total Revenue | 2,538,321 | 1,258,681 | 4,986,829 | 5,020,674 | 5,092,019 | 4,828,984 | 4,364,518 | 3,960,069 |
| EBITDA | 614,845 | 279,766 | 1,022,703 | 1,133,906 | 856,362 | 1,295,820 | 949,267 | 1,109,761 |
| Depn & Amortn | 387,269 | 192,518 | 734,800 | 724,100 | 694,400 | 692,900 | 681,200 | 655,800 |
| Income Before Taxes | 158,777 | 61,773 | 183,191 | 296,370 | 63,194 | 593,619 | 228,168 | 396,139 |
| Income Taxes | 39,833 | 28,917 | 92,283 | 133,376 | 30,093 | 269,054 | 116,459 | 140,572 |
| Net Income | 132,685 | 41,622 | 143,856 | 193,902 | 93,541 | 386,112 | 161,759 | 222,544 |
| Average Shares | 104,062 | 104,554 | 105,506 | 109,577 | 116,255 | 119,126 | 116,844 | 116,081 |
| **Balance Sheet** | | | | | | | | |
| Current Assets | 1,758,925 | 1,939,063 | 1,596,076 | 1,644,142 | 1,628,936 | 3,875,588 | 2,973,084 | 1,778,969 |
| Total Assets | 7,920,908 | 8,071,301 | 7,762,519 | 7,608,784 | 7,652,416 | 9,894,143 | 10,599,514 | 10,404,565 |
| Current Liabilities | 763,736 | 1,026,529 | 810,633 | 780,296 | 773,287 | 2,799,519 | 2,084,731 | 1,056,104 |
| Long-Term Obligations | 1,530,369 | 1,517,176 | 1,499,862 | 1,492,908 | 1,621,422 | 1,632,226 | 1,633,308 | 1,633,519 |
| Total Liabilities | 4,015,921 | 4,231,274 | 3,947,767 | 3,830,647 | 3,884,077 | 5,966,945 | 7,028,231 | 7,050,089 |
| Stockholders' Equity | 3,904,987 | 3,840,027 | 3,814,752 | 3,778,137 | 3,768,339 | 3,927,198 | 3,571,283 | 3,354,476 |
| Shares Outstanding | 103,323 | 103,610 | 103,936 | 106,022 | 112,198 | 117,824 | 116,592 | 115,556 |
| **Statistical Record** | | | | | | | | |
| Return on Assets % | 2.42 | 1.75 | 1.87 | 2.54 | 1.06 | 3.77 | 1.54 | 2.08 |
| Return on Equity % | 4.87 | 3.59 | 3.79 | 5.14 | 2.42 | 10.30 | 4.67 | 6.80 |
| EBITDA Margin % | 24.22 | 22.23 | 20.51 | 22.58 | 16.82 | 26.83 | 21.75 | 28.02 |
| Net Margin % | 5.23 | 3.31 | 2.88 | 3.86 | 1.84 | 8.00 | 3.71 | 5.62 |
| Asset Turnover | 0.65 | 0.64 | 0.65 | 0.66 | 0.58 | 0.47 | 0.42 | 0.37 |
| Current Ratio | 2.30 | 1.89 | 1.97 | 2.11 | 2.11 | 1.38 | 1.43 | 1.68 |
| Debt to Equity | 0.39 | 0.40 | 0.39 | 0.40 | 0.43 | 0.42 | 0.46 | 0.49 |
| Price Range | 37.72-28.89 | 37.72-28.89 | 37.72-28.89 | 35.23-24.24 | 63.60-22.39 | 73.26-53.43 | 55.01-35.40 | 44.31-36.03 |
| P/E Ratio | 21.07-16.14 | 29.02-22.22 | 27.74-21.24 | 19.90-13.69 | 79.50-27.99 | 22.75-16.59 | 40.15-25.84 | 23.20-18.86 |
| Average Yield % | 1.37 | 1.35 | 1.35 | 1.44 | 1.00 | 0.63 | 0.88 | 1.10 |

| | | |
|---|---|---|
| **Address:** 30 North LaSalle Street, Chicago, IL 60602 | **Officers:** LeRoy T. Carlson - Chairman Emeritus<br>LeRoy T. Carlson - President, Chief Executive Officer | **Investor Contact:** 312-592-5341 |
| **Telephone:** 312-630-1900 | **Transfer Agents:** ComputerShare Investor Services, Chicago, IL | **No of Institutions:** 306 |
| **Web Site:** www.teldta.com | | **Shares:** 47,885,896 **% Held:** 87.08 |

# TENNANT CO.

| Exchange | Symbol | Price | 52Wk Range | Yield | P/E |
|---|---|---|---|---|---|
| NYS | TNC | $43.96 (8/31/2011) | 44.25-28.82 | 1.55 | 23.51 |

*7 Year Price Score 129.97 *NYSE Composite Index=100 *12 Month Price Score 108.93

**Interim Earnings (Per Share)**

| Qtr. | Mar | Jun | Sep | Dec |
|---|---|---|---|---|
| 2008 | 0.28 | 0.44 | 0.76 | (0.91) |
| 2009 | (2.29) | 0.16 | 0.31 | 0.36 |
| 2010 | 0.21 | 0.33 | 0.39 | 0.88 |
| 2011 | 0.30 | 0.30 | ... | ... |

**Interim Dividends (Per Share)**

| Amt | Decl | Ex | Rec | Pay |
|---|---|---|---|---|
| 0.17Q | 11/09/2010 | 11/26/2010 | 11/30/2010 | 12/15/2010 |
| 0.17Q | 02/16/2011 | 02/24/2011 | 02/28/2011 | 03/15/2011 |
| 0.17Q | 04/28/2011 | 05/26/2011 | 05/31/2011 | 06/15/2011 |
| 0.17Q | 08/17/2011 | 08/29/2011 | 08/31/2011 | 09/15/2011 |

**Indicated Div: $0.68 (Div. Reinv. Plan)**

**Valuation Analysis**

Forecast EPS $2.00 (09/02/2011)
Market Cap $831.9 Million Book Value $223.4 Million
Price/Book 3.72 Price/Sales 1.15

**Dividend Achiever Status**

**10 Year Growth Rate** 3.96%
**Total Years of Dividend Growth** 38

**Business Summary:** Industrial Machinery & Equipment (MIC: 7.2.1 SIC: 3589 NAIC: 333319)

Tennant is engaged in designing, manufacturing and marketing a range of products used to clean and coat surfaces in factories, office buildings, parking lots and streets, airports, hospitals, schools, warehouses, shopping centers and other retail environments. Co.'s products include: equipment for maintaining surfaces in industrial, commercial and outdoor environments; cleaning technologies; and surface coatings for protecting, repairing and upgrading floors. Co. sells its products through its direct sales and service organization and a network of authorized distributors worldwide. Co.'s customers are located in North America, Latin America, Europe, the Middle East, Africa and Asia Pacific.

**Recent Developments:** For the quarter ended June 30 2011, net income decreased 5.2% to US$5.9 million from US$6.2 million in the year-earlier quarter. Revenues were US$201.3 million, up 21.1% from US$166.1 million the year before. Operating income was US$10.2 million versus US$10.6 million in the prior-year quarter, a decrease of 3.7%. Direct operating expenses rose 24.5% to US$117.8 million from US$94.6 million in the comparable period the year before. Indirect operating expenses increased 20.2% to US$73.2 million from US$60.9 million in the equivalent prior-year period.

**Prospects:** Our evaluation of Tennant Co. as of Sep. 6, 2011 is the result of our systematic analysis on three basic characteristics: earnings strength, relative valuation, and recent stock price movement. The company has produced a positive trend in earnings per share over the past 5 quarters and while recent estimates for the company have remained steady, TNC has posted better than expected results. Based on operating earnings yield, the company is about fairly valued when compared to all of the companies in our coverage universe. Share price changes over the past year indicates that TNC will perform poorly over the near term.

**Financial Data**

| (US$ in Thousands) | 6 Mos | 3 Mos | 12/31/2010 | 12/31/2009 | 12/31/2008 | 12/31/2007 | 12/31/2006 | 12/31/2005 |
|---|---|---|---|---|---|---|---|---|
| Earnings Per Share | 1.87 | 1.90 | 1.80 | (1.42) | 0.57 | 2.08 | 1.57 | 1.26 |
| Cash Flow Per Share | 1.63 | 1.12 | 2.26 | 4.06 | 2.05 | 2.13 | 2.17 | 2.45 |
| Tang Book Value Per Share | 9.25 | 9.32 | 8.95 | 7.19 | 6.51 | 11.78 | 10.60 | 9.21 |
| Dividends Per Share | 0.650 | 0.620 | 0.590 | 0.530 | 0.520 | 0.480 | 0.460 | 0.440 |
| Dividend Payout % | 34.76 | 32.63 | 32.78 | ... | 91.23 | 23.08 | 29.30 | 34.92 |
| **Income Statement** | | | | | | | | |
| Total Revenue | 373,849 | 172,591 | 667,667 | 595,875 | 701,405 | 664,218 | 598,981 | 552,908 |
| EBITDA | 30,204 | 13,973 | 54,239 | (2,251) | 40,837 | 73,657 | 55,052 | 46,906 |
| Depn & Amortn | 10,368 | 5,223 | 18,026 | 19,632 | 20,360 | 16,901 | 13,711 | 13,039 |
| Income Before Taxes | 19,128 | 8,403 | 34,727 | (24,320) | 17,575 | 57,712 | 43,302 | 34,994 |
| Income Taxes | 7,407 | 2,537 | (76) | 1,921 | 6,951 | 17,845 | 13,493 | 12,058 |
| Net Income | 11,721 | 5,866 | 34,803 | (26,241) | 10,624 | 39,867 | 29,809 | 22,936 |
| Average Shares | 19,467 | 19,556 | 19,332 | 18,507 | 18,581 | 19,146 | 18,989 | 18,210 |
| **Balance Sheet** | | | | | | | | |
| Current Assets | 276,092 | 259,794 | 248,269 | 215,912 | 250,419 | 240,724 | 235,404 | 211,601 |
| Total Assets | 429,290 | 412,095 | 403,668 | 377,726 | 456,604 | 382,070 | 354,250 | 311,472 |
| Current Liabilities | 126,618 | 107,485 | 116,144 | 116,152 | 107,159 | 96,673 | 94,804 | 88,965 |
| Long-Term Obligations | 37,254 | 37,087 | 27,674 | 30,192 | 91,393 | 2,470 | 1,907 | 1,608 |
| Total Liabilities | 205,862 | 187,727 | 187,535 | 193,447 | 246,700 | 129,639 | 124,586 | 118,370 |
| Stockholders' Equity | 223,428 | 224,368 | 216,133 | 184,279 | 209,904 | 252,431 | 229,664 | 193,102 |
| Shares Outstanding | 18,922 | 19,143 | 19,038 | 18,750 | 18,284 | 18,499 | 18,753 | 18,382 |
| **Statistical Record** | | | | | | | | |
| Return on Assets % | 9.01 | 9.40 | 8.91 | N.M. | 2.53 | 10.83 | 8.96 | 7.68 |
| Return on Equity % | 17.52 | 17.90 | 17.38 | N.M. | 4.58 | 16.54 | 14.10 | 12.49 |
| EBITDA Margin % | 8.08 | 8.10 | 8.12 | N.M. | 5.82 | 11.09 | 9.19 | 8.48 |
| Net Margin % | 3.14 | 3.40 | 5.21 | N.M. | 1.51 | 6.00 | 4.98 | 4.15 |
| Asset Turnover | 1.80 | 1.77 | 1.71 | 1.43 | 1.67 | 1.80 | 1.80 | 1.85 |
| Current Ratio | 2.18 | 2.42 | 2.14 | 1.86 | 2.34 | 2.49 | 2.48 | 2.38 |
| Debt to Equity | 0.17 | 0.17 | 0.13 | 0.16 | 0.44 | 0.01 | 0.01 | 0.01 |
| Price Range | 43.24-28.82 | 43.24-27.17 | 38.82-21.84 | 31.92-7.74 | 45.41-15.33 | 49.32-27.84 | 29.88-21.70 | 26.00-17.41 |
| P/E Ratio | 23.12-15.41 | 22.76-14.30 | 21.57-12.13 | ... | 79.67-26.89 | 23.71-13.38 | 19.03-13.82 | 20.63-13.82 |
| Average Yield % | 1.78 | 1.76 | 1.86 | 2.61 | 1.65 | 1.27 | 1.78 | 2.20 |

**Address:** 701 North Lilac Drive, P.O. Box 1452, Minneapolis, MN 55440
**Telephone:** 763-540-1200
**Web Site:** www.tennantco.com

**Officers:** H. Chris Killingstad - President, Chief Executive Officer Thomas Poulson - Vice President, Chief Financial Officer **Transfer Agents:** Wells Fargo Bank, N.A., South St. Paul, MN

**Investor Contact:** 763-540-1553
**No of Institutions:** 133
**Shares:** 15,771,895 **% Held:** 79.79

# 3M CO

| Exchange | Symbol | Price | 52Wk Range | Yield | P/E |
|---|---|---|---|---|---|
| NYS | MMM | $82.98 (8/31/2011) | 97.97-76.87 | 2.65 | 14.09 |

***7 Year Price Score 112.75** *NYSE Composite Index=100 ***12 Month Price Score 98.94**

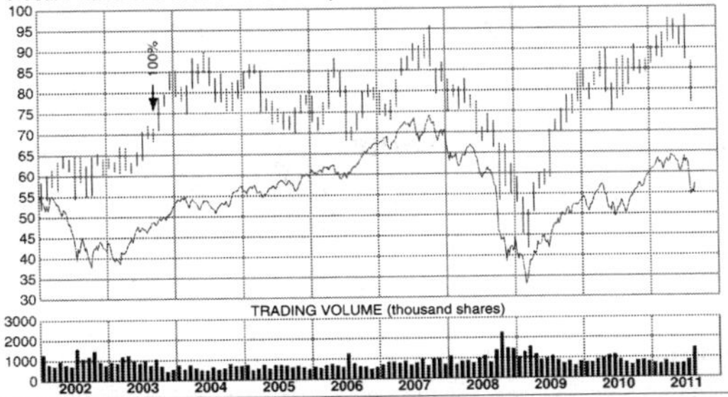


**Interim Earnings (Per Share)**

| Qtr. | Mar | Jun | Sep | Dec |
|---|---|---|---|---|
| 2008 | 1.38 | 1.33 | 1.41 | 0.78 |
| 2009 | 0.74 | 1.12 | 1.35 | 1.31 |
| 2010 | 1.29 | 1.54 | 1.53 | 1.27 |
| 2011 | 1.49 | 1.60 | ... | ... |

**Interim Dividends (Per Share)**

| Amt | Decl | Ex | Rec | Pay |
|---|---|---|---|---|
| 0.525Q | 11/08/2010 | 11/17/2010 | 11/19/2010 | 12/12/2010 |
| 0.55Q | 02/08/2011 | 02/16/2011 | 02/18/2011 | 03/12/2011 |
| 0.55Q | 05/10/2011 | 05/18/2011 | 05/20/2011 | 06/12/2011 |
| 0.55Q | 08/08/2011 | 08/17/2011 | 08/19/2011 | 09/12/2011 |

**Indicated Div: $2.20 (Div. Reinv. Plan)**

**Valuation Analysis**

| | | | |
|---|---|---|---|
| Forecast EPS | $6.20 (09/05/2011) | | |
| Market Cap | $58.9 Billion | Book Value | $17.3 Billion |
| Price/Book | 3.40 | Price/Sales | 2.06 |

**Dividend Achiever Status**

| | |
|---|---|
| **10 Year Growth Rate** | 5.76% |
| **Total Years of Dividend Growth** | 52 |

**Business Summary:** Medical Instruments & Equipment (MIC: 4.3.1 SIC: 3841 NAIC: 339112)

3M manufactures and sells of a range of products. Co. has six segments: Industrial and Transportation, which provides abrasives, adhesives, specialty materials and filtration products; Health Care, which provides medical and surgical supplies, and dental and orthodontic products; Display and Graphics, which includes optical film applications, computer screen filters, and reflective sheeting; Consumer and Office, which include office supply and stationery products; Safety, Security and Protection Services, which provides personal protection and safety and security products; and Electro and Communications, which include electronic and interconnect applications and telecommunications products.

**Recent Developments:** For the quarter ended June 30 2011, net income increased 3.2% to US$1.18 billion from US$1.14 billion in the year-earlier quarter. Revenues were US$7.68 billion, up 14.1% from US$6.73 billion the year before. Operating income was US$1.66 billion versus US$1.60 billion in the prior-year quarter, an increase of 3.7%. Direct operating expenses rose 17.6% to US$4.04 billion from US$3.44 billion in the comparable period the year before. Indirect operating expenses increased 16.8% to US$1.99 billion from US$1.70 billion in the equivalent prior-year period.

**Prospects:** Our evaluation of 3M Co as of Sep. 6, 2011 is the result of our systematic analysis on three basic characteristics: earnings strength, relative valuation, and recent stock price movement. The company has managed to produce a neutral trend in earnings per share over the past 5 quarters. However, while recent estimates for the company have been lowered by analysts, MMM has posted better than expected results. Based on operating earnings yield, the company is undervalued when compared to all of the companies in our coverage universe. Share price changes over the past year indicates that MMM will perform poorly over the near term.

| **Financial Data** (US$ in Millions) | 6 Mos | 3 Mos | 12/31/2010 | 12/31/2009 | 12/31/2008 | 12/31/2007 | 12/31/2006 | 12/31/2005 |
|---|---|---|---|---|---|---|---|---|
| Earnings Per Share | 5.89 | 5.83 | 5.63 | 4.52 | 4.89 | 5.60 | 5.06 | 4.12 |
| Cash Flow Per Share | 7.20 | 6.78 | 7.25 | 7.05 | 6.47 | 5.95 | 5.14 | 5.57 |
| Tang Book Value Per Share | 11.38 | 10.37 | 9.86 | 7.87 | 3.93 | 8.96 | 7.04 | 8.14 |
| Dividends Per Share | 2.150 | 2.125 | 2.100 | 2.040 | 2.000 | 1.920 | 1.840 | 1.680 |
| Dividend Payout % | 36.50 | 36.45 | 37.30 | 45.13 | 40.90 | 34.29 | 36.36 | 40.78 |
| **Income Statement** | | | | | | | | |
| Total Revenue | 14,991 | 7,311 | 26,662 | 23,123 | 25,269 | 24,462 | 22,923 | 21,167 |
| EBITDA | 3,841 | 1,867 | 7,038 | 5,971 | 6,371 | 7,265 | 6,775 | 5,995 |
| Depn & Amortn | 608 | 289 | 1,120 | 1,157 | 1,153 | 1,072 | 1,079 | 986 |
| Income Before Taxes | 3,159 | 1,545 | 5,755 | 4,632 | 5,108 | 6,115 | 5,625 | 4,983 |
| Income Taxes | 879 | 442 | 1,592 | 1,388 | 1,588 | 1,964 | 1,723 | 1,694 |
| Net Income | 2,241 | 1,081 | 4,085 | 3,193 | 3,460 | 4,096 | 3,851 | 3,199 |
| Average Shares | 726 | 726 | 725 | 706 | 707 | 732 | 761 | 776 |
| **Balance Sheet** | | | | | | | | |
| Current Assets | 13,537 | 12,645 | 12,215 | 10,795 | 9,598 | 9,838 | 8,946 | 7,115 |
| Total Assets | 32,282 | 31,129 | 30,156 | 27,250 | 25,547 | 24,694 | 21,294 | 20,513 |
| Current Liabilities | 6,203 | 5,900 | 6,089 | 4,897 | 5,839 | 5,362 | 7,323 | 5,238 |
| Long-Term Obligations | 4,484 | 4,486 | 4,277 | 5,204 | 5,224 | 4,088 | 1,112 | 1,368 |
| Total Liabilities | 14,952 | 14,635 | 14,493 | 14,486 | 15,668 | 12,947 | 11,335 | 10,413 |
| Stockholders' Equity | 17,330 | 16,494 | 15,663 | 12,764 | 9,879 | 11,747 | 9,959 | 10,100 |
| Shares Outstanding | 709 | 710 | 711 | 710 | 693 | 709 | 734 | 754 |
| **Statistical Record** | | | | | | | | |
| Return on Assets % | 14.07 | 14.32 | 14.23 | 12.10 | 13.74 | 17.81 | 18.42 | 15.52 |
| Return on Equity % | 27.32 | 28.18 | 28.74 | 28.20 | 31.91 | 37.74 | 38.40 | 31.24 |
| EBITDA Margin % | 25.62 | 25.54 | 26.40 | 25.82 | 25.21 | 29.70 | 29.56 | 28.32 |
| Net Margin % | 14.95 | 14.79 | 15.32 | 13.81 | 13.69 | 16.74 | 16.80 | 15.11 |
| Asset Turnover | 0.94 | 0.93 | 0.93 | 0.88 | 1.00 | 1.06 | 1.10 | 1.03 |
| Current Ratio | 2.18 | 2.14 | 2.01 | 2.20 | 1.64 | 1.83 | 1.22 | 1.36 |
| Debt to Equity | 0.26 | 0.27 | 0.27 | 0.41 | 0.53 | 0.35 | 0.11 | 0.14 |
| Price Range | 97.23-77.67 | 93.75-74.74 | 90.90-74.74 | 84.13-41.83 | 84.32-53.50 | 95.85-73.01 | 88.13-68.11 | 86.80-70.07 |
| P/E Ratio | 16.51-13.19 | 16.08-12.82 | 16.15-13.28 | 18.61-9.25 | 17.24-10.94 | 17.12-13.04 | 17.42-13.46 | 21.07-17.01 |
| Average Yield % | 2.43 | 2.48 | 2.51 | 3.19 | 2.79 | 2.29 | 2.39 | 2.16 |

**Address:** 3M Center, St. Paul, MN 55144
**Telephone:** 651-733-1110
**Web Site:** www.3M.com

**Officers:** George W. Buckley - Chairman, President, Chief Executive Officer Frederick J. Palensky - Executive Vice President, Chief Technology Officer
**Transfer Agents:** Wells Fargo Shareowner Services, St. Paul, MN

**Investor Contact:** 651-733-8206
**No of Institutions:** 1597
**Shares:** 538,258,304 **% Held:** 68.72

# TJX COMPANIES, INC.

| Exchange | Symbol | Price | 52Wk Range | Yield | P/E |
|---|---|---|---|---|---|
| NYS | TJX | $54.62 (8/31/2011) | 56.33-39.69 | 1.39 | 16.40 |

*7 Year Price Score 151.07 *NYSE Composite Index=100 *12 Month Price Score 111.35

**Interim Earnings (Per Share)**

| Qtr. | Apr | Jul | Oct | Jan |
|---|---|---|---|---|
| 2008-09 | 0.43 | 0.45 | 0.54 | 0.58 |
| 2009-10 | 0.49 | 0.61 | 0.81 | 0.93 |
| 2010-11 | 0.80 | 0.74 | 0.92 | 0.84 |
| 2011-12 | 0.67 | 0.90 | ... | ... |

**Interim Dividends (Per Share)**

| Amt | Decl | Ex | Rec | Pay |
|---|---|---|---|---|
| 0.15Q | 09/09/2010 | 11/08/2010 | 11/11/2010 | 12/02/2010 |
| 0.15Q | 11/30/2010 | 02/08/2011 | 02/10/2011 | 03/03/2011 |
| 0.19Q | 04/05/2011 | 05/10/2011 | 05/12/2011 | 06/02/2011 |
| 0.19Q | 06/14/2011 | 08/09/2011 | 08/11/2011 | 09/01/2011 |

**Indicated Div: $0.76**

**Valuation Analysis**

| | | | |
|---|---|---|---|
| Forecast EPS | $3.97 (09/03/2011) | | |
| Market Cap | $20.8 Billion | Book Value | $3.1 Billion |
| Price/Book | 6.70 | Price/Sales | 0.92 |

**Dividend Achiever Status**

| | |
|---|---|
| **10 Year Growth Rate** | 20.61% |
| **Total Years of Dividend Growth** | 14 |

**Business Summary:** Retail - Apparel and Accessories (MIC: 2.1.5 SIC: 5651 NAIC: 448140)

TJX Companies is an apparel and home fashions retailer. In the U.S., Co.'s retail chains include T.J. Maxx and Marshalls and HomeGoods. Outside the U.S., Co.'s store chains are Winners, Marshalls and HomeSense in Canada, as well as T.K. Maxx and HomeSense in Europe. As of Jan 29 2011, Co. operated five business segments: three in the U.S. and one in each of Canada and Europe. As of the same date, Co. operated a total of 2,859 stores, which consisted of 923 T.J. Maxx stores, 830 Marshalls stores, 336 HomeGoods stores and 142 A.J. Wright Stores in the U.S., as well as 215 Winners stores and 82 HomeSense stores in Canada, along with 307 T.K. Maxx stores and 24 HomeSense stores in Europe.

**Recent Developments:** For the quarter ended July 30 2011, net income increased 14.2% to US$348.3 million from US$305.0 million in the year-earlier quarter. Revenues were US$5.47 billion, up 7.9% from US$5.07 billion the year before. Direct operating expenses rose 6.9% to US$3.98 billion from US$3.72 billion in the comparable period the year before. Indirect operating expenses increased 9.7% to US$923.7 million from US$842.3 million in the equivalent prior-year period.

**Prospects:** Our evaluation of TJX Companies Inc. as of Sep. 6, 2011 is the result of our systematic analysis on three basic characteristics: earnings strength, relative valuation, and recent stock price movement. The company has produced a positive trend in earnings per share over the past 5 quarters and while recent estimates for the company have been raised by analysts, TJX has posted better than expected results. Based on operating earnings yield, the company is undervalued when compared to all of the companies in our coverage universe. Share price changes over the past year indicates that TJX will perform poorly over the near term.

**Financial Data**

| (US$ in Thousands) | 6 Mos | 3 Mos | 01/29/2011 | 01/30/2010 | 01/31/2009 | 01/26/2008 | 01/27/2007 | 01/28/2006 |
|---|---|---|---|---|---|---|---|---|
| Earnings Per Share | 3.33 | 3.17 | 3.30 | 2.84 | 2.00 | 1.66 | 1.55 | 1.41 |
| Cash Flow Per Share | 4.28 | 4.10 | 4.95 | 5.45 | 2.71 | 3.08 | 2.64 | 2.49 |
| Tang Book Value Per Share | 7.68 | 7.62 | 7.49 | 6.62 | 4.74 | 4.56 | 4.65 | 3.71 |
| Dividends Per Share | 0.640 | 0.600 | 0.570 | 0.470 | 0.420 | 0.340 | 0.270 | 0.225 |
| Dividend Payout % | 19.22 | 18.93 | 17.27 | 16.55 | 21.00 | 20.48 | 17.42 | 15.96 |
| **Income Statement** | | | | | | | | |
| Total Revenue | 10,688,569 | 5,220,295 | 21,942,193 | 20,288,444 | 18,999,505 | 18,647,126 | 17,404,637 | 16,057,935 |
| EBITDA | 1,243,551 | 554,791 | 2,205,429 | 1,993,271 | 1,467,431 | 1,243,291 | 1,264,614 | 1,444,434 |
| Depn & Amortn | 236,442 | 116,228 | 2,200 | 2,200 | 2,200 | 2,200 | 2,200 | 405,475 |
| Income Before Taxes | 989,083 | 429,646 | 2,164,092 | 1,951,562 | 1,450,940 | 1,242,689 | 1,246,848 | 1,009,327 |
| Income Taxes | 374,794 | 163,695 | 824,562 | 737,990 | 536,054 | 470,939 | 470,092 | 318,904 |
| Net Income | 614,289 | 265,951 | 1,343,141 | 1,213,572 | 880,617 | 771,750 | 738,039 | 690,423 |
| Average Shares | 387,625 | 394,004 | 406,413 | 427,619 | 442,255 | 468,046 | 480,045 | 491,500 |
| **Balance Sheet** | | | | | | | | |
| Current Assets | 5,029,069 | 5,008,421 | 5,099,527 | 4,803,856 | 3,626,129 | 3,992,294 | 3,748,813 | 3,140,127 |
| Total Assets | 8,097,126 | 7,984,470 | 7,971,763 | 7,463,977 | 6,178,242 | 6,599,934 | 6,085,700 | 5,496,305 |
| Current Liabilities | 3,191,344 | 3,101,855 | 3,133,121 | 2,894,986 | 2,767,891 | 2,760,993 | 2,382,980 | 2,251,851 |
| Long-Term Obligations | 786,100 | 786,816 | 787,517 | 790,169 | 383,782 | 853,460 | 808,027 | 807,150 |
| Total Liabilities | 4,992,137 | 4,861,076 | 4,871,864 | 4,574,701 | 4,043,685 | 4,468,689 | 3,795,579 | 3,603,651 |
| Stockholders' Equity | 3,104,989 | 3,123,394 | 3,099,899 | 2,889,276 | 2,134,557 | 2,131,245 | 2,290,121 | 1,892,654 |
| Shares Outstanding | 380,980 | 386,107 | 389,657 | 409,386 | 412,821 | 427,949 | 453,649 | 460,967 |
| **Statistical Record** | | | | | | | | |
| Return on Assets % | 16.74 | 16.24 | 17.45 | 17.84 | 13.56 | 12.20 | 12.78 | 13.10 |
| Return on Equity % | 43.46 | 41.46 | 44.98 | 48.45 | 40.62 | 35.01 | 35.39 | 39.05 |
| EBITDA Margin % | 11.63 | 10.63 | 10.05 | 9.82 | 7.72 | 6.67 | 7.27 | 9.00 |
| Net Margin % | 5.75 | 5.09 | 6.12 | 5.98 | 4.63 | 4.14 | 4.24 | 4.30 |
| Asset Turnover | 2.86 | 2.81 | 2.85 | 2.98 | 2.93 | 2.95 | 3.01 | 3.05 |
| Current Ratio | 1.58 | 1.61 | 1.63 | 1.66 | 1.31 | 1.45 | 1.57 | 1.39 |
| Debt to Equity | 0.25 | 0.25 | 0.25 | 0.27 | 0.18 | 0.40 | 0.35 | 0.43 |
| Price Range | 56.33-39.69 | 53.72-39.69 | 48.61-37.52 | 40.22-19.47 | 37.00-18.42 | 31.87-26.00 | 30.04-22.23 | 25.89-20.26 |
| P/E Ratio | 16.92-11.92 | 16.95-12.52 | 14.73-11.37 | 14.16-6.86 | 18.50-9.21 | 19.20-15.66 | 19.38-14.34 | 18.36-14.37 |
| Average Yield % | 1.34 | 1.31 | 1.30 | 1.44 | 1.43 | 1.19 | 1.03 | 0.97 |

**Address:** 770 Cochituate Road, Framingham, MA 01701
**Telephone:** 508-390-1000
**Web Site:** www.tjx.com

**Officers:** Bernard Cammarata - Chairman Ernie Herrman - President **Transfer Agents:** BNY Mellon Shareowner Services, Pittsburgh, PA

**Investor Contact:** 508-390-2323
**No of Institutions:** 836
**Shares:** 393,727,744 % **Held:** 84.15

# TOOTSIE ROLL INDUSTRIES INC

| Exchange | Symbol | Price | 52Wk Range | Yield | P/E |
|---|---|---|---|---|---|
| NYS | TR | $25.34 (8/31/2011) | 29.80-22.92 | 1.26 | 29.47 |

*7 Year Price Score 107.83 *NYSE Composite Index=100 *12 Month Price Score 102.07

**Interim Earnings (Per Share)**

| Qtr. | Mar | Jun | Sep | Dec |
|---|---|---|---|---|
| 2008 | 0.11 | 0.12 | 0.33 | 0.08 |
| 2009 | 0.14 | 0.17 | 0.46 | 0.12 |
| 2010 | 0.16 | 0.15 | 0.47 | 0.15 |
| 2011 | 0.14 | 0.11 | ... | ... |

**Interim Dividends (Per Share)**

| Amt | Decl | Ex | Rec | Pay |
|---|---|---|---|---|
| 0.078Q | 12/07/2010 | 12/16/2010 | 12/20/2010 | 01/03/2011 |
| 3% | 02/22/2011 | 03/04/2011 | 03/08/2011 | 04/07/2011 |
| 0.078Q | 02/22/2011 | 03/04/2011 | 03/08/2011 | 03/30/2011 |
| 0.08Q | 06/13/2011 | 06/21/2011 | 06/23/2011 | 07/08/2011 |

**Indicated Div: $0.32**

**Valuation Analysis**

| | | | |
|---|---|---|---|
| Forecast EPS | $0.89 (09/02/2011) | | |
| Market Cap | $1.5 Billion | Book Value | $663.9 Million |
| Price/Book | 2.21 | Price/Sales | 2.79 |

**Dividend Achiever Status**

| | |
|---|---|
| **10 Year Growth Rate** | 4.08% |
| **Total Years of Dividend Growth** | 47 |

**Business Summary:** Food (MIC: 1.2.1 SIC: 2064 NAIC: 311340)

Tootsie Roll Industries and its consolidated subsidiaries are engaged in the manufacture and sale of confectionery products. The majority of the Company's products are sold under the TOOTSIE ROLL, TOOTSIE ROLL POPS, CHILD'S PLAY, CARAMEL APPLE POPS, CHARMS, BLOW-POP, BLUE RAZZ, ZIP-A-DEE POPS, CELLA'S, MASON DOTS, MASON CROWS, JUNIOR MINT, CHARLESTON CHEW, SUGAR DADDY, SUGAR BABIES, ANDES, FLUFFY STUFF, DUBBLE BUBBLE, RAZZLES, CRY BABY and NIK-L-NIP registered trademarks. At Dec 31 2010, Co.'s products were distributed through about 100 candy and grocery brokers and by Co. to customers throughout the U.S. Co.'s principal markets are in the U.S., Canada and Mexico.

**Recent Developments:** For the quarter ended July 2 2011, net income decreased 27.0% to US$6.2 million from US$8.4 million in the year-earlier quarter. Revenues were US$105.8 million, down 0.2% from US$106.0 million the year before. Operating income was US$7.9 million versus US$13.9 million in the prior-year quarter, a decrease of 42.9%. Direct operating expenses rose 3.0% to US$71.7 million from US$69.6 million in the comparable period the year before. Indirect operating expenses increased 16.1% to US$26.2 million from US$22.5 million in the equivalent prior-year period.

**Prospects:** Our evaluation of Tootsie Roll Industries Inc. as of Sep. 6, 2011 is the result of our systematic analysis on three basic characteristics: earnings strength, relative valuation, and recent stock price movement. The company has enjoyed a very positive trend in earnings per share over the past 5 quarters and while recent estimates for the company have remained steady, TR has posted results that fell short of analysts expectations. Based on operating earnings yield, the company is overvalued when compared to all of the companies in our coverage universe. Share price changes over the past year indicates that TR will perform in line with the market over the near term.

| **Financial Data** (US$ in Thousands) | 6 Mos | 3 Mos | 12/31/2010 | 12/31/2009 | 12/31/2008 | 12/31/2007 | 12/31/2006 | 12/31/2005 |
|---|---|---|---|---|---|---|---|---|
| Earnings Per Share | 0.86 | 0.90 | 0.91 | 0.90 | 0.64 | 0.84 | 1.05 | 1.24 |
| Cash Flow Per Share | 1.25 | 1.47 | 1.41 | 1.27 | 0.94 | 1.46 | 0.89 | 1.33 |
| Tang Book Value Per Share | 7.18 | 7.21 | 7.23 | 6.85 | 6.20 | 6.16 | 5.90 | 5.74 |
| Dividends Per Share | 0.313 | 0.311 | 0.308 | 0.299 | 0.291 | 0.282 | 0.274 | 0.241 |
| Dividend Payout % | 36.33 | 34.63 | 33.80 | 33.44 | 45.38 | 33.80 | 26.04 | 19.42 |
| **Income Statement** | | | | | | | | |
| Total Revenue | 215,215 | 109,395 | 521,448 | 499,331 | 496,016 | 497,717 | 495,990 | 487,739 |
| EBITDA | 21,547 | 12,281 | 92,510 | 86,917 | 73,800 | 93,379 | 110,336 | 129,958 |
| Depn & Amortn | 513 | 169 | 18,279 | 17,862 | 17,036 | 15,859 | 15,816 | 14,687 |
| Income Before Taxes | 21,034 | 12,112 | 74,089 | 68,812 | 56,386 | 76,985 | 93,794 | 112,734 |
| Income Taxes | 6,869 | 4,112 | 20,375 | 10,704 | 17,132 | 25,542 | 28,796 | 36,425 |
| Net Income | 14,165 | 8,000 | 53,714 | 53,475 | 38,777 | 51,625 | 65,919 | 77,227 |
| Average Shares | 58,012 | 58,093 | 58,706 | 59,486 | 60,271 | 61,880 | 62,826 | 62,069 |
| **Balance Sheet** | | | | | | | | |
| Current Assets | 200,989 | 216,202 | 237,591 | 211,878 | 187,979 | 199,726 | 190,917 | 246,596 |
| Total Assets | 858,910 | 857,474 | 860,383 | 838,247 | 812,092 | 812,725 | 791,639 | 813,696 |
| Current Liabilities | 59,701 | 56,035 | 58,505 | 56,066 | 59,252 | 57,972 | 62,211 | 113,656 |
| Long-Term Obligations | 7,500 | 7,500 | 7,500 | 7,500 | 7,500 | 7,500 | 7,500 | 7,500 |
| Total Liabilities | 195,009 | 189,835 | 191,429 | 185,762 | 177,322 | 174,495 | 160,958 | 196,291 |
| Stockholders' Equity | 663,901 | 667,639 | 668,954 | 652,485 | 634,770 | 638,230 | 630,681 | 617,405 |
| Shares Outstanding | 57,859 | 58,137 | 58,147 | 59,043 | 60,045 | 61,039 | 62,243 | 61,667 |
| **Statistical Record** | | | | | | | | |
| Return on Assets % | 5.93 | 6.18 | 6.32 | 6.48 | 4.76 | 6.44 | 8.21 | 9.50 |
| Return on Equity % | 7.67 | 7.96 | 8.13 | 8.31 | 6.08 | 8.14 | 10.56 | 13.01 |
| EBITDA Margin % | 10.01 | 11.23 | 17.74 | 17.41 | 14.88 | 18.76 | 22.25 | 26.64 |
| Net Margin % | 6.58 | 7.31 | 10.30 | 10.71 | 7.82 | 10.37 | 13.29 | 15.83 |
| Asset Turnover | 0.62 | 0.62 | 0.61 | 0.61 | 0.61 | 0.62 | 0.62 | 0.60 |
| Current Ratio | 3.37 | 3.86 | 4.06 | 3.78 | 3.17 | 3.45 | 3.07 | 2.17 |
| Debt to Equity | 0.01 | 0.01 | 0.01 | 0.01 | 0.01 | 0.01 | 0.01 | 0.01 |
| Price Range | 29.68-22.66 | 28.97-22.66 | 28.97-22.66 | 26.45-18.09 | 28.69-19.63 | 28.20-20.92 | 28.69-22.73 | 28.16-24.23 |
| P/E Ratio | 34.51-26.35 | 32.19-25.18 | 31.84-24.90 | 29.39-20.10 | 44.83-30.67 | 33.57-24.91 | 27.32-21.65 | 22.71-19.54 |
| Average Yield % | 1.18 | 1.21 | 1.22 | 1.34 | 1.25 | 1.14 | 1.08 | 0.94 |

**Address:** 7401 South Cicero Avenue, Chicago, IL 60629
**Telephone:** 773-838-3400
**Web Site:** www.tootsie.com

**Officers:** Melvin J. Gordon - Chairman, Chief Executive Officer Ellen R. Gordon - President, Chief Operating Officer **Transfer Agents:** American Stock & Trust Company, New York, NY

**No of Institutions:** 154
**Shares:** 14,654,265 **% Held:** 24.75

# TRANSATLANTIC HOLDINGS, INC.

| Exchange | Symbol | Price | 52Wk Range | Yield | P/E |
|---|---|---|---|---|---|
| NYS | TRH | $50.63 (8/31/2011) | 54.00-44.01 | 1.74 | 20.17 |

***7 Year Price Score 87.65** *NYSE Composite Index=100 ***12 Month Price Score 99.98**

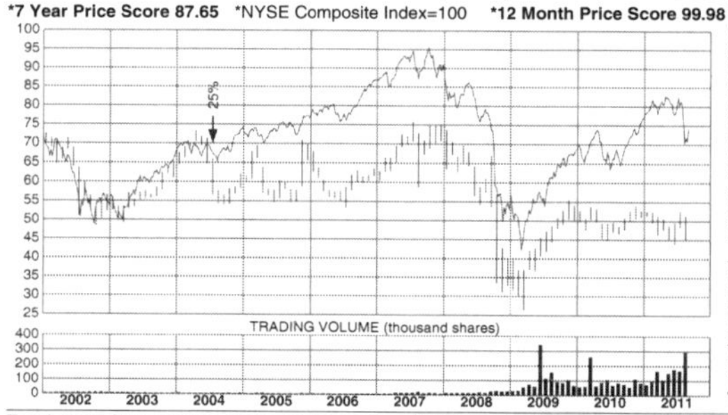


**Interim Earnings (Per Share)**

| Qtr. | Mar | Jun | Sep | Dec |
|---|---|---|---|---|
| 2008 | 1.73 | 1.34 | (1.62) | 0.06 |
| 2009 | 1.13 | 1.68 | 2.28 | 2.05 |
| 2010 | 0.24 | 1.70 | 2.08 | 2.20 |
| 2011 | (3.05) | 1.28 | ... | ... |

**Interim Dividends (Per Share)**

| Amt | Decl | Ex | Rec | Pay |
|---|---|---|---|---|
| 0.21Q | 09/30/2010 | 11/17/2010 | 11/19/2010 | 12/03/2010 |
| 0.21Q | 12/16/2010 | 02/25/2011 | 03/01/2011 | 03/15/2011 |
| 0.21Q | 03/17/2011 | 06/01/2011 | 06/03/2011 | 06/17/2011 |
| 0.22Q | 05/26/2011 | 08/31/2011 | 09/02/2011 | 09/16/2011 |

**Indicated Div: $0.88**

**Valuation Analysis**

Forecast EPS $0.75 (09/02/2011)

| | | | |
|---|---|---|---|
| Market Cap | $3.2 Billion | Book Value | $4.2 Billion |
| Price/Book | 0.75 | Price/Sales | 0.73 |

**Dividend Achiever Status**

**10 Year Growth Rate** 10.67%

**Total Years of Dividend Growth** 20

**Business Summary:** General Insurance (MIC: 5.2.1 SIC: 6331 NAIC: 524126)

Transatlantic Holdings is a holding company. Through its wholly-owned subsidiaries, Transatlantic Reinsurance Company®, Trans Re Zurich Reinsurance Company Ltd., and Putnam Reinsurance Company, Co. provides reinsurance capacity for a range of property and casualty products, directly and through brokers, to insurance and reinsurance companies, in both the domestic and international markets on both a treaty and facultative basis. Co. provides two types of reinsurance based on the underlying insurance coverage: casualty insurance and property insurance. Co. provides reinsurance for most major lines of insurance on both pro rata and excess-of-loss bases.

**Recent Developments:** For the quarter ended June 30 2011, net income decreased 26.8% to US$80.9 million from US$110.5 million in the year-earlier quarter. Revenues were US$1.07 billion, down 2.2% from US$1.10 billion the year before. Net premiums earned were US$954.9 million versus US$973.8 million in the prior-year quarter, a decrease of 1.9%. Net investment income rose 3.2% to US$119.5 million from US$115.8 million a year ago.

**Prospects:** Our evaluation of Transatlantic Holdings Inc. as of Sep. 6, 2011 is the result of our systematic analysis on three basic characteristics: earnings strength, relative valuation, and recent stock price movement. The company has managed to produce a neutral trend in earnings per share over the past 5 quarters and while recent estimates for the company have been raised by analysts, TRH has posted results that fell short of analysts expectations. Based on operating earnings yield, the company is overvalued when compared to all of the companies in our coverage universe. Share price changes over the past year indicates that TRH will perform very poorly over the near term.

**Financial Data**

| (US$ in Thousands) | 6 Mos | 3 Mos | 12/31/2010 | 12/31/2009 | 12/31/2008 | 12/31/2007 | 12/31/2006 | 12/31/2005 |
|---|---|---|---|---|---|---|---|---|
| Earnings Per Share | 2.51 | 2.93 | 6.19 | 7.15 | 1.53 | 7.31 | 6.46 | 0.57 |
| Cash Flow Per Share | 16.08 | 16.42 | 16.55 | 14.33 | 16.50 | 15.53 | 12.82 | 9.57 |
| Tang Book Value Per Share | 67.76 | 64.69 | 68.83 | 60.77 | 48.19 | 50.56 | 44.80 | 38.60 |
| Dividends Per Share | 0.840 | 0.830 | 0.820 | 0.780 | 0.700 | 0.590 | 0.510 | 0.440 |
| Dividend Payout % | 33.47 | 28.33 | 13.25 | 10.91 | 45.75 | 8.07 | 7.89 | 77.19 |
| **Income Statement** | | | | | | | | |
| Premium Income | 1,911,758 | 956,829 | 3,858,620 | 4,039,082 | 4,067,389 | 3,902,669 | 3,604,094 | 3,384,994 |
| Total Revenue | 2,191,573 | 1,117,902 | 4,362,153 | 4,445,712 | 4,082,549 | 4,381,830 | 4,049,496 | 3,768,125 |
| Benefits & Claims | 1,850,178 | 1,169,052 | 2,681,774 | 2,679,171 | 2,907,227 | 2,638,033 | 2,462,666 | 2,877,042 |
| Income Before Taxes | (226,025) | (320,762) | 472,788 | 596,033 | 3,223 | 595,752 | 539,908 | (46,098) |
| Income Taxes | (116,755) | (130,610) | 70,587 | 118,371 | (99,031) | 108,611 | 111,756 | (84,008) |
| Net Income | (109,270) | (190,152) | 402,201 | 477,662 | 102,254 | 487,141 | 428,152 | 37,910 |
| Average Shares | 63,340 | 62,365 | 64,930 | 66,802 | 66,722 | 66,654 | 66,266 | 66,169 |
| **Balance Sheet** | | | | | | | | |
| Total Assets | 16,706,353 | 16,335,382 | 15,705,354 | 14,943,659 | 13,376,938 | 15,484,327 | 14,268,464 | 12,364,676 |
| Total Liabilities | 12,472,421 | 12,294,009 | 11,420,895 | 10,909,279 | 10,178,718 | 12,135,285 | 11,310,194 | 9,820,725 |
| Stockholders' Equity | 4,233,932 | 4,041,373 | 4,284,459 | 4,034,380 | 3,198,220 | 3,349,042 | 2,958,270 | 2,543,951 |
| Shares Outstanding | 62,483 | 62,475 | 62,248 | 66,382 | 66,364 | 66,233 | 66,037 | 65,911 |
| **Statistical Record** | | | | | | | | |
| Return on Assets % | 1.04 | 1.25 | 2.62 | 3.37 | 0.71 | 3.27 | 3.22 | 0.33 |
| Return on Equity % | 4.02 | 4.89 | 9.67 | 13.21 | 3.12 | 15.45 | 15.56 | 1.48 |
| Loss Ratio % | 96.78 | 122.18 | 69.50 | 66.33 | 71.48 | 67.60 | 68.33 | 84.99 |
| Net Margin % | (4.99) | (17.01) | 9.22 | 10.74 | 2.50 | 11.12 | 10.57 | 1.01 |
| Price Range | 54.00-44.01 | 54.00-44.74 | 54.00-44.74 | 55.59-26.52 | 73.70-31.16 | 75.78-58.84 | 68.00-53.28 | 70.94-54.60 |
| P/E Ratio | 21.51-17.53 | 18.43-15.27 | 8.72-7.23 | 7.77-3.71 | 48.17-20.37 | 10.37-8.05 | 10.53-8.25 | 124.46-95.79 |
| Average Yield % | 1.69 | 1.66 | 1.64 | 1.79 | 1.22 | 0.85 | 0.85 | 0.72 |

**Address:** 80 Pine Street, New York, NY 10005
**Telephone:** 212-365-2200
**Web Site:** www.transre.com

**Officers:** Robert F. Orlich - Chairman, President, Chief Executive Officer Kenneth Apfel - Executive Vice President, Chief Actuary **Transfer Agents:** American Stock Transfer & Trust Company, New York, NY

**Investor Contact:** 212-770-2040
**No of Institutions:** 317
**Shares:** 61,476,772 **% Held:** 95.44

# UMB FINANCIAL CORP

| Exchange | Symbol | Price | 52Wk Range | Yield | P/E |
|---|---|---|---|---|---|
| NMS | UMBF | $38.78 (8/31/2011) | 45.20-31.88 | 2.01 | 15.76 |

***7 Year Price Score 102.25** *NYSE Composite Index=100 ***12 Month Price Score 103.65**

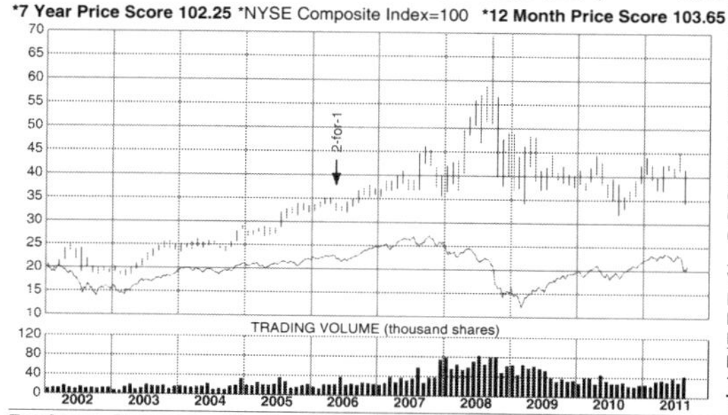

**Interim Earnings (Per Share)**

| Qtr. | Mar | Jun | Sep | Dec |
|---|---|---|---|---|
| 2008 | 0.78 | 0.58 | 0.53 | 0.49 |
| 2009 | 0.55 | 0.47 | 0.59 | 0.59 |
| 2010 | 0.65 | 0.57 | 0.57 | 0.48 |
| 2011 | 0.76 | 0.65 | ... | ... |

**Interim Dividends (Per Share)**

| Amt | Decl | Ex | Rec | Pay |
|---|---|---|---|---|
| 0.195Q | 10/26/2010 | 12/08/2010 | 12/10/2010 | 12/30/2010 |
| 0.195Q | 01/26/2011 | 03/09/2011 | 03/11/2011 | 04/01/2011 |
| 0.195Q | 04/26/2011 | 06/08/2011 | 06/10/2011 | 07/01/2011 |
| 0.195Q | 07/26/2011 | 09/07/2011 | 09/09/2011 | 10/03/2011 |

**Indicated Div: $0.78 (Div. Reinv. Plan)**

**Valuation Analysis**

| | | | |
|---|---|---|---|
| Forecast EPS | $2.70 (09/03/2011) | | |
| Market Cap | $1.6 Billion | Book Value | $1.1 Billion |
| Price/Book | 1.39 | Price/Sales | N/A |

**Dividend Achiever Status**

| | |
|---|---|
| 10 Year Growth Rate | 9.39% |
| Total Years of Dividend Growth | 19 |

**Business Summary:** Banking (MIC: 5.1.1 SIC: 6021 NAIC: 522110)

UMB Financial is a bank holding company. Co. owns all of the outstanding stock of four commercial banks and 19 other subsidiaries. These banks are engaged in providing a range of banking services to commercial, retail, government and correspondent bank customers. In addition, Co.'s UMB Bank, n.a. subsidiary provides international banking services, investment and cash management services, and a range of trust activities for individuals, estates, business corporations, governmental bodies and public authorities. Co. has three segments: Commercial Financial Services, Institutional Financial Services and Personal Financial Services. As of Dec 31 2010, Co. had total assets of $12.40 billion.

**Recent Developments:** For the quarter ended June 30 2011, net income increased 14.4% to US$26.3 million from US$23.0 million in the year-earlier quarter. Net interest income increased 2.9% to US$79.9 million from US$77.7 million in the year-earlier quarter. Provision for loan losses was US$5.6 million versus US$8.1 million in the prior-year quarter, a decrease of 30.9%. Non-interest income rose 21.1% to US$107.9 million from US$89.1 million, while non-interest expense advanced 15.4% to US$145.6 million.

**Prospects:** Our evaluation of UMB Financial Corp. as of Sep. 6, 2011 is the result of our systematic analysis on three basic characteristics: earnings strength, relative valuation, and recent stock price movement. The company has produced a positive trend in earnings per share over the past 5 quarters. However, while recent estimates for the company have been lowered by analysts, UMBF has posted better than expected results. Based on operating earnings yield, the company is undervalued when compared to all of the companies in our coverage universe. Share price changes over the past year indicates that UMBF will perform well over the near term.

**Financial Data**

| (US$ in Thousands) | 6 Mos | 3 Mos | 12/31/2010 | 12/31/2009 | 12/31/2008 | 12/31/2007 | 12/31/2006 | 12/31/2005 |
|---|---|---|---|---|---|---|---|---|
| Earnings Per Share | 2.46 | 2.38 | 2.26 | 2.20 | 2.38 | 1.77 | 1.40 | 1.30 |
| Cash Flow Per Share | 5.14 | 5.13 | 4.49 | 3.64 | 3.28 | 3.15 | 3.02 | 2.44 |
| Tang Book Value Per Share | 20.49 | 19.24 | 18.73 | 20.69 | 20.80 | 18.86 | 17.41 | 17.91 |
| Dividends Per Share | 0.770 | 0.760 | 0.750 | 0.710 | 0.655 | 0.570 | 0.515 | 0.455 |
| Dividend Payout % | 31.30 | 31.93 | 33.19 | 32.27 | 27.52 | 32.20 | 36.79 | 35.00 |
| **Income Statement** | | | | | | | | |
| Interest Income | 172,524 | 85,973 | 346,507 | 356,217 | 387,973 | 414,413 | 369,083 | 271,911 |
| Interest Expense | 14,158 | 7,525 | 35,894 | 53,232 | 112,922 | 181,729 | 151,859 | 83,621 |
| Net Interest Income | 158,366 | 78,448 | 310,613 | 302,985 | 275,051 | 232,684 | 217,224 | 188,290 |
| Provision for Losses | 12,700 | 7,100 | 31,510 | 32,100 | 17,850 | 9,333 | 8,734 | 5,775 |
| Non-Interest Income | 215,606 | 107,750 | 360,370 | 310,176 | 312,783 | 288,788 | 254,945 | 251,873 |
| Non-Interest Expense | 281,097 | 135,516 | 512,622 | 460,585 | 430,153 | 407,164 | 381,417 | 358,069 |
| Income Before Taxes | 80,175 | 43,582 | 126,851 | 120,476 | 139,831 | 104,975 | 82,018 | 76,319 |
| Income Taxes | 22,984 | 12,712 | 35,849 | 30,992 | 41,756 | 30,762 | 22,251 | 20,001 |
| Net Income | 57,191 | 30,870 | 91,002 | 89,484 | 98,075 | 74,213 | 59,767 | 56,318 |
| Average Shares | 40,403 | 40,070 | 40,071 | 40,626 | 41,138 | 42,006 | 42,813 | 43,312 |
| **Balance Sheet** | | | | | | | | |
| Net Loans & Leases | 4,665,442 | 4,601,590 | 4,524,145 | 4,268,089 | 4,357,737 | 3,883,379 | 3,722,639 | 3,352,579 |
| Total Assets | 12,770,576 | 13,352,320 | 12,404,932 | 11,663,355 | 10,976,596 | 9,342,959 | 8,917,765 | 8,247,789 |
| Total Deposits | 9,913,801 | 10,372,756 | 9,028,741 | 8,534,488 | 7,725,326 | 6,550,802 | 6,308,964 | 5,920,822 |
| Total Liabilities | 11,637,620 | 12,273,331 | 11,344,072 | 10,647,804 | 10,001,785 | 8,452,385 | 8,068,890 | 7,414,326 |
| Stockholders' Equity | 1,132,956 | 1,078,989 | 1,060,860 | 1,015,551 | 974,811 | 890,574 | 848,875 | 833,463 |
| Shares Outstanding | 40,499 | 40,526 | 40,430 | 40,439 | 40,947 | 41,327 | 42,266 | 42,981 |
| **Statistical Record** | | | | | | | | |
| Return on Assets % | 0.83 | 0.79 | 0.76 | 0.79 | 0.96 | 0.81 | 0.70 | 0.70 |
| Return on Equity % | 8.99 | 9.08 | 8.77 | 8.99 | 10.49 | 8.53 | 7.11 | 6.82 |
| Net Interest Margin % | 92.34 | 91.25 | 89.64 | 85.06 | 70.89 | 56.15 | 58.86 | 69.25 |
| Efficiency Ratio % | 74.88 | 69.95 | 72.52 | 69.12 | 61.38 | 57.90 | 61.12 | 68.36 |
| Loans to Deposits | 0.47 | 0.44 | 0.50 | 0.50 | 0.56 | 0.59 | 0.59 | 0.57 |
| Price Range | 44.21-31.88 | 44.51-31.88 | 44.51-31.88 | 49.14-34.11 | 69.50-36.57 | 46.17-35.50 | 37.99-32.05 | 34.00-26.70 |
| P/E Ratio | 17.97-12.96 | 18.70-13.39 | 19.69-14.11 | 22.34-15.50 | 29.20-15.37 | 26.08-20.06 | 27.14-22.89 | 26.15-20.53 |
| Average Yield % | 1.99 | 1.97 | 1.96 | 1.74 | 1.39 | 1.45 | 1.49 | 1.52 |

**Address:** 1010 Grand Boulevard, Kansas City, MO 64106
**Telephone:** 816-860-7000
**Web Site:** www.umb.com

**Officers:** J. Mariner Kemper - Chairman, Chief Executive Officer, Region Officer Peter J. Genovese - Vice-Chairman, Region Officer **Transfer Agents:** Computershare Trust Company NA, Canton, MA

**Investor Contact:** 800-892-2434
**No of Institutions:** 199
**Shares:** 27,166,556 **% Held:** 63.33

# UNISOURCE ENERGY CORP.

| Exchange | Symbol | Price | 52Wk Range | Yield | P/E |
|---|---|---|---|---|---|
| NYS | UNS | $37.86 (8/31/2011) | 38.71-32.41 | 4.44 | 13.52 |

***7 Year Price Score 112.94** *NYSE Composite Index=100 ***12 Month Price Score 103.45**

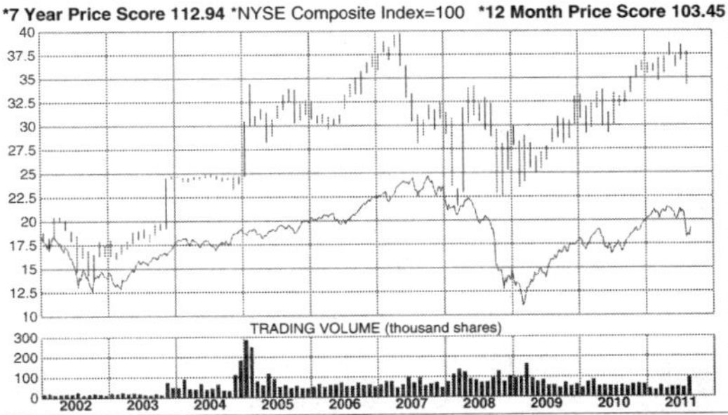


**Interim Earnings (Per Share)**

| Qtr. | Mar | Jun | Sep | Dec |
|---|---|---|---|---|
| 2008 | (0.07) | 0.13 | (0.31) | 0.64 |
| 2009 | 0.14 | 0.80 | 1.45 | 0.29 |
| 2010 | 0.52 | 0.65 | 1.36 | 0.29 |
| 2011 | 0.44 | 0.71 | ... | ... |

**Interim Dividends (Per Share)**

| Amt | Decl | Ex | Rec | Pay |
|---|---|---|---|---|
| 0.39Q | 12/03/2010 | 12/14/2010 | 12/16/2010 | 12/28/2010 |
| 0.42Q | 02/28/2011 | 03/09/2011 | 03/11/2011 | 03/23/2011 |
| 0.42Q | 05/06/2011 | 05/17/2011 | 05/19/2011 | 06/06/2011 |
| 0.42Q | 08/05/2011 | 08/16/2011 | 08/18/2011 | 09/01/2011 |

**Indicated Div: $1.68 (Div. Reinv. Plan)**

**Valuation Analysis**

| | | | |
|---|---|---|---|
| Forecast EPS | $2.77 (09/02/2011) | | |
| Market Cap | $1.4 Billion | Book Value | $847.1 Million |
| Price/Book | 1.65 | Price/Sales | 0.92 |

**Dividend Achiever Status**

| | |
|---|---|
| **10 Year Growth Rate** | 14.58% |
| **Total Years of Dividend Growth** | 10 |

**Business Summary:** Electric Utilities (MIC: 3.1.1 SIC: 4911 NAIC: 221111)

UniSource Energy is a holding company. As of Dec 31 2010, Co. conducted its business in four primary business segments: Tucson Electric Power Company (TEP), UNS Gas, Inc. (UNS Gas), UNS Electric, Inc. (UNS Electric), and Millennium Energy Holdings, Inc. (Millennium). TEP is an electric utility which provides electric service to the community of Tucson, AZ. UNS Gas and UNS Electric provide gas and electric service to 30 communities in northern and southern Arizona. Millennium had investments in unregulated businesses. As of Dec 31 2010, TEP provided electric service to approximately 403,000 retail customers.

**Recent Developments:** For the quarter ended June 30 2011, net income increased 10.4% to US$28.6 million from US$25.9 million in the year-earlier quarter. Revenues were US$369.7 million, up 9.0% from US$339.1 million the year before. Operating income was US$71.2 million versus US$72.3 million in the prior-year quarter, a decrease of 1.5%. Direct operating expenses rose 13.9% to US$245.6 million from US$215.6 million in the comparable period the year before. Indirect operating expenses increased 3.1% to US$52.8 million from US$51.2 million in the equivalent prior-year period.

**Prospects:** Our evaluation of UniSource Energy Corp. as of Sep. 6, 2011 is the result of our systematic analysis on three basic characteristics: earnings strength, relative valuation, and recent stock price movement. The company has produced a positive trend in earnings per share over the past 5 quarters. However, while recent estimates for the company have been mixed, UNS has posted results that fell short of analysts expectations. Based on operating earnings yield, the company is undervalued when compared to all of the companies in our coverage universe. Share price changes over the past year indicates that UNS will perform very poorly over the near term.

| **Financial Data** (US$ in Thousands) | 6 Mos | 3 Mos | 12/31/2010 | 12/31/2009 | 12/31/2008 | 12/31/2007 | 12/31/2006 | 12/31/2005 |
|---|---|---|---|---|---|---|---|---|
| Earnings Per Share | 2.80 | 2.74 | 2.82 | 2.69 | 0.39 | 1.57 | 1.80 | 1.28 |
| Cash Flow Per Share | 9.49 | 9.70 | 9.40 | 9.69 | 7.75 | 9.10 | 8.02 | 7.94 |
| Tang Book Value Per Share | 22.98 | 22.49 | 22.46 | 20.94 | 19.16 | 19.54 | 18.59 | 17.68 |
| Dividends Per Share | 1.620 | 1.590 | 1.560 | 1.160 | 0.960 | 0.900 | 0.840 | 0.760 |
| Dividend Payout % | 57.86 | 58.03 | 55.32 | 43.12 | 246.15 | 57.32 | 46.67 | 59.38 |
| **Income Statement** | | | | | | | | |
| Total Revenue | 714,439 | 344,633 | 1,453,677 | 1,394,424 | 1,397,511 | 1,381,373 | 1,316,869 | 1,229,535 |
| EBITDA | 202,828 | 88,219 | 421,003 | 450,222 | 325,749 | 445,194 | 454,425 | 422,988 |
| Depn & Amortn | 82,801 | 41,212 | 128,215 | 185,118 | 181,993 | 229,047 | 208,713 | 203,200 |
| Income Before Taxes | 66,721 | 20,901 | 189,743 | 168,606 | 30,997 | 97,452 | 113,179 | 79,330 |
| Income Taxes | 24,731 | 3,909 | 78,266 | 64,348 | 16,976 | 39,079 | 43,936 | 32,560 |
| Net Income | 41,990 | 16,992 | 111,477 | 104,258 | 14,021 | 58,373 | 67,447 | 46,144 |
| Average Shares | 41,555 | 41,405 | 36,415 | 35,858 | 35,632 | 35,486 | 35,264 | 38,851 |
| **Balance Sheet** | | | | | | | | |
| Current Assets | 492,226 | 389,422 | 420,950 | 446,305 | 481,651 | 430,240 | 455,910 | 444,514 |
| Total Assets | 3,859,945 | 3,744,499 | 3,779,323 | 3,601,242 | 3,508,331 | 3,185,716 | 3,187,409 | 3,126,780 |
| Current Liabilities | 534,457 | 490,231 | 463,424 | 385,618 | 351,623 | 547,681 | 395,920 | 344,033 |
| Long-Term Obligations | 1,735,250 | 1,713,427 | 1,782,051 | 1,796,144 | 1,827,132 | 1,524,843 | 1,759,941 | 1,878,157 |
| Total Liabilities | 3,012,850 | 2,920,372 | 2,958,537 | 2,850,377 | 2,829,057 | 2,495,641 | 2,533,260 | 2,510,039 |
| Stockholders' Equity | 847,095 | 824,127 | 820,786 | 750,865 | 679,274 | 690,075 | 654,149 | 616,741 |
| Shares Outstanding | 36,856 | 36,641 | 36,541 | 35,851 | 35,457 | 35,314 | 35,189 | 34,874 |
| **Statistical Record** | | | | | | | | |
| Return on Assets % | 2.96 | 2.94 | 3.02 | 2.93 | 0.42 | 1.83 | 2.14 | 1.46 |
| Return on Equity % | 13.77 | 13.72 | 14.19 | 14.58 | 2.04 | 8.69 | 10.61 | 7.71 |
| EBITDA Margin % | 28.39 | 25.60 | 28.96 | 32.29 | 23.31 | 32.23 | 34.51 | 34.40 |
| Net Margin % | 5.88 | 4.93 | 7.67 | 7.48 | 1.00 | 4.23 | 5.12 | 3.75 |
| Asset Turnover | 0.40 | 0.40 | 0.39 | 0.39 | 0.42 | 0.43 | 0.42 | 0.39 |
| Current Ratio | 0.92 | 0.79 | 0.91 | 1.16 | 1.37 | 0.79 | 1.15 | 1.29 |
| Debt to Equity | 2.05 | 2.08 | 2.17 | 2.39 | 2.69 | 2.21 | 2.69 | 3.05 |
| Price Range | 38.71-30.08 | 37.11-29.18 | 36.77-29.14 | 33.11-23.50 | 34.17-21.56 | 39.76-28.09 | 37.32-29.62 | 34.45-24.11 |
| P/E Ratio | 13.83-10.74 | 13.54-10.65 | 13.04-10.33 | 12.31-8.74 | 87.62-55.28 | 25.32-17.89 | 20.73-16.46 | 26.91-18.84 |
| Average Yield % | 4.61 | 4.70 | 4.77 | 4.13 | 3.33 | 2.64 | 2.57 | 2.45 |

**Address:** One South Church Avenue, Suite 100, Tucson, AZ 85701
**Telephone:** 520-571-4000
**Web Site:** www.UNS.com

**Officers:** Paul J. Bonavia - Chairman, President, Chief Executive Officer Michael J. DeConcini - Senior Vice President, Chief Operating Officer **Transfer Agents:** BNY Mellon Shareholder Services, Jersey City, NJ

**Investor Contact:** 520-884-3650
**No of Institutions:** 204
**Shares:** 35,502,008 **% Held:** 91.78

# UNITED BANKSHARES, INC.

| Exchange | Symbol | Price | 52Wk Range | Yield | P/E |
|---|---|---|---|---|---|
| NMS | UBSI | $22.47 (8/31/2011) | 30.56-19.64 | 5.34 | 13.62 |

*7 Year Price Score 85.86 *NYSE Composite Index=100 *12 Month Price Score 89.67

**Interim Earnings (Per Share)**

| Qtr. | Mar | Jun | Sep | Dec |
|---|---|---|---|---|
| 2008 | 0.59 | 0.58 | 0.45 | 0.38 |
| 2009 | 0.68 | 0.19 | 0.28 | 0.40 |
| 2010 | 0.40 | 0.41 | 0.40 | 0.44 |
| 2011 | 0.41 | 0.40 | ... | ... |

**Interim Dividends (Per Share)**

| Amt | Decl | Ex | Rec | Pay |
|---|---|---|---|---|
| 0.30Q | 11/22/2010 | 12/08/2010 | 12/10/2010 | 01/03/2011 |
| 0.30Q | 02/28/2011 | 03/09/2011 | 03/11/2011 | 04/01/2011 |
| 0.30Q | 05/17/2011 | 06/08/2011 | 06/10/2011 | 07/01/2011 |
| 0.30Q | 08/29/2011 | 09/07/2011 | 09/09/2011 | 10/03/2011 |

**Indicated Div: $1.20 (Div. Reinv. Plan)**

**Valuation Analysis**

| | | | |
|---|---|---|---|
| Forecast EPS | $1.63 (09/02/2011) | | |
| Market Cap | $980.7 Million | Book Value | $804.2 Million |
| Price/Book | 1.22 | Price/Sales | N/A |

**Dividend Achiever Status**

| | |
|---|---|
| 10 Year Growth Rate | 3.03% |
| Total Years of Dividend Growth | 29 |

**Business Summary:** Banking (MIC: 5.1.1 SIC: 6022 NAIC: 522110)

United Bankshares is a bank holding company. Through its banking subsidiaries, Co. provides a range of commercial and retail banking services and products including the acceptance of deposits in checking, savings, time and money market accounts; the making and servicing of personal, commercial, floor plan and student loans; and the making of construction and real estate loans. Co. also owns nonbank subsidiaries which engage in other community banking services such as asset management, real property title insurance, investment banking, financial planning, and brokerage services. As of Dec 31 2010, Co. had total assets of $7.16 billion and total deposits of $5.71 billion.

**Recent Developments:** For the quarter ended June 30 2011, net income decreased 2.6% to US$17.5 million from US$17.9 million in the year-earlier quarter. Net interest income decreased 2.6% to US$58.6 million from US$60.2 million in the year-earlier quarter. Provision for loan losses was US$4.8 million versus US$6.4 million in the prior-year quarter, a decrease of 25.0%. Non-interest income fell 24.2% to US$13.3 million from US$17.6 million, while non-interest expense declined 7.8% to US$41.7 million.

**Prospects:** Our evaluation of United Bankshares Inc. as of Sep. 6, 2011 is the result of our systematic analysis on three basic characteristics: earnings strength, relative valuation, and recent stock price movement. The company has managed to produce a neutral trend in earnings per share over the past 5 quarters. However, while recent estimates for the company have been mixed, UBSI has posted results that were in line with analysts expectations. Based on operating earnings yield, the company is undervalued when compared to all of the companies in our coverage universe. Share price changes over the past year indicates that UBSI will perform poorly over the near term.

**Financial Data**

| (US$ in Thousands) | 6 Mos | 3 Mos | 12/31/2010 | 12/31/2009 | 12/31/2008 | 12/31/2007 | 12/31/2006 | 12/31/2005 |
|---|---|---|---|---|---|---|---|---|
| Earnings Per Share | 1.65 | 1.66 | 1.65 | 1.55 | 2.00 | 2.15 | 2.13 | 2.33 |
| Cash Flow Per Share | 2.12 | 2.28 | 2.32 | 1.24 | 2.63 | 1.94 | 2.15 | 2.66 |
| Tang Book Value Per Share | 11.29 | 11.18 | 11.03 | 10.35 | 9.78 | 10.39 | 11.37 | 11.13 |
| Dividends Per Share | 1.200 | 1.200 | 1.200 | 1.170 | 1.160 | 1.130 | 1.090 | 1.050 |
| Dividend Payout % | 72.73 | 72.29 | 72.73 | 75.48 | 58.00 | 52.56 | 51.17 | 45.06 |
| **Income Statement** | | | | | | | | |
| Interest Income | 146,292 | 73,857 | 323,382 | 365,845 | 429,911 | 438,729 | 400,683 | 345,278 |
| Interest Expense | 28,308 | 14,494 | 85,196 | 120,374 | 177,119 | 213,310 | 181,090 | 124,451 |
| Net Interest Income | 117,984 | 59,363 | 238,186 | 245,471 | 252,792 | 225,419 | 219,593 | 220,827 |
| Provision for Losses | 9,236 | 4,436 | 13,773 | 46,065 | 25,155 | 5,330 | 1,437 | 5,618 |
| Non-Interest Income | 27,985 | 14,651 | 62,203 | 53,970 | 67,303 | 57,749 | 49,033 | 52,625 |
| Non-Interest Expense | 85,146 | 43,469 | 182,212 | 175,127 | 171,073 | 147,929 | 137,173 | 121,160 |
| Income Before Taxes | 51,587 | 26,109 | 104,404 | 78,249 | 123,867 | 129,909 | 130,016 | 146,674 |
| Income Taxes | 16,250 | 8,224 | 32,457 | 10,951 | 36,913 | 39,235 | 40,767 | 46,265 |
| Net Income | 35,337 | 17,885 | 71,947 | 67,298 | 86,954 | 90,674 | 89,249 | 100,409 |
| Average Shares | 43,676 | 43,700 | 43,625 | 43,456 | 43,434 | 42,222 | 41,942 | 43,024 |
| **Balance Sheet** | | | | | | | | |
| Net Loans & Leases | 5,180,021 | 5,150,874 | 5,194,162 | 5,674,240 | 5,953,529 | 5,744,298 | 4,765,159 | 4,609,015 |
| Total Assets | 7,133,983 | 7,191,336 | 7,155,719 | 7,805,101 | 8,102,091 | 7,994,739 | 6,717,598 | 6,728,492 |
| Total Deposits | 5,728,536 | 5,711,923 | 5,713,534 | 5,971,100 | 5,647,954 | 5,349,750 | 4,828,192 | 4,617,452 |
| Total Liabilities | 6,329,742 | 6,391,873 | 6,362,707 | 7,043,551 | 7,365,379 | 7,233,540 | 6,083,506 | 6,093,287 |
| Stockholders' Equity | 804,241 | 799,463 | 793,012 | 761,550 | 736,712 | 761,199 | 634,092 | 635,205 |
| Shares Outstanding | 43,645 | 43,645 | 43,621 | 43,437 | 43,403 | 43,234 | 41,058 | 42,008 |
| **Statistical Record** | | | | | | | | |
| Return on Assets % | 0.99 | 0.98 | 0.96 | 0.85 | 1.08 | 1.23 | 1.33 | 1.53 |
| Return on Equity % | 9.10 | 9.23 | 9.26 | 8.98 | 11.58 | 13.00 | 14.06 | 15.85 |
| Net Interest Margin % | 80.93 | 80.38 | 73.65 | 67.10 | 58.80 | 51.38 | 54.80 | 63.96 |
| Efficiency Ratio % | 48.59 | 49.11 | 47.26 | 41.72 | 34.41 | 29.80 | 30.50 | 30.45 |
| Loans to Deposits | 0.90 | 0.90 | 0.91 | 0.95 | 1.05 | 1.07 | 0.99 | 1.00 |
| Price Range | 30.56-22.57 | 31.54-22.75 | 31.54-19.97 | 33.22-13.79 | 36.00-19.48 | 39.14-25.84 | 39.46-34.50 | 38.48-30.00 |
| P/E Ratio | 18.52-13.68 | 19.00-13.70 | 19.12-12.10 | 21.43-8.90 | 18.00-9.74 | 18.20-12.02 | 18.53-16.20 | 16.52-12.88 |
| Average Yield % | 4.59 | 4.46 | 4.61 | 5.91 | 4.14 | 3.48 | 2.94 | 3.01 |

**Address:** 300 United Center, 500 Virginia Street East, Charleston, WV 25301
**Telephone:** 304-424-8800
**Web Site:** www.ubsi-wv.com

**Officers:** Richard M. Adams - Chairman, Chief Executive Officer Steven E. Wilson - Executive Vice President, Chief Financial Officer, Chief Accounting Officer, Treasurer, Secretary **Transfer Agents:** Mellon Investor Services LLC, Ridgefield Park, NJ

**Investor Contact:** 304-424-8704
**No of Institutions:** 175
**Shares:** 24,692,482 **% Held:** 53.83

# UNITED TECHNOLOGIES CORP.

| Exchange | Symbol | Price | 52Wk Range | Yield | P/E |
|---|---|---|---|---|---|
| NYS | UTX | $74.25 (8/31/2011) | 91.39-65.21 | 2.59 | 14.36 |

***7 Year Price Score 124.14** *NYSE Composite Index=100 ***12 Month Price Score 101.98**

**Interim Earnings (Per Share)**

| Qtr. | Mar | Jun | Sep | Dec |
|---|---|---|---|---|
| 2008 | 1.03 | 1.32 | 1.33 | 1.22 |
| 2009 | 0.78 | 1.05 | 1.14 | 1.15 |
| 2010 | 0.93 | 1.20 | 1.30 | 1.31 |
| 2011 | 1.11 | 1.45 | ... | ... |

**Interim Dividends (Per Share)**

| Amt | Decl | Ex | Rec | Pay |
|---|---|---|---|---|
| 0.425Q | 10/13/2010 | 11/17/2010 | 11/19/2010 | 12/10/2010 |
| 0.425Q | 02/07/2011 | 02/16/2011 | 02/18/2011 | 03/10/2011 |
| 0.48Q | 04/13/2011 | 05/18/2011 | 05/20/2011 | 06/10/2011 |
| 0.48Q | 06/08/2011 | 08/17/2011 | 08/19/2011 | 09/10/2011 |

**Indicated Div: $1.92 (Div. Reinv. Plan)**

**Valuation Analysis**

| | | | |
|---|---|---|---|
| Forecast EPS | $5.45 (09/05/2011) | | |
| Market Cap | $67.5 Billion | Book Value | $22.7 Billion |
| Price/Book | 2.97 | Price/Sales | 1.19 |

**Dividend Achiever Status**

| | |
|---|---|
| **10 Year Growth Rate** | 14.22% |
| **Total Years of Dividend Growth** | 17 |

**Business Summary:** Aerospace (MIC: 7.1.1 SIC: 3724 NAIC: 336412)

United Technologies operates through six principal segments. Otis products include elevators, escalators and moving walkways. Carrier products include heating, ventilating, air conditioning and refrigeration systems, controls, services and products. UTC Fire & Security products include fire and special hazard and suppression systems and firefighting equipment. Pratt & Whitney products include commercial, military, business jet and general aviation aircraft engines, parts and services. Hamilton Sundstrand provides aerospace and industrial products and aftermarket services. Sikorsky products include military and commercial helicopters, aftermarket helicopter and aircraft parts and services.

**Recent Developments:** For the quarter ended June 30 2011, net income increased 18.0% to US$1.43 billion from US$1.21 billion in the year-earlier quarter. Revenues were US$15.08 billion, up 9.2% from US$13.80 billion the year before. Operating income was US$2.22 billion versus US$1.88 billion in the prior-year quarter, an increase of 18.0%. Direct operating expenses rose 8.9% to US$10.91 billion from US$10.02 billion in the comparable period the year before. Indirect operating expenses increased 2.4% to US$1.95 billion from US$1.91 billion in the equivalent prior-year period.

**Prospects:** Our evaluation of United Technologies Corp. as of Sep. 6, 2011 is the result of our systematic analysis on three basic characteristics: earnings strength, relative valuation, and recent stock price movement. The company has managed to produce a neutral trend in earnings per share over the past 5 quarters. However, while recent estimates for the company have been lowered by analysts, UTX has posted better than expected results. Based on operating earnings yield, the company is undervalued when compared to all of the companies in our coverage universe. Share price changes over the past year indicates that UTX will perform in line with the market over the near term.

**Financial Data**

| (US$ in Millions) | 6 Mos | 3 Mos | 12/31/2010 | 12/31/2009 | 12/31/2008 | 12/31/2007 | 12/31/2006 | 12/31/2005 |
|---|---|---|---|---|---|---|---|---|
| Earnings Per Share | 5.17 | 4.92 | 4.74 | 4.12 | 4.90 | 4.27 | 3.71 | 3.03 |
| Cash Flow Per Share | 6.69 | 6.80 | 6.51 | 5.83 | 6.55 | 5.53 | 4.90 | 4.37 |
| Tang Book Value Per Share | 0.30 | N.M. | N.M. | 0.25 | N.M. | 1.50 | N.M. | 0.91 |
| Dividends Per Share | 1.755 | 1.700 | 1.700 | 1.540 | 1.345 | 1.170 | 1.015 | 0.880 |
| Dividend Payout % | 33.95 | 34.55 | 35.86 | 37.38 | 27.45 | 27.40 | 27.36 | 29.04 |
| **Income Statement** | | | | | | | | |
| Total Revenue | 28,420 | 13,344 | 54,326 | 52,920 | 58,681 | 54,759 | 47,829 | 42,725 |
| EBITDA | 4,676 | 2,112 | 8,086 | 7,317 | 8,490 | 7,820 | 6,822 | 5,891 |
| Depn & Amortn | 677 | 333 | 900 | 852 | 865 | 770 | 724 | 709 |
| Income Before Taxes | 3,709 | 1,630 | 6,538 | 5,760 | 6,936 | 6,384 | 5,492 | 4,684 |
| Income Taxes | 1,178 | 529 | 1,827 | 1,581 | 1,883 | 1,836 | 1,494 | 1,253 |
| Net Income | 2,330 | 1,012 | 4,373 | 3,829 | 4,689 | 4,224 | 3,732 | 3,069 |
| Average Shares | 909 | 914 | 922 | 928 | 956 | 988 | 1,005 | 1,014 |
| **Balance Sheet** | | | | | | | | |
| Current Assets | 26,429 | 25,005 | 23,510 | 23,194 | 24,099 | 22,071 | 18,844 | 17,206 |
| Total Assets | 62,147 | 60,664 | 58,493 | 55,762 | 56,469 | 54,575 | 47,141 | 45,925 |
| Current Liabilities | 20,214 | 18,916 | 17,732 | 17,913 | 19,434 | 17,469 | 15,208 | 15,345 |
| Long-Term Obligations | 9,492 | 9,986 | 10,010 | 8,257 | 9,337 | 8,015 | 7,037 | 5,935 |
| Total Liabilities | 39,424 | 38,538 | 37,108 | 35,696 | 40,552 | 33,220 | 29,844 | 28,934 |
| Stockholders' Equity | 22,723 | 22,126 | 21,385 | 20,066 | 15,917 | 21,355 | 17,297 | 16,991 |
| Shares Outstanding | 908 | 915 | 921 | 936 | 943 | 983 | 955 | 1,013 |
| **Statistical Record** | | | | | | | | |
| Return on Assets % | 7.85 | 7.59 | 7.65 | 6.82 | 8.42 | 8.31 | 8.02 | 7.14 |
| Return on Equity % | 22.16 | 21.47 | 21.10 | 21.28 | 25.09 | 21.86 | 21.77 | 19.80 |
| EBITDA Margin % | 16.45 | 15.83 | 14.88 | 13.83 | 14.47 | 14.28 | 14.26 | 13.79 |
| Net Margin % | 8.20 | 7.58 | 8.05 | 7.24 | 7.99 | 7.71 | 7.80 | 7.18 |
| Asset Turnover | 0.94 | 0.93 | 0.95 | 0.94 | 1.05 | 1.08 | 1.03 | 0.99 |
| Current Ratio | 1.31 | 1.32 | 1.33 | 1.29 | 1.24 | 1.26 | 1.24 | 1.12 |
| Debt to Equity | 0.42 | 0.45 | 0.47 | 0.41 | 0.59 | 0.38 | 0.41 | 0.35 |
| Price Range | 90.00-64.29 | 85.21-63.22 | 79.52-63.22 | 70.49-37.56 | 76.54-43.22 | 82.07-62.47 | 66.79-54.47 | 58.03-48.77 |
| P/E Ratio | 17.41-12.44 | 17.32-12.85 | 16.78-13.34 | 17.11-9.12 | 15.62-8.82 | 19.22-14.63 | 18.00-14.68 | 19.15-16.10 |
| Average Yield % | 2.25 | 2.29 | 2.38 | 2.79 | 2.10 | 1.63 | 1.65 | 1.70 |

| | | |
|---|---|---|
| **Address:** One Financial Plaza, Hartford, CT 06103<br>**Telephone:** 860-728-7000<br>**Web Site:** www.utc.com | **Officers:** Louis R. Chênevert - Chairman, Chief Executive Officer Gregory J. Hayes - Senior Vice President, Chief Financial Officer **Transfer Agents:** Computershare Trust Company, N.A., Canton, MA | **No of Institutions:** 1492<br>**Shares:** 825,729,344 **% Held:** 77.85 |

# UNIVERSAL CORP.

| Exchange | Symbol | Price | 52Wk Range | Yield | P/E |
|---|---|---|---|---|---|
| NYS | UVV | $40.70 (8/31/2011) | 45.72-35.11 | 4.72 | 8.01 |

*7 Year Price Score 88.95 *NYSE Composite Index=100 *12 Month Price Score 94.20

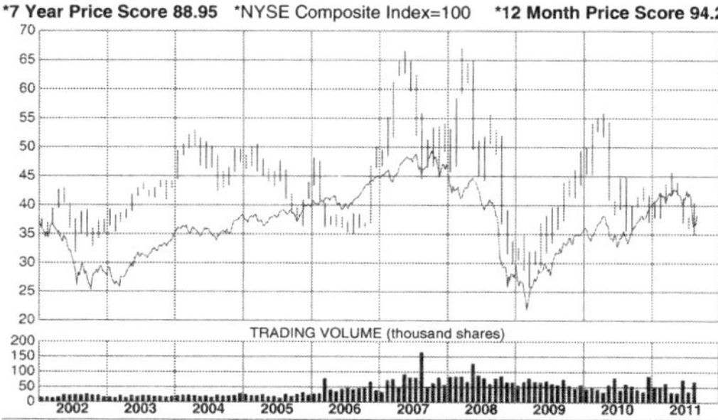


**Interim Earnings (Per Share)**

| Qtr. | Jun | Sep | Dec | Mar |
|---|---|---|---|---|
| 2008-09 | 0.64 | 1.38 | 1.78 | 0.79 |
| 2009-10 | 1.47 | 1.77 | 1.54 | 0.90 |
| 2010-11 | 0.87 | 1.78 | 1.82 | 0.96 |
| 2011-12 | 0.52 | ... | ... | ... |

**Interim Dividends (Per Share)**

| Amt | Decl | Ex | Rec | Pay |
|---|---|---|---|---|
| 0.48Q | 11/04/2010 | 01/06/2011 | 01/10/2011 | 02/14/2011 |
| 0.48Q | 02/08/2011 | 04/07/2011 | 04/11/2011 | 05/09/2011 |
| 0.48Q | 05/19/2011 | 07/07/2011 | 07/11/2011 | 08/08/2011 |
| 0.48Q | 08/04/2011 | 10/06/2011 | 10/11/2011 | 11/14/2011 |

**Indicated Div: $1.92 (Div. Reinv. Plan)**

**Valuation Analysis**

| | | | |
|---|---|---|---|
| Forecast EPS | $4.00 (09/02/2011) | | |
| Market Cap | $945.3 Million | Book Value | $1.2 Billion |
| Price/Book | 0.79 | Price/Sales | 0.38 |

**Dividend Achiever Status**

| | |
|---|---|
| **10 Year Growth Rate** | 3.92% |
| **Total Years of Dividend Growth** | 40 |

**Business Summary:** Tobacco Products (MIC: 1.3.1 SIC: 5159 NAIC: 424590)

Universal is a holding company. Through its subsidiaries, Co. is a leaf tobacco merchant and processor. Co. is engaged in the procurement, processing, packing, and supply of flue-cured and burley leaf tobacco to manufacturers of consumer tobacco products. Co. also provides services to customers, including blending, chemical and physical testing of tobacco, managing inventory, and manufacturing reconstituted sheet tobacco. The segments for its flue-cured and burley tobacco operations are North America and Other Regions. Co. also has a third segment: Other Tobacco Operations, which comprises its dark tobacco business, its oriental tobacco joint venture, and certain tobacco-related services.

**Recent Developments:** For the quarter ended June 30 2011, net income decreased 29.1% to US$17.3 million from US$24.4 million in the year-earlier quarter. Revenues were US$479.5 million, down 11.0% from US$538.9 million the year before. Operating income was US$35.5 million versus US$41.1 million in the prior-year quarter, a decrease of 13.6%. Direct operating expenses declined 11.8% to US$385.1 million from US$436.7 million in the comparable period the year before. Indirect operating expenses decreased 3.7% to US$58.8 million from US$61.1 million in the equivalent prior-year period.

**Prospects:** Our evaluation of Universal Corp. as of Sep. 6, 2011 is the result of our systematic analysis on three basic characteristics: earnings strength, relative valuation, and recent stock price movement. The company has generated a negative trend in earnings per share over the past 5 quarters. Because the company lacks sufficient analyst estimate data, we place greater weight on the historical EPS trend as the measure of earnings strength. Based on operating earnings yield, the company is undervalued when compared to all of the companies in our coverage universe. Share price changes over the past year indicates that UVV will perform very poorly over the near term.

**Financial Data**

| (US$ in Thousands) | 3 Mos | 03/31/2011 | 03/31/2010 | 03/31/2009 | 03/31/2008 | 03/31/2007 | 03/31/2006 | 03/31/2005 |
|---|---|---|---|---|---|---|---|---|
| Earnings Per Share | 5.08 | 5.42 | 5.68 | 4.57 | 3.70 | 1.13 | 0.31 | 3.73 |
| Cash Flow Per Share | 7.41 | 2.27 | 6.56 | 3.87 | 3.31 | 9.48 | 2.46 | (3.41) |
| Tang Book Value Per Share | 37.76 | 37.57 | 33.05 | 28.42 | 29.30 | 26.47 | 24.67 | 26.66 |
| Dividends Per Share | 1.900 | 1.890 | 1.850 | 1.810 | 1.770 | 1.730 | 1.690 | 1.590 |
| Dividend Payout % | 37.40 | 34.87 | 32.57 | 39.61 | 47.84 | 153.10 | 545.16 | 42.63 |
| **Income Statement** | | | | | | | | |
| Total Revenue | 479,465 | 2,571,527 | 2,491,738 | 2,554,659 | 2,145,822 | 2,007,272 | 3,511,332 | 3,276,057 |
| EBITDA | 46,940 | 298,254 | 298,497 | 250,693 | 232,896 | 210,014 | 169,106 | 277,965 |
| Depn & Amortn | 11,427 | 43,654 | 41,288 | 40,761 | 41,383 | 46,423 | 64,753 | 69,409 |
| Income Before Taxes | 30,337 | 234,265 | 234,252 | 176,606 | 166,783 | 120,642 | 23,060 | 150,304 |
| Income Taxes | 9,526 | 78,349 | 86,283 | 64,588 | 63,799 | 61,126 | 34,403 | 68,197 |
| Net Income | 15,888 | 156,565 | 168,397 | 131,739 | 119,156 | 44,352 | 7,940 | 96,013 |
| Average Shares | 23,513 | 28,888 | 29,662 | 25,570 | 32,186 | 26,051 | 25,957 | 25,717 |
| **Balance Sheet** | | | | | | | | |
| Current Assets | 1,795,128 | 1,578,234 | 1,693,076 | 1,503,919 | 1,417,060 | 1,545,365 | 1,802,598 | 1,788,808 |
| Total Assets | 2,397,625 | 2,227,867 | 2,371,040 | 2,138,176 | 2,134,112 | 2,328,822 | 2,901,341 | 2,885,324 |
| Current Liabilities | 674,911 | 512,351 | 614,999 | 549,875 | 402,326 | 692,974 | 937,806 | 969,761 |
| Long-Term Obligations | 321,612 | 320,193 | 414,764 | 331,808 | 402,942 | 398,952 | 762,201 | 838,687 |
| Total Liabilities | 1,208,129 | 1,042,261 | 1,248,470 | 1,108,703 | 1,018,481 | 1,298,089 | 1,936,470 | 2,062,936 |
| Stockholders' Equity | 1,189,496 | 1,185,606 | 1,122,570 | 1,029,473 | 1,115,631 | 1,030,733 | 964,871 | 822,388 |
| Shares Outstanding | 23,226 | 23,240 | 24,325 | 24,999 | 27,162 | 26,948 | 25,748 | 25,668 |
| **Statistical Record** | | | | | | | | |
| Return on Assets % | 6.06 | 6.81 | 7.47 | 6.17 | 5.33 | 1.70 | 0.27 | 3.58 |
| Return on Equity % | 12.79 | 13.57 | 15.65 | 12.28 | 11.07 | 4.44 | 0.89 | 12.14 |
| EBITDA Margin % | 9.79 | 11.60 | 11.98 | 9.81 | 10.85 | 10.46 | 4.82 | 8.48 |
| Net Margin % | 3.31 | 6.09 | 6.76 | 5.16 | 5.55 | 2.21 | 0.23 | 2.93 |
| Asset Turnover | 1.03 | 1.12 | 1.11 | 1.20 | 0.96 | 0.77 | 1.21 | 1.22 |
| Current Ratio | 2.66 | 3.08 | 2.75 | 2.74 | 3.52 | 2.23 | 1.92 | 1.84 |
| Debt to Equity | 0.27 | 0.27 | 0.37 | 0.32 | 0.36 | 0.39 | 0.79 | 1.02 |
| Price Range | 45.72-35.44 | 55.92-35.44 | 55.19-29.27 | 65.53-25.82 | 67.08-44.48 | 61.35-35.02 | 48.21-36.17 | 53.01-42.25 |
| P/E Ratio | 9.00-6.98 | 10.32-6.54 | 9.72-5.15 | 14.34-5.65 | 18.13-12.02 | 54.29-30.99 | 155.52-116.68 | 14.21-11.33 |
| Average Yield % | 4.68 | 4.48 | 4.43 | 4.11 | 3.19 | 4.11 | 3.97 | 3.34 |

**Address:** 9201 Forest Hill Avenue, Richmond, VA 23235
**Telephone:** 804-359-9311
**Web Site:** www.universalcorp.com

**Officers:** George C. Freeman - Chairman, President, Chief Executive Officer W. K. Brewer - Executive Vice President, Chief Operating Officer **Transfer Agents:** Wells Fargo Bank, N.A., St. Paul, MN

**Investor Contact:** 804-359-9311
**No of Institutions:** 212
**Shares:** 22,425,030 **% Held:** 87.05

# UNIVERSAL FOREST PRODUCTS INC.

| Exchange | Symbol | Price | 52Wk Range | Yield | P/E |
|---|---|---|---|---|---|
| NMS | UFPI | $30.56 (8/31/2011) | 39.70-23.76 | 1.31 | 191.00 |

***7 Year Price Score 79.75** *NYSE Composite Index=100 ***12 Month Price Score 88.27**

**Interim Earnings (Per Share)**

| Qtr. | Mar | Jun | Sep | Dec |
|---|---|---|---|---|
| 2008 | (0.24) | 0.61 | (0.10) | (0.04) |
| 2009 | (0.06) | 0.83 | 0.51 | (0.03) |
| 2010 | 0.05 | 0.70 | 0.13 | 0.00 |
| 2011 | (0.19) | 0.22 | ... | ... |

**Interim Dividends (Per Share)**

| Amt | Decl | Ex | Rec | Pay |
|---|---|---|---|---|
| 0.20S | 10/15/2009 | 11/27/2009 | 12/01/2009 | 12/15/2009 |
| 0.20S | 04/14/2010 | 05/27/2010 | 06/01/2010 | 06/15/2010 |
| 0.20S | 10/14/2010 | 11/29/2010 | 12/01/2010 | 12/15/2010 |
| 0.20S | 04/13/2011 | 05/27/2011 | 06/01/2011 | 06/15/2011 |

**Indicated Div: $0.40**

**Valuation Analysis**

| | | | |
|---|---|---|---|
| Forecast EPS | $0.39 (09/02/2011) | | |
| Market Cap | $596.7 Million | Book Value | $574.3 Million |
| Price/Book | 1.04 | Price/Sales | 0.33 |

**Dividend Achiever Status**

| | |
|---|---|
| **10 Year Growth Rate** | 16.75% |
| **Total Years of Dividend Growth** | 17 |

**Business Summary:** Paper & Forest Products (MIC: 8.1.2 SIC: 2421 NAIC: 321113)

Universal Forest Products is a holding company. Through its subsidiaries, Co. designs, manufactures and markets wood and wood-alternative products for the do-it-yourself/retail home centers and other retailers, structural lumber products for the manufactured housing industry, engineered wood components for the site-built construction market, and wood packaging and components for various industries. Co.'s products include preservative-treated wood, remanufactured lumber, lattice, fence panels, deck components, packaging, engineered trusses, wall panels, and other building products. Co. also provides framing services for the site-built market and forming products for concrete construction.

**Recent Developments:** For the quarter ended June 25 2011, net income decreased 69.0% to US$4.5 million from US$14.5 million in the year-earlier quarter. Revenues were US$544.1 million, down 14.8% from US$638.6 million the year before. Operating income was US$7.8 million versus US$23.6 million in the prior-year quarter, a decrease of 67.1%. Direct operating expenses declined 13.1% to US$487.6 million from US$560.7 million in the comparable period the year before. Indirect operating expenses decreased 10.0% to US$48.8 million from US$54.3 million in the equivalent prior-year period.

**Prospects:** Our evaluation of Universal Forest Products Inc. as of Sep. 6, 2011 is the result of our systematic analysis on three basic characteristics: earnings strength, relative valuation, and recent stock price movement. The company has managed to produce a neutral trend in earnings per share over the past 5 quarters and while recent estimates for the company have remained steady, UFPI has posted better than expected results. Based on operating earnings yield, the company is overvalued when compared to all of the companies in our coverage universe. Share price changes over the past year indicates that UFPI will perform very poorly over the near term.

**Financial Data**

| (US$ in Thousands) | 6 Mos | 3 Mos | 12/25/2010 | 12/26/2009 | 12/27/2008 | 12/29/2007 | 12/30/2006 | 12/31/2005 |
|---|---|---|---|---|---|---|---|---|
| Earnings Per Share | 0.16 | 0.64 | 0.89 | 1.25 | 0.23 | 1.09 | 3.62 | 3.53 |
| Cash Flow Per Share | 1.12 | (0.10) | 1.53 | 6.68 | 4.66 | 4.58 | 8.12 | 3.97 |
| Tang Book Value Per Share | 20.70 | 20.57 | 20.77 | 20.20 | 18.85 | 19.17 | 17.72 | 15.72 |
| Dividends Per Share | 0.400 | 0.400 | 0.400 | 0.260 | 0.120 | 0.115 | 0.110 | 0.105 |
| Dividend Payout % | 250.00 | 62.50 | 44.94 | 20.80 | 52.17 | 10.55 | 3.04 | 2.97 |
| **Income Statement** | | | | | | | | |
| Total Revenue | 931,372 | 387,233 | 1,890,851 | 1,673,000 | 2,232,394 | 2,513,178 | 2,664,572 | 2,691,522 |
| EBITDA | 20,021 | 3,262 | 67,637 | 84,042 | 65,772 | 101,073 | 163,267 | 159,641 |
| Depn & Amortn | 17,325 | 8,343 | 37,348 | 41,225 | 47,367 | 47,581 | 39,522 | 34,796 |
| Income Before Taxes | 1,264 | (5,716) | 27,041 | 38,597 | 7,146 | 38,609 | 112,135 | 110,772 |
| Income Taxes | 215 | (2,287) | 7,200 | 13,852 | 1,686 | 15,396 | 38,760 | 41,050 |
| Net Income | 607 | (3,670) | 17,411 | 24,272 | 4,343 | 21,045 | 70,125 | 67,373 |
| Average Shares | 19,546 | 19,306 | 19,476 | 19,468 | 19,225 | 19,362 | 19,370 | 19,106 |
| **Balance Sheet** | | | | | | | | |
| Current Assets | 434,225 | 456,042 | 381,999 | 383,349 | 380,908 | 500,525 | 475,135 | 502,178 |
| Total Assets | 832,853 | 856,076 | 788,580 | 791,677 | 816,019 | 957,000 | 913,441 | 876,920 |
| Current Liabilities | 164,278 | 190,686 | 119,894 | 135,184 | 150,600 | 162,725 | 192,222 | 204,151 |
| Long-Term Obligations | 52,200 | 52,474 | 54,579 | 53,181 | 85,684 | 205,126 | 169,417 | 209,039 |
| Total Liabilities | 258,531 | 282,819 | 214,071 | 228,459 | 274,136 | 420,332 | 398,699 | 445,068 |
| Stockholders' Equity | 574,322 | 573,257 | 574,509 | 563,218 | 541,883 | 536,668 | 514,742 | 431,852 |
| Shares Outstanding | 19,525 | 19,524 | 19,333 | 19,284 | 19,088 | 18,907 | 18,858 | 18,402 |
| **Statistical Record** | | | | | | | | |
| Return on Assets % | 0.39 | 1.51 | 2.21 | 3.03 | 0.49 | 2.26 | 7.86 | 8.09 |
| Return on Equity % | 0.58 | 2.24 | 3.07 | 4.40 | 0.81 | 4.01 | 14.86 | 16.81 |
| EBITDA Margin % | 2.15 | 0.84 | 3.58 | 5.02 | 2.95 | 4.02 | 6.13 | 5.93 |
| Net Margin % | 0.07 | N.M. | 0.92 | 1.45 | 0.19 | 0.84 | 2.63 | 2.50 |
| Asset Turnover | 2.11 | 2.23 | 2.40 | 2.09 | 2.53 | 2.69 | 2.98 | 3.23 |
| Current Ratio | 2.64 | 2.39 | 3.19 | 2.84 | 2.53 | 3.08 | 2.47 | 2.46 |
| Debt to Equity | 0.09 | 0.09 | 0.10 | 0.09 | 0.16 | 0.38 | 0.33 | 0.48 |
| Price Range | 39.70-25.92 | 45.08-25.92 | 45.08-25.92 | 46.94-19.14 | 37.37-15.37 | 54.46-28.22 | 79.96-43.81 | 60.40-37.37 |
| P/E Ratio | 248.13-162.00 | 70.44-40.50 | 50.65-29.12 | 37.55-15.31 | 162.48-66.83 | 49.96-25.89 | 22.09-12.10 | 17.11-10.59 |
| Average Yield % | 1.23 | 1.16 | 1.17 | 0.77 | 0.41 | 0.28 | 0.19 | 0.22 |

| | | |
|---|---|---|
| **Address:** 2801 East Beltline NE, Grand Rapids, MI 49525<br>**Telephone:** 616-364-6161<br>**Web Site:** www.ufpi.com | **Officers:** Patrick M. Webster - President, Chief Operating Officer Matthew J. Missad - Chief Executive Officer **Transfer Agents:**<br>American Stock Transfer & Trust Company, New York, NY | **No of Institutions:** 133<br>**Shares:** 15,363,152 **% Held:** 75.16 |

# UNIVERSAL HEALTH REALTY INCOME TRUST

| Exchange | Symbol | Price | 52Wk Range | Yield | P/E |
|---|---|---|---|---|---|
| NYS | UHT | $37.42 (8/31/2011) | 43.38-31.81 | 6.47 | 30.67 |

***7 Year Price Score 110.24** *NYSE Composite Index=100 ***12 Month Price Score 103.53**

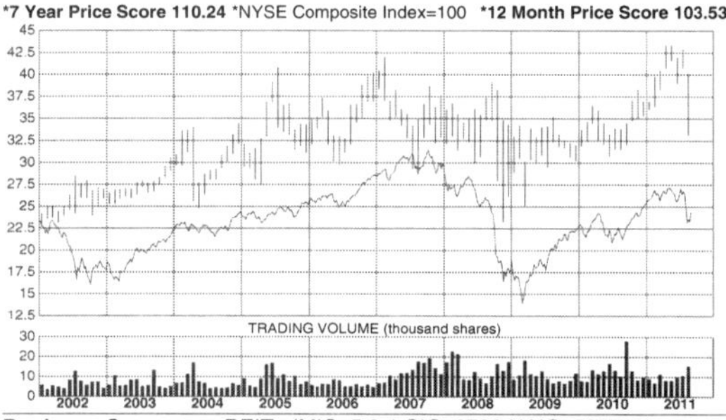


**Interim Earnings (Per Share)**

| Qtr. | Mar | Jun | Sep | Dec |
|---|---|---|---|---|
| 2008 | 0.35 | 0.35 | 0.35 | (0.07) |
| 2009 | 0.39 | 0.40 | 0.38 | 0.38 |
| 2010 | 0.37 | 0.35 | 0.27 | 0.33 |
| 2011 | 0.33 | 0.29 | ... | ... |

**Interim Dividends (Per Share)**

| Amt | Decl | Ex | Rec | Pay |
|---|---|---|---|---|
| 0.605Q | 09/02/2010 | 09/14/2010 | 09/16/2010 | 09/30/2010 |
| 0.605Q | 12/02/2010 | 12/14/2010 | 12/16/2010 | 12/30/2010 |
| 0.605Q | 03/02/2011 | 03/14/2011 | 03/16/2011 | 03/31/2011 |
| 0.605Q | 06/02/2011 | 06/14/2011 | 06/16/2011 | 06/30/2011 |

**Indicated Div: $2.42 (Div. Reinv. Plan)**

**Valuation Analysis**

| | | | |
|---|---|---|---|
| Forecast EPS | N/A | | |
| Market Cap | $473.9 Million | Book Value | $138.2 Million |
| Price/Book | 3.43 | Price/Sales | 17.42 |

**Dividend Achiever Status**

| | |
|---|---|
| **10 Year Growth Rate** | 2.56% |
| **Total Years of Dividend Growth** | 23 |

**Business Summary:** REITs (MIC: 5.3.1 SIC: 6798 NAIC: 525930)

Universal Health Realty Income Trust is real estate investment trust. Co. invests in health care and human service related facilities, including acute care hospitals, behavioral healthcare facilities, rehabilitation hospitals, sub-acute facilities, surgery centers, childcare centers and medical office buildings (MOBs). As of Dec 31 2010, Co. had 52 real estate investments or commitments located in 15 states in the U.S. consisting of: seven hospital facilities, including three acute care, one behavioral healthcare, one rehabilitation and two sub-acute; 41 MOBs, including 32 owned by various limited liability companies; and four preschool and childcare centers.

**Recent Developments:** For the quarter ended June 30 2011, net income decreased 13.6% to US$3.7 million from US$4.3 million in the year-earlier quarter. Revenues were US$6.8 million, down 9.5% from US$7.5 million the year before.

**Prospects:** Our evaluation of Universal Health Realty Income Trust as of Sep. 6, 2011 is the result of our systematic analysis on three basic characteristics: earnings strength, relative valuation, and recent stock price movement. The company has managed to produce a neutral trend in earnings per share over the past 5 quarters. Because the company lacks sufficient analyst estimate data, we place greater weight on the historical EPS trend as the measure of earnings strength. Based on operating earnings yield, the company is overvalued when compared to all of the companies in our coverage universe. Share price changes over the past year indicates that UHT will perform in line with the market over the nea

**Financial Data**

| (US$ in Thousands) | 6 Mos | 3 Mos | 12/31/2010 | 12/31/2009 | 12/31/2008 | 12/31/2007 | 12/31/2006 | 12/31/2005 |
|---|---|---|---|---|---|---|---|---|
| Earnings Per Share | 1.22 | 1.28 | 1.33 | 1.56 | 0.98 | 1.87 | 2.92 | 2.15 |
| Cash Flow Per Share | 1.67 | 1.75 | 1.88 | 2.10 | 1.84 | 1.93 | 2.10 | 2.15 |
| Tang Book Value Per Share | 10.91 | 11.22 | 11.49 | 11.66 | 12.21 | 13.54 | 13.92 | 13.20 |
| Dividends Per Share | 2.420 | 2.420 | 2.415 | 2.380 | 2.340 | 2.300 | 2.260 | 2.175 |
| Dividend Payout % | 198.36 | 189.06 | 181.58 | 152.56 | 238.78 | 122.99 | 77.40 | 101.16 |
| **Income Statement** | | | | | | | | |
| Total Revenue | 13,442 | 6,676 | 28,878 | 31,914 | 29,184 | 27,960 | 32,509 | 33,338 |
| EBITDA | 9,350 | 4,837 | 20,578 | 23,687 | 18,235 | 20,981 | 22,580 | 23,947 |
| Depn & Amortn | 3,042 | 1,503 | 6,286 | 6,399 | 5,904 | 5,209 | 5,757 | 5,825 |
| Income Before Taxes | 5,562 | 2,956 | 12,353 | 14,840 | 9,940 | 14,023 | 14,540 | 14,824 |
| Net Income | 7,820 | 4,128 | 16,310 | 18,576 | 11,653 | 22,191 | 34,697 | 25,423 |
| Average Shares | 12,651 | 12,642 | 12,262 | 11,897 | 11,882 | 11,875 | 11,866 | 11,841 |
| **Balance Sheet** | | | | | | | | |
| Current Assets | 3,857 | 4,058 | 3,863 | 6,057 | 3,545 | 2,837 | 2,637 | 13,166 |
| Total Assets | 227,741 | 221,686 | 216,135 | 228,825 | 221,056 | 199,749 | 194,139 | 196,889 |
| Current Liabilities | 71,799 | 62,094 | 113 | 142 | 190 | 125 | 84 | 357 |
| Long-Term Obligations | 14,823 | 14,897 | 67,563 | 84,267 | 71,692 | 36,617 | 26,337 | 35,548 |
| Total Liabilities | 89,575 | 79,667 | 70,722 | 87,863 | 76,128 | 39,444 | 29,942 | 41,439 |
| Stockholders' Equity | 138,166 | 142,019 | 145,413 | 140,962 | 144,928 | 160,305 | 164,197 | 155,450 |
| Shares Outstanding | 12,663 | 12,654 | 12,653 | 12,089 | 11,865 | 11,841 | 11,791 | 11,777 |
| **Statistical Record** | | | | | | | | |
| Return on Assets % | 6.76 | 7.15 | 7.33 | 8.26 | 5.52 | 11.27 | 17.75 | 12.66 |
| Return on Equity % | 11.02 | 11.35 | 11.39 | 13.00 | 7.61 | 13.68 | 21.71 | 16.43 |
| EBITDA Margin % | 69.56 | 72.45 | 71.26 | 74.22 | 62.48 | 75.04 | 69.46 | 71.83 |
| Net Margin % | 58.18 | 61.83 | 56.48 | 58.21 | 39.93 | 79.37 | 106.73 | 76.26 |
| Asset Turnover | 0.12 | 0.13 | 0.13 | 0.14 | 0.14 | 0.14 | 0.17 | 0.17 |
| Current Ratio | 0.05 | 0.07 | 34.19 | 42.65 | 18.66 | 22.70 | 31.39 | 36.88 |
| Debt to Equity | 0.11 | 0.10 | 0.46 | 0.60 | 0.49 | 0.23 | 0.16 | 0.23 |
| Price Range | 43.38-31.50 | 40.53-30.79 | 38.40-30.79 | 35.28-25.11 | 39.14-23.27 | 42.05-29.23 | 40.24-29.72 | 40.80-27.47 |
| P/E Ratio | 35.56-25.82 | 31.66-24.05 | 28.87-23.15 | 22.62-16.10 | 39.94-23.74 | 22.49-15.63 | 13.78-10.18 | 18.98-12.78 |
| Average Yield % | 6.53 | 6.91 | 7.08 | 7.51 | 6.97 | 6.48 | 6.50 | 6.56 |

**Address:** Universal Corporate Center, 367 South Gulph Road, King of Prussia, PA 19406
**Telephone:** 610-265-0688
**Web Site:** www.uhrit.com

**Officers:** Alan B. Miller - Chairman, President, Chief Executive Officer Charles F. Boyle - Vice President, Chief Financial Officer **Transfer Agents:** EquiServe Trust Company, N.A., Providence, RI

**No of Institutions:** 142
**Shares:** 6,571,694 **% Held:** 51.92

# URSTADT BIDDLE PROPERTIES INC

| Exchange | Symbol | Price | 52Wk Range | Yield | P/E |
|---|---|---|---|---|---|
| NYS | UBA | $16.81 (8/31/2011) | 20.05-15.31 | 5.83 | 25.86 |

*7 Year Price Score 110.51 *NYSE Composite Index=100 *12 Month Price Score 94.54

**Interim Earnings (Per Share)**

| Qtr. | Jan | Apr | Jul | Oct |
|---|---|---|---|---|
| 2007-08 | 0.16 | 0.15 | 0.16 | 0.11 |
| 2008-09 | 0.13 | 0.15 | 0.14 | 0.12 |
| 2009-10 | 0.11 | 0.10 | 0.16 | 0.14 |
| 2010-11 | 0.23 | 0.12 | ... | ... |

**Interim Dividends (Per Share)**

| Amt | Decl | Ex | Rec | Pay |
|---|---|---|---|---|
| 0.242Q | 09/15/2010 | 09/29/2010 | 10/01/2010 | 10/15/2010 |
| 0.245Q | 12/16/2010 | 01/05/2011 | 01/07/2011 | 01/21/2011 |
| 0.245Q | 03/10/2011 | 03/30/2011 | 04/01/2011 | 04/15/2011 |
| 0.245Q | 06/07/2011 | 06/29/2011 | 07/01/2011 | 07/15/2011 |

**Indicated Div: $0.98**

**Valuation Analysis**

Forecast EPS $0.69 (09/02/2011)
Market Cap $496.8 Million Book Value $402.6 Million
Price/Book 1.23 Price/Sales 5.50

**Dividend Achiever Status**

**10 Year Growth Rate** 1.95%
**Total Years of Dividend Growth** 12

**Business Summary:** REITs (MIC: 5.3.1 SIC: 6798 NAIC: 525930)

Urstadt Biddle Properties is a real estate investment trust engaged in the acquisition, ownership and management of commercial real estate, mainly neighborhood and community shopping centers in the northeastern part of the U.S. Other real estate assets include office and industrial properties. Co.'s major tenants include supermarket chains and other retailers who sell basic necessities. At Oct 31 2010, Co. owned or had equity interests in 50 properties comprised of neighborhood and community shopping centers, office buildings, office/retail mixed use and industrial facilities located in seven states throughout the U.S., containing a total of 4.6 million square feet of gross leasable area.

**Recent Developments:** For the quarter ended Apr 30 2011, net income increased 12.1% to US$7.0 million from US$6.2 million in the year-earlier quarter. Revenues were US$22.4 million, up 5.7% from US$21.1 million the year before. Revenues from property income rose 3.7% to US$21.7 million from US$20.9 million in the corresponding quarter a year earlier.

**Prospects:** Our evaluation of Urstadt Biddle Properties Inc. as of Sep. 6, 2011 is the result of our systematic analysis on three basic characteristics: earnings strength, relative valuation, and recent stock price movement. The company has generated a negative trend in earnings per share over the past 5 quarters. Because the company lacks sufficient analyst estimate data, we place greater weight on the historical EPS trend as the measure of earnings strength. Based on operating earnings yield, the company is about fairly valued when compared to all of the companies in our coverage universe. Share price changes over the past year indicates that UBA will perform poorly over the near term.

| **Financial Data** (US$ in Thousands) | 6 Mos | 3 Mos | 10/31/2010 | 10/31/2009 | 10/31/2008 | 10/31/2007 | 10/31/2006 | 10/31/2005 |
|---|---|---|---|---|---|---|---|---|
| Earnings Per Share | 0.65 | 0.63 | 0.52 | 0.54 | 0.58 | 1.25 | 0.57 | 0.87 |
| Cash Flow Per Share | 1.63 | 1.64 | 1.78 | 1.71 | 1.78 | 1.95 | 1.42 | 1.40 |
| Tang Book Value Per Share | 11.55 | 11.63 | 11.69 | 11.66 | 12.03 | 10.74 | 10.29 | 10.57 |
| Dividends Per Share | 0.975 | 0.973 | 0.970 | 0.960 | 0.950 | 0.920 | 0.900 | 0.880 |
| Dividend Payout % | 150.00 | 154.37 | 186.54 | 177.78 | 163.79 | 73.60 | 157.89 | 101.15 |
| **Income Statement** | | | | | | | | |
| Total Revenue | 46,879 | 24,526 | 85,149 | 82,572 | 80,856 | 81,880 | 73,249 | 69,964 |
| EBITDA | 31,299 | 17,303 | 57,725 | 56,756 | 56,921 | 61,600 | 54,277 | 46,692 |
| Depn & Amortn | 7,593 | 3,787 | 15,066 | 15,366 | 14,374 | 13,482 | 13,243 | 14,016 |
| Income Before Taxes | 20,321 | 11,810 | 35,074 | 34,695 | 35,535 | 40,345 | 32,747 | 24,174 |
| Net Income | 17,062 | 10,149 | 27,542 | 27,743 | 28,525 | 44,388 | 25,032 | 30,985 |
| Average Shares | 28,673 | 28,448 | 26,118 | 25,418 | 25,759 | 25,987 | 25,872 | 25,907 |
| **Balance Sheet** | | | | | | | | |
| Current Assets | 25,304 | 29,687 | 37,972 | 31,808 | 20,862 | 23,135 | 22,576 | 44,589 |
| Total Assets | 557,970 | 554,161 | 557,053 | 504,539 | 506,117 | 471,770 | 451,350 | 464,439 |
| Current Liabilities | 17,708 | 15,316 | 1,397 | 771 | 606 | 3,970 | 1,785 | 3,991 |
| Long-Term Obligations | 122,676 | 118,326 | 129,802 | 116,417 | 110,054 | 108,482 | 104,341 | 111,786 |
| Total Liabilities | 155,414 | 149,413 | 153,399 | 134,755 | 129,617 | 124,820 | 118,147 | 126,845 |
| Stockholders' Equity | 402,556 | 404,748 | 403,654 | 369,784 | 376,500 | 346,950 | 333,203 | 337,594 |
| Shares Outstanding | 29,554 | 29,537 | 29,281 | 26,463 | 26,198 | 26,610 | 26,440 | 26,135 |
| **Statistical Record** | | | | | | | | |
| Return on Assets % | 6.00 | 5.94 | 5.19 | 5.49 | 5.82 | 9.62 | 5.47 | 7.21 |
| Return on Equity % | 8.35 | 8.11 | 7.12 | 7.43 | 7.86 | 13.05 | 7.46 | 10.12 |
| EBITDA Margin % | 66.77 | 70.55 | 67.79 | 68.74 | 70.40 | 75.23 | 74.10 | 66.74 |
| Net Margin % | 36.40 | 41.38 | 32.35 | 33.60 | 35.28 | 54.21 | 34.17 | 44.29 |
| Asset Turnover | 0.17 | 0.17 | 0.16 | 0.16 | 0.16 | 0.18 | 0.16 | 0.16 |
| Current Ratio | 1.43 | 1.94 | 27.18 | 41.26 | 34.43 | 5.83 | 12.65 | 11.17 |
| Debt to Equity | 0.30 | 0.29 | 0.32 | 0.31 | 0.29 | 0.31 | 0.31 | 0.33 |
| Price Range | 20.05-15.72 | 19.97-14.49 | 19.55-13.72 | 17.39-10.08 | 19.28-12.79 | 19.62-14.97 | 19.44-15.58 | 18.75-14.26 |
| P/E Ratio | 30.85-24.18 | 31.70-23.00 | 37.60-26.38 | 32.20-18.67 | 33.24-22.05 | 15.70-11.98 | 34.11-27.33 | 21.55-16.39 |
| Average Yield % | 5.30 | 5.50 | 5.84 | 6.55 | 5.84 | 5.16 | 5.29 | 5.37 |

**Address:** 321 Railroad Avenue, Greenwich, CT 06830
**Telephone:** 203-863-8200
**Web Site:** www.ubproperties.com

**Officers:** Charles J. Urstadt - Chairman, Chief Executive Officer Robert R. Douglass - Vice-Chairman **Transfer Agents:** The Bank of New York Mellon, New York, NY

**Investor Contact:** 203-863-8200
**No of Institutions:** 36
**Shares:** 1,111,700 **% Held:** 3.93

# VALSPAR CORP.

| Exchange | Symbol | Price | 52Wk Range | Yield | P/E |
|---|---|---|---|---|---|
| NYS | VAL | $32.29 (8/31/2011) | 40.18-27.59 | 2.23 | 14.88 |

***7 Year Price Score 131.62** *NYSE Composite Index=100 ***12 Month Price Score 93.39**

**Interim Earnings (Per Share)**

| Qtr. | Jan | Apr | Jul | Oct |
|---|---|---|---|---|
| 2007-08 | 0.21 | 0.38 | 0.44 | 0.35 |
| 2008-09 | 0.11 | 0.28 | 0.61 | 0.49 |
| 2009-10 | 0.34 | 0.61 | 0.74 | 0.51 |
| 2010-11 | 0.34 | 0.58 | ... | ... |

**Interim Dividends (Per Share)**

| Amt | Decl | Ex | Rec | Pay |
|---|---|---|---|---|
| 0.16Q | 09/20/2010 | 09/29/2010 | 10/01/2010 | 10/15/2010 |
| 0.18Q | 12/08/2010 | 12/22/2010 | 12/27/2010 | 01/14/2011 |
| 0.18Q | 02/17/2011 | 03/30/2011 | 04/01/2011 | 04/15/2011 |
| 0.18Q | 06/08/2011 | 06/29/2011 | 07/01/2011 | 07/15/2011 |

**Indicated Div: $0.72 (Div. Reinv. Plan)**

**Valuation Analysis**

| | | | |
|---|---|---|---|
| Forecast EPS | $2.52 (09/02/2011) | | |
| Market Cap | $3.0 Billion | Book Value | $1.5 Billion |
| Price/Book | 1.97 | Price/Sales | 0.84 |

**Dividend Achiever Status**

| | |
|---|---|
| 10 Year Growth Rate | 9.01% |
| Total Years of Dividend Growth | 32 |

**Business Summary:** Specialty Chemicals (MIC: 8.3.2 SIC: 2851 NAIC: 325510)

Valspar is a coatings and paints manufacturer and distributor. Co. operates through two segments: Coatings and Paints. Co.'s Coatings segment includes decorative and protective coatings for metal, wood and plastic, primarily for sale to original equipment manufacturing customers. Products within Co.'s Coatings segment include primers, top coats, varnishes, sprays, stains, fillers and other coatings. Co.'s Paints segment includes a range of products such as paints, primers, topcoats and aerosol spray paints sold primarily through retailers and distribution networks. This segment includes Co.'s consumer paints and automotive refinish product lines.

**Recent Developments:** For the quarter ended Apr 29 2011, net income decreased 8.7% to US$56.3 million from US$61.7 million in the year-earlier quarter. Revenues were US$992.7 million, up 23.5% from US$803.6 million the year before. Operating income was US$99.5 million versus US$104.3 million in the prior-year quarter, a decrease of 4.6%. Direct operating expenses rose 27.7% to US$677.2 million from US$530.2 million in the comparable period the year before. Indirect operating expenses increased 27.8% to US$216.0 million from US$169.1 million in the equivalent prior-year period.

**Prospects:** Our evaluation of Valspar Corp. as of Sep. 6, 2011 is the result of our systematic analysis on three basic characteristics: earnings strength, relative valuation, and recent stock price movement. The company has enjoyed a very positive trend in earnings per share over the past 5 quarters. However, while recent estimates for the company have been lowered by analysts, VAL has posted results that were in line with analysts expectations. Based on operating earnings yield, the company is undervalued when compared to all of the companies in our coverage universe. Share price changes over the past year indicates that VAL will perform poorly over the near term.

**Financial Data**

| (US$ in Thousands) | 6 Mos | 3 Mos | 10/29/2010 | 10/30/2009 | 10/31/2008 | 10/26/2007 | 10/27/2006 | 10/28/2005 |
|---|---|---|---|---|---|---|---|---|
| Earnings Per Share | 2.17 | 2.20 | 2.20 | 1.49 | 1.38 | 1.50 | 1.71 | 1.42 |
| Cash Flow Per Share | 1.62 | 2.49 | 2.71 | 3.38 | 2.61 | 1.89 | 2.82 | 2.27 |
| Dividends Per Share | 0.680 | 0.660 | 0.640 | 0.600 | 0.560 | 0.520 | 0.440 | 0.400 |
| Dividend Payout % | 31.34 | 30.00 | 29.09 | 40.27 | 40.58 | 34.67 | 25.73 | 28.17 |
| **Income Statement** | | | | | | | | |
| Total Revenue | 1,835,133 | 842,404 | 3,226,687 | 2,879,042 | 3,482,378 | 3,249,287 | 2,978,062 | 2,713,950 |
| EBITDA | 207,537 | 84,862 | 451,503 | 371,584 | 367,273 | 393,244 | 372,354 | 338,637 |
| Depn & Amortn | 45,180 | 22,038 | 74,039 | 82,862 | 80,831 | 71,811 | 68,716 | 68,395 |
| Income Before Taxes | 131,312 | 47,265 | 319,197 | 238,328 | 228,697 | 259,771 | 257,432 | 225,720 |
| Income Taxes | 41,577 | 13,838 | 97,141 | 78,175 | 77,931 | 87,656 | 82,180 | 78,102 |
| Net Income | 89,735 | 33,427 | 222,056 | 160,153 | 150,766 | 172,115 | 175,252 | 147,618 |
| Average Shares | 97,497 | 99,600 | 100,866 | 100,921 | 100,326 | 102,617 | 102,726 | 104,149 |
| **Balance Sheet** | | | | | | | | |
| Current Assets | 1,406,001 | 1,264,209 | 1,284,922 | 1,062,466 | 1,047,020 | 1,029,642 | 967,123 | 865,204 |
| Total Assets | 4,039,902 | 3,851,792 | 3,867,936 | 3,511,024 | 3,520,042 | 3,452,281 | 3,188,253 | 2,761,163 |
| Current Liabilities | 1,183,211 | 920,665 | 884,851 | 711,479 | 880,343 | 1,029,147 | 1,195,683 | 625,631 |
| Long-Term Obligations | 903,031 | 949,795 | 943,216 | 873,095 | 763,129 | 648,988 | 350,267 | 706,415 |
| Total Liabilities | 2,505,061 | 2,282,050 | 2,237,571 | 2,006,517 | 2,033,597 | 2,034,142 | 1,929,467 | 1,700,071 |
| Stockholders' Equity | 1,534,841 | 1,569,742 | 1,630,365 | 1,504,507 | 1,486,445 | 1,418,139 | 1,258,786 | 1,061,092 |
| Shares Outstanding | 93,620 | 95,944 | 98,027 | 99,482 | 99,992 | 100,634 | 101,904 | 100,432 |
| **Statistical Record** | | | | | | | | |
| Return on Assets % | 5.72 | 6.13 | 6.04 | 4.57 | 4.25 | 5.20 | 5.91 | 5.49 |
| Return on Equity % | 14.05 | 14.37 | 14.21 | 10.74 | 10.21 | 12.89 | 15.15 | 14.36 |
| EBITDA Margin % | 11.31 | 10.07 | 13.99 | 12.91 | 10.55 | 12.10 | 12.50 | 12.48 |
| Net Margin % | 4.89 | 3.97 | 6.88 | 5.56 | 4.33 | 5.30 | 5.88 | 5.44 |
| Asset Turnover | 0.95 | 0.94 | 0.88 | 0.82 | 0.98 | 0.98 | 1.00 | 1.01 |
| Current Ratio | 1.19 | 1.37 | 1.45 | 1.49 | 1.19 | 1.00 | 0.81 | 1.38 |
| Debt to Equity | 0.59 | 0.61 | 0.58 | 0.58 | 0.51 | 0.46 | 0.28 | 0.67 |
| Price Range | 40.18-29.50 | 37.33-25.25 | 32.91-25.25 | 28.35-14.57 | 26.04-16.96 | 29.22-24.57 | 29.42-21.80 | 25.38-20.57 |
| P/E Ratio | 18.52-13.59 | 16.97-11.48 | 14.96-11.48 | 19.03-9.78 | 18.87-12.29 | 19.48-16.38 | 17.20-12.75 | 17.87-14.49 |
| Average Yield % | 2.02 | 2.11 | 2.16 | 2.75 | 2.59 | 1.88 | 1.68 | 1.71 |

**Address:** 901 3rd Avenue South, Minneapolis, MN 55402
**Telephone:** 612-851-7000
**Web Site:** www.valsparglobal.com

**Officers:** William L. Mansfield - Chairman Gary E. Hendrickson - President, Chief Executive Officer
**Transfer Agents:** BNY Mellon Shareholder Services, Jersey City, NJ

**No of Institutions:** 286
**Shares:** 77,549,464 **% Held:** 64.02

# VECTOR GROUP LTD

| Exchange | Symbol | Price | 52Wk Range | Yield | P/E |
|---|---|---|---|---|---|
| NYS | VGR | $18.68 (8/31/2011) | 19.80-15.88 | 8.57 | 20.53 |

***7 Year Price Score 117.64** *NYSE Composite Index=100 ***12 Month Price Score 100.69**

**Interim Earnings (Per Share)**

| Qtr. | Mar | Jun | Sep | Dec |
|---|---|---|---|---|
| 2008 | 0.19 | 0.22 | 0.19 | 0.09 |
| 2009 | 0.04 | (0.11) | 0.21 | 0.17 |
| 2010 | 0.14 | 0.19 | 0.14 | 0.16 |
| 2011 | 0.25 | 0.36 | ... | ... |

**Interim Dividends (Per Share)**

| Amt | Decl | Ex | Rec | Pay |
|---|---|---|---|---|
| 0.40Q | 03/07/2011 | 03/16/2011 | 03/18/2011 | 03/29/2011 |
| 0.40Q | 06/08/2011 | 06/15/2011 | 06/17/2011 | 06/29/2011 |
| 0.40Q | 09/01/2011 | 09/16/2011 | 09/20/2011 | 09/29/2011 |
| 5% | 09/01/2011 | 09/16/2011 | 09/20/2011 | 09/29/2011 |

**Indicated Div: $1.60 (Div. Reinv. Plan)**

**Valuation Analysis**

| | | | |
|---|---|---|---|
| Forecast EPS | N/A | | |
| Market Cap | $1.4 Billion | Book Value | N/A |
| Price/Book | N/A | Price/Sales | 1.26 |

**Dividend Achiever Status**

| | |
|---|---|
| **10 Year Growth Rate** | 4.49% |
| **Total Years of Dividend Growth** | 12 |

**Business Summary:** Tobacco Products (MIC: 1.3.1 SIC: 2111 NAIC: 312221)

Vector Group is a holding company. Co. operates through two segments: Tobacco and Real Estate. The Tobacco segment consists of the manufacture and sale of cigarettes in the U.S. through Co.'s subsidiaries, Liggett Group, LLC. (Liggett), and Vector Tobacco, Inc. Liggett's brand portfolio includes PYRAMID, GRAND PRIX; LIGGETT SELECT, EVE; PYRAMID; and USA. The Real Estate segment includes Co.'s investment in the 450-acre approved master planned community in Palm Springs, CA and investments in non-consolidated real estate businesses. Co. conducts its real estate business through its subsidiary, New Valley, LLC.

**Recent Developments:** For the quarter ended June 30 2011, net income increased 57.6% to US$30.3 million from US$19.2 million in the year-earlier quarter. Revenues were US$291.2 million, up 8.5% from US$268.5 million the year before. Operating income was US$38.0 million versus US$21.1 million in the prior-year quarter, an increase of 80.1%. Direct operating expenses rose 9.5% to US$231.1 million from US$211.0 million in the comparable period the year before. Indirect operating expenses decreased 39.2% to US$22.1 million from US$36.4 million in the equivalent prior-year period.

**Prospects:** Our evaluation of Vector Group Ltd. as of Sep. 6, 2011 is the result of our systematic analysis on three basic characteristics: earnings strength, relative valuation, and recent stock price movement. The company has generated a negative trend in earnings per share over the past 5 quarters. Because the company lacks sufficient analyst estimate data, we place greater weight on the historical EPS trend as the measure of earnings strength. Based on operating earnings yield, the company is overvalued when compared to all of the companies in our coverage universe. Share price changes over the past year indicates that VGR will perform very poorly over the near term.

**Financial Data**

| (US$ in Thousands) | 6 Mos | 3 Mos | 12/31/2010 | 12/31/2009 | 12/31/2008 | 12/31/2007 | 12/31/2006 | 12/31/2005 |
|---|---|---|---|---|---|---|---|---|
| Earnings Per Share | 0.91 | 0.74 | 0.71 | 0.32 | 0.73 | 0.98 | 0.58 | 0.83 |
| Cash Flow Per Share | 0.64 | 0.73 | 0.90 | 0.08 | 1.28 | 1.58 | 0.70 | 1.21 |
| Dividends Per Share | 1.581 | 1.562 | 1.543 | 1.469 | 1.399 | 1.333 | 1.269 | 1.209 |
| Dividend Payout % | 173.73 | 210.93 | 217.30 | 453.79 | 192.86 | 136.54 | 217.31 | 145.54 |
| **Income Statement** | | | | | | | | |
| Total Revenue | 551,558 | 260,378 | 1,063,289 | 801,494 | 565,186 | 555,430 | 506,252 | 478,427 |
| EBITDA | 119,777 | 52,046 | 156,493 | 91,720 | 136,701 | 156,427 | 98,058 | 110,994 |
| Depn & Amortn | ... | ... | 10,790 | 10,398 | 10,057 | 10,202 | 9,888 | 11,349 |
| Income Before Taxes | 69,767 | 27,118 | 61,607 | 13,324 | 70,173 | 110,360 | 59,394 | 73,275 |
| Income Taxes | 31,194 | 12,649 | 31,486 | 3,731 | 34,068 | 52,800 | 25,768 | 40,352 |
| Net Income | 49,674 | 19,373 | 54,084 | 24,806 | 60,504 | 73,803 | 42,712 | 49,082 |
| Average Shares | 81,697 | 74,760 | 74,693 | 73,059 | 78,415 | 70,938 | 67,683 | 59,210 |
| **Balance Sheet** | | | | | | | | |
| Current Assets | 564,816 | 515,031 | 526,763 | 389,208 | 355,283 | 395,626 | 303,156 | 319,099 |
| Total Assets | 941,159 | 924,561 | 949,595 | 735,542 | 717,712 | 785,289 | 637,462 | 603,130 |
| Current Liabilities | 307,203 | 220,191 | 226,872 | 149,008 | 296,159 | 109,337 | 168,786 | 128,100 |
| Long-Term Obligations | 486,989 | 501,751 | 506,052 | 334,920 | 210,301 | 277,178 | 103,304 | 243,590 |
| Total Liabilities | 991,228 | 985,916 | 995,829 | 740,224 | 684,107 | 684,437 | 542,485 | 569,727 |
| Stockholders' Equity | (50,069) | (61,355) | (46,234) | (4,682) | 33,605 | 100,852 | 94,977 | 33,403 |
| Shares Outstanding | 75,719 | 74,997 | 74,939 | 74,825 | 72,780 | 69,875 | 69,321 | 63,622 |
| **Statistical Record** | | | | | | | | |
| Return on Assets % | 8.11 | 7.38 | 6.42 | 3.41 | 8.03 | 10.37 | 6.89 | 8.62 |
| Return on Equity % | ... | ... | ... | 171.53 | 89.75 | 75.37 | 66.54 | ... |
| EBITDA Margin % | 21.72 | 19.99 | 14.72 | 11.44 | 24.19 | 28.16 | 19.37 | 23.20 |
| Net Margin % | 9.01 | 7.44 | 5.09 | 3.09 | 10.71 | 13.29 | 8.44 | 10.26 |
| Asset Turnover | 1.26 | 1.32 | 1.26 | 1.10 | 0.75 | 0.78 | 0.82 | 0.84 |
| Current Ratio | 1.84 | 2.34 | 2.32 | 2.61 | 1.20 | 3.62 | 1.80 | 2.49 |
| Debt to Equity | ... | ... | ... | ... | 6.26 | 2.75 | 1.09 | 7.29 |
| Price Range | 19.80-15.88 | 19.80-14.63 | 19.80-13.03 | 15.15-10.22 | 17.33-12.05 | 20.33-14.30 | 15.11-12.41 | 16.16-11.22 |
| P/E Ratio | 21.76-17.45 | 26.76-19.77 | 27.89-18.35 | 47.34-31.94 | 23.74-16.50 | 20.74-14.59 | 26.05-21.40 | 19.47-13.52 |
| Average Yield % | 8.87 | 9.12 | 9.39 | 11.10 | 9.30 | 7.77 | 9.17 | 8.91 |

| | | |
|---|---|---|
| **Address:** 100 S.E. Second Street, Miami, FL 33131<br>**Telephone:** 305-579-8000<br>**Web Site:** www.vectorgroupltd.com | **Officers:** Bennett S. LeBow - Chairman Howard M. Lorber - President, Chief Executive Officer **Transfer Agents:** American Stock Transfer & Trust Company, New York, NY | **No of Institutions:** 127<br>**Shares:** 37,463,340 **% Held:** 46.07 |

# UGI CORP.

| Exchange | Symbol | Price | 52Wk Range | Yield | P/E |
|---|---|---|---|---|---|
| NYS | UGI | $29.76 (8/31/2011) | 33.30-25.93 | 3.49 | 13.05 |

***7 Year Price Score 118.16** *NYSE Composite Index=100 ***12 Month Price Score 97.18**

**Interim Earnings (Per Share)**

| Qtr. | Dec | Mar | Jun | Sep |
|---|---|---|---|---|
| 2007-08 | 0.74 | 1.17 | 0.14 | (0.06) |
| 2008-09 | 1.05 | 1.45 | (0.03) | (0.11) |
| 2009-10 | 0.90 | 1.43 | 0.03 | 0.01 |
| 2010-11 | 1.01 | 1.32 | (0.06) | ... |

**Interim Dividends (Per Share)**

| Amt | Decl | Ex | Rec | Pay |
|---|---|---|---|---|
| 0.25Q | 11/19/2010 | 12/13/2010 | 12/15/2010 | 01/01/2011 |
| 0.25Q | 01/20/2011 | 03/11/2011 | 03/15/2011 | 04/01/2011 |
| 0.26Q | 04/28/2011 | 06/13/2011 | 06/15/2011 | 07/01/2011 |
| 0.26Q | 07/26/2011 | 09/13/2011 | 09/15/2011 | 10/01/2011 |

**Indicated Div: $1.04 (Div. Reinv. Plan)**

**Valuation Analysis**

| | | | |
|---|---|---|---|
| Forecast EPS | $2.18 (09/05/2011) | | |
| Market Cap | $3.3 Billion | Book Value | $2.1 Billion |
| Price/Book | 1.58 | Price/Sales | 0.56 |

**Dividend Achiever Status**

| | |
|---|---|
| 10 Year Growth Rate | 5.54% |
| Total Years of Dividend Growth | 23 |

**Business Summary:** Gas Utilities (MIC: 3.3.1 SIC: 4932 NAIC: 221210)

UGI is a holding company. Through its subsidiaries, Co. distributes and markets energy products and related services. Co. is a retail distributor of propane and butane; a provider of natural gas and electric service through regulated local distribution utilities; a generator of electricity; a marketer of energy commodities; a manager of midstream assets; and a provider of heating, ventilation, air conditioning, refrigeration and electrical contracting services. Co.'s subsidiaries and affiliates operate principally in the following six business segments: AmeriGas Propane; International Propane - Antargaz; International Propane - Other; Gas Utility; Electric Utility; and Midstream & Marketing.

**Recent Developments:** For the quarter ended June 30 2011, net loss amounted to US$13.5 million versus a net loss of US$4.2 million in the year-earlier quarter. Revenues were US$1.11 billion, up 14.9% from US$961.9 million the year before. Operating income was US$17.2 million versus US$31.2 million in the prior-year quarter, a decrease of 44.9%. Direct operating expenses rose 18.8% to US$731.0 million from US$615.5 million in the comparable period the year before. Indirect operating expenses increased 13.3% to US$357.2 million from US$315.2 million in the equivalent prior-year period.

**Prospects:** Our evaluation of UGI Corp. as of Sep. 6, 2011 is the result of our systematic analysis on three basic characteristics: earnings strength, relative valuation, and recent stock price movement. The company has generated a negative trend in earnings per share over the past 5 quarters. However, while recent estimates for the company have been mixed, UGI has posted results that fell short of analysts expectations. Based on operating earnings yield, the company is undervalued when compared to all of the companies in our coverage universe. Share price changes over the past year indicates that UGI will perform very poorly over the near term.

| **Financial Data** (US$ in Thousands) | 9 Mos | 6 Mos | 3 Mos | 09/30/2010 | 09/30/2009 | 09/30/2008 | 09/30/2007 | 09/30/2006 |
|---|---|---|---|---|---|---|---|---|
| Earnings Per Share | 2.28 | 2.37 | 2.48 | 2.36 | 2.36 | 1.99 | 1.89 | 1.65 |
| Cash Flow Per Share | 4.90 | 5.25 | 4.92 | 5.46 | 6.13 | 4.31 | 4.29 | 2.65 |
| Tang Book Value Per Share | 3.04 | 3.38 | 2.11 | 1.01 | N.M. | N.M. | N.M. | N.M. |
| Dividends Per Share | 1.010 | 1.000 | 0.950 | 0.900 | 0.785 | 0.755 | 0.723 | 0.690 |
| Dividend Payout % | 44.30 | 42.19 | 38.31 | 38.14 | 33.26 | 37.94 | 38.23 | 41.82 |
| **Income Statement** | | | | | | | | |
| Total Revenue | 5,052,000 | 3,946,600 | 1,765,600 | 5,591,400 | 5,737,800 | 6,648,200 | 5,476,900 | 5,221,000 |
| EBITDA | 770,100 | 698,500 | 305,900 | 843,900 | 860,500 | 756,200 | 737,300 | 580,800 |
| Depn & Amortn | 149,000 | 98,200 | 49,200 | 187,600 | 180,200 | 182,600 | 167,500 | 147,400 |
| Income Before Taxes | 518,500 | 532,700 | 223,400 | 525,400 | 544,200 | 442,700 | 441,700 | 325,600 |
| Income Taxes | 160,600 | 161,500 | 68,200 | 167,600 | 159,100 | 134,500 | 126,700 | 98,500 |
| Net Income | 255,300 | 262,500 | 113,100 | 261,000 | 258,500 | 215,500 | 204,300 | 176,200 |
| Average Shares | 112,020 | 113,160 | 112,416 | 110,511 | 109,339 | 108,521 | 107,941 | 106,727 |
| **Balance Sheet** | | | | | | | | |
| Current Assets | 1,290,200 | 1,579,100 | 1,635,100 | 1,220,100 | 1,185,100 | 1,338,600 | 1,173,600 | 1,040,600 |
| Total Assets | 6,673,700 | 6,894,400 | 6,807,800 | 6,374,300 | 6,042,600 | 5,685,000 | 5,502,700 | 5,080,500 |
| Current Liabilities | 1,034,900 | 1,227,900 | 2,024,100 | 1,674,700 | 1,097,300 | 1,184,200 | 1,057,500 | 1,026,600 |
| Long-Term Obligations | 2,039,500 | 2,028,000 | 1,448,400 | 1,432,200 | 2,038,600 | 1,987,300 | 2,038,800 | 1,965,000 |
| Total Liabilities | 4,562,500 | 4,755,200 | 4,859,000 | 4,549,800 | 4,451,200 | 4,267,300 | 4,180,800 | 3,980,900 |
| Stockholders' Equity | 2,111,200 | 2,139,200 | 1,948,800 | 1,824,500 | 1,591,400 | 1,417,700 | 1,321,900 | 1,099,600 |
| Shares Outstanding | 111,804 | 115,501 | 111,111 | 110,373 | 108,746 | 107,860 | 106,646 | 105,454 |
| **Statistical Record** | | | | | | | | |
| Return on Assets % | 4.12 | 4.06 | 4.16 | 4.20 | 4.41 | 3.84 | 3.86 | 3.65 |
| Return on Equity % | 13.40 | 13.67 | 15.19 | 15.28 | 17.18 | 15.69 | 16.87 | 16.80 |
| EBITDA Margin % | 15.24 | 17.70 | 17.33 | 15.09 | 15.00 | 11.37 | 13.46 | 11.12 |
| Net Margin % | 5.05 | 6.65 | 6.41 | 4.67 | 4.51 | 3.24 | 3.73 | 3.37 |
| Asset Turnover | 0.95 | 0.88 | 0.87 | 0.90 | 0.98 | 1.19 | 1.04 | 1.08 |
| Current Ratio | 1.25 | 1.29 | 0.81 | 0.73 | 1.08 | 1.13 | 1.11 | 1.01 |
| Debt to Equity | 0.97 | 0.95 | 0.74 | 0.78 | 1.28 | 1.40 | 1.54 | 1.79 |
| Price Range | 33.30-25.25 | 33.22-24.95 | 32.16-24.01 | 28.79-23.36 | 27.23-19.93 | 28.71-24.67 | 29.30-23.78 | 28.15-20.46 |
| P/E Ratio | 14.61-11.07 | 14.02-10.53 | 12.97-9.68 | 12.20-9.90 | 11.54-8.44 | 14.43-12.40 | 15.50-12.58 | 17.06-12.40 |
| Average Yield % | 3.32 | 3.44 | 3.47 | 3.48 | 3.23 | 2.86 | 2.70 | 2.99 |

| | | |
|---|---|---|
| **Address:** 460 North Gulph Road, King of Prussia, PA 19406<br>**Telephone:** 610-337-1000<br>**Web Site:** www.ugicorp.com | **Officers:** Lon R. Greenberg - Chairman, Chief Executive Officer John L. Walsh - President, Chief Operating Officer **Transfer Agents:** ComputerShare Investor Services, Providence, RI | **Investor Contact:** 610-337-1000<br>**No of Institutions:** 342<br>**Shares:** 89,381,896 **% Held:** 74.30 |

# VECTREN CORP

| Exchange | Symbol | Price | 52Wk Range | Yield | P/E |
|---|---|---|---|---|---|
| NYS | VVC | $27.37 (8/31/2011) | 28.73-23.90 | 5.04 | 18.49 |

***7 Year Price Score 99.36** *NYSE Composite Index=100 ***12 Month Price Score 100.81**

**Interim Earnings (Per Share)**

| Qtr. | Mar | Jun | Sep | Dec |
|---|---|---|---|---|
| 2008 | 0.84 | 0.06 | 0.29 | 0.46 |
| 2009 | 0.90 | (0.08) | 0.15 | 0.67 |
| 2010 | 0.78 | 0.11 | 0.20 | 0.55 |
| 2011 | 0.55 | 0.18 | ... | ... |

**Interim Dividends (Per Share)**

| Amt | Decl | Ex | Rec | Pay |
|---|---|---|---|---|
| 0.345Q | 11/05/2010 | 11/10/2010 | 11/15/2010 | 12/01/2010 |
| 0.345Q | 02/02/2011 | 02/11/2011 | 02/15/2011 | 03/01/2011 |
| 0.345Q | 04/06/2011 | 05/11/2011 | 05/13/2011 | 06/01/2011 |
| 0.345Q | 08/03/2011 | 08/11/2011 | 08/15/2011 | 09/01/2011 |

**Indicated Div: $1.38 (Div. Reinv. Plan)**

**Valuation Analysis**

| | | | |
|---|---|---|---|
| Forecast EPS | $1.74 (09/02/2011) | | |
| Market Cap | $2.2 Billion | Book Value | $1.4 Billion |
| Price/Book | 1.55 | Price/Sales | 1.04 |

**Dividend Achiever Status**

| | |
|---|---|
| **10 Year Growth Rate** | 2.86% |
| **Total Years of Dividend Growth** | 35 |

**Business Summary:** Electric Utilities (MIC: 3.1.1 SIC: 4932 NAIC: 221210)

Vectren is an energy holding company. Through its subsidiary, Vectren Utility Holdings, Inc., Co. serves as the intermediate holding company for three public utilities: Indiana Gas Company, Inc., Southern Indiana Gas and Electric Company, and the Ohio operations. Also, through Vectren Enterprises, Inc., Co. is involved in nonutility activities in four primary business areas: Infrastructure Services, which provides underground construction and repair services; Energy Services, which provides performance contracting and renewable energy services; Coal Mining, which mines and sells coal; and Energy Marketing, which markets and supplies natural gas and provides energy management services.

**Recent Developments:** For the quarter ended June 30 2011, net income increased 73.6% to US$15.1 million from US$8.7 million in the year-earlier quarter. Revenues were US$475.8 million, up 18.2% from US$402.4 million the year before. Operating income was US$61.6 million versus US$52.1 million in the prior-year quarter, an increase of 18.2%. Direct operating expenses rose 19.4% to US$177.6 million from US$148.7 million in the comparable period the year before. Indirect operating expenses increased 17.4% to US$236.6 million from US$201.6 million in the equivalent prior-year period.

**Prospects:** Our evaluation of Vectren Corp. as of Sep. 6, 2011 is the result of our systematic analysis on three basic characteristics: earnings strength, relative valuation, and recent stock price movement. The company has enjoyed a very positive trend in earnings per share over the past 5 quarters. However, while recent estimates for the company have been mixed, VVC has posted better than expected results. Based on operating earnings yield, the company is about fairly valued when compared to all of the companies in our coverage universe. Share price changes over the past year indicates that VVC will perform very poorly over the near term.

**Financial Data**

| (US$ in Thousands) | 6 Mos | 3 Mos | 12/31/2010 | 12/31/2009 | 12/31/2008 | 12/31/2007 | 12/31/2006 | 12/31/2005 |
|---|---|---|---|---|---|---|---|---|
| Earnings Per Share | 1.48 | 1.41 | 1.64 | 1.64 | 1.63 | 1.87 | 1.43 | 1.80 |
| Cash Flow Per Share | 4.84 | 4.53 | 4.74 | 5.57 | 5.39 | 3.93 | 4.10 | 3.55 |
| Tang Book Value Per Share | 14.48 | 14.61 | 14.65 | 14.24 | 13.72 | 13.05 | 12.30 | 12.32 |
| Dividends Per Share | 1.375 | 1.370 | 1.365 | 1.345 | 1.310 | 1.270 | 1.230 | 1.190 |
| Dividend Payout % | 92.91 | 97.16 | 83.23 | 82.01 | 80.37 | 67.91 | 86.01 | 66.11 |
| **Income Statement** | | | | | | | | |
| Total Revenue | 1,158,400 | 682,600 | 2,129,500 | 2,088,900 | 2,484,700 | 2,281,900 | 2,041,600 | 2,028,000 |
| EBITDA | 290,400 | 164,800 | 545,500 | 497,000 | 455,500 | 479,200 | 386,100 | 373,700 |
| Depn & Amortn | 120,300 | 59,100 | 229,100 | 211,900 | 192,300 | 184,800 | 172,300 | 158,200 |
| Income Before Taxes | 116,500 | 79,100 | 217,000 | 193,800 | 167,700 | 196,300 | 122,200 | 135,400 |
| Income Taxes | 33,900 | 23,600 | 74,700 | 64,100 | 76,100 | 76,000 | 30,300 | 44,100 |
| Net Income | 59,700 | 44,600 | 133,700 | 133,100 | 129,000 | 143,100 | 108,800 | 136,800 |
| Average Shares | 81,800 | 81,700 | 81,300 | 81,000 | 78,900 | 76,600 | 76,200 | 76,100 |
| **Balance Sheet** | | | | | | | | |
| Current Assets | 512,800 | 554,300 | 645,200 | 581,900 | 775,600 | 699,600 | 715,900 | 725,200 |
| Total Assets | 4,720,100 | 4,741,800 | 4,764,200 | 4,671,800 | 4,632,900 | 4,296,400 | 4,091,600 | 3,868,100 |
| Current Liabilities | 644,100 | 626,100 | 820,700 | 747,700 | 1,120,300 | 1,027,400 | 961,400 | 839,500 |
| Long-Term Obligations | 1,551,400 | 1,587,400 | 1,435,200 | 1,540,500 | 1,247,900 | 1,245,400 | 1,208,000 | 1,198,000 |
| Total Liabilities | 3,273,800 | 3,285,600 | 3,325,300 | 3,274,600 | 3,281,300 | 3,062,700 | 2,917,400 | 2,724,800 |
| Stockholders' Equity | 1,446,300 | 1,456,200 | 1,438,900 | 1,397,200 | 1,351,600 | 1,233,700 | 1,174,200 | 1,143,300 |
| Shares Outstanding | 81,800 | 81,700 | 81,700 | 81,100 | 81,000 | 76,300 | 76,100 | 76,000 |
| **Statistical Record** | | | | | | | | |
| Return on Assets % | 2.62 | 2.46 | 2.83 | 2.86 | 2.88 | 3.41 | 2.73 | 3.67 |
| Return on Equity % | 8.48 | 7.98 | 9.43 | 9.68 | 9.95 | 11.89 | 9.39 | 12.22 |
| EBITDA Margin % | 25.07 | 24.14 | 25.62 | 23.79 | 18.33 | 21.00 | 18.91 | 18.43 |
| Net Margin % | 5.15 | 6.53 | 6.28 | 6.37 | 5.19 | 6.27 | 5.33 | 6.75 |
| Asset Turnover | 0.46 | 0.44 | 0.45 | 0.45 | 0.56 | 0.54 | 0.51 | 0.54 |
| Current Ratio | 0.80 | 0.89 | 0.79 | 0.78 | 0.69 | 0.68 | 0.74 | 0.86 |
| Debt to Equity | 1.07 | 1.09 | 1.00 | 1.10 | 0.92 | 1.01 | 1.03 | 1.05 |
| Price Range | 28.73-23.18 | 27.74-22.41 | 27.74-22.41 | 26.72-18.27 | 32.10-21.60 | 30.41-24.96 | 29.25-25.61 | 29.32-25.39 |
| P/E Ratio | 19.41-15.66 | 19.67-15.89 | 16.91-13.66 | 16.29-11.14 | 19.69-13.25 | 16.26-13.35 | 20.45-17.91 | 16.29-14.11 |
| Average Yield % | 5.24 | 5.40 | 5.52 | 5.83 | 4.80 | 4.52 | 4.52 | 4.35 |

**Address:** One Vectren Square, Evansville, IN 47708
**Telephone:** 812-491-4000
**Web Site:** www.vectren.com

**Officers:** Carl L. Chapman - President, Chief Executive Officer Jerome A. Benkert - Executive Vice President, Chief Financial Officer **Transfer Agents:** Wells Fargo Shareowner Services, St. Paul, MN

**Investor Contact:** 800-227-8625
**No of Institutions:** 272
**Shares:** 46,961,748 **% Held:** 53.39

# VF CORP.

| Exchange | Symbol | Price | 52Wk Range | Yield | P/E |
|---|---|---|---|---|---|
| NYS | VFC | $117.06 (8/31/2011) | 121.05-70.57 | 2.15 | 20.50 |

***7 Year Price Score 129.07** *NYSE Composite Index=100 ***12 Month Price Score 121.65**

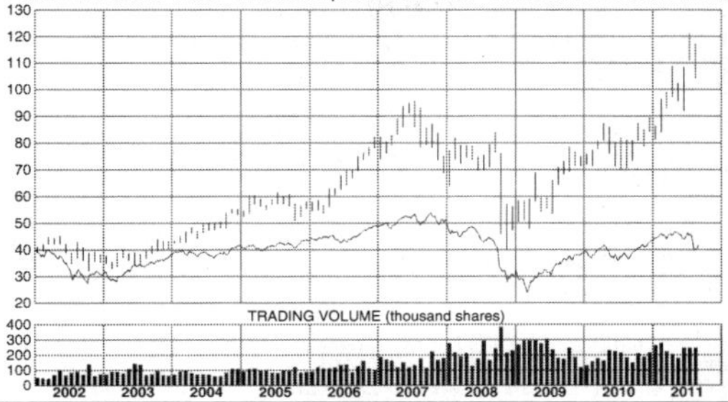


**Interim Earnings (Per Share)**

| Qtr. | Mar | Jun | Sep | Dec |
|---|---|---|---|---|
| 2008 | 1.33 | 0.94 | 2.10 | 1.05 |
| 2009 | 0.91 | 0.68 | 1.94 | 0.59 |
| 2010 | 1.46 | 1.00 | 2.22 | 0.50 |
| 2011 | 1.82 | 1.17 | ... | ... |

**Interim Dividends (Per Share)**

| Amt | Decl | Ex | Rec | Pay |
|---|---|---|---|---|
| 0.63Q | 10/21/2010 | 12/08/2010 | 12/10/2010 | 12/20/2010 |
| 0.63Q | 02/22/2011 | 03/09/2011 | 03/11/2011 | 03/21/2011 |
| 0.63Q | 04/29/2011 | 06/08/2011 | 06/10/2011 | 06/20/2011 |
| 0.63Q | 07/21/2011 | 09/07/2011 | 09/09/2011 | 09/19/2011 |

**Indicated Div: $2.52 (Div. Reinv. Plan)**

**Valuation Analysis**

| | | | |
|---|---|---|---|
| Forecast EPS | $7.53 (09/05/2011) | | |
| Market Cap | $12.8 Billion | Book Value | $4.3 Billion |
| Price/Book | 3.01 | Price/Sales | 1.57 |

**Dividend Achiever Status**

| | |
|---|---|
| **10 Year Growth Rate** | 10.08% |
| **Total Years of Dividend Growth** | 38 |

**Business Summary:** Apparel, Footwear & Accessories (MIC: 1.4.2 SIC: 2329 NAIC: 315228)

VF is a global apparel company with brands in the jeanswear, outerwear, packs, luggage, footwear, sportswear, occupational and performance apparel categories. Co.'s businesses are organized into product categories as follows: Outdoor & Action Sports, a group of outdoor and activity-based businesses that represent a range of brands; Jeanswear, which markets jeanswear and related casual products; Imagewear, which operates the Image and Licensed Sports businesses; Sportswear, which includes the Nautica® product lines and Kipling® business; and Contemporary Brands, which is comprised of the 7 For All Mankind®, John Varvatos®, Splendid® and Ella Moss® brands.

**Recent Developments:** For the quarter ended June 30 2011, net income increased 16.2% to US$129.6 million from US$111.5 million in the year-earlier quarter. Revenues were US$1.84 billion, up 15.4% from US$1.59 billion the year before. Operating income was US$188.7 million versus US$169.5 million in the prior-year quarter, an increase of 11.3%. Direct operating expenses rose 18.1% to US$994.6 million from US$842.5 million in the comparable period the year before. Indirect operating expenses increased 12.8% to US$656.9 million from US$582.1 million in the equivalent prior-year period.

**Prospects:** Our evaluation of VF Corp. as of Sep. 6, 2011 is the result of our systematic analysis on three basic characteristics: earnings strength, relative valuation, and recent stock price movement. The company has managed to produce a neutral trend in earnings per share over the past 5 quarters and while recent estimates for the company have been mixed, VFC has posted better than expected results. Based on operating earnings yield, the company is about fairly valued when compared to all of the companies in our coverage universe. Share price changes over the past year indicates that VFC will perform poorly over the near term.

**Financial Data**

| (US$ in Thousands) | 6 Mos | 3 Mos | 12/31/2010 | 01/02/2010 | 01/03/2009 | 12/29/2007 | 12/30/2006 | 12/31/2005 |
|---|---|---|---|---|---|---|---|---|
| Earnings Per Share | 5.71 | 5.54 | 5.18 | 4.13 | 5.42 | 5.22 | 4.72 | 4.44 |
| Cash Flow Per Share | 5.96 | 7.25 | 9.26 | 8.84 | 6.11 | 7.45 | 4.45 | 5.06 |
| Tang Book Value Per Share | 13.86 | 12.67 | 10.75 | 7.90 | 7.54 | 7.38 | 12.62 | 7.98 |
| Dividends Per Share | 2.490 | 2.460 | 2.430 | 2.370 | 2.330 | 2.230 | 1.940 | 1.100 |
| Dividend Payout % | 43.61 | 44.40 | 46.91 | 57.38 | 42.99 | 42.72 | 41.10 | 24.77 |
| **Income Statement** | | | | | | | | |
| Total Revenue | 3,798,922 | 1,958,799 | 7,702,589 | 7,220,286 | 7,642,600 | 7,219,359 | 6,215,794 | 6,502,377 |
| EBITDA | 546,403 | 317,653 | 981,824 | 892,052 | 1,080,378 | 1,090,028 | 936,880 | 949,470 |
| Depn & Amortn | 87,755 | 44,941 | 156,210 | 153,707 | 144,486 | 121,646 | 108,377 | 116,233 |
| Income Before Taxes | 429,222 | 257,738 | 750,212 | 654,673 | 847,957 | 905,570 | 777,238 | 770,813 |
| Income Taxes | 98,235 | 56,318 | 176,700 | 196,215 | 245,209 | 292,324 | 242,187 | 252,278 |
| Net Income | 330,071 | 200,703 | 571,362 | 461,271 | 602,748 | 591,621 | 533,516 | 506,702 |
| Average Shares | 110,890 | 110,040 | 110,328 | 111,605 | 111,255 | 113,348 | 113,040 | 114,192 |
| **Balance Sheet** | | | | | | | | |
| Current Assets | 3,045,908 | 2,950,028 | 2,826,060 | 2,629,356 | 2,653,010 | 2,645,129 | 2,578,010 | 2,365,376 |
| Total Assets | 6,800,446 | 6,693,138 | 6,457,556 | 6,470,657 | 6,433,868 | 6,446,685 | 5,465,693 | 5,171,071 |
| Current Liabilities | 1,013,914 | 1,036,846 | 1,109,475 | 1,092,583 | 1,012,182 | 1,134,387 | 1,014,848 | 1,152,143 |
| Long-Term Obligations | 934,600 | 935,244 | 935,882 | 938,494 | 1,141,546 | 1,144,810 | 635,359 | 647,728 |
| Total Liabilities | 2,531,153 | 2,567,631 | 2,596,337 | 2,655,506 | 2,877,976 | 2,869,856 | 2,200,521 | 2,339,532 |
| Stockholders' Equity | 4,269,293 | 4,125,507 | 3,861,219 | 3,815,151 | 3,555,892 | 3,576,829 | 3,265,172 | 2,831,539 |
| Shares Outstanding | 109,597 | 109,013 | 107,938 | 110,285 | 109,847 | 109,797 | 112,184 | 110,107 |
| **Statistical Record** | | | | | | | | |
| Return on Assets % | 9.56 | 9.25 | 8.89 | 7.17 | 9.21 | 9.96 | 10.06 | 9.99 |
| Return on Equity % | 15.84 | 15.31 | 14.97 | 12.55 | 16.63 | 17.34 | 17.55 | 18.92 |
| EBITDA Margin % | 14.38 | 16.22 | 12.75 | 12.35 | 14.14 | 15.10 | 15.07 | 14.60 |
| Net Margin % | 8.69 | 10.25 | 7.42 | 6.39 | 7.89 | 8.19 | 8.58 | 7.79 |
| Asset Turnover | 1.24 | 1.20 | 1.20 | 1.12 | 1.17 | 1.22 | 1.17 | 1.28 |
| Current Ratio | 3.00 | 2.85 | 2.55 | 2.41 | 2.62 | 2.33 | 2.54 | 2.05 |
| Debt to Equity | 0.22 | 0.23 | 0.24 | 0.25 | 0.32 | 0.32 | 0.19 | 0.23 |
| Price Range | 108.66-69.91 | 99.17-69.91 | 89.32-69.91 | 78.49-47.65 | 84.34-39.88 | 95.65-68.90 | 82.60-53.66 | 61.52-50.85 |
| P/E Ratio | 19.03-12.24 | 17.90-12.62 | 17.24-13.50 | 19.00-11.54 | 15.56-7.36 | 18.32-13.20 | 17.50-11.37 | 13.86-11.45 |
| Average Yield % | 2.84 | 2.97 | 3.06 | 3.73 | 3.32 | 2.68 | 2.92 | 1.93 |

**Address:** 105 Corporate Center Boulevard, Greensboro, NC 27408
**Telephone:** 336-424-6000
**Web Site:** www.vfc.com

**Officers:** Eric C. Wiseman - Chairman, President, Chief Executive Officer Robert K. Shearer - Senior Vice President, Chief Financial Officer **Transfer Agents:**Computershare Trust Company, N.A, Providence, RI

**No of Institutions:** 685
**Shares:** 104,720,752 **% Held:** 87.75

# WAL-MART STORES, INC.

| Exchange | Symbol | Price | 52Wk Range | Yield | P/E |
|---|---|---|---|---|---|
| NYS | WMT | $53.19 (8/31/2011) | 57.57-48.41 | 2.74 | 11.34 |

***7 Year Price Score 104.33** *NYSE Composite Index=100 ***12 Month Price Score 98.35**

**Interim Earnings (Per Share)**

| Qtr. | Apr | Jul | Oct | Jan |
|---|---|---|---|---|
| 2008-09 | 0.76 | 0.87 | 0.80 | 0.96 |
| 2009-10 | 0.77 | 0.88 | 0.84 | 1.21 |
| 2010-11 | 0.88 | 0.97 | 0.95 | 1.68 |
| 2011-12 | 0.97 | 1.09 | ... | ... |

**Interim Dividends (Per Share)**

| Amt | Decl | Ex | Rec | Pay |
|---|---|---|---|---|
| 0.365Q | 03/03/2011 | 08/10/2011 | 08/12/2011 | 09/06/2011 |
| 0.365Q | 03/03/2011 | 12/07/2011 | 12/09/2011 | 01/03/2012 |
| 0.365Q | 03/03/2011 | 03/09/2011 | 03/11/2011 | 04/04/2011 |
| 0.365Q | 03/03/2011 | 05/11/2011 | 05/13/2011 | 06/06/2011 |

**Indicated Div: $1.46 (Div. Reinv. Plan)**

**Valuation Analysis**

| | | | |
|---|---|---|---|
| Forecast EPS | $4.48 (09/03/2011) | | |
| Market Cap | $184.1 Billion | Book Value | $67.9 Billion |
| Price/Book | 2.71 | Price/Sales | 0.43 |

**Dividend Achiever Status**

| | |
|---|---|
| **10 Year Growth Rate** | 15.89% |
| **Total Years of Dividend Growth** | 35 |

**Business Summary:** Retail - General Merchandise/Department Stores (MIC: 2.1.1 SIC: 5311 NAIC: 452111)

Wal-Mart Stores operates retail stores in a range of formats. Co.'s operations comprise three business segments: Walmart U.S., which operates retail stores in different formats in the U.S. under the Walmart or Wal-Mart brand, as well as Walmart's online retail operations, walmart.com; International, which consists of retail operations in 14 countries, and comprises of retail stores and restaurants including discount stores, supercenters and Sam's Clubs; and Sam's Club, which consists of membership warehouse clubs in the U.S. and the segment's online retail operations, samsclub.com. As of Jan 31 2011, Co. had a total of 4,413 domestic stores and 4,557 international stores.

**Recent Developments:** For the quarter ended July 31 2011, income from continuing operations increased 5.1% to US$3.94 billion from US$3.75 billion in the year-earlier quarter. Net income increased 5.1% to US$3.94 billion from US$3.75 billion in the year-earlier quarter. Revenues were US$109.37 billion, up 5.4% from US$103.73 billion the year before. Operating income was US$6.38 billion versus US$6.19 billion in the prior-year quarter, an increase of 3.1%. Direct operating expenses rose 5.6% to US$81.77 billion from US$77.44 billion in the comparable period the year before. Indirect operating expenses increased 5.5% to US$21.21 billion from US$20.10 billion in the equivalent prior-year period.

**Prospects:** Our evaluation of Wal-Mart Stores Inc. as of Sep. 6, 2011 is the result of our systematic analysis on three basic characteristics: earnings strength, relative valuation, and recent stock price movement. The company has managed to produce a neutral trend in earnings per share over the past 5 quarters. However, while recent estimates for the company have been mixed, WMT has posted better than expected results. Based on operating earnings yield, the company is undervalued when compared to all of the companies in our coverage universe. Share price changes over the past year indicates that WMT will perform very poorly over the near term.

**Financial Data**

| (US$ in Thousands) | 6 Mos | 3 Mos | 01/31/2011 | 01/31/2010 | 01/31/2009 | 01/31/2008 | 01/31/2007 | 01/31/2006 |
|---|---|---|---|---|---|---|---|---|
| Earnings Per Share | 4.69 | 4.57 | 4.47 | 3.70 | 3.39 | 3.13 | 2.71 | 2.68 |
| Cash Flow Per Share | 6.72 | 7.05 | 6.47 | 6.79 | 5.86 | 5.01 | 4.84 | 4.22 |
| Tang Book Value Per Share | 13.41 | 13.83 | 14.73 | 14.43 | 12.75 | 12.22 | 11.57 | 9.84 |
| Dividends Per Share | 1.335 | 1.273 | 1.210 | 1.090 | 0.950 | 0.880 | 0.670 | 0.600 |
| Dividend Payout % | 28.46 | 27.84 | 27.07 | 29.46 | 28.02 | 28.12 | 24.72 | 22.39 |
| **Income Statement** | | | | | | | | |
| Total Revenue | 213,555,000 | 104,189,000 | 421,849,000 | 408,214,000 | 405,607,000 | 378,799,000 | 348,650,000 | 315,654,000 |
| EBITDA | 16,306,000 | 7,881,000 | 33,142,000 | 31,150,000 | 29,498,000 | 28,296,000 | 25,997,000 | 23,230,000 |
| Depn & Amortn | 4,027,000 | 1,985,000 | 7,600,000 | 7,200,000 | 6,700,000 | 6,300,000 | 5,500,000 | 4,700,000 |
| Income Before Taxes | 11,183,000 | 5,378,000 | 23,538,000 | 22,066,000 | 20,898,000 | 20,198,000 | 18,968,000 | 17,358,000 |
| Income Taxes | 3,668,000 | 1,800,000 | 7,579,000 | 7,139,000 | 7,145,000 | 6,908,000 | 6,365,000 | 5,803,000 |
| Net Income | 7,200,000 | 3,399,000 | 16,389,000 | 14,335,000 | 13,400,000 | 12,731,000 | 11,284,000 | 11,231,000 |
| Average Shares | 3,485,000 | 3,513,000 | 3,670,000 | 3,877,000 | 3,951,000 | 4,072,000 | 4,168,000 | 4,188,000 |
| **Balance Sheet** | | | | | | | | |
| Current Assets | 55,414,000 | 55,958,000 | 51,893,000 | 48,331,000 | 48,949,000 | 47,585,000 | 46,588,000 | 43,824,000 |
| Total Assets | 193,656,000 | 186,065,000 | 180,663,000 | 170,706,000 | 163,429,000 | 163,514,000 | 151,193,000 | 138,187,000 |
| Current Liabilities | 64,624,000 | 62,051,000 | 58,484,000 | 55,561,000 | 55,390,000 | 58,454,000 | 51,754,000 | 48,826,000 |
| Long-Term Obligations | 48,452,000 | 48,697,000 | 43,842,000 | 36,401,000 | 34,549,000 | 33,402,000 | 30,735,000 | 30,171,000 |
| Total Liabilities | 125,715,000 | 121,059,000 | 112,121,000 | 99,957,000 | 98,144,000 | 98,906,000 | 89,620,000 | 85,016,000 |
| Stockholders' Equity | 67,941,000 | 65,006,000 | 68,542,000 | 70,749,000 | 65,285,000 | 64,608,000 | 61,573,000 | 53,171,000 |
| Shares Outstanding | 3,462,000 | 3,479,000 | 3,516,000 | 3,786,000 | 3,925,000 | 3,973,000 | 4,131,000 | 4,165,000 |
| **Statistical Record** | | | | | | | | |
| Return on Assets % | 9.01 | 9.15 | 9.33 | 8.58 | 8.17 | 8.09 | 7.80 | 8.69 |
| Return on Equity % | 25.18 | 25.11 | 23.53 | 21.08 | 20.58 | 20.18 | 19.67 | 21.90 |
| EBITDA Margin % | 7.64 | 7.56 | 7.86 | 7.63 | 7.27 | 7.47 | 7.46 | 7.36 |
| Net Margin % | 3.37 | 3.26 | 3.89 | 3.51 | 3.30 | 3.36 | 3.24 | 3.56 |
| Asset Turnover | 2.33 | 2.37 | 2.40 | 2.44 | 2.47 | 2.41 | 2.41 | 2.44 |
| Current Ratio | 0.86 | 0.90 | 0.89 | 0.87 | 0.88 | 0.81 | 0.90 | 0.90 |
| Debt to Equity | 0.71 | 0.75 | 0.64 | 0.51 | 0.53 | 0.52 | 0.50 | 0.57 |
| Price Range | 57.57-50.06 | 57.57-48.00 | 57.57-48.00 | 55.01-46.42 | 63.17-47.86 | 51.21-42.27 | 51.75-43.02 | 53.51-42.49 |
| P/E Ratio | 12.28-10.67 | 12.60-10.50 | 12.88-10.74 | 14.87-12.55 | 18.63-14.12 | 16.36-13.50 | 19.10-15.87 | 19.97-15.85 |
| Average Yield % | 2.49 | 2.41 | 2.28 | 2.15 | 1.72 | 1.87 | 1.43 | 1.25 |

| | | |
|---|---|---|
| **Address:** 702 S.W. 8th Street, Bentonville, AR 72716<br>**Telephone:** 479-273-4000<br>**Web Site:** www.walmartstores.com | **Officers:** S. Robson Walton - Chairman Eduardo Castro-Wright - Vice-Chairman, Division Officer<br>**Transfer Agents:**Computershare Trust Company, N.A., Providence, RI | **No of Institutions:** 1667<br>**Shares:** 1,225,229,952 **% Held:** 29.56 |

# WALGREEN CO.

| Exchange | Symbol | Price | 52Wk Range | Yield | P/E |
|---|---|---|---|---|---|
| NYS | WAG | $35.21 (8/31/2011) | 45.18-26.88 | 2.56 | 13.81 |

*7 Year Price Score 99.52 *NYSE Composite Index=100 *12 Month Price Score 101.16

**Interim Earnings (Per Share)**

| Qtr. | Nov | Feb | May | Aug |
|---|---|---|---|---|
| 2007-08 | 0.46 | 0.69 | 0.58 | 0.45 |
| 2008-09 | 0.41 | 0.65 | 0.53 | 0.44 |
| 2009-10 | 0.49 | 0.68 | 0.47 | 0.48 |
| 2010-11 | 0.62 | 0.80 | 0.65 | ... |

**Interim Dividends (Per Share)**

| Amt | Decl | Ex | Rec | Pay |
|---|---|---|---|---|
| 0.175Q | 10/13/2010 | 11/10/2010 | 11/15/2010 | 12/11/2010 |
| 0.175Q | 01/13/2011 | 02/16/2011 | 02/18/2011 | 03/12/2011 |
| 0.175Q | 04/11/2011 | 05/18/2011 | 05/20/2011 | 06/11/2011 |
| 0.225Q | 07/13/2011 | 08/17/2011 | 08/19/2011 | 09/12/2011 |

**Indicated Div: $0.90 (Div. Reinv. Plan)**

**Valuation Analysis**

| | | | |
|---|---|---|---|
| Forecast EPS | $2.63 (09/05/2011) | | |
| Market Cap | $31.9 Billion | Book Value | $14.7 Billion |
| Price/Book | 2.17 | Price/Sales | 0.45 |

**Dividend Achiever Status**

| | |
|---|---|
| 10 Year Growth Rate | 16.04% |
| Total Years of Dividend Growth | 35 |

**Business Summary:** Retail - Food & Beverage, Drug & Tobacco (MIC: 2.1.2 SIC: 5912 NAIC: 446110)

Walgreen operates a drugstore chain that sells prescription and non-prescription drugs and general merchandise such as household items, convenience foods, personal care, beauty care, candy, photofinishing and other items. Co.'s pharmacy services include retail, infusion, medical facility, long- term care and mail service, pharmacy benefit services and respiratory services. Co. provides its products and services through drugstores, mail, telephone, and the Internet. Also, Co.'s Take Care Health Systems, Inc. subsidiary manages worksite health centers and in-store convenient care clinics. At Aug 31 2010, Co. operated 8,046 locations in 50 states, the District of Columbia, Puerto Rico and Guam.

**Recent Developments:** For the quarter ended May 31 2011, net income increased 30.2% to US$603.0 million from US$463.0 million in the year-earlier quarter. Revenues were US$18.37 billion, up 6.8% from US$17.20 billion the year before. Operating income was US$951.0 million versus US$829.0 million in the prior-year quarter, an increase of 14.7%. Direct operating expenses rose 6.2% to US$13.22 billion from US$12.45 billion in the comparable period the year before. Indirect operating expenses increased 7.2% to US$4.20 billion from US$3.92 billion in the equivalent prior-year period.

**Prospects:** Our evaluation of Walgreen Co. as of Sep. 6, 2011 is the result of our systematic analysis on three basic characteristics: earnings strength, relative valuation, and recent stock price movement. The company has managed to produce a neutral trend in earnings per share over the past 5 quarters. However, while recent estimates for the company have been lowered by analysts, WAG has posted better than expected results. Based on operating earnings yield, the company is undervalued when compared to all of the companies in our coverage universe. Share price changes over the past year indicates that WAG will perform well over the near term.

**Financial Data**

| (US$ in Thousands) | 9 Mos | 6 Mos | 3 Mos | 08/31/2010 | 08/31/2009 | 08/31/2008 | 08/31/2007 | 08/31/2006 |
|---|---|---|---|---|---|---|---|---|
| Earnings Per Share | 2.55 | 2.37 | 2.25 | 2.12 | 2.02 | 2.17 | 2.03 | 1.72 |
| Cash Flow Per Share | 4.62 | 4.39 | 4.03 | 3.81 | 4.15 | 3.06 | 2.36 | 2.41 |
| Tang Book Value Per Share | 14.16 | 13.96 | 13.52 | 12.14 | 13.06 | 11.56 | 10.13 | 10.04 |
| Dividends Per Share | 0.700 | 0.662 | 0.625 | 0.588 | 0.475 | 0.398 | 0.328 | 0.273 |
| Dividend Payout % | 27.45 | 27.95 | 27.78 | 27.71 | 23.51 | 18.32 | 16.13 | 15.84 |
| **Income Statement** | | | | | | | | |
| Total Revenue | 54,217,000 | 35,846,000 | 17,344,000 | 67,420,000 | 63,335,000 | 59,034,000 | 53,762,000 | 47,409,000 |
| EBITDA | 3,701,000 | 2,677,000 | 1,214,000 | 4,262,000 | 4,222,000 | 4,281,000 | 3,826,600 | 3,273,700 |
| Depn & Amortn | 602,000 | 529,000 | 273,000 | 804,000 | 975,000 | 840,000 | 675,900 | 572,200 |
| Income Before Taxes | 3,043,000 | 2,110,000 | 921,000 | 3,373,000 | 3,164,000 | 3,430,000 | 3,189,100 | 2,754,100 |
| Income Taxes | 1,121,000 | 791,000 | 341,000 | 1,282,000 | 1,158,000 | 1,273,000 | 1,147,800 | 1,003,500 |
| Net Income | 1,922,000 | 1,319,000 | 580,000 | 2,091,000 | 2,006,000 | 2,157,000 | 2,041,300 | 1,750,600 |
| Average Shares | 922,200 | 928,000 | 934,300 | 987,900 | 991,330 | 995,543 | 1,006,340 | 1,019,400 |
| **Balance Sheet** | | | | | | | | |
| Current Assets | 13,005,000 | 12,537,000 | 12,663,000 | 11,922,000 | 12,049,000 | 10,433,000 | 9,510,500 | 9,705,400 |
| Total Assets | 27,316,000 | 26,878,000 | 27,044,000 | 26,275,000 | 25,142,000 | 22,410,000 | 19,313,600 | 17,131,100 |
| Current Liabilities | 7,918,000 | 7,544,000 | 8,149,000 | 7,433,000 | 6,769,000 | 6,644,000 | 6,744,300 | 5,755,300 |
| Long-Term Obligations | 2,384,000 | 2,380,000 | 2,389,000 | 2,389,000 | 2,336,000 | 1,337,000 | ... | ... |
| Total Liabilities | 12,593,000 | 12,197,000 | 12,681,000 | 11,875,000 | 10,766,000 | 9,541,000 | 8,209,300 | 7,015,300 |
| Stockholders' Equity | 14,723,000 | 14,681,000 | 14,363,000 | 14,400,000 | 14,376,000 | 12,869,000 | 11,104,300 | 10,115,800 |
| Shares Outstanding | 905,418 | 915,459 | 922,415 | 938,605 | 988,561 | 989,176 | 991,141 | 1,007,862 |
| **Statistical Record** | | | | | | | | |
| Return on Assets % | 8.86 | 8.46 | 8.14 | 8.13 | 8.44 | 10.31 | 11.20 | 11.03 |
| Return on Equity % | 16.03 | 15.20 | 15.06 | 14.53 | 14.73 | 17.95 | 19.24 | 18.42 |
| EBITDA Margin % | 6.83 | 7.47 | 7.00 | 6.32 | 6.67 | 7.25 | 7.12 | 6.91 |
| Net Margin % | 3.55 | 3.68 | 3.34 | 3.10 | 3.17 | 3.65 | 3.80 | 3.69 |
| Asset Turnover | 2.63 | 2.63 | 2.55 | 2.62 | 2.66 | 2.82 | 2.95 | 2.99 |
| Current Ratio | 1.64 | 1.66 | 1.55 | 1.60 | 1.78 | 1.57 | 1.41 | 1.69 |
| Debt to Equity | 0.16 | 0.16 | 0.17 | 0.17 | 0.16 | 0.10 | ... | ... |
| Price Range | 45.12-26.36 | 43.34-26.36 | 39.37-26.36 | 40.37-26.36 | 36.67-21.40 | 47.93-31.39 | 51.48-40.10 | 49.69-39.80 |
| P/E Ratio | 17.69-10.34 | 18.29-11.12 | 17.50-11.72 | 19.04-12.43 | 18.15-10.59 | 22.09-14.47 | 25.36-19.75 | 28.89-23.14 |
| Average Yield % | 1.95 | 1.94 | 1.88 | 1.71 | 1.70 | 1.07 | 0.73 | 0.61 |

**Address:** 200 Wilmot Road, Deerfield, IL 60015
**Telephone:** 847-914-2500
**Web Site:** www.walgreens.com

**Officers:** Alan G. McNally - Chairman Gregory D. Wasson - President, Chief Executive Officer **Transfer Agents:** Wells Fargo Bank, N.A., South St. Paul, MN

**No of Institutions:** 1253
**Shares:** 690,814,272 **% Held:** 65.28

# WASHINGTON REAL ESTATE INVESTMENT TRUST

| Exchange | Symbol | Price | 52Wk Range | Yield | P/E |
|---|---|---|---|---|---|
| NYS | WRE | $30.94 (8/31/2011) | 34.53-25.51 | 5.61 | 70.32 |

*7 Year Price Score 98.15 *NYSE Composite Index=100 *12 Month Price Score 99.35

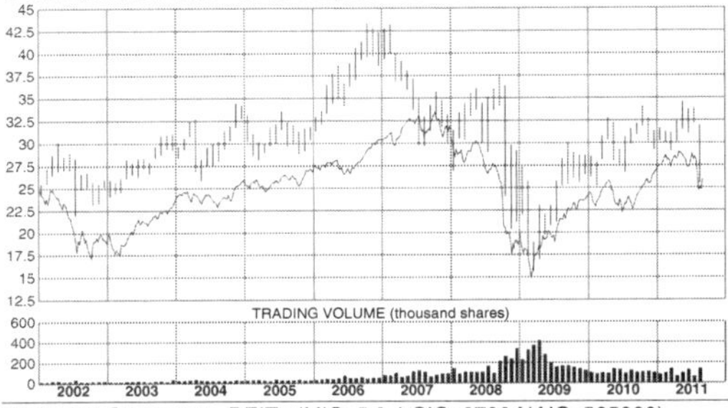

**Interim Earnings (Per Share)**

| Qtr. | Mar | Jun | Sep | Dec |
|---|---|---|---|---|
| 2008 | (0.03) | 0.44 | 0.12 | 0.14 |
| 2009 | 0.20 | 0.23 | 0.16 | 0.11 |
| 2010 | 0.09 | 0.24 | 0.10 | 0.17 |
| 2011 | 0.07 | 0.10 | ... | ... |

**Interim Dividends (Per Share)**

| Amt | Decl | Ex | Rec | Pay |
|---|---|---|---|---|
| 0.434Q | 10/27/2010 | 12/13/2010 | 12/15/2010 | 12/30/2010 |
| 0.434Q | 02/17/2011 | 03/10/2011 | 03/14/2011 | 03/31/2011 |
| 0.434Q | 04/28/2011 | 06/13/2011 | 06/15/2011 | 06/30/2011 |
| 0.434Q | 07/28/2011 | 09/13/2011 | 09/15/2011 | 09/30/2011 |

**Indicated Div: $1.74 (Div. Reinv. Plan)**

**Valuation Analysis**

| | | | |
|---|---|---|---|
| Forecast EPS | $0.44 (09/02/2011) | | |
| Market Cap | $2.0 Billion | Book Value | $817.7 Million |
| Price/Book | 2.50 | Price/Sales | 6.69 |

**Dividend Achiever Status**

| | |
|---|---|
| 10 Year Growth Rate | 2.83% |
| Total Years of Dividend Growth | 41 |

**Business Summary:** REITs (MIC: 5.3.1 SIC: 6798 NAIC: 525930)

Washington Real Estate Investment Trust is a self-administered, self-managed, equity real estate investment trust. Co.'s business consists of the ownership and operation of income-producing real property in the Washington metro region. As of Dec 31 2010, Co. owned a portfolio of 85 properties, totaling approximately 10.7 million square feet of commercial space and 2,540 residential units, and land held for development. These 85 properties consisted of 25 office properties, 18 medical office properties, 15 retail centers, 11 multifamily properties and 16 industrial/flex properties. Co. has five reportable segments: office; medical office; retail; multifamily; and industrial/flex properties.

**Recent Developments:** For the quarter ended June 30 2011, income from continuing operations increased 27.0% to US$7.7 million from US$6.1 million in the year-earlier quarter. Net income decreased 56.4% to US$6.6 million from US$15.0 million in the year-earlier quarter. Revenues were US$80.6 million, up 11.3% from US$72.4 million the year before.

**Prospects:** Our evaluation of Washington Real Estate Investment Trust as of Sep. 6, 2011 is the result of our systematic analysis on three basic characteristics: earnings strength, relative valuation, and recent stock price movement. The company has produced a positive trend in earnings per share over the past 5 quarters. Because the company lacks sufficient analyst estimate data, we place greater weight on the historical EPS trend as the measure of earnings strength. Based on operating earnings yield, the company is overvalued when compared to all of the companies in our coverage universe. Share price changes over the past year indicates that WRE will perform very poorly over the near term.

| **Financial Data** (US$ in Thousands) | 6 Mos | 3 Mos | 12/31/2010 | 12/31/2009 | 12/31/2008 | 12/31/2007 | 12/31/2006 | 12/31/2005 |
|---|---|---|---|---|---|---|---|---|
| Earnings Per Share | 0.44 | 0.58 | 0.60 | 0.71 | 0.67 | 1.34 | 0.88 | 1.84 |
| Cash Flow Per Share | 1.67 | 1.75 | 1.80 | 1.81 | 1.97 | 2.52 | 1.98 | 2.08 |
| Tang Book Value Per Share | 12.39 | 12.68 | 13.01 | 12.46 | 11.95 | 10.42 | 9.81 | 9.03 |
| Dividends Per Share | 1.734 | 1.732 | 1.731 | 1.730 | 1.720 | 1.680 | 1.640 | 1.600 |
| Dividend Payout % | 394.03 | 298.71 | 288.54 | 243.66 | 256.72 | 125.37 | 186.36 | 86.96 |
| **Income Statement** | | | | | | | | |
| Total Revenue | 158,725 | 78,155 | 297,977 | 306,929 | 282,312 | 255,655 | 219,662 | 190,046 |
| EBITDA | 51,239 | 24,107 | 158,020 | 176,822 | 154,323 | 150,345 | 134,107 | 119,986 |
| Depn & Amortn | 4,131 | 1,835 | 76,500 | 75,800 | 69,200 | 56,300 | 47,600 | 41,800 |
| Income Before Taxes | 12,885 | 5,146 | 13,131 | 26,021 | 15,214 | 32,139 | 38,661 | 40,443 |
| Net Income | 11,187 | 4,665 | 37,426 | 40,745 | 32,841 | 61,881 | 38,661 | 77,638 |
| Average Shares | 65,989 | 65,907 | 62,264 | 56,968 | 49,373 | 46,115 | 43,874 | 42,203 |
| **Balance Sheet** | | | | | | | | |
| Current Assets | 122,897 | 90,074 | 155,495 | 80,898 | 76,136 | 64,113 | 45,504 | 31,960 |
| Total Assets | 2,187,176 | 2,216,212 | 2,167,881 | 2,045,225 | 2,111,391 | 1,898,326 | 1,531,265 | 1,141,285 |
| Current Liabilities | 326,052 | 242,891 | 122,135 | 149,150 | 86,442 | 212,856 | 76,976 | 36,965 |
| Long-Term Obligations | 1,038,403 | 1,133,025 | 1,133,758 | 1,094,363 | 1,324,186 | 1,131,607 | 965,328 | 689,617 |
| Total Liabilities | 1,369,462 | 1,380,172 | 1,310,801 | 1,299,970 | 1,484,998 | 1,411,782 | 1,089,334 | 760,980 |
| Stockholders' Equity | 817,714 | 836,040 | 857,080 | 745,255 | 626,393 | 486,544 | 441,931 | 380,305 |
| Shares Outstanding | 66,017 | 65,941 | 65,870 | 59,811 | 52,434 | 46,682 | 45,042 | 42,139 |
| **Statistical Record** | | | | | | | | |
| Return on Assets % | 1.34 | 1.74 | 1.78 | 1.96 | 1.63 | 3.61 | 2.89 | 7.21 |
| Return on Equity % | 3.54 | 4.66 | 4.67 | 5.94 | 5.89 | 13.33 | 9.40 | 20.81 |
| EBITDA Margin % | 32.28 | 30.85 | 53.03 | 57.61 | 54.66 | 58.81 | 61.05 | 63.14 |
| Net Margin % | 7.05 | 5.97 | 12.56 | 13.28 | 11.63 | 24.20 | 17.60 | 40.85 |
| Asset Turnover | 0.14 | 0.14 | 0.14 | 0.15 | 0.14 | 0.15 | 0.16 | 0.18 |
| Current Ratio | 0.38 | 0.37 | 1.27 | 0.54 | 0.88 | 0.30 | 0.59 | 0.86 |
| Debt to Equity | 1.27 | 1.36 | 1.32 | 1.47 | 2.11 | 2.33 | 2.18 | 1.81 |
| Price Range | 34.53-26.67 | 34.05-26.67 | 34.05-25.09 | 30.02-15.60 | 37.61-20.33 | 43.20-29.65 | 43.30-31.26 | 33.87-28.15 |
| P/E Ratio | 78.48-60.61 | 58.71-45.98 | 56.75-41.82 | 42.28-21.97 | 56.13-30.34 | 32.24-22.13 | 49.20-35.52 | 18.41-15.30 |
| Average Yield % | 5.58 | 5.66 | 5.78 | 7.21 | 5.43 | 4.72 | 4.39 | 5.24 |

| | | |
|---|---|---|
| **Address:** 6110 Executive Boulevard, Suite 800, Rockville, MD 20852<br>**Telephone:** 301-984-9400<br>**Web Site:** www.writ.com | **Officers:** John P. McDaniel - Chairman George F. McKenzie - President, Chief Executive Officer<br>**Transfer Agents:**Computershare Trust Company, N.A., Providence, RI | **No of Institutions:** 279<br>**Shares:** 51,665,016 **% Held:** 76.52 |

# WEST PHARMACEUTICAL SERVICES, INC.

| Exchange | Symbol | Price | 52Wk Range | Yield | P/E |
|---|---|---|---|---|---|
| NYS | WST | $40.12 (8/31/2011) | 47.44-33.04 | 1.69 | 21.92 |

***7 Year Price Score 108.12** *NYSE Composite Index=100 ***12 Month Price Score 105.46**

**Interim Earnings (Per Share)**

| Qtr. | Mar | Jun | Sep | Dec |
|---|---|---|---|---|
| 2008 | 0.76 | 0.82 | 0.40 | 0.52 |
| 2009 | 0.46 | 0.57 | 0.50 | 0.59 |
| 2010 | 0.57 | 0.62 | 0.51 | 0.19 |
| 2011 | 0.56 | 0.57 | ... | ... |

**Interim Dividends (Per Share)**

| Amt | Decl | Ex | Rec | Pay |
|---|---|---|---|---|
| 0.17Q | 10/04/2010 | 10/18/2010 | 10/20/2010 | 11/03/2010 |
| 0.17Q | 12/16/2010 | 01/14/2011 | 01/19/2011 | 02/02/2011 |
| 0.17Q | 02/24/2011 | 04/18/2011 | 04/20/2011 | 05/04/2011 |
| 0.17Q | 05/06/2011 | 07/18/2011 | 07/20/2011 | 08/03/2011 |

**Indicated Div: $0.68 (Div. Reinv. Plan)**

**Valuation Analysis**

| | | | |
|---|---|---|---|
| Forecast EPS | $2.35 (09/02/2011) | | |
| Market Cap | $1.4 Billion | Book Value | $696.0 Million |
| Price/Book | 1.98 | Price/Sales | 1.20 |

**Dividend Achiever Status**

| | |
|---|---|
| **10 Year Growth Rate** | 5.94% |
| **Total Years of Dividend Growth** | 18 |

**Business Summary:** Medical Instruments & Equipment (MIC: 4.3.1 SIC: 3069 NAIC: 326299)

West Pharmaceutical Services is a manufacturer of components and systems for the packaging and delivery of injectable drugs as well as delivery system components for the pharmaceutical, healthcare and consumer products industries. Co.'s products include stoppers and seals for vials, prefillable syringe components and systems, components for intravenous and blood collection systems, safety and administration systems, and contract design and manufacturing services. Co.'s customers include producers and distributors of pharmaceuticals, biologics, medical devices and personal care products. Co. operates through two segments: Pharmaceutical Packaging Systems and Pharmaceutical Delivery Systems.

**Recent Developments:** For the quarter ended June 30 2011, net income decreased 7.4% to US$20.1 million from US$21.7 million in the year-earlier quarter. Revenues were US$307.9 million, up 9.3% from US$281.8 million the year before. Operating income was US$27.8 million versus US$30.5 million in the prior-year quarter, a decrease of 8.9%. Direct operating expenses rose 12.4% to US$223.3 million from US$198.6 million in the comparable period the year before. Indirect operating expenses increased 7.8% to US$56.8 million from US$52.7 million in the equivalent prior-year period.

**Prospects:** Our evaluation of West Pharmaceutical Services Inc. as of Sep. 6, 2011 is the result of our systematic analysis on three basic characteristics: earnings strength, relative valuation, and recent stock price movement. The company has enjoyed a very positive trend in earnings per share over the past 5 quarters. However, while recent estimates for the company have been lowered by analysts, WST has posted results that fell short of analysts expectations. Based on operating earnings yield, the company is about fairly valued when compared to all of the companies in our coverage universe. Share price changes over the past year indicates that WST will perform in line with the market over the near te

**Financial Data**

| (US$ in Thousands) | 6 Mos | 3 Mos | 12/31/2010 | 12/31/2009 | 12/31/2008 | 12/31/2007 | 12/31/2006 | 12/31/2005 |
|---|---|---|---|---|---|---|---|---|
| Earnings Per Share | 1.83 | 1.88 | 1.89 | 2.12 | 2.50 | 2.05 | 2.00 | 1.40 |
| Cash Flow Per Share | 4.30 | 4.08 | 4.15 | 4.20 | 4.12 | 3.95 | 4.33 | 2.75 |
| Tang Book Value Per Share | 15.33 | 14.75 | 13.76 | 12.40 | 10.15 | 9.97 | 7.46 | 5.49 |
| Dividends Per Share | 0.670 | 0.660 | 0.650 | 0.610 | 0.570 | 0.530 | 0.490 | 0.450 |
| Dividend Payout % | 36.61 | 35.11 | 34.39 | 28.77 | 22.80 | 25.85 | 24.50 | 32.14 |
| **Income Statement** | | | | | | | | |
| Total Revenue | 603,300 | 295,400 | 1,104,700 | 1,055,700 | 1,051,100 | 1,020,100 | 913,300 | 699,700 |
| EBITDA | 95,300 | 48,300 | 159,500 | 161,400 | 180,200 | 146,500 | 143,200 | 114,800 |
| Depn & Amortn | 38,800 | 19,500 | 68,800 | 63,900 | 56,100 | 51,600 | 48,100 | 42,600 |
| Income Before Taxes | 47,700 | 24,300 | 74,500 | 83,100 | 109,500 | 86,400 | 84,500 | 60,200 |
| Income Taxes | 11,300 | 6,100 | 13,600 | 13,500 | 23,700 | 17,200 | 24,600 | 17,300 |
| Net Income | 39,700 | 19,600 | 65,300 | 72,600 | 86,000 | 70,700 | 67,100 | 45,600 |
| Average Shares | 37,000 | 36,800 | 36,700 | 36,300 | 36,200 | 36,200 | 33,600 | 32,525 |
| **Balance Sheet** | | | | | | | | |
| Current Assets | 510,400 | 481,100 | 436,600 | 397,200 | 366,200 | 412,300 | 281,700 | 237,200 |
| Total Assets | 1,415,300 | 1,366,100 | 1,294,300 | 1,271,000 | 1,168,700 | 1,185,600 | 918,200 | 823,600 |
| Current Liabilities | 192,700 | 182,800 | 169,700 | 171,100 | 159,100 | 182,900 | 156,900 | 124,800 |
| Long-Term Obligations | 367,200 | 364,700 | 358,100 | 379,100 | 382,100 | 394,600 | 235,800 | 280,700 |
| Total Liabilities | 719,300 | 703,000 | 668,600 | 691,900 | 681,600 | 700,300 | 503,700 | 490,100 |
| Stockholders' Equity | 696,000 | 663,100 | 625,700 | 579,100 | 487,100 | 485,300 | 414,500 | 333,500 |
| Shares Outstanding | 34,300 | 33,400 | 33,300 | 33,000 | 32,700 | 32,200 | 32,900 | 31,772 |
| **Statistical Record** | | | | | | | | |
| Return on Assets % | 4.82 | 4.97 | 5.09 | 5.95 | 7.29 | 6.72 | 7.70 | 6.15 |
| Return on Equity % | 10.02 | 10.48 | 10.84 | 13.62 | 17.64 | 15.71 | 17.94 | 14.37 |
| EBITDA Margin % | 15.80 | 16.35 | 14.44 | 15.29 | 17.14 | 14.36 | 15.68 | 16.41 |
| Net Margin % | 6.58 | 6.64 | 5.91 | 6.88 | 8.18 | 6.93 | 7.35 | 6.52 |
| Asset Turnover | 0.87 | 0.86 | 0.86 | 0.87 | 0.89 | 0.97 | 1.05 | 0.94 |
| Current Ratio | 2.65 | 2.63 | 2.57 | 2.32 | 2.30 | 2.25 | 1.80 | 1.90 |
| Debt to Equity | 0.53 | 0.55 | 0.57 | 0.65 | 0.78 | 0.81 | 0.57 | 0.84 |
| Price Range | 47.44-33.04 | 44.77-33.04 | 44.57-33.04 | 41.52-28.12 | 51.66-31.13 | 52.14-36.12 | 52.13-25.30 | 29.83-23.10 |
| P/E Ratio | 25.92-18.05 | 23.81-17.57 | 23.58-17.48 | 19.58-13.26 | 20.66-12.45 | 25.43-17.62 | 26.07-12.65 | 21.31-16.50 |
| Average Yield % | 1.69 | 1.71 | 1.71 | 1.69 | 1.33 | 1.19 | 1.30 | 1.70 |

| | | |
|---|---|---|
| **Address:** 101 Gordon Drive, P.O. Box 645, Lionville, PA 19341-0645<br>**Telephone:** 610-594-2900<br>**Web Site:** www.westpharma.com | **Officers:** Donald E. Morel - Chairman, Chief Executive Officer William J. Federici - Vice President, Chief Financial Officer **Transfer Agents:** American Stock Transfer and Trust Company, New York, NY | **Investor Contact:** 610-594-3345<br>**No of Institutions:** 197<br>**Shares:** 35,240,660 **% Held:** 88.81 |

# WESTAMERICA BANCORPORATION

| Exchange | Symbol | Price | 52Wk Range | Yield | P/E |
|---|---|---|---|---|---|
| NMS | WABC | $42.41 (8/31/2011) | 56.55-37.00 | 3.40 | 13.55 |

*7 Year Price Score 96.95 *NYSE Composite Index=100 *12 Month Price Score 90.53

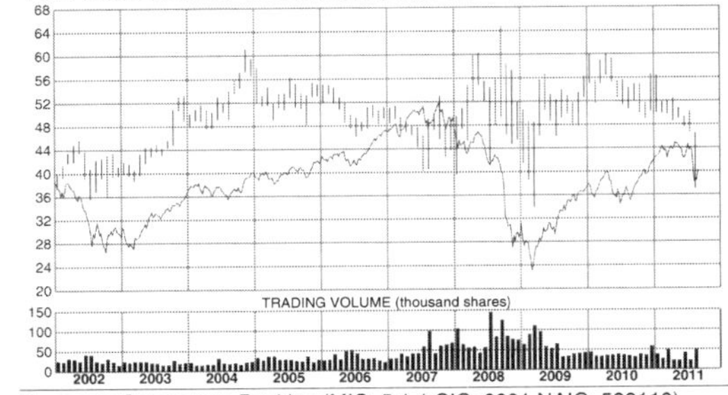


**Interim Earnings (Per Share)**

| Qtr. | Mar | Jun | Sep | Dec |
|---|---|---|---|---|
| 2008 | 0.92 | 0.42 | 0.00 | 0.71 |
| 2009 | 1.80 | 0.75 | 0.81 | 0.79 |
| 2010 | 0.80 | 0.80 | 0.81 | 0.81 |
| 2011 | 0.77 | 0.74 | ... | ... |

**Interim Dividends (Per Share)**

| Amt | Decl | Ex | Rec | Pay |
|---|---|---|---|---|
| 0.36Q | 10/28/2010 | 11/04/2010 | 11/08/2010 | 11/19/2010 |
| 0.36Q | 01/27/2011 | 02/03/2011 | 02/07/2011 | 02/18/2011 |
| 0.36Q | 04/28/2011 | 05/05/2011 | 05/09/2011 | 05/20/2011 |
| 0.36Q | 07/28/2011 | 08/04/2011 | 08/08/2011 | 08/19/2011 |

**Indicated Div: $1.44 (Div. Reinv. Plan)**

**Valuation Analysis**

| | | | |
|---|---|---|---|
| Forecast EPS | $3.12 (09/02/2011) | | |
| Market Cap | $1.2 Billion | Book Value | $549.3 Million |
| Price/Book | 2.20 | Price/Sales | N/A |

**Dividend Achiever Status**

| | |
|---|---|
| 10 Year Growth Rate | 5.79% |
| Total Years of Dividend Growth | 21 |

**Business Summary:** Banking (MIC: 5.1.1 SIC: 6021 NAIC: 522110)

Westamerica is a bank holding company. Through its subsidiary bank, Westamerica Bank (the Bank), Co. is engaged in providing a range of banking services to corporate and individual customers in Northern and Central California. The principal communities served are located in Northern and Central California, from Mendocino, Lake and Nevada Counties in the north to Kern County in the south. In addition, the Bank owns 100.0% of the capital stock of Community Banker Services Corporation, a company engaged in providing Co. and its subsidiaries with data processing services and other support functions. As of Dec 31 2010, Co. had total assets of $4.93 billion and total deposits of $4.13 billion.

**Recent Developments:** For the quarter ended June 30 2011, net income decreased 9.7% to US$21.3 million from US$23.6 million in the year-earlier quarter. Net interest income decreased 1.9% to US$50.9 million from US$51.9 million in the year-earlier quarter. Provision for loan losses was unchanged at US$2.8 million versus the prior-year quarter. Non-interest income fell 3.0% to US$15.3 million from US$15.8 million, while non-interest expense advanced 6.9% to US$34.3 million.

**Prospects:** Our evaluation of WestAmerica Bancorporation as of Sep. 6, 2011 is the result of our systematic analysis on three basic characteristics: earnings strength, relative valuation, and recent stock price movement. The company has managed to produce a neutral trend in earnings per share over the past 5 quarters. However, while recent estimates for the company have been mixed, WABC has posted results that fell short of analysts expectations. Based on operating earnings yield, the company is undervalued when compared to all of the companies in our coverage universe. Share price changes over the past year indicates that WABC will perform poorly over the near term.

**Financial Data**

| (US$ in Thousands) | 6 Mos | 3 Mos | 12/31/2010 | 12/31/2009 | 12/31/2008 | 12/31/2007 | 12/31/2006 | 12/31/2005 |
|---|---|---|---|---|---|---|---|---|
| Earnings Per Share | 3.13 | 3.19 | 3.21 | 4.14 | 2.04 | 2.98 | 3.11 | 3.27 |
| Cash Flow Per Share | 4.83 | 3.86 | 3.94 | 5.12 | 3.22 | 3.64 | 3.46 | 3.70 |
| Tang Book Value Per Share | 13.88 | 13.70 | 13.37 | 11.92 | 9.45 | 8.77 | 9.18 | 8.74 |
| Dividends Per Share | 1.440 | 1.440 | 1.440 | 1.410 | 1.390 | 1.360 | 1.300 | 1.220 |
| Dividend Payout % | 46.01 | 45.14 | 44.86 | 34.06 | 68.14 | 45.64 | 41.80 | 37.31 |
| **Income Statement** | | | | | | | | |
| Interest Income | 105,582 | 52,494 | 221,155 | 241,949 | 208,469 | 235,872 | 246,515 | 242,797 |
| Interest Expense | 4,456 | 2,303 | 12,840 | 19,380 | 33,243 | 72,555 | 65,268 | 43,649 |
| Net Interest Income | 101,126 | 50,191 | 208,315 | 222,569 | 175,226 | 163,317 | 181,247 | 199,148 |
| Provision for Losses | 5,600 | 2,800 | 11,200 | 10,500 | 2,700 | 700 | 445 | 900 |
| Non-Interest Income | 30,035 | 14,743 | 61,454 | 112,011 | (2,056) | 59,278 | 55,347 | 54,540 |
| Non-Interest Expense | 65,632 | 31,323 | 127,147 | 140,776 | 100,761 | 101,428 | 101,724 | 104,856 |
| Income Before Taxes | 59,929 | 30,811 | 131,422 | 183,304 | 69,709 | 120,467 | 134,425 | 147,932 |
| Income Taxes | 16,278 | 8,429 | 36,845 | 57,878 | 9,874 | 30,691 | 35,619 | 40,491 |
| Net Income | 43,651 | 22,382 | 94,577 | 125,426 | 59,835 | 89,776 | 98,806 | 107,441 |
| Average Shares | 28,923 | 29,225 | 29,471 | 29,353 | 29,273 | 30,165 | 31,739 | 32,897 |
| **Balance Sheet** | | | | | | | | |
| Net Loans & Leases | 2,718,205 | 2,800,314 | 2,886,448 | 3,015,346 | 2,337,956 | 2,450,470 | 2,476,404 | 2,616,372 |
| Total Assets | 4,876,731 | 4,937,429 | 4,931,524 | 4,975,501 | 4,032,934 | 4,558,959 | 4,769,335 | 5,149,209 |
| Total Deposits | 4,088,385 | 4,140,373 | 4,132,961 | 4,060,208 | 3,095,054 | 3,264,790 | 3,516,734 | 3,846,101 |
| Total Liabilities | 4,327,391 | 4,386,514 | 4,386,237 | 4,470,053 | 3,623,082 | 4,164,356 | 4,345,100 | 4,722,495 |
| Stockholders' Equity | 549,340 | 550,915 | 545,287 | 505,448 | 409,852 | 394,603 | 424,235 | 426,714 |
| Shares Outstanding | 28,540 | 28,920 | 29,090 | 29,208 | 28,880 | 29,018 | 30,547 | 31,882 |
| **Statistical Record** | | | | | | | | |
| Return on Assets % | 1.90 | 1.93 | 1.91 | 2.78 | 1.39 | 1.92 | 1.99 | 2.17 |
| Return on Equity % | 16.92 | 17.45 | 18.00 | 27.41 | 14.84 | 21.93 | 23.22 | 27.36 |
| Net Interest Margin % | 95.94 | 95.61 | 94.19 | 91.99 | 84.05 | 69.24 | 73.52 | 82.02 |
| Efficiency Ratio % | 50.17 | 46.59 | 44.99 | 39.77 | 48.82 | 34.36 | 33.70 | 35.27 |
| Loans to Deposits | 0.66 | 0.68 | 0.70 | 0.74 | 0.76 | 0.75 | 0.70 | 0.68 |
| Price Range | 56.55-47.48 | 59.94-48.88 | 59.94-48.88 | 56.78-33.88 | 64.68-39.53 | 53.01-40.25 | 55.10-46.14 | 58.31-48.16 |
| P/E Ratio | 18.07-15.17 | 18.79-15.32 | 18.67-15.23 | 13.71-8.18 | 31.71-19.38 | 17.79-13.51 | 17.72-14.84 | 17.83-14.73 |
| Average Yield % | 2.78 | 2.69 | 2.64 | 2.86 | 2.69 | 2.88 | 2.57 | 2.31 |

**Address:** 1108 Fifth Avenue, San Rafael, CA 94901
**Telephone:** 707-863-6000
**Web Site:** www.westamerica.com

**Officers:** David L. Payne - Chairman, President, Chief Executive Officer John A. Thorson - Senior Vice President, Chief Financial Officer **Transfer Agents:** Computershare Investor Services LLC

**No of Institutions:** 179
**Shares:** 24,054,704 **% Held:** 68.75

# WGL HOLDINGS, INC.

| Exchange | Symbol | Price | 52Wk Range | Yield | P/E |
|---|---|---|---|---|---|
| NYS | WGL | $41.36 (8/31/2011) | 41.36-35.06 | 3.75 | 17.53 |

***7 Year Price Score 113.10 *NYSE Composite Index=100 *12 Month Price Score 103.98**

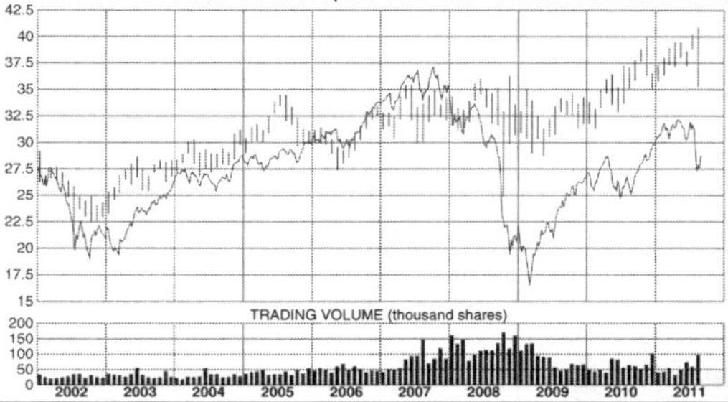


**Interim Earnings (Per Share)**

| Qtr. | Dec | Mar | Jun | Sep |
|---|---|---|---|---|
| 2007-08 | 0.95 | 1.63 | (0.01) | (0.23) |
| 2008-09 | 1.09 | 1.49 | 0.04 | (0.22) |
| 2009-10 | 0.94 | 1.56 | 0.19 | (0.53) |
| 2010-11 | 1.28 | 1.55 | 0.06 | ... |

**Interim Dividends (Per Share)**

| Amt | Decl | Ex | Rec | Pay |
|---|---|---|---|---|
| 0.378Q | 09/29/2010 | 10/06/2010 | 10/08/2010 | 11/01/2010 |
| 0.378Q | 12/17/2010 | 01/06/2011 | 01/10/2011 | 02/01/2011 |
| 0.388Q | 03/03/2011 | 04/06/2011 | 04/08/2011 | 05/01/2011 |
| 0.388Q | 06/30/2011 | 07/18/2011 | 07/20/2011 | 08/01/2011 |

**Indicated Div: $1.55 (Div. Reinv. Plan)**

**Valuation Analysis**

| | | | |
|---|---|---|---|
| Forecast EPS | $2.16 (09/05/2011) | | |
| Market Cap | $2.1 Billion | Book Value | $1.3 Billion |
| Price/Book | 1.66 | Price/Sales | 0.77 |

**Dividend Achiever Status**

| | |
|---|---|
| **10 Year Growth Rate** | 1.80% |
| **Total Years of Dividend Growth** | 34 |

**Business Summary:** Gas Utilities (MIC: 3.3.1 SIC: 4924 NAIC: 221210)

WGL Holdings is a holding company. Through its subsidiaries, Co. sells and delivers natural gas and provides a range of energy-related products and services to customers primarily in the District of Columbia and the surrounding metropolitan areas in Maryland and Virginia. Co. has three operating segments: regulated utility, which delivers natural gas to retail customers; retail energy-marketing, which sells natural gas and/or electricity directly to residential, commercial and industrial customers; and design-build energy systems, which provides design-build energy efficiency and sustainability applications to governmental and commercial clients.

**Recent Developments:** For the quarter ended June 30 2011, net income decreased 67.2% to US$3.3 million from US$10.0 million in the year-earlier quarter. Revenues were US$490.3 million, up 6.7% from US$459.7 million the year before. Operating income was US$15.2 million versus US$27.2 million in the prior-year quarter, a decrease of 44.1%. Direct operating expenses rose 9.7% to US$446.2 million from US$406.7 million in the comparable period the year before. Indirect operating expenses increased 12.0% to US$28.8 million from US$25.8 million in the equivalent prior-year period.

**Prospects:** Our evaluation of WGL Holdings Inc. as of Sep. 6, 2011 is the result of our systematic analysis on three basic characteristics: earnings strength, relative valuation, and recent stock price movement. The company has managed to produce a neutral trend in earnings per share over the past 5 quarters and while recent estimates for the company have been mixed, WGL has posted better than expected results. Based on operating earnings yield, the company is about fairly valued when compared to all of the companies in our coverage universe. Share price changes over the past year indicates that WGL will perform very poorly over the near term.

**Financial Data**

| (US$ in Thousands) | 9 Mos | 6 Mos | 3 Mos | 09/30/2010 | 09/30/2009 | 09/30/2008 | 09/30/2007 | 09/30/2006 |
|---|---|---|---|---|---|---|---|---|
| Earnings Per Share | 2.36 | 2.49 | 2.50 | 2.16 | 2.39 | 2.33 | 2.19 | 1.79 |
| Cash Flow Per Share | 5.57 | 7.88 | 5.43 | 5.76 | 6.13 | 1.25 | 4.34 | 1.76 |
| Tang Book Value Per Share | 24.96 | 25.22 | 24.05 | 22.63 | 21.89 | 20.99 | 19.89 | 18.86 |
| Dividends Per Share | 1.520 | 1.510 | 1.500 | 1.490 | 1.445 | 1.395 | 1.360 | 1.340 |
| Dividend Payout % | 64.41 | 60.64 | 60.00 | 68.98 | 60.46 | 59.87 | 62.10 | 74.86 |
| **Income Statement** | | | | | | | | |
| Total Revenue | 2,303,376 | 1,813,095 | 795,874 | 2,708,876 | 2,706,856 | 2,628,194 | 2,646,008 | 2,637,883 |
| EBITDA | 280,431 | 263,554 | 119,782 | 446,089 | 456,096 | 433,953 | 420,184 | 396,445 |
| Depn & Amortn | 3,419 | 2,264 | 1,117 | 98,464 | 99,492 | 98,598 | 93,256 | 95,947 |
| Income Before Taxes | 246,462 | 240,972 | 108,719 | 307,558 | 311,701 | 288,558 | 278,060 | 252,194 |
| Income Taxes | 97,860 | 95,652 | 43,157 | 196,353 | 191,328 | 172,035 | 170,160 | 157,500 |
| Net Income | 148,602 | 145,320 | 65,562 | 111,205 | 120,373 | 116,523 | 107,900 | 87,578 |
| Average Shares | 51,314 | 51,242 | 51,143 | 50,765 | 50,382 | 49,912 | 49,377 | 48,905 |
| **Balance Sheet** | | | | | | | | |
| Current Assets | 822,856 | 920,282 | 1,025,027 | 717,265 | 683,514 | 742,349 | 573,725 | 562,022 |
| Total Assets | 3,796,677 | 3,869,699 | 4,028,258 | 3,643,894 | 3,349,890 | 3,243,543 | 3,046,361 | 2,791,406 |
| Current Liabilities | 575,513 | 610,308 | 787,309 | 544,051 | 634,616 | 748,479 | 557,056 | 560,842 |
| Long-Term Obligations | 587,239 | 614,930 | 637,857 | 592,875 | 561,830 | 603,738 | 616,419 | 576,139 |
| Total Liabilities | 2,516,328 | 2,577,518 | 2,798,427 | 2,462,326 | 2,224,019 | 2,167,806 | 2,037,421 | 1,841,426 |
| Stockholders' Equity | 1,280,349 | 1,292,181 | 1,229,831 | 1,181,568 | 1,125,871 | 1,075,737 | 1,008,940 | 949,980 |
| Shares Outstanding | 51,292 | 51,226 | 51,127 | 50,974 | 50,143 | 49,916 | 49,316 | 48,878 |
| **Statistical Record** | | | | | | | | |
| Return on Assets % | 3.40 | 3.46 | 3.37 | 3.18 | 3.65 | 3.69 | 3.70 | 3.25 |
| Return on Equity % | 9.82 | 10.29 | 10.80 | 9.64 | 10.94 | 11.15 | 11.02 | 9.36 |
| EBITDA Margin % | 12.17 | 14.54 | 15.05 | 16.47 | 16.85 | 16.51 | 15.88 | 15.03 |
| Net Margin % | 6.45 | 8.02 | 8.24 | 4.11 | 4.45 | 4.43 | 4.08 | 3.32 |
| Asset Turnover | 0.77 | 0.73 | 0.73 | 0.77 | 0.82 | 0.83 | 0.91 | 0.98 |
| Current Ratio | 1.43 | 1.51 | 1.30 | 1.32 | 1.08 | 0.99 | 1.03 | 1.00 |
| Debt to Equity | 0.46 | 0.48 | 0.52 | 0.50 | 0.50 | 0.56 | 0.61 | 0.61 |
| Price Range | 39.98-33.59 | 39.98-32.89 | 39.98-31.27 | 37.78-31.27 | 36.29-24.84 | 36.01-30.76 | 35.46-29.94 | 32.31-27.38 |
| P/E Ratio | 16.94-14.23 | 16.06-13.21 | 15.99-12.51 | 17.49-14.48 | 15.18-10.39 | 15.45-13.20 | 16.19-13.67 | 18.05-15.30 |
| Average Yield % | 4.07 | 4.14 | 4.24 | 4.35 | 4.55 | 4.18 | 4.17 | 4.47 |

**Address:** 101 Constitution Avenue, N.W., Washington, DC 20080
**Telephone:** 703-750-2000
**Web Site:** www.wglholdings.com

**Officers:** Terry D. McCallister - Chairman, Chief Executive Officer Adrian P. Chapman - President, Chief Operating Officer **Transfer Agents:** BNY Mellon Shareowner Services, Pittsburgh, PA

**No of Institutions:** 252
**Shares:** 38,588,976 **% Held:** 59.21

# W.P. CAREY & CO. LLC

| Exchange | Symbol | Price | 52Wk Range | Yield | P/E |
|---|---|---|---|---|---|
| NYS | WPC | $40.92 (8/31/2011) | 41.94-28.13 | 5.08 | 11.93 |

*7 Year Price Score 114.02 *NYSE Composite Index=100 *12 Month Price Score 114.55

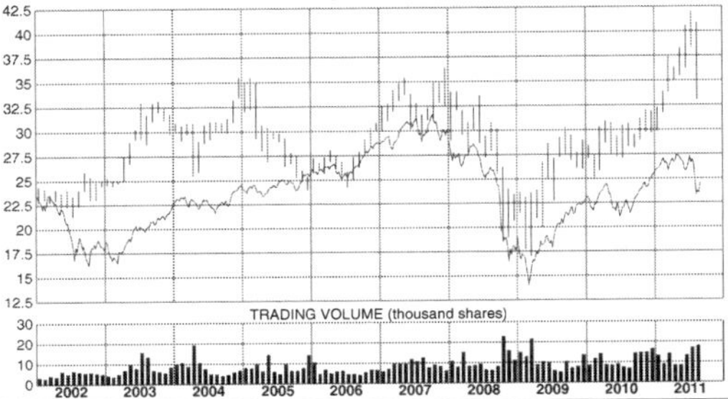

**Interim Earnings (Per Share)**

| Qtr. | Mar | Jun | Sep | Dec |
|---|---|---|---|---|
| 2008 | 0.43 | 0.50 | 0.48 | 0.55 |
| 2009 | 0.44 | 0.37 | 0.34 | 0.59 |
| 2010 | 0.36 | 0.59 | 0.41 | 0.50 |
| 2011 | 0.58 | 1.94 | ... | ... |

**Interim Dividends (Per Share)**

| Amt | Decl | Ex | Rec | Pay |
|---|---|---|---|---|
| 0.508Q | 09/17/2010 | 09/28/2010 | 09/30/2010 | 10/15/2010 |
| 0.51Q | 12/09/2010 | 12/29/2010 | 12/31/2010 | 01/14/2011 |
| 0.512Q | 03/21/2011 | 03/29/2011 | 03/31/2011 | 04/15/2011 |
| 0.55Q | 06/16/2011 | 06/28/2011 | 06/30/2011 | 07/15/2011 |

**Indicated Div: $2.08 (Div. Reinv. Plan)**

**Valuation Analysis**

| | | | |
|---|---|---|---|
| Forecast EPS | $2.73 (09/05/2011) | | |
| Market Cap | $1.6 Billion | Book Value | $693.3 Million |
| Price/Book | 2.34 | Price/Sales | 4.82 |

**Dividend Achiever Status**

| | |
|---|---|
| 10 Year Growth Rate | 1.76% |
| Total Years of Dividend Growth | 12 |

**Business Summary:** Property, Real Estate & Development (MIC: 5.3.2 SIC: 6531 NAIC: 531390)

W. P. Carey & Co. provides long-term sale-leaseback and build-to-suit transactions for companies worldwide and manages a global investment portfolio. Co. has two primary business segments: investment management, in which Co. structures and negotiates investments and debt placement transactions for the Corporate Property Associates® real estate investment trusts, and manages their portfolios of real estate investments; and real estate ownership, in which Co. owns and invests in commercial properties in the U.S. and the European Union that are then leased to companies. As of Dec 31 2010, Co. owned and managed 955 properties domestically and internationally, including its owned portfolio.

**Recent Developments:** For the quarter ended June 30 2011, income from continuing operations increased 226.0% to US$78.9 million from US$24.2 million in the year-earlier quarter. Net income increased 231.9% to US$78.7 million from US$23.7 million in the year-earlier quarter. Revenues were US$118.4 million, up 69.1% from US$70.0 million the year before. Revenues from property income rose 16.3% to US$23.5 million from US$20.2 million in the corresponding quarter a year earlier.

**Prospects:** Our evaluation of W.P. Carey & Co. LLC as of Sep. 6, 2011 is the result of our systematic analysis on three basic characteristics: earnings strength, relative valuation, and recent stock price movement. The company has managed to produce a neutral trend in earnings per share over the past 5 quarters. Because the company lacks sufficient analyst estimate data, we place greater weight on the historical EPS trend as the measure of earnings strength. Based on operating earnings yield, the company is undervalued when compared to all of the companies in our coverage universe. Share price changes over the past year indicates that WPC will perform poorly over the near term.

| Financial Data (US$ in Thousands) | 6 Mos | 3 Mos | 12/31/2010 | 12/31/2009 | 12/31/2008 | 12/31/2007 | 12/31/2006 | 12/31/2005 |
|---|---|---|---|---|---|---|---|---|
| Earnings Per Share | 3.43 | 2.08 | 1.86 | 1.74 | 1.96 | 2.05 | 2.22 | 1.25 |
| Cash Flow Per Share | 2.42 | 2.00 | 2.19 | 1.91 | 1.61 | 1.25 | 3.18 | 1.40 |
| Tang Book Value Per Share | 14.18 | 13.83 | 13.62 | 13.79 | 14.01 | 13.63 | 13.71 | 13.34 |
| Dividends Per Share | 2.080 | 2.036 | 2.028 | 2.296 | 1.955 | 2.148 | 1.820 | 1.788 |
| Dividend Payout % | 60.64 | 97.88 | 109.03 | 131.95 | 99.74 | 104.78 | 81.98 | 143.04 |
| **Income Statement** | | | | | | | | |
| Total Revenue | 195,930 | 77,532 | 273,910 | 235,876 | 243,873 | 263,129 | 273,258 | 174,117 |
| EBITDA | 122,283 | 33,266 | 113,818 | 107,754 | 127,357 | 147,487 | 168,162 | 82,548 |
| Depn & Amortn | (1,573) | 5,457 | 24,443 | 24,476 | 27,197 | 27,321 | 27,207 | 11,939 |
| Income Before Taxes | 115,255 | 24,044 | 74,409 | 69,803 | 83,755 | 106,128 | 126,249 | 57,333 |
| Income Taxes | 32,334 | 7,574 | 25,822 | 22,793 | 23,521 | 51,739 | 45,491 | 19,390 |
| Net Income | 102,455 | 23,343 | 73,972 | 69,023 | 78,047 | 79,252 | 86,303 | 48,604 |
| Average Shares | 40,243 | 40,242 | 40,007 | 39,712 | 40,221 | 39,868 | 39,093 | 39,020 |
| **Balance Sheet** | | | | | | | | |
| Current Assets | 58,475 | 69,419 | 103,486 | 54,448 | 69,873 | 100,466 | 110,992 | 95,947 |
| Total Assets | 1,459,706 | 1,144,202 | 1,172,326 | 1,093,336 | 1,111,136 | 1,153,284 | 1,093,010 | 983,262 |
| Current Liabilities | 144,797 | 89,486 | 102,324 | 126,906 | 119,902 | 166,193 | 120,740 | 50,020 |
| Long-Term Obligations | 576,101 | 372,747 | 396,982 | 326,330 | 326,874 | 316,751 | 278,653 | 246,113 |
| Total Liabilities | 766,357 | 509,925 | 547,313 | 467,703 | 463,000 | 519,013 | 461,025 | 375,794 |
| Stockholders' Equity | 693,349 | 634,277 | 625,013 | 625,633 | 648,136 | 634,271 | 631,985 | 607,468 |
| Shares Outstanding | 39,707 | 39,614 | 39,454 | 39,204 | 39,589 | 39,216 | 38,262 | 37,706 |
| **Statistical Record** | | | | | | | | |
| Return on Assets % | 10.73 | 7.42 | 6.53 | 6.26 | 6.87 | 7.06 | 8.31 | 4.87 |
| Return on Equity % | 21.15 | 13.26 | 11.83 | 10.84 | 12.14 | 12.52 | 13.93 | 7.93 |
| EBITDA Margin % | 62.41 | 42.91 | 41.55 | 45.68 | 52.22 | 56.05 | 61.54 | 47.41 |
| Net Margin % | 52.29 | 30.11 | 27.01 | 29.26 | 32.00 | 30.12 | 31.58 | 27.91 |
| Asset Turnover | 0.26 | 0.26 | 0.24 | 0.21 | 0.21 | 0.23 | 0.26 | 0.17 |
| Current Ratio | 0.40 | 0.78 | 1.01 | 0.43 | 0.58 | 0.60 | 0.92 | 1.92 |
| Debt to Equity | 0.83 | 0.59 | 0.64 | 0.52 | 0.50 | 0.50 | 0.44 | 0.41 |
| Price Range | 40.54-27.05 | 37.45-27.05 | 31.96-25.00 | 30.27-17.00 | 34.00-18.45 | 36.43-29.62 | 30.82-24.20 | 35.52-23.95 |
| P/E Ratio | 11.82-7.89 | 18.00-13.00 | 17.18-13.44 | 17.40-9.77 | 17.35-9.41 | 17.77-14.45 | 13.88-10.90 | 28.42-19.16 |
| Average Yield % | 6.47 | 6.73 | 7.01 | 9.09 | 6.93 | 6.59 | 6.71 | 6.19 |

**Address:** 50 Rockefeller Plaza, New York, NY 10020
**Telephone:** 212-492-1100
**Web Site:** www.wpcarey.com

**Officers:** Polk Carey - Chairman Trevor P. Bond - President, Chief Executive Officer **Transfer Agents:** Mellon Investor Services LLC, Jersey City, NJ

**No of Institutions:** 107
**Shares:** 6,168,229 **% Held:** 12.77

# WILEY (JOHN) & SONS INC.

| Exchange | Symbol | Price | 52Wk Range | Yield | P/E |
|---|---|---|---|---|---|
| NYS | JW A | $48.79 (8/31/2011) | 53.00-35.59 | 1.64 | 17.43 |

*7 Year Price Score 117.13 *NYSE Composite Index=100 *12 Month Price Score 105.44

**Interim Earnings (Per Share)**

| Qtr. | Jul | Oct | Jan | Apr |
|---|---|---|---|---|
| 2006-07 | 0.38 | 0.52 | 0.57 | 0.24 |
| 2007-08 | 0.68 | 0.65 | 0.67 | 0.49 |
| 2008-09 | 0.50 | 0.67 | 0.57 | 0.41 |
| 2009-10 | 0.45 | 0.78 | 0.71 | 0.46 |
| 2010-11 | 0.72 | 0.88 | 0.74 | 0.46 |

**Interim Dividends (Per Share)**

| Amt | Decl | Ex | Rec | Pay |
|---|---|---|---|---|
| 0.16Q | 09/16/2010 | 09/29/2010 | 10/01/2010 | 10/13/2010 |
| 0.16Q | 12/15/2010 | 12/28/2010 | 12/30/2010 | 01/14/2011 |
| 0.16Q | 03/16/2011 | 03/30/2011 | 04/01/2011 | 04/14/2011 |
| 0.20Q | 06/16/2011 | 06/30/2011 | 07/05/2011 | 07/14/2011 |

**Indicated Div: $0.80**

**Valuation Analysis**

| | | | |
|---|---|---|---|
| Forecast EPS | $3.13 (09/02/2011) | | |
| Market Cap | $3.0 Billion | Book Value | $977.9 Million |
| Price/Book | 3.03 | Price/Sales | 1.70 |

**Dividend Achiever Status**

| | |
|---|---|
| 10 Year Growth Rate | 13.44% |
| Total Years of Dividend Growth | 17 |

**Business Summary:** Publishing (MIC: 2.3.3 SIC: 2731 NAIC: 511130)

John Wiley & Sons is a publisher of print and electronic products. Co.'s businesses produce scientific, technical, medical and scholarly journals, encyclopedias, books, online products and services; professional and consumer books, subscription products, certification and training materials, online applications and websites; and educational materials, including integrated online teaching and learning resources, for undergraduate, graduate and advanced placement students, educators, and lifelong learners as well as secondary school students in Australia. Co. operates in three reportable segments: Scientific, Technical, Medical and Scholarly, Professional/Trade and Higher Education.

**Recent Developments:** For the year ended Apr 30 2011, net income increased 19.7% to US$171.9 million from US$143.5 million in the prior year. Revenues were US$1.74 billion, up 2.6% from US$1.70 billion the year before. Operating income was US$248.1 million versus US$242.6 million in the prior year, an increase of 2.3%. Direct operating expenses rose 0.9% to US$539.0 million from US$534.0 million in the comparable period the year before. Indirect operating expenses increased 3.6% to US$955.4 million from US$922.5 million in the equivalent prior-year period.

**Prospects:** Our evaluation of Wiley (John) & Sons Inc. as of Sep. 6, 2011 is the result of our systematic analysis on three basic characteristics: earnings strength, relative valuation, and recent stock price movement. The company has produced a positive trend in earnings per share over the past 5 quarters. However, while recent estimates for the company have been lowered by analysts, JW.A has posted results that fell short of analysts expectations. Based on operating earnings yield, the company is about fairly valued when compared to all of the companies in our coverage universe. Share price changes over the past year indicates that JW.A will perform in line with the market over the near term.

**Financial Data**

| (US$ in Thousands) | 04/30/2011 | 04/30/2010 | 04/30/2009 | 04/30/2008 | 04/30/2007 | 04/30/2006 | 04/30/2005 | 04/30/2004 |
|---|---|---|---|---|---|---|---|---|
| Earnings Per Share | 2.80 | 2.41 | 2.15 | 2.49 | 1.71 | 1.85 | 1.35 | 1.41 |
| Cash Flow Per Share | 6.24 | 7.16 | 5.84 | 4.82 | 3.87 | 4.18 | 4.01 | 3.43 |
| Dividends Per Share | 0.640 | 0.560 | 0.520 | 0.440 | 0.400 | 0.360 | 0.300 | 0.260 |
| Dividend Payout % | 22.86 | 23.24 | 24.19 | 17.67 | 23.39 | 19.46 | 22.22 | 18.44 |
| **Income Statement** | | | | | | | | |
| Total Revenue | 1,742,551 | 1,699,062 | 1,611,390 | 1,673,734 | 1,234,936 | 1,044,185 | 974,048 | 922,962 |
| EBITDA | 327,045 | 307,148 | 278,697 | 295,300 | 210,881 | 198,208 | 183,709 | 168,894 |
| Depn & Amortn | 81,085 | 75,439 | 71,978 | 72,310 | 49,602 | 45,529 | 42,328 | 39,515 |
| Income Before Taxes | 231,060 | 200,209 | 164,475 | 161,528 | 139,502 | 143,844 | 135,663 | 125,110 |
| Income Taxes | 59,171 | 56,666 | 36,217 | 13,992 | 39,883 | 33,516 | 51,822 | 36,270 |
| Net Income | 171,889 | 143,543 | 128,258 | 147,536 | 99,619 | 110,328 | 83,841 | 88,840 |
| Average Shares | 61,359 | 59,679 | 59,610 | 59,323 | 58,287 | 59,792 | 62,093 | 63,226 |
| **Balance Sheet** | | | | | | | | |
| Current Assets | 527,490 | 485,714 | 439,569 | 447,580 | 405,437 | 326,308 | 338,918 | 324,006 |
| Total Assets | 2,430,141 | 2,316,202 | 2,223,708 | 2,588,814 | 2,531,115 | 1,026,009 | 1,032,569 | 1,014,582 |
| Current Liabilities | 756,365 | 674,372 | 596,967 | 691,161 | 598,883 | 362,109 | 341,311 | 306,365 |
| Long-Term Obligations | 330,500 | 559,000 | 754,900 | 797,318 | 977,721 | 160,496 | 196,214 | 200,000 |
| Total Liabilities | 1,452,252 | 1,593,766 | 1,710,192 | 1,899,696 | 2,001,607 | 624,169 | 635,995 | 599,518 |
| Stockholders' Equity | 977,889 | 722,436 | 513,516 | 689,118 | 529,508 | 401,840 | 396,574 | 415,064 |
| Shares Outstanding | 60,709 | 60,017 | 58,380 | 58,626 | 57,552 | 57,145 | 59,331 | 61,694 |
| **Statistical Record** | | | | | | | | |
| Return on Assets % | 7.24 | 6.32 | 5.33 | 5.75 | 5.60 | 10.72 | 8.19 | 8.99 |
| Return on Equity % | 20.22 | 23.23 | 21.33 | 24.15 | 21.39 | 27.64 | 20.66 | 23.34 |
| EBITDA Margin % | 18.77 | 18.08 | 17.30 | 17.64 | 17.08 | 18.98 | 18.86 | 18.30 |
| Net Margin % | 9.86 | 8.45 | 7.96 | 8.81 | 8.07 | 10.57 | 8.61 | 9.63 |
| Asset Turnover | 0.73 | 0.75 | 0.67 | 0.65 | 0.69 | 1.01 | 0.95 | 0.93 |
| Current Ratio | 0.70 | 0.72 | 0.74 | 0.65 | 0.68 | 0.90 | 0.99 | 1.06 |
| Debt to Equity | 0.34 | 0.77 | 1.47 | 1.16 | 1.85 | 0.40 | 0.49 | 0.48 |
| Price Range | 52.64-35.59 | 43.95-29.77 | 49.76-26.21 | 49.35-35.98 | 41.00-31.86 | 44.90-35.73 | 36.91-29.27 | 31.58-24.07 |
| P/E Ratio | 18.80-12.71 | 18.24-12.35 | 23.14-12.19 | 19.82-14.45 | 23.98-18.63 | 24.27-19.31 | 27.34-21.68 | 22.40-17.07 |
| Average Yield % | 1.48 | 1.51 | 1.36 | 1.04 | 1.10 | 0.91 | 0.90 | 0.97 |

**Address:** 111 River Street, Hoboken, NJ 07030
**Telephone:** 201-748-6000
**Web Site:** www.wiley.com

**Officers:** Peter Booth Wiley - Chairman William J. Pesce - President, Chief Executive Officer **Transfer Agents:** Registrar and Transfer Company, Cranford, NJ

**No of Institutions:** 294
**Shares:** 46,863,840 **% Held:** 68.93

This page left intentionally blank.

# 2011 Fall Dividend Achiever Canadian Companies

# AG GROWTH INTERNATIONAL INC.

| Exchange | Symbol | Price | 52Wk Range | Yield | P/E |
|---|---|---|---|---|---|
| TSX | AFN | C$40.38 (8/31/2011) | 55.51-36.30 | 5.94 | 15.18 |

*7 Year Price Score 182.64 *NYSE Composite Index=100 *12 Month Price Score 96.24

**Interim Earnings (Per Share) Can$**

| Qtr. | Mar | Jun | Sep | Dec |
|---|---|---|---|---|
| 2009 | 0.79 | 1.27 | 1.17 | 0.21 |
| 2010 | 0.33 | 0.86 | 1.13 | 0.24 |
| 2011 | 0.38 | 0.91 | ... | ... |

**Interim Dividends (Per Share)**

| Amt | Decl | Ex | Rec | Pay |
|---|---|---|---|---|
| 0.20M | 06/09/2011 | 08/29/2011 | 08/31/2011 | 09/30/2011 |
| 0.20M | 08/12/2011 | 10/27/2011 | 10/31/2011 | 11/30/2011 |
| 0.20M | 08/12/2011 | 11/28/2011 | 11/30/2011 | 12/30/2011 |
| 0.20M | 08/12/2011 | 09/28/2011 | 09/30/2011 | 10/28/2011 |

**Indicated Div: $2.40**

**Valuation Analysis**

Forecast EPS $2.55 (09/02/2011)

Market Cap C$500.5 Million Book Value $207.9 Million

Price/Book 2.41 Price/Sales N/A

**Dividend Achiever Status**

**5 Year Growth Rate** 7.98%

**Total Years of Dividend Growth** 6

**Business Summary:** Industrial Machinery & Equipment (MIC: 7.2.1 SIC: 3523 NAIC: 333111)

AG Growth International is a manufacturer of portable and stationary grain handling, storage and conditioning equipment. Co.'s divisions include: Batco Manufacturing, which manufactures portable belt conveyors; Union Iron, which manufactures material-handling and storage equipment; Edwards Group, which manufactures natural air grain drying equipment; Wheatheart Manufacturing, which manufactures portable grain augers, grain-handling accessories and fencing equipment; Hi Roller, which manufactures dust-tight and self-reloading conveyors; Twister, which manufactures corrugated steel bins; and Applegate Livestock Equipment Inc., which manufactures cattle-handling and containment equipment.

**Recent Developments:** For the quarter ended June 30 2011, net income increased 3.1% to C$12.0 million from C$11.6 million in the year-earlier quarter. Revenues were C$88.1 million, up 14.8% from C$76.7 million the year before. Operating income was C$17.9 million versus C$19.9 million in the prior-year quarter, a decrease of 9.8%. Direct operating expenses rose 26.2% to C$57.3 million from C$45.4 million in the comparable period the year before. Indirect operating expenses increased 11.1% to C$12.9 million from C$11.6 million in the equivalent prior-year period.

**Prospects:** Co. anticipates a number of challenges in the second half of 2011, mainly gross margin pressures due to high steel costs and the effect of its effort to address the start-up issues at the new storage bin plant in Alberta. However, Co. foresees that the challenges at the Alberta bin plant will be resolved by end of 2011 and thus, retain a positive outlook for contributions from this plant in 2012 and beyond. Co. is also seeing growing demand for storage bins and commercial grain handling equipment domestically and overseas. Thus, Co. expects its investment in grain storage bin capacity will allow it to capitalize on international sales opportunities and to increase sales in North America.

| **Financial Data** (Can$ in Thousands) | 6 Mos | 3 Mos | 12/31/2010 | 12/31/2009 | 12/31/2008 | 12/31/2007 | 12/31/2006 | 12/31/2005 |
|---|---|---|---|---|---|---|---|---|
| Earnings Per Share | 2.66 | 2.61 | 2.78 | 3.45 | 1.64 | 1.06 | 1.70 | 1.82 |
| Cash Flow Per Share | ... | ... | 3.21 | 4.24 | 0.84 | 3.18 | 2.25 | 1.97 |
| Tang Book Value Per Share | 6.04 | 5.70 | 1.96 | 4.26 | 0.10 | 1.53 | N.M. | 1.42 |
| Dividends Per Share | 2.280 | 2.190 | 2.100 | 2.040 | 1.800 | 1.680 | 1.670 | 1.410 |
| Dividend Payout % | 85.71 | 83.91 | 75.54 | 59.13 | 109.76 | 158.49 | 98.23 | 77.47 |
| **Income Statement** | | | | | | | | |
| Total Revenue | 155,176 | 67,065 | 262,077 | 237,294 | 199,341 | 130,702 | 81,525 | 84,034 |
| EBITDA | ... | 7,754 | 60,692 | 54,878 | 29,017 | 28,618 | 21,673 | 22,238 |
| Depn & Amortn | 1,940 | (173) | 5,427 | 5,388 | 2,980 | 2,368 | 1,576 | 1,673 |
| Income Before Taxes | ... | 7,927 | 44,074 | 45,410 | 23,304 | 24,056 | 19,322 | 19,967 |
| Income Taxes | 6,219 | 3,221 | 7,918 | 107 | 2,092 | 11,690 | 279 | 315 |
| Net Income | 16,700 | 4,706 | 36,156 | 45,303 | 21,212 | 12,366 | 19,044 | 19,652 |
| Average Shares | 15,054 | 12,498 | 15,520 | 13,459 | 12,923 | 11,651 | 11,225 | 10,801 |
| **Balance Sheet** | | | | | | | | |
| Current Assets | 133,993 | 124,288 | 151,061 | 193,809 | 75,165 | 62,753 | 44,180 | 37,192 |
| Total Assets | 390,737 | 380,009 | 391,563 | 387,850 | 228,464 | 210,683 | 170,233 | 144,353 |
| Current Liabilities | 44,703 | 37,683 | 58,858 | 37,027 | 37,712 | 26,630 | 17,708 | 13,556 |
| Long-Term Obligations | 129,898 | 129,494 | 129,796 | 128,510 | 52,791 | 25,623 | 41,560 | 20,018 |
| Total Liabilities | 182,871 | 175,752 | 230,847 | 211,051 | 102,928 | 64,029 | 59,268 | 33,574 |
| Stockholders' Equity | 207,866 | 204,257 | 160,716 | 176,799 | 125,536 | 146,655 | 110,965 | 110,779 |
| Shares Outstanding | 12,394 | 12,394 | 12,399 | 13,020 | 12,684 | 12,955 | 11,225 | 11,225 |
| **Statistical Record** | | | | | | | | |
| Return on Assets % | ... | ... | 9.28 | 14.70 | 9.63 | 6.49 | 12.11 | 14.83 |
| Return on Equity % | ... | ... | 21.42 | 29.97 | 15.54 | 9.60 | 17.18 | 19.62 |
| EBITDA Margin % | ... | 11.56 | 23.16 | 23.13 | 14.56 | 21.90 | 26.58 | 26.46 |
| Net Margin % | 10.76 | 7.02 | 13.80 | 19.09 | 10.64 | 9.46 | 23.36 | 23.39 |
| Asset Turnover | ... | ... | 0.67 | 0.77 | 0.91 | 0.69 | 0.52 | 0.63 |
| Current Ratio | 3.00 | 3.30 | 2.57 | 5.23 | 1.99 | 2.36 | 2.49 | 2.74 |
| Debt to Equity | 0.62 | 0.63 | 0.81 | 0.73 | 0.42 | 0.17 | 0.37 | 0.18 |
| Price Range | 55.51-32.36 | 55.51-30.56 | 54.05-30.56 | 34.92-13.53 | 37.99-13.19 | 33.90-13.97 | 16.96-11.04 | 17.05-9.85 |
| P/E Ratio | 20.87-12.17 | 21.27-11.71 | 19.44-10.99 | 10.12-3.92 | 23.16-8.04 | 31.98-13.18 | 9.98-6.49 | 9.37-5.41 |
| Average Yield % | 5.19 | 5.09 | 5.49 | 4.45 | 6.41 | 4.43 | 12.14 | 13.53 |

**Address:** 1301 Kenaston Blvd., Winnipeg, R3P 2P2
**Telephone:** 204-489-1855
**Web Site:** www.aggrowth.com

**Officers:** Gary Anderson - President, Chief Executive Officer Steve Sommerfeld - Chief Financial Officer, Corporate Secretary **Transfer Agents:** Computershare Investor Services Inc., Toronto, Ontario, Canada

**Investor Contact:** 204-489-1855
**No of Institutions:** N/A
**Shares:** N/A **% Held:** N/A

# AGF MANAGEMENT LTD

| Exchange | Symbol | Price | 52Wk Range | Yield | P/E |
|---|---|---|---|---|---|
| TSX | AGF B | C$16.65 (8/31/2011) | 20.42-13.61 | 6.49 | 12.81 |

***7 Year Price Score 88.04** *NYSE Composite Index=100 ***12 Month Price Score 95.40**

**Interim Earnings (Per Share) Can$**

| Qtr. | Feb | May | Aug | Nov |
|---|---|---|---|---|
| 2007-08 | 0.70 | 0.49 | 0.46 | (0.24) |
| 2008-09 | 0.14 | 0.19 | 0.25 | 0.51 |
| 2009-10 | 0.34 | 0.30 | 0.31 | 0.35 |
| 2010-11 | 0.30 | 0.34 | ... | ... |

**Interim Dividends (Per Share)**

| Amt | Decl | Ex | Rec | Pay |
|---|---|---|---|---|
| 0.26Q | 09/28/2010 | 10/06/2010 | 10/08/2010 | 10/20/2010 |
| 0.26Q | 12/08/2010 | 01/07/2011 | 01/11/2011 | 01/24/2011 |
| 0.26Q | 03/29/2011 | 04/06/2011 | 04/08/2011 | 04/20/2011 |
| 0.27Q | 06/21/2011 | 07/06/2011 | 07/08/2011 | 07/20/2011 |

**Indicated Div: $1.08**

**Valuation Analysis**

| | | | |
|---|---|---|---|
| Forecast EPS | $1.47 (09/02/2011) | | |
| Market Cap | C$1.6 Billion | Book Value | $1.3 Billion |
| Price/Book | 1.25 | Price/Sales | N/A |

**Dividend Achiever Status**

| | |
|---|---|
| **5 Year Growth Rate** | 12.96% |
| **Total Years of Dividend Growth** | 14 |

**Business Summary:** Wealth Management (MIC: 5.5.2 SIC: 6163 NAIC: 522310)

AGF Management is an integrated, global wealth management corporation whose principal subsidiaries provide investment management for mutual funds, institutions and corporations, as well as high-net-worth clients; and trust products and services (including real estate secured loans and investment loans and Guaranteed Investment Certificates (GICs)). Co. conducts the management and distribution of mutual funds in Canada under the brand names AGF, Elements and Harmony (collectively, AGF Funds). Co. conducts its trust business under the name AGF Trust Company (AGF Trust).

**Recent Developments:** For the quarter ended May 31 2011, net income increased 19.0% to C$32.9 million from C$27.7 million in the year-earlier quarter. Non-interest income rose 17.1% to C$180.1 million from C$153.8 million, while non-interest expense advanced 16.6% to C$134.4 million.

**Prospects:** Our evaluation of AGF Management Limited as of Sep. 6, 2011 is the result of our systematic analysis on three basic characteristics: earnings strength, relative valuation, and recent stock price movement. The company has enjoyed a very positive trend in earnings per share over the past 5 quarters. However, while recent estimates for the company have been lowered by analysts, C.AGF.B has posted results that fell short of analysts expectations. Based on operating earnings yield, the company is undervalued when compared to all of the companies in our coverage universe. Share price changes over the past year indicates that C.AGF.B will perform in line with the market over the near term.

| **Financial Data** (Can$ in Thousands) | 6 Mos | 3 Mos | 11/30/2010 | 11/30/2009 | 11/30/2008 | 11/30/2007 | 11/30/2006 | 11/30/2005 |
|---|---|---|---|---|---|---|---|---|
| Earnings Per Share | 1.30 | 1.26 | 1.30 | 1.09 | 1.41 | 1.96 | 1.25 | 1.01 |
| Cash Flow Per Share | ... | ... | 2.00 | 2.13 | 3.92 | 4.43 | 2.49 | 2.60 |
| Tang Book Value Per Share | N.M. | N.M. | 11.00 | 10.71 | 10.48 | 9.90 | 9.48 | 8.78 |
| Dividends Per Share | 1.040 | 1.040 | 1.030 | 1.000 | 0.950 | 0.780 | 0.690 | 0.560 |
| Dividend Payout % | 80.00 | 82.54 | 79.23 | 91.74 | 67.38 | 39.80 | 55.20 | 55.45 |
| **Income Statement** | | | | | | | | |
| Total Revenue | 343,015 | 162,894 | 614,578 | 586,114 | 725,570 | 780,320 | 703,481 | 594,446 |
| EBITDA | ... | 63,969 | 251,034 | 213,555 | 255,832 | 347,263 | 248,090 | 240,743 |
| Depn & Amortn | 48,696 | 22,627 | 87,204 | 96,702 | 113,997 | 123,827 | 134,774 | 139,013 |
| Income Before Taxes | ... | 39,413 | 163,830 | 116,853 | 141,835 | 223,436 | 113,316 | 101,730 |
| Income Taxes | 24,168 | 11,430 | 46,062 | 18,577 | 12,686 | 46,689 | 11,081 | 29,018 |
| Net Income | 60,397 | 27,705 | 116,775 | 97,694 | 128,592 | 178,687 | 112,657 | 91,872 |
| Average Shares | 96,794 | 92,010 | 90,157 | 89,660 | 91,333 | 91,295 | 89,840 | 90,659 |
| **Balance Sheet** | | | | | | | | |
| Current Assets | 1,282,841 | 1,349,004 | 1,510,347 | 1,465,328 | 1,463,337 | 1,447,421 | 828,492 | 233,165 |
| Total Assets | 5,239,201 | 5,402,284 | 5,253,861 | 5,675,922 | 6,533,959 | 5,876,812 | 3,919,768 | 2,709,667 |
| Current Liabilities | 1,832,323 | 1,885,992 | 2,091,453 | 2,203,551 | 2,840,880 | 2,182,524 | 1,243,319 | 117,726 |
| Long-Term Obligations | 308,763 | 344,621 | 143,678 | 143,648 | 123,740 | 184,486 | ... | 17,364 |
| Total Liabilities | 3,963,020 | 4,137,630 | 4,102,670 | 4,545,111 | 5,426,334 | 4,807,419 | 2,939,997 | 1,791,341 |
| Stockholders' Equity | 1,276,181 | 1,264,654 | 1,150,694 | 1,130,403 | 1,107,422 | 1,069,002 | 979,771 | 918,326 |
| Shares Outstanding | 95,618 | 95,477 | 88,663 | 89,155 | 88,537 | 88,979 | 89,229 | 89,180 |
| **Statistical Record** | | | | | | | | |
| Return on Assets % | ... | ... | 2.14 | 1.60 | 2.07 | 3.65 | 3.40 | 3.77 |
| Return on Equity % | ... | ... | 10.24 | 8.73 | 11.78 | 17.44 | 11.87 | 10.03 |
| EBITDA Margin % | ... | 39.27 | 40.85 | 36.44 | 35.26 | 44.50 | 35.27 | 40.50 |
| Net Margin % | 17.61 | 17.01 | 19.00 | 16.67 | 17.72 | 22.90 | 16.01 | 15.46 |
| Asset Turnover | ... | ... | 0.11 | 0.10 | 0.12 | 0.16 | 0.21 | 0.24 |
| Current Ratio | 0.70 | 0.72 | 0.72 | 0.66 | 0.52 | 0.66 | 0.67 | 1.98 |
| Debt to Equity | 0.24 | 0.27 | 0.12 | 0.13 | 0.11 | 0.17 | ... | 0.02 |
| Price Range | 20.42-12.95 | 20.13-12.95 | 18.77-12.95 | 17.15-6.80 | 31.85-7.47 | 39.59-25.10 | 25.91-19.10 | 23.38-15.59 |
| P/E Ratio | 15.71-9.96 | 15.98-10.28 | 14.44-9.96 | 15.73-6.24 | 22.59-5.30 | 20.20-12.81 | 20.73-15.28 | 23.15-15.44 |
| Average Yield % | 6.23 | 6.29 | 6.43 | 8.25 | 4.39 | 2.35 | 3.07 | 3.13 |

**Address:** Suite 3100, 66 Wellington Street West, Toronto-Dominion Bank Tower, Toronto-Dominion Centre, Toronto, M5K 1E9
**Telephone:** 416-367-1900
**Web Site:** www.agf.com

**Officers:** Blake C. Goldring - Chairman, Chief Executive Officer W. Robert Farquharson - Vice-Chairman **Transfer Agents:** Computershare Trust Company of Canada, Canada

**No of Institutions:** N/A
**Shares:** N/A **% Held:** N/A

# ATCO LTD

| Exchange | Symbol | Price | 52Wk Range | Yield | P/E |
|---|---|---|---|---|---|
| TSX | ACO X | C$64.00 (8/31/2011) | 65.95-50.90 | 1.75 | 11.90 |

***7 Year Price Score 127.92** *NYSE Composite Index=100 ***12 Month Price Score 105.19**

**Interim Earnings (Per Share) Can$**

| Qtr. | Mar | Jun | Sep | Dec |
|---|---|---|---|---|
| 2008 | 1.58 | 0.90 | 0.90 | 1.28 |
| 2009 | 1.63 | 0.85 | 1.05 | 1.35 |
| 2010 | 1.54 | 1.01 | 1.02 | 1.41 |
| 2011 | 1.89 | 1.06 | ... | ... |

**Interim Dividends (Per Share)**

| Amt | Decl | Ex | Rec | Pay |
|---|---|---|---|---|
| 0.265Q | 10/22/2010 | 12/08/2010 | 12/10/2010 | 12/31/2010 |
| 0.285Q | 01/13/2011 | 03/08/2011 | 03/10/2011 | 03/31/2011 |
| 0.285Q | 04/13/2011 | 06/07/2011 | 06/09/2011 | 06/30/2011 |
| 0.285Q | 07/13/2011 | 09/07/2011 | 09/09/2011 | 09/30/2011 |

**Indicated Div: $1.12**

**Valuation Analysis**

| | | | |
|---|---|---|---|
| Forecast EPS | $5.32 (09/02/2011) | | |
| Market Cap | C$3.7 Billion | Book Value | $2.1 Billion |
| Price/Book | 1.76 | Price/Sales | N/A |

**Dividend Achiever Status**

| | |
|---|---|
| **5 Year Growth Rate** | 6.88% |
| **Total Years of Dividend Growth** | 17 |

**Business Summary:** Electric Utilities (MIC: 3.1.1 SIC: 4911 NAIC: 221122)

Atco is a holding company. Co.'s Utilities segment includes the regulated distribution of natural gas by ATCO Gas, the regulated transmission of natural gas by ATCO Pipelines, and regulated distribution and transmission of electric energy by ATCO Electric. Co.'s Energy segment includes the non-regulated supply of electricity and cogeneration steam by ATCO Power and ATCO Resources, the regulated supply of electricity by Alberta Power and the non-regulated natural gas gathering, processing, storage and natural gas liquids extraction by ATCO Midstream. Co.'s Structures & Logistics segment includes the manufacture, sale and lease of transportable workforce housing and space rentals products.

**Recent Developments:** For the quarter ended June 30 2011, net income increased 10.6% to C$115.0 million from C$104.0 million in the year-earlier quarter. Revenues were C$879.0 million, up 3.3% from C$851.0 million the year before. Operating income was C$209.0 million versus C$186.0 million in the prior-year quarter, an increase of 12.4%. Direct operating expenses declined 3.6% to C$240.0 million from C$249.0 million in the comparable period the year before. Indirect operating expenses increased 4.9% to C$430.0 million from C$410.0 million in the equivalent prior-year period.

**Prospects:** Our evaluation of ATCO Limited as of Sep. 6, 2011 is the result of our systematic analysis on three basic characteristics: earnings strength, relative valuation, and recent stock price movement. The company has managed to produce a neutral trend in earnings per share over the past 5 quarters. However, while recent estimates for the company have been mixed, C.ACO.X has posted results that fell short of analysts expectations. Based on operating earnings yield, the company is undervalued when compared to all of the companies in our coverage universe. Share price changes over the past year indicates that C.ACO.X will perform poorly over the near term.

**Financial Data**

| (Can$ in Thousands) | 6 Mos | 3 Mos | 12/31/2010 | 12/31/2009 | 12/31/2008 | 12/31/2007 | 12/31/2006 | 12/31/2005 |
|---|---|---|---|---|---|---|---|---|
| Earnings Per Share | 5.38 | 5.33 | 5.02 | 4.88 | 4.66 | 4.26 | 3.45 | 2.46 |
| Cash Flow Per Share | ... | ... | 16.20 | 15.22 | 15.80 | 14.17 | 12.34 | 13.73 |
| Tang Book Value Per Share | 30.50 | 29.50 | 32.24 | 28.90 | 29.43 | 25.99 | 23.28 | 21.03 |
| Dividends Per Share | 1.100 | 1.080 | 1.060 | 1.000 | 0.940 | 0.880 | 0.820 | 0.760 |
| Dividend Payout % | 20.45 | 20.26 | 21.12 | 20.49 | 20.17 | 20.66 | 23.77 | 30.89 |
| **Income Statement** | | | | | | | | |
| Total Revenue | 1,900,000 | 1,021,000 | 3,445,400 | 3,108,900 | 3,265,600 | 2,901,800 | 2,860,900 | 2,859,600 |
| EBITDA | ... | 422,000 | 1,072,200 | 1,052,800 | 1,087,000 | 945,000 | 965,700 | 838,800 |
| Depn & Amortn | 198,000 | 97,000 | 393,900 | 375,100 | 425,600 | 383,100 | 378,600 | 337,900 |
| Income Before Taxes | ... | 271,000 | 678,300 | 677,700 | 661,400 | 561,900 | 587,100 | 500,900 |
| Income Taxes | 115,000 | 69,000 | 133,000 | 144,200 | 160,000 | 92,000 | 188,700 | 187,700 |
| Net Income | 171,000 | 110,000 | 292,900 | 283,300 | 271,500 | 250,800 | 207,000 | 149,000 |
| Average Shares | 57,975 | 58,116 | 58,326 | 58,071 | 58,238 | 58,868 | 60,030 | 60,700 |
| **Balance Sheet** | | | | | | | | |
| Current Assets | 1,145,000 | 1,415,000 | 1,392,100 | 1,706,000 | 1,592,700 | 1,446,600 | 1,483,500 | 1,480,700 |
| Total Assets | 10,215,000 | 10,249,000 | 10,239,800 | 9,954,600 | 8,673,600 | 7,999,900 | 7,698,500 | 7,461,400 |
| Current Liabilities | 547,000 | 722,000 | 620,800 | 745,000 | 738,800 | 559,000 | 546,500 | 550,700 |
| Long-Term Obligations | 3,359,000 | 3,347,000 | 3,460,200 | 3,577,900 | 3,394,200 | 3,232,500 | 3,207,800 | 3,077,800 |
| Total Liabilities | 8,113,000 | 8,198,000 | 8,025,900 | 7,945,000 | 6,901,800 | 6,426,700 | 6,266,400 | 6,130,300 |
| Stockholders' Equity | 2,102,000 | 2,051,000 | 2,213,900 | 2,009,600 | 1,771,800 | 1,573,200 | 1,432,100 | 1,331,100 |
| Shares Outstanding | 57,700 | 57,798 | 57,924 | 58,220 | 57,779 | 57,801 | 58,452 | 59,920 |
| **Statistical Record** | | | | | | | | |
| Return on Assets % | ... | ... | 2.90 | 3.04 | 3.25 | 3.20 | 2.73 | 2.06 |
| Return on Equity % | ... | ... | 13.87 | 14.98 | 16.19 | 16.69 | 14.98 | 11.57 |
| EBITDA Margin % | ... | 41.33 | 31.12 | 33.86 | 33.29 | 32.57 | 33.76 | 29.33 |
| Net Margin % | 9.00 | 10.77 | 8.50 | 9.11 | 8.31 | 8.64 | 7.24 | 5.21 |
| Asset Turnover | ... | ... | 0.34 | 0.33 | 0.39 | 0.37 | 0.38 | 0.39 |
| Current Ratio | 2.09 | 1.96 | 2.24 | 2.29 | 2.16 | 2.59 | 2.71 | 2.69 |
| Debt to Equity | 1.60 | 1.63 | 1.56 | 1.78 | 1.92 | 2.05 | 2.24 | 2.31 |
| Price Range | 65.95-47.20 | 62.09-46.67 | 60.48-44.86 | 46.42-33.26 | 55.21-34.00 | 64.23-44.19 | 50.99-33.56 | 42.45-28.50 |
| P/E Ratio | 12.26-8.77 | 11.65-8.76 | 12.05-8.94 | 9.51-6.82 | 11.85-7.30 | 15.08-10.37 | 14.78-9.73 | 17.26-11.59 |
| Average Yield % | 1.94 | 1.99 | 2.08 | 2.55 | 2.02 | 1.64 | 2.07 | 2.15 |

**Address:** 1400, 909-11th Avenue S.W., Calgary, T2R 1N6
**Telephone:** 403-292-7500
**Web Site:** www.atco.com

**Officers:** Ronald D. Southern - Chairman Nancy C. Southern - Deputy Chairman, President, Chief Executive Officer **Transfer Agents:** CIBC Mellon Trust Company, Calgary, Alberta; Montreal, Quebec; Toronto, Ontario; Vancouver, British Columbia, Canada

**No of Institutions:** N/A
**Shares:** N/A **% Held:** N/A

# CAMECO CORP.

| Exchange | Symbol | Price | 52Wk Range | Yield | P/E |
|---|---|---|---|---|---|
| TSX | CCO | C$22.73 (8/31/2011) | 43.14-20.55 | 1.76 | 19.94 |

*7 Year Price Score 93.89 *NYSE Composite Index=100 *12 Month Price Score 77.65

**Interim Earnings (Per Share) Can$**

| Qtr. | Mar | Jun | Sep | Dec |
|---|---|---|---|---|
| 2008 | 0.37 | 0.42 | 0.39 | 0.07 |
| 2009 | 0.22 | 0.63 | 0.44 | 1.53 |
| 2010 | 0.36 | 0.18 | 0.25 | 0.52 |
| 2011 | 0.23 | 0.14 | ... | ... |

**Interim Dividends (Per Share)**

| Amt | Decl | Ex | Rec | Pay |
|---|---|---|---|---|
| 0.07Q | 12/02/2010 | 12/29/2010 | 12/31/2010 | 01/14/2011 |
| 0.10Q | 02/11/2011 | 03/29/2011 | 03/31/2011 | 04/15/2011 |
| 0.10Q | 05/06/2011 | 06/28/2011 | 06/30/2011 | 07/15/2011 |
| 0.10Q | 08/04/2011 | 09/28/2011 | 09/30/2011 | 10/14/2011 |

**Indicated Div: $0.40**

**Valuation Analysis**

| | | | |
|---|---|---|---|
| Forecast EPS | $1.10 (09/05/2011) | | |
| Market Cap | C$9.0 Billion | Book Value | $4.7 Billion |
| Price/Book | 1.89 | Price/Sales | N/A |

**Dividend Achiever Status**

| | |
|---|---|
| 5 Year Growth Rate | 18.61% |
| Total Years of Dividend Growth | 8 |

**Business Summary:** Mining (MIC: 8.2.4 SIC: 1094 NAIC: 212291)

Cameco and its subsidiaries are engaged in the exploration for and the development, mining, refining, conversion and fabrication of uranium for sale as fuel for generating electricity in nuclear power reactors in Canada and other countries. Co. has three reportable segments: uranium, which explores for, mines, mills, purchases, and sells uranium concentrate; fuel services, which refines, converts and fabricates uranium concentrate, and purchases and sells conversion services; and electricity, which generates and sells electricity through its 31.6% interest in the Bruce Power Limited Partnership, which operates four nuclear reactors and manages the overall site in southern Ontario.

**Recent Developments:** For the quarter ended June 30 2011, net income decreased 24.8% to C$51.2 million from C$68.1 million in the year-earlier quarter. Revenues were C$425.7 million, down 22.0% from C$546.1 million the year before. Operating income was C$53.7 million versus C$127.2 million in the prior-year quarter, a decrease of 57.8%. Direct operating expenses declined 13.2% to C$317.8 million from C$366.2 million in the comparable period the year before. Indirect operating expenses increased 1.4% to C$53.5 million from C$52.7 million in the equivalent prior-year period.

**Prospects:** Our evaluation of Cameco Corp. as of Sep. 6, 2011 is the result of our systematic analysis on three basic characteristics: earnings strength, relative valuation, and recent stock price movement. The company has produced a positive trend in earnings per share over the past 5 quarters. However, while recent estimates for the company have been lowered by analysts, CCJ has posted results that fell short of analysts expectations. Based on operating earnings yield, the company is about fairly valued when compared to all of the companies in our coverage universe. Share price changes over the past year indicates that CCJ will perform in line with the market over the near term.

| **Financial Data** (Can$ in Thousands) | 6 Mos | 3 Mos | 12/31/2010 | 12/31/2009 | 12/31/2008 | 12/31/2007 | 12/31/2006 | 12/31/2005 |
|---|---|---|---|---|---|---|---|---|
| Earnings Per Share | 1.14 | 1.18 | 1.30 | 2.82 | 1.28 | 1.13 | 1.02 | 0.60 |
| Cash Flow Per Share | ... | ... | 1.29 | 1.78 | 2.02 | 2.28 | 1.19 | 0.80 |
| Tang Book Value Per Share | 11.77 | 11.74 | 12.99 | 12.08 | 8.84 | 7.23 | 7.27 | 6.25 |
| Dividends Per Share | 0.340 | 0.310 | 0.280 | 0.240 | 0.240 | 0.200 | 0.160 | 0.120 |
| Dividend Payout % | 29.82 | 26.27 | 21.54 | 8.51 | 18.75 | 17.70 | 15.69 | 20.00 |
| **Income Statement** | | | | | | | | |
| Total Revenue | 879,965 | 454,260 | 2,123,655 | 2,314,985 | 2,859,158 | 2,309,741 | 1,831,690 | 1,312,655 |
| EBITDA | ... | 159,739 | 531,648 | 766,859 | 484,897 | 465,932 | 345,426 | 274,626 |
| Depn & Amortn | 98,871 | 49,113 | ... | ... | ... | ... | ... | ... |
| Income Before Taxes | ... | 95,961 | 531,648 | 766,859 | 484,897 | 465,932 | 345,426 | 274,626 |
| Income Taxes | 2,934 | 3,807 | 27,251 | 52,897 | (24,755) | 29,468 | (68,843) | 30,257 |
| Net Income | 145,226 | 91,487 | 514,749 | 1,099,422 | 450,117 | 416,112 | 375,715 | 217,631 |
| Average Shares | 395,373 | 396,311 | 395,019 | 389,933 | 352,112 | 376,871 | 376,835 | 373,692 |
| **Balance Sheet** | | | | | | | | |
| Current Assets | 2,417,208 | 2,526,213 | 2,573,299 | 2,527,741 | 1,659,938 | 1,291,144 | 1,354,424 | 1,524,459 |
| Total Assets | 7,156,579 | 7,176,479 | 7,671,368 | 7,342,102 | 7,010,601 | 5,371,382 | 5,140,429 | 4,772,775 |
| Current Liabilities | 528,989 | 551,160 | 604,709 | 763,057 | 888,917 | 684,464 | 501,968 | 609,048 |
| Long-Term Obligations | 933,376 | 936,878 | 940,317 | 952,853 | 1,212,982 | 717,130 | 696,691 | 702,109 |
| Total Liabilities | 2,409,488 | 2,450,651 | 2,455,041 | 2,498,274 | 3,495,678 | 2,627,521 | 2,399,047 | 2,409,144 |
| Stockholders' Equity | 4,747,091 | 4,725,828 | 5,216,327 | 4,843,828 | 3,514,923 | 2,743,861 | 2,741,382 | 2,363,631 |
| Shares Outstanding | 394,711 | 394,699 | 394,351 | 392,838 | 365,718 | 344,398 | 352,292 | 349,570 |
| **Statistical Record** | | | | | | | | |
| Return on Assets % | ... | ... | 6.86 | 15.32 | 7.25 | 7.92 | 7.58 | 4.93 |
| Return on Equity % | ... | ... | 10.23 | 26.31 | 14.34 | 15.17 | 14.72 | 9.62 |
| EBITDA Margin % | ... | 35.16 | 25.03 | 33.13 | 16.96 | 20.17 | 18.86 | 20.92 |
| Net Margin % | 16.50 | 20.14 | 24.24 | 47.49 | 15.74 | 18.02 | 20.51 | 16.58 |
| Asset Turnover | ... | ... | 0.28 | 0.32 | 0.46 | 0.44 | 0.37 | 0.30 |
| Current Ratio | 4.57 | 4.58 | 4.26 | 3.31 | 1.87 | 1.89 | 2.70 | 2.50 |
| Debt to Equity | 0.20 | 0.20 | 0.18 | 0.20 | 0.35 | 0.26 | 0.25 | 0.30 |
| Price Range | 43.14-21.81 | 43.14-21.81 | 40.35-21.81 | 34.50-16.22 | 43.80-15.46 | 59.46-35.49 | 48.67-20.36 | 37.48-6.37 |
| P/E Ratio | 37.84-19.13 | 36.56-18.48 | 31.04-16.78 | 12.23-5.75 | 34.22-12.08 | 52.62-31.41 | 47.72-19.96 | 62.47-10.62 |
| Average Yield % | 1.05 | 0.95 | 0.97 | 0.88 | 0.75 | 0.43 | 0.38 | 0.44 |

**Address:** 2121 - 11th Street West, Saskatoon, S7M 1J3
**Telephone:** 306-956-6200
**Web Site:** www.cameco.com

**Officers:** Victor J. Zaleschuk - Chairman Timothy S. Gitzel - President **Transfer Agents:** CIBC Mellon Trust Company, Toronto, Ontario, Canada

**No of Institutions:** 384
**Shares:** 270,571,936 **% Held:** 62.11

# CANADIAN NATIONAL RAILWAY CO.

| Exchange | Symbol | Price | 52Wk Range | Yield | P/E |
|---|---|---|---|---|---|
| TSX | CNR | C$72.03 (8/31/2011) | 77.84-64.13 | 1.80 | 14.67 |

*7 Year Price Score 132.78 *NYSE Composite Index=100 *12 Month Price Score 103.78

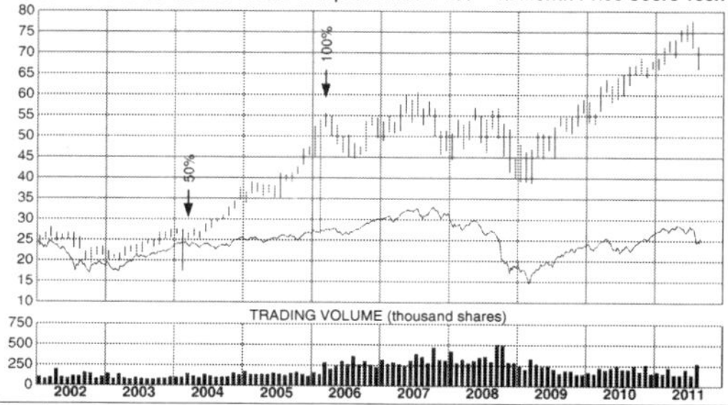


**Interim Earnings (Per Share) Can$**

| Qtr. | Mar | Jun | Sep | Dec |
|---|---|---|---|---|
| 2008 | 0.64 | 0.95 | 1.16 | 1.21 |
| 2009 | 0.90 | 0.82 | 0.97 | 1.23 |
| 2010 | 1.08 | 1.13 | 1.19 | 1.09 |
| 2011 | 1.45 | 1.18 | ... | ... |

**Interim Dividends (Per Share)**

| Amt | Decl | Ex | Rec | Pay |
|---|---|---|---|---|
| 0.27Q | 10/26/2010 | 12/08/2010 | 12/10/2010 | 12/31/2010 |
| 0.325Q | 01/25/2011 | 03/08/2011 | 03/10/2011 | 03/31/2011 |
| 0.325Q | 04/26/2011 | 06/07/2011 | 06/09/2011 | 06/30/2011 |
| 0.325Q | 07/25/2011 | 09/07/2011 | 09/09/2011 | 09/30/2011 |

**Indicated Div: $1.30**

**Valuation Analysis**

| | | | |
|---|---|---|---|
| Forecast EPS | $4.78 (09/03/2011) | | |
| Market Cap | C$32.5 Billion | Book Value | $11.5 Billion |
| Price/Book | 2.83 | Price/Sales | N/A |

**Dividend Achiever Status**

| | |
|---|---|
| 5 Year Growth Rate | 16.65% |
| Total Years of Dividend Growth | 14 |

**Business Summary:** Rail (MIC: 7.4.3 SIC: 4011 NAIC: 482111)

Canadian National Railway is engaged in the rail and related transportation business. Co.'s network of approx. 21,100 route miles spans Canada and mid-America, from the Atlantic and Pacific oceans to the Gulf of Mexico, serving the ports of Vancouver, Prince Rupert, British Columbia, Montreal, Halifax, New Orleans, and Mobile, AL and the areas of Toronto, Buffalo, Chicago, Detroit, Duluth, Minnesota/Superior and Green Bay, WI, Minneapolis/St. Paul, Memphis and Jackson, MS, in North America. Co.'s extensive network, and its co-production agreements, routing protocols, marketing alliances and interline agreements, provide Co. customers access to all three North American Free Trade nations.

**Recent Developments:** For the quarter ended June 30 2011, net income increased 0.7% to C$538.0 million from C$534.0 million in the year-earlier quarter. Revenues were C$2.26 billion, up 8.0% from C$2.09 billion the year before. Operating income was C$874.0 million versus C$813.0 million in the prior-year quarter, an increase of 7.5%. Indirect operating expenses increased 8.3% to C$1.39 billion from C$1.28 billion in the equivalent prior-year period.

**Prospects:** Our evaluation of Canadian National Railway Co. as of Sep. 6, 2011 is the result of our systematic analysis on three basic characteristics: earnings strength, relative valuation, and recent stock price movement. The company has managed to produce a neutral trend in earnings per share over the past 5 quarters. However, while recent estimates for the company have been mixed, CNI has posted results that were in line with analysts expectations. Based on operating earnings yield, the company is about fairly valued when compared to all of the companies in our coverage universe. Share price changes over the past year indicates that CNI will perform poorly over the near term.

**Financial Data**

| (Can$ in Thousands) | 6 Mos | 3 Mos | 12/31/2010 | 12/31/2009 | 12/31/2008 | 12/31/2007 | 12/31/2006 | 12/31/2005 |
|---|---|---|---|---|---|---|---|---|
| Earnings Per Share | 4.91 | 4.86 | 4.48 | 3.92 | 3.95 | 4.25 | 3.91 | 2.77 |
| Cash Flow Per Share | 6.48 | 6.33 | 6.43 | 4.86 | 4.27 | 4.82 | 5.61 | 4.90 |
| Tang Book Value Per Share | 25.46 | ... | 24.56 | 23.85 | 22.55 | 20.97 | 19.17 | 17.23 |
| Dividends Per Share | 1.190 | 1.135 | 1.080 | 1.010 | 0.920 | 0.840 | 0.650 | 0.500 |
| Dividend Payout % | 24.24 | 23.35 | 24.11 | 25.77 | 23.29 | 19.76 | 16.62 | 18.05 |
| **Income Statement** | | | | | | | | |
| Total Revenue | 4,344,000 | 2,084,000 | 8,297,000 | 7,367,000 | 8,482,000 | 7,897,000 | 7,716,000 | 7,240,000 |
| EBITDA | 2,264,000 | 1,163,000 | 4,070,000 | 3,463,000 | 3,645,000 | 3,720,000 | 3,694,000 | 3,266,000 |
| Depn & Amortn | 435,000 | 218,000 | 834,000 | 790,000 | 725,000 | 678,000 | 653,000 | 630,000 |
| Income Before Taxes | 1,658,000 | 859,000 | 2,876,000 | 2,261,000 | 2,545,000 | 2,706,000 | 2,729,000 | 2,337,000 |
| Income Taxes | 452,000 | 191,000 | 772,000 | 407,000 | 650,000 | 548,000 | 642,000 | 781,000 |
| Net Income | 1,206,000 | 668,000 | 2,104,000 | 1,854,000 | 1,895,000 | 2,158,000 | 2,087,000 | 1,556,000 |
| Average Shares | 457,100 | 461,800 | 470,100 | 473,500 | 480,000 | 508,000 | 534,300 | 562,200 |
| **Balance Sheet** | | | | | | | | |
| Current Assets | 1,841,000 | 1,714,000 | 1,590,000 | 1,490,000 | 1,756,000 | 1,048,000 | 1,336,000 | 1,149,000 |
| Total Assets | 25,470,000 | 25,212,000 | 25,206,000 | 25,176,000 | 26,720,000 | 23,460,000 | 24,004,000 | 22,188,000 |
| Current Liabilities | 1,982,000 | 1,815,000 | 1,906,000 | 1,237,000 | 1,892,000 | 1,590,000 | 2,114,000 | 1,958,000 |
| Long-Term Obligations | 5,432,000 | 5,451,000 | 5,531,000 | 6,391,000 | 7,405,000 | 5,363,000 | 5,386,000 | 4,677,000 |
| Total Liabilities | 13,999,000 | 13,754,000 | 13,922,000 | 13,943,000 | 16,161,000 | 13,283,000 | 14,180,000 | 12,939,000 |
| Stockholders' Equity | 11,471,000 | 11,458,000 | 11,284,000 | 11,233,000 | 10,559,000 | 10,177,000 | 9,824,000 | 9,249,000 |
| Shares Outstanding | 450,600 | ... | 459,356 | 471,000 | 468,200 | 485,200 | 512,400 | 536,800 |
| **Statistical Record** | | | | | | | | |
| Return on Assets % | 8.78 | 8.94 | 8.35 | 7.15 | 7.53 | 9.09 | 9.04 | 7.51 |
| Return on Equity % | 19.57 | 19.69 | 18.69 | 17.02 | 18.23 | 21.58 | 21.88 | 18.75 |
| EBITDA Margin % | 52.12 | 55.81 | 49.05 | 47.01 | 42.97 | 47.11 | 47.87 | 45.11 |
| Net Margin % | 27.76 | 32.05 | 25.36 | 25.17 | 22.34 | 27.33 | 27.05 | 21.49 |
| Asset Turnover | ... | ... | 0.33 | 0.28 | 0.34 | 0.33 | 0.33 | 0.35 |
| Current Ratio | 0.93 | 0.94 | 0.83 | 1.20 | 0.93 | 0.66 | 0.63 | 0.59 |
| Debt to Equity | 0.47 | 0.48 | 0.49 | 0.57 | 0.70 | 0.53 | 0.55 | 0.51 |
| Price Range | 77.14-59.91 | 73.15-58.16 | 68.87-52.91 | 58.96-38.74 | 57.00-40.06 | 60.65-45.62 | 55.52-26.60 | 47.52-33.75 |
| P/E Ratio | 15.71-12.20 | 15.05-11.97 | 15.37-11.81 | 15.04-9.88 | 14.43-10.14 | 14.27-10.73 | 14.20-6.80 | 17.16-12.18 |
| Average Yield % | 1.74 | 1.73 | 1.74 | 2.03 | 1.83 | 1.57 | 1.32 | 1.27 |

**Address:** 935 de La Gauchetiere Street West, Montreal, H3B 2M9
**Telephone:** 514-399-4821
**Web Site:** www.cn.ca

**Officers:** Claude Mongeau - President, Chief Executive Officer Keith E. Creel - Executive Vice President, Chief Operating Officer **Transfer Agents:** Computershare Trust Company, N.A., Providence, RI

**No of Institutions:** 511
**Shares:** 312,733,824 **% Held:** 53.39

# CANADIAN NATURAL RESOURCES LTD.

| Exchange | Symbol | Price | 52Wk Range | Yield | P/E |
|---|---|---|---|---|---|
| TSX | CNQ | C$37.00 (8/31/2011) | 49.73-32.90 | 0.97 | 35.92 |

*7 Year Price Score 127.44 *NYSE Composite Index=100 *12 Month Price Score 92.76

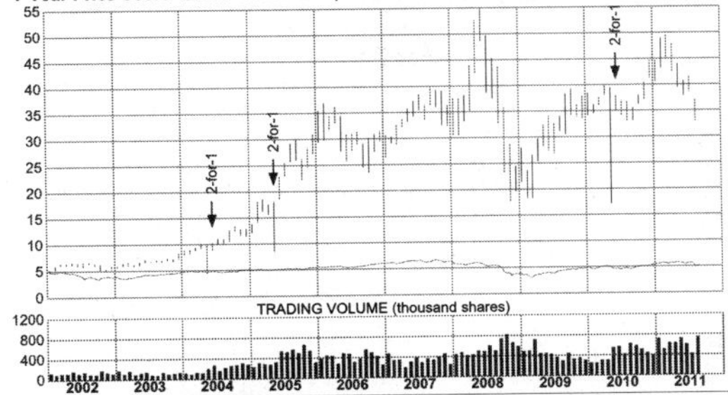


**Interim Earnings (Per Share) Can$**

| Qtr. | Mar | Jun | Sep | Dec |
|---|---|---|---|---|
| 2008 | 0.68 | (0.33) | 2.63 | 1.64 |
| 2009 | 0.28 | 0.15 | 0.60 | 0.42 |
| 2010 | 0.67 | 0.60 | 0.53 | (0.38) |
| 2011 | 0.04 | 0.84 | ... | ... |

**Interim Dividends (Per Share)**

| Amt | Decl | Ex | Rec | Pay |
|---|---|---|---|---|
| 0.075Q | 11/04/2010 | 12/15/2010 | 12/17/2010 | 01/01/2011 |
| 0.09Q | 03/03/2011 | 03/16/2011 | 03/18/2011 | 04/01/2011 |
| 0.09Q | 05/05/2011 | 06/15/2011 | 06/17/2011 | 07/01/2011 |
| 0.09Q | 08/04/2011 | 09/14/2011 | 09/16/2011 | 10/01/2011 |

**Indicated Div: $0.36**

**Valuation Analysis**

| | | | |
|---|---|---|---|
| Forecast EPS | $2.10 (09/05/2011) | | |
| Market Cap | C$40.6 Billion | Book Value | $21.5 Billion |
| Price/Book | 1.89 | Price/Sales | N/A |

**Dividend Achiever Status**

| | |
|---|---|
| 5 Year Growth Rate | 19.66% |
| Total Years of Dividend Growth | 8 |

**Business Summary:** Production & Extraction (MIC: 9.1.1 SIC: 1311 NAIC: 211111)

Canadian Natural Resources is a senior independent crude oil and natural gas exploration, development and production company. Co.'s exploration and production operations are focused in North America, Western Canada; the United Kingdom portion of the North Sea; and Cote d'Ivoire and Gabon in Offshore West Africa. The Horizon Oil Sands Mining and Upgrading segment ("Horizon") produces synthetic crude oil through bitumen mining and upgrading operations. Also within Western Canada, Co. maintains certain midstream activities that include pipeline operations and an electricity co-generation system.

**Recent Developments:** For the quarter ended June 30 2011, net income increased 42.7% to C$929.0 million from C$651.0 million in the year-earlier quarter. Revenues were C$3.33 billion, up 1.3% from C$3.29 billion the year before. Operating income was C$1.31 billion versus C$1.05 billion in the prior-year quarter, an increase of 24.8%. Direct operating expenses rose 2.6% to C$833.0 million from C$812.0 million in the comparable period the year before. Indirect operating expenses increased 7.7% to C$1.36 billion from C$1.27 billion in the equivalent prior-year period.

**Prospects:** Our evaluation of Canadian Natural Resources Ltd. as of Sep. 6, 2011 is the result of our systematic analysis on three basic characteristics: earnings strength, relative valuation, and recent stock price movement. The company has produced a positive trend in earnings per share over the past 5 quarters. However, while recent estimates for the company have been mixed, CNQ has posted better than expected results. Based on operating earnings yield, the company is about fairly valued when compared to all of the companies in our coverage universe. Share price changes over the past year indicates that CNQ will perform in line with the market over the near term.

| **Financial Data** (Can$ in Thousands) | 6 Mos | 3 Mos | 12/31/2010 | 12/31/2009 | 12/31/2008 | 12/31/2007 | 12/31/2006 | 12/31/2005 |
|---|---|---|---|---|---|---|---|---|
| Earnings Per Share | 1.03 | 0.79 | 1.56 | 1.46 | 4.61 | 2.42 | 2.35 | 0.97 |
| Cash Flow Per Share | ... | ... | 5.78 | 5.36 | 6.24 | 5.39 | 3.89 | 4.47 |
| Tang Book Value Per Share | 19.55 | 18.78 | 19.24 | 17.91 | 16.98 | 12.34 | 9.94 | 7.68 |
| Dividends Per Share | 0.330 | 0.315 | 0.300 | 0.210 | 0.200 | 0.170 | 0.150 | 0.118 |
| Dividend Payout % | 32.04 | 39.87 | 19.23 | 14.38 | 4.34 | 7.02 | 6.38 | 12.12 |
| **Income Statement** | | | | | | | | |
| Total Revenue | 6,284,000 | 2,951,000 | 12,901,000 | 10,142,000 | 14,156,000 | 11,152,000 | 10,398,000 | 8,741,000 |
| EBITDA | ... | 1,246,000 | 6,914,000 | 4,794,000 | 9,954,000 | 5,560,000 | 6,045,000 | 3,896,000 |
| Depn & Amortn | 1,783,000 | 882,000 | 4,036,000 | 2,819,000 | 2,683,000 | 2,863,000 | 2,391,000 | 2,013,000 |
| Income Before Taxes | ... | 270,000 | 2,878,000 | 1,975,000 | 7,271,000 | 2,697,000 | 3,654,000 | 1,883,000 |
| Income Taxes | 506,000 | 224,000 | 1,181,000 | 395,000 | 2,286,000 | 89,000 | 1,130,000 | 833,000 |
| Net Income | 975,000 | 46,000 | 1,697,000 | 1,580,000 | 4,985,000 | 2,608,000 | 2,524,000 | 1,050,000 |
| Average Shares | 1,105,305 | 1,105,677 | 1,088,096 | 1,083,850 | 1,081,294 | 1,078,672 | 1,074,678 | 1,076,850 |
| **Balance Sheet** | | | | | | | | |
| Current Assets | 2,623,000 | 2,278,000 | 2,172,000 | 1,891,000 | 3,392,000 | 2,181,000 | 2,239,000 | 2,051,000 |
| Total Assets | 44,658,000 | 43,841,000 | 42,669,000 | 41,024,000 | 42,650,000 | 36,114,000 | 33,160,000 | 21,852,000 |
| Current Liabilities | 4,041,000 | 4,324,000 | 3,156,000 | 2,405,000 | 3,420,000 | 3,563,000 | 3,071,000 | 3,825,000 |
| Long-Term Obligations | 8,238,000 | 8,079,000 | 8,499,000 | 9,658,000 | 12,596,000 | 10,940,000 | 11,043,000 | 3,321,000 |
| Total Liabilities | 23,206,000 | 23,246,000 | 21,684,000 | 21,598,000 | 24,276,000 | 22,793,000 | 22,470,000 | 13,615,000 |
| Stockholders' Equity | 21,452,000 | 20,595,000 | 20,985,000 | 19,426,000 | 18,374,000 | 13,321,000 | 10,690,000 | 8,237,000 |
| Shares Outstanding | 1,097,078 | 1,096,360 | 1,090,848 | 1,084,654 | 1,081,982 | 1,079,458 | 1,075,806 | 1,072,696 |
| **Statistical Record** | | | | | | | | |
| Return on Assets % | ... | ... | 4.06 | 3.78 | 12.62 | 7.53 | 9.18 | 5.22 |
| Return on Equity % | ... | ... | 8.40 | 8.36 | 31.37 | 21.72 | 26.67 | 13.50 |
| EBITDA Margin % | ... | 42.22 | 53.59 | 47.27 | 70.32 | 49.86 | 58.14 | 44.57 |
| Net Margin % | 15.52 | 1.56 | 13.15 | 15.58 | 35.21 | 23.39 | 24.27 | 12.01 |
| Asset Turnover | ... | ... | 0.31 | 0.24 | 0.36 | 0.32 | 0.38 | 0.43 |
| Current Ratio | 0.65 | 0.53 | 0.69 | 0.79 | 0.99 | 0.61 | 0.73 | 0.54 |
| Debt to Equity | 0.38 | 0.39 | 0.41 | 0.50 | 0.69 | 0.82 | 1.03 | 0.40 |
| Price Range | 49.73-32.91 | 49.73-17.14 | 44.70-17.14 | 39.29-18.27 | 54.85-17.72 | 39.88-26.34 | 36.95-23.48 | 31.00-8.41 |
| P/E Ratio | 48.28-31.95 | 62.95-21.70 | 28.65-10.98 | 26.91-12.51 | 11.90-3.84 | 16.48-10.88 | 15.73-9.99 | 31.96-8.67 |
| Average Yield % | 0.80 | 0.94 | 0.82 | 0.69 | 0.54 | 0.50 | 0.50 | 0.55 |

**Address:** 2500, 855 - 2 Street S.W., Calgary, T2P 4J8
**Telephone:** 403-517-6700
**Web Site:** www.cnrl.com

**Officers:** Allan P. Markin - Chairman Steve W. Laut - President **Transfer Agents:** Computershare Shareholder Services, Inc., New York, NY, United States

**No of Institutions:** 510
**Shares:** 716,090,880 **% Held:** 63.03

# CANADIAN PACIFIC RAILWAY LTD.

| Exchange | Symbol | Price | 52Wk Range | Yield | P/E |
|---|---|---|---|---|---|
| TSX | CP | C$57.42 (8/31/2011) | 69.44-54.29 | 2.09 | 17.83 |

***7 Year Price Score 121.23** *NYSE Composite Index=100 ***12 Month Price Score 96.27**

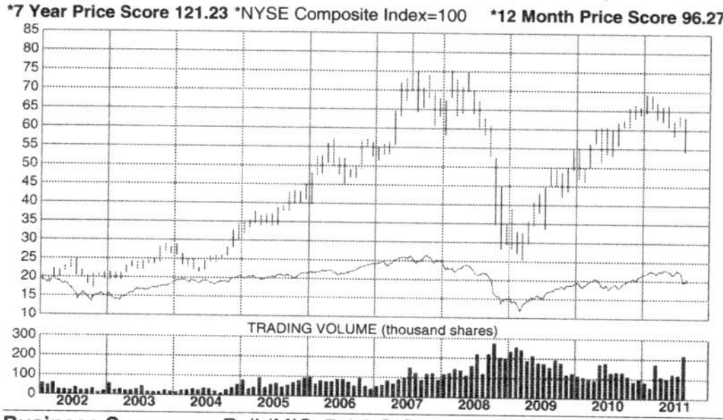


**Interim Earnings (Per Share) Can$**

| Qtr. | Mar | Jun | Sep | Dec |
|---|---|---|---|---|
| 2008 | 0.59 | 1.00 | 1.11 | 1.28 |
| 2009 | 0.39 | 0.93 | 1.16 | 1.17 |
| 2010 | 0.59 | 1.96 | 1.17 | 1.10 |
| 2011 | 0.20 | 0.75 | ... | ... |

**Interim Dividends (Per Share)**

| Amt | Decl | Ex | Rec | Pay |
|---|---|---|---|---|
| 0.27Q | 12/14/2010 | 12/29/2010 | 12/31/2010 | 01/31/2011 |
| 0.27Q | 02/24/2011 | 03/23/2011 | 03/25/2011 | 04/25/2011 |
| 0.30Q | 05/11/2011 | 06/22/2011 | 06/24/2011 | 07/25/2011 |
| 0.30Q | 08/05/2011 | 09/28/2011 | 09/30/2011 | 10/31/2011 |

**Indicated Div: $1.20**

**Valuation Analysis**

| | | | |
|---|---|---|---|
| Forecast EPS | $3.44 (09/05/2011) | | |
| Market Cap | C$9.7 Billion | Book Value | $5.0 Billion |
| Price/Book | 1.94 | Price/Sales | N/A |

**Dividend Achiever Status**

| | |
|---|---|
| **5 Year Growth Rate** | 12.87% |
| **Total Years of Dividend Growth** | 7 |

**Business Summary:** Rail (MIC: 7.4.3 SIC: 4011 NAIC: 482111)

Canadian Pacific Railway and its subsidiaries are engaged in the operation of a transcontinental railway in Canada and the U.S. Co. provides rail and intermodal transportation services from Montreal, Quebec, to Vancouver, British Columbia, and the U.S. Northeast and Midwest regions. Co. also transports bulk commodities, merchandise freight and intermodal traffic. Bulk commodities include grain, coal, sulphur and fertilizers. Merchandise freight consists of finished vehicles and automotive parts, forest and industrial and consumer products. Intermodal traffic consists primarily retail goods.

**Recent Developments:** For the quarter ended June 30 2011, net income decreased 23.2% to C$128.0 million from C$166.6 million in the year-earlier quarter. Revenues were C$1.26 billion, up 2.5% from C$1.23 billion the year before. Operating income was C$230.5 million versus C$274.1 million in the prior-year quarter, a decrease of 15.9%. Direct operating expenses rose 28.8% to C$294.8 million from C$228.9 million in the comparable period the year before. Indirect operating expenses increased 1.1% to C$739.2 million from C$731.2 million in the equivalent prior-year period.

**Prospects:** Our evaluation of Canadian Pacific Railway Ltd. as of Sep. 6, 2011 is the result of our systematic analysis on three basic characteristics: earnings strength, relative valuation, and recent stock price movement. The company has generated a negative trend in earnings per share over the past 5 quarters. Because the company lacks sufficient analyst estimate data, we place greater weight on the historical EPS trend as the measure of earnings strength. Based on operating earnings yield, the company is about fairly valued when compared to all of the companies in our coverage universe. Share price changes over the past year indicates that CP will perform poorly over the near term.

**Financial Data**

| (Can$ in Thousands) | 6 Mos | 3 Mos | 12/31/2010 | 12/31/2009 | 12/31/2008 | 12/31/2007 | 12/31/2006 | 12/31/2005 |
|---|---|---|---|---|---|---|---|---|
| Earnings Per Share | 3.22 | 4.43 | 3.85 | 3.67 | 3.98 | 6.08 | 5.02 | 3.39 |
| Cash Flow Per Share | 2.82 | 3.78 | 2.97 | 3.32 | 7.00 | 8.54 | 6.68 | 6.63 |
| Tang Book Value Per Share | 28.46 | 27.84 | 27.40 | 38.60 | 37.43 | 35.60 | 31.23 | 27.72 |
| Dividends Per Share | 1.110 | 1.080 | 1.058 | 0.990 | 0.990 | 0.900 | 0.750 | 0.583 |
| Dividend Payout % | 34.47 | 24.38 | 27.47 | 26.98 | 24.87 | 14.80 | 14.94 | 17.18 |
| **Income Statement** | | | | | | | | |
| Total Revenue | 2,427,900 | 1,163,400 | 4,981,500 | 4,303,200 | 4,931,600 | 4,707,600 | 4,583,200 | 4,391,600 |
| EBITDA | 589,700 | 232,000 | 1,617,700 | 1,485,400 | 2,527,500 | 2,526,100 | 2,231,800 | 2,070,300 |
| Depn & Amortn | 244,500 | 122,300 | 489,600 | 498,400 | 501,400 | 484,100 | 480,600 | 464,600 |
| Income Before Taxes | 218,500 | 45,500 | 870,800 | 713,900 | 1,765,000 | 1,837,700 | 1,556,700 | 1,401,500 |
| Income Taxes | 56,800 | 11,800 | 220,100 | 101,500 | 140,200 | 144,700 | 109,900 | 270,600 |
| Net Income | 161,700 | 33,700 | 650,700 | 612,400 | 619,000 | 946,200 | 796,300 | 542,900 |
| Average Shares | 170,700 | 170,700 | 169,200 | 166,800 | 155,500 | 155,600 | 158,800 | 160,100 |
| **Balance Sheet** | | | | | | | | |
| Current Assets | 1,107,600 | 1,154,200 | 1,203,800 | 1,427,400 | 1,123,000 | 1,167,700 | 1,004,900 | 893,900 |
| Total Assets | 13,555,800 | 13,523,300 | 13,675,900 | 15,531,400 | 15,469,800 | 13,365,000 | 11,415,900 | 10,891,100 |
| Current Liabilities | 1,270,100 | 1,309,000 | 1,289,500 | 1,383,000 | 1,309,300 | 1,344,800 | 1,239,000 | 1,116,700 |
| Long-Term Obligations | 3,918,800 | 3,940,900 | 4,033,200 | 4,102,700 | 4,685,800 | 4,146,200 | 2,813,500 | 2,970,800 |
| Total Liabilities | 8,551,200 | 8,622,600 | 8,851,200 | 8,825,400 | 9,476,400 | 7,907,100 | 6,559,400 | 6,505,400 |
| Stockholders' Equity | 5,004,600 | 4,900,700 | 4,824,700 | 6,706,000 | 5,993,400 | 5,457,900 | 4,856,500 | 4,385,700 |
| Shares Outstanding | 169,400 | 169,400 | 169,175 | 168,500 | 153,800 | 153,300 | 155,500 | 158,200 |
| **Statistical Record** | | | | | | | | |
| Return on Assets % | 3.99 | 5.42 | 4.46 | 3.95 | 4.28 | 7.64 | 7.14 | 5.08 |
| Return on Equity % | 11.02 | 15.47 | 11.29 | 9.64 | 10.78 | 18.35 | 17.23 | 12.98 |
| EBITDA Margin % | 24.29 | 19.94 | 32.47 | 34.52 | 51.25 | 53.66 | 48.70 | 47.14 |
| Net Margin % | 6.66 | 2.90 | 13.06 | 14.23 | 12.55 | 20.10 | 17.37 | 12.36 |
| Asset Turnover | ... | ... | 0.34 | 0.28 | 0.34 | 0.38 | 0.41 | 0.41 |
| Current Ratio | 0.87 | 0.88 | 0.93 | 1.03 | 0.86 | 0.87 | 0.81 | 0.80 |
| Debt to Equity | 0.78 | 0.80 | 0.84 | 0.61 | 0.78 | 0.76 | 0.58 | 0.68 |
| Price Range | 69.44-53.14 | 69.44-51.38 | 66.48-46.24 | 55.02-25.53 | 75.28-28.28 | 85.00-51.53 | 57.22-39.63 | 44.88-31.80 |
| P/E Ratio | 21.57-16.50 | 15.67-11.60 | 17.27-12.01 | 14.99-6.96 | 18.91-7.11 | 13.98-8.48 | 11.40-7.89 | 13.24-9.38 |
| Average Yield % | 1.76 | 1.75 | 1.82 | 2.44 | 1.70 | 1.39 | 1.48 | 1.55 |

**Address:** Suite 500, 401 - 9th Avenue S.W., Calgary, T2P 4Z4
**Telephone:** 403-319-6171
**Web Site:** www.cpr.ca

**Officers:** John E. Cleghorn - Chairman Frederic J. Green - President, Chief Executive Officer **Transfer Agents:** Computershare Trust Company NA, Denver, CO

**No of Institutions:** 276
**Shares:** 103,841,280 **% Held:** 61.25

# CANADIAN REAL ESTATE INVESTMENT TRUST

| Exchange | Symbol | Price | 52Wk Range | Yield | P/E |
|---|---|---|---|---|---|
| TSX | REF UN | C$34.85 (8/31/2011) | 34.85-30.15 | 4.13 | 16.44 |

*7 Year Price Score 122.74 *NYSE Composite Index=100 *12 Month Price Score 103.17

**Interim Earnings (Per Share) Can$**

| Qtr. | Mar | Jun | Sep | Dec |
|---|---|---|---|---|
| 2008 | 0.30 | 0.31 | 0.31 | 0.21 |
| 2009 | 0.47 | 0.31 | 0.46 | 0.57 |
| 2010 | 0.35 | 0.35 | 0.32 | 1.46 |
| 2011 | 0.20 | 0.14 | ... | ... |

**Interim Dividends (Per Share)**

| Amt | Decl | Ex | Rec | Pay |
|---|---|---|---|---|
| 0.12M | 05/16/2011 | 05/27/2011 | 05/31/2011 | 06/14/2011 |
| 0.12M | 06/15/2011 | 06/28/2011 | 06/30/2011 | 07/15/2011 |
| 0.12M | 07/14/2011 | 07/27/2011 | 07/29/2011 | 08/15/2011 |
| 0.12M | 08/16/2011 | 08/29/2011 | 08/31/2011 | 09/15/2011 |

**Indicated Div: $1.44**

**Valuation Analysis**

| | | | |
|---|---|---|---|
| Forecast EPS | $0.70 (09/02/2011) | | |
| Market Cap | C$2.3 Billion | Book Value | $1.7 Billion |
| Price/Book | 1.36 | Price/Sales | N/A |

**Dividend Achiever Status**

| | |
|---|---|
| **5 Year Growth Rate** | 1.89% |
| **Total Years of Dividend Growth** | 8 |

**Business Summary:** REITs (MIC: 5.3.1 SIC: 6798 NAIC: 525930)

Canadian Real Estate Investment Trust is a closed-ended real estate investment trust created for the benefit of unitholders. Co. owns and manages a diversified real estate portfolio of office, industrial and retail properties throughout Canada and one property in the Chicago, IL.

**Recent Developments:** For the quarter ended June 30 2011, net income amounted to C$9.3 million versus a net loss of C$214.0 million in the year-earlier quarter. Revenues were C$55.2 million, up 1.2% from C$54.6 million the year before. Operating income was C$26.7 million versus a loss of C$3.3 million in the prior-year quarter. Indirect operating expenses were unchanged at C$32.4 million versus the equivalent prior-year period. Revenues from property income rose 0.4% to C$80.3 million from C$79.9 million in the corresponding quarter a year earlier.

**Prospects:** Co. continues to be negatively affected by slower activity levels for its mezzanine loan program as well as declines in the investment in mortgages, a trend which is expected to persist during 2011 due to repayments of mortgages. Notwithstanding, Co. foresees declining market vacancies, rising rental rates (mainly in industrial real estate in Alberta and the Greater Toronto Area) and the commencement of a new development cycle in 2011 following the recent increase in demand for investment property. Separately, on May 19, 2011, Co. announced an agreement to acquire two retail power centres in Mississauga, Ontario for about C$171.0 million. Co. plans to complete the transaction by June 2011.

| **Financial Data** (Can$ in Thousands) | 6 Mos | 3 Mos | 12/31/2010 | 12/31/2009 | 12/31/2008 | 12/31/2007 | 12/31/2006 | 12/31/2005 |
|---|---|---|---|---|---|---|---|---|
| Earnings Per Share | 2.12 | 2.33 | 2.48 | 1.81 | 1.13 | 0.46 | 1.12 | 1.04 |
| Cash Flow Per Share | ... | ... | 2.23 | 2.23 | 1.99 | 1.88 | 1.72 | 1.39 |
| Tang Book Value Per Share | 25.56 | 25.85 | 12.21 | 11.02 | 9.72 | 10.05 | 9.98 | 10.25 |
| Dividends Per Share | 1.408 | 1.405 | 1.398 | 1.363 | 1.347 | 1.317 | 1.292 | 1.272 |
| Dividend Payout % | 66.39 | 60.30 | 56.35 | 75.30 | 119.21 | 286.33 | 115.32 | 122.30 |
| **Income Statement** | | | | | | | | |
| Total Revenue | 109,463 | 54,243 | 329,024 | 329,802 | 319,723 | 291,715 | 269,753 | 241,762 |
| EBITDA | ... | 56,511 | 149,335 | 152,042 | 122,137 | 123,967 | 99,883 | 92,516 |
| Depn & Amortn | 52,234 | 25,887 | 59,708 | 60,998 | 42,620 | 40,223 | 38,924 | 37,646 |
| Income Before Taxes | ... | 13,294 | 89,627 | 91,044 | 79,517 | 83,744 | 60,959 | 54,870 |
| Income Taxes | 942 | 129 | (67,696) | (1,985) | 10,627 | 56,486 | 676 | 609 |
| Net Income | 22,499 | 13,165 | 164,929 | 117,398 | 68,890 | 27,235 | 64,209 | 59,012 |
| Average Shares | ... | ... | 66,503 | 64,882 | 60,904 | 59,189 | 57,526 | 56,894 |
| **Balance Sheet** | | | | | | | | |
| Current Assets | ... | ... | 44,748 | 39,128 | 53,478 | 51,050 | 48,445 | 38,918 |
| Total Assets | 3,222,711 | 3,049,559 | 2,164,585 | 2,158,935 | 2,195,638 | 1,979,595 | 1,805,382 | 1,591,787 |
| Current Liabilities | ... | ... | 64,756 | 143,588 | 300,201 | 161,212 | 174,496 | 120,484 |
| Long-Term Obligations | ... | ... | 1,216,869 | 1,161,618 | 1,173,193 | 1,099,962 | 1,011,149 | 861,325 |
| Total Liabilities | 1,507,152 | 1,320,118 | 1,313,653 | 1,392,704 | 1,563,784 | 1,337,823 | 1,199,729 | 989,025 |
| Stockholders' Equity | 1,715,559 | 1,729,441 | 846,651 | 766,231 | 631,854 | 641,772 | 605,653 | 602,762 |
| Shares Outstanding | 67,123 | 66,905 | 66,733 | 66,287 | 61,098 | 60,672 | 57,726 | 56,986 |
| **Statistical Record** | | | | | | | | |
| Return on Assets % | ... | ... | 7.63 | 5.39 | 3.29 | 1.44 | 3.78 | 3.86 |
| Return on Equity % | ... | ... | 20.45 | 16.79 | 10.79 | 4.37 | 10.63 | 9.77 |
| EBITDA Margin % | ... | 104.18 | 45.39 | 46.10 | 38.20 | 42.50 | 37.03 | 38.27 |
| Net Margin % | 20.55 | 24.27 | 50.13 | 35.60 | 21.55 | 9.34 | 23.80 | 24.41 |
| Asset Turnover | ... | ... | 0.15 | 0.15 | 0.15 | 0.15 | 0.16 | 0.16 |
| Current Ratio | ... | ... | 0.69 | 0.27 | 0.18 | 0.32 | 0.28 | 0.32 |
| Debt to Equity | ... | ... | 1.44 | 1.52 | 1.86 | 1.71 | 1.67 | 1.43 |
| Price Range | 34.65-27.78 | 34.65-26.95 | 33.19-26.61 | 29.00-19.00 | 31.24-19.57 | 33.59-27.30 | 31.91-21.00 | 23.08-17.10 |
| P/E Ratio | 16.34-13.10 | 14.87-11.57 | 13.38-10.73 | 16.02-10.50 | 27.65-17.32 | 73.02-59.35 | 28.49-18.75 | 22.19-16.44 |
| Average Yield % | 4.51 | 4.56 | 4.77 | 5.82 | 4.97 | 4.34 | 5.14 | 6.41 |

**Address:** 175 Bloor Street East, North Tower, Suite 500, Toronto, M4W 3R8
**Telephone:** 416-628-7771
**Web Site:** www.creit.ca

**Officers:** F. Robert Hewett - Chairman Stephen E. Johnson - President, Chief Executive Officer **Transfer Agents:** CIBC Mellon Trust Company, Toronto, Ontario, Canada

**No of Institutions:** N/A
**Shares:** N/A **% Held:** N/A

# CANADIAN UTILITIES LIMITED

| Exchange | Symbol | Price | 52Wk Range | Yield | P/E |
|---|---|---|---|---|---|
| TSX | CU | C$60.00 (8/31/2011) | 60.00-47.70 | 2.64 | 16.17 |

*7 Year Price Score 123.09 *NYSE Composite Index=100 *12 Month Price Score 107.52

**Interim Earnings (Per Share) Can$**

| Qtr. | Mar | Jun | Sep | Dec |
|---|---|---|---|---|
| 2008 | 1.20 | 0.65 | 0.53 | 0.91 |
| 2009 | 1.16 | 0.58 | 0.96 | 1.01 |
| 2010 | 1.14 | 0.55 | 0.66 | 1.02 |
| 2011 | 1.33 | 0.70 | ... | ... |

**Interim Dividends (Per Share)**

| Amt | Decl | Ex | Rec | Pay |
|---|---|---|---|---|
| 0.378Q | 10/22/2010 | 11/08/2010 | 11/10/2010 | 12/01/2010 |
| 0.403Q | 01/13/2011 | 02/03/2011 | 02/07/2011 | 03/01/2011 |
| 0.403Q | 04/13/2011 | 05/06/2011 | 05/10/2011 | 06/01/2011 |
| 0.403Q | 07/13/2011 | 08/09/2011 | 08/11/2011 | 09/01/2011 |

**Indicated Div: $1.59**

**Valuation Analysis**

| | | | |
|---|---|---|---|
| Forecast EPS | $3.60 (09/02/2011) | | |
| Market Cap | C$7.6 Billion | Book Value | $4.0 Billion |
| Price/Book | 1.93 | Price/Sales | N/A |

**Dividend Achiever Status**

| | |
|---|---|
| 5 Year Growth Rate | 6.54% |
| Total Years of Dividend Growth | 28 |

**Business Summary:** Gas Utilities (MIC: 3.3.1 SIC: 4925 NAIC: 221210)

Canadian Utilities is a holding company. Through its principal subsidiaries, Co. is engaged in the delivering of service and business applications with companies engaged in Utilities (pipelines, natural gas and electricity transmission and distribution), Energy (power generation, natural gas gathering, processing, storage and liquid extraction) and Technologies (business systems solutions). Co. operates in the following segments, Utilities, Energy and Corporate and Other.

**Recent Developments:** For the quarter ended June 30 2011, net income increased 26.3% to C$101.0 million from C$80.0 million in the year-earlier quarter. Revenues were C$663.0 million, up 1.1% from C$656.0 million the year before. Operating income was C$187.0 million versus C$154.0 million in the prior-year quarter, an increase of 21.4%. Direct operating expenses declined 19.9% to C$169.0 million from C$211.0 million in the comparable period the year before. Indirect operating expenses increased 8.7% to C$312.0 million from C$287.0 million in the equivalent prior-year period.

**Prospects:** Our evaluation of Canadian Utilities Limited as of Sep. 6, 2011 is the result of our systematic analysis on three basic characteristics: earnings strength, relative valuation, and recent stock price movement. The company has managed to produce a neutral trend in earnings per share over the past 5 quarters and while recent estimates for the company have been mixed, C.CU has posted better than expected results. Based on operating earnings yield, the company is about fairly valued when compared to all of the companies in our coverage universe. Share price changes over the past year indicates that C.CU will perform very poorly over the near term.

**Financial Data**

| (Can$ in Thousands) | 6 Mos | 3 Mos | 12/31/2010 | 12/31/2009 | 12/31/2008 | 12/31/2007 | 12/31/2006 | 12/31/2005 |
|---|---|---|---|---|---|---|---|---|
| Earnings Per Share | 3.71 | 3.56 | 3.45 | 3.71 | 3.28 | 3.07 | 2.56 | 2.08 |
| Cash Flow Per Share | ... | ... | 6.07 | 5.88 | 6.30 | 5.64 | 4.90 | 5.91 |
| Tang Book Value Per Share | 22.42 | 21.92 | 17.12 | 16.04 | 16.94 | 15.14 | 18.54 | 17.52 |
| Dividends Per Share | 1.560 | 1.535 | 1.510 | 1.410 | 1.330 | 1.250 | 1.400 | 1.100 |
| Dividend Payout % | 42.05 | 43.12 | 43.77 | 38.01 | 40.55 | 40.72 | 54.69 | 52.88 |
| **Income Statement** | | | | | | | | |
| Total Revenue | 1,472,000 | 809,000 | 2,657,200 | 2,584,000 | 2,778,900 | 2,404,900 | 2,430,400 | 2,515,800 |
| EBITDA | ... | 402,000 | 864,200 | 911,300 | 909,900 | 785,900 | 816,800 | 751,900 |
| Depn & Amortn | 177,000 | 106,000 | 335,500 | 329,700 | 389,100 | 351,500 | 348,500 | 311,500 |
| Income Before Taxes | ... | 243,000 | 568,000 | 624,900 | 579,900 | 498,700 | 526,800 | 477,000 |
| Income Taxes | 98,000 | 61,000 | 109,200 | 125,400 | 134,300 | 77,700 | 167,100 | 175,600 |
| Net Income | 274,000 | 176,000 | 478,500 | 507,300 | 445,600 | 421,000 | 359,700 | 301,400 |
| Average Shares | 127,691 | 127,637 | 125,971 | 125,774 | 125,784 | 125,934 | 126,687 | 127,452 |
| **Balance Sheet** | | | | | | | | |
| Current Assets | 798,000 | 1,099,000 | 1,082,000 | 1,327,900 | 1,335,100 | 1,263,700 | 1,294,500 | 1,302,900 |
| Total Assets | 9,578,000 | 9,654,000 | 9,415,300 | 9,083,600 | 7,864,400 | 7,285,400 | 6,993,500 | 6,815,700 |
| Current Liabilities | 400,000 | 578,000 | 467,000 | 462,900 | 603,600 | 445,900 | 421,600 | 434,900 |
| Long-Term Obligations | 3,323,000 | 3,327,000 | 3,363,100 | 3,457,100 | 3,256,700 | 3,081,300 | 3,038,200 | 2,904,800 |
| Total Liabilities | 5,615,000 | 5,753,000 | 5,280,100 | 5,252,500 | 4,487,700 | 4,138,700 | 4,032,300 | 3,955,700 |
| Stockholders' Equity | 3,963,000 | 3,901,000 | 3,275,200 | 3,046,100 | 2,751,700 | 2,521,700 | 2,961,200 | 2,860,000 |
| Shares Outstanding | 127,493 | 127,482 | 125,930 | 125,859 | 125,510 | 125,294 | 125,388 | 126,892 |
| **Statistical Record** | | | | | | | | |
| Return on Assets % | ... | ... | 5.17 | 5.99 | 5.87 | 5.90 | 5.21 | 4.54 |
| Return on Equity % | ... | ... | 15.14 | 17.50 | 16.85 | 15.36 | 12.36 | 10.74 |
| EBITDA Margin % | ... | 49.69 | 32.52 | 35.27 | 32.74 | 32.68 | 33.61 | 29.89 |
| Net Margin % | 18.61 | 21.76 | 18.01 | 19.63 | 16.04 | 17.51 | 14.80 | 11.98 |
| Asset Turnover | ... | ... | 0.29 | 0.30 | 0.37 | 0.34 | 0.35 | 0.38 |
| Current Ratio | 2.00 | 1.90 | 2.32 | 2.87 | 2.21 | 2.83 | 3.07 | 3.00 |
| Debt to Equity | 0.84 | 0.85 | 1.03 | 1.13 | 1.18 | 1.22 | 1.03 | 1.02 |
| Price Range | 59.48-45.11 | 54.49-42.26 | 54.49-41.97 | 45.15-34.10 | 50.23-35.03 | 54.36-42.09 | 48.25-35.64 | 46.20-29.81 |
| P/E Ratio | 16.03-12.16 | 15.31-11.87 | 15.79-12.17 | 12.17-9.19 | 15.31-10.68 | 17.71-13.71 | 18.85-13.92 | 22.21-14.33 |
| Average Yield % | 2.98 | 3.17 | 3.21 | 3.69 | 3.08 | 2.68 | 3.45 | 3.12 |

**Address:** 1600, 909 - 11th Avenue S.W., Calgary, T2R 1N6
**Telephone:** 403-292-7500
**Web Site:** www.canadian-utilities.com

**Officers:** Ronald D. Southern - Chairman Nancy C. Southern - Deputy Chairman, President, Chief Executive Officer **Transfer Agents:** CIBC Mellon Trust Company, Calgary, Montreal, Toronto, Vancouver, Canada

**No of Institutions:** N/A
**Shares:** N/A **% Held:** N/A

# CCL INDUSTRIES INC.

| Exchange | Symbol | Price | 52Wk Range | Yield | P/E |
|---|---|---|---|---|---|
| TSX | CCL B | C$30.81 (8/31/2011) | 34.95-28.10 | 2.27 | 13.28 |

***7 Year Price Score 104.16** *NYSE Composite Index=100 ***12 Month Price Score 102.12**

**Interim Earnings (Per Share) Can$**

| Qtr. | Mar | Jun | Sep | Dec |
|---|---|---|---|---|
| 2008 | 0.82 | 0.73 | 0.68 | (0.77) |
| 2009 | 0.51 | 0.27 | 0.51 | 0.00 |
| 2010 | 0.74 | 0.52 | 0.45 | 0.43 |
| 2011 | 0.80 | 0.64 | ... | ... |

**Interim Dividends (Per Share)**

| Amt | Decl | Ex | Rec | Pay |
|---|---|---|---|---|
| 0.175Q | 11/04/2010 | 12/10/2010 | 12/14/2010 | 01/04/2011 |
| 0.175Q | 02/24/2011 | 03/15/2011 | 03/17/2011 | 03/31/2011 |
| 0.175Q | 05/05/2011 | 06/14/2011 | 06/16/2011 | 06/30/2011 |
| 0.175Q | 08/04/2011 | 09/14/2011 | 09/16/2011 | 09/30/2011 |

**Indicated Div: $0.70**

**Valuation Analysis**

Forecast EPS $2.54 (09/02/2011)

| | | | |
|---|---|---|---|
| Market Cap | C$1.0 Billion | Book Value | $818.4 Million |
| Price/Book | 1.24 | Price/Sales | N/A |

**Dividend Achiever Status**

| | |
|---|---|
| **5 Year Growth Rate** | 9.51% |
| **Total Years of Dividend Growth** | 9 |

**Business Summary:** Metal Products (MIC: 8.2.3 SIC: 3411 NAIC: 332431)

CCL Industries is the provider of packaging solutions to global customers in the personal care, cosmetic, healthcare, household, specialty food, beverage, automotive and consumer durable markets. Co.'s businesses are divided into three segments: label, container and tube. The label segment product lines include pressure sensitive, shrink sleeve, stretch sleeve, in-mould and expanded content labels and pharmaceutical instructional leaflets. The container segment manufactures aluminum specialty containers, and the tube segment manufactures plastic tubes.

**Recent Developments:** For the quarter ended June 30 2011, net income increased 24.9% to C$21.8 million from C$17.5 million in the year-earlier quarter. Revenues were C$318.9 million, up 5.5% from C$302.2 million the year before. Operating income was C$35.9 million versus C$34.5 million in the prior-year quarter, an increase of 4.1%. Direct operating expenses rose 5.9% to C$243.7 million from C$230.1 million in the comparable period the year before. Indirect operating expenses increased 4.7% to C$39.4 million from C$37.6 million in the equivalent prior-year period.

**Prospects:** Our evaluation of CCL Industries Inc. as of Sep. 6, 2011 is the result of our systematic analysis on three basic characteristics: earnings strength, relative valuation, and recent stock price movement. The company has enjoyed a very positive trend in earnings per share over the past 5 quarters. However, while recent estimates for the company have been lowered by analysts, C.CCL.B has posted results that fell short of analysts expectations. Based on operating earnings yield, the company is undervalued when compared to all of the companies in our coverage universe. Share price changes over the past year indicates that C.CCL.B will perform poorly over the near term.

**Financial Data**

| (Can$ in Thousands) | 6 Mos | 3 Mos | 12/31/2010 | 12/31/2009 | 12/31/2008 | 12/31/2007 | 12/31/2006 | 12/31/2005 |
|---|---|---|---|---|---|---|---|---|
| Earnings Per Share | 2.32 | 2.20 | 2.13 | 1.29 | 1.46 | 4.42 | 2.33 | 4.97 |
| Cash Flow Per Share | ... | ... | 5.13 | 4.65 | 6.72 | 4.87 | 5.04 | 3.48 |
| Tang Book Value Per Share | 12.96 | 12.33 | 12.09 | 10.64 | 9.94 | 9.64 | 6.87 | 5.11 |
| Dividends Per Share | 0.685 | 0.670 | 0.655 | 0.600 | 0.560 | 0.480 | 0.430 | 0.400 |
| Dividend Payout % | 29.53 | 30.45 | 30.75 | 46.51 | 38.36 | 10.86 | 18.45 | 8.05 |
| **Income Statement** | | | | | | | | |
| Total Revenue | 634,519 | 315,625 | 1,192,318 | 1,198,984 | 1,189,025 | 1,144,260 | 1,212,229 | 1,110,144 |
| EBITDA | ... | 60,189 | 218,747 | 200,562 | 181,956 | 211,041 | 168,689 | 132,830 |
| Depn & Amortn | 48,942 | 23,950 | 94,034 | 100,004 | 85,144 | 75,912 | 74,605 | 65,424 |
| Income Before Taxes | ... | 36,239 | 99,651 | 71,235 | 72,863 | 111,972 | 94,084 | 67,406 |
| Income Taxes | 18,126 | 9,419 | 28,514 | 29,061 | 24,877 | 18,466 | 16,664 | 17,454 |
| Net Income | 48,652 | 26,820 | 71,137 | 42,174 | 47,986 | 147,915 | 77,420 | 163,836 |
| Average Shares | 33,735 | 33,734 | 33,414 | 32,853 | 32,982 | 33,492 | 33,259 | 33,010 |
| **Balance Sheet** | | | | | | | | |
| Current Assets | 402,757 | 379,578 | 432,566 | 399,154 | 407,947 | 391,023 | 424,897 | 405,213 |
| Total Assets | 1,601,567 | 1,564,265 | 1,622,411 | 1,645,497 | 1,766,674 | 1,488,190 | 1,542,590 | 1,368,850 |
| Current Liabilities | 252,216 | 237,839 | 309,716 | 266,743 | 276,711 | 244,966 | 322,996 | 299,844 |
| Long-Term Obligations | 337,461 | 338,427 | 347,733 | 448,849 | 566,575 | 382,166 | 413,552 | 376,458 |
| Total Liabilities | 783,192 | 768,136 | 833,414 | 892,740 | 1,016,156 | 770,331 | 889,989 | 803,032 |
| Stockholders' Equity | 818,375 | 796,129 | 788,997 | 752,757 | 750,518 | 717,859 | 652,601 | 565,818 |
| Shares Outstanding | 33,063 | 33,300 | 33,287 | 33,049 | 32,556 | 32,879 | 32,602 | 32,510 |
| **Statistical Record** | | | | | | | | |
| Return on Assets % | ... | ... | 4.35 | 2.47 | 2.94 | 9.76 | 5.32 | 12.40 |
| Return on Equity % | ... | ... | 9.23 | 5.61 | 6.52 | 21.59 | 12.71 | 32.29 |
| EBITDA Margin % | ... | 19.07 | 18.35 | 16.73 | 15.30 | 18.44 | 13.92 | 11.97 |
| Net Margin % | 7.67 | 8.50 | 5.97 | 3.52 | 4.04 | 12.93 | 6.39 | 14.76 |
| Asset Turnover | ... | ... | 0.73 | 0.70 | 0.73 | 0.76 | 0.83 | 0.84 |
| Current Ratio | 1.60 | 1.60 | 1.40 | 1.50 | 1.47 | 1.60 | 1.32 | 1.35 |
| Debt to Equity | 0.41 | 0.43 | 0.44 | 0.60 | 0.75 | 0.53 | 0.63 | 0.67 |
| Price Range | 34.09-25.85 | 34.09-25.85 | 31.54-24.90 | 28.60-19.52 | 40.24-24.00 | 47.04-28.50 | 35.00-27.05 | 31.47-18.25 |
| P/E Ratio | 14.69-11.14 | 15.50-11.75 | 14.81-11.69 | 22.17-15.13 | 27.56-16.44 | 10.64-6.45 | 15.02-11.61 | 6.33-3.67 |
| Average Yield % | 2.29 | 2.24 | 2.28 | 2.58 | 1.80 | 1.21 | 1.42 | 1.53 |

**Address:** 105 Gordon Baker Road, Suite 500, Willowdale, M2H 3P8
**Telephone:** 416-756-8500
**Web Site:** www.cclind.com

**Officers:** Donald G. Lang - Chairman Geoffrey T. Martin - President, Chief Executive Officer **Transfer Agents:** CIBC Mellon Trust Company, Toronto, Ontario, Canada

**Investor Contact:** 416-756-8526
**No of Institutions:** N/A
**Shares:** N/A **% Held:** N/A

# COGECO CABLE INC.

| Exchange | Symbol | Price | 52Wk Range | Yield | P/E |
|---|---|---|---|---|---|
| TSX | CCA | C$46.25 (8/31/2011) | 48.08-34.95 | 1.73 | N/A |

*7 Year Price Score 121.08 *NYSE Composite Index=100 *12 Month Price Score 109.99

**Interim Earnings (Per Share) Can$**

| Qtr. | Nov | Feb | May | Aug |
|---|---|---|---|---|
| 2007-08 | 0.42 | 1.02 | 0.64 | 0.65 |
| 2008-09 | 0.48 | (7.39) | 0.65 | 0.96 |
| 2009-10 | 1.16 | 0.61 | 0.64 | 0.81 |
| 2010-11 | 0.69 | 0.64 | (3.74) | ... |

**Interim Dividends (Per Share)**

| Amt | Decl | Ex | Rec | Pay |
|---|---|---|---|---|
| 0.17Q | 10/27/2010 | 11/08/2010 | 11/10/2010 | 11/24/2010 |
| 0.17Q | 01/12/2011 | 01/24/2011 | 01/26/2011 | 02/09/2011 |
| 0.17Q | 04/07/2011 | 04/19/2011 | 04/21/2011 | 05/05/2011 |
| 0.20Q | 07/06/2011 | 07/18/2011 | 07/20/2011 | 08/03/2011 |

**Indicated Div: $0.80**

**Valuation Analysis**

| | | | |
|---|---|---|---|
| Forecast EPS | $3.15 (09/05/2011) | | |
| Market Cap | C$2.3 Billion | Book Value | $1.0 Billion |
| Price/Book | 2.25 | Price/Sales | N/A |

**Dividend Achiever Status**

| | |
|---|---|
| 5 Year Growth Rate | 37.51% |
| Total Years of Dividend Growth | 6 |

**Business Summary:** Radio & Television (MIC: 2.3.1 SIC: 4841 NAIC: 517510)

Cogeco Cable is engaged in the business of providing cable television, high-speed internet ("HSI") access, telephony services and other telecommunications services in Canada and in Portugal which supported by hybrid fibre and co-axial cable and fibre optic broadband networks. Co. provides its residential customers with Audio, Analogue and Digital Television as well as HSI and Telephony services. Co. also provides its business customers with data networking, e-business applications, video conferencing, hosting services, Ethernet, private line, voice over IP, HSI access, dark fibre, data storage, data security and co-location services and other communications services.

**Recent Developments:** For the quarter ended May 31 2011, net loss amounted to C$182.0 million versus net income of C$31.2 million in the year-earlier quarter. Revenues were C$342.9 million, up 7.4% from C$319.3 million the year before. Operating income was C$78.4 million versus C$62.9 million in the prior-year quarter, an increase of 24.7%. Indirect operating expenses increased 3.2% to C$264.5 million from C$256.4 million in the equivalent prior-year period.

**Prospects:** Our evaluation of Cogeco Cable Inc. as of Sep. 6, 2011 is the result of our systematic analysis on three basic characteristics: earnings strength, relative valuation, and recent stock price movement. The company has produced a positive trend in earnings per share over the past 5 quarters and while recent estimates for the company have remained steady, C.CCA has posted better than expected results. Based on operating earnings yield, the company is undervalued when compared to all of the companies in our coverage universe. Share price changes over the past year indicates that C.CCA will perform poorly over the near term.

**Financial Data**

| (Can$ in Thousands) | 9 Mos | 6 Mos | 3 Mos | 08/31/2010 | 08/31/2009 | 08/31/2008 | 08/31/2007 | 08/31/2006 |
|---|---|---|---|---|---|---|---|---|
| Earnings Per Share | (1.60) | 2.78 | 2.75 | 3.23 | (5.29) | 2.73 | 1.94 | 1.63 |
| Cash Flow Per Share | 10.08 | 9.37 | 9.81 | 8.60 | 8.89 | 8.08 | 4.90 | 4.90 |
| Tang Book Value Per Share | N.M. | 0.52 | N.M. | N.M. | N.M. | N.M. | N.M. | N.M. |
| Dividends Per Share | 0.650 | 0.620 | 0.590 | 0.560 | 0.480 | 0.400 | 0.240 | 0.160 |
| Dividend Payout % | ... | 22.30 | 21.45 | 17.34 | ... | 14.65 | 12.37 | 9.82 |
| **Income Statement** | | | | | | | | |
| Total Revenue | 1,010,998 | 668,088 | 331,519 | 1,281,376 | 1,217,837 | 1,076,787 | 938,880 | 620,001 |
| EBITDA | 127,398 | 224,571 | 113,459 | 448,978 | 73,743 | 379,531 | 288,410 | 196,752 |
| Depn & Amortn | 195,964 | 129,665 | 63,721 | 262,657 | 273,005 | 231,517 | 191,549 | 121,922 |
| Income Before Taxes | (68,566) | 94,906 | 49,738 | 186,321 | (199,262) | 148,014 | 96,861 | 74,830 |
| Income Taxes | 48,665 | 30,118 | 16,101 | 29,018 | 57,413 | 14,732 | 12,170 | 9,274 |
| Net Income | (117,231) | 64,788 | 33,637 | 157,303 | (256,675) | 133,282 | 84,691 | 65,556 |
| Average Shares | 48,641 | 48,822 | 48,751 | 48,699 | 48,545 | 48,760 | 43,595 | 40,163 |
| **Balance Sheet** | | | | | | | | |
| Current Assets | 225,744 | 167,536 | 326,014 | 167,508 | 122,821 | 119,773 | 137,857 | 122,078 |
| Total Assets | 2,543,743 | 2,694,331 | 2,847,210 | 2,702,819 | 2,665,403 | 3,019,155 | 2,714,339 | 2,602,603 |
| Current Liabilities | 352,588 | 324,653 | 490,259 | 362,999 | 363,744 | 727,609 | 258,578 | 437,034 |
| Long-Term Obligations | 932,442 | 929,534 | 953,158 | 952,687 | 1,009,788 | 718,234 | 1,010,634 | 1,190,126 |
| Total Liabilities | 1,541,487 | 1,509,073 | 1,687,225 | 1,566,518 | 1,633,740 | 1,714,076 | 1,548,673 | 1,857,412 |
| Stockholders' Equity | 1,002,256 | 1,185,258 | 1,159,985 | 1,136,301 | 1,031,663 | 1,305,079 | 1,165,666 | 745,191 |
| Shares Outstanding | 48,764 | 48,636 | 48,473 | 48,519 | 48,558 | 48,517 | 48,354 | 39,999 |
| **Statistical Record** | | | | | | | | |
| Return on Assets % | N.M. | 5.10 | 4.90 | 5.86 | N.M. | 4.64 | 3.19 | 3.01 |
| Return on Equity % | N.M. | 11.99 | 12.10 | 14.51 | N.M. | 10.76 | 8.86 | 9.14 |
| EBITDA Margin % | 12.60 | 33.61 | 34.22 | 35.04 | 6.06 | 35.25 | 30.72 | 31.73 |
| Net Margin % | N.M. | 9.70 | 10.15 | 12.28 | N.M. | 12.38 | 9.02 | 10.57 |
| Asset Turnover | ... | ... | ... | 0.48 | 0.43 | 0.37 | 0.35 | 0.28 |
| Current Ratio | 0.64 | 0.52 | 0.66 | 0.46 | 0.34 | 0.16 | 0.53 | 0.28 |
| Debt to Equity | 0.93 | 0.78 | 0.82 | 0.84 | 0.98 | 0.55 | 0.87 | 1.60 |
| Price Range | 46.70-32.82 | 43.81-32.72 | 43.81-32.72 | 43.81-26.51 | 43.90-26.65 | 50.17-32.79 | 51.98-24.60 | 32.60-20.35 |
| P/E Ratio | ... | 15.76-11.77 | 15.93-11.90 | 13.56-8.21 | ... | 18.38-12.01 | 26.79-12.68 | 20.00-12.48 |
| Average Yield % | 1.64 | 1.64 | 1.60 | 1.59 | 1.51 | 0.97 | 0.63 | 0.60 |

**Address:** 5 Place Ville Marie, Suite 1700, Montreal, H3B 0B3
**Telephone:** 514-764-4700
**Web Site:** www.cogeco.ca

**Officers:** Jan Peeters - Chairman Louis Audet - President, Chief Executive Officer **Transfer Agents:** Computershare Trust Company of Canada, Toronto, Ontario, Canada

**No of Institutions:** N/A
**Shares:** N/A **% Held:** N/A

# COMPUTER MODELLING GROUP, LTD.

| Exchange | Symbol | Price | 52Wk Range | Yield | P/E |
|---|---|---|---|---|---|
| TSX | CMG | C$13.05 (8/31/2011) | 15.28-8.63 | 3.37 | 27.77 |

***7 Year Price Score 238.89** *NYSE Composite Index=100 ***12 Month Price Score 106.44**

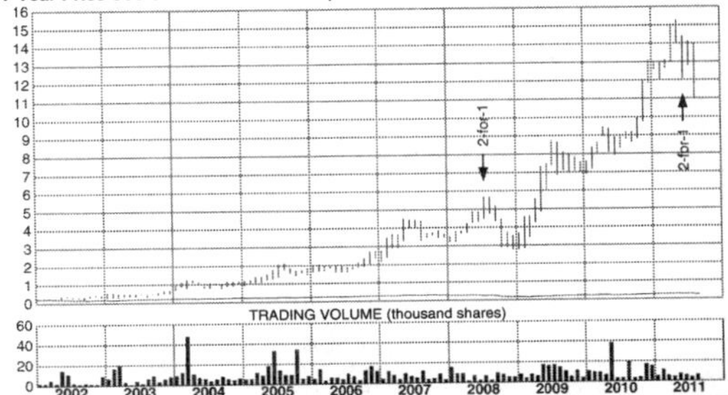

**Interim Earnings (Per Share) Can$**

| Qtr. | Jun | Sep | Dec | Mar |
|---|---|---|---|---|
| 2003-04 | 0.00 | 0.02 | 0.04 | 0.02 |
| 2007-08 | 0.03 | 0.04 | 0.06 | 0.08 |
| 2008-09 | 0.07 | 0.09 | 0.14 | 0.17 |
| 2009-10 | 0.07 | 0.07 | 0.11 | 0.14 |
| 2010-11 | 0.12 | 0.13 | 0.10 | 0.13 |

**Interim Dividends (Per Share)**

| Amt | Decl | Ex | Rec | Pay |
|---|---|---|---|---|
| 2-for-1 | 05/25/2011 | 06/20/2011 | 06/22/2011 | 06/30/2011 |
| 0.105Q | 05/25/2011 | 06/07/2011 | 06/09/2011 | 06/15/2011 |
| 0.10Q | 05/25/2011 | 06/07/2011 | 06/09/2011 | 06/15/2011 |
| 0.11Q | 08/22/2011 | 09/06/2011 | 09/08/2011 | 09/15/2011 |

**Indicated Div: $0.44**

**Valuation Analysis**

| | | | |
|---|---|---|---|
| Forecast EPS | $0.59 (09/05/2011) | | |
| Market Cap | C$475.4 Million | Book Value | $35.8 Million |
| Price/Book | 13.29 | Price/Sales | N/A |

**Dividend Achiever Status**

| | |
|---|---|
| 5 Year Growth Rate | 51.17% |
| Total Years of Dividend Growth | 6 |

**Business Summary:** Internet & Software (MIC: 6.3.2 SIC: 7373 NAIC: 541512)

Computer Modelling Group is a computer software technology and consulting firm engaged in the development, sale and technology transfer of reservoir simulation software. As of Mar 31 2011, Co. sold reservoir simulation software licenses to approximately 450 oil and gas companies, consulting firms and research institutions in over 50 countries. In combination with its principal business of selling software licenses, Co. also performs consulting services that include reservoir simulation modelling, advisory services and training, and funded research for its clients.

**Recent Developments:** For the year ended Mar 31 2011, net income increased 18.7% to C$17.2 million from C$14.5 million in the prior year. Revenues were C$51.8 million, up 14.4% from C$45.3 million the year before. Direct operating expenses rose 17.3% to C$11.4 million from C$9.7 million in the comparable period the year before. Indirect operating expenses increased 2.7% to C$15.3 million from C$14.9 million in the equivalent prior-year period.

**Prospects:** Our evaluation of Computer Modelling Group Ltd. as of Sep. 6, 2011 is the result of our systematic analysis on three basic characteristics: earnings strength, relative valuation, and recent stock price movement. The company has produced a positive trend in earnings per share over the past 5 quarters and while recent estimates for the company have been raised by analysts, C.CMG has posted better than expected results. Based on operating earnings yield, the company is about fairly valued when compared to all of the companies in our coverage universe. Share price changes over the past year indicates that C.CMG will perform in line with the market over the near term.

| **Financial Data** (Can$ in Thousands) | 03/31/2011 | 03/31/2010 | 03/31/2009 | 03/31/2008 | 03/31/2007 | 03/31/2006 | 03/31/2005 | 03/31/2004 |
|---|---|---|---|---|---|---|---|---|
| Earnings Per Share | 0.47 | 0.40 | 0.47 | 0.21 | 0.20 | 0.12 | 0.10 | 0.08 |
| Cash Flow Per Share | 0.76 | 0.26 | 0.63 | 0.29 | 0.20 | 0.13 | 0.09 | 0.12 |
| Tang Book Value Per Share | 0.98 | 0.85 | 0.80 | 0.56 | 0.54 | 0.44 | 0.40 | 0.34 |
| Dividends Per Share | 0.470 | 0.470 | 0.318 | 0.207 | 0.133 | 0.100 | 0.040 | 0.010 |
| Dividend Payout % | 101.08 | 117.50 | 66.84 | 97.92 | 67.05 | 85.69 | 39.06 | 12.72 |
| **Income Statement** | | | | | | | | |
| Total Revenue | 51,827 | 45,303 | 43,942 | 27,993 | 23,715 | 17,220 | 15,164 | 12,307 |
| EBITDA | 26,181 | 21,592 | 24,408 | 11,699 | 10,689 | 6,405 | 5,224 | 4,265 |
| Depn & Amortn | 1,037 | 887 | 716 | 677 | 517 | 367 | 290 | 281 |
| Income Before Taxes | 25,434 | 20,846 | 24,247 | 11,863 | 10,812 | 6,405 | 5,203 | 3,984 |
| Income Taxes | 8,268 | 6,383 | 7,631 | 4,263 | 3,855 | 2,419 | 1,729 | 1,401 |
| Net Income | 17,166 | 14,463 | 16,616 | 7,600 | 6,957 | 3,986 | 3,474 | 2,583 |
| Average Shares | 36,868 | 36,032 | 34,805 | 36,013 | 35,091 | 34,040 | 33,603 | 31,397 |
| **Balance Sheet** | | | | | | | | |
| Current Assets | 56,135 | 47,473 | 46,880 | 32,047 | 29,080 | 23,518 | 19,687 | 16,083 |
| Total Assets | 58,689 | 49,906 | 48,044 | 33,339 | 30,414 | 24,668 | 20,249 | 16,717 |
| Current Liabilities | 22,716 | 19,463 | 20,384 | 13,352 | 11,775 | 9,778 | 7,068 | 5,579 |
| Total Liabilities | 22,919 | 19,463 | 20,384 | 13,352 | 11,775 | 9,778 | 7,068 | 5,579 |
| Stockholders' Equity | 35,770 | 30,443 | 27,660 | 19,987 | 18,639 | 14,889 | 13,181 | 11,138 |
| Shares Outstanding | 36,426 | 35,660 | 34,519 | 35,418 | 34,771 | 33,930 | 32,571 | 32,663 |
| **Statistical Record** | | | | | | | | |
| Return on Assets % | 31.62 | 29.53 | 40.83 | 23.78 | 25.26 | 17.75 | 18.79 | 17.21 |
| Return on Equity % | 51.85 | 49.78 | 69.75 | 39.24 | 41.50 | 28.40 | 28.57 | 26.13 |
| EBITDA Margin % | 50.52 | 47.66 | 55.55 | 41.79 | 45.07 | 37.19 | 34.45 | 34.65 |
| Net Margin % | 33.12 | 31.93 | 37.81 | 27.15 | 29.34 | 23.15 | 22.91 | 20.99 |
| Asset Turnover | 0.95 | 0.93 | 1.08 | 0.88 | 0.86 | 0.77 | 0.82 | 0.82 |
| Current Ratio | 2.47 | 2.44 | 2.30 | 2.40 | 2.47 | 2.41 | 2.79 | 2.88 |
| Price Range | 13.15-7.91 | 8.75-4.26 | 5.67-2.77 | 4.53-2.88 | 3.68-1.57 | 2.12-1.09 | 1.40-0.77 | 1.25-0.31 |
| P/E Ratio | 27.98-16.84 | 21.88-10.65 | 12.07-5.90 | 21.55-13.74 | 18.40-7.84 | 17.67-9.06 | 13.98-7.65 | 15.69-3.91 |
| Average Yield % | 4.53 | 6.37 | 7.49 | 5.55 | 5.61 | 5.83 | 3.67 | 1.44 |

**Address:** 150, 3553 - 31 Street NW, Calgary, T2L 2K7
**Telephone:** 403-531-1300
**Web Site:** www.cmgl.ca

**Officers:** Frank L. Meyer - Chairman Kenneth M. Dedeluk - President, Chief Executive Officer
**Transfer Agents:** Computershare Trust Company of Canada, Calgary, Alberta; Toronto, Ontario, Canada

**No of Institutions:** N/A
**Shares:** N/A **% Held:** N/A

# CORUS ENTERTAINMENT, INC.

| Exchange | Symbol | Price | 52Wk Range | Yield | P/E |
|---|---|---|---|---|---|
| TSX | CJR B | C$20.96 (8/31/2011) | 23.99-18.26 | 4.15 | 14.07 |

***7 Year Price Score 113.05** *NYSE Composite Index=100 ***12 Month Price Score 100.44**

**Interim Earnings (Per Share) Can$**

| Qtr. | Nov | Feb | May | Aug |
|---|---|---|---|---|
| 2007-08 | 0.91 | 0.41 | 0.45 | 0.19 |
| 2008-09 | 0.50 | 0.36 | (1.81) | 0.23 |
| 2009-10 | 0.91 | 0.18 | 0.39 | 0.08 |
| 2010-11 | 0.56 | 0.38 | 0.47 | ... |

**Interim Dividends (Per Share)**

| Amt | Decl | Ex | Rec | Pay |
|---|---|---|---|---|
| 0.063M | 04/14/2011 | 07/13/2011 | 07/15/2011 | 07/29/2011 |
| 0.072M | 07/14/2011 | 09/13/2011 | 09/15/2011 | 09/30/2011 |
| 0.072M | 07/14/2011 | 10/12/2011 | 10/14/2011 | 10/31/2011 |
| 0.072M | 07/14/2011 | 08/11/2011 | 08/15/2011 | 08/31/2011 |

**Indicated Div: $0.87**

**Valuation Analysis**

| | | | |
|---|---|---|---|
| Forecast EPS | $1.70 (09/05/2011) | | |
| Market Cap | C$1.7 Billion | Book Value | $1.0 Billion |
| Price/Book | 1.65 | Price/Sales | N/A |

**Dividend Achiever Status**

| | |
|---|---|
| 5 Year Growth Rate | 65.72% |
| Total Years of Dividend Growth | 7 |

**Business Summary:** Radio & Television (MIC: 2.3.1 SIC: 4832 NAIC: 334220)

Corus Entertainment is a Canadian media and entertainment company with a global distribution network for the programming Co. produces, in radio broadcasting, television broadcasting, and the production and distribution of children's media content. Co. has two brands of businesses: Radio and Television. Co. has 49 radio stations; a variety television networks focused on children and adult genres; and western Canada's premium television services. Co. also owns Nelvana Limited, an international producer and distributor of children's programming and merchandise products; Kids Can Press, the Canadian-owned English language publisher of children's books, and three broadcast television stations.

**Recent Developments:** For the quarter ended May 31 2011, net income increased 24.9% to C$39.2 million from C$31.4 million in the year-earlier quarter. Revenues were C$211.8 million, up 6.8% from C$198.4 million the year before. Indirect operating expenses increased 4.6% to C$155.5 million from C$148.7 million in the equivalent prior-year period.

**Prospects:** Our evaluation of Corus Entertainment, Inc. as of Sep. 6, 2011 is the result of our systematic analysis on three basic characteristics: earnings strength, relative valuation, and recent stock price movement. The company has enjoyed a very positive trend in earnings per share over the past 5 quarters and while recent estimates for the company have remained steady, C.CJR.B has posted better than expected results. Based on operating earnings yield, the company is undervalued when compared to all of the companies in our coverage universe. Share price changes over the past year indicates that C.CJR.B will perform poorly over the near term.

**Financial Data**

| (Can$ in Thousands) | 9 Mos | 6 Mos | 3 Mos | 08/31/2010 | 08/31/2009 | 08/31/2008 | 08/31/2007 | 08/31/2006 |
|---|---|---|---|---|---|---|---|---|
| Earnings Per Share | 1.49 | 1.41 | 1.21 | 1.56 | (0.71) | 1.54 | 1.24 | 0.41 |
| Cash Flow Per Share | 1.66 | 1.67 | 1.57 | 1.78 | 1.41 | 1.57 | 1.22 | 1.31 |
| Dividends Per Share | 0.688 | 0.650 | 0.613 | 0.600 | 0.600 | 0.558 | 0.531 | 0.125 |
| Dividend Payout % | 46.14 | 46.10 | 50.62 | 38.46 | ... | 36.25 | 42.98 | 30.49 |
| **Income Statement** | | | | | | | | |
| Total Revenue | 625,020 | 413,232 | 240,651 | 836,221 | 788,718 | 787,156 | 768,743 | 726,270 |
| EBITDA | 341,345 | 224,754 | 128,309 | 404,261 | 222,036 | 379,002 | 368,277 | 191,956 |
| Depn & Amortn | 178,833 | 119,499 | 59,676 | 189,301 | 180,236 | 167,715 | 160,267 | 145,629 |
| Income Before Taxes | 162,512 | 105,255 | 68,633 | 167,737 | 4,374 | 169,974 | 172,172 | 3,222 |
| Income Taxes | 45,212 | 30,312 | 20,592 | 35,119 | 56,350 | 35,519 | 59,813 | (36,005) |
| Net Income | 117,087 | 77,858 | 46,221 | 126,734 | (56,635) | 129,835 | 107,018 | 35,471 |
| Average Shares | 82,611 | 82,309 | 81,912 | 81,355 | 80,067 | 84,519 | 86,656 | 86,494 |
| **Balance Sheet** | | | | | | | | |
| Current Assets | 411,652 | 407,342 | 424,496 | 369,041 | 327,333 | 329,726 | 334,234 | 313,160 |
| Total Assets | 2,101,526 | 2,066,045 | 2,144,961 | 2,059,255 | 1,874,703 | 2,033,653 | 1,936,967 | 1,842,209 |
| Current Liabilities | 226,024 | 216,917 | 228,488 | 203,422 | 171,055 | 196,026 | 167,557 | 180,967 |
| Long-Term Obligations | 620,114 | 648,587 | 722,816 | 691,891 | 651,767 | 692,750 | 610,697 | 596,362 |
| Total Liabilities | 1,037,730 | 1,035,658 | 1,138,823 | 1,085,252 | 999,024 | 1,036,411 | 961,074 | 924,711 |
| Stockholders' Equity | 1,044,849 | 1,012,870 | 990,469 | 955,948 | 854,278 | 977,005 | 975,893 | 917,498 |
| Shares Outstanding | 82,368 | 81,859 | 81,409 | 81,139 | 80,052 | 80,807 | 84,470 | 84,010 |
| **Statistical Record** | | | | | | | | |
| Return on Assets % | 5.99 | 5.71 | 4.79 | 6.44 | N.M. | 6.52 | 5.66 | 1.88 |
| Return on Equity % | 12.37 | 11.92 | 10.39 | 14.00 | N.M. | 13.26 | 11.30 | 3.84 |
| EBITDA Margin % | 54.61 | 54.39 | 53.32 | 48.34 | 28.15 | 48.15 | 47.91 | 26.43 |
| Net Margin % | 18.73 | 18.84 | 19.21 | 15.16 | N.M. | 16.49 | 13.92 | 4.88 |
| Asset Turnover | ... | ... | ... | 0.43 | 0.40 | 0.40 | 0.41 | 0.39 |
| Current Ratio | 1.82 | 1.88 | 1.86 | 1.81 | 1.91 | 1.68 | 1.99 | 1.73 |
| Debt to Equity | 0.59 | 0.64 | 0.73 | 0.72 | 0.76 | 0.71 | 0.63 | 0.65 |
| Price Range | 23.99-17.55 | 23.99-17.55 | 22.34-17.55 | 21.00-14.70 | 20.00-10.95 | 25.52-15.99 | 25.93-19.31 | 20.00-14.50 |
| P/E Ratio | 16.10-11.78 | 17.01-12.45 | 18.46-14.50 | 13.46-9.42 | ... | 16.57-10.38 | 20.92-15.57 | 48.78-35.37 |
| Average Yield % | 3.30 | 3.17 | 3.11 | 3.20 | 4.06 | 2.64 | 2.33 | 0.72 |

| | | |
|---|---|---|
| **Address:** Corus Quay, 25 Dockside Drive, Toronto, M5A 0B5<br>**Telephone:** 416-479-6534<br>**Web Site:** www.corusent.com | **Officers:** Heather A. Shaw - Chairman John M. Cassaday - President, Chief Executive Officer<br>**Transfer Agents:**CIBC Mellon Trust Company, Toronto, Ontario, Canada | **No of Institutions:** 11<br>**Shares:** 718,425 **% Held:** 0.57 |

# EMPiRE CO LTD

| Exchange | Symbol | Price | 52Wk Range | Yield | P/E |
|---|---|---|---|---|---|
| TSX | EMP A | C$57.19 (8/31/2011) | 61.55-51.20 | 1.57 | 10.55 |

***7 Year Price Score 122.68** *NYSE Composite Index=100 ***12 Month Price Score 104.81**

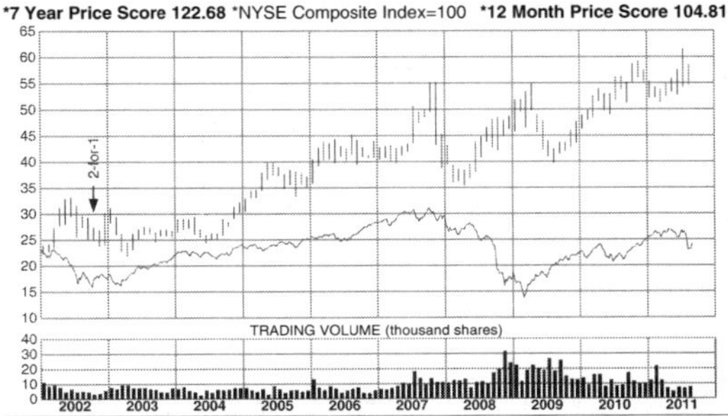


**Interim Earnings (Per Share) Can$**

| Qtr. | Jul | Oct | Jan | Apr |
|---|---|---|---|---|
| 2006-07 | 0.81 | 0.87 | 0.53 | 0.98 |
| 2007-08 | 2.16 | 0.89 | 0.74 | 1.01 |
| 2008-09 | 1.14 | 1.00 | 0.94 | 0.96 |
| 2009-10 | 1.31 | 1.03 | 0.99 | 1.07 |
| 2010-11 | 1.19 | 1.94 | 0.92 | 1.37 |

**Interim Dividends (Per Share)**

| Amt | Decl | Ex | Rec | Pay |
|---|---|---|---|---|
| 0.20Q | 09/10/2010 | 10/13/2010 | 10/15/2010 | 10/29/2010 |
| 0.20Q | 12/09/2010 | 01/12/2011 | 01/14/2011 | 01/31/2011 |
| 0.20Q | 03/08/2011 | 04/13/2011 | 04/15/2011 | 04/29/2011 |
| 0.225Q | 06/30/2011 | 07/13/2011 | 07/15/2011 | 07/29/2011 |

**Indicated Div: $0.90**

**Valuation Analysis**

| | | | |
|---|---|---|---|
| Forecast EPS | $4.66 (09/02/2011) | | |
| Market Cap | C$3.9 Billion | Book Value | $3.2 Billion |
| Price/Book | 1.20 | Price/Sales | N/A |

**Dividend Achiever Status**

| | |
|---|---|
| **5 Year Growth Rate** | 8.17% |
| **Total Years of Dividend Growth** | 16 |

**Business Summary:** Retail - Food & Beverage, Drug & Tobacco (MIC: 2.1.2 SIC: 5149 NAIC: 424490)

Empire is a diversified company whose key businesses include food retailing, real estate, and investments and other operations. Food retailing is carried out through wholly-owned Sobeys Inc. The real estate business is carried out through a wholly-owned operating subsidiary ECL Properties Limited, which at fiscal year-end on May 7, 2011 included a 46.4% ownership interest in Crombie REIT as well as a 40.7% ownership interest in Genstar Development Partnership, a 44.8% interest in Genstar Development Partnership II, and 42.1 percent interests in each of GDC Investments 4, L.P., GDC Investments 5, L.P. and GDC Investments 6, L.P. (collectively referred to as "Genstar").

**Recent Developments:** For the year ended May 7 2011, net income increased 22.4% to C$369.5 million from C$301.9 million in the prior year. Revenues were C$16.03 billion, up 3.3% from C$15.52 billion the year before. Direct operating expenses rose 3.2% to C$15.20 billion from C$14.73 billion in the comparable period the year before. Indirect operating expenses increased 6.6% to C$362.1 million from C$339.7 million in the equivalent prior-year period.

**Prospects:** Our evaluation of Empire Company Ltd. as of Sep. 6, 2011 is the result of our systematic analysis on three basic characteristics: earnings strength, relative valuation, and recent stock price movement. The company has produced a positive trend in earnings per share over the past 5 quarters and while recent estimates for the company have remained steady, C.EMP.A has posted better than expected results. Based on operating earnings yield, the company is undervalued when compared to all of the companies in our coverage universe. Share price changes over the past year indicates that C.EMP.A will perform poorly over the near term.

| **Financial Data** (Can$ in Thousands) | 05/07/2011 | 05/01/2010 | 05/02/2009 | 05/03/2008 | 05/05/2007 | 05/06/2006 | 05/07/2005 | 04/30/2004 |
|---|---|---|---|---|---|---|---|---|
| Earnings Per Share | 5.42 | 4.40 | 4.04 | 4.80 | 3.19 | 4.51 | 2.83 | 2.63 |
| Cash Flow Per Share | 9.93 | 11.49 | 10.05 | 9.84 | 6.87 | 9.59 | 7.26 | 7.08 |
| Tang Book Value Per Share | 23.74 | 19.29 | 16.98 | 13.23 | 20.40 | 18.64 | 15.45 | 13.83 |
| Dividends Per Share | 0.800 | 0.740 | 0.700 | 0.660 | 0.600 | 0.560 | 0.480 | 0.400 |
| Dividend Payout % | 14.76 | 16.82 | 17.33 | 13.75 | 18.81 | 12.42 | 16.96 | 15.21 |
| **Income Statement** | | | | | | | | |
| Total Revenue | 16,029,200 | 15,516,200 | 15,015,100 | 14,065,000 | 13,366,700 | 13,161,100 | 12,435,200 | 11,284,000 |
| EBITDA | 920,800 | 818,800 | 798,900 | 870,000 | 735,700 | 862,400 | 703,600 | 607,100 |
| Depn & Amortn | 362,100 | 339,700 | 328,000 | 309,700 | 288,300 | 261,600 | 235,500 | 171,900 |
| Income Before Taxes | 487,400 | 406,600 | 390,300 | 454,500 | 387,300 | 517,000 | 381,400 | 343,600 |
| Income Taxes | 108,900 | 99,100 | 116,100 | 125,900 | 120,200 | 153,100 | 131,200 | 111,600 |
| Net Income | 369,500 | 301,900 | 265,900 | 315,800 | 210,100 | 296,800 | 186,600 | 173,100 |
| Average Shares | 68,200 | 68,500 | 65,800 | 65,700 | 65,700 | 65,700 | 62,750 | 65,772 |
| **Balance Sheet** | | | | | | | | |
| Current Assets | 2,026,800 | 1,794,100 | 1,524,600 | 1,408,600 | 1,434,200 | 1,362,300 | 1,246,400 | 1,073,900 |
| Total Assets | 6,555,400 | 6,248,300 | 5,898,000 | 5,706,900 | 5,224,900 | 5,051,500 | 4,929,200 | 4,681,700 |
| Current Liabilities | 1,806,100 | 2,089,200 | 1,708,700 | 1,529,700 | 1,420,100 | 1,524,800 | 1,667,900 | 1,420,400 |
| Long-Term Obligations | 1,095,400 | 829,000 | 1,124,000 | 1,414,600 | 829,500 | 728,100 | 739,700 | 903,900 |
| Total Liabilities | 3,306,400 | 3,295,900 | 3,214,500 | 3,324,600 | 3,089,500 | 3,086,300 | 3,220,200 | 3,104,900 |
| Stockholders' Equity | 3,249,000 | 2,952,400 | 2,683,500 | 2,382,300 | 2,135,400 | 1,965,200 | 1,709,000 | 1,576,800 |
| Shares Outstanding | 67,948 | 68,458 | 68,458 | 65,745 | 65,734 | 65,735 | 65,735 | 65,754 |
| **Statistical Record** | | | | | | | | |
| Return on Assets % | 5.68 | 4.98 | 4.60 | 5.79 | 4.10 | 5.96 | 3.81 | 3.75 |
| Return on Equity % | 11.72 | 10.74 | 10.53 | 14.02 | 10.28 | 16.20 | 11.14 | 11.49 |
| EBITDA Margin % | 5.74 | 5.28 | 5.32 | 6.19 | 5.50 | 6.55 | 5.66 | 5.38 |
| Net Margin % | 2.31 | 1.95 | 1.77 | 2.25 | 1.57 | 2.26 | 1.50 | 1.53 |
| Asset Turnover | 2.46 | 2.56 | 2.59 | 2.58 | 2.61 | 2.64 | 2.54 | 2.45 |
| Current Ratio | 1.12 | 0.86 | 0.89 | 0.92 | 1.01 | 0.89 | 0.75 | 0.76 |
| Debt to Equity | 0.34 | 0.28 | 0.42 | 0.59 | 0.39 | 0.37 | 0.43 | 0.57 |
| Price Range | 59.12-48.91 | 53.95-39.70 | 54.78-36.64 | 55.19-35.40 | 45.25-39.49 | 44.35-33.37 | 38.00-24.25 | 29.50-23.10 |
| P/E Ratio | 10.91-9.02 | 12.26-9.02 | 13.56-9.07 | 11.50-7.38 | 14.18-12.38 | 9.83-7.40 | 13.43-8.57 | 11.22-8.78 |
| Average Yield % | 1.47 | 1.61 | 1.51 | 1.49 | 1.44 | 1.46 | 1.62 | 1.50 |

| | | |
|---|---|---|
| **Address:** 115 King Street, Stellarton, B0K 1S0<br>**Telephone:** 902-755-4440<br>**Web Site:** www.empireco.ca | **Officers:** Robert P. Dexter - Chairman Paul D. Sobey - President, Chief Executive Officer **Transfer Agents:** CIBC Mellon Trust Company, Toronto, Ontario, Canada | **No of Institutions:** N/A<br>**Shares:** N/A **% Held:** N/A |

# ENBRIDGE INC

| Exchange | Symbol | Price | 52Wk Range | Yield | P/E |
|---|---|---|---|---|---|
| TSX | ENB | C$32.50 (8/31/2011) | 32.50-25.65 | 3.02 | 38.24 |

***7 Year Price Score 139.98** *NYSE Composite Index=100 ***12 Month Price Score 106.72**

**Interim Earnings (Per Share) Can$**

| Qtr. | Mar | Jun | Sep | Dec |
|---|---|---|---|---|
| 2008 | 0.70 | 1.81 | 0.41 | (1.10) |
| 2009 | 1.53 | 1.08 | 0.83 | (1.30) |
| 2010 | 0.92 | 0.37 | 0.42 | (0.42) |
| 2011 | 0.52 | 0.34 | ... | ... |

**Interim Dividends (Per Share)**

| Amt | Decl | Ex | Rec | Pay |
|---|---|---|---|---|
| 0.245Q | 12/01/2010 | 02/11/2011 | 02/15/2011 | 03/01/2011 |
| 2-for-1 | 02/22/2011 | 06/01/2011 | 05/25/2011 | 05/31/2011 |
| 0.245Q | 04/28/2011 | 05/11/2011 | 05/13/2011 | 06/01/2011 |
| 0.245Q | 08/04/2011 | 08/11/2011 | 08/15/2011 | 09/01/2011 |

**Indicated Div: $0.98 (Div. Reinv. Plan)**

**Valuation Analysis**

| | | | |
|---|---|---|---|
| Forecast EPS | $1.45 (09/05/2011) | | |
| Market Cap | C$25.2 Billion | Book Value | $7.9 Billion |
| Price/Book | 3.20 | Price/Sales | N/A |

**Dividend Achiever Status**

| | |
|---|---|
| **5 Year Growth Rate** | 10.38% |
| **Total Years of Dividend Growth** | 15 |

**Business Summary:** Equipment & Services (MIC: 9.1.3 SIC: 4619 NAIC: 486110)

Enbridge is a publicly traded energy transportation and distribution company. Co. conducts its business through five operating segments: Liquids Pipelines, Gas Distributions, Gas Pipelines, Processing and Energy Services, Sponsored Investments and Corporate.

**Recent Developments:** For the quarter ended June 30 2011, net income increased 76.6% to C$272.0 million from C$154.0 million in the year-earlier quarter. Revenues were C$4.98 billion, up 42.1% from C$3.51 billion the year before. Operating income was C$463.0 million versus C$392.0 million in the prior-year quarter, an increase of 18.1%. Direct operating expenses rose 53.1% to C$3.91 billion from C$2.56 billion in the comparable period the year before. Indirect operating expenses increased 8.4% to C$604.0 million from C$557.0 million in the equivalent prior-year period.

**Prospects:** Our evaluation of Enbridge Inc. as of Sep. 6, 2011 is the result of our systematic analysis on three basic characteristics: earnings strength, relative valuation, and recent stock price movement. The company has suffered a very negative trend in earnings per share over the past 5 quarters. However, while recent estimates for the company have been mixed, ENB has posted better than expected results. Based on operating earnings yield, the company is about fairly valued when compared to all of the companies in our coverage universe. Share price changes over the past year indicates that ENB will perform poorly over the near term.

**Financial Data**

| (Can$ in Thousands) | 6 Mos | 3 Mos | 12/31/2010 | 12/31/2009 | 12/31/2008 | 12/31/2007 | 12/31/2006 | 12/31/2005 |
|---|---|---|---|---|---|---|---|---|
| Earnings Per Share | 0.85 | 0.89 | 1.28 | 2.13 | 1.82 | 0.97 | 0.90 | 0.81 |
| Cash Flow Per Share | 2.97 | 5.58 | 2.50 | 2.77 | 1.92 | 1.94 | 1.91 | 1.34 |
| Tang Book Value Per Share | 8.92 | 17.71 | 8.54 | 8.30 | 7.88 | 6.17 | 5.47 | 5.05 |
| Dividends Per Share | 0.915 | 0.882 | 0.850 | 0.740 | 0.660 | 0.615 | 0.575 | 0.519 |
| Dividend Payout % | 107.02 | 99.72 | 66.15 | 34.82 | 36.26 | 63.08 | 64.25 | 63.65 |
| **Income Statement** | | | | | | | | |
| Total Revenue | 9,694,000 | 4,713,000 | 15,127,000 | 12,466,000 | 16,131,300 | 11,919,400 | 10,644,500 | 8,453,100 |
| EBITDA | 9,243,000 | ... | 2,772,000 | 3,229,000 | 3,045,900 | 2,063,200 | 1,969,100 | 1,898,700 |
| Depn & Amortn | 456,000 | 230,000 | 864,000 | 764,000 | 658,500 | 596,900 | 587,400 | 575,300 |
| Income Before Taxes | 8,425,000 | ... | 1,221,000 | 1,868,000 | 1,836,600 | 916,300 | 814,600 | 784,200 |
| Income Taxes | 236,000 | 114,000 | 251,000 | 306,000 | 508,900 | 209,200 | 192,300 | 221,300 |
| Net Income | 675,000 | 403,000 | 970,000 | 1,562,000 | 1,327,700 | 707,100 | 622,300 | 562,900 |
| Average Shares | 760,000 | 404,173 | 748,000 | 732,000 | 726,200 | 716,600 | 686,600 | 682,400 |
| **Balance Sheet** | | | | | | | | |
| Current Assets | 3,309,000 | 3,270,000 | 3,761,000 | 3,595,000 | 3,708,900 | 3,264,800 | 3,054,200 | 3,075,600 |
| Total Assets | 30,123,000 | 29,663,000 | 30,120,000 | 28,169,000 | 24,701,400 | 19,907,400 | 18,379,300 | 17,210,900 |
| Current Liabilities | 2,764,000 | 2,652,000 | 3,355,000 | 3,789,000 | 4,106,500 | 3,514,800 | 3,223,900 | 3,250,700 |
| Long-Term Obligations | 14,638,000 | 14,500,000 | 14,622,000 | 12,974,000 | 11,628,900 | 9,237,400 | 8,676,000 | 7,899,000 |
| Total Liabilities | 21,605,000 | 21,185,000 | 21,897,000 | 20,181,000 | 18,082,600 | 14,632,200 | 13,768,700 | 12,941,400 |
| Stockholders' Equity | 7,889,000 | 7,826,000 | 7,565,000 | 7,261,000 | 6,618,800 | 5,275,200 | 4,610,600 | 4,269,500 |
| Shares Outstanding | 776,441 | 387,172 | 770,000 | 756,000 | 746,000 | 737,000 | 703,600 | 697,800 |
| **Statistical Record** | | | | | | | | |
| Return on Assets % | 3.94 | 3.56 | 3.33 | 5.91 | 5.94 | 3.69 | 3.50 | 3.51 |
| Return on Equity % | 15.06 | 13.53 | 13.09 | 22.51 | 22.26 | 14.31 | 14.02 | 13.65 |
| EBITDA Margin % | 95.35 | ... | 18.32 | 25.90 | 18.88 | 17.31 | 18.50 | 22.46 |
| Net Margin % | 6.96 | 8.55 | 6.41 | 12.53 | 8.23 | 5.93 | 5.85 | 6.66 |
| Asset Turnover | ... | ... | 0.52 | 0.47 | 0.72 | 0.62 | 0.60 | 0.53 |
| Current Ratio | 1.20 | 1.23 | 1.12 | 0.95 | 0.90 | 0.93 | 0.95 | 0.95 |
| Debt to Equity | 1.86 | 1.85 | 1.93 | 1.79 | 1.76 | 1.75 | 1.88 | 1.85 |
| Price Range | 32.47-24.57 | 29.85-23.20 | 28.91-23.05 | 24.32-17.80 | 23.02-17.20 | 20.48-17.29 | 20.62-15.98 | 19.03-8.40 |
| P/E Ratio | 38.20-28.91 | 33.54-26.06 | 22.59-18.01 | 11.42-8.36 | 12.65-9.45 | 21.11-17.82 | 22.91-17.75 | 23.49-10.38 |
| Average Yield % | 3.23 | 3.30 | 3.34 | 3.65 | 3.20 | 3.28 | 3.22 | 3.12 |

| | | |
|---|---|---|
| **Address:** 3000 Fifth Avenue Place, 425 ¿ 1st Street S.W, Calgary, T2P 3L8<br>**Telephone:** 403-231-3900<br>**Web Site:** www.enbridge.com | **Officers:** Patrick D. Daniel - President, Chief Executive Officer Al Monaco - President **Transfer Agents:** BNY Mellon Shareowner Services, Jersey City, NJ | **No of Institutions:** 265<br>**Shares:** 508,774,400 **% Held:** 55.02 |

# ENSIGN ENERGY SERVICES INC

| Exchange | Symbol | Price | 52Wk Range | Yield | P/E |
|---|---|---|---|---|---|
| TSX | ESI | C$17.25 (8/31/2011) | 21.16-11.57 | 2.20 | 15.83 |

***7 Year Price Score 94.04** *NYSE Composite Index=100 ***12 Month Price Score 118.14**

**Interim Earnings (Per Share) Can$**

| Qtr. | Mar | Jun | Sep | Dec |
|---|---|---|---|---|
| 2008 | 0.53 | 0.21 | 0.47 | 0.48 |
| 2009 | 0.47 | 0.09 | 0.11 | 0.15 |
| 2010 | 0.25 | 0.10 | 0.20 | 0.27 |
| 2011 | 0.52 | 0.11 | ... | ... |

**Interim Dividends (Per Share)**

| Amt | Decl | Ex | Rec | Pay |
|---|---|---|---|---|
| 0.095Q | 11/08/2010 | 12/17/2010 | 12/21/2010 | 01/05/2011 |
| 0.095Q | 03/14/2011 | 03/23/2011 | 03/25/2011 | 04/05/2011 |
| 0.095Q | 05/09/2011 | 06/17/2011 | 06/21/2011 | 07/06/2011 |
| 0.095Q | 08/04/2011 | 09/16/2011 | 09/20/2011 | 10/05/2011 |

**Indicated Div: $0.38**

**Valuation Analysis**

| | | | |
|---|---|---|---|
| Forecast EPS | $1.38 (09/05/2011) | | |
| Market Cap | C$2.6 Billion | Book Value | $1.6 Billion |
| Price/Book | 1.66 | Price/Sales | N/A |

**Dividend Achiever Status**

| | |
|---|---|
| **5 Year Growth Rate** | 16.95% |
| **Total Years of Dividend Growth** | 15 |

**Business Summary:** Production & Extraction (MIC: 9.1.1 SIC: 1381 NAIC: 213111)

Ensign Energy Services is engaged in the provision of oilfield services to the crude oil and natural gas industry primarily in northern and central Alberta and northeastern British Columbia and in the U.S. Co. services include drilling services for shallow, intermediate and deep oil and natural gas wells; horizontal, under-balanced and horizontal re-entry drilling services; and slickline, braided line and production testing services. In additions, Co. also provides drilling services in Australia, Southeast Asia, the Middle East, Africa, Argentina and New Zealand.

**Recent Developments:** For the quarter ended June 30 2011, net income increased 0.4% to C$16.1 million from C$16.0 million in the year-earlier quarter. Revenues were C$334.4 million, up 29.8% from C$257.6 million the year before. Operating income was C$25.7 million versus C$26.5 million in the prior-year quarter, a decrease of 3.3%. Direct operating expenses rose 29.7% to C$254.6 million from C$196.2 million in the comparable period the year before. Indirect operating expenses increased 55.8% to C$54.2 million from C$34.8 million in the equivalent prior-year period.

**Prospects:** Our evaluation of Ensign Energy Services Inc. as of Sep. 6, 2011 is the result of our systematic analysis on three basic characteristics: earnings strength, relative valuation, and recent stock price movement. The company has generated a negative trend in earnings per share over the past 5 quarters and while recent estimates for the company have been mixed, C.ESI has posted results that fell short of analysts expectations. Based on operating earnings yield, the company is undervalued when compared to all of the companies in our coverage universe. Share price changes over the past year indicates that C.ESI will perform very well over the near term.

**Financial Data**

| (Can$ in Thousands) | 6 Mos | 3 Mos | 12/31/2010 | 12/31/2009 | 12/31/2008 | 12/31/2007 | 12/31/2006 | 12/31/2005 |
|---|---|---|---|---|---|---|---|---|
| Earnings Per Share | 1.09 | 1.10 | 0.79 | 0.82 | 1.68 | 1.62 | 2.18 | 1.09 |
| Cash Flow Per Share | ... | ... | 1.76 | 1.87 | 2.16 | 2.03 | 2.60 | 1.96 |
| Tang Book Value Per Share | 10.41 | 10.43 | 10.25 | 9.99 | 10.13 | 8.13 | 7.27 | 5.10 |
| Dividends Per Share | 0.373 | 0.365 | 0.357 | 0.343 | 0.333 | 0.323 | 0.280 | 0.170 |
| Dividend Payout % | 34.17 | 33.18 | 45.25 | 41.77 | 19.79 | 19.91 | 12.84 | 15.67 |
| **Income Statement** | | | | | | | | |
| Total Revenue | 836,656 | 502,211 | 1,355,683 | 1,137,575 | 1,705,579 | 1,577,601 | 1,807,230 | 1,520,724 |
| EBITDA | ... | 158,076 | 323,838 | 298,718 | 488,928 | 470,312 | 594,257 | 345,925 |
| Depn & Amortn | 75,859 | 40,778 | 135,799 | 111,015 | 125,809 | 92,636 | 80,921 | 74,917 |
| Income Before Taxes | ... | 116,879 | 188,039 | 187,703 | 363,119 | 377,676 | 513,336 | 271,008 |
| Income Taxes | 46,584 | 37,188 | 66,613 | 62,267 | 103,160 | 127,911 | 172,052 | 101,343 |
| Net Income | 95,764 | 79,691 | 121,426 | 125,436 | 259,959 | 249,765 | 341,284 | 169,665 |
| Average Shares | 152,953 | 153,208 | 153,172 | 153,260 | 154,408 | 154,306 | 156,228 | 156,223 |
| **Balance Sheet** | | | | | | | | |
| Current Assets | 467,738 | 546,430 | 488,508 | 445,339 | 518,255 | 395,780 | 467,883 | 492,097 |
| Total Assets | 2,284,892 | 2,291,109 | 2,244,220 | 2,128,090 | 2,228,836 | 1,786,560 | 1,762,149 | 1,522,339 |
| Current Liabilities | 384,607 | 398,966 | 392,579 | 337,445 | 411,231 | 335,508 | 404,721 | 503,975 |
| Long-Term Obligations | ... | ... | ... | ... | 20,000 | ... | ... | ... |
| Total Liabilities | 694,428 | 696,243 | 673,380 | 597,293 | 677,685 | 542,354 | 654,544 | 750,437 |
| Stockholders' Equity | 1,590,464 | 1,594,866 | 1,570,840 | 1,530,797 | 1,551,151 | 1,244,206 | 1,107,605 | 771,902 |
| Shares Outstanding | 152,728 | 152,955 | 153,210 | 153,228 | 153,135 | 153,041 | 152,267 | 151,412 |
| **Statistical Record** | | | | | | | | |
| Return on Assets % | ... | ... | 5.55 | 5.76 | 12.91 | 14.08 | 20.78 | 12.75 |
| Return on Equity % | ... | ... | 7.83 | 8.14 | 18.55 | 21.24 | 36.32 | 23.87 |
| EBITDA Margin % | ... | 31.48 | 23.89 | 26.26 | 28.67 | 29.81 | 32.88 | 22.75 |
| Net Margin % | 11.45 | 15.87 | 8.96 | 11.03 | 15.24 | 15.83 | 18.88 | 11.16 |
| Asset Turnover | ... | ... | 0.62 | 0.52 | 0.85 | 0.89 | 1.10 | 1.14 |
| Current Ratio | 1.22 | 1.37 | 1.24 | 1.32 | 1.26 | 1.18 | 1.16 | 0.98 |
| Debt to Equity | ... | ... | ... | ... | 0.01 | ... | ... | ... |
| Price Range | 19.40-11.57 | 18.26-11.57 | 16.89-11.57 | 18.06-9.00 | 24.60-11.06 | 23.43-14.28 | 26.45-16.85 | 24.00-11.92 |
| P/E Ratio | 17.80-10.61 | 16.60-10.52 | 21.38-14.65 | 22.02-10.98 | 14.64-6.58 | 14.46-8.81 | 12.13-7.73 | 22.02-10.94 |
| Average Yield % | 2.41 | 2.45 | 2.62 | 2.37 | 1.83 | 1.73 | 1.31 | 1.05 |

**Address:** 1000, 400 - 5th Avenue S.W., Calgary, T2P 0L6
**Telephone:** 403-262-1361
**Web Site:** www.ensigngroup.com

**Officers:** N. Murray Edwards - Chairman Selby W. Porter - Vice-Chairman **Transfer Agents:** Computershare Trust Company of Canada, Toronto, Ontario, Canada

**No of Institutions:** N/A
**Shares:** N/A **% Held:** N/A

# FINNING INTERNATIONAL INC

| Exchange | Symbol | Price | 52Wk Range | Yield | P/E |
|---|---|---|---|---|---|
| TSX | FTT | C$25.01 (8/31/2011) | 30.25-20.60 | 2.08 | 16.35 |

*7 Year Price Score 122.12 *NYSE Composite Index=100 *12 Month Price Score 101.13

**Interim Earnings (Per Share) Can$**

| Qtr. | Mar | Jun | Sep | Dec |
|---|---|---|---|---|
| 2008 | 0.40 | 0.39 | 0.37 | (0.61) |
| 2009 | 0.26 | 0.28 | 0.13 | 0.10 |
| 2010 | 0.14 | (0.51) | 0.36 | 0.29 |
| 2011 | 0.41 | 0.47 | ... | ... |

**Interim Dividends (Per Share)**

| Amt | Decl | Ex | Rec | Pay |
|---|---|---|---|---|
| 0.12Q | 11/10/2010 | 11/24/2010 | 11/26/2010 | 12/10/2010 |
| 0.12Q | 02/16/2011 | 03/02/2011 | 03/04/2011 | 03/18/2011 |
| 0.13Q | 05/11/2011 | 05/25/2011 | 05/27/2011 | 06/10/2011 |
| 0.13Q | 08/12/2011 | 08/24/2011 | 08/26/2011 | 09/09/2011 |

**Indicated Div: $0.52**

**Valuation Analysis**

| | | | |
|---|---|---|---|
| Forecast EPS | $1.80 (09/05/2011) | | |
| Market Cap | C$4.3 Billion | Book Value | $1.3 Billion |
| Price/Book | 3.32 | Price/Sales | N/A |

**Dividend Achiever Status**

| | |
|---|---|
| 5 Year Growth Rate | 16.40% |
| Total Years of Dividend Growth | 9 |

**Business Summary:** Industrial Machinery & Equipment (MIC: 7.2.1 SIC: 5082 NAIC: 423810)

Finning International is engaged in the selling, rental and provision of customer support services for Caterpillar Inc.'s equipment and engines in Western Canada, the U.K., and South America. Co.'s operating units are comprised of: Finning (Canada), which conducts its operations in British Columbia, Alberta, the Yukon Territory, the Northwest Territories, and a portion of Nunavut; Finning South America, which conducts its operations in Chile, Argentina, Uruguay, and Bolivia; and Finning UK Group, which conducts its operations in England, Scotland, Wales, Falkland Islands, and the Channel Islands.

**Recent Developments:** For the quarter ended June 30 2011, net income amounted to C$81.8 million versus a net loss of C$87.6 million in the year-earlier quarter. Revenues were C$1.48 billion, up 39.0% from C$1.06 billion the year before. Operating income was C$118.6 million versus C$61.8 million in the prior-year quarter, an increase of 91.9%. Direct operating expenses rose 41.6% to C$1.04 billion from C$734.9 million in the comparable period the year before. Indirect operating expenses increased 19.8% to C$321.4 million from C$268.3 million in the equivalent prior-year period.

**Prospects:** Our evaluation of Finning International Inc. as of Sep. 6, 2011 is the result of our systematic analysis on three basic characteristics: earnings strength, relative valuation, and recent stock price movement. The company has generated a negative trend in earnings per share over the past 5 quarters and while recent estimates for the company have been raised by analysts, C.FTT has posted better than expected results. Based on operating earnings yield, the company is undervalued when compared to all of the companies in our coverage universe. Share price changes over the past year indicates that C.FTT will perform well over the near term.

**Financial Data**

| (Can$ in Thousands) | 6 Mos | 3 Mos | 12/31/2010 | 12/31/2009 | 12/31/2008 | 12/31/2007 | 12/31/2006 | 12/31/2005 |
|---|---|---|---|---|---|---|---|---|
| Earnings Per Share | 1.53 | 0.55 | (0.46) | 0.77 | 0.55 | 1.54 | 1.14 | 0.92 |
| Cash Flow Per Share | ... | ... | 1.89 | 3.30 | 0.42 | (0.32) | 0.54 | 0.89 |
| Tang Book Value Per Share | 6.70 | 6.45 | 7.29 | 8.08 | 8.39 | 7.62 | 6.80 | 5.78 |
| Dividends Per Share | 0.490 | 0.480 | 0.470 | 0.440 | 0.430 | 0.360 | 0.275 | 0.220 |
| Dividend Payout % | 32.03 | 87.27 | ... | 57.14 | 78.18 | 23.38 | 24.23 | 24.04 |
| **Income Statement** | | | | | | | | |
| Total Revenue | 2,755,170 | 1,274,636 | 4,641,302 | 4,737,541 | 5,991,425 | 5,662,244 | 5,047,330 | 4,834,578 |
| EBITDA | ... | 145,461 | 396,016 | 410,519 | 479,205 | 734,294 | 670,170 | 565,256 |
| Depn & Amortn | 82,406 | 41,418 | 179,754 | 271,107 | 326,095 | 351,289 | 358,089 | 356,834 |
| Income Before Taxes | ... | 91,839 | 216,262 | 139,412 | 153,110 | 383,005 | 312,081 | 208,422 |
| Income Taxes | 44,864 | 21,074 | 45,546 | 8,589 | 57,114 | 102,898 | 71,343 | 44,392 |
| Net Income | 153,367 | 71,539 | (78,373) | 130,823 | 95,996 | 278,057 | 204,076 | 164,030 |
| Average Shares | 172,499 | 172,493 | 171,718 | 170,993 | 173,318 | 180,459 | 179,798 | 179,789 |
| **Balance Sheet** | | | | | | | | |
| Current Assets | 2,463,965 | 2,352,290 | 2,378,516 | 2,083,661 | 2,814,795 | 2,248,942 | 2,232,027 | 1,814,777 |
| Total Assets | 3,645,042 | 3,511,009 | 3,613,641 | 3,671,435 | 4,720,375 | 4,134,163 | 4,200,753 | 3,736,388 |
| Current Liabilities | 1,439,698 | 1,321,376 | 1,308,101 | 944,982 | 1,516,283 | 1,725,437 | 1,637,732 | 1,324,023 |
| Long-Term Obligations | 710,955 | 711,680 | 736,056 | 991,732 | 1,410,727 | 590,382 | 735,926 | 844,638 |
| Total Liabilities | 2,354,148 | 2,266,592 | 2,227,054 | 2,155,749 | 3,153,271 | 2,516,366 | 2,576,347 | 2,323,410 |
| Stockholders' Equity | 1,290,894 | 1,244,417 | 1,386,587 | 1,515,686 | 1,567,104 | 1,617,797 | 1,624,406 | 1,412,978 |
| Shares Outstanding | 171,569 | 171,527 | 171,431 | 170,746 | 170,445 | 176,131 | 179,090 | 178,403 |
| **Statistical Record** | | | | | | | | |
| Return on Assets % | ... | ... | N.M. | 3.12 | 2.16 | 6.67 | 5.14 | 4.35 |
| Return on Equity % | ... | ... | N.M. | 8.49 | 6.01 | 17.15 | 13.44 | 11.98 |
| EBITDA Margin % | ... | 11.41 | 8.53 | 8.67 | 8.00 | 12.97 | 13.28 | 11.69 |
| Net Margin % | 5.57 | 5.61 | N.M. | 2.76 | 1.60 | 4.91 | 4.04 | 3.39 |
| Asset Turnover | ... | ... | 1.27 | 1.13 | 1.35 | 1.36 | 1.27 | 1.28 |
| Current Ratio | 1.71 | 1.78 | 1.82 | 2.20 | 1.86 | 1.30 | 1.36 | 1.37 |
| Debt to Equity | 0.55 | 0.57 | 0.53 | 0.65 | 0.90 | 0.36 | 0.45 | 0.60 |
| Price Range | 29.63-17.51 | 29.63-16.76 | 27.40-16.54 | 19.06-10.15 | 31.15-12.09 | 33.50-23.10 | 23.90-18.05 | 20.63-16.13 |
| P/E Ratio | 19.37-11.44 | 53.81-30.47 | ... | 24.75-13.18 | 56.64-21.98 | 21.75-15.00 | 20.96-15.83 | 22.42-17.53 |
| Average Yield % | 2.08 | 2.07 | 2.30 | 2.91 | 1.80 | 1.26 | 1.39 | 1.21 |

**Address:** Suite 1000-666 Burrard Street, Vancouver, V6C 2X8
**Telephone:** 604-691-6444
**Web Site:** www.finning.com

**Officers:** Douglas W. G. Whitehead - Chairman
Michael T. Waites - President, Chief Executive Officer
**Transfer Agents:**Computershare Trust Company of Canada, Vancouver, British Columbia; Toronto, Ontario, Canada

**No of Institutions:** N/A
**Shares:** N/A **% Held:** N/A

# FORTIS INC.

| Exchange | Symbol | Price | 52Wk Range | Yield | P/E |
|---|---|---|---|---|---|
| TSX | FTS | C$32.66 (8/31/2011) | 35.15-29.11 | 3.55 | 19.10 |

***7 Year Price Score 124.94** *NYSE Composite Index=100 ***12 Month Price Score 97.97**

**Interim Earnings (Per Share) Can$**

| Qtr. | Mar | Jun | Sep | Dec |
|---|---|---|---|---|
| 2008 | 0.55 | 0.18 | 0.31 | 0.46 |
| 2009 | 0.52 | 0.31 | 0.21 | 0.46 |
| 2010 | 0.56 | 0.32 | 0.26 | 0.47 |
| 2011 | 0.65 | 0.33 | ... | ... |

**Interim Dividends (Per Share)**

| Amt | Decl | Ex | Rec | Pay |
|---|---|---|---|---|
| 0.28Q | 09/28/2010 | 11/09/2010 | 11/12/2010 | 12/01/2010 |
| 0.29Q | 12/14/2010 | 02/09/2011 | 02/11/2011 | 03/01/2011 |
| 0.29Q | 03/02/2011 | 05/11/2011 | 05/13/2011 | 06/01/2011 |
| 0.29Q | 05/05/2011 | 08/10/2011 | 08/12/2011 | 09/01/2011 |

**Indicated Div: $1.16**

**Valuation Analysis**

| | | | |
|---|---|---|---|
| Forecast EPS | $1.70 (09/05/2011) | | |
| Market Cap | C$6.0 Billion | Book Value | $4.3 Billion |
| Price/Book | 1.40 | Price/Sales | 1.60 |

**Dividend Achiever Status**

| | |
|---|---|
| **5 Year Growth Rate** | 13.77% |
| **Total Years of Dividend Growth** | 22 |

**Business Summary:** Electric Utilities (MIC: 3.1.1 SIC: 4911 NAIC: 221122)

Fortis is a distribution utility holding company. Co. segments its utility operations by franchise area and, depending on regulatory requirements, by the nature of the assets. Co. also holds investments in non-regulated generation assets, and commercial office and retail space and hotels, which are treated as two separate segments. Co.'s regulated utilities include: Regulated Gas Utilities - Canadian; Regulated Electric Utilities - Canadian; and Regulated Electric Utilities - Caribbean. Non-Regulated - Fortis Generation consists of Belize, Ontario, Central Newfoundland, British Columbia and Upper New York State. Also, Fortis Properties owns and operates 21 hotels in eight Canadian provinces.

**Recent Developments:** For the quarter ended June 30 2011, net income increased 4.5% to C$69.0 million from C$66.0 million in the year-earlier quarter. Revenues were C$850.0 million, up 1.8% from C$835.0 million the year before. Operating income was C$176.0 million versus C$169.0 million in the prior-year quarter, an increase of 4.1%. Direct operating expenses declined 2.5% to C$358.0 million from C$367.0 million in the comparable period the year before. Indirect operating expenses increased 5.7% to C$316.0 million from C$299.0 million in the equivalent prior-year period.

**Prospects:** Our evaluation of Fortis Inc. as of Sep. 6, 2011 is the result of our systematic analysis on three basic characteristics: earnings strength, relative valuation, and recent stock price movement. The company has generated a negative trend in earnings per share over the past 5 quarters. However, while recent estimates for the company have been lowered by analysts, C.FTS has posted results that fell short of analysts expectations. Based on operating earnings yield, the company is about fairly valued when compared to all of the companies in our coverage universe. Share price changes over the past year indicates that C.FTS will perform very poorly over the near term.

| **Financial Data** (Can$ in Thousands) | 6 Mos | 3 Mos | 12/31/2010 | 12/31/2009 | 12/31/2008 | 12/31/2007 | 12/31/2006 |
|---|---|---|---|---|---|---|---|
| Earnings Per Share | 1.71 | 1.70 | 1.62 | 1.51 | 1.52 | 1.32 | 1.37 |
| Cash Flow Per Share | ... | ... | 4.23 | 4.00 | 4.20 | 2.71 | 2.54 |
| Tang Book Value Per Share | 10.07 | 8.68 | 8.19 | 7.87 | 8.64 | 6.70 | 5.81 |
| Dividends Per Share | 1.140 | 1.130 | 1.120 | 1.040 | 1.000 | 0.820 | 0.670 |
| Dividend Payout % | 66.67 | 66.47 | 69.14 | 68.87 | 65.79 | 62.12 | 48.91 |
| **Income Statement** | | | | | | | |
| Total Revenue | 2,014,000 | 1,164,000 | 3,664,000 | 3,643 | 3,903,000 | 2,718,000 | 1,471,736 |
| EBITDA | ... | 348,000 | 800,000 | 705 | 685,000 | 523,000 | 366,423 |
| Depn & Amortn | 206,000 | 103,000 | 410,000 | 364 | 348,000 | 273,000 | 177,511 |
| Income Before Taxes | ... | 155,000 | 390,000 | 341 | 337,000 | 250,000 | 188,912 |
| Income Taxes | 45,000 | 30,000 | 67,000 | 49 | 65,000 | 36,000 | 32,538 |
| Net Income | 175,000 | 117,000 | 285,000 | 262 | 259,000 | 199,000 | 148,772 |
| Average Shares | 178,300 | 187,700 | 187,100 | 184,800 | 173,700 | 159,500 | 120,962 |
| **Balance Sheet** | | | | | | | |
| Current Assets | 1,235,000 | 1,109,000 | 1,204,000 | 1,124,000 | 1,150,000 | 1,064,000 | 409,139 |
| Total Assets | 13,177,000 | 12,977,000 | 12,903,000 | 12,139,000 | 11,178,000 | 10,273,000 | 5,447,441 |
| Current Liabilities | 1,495,000 | 1,445,000 | 1,517,000 | 1,592,000 | 1,697,000 | 1,804,000 | 565,254 |
| Long-Term Obligations | 5,699,000 | 5,921,000 | 5,609,000 | 5,276,000 | 4,884,000 | 4,623,000 | 2,558,463 |
| Total Liabilities | 8,847,000 | 8,988,000 | 9,006,000 | 8,599,000 | 7,785,000 | 7,550,000 | 4,049,339 |
| Stockholders' Equity | 4,330,000 | 3,989,000 | 3,897,000 | 3,540,000 | 3,393,000 | 2,723,000 | 1,398,102 |
| Shares Outstanding | 185,059 | 175,422 | 174,393 | 171,256 | 169,190 | 155,521 | 104,091 |
| **Statistical Record** | | | | | | | |
| Return on Assets % | 2.39 | 2.39 | 2.28 | ... | 2.41 | 2.53 | 3.05 |
| Return on Equity % | 7.47 | 7.75 | 7.66 | ... | 8.45 | 9.66 | 11.39 |
| EBITDA Margin % | ... | 29.90 | 21.83 | 19.35 | 17.55 | 19.24 | 24.90 |
| Net Margin % | 8.69 | 10.05 | 7.78 | 7.19 | 6.64 | 7.32 | 10.11 |
| Asset Turnover | 0.30 | 0.30 | 0.29 | ... | 0.36 | 0.35 | 0.30 |
| Current Ratio | 0.83 | 0.77 | 0.79 | 0.71 | 0.68 | 0.59 | 0.72 |
| Debt to Equity | 1.32 | 1.48 | 1.44 | 1.49 | 1.44 | 1.70 | 1.83 |
| Price Range | 35.15-26.89 | 35.15-25.76 | 34.20-25.76 | 28.86-21.62 | 29.75-21.05 | 29.55-24.80 | 29.85-20.75 |
| P/E Ratio | 20.56-15.73 | 20.68-15.15 | 21.11-15.90 | 19.11-14.32 | 19.57-13.85 | 22.39-18.79 | 21.79-15.15 |
| Average Yield % | 3.68 | 3.71 | 3.81 | 4.22 | 3.76 | 3.01 | 2.80 |


**Address:** 12th. Floor, Fortis Building, 139 Water Street, P.O. Box 8837, St. John's, A1B 3T2
**Telephone:** 709-737-2800
**Web Site:** www.fortisinc.com

**Officers:** H. Stanley Marshall - President, Chief Executive Officer Barry V. Perry - Vice President, Chief Financial Officer **Transfer Agents:** Computershare Trust Company of Canada, Toronto, Ontario, Canada

**Investor Contact:** 709-737-2800
**No of Institutions:** N/A
**Shares:** N/A **% Held:** N/A

# HOME CAPITAL GROUP INC

| Exchange | Symbol | Price | 52Wk Range | Yield | P/E |
|---|---|---|---|---|---|
| TSX | HCG | C$49.09 (8/31/2011) | 59.41-43.12 | 1.63 | 9.12 |

***7 Year Price Score 138.37** *NYSE Composite Index=100 ***12 Month Price Score 97.12**

**Interim Earnings (Per Share) Can$**

| Qtr. | Mar | Jun | Sep | Dec |
|---|---|---|---|---|
| 2008 | 0.72 | 0.76 | 0.81 | 0.84 |
| 2009 | 0.91 | 0.99 | 1.10 | 1.15 |
| 2010 | 1.03 | 1.19 | 1.31 | 1.45 |
| 2011 | 1.24 | 1.38 | ... | ... |

**Interim Dividends (Per Share)**

| Amt | Decl | Ex | Rec | Pay |
|---|---|---|---|---|
| 0.18Q | 11/02/2010 | 11/10/2010 | 11/15/2010 | 12/01/2010 |
| 0.18Q | 02/09/2011 | 02/16/2011 | 02/18/2011 | 03/01/2011 |
| 0.18Q | 05/04/2011 | 05/11/2011 | 05/13/2011 | 06/01/2011 |
| 0.20Q | 08/03/2011 | 08/11/2011 | 08/15/2011 | 09/01/2011 |

**Indicated Div: $0.80**

**Valuation Analysis**

| | | | |
|---|---|---|---|
| Forecast EPS | $5.41 (09/02/2011) | | |
| Market Cap | C$1.7 Billion | Book Value | $701.9 Million |
| Price/Book | 2.43 | Price/Sales | N/A |

**Dividend Achiever Status**

| | |
|---|---|
| **5 Year Growth Rate** | 31.17% |
| **Total Years of Dividend Growth** | 11 |

**Business Summary:** Credit & Lending (MIC: 5.4.1 SIC: 6141 NAIC: 522210)

Home Capital Group is engaged in a federally regulated financial institution that provides deposit services, residential and non-residential mortgage lending, securitization of insured residential first mortgages, consumer lending and payment card services. Co. also focuses on providing residential first mortgages to borrowers that fail to meet all of the major banks' lending requirements, as well as borrowers who meet the criteria for insured mortgage products. Co. operates two segments: Mortgage Lending and Consumer Lending. As of Dec 31 2010, Co. had total assets of C$7,712,239,000 and total deposits of C$6,522,850,000.

**Recent Developments:** For the quarter ended June 30 2011, net income increased 16.7% to C$48.2 million from C$41.3 million in the year-earlier quarter. Net interest income increased 30.7% to C$81.3 million from C$62.2 million in the year-earlier quarter. Provision for loan losses was C$1.2 million versus C$537,000 in the prior-year quarter, an increase of 126.6%. Non-interest income rose 21.3% to C$8.6 million from C$7.1 million, while non-interest expense advanced 103.8% to C$24.1 million.

**Prospects:** Our evaluation of Home Capital Group Inc. as of Sep. 6, 2011 is the result of our systematic analysis on three basic characteristics: earnings strength, relative valuation, and recent stock price movement. The company has managed to produce a neutral trend in earnings per share over the past 5 quarters. However, while recent estimates for the company have been mixed, C.HCG has posted better than expected results. Based on operating earnings yield, the company is undervalued when compared to all of the companies in our coverage universe. Share price changes over the past year indicates that C.HCG will perform poorly over the near term.

**Financial Data**

| (Can$ in Thousands) | 6 Mos | 3 Mos | 12/31/2010 | 12/31/2009 | 12/31/2008 | 12/31/2007 | 12/31/2006 | 12/31/2005 |
|---|---|---|---|---|---|---|---|---|
| Earnings Per Share | 5.38 | 5.19 | 5.20 | 4.15 | 3.13 | 2.59 | 1.95 | 1.72 |
| Cash Flow Per Share | ... | ... | 4.75 | 3.18 | 3.32 | 3.30 | 2.02 | 2.61 |
| Tang Book Value Per Share | 18.16 | 17.20 | 21.42 | 17.00 | 12.57 | 10.08 | 8.10 | 6.44 |
| Dividends Per Share | 0.700 | 0.680 | 0.660 | 0.580 | 0.500 | 0.410 | 0.270 | 0.170 |
| Dividend Payout % | 13.01 | 13.10 | 12.69 | 13.98 | 15.97 | 15.83 | 13.85 | 9.88 |
| **Income Statement** | | | | | | | | |
| Interest Income | 157,928 | 76,606 | 382,232 | 365,104 | 374,003 | 320,814 | 241,148 | 199,098 |
| Interest Expense | ... | ... | 188,370 | 200,093 | 223,428 | 174,556 | 122,549 | 96,420 |
| Net Interest Income | ... | ... | 193,862 | 165,011 | 150,575 | 146,258 | 118,599 | 102,678 |
| Provision for Losses | 2,191 | 974 | 9,411 | 11,526 | 6,638 | 6,042 | 4,398 | 3,128 |
| Non-Interest Income | 19,563 | 7,109 | 151,705 | 124,075 | 80,692 | 48,067 | 50,140 | 44,008 |
| Non-Interest Expense | 51,859 | 25,216 | (57,766) | (45,474) | (14,681) | 6,131 | 12,291 | 8,093 |
| Income Before Taxes | ... | ... | 242,217 | 198,959 | 158,618 | 134,085 | 101,910 | 91,457 |
| Income Taxes | 32,057 | 14,347 | 61,273 | 54,466 | 49,931 | 43,844 | 34,095 | 30,596 |
| Net Income | 91,384 | 43,178 | 180,944 | 144,493 | 108,687 | 90,241 | 67,815 | 60,861 |
| Average Shares | 34,843 | 34,872 | 34,776 | 34,795 | 34,669 | 34,856 | 34,801 | 35,450 |
| **Balance Sheet** | | | | | | | | |
| Net Loans & Leases | 15,289,755 | 14,927,512 | 5,832,569 | 5,440,747 | 4,506,391 | 4,022,171 | 3,309,214 | 2,796,873 |
| Total Assets | 16,434,599 | 16,010,923 | 7,712,239 | 7,360,874 | 5,809,713 | 4,973,307 | 3,902,316 | 3,284,829 |
| Total Deposits | 6,806,499 | 6,404,418 | 6,522,850 | 6,409,822 | 5,102,781 | 4,413,984 | 3,443,640 | 2,895,461 |
| Total Liabilities | 15,732,664 | 15,346,461 | 6,969,959 | 6,770,586 | 5,376,960 | 4,625,267 | 3,625,450 | 3,065,944 |
| Stockholders' Equity | 701,935 | 664,462 | 742,280 | 590,288 | 432,753 | 348,040 | 276,866 | 218,885 |
| Shares Outstanding | 34,684 | 34,720 | 34,645 | 34,713 | 34,433 | 34,532 | 34,166 | 34,012 |
| **Statistical Record** | | | | | | | | |
| Return on Assets % | ... | ... | 2.40 | 2.19 | 2.01 | 2.03 | 1.89 | 2.08 |
| Return on Equity % | ... | ... | 27.16 | 28.25 | 27.76 | 28.88 | 27.36 | 31.94 |
| Net Interest Margin % | ... | ... | 50.72 | 45.20 | 40.26 | 45.59 | 49.18 | 51.57 |
| Efficiency Ratio % | 28.41 | 30.12 | N.M. | N.M. | N.M. | 1.91 | 5.10 | 4.06 |
| Loans to Deposits | 2.25 | 2.33 | 0.89 | 0.85 | 0.88 | 0.91 | 0.96 | 0.97 |
| Price Range | 59.41-40.29 | 59.41-40.29 | 52.00-39.00 | 42.92-15.70 | 41.90-15.00 | 42.24-32.07 | 42.65-26.21 | 41.19-28.90 |
| P/E Ratio | 11.04-7.49 | 11.45-7.76 | 10.00-7.50 | 10.34-3.78 | 13.39-4.79 | 16.31-12.38 | 21.87-13.44 | 23.95-16.80 |
| Average Yield % | 1.40 | 1.36 | 1.49 | 1.86 | 1.50 | 1.11 | 0.83 | 0.48 |

**Address:** Suite 2300, 145 King Street West, Toronto, M5H 1J8
**Telephone:** 416-360-4663
**Web Site:** www.homecapital.com

**Officers:** Norman F. Angus - Chairman Gerald M. Soloway - Chief Executive Officer **Transfer Agents:** Computershare Investor Services Inc., Toronto, Ontario, Canada

**Investor Contact:** 416-360-4663
**No of Institutions:** N/A
**Shares:** N/A **% Held:** N/A

# IMPERIAL OIL LTD.

| Exchange | Symbol | Price | 52Wk Range | Yield | P/E |
|---|---|---|---|---|---|
| TSX | IMO | C$40.16 (8/31/2011) | 52.67-37.25 | 1.10 | 12.59 |

*7 Year Price Score 103.99 *NYSE Composite Index=100 *12 Month Price Score 97.34

**Interim Earnings (Per Share) Can$**

| Qtr. | Mar | Jun | Sep | Dec |
|---|---|---|---|---|
| 2008 | 0.76 | 1.28 | 1.57 | 0.76 |
| 2009 | 0.33 | 0.25 | 0.64 | 0.62 |
| 2010 | 0.56 | 0.60 | 0.49 | 0.94 |
| 2011 | 0.91 | 0.85 | ... | ... |

**Interim Dividends (Per Share)**

| Amt | Decl | Ex | Rec | Pay |
|---|---|---|---|---|
| 0.11Q | 11/01/2010 | 12/01/2010 | 12/03/2010 | 01/01/2011 |
| 0.11Q | 01/31/2011 | 03/01/2011 | 03/03/2011 | 04/01/2011 |
| 0.11Q | 04/28/2011 | 05/31/2011 | 06/02/2011 | 07/01/2011 |
| 0.11Q | 07/28/2011 | 08/31/2011 | 09/02/2011 | 10/01/2011 |

**Indicated Div: $0.44 (Div. Reinv. Plan)**

**Valuation Analysis**

| | | | |
|---|---|---|---|
| Forecast EPS | $3.70 (09/05/2011) | | |
| Market Cap | C$34.0 Billion | Book Value | $12.4 Billion |
| Price/Book | 2.75 | Price/Sales | N/A |

**Dividend Achiever Status**

| | |
|---|---|
| 5 Year Growth Rate | 6.49% |
| Total Years of Dividend Growth | 16 |

**Business Summary:** Refining & Marketing (MIC: 9.1.2 SIC: 2911 NAIC: 324110)

Imperial Oil is engaged in the exploration, production, transportation and sale of crude oil and natural gas and the manufacture, transportation and sale of petroleum products. Co. is also a manufacturer and marketer of petrochemicals. Co.'s Upstream operations include the exploration for, and production of, conventional crude oil, natural gas, synthetic oil and bitumen. Downstream operations consist of the transportation and refining of crude oil, blending of refined products, and the distribution and marketing of those products. Chemicals consist of the manufacturing and marketing of various petrochemicals. At Dec 31 2010, Co. had 2.55 billion oil-equivalent barrels of net proved reserves.

**Recent Developments:** For the quarter ended June 30 2011, net income increased 40.4% to C$726.0 million from C$517.0 million in the year-earlier quarter. Revenues were C$7.77 billion, up 26.6% from C$6.14 billion the year before. Indirect operating expenses increased 24.9% to C$6.82 billion from C$5.46 billion in the equivalent prior-year period.

**Prospects:** Our evaluation of Imperial Oil Ltd. as of Sep. 6, 2011 is the result of our systematic analysis on three basic characteristics: earnings strength, relative valuation, and recent stock price movement. The company has managed to produce a neutral trend in earnings per share over the past 5 quarters. Because the company lacks sufficient analyst estimate data, we place greater weight on the historical EPS trend as the measure of earnings strength. Based on operating earnings yield, the company is undervalued when compared to all of the companies in our coverage universe. Share price changes over the past year indicates that IMO will perform in line with the market over the near term.

**Financial Data**

| (Can$ in Millions) | 6 Mos | 3 Mos | 12/31/2010 | 12/31/2009 | 12/31/2008 | 12/31/2007 | 12/31/2006 | 12/31/2005 |
|---|---|---|---|---|---|---|---|---|
| Earnings Per Share | 3.19 | 2.94 | 2.59 | 1.84 | 4.36 | 3.41 | 3.11 | 2.53 |
| Cash Flow Per Share | 4.23 | 3.84 | 3.78 | 1.87 | 4.82 | 3.91 | 3.68 | 3.37 |
| Tang Book Value Per Share | 14.27 | 13.56 | 12.87 | 10.82 | 10.24 | 8.48 | 7.49 | 6.29 |
| Dividends Per Share | 0.440 | 0.440 | 0.430 | 0.400 | 0.380 | 0.350 | 0.320 | 0.313 |
| Dividend Payout % | 13.79 | 14.97 | 16.60 | 21.74 | 8.72 | 10.26 | 10.29 | 12.38 |
| **Income Statement** | | | | | | | | |
| Total Revenue | 14,645 | 6,871 | 25,092 | 21,398 | 31,579 | 25,443 | 24,788 | 28,214 |
| EBITDA | 2,388 | 1,239 | 3,701 | 2,981 | 6,004 | 5,159 | 4,931 | 4,813 |
| Depn & Amortn | 378 | 188 | 747 | 781 | 728 | 780 | 831 | 895 |
| Income Before Taxes | 2,010 | 1,051 | 2,954 | 2,200 | 5,276 | 4,379 | 4,100 | 3,918 |
| Income Taxes | 503 | 270 | 744 | 621 | 1,398 | 1,191 | 1,056 | 1,318 |
| Net Income | 1,507 | 781 | 2,210 | 1,579 | 3,878 | 3,188 | 3,044 | 2,600 |
| Average Shares | 853 | 854 | 854 | 856 | 889 | 934 | 979 | 1,028 |
| **Balance Sheet** | | | | | | | | |
| Current Assets | 4,609 | 4,356 | 3,538 | 3,505 | 4,643 | 4,694 | 5,309 | 4,966 |
| Total Assets | 22,966 | 22,008 | 20,580 | 17,473 | 17,035 | 16,287 | 16,141 | 15,582 |
| Current Liabilities | 5,472 | 5,326 | 4,577 | 3,768 | 4,149 | 4,941 | 5,348 | 5,145 |
| Long-Term Obligations | 845 | 526 | 527 | 31 | 34 | 38 | 359 | 863 |
| Total Liabilities | 10,602 | 10,244 | 9,403 | 8,034 | 7,970 | 8,364 | 8,735 | 8,949 |
| Stockholders' Equity | 12,364 | 11,764 | 11,177 | 9,439 | 9,065 | 7,923 | 7,406 | 6,633 |
| Shares Outstanding | 847 | 847 | 847 | 848 | 859 | 903 | 952 | 997 |
| **Statistical Record** | | | | | | | | |
| Return on Assets % | 13.18 | 12.47 | 11.62 | 9.15 | 23.21 | 19.66 | 19.19 | 17.58 |
| Return on Equity % | 23.94 | 23.17 | 21.44 | 17.07 | 45.53 | 41.59 | 43.36 | 39.18 |
| EBITDA Margin % | 16.31 | 18.03 | 14.75 | 13.93 | 19.01 | 20.28 | 19.89 | 17.06 |
| Net Margin % | 10.29 | 11.37 | 8.81 | 7.38 | 12.28 | 12.53 | 12.28 | 9.22 |
| Asset Turnover | ... | ... | 1.32 | 1.24 | 1.89 | 1.57 | 1.56 | 1.91 |
| Current Ratio | 0.84 | 0.82 | 0.77 | 0.93 | 1.12 | 0.95 | 0.99 | 0.97 |
| Debt to Equity | 0.07 | 0.04 | 0.05 | N.M. | N.M. | N.M. | 0.05 | 0.13 |
| Price Range | 52.67-37.25 | 52.46-37.25 | 43.50-37.25 | 48.00-35.95 | 61.16-31.00 | 55.25-37.52 | 45.02-12.50 | 44.98-22.79 |
| P/E Ratio | 16.51-11.68 | 17.84-12.67 | 16.80-14.38 | 26.09-19.54 | 14.03-7.11 | 16.20-11.00 | 14.48-4.02 | 17.78-9.01 |
| Average Yield % | 1.02 | 1.06 | 1.08 | 0.96 | 0.76 | 0.75 | 0.81 | 0.94 |

**Address:** 237 Fourth Avenue S.W., Calgary, T2P 3M9
**Telephone:** 416-968-8145
**Web Site:** www.imperialoil.ca

**Officers:** Bruce H. March - Chairman, President, Chief Executive Officer Paul J. Masschelin - Senior Vice President, Treasurer **Transfer Agents:** BNY Mellon Shareowner Service, Jersey City, NJ, United States

**No of Institutions:** 259
**Shares:** 143,089,120 **% Held:** 15.55

# INTACT FINANCIAL CORP

| Exchange | Symbol | Price | 52Wk Range | Yield | P/E |
|---|---|---|---|---|---|
| TSX | IFC | C$25.00 (8/31/2011) | 25.00-24.88 | 5.92 | 6.05 |

*7 Year Price Score N/A *NYSE Composite Index=100 *12 Month Price Score N/A

**Interim Earnings (Per Share) Can$**

| Qtr. | Mar | Jun | Sep | Dec |
|---|---|---|---|---|
| 2008 | 0.19 | 0.91 | 0.47 | (0.52) |
| 2009 | (0.30) | 0.62 | (0.07) | 0.81 |
| 2010 | 0.34 | 1.22 | 0.72 | 0.87 |
| 2011 | 1.42 | 1.12 | ... | ... |

**Interim Dividends (Per Share)**

| Amt | Decl | Ex | Rec | Pay |
|---|---|---|---|---|
| 0.34Q | 11/03/2010 | 12/13/2010 | 12/15/2010 | 12/31/2010 |
| 0.37Q | 02/09/2011 | 03/11/2011 | 03/15/2011 | 03/31/2011 |
| 0.37Q | 05/04/2011 | 06/13/2011 | 06/15/2011 | 06/30/2011 |
| 0.37Q | 08/04/2011 | 09/13/2011 | 09/15/2011 | 09/30/2011 |

**Indicated Div: $1.48**

**Valuation Analysis**

| | | | |
|---|---|---|---|
| Forecast EPS | N/A | | |
| Market Cap | C$2.7 Billion | Book Value | $2.9 Billion |
| Price/Book | 0.93 | Price/Sales | N/A |

**Dividend Achiever Status**

| | |
|---|---|
| 5 Year Growth Rate | 15.91% |
| Total Years of Dividend Growth | 5 |

**Business Summary:** General Insurance (MIC: 5.2.1 SIC: 6331 NAIC: 524126)

Intact Financial is a holding company. Through its subsidiaries, Co. provides automobile, home and business insurance in Canada. Co. distributes insurance under the Intact Insurance brand through a network of brokers and its wholly-owned subsidiary, Canada BrokerLink Inc. Co. also distributes insurance direct-to-consumers through belairdirect and Grey Power brands. Co. has two reportable segments, the underwriting segment and the corporate and distribution segment. The underwriting segment includes two lines of business: personal lines and commercial lines. As of Dec 31 2010, Co. had total assets of C$12.15 billion.

**Recent Developments:** For the quarter ended June 30 2011, net income decreased 12.8% to C$123.0 million from C$141.0 million in the year-earlier quarter. Revenues were C$1.24 billion, up 2.1% from C$1.22 billion the year before. Net premiums earned were C$1.08 billion versus C$1.05 billion in the prior-year quarter, an increase of 2.0%. Net investment income rose 5.0% to C$146.0 million from C$139.0 million a year ago.

**Prospects:** Our evaluation of Intact Financial Corp. as of Aug. 14, 2011 is the result of our systematic analysis on three basic characteristics: earnings strength, relative valuation, and recent stock price movement. The company has produced a positive trend in earnings per share over the past 5 quarters and while recent estimates for the company have been raised by analysts, C.IFC has posted better than expected results. Based on operating earnings yield, the company is undervalued when compared to all of the companies in our coverage universe. Share price changes over the past year indicates that C.IFC will perform poorly over the near term.

**Financial Data**

| (Can$ in Thousands) | 6 Mos | 3 Mos | 12/31/2010 | 12/31/2009 | 12/31/2008 | 12/31/2007 | 12/31/2006 | 12/31/2005 |
|---|---|---|---|---|---|---|---|---|
| Earnings Per Share | 4.13 | 4.23 | 3.65 | 1.06 | 1.05 | 4.01 | 4.92 | 5.85 |
| Cash Flow Per Share | ... | ... | 4.35 | 4.49 | 5.07 | 4.90 | 3.22 | 4.77 |
| Tang Book Value Per Share | 23.30 | 23.36 | 23.97 | 22.05 | 20.14 | 23.70 | 23.97 | 20.54 |
| Dividends Per Share | 1.420 | 1.390 | 1.360 | 1.280 | 1.240 | 1.080 | ... | 0.650 |
| Dividend Payout % | 34.28 | 32.86 | 37.26 | 120.75 | 118.10 | 26.93 | ... | 11.11 |
| **Income Statement** | | | | | | | | |
| Total Revenue | 2,462,000 | 1,219,000 | 4,668,900 | 4,241,300 | 4,131,700 | 4,439,900 | 4,406,376 | 4,446,068 |
| EBITDA | ... | 218,000 | 586,200 | 170,200 | 131,600 | 679,600 | 965,893 | 1,137,165 |
| Depn & Amortn | 23,000 | 11,000 | 33,100 | 24,800 | 8,000 | 8,000 | 8,577 | 38,249 |
| Income Before Taxes | ... | 207,000 | 524,800 | 139,800 | 123,600 | 671,600 | 952,007 | 1,090,953 |
| Income Taxes | 80,000 | 50,000 | 105,000 | 13,100 | (4,600) | 163,300 | 293,954 | 309,170 |
| Net Income | 280,000 | 157,000 | 419,800 | 126,700 | 128,200 | 508,300 | 658,053 | 781,783 |
| Average Shares | 109,000 | 111,000 | 115,100 | 119,900 | 122,000 | 126,700 | 133,732 | 133,546 |
| **Balance Sheet** | | | | | | | | |
| Current Assets | 23,000 | 88,000 | 2,243,300 | 2,028,900 | 2,482,500 | 1,928,300 | 2,149,710 | 2,296,182 |
| Total Assets | 12,269,000 | 11,906,000 | 12,148,900 | 11,351,300 | 9,773,400 | 10,389,700 | 10,377,269 | 9,926,535 |
| Current Liabilities | ... | ... | 131,800 | 128,300 | 7,400 | 32,500 | 23,984 | 70,673 |
| Long-Term Obligations | ... | ... | 496,100 | 397,700 | ... | ... | ... | 127,000 |
| Total Liabilities | 9,327,000 | 8,958,000 | 9,078,800 | 8,368,700 | 7,140,800 | 7,217,600 | 6,956,514 | 7,033,922 |
| Stockholders' Equity | 2,942,000 | 2,948,000 | 3,070,100 | 2,982,600 | 2,632,600 | 3,172,100 | 3,420,755 | 2,892,613 |
| Shares Outstanding | 109,428 | 109,555 | 112,179 | 119,906 | 119,906 | 124,472 | 133,732 | 133,732 |
| **Statistical Record** | | | | | | | | |
| Return on Assets % | ... | ... | 3.57 | 1.20 | 1.27 | 4.90 | 6.48 | 7.98 |
| Return on Equity % | ... | ... | 13.87 | 4.51 | 4.41 | 15.42 | 20.85 | 31.57 |
| EBITDA Margin % | ... | 17.88 | 12.56 | 4.01 | 3.19 | 15.31 | 21.92 | 25.58 |
| Net Margin % | 11.37 | 12.88 | 8.99 | 2.99 | 3.10 | 11.45 | 14.93 | 17.58 |
| Asset Turnover | ... | ... | 0.40 | 0.40 | 0.41 | 0.43 | 0.43 | 0.45 |
| Current Ratio | ... | ... | 17.02 | 15.81 | 335.47 | 59.33 | 89.63 | 32.49 |
| Debt to Equity | ... | ... | 0.16 | 0.13 | ... | ... | ... | 0.04 |

**Address:** 700 University Avenue, Suite 1500, Toronto, M5G 0A1
**Telephone:** 416-217-7206
**Web Site:** www.ingcanada.com

**Officers:** Charles Brindamour - President, Chief Executive Officer Susan Black - Chief Human Resources Officer **Transfer Agents:** Computershare Investor Services Inc., Toronto, Ontario, Canada

**Investor Contact:** 416-341-1464
**No of Institutions:** N/A
**Shares:** N/A **% Held:** N/A

# METRO INC

| Exchange | Symbol | Price | 52Wk Range | Yield | P/E |
|---|---|---|---|---|---|
| TSX | MRU A | C$46.61 (8/31/2011) | 49.25-42.47 | 1.65 | 12.36 |

***7 Year Price Score 131.03** *NYSE Composite Index=100 ***12 Month Price Score 103.42**

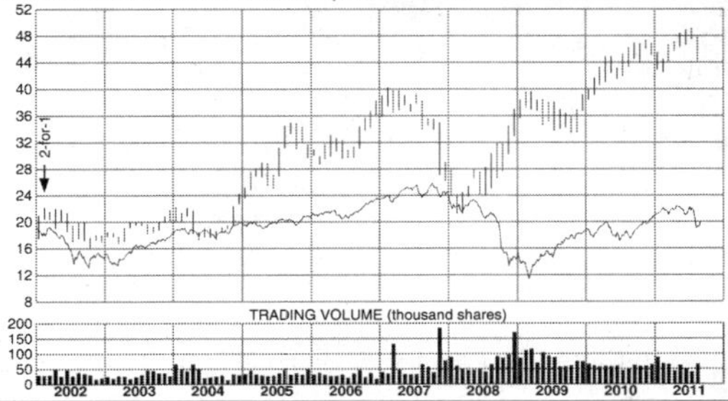


**Interim Earnings (Per Share) Can$**

| Qtr. | Dec | Mar | Jun | Sep |
|---|---|---|---|---|
| 2007-08 | 0.61 | 0.51 | 0.82 | 0.64 |
| 2008-09 | 0.73 | 0.68 | 1.01 | 0.77 |
| 2009-10 | 0.91 | 0.74 | 1.12 | 0.88 |
| 2010-11 | 0.88 | 0.80 | 1.21 | ... |

**Interim Dividends (Per Share)**

| Amt | Decl | Ex | Rec | Pay |
|---|---|---|---|---|
| 0.17Q | 09/21/2010 | 10/22/2010 | 10/26/2010 | 11/16/2010 |
| 0.193Q | 01/24/2011 | 02/09/2011 | 02/11/2011 | 03/08/2011 |
| 0.193Q | 04/19/2011 | 05/12/2011 | 05/16/2011 | 06/07/2011 |
| 0.193Q | 08/09/2011 | 08/22/2011 | 08/24/2011 | 09/07/2011 |

**Indicated Div: $0.77**

**Valuation Analysis**

| | | | |
|---|---|---|---|
| Forecast EPS | $3.84 (09/02/2011) | | |
| Market Cap | C$4.8 Billion | Book Value | $2.6 Billion |
| Price/Book | 1.87 | Price/Sales | N/A |

**Dividend Achiever Status**

| | |
|---|---|
| **5 Year Growth Rate** | 11.20% |
| **Total Years of Dividend Growth** | 15 |

**Business Summary:** Retail - Food & Beverage, Drug & Tobacco (MIC: 2.1.2 SIC: 5141 NAIC: 424410)

Metro is a food and pharmaceutical retailer and distributor. Co. operates a network of supermarkets, discount stores and drugstores in Quebec and Ontario. Co. operates supermarkets under the banners Metro and Metro Plus and discount stores under the Super C and Food Basics banners. Co. also acts as a distributor by providing small-surface food stores and convenience stores with banners. Co. also acts as franchisor and distributor for the franchised Brunet and Clini Plus drugstores, owned by independent pharmacists. Co. also operates drugstores under the banners Pharmacy and Drug Basics.

**Recent Developments:** For the quarter ended July 2 2011, net income increased 4.1% to C$124.9 million from C$120.0 million in the year-earlier quarter. Revenues were C$3.58 billion, up 0.4% from C$3.57 billion the year before. Operating income was C$187.7 million versus C$185.5 million in the prior-year quarter, an increase of 1.2%. Direct operating expenses rose 0.4% to C$3.34 billion from C$3.32 billion in the comparable period the year before. Indirect operating expenses decreased 3.1% to C$60.3 million from C$62.2 million in the equivalent prior-year period.

**Prospects:** Our evaluation of Metro Inc. as of Sep. 6, 2011 is the result of our systematic analysis on three basic characteristics: earnings strength, relative valuation, and recent stock price movement. The company has enjoyed a very positive trend in earnings per share over the past 5 quarters. However, while recent estimates for the company have been mixed, C.MRU.A has posted results that fell short of analysts expectations. Based on operating earnings yield, the company is undervalued when compared to all of the companies in our coverage universe. Share price changes over the past year indicates that C.MRU.A will perform very poorly over the near term.

**Financial Data**

| (Can$ in Thousands) | 9 Mos | 6 Mos | 3 Mos | 09/25/2010 | 09/26/2009 | 09/27/2008 | 09/29/2007 | 09/30/2006 |
|---|---|---|---|---|---|---|---|---|
| Earnings Per Share | 3.77 | 3.68 | 3.62 | 3.65 | 3.19 | 2.58 | 2.37 | 2.18 |
| Cash Flow Per Share | 5.23 | 5.40 | 5.39 | 5.14 | 4.72 | 4.01 | 3.17 | 3.37 |
| Tang Book Value Per Share | 5.82 | 5.60 | 5.23 | 4.98 | 4.24 | 2.19 | 0.87 | N.M. |
| Dividends Per Share | 0.725 | 0.703 | 0.680 | 0.647 | 0.537 | 0.490 | 0.450 | 0.415 |
| Dividend Payout % | 19.23 | 19.09 | 18.78 | 17.74 | 16.85 | 18.99 | 18.99 | 19.04 |
| **Income Statement** | | | | | | | | |
| Total Revenue | 8,801,300 | 5,217,900 | 2,644,100 | 11,383,300 | 11,233,400 | 10,742,800 | 10,669,900 | 10,944,000 |
| EBITDA | 568,800 | 332,900 | 171,000 | 744,100 | 695,600 | 583,400 | 627,500 | 613,300 |
| Depn & Amortn | 150,400 | 90,000 | 44,500 | 203,000 | 191,100 | 178,400 | 167,700 | 180,700 |
| Income Before Taxes | 418,400 | 242,900 | 126,500 | 541,100 | 504,500 | 405,000 | 398,200 | 363,900 |
| Income Taxes | 118,200 | 67,600 | 34,500 | 149,300 | 150,100 | 114,200 | 125,200 | 107,000 |
| Net Income | 300,200 | 175,300 | 92,000 | 391,800 | 354,400 | 292,700 | 276,600 | 253,000 |
| Average Shares | 103,300 | 103,800 | 105,100 | 107,400 | 111,100 | 113,300 | 116,600 | 115,900 |
| **Balance Sheet** | | | | | | | | |
| Current Assets | 1,273,300 | 1,219,800 | 1,301,500 | 1,249,000 | 1,283,200 | 1,148,000 | 1,054,700 | 1,061,300 |
| Total Assets | 4,911,700 | 4,816,600 | 4,888,700 | 4,821,600 | 4,666,200 | 4,411,100 | 4,273,900 | 4,163,900 |
| Current Liabilities | 1,118,700 | 1,076,100 | 1,183,700 | 1,142,600 | 1,152,400 | 1,126,800 | 1,069,100 | 1,093,900 |
| Long-Term Obligations | 1,012,700 | 1,011,700 | 1,004,200 | 1,004,300 | 1,004,300 | 1,005,000 | 1,038,900 | 1,116,600 |
| Total Liabilities | 2,360,500 | 2,319,500 | 2,430,700 | 2,378,800 | 2,402,100 | 2,350,000 | 2,341,600 | 2,440,100 |
| Stockholders' Equity | 2,551,200 | 2,497,100 | 2,458,000 | 2,442,800 | 2,264,100 | 2,061,100 | 1,932,300 | 1,723,800 |
| Shares Outstanding | 102,170 | 103,239 | 103,711 | 105,069 | 108,548 | 110,556 | 114,487 | 114,732 |
| **Statistical Record** | | | | | | | | |
| Return on Assets % | 8.16 | 8.19 | 8.00 | 8.28 | 7.83 | 6.76 | 6.57 | 6.15 |
| Return on Equity % | 15.90 | 16.00 | 16.15 | 16.69 | 16.43 | 14.70 | 15.17 | 15.38 |
| EBITDA Margin % | 6.46 | 6.38 | 6.47 | 6.54 | 6.19 | 5.43 | 5.88 | 5.60 |
| Net Margin % | 3.41 | 3.36 | 3.48 | 3.44 | 3.15 | 2.72 | 2.59 | 2.31 |
| Asset Turnover | ... | ... | ... | 2.41 | 2.48 | 2.48 | 2.54 | 2.66 |
| Current Ratio | 1.14 | 1.13 | 1.10 | 1.09 | 1.11 | 1.02 | 0.99 | 0.97 |
| Debt to Equity | 0.40 | 0.41 | 0.41 | 0.41 | 0.44 | 0.49 | 0.54 | 0.65 |
| Price Range | 48.90-41.78 | 47.40-41.01 | 47.40-37.50 | 46.92-33.30 | 39.65-27.67 | 35.53-21.13 | 40.25-33.77 | 34.86-28.70 |
| P/E Ratio | 12.97-11.08 | 12.88-11.14 | 13.09-10.36 | 12.85-9.12 | 12.43-8.67 | 13.77-8.19 | 16.98-14.25 | 15.99-13.17 |
| Average Yield % | 1.60 | 1.59 | 1.57 | 1.58 | 1.50 | 1.80 | 1.22 | 1.32 |

| | | |
|---|---|---|
| **Address:** 11011 Maurice-Duplessis, Montreal, H1C 1V6<br>**Telephone:** 514-643-1245<br>**Web Site:** www.metro.ca | **Officers:** Pierre H. Lessard - Chairman Paul Gobeil - Vice-Chairman **Transfer Agents:** Computershare Investor Services, Canada | **No of Institutions:** N/A<br>**Shares:** N/A **% Held:** N/A |

# NORTH WEST CO INC.

| Exchange | Symbol | Price | 52Wk Range | Yield | P/E |
|---|---|---|---|---|---|
| TSX | NWC | C$20.28 (8/31/2011) | 23.11-18.59 | 4.73 | N/A |

*7 Year Price Score 128.76 *NYSE Composite Index=100 *12 Month Price Score 99.22

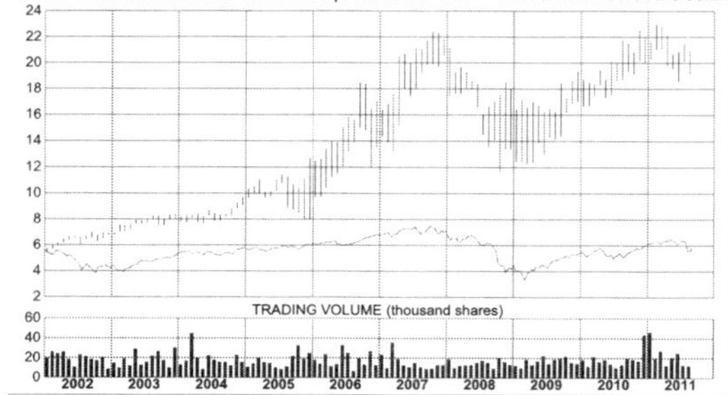


**Interim Earnings (Per Share) Can$**

| Qtr. | Apr | Jul | Oct | Jan |
|---|---|---|---|---|
| 2008-09 | 0.32 | 0.38 | 0.46 | 0.40 |
| 2009-10 | 0.33 | 0.43 | 0.51 | 0.42 |
| 2010-11 | 0.37 | 0.41 | 0.45 | 0.36 |
| 2011-12 | 0.26 | ... | ... | ... |

**Interim Dividends (Per Share)**

| Amt | Decl | Ex | Rec | Pay |
|---|---|---|---|---|
| 0.24Q | 03/16/2011 | 03/29/2011 | 03/31/2011 | 04/15/2011 |
| 0.24Q | 06/14/2011 | 06/28/2011 | 06/30/2011 | 07/15/2011 |

**Indicated Div: $0.96**

**Valuation Analysis**

| | | | |
|---|---|---|---|
| Forecast EPS | $1.30 (09/03/2011) | | |
| Market Cap | C$981.1 Million | Book Value | $285.9 Million |
| Price/Book | 3.43 | Price/Sales | N/A |

**Dividend Achiever Status**

| | |
|---|---|
| 5 Year Growth Rate | 17.01% |
| Total Years of Dividend Growth | 7 |

**Business Summary:** Retail - Food & Beverage, Drug & Tobacco (MIC: 2.1.2 SIC: 6722 NAIC: 525910)

North West Company is a retailer to rural communities and urban neighbourhood markets in northern Canada, western Canada, rural Alaska, the South Pacific and the Caribbean. Co. offers a range of products and services with an emphasis on food and as of Jan 31 2011, operated 230 stores.

**Recent Developments:** For the year ended Jan 31 2011, net income decreased 6.4% to C$76.6 million from C$81.8 million in the prior year. Revenues were C$1.45 billion, up 0.3% from C$1.44 billion the year before.

**Prospects:** Our evaluation of North West Co Inc. as of Sep. 6, 2011 is the result of our systematic analysis on three basic characteristics: earnings strength, relative valuation, and recent stock price movement. The company has managed to produce a neutral trend in earnings per share over the past 5 quarters and while recent estimates for the company have remained steady, C.NWC has posted results that fell short of analysts expectations. Based on operating earnings yield, the company is undervalued when compared to all of the companies in our coverage universe. Share price changes over the past year indicates that C.NWC will perform very poorly over the near term.

**Financial Data**

| (Can$ in Thousands) | 3 Mos | 01/31/2011 | 01/31/2010 | 01/31/2009 | 01/31/2008 | 01/31/2007 | 01/28/2006 | 01/29/2005 |
|---|---|---|---|---|---|---|---|---|
| Earnings Per Share | 1.48 | 1.58 | 1.69 | 1.56 | 1.31 | 1.12 | 0.89 | 0.77 |
| Cash Flow Per Share | ... | 2.30 | 2.26 | 1.88 | 1.96 | 1.70 | 1.58 | 1.03 |
| Tang Book Value Per Share | 5.07 | 5.36 | 5.02 | 4.67 | 4.74 | 5.21 | 5.01 | 4.88 |
| Dividends Per Share | 1.250 | 1.360 | 1.360 | 1.300 | 1.230 | 0.980 | 0.740 | 0.852 |
| Dividend Payout % | 84.46 | 86.08 | 80.47 | 83.33 | 93.89 | 87.50 | 83.15 | 110.58 |
| **Income Statement** | | | | | | | | |
| Total Revenue | 346,262 | 1,448,104 | 1,444,366 | 1,392,634 | 1,064,490 | 944,924 | 849,653 | 788,693 |
| EBITDA | 28,442 | 125,519 | 130,519 | 122,443 | 106,743 | 96,555 | 85,688 | 76,792 |
| Depn & Amortn | 9,057 | 35,709 | 35,395 | 32,240 | 27,136 | 26,358 | 25,199 | 24,091 |
| Income Before Taxes | 17,888 | 83,935 | 89,654 | 81,896 | 72,142 | 63,353 | 54,369 | 46,940 |
| Income Taxes | 5,463 | 7,341 | 7,841 | 6,518 | 9,151 | 9,693 | 11,479 | 9,675 |
| Net Income | 12,425 | 76,594 | 81,813 | 75,378 | 62,991 | 53,660 | 42,890 | 37,265 |
| Average Shares | 48,533 | 48,512 | 48,462 | 48,431 | 48,410 | 48,389 | 48,378 | 48,378 |
| **Balance Sheet** | | | | | | | | |
| Current Assets | 290,820 | 289,303 | 285,843 | 285,088 | 254,061 | 226,164 | 218,742 | 207,642 |
| Total Assets | 614,797 | 620,482 | 623,800 | 609,173 | 529,670 | 441,869 | 423,849 | 413,637 |
| Current Liabilities | 197,806 | 185,377 | 171,946 | 175,301 | 134,899 | 122,783 | 95,467 | 87,444 |
| Long-Term Obligations | 112,045 | 124,339 | 152,519 | 157,725 | 136,864 | 65,631 | 84,524 | 88,803 |
| Total Liabilities | 328,918 | 317,985 | 333,874 | 334,763 | 273,369 | 189,839 | 181,276 | 177,352 |
| Stockholders' Equity | 285,879 | 302,497 | 289,926 | 274,410 | 256,301 | 252,030 | 242,573 | 236,285 |
| Shares Outstanding | 48,378 | 48,378 | 48,378 | 48,378 | 48,378 | 48,378 | 48,378 | 48,378 |
| **Statistical Record** | | | | | | | | |
| Return on Assets % | ... | 12.31 | 13.27 | 13.20 | 12.97 | 12.30 | 10.27 | 9.08 |
| Return on Equity % | ... | 25.86 | 28.99 | 28.33 | 24.78 | 21.52 | 17.96 | 16.04 |
| EBITDA Margin % | 8.21 | 8.67 | 9.04 | 8.79 | 10.03 | 10.22 | 10.09 | 9.74 |
| Net Margin % | 3.59 | 5.29 | 5.66 | 5.41 | 5.92 | 5.68 | 5.05 | 4.72 |
| Asset Turnover | ... | 2.33 | 2.34 | 2.44 | 2.19 | 2.17 | 2.03 | 1.92 |
| Current Ratio | 1.47 | 1.56 | 1.66 | 1.63 | 1.88 | 1.84 | 2.29 | 2.37 |
| Debt to Equity | 0.39 | 0.41 | 0.53 | 0.57 | 0.53 | 0.26 | 0.35 | 0.38 |
| Price Range | 23.11-17.33 | 22.48-16.68 | 19.35-12.28 | 19.63-11.72 | 22.41-13.10 | 18.45-9.75 | 12.70-7.97 | 10.35-7.70 |
| P/E Ratio | 15.61-11.71 | 14.23-10.56 | 11.45-7.27 | 12.58-7.51 | 17.11-10.00 | 16.47-8.71 | 14.27-8.96 | 13.44-10.00 |
| Average Yield % | 6.18 | 6.95 | 8.60 | 8.29 | 6.93 | 6.95 | 7.16 | 9.43 |


**Address:** Gibraltar House, 77 Main Street, Winnipeg, R3C 2R1
**Telephone:** 204-934-1756
**Web Site:** www.northwest.ca


**Officers:** Edward S. Kennedy - President, Chief Executive Officer Dalbir S. Bains - Vice President
**Transfer Agents:** CIBC Mellon Trust Company, Calgary and Toronto, Canada

**No of Institutions:** N/A
**Shares:** N/A **% Held:** N/A

# PASON SYSTEMS, INC

| Exchange | Symbol | Price | 52Wk Range | Yield | P/E |
|---|---|---|---|---|---|
| TSX | PSI | C$13.09 (8/31/2011) | 16.42-11.54 | 2.75 | 22.96 |

***7 Year Price Score 105.54** *NYSE Composite Index=100 ***12 Month Price Score 102.33**

**Interim Earnings (Per Share) Can$**

| Qtr. | Mar | Jun | Sep | Dec |
|---|---|---|---|---|
| 2008 | 0.26 | 0.08 | 0.26 | 0.16 |
| 2009 | 0.06 | (0.11) | (0.05) | 0.03 |
| 2010 | 0.10 | 0.08 | 0.16 | 0.10 |
| 2011 | 0.22 | 0.09 | ... | ... |

**Interim Dividends (Per Share)**

| Amt | Decl | Ex | Rec | Pay |
|---|---|---|---|---|
| 0.14S | 11/04/2009 | 12/11/2009 | 12/15/2009 | 01/04/2010 |
| 0.16S | 05/04/2010 | 06/11/2010 | 06/15/2010 | 07/02/2010 |
| 0.17S | 11/02/2010 | 12/13/2010 | 12/15/2010 | 01/03/2011 |
| 0.18S | 05/04/2011 | 06/13/2011 | 06/15/2011 | 07/04/2011 |

**Indicated Div: $0.36**

**Valuation Analysis**

| | | | |
|---|---|---|---|
| Forecast EPS | $0.84 (09/02/2011) | | |
| Market Cap | C$1.1 Billion | Book Value | $322.1 Million |
| Price/Book | 3.33 | Price/Sales | N/A |

**Dividend Achiever Status**

| | |
|---|---|
| **5 Year Growth Rate** | 30.41% |
| **Total Years of Dividend Growth** | 7 |

**Business Summary:** Equipment & Services (MIC: 9.1.3 SIC: 1382 NAIC: 213112)

Pason Systems is an international oil services company. Co. provides instrumentation systems for rent or sale to land-based and offshore drilling operations in the oil and gas industry. Co.'s customers include oil and gas companies and drilling contractors. Co.'s products provide an integrated package of services including; data acquisition, well site reporting, remote communications and Internet information management tools. Co.'s rental oilfield instrumentation and data acquisition systems, such as its industry-standard Electronic Drilling Recorder and automatically aiming Satellite System, bridge the physical separation between the remote wellsite and the office.

**Recent Developments:** For the quarter ended June 30 2011, net income increased 33.5% to C$8.2 million from C$6.2 million in the year-earlier quarter. Revenues were C$62.4 million, up 22.3% from C$51.0 million the year before. Operating income was C$19.5 million versus C$14.0 million in the prior-year quarter, an increase of 38.9%. Indirect operating expenses increased 16.0% to C$42.9 million from C$37.0 million in the equivalent prior-year period.

**Prospects:** Our evaluation of Pason Systems, Inc. as of Sep. 6, 2011 is the result of our systematic analysis on three basic characteristics: earnings strength, relative valuation, and recent stock price movement. The company has generated a negative trend in earnings per share over the past 5 quarters. However, while recent estimates for the company have been lowered by analysts, C.PSI has posted results that fell short of analysts expectations. Based on operating earnings yield, the company is about fairly valued when compared to all of the companies in our coverage universe. Share price changes over the past year indicates that C.PSI will perform well over the near term.

**Financial Data**

| (Can$ in Thousands) | 6 Mos | 3 Mos | 12/31/2010 | 12/31/2009 | 12/31/2008 | 12/31/2007 | 12/31/2006 | 12/31/2005 |
|---|---|---|---|---|---|---|---|---|
| Earnings Per Share | 0.57 | 0.56 | 0.44 | (0.07) | 0.75 | 0.68 | 0.81 | 0.64 |
| Cash Flow Per Share | ... | ... | 0.97 | 1.05 | 1.71 | 1.06 | 1.32 | 0.74 |
| Tang Book Value Per Share | 3.46 | 3.51 | 3.36 | 3.47 | 4.35 | 3.37 | 2.94 | 2.12 |
| Dividends Per Share | 0.350 | 0.330 | 0.330 | 0.260 | 0.220 | 0.160 | 0.125 | 0.087 |
| Dividend Payout % | 61.40 | 58.93 | 75.00 | ... | 29.33 | 23.53 | 15.43 | 13.67 |
| **Income Statement** | | | | | | | | |
| Total Revenue | 147,165 | 84,745 | 249,562 | 145,861 | 292,528 | 236,439 | 240,584 | 177,929 |
| EBITDA | ... | 39,282 | 105,349 | 40,966 | 137,149 | 122,697 | 138,019 | 103,534 |
| Depn & Amortn | 27,192 | 12,945 | 55,764 | 55,842 | 55,719 | 42,797 | 39,923 | 27,197 |
| Income Before Taxes | ... | 26,337 | 49,585 | (14,876) | 81,430 | 79,900 | 98,096 | 76,336 |
| Income Taxes | 12,196 | 8,580 | 14,053 | (9,366) | 20,109 | 24,848 | 33,565 | 26,056 |
| Net Income | 25,974 | 17,757 | 35,532 | (5,510) | 61,321 | 55,052 | 64,531 | 50,280 |
| Average Shares | 82,699 | 82,539 | 81,525 | 81,476 | 81,936 | 80,630 | 80,087 | 78,544 |
| **Balance Sheet** | | | | | | | | |
| Current Assets | 191,765 | 185,170 | 207,320 | 162,332 | 202,893 | 101,252 | 93,846 | 68,418 |
| Total Assets | 405,437 | 396,792 | 424,172 | 373,097 | 427,016 | 301,570 | 270,860 | 218,197 |
| Current Liabilities | 75,733 | 63,634 | 79,753 | 42,508 | 50,556 | 24,469 | 35,351 | 44,734 |
| Long-Term Obligations | ... | ... | ... | ... | ... | ... | ... | 4,286 |
| Total Liabilities | 83,355 | 71,133 | 111,805 | 64,762 | 72,427 | 30,853 | 39,651 | 55,038 |
| Stockholders' Equity | 322,082 | 325,659 | 312,367 | 308,335 | 354,589 | 270,717 | 231,209 | 163,159 |
| Shares Outstanding | 81,893 | 81,835 | 81,714 | 81,487 | 81,456 | 80,346 | 78,738 | 77,045 |
| **Statistical Record** | | | | | | | | |
| Return on Assets % | ... | ... | 8.91 | N.M. | 16.79 | 19.23 | 26.39 | 28.15 |
| Return on Equity % | ... | ... | 11.45 | N.M. | 19.56 | 21.94 | 32.73 | 36.19 |
| EBITDA Margin % | ... | 46.35 | 42.21 | 28.09 | 46.88 | 51.89 | 57.37 | 58.19 |
| Net Margin % | 17.65 | 20.95 | 14.24 | N.M. | 20.96 | 23.28 | 26.82 | 28.26 |
| Asset Turnover | ... | ... | 0.63 | 0.36 | 0.80 | 0.83 | 0.98 | 1.00 |
| Current Ratio | 2.53 | 2.91 | 2.60 | 3.82 | 4.01 | 4.14 | 2.65 | 1.53 |
| Debt to Equity | ... | ... | ... | ... | ... | ... | ... | 0.03 |
| Price Range | 16.42-10.72 | 15.75-10.51 | 14.70-10.51 | 14.18-8.82 | 18.20-10.00 | 17.74-11.61 | 19.00-13.26 | 15.10-8.93 |
| P/E Ratio | 28.81-18.81 | 28.13-18.77 | 33.41-23.89 | ... | 24.27-13.33 | 26.09-17.07 | 23.46-16.37 | 23.59-13.95 |
| Average Yield % | 2.58 | 2.51 | 2.75 | 2.42 | 1.56 | 1.08 | 0.78 | 0.77 |

| | | |
|---|---|---|
| **Address:** 6130 Third Street S.E., Calgary, T2H 1K4<br>**Telephone:** 403-301-3400<br>**Web Site:** www.pason.com | **Officers:** James D. Hill - Chairman, President, Chief Executive Officer David Elliott - Chief Financial Officer, Treasurer **Transfer Agents:** Valiant Trust Company, Calgary, Alberta, Canada | **No of Institutions:** N/A<br>**Shares:** N/A **% Held:** N/A |

# RITCHIE BROS. AUCTIONEERS, INC.

| Exchange | Symbol | Price | 52Wk Range | Yield | P/E |
|---|---|---|---|---|---|
| TSX | RBA | C$22.99 (8/31/2011) | 31.27-18.23 | 1.96 | 34.31 |

*7 Year Price Score 122.31 *NYSE Composite Index=100 *12 Month Price Score 107.42

**Interim Earnings (Per Share)**

| Qtr. | Mar | Jun | Sep | Dec |
|---|---|---|---|---|
| 2008 | 0.16 | 0.43 | 0.11 | 0.26 |
| 2009 | 0.19 | 0.37 | 0.12 | 0.20 |
| 2010 | 0.12 | 0.25 | 0.13 | 0.13 |
| 2011 | 0.16 | 0.25 | ... | ... |

**Interim Dividends (Per Share)**

| Amt | Decl | Ex | Rec | Pay |
|---|---|---|---|---|
| 0.105Q | 11/02/2010 | 11/17/2010 | 11/19/2010 | 12/10/2010 |
| 0.105Q | 01/24/2011 | 02/16/2011 | 02/18/2011 | 03/11/2011 |
| 0.105Q | 05/03/2011 | 05/18/2011 | 05/20/2011 | 06/10/2011 |
| 0.113Q | 08/05/2011 | 08/17/2011 | 08/19/2011 | 09/09/2011 |

**Indicated Div: $0.45**

**Valuation Analysis**

| | | | |
|---|---|---|---|
| Forecast EPS | $0.73 (09/02/2011) | | |
| Market Cap | $2.4 Billion | Book Value | $630.4 Million |
| Price/Book | 3.88 | Price/Sales | N/A |

**Dividend Achiever Status**

| | |
|---|---|
| 5 Year Growth Rate | 16.22% |
| Total Years of Dividend Growth | 7 |

**Business Summary:** Business Services (MIC: 7.5.2 SIC: 7389 NAIC: 561990)

Ritchie Bros. Auctioneers is engaged in the auction of industrial equipment. Through unreserved public auctions, Co. sells a range of used and unused industrial assets, including equipment, trucks and other assets utilized in the construction, transportation, agricultural, material handling, mining, forestry, petroleum, and marine industries. Co.'s purpose is to use unreserved auctions to create a global marketplace for its customers. As of Dec 31 2010, Co. operated from over 110 locations in more than 25 countries, including 43 auction sites globally.

**Recent Developments:** For the quarter ended June 30 2011, net income increased 2.7% to US$26.8 million from US$26.1 million in the year-earlier quarter. Revenues were US$114.5 million, up 10.9% from US$103.3 million the year before. Operating income was US$38.0 million versus US$37.3 million in the prior-year quarter, an increase of 1.9%. Direct operating expenses rose 5.6% to US$15.3 million from US$14.5 million in the comparable period the year before. Indirect operating expenses increased 16.1% to US$62.5 million from US$53.8 million in the equivalent prior-year period.

**Prospects:** Our evaluation of Ritchie Bros. Auctioneers Inc. as of Sep. 6, 2011 is the result of our systematic analysis on three basic characteristics: earnings strength, relative valuation, and recent stock price movement. The company has enjoyed a very positive trend in earnings per share over the past 5 quarters. However, while recent estimates for the company have been lowered by analysts, RBA has posted results that fell short of analysts expectations. Based on operating earnings yield, the company is overvalued when compared to all of the companies in our coverage universe. Share price changes over the past year indicates that RBA will perform very well over the near term.

**Financial Data**

| (US$ in Thousands) | 6 Mos | 3 Mos | 12/31/2010 | 12/31/2009 | 12/31/2008 | 12/31/2007 | 12/31/2006 | 12/31/2005 |
|---|---|---|---|---|---|---|---|---|
| Earnings Per Share | 0.67 | 0.67 | 0.62 | 0.88 | 0.96 | 0.72 | 0.55 | 0.51 |
| Cash Flow Per Share | ... | ... | 0.38 | 1.32 | 0.86 | 0.97 | 0.63 | 0.83 |
| Tang Book Value Per Share | 5.49 | 5.26 | 5.03 | 4.73 | 4.05 | 3.76 | 3.16 | 2.78 |
| Dividends Per Share | 0.420 | 0.415 | 0.410 | 0.380 | 0.340 | 0.300 | 0.260 | 0.193 |
| Dividend Payout % | 62.69 | 61.94 | 66.13 | 43.18 | 35.42 | 41.47 | 47.56 | 37.66 |
| **Income Statement** | | | | | | | | |
| Total Revenue | 202,987 | 88,463 | 357,369 | 377,211 | 354,818 | 315,231 | 261,040 | 212,633 |
| EBITDA | ... | 32,716 | 131,840 | 161,428 | 159,913 | 132,518 | 108,255 | 97,910 |
| Depn & Amortn | 21,105 | 10,312 | 37,813 | 31,761 | 24,764 | 19,417 | 15,017 | 13,172 |
| Income Before Taxes | ... | 22,404 | 90,846 | 131,523 | 139,284 | 111,895 | 92,066 | 82,514 |
| Income Taxes | 16,234 | 5,834 | 24,933 | 38,071 | 37,884 | 35,912 | 34,848 | 28,934 |
| Net Income | 43,333 | 16,570 | 65,913 | 93,452 | 101,400 | 75,983 | 57,218 | 53,580 |
| Average Shares | 106,960 | 106,611 | 106,169 | 105,773 | 104,713 | 105,262 | 104,556 | 104,195 |
| **Balance Sheet** | | | | | | | | |
| Current Assets | 430,628 | 416,852 | 182,468 | 198,707 | 193,940 | 237,185 | 228,067 | 209,457 |
| Total Assets | 1,151,058 | 1,123,237 | 870,818 | 857,821 | 689,488 | 672,887 | 554,227 | 500,896 |
| Current Liabilities | 357,835 | 360,058 | 137,135 | 168,197 | 146,831 | 178,978 | 133,698 | 125,349 |
| Long-Term Obligations | 139,157 | 138,537 | 135,886 | 130,394 | 67,411 | 44,844 | 43,081 | 43,322 |
| Total Liabilities | 520,675 | 519,158 | 292,691 | 313,410 | 224,326 | 237,771 | 185,590 | 175,713 |
| Stockholders' Equity | 630,383 | 604,079 | 578,127 | 544,411 | 465,162 | 435,116 | 368,637 | 325,183 |
| Shares Outstanding | 106,311 | 106,043 | 105,648 | 105,378 | 104,887 | 104,438 | 104,019 | 103,271 |
| **Statistical Record** | | | | | | | | |
| Return on Assets % | ... | ... | 7.63 | 12.08 | 14.85 | 12.38 | 10.85 | 11.36 |
| Return on Equity % | ... | ... | 11.74 | 18.51 | 22.46 | 18.91 | 16.49 | 17.44 |
| EBITDA Margin % | ... | 36.98 | 36.89 | 42.80 | 45.07 | 42.04 | 41.47 | 46.05 |
| Net Margin % | 21.35 | 18.73 | 18.44 | 24.77 | 28.58 | 24.10 | 21.92 | 25.20 |
| Asset Turnover | ... | ... | 0.41 | 0.49 | 0.52 | 0.51 | 0.49 | 0.45 |
| Current Ratio | 1.20 | 1.16 | 1.33 | 1.18 | 1.32 | 1.33 | 1.71 | 1.67 |
| Debt to Equity | 0.22 | 0.23 | 0.24 | 0.24 | 0.14 | 0.10 | 0.12 | 0.13 |
| Price Range | 31.27-17.52 | 28.15-17.52 | 23.60-17.52 | 26.04-14.14 | 29.47-16.59 | 28.29-17.64 | 19.84-14.12 | 15.02-10.05 |
| P/E Ratio | 46.67-26.15 | 42.01-26.15 | 38.06-28.26 | 29.59-16.07 | 30.70-17.28 | 39.29-24.50 | 36.08-25.67 | 29.44-19.71 |
| Average Yield % | 1.72 | 1.82 | 2.00 | 1.71 | 1.39 | 1.41 | 1.52 | 1.56 |

| | | |
|---|---|---|
| **Address:** 9500 Glenlyon Parkway, Burnaby, V5J 0C6 **Telephone:** 778-331-5500 **Web Site:** www.rbauction.com | **Officers:** Robert W. Murdoch - Chairman Peter J. Blake - Chief Executive Officer **Transfer Agents:** Computershare Trust Company of Canada, Vancouver, British Columbia; Toronto, Ontario, Canada | **Investor Contact:** 778-331-5500 **No of Institutions:** 182 **Shares:** 96,570,336 **% Held:** 81.50 |

# ROGERS COMMUNICATIONS INC.

| Exchange | Symbol | Price | 52Wk Range | Yield | P/E |
|---|---|---|---|---|---|
| TSX | RCI A | C$38.89 (8/31/2011) | 41.31-33.53 | 3.65 | 15.07 |

***7 Year Price Score 113.01** *NYSE Composite Index=100 ***12 Month Price Score 103.76**

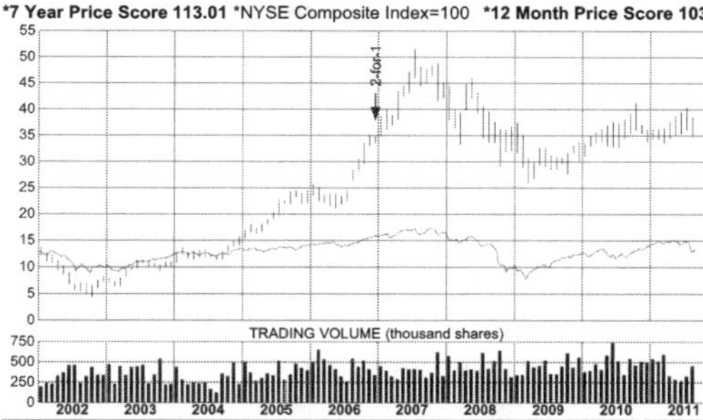


**Interim Earnings (Per Share) Can$**

| Qtr. | Mar | Jun | Sep | Dec |
|---|---|---|---|---|
| 2008 | 0.54 | 0.47 | 0.78 | (0.22) |
| 2009 | 0.49 | 0.59 | 0.79 | 0.52 |
| 2010 | 0.62 | 0.77 | 0.64 | 0.59 |
| 2011 | 0.60 | 0.75 | ... | ... |

**Interim Dividends (Per Share)**

| Amt | Decl | Ex | Rec | Pay |
|---|---|---|---|---|
| 0.32Q | 10/26/2010 | 11/16/2010 | 11/18/2010 | 01/04/2011 |
| 0.355Q | 02/16/2011 | 03/16/2011 | 03/18/2011 | 04/01/2011 |
| 0.355Q | 04/27/2011 | 06/13/2011 | 06/15/2011 | 07/04/2011 |
| 0.355Q | 08/17/2011 | 09/13/2011 | 09/15/2011 | 10/03/2011 |

**Indicated Div: $1.42**

**Valuation Analysis**

| | | | |
|---|---|---|---|
| Forecast EPS | $3.11 (09/08/2011) | | |
| Market Cap | C$21.3 Billion | Book Value | $3.9 Billion |
| Price/Book | 5.46 | Price/Sales | N/A |

**Dividend Achiever Status**

| | |
|---|---|
| **5 Year Growth Rate** | 90.37% |
| **Total Years of Dividend Growth** | 6 |

**Business Summary:** Services (MIC: 6.1.2 SIC: 4812 NAIC: 517212)

Rogers Communications is a holding company. Co. is a diversified Canadian communications and media company, with substantially all of its operations and sales in Canada. Co. is engaged in wireless voice and data communications services through its wireless segment; cable television, high-speed internet access, telephony, data networking and retailing of wireless, cable and video products and services through its cable segment; and radio and television broadcasting, televised shopping, magazines and trade publications, and sports entertainment through its media segment.

**Recent Developments:** For the quarter ended June 30 2011, net income decreased 9.3% to C$410.0 million from C$452.0 million in the year-earlier quarter. Revenues were C$3.12 billion, up 3.2% from C$3.02 billion the year before. Operating income was C$727.0 million versus C$772.0 million in the prior-year quarter, a decrease of 5.8%. Indirect operating expenses increased 6.4% to C$2.39 billion from C$2.25 billion in the equivalent prior-year period.

**Prospects:** Our evaluation of Rogers Communications Inc. as of Sep. 6, 2011 is the result of our systematic analysis on three basic characteristics: earnings strength, relative valuation, and recent stock price movement. The company has managed to produce a neutral trend in earnings per share over the past 5 quarters and while recent estimates for the company have been mixed, RCI has posted better than expected results. Based on operating earnings yield, the company is undervalued when compared to all of the companies in our coverage universe. Share price changes over the past year indicates that RCI will perform very poorly over the near term.

**Financial Data**

| (Can$ in Thousands) | 6 Mos | 3 Mos | 12/31/2010 | 12/31/2009 | 12/31/2008 | 12/31/2007 | 12/31/2006 | 12/31/2005 |
|---|---|---|---|---|---|---|---|---|
| Earnings Per Share | 2.58 | 2.60 | 2.65 | 2.38 | 1.57 | 0.99 | 0.97 | (0.07) |
| Cash Flow Per Share | ... | ... | 6.28 | 6.10 | 5.17 | 4.43 | 3.90 | 2.13 |
| Dividends Per Share | 1.350 | 1.315 | 1.280 | 1.160 | 1.000 | 0.415 | 0.077 | 0.063 |
| Dividend Payout % | 52.33 | 50.58 | 48.30 | 48.74 | 63.69 | 41.92 | 7.99 | ... |
| **Income Statement** | | | | | | | | |
| Total Revenue | 6,102,000 | 2,987,000 | 12,186,000 | 11,731,000 | 11,335,000 | 10,123,000 | 8,838,000 | 7,482,154 |
| EBITDA | ... | 926,000 | 4,671,000 | 4,526,000 | 3,902,000 | 3,154,000 | 2,946,000 | 2,220,864 |
| Depn & Amortn | 963,000 | 469,000 | 1,864,000 | 1,899,000 | 1,901,000 | 1,689,000 | 1,648,000 | 1,553,288 |
| Income Before Taxes | ... | 457,000 | 2,138,000 | 1,980,000 | 1,426,000 | 886,000 | 678,000 | (42,503) |
| Income Taxes | 281,000 | 125,000 | 610,000 | 502,000 | 424,000 | 249,000 | 56,000 | 2,155 |
| Net Income | 745,000 | 335,000 | 1,528,000 | 1,478,000 | 1,002,000 | 637,000 | 622,000 | (44,658) |
| Average Shares | 550,000 | 557,000 | 576,000 | 621,000 | 638,000 | 642,000 | 641,900 | 577,336 |
| **Balance Sheet** | | | | | | | | |
| Current Assets | 2,039,000 | 1,867,000 | 2,005,000 | 2,255,000 | 2,291,000 | 2,143,000 | 1,734,000 | 1,301,697 |
| Total Assets | 17,923,000 | 17,650,000 | 17,330,000 | 17,018,000 | 17,093,000 | 15,325,000 | 14,105,000 | 13,834,289 |
| Current Liabilities | 2,935,000 | 2,742,000 | 3,013,000 | 2,748,000 | 2,716,000 | 2,742,000 | 2,496,000 | 1,991,511 |
| Long-Term Obligations | 9,558,000 | 9,726,000 | 8,718,000 | 8,463,000 | 8,506,000 | 6,032,000 | 6,537,000 | 7,453,412 |
| Total Liabilities | 14,028,000 | 13,955,000 | 13,371,000 | 12,745,000 | 12,366,000 | 10,701,000 | 9,905,000 | 10,306,674 |
| Stockholders' Equity | 3,895,000 | 3,695,000 | 3,959,000 | 4,273,000 | 4,727,000 | 4,624,000 | 4,200,000 | 3,527,615 |
| Shares Outstanding | 546,570 | 546,553 | 555,534 | 592,410 | 635,892 | 639,467 | 635,700 | 627,872 |
| **Statistical Record** | | | | | | | | |
| Return on Assets % | ... | ... | 8.90 | 8.67 | 6.16 | 4.33 | 4.45 | N.M. |
| Return on Equity % | ... | ... | 37.12 | 32.84 | 21.37 | 14.44 | 16.10 | N.M. |
| EBITDA Margin % | ... | 31.00 | 38.33 | 38.58 | 34.42 | 31.16 | 33.33 | 29.68 |
| Net Margin % | 12.21 | 11.22 | 12.54 | 12.60 | 8.84 | 6.29 | 7.04 | N.M. |
| Asset Turnover | ... | ... | 0.71 | 0.69 | 0.70 | 0.69 | 0.63 | 0.55 |
| Current Ratio | 0.69 | 0.68 | 0.67 | 0.82 | 0.84 | 0.78 | 0.69 | 0.65 |
| Debt to Equity | 2.45 | 2.63 | 2.20 | 1.98 | 1.80 | 1.30 | 1.56 | 2.11 |
| Price Range | 41.31-32.59 | 41.31-32.59 | 41.31-30.95 | 37.45-25.84 | 46.06-29.07 | 51.58-34.88 | 34.98-21.16 | 24.64-15.41 |
| P/E Ratio | 16.04-12.63 | 15.89-12.53 | 15.59-11.68 | 15.74-10.86 | 29.34-18.52 | 52.10-35.23 | 36.07-21.81 | ... |
| Average Yield % | 3.65 | 3.56 | 3.57 | 3.77 | 2.64 | 0.96 | 0.29 | 0.31 |

| | | |
|---|---|---|
| **Address:** 333 Bloor Street East, Toronto, M4W IG9<br>**Telephone:** 416-935-7777<br>**Web Site:** www.rogers.com | **Officers:** Alan D. Horn - Chairman Philip B. Lind - Vice-Chairman, Executive Vice President **Transfer Agents:**Computershare Investor Services Inc., Toronto, Ontario, Canada | **No of Institutions:** 275<br>**Shares:** 314,122,272 **% Held:** 48.10 |

# SAPUTO INC

| Exchange | Symbol | Price | 52Wk Range | Yield | P/E |
|---|---|---|---|---|---|
| TSX | SAP | C$40.38 (8/31/2011) | 48.02-33.93 | 1.88 | 18.03 |

*7 Year Price Score 160.74 *NYSE Composite Index=100 *12 Month Price Score 106.07

**Interim Earnings (Per Share) Can$**

| Qtr. | Jun | Sep | Dec | Mar |
|---|---|---|---|---|
| 2008-09 | 0.40 | 0.33 | 0.28 | 0.33 |
| 2009-10 | 0.41 | 0.45 | 0.50 | 0.47 |
| 2010-11 | 0.53 | 0.60 | 0.54 | 0.49 |
| 2011-12 | 0.61 | ... | ... | ... |

**Interim Dividends (Per Share)**

| Amt | Decl | Ex | Rec | Pay |
|---|---|---|---|---|
| 0.16Q | 11/01/2010 | 12/03/2010 | 12/07/2010 | 12/17/2010 |
| 0.16Q | 02/03/2011 | 03/03/2011 | 03/07/2011 | 03/18/2011 |
| 0.16Q | 06/07/2011 | 07/07/2011 | 07/11/2011 | 07/22/2011 |
| 0.19Q | 08/02/2011 | 09/06/2011 | 09/08/2011 | 09/19/2011 |

**Indicated Div: $0.76**

**Valuation Analysis**

| | | | |
|---|---|---|---|
| Forecast EPS | $2.46 (09/10/2011) | | |
| Market Cap | C$8.2 Billion | Book Value | $2.1 Billion |
| Price/Book | 3.83 | Price/Sales | N/A |

**Dividend Achiever Status**

| | |
|---|---|
| **5 Year Growth Rate** | 13.07% |
| **Total Years of Dividend Growth** | 12 |

**Business Summary:** Food (MIC: 1.2.1 SIC: 5143 NAIC: 424430)

Saputo is engaged in the business of producing, marketing and distributing cheese, fluid milk, yogurt, dairy ingredients and snack-cakes. Co. products are sold under brands such as Saputo, Alexis de Portneuf, Armstrong, Baxter, Dairyland, Danscorella, De Lucia, Dragone, DuVillage 1860, Frigo Cheese Heads, Kingsey, La Paulina, Neilson, Nutrilait, Ricrem, Stella, Treasure Cave, HOP&GO!, Rondeau and Vachon. Co. operates its business through two sectors, the Dairy Products Sector - production and distribution of cheeses, fluid milk and dairy ingredients; and the Grocery Products Sector - production and distribution mainly of snack-cakes.

**Recent Developments:** For the quarter ended June 30 2011, net income increased 13.3% to C$126.6 million from C$111.7 million in the year-earlier quarter. Revenues were C$1.64 billion, up 14.1% from C$1.44 billion the year before. Operating income was C$185.0 million versus C$165.0 million in the prior-year quarter, an increase of 12.2%. Direct operating expenses rose 16.7% to C$1.13 billion from C$974.2 million in the comparable period the year before. Indirect operating expenses increased 7.0% to C$319.2 million from C$298.3 million in the equivalent prior-year period.

**Prospects:** Our evaluation of Saputo Inc. as of Sep. 11, 2011 is the result of our systematic analysis on three basic characteristics: earnings strength, relative valuation, and recent stock price movement. The company has produced a positive trend in earnings per share over the past 5 quarters. However, while recent estimates for the company have been lowered by analysts, C.SAP has posted results that fell short of analysts expectations. Based on operating earnings yield, the company is about fairly valued when compared to all of the companies in our coverage universe. Share price changes over the past year indicates that C.SAP will perform well over the near term.

**Financial Data**

| (Can$ in Thousands) | 3 Mos | 03/31/2011 | 03/31/2010 | 03/31/2009 | 03/31/2008 | 03/31/2007 | 03/31/2006 | 03/31/2005 |
|---|---|---|---|---|---|---|---|---|
| Earnings Per Share | 2.24 | 2.16 | 1.83 | 1.34 | 1.38 | 1.14 | 0.91 | 1.10 |
| Cash Flow Per Share | ... | 2.87 | 2.82 | 2.26 | 1.41 | 1.66 | 1.43 | 1.33 |
| Tang Book Value Per Share | 4.74 | 4.61 | 4.80 | 4.27 | 5.14 | 4.60 | 3.97 | 3.75 |
| Dividends Per Share | 0.625 | 0.625 | 0.575 | 0.540 | 0.460 | 0.390 | 0.345 | 0.285 |
| Dividend Payout % | 27.90 | 28.94 | 31.42 | 40.30 | 33.33 | 34.21 | 37.91 | 25.91 |
| **Income Statement** | | | | | | | | |
| Total Revenue | 1,638,995 | 6,025,470 | 5,810,582 | 5,793,263 | 5,058,900 | 4,000,980 | 4,022,210 | 3,883,069 |
| EBITDA | 209,081 | 775,877 | 686,910 | 536,768 | 519,506 | 429,830 | 356,609 | 406,695 |
| Depn & Amortn | 24,609 | 104,832 | 113,506 | 108,284 | 79,434 | 72,116 | 69,361 | 66,065 |
| Income Before Taxes | 178,753 | 647,834 | 543,503 | 407,800 | 421,266 | 335,111 | 262,774 | 312,604 |
| Income Taxes | 52,187 | 196,715 | 160,789 | 128,852 | 133,066 | 96,644 | 70,672 | 80,459 |
| Net Income | 126,566 | 451,119 | 382,714 | 278,948 | 288,200 | 238,467 | 192,102 | 232,145 |
| Average Shares | 207,626 | 208,795 | 208,844 | 208,315 | 208,299 | 208,895 | 211,023 | 211,397 |
| **Balance Sheet** | | | | | | | | |
| Current Assets | 1,271,153 | 1,312,098 | 1,046,378 | 1,125,672 | 1,179,500 | 1,090,985 | 891,872 | 836,006 |
| Total Assets | 3,549,327 | 3,664,309 | 3,253,451 | 3,499,103 | 2,733,476 | 2,488,367 | 2,253,933 | 2,133,072 |
| Current Liabilities | 837,836 | 971,205 | 690,694 | 958,944 | 763,208 | 569,871 | 468,249 | 383,371 |
| Long-Term Obligations | 378,225 | 378,480 | 380,790 | 403,065 | 225,830 | 254,012 | 256,833 | 302,521 |
| Total Liabilities | 1,400,436 | 1,538,668 | 1,224,853 | 1,526,755 | 1,114,316 | 955,349 | 851,390 | 817,222 |
| Stockholders' Equity | 2,148,891 | 2,125,641 | 2,028,598 | 1,972,348 | 1,619,160 | 1,533,018 | 1,402,543 | 1,315,850 |
| Shares Outstanding | 203,933 | 203,830 | 207,425 | 207,087 | 205,962 | 207,353 | 208,229 | 209,054 |
| **Statistical Record** | | | | | | | | |
| Return on Assets % | ... | 13.04 | 11.34 | 8.95 | 11.01 | 10.06 | 8.76 | 11.05 |
| Return on Equity % | ... | 21.72 | 19.13 | 15.53 | 18.24 | 16.25 | 14.13 | 18.78 |
| EBITDA Margin % | 12.76 | 12.88 | 11.82 | 9.27 | 10.27 | 10.74 | 8.87 | 10.47 |
| Net Margin % | 7.72 | 7.49 | 6.59 | 4.82 | 5.70 | 5.96 | 4.78 | 5.98 |
| Asset Turnover | ... | 1.74 | 1.72 | 1.86 | 1.93 | 1.69 | 1.83 | 1.85 |
| Current Ratio | 1.52 | 1.35 | 1.51 | 1.17 | 1.55 | 1.91 | 1.90 | 2.18 |
| Debt to Equity | 0.18 | 0.18 | 0.19 | 0.20 | 0.14 | 0.17 | 0.18 | 0.23 |
| Price Range | 48.02-30.40 | 43.76-27.49 | 31.02-20.94 | 29.85-18.75 | 30.77-20.32 | 23.09-16.04 | 19.57-16.26 | 19.07-15.57 |
| P/E Ratio | 21.44-13.57 | 20.26-12.73 | 16.95-11.44 | 22.28-13.99 | 22.30-14.73 | 20.25-14.07 | 21.51-17.87 | 17.34-14.15 |
| Average Yield % | 1.59 | 1.78 | 2.18 | 2.19 | 1.80 | 2.11 | 1.93 | 1.69 |

**Address:** 6869 Metropolitain Blvd. East, St-Léonard, H1P 1X8
**Telephone:** 514-328-6662
**Web Site:** www.saputo.com

**Officers:** Emanuele Saputo - Chairman Lino A. Saputo - President, Chief Executive Officer, Vice-Chairman **Transfer Agents:** Computershare Trust Company of Canada, Montreal, Quebec, Canada

**No of Institutions:** N/A
**Shares:** N/A **% Held:** N/A

# SHAW COMMUNICATIONS INC

| Exchange | Symbol | Price | 52Wk Range | Yield | P/E |
|---|---|---|---|---|---|
| TSX | SJR B | C$22.82 (8/31/2011) | 23.04-19.97 | 4.03 | 20.02 |

***7 Year Price Score 123.15** *NYSE Composite Index=100 ***12 Month Price Score 104.16**

**Interim Earnings (Per Share) Can$**

| Qtr. | Nov | Feb | May | Aug |
|---|---|---|---|---|
| 2007-08 | 0.26 | 0.69 | 0.30 | 0.31 |
| 2008-09 | 0.29 | 0.36 | 0.31 | 0.29 |
| 2009-10 | 0.26 | 0.32 | 0.37 | 0.28 |
| 2010-11 | 0.04 | 0.37 | 0.45 | ... |

**Interim Dividends (Per Share)**

| Amt | Decl | Ex | Rec | Pay |
|---|---|---|---|---|
| 0.077M | 04/13/2011 | 08/11/2011 | 08/15/2011 | 08/30/2011 |
| 0.077M | 06/29/2011 | 10/12/2011 | 10/15/2011 | 10/28/2011 |
| 0.077M | 06/29/2011 | 11/10/2011 | 11/15/2011 | 11/29/2011 |
| 0.077M | 06/29/2011 | 09/13/2011 | 09/15/2011 | 09/29/2011 |

**Indicated Div: $0.92**

**Valuation Analysis**

Forecast EPS $1.53 (09/05/2011)

| Market Cap | C$9.9 Billion | Book Value | $3.4 Billion |
|---|---|---|---|
| Price/Book | 2.89 | Price/Sales | N/A |

**Dividend Achiever Status**

| | |
|---|---|
| 5 Year Growth Rate | 35.91% |
| Total Years of Dividend Growth | 8 |

**Business Summary:** Radio & Television (MIC: 2.3.1 SIC: 4841 NAIC: 517510)

Shaw Communications is a communications, engaged in providing broadband cable television, Internet, Digital Phone, telecommunications services (through Shaw Business service) and satellite direct-to-home services (through Shaw Direct) and engaging programming content (through Shaw Media). Co. has four main business segments: cable segment, which is comprised of cable television, Internet, Digital Phone and Internet infrastructure service businesses; satellite segment, which comprised of direct-to-home ("DTH") and Satellite Services; wireless segment, which is in the development and construction stage; and media segment, which includes television broadcasting.

**Recent Developments:** For the quarter ended May 31 2011, net income increased 28.1% to C$202.7 million from C$158.2 million in the year-earlier quarter. Revenues were C$1.28 billion, up 36.1% from C$943.6 million the year before. Operating income was C$401.0 million versus C$277.3 million in the prior-year quarter, an increase of 44.6%. Direct operating expenses rose 38.9% to C$705.1 million from C$507.8 million in the comparable period the year before. Indirect operating expenses increased 12.6% to C$178.6 million from C$158.5 million in the equivalent prior-year period.

**Prospects:** Our evaluation of Shaw Communications Inc. as of Sep. 6, 2011 is the result of our systematic analysis on three basic characteristics: earnings strength, relative valuation, and recent stock price movement. The company has managed to produce a neutral trend in earnings per share over the past 5 quarters and while recent estimates for the company have been mixed, SJR has posted better than expected results. Based on operating earnings yield, the company is undervalued when compared to all of the companies in our coverage universe. Share price changes over the past year indicates that SJR will perform very poorly over the near term.

**Financial Data**

| (Can$ in Thousands) | 9 Mos | 6 Mos | 3 Mos | 08/31/2010 | 08/31/2009 | 08/31/2008 | 08/31/2007 | 08/31/2006 |
|---|---|---|---|---|---|---|---|---|
| Earnings Per Share | 1.14 | 1.06 | 1.01 | 1.23 | 1.24 | 1.55 | 0.89 | 1.04 |
| Cash Flow Per Share | 2.71 | 2.63 | 2.73 | 3.37 | 3.22 | 2.87 | 2.31 | 1.95 |
| Dividends Per Share | 0.890 | 0.880 | 0.870 | 0.860 | 0.820 | 0.705 | 0.465 | 0.237 |
| Dividend Payout % | 78.07 | 83.02 | 86.14 | 69.92 | 66.13 | 45.48 | 52.25 | 22.73 |
| **Income Statement** | | | | | | | | |
| Total Revenue | 3,560,204 | 2,275,516 | 1,078,905 | 3,717,580 | 3,390,913 | 3,104,859 | 2,774,445 | 2,459,284 |
| EBITDA | 1,318,499 | 776,310 | 277,535 | 1,635,373 | 1,550,339 | 1,426,981 | 1,249,145 | 1,127,198 |
| Depn & Amortn | 550,542 | 371,973 | 180,742 | 660,243 | 587,180 | 508,760 | 473,115 | 498,351 |
| Income Before Taxes | 524,314 | 250,405 | 28,098 | 727,119 | 726,112 | 687,633 | 530,987 | 374,544 |
| Income Taxes | 148,102 | 76,608 | 21,391 | 183,137 | 190,774 | 16,366 | 142,871 | (83,662) |
| Net Income | 390,301 | 187,631 | 20,332 | 532,732 | 535,239 | 671,562 | 388,479 | 458,250 |
| Average Shares | 434,816 | 434,573 | 435,153 | 433,882 | 430,781 | 433,867 | 435,742 | 435,332 |
| **Balance Sheet** | | | | | | | | |
| Current Assets | 1,536,857 | 1,284,170 | 820,716 | 595,523 | 757,669 | 404,467 | 590,244 | 213,006 |
| Total Assets | 12,760,027 | 12,547,796 | 12,295,711 | 10,153,965 | 8,938,069 | 8,357,801 | 8,163,739 | 7,522,543 |
| Current Liabilities | 1,066,301 | 1,155,047 | 1,068,427 | 1,019,439 | 1,377,017 | 828,645 | 861,901 | 593,345 |
| Long-Term Obligations | 5,574,181 | 5,651,081 | 5,394,410 | 3,981,671 | 2,668,749 | 2,706,534 | 2,771,316 | 2,995,936 |
| Total Liabilities | 9,320,838 | 9,517,265 | 9,344,727 | 7,383,433 | 6,440,085 | 6,102,609 | 6,169,699 | 5,712,838 |
| Stockholders' Equity | 3,439,189 | 3,030,531 | 2,950,984 | 2,770,532 | 2,497,984 | 2,255,192 | 1,994,040 | 1,809,705 |
| Shares Outstanding | 435,537 | 434,572 | 434,178 | 433,142 | 430,237 | 428,432 | 431,333 | 429,883 |
| **Statistical Record** | | | | | | | | |
| Return on Assets % | 4.52 | 4.16 | 3.96 | 5.58 | 6.19 | 8.11 | 4.95 | 6.13 |
| Return on Equity % | 16.62 | 16.49 | 15.64 | 20.22 | 22.52 | 31.52 | 20.43 | 23.73 |
| EBITDA Margin % | 37.03 | 34.12 | 25.72 | 43.99 | 45.72 | 45.96 | 45.02 | 45.83 |
| Net Margin % | 10.96 | 8.25 | 1.88 | 14.33 | 15.78 | 21.63 | 14.00 | 18.63 |
| Asset Turnover | ... | ... | ... | 0.39 | 0.39 | 0.37 | 0.35 | 0.33 |
| Current Ratio | 1.44 | 1.11 | 0.77 | 0.58 | 0.55 | 0.49 | 0.68 | 0.36 |
| Debt to Equity | 1.62 | 1.86 | 1.83 | 1.44 | 1.07 | 1.20 | 1.39 | 1.66 |
| Price Range | 22.85-17.90 | 22.85-17.35 | 22.85-17.35 | 20.91-16.93 | 22.39-13.55 | 28.21-17.16 | 25.43-14.20 | 15.20-9.87 |
| P/E Ratio | 20.04-15.70 | 21.56-16.37 | 22.62-17.18 | 17.00-13.76 | 18.06-10.93 | 18.20-11.07 | 28.57-15.96 | 14.62-9.49 |
| Average Yield % | 4.29 | 4.33 | 4.36 | 4.49 | 4.82 | 3.21 | 2.52 | 1.93 |

**Address:** Suite 900, 630 - 3rd Avenue S.W., Calgary, T2P 4L4
**Telephone:** 403-750-4570
**Web Site:** www.shaw.ca

**Officers:** James R. Shaw - Chairman Jim Shaw - Vice-Chairman, Chief Executive Officer **Transfer Agents:** CIMB Mellon Trust Company, Vancouver, British Columbia; Calgary, Alberta; Toronto, Ontario; Halifax, Nova Scotia, Canada

**No of Institutions:** 169
**Shares:** 226,636,800 **% Held:** 48.65

# SHAWCOR LTD.

| Exchange | Symbol | Price | 52Wk Range | Yield | P/E |
|---|---|---|---|---|---|
| TSX | SCL A | C$25.16 (8/31/2011) | 37.44-24.26 | 1.27 | 15.34 |

*7 Year Price Score 128.96 *NYSE Composite Index=100 *12 Month Price Score 91.02

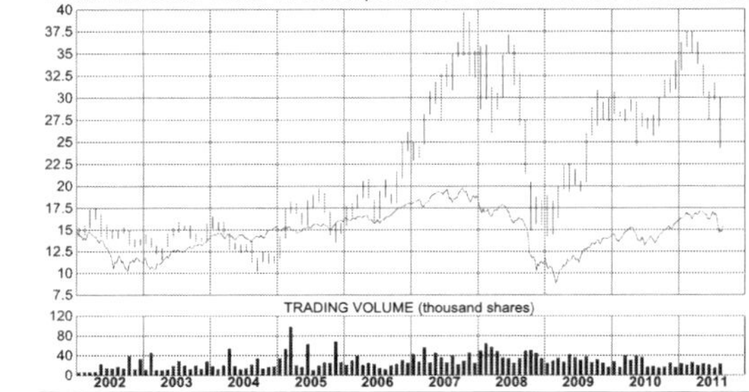


**Interim Earnings (Per Share) Can$**

| Qtr. | Mar | Jun | Sep | Dec |
|---|---|---|---|---|
| 2008 | 0.38 | 0.46 | 0.46 | 0.81 |
| 2009 | 0.45 | 0.49 | 0.48 | 0.43 |
| 2010 | 0.16 | 0.17 | 0.47 | 0.71 |
| 2011 | 0.29 | 0.21 | ... | ... |

**Interim Dividends (Per Share)**

| Amt | Decl | Ex | Rec | Pay |
|---|---|---|---|---|
| 0.075Q | 11/02/2010 | 11/15/2010 | 11/17/2010 | 11/30/2010 |
| 0.075Q | 03/03/2011 | 03/16/2011 | 03/18/2011 | 03/31/2011 |
| 0.08Q | 05/12/2011 | 05/19/2011 | 05/24/2011 | 05/31/2011 |
| 0.08Q | 08/10/2011 | 08/17/2011 | 08/19/2011 | 08/31/2011 |

**Indicated Div: $0.32**

**Valuation Analysis**

| | | | |
|---|---|---|---|
| Forecast EPS | $1.14 (09/05/2011) | | |
| Market Cap | C$1.8 Billion | Book Value | $862.5 Million |
| Price/Book | 2.06 | Price/Sales | N/A |

**Dividend Achiever Status**

| | |
|---|---|
| 5 Year Growth Rate | 26.80% |
| Total Years of Dividend Growth | 6 |

**Business Summary:** Equipment & Services (MIC: 9.1.3 SIC: 3533 NAIC: 333132)

ShawCor is an energy services company. Co. operates two business segments: Pipeline and Pipe Services, which provides pipe-coating, lining and insulation products, spoolable composite pipe systems, heat shrinkable sleeves, adhesives and liquid coatings for pipeline joint protection applications, ultrasonic and radio - graphic weld inspection services for land and marine pipeline construction, oilfield tubular management services, as well as inspection, testing and refurbishment of oilfield tubulars; and Petrochemical and Industrial, which manufactures wire and cable for process instrumentation and control applications as well as heat shrinkable tubing for automotive and utility applications.

**Recent Developments:** For the quarter ended June 30 2011, net income increased 30.5% to C$15.7 million from C$12.0 million in the year-earlier quarter. Revenues were C$264.5 million, up 12.8% from C$234.5 million the year before. Operating income was C$22.7 million versus C$18.9 million in the prior-year quarter, an increase of 19.6%. Direct operating expenses rose 19.8% to C$169.9 million from C$141.8 million in the comparable period the year before. Indirect operating expenses increased 6.8% to C$76.4 million from C$71.5 million in the equivalent prior-year period.

**Prospects:** Our evaluation of ShawCor Ltd. as of Sep. 6, 2011 is the result of our systematic analysis on three basic characteristics: earnings strength, relative valuation, and recent stock price movement. The company has generated a negative trend in earnings per share over the past 5 quarters. However, while recent estimates for the company have been lowered by analysts, C.SCL.A has posted results that fell short of analysts expectations. Based on operating earnings yield, the company is about fairly valued when compared to all of the companies in our coverage universe. Share price changes over the past year indicates that C.SCL.A will perform well over the near term.

**Financial Data**

| (Can$ in Thousands) | 6 Mos | 3 Mos | 12/31/2010 | 12/31/2009 | 12/31/2008 | 12/31/2007 | 12/31/2006 | 12/31/2005 |
|---|---|---|---|---|---|---|---|---|
| Earnings Per Share | 1.64 | 1.68 | 1.48 | 1.85 | 2.09 | 1.19 | 1.25 | 1.85 |
| Cash Flow Per Share | ... | ... | 0.75 | 4.08 | 2.49 | 1.34 | 2.48 | 1.06 |
| Tang Book Value Per Share | 7.75 | 7.79 | 7.52 | 7.28 | 6.21 | 5.88 | 6.14 | 4.97 |
| Dividends Per Share | 0.305 | 0.300 | 0.295 | 0.535 | 0.253 | 0.230 | 0.135 | 0.090 |
| Dividend Payout % | 18.60 | 17.86 | 19.93 | 28.92 | 12.08 | 19.33 | 10.80 | 4.86 |
| **Income Statement** | | | | | | | | |
| Total Revenue | 544,007 | 279,466 | 1,034,163 | 1,183,978 | 1,379,577 | 1,048,099 | 1,059,619 | 1,004,119 |
| EBITDA | ... | 40,264 | 200,110 | 256,332 | 286,639 | 202,166 | 185,525 | 137,649 |
| Depn & Amortn | 24,848 | 11,889 | 55,626 | 63,241 | 84,921 | 42,165 | 46,745 | 43,731 |
| Income Before Taxes | ... | 27,647 | 140,526 | 187,503 | 196,059 | 164,382 | 141,584 | 90,539 |
| Income Taxes | 9,336 | 7,162 | 35,136 | 56,397 | 57,590 | 47,205 | 46,840 | 10,109 |
| Net Income | 36,188 | 20,485 | 105,390 | 131,450 | 149,728 | 87,357 | 92,635 | 138,840 |
| Average Shares | 71,684 | 71,761 | 71,444 | 70,967 | 71,552 | 73,428 | 74,113 | 74,988 |
| **Balance Sheet** | | | | | | | | |
| Current Assets | 539,362 | 580,492 | 559,799 | 586,085 | 577,678 | 516,164 | 595,195 | 515,635 |
| Total Assets | 1,246,565 | 1,283,013 | 1,231,182 | 1,185,977 | 1,228,466 | 960,326 | 1,008,026 | 915,683 |
| Current Liabilities | 239,396 | 273,894 | 268,391 | 278,518 | 350,366 | 260,539 | 249,187 | 251,616 |
| Long-Term Obligations | 225 | 267 | 339 | 26,544 | 60,554 | 72,726 | 87,480 | 87,210 |
| Total Liabilities | 384,064 | 423,585 | 388,431 | 395,555 | 494,891 | 377,011 | 378,099 | 380,445 |
| Stockholders' Equity | 862,501 | 859,428 | 842,751 | 790,422 | 733,575 | 580,032 | 629,927 | 535,238 |
| Shares Outstanding | 70,636 | 70,736 | 70,636 | 70,518 | 70,418 | 71,312 | 73,992 | 74,094 |
| **Statistical Record** | | | | | | | | |
| Return on Assets % | ... | ... | 8.72 | 10.89 | 13.64 | 8.88 | 9.63 | 16.41 |
| Return on Equity % | ... | ... | 12.91 | 17.25 | 22.73 | 14.44 | 15.90 | 28.37 |
| EBITDA Margin % | ... | 14.41 | 19.35 | 21.65 | 20.78 | 19.29 | 17.51 | 13.71 |
| Net Margin % | 6.65 | 7.33 | 10.19 | 11.10 | 10.85 | 8.33 | 8.74 | 13.83 |
| Asset Turnover | ... | ... | 0.86 | 0.98 | 1.26 | 1.06 | 1.10 | 1.19 |
| Current Ratio | 2.25 | 2.12 | 2.09 | 2.10 | 1.65 | 1.98 | 2.39 | 2.05 |
| Debt to Equity | N.M. | N.M. | N.M. | 0.03 | 0.08 | 0.13 | 0.14 | 0.16 |
| Price Range | 37.44-25.65 | 37.44-24.51 | 34.23-24.51 | 30.82-14.12 | 37.11-14.88 | 39.73-22.93 | 26.15-15.40 | 19.75-11.72 |
| P/E Ratio | 22.83-15.64 | 22.29-14.59 | 23.13-16.56 | 16.66-7.63 | 17.76-7.12 | 33.39-19.27 | 20.92-12.32 | 10.68-6.34 |
| Average Yield % | 0.97 | 0.97 | 1.03 | 2.38 | 0.92 | 0.74 | 0.70 | 0.55 |

**Address:** 25 Bethridge Road, Toronto, M9W 1M7
**Telephone:** 416-743-7111
**Web Site:** www.shawcor.com

**Officers:** Virginia L. Shaw - Chairman Leslie W. J. Hutchison - Vice-Chairman **Transfer Agents:** CIBC Mellon Trust Company, Toronto, Ontario, Canada

**No of Institutions:** N/A
**Shares:** N/A **% Held:** N/A

# SHOPPERS DRUG MART CORP.

| Exchange | Symbol | Price | 52Wk Range | Yield | P/E |
|---|---|---|---|---|---|
| TSX | SC | C$39.77 (8/31/2011) | 42.48-36.18 | 2.51 | 14.62 |

*7 Year Price Score 87.51 *NYSE Composite Index=100 *12 Month Price Score 101.49

**Interim Earnings (Per Share) Can$**

| Qtr. | Mar | Jun | Oct | Dec |
|---|---|---|---|---|
| 2009 | 0.49 | 0.63 | 0.79 | 0.79 |
| 2010 | 0.56 | 0.66 | 0.73 | 0.79 |
| 2011 | 0.54 | ... | ... | ... |

**Interim Dividends (Per Share)**

| Amt | Decl | Ex | Rec | Pay |
|---|---|---|---|---|
| 0.225Q | 11/10/2010 | 12/29/2010 | 12/31/2010 | 01/14/2011 |
| 0.25Q | 02/10/2011 | 03/29/2011 | 03/31/2011 | 04/15/2011 |
| 0.25Q | 04/27/2011 | 06/28/2011 | 06/30/2011 | 07/15/2011 |
| 0.25Q | 07/21/2011 | 09/28/2011 | 09/30/2011 | 10/14/2011 |

**Indicated Div: $1.00**

**Valuation Analysis**

| | | | |
|---|---|---|---|
| Forecast EPS | $2.85 (09/10/2011) | | |
| Market Cap | C$8.6 Billion | Book Value | $4.2 Billion |
| Price/Book | 2.08 | Price/Sales | N/A |

**Dividend Achiever Status**

| | |
|---|---|
| 5 Year Growth Rate | 24.30% |
| Total Years of Dividend Growth | 5 |

**Business Summary:** Retail - Food & Beverage, Drug & Tobacco (MIC: 2.1.2 SIC: 5912 NAIC: 446110)

Shoppers Drug Mart is a licensor of retail drug stores operating under the name Shoppers Drug Mart® (Pharmaprix® in Quebec). In addition, Co. owns and operates Shoppers Home Health Care® stores, which are engaged in the sale and service of assisted-living devices, medical equipment, home-care products and mobility equipment to institutional and retail customers. In addition to its retail store network, Co. owns Shoppers Drug Mart Specialty Health Network Inc., a provider of specialty drug distribution, pharmacy and patient support services, and MediSystem Technologies Inc., a provider of pharmaceutical products and services to long-term care facilities in Ontario and Alberta.

**Recent Developments:** For the quarter ended June 18 2011, net income increased 1.3% to C$147.9 million from C$146.0 million in the year-earlier quarter. Revenues were C$2.39 billion, up 1.4% from C$2.36 billion the year before. Operating income was C$220.3 million versus C$218.9 million in the prior-year quarter, an increase of 0.6%. Direct operating expenses was unchanged at C$1.46 billion versus the comparable period the year before. Indirect operating expenses increased 5.0% to C$711.0 million from C$677.3 million in the equivalent prior-year period.

**Prospects:** Our evaluation of Shoppers Drug Mart Corporation as of Sep. 11, 2011 is the result of our systematic analysis on three basic characteristics: earnings strength, relative valuation, and recent stock price movement. The company has enjoyed a very positive trend in earnings per share over the past 5 quarters and while recent estimates for the company have remained steady, C.SC has posted better than expected results. Based on operating earnings yield, the company is undervalued when compared to all of the companies in our coverage universe. Share price changes over the past year indicates that C.SC will perform very poorly over the near term.

| **Financial Data** (Can$ in Thousands) | 3 Mos | 01/01/2011 | 01/02/2010 | 01/03/2009 | 12/29/2007 | 12/30/2006 | 12/31/2005 | 01/01/2005 |
|---|---|---|---|---|---|---|---|---|
| Earnings Per Share | 2.72 | 2.72 | 2.69 | 2.60 | 2.27 | 1.95 | 1.69 | 1.47 |
| Cash Flow Per Share | ... | 3.84 | 3.20 | 2.17 | 2.62 | 2.71 | 2.13 | 1.82 |
| Tang Book Value Per Share | 6.38 | 6.71 | 4.99 | 4.30 | 3.66 | 2.59 | 1.64 | 0.69 |
| Dividends Per Share | 0.925 | 0.900 | 0.860 | 0.860 | 0.640 | 0.480 | 0.400 | ... |
| Dividend Payout % | 34.01 | 33.09 | 31.97 | 33.08 | 28.19 | 24.62 | 23.67 | ... |
| **Income Statement** | | | | | | | | |
| Total Revenue | 2,347,021 | 10,376,067 | 9,985,600 | 9,422,911 | 8,478,382 | 7,786,436 | 7,151,115 | 4,723,119 |
| EBITDA | 230,311 | 1,180,352 | 1,145,838 | 1,102,457 | 971,434 | 833,614 | 727,775 | 636,389 |
| Depn & Amortn | 67,060 | 283,401 | 250,202 | 219,955 | 181,418 | 150,088 | 128,530 | 99,520 |
| Income Before Taxes | 163,251 | 840,915 | 837,421 | 818,550 | 737,143 | 633,654 | 550,596 | 489,419 |
| Income Taxes | 45,710 | 250,172 | 252,513 | 253,338 | 243,515 | 211,163 | 186,102 | 173,549 |
| Net Income | 117,541 | 590,743 | 584,908 | 565,212 | 493,628 | 422,491 | 364,494 | 315,870 |
| Average Shares | 217,540 | 217,537 | 217,501 | 217,450 | 217,220 | 216,668 | 216,088 | 214,942 |
| **Balance Sheet** | | | | | | | | |
| Current Assets | 2,502,114 | 2,623,296 | 2,529,595 | 2,384,464 | 2,172,199 | 1,821,423 | 1,564,911 | 870,899 |
| Total Assets | 7,013,420 | 7,122,210 | 6,852,454 | 6,419,306 | 5,644,039 | 4,929,014 | 4,375,383 | 3,499,693 |
| Current Liabilities | 1,541,712 | 1,367,259 | 1,559,248 | 1,843,860 | 2,159,045 | 1,577,784 | 1,392,501 | 761,884 |
| Long-Term Obligations | 694,521 | 943,412 | 946,098 | 647,250 | ... | 300,000 | 325,000 | 554,943 |
| Total Liabilities | 2,858,544 | 2,759,314 | 2,896,155 | 2,841,215 | 2,433,873 | 2,088,411 | 1,872,374 | 1,342,390 |
| Stockholders' Equity | 4,154,876 | 4,223,903 | 3,826,110 | 3,459,413 | 3,097,047 | 2,723,954 | 2,386,508 | 2,157,303 |
| Shares Outstanding | 217,500 | 217,452 | 217,431 | 217,250 | 216,788 | 214,975 | 213,430 | 209,990 |
| **Statistical Record** | | | | | | | | |
| Return on Assets % | ... | 8.48 | 8.84 | 9.22 | 9.36 | 9.11 | 9.28 | 9.31 |
| Return on Equity % | ... | 14.72 | 16.10 | 16.96 | 17.01 | 16.58 | 16.09 | 15.82 |
| EBITDA Margin % | 9.81 | 11.38 | 11.47 | 11.70 | 11.46 | 10.71 | 10.18 | 13.47 |
| Net Margin % | 5.01 | 5.69 | 5.86 | 6.00 | 5.82 | 5.43 | 5.10 | 6.69 |
| Asset Turnover | ... | 1.49 | 1.51 | 1.54 | 1.61 | 1.68 | 1.82 | 1.39 |
| Current Ratio | 1.62 | 1.92 | 1.62 | 1.29 | 1.01 | 1.15 | 1.12 | 1.14 |
| Debt to Equity | 0.17 | 0.22 | 0.25 | 0.19 | ... | 0.11 | 0.14 | 0.26 |
| Price Range | 43.69-32.70 | 45.96-32.70 | 49.99-41.55 | 57.74-41.63 | 56.01-48.00 | 51.08-40.23 | 44.70-36.81 | 37.95-28.86 |
| P/E Ratio | 16.06-12.02 | 16.90-12.02 | 18.58-15.45 | 22.21-16.01 | 24.67-21.15 | 26.19-20.63 | 26.45-21.78 | 25.82-19.63 |
| Average Yield % | 2.42 | 2.33 | 1.94 | 1.68 | 1.23 | 1.07 | 0.98 | ... |

**Address:** 243 Consumers Road, Toronto, M2J 4W8
**Telephone:** 416-493-1220
**Web Site:** www.shoppersdrugmart.ca

**Officers:** David M. Williams - Interim President, Chief Executive Officer Mary Kelly - Executive Vice President **Transfer Agents:** CIBC Mellon Trust Company, Toronto, Ontario, Canada

**Investor Contact:** 416-493-1220
**No of Institutions:** N/A
**Shares:** N/A **% Held:** N/A

# SNC - LAVALIN GROUP INC

| Exchange | Symbol | Price | 52Wk Range | Yield | P/E |
|---|---|---|---|---|---|
| TSX | SNC | C$52.38 (8/31/2011) | 62.07-47.99 | 1.60 | 18.06 |

***7 Year Price Score 139.70** *NYSE Composite Index=100 ***12 Month Price Score 97.95**

**Interim Earnings (Per Share) Can$**

| Qtr. | Mar | Jun | Sep | Dec |
|---|---|---|---|---|
| 2008 | 0.47 | 0.49 | 0.60 | 0.49 |
| 2009 | 0.51 | 0.53 | 0.68 | 0.64 |
| 2010 | 0.55 | 0.78 | 0.84 | 0.91 |
| 2011 | 0.49 | 0.66 | ... | ... |

**Interim Dividends (Per Share)**

| Amt | Decl | Ex | Rec | Pay |
|---|---|---|---|---|
| 0.17Q | 11/05/2010 | 11/17/2010 | 11/19/2010 | 12/03/2010 |
| 0.21Q | 03/04/2011 | 03/16/2011 | 03/18/2011 | 04/01/2011 |
| 0.21Q | 05/05/2011 | 05/17/2011 | 05/19/2011 | 06/02/2011 |
| 0.21Q | 08/05/2011 | 08/17/2011 | 08/19/2011 | 09/02/2011 |

**Indicated Div: $0.84**

**Valuation Analysis**

| | | | |
|---|---|---|---|
| Forecast EPS | $2.79 (09/05/2011) | | |
| Market Cap | C$7.9 Billion | Book Value | $1.9 Billion |
| Price/Book | 4.08 | Price/Sales | N/A |

**Dividend Achiever Status**

| | |
|---|---|
| **5 Year Growth Rate** | 26.09% |
| **Total Years of Dividend Growth** | 10 |

**Business Summary:** Construction Services (MIC: 7.5.4 SIC: 8711 NAIC: 541330)

SNC - Lavalin Group is engaged in the provision of engineering and construction, and operations and maintenance expertise through its network of offices located across Canada and in over 35 other countries, and is working on projects around the world. Co. reports its revenues under four categories of activities: services, packages, operations and maintenance, and infrastructure concession investments. Services and packages relate to engineering and construction operations. Operations and maintenance activities consists of providing operations, maintenance and logistics solutions. Infrastructure concession investments regroups Co.'s investments in infrastructure concessions.

**Recent Developments:** For the quarter ended June 30 2011, net income decreased 15.9% to C$103.4 million from C$122.9 million in the year-earlier quarter. Revenues were C$1.67 billion, up 22.9% from C$1.36 billion the year before. Operating income was C$148.6 million versus C$180.6 million in the prior-year quarter, a decrease of 17.7%. Direct operating expenses rose 31.2% to C$1.35 billion from C$1.03 billion in the comparable period the year before. Indirect operating expenses increased 13.8% to C$166.1 million from C$146.0 million in the equivalent prior-year period.

**Prospects:** Our evaluation of SNC-Lavalin Group as of Sep. 6, 2011 is the result of our systematic analysis on three basic characteristics: earnings strength, relative valuation, and recent stock price movement. The company has managed to produce a neutral trend in earnings per share over the past 5 quarters. However, while recent estimates for the company have been mixed, C.SNC has posted results that were in line with analysts expectations. Based on operating earnings yield, the company is about fairly valued when compared to all of the companies in our coverage universe. Share price changes over the past year indicates that C.SNC will perform poorly over the near term.

**Financial Data**

| (Can$ in Thousands) | 6 Mos | 3 Mos | 12/31/2010 | 12/31/2009 | 12/31/2008 | 12/31/2007 | 12/31/2006 | 12/31/2005 |
|---|---|---|---|---|---|---|---|---|
| Earnings Per Share | 2.90 | 3.02 | 2.87 | 2.36 | 2.05 | 1.00 | 1.04 | 0.85 |
| Cash Flow Per Share | ... | ... | 3.24 | 2.64 | 2.07 | 3.06 | (0.40) | 3.30 |
| Tang Book Value Per Share | 9.15 | 8.80 | 7.71 | 6.05 | 3.97 | 2.96 | 3.83 | 4.43 |
| Dividends Per Share | 0.760 | 0.720 | 0.680 | 0.600 | 0.480 | 0.360 | 0.280 | 0.213 |
| Dividend Payout % | 26.21 | 23.84 | 23.69 | 25.42 | 23.41 | 36.00 | 26.92 | 25.10 |
| **Income Statement** | | | | | | | | |
| Total Revenue | 3,307,604 | 1,640,759 | 6,314,990 | 6,101,737 | 7,106,869 | 6,731,464 | 5,150,406 | 3,787,809 |
| EBITDA | ... | 122,812 | 704,590 | 607,331 | 533,240 | 214,552 | 280,314 | 239,284 |
| Depn & Amortn | 61,482 | 29,648 | 133,396 | 130,078 | 130,045 | 112,627 | 81,293 | 48,523 |
| Income Before Taxes | ... | 93,164 | 571,194 | 477,253 | 403,195 | 101,925 | 199,021 | 190,761 |
| Income Taxes | 35,364 | 16,538 | 123,422 | 108,141 | 85,114 | 23,650 | 55,081 | 60,849 |
| Net Income | 174,619 | 73,880 | 437,014 | 359,394 | 312,520 | 153,202 | 158,372 | 129,912 |
| Average Shares | 151,956 | 152,295 | 152,221 | 151,992 | 152,265 | 152,697 | 152,685 | 153,143 |
| **Balance Sheet** | | | | | | | | |
| Current Assets | 3,530,719 | 3,605,068 | 4,171,327 | 3,393,023 | 3,552,423 | 3,421,021 | 3,599,701 | 2,587,171 |
| Total Assets | 7,820,518 | 7,694,841 | 8,603,223 | 7,206,283 | 6,777,392 | 6,485,386 | 6,238,987 | 4,026,461 |
| Current Liabilities | 3,046,526 | 3,002,586 | 2,924,909 | 2,848,951 | 3,276,027 | 3,150,818 | 3,299,363 | 2,222,030 |
| Long-Term Obligations | 1,871,588 | 1,876,857 | 3,329,652 | 2,353,533 | 2,108,012 | 2,075,548 | 1,781,216 | 918,523 |
| Total Liabilities | 5,882,587 | 5,825,549 | 6,792,202 | 5,691,558 | 5,614,653 | 5,485,805 | 5,267,464 | 3,236,754 |
| Stockholders' Equity | 1,937,931 | 1,869,292 | 1,708,426 | 1,434,692 | 1,095,007 | 928,289 | 905,956 | 789,707 |
| Shares Outstanding | 150,893 | 150,815 | 151,034 | 151,033 | 151,033 | 151,038 | 151,033 | 151,282 |
| **Statistical Record** | | | | | | | | |
| Return on Assets % | ... | ... | 5.53 | 5.14 | 4.70 | 2.41 | 3.09 | 3.61 |
| Return on Equity % | ... | ... | 27.81 | 28.41 | 30.81 | 16.70 | 18.68 | 17.23 |
| EBITDA Margin % | ... | 7.49 | 11.16 | 9.95 | 7.50 | 3.19 | 5.44 | 6.32 |
| Net Margin % | 5.28 | 4.50 | 6.92 | 5.89 | 4.40 | 2.28 | 3.07 | 3.43 |
| Asset Turnover | ... | ... | 0.80 | 0.87 | 1.07 | 1.06 | 1.00 | 1.05 |
| Current Ratio | 1.16 | 1.20 | 1.43 | 1.19 | 1.08 | 1.09 | 1.09 | 1.16 |
| Debt to Equity | 0.97 | 1.00 | 1.95 | 1.64 | 1.93 | 2.24 | 1.97 | 1.16 |
| Price Range | 62.07-42.00 | 62.07-42.00 | 59.77-42.00 | 53.99-27.00 | 61.65-26.00 | 49.95-30.40 | 32.90-25.42 | 26.26-18.59 |
| P/E Ratio | 21.40-14.48 | 20.55-13.91 | 20.83-14.63 | 22.88-11.44 | 30.07-12.68 | 49.95-30.40 | 31.63-24.44 | 30.89-21.87 |
| Average Yield % | 1.46 | 1.38 | 1.35 | 1.43 | 1.06 | 0.90 | 0.94 | 0.92 |

**Address:** 455 René-Lévesque Blvd. West, Montreal, H2Z 1Z3
**Telephone:** 514-393-1000
**Web Site:** www.snclavalin.com

**Officers:** Gilles Lamarre - Executive Vice President, Chief Financial Officer Louis Dagenais - Senior Vice President **Transfer Agents:** Computershare Investor Services Inc., Toronto, Ontario, Canada

**Investor Contact:** 514-393-1000
**No of Institutions:** N/A
**Shares:** N/A **% Held:** N/A

# SUNCOR ENERGY INC.

| Exchange | Symbol | Price | 52Wk Range | Yield | P/E |
|---|---|---|---|---|---|
| TSX | SU | C$31.90 (8/31/2011) | 47.73-29.14 | 1.38 | 12.91 |

***7 Year Price Score 146.81** *NYSE Composite Index=100 ***12 Month Price Score 95.97**

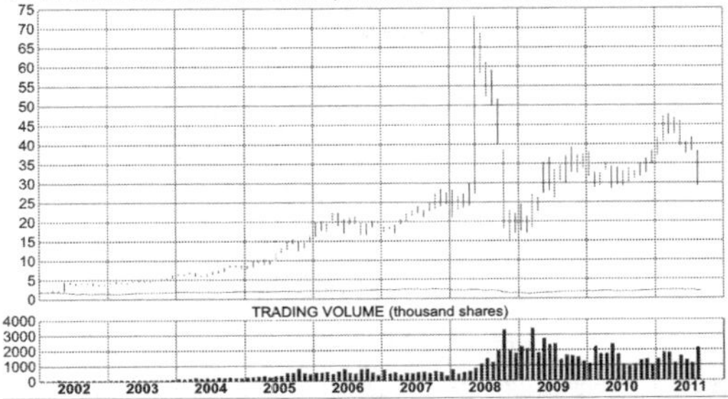


**Interim Earnings (Per Share) Can$**

| Qtr. | Mar | Jun | Sep | Dec |
|---|---|---|---|---|
| 2008 | 0.75 | 0.87 | 0.86 | (0.22) |
| 2009 | (0.20) | (0.06) | 0.74 | 0.31 |
| 2010 | 0.46 | 0.34 | 0.65 | 0.86 |
| 2011 | 0.65 | 0.31 | ... | ... |

**Interim Dividends (Per Share)**

| Amt | Decl | Ex | Rec | Pay |
|---|---|---|---|---|
| 0.10Q | 11/09/2010 | 12/01/2010 | 12/03/2010 | 12/24/2010 |
| 0.10Q | 02/01/2011 | 03/02/2011 | 03/04/2011 | 03/25/2011 |
| 0.11Q | 05/02/2011 | 06/01/2011 | 06/03/2011 | 06/24/2011 |
| 0.11Q | 07/26/2011 | 09/01/2011 | 09/06/2011 | 09/26/2011 |

**Indicated Div: $0.44**

**Valuation Analysis**

| | | | |
|---|---|---|---|
| Forecast EPS | $3.04 (09/05/2011) | | |
| Market Cap | C$50.2 Billion | Book Value | $36.8 Billion |
| Price/Book | 1.36 | Price/Sales | N/A |

**Dividend Achiever Status**

| | |
|---|---|
| **5 Year Growth Rate** | 27.23% |
| **Total Years of Dividend Growth** | 8 |

**Business Summary:** Refining & Marketing (MIC: 9.1.2 SIC: 2911 NAIC: 324110)

Suncor Energy is an integrated energy company focused on developing petroleum resource basins, primarily Canada's Athabasca oil sands. In addition, Co. explores for, acquires, develops, produces and markets crude oil and natural gas; transports and refines crude oil; and markets petroleum and petrochemical products. Co. also markets third party petroleum products and carries on energy trading activities. As of Dec 31 2010, Co. had total gross proved reserves of 2,906 million barrels of synthetic crude oil, 397 million barrels of bitumen, 348 million barrels of light and medium oil, 1,235 billion cubic feet of natural gas and 17 million barrels of natural gas liquids.

**Recent Developments:** For the quarter ended June 30 2011, net income increased 4.1% to C$562.0 million from C$540.0 million in the year-earlier quarter. Revenues were C$9.59 billion, up 13.3% from C$8.46 billion the year before. Operating income was C$1.06 billion versus C$1.52 billion in the prior-year quarter, a decrease of 30.2%. Direct operating expenses rose 29.1% to C$5.08 billion from C$3.94 billion in the comparable period the year before. Indirect operating expenses increased 11.1% to C$3.50 billion from C$3.15 billion in the equivalent prior-year period.

**Prospects:** Our evaluation of Suncor Energy Inc. as of Sep. 6, 2011 is the result of our systematic analysis on three basic characteristics: earnings strength, relative valuation, and recent stock price movement. The company has generated a negative trend in earnings per share over the past 5 quarters. However, while recent estimates for the company have been lowered by analysts, SU has posted results that fell short of analysts expectations. Based on operating earnings yield, the company is undervalued when compared to all of the companies in our coverage universe. Share price changes over the past year indicates that SU will perform well over the near term.

| **Financial Data** (Can$ in Millions) | 6 Mos | 3 Mos | 12/31/2010 | 12/31/2009 | 12/31/2008 | 12/31/2007 | 12/31/2006 | 12/31/2005 |
|---|---|---|---|---|---|---|---|---|
| Earnings Per Share | 2.47 | 2.50 | 2.27 | 0.95 | 2.26 | 3.01 | 3.16 | 1.34 |
| Cash Flow Per Share | ... | ... | 3.51 | 2.15 | 4.77 | 4.22 | 4.97 | 2.65 |
| Tang Book Value Per Share | 21.38 | 21.14 | 21.41 | 19.82 | 15.52 | 12.55 | 9.73 | 6.70 |
| Dividends Per Share | 0.410 | 0.400 | 0.400 | 0.300 | 0.200 | 0.190 | 0.150 | 0.120 |
| Dividend Payout % | 16.60 | 16.00 | 17.62 | 31.58 | 8.85 | 6.31 | 4.75 | 8.96 |
| **Income Statement** | | | | | | | | |
| Total Revenue | 18,975 | 9,845 | 34,350 | 25,480 | 30,089 | 17,933 | 15,829 | 11,086 |
| EBITDA | ... | 2,107 | 8,060 | 3,595 | 4,181 | 4,209 | 4,501 | 2,707 |
| Depn & Amortn | ... | ... | 3,813 | 2,306 | 1,049 | 864 | 695 | 720 |
| Income Before Taxes | ... | 2,046 | 4,247 | 1,289 | 3,132 | 3,345 | 3,806 | 1,987 |
| Income Taxes | 1,497 | 1,018 | 1,559 | 143 | 995 | 513 | 835 | 742 |
| Net Income | 1,590 | 1,028 | 3,571 | 1,146 | 2,137 | 2,832 | 2,971 | 1,245 |
| Average Shares | 1,587 | 1,581 | 1,574 | 1,211 | 945 | 942 | 940 | 932 |
| **Balance Sheet** | | | | | | | | |
| Current Assets | 12,107 | 13,055 | 10,513 | 8,331 | 3,237 | 2,818 | 2,302 | 1,916 |
| Total Assets | 69,343 | 69,643 | 70,169 | 69,746 | 32,528 | 24,167 | 18,781 | 15,351 |
| Current Liabilities | 9,517 | 10,414 | 8,526 | 7,848 | 3,529 | 3,097 | 2,158 | 1,935 |
| Long-Term Obligations | 9,570 | 9,637 | 11,720 | 13,900 | 7,931 | 3,850 | 2,385 | 3,007 |
| Total Liabilities | 32,554 | 33,243 | 33,448 | 35,635 | 18,005 | 12,554 | 9,829 | 9,221 |
| Stockholders' Equity | 36,789 | 36,400 | 36,721 | 34,111 | 14,523 | 11,613 | 8,952 | 6,130 |
| Shares Outstanding | 1,573 | 1,572 | 1,565 | 1,559 | 935 | 925 | 919 | 915 |
| **Statistical Record** | | | | | | | | |
| Return on Assets % | ... | ... | 5.10 | 2.24 | 7.52 | 13.19 | 17.41 | 9.17 |
| Return on Equity % | ... | ... | 10.08 | 4.71 | 16.31 | 27.54 | 39.40 | 22.58 |
| EBITDA Margin % | ... | 21.40 | 23.46 | 14.11 | 13.90 | 23.47 | 28.44 | 24.42 |
| Net Margin % | 8.38 | 10.44 | 10.40 | 4.50 | 7.10 | 15.79 | 18.77 | 11.23 |
| Asset Turnover | ... | ... | 0.49 | 0.50 | 1.06 | 0.84 | 0.93 | 0.82 |
| Current Ratio | 1.27 | 1.25 | 1.23 | 1.06 | 0.92 | 0.91 | 1.07 | 0.99 |
| Debt to Equity | 0.26 | 0.26 | 0.32 | 0.41 | 0.55 | 0.33 | 0.27 | 0.49 |
| Price Range | 47.73-29.17 | 47.73-28.51 | 38.29-28.51 | 39.28-17.00 | 72.95-14.66 | 28.36-16.96 | 22.32-16.15 | 16.34-7.97 |
| P/E Ratio | 19.32-11.81 | 19.09-11.40 | 16.87-12.56 | 41.35-17.89 | 32.28-6.49 | 9.42-5.63 | 7.06-5.11 | 12.20-5.95 |
| Average Yield % | 1.07 | 1.05 | 1.22 | 1.07 | 0.46 | 0.84 | 0.78 | 0.99 |

**Address:** 150 - 6th Avenue S.W., Box 2844, Calgary, T2P 3E3
**Telephone:** 403-296-8000
**Web Site:** www.suncor.com

**Officers:** Richard L. George - President, Chief Executive Officer Steven W. Williams - Chief Operating Officer **Transfer Agents:** Computershare Trust Company of Canada, Calgary, Alberta; Toronto, Ontario; Montreal, Quebec; Vancouver, British Columbia, Canada

**No of Institutions:** 717
**Shares:** 996,374,976 **% Held:** N/A

# TALISMAN ENERGY, INC.

| Exchange | Symbol | Price | 52Wk Range | Yield | P/E |
|---|---|---|---|---|---|
| TSX | TLM | C$16.70 (8/31/2011) | 25.11-15.23 | 1.62 | ... |

***7 Year Price Score 123.37** *NYSE Composite Index=100 ***12 Month Price Score 89.44**

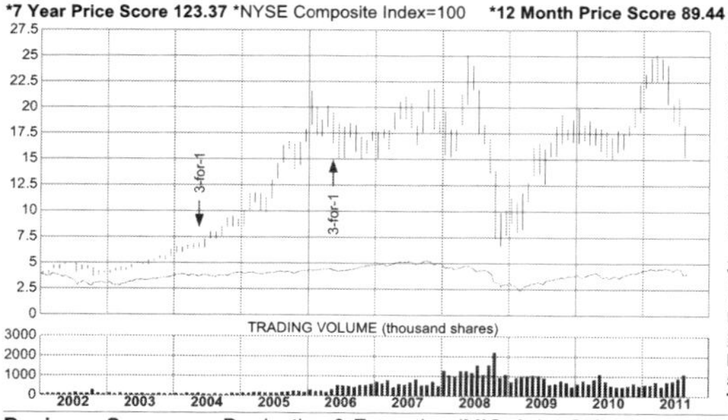


**Interim Earnings (Per Share) Can$**

| Qtr. | Mar | Jun | Sep | Dec |
|---|---|---|---|---|
| 2008 | 0.46 | 0.41 | 1.38 | 1.17 |
| 2009 | 0.45 | 0.06 | 0.03 | (0.11) |
| 2010 | 0.36 | 0.50 | 0.12 | (0.30) |
| 2011 | (0.32) | 0.50 | ... | ... |

**Interim Dividends (Per Share)**

| Amt | Decl | Ex | Rec | Pay |
|---|---|---|---|---|
| 0.113S | 10/05/2009 | 12/09/2009 | 12/11/2009 | 12/31/2009 |
| 0.125S | 05/05/2010 | 06/02/2010 | 06/04/2010 | 06/30/2010 |
| 0.125S | 10/05/2010 | 12/08/2010 | 12/10/2010 | 12/31/2010 |
| 0.135S | 05/04/2011 | 06/01/2011 | 06/03/2011 | 06/30/2011 |

**Indicated Div: $0.27**

**Valuation Analysis**

Forecast EPS $0.85 (09/05/2011)

| Market Cap | C$17.1 Billion | Book Value | $9.6 Billion |
|---|---|---|---|
| Price/Book | 1.78 | Price/Sales | N/A |

**Dividend Achiever Status**

| 5 Year Growth Rate | 17.14% |
|---|---|
| Total Years of Dividend Growth | 8 |

**Business Summary:** Production & Extraction (MIC: 9.1.1 SIC: 1311 NAIC: 213112)

Talisman Energy is engaged in the exploration, development, production and sale of crude oil, natural gas and natural gas liquids. Co. operates mainly in America, which includes operations in Canada and the U.S.; U.K.; Scandinavia; Southeast Asia, which includes exploration and operations in Indonesia, Malaysia, Vietnam and Australia and exploration activities in Papua New Guinea; and other countries, which includes operations in Algeria and exploration activities in Peru, Colombia and the Kurdistan region of northern Iraq. As of Dec 31 2010, total net proved reserves for oil and liquids was 447.6 million barrels and total net proved reserves for natural gas was 4,210.8 billion cubic feet.

**Recent Developments:** For the quarter ended June 30 2011, net income increased 22.0% to US$698.0 million from US$572.0 million in the year-earlier quarter. Revenues were US$2.23 billion, up 39.6% from US$1.60 billion the year before. Operating income was US$1.15 billion versus US$819.0 million in the prior-year quarter, an increase of 40.5%. Indirect operating expenses increased 15.0% to US$1.27 billion from US$1.11 billion in the equivalent prior-year period.

**Prospects:** Our evaluation of Talisman Energy Inc. as of Sep. 6, 2011 is the result of our systematic analysis on three basic characteristics: earnings strength, relative valuation, and recent stock price movement. The company has enjoyed a very positive trend in earnings per share over the past 5 quarters. However, while recent estimates for the company have been lowered by analysts, TLM has posted results that fell short of analysts expectations. Based on operating earnings yield, the company is overvalued when compared to all of the companies in our coverage universe. Share price changes over the past year indicates that TLM will perform in line with the market over the near term.

**Financial Data**

| (Can$ in Thousands) | 6 Mos | 3 Mos | 12/31/2010 | 12/31/2009 | 12/31/2008 | 12/31/2007 | 12/31/2006 | 12/31/2005 |
|---|---|---|---|---|---|---|---|---|
| Earnings Per Share | 0.00 | 0.00 | 0.62 | 0.43 | 3.40 | 1.97 | 1.79 | 1.38 |
| Cash Flow Per Share | ... | ... | 3.40 | 3.55 | 6.03 | 3.94 | 4.01 | 4.41 |
| Tang Book Value Per Share | 8.15 | 7.61 | 9.15 | 9.73 | 9.72 | 6.43 | 5.42 | 3.85 |
| Dividends Per Share | 0.260 | 0.250 | 0.250 | 0.225 | 0.200 | 0.175 | 0.150 | 0.113 |
| Dividend Payout % | ... | ... | 40.32 | 52.33 | 5.88 | 8.88 | 8.38 | 8.21 |
| **Income Statement** | | | | | | | | |
| Total Revenue | 4,234,000 | 2,000,000 | 6,912,000 | 6,488,000 | 9,806,000 | 7,919,000 | 7,944,000 | 8,047,000 |
| EBITDA | ... | 599,000 | 3,463,000 | 2,108,000 | 8,107,000 | 4,333,000 | 5,051,000 | 4,827,000 |
| Depn & Amortn | 948,000 | 469,000 | 2,164,000 | 2,674,000 | 2,979,000 | 2,316,000 | 2,005,000 | 1,843,000 |
| Income Before Taxes | ... | 130,000 | 1,299,000 | (566,000) | 5,128,000 | 2,017,000 | 3,046,000 | 2,984,000 |
| Income Taxes | 909,000 | 456,000 | 891,000 | 142,000 | 1,792,000 | 971,000 | 1,594,000 | 1,423,000 |
| Net Income | 372,000 | (326,000) | 648,000 | 437,000 | 3,519,000 | 2,078,000 | 2,005,000 | 1,561,000 |
| Average Shares | 1,044,000 | 1,022,000 | 1,037,000 | 1,015,000 | 1,034,000 | 1,056,000 | 1,122,000 | 1,131,000 |
| **Balance Sheet** | | | | | | | | |
| Current Assets | 2,669,000 | 3,084,000 | 3,208,000 | 3,154,000 | 2,928,000 | 1,875,000 | 2,075,000 | 1,631,000 |
| Total Assets | 23,037,000 | 22,519,000 | 24,193,000 | 23,618,000 | 24,275,000 | 21,443,000 | 21,461,000 | 18,339,000 |
| Current Liabilities | 3,963,000 | 4,014,000 | 3,401,000 | 2,601,000 | 2,818,000 | 2,329,000 | 3,163,000 | 3,032,000 |
| Long-Term Obligations | 3,851,000 | 3,853,000 | 3,824,000 | 3,770,000 | 3,961,000 | 4,862,000 | 4,560,000 | 4,263,000 |
| Total Liabilities | 13,429,000 | 13,499,000 | 13,714,000 | 12,507,000 | 13,125,000 | 13,480,000 | 14,154,000 | 12,544,000 |
| Stockholders' Equity | 9,608,000 | 9,020,000 | 10,479,000 | 11,111,000 | 11,150,000 | 7,963,000 | 7,307,000 | 5,729,000 |
| Shares Outstanding | 1,024,656 | 1,024,035 | 1,019,290 | 1,014,876 | 1,014,708 | 1,018,590 | 1,063,928 | 1,098,783 |
| **Statistical Record** | | | | | | | | |
| Return on Assets % | ... | ... | 2.71 | 1.82 | 15.35 | 9.69 | 10.08 | 10.15 |
| Return on Equity % | ... | ... | 6.00 | 3.93 | 36.72 | 27.22 | 30.76 | 29.56 |
| EBITDA Margin % | ... | 29.95 | 50.10 | 32.49 | 82.67 | 54.72 | 63.58 | 59.99 |
| Net Margin % | 8.79 | N.M. | 9.38 | 6.74 | 35.89 | 26.24 | 25.24 | 19.40 |
| Asset Turnover | ... | ... | 0.29 | 0.27 | 0.43 | 0.37 | 0.40 | 0.52 |
| Current Ratio | 0.67 | 0.77 | 0.94 | 1.21 | 1.04 | 0.81 | 0.66 | 0.54 |
| Debt to Equity | 0.40 | 0.43 | 0.36 | 0.34 | 0.36 | 0.61 | 0.62 | 0.74 |
| Price Range | 25.11-15.09 | 25.11-15.09 | 22.25-15.09 | 19.33-7.98 | 25.09-6.68 | 21.87-15.09 | 21.61-15.01 | 17.89-8.57 |
| P/E Ratio | ... | ... | 35.89-24.34 | 44.95-18.56 | 7.38-1.96 | 11.10-7.66 | 12.07-8.39 | 12.96-6.21 |
| Average Yield % | 1.29 | 1.24 | 1.42 | 1.56 | 1.22 | 0.94 | 0.86 | 0.86 |

**Address:** Suite 2000, 888-3rd Street S.W., Calgary, T2P 5C5
**Telephone:** 403-920-8285
**Web Site:** www.talisman-energy.com

**Officers:** John A. Manzoni - President, Chief Executive Officer L. Scott Thomson - Executive Vice President, Chief Financial Officer **Transfer Agents:** Computershare Investor Services Inc., Calgary, Alberta, Canada

**No of Institutions:** 306
**Shares:** 730,339,712 **% Held:** 65.91

# TELUS CORP.

| Exchange | Symbol | Price | 52Wk Range | Yield | P/E |
|---|---|---|---|---|---|
| TSX | T | C$53.98 (8/31/2011) | 54.83-42.99 | 4.08 | 15.69 |

*7 Year Price Score 108.82 *NYSE Composite Index=100 *12 Month Price Score 108.93

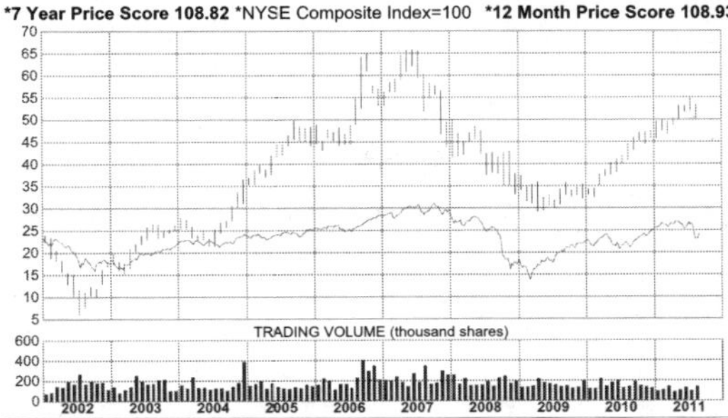


**Interim Earnings (Per Share) Can$**

| Qtr. | Mar | Jun | Sep | Dec |
|---|---|---|---|---|
| 2008 | 0.90 | 0.83 | 0.89 | 0.90 |
| 2009 | 1.01 | 0.77 | 0.87 | 0.49 |
| 2010 | 0.84 | 0.92 | 0.76 | 0.70 |
| 2011 | 1.00 | 0.98 | ... | ... |

**Interim Dividends (Per Share)**

| Amt | Decl | Ex | Rec | Pay |
|---|---|---|---|---|
| 0.525Q | 11/05/2010 | 12/08/2010 | 12/10/2010 | 01/04/2011 |
| 0.525Q | 02/11/2011 | 03/09/2011 | 03/11/2011 | 04/01/2011 |
| 0.55Q | 05/05/2011 | 06/08/2011 | 06/10/2011 | 07/04/2011 |
| 0.55Q | 08/05/2011 | 09/07/2011 | 09/09/2011 | 10/03/2011 |

**Indicated Div: $2.20**

**Valuation Analysis**

| | | | |
|---|---|---|---|
| Forecast EPS | $3.79 (09/02/2011) | | |
| Market Cap | C$17.5 Billion | Book Value | $8.1 Billion |
| Price/Book | 2.17 | Price/Sales | N/A |

**Dividend Achiever Status**

| | |
|---|---|
| **5 Year Growth Rate** | 19.51% |
| **Total Years of Dividend Growth** | 6 |

**Business Summary:** Services (MIC: 6.1.2 SIC: 4813 NAIC: 517110)

TELUS is a telecommunications company. Co. provides a range of wireline and wireless communications products and services including data, voice, entertainment and video. Co. operates two segments: Wireless, which includes digital personal communications services, equipment sales and wireless Internet services; and Wireline, which includes voice local, voice long distance, data including TELUS TV, and other telecommunications services excluding wireless. As of Dec 31 2010, Co. had approximately 12.3 million subscriber connections, including 7.0 million wireless subscribers, 3.7 million wireline network access lines, 1.2 million Internet subscribers and more than 300,000 TELUS TV subscribers.

**Recent Developments:** For the quarter ended June 30 2011, net income increased 7.3% to C$324.0 million from C$302.0 million in the year-earlier quarter. Revenues were C$2.54 billion, up 6.5% from C$2.39 billion the year before. Operating income was C$508.0 million versus C$516.0 million in the prior-year quarter, a decrease of 1.6%. Indirect operating expenses increased 8.6% to C$2.05 billion from C$1.88 billion in the equivalent prior-year period.

**Prospects:** Co.'s top-line results are being positively affected by an increase in wireless revenue as well as higher wireline revenue, both driven by data growth. In view of that, Co. has revised its consolidated revenues guidance range for the full year of 2011 to C$10.23 billion to C$10.43 billion, compared with its previous guidance range of C$9.93 billion to C$10.23 billion. Meanwhile, Co. continues to focus on its business growth by expanding its data and wireless operations. Notably, for the full year of 2011, Co. plans to invest C$650.0 million in Alberta to expand and improve its fourth generation (4G) wireless and wireline networks.

| **Financial Data** (Can$ in Thousands) | 6 Mos | 3 Mos | 12/31/2010 | 12/31/2009 | 12/31/2008 | 12/31/2007 | 12/31/2006 | 12/31/2005 |
|---|---|---|---|---|---|---|---|---|
| Earnings Per Share | 3.44 | 3.38 | 3.22 | 3.14 | 3.51 | 3.76 | 3.23 | 1.94 |
| Cash Flow Per Share | ... | ... | 7.96 | 9.13 | 8.79 | 9.56 | 8.16 | 8.16 |
| Tang Book Value Per Share | N.M. | N.M. | N.M. | N.M. | N.M. | N.M. | 0.72 | 0.32 |
| Dividends Per Share | 2.100 | 2.050 | 2.000 | 1.900 | 1.825 | 1.575 | 1.200 | 0.875 |
| Dividend Payout % | 61.05 | 60.65 | 62.11 | 60.51 | 51.99 | 41.89 | 37.15 | 45.10 |
| **Income Statement** | | | | | | | | |
| Total Revenue | 5,050,000 | 2,506,000 | 9,779,000 | 9,606,000 | 9,653,000 | 9,074,400 | 8,681,000 | 8,142,700 |
| EBITDA | ... | 988,000 | 3,101,000 | 2,927,000 | 3,280,000 | 3,113,100 | 3,057,600 | 2,653,800 |
| Depn & Amortn | (886,000) | 444,000 | 1,735,000 | 1,722,000 | 1,713,000 | 1,615,000 | 1,575,600 | 1,623,700 |
| Income Before Taxes | ... | 438,000 | 1,366,000 | 1,205,000 | 1,567,000 | 1,498,100 | 1,482,000 | 1,030,100 |
| Income Taxes | 200,000 | 110,000 | 328,000 | 203,000 | 436,000 | 233,600 | 351,000 | 322,000 |
| Net Income | 648,000 | 327,000 | 1,038,000 | 1,002,000 | 1,128,000 | 1,257,900 | 1,122,500 | 700,300 |
| Average Shares | 326,000 | 326,000 | 321,000 | 318,000 | 322,000 | 334,200 | 347,400 | 361,000 |
| **Balance Sheet** | | | | | | | | |
| Current Assets | 2,133,000 | 1,931,000 | 1,390,000 | 1,127,000 | 1,558,000 | 1,340,700 | 1,344,900 | 1,242,500 |
| Total Assets | 20,152,000 | 20,053,000 | 19,599,000 | 19,219,000 | 19,160,000 | 16,987,600 | 16,508,200 | 16,222,300 |
| Current Liabilities | 3,981,000 | 4,520,000 | 3,949,000 | 2,964,000 | 3,057,000 | 2,686,000 | 3,738,200 | 2,027,600 |
| Long-Term Obligations | 5,503,000 | 4,910,000 | 5,313,000 | 6,090,000 | 6,348,000 | 4,583,500 | 3,493,700 | 4,639,900 |
| Total Liabilities | 12,093,000 | 12,013,000 | 11,398,000 | 11,644,000 | 11,978,000 | 10,061,400 | 9,580,100 | 9,352,300 |
| Stockholders' Equity | 8,059,000 | 8,040,000 | 8,201,000 | 7,575,000 | 7,182,000 | 6,926,200 | 6,928,100 | 6,870,000 |
| Shares Outstanding | 324,454 | 324,203 | 322,364 | 317,694 | 317,649 | 324,347 | 337,908 | 350,097 |
| **Statistical Record** | | | | | | | | |
| Return on Assets % | ... | ... | 5.35 | 5.22 | 6.22 | 7.51 | 6.86 | 4.11 |
| Return on Equity % | ... | ... | 13.16 | 13.58 | 15.95 | 18.16 | 16.27 | 10.08 |
| EBITDA Margin % | ... | 39.43 | 31.71 | 30.47 | 33.98 | 34.31 | 35.22 | 32.59 |
| Net Margin % | 12.83 | 13.05 | 10.61 | 10.43 | 11.69 | 13.86 | 12.93 | 8.60 |
| Asset Turnover | ... | ... | 0.50 | 0.50 | 0.53 | 0.54 | 0.53 | 0.48 |
| Current Ratio | 0.54 | 0.43 | 0.35 | 0.38 | 0.51 | 0.50 | 0.36 | 0.61 |
| Debt to Equity | 0.68 | 0.61 | 0.65 | 0.80 | 0.88 | 0.66 | 0.50 | 0.68 |
| Price Range | 53.19-40.17 | 49.93-37.15 | 47.71-32.34 | 37.41-29.15 | 49.85-33.00 | 65.86-43.91 | 64.93-43.00 | 49.87-35.30 |
| P/E Ratio | 15.46-11.68 | 14.77-10.99 | 14.82-10.04 | 11.91-9.28 | 14.20-9.40 | 17.52-11.68 | 20.10-13.31 | 25.71-18.20 |
| Average Yield % | 4.50 | 4.71 | 4.93 | 5.76 | 4.34 | 2.75 | 2.37 | 2.06 |

**Address:** Floor 8, 555 Robson Street, Vancouver, V6B 3K9
**Telephone:** 604-432-2151
**Web Site:** telus.com/investors

**Officers:** Brian A. Canfield - Chairman Darren Entwistle - President, Chief Executive Officer
**Transfer Agents:** Computershare Trust Company of Canada, Canada

**Investor Contact:** 604-643-4113
**No of Institutions:** 178
**Shares:** 104,611,176 **% Held:** 31.57

# THOMSON REUTERS CORP

| Exchange | Symbol | Price | 52Wk Range | Yield | P/E |
|---|---|---|---|---|---|
| NYS | TRI | $30.29 (8/31/2011) | 41.49-29.21 | 4.09 | 19.54 |

***7 Year Price Score 93.36** *NYSE Composite Index=100 ***12 Month Price Score 87.70**

**Interim Earnings (Per Share)**

| Qtr. | Mar | Jun | Sep | Dec |
|---|---|---|---|---|
| 2008 | 0.30 | 0.19 | 0.49 | 0.70 |
| 2009 | 0.23 | 0.38 | 0.19 | 0.21 |
| 2010 | 0.15 | 0.35 | 0.32 | 0.26 |
| 2011 | 0.30 | 0.67 | ... | ... |

**Interim Dividends (Per Share)**

| Amt | Decl | Ex | Rec | Pay |
|---|---|---|---|---|
| 0.29Q | 10/28/2010 | 11/16/2010 | 11/18/2010 | 12/15/2010 |
| 0.31Q | 02/10/2011 | 02/17/2011 | 02/22/2011 | 03/15/2011 |
| 0.31Q | 04/28/2011 | 05/17/2011 | 05/19/2011 | 06/15/2011 |
| 0.31Q | 07/28/2011 | 08/16/2011 | 08/18/2011 | 09/15/2011 |

**Indicated Div: $1.24**

**Valuation Analysis**

| | | | |
|---|---|---|---|
| Forecast EPS | $2.00 (09/05/2011) | | |
| Market Cap | $25.3 Billion | Book Value | $20.2 Billion |
| Price/Book | 1.26 | Price/Sales | 1.88 |

**Dividend Achiever Status**

| | |
|---|---|
| **5 Year Growth Rate** | 7.99% |
| **Total Years of Dividend Growth** | 17 |

**Business Summary:** Publishing (MIC: 2.3.3 SIC: 2721 NAIC: 511120)

Thomson Reuters is engaged in the provision of information for the world's businesses and professionals. Co. delivers its insight to the financial, legal, tax and accounting, healthcare, science and media markets. Co.'s businesses are organized into the following two divisions: Professional, which consists of legal, tax and accounting, healthcare and science businesses; and Markets, which consists of financial and media businesses.

**Recent Developments:** For the quarter ended June 30 2011, net income increased 92.6% to US$572.0 million from US$297.0 million in the year-earlier quarter. Revenues were US$3.45 billion, up 7.2% from US$3.22 billion the year before. Operating income was US$833.0 million versus US$435.0 million in the prior-year quarter, an increase of 91.5%. Indirect operating expenses increased 5.6% to US$2.90 billion from US$2.75 billion in the equivalent prior-year period.

**Prospects:** Our evaluation of Thomson Reuters Corp as of Sep. 6, 2011 is the result of our systematic analysis on three basic characteristics: earnings strength, relative valuation, and recent stock price movement. The company has managed to produce a neutral trend in earnings per share over the past 5 quarters and while recent estimates for the company have been mixed, TRI has posted better than expected results. Based on operating earnings yield, the company is about fairly valued when compared to all of the companies in our coverage universe. Share price changes over the past year indicates that TRI will perform poorly over the near term.

**Financial Data**

| (US$ in Thousands) | 6 Mos | 3 Mos | 12/31/2010 | 12/31/2009 | 12/31/2008 | 12/31/2007 | 12/31/2006 |
|---|---|---|---|---|---|---|---|
| Earnings Per Share | 1.55 | 1.23 | 1.08 | 1.01 | 1.68 | 6.20 | 1.73 |
| Cash Flow Per Share | ... | ... | 3.19 | 3.21 | 3.57 | 2.83 | 3.30 |
| Tang Book Value Per Share | N.M. | N.M. | N.M. | N.M. | N.M. | 4.83 | 0.56 |
| Dividends Per Share | 1.200 | 1.180 | 1.160 | 1.120 | 1.080 | 0.930 | 0.880 |
| Dividend Payout % | 77.42 | 95.93 | 107.41 | 110.89 | 64.28 | 15.81 | 50.87 |
| **Income Statement** | | | | | | | |
| Total Revenue | 6,777,000 | 3,330,000 | 13,070,000 | 12,997,000 | 11,707,000 | 7,296,000 | 6,641,000 |
| EBITDA | ... | ... | 3,036,000 | 2,519,000 | 3,390,000 | 7,262,000 | 6,642,000 |
| Depn & Amortn | 837,000 | 415,000 | 1,574,000 | 1,556,000 | 1,321,000 | 724,000 | 681,000 |
| Income Before Taxes | ... | ... | 1,056,000 | 531,000 | 1,680,000 | 6,526,000 | 5,740,000 |
| Income Taxes | 226,000 | 52,000 | 139,000 | (299,000) | 350,000 | 155,000 | 119,000 |
| Net Income | 813,000 | 250,000 | 909,000 | 844,000 | 1,307,000 | 4,004,000 | 1,120,000 |
| Average Shares | 839,846 | 839,706 | 836,447 | 832,942 | 775,179 | 644,430 | 646,026 |
| **Balance Sheet** | | | | | | | |
| Current Assets | 4,269,000 | 3,693,000 | 3,659,000 | 3,663,000 | 3,686,000 | 9,678,000 | 3,265,000 |
| Total Assets | 35,984,000 | 35,541,000 | 35,531,000 | 34,573,000 | 34,589,000 | 22,831,000 | 20,132,000 |
| Current Liabilities | 4,695,000 | 4,731,000 | 5,011,000 | 4,712,000 | 4,645,000 | 3,239,000 | 3,739,000 |
| Long-Term Obligations | 6,955,000 | 6,931,000 | 6,873,000 | 6,821,000 | 6,783,000 | 4,264,000 | 3,681,000 |
| Total Liabilities | 15,831,000 | 15,916,000 | 16,209,000 | 15,306,000 | 16,173,000 | 9,260,000 | 9,651,000 |
| Stockholders' Equity | 20,153,000 | 19,625,000 | 19,322,000 | 19,267,000 | 18,416,000 | 13,571,000 | 10,481,000 |
| Shares Outstanding | 836,797 | 835,647 | 833,396 | 829,758 | 827,275 | 638,682 | 640,437 |
| **Statistical Record** | | | | | | | |
| Return on Assets % | 3.76 | 2.97 | 2.59 | 2.44 | ... | 18.64 | 5.66 |
| Return on Equity % | 6.78 | 5.37 | 4.71 | 4.48 | ... | 33.29 | 10.96 |
| EBITDA Margin % | ... | ... | 23.23 | 19.38 | 28.96 | 99.53 | 100.02 |
| Net Margin % | 12.00 | 7.51 | 6.95 | 6.49 | 11.16 | 54.88 | 16.86 |
| Asset Turnover | 0.39 | 0.38 | 0.37 | 0.38 | ... | 0.34 | 0.34 |
| Current Ratio | 0.91 | 0.78 | 0.73 | 0.78 | 0.79 | 2.99 | 0.87 |
| Debt to Equity | 0.35 | 0.35 | 0.36 | 0.35 | 0.37 | 0.31 | 0.35 |
| Price Range | 41.49-35.48 | 41.49-36.15 | 39.90-33.60 | 37.95-28.25 | 40.51-25.86 | 51.25-37.11 | 49.18-39.69 |
| P/E Ratio | 26.77-22.89 | 33.93-29.39 | 36.94-31.11 | 37.57-27.97 | 24.11-15.39 | 8.27-5.99 | 28.43-22.94 |
| Average Yield % | 4.03 | 3.04 | 3.10 | 3.38 | 3.25 | 2.18 | 1.97 |

**Address:** 3 Times Square, New York, NY 10036
**Telephone:** 646-223-4000
**Web Site:** www.thomsonreuters.com

**Officers:** Thomas H. Glocer - Chief Executive Officer Robert D. Daleo - Executive Vice President, Chief Financial Officer **Transfer Agents:** Computershare Trust Company of Canada, Toronto, Montreal, Calgary, Vancouver, Canada

**No of Institutions:** 266
**Shares:** 286,210,656 **% Held:** 32.96

# TOROMONT INDUSTRIES LTD

| Exchange | Symbol | Price | 52Wk Range | Yield | P/E |
|---|---|---|---|---|---|
| TSX | TIH | C$18.10 (8/31/2011) | 20.32-16.12 | 2.43 | 5.76 |

***7 Year Price Score 116.68** *NYSE Composite Index=100 ***12 Month Price Score 98.20**

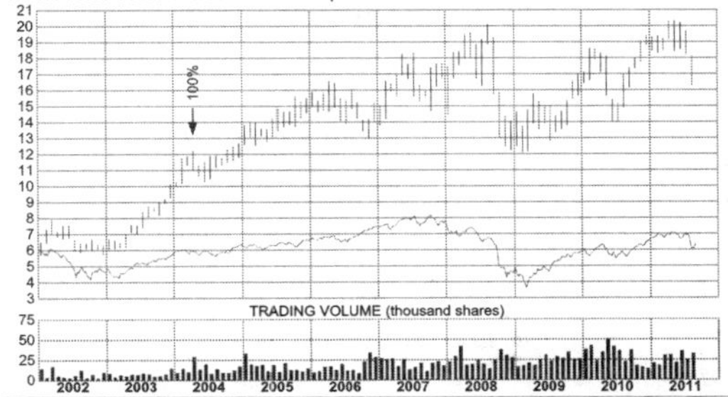


**Interim Earnings (Per Share) Can$**

| Qtr. | Mar | Jun | Sep | Dec |
|---|---|---|---|---|
| 2008 | 0.25 | 0.58 | 0.56 | 0.76 |
| 2009 | 0.37 | 0.51 | 0.50 | 0.48 |
| 2010 | 0.21 | 0.28 | 0.34 | 0.46 |
| 2011 | 0.28 | 2.06 | ... | ... |

**Interim Dividends (Per Share)**

| Amt | Decl | Ex | Rec | Pay |
|---|---|---|---|---|
| 0.16Q | 02/25/2011 | 03/09/2011 | 03/11/2011 | 04/01/2011 |
| 0.10Q | 04/21/2011 | 06/08/2011 | 06/10/2011 | 07/01/2011 |
| 0.00Q | ... | 06/03/2011 | 06/07/2011 | 06/08/2011 |
| 0.11Q | 08/12/2011 | 09/13/2011 | 09/15/2011 | 10/03/2011 |

**Indicated Div: $0.44**

**Valuation Analysis**

| | | | |
|---|---|---|---|
| Forecast EPS | $1.18 (09/05/2011) | | |
| Market Cap | C$1.4 Billion | Book Value | $369.2 Million |
| Price/Book | 3.79 | Price/Sales | 0.62 |

**Dividend Achiever Status**

| | |
|---|---|
| **5 Year Growth Rate** | 14.87% |
| **Total Years of Dividend Growth** | 21 |

**Business Summary:** Construction Services (MIC: 7.5.4 SIC: 7353 NAIC: 532412)

Toromont Industries operates through two business segments, the Equipment Group and the Compression Group. The Equipment Group sell, rent and service a range of mobile equipment and industrial engines through its Caterpillar dealership and Battlefield – The CAT Rental Store in Ontario, Manitoba, Newfoundland, and most of Labrador and Nunavut. The Compression Group design, engineer, fabricate, install and service natural gas compression units and hydrocarbon and petrochemical process systems through Enerflex Ltd. and industrial and recreational refrigeration systems through CIMCO Refrigeration Inc.

**Recent Developments:** For the quarter ended June 30 2011, net income increased 628.4% to C$159.7 million from C$21.9 million in the year-earlier quarter. Revenues were C$344.6 million, up 9.3% from C$315.3 million the year before. Operating income was C$34.5 million versus C$30.7 million in the prior-year quarter, an increase of 12.1%. Direct operating expenses rose 7.8% to C$260.9 million from C$242.0 million in the comparable period the year before. Indirect operating expenses increased 15.7% to C$49.3 million from C$42.6 million in the equivalent prior-year period.

**Prospects:** Our evaluation of Toromont Industries Ltd. as of Sep. 6, 2011 is the result of our systematic analysis on three basic characteristics: earnings strength, relative valuation, and recent stock price movement. The company has generated a negative trend in earnings per share over the past 5 quarters and while recent estimates for the company have been mixed, C.TIH has posted better than expected results. Based on operating earnings yield, the company is undervalued when compared to all of the companies in our coverage universe. Share price changes over the past year indicates that C.TIH will perform poorly over the near term.

| **Financial Data** (Can$ in Thousands) | 6 Mos | 3 Mos | 12/31/2010 | 12/31/2009 | 12/31/2008 | 12/31/2007 | 12/31/2006 |
|---|---|---|---|---|---|---|---|
| Earnings Per Share | 3.14 | 1.36 | 1.29 | 1.86 | 2.15 | 1.88 | 1.54 |
| Cash Flow Per Share | ... | ... | 3.36 | 3.03 | 2.53 | 2.74 | 1.49 |
| Tang Book Value Per Share | 4.61 | 8.76 | 8.77 | 12.63 | 11.52 | 9.55 | 8.25 |
| Dividends Per Share | 0.580 | 0.630 | 0.620 | 0.600 | 0.560 | 0.480 | 0.400 |
| Dividend Payout % | 18.47 | 46.32 | 48.06 | 32.26 | 26.05 | 25.53 | 25.97 |
| **Income Statement** | | | | | | | |
| Total Revenue | 606,253 | 588,015 | 2,332,247 | 1,824,592 | 2,121,209 | 1,902,980 | 1,764,833 |
| EBITDA | ... | 57,310 | 175,149 | 188,707 | 263,924 | 249,444 | 214,871 |
| Depn & Amortn | 21,235 | 20,002 | ... | ... | 56,070 | 52,702 | 48,498 |
| Income Before Taxes | ... | 32,695 | 148,073 | 179,892 | 211,100 | 187,411 | 155,263 |
| Income Taxes | 14,387 | 12,538 | 48,393 | 59,376 | 70,247 | 65,131 | 55,842 |
| Net Income | 181,306 | 21,841 | 98,650 | 120,516 | 140,524 | 122,280 | 99,421 |
| Average Shares | 77,601 | 77,492 | 76,361 | 64,830 | 65,439 | 65,067 | 64,693 |
| **Balance Sheet** | | | | | | | |
| Current Assets | 506,663 | 996,761 | 1,143,985 | 882,156 | 1,073,288 | 939,722 | 893,214 |
| Total Assets | 823,873 | 2,164,335 | 2,269,238 | 1,364,667 | 1,533,450 | 1,356,861 | 1,299,992 |
| Current Liabilities | 287,886 | 557,901 | 624,213 | 342,892 | 564,012 | 472,863 | 423,576 |
| Long-Term Obligations | 133,046 | 368,099 | 413,040 | 144,051 | 158,112 | 203,425 | 238,468 |
| Total Liabilities | 454,681 | 961,602 | 1,063,546 | 510,604 | 754,347 | 702,131 | 734,436 |
| Stockholders' Equity | 369,192 | 1,202,733 | 1,205,692 | 854,063 | 779,103 | 654,730 | 565,556 |
| Shares Outstanding | 77,223 | 77,179 | 77,149 | 64,867 | 64,620 | 64,943 | 64,310 |
| **Statistical Record** | | | | | | | |
| Return on Assets % | 15.25 | 4.75 | 5.43 | ... | 9.70 | 9.20 | 8.14 |
| Return on Equity % | 31.47 | 8.96 | 9.58 | ... | 19.55 | 20.04 | 18.98 |
| EBITDA Margin % | ... | 9.75 | 7.51 | 10.34 | 12.44 | 13.11 | 12.18 |
| Net Margin % | 29.91 | 3.71 | 4.23 | 6.61 | 6.62 | 6.43 | 5.63 |
| Asset Turnover | 1.42 | 1.13 | 1.28 | ... | 1.46 | 1.43 | 1.44 |
| Current Ratio | 1.76 | 1.79 | 1.83 | 2.57 | 1.90 | 1.99 | 2.11 |
| Debt to Equity | 0.36 | 0.31 | 0.34 | 0.17 | 0.20 | 0.31 | 0.42 |
| Price Range | 20.32-14.03 | 19.40-14.03 | 19.40-14.03 | 16.99-12.08 | 20.10-12.23 | 18.34-13.75 | 16.57-12.97 |
| P/E Ratio | 6.47-4.47 | 14.26-10.32 | 15.04-10.87 | 9.13-6.50 | 9.35-5.69 | 9.75-7.31 | 10.76-8.42 |
| Average Yield % | 3.38 | 3.77 | 3.65 | 4.17 | 3.33 | 2.94 | 2.68 |

| | | |
|---|---|---|
| **Address:** 3131 Highway 7 West, P.O. Box 5511, Concord, L4K 1B7<br>**Telephone:** 416-667-5511<br>**Web Site:** www.toromont.com | **Officers:** Robert M. Ogilvie - Chairman, Chief Executive Officer Paul R. Jewer - Vice President, Chief Financial Officer **Transfer Agents:** CIBC Mellon Trust Company, Toronto, Ontario, Canada | **Investor Contact:** 416-667-5511<br>**No of Institutions:** N/A<br>**Shares:** N/A **% Held:** N/A |

# TRANSCANADA CORP

| Exchange | Symbol | Price | 52Wk Range | Yield | P/E |
|---|---|---|---|---|---|
| TSX | TRP | C$43.15 (8/31/2011) | 44.83-35.08 | 3.89 | 21.47 |

***7 Year Price Score 119.50** *NYSE Composite Index=100 ***12 Month Price Score 105.93**

**Interim Earnings (Per Share) Can$**

| Qtr. | Mar | Jun | Sep | Dec |
|---|---|---|---|---|
| 2008 | 0.83 | 0.58 | 0.67 | 0.45 |
| 2009 | 0.54 | 0.50 | 0.50 | 0.56 |
| 2010 | 0.43 | 0.41 | 0.54 | 0.38 |
| 2011 | 0.59 | 0.50 | ... | ... |

**Interim Dividends (Per Share)**

| Amt | Decl | Ex | Rec | Pay |
|---|---|---|---|---|
| 0.40Q | 11/03/2010 | 12/29/2010 | 12/31/2010 | 01/31/2011 |
| 0.42Q | 02/15/2011 | 03/29/2011 | 03/31/2011 | 04/29/2011 |
| 0.42Q | 04/29/2011 | 06/28/2011 | 06/30/2011 | 07/29/2011 |
| 0.42Q | 07/28/2011 | 09/28/2011 | 09/30/2011 | 10/31/2011 |

**Indicated Div: $1.68**

**Valuation Analysis**

| | | | |
|---|---|---|---|
| Forecast EPS | $2.21 (09/05/2011) | | |
| Market Cap | C$30.3 Billion | Book Value | $17.1 Billion |
| Price/Book | 1.78 | Price/Sales | N/A |

**Dividend Achiever Status**

| | |
|---|---|
| 5 Year Growth Rate | 5.57% |
| Total Years of Dividend Growth | 9 |

**Business Summary:** Equipment & Services (MIC: 9.1.3 SIC: 4922 NAIC: 486210)

TransCanada is an energy company. Co. operates three business segments, Natural Gas Pipelines, Oil Pipelines and Energy. The Natural Gas Pipelines segment consists of Co.'s investments in regulated natural gas pipelines and regulated natural gas storage facilities. The Oil Pipelines segment consists of a wholly owned and operated crude oil pipeline extending from Hardisty, Alberta to U.S. markets at Wood River and Patoka in Illinois (Wood River/Patoka) and from Steele City, Nebraska to Cushing, Oklahoma (Cushing Extension). The Energy segment primarily consists of Co.'s investments in electrical power generation plants and non-regulated natural gas storage facilities.

**Recent Developments:** For the quarter ended June 30 2011, net income increased 24.6% to C$395.0 million from C$317.0 million in the year-earlier quarter. Revenues were C$2.14 billion, up 11.4% from C$1.92 billion the year before. Operating income was C$757.0 million versus C$602.0 million in the prior-year quarter, an increase of 25.7%. Direct operating expenses rose 2.8% to C$1.01 billion from C$980.0 million in the comparable period the year before. Indirect operating expenses increased 11.1% to C$379.0 million from C$341.0 million in the equivalent prior-year period.

**Prospects:** Our evaluation of Transcanada Corp. as of Sep. 6, 2011 is the result of our systematic analysis on three basic characteristics: earnings strength, relative valuation, and recent stock price movement. The company has managed to produce a neutral trend in earnings per share over the past 5 quarters. Because the company lacks sufficient analyst estimate data, we place greater weight on the historical EPS trend as the measure of earnings strength. Based on operating earnings yield, the company is about fairly valued when compared to all of the companies in our coverage universe. Share price changes over the past year indicates that TRP will perform very poorly over the near term.

**Financial Data**

| (Can$ in Thousands) | 6 Mos | 3 Mos | 12/31/2010 | 12/31/2009 | 12/31/2008 | 12/31/2007 | 12/31/2006 | 12/31/2005 |
|---|---|---|---|---|---|---|---|---|
| Earnings Per Share | 2.01 | 1.92 | 1.77 | 2.11 | 2.52 | 2.30 | 2.20 | 2.47 |
| Cash Flow Per Share | ... | ... | 4.46 | 4.59 | 4.97 | 5.35 | 4.25 | 3.91 |
| Tang Book Value Per Share | 17.62 | 17.42 | 17.14 | 16.74 | 13.79 | 13.25 | 15.17 | 14.79 |
| Dividends Per Share | 1.640 | 1.620 | 1.600 | 1.520 | 1.440 | 1.360 | 1.280 | 1.220 |
| Dividend Payout % | 81.59 | 84.38 | 90.40 | 72.04 | 57.14 | 59.13 | 58.18 | 49.39 |
| **Income Statement** | | | | | | | | |
| Total Revenue | 4,386,000 | 2,243,000 | 8,064,000 | 8,966,000 | 8,619,000 | 8,828,000 | 7,520,000 | 6,124,000 |
| EBITDA | ... | 1,240,000 | 3,881,000 | 4,258,000 | 3,361,000 | 2,989,000 | 2,664,000 | 2,920,000 |
| Depn & Amortn | 749,000 | 370,000 | 1,354,000 | 1,377,000 | 1,189,000 | 1,179,000 | 1,059,000 | 1,017,000 |
| Income Before Taxes | ... | 643,000 | 1,767,000 | 1,863,000 | 2,172,000 | 1,810,000 | 1,605,000 | 1,903,000 |
| Income Taxes | 317,000 | 178,000 | 380,000 | 387,000 | 602,000 | 490,000 | 476,000 | 610,000 |
| Net Income | 796,000 | 429,000 | 1,272,000 | 1,380,000 | 1,440,000 | 1,223,000 | 1,079,000 | 1,209,000 |
| Average Shares | 703,000 | 699,000 | 691,700 | 652,800 | 571,500 | 532,500 | 490,600 | 489,100 |
| **Balance Sheet** | | | | | | | | |
| Current Assets | 2,754,000 | 2,834,000 | 3,237,000 | 3,175,000 | 3,600,000 | 2,305,000 | 2,092,000 | 1,566,000 |
| Total Assets | 45,887,000 | 45,991,000 | 46,589,000 | 43,841,000 | 39,414,000 | 30,330,000 | 25,909,000 | 24,113,000 |
| Current Liabilities | 4,555,000 | 5,126,000 | 5,661,000 | 4,949,000 | 4,930,000 | 3,035,000 | 2,989,000 | 3,112,000 |
| Long-Term Obligations | 18,438,000 | 18,500,000 | 18,814,000 | 17,975,000 | 17,450,000 | 14,225,000 | 12,023,000 | 10,577,000 |
| Total Liabilities | 28,816,000 | 29,088,000 | 28,705,000 | 26,908,000 | 25,322,000 | 19,546,000 | 17,453,000 | 16,124,000 |
| Stockholders' Equity | 17,071,000 | 16,903,000 | 16,727,000 | 15,759,000 | 12,898,000 | 9,785,000 | 7,701,000 | 7,206,000 |
| Shares Outstanding | 703,000 | 700,000 | 696,230 | 684,359 | 616,471 | 539,765 | 488,975 | 487,236 |
| **Statistical Record** | | | | | | | | |
| Return on Assets % | ... | ... | 2.81 | 3.32 | 4.12 | 4.35 | 4.31 | 5.23 |
| Return on Equity % | ... | ... | 7.83 | 9.63 | 12.66 | 13.99 | 14.48 | 17.56 |
| EBITDA Margin % | ... | 55.28 | 48.13 | 47.49 | 39.00 | 33.86 | 35.43 | 47.68 |
| Net Margin % | 18.15 | 19.13 | 15.77 | 15.39 | 16.71 | 13.85 | 14.35 | 19.74 |
| Asset Turnover | ... | ... | 0.18 | 0.22 | 0.25 | 0.31 | 0.30 | 0.26 |
| Current Ratio | 0.60 | 0.55 | 0.57 | 0.64 | 0.73 | 0.76 | 0.70 | 0.50 |
| Debt to Equity | 1.08 | 1.09 | 1.12 | 1.14 | 1.35 | 1.45 | 1.56 | 1.47 |
| Price Range | 44.83-33.32 | 40.53-32.17 | 38.39-31.85 | 34.37-22.54 | 41.36-24.72 | 43.59-31.79 | 35.34-27.67 | 32.24-23.53 |
| P/E Ratio | 22.30-16.58 | 21.11-16.76 | 21.69-17.99 | 16.29-10.68 | 16.41-9.81 | 18.95-13.82 | 16.06-12.58 | 13.05-9.53 |
| Average Yield % | 4.20 | 4.46 | 4.50 | 5.35 | 4.05 | 3.79 | 4.14 | 4.53 |

**Address:** TransCanada Tower, 450 - 1st Street S.W., Calgary, T2P 5H1
**Telephone:** 403-920-6411
**Web Site:** www.transcanada.com

**Officers:** S. Barry Jackson - Chairman Gregory A. Lohnes - Executive Vice President, Chief Financial Officer **Transfer Agents:**
Computershare Trust Company of Canada, Montreal, Quebec, Canada

**Investor Contact:** 800-361-6522
**No of Institutions:** 314
**Shares:** 362,622,400 **% Held:** 47.80

# TRANSCONTINENTAL INC

| Exchange | Symbol | Price | 52Wk Range | Yield | P/E |
|---|---|---|---|---|---|
| TSX | TCL A | C$14.06 (8/31/2011) | 17.15-12.15 | 3.84 | 9.97 |

***7 Year Price Score 86.94** *NYSE Composite Index=100 ***12 Month Price Score 99.20**

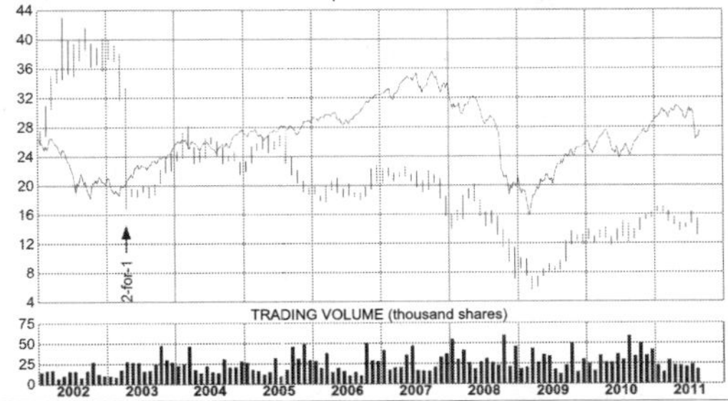


**Interim Earnings (Per Share) Can$**

| Qtr. | Jan | Apr | Jul | Oct |
|---|---|---|---|---|
| 2007-08 | 0.41 | 0.46 | 0.37 | (1.14) |
| 2008-09 | (0.08) | (1.79) | 0.31 | 0.53 |
| 2009-10 | 0.32 | 0.83 | 0.35 | 0.55 |
| 2010-11 | 0.32 | 0.41 | 0.13 | ... |

**Interim Dividends (Per Share)**

| Amt | Decl | Ex | Rec | Pay |
|---|---|---|---|---|
| 0.11Q | 12/10/2010 | 01/05/2011 | 01/07/2011 | 01/21/2011 |
| 0.11Q | 03/09/2011 | 03/31/2011 | 04/04/2011 | 04/21/2011 |
| 0.135Q | 06/08/2011 | 06/29/2011 | 07/04/2011 | 07/22/2011 |
| 0.135Q | 09/07/2011 | 09/29/2011 | 10/03/2011 | 10/21/2011 |

**Indicated Div: $0.54**

**Valuation Analysis**

| | | | |
|---|---|---|---|
| Forecast EPS | $1.89 (09/11/2011) | | |
| Market Cap | C$1.1 Billion | Book Value | $1.3 Billion |
| Price/Book | 0.87 | Price/Sales | N/A |

**Dividend Achiever Status**

| | |
|---|---|
| 5 Year Growth Rate | 10.76% |
| Total Years of Dividend Growth | 9 |

**Business Summary:** Printing (MIC: 7.5.5 SIC: 2711 NAIC: 511110)

Transcontinental provides printing, publishing and marketing services. The Printing Sector include activities such as printing of marketing products, newspapers, flyers, books, catalogues and magazines. The Media Sector publishes consumer magazines, French-language educational resources, and community newspaper, and has a digital platform that delivers content through more than 120 websites. The Marketing Communications Sector provides advertising services and marketing products using communications platforms supported by database analytics, premedia, e-flyers, email marketing and custom communications.

**Recent Developments:** For the quarter ended Apr 30 2011, net income decreased 49.5% to C$34.7 million from C$68.7 million in the year-earlier quarter. Revenues were C$514.7 million, up 0.9% from C$510.0 million the year before. Operating income was C$57.2 million versus C$55.5 million in the prior-year quarter, an increase of 3.1%. Direct operating expenses rose 1.7% to C$362.1 million from C$356.2 million in the comparable period the year before. Indirect operating expenses decreased 3.0% to C$95.4 million from C$98.3 million in the equivalent prior-year period.

**Prospects:** Our evaluation of Transcontinental Inc. as of Sep. 11, 2011 is the result of our systematic analysis on three basic characteristics: earnings strength, relative valuation, and recent stock price movement. The company has generated a negative trend in earnings per share over the past 5 quarters. However, while recent estimates for the company have been lowered by analysts, C.TCL.A has posted results that fell short of analysts expectations. Based on operating earnings yield, the company is undervalued when compared to all of the companies in our coverage universe. Share price changes over the past year indicates that C.TCL.A will perform very well over the near term.

**Financial Data**
**(Can$ in Thousands)**

| | 9 Mos | 6 Mos | 3 Mos | 10/31/2010 | 10/31/2009 | 10/31/2008 | 10/31/2007 | 10/31/2006 |
|---|---|---|---|---|---|---|---|---|
| Earnings Per Share | 1.41 | 1.63 | 2.05 | 2.06 | (1.02) | 0.10 | 1.42 | 1.58 |
| Cash Flow Per Share | 2.90 | 3.35 | 2.01 | 2.03 | 0.98 | 3.50 | 2.84 | 2.45 |
| Tang Book Value Per Share | 5.51 | 5.26 | 4.98 | 3.62 | 2.03 | 1.21 | 0.84 | 1.27 |
| Dividends Per Share | 0.445 | 0.400 | 0.380 | 0.350 | 0.320 | 0.310 | 0.275 | 0.250 |
| Dividend Payout % | 31.56 | 24.54 | 18.54 | 16.99 | ... | 310.00 | 19.37 | 15.82 |
| **Income Statement** | | | | | | | | |
| Total Revenue | 1,506,100 | 1,044,800 | 530,100 | 2,091,600 | 2,294,600 | 2,429,300 | 2,326,200 | 2,196,000 |
| EBITDA | 231,000 | 153,900 | 72,400 | 335,000 | 77,500 | 127,300 | 323,500 | 306,300 |
| Depn & Amortn | 110,000 | 77,200 | 38,500 | 154,100 | 161,700 | 150,800 | 149,000 | 129,500 |
| Income Before Taxes | 121,000 | 76,700 | 33,900 | 180,900 | (84,200) | (23,500) | 174,500 | 176,800 |
| Income Taxes | 25,300 | 13,300 | 5,700 | 34,000 | (2,700) | (31,000) | 53,600 | 38,400 |
| Net Income | 74,900 | 62,600 | 27,900 | 173,400 | (81,800) | 7,900 | 120,600 | 137,900 |
| Average Shares | 81,100 | 81,100 | 81,100 | 80,900 | 80,800 | 81,800 | 85,000 | 87,400 |
| **Balance Sheet** | | | | | | | | |
| Current Assets | 584,500 | 532,000 | 591,300 | 633,000 | 482,600 | 445,800 | 367,900 | 384,300 |
| Total Assets | 2,450,700 | 2,423,700 | 2,528,600 | 2,594,700 | 2,549,700 | 2,620,400 | 2,369,600 | 2,274,700 |
| Current Liabilities | 324,900 | 335,000 | 367,500 | 445,900 | 457,100 | 745,000 | 499,900 | 537,600 |
| Long-Term Obligations | 642,200 | 619,900 | 706,200 | 712,900 | 819,000 | 602,100 | 523,300 | 467,900 |
| Total Liabilities | 1,146,500 | 1,140,100 | 1,265,000 | 1,346,900 | 1,434,400 | 1,513,700 | 1,189,800 | 1,117,600 |
| Stockholders' Equity | 1,303,400 | 1,282,800 | 1,263,300 | 1,247,000 | 1,115,200 | 1,106,600 | 1,177,600 | 1,156,300 |
| Shares Outstanding | 81,021 | 81,021 | 81,000 | 81,003 | 80,794 | 80,778 | 83,614 | 86,047 |
| **Statistical Record** | | | | | | | | |
| Return on Assets % | 4.92 | 5.68 | 6.87 | 6.74 | N.M. | 0.32 | 5.19 | 6.10 |
| Return on Equity % | 9.64 | 11.26 | 14.49 | 14.68 | N.M. | 0.69 | 10.33 | 12.19 |
| EBITDA Margin % | 15.34 | 14.73 | 13.66 | 16.02 | 3.38 | 5.24 | 13.91 | 13.95 |
| Net Margin % | 4.97 | 5.99 | 5.26 | 8.29 | N.M. | 0.33 | 5.18 | 6.28 |
| Asset Turnover | ... | ... | ... | 0.81 | 0.89 | 0.97 | 1.00 | 0.97 |
| Current Ratio | 1.80 | 1.59 | 1.61 | 1.42 | 1.06 | 0.60 | 0.74 | 0.71 |
| Debt to Equity | 0.49 | 0.48 | 0.56 | 0.57 | 0.73 | 0.54 | 0.44 | 0.40 |
| Price Range | 17.15-12.15 | 17.15-11.66 | 17.15-11.66 | 15.45-11.66 | 13.70-5.58 | 20.99-11.24 | 22.75-19.05 | 21.14-17.70 |
| P/E Ratio | 12.16-8.62 | 10.52-7.15 | 8.37-5.69 | 7.50-5.66 | ... | 209.90-112.40 | 16.02-13.42 | 13.38-11.20 |
| Average Yield % | 2.96 | 2.73 | 2.70 | 2.63 | 3.52 | 1.89 | 1.30 | 1.31 |

**Address:** 1, Place Ville Marie, Bureau 3315, Montreal, H3B 3N2
**Telephone:** 514-954-2822
**Web Site:** www.transcontinental.com

**Officers:** Remi Marcoux - Chairman, President, Chief Executive Officer Isabelle Marcoux - Vice-Chairman, Vice President **Transfer Agents:** CIBC Mellon Trust Company, Montreal, Quebec, Canada

**No of Institutions:** N/A
**Shares:** N/A **% Held:** N/A

This page left intentionally blank.

# Non-Liquidity Section

## Companies in this section are those that do not meet the Index methodology.

# Index Description

The Broad Dividend Achievers™ Index is comprised of companies incorporated in the United States or its territories, trade on the NYSE or NASDAQ, and have increased their annual regular dividend payments for the last ten or more consecutive years. In addition, Mergent requires that a stock's average daily cash volume exceed $500,000 per day in the November and December prior to the annual reconstitution date on the last trading date in January. The Index is calculated using a modified market capitalization weighting methodology and has been published by the NYSE or the American Stock Exchange under the ticker symbol DAA since December 5, 2003.

# Index Methodology

**Universe Selection**

Select US companies with at least ten consecutive years of increasing regular dividends. US companies must be listed on the NYSE or NASDAQ. US Companies must have a minimum average daily cash volume of US$500,000 per day for the November and December prior to each Annual Reconstitution Date.

# ARROW FINANCIAL CORP.

| Exchange | Symbol | Price | 52Wk Range | Yield | P/E |
|---|---|---|---|---|---|
| NMS | AROW | $23.71 (8/31/2011) | 28.35-22.14 | 4.22 | 12.22 |

*7 Year Price Score 104.09 *NYSE Composite Index=100 *12 Month Price Score 97.70

**Interim Earnings (Per Share)**

| Qtr. | Mar | Jun | Sep | Dec |
|---|---|---|---|---|
| 2008 | 0.44 | 0.48 | 0.44 | 0.44 |
| 2009 | 0.59 | 0.43 | 0.45 | 0.46 |
| 2010 | 0.48 | 0.50 | 0.50 | 0.46 |
| 2011 | 0.47 | 0.51 | ... | ... |

**Interim Dividends (Per Share)**

| Amt | Decl | Ex | Rec | Pay |
|---|---|---|---|---|
| 0.25Q | 01/26/2011 | 03/01/2011 | 03/03/2011 | 03/15/2011 |
| 0.25Q | 04/27/2011 | 06/01/2011 | 06/03/2011 | 06/15/2011 |
| 0.25Q | 07/27/2011 | 08/31/2011 | 09/02/2011 | 09/15/2011 |
| 3% | 08/31/2011 | 09/19/2011 | 09/21/2011 | 09/29/2011 |

**Indicated Div: $1.00 (Div. Reinv. Plan)**

| Valuation Analysis | | Institutional Holding |
|---|---|---|
| Forecast EPS | $1.80 (09/02/2011) | No of Institutions 75 |
| Market Cap | $274.8 Million | Shares |
| Book Value | $163.6 Million | 5,576,621 |
| Price/Book | 1.68 | % Held |
| Price/Sales | N/A | 37.43 |

**Business Summary:** Banking (MIC: 5.1.1 SIC: 6021 NAIC: 522110)

Arrow Financial is a bank holding company. Through its subsidiaries, Co. provides a range of commercial and consumer banking and financial products. Co. engages in a range of lending activities, including commercial and industrial lending primarily to small and mid-sized companies; mortgage lending for residential and commercial properties; and consumer installment and home equity financing. Co. operates primarily in the northeastern region of New York State in Warren, Washington, Saratoga, Essex and Clinton counties and surrounding areas. As of Dec 31 2010, Co. had total assets of $1.91 billion and total deposits of $1.53 billion.

**Recent Developments:** For the quarter ended June 30 2011, net income increased 2.4% to US$5.8 million from US$5.7 million in the year-earlier quarter. Net interest income decreased 6.9% to US$14.6 million from US$15.7 million in the year-earlier quarter. Provision for loan losses was US$170,000 versus US$375,000 in the prior-year quarter, a decrease of 54.7%. Non-interest income rose 23.9% to US$6.2 million from US$5.0 million, while non-interest expense advanced 1.4% to US$12.2 million.

**Prospects:** Our evaluation of Arrow Financial Corp. as of Sep. 6, 2011 is the result of our systematic analysis on three basic characteristics: earnings strength, relative valuation, and recent stock price movement. The company has produced a positive trend in earnings per share over the past 5 quarters. Because the company lacks sufficient analyst estimate data, we place greater weight on the historical EPS trend as the measure of earnings strength. Based on operating earnings yield, the company is undervalued when compared to all of the companies in our coverage universe. Share price changes over the past year indicates that AROW will perform poorly over the near term.

**Financial Data**

| (US$ in Thousands) | 6 Mos | 3 Mos | 12/31/2010 | 12/31/2009 | 12/31/2008 | 12/31/2007 | 12/31/2006 | 12/31/2005 |
|---|---|---|---|---|---|---|---|---|
| Earnings Per Share | 1.94 | 1.93 | 1.94 | 1.93 | 1.81 | 1.52 | 1.44 | 1.56 |
| Cash Flow Per Share | 2.17 | 2.10 | 0.88 | 1.69 | 2.28 | 1.87 | 2.00 | 2.02 |
| Tang Book Value Per Share | 11.95 | 11.65 | 11.86 | 10.93 | 9.67 | 9.28 | 8.70 | 8.51 |
| Dividends Per Share | 0.993 | 0.985 | 0.978 | 0.950 | 0.924 | 0.885 | 0.859 | 0.817 |
| Dividend Payout % | 51.17 | 50.93 | 50.42 | 49.15 | 51.04 | 58.32 | 59.81 | 52.25 |
| **Income Statement** | | | | | | | | |
| Interest Income | 39,447 | 19,891 | 84,972 | 86,857 | 89,508 | 86,577 | 80,611 | 72,127 |
| Interest Expense | 10,312 | 5,337 | 23,695 | 26,492 | 32,277 | 40,283 | 34,743 | 24,114 |
| Net Interest Income | 29,135 | 14,554 | 61,277 | 60,365 | 57,231 | 46,294 | 45,868 | 48,013 |
| Provision for Losses | 390 | 220 | 1,302 | 1,783 | 1,671 | 513 | 826 | 1,030 |
| Non-Interest Income | 11,848 | 5,620 | 19,089 | 19,592 | 16,269 | 16,288 | 15,781 | 14,948 |
| Non-Interest Expense | 24,490 | 12,319 | 47,418 | 46,592 | 42,393 | 37,930 | 36,807 | 35,189 |
| Income Before Taxes | 16,103 | 7,635 | 31,646 | 31,582 | 29,436 | 24,139 | 24,016 | 26,742 |
| Income Taxes | 4,973 | 2,354 | 9,754 | 9,790 | 8,999 | 6,807 | 7,124 | 8,103 |
| Net Income | 11,130 | 5,281 | 21,892 | 21,792 | 20,437 | 17,332 | 16,892 | 18,639 |
| Average Shares | 11,399 | 11,347 | 11,300 | 11,281 | 11,268 | 11,442 | 11,741 | 11,925 |
| **Balance Sheet** | | | | | | | | |
| Net Loans & Leases | 1,105,276 | 1,120,998 | 1,130,819 | 1,098,136 | 1,096,540 | 1,026,443 | 996,721 | 984,304 |
| Total Assets | 1,901,774 | 1,978,404 | 1,908,336 | 1,841,627 | 1,665,086 | 1,584,846 | 1,520,217 | 1,519,603 |
| Total Deposits | 1,541,859 | 1,608,119 | 1,534,004 | 1,443,566 | 1,275,063 | 1,204,200 | 1,186,397 | 1,165,763 |
| Total Liabilities | 1,738,185 | 1,819,216 | 1,756,077 | 1,700,809 | 1,539,284 | 1,462,590 | 1,402,087 | 1,402,182 |
| Stockholders' Equity | 163,589 | 159,188 | 152,259 | 140,818 | 125,802 | 122,256 | 118,130 | 117,421 |
| Shares Outstanding | 11,591 | 11,524 | 11,388 | 11,353 | 11,318 | 11,391 | 11,637 | 11,759 |
| **Statistical Record** | | | | | | | | |
| Return on Assets % | 1.17 | 1.13 | 1.17 | 1.24 | 1.25 | 1.12 | 1.11 | 1.29 |
| Return on Equity % | 13.84 | 14.27 | 14.94 | 16.35 | 16.43 | 14.42 | 14.34 | 15.83 |
| Net Interest Margin % | 74.56 | 73.17 | 72.11 | 69.50 | 63.94 | 53.47 | 56.90 | 66.57 |
| Efficiency Ratio % | 47.20 | 48.29 | 45.57 | 43.77 | 40.08 | 36.87 | 38.18 | 40.41 |
| Loans to Deposits | 0.72 | 0.70 | 0.74 | 0.76 | 0.86 | 0.85 | 0.84 | 0.84 |
| Price Range | 28.35-21.41 | 28.38-21.41 | 28.38-21.41 | 27.94-18.94 | 27.72-17.09 | 23.03-18.55 | 24.82-21.49 | 26.74-21.05 |
| P/E Ratio | 14.61-11.03 | 14.70-11.09 | 14.63-11.03 | 14.48-9.81 | 15.32-9.44 | 15.15-12.20 | 17.24-14.93 | 17.14-13.49 |
| Average Yield % | 4.01 | 3.92 | 3.89 | 3.91 | 4.21 | 4.29 | 3.68 | 3.39 |

**Address:** 250 Glen Street, Glens Falls, NY 12801
**Telephone:** 518-745-1000

**Web Site:** www.arrowfinancial.com
**Officers:** Thomas L. Hoy - Chairman, President, Chief Executive Officer Thomas J. Murphy - Senior Executive Vice President, Secretary

**Auditors:** KPMG LLP
**Investor Contact:** 518-793-4121
**Transfer Agents:** American Stock Transfer and Trust Company

# ARTESIAN RESOURCES CORP.

| Exchange | Symbol | Price | 52Wk Range | Yield | P/E |
|---|---|---|---|---|---|
| NMS | ARTN A | $18.22 (8/31/2011) | 19.91-17.09 | 4.18 | 20.02 |

***7 Year Price Score 101.21** *NYSE Composite Index=100 ***12 Month Price Score 97.79**

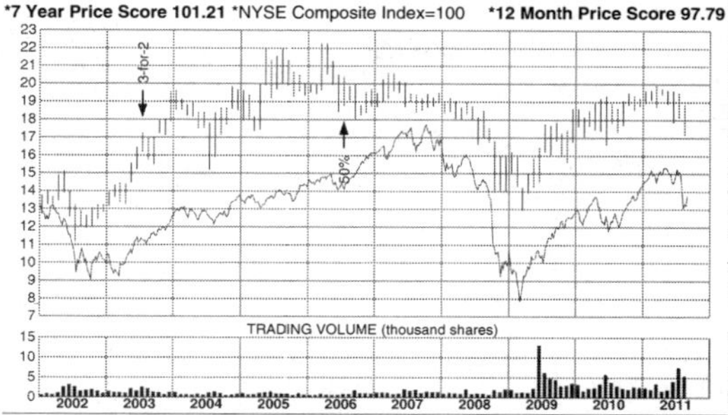


**Interim Earnings (Per Share)**

| Qtr. | Mar | Jun | Sep | Dec |
|---|---|---|---|---|
| 2008 | 0.13 | 0.21 | 0.35 | 0.17 |
| 2009 | 0.22 | 0.27 | 0.28 | 0.21 |
| 2010 | 0.22 | 0.24 | 0.38 | 0.17 |
| 2011 | 0.13 | 0.23 | ... | ... |

**Interim Dividends (Per Share)**

| Amt | Decl | Ex | Rec | Pay |
|---|---|---|---|---|
| 0.189Q | 10/06/2010 | 11/04/2010 | 11/08/2010 | 11/19/2010 |
| 0.189Q | 01/26/2011 | 02/04/2011 | 02/08/2011 | 02/18/2011 |
| 0.19Q | 04/27/2011 | 05/06/2011 | 05/10/2011 | 05/20/2011 |
| 0.19Q | 07/27/2011 | 08/04/2011 | 08/08/2011 | 08/19/2011 |

**Indicated Div: $0.76 (Div. Reinv. Plan)**

| Valuation Analysis | | Institutional Holding |
|---|---|---|
| Forecast EPS | $0.94 (09/02/2011) | No of Institutions 62 |
| Market Cap | $154.5 Million | Shares |
| Book Value | $95.7 Million | 2,329,802 |
| Price/Book | 1.61 | % Held |
| Price/Sales | 2.37 | 31.25 |

**Business Summary:** Water Utilities (MIC: 3.2.1 SIC: 4941 NAIC: 221310)

Artesian Resources is a holding company. Through its subsidiaries, Co. provides water, wastewater and other services on the Delmarva Peninsula. Co. distributes and sells water, including water for public and private fire protection to residential, commercial, industrial, municipal and utility customers throughout Delaware, Maryland and Pennsylvania. Co. also provides wastewater services to customers in Delaware. In addition, Co. provides contract water and wastewater operations, water and sewer Service Line Protection Plans, wastewater management services, and design, construction and engineering services. At Dec 31 2010, Co. had about 78,400 metered customers and 1,131 miles of water main.

**Recent Developments:** For the quarter ended June 30 2011, net income was unchanged at US$1.8 million versus US$1.8 million the year-earlier quarter. Revenues were US$16.5 million, up 3.2% from US$16.0 million the year before. Operating income was unchanged at US$3.6 million versus the prior-year quarter. Direct operating expenses rose 9.0% to US$8.1 million from US$7.5 million in the comparable period the year before. Indirect operating expenses decreased 2.7% to US$4.8 million from US$4.9 million in the equivalent prior-year period.

**Prospects:** Our evaluation of Artesian Resources Corp. as of Sep. 6, 2011 is the result of our systematic analysis on three basic characteristics: earnings strength, relative valuation, and recent stock price movement. The company has produced a positive trend in earnings per share over the past 5 quarters. However, while recent estimates for the company have been mixed, ARTNA has posted better than expected results. Based on operating earnings yield, the company is about fairly valued when compared to all of the companies in our coverage universe. Share price changes over the past year indicates that ARTNA will perform very poorly over the near term.

**Financial Data**
(US$ in Thousands)

| | 6 Mos | 3 Mos | 12/31/2010 | 12/31/2009 | 12/31/2008 | 12/31/2007 | 12/31/2006 | 12/31/2005 |
|---|---|---|---|---|---|---|---|---|
| Earnings Per Share | 0.91 | 0.92 | 1.00 | 0.97 | 0.86 | 0.90 | 0.97 | 0.81 |
| Cash Flow Per Share | 2.41 | 2.37 | 2.40 | 1.79 | 2.47 | 1.71 | 2.10 | 2.32 |
| Tang Book Value Per Share | 11.24 | 12.37 | 12.41 | 12.10 | 11.81 | 11.66 | 10.15 | 9.60 |
| Dividends Per Share | 0.757 | 0.755 | 0.753 | 0.723 | 0.707 | 0.664 | 0.613 | 0.580 |
| Dividend Payout % | 83.16 | 82.04 | 75.29 | 74.48 | 82.23 | 73.78 | 63.24 | 71.37 |
| **Income Statement** | | | | | | | | |
| Total Revenue | 31,267 | 14,757 | 64,885 | 60,912 | 56,185 | 52,524 | 48,587 | 45,285 |
| EBITDA | 10,085 | 4,661 | 21,947 | 21,036 | 18,813 | 17,730 | 17,017 | 15,520 |
| Depn & Amortn | 3,633 | 1,810 | 7,032 | 6,556 | 5,782 | 5,162 | 4,609 | 4,364 |
| Income Before Taxes | 2,762 | 1,009 | 7,620 | 7,262 | 6,418 | 6,263 | 6,071 | 5,035 |
| Net Income | 2,762 | 1,009 | 7,620 | 7,262 | 6,418 | 6,263 | 6,071 | 5,035 |
| Average Shares | 7,714 | 7,699 | 7,618 | 7,512 | 7,427 | 6,936 | 6,235 | 6,181 |
| **Balance Sheet** | | | | | | | | |
| Current Assets | 11,339 | 11,779 | 14,033 | 13,243 | 13,472 | 14,324 | 10,245 | 10,406 |
| Total Assets | 371,813 | 370,299 | 371,529 | 358,895 | 348,706 | 294,589 | 269,360 | 243,854 |
| Current Liabilities | 38,253 | 38,229 | 41,885 | 36,521 | 34,377 | 11,844 | 19,122 | 12,238 |
| Long-Term Obligations | 106,729 | 106,920 | 105,061 | 106,025 | 107,555 | 91,757 | 92,073 | 92,379 |
| Total Liabilities | 276,108 | 275,095 | 276,383 | 267,721 | 260,912 | 209,457 | 207,560 | 186,041 |
| Stockholders' Equity | 95,705 | 95,204 | 95,146 | 91,174 | 87,794 | 85,132 | 61,800 | 57,813 |
| Shares Outstanding | 8,480 | 7,667 | 7,637 | 7,507 | 7,401 | 7,300 | 6,086 | 6,021 |
| **Statistical Record** | | | | | | | | |
| Return on Assets % | 1.90 | 1.92 | 2.09 | 2.05 | 1.99 | 2.22 | 2.37 | 2.14 |
| Return on Equity % | 7.37 | 7.48 | 8.18 | 8.12 | 7.40 | 8.53 | 10.15 | 8.93 |
| EBITDA Margin % | 32.25 | 31.59 | 33.82 | 34.54 | 33.48 | 33.76 | 35.02 | 34.27 |
| Net Margin % | 8.83 | 6.84 | 11.74 | 11.92 | 11.42 | 11.92 | 12.50 | 11.12 |
| Asset Turnover | 0.18 | 0.18 | 0.18 | 0.17 | 0.17 | 0.19 | 0.19 | 0.19 |
| Current Ratio | 0.30 | 0.31 | 0.34 | 0.36 | 0.39 | 1.21 | 0.54 | 0.85 |
| Debt to Equity | 1.12 | 1.12 | 1.10 | 1.16 | 1.23 | 1.08 | 1.49 | 1.60 |
| Price Range | 19.91-17.31 | 19.91-16.61 | 19.50-16.61 | 18.61-12.95 | 19.24-13.95 | 20.60-18.41 | 22.27-18.03 | 21.99-17.35 |
| P/E Ratio | 21.88-19.02 | 21.64-18.05 | 19.50-16.61 | 19.19-13.35 | 22.37-16.22 | 22.89-20.46 | 22.96-18.59 | 27.15-21.42 |
| Average Yield % | 4.01 | 4.06 | 4.12 | 4.53 | 4.08 | 3.43 | 3.12 | 2.95 |

**Address:** 664 Churchmans Road, Newark, DE 19702
**Telephone:** 302-453-6900
**Fax:** 302-453-6957

**Web Site:** www.artesianwater.com
**Officers:** Dian C. Taylor - Chairperson, President, Chief Executive Officer Joseph A. DiNunzio - Executive Vice President, Corporate Secretary

**Auditors:** BDO USA, LLP
**Investor Contact:** 302-453-6943
**Transfer Agents:** Registrar and Transfer Company, Cranford, NJ

# BOWL AMERICA INC.

| Exchange | Symbol | Price | 52Wk Range | Yield | P/E |
|---|---|---|---|---|---|
| ASE | BWL A | $12.55 (8/31/2011) | 15.02-11.14 | 5.10 | 40.48 |

***7 Year Price Score 91.82** *NYSE Composite Index=100 ***12 Month Price Score 98.35**

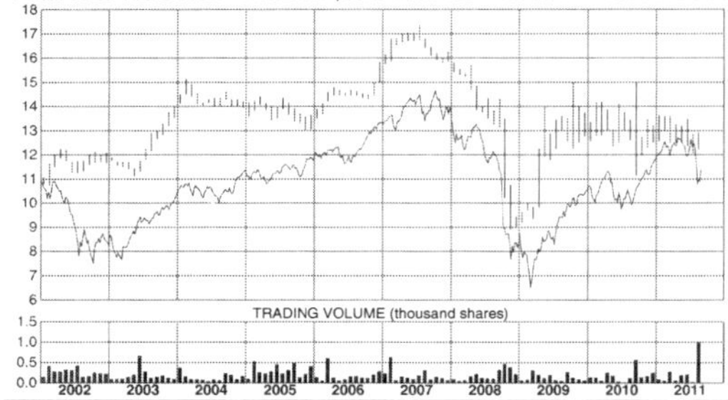


**Interim Earnings (Per Share)**

| Qtr. | Sep | Dec | Mar | Jun |
|---|---|---|---|---|
| 2007-08 | 0.05 | 0.22 | 0.31 | 0.11 |
| 2008-09 | 0.02 | 0.15 | 0.35 | 0.08 |
| 2009-10 | 0.00 | 0.08 | 0.24 | 0.04 |
| 2010-11 | (0.04) | 0.06 | 0.25 | ... |

**Interim Dividends (Per Share)**

| Amt | Decl | Ex | Rec | Pay |
|---|---|---|---|---|
| 0.155Q | 09/24/2010 | 10/15/2010 | 10/19/2010 | 11/10/2010 |
| 0.16Q | 12/07/2010 | 01/06/2011 | 01/10/2011 | 02/09/2011 |
| 0.16Q | 03/22/2011 | 04/12/2011 | 04/14/2011 | 05/11/2011 |
| 0.16Q | 06/21/2011 | 07/22/2011 | 07/26/2011 | 08/17/2011 |

**Indicated Div: $0.64**

| Valuation Analysis | | Institutional Holding |
|---|---|---|
| Forecast EPS | N/A | No of Institutions 18 |
| Market Cap | $64.6 Million | Shares |
| Book Value | $35.7 Million | 871,316 |
| Price/Book | 1.81 | % Held |
| Price/Sales | 2.46 | 16.27 |

**Business Summary:** Sporting & Recreational (MIC: 2.2.4 SIC: 7933 NAIC: 713950)

Bowl America is engaged in the entertainment business. As of Sept 1 2010 Co. operated 10 bowling centers in the greater metropolitan area of Washington, D.C., one bowling center in the greater metropolitan area of Baltimore, MD, one bowling center in Orlando, FL, three bowling centers in the greater metropolitan area of Jacksonville, FL, and four bowling centers in the greater metropolitan area of Richmond, VA. These establishments are fully air-conditioned with facilities for service of food and beverages, game rooms, rental lockers, and meeting room facilities. All centers provide shoes for rental, and bowling balls are provided free. In addition, each center retails bowling accessories.

**Recent Developments:** For the quarter ended Mar 27 2011, net income increased 5.7% to US$1.3 million from US$1.2 million in the year-earlier quarter. Revenues were US$8.3 million, unchanged from the year before. Operating income was US$1.9 million versus US$1.7 million in the prior-year quarter, an increase of 9.1%. Direct operating expenses declined 3.4% to US$2.6 million from US$2.7 million in the comparable period the year before. Indirect operating expenses decreased 2.1% to US$3.8 million from US$3.9 million in the equivalent prior-year period.

**Prospects:** Our evaluation of Bowl America Inc. as of Sep. 6, 2011 is the result of our systematic analysis on three basic characteristics: earnings strength, relative valuation, and recent stock price movement. The company has enjoyed a very positive trend in earnings per share over the past 5 quarters. Because the company lacks sufficient analyst estimate data, we place greater weight on the historical EPS trend as the measure of earnings strength. Based on operating earnings yield, the company is overvalued when compared to all of the companies in our coverage universe. Share price changes over the past year indicates that BWL.A will perform very poorly over the near term.

**Financial Data**

| (US$ in Thousands) | 9 Mos | 6 Mos | 3 Mos | 06/27/2010 | 06/28/2009 | 06/29/2008 | 07/01/2007 | 07/02/2006 |
|---|---|---|---|---|---|---|---|---|
| Earnings Per Share | 0.31 | 0.30 | 0.32 | 0.36 | 0.60 | 0.69 | 0.82 | 0.71 |
| Cash Flow Per Share | 0.63 | 0.58 | 0.63 | 0.57 | 1.27 | 0.68 | 1.19 | 0.84 |
| Tang Book Value Per Share | 6.93 | 6.85 | 6.93 | 7.07 | 7.31 | 7.44 | 7.66 | 7.22 |
| Dividends Per Share | 0.625 | 0.620 | 0.620 | 0.620 | 0.605 | 0.690 | 0.570 | 0.560 |
| Dividend Payout % | 201.61 | 206.67 | 193.75 | 172.22 | 100.83 | 100.00 | 69.51 | 78.87 |
| **Income Statement** | | | | | | | | |
| Total Revenue | 20,405 | 12,130 | 5,650 | 27,127 | 29,711 | 30,104 | 31,974 | 30,320 |
| EBITDA | 2,989 | 664 | (29) | 4,020 | 5,741 | 6,390 | 7,423 | 6,599 |
| Depn & Amortn | 1,305 | 868 | 436 | 1,687 | 1,727 | 1,764 | 1,919 | 1,666 |
| Income Before Taxes | 2,132 | 126 | (320) | 2,863 | 4,694 | 5,437 | 6,369 | 5,589 |
| Income Taxes | 768 | 45 | (115) | 1,012 | 1,636 | 1,902 | 2,180 | 1,949 |
| Net Income | 1,365 | 81 | (205) | 1,851 | 3,057 | 3,535 | 4,189 | 3,640 |
| Average Shares | 5,146 | 5,146 | 5,146 | 5,141 | 5,133 | 5,135 | 5,136 | 5,136 |
| **Balance Sheet** | | | | | | | | |
| Current Assets | 12,587 | 11,153 | 10,944 | 11,311 | 12,410 | 11,558 | 13,207 | 10,860 |
| Total Assets | 43,013 | 41,750 | 41,205 | 41,410 | 42,967 | 44,057 | 45,835 | 43,130 |
| Current Liabilities | 4,997 | 4,163 | 3,220 | 2,890 | 3,167 | 3,170 | 3,062 | 3,240 |
| Total Liabilities | 7,333 | 6,511 | 5,515 | 5,007 | 5,387 | 5,842 | 6,497 | 6,041 |
| Stockholders' Equity | 35,680 | 35,239 | 35,691 | 36,404 | 37,579 | 38,215 | 39,337 | 37,089 |
| Shares Outstanding | 5,146 | 5,146 | 5,146 | 5,146 | 5,141 | 5,135 | 5,135 | 5,136 |
| **Statistical Record** | | | | | | | | |
| Return on Assets % | ... | ... | ... | 4.40 | 7.05 | 7.89 | 9.44 | 8.52 |
| Return on Equity % | ... | ... | ... | 5.02 | 8.09 | 9.14 | 10.99 | 9.96 |
| EBITDA Margin % | 14.65 | 5.47 | N.M. | 14.82 | 19.32 | 21.23 | 23.22 | 21.76 |
| Net Margin % | 6.69 | 0.66 | N.M. | 6.82 | 10.29 | 11.74 | 13.10 | 12.00 |
| Asset Turnover | 0.60 | 0.62 | 0.64 | 0.64 | 0.68 | 0.67 | 0.72 | 0.71 |
| Current Ratio | 2.52 | 2.68 | 3.40 | 3.91 | 3.92 | 3.65 | 4.31 | 3.35 |
| Price Range | 15.02-11.14 | 15.02-11.14 | 15.02-11.14 | 14.99-12.07 | 14.35-8.90 | 17.35-13.75 | 17.05-14.31 | 14.79-13.03 |
| P/E Ratio | 48.45-35.94 | 50.07-37.13 | 46.94-34.81 | 41.64-33.53 | 23.92-14.83 | 25.14-19.93 | 20.79-17.45 | 20.83-18.35 |
| Average Yield % | 4.83 | 4.78 | 4.74 | 4.76 | 5.35 | 4.42 | 3.64 | 4.02 |

**Address:** 6446 Edsall Road, Alexandria, VA 22312
**Telephone:** 703-941-6300

**Web Site:** www.bowlamericainc.com
**Officers:** Leslie H. Goldberg - President, Chief Executive Officer Ruth E. Macklin - Senior Vice President, Treasurer

**Auditors:** Aronson & Company
**Transfer Agents:** American Stock Transfer & Trust Co.

# CAMBRIDGE BANCORP

| Exchange | Symbol | Price | 52Wk Range | Yield | P/E |
|---|---|---|---|---|---|
| OTC | CATC | $34.10 (8/31/2011) | 37.00-31.25 | 4.11 | 9.72 |

***7 Year Price Score 115.00** *NYSE Composite Index=100 ***12 Month Price Score 104.28**

**Interim Earnings (Per Share)**

| Qtr. | Mar | June | Sept | Dec |
|---|---|---|---|---|
| 2009 | 0.54 | 0.67 | 0.84 | 0.70 |
| 2010 | 0.73 | 1.24 | 0.84 | 0.70 |

**Interim Dividends (Per Share)**

| Amt | Decl | Ex | Rec | Pay |
|---|---|---|---|---|
| 0.35Q | 11/16/2010 | 12/08/2010 | 12/10/2010 | 01/03/2011 |
| 0.35Q | 02/23/2011 | 03/08/2011 | 03/10/2011 | 04/01/2011 |
| 0.35Q | 05/17/2011 | 06/08/2011 | 06/10/2011 | 07/01/2011 |
| 0.35Q | 08/15/2011 | 09/08/2011 | 09/12/2011 | 10/03/2011 |

**Indicated Div: $1.40**

| Valuation Analysis | | Institutional Holding |
|---|---|---|
| Forecast EPS | N/A | No of Institutions |
| | | N/A |
| Market Cap | $128.2 Million | Shares |
| Book Value | $89.2 Million | N/A |
| Price/Book | 1.44 | % Held |
| Price/Sales | 1.93 | N/A |

**Business Summary:** Banking (MIC: 5.1.1 SIC: 6035 NAIC: 522120)

Cambridge Bancorp is a bank holding company for Cambridge Trust Company (the Bank). The Bank provides a range of commercial and consumer banking services through its network of banking offices in Massachusetts. The Bank is engaged principally in the business of accepting deposits from the public and investing those deposits. The Bank invests those funds in various types of loans, including residential, commercial real estate, and a variety of commercial and consumer loans. The Bank also invests its deposits and borrowed funds in investment securities. As of Dec 31 2010, Co. had total assets of $1.13 billion and total deposits of $993.8 million.

**Recent Developments:** For the year ended Dec 31 2010, net income increased 29.0% to US$13.3 million from US$10.3 million in the prior year. Net interest income increased 7.0% to US$41.8 million from US$39.0 million in the prior year. Provision for loan losses was US$550,000 versus US$1.2 million in the prior year, a decrease of 54.2%. Non-interest income rose 19.6% to US$19.9 million from US$16.6 million, while non-interest expense advanced 4.6% to US$41.4 million.

**Prospects:** Co. is experiencing a decrease in its bottom-line results primarily attributable to the sale of its Cambridge Trust Company (the Bank) subsidiary's Merchant Services portfolio during the second quarter of 2010. Nevertheless, Co. noted an increase in net interest income driven by growth in commercial and residential mortgage loans. Notably, Co. stated that while ongoing low interest rates continue to put pressure on the Bank's net interest margin, total loans outstanding has increased from the prior year, with growth primarily from a combination of commercial loan and residential mortgage loans. In addition, Co. is seeing an increase in fee income from its Wealth Management segment.

**Financial Data**

| (US$ in Thousands) | 12/31/2010 | 12/31/2009 | 12/31/2008 | 12/31/2007 | 12/31/2006 | 12/31/2005 | 12/31/2004 | 12/31/2003 |
|---|---|---|---|---|---|---|---|---|
| Earnings Per Share | 3.51 | 2.75 | 2.56 | 2.41 | 2.24 | 1.94 | 2.04 | 1.49 |
| Cash Flow Per Share | 3.67 | 2.62 | 3.39 | 3.19 | 2.84 | 2.44 | 1.88 | 4.34 |
| Tang Book Value Per Share | 23.73 | 21.95 | 20.29 | 18.49 | 16.44 | 15.65 | 15.66 | 15.24 |
| Dividends Per Share | 1.400 | 1.340 | 1.280 | 1.180 | 1.060 | 1.010 | 0.940 | 0.880 |
| Dividend Payout % | 39.89 | 48.73 | 50.00 | 48.96 | 47.32 | 52.06 | 46.08 | 59.06 |
| **Income Statement** | | | | | | | | |
| Interest Income | 46,556 | 46,158 | 44,783 | 42,547 | 39,019 | 34,685 | 31,243 | 30,471 |
| Interest Expense | 4,806 | 7,149 | 10,447 | 11,953 | 8,587 | 4,564 | 2,836 | 3,737 |
| Net Interest Income | 41,750 | 39,009 | 34,336 | 30,594 | 30,432 | 30,121 | 28,407 | 26,734 |
| Provision for Losses | 550 | 1,200 | 1,000 | 700 | 265 | 200 | 475 | 700 |
| Non-Interest Income | 19,877 | 16,618 | 16,848 | 17,061 | 15,882 | 14,664 | 19,404 | 17,136 |
| Non-Interest Expense | 41,444 | 39,627 | 36,267 | 33,583 | 33,166 | 32,638 | 34,472 | 34,320 |
| Income Before Taxes | 19,633 | 14,800 | 13,917 | 13,372 | 12,883 | 11,947 | 12,864 | 8,850 |
| Income Taxes | 6,379 | 4,523 | 4,304 | 4,129 | 4,203 | 4,224 | 4,680 | 2,747 |
| Net Income | 13,254 | 10,277 | 9,613 | 9,243 | 8,680 | 7,723 | 8,184 | 6,103 |
| Average Shares | 3,776 | 3,739 | 3,758 | 3,837 | 3,875 | 3,989 | 4,012 | 4,107 |
| **Balance Sheet** | | | | | | | | |
| Net Loans & Leases | 559,683 | 529,204 | 464,118 | 412,089 | 350,009 | 326,736 | 287,257 | 281,985 |
| Total Assets | 1,130,988 | 1,018,949 | 917,212 | 849,588 | 773,013 | 743,124 | 723,195 | 693,187 |
| Total Deposits | 993,808 | 872,767 | 767,654 | 698,625 | 663,437 | 663,150 | 648,741 | 606,648 |
| Total Liabilities | 1,041,770 | 937,241 | 841,168 | 779,896 | 709,760 | 682,708 | 661,670 | 633,582 |
| Stockholders' Equity | 89,218 | 81,708 | 76,044 | 69,692 | 63,253 | 60,416 | 61,525 | 59,605 |
| Shares Outstanding | 3,759 | 3,722 | 3,748 | 3,768 | 3,848 | 3,861 | 3,929 | 3,911 |
| **Statistical Record** | | | | | | | | |
| Return on Assets % | 1.23 | 1.06 | 1.09 | 1.14 | 1.15 | 1.05 | 1.15 | 0.90 |
| Return on Equity % | 15.51 | 13.03 | 13.16 | 13.90 | 14.04 | 12.67 | 13.48 | 10.28 |
| Net Interest Margin % | 89.68 | 84.51 | 76.67 | 71.91 | 77.99 | 86.84 | 90.92 | 87.74 |
| Efficiency Ratio % | 62.38 | 63.12 | 58.85 | 56.34 | 60.41 | 66.14 | 68.06 | 72.09 |
| Loans to Deposits | 0.56 | 0.61 | 0.60 | 0.59 | 0.53 | 0.49 | 0.44 | 0.46 |
| Price Range | 34.65-28.50 | 31.45-20.00 | 30.04-23.01 | 33.30-27.00 | 29.95-25.65 | 33.80-26.57 | 32.75-29.20 | 35.00-30.25 |
| P/E Ratio | 9.87-8.12 | 11.44-7.27 | 11.73-8.99 | 13.82-11.20 | 13.37-11.45 | 17.42-13.70 | 16.05-14.31 | 23.49-20.30 |
| Average Yield % | 4.42 | 5.31 | 4.71 | 3.98 | 3.90 | 3.37 | 3.05 | 2.75 |

**Address:** 1336 Massachusetts Avenue, Cambridge, MA 02138
**Telephone:** 617-876-2790
**Fax:** 617-441-1421

**Web Site:** www.cambridgetrust.com
**Officers:** Joseph V. Roller - President, Chief Executive Officer

**Auditors:** KMPG LLP
**Investor Contact:** 617-441-1516
**Transfer Agents:** American Stock Transfer and Trust Company LLC, Brooklyn, NY

# CCFNB BANCORP INC.

| Exchange | Symbol | Price | 52Wk Range | Yield | P/E |
|---|---|---|---|---|---|
| OTC | CCFN | $35.00 (8/31/2011) | 37.75-26.45 | 3.54 | 11.90 |

***7 Year Price Score 116.87** *NYSE Composite Index=100 ***12 Month Price Score 111.58**

**Interim Earnings (Per Share)**

| Qtr. | Mar | Jun | Sep | Dec |
|---|---|---|---|---|
| 2009 | 0.69 | 0.68 | 0.65 | 0.59 |
| 2010 | 0.69 | 0.74 | 0.76 | 0.63 |
| 2011 | 0.72 | 0.83 | ... | ... |

**Interim Dividends (Per Share)**

| Amt | Decl | Ex | Rec | Pay |
|---|---|---|---|---|
| 0.30Q | ... | 12/03/2010 | 12/07/2010 | 12/23/2010 |
| 0.31Q | ... | 02/25/2011 | 03/01/2011 | 03/24/2011 |
| 0.31Q | 05/10/2011 | 05/20/2011 | 05/24/2011 | 06/16/2011 |
| 0.31Q | 08/23/2011 | 09/01/2011 | 09/06/2011 | 09/22/2011 |

**Indicated Div: $1.24**

| **Valuation Analysis** | | **Institutional Holding** |
|---|---|---|
| Forecast EPS | N/A | No of Institutions 5 |
| Market Cap | $78.0 Million | Shares 104,632 |
| Book Value | $70.4 Million | |
| Price/Book | 1.11 | % Held |
| Price/Sales | N/A | 3.25 |

**Business Summary:** Banking (MIC: 5.1.1 SIC: 6022 NAIC: 522110)

CCFNB Bancorp is a bank and financial holding company for First Columbia Bank & Trust Co. (the Bank). The Bank is a commercial bank providing a range of services and products, including time and demand deposit accounts, consumer, commercial and mortgage loans to individuals and small to medium-sized businesses in its Northcentral Pennsylvania market area. As of Dec 31 2010, the Bank had 14 branch banking offices which are located in the Pennsylvania counties of Columbia, Luzerne, and Northumberland. Also, Co. holds a 50% interest in a local insurance agency, Neighborhood Group, Inc., which sells insurance products and services. As of the date above, Co. had total assets of $614.3 million.

**Recent Developments:** For the quarter ended June 30 2011, net income increased 10.8% to US$1.8 million from US$1.7 million in the year-earlier quarter. Net interest income decreased 3.5% to US$4.9 million from US$5.1 million in the year-earlier quarter. Provision for loan losses was US$330,000 versus US$160,000 in the prior-year quarter, an increase of 106.3%. Non-interest income rose 42.8% to US$2.0 million from US$1.4 million, while non-interest expense advanced 1.9% to US$4.1 million.

**Prospects:** Co.'s near-term outlook appears somewhat uncertain. On one hand, Co. continues to experience a decline in its net interest income as a result of lower interest income due to maturing and called investment securities re-priced throughout the previous year. Further, Co. is seeing a decrease in its net interest margin, attributable to unfavorable yield on investment securities and loans, partially offset by lower deposit yields and other borrowings. On the other hand, Co. is encouraged by the improvement in its non-interest income, resulting from elevated gains on sale of loans and trust income, partially offset by the decline in service charges and fees and lower brokerage income.

**Financial Data**
(US$ in Thousands)

| | 6 Mos | 3 Mos | 12/31/2010 | 12/31/2009 | 12/31/2008 | 12/31/2007 | 12/31/2006 |
|---|---|---|---|---|---|---|---|
| Earnings Per Share | 2.94 | 2.85 | 2.82 | 2.61 | 1.82 | 2.15 | 1.93 |
| Cash Flow Per Share | 3.92 | 3.83 | 3.83 | 2.87 | 3.23 | 2.01 | ... |
| Tang Book Value Per Share | 27.18 | 26.25 | 25.93 | 24.19 | 21.94 | 24.97 | ... |
| Dividends Per Share | 1.220 | 1.200 | 1.180 | 1.030 | 0.900 | 0.820 | 0.780 |
| Dividend Payout % | 41.50 | 42.11 | 41.84 | 39.46 | 49.45 | 38.14 | 40.41 |
| **Income Statement** | | | | | | | |
| Total Revenue | 15,979 | 7,760 | 32,899 | 33,485 | 24,400 | 16,788 | 15,102 |
| Income Before Taxes | 4,628 | 2,165 | 8,630 | 7,932 | 3,974 | 3,535 | 3,189 |
| Income Taxes | 1,178 | 555 | 2,326 | 2,055 | 896 | 888 | 777 |
| Net Income | 3,450 | 1,610 | 6,304 | 5,877 | 3,078 | 2,647 | 2,412 |
| Average Shares | 2,227 | 2,226 | 2,232 | 2,253 | 1,688 | 1,233 | 1,249 |
| **Balance Sheet** | | | | | | | |
| Total Assets | 599,546 | 620,106 | 614,299 | 602,489 | 568,319 | 245,324 | ... |
| Total Liabilities | 529,132 | 551,563 | 546,445 | 537,403 | 507,544 | 213,697 | ... |
| Stockholders' Equity | 70,414 | 68,543 | 67,854 | 65,086 | 60,775 | 31,627 | ... |
| Shares Outstanding | 2,229 | 2,229 | 2,225 | 2,248 | 2,253 | 1,266 | 1,241 |
| **Statistical Record** | | | | | | | |
| Return on Assets % | 1.08 | 1.04 | 1.04 | 1.00 | 0.75 | ... | ... |
| Return on Equity % | 9.53 | 9.48 | 9.48 | 9.34 | 6.64 | ... | ... |
| Net Margin % | 21.59 | 20.75 | 19.16 | 17.55 | 12.61 | 15.77 | 15.97 |
| Asset Turnover | ... | ... | 0.05 | 0.06 | 0.06 | ... | ... |
| Price Range | 37.75-26.30 | 33.00-26.25 | 30.00-26.05 | 27.50-14.05 | 26.00-18.50 | 30.00-24.40 | 30.00-27.10 |
| P/E Ratio | 12.84-8.95 | 11.58-9.21 | 10.64-9.24 | 10.54-5.38 | 14.29-10.16 | 13.95-11.35 | 15.54-14.04 |
| Average Yield % | 4.08 | 4.24 | 4.26 | 4.66 | 4.02 | 3.06 | 2.79 |

**Address:** 232 East Street, Bloomsburg, PA 17815
**Telephone:** 570-784-4400

**Web Site:** www.firstcolumbiabank.com
**Officers:** Glenn E. Halterman - Chairman

**Auditors:** J. H. Williams & Co., LLP

# CITIZENS FINANCIAL SERVICES, INC

| Exchange | Symbol | Price | 52Wk Range | Yield | P/E |
|---|---|---|---|---|---|
| OTC | CZFS | $37.00 (8/31/2011) | 40.59-29.70 | 2.86 | 9.14 |

*7 Year Price Score 148.75 *NYSE Composite Index=100 *12 Month Price Score 105.88

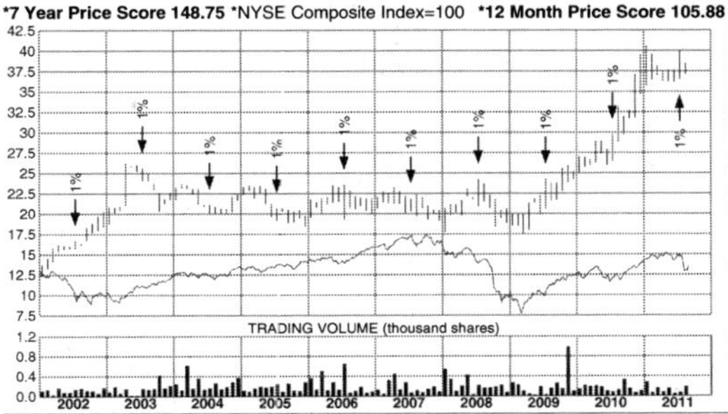


**Interim Earnings (Per Share)**

| Qtr. | Mar | Jun | Sep | Dec |
|---|---|---|---|---|
| 2008 | 0.69 | 0.84 | (0.36) | 1.18 |
| 2009 | 0.80 | 0.85 | 0.81 | 0.90 |
| 2010 | 0.94 | 1.01 | 0.99 | 1.00 |
| 2011 | 0.97 | 1.09 | ... | ... |

**Interim Dividends (Per Share)**

| Amt | Decl | Ex | Rec | Pay |
|---|---|---|---|---|
| 0.26Q | 01/04/2011 | 01/12/2011 | 01/14/2011 | 01/28/2011 |
| 0.265Q | 04/11/2011 | 04/13/2011 | 04/15/2011 | 04/29/2011 |
| 0.265Q | 07/05/2011 | 07/13/2011 | 07/15/2011 | 07/29/2011 |
| 1% | 07/05/2011 | 07/13/2011 | 07/15/2011 | 07/29/2011 |

**Indicated Div: $1.06**

| **Valuation Analysis** | | **Institutional Holding** |
|---|---|---|
| Forecast EPS | N/A | No of Institutions |
| | | 3 |
| Market Cap | $106.9 Million | Shares |
| Book Value | $75.3 Million | 36,874 |
| Price/Book | 1.42 | % Held |
| Price/Sales | N/A | 1.30 |

**Business Summary:** Banking (MIC: 5.1.1 SIC: 6022 NAIC: 522110)

Citizens Financial Services is a bank holding company for First Citizens National Bank (the Bank). The Bank is engaged in a range of banking activities and services for individual, business, governmental and institutional customers. These activities and services include checking, savings, time and deposit accounts; real estate, commercial, industrial, residential and consumer loans; and other financial services. The Bank's Trust and Investment division provides a range of client investment, estate and retirement services through the Bank's insurance agency subsidiary. As of Dec 31 2010, Co. had total assets of $812.5 million and total deposits of $680.7 million.

**Recent Developments:** For the quarter ended June 30 2011, net income increased 7.5% to US$3.1 million from US$2.9 million in the year-earlier quarter. Net interest income increased 3.9% to US$7.1 million from US$6.8 million in the year-earlier quarter. Provision for loan losses was US$150,000 versus US$235,000 in the prior-year quarter, a decrease of 36.2%. Non-interest income rose 9.7% to US$1.7 million from US$1.5 million, while non-interest expense advanced 5.2% to US$4.6 million.

**Prospects:** Our evaluation of Citizens Financial Services Inc. as of Sep. 6, 2011 is the result of our systematic analysis on three basic characteristics: earnings strength, relative valuation, and recent stock price movement. The company has managed to produce a neutral trend in earnings per share over the past 5 quarters. Because the company lacks sufficient analyst estimate data, we place greater weight on the historical EPS trend as the measure of earnings strength. Based on operating earnings yield, the company is undervalued when compared to all of the companies in our coverage universe. Share price changes over the past year indicates that CZFS will perform in line with the market over the near

| **Financial Data** (US$ in Thousands) | 6 Mos | 3 Mos | 12/31/2010 | 12/31/2009 | 12/31/2008 | 12/31/2007 | 12/31/2006 | 12/31/2005 |
|---|---|---|---|---|---|---|---|---|
| Earnings Per Share | 4.05 | 3.97 | 3.93 | 3.36 | 2.35 | 2.28 | 1.94 | 1.74 |
| Cash Flow Per Share | 4.96 | 4.70 | 4.38 | 3.39 | 3.52 | 2.73 | 2.35 | 2.58 |
| Tang Book Value Per Share | 22.51 | 20.85 | 20.00 | 17.50 | 14.49 | 13.58 | 11.77 | 10.68 |
| Dividends Per Share | 1.112 | 1.100 | 1.087 | 1.013 | 0.964 | 0.867 | 0.820 | 0.774 |
| Dividend Payout % | 27.47 | 27.70 | 27.67 | 30.12 | 41.03 | 38.07 | 42.26 | 44.44 |
| **Income Statement** | | | | | | | | |
| Interest Income | 19,034 | 9,469 | 39,000 | 38,615 | 37,238 | 36,024 | 32,851 | 28,699 |
| Interest Expense | 5,022 | 2,533 | 11,340 | 13,231 | 14,058 | 16,922 | 14,953 | 11,000 |
| Net Interest Income | 14,012 | 6,936 | 27,660 | 25,384 | 23,180 | 19,102 | 17,898 | 17,699 |
| Provision for Losses | 375 | 225 | 1,255 | 925 | 330 | 365 | 330 | 60 |
| Non-Interest Income | 3,187 | 1,515 | 6,010 | 5,847 | 1,156 | 5,085 | 4,716 | 4,688 |
| Non-Interest Expense | 9,260 | 4,676 | 17,757 | 17,759 | 15,877 | 15,314 | 15,027 | 15,387 |
| Income Before Taxes | 7,564 | 3,550 | 14,658 | 12,547 | 8,129 | 8,508 | 7,257 | 6,940 |
| Income Taxes | 1,587 | 720 | 3,156 | 2,683 | 1,224 | 1,772 | 1,457 | 1,666 |
| Net Income | 5,977 | 2,830 | 11,502 | 9,864 | 6,905 | 6,736 | 5,800 | 5,274 |
| Average Shares | 2,887 | 2,917 | 2,924 | 2,931 | 2,937 | 2,956 | 2,989 | 3,032 |
| **Balance Sheet** | | | | | | | | |
| Net Loans & Leases | 470,749 | 460,700 | 467,602 | 451,496 | 428,436 | 419,182 | 410,897 | 379,139 |
| Total Assets | 852,982 | 840,248 | 812,526 | 729,477 | 668,612 | 591,029 | 572,168 | 529,241 |
| Total Deposits | 713,127 | 704,529 | 680,711 | 605,559 | 546,680 | 456,028 | 446,515 | 429,799 |
| Total Liabilities | 777,683 | 769,205 | 743,836 | 667,950 | 615,842 | 542,501 | 528,668 | 487,680 |
| Stockholders' Equity | 75,299 | 71,043 | 68,690 | 61,527 | 52,770 | 48,528 | 43,500 | 41,561 |
| Shares Outstanding | 2,889 | 2,915 | 2,921 | 2,929 | 2,933 | 2,940 | 2,963 | 3,021 |
| **Statistical Record** | | | | | | | | |
| Return on Assets % | 1.45 | 1.46 | 1.49 | 1.41 | 1.09 | 1.16 | 1.05 | 1.03 |
| Return on Equity % | 16.64 | 17.19 | 17.67 | 17.26 | 13.60 | 14.64 | 13.64 | 12.81 |
| Net Interest Margin % | 73.98 | 73.25 | 70.92 | 65.74 | 62.25 | 53.03 | 54.48 | 61.67 |
| Efficiency Ratio % | 40.79 | 42.57 | 39.45 | 39.94 | 41.35 | 37.25 | 40.00 | 46.09 |
| Loans to Deposits | 0.66 | 0.65 | 0.69 | 0.75 | 0.78 | 0.92 | 0.92 | 0.88 |
| Price Range | 40.59-26.47 | 40.59-25.98 | 39.60-25.00 | 25.98-17.52 | 24.26-17.73 | 23.31-19.12 | 23.55-19.27 | 23.50-18.46 |
| P/E Ratio | 10.02-6.54 | 10.23-6.54 | 10.08-6.36 | 7.73-5.21 | 10.33-7.54 | 10.22-8.39 | 12.14-9.93 | 13.51-10.61 |
| Average Yield % | 3.24 | 3.42 | 3.71 | 4.64 | 4.63 | 4.08 | 3.81 | 3.67 |

**Address:** 15 South Main Street, Mansfield, PA 16933
**Telephone:** 570-662-2121
**Fax:** 717-662-2365

**Web Site:** www.firstcitizensbank.com
**Officers:** R. Lowell Coolidge - Chairman Randall E. Black - President, Chief Executive Officer

**Auditors:** S.R. Snodgrass, A.C.
**Investor Contact:** 570-662-2121
**Transfer Agents:** Citizens Financial Services, Inc.

# CITIZENS HOLDING CO

| Exchange | Symbol | Price | 52Wk Range | Yield | P/E |
|---|---|---|---|---|---|
| NMS | CIZN | $18.30 (8/31/2011) | 21.50-17.96 | 4.81 | 12.12 |

*7 Year Price Score N/A  *NYSE Composite Index=100  *12 Month Price Score 97.81

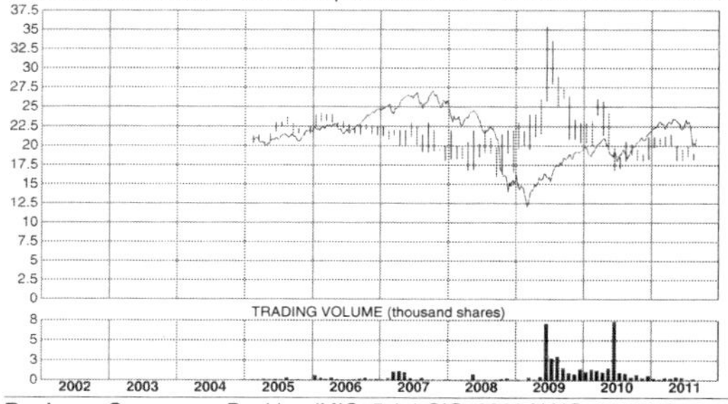

**Interim Earnings (Per Share)**

| Qtr. | Mar | Jun | Sep | Dec |
|---|---|---|---|---|
| 2008 | 0.33 | 0.51 | 0.43 | 0.42 |
| 2009 | 0.38 | 0.37 | 0.35 | 0.34 |
| 2010 | 0.41 | 0.35 | 0.37 | 0.36 |
| 2011 | 0.40 | 0.38 | ... | ... |

**Interim Dividends (Per Share)**

| Amt | Decl | Ex | Rec | Pay |
|---|---|---|---|---|
| 0.22Q | 11/30/2010 | 12/13/2010 | 12/15/2010 | 12/31/2010 |
| 0.22Q | 03/01/2011 | 03/11/2011 | 03/15/2011 | 03/31/2011 |
| 0.22Q | 05/26/2011 | 06/13/2011 | 06/15/2011 | 06/30/2011 |
| 0.22Q | 08/25/2011 | 09/13/2011 | 09/15/2011 | 09/30/2011 |

**Indicated Div: $0.88 (Div. Reinv. Plan)**

| Valuation Analysis | | Institutional Holding |
|---|---|---|
| Forecast EPS | N/A | No of Institutions 14 |
| Market Cap | $88.6 Million | Shares 330,956 |
| Book Value | $83.3 Million | |
| Price/Book | 1.06 | % Held 6.43 |
| Price/Sales | N/A | |

**Business Summary:** Banking (MIC: 5.1.1 SIC: 6022 NAIC: 522110)

Citizens Holding is a bank holding company. Through its subsidiary, The Citizens Bank of Philadelphia, Mississippi (the Bank), Co. engages in a range of commercial and personal banking activities, including accepting demand deposits, savings and time deposit accounts, making secured and unsecured loans, issuing letters of credit, originating mortgage loans, and providing personal and corporate trust services. Co.'s market consists principally of Neshoba, Newton, Leake, Scott, Attala, Lauderdale, Oktibbeha, Winston and Kemper counties in Mississippi. As of Dec 31 2010, Co. had total assets of $818.2 million and total deposits of $537.4 million.

**Recent Developments:** For the quarter ended June 30 2011, net income increased 9.3% to US$1.9 million from US$1.7 million in the year-earlier quarter. Net interest income increased 7.6% to US$7.8 million from US$7.2 million in the year-earlier quarter. Provision for loan losses was US$682,773 versus US$695,255 in the prior-year quarter, a decrease of 1.8%. Non-interest income fell 11.3% to US$1.5 million from US$1.7 million, while non-interest expense advanced 2.2% to US$6.2 million.

**Prospects:** Our evaluation of Citizens Holding Co as of Sep. 6, 2011 is the result of our systematic analysis on three basic characteristics: earnings strength, relative valuation, and recent stock price movement. The company has enjoyed a very positive trend in earnings per share over the past 5 quarters. Because the company lacks sufficient analyst estimate data, we place greater weight on the historical EPS trend as the measure of earnings strength. Based on operating earnings yield, the company is undervalued when compared to all of the companies in our coverage universe. Share price changes over the past year indicates that CIZN will perform very poorly over the near term.

**Financial Data**

| (US$ in Thousands) | 6 Mos | 3 Mos | 12/31/2010 | 12/31/2009 | 12/31/2008 | 12/31/2007 | 12/31/2006 | 12/31/2005 |
|---|---|---|---|---|---|---|---|---|
| Earnings Per Share | 1.51 | 1.48 | 1.48 | 1.45 | 1.69 | 1.39 | 1.65 | 1.57 |
| Cash Flow Per Share | 3.13 | 3.10 | 3.62 | 2.02 | 2.09 | 1.97 | 2.71 | 2.66 |
| Tang Book Value Per Share | 16.52 | 15.59 | 15.06 | 14.68 | 13.94 | 13.16 | 12.93 | 11.68 |
| Dividends Per Share | 0.870 | 0.860 | 0.850 | 0.810 | 0.770 | 0.730 | 0.690 | 0.650 |
| Dividend Payout % | 57.62 | 58.11 | 57.43 | 55.86 | 45.56 | 52.52 | 41.82 | 41.40 |
| **Income Statement** | | | | | | | | |
| Interest Income | 18,789 | 9,345 | 38,138 | 40,889 | 39,558 | 38,100 | 36,487 | 33,044 |
| Interest Expense | 3,449 | 1,767 | 8,726 | 11,336 | 13,775 | 16,763 | 13,182 | 9,847 |
| Net Interest Income | 15,340 | 7,578 | 29,412 | 29,553 | 25,783 | 21,337 | 23,306 | 23,196 |
| Provision for Losses | 927 | 244 | 2,456 | 3,013 | 1,224 | 784 | (361) | 1,084 |
| Non-Interest Income | 3,101 | 1,584 | 7,409 | 8,058 | 7,863 | 7,779 | 6,188 | 5,737 |
| Non-Interest Expense | 12,635 | 6,387 | 24,432 | 24,138 | 21,859 | 19,449 | 18,623 | 17,517 |
| Income Before Taxes | 4,868 | 2,518 | 9,245 | 8,770 | 10,563 | 8,882 | 11,416 | 10,531 |
| Income Taxes | 1,058 | 563 | 2,082 | 1,631 | 2,289 | 1,968 | 2,836 | 2,366 |
| Net Income | 3,809 | 1,955 | 7,163 | 7,139 | 8,274 | 6,914 | 8,395 | 7,966 |
| Average Shares | 4,854 | 4,856 | 4,852 | 4,913 | 4,895 | 4,964 | 5,080 | 5,066 |
| **Balance Sheet** | | | | | | | | |
| Net Loans & Leases | 406,073 | 407,084 | 415,497 | 441,695 | 424,226 | 368,025 | 369,281 | 374,964 |
| Total Assets | 845,253 | 832,143 | 818,233 | 840,004 | 766,047 | 680,904 | 621,197 | 607,709 |
| Total Deposits | 547,150 | 546,731 | 537,430 | 569,803 | 545,927 | 477,232 | 471,847 | 473,812 |
| Total Liabilities | 761,909 | 753,353 | 741,938 | 765,406 | 694,648 | 612,712 | 551,532 | 543,935 |
| Stockholders' Equity | 83,343 | 78,789 | 76,295 | 74,597 | 71,400 | 68,191 | 69,665 | 63,774 |
| Shares Outstanding | 4,843 | 4,839 | 4,838 | 4,838 | 4,849 | 4,863 | 5,020 | 5,009 |
| **Statistical Record** | | | | | | | | |
| Return on Assets % | 0.87 | 0.85 | 0.86 | 0.89 | 1.14 | 1.06 | 1.37 | 1.33 |
| Return on Equity % | 9.01 | 9.15 | 9.49 | 9.78 | 11.82 | 10.03 | 12.58 | 12.85 |
| Net Interest Margin % | 82.19 | 81.09 | 77.12 | 72.28 | 65.18 | 56.00 | 63.87 | 70.20 |
| Efficiency Ratio % | 57.00 | 58.44 | 53.64 | 49.31 | 46.10 | 42.39 | 43.64 | 45.17 |
| Loans to Deposits | 0.74 | 0.74 | 0.77 | 0.78 | 0.78 | 0.77 | 0.78 | 0.79 |
| Price Range | 21.50-17.04 | 25.72-16.79 | 26.00-16.79 | 35.41-19.46 | 22.00-16.01 | 23.00-18.00 | 24.15-21.33 | 23.75-20.00 |
| P/E Ratio | 14.24-11.28 | 17.38-11.34 | 17.57-11.34 | 24.42-13.42 | 13.02-9.47 | 16.55-12.95 | 14.64-12.93 | 15.13-12.74 |
| Average Yield % | 4.52 | 4.32 | 4.13 | 3.25 | 3.99 | 3.48 | 3.04 | 2.98 |

**Address:** 521 Main Street, Philadelphia, MS 39350
**Telephone:** 601-656-4692

**Web Site:** www.thecitizensbankphila.com
**Officers:** Herbert A. King - Chairman Greg L. McKee - Chief Executive Officer

**Auditors:** Horne LLP
**Investor Contact:** 601-656-4692
**Transfer Agents:** American Stock Transfer & Trust Company, New York, NY

# COMPUTER SERVICES, INC.

| Exchange | Symbol | Price | 52Wk Range | Yield | P/E |
|---|---|---|---|---|---|
| NBB | CSVI | $28.25 (8/31/2011) | 31.48-20.53 | 1.77 | 17.33 |

*7 Year Price Score 148.73 *NYSE Composite Index=100 *12 Month Price Score 113.39

**Interim Earnings (Per Share)**

| Qtr. | May | Aug | Nov | Feb |
|---|---|---|---|---|
| 2008-09 | 0.28 | 0.28 | 0.32 | 0.45 |
| 2009-10 | 0.33 | 0.34 | 0.32 | 0.44 |
| 2010-11 | 0.36 | 0.41 | 0.39 | 0.45 |
| 2011-12 | 0.38 | ... | ... | ... |

**Interim Dividends (Per Share)**

| Amt | Decl | Ex | Rec | Pay |
|---|---|---|---|---|
| 0.11Q | ... | 11/29/2010 | 12/01/2010 | 12/24/2010 |
| 0.11Q | 03/02/2011 | 03/14/2011 | 03/16/2011 | 03/31/2011 |
| 0.11Q | 03/29/2011 | 05/27/2011 | 06/01/2011 | 06/24/2011 |
| 0.125Q | 07/01/2011 | 08/30/2011 | 09/01/2011 | 09/26/2011 |

**Indicated Div: $0.50**

| Valuation Analysis | | Institutional Holding |
|---|---|---|
| Forecast EPS | N/A | No of Institutions N/A |
| Market Cap | $412.6 Million | Shares |
| Book Value | $111.3 Million | N/A |
| Price/Book | 3.71 | % Held |
| Price/Sales | 2.51 | N/A |

**Business Summary:** IT Services (MIC: 6.3.1 SIC: 7374 NAIC: 518210)

Computer Services provides service and software applications for financial institutions in a service bureau and an in-house environment. Co.'s integrated banking applications include check imaging; cash management; branch and merchant capture; Internet banking; print and mail, and online document delivery; corporate intranets; web hosting; emessaging; teller and platform services; automated teller machine and debit card services; risk assessment; network management; and compliance software and services for regulatory compliance, homeland security and fraud prevention. Co.'s customers include community and regional banks and multi-bank holding companies, and various business enterprises.

**Recent Developments:** For the quarter ended May 31 2011, net income increased 5.7% to US$5.6 million from US$5.3 million in the year-earlier quarter. Revenues were US$40.4 million, up 1.8% from US$39.7 million the year before. Operating income was US$9.3 million versus US$8.9 million in the prior-year quarter, an increase of 4.8%. Indirect operating expenses increased 0.9% to US$31.1 million from US$30.9 million in the equivalent prior-year period.

**Prospects:** Co.'s near-term outlook appears encouraging as it remains focused on implementing its Strategic Growth Initiative, which emphasizes on growing its existing products and services, capitalizing on new growth opportunities in the regulatory and compliance area, as well as exploring new acquisition and investment opportunities. For instance, on Sep 1 2011, Co. announced that it has completed the acquisition of HEIT, a provider of cloud-based managed compliance, security and Information Technology services and programs. Specifically, Co. believes that this acquisition will further accelerate its capability as a provider of cloud and managed services for financial institutions nationwide.

**Financial Data**

| (US$ in Thousands) | 3 Mos | 02/28/2011 | 02/28/2010 | 02/28/2009 | 02/29/2008 | 02/28/2007 | 02/28/2006 | 02/28/2005 |
|---|---|---|---|---|---|---|---|---|
| Earnings Per Share | 1.63 | 1.61 | 1.44 | 1.31 | 1.10 | 0.94 | 0.85 | 0.71 |
| Cash Flow Per Share | 2.70 | 2.64 | 2.43 | 2.28 | 1.69 | 1.75 | 1.52 | 1.47 |
| Tang Book Value Per Share | 3.03 | 2.62 | 2.01 | 2.12 | 2.07 | 1.78 | 1.84 | 2.80 |
| Dividends Per Share | 0.440 | 0.410 | 0.360 | 0.330 | 0.290 | 0.250 | 0.210 | 0.160 |
| Dividend Payout % | 26.99 | 25.47 | 25.09 | 25.19 | 26.36 | 26.46 | 24.71 | 22.38 |
| **Income Statement** | | | | | | | | |
| Total Revenue | 40,432 | 163,776 | 153,985 | 150,649 | 145,618 | 124,501 | 104,980 | 94,181 |
| EBITDA | 12,527 | 45,854 | 41,857 | 40,218 | 35,251 | 31,559 | 28,943 | 25,664 |
| Depn & Amortn | 3,229 | 5,976 | 6,125 | 6,010 | 6,386 | 6,366 | 5,305 | 5,204 |
| Income Before Taxes | 9,274 | 39,696 | 35,468 | 33,937 | 28,182 | 24,821 | 23,784 | 20,716 |
| Income Taxes | 3,640 | 15,680 | 13,833 | 13,235 | 10,516 | 9,513 | 9,680 | 8,594 |
| Net Income | 5,634 | 24,016 | 21,635 | 20,714 | 18,093 | 15,592 | 14,104 | 12,122 |
| Average Shares | 14,818 | 14,875 | 15,077 | 15,810 | 16,434 | 16,514 | 16,632 | 16,902 |
| **Balance Sheet** | | | | | | | | |
| Current Assets | 32,154 | 30,520 | 27,993 | 24,526 | 22,332 | 21,960 | 18,960 | 29,313 |
| Total Assets | 136,420 | 136,122 | 125,920 | 108,685 | 106,713 | 102,974 | 85,566 | 64,465 |
| Current Liabilities | 20,113 | 21,037 | 20,251 | 15,365 | 12,882 | 13,779 | 9,142 | 7,301 |
| Long-Term Obligations | 55 | 3,099 | 8,340 | 5,000 | 9,990 | 12,787 | 10,169 | ... |
| Total Liabilities | 25,108 | 29,419 | 32,478 | 24,452 | 25,324 | 29,548 | 23,167 | 9,608 |
| Stockholders' Equity | 111,312 | 106,703 | 93,442 | 84,233 | 81,389 | 73,426 | 62,399 | 54,857 |
| Shares Outstanding | 14,605 | 14,581 | 14,639 | 14,801 | 15,627 | 15,856 | 15,721 | 15,754 |
| **Statistical Record** | | | | | | | | |
| Return on Assets % | 18.34 | 18.33 | 18.44 | 19.23 | 17.21 | 16.54 | 18.80 | 19.51 |
| Return on Equity % | 23.23 | 24.00 | 24.35 | 25.01 | 23.31 | 22.96 | 24.06 | 22.67 |
| EBITDA Margin % | 30.98 | 28.00 | 27.18 | 26.70 | 24.21 | 25.35 | 27.57 | 27.25 |
| Net Margin % | 13.93 | 14.66 | 14.05 | 13.75 | 12.42 | 12.52 | 13.43 | 12.87 |
| Asset Turnover | 1.24 | 1.25 | 1.31 | 1.40 | 1.39 | 1.32 | 1.40 | 1.52 |
| Current Ratio | 1.60 | 1.45 | 1.38 | 1.60 | 1.73 | 1.59 | 2.07 | 4.01 |
| Debt to Equity | N.M. | 0.03 | 0.09 | 0.06 | 0.12 | 0.17 | 0.16 | ... |
| Price Range | 29.75-19.15 | 29.75-18.00 | 18.95-12.25 | 17.95-10.63 | 20.75-14.38 | 15.50-14.50 | 18.75-14.81 | 17.63-8.06 |
| P/E Ratio | 18.25-11.75 | 18.48-11.18 | 13.16-8.51 | 13.70-8.11 | 18.86-13.07 | 16.49-15.43 | 22.06-17.42 | 24.82-11.36 |
| Average Yield % | 1.83 | 1.85 | 2.19 | 2.24 | 1.69 | 1.68 | 1.31 | 1.38 |

**Address:** 3901 Technology Drive, Paducah, KY 42001-5201
**Telephone:** 270-442-7361
**Fax:** 270-442-9905

**Web Site:** www.csiweb.com
**Officers:** John A. Williams - Chairman R. Stanley Eckenberg - President, Chief Operating Officer

**Auditors:** McGladrey & Pullen, LLP
**Investor Contact:** 270-442-7361x10126
**Transfer Agents:** BNY Mellon Shareowner Services, Pittsburgh, PA

# CONNECTICUT WATER SERVICE, INC.

| Exchange | Symbol | Price | 52Wk Range | Yield | P/E |
|---|---|---|---|---|---|
| NMS | CTWS | $26.56 (8/31/2011) | 28.16-22.52 | 3.58 | 18.97 |

***7 Year Price Score 103.77** *NYSE Composite Index=100 ***12 Month Price Score 104.30**

**Interim Earnings (Per Share)**

| Qtr. | Mar | Jun | Sep | Dec |
|---|---|---|---|---|
| 2008 | 0.20 | 0.35 | 0.34 | 0.22 |
| 2009 | 0.13 | 0.27 | 0.67 | 0.12 |
| 2010 | 0.12 | 0.27 | 0.54 | 0.20 |
| 2011 | 0.26 | 0.40 | ... | ... |

**Interim Dividends (Per Share)**

| Amt | Decl | Ex | Rec | Pay |
|---|---|---|---|---|
| 0.233Q | 11/12/2010 | 11/29/2010 | 12/01/2010 | 12/15/2010 |
| 0.233Q | 01/27/2011 | 02/25/2011 | 03/01/2011 | 03/15/2011 |
| 0.233Q | 05/13/2011 | 05/27/2011 | 06/01/2011 | 06/15/2011 |
| 0.237Q | 08/05/2011 | 08/30/2011 | 09/01/2011 | 09/15/2011 |

**Indicated Div: $0.95 (Div. Reinv. Plan)**

| Valuation Analysis | | Institutional Holding |
|---|---|---|
| Forecast EPS | $1.28 (09/02/2011) | No of Institutions 80 |
| Market Cap | $231.7 Million | Shares |
| Book Value | $116.6 Million | 2,865,007 |
| Price/Book | 1.99 | % Held |
| Price/Sales | 3.31 | 32.41 |

**Business Summary:** Water Utilities (MIC: 3.2.1 SIC: 4941 NAIC: 221310)

Connecticut Water Service is a holding company. Through its regulated utility and unregulated subsidiaries, Co. operates its business in three segments: Water Activities, which is comprised of its regulated water activities to supply public drinking water to customers; Real Estate Transactions, which involves the sale or donation for income tax benefits of its real estate holdings; and Services and Rentals, which provides contracted services to water and wastewater utilities and other clients and leases certain of its properties to third parties. At Dec 31 2010, Co.'s primary regulated subsidiary, The Connecticut Water Company, supplied water to 89,402 customers in 55 towns in Connecticut.

**Recent Developments:** For the quarter ended June 30 2011, net income increased 50.1% to US$3.5 million from US$2.3 million in the year-earlier quarter. Revenues were US$17.4 million, up 9.2% from US$15.9 million the year before. Operating income was US$4.6 million versus US$3.7 million in the prior-year quarter, an increase of 23.3%. Direct operating expenses declined 2.2% to US$7.8 million from US$8.0 million in the comparable period the year before. Indirect operating expenses increased 18.3% to US$5.0 million from US$4.2 million in the equivalent prior-year period.

**Prospects:** Our evaluation of Connecticut Water Service Inc. as of Sep. 6, 2011 is the result of our systematic analysis on three basic characteristics: earnings strength, relative valuation, and recent stock price movement. The company has generated a negative trend in earnings per share over the past 5 quarters and while recent estimates for the company have been raised by analysts, CTWS has posted better than expected results. Based on operating earnings yield, the company is about fairly valued when compared to all of the companies in our coverage universe. Share price changes over the past year indicates that CTWS will perform very poorly over the near term.

**Financial Data**

| (US$ in Thousands) | 6 Mos | 3 Mos | 12/31/2010 | 12/31/2009 | 12/31/2008 | 12/31/2007 | 12/31/2006 | 12/31/2005 |
|---|---|---|---|---|---|---|---|---|
| Earnings Per Share | 1.40 | 1.27 | 1.13 | 1.19 | 1.11 | 1.05 | 0.84 | 1.26 |
| Cash Flow Per Share | 2.70 | 2.05 | 1.97 | 2.45 | 1.87 | 1.88 | 1.21 | 1.55 |
| Tang Book Value Per Share | 12.86 | 12.67 | 12.72 | 12.33 | 11.89 | 11.61 | 11.26 | 11.18 |
| Dividends Per Share | 0.930 | 0.925 | 0.920 | 0.900 | 0.880 | 0.865 | 0.855 | 0.845 |
| Dividend Payout % | 66.43 | 72.83 | 81.42 | 75.63 | 79.28 | 82.38 | 101.79 | 67.06 |
| **Income Statement** | | | | | | | | |
| Total Revenue | 33,348 | 15,989 | 66,408 | 59,391 | 61,270 | 59,026 | 46,945 | 47,453 |
| EBITDA | 15,581 | 6,803 | 28,868 | 24,585 | 25,220 | 24,560 | 19,501 | 19,433 |
| Depn & Amortn | 4,187 | 2,073 | 7,894 | 7,166 | 7,080 | 7,173 | 6,277 | 5,912 |
| Income Before Taxes | 8,623 | 3,370 | 15,121 | 12,675 | 12,942 | 12,976 | 8,763 | 9,504 |
| Income Taxes | 2,885 | 1,102 | 5,323 | 2,466 | 3,518 | 4,195 | 2,055 | 2,338 |
| Net Income | 5,738 | 2,268 | 9,798 | 10,209 | 9,424 | 8,781 | 6,951 | 10,324 |
| Average Shares | 8,710 | 8,694 | 8,633 | 8,523 | 8,430 | 8,333 | 8,237 | 8,143 |
| **Balance Sheet** | | | | | | | | |
| Current Assets | 20,428 | 21,205 | 20,428 | 19,962 | 15,780 | 22,971 | 14,150 | 26,146 |
| Total Assets | 430,732 | 427,049 | 425,211 | 415,276 | 372,431 | 360,813 | 315,193 | 306,035 |
| Current Liabilities | 34,739 | 34,100 | 35,102 | 33,056 | 19,070 | 14,913 | 12,970 | 13,229 |
| Long-Term Obligations | 111,385 | 111,485 | 111,675 | 111,955 | 92,227 | 92,285 | 77,347 | 77,404 |
| Total Liabilities | 314,174 | 312,361 | 311,248 | 305,935 | 268,183 | 259,943 | 218,483 | 211,112 |
| Stockholders' Equity | 116,558 | 114,688 | 113,963 | 109,341 | 104,248 | 100,870 | 96,710 | 94,923 |
| Shares Outstanding | 8,722 | 8,704 | 8,676 | 8,573 | 8,463 | 8,376 | 8,270 | 8,169 |
| **Statistical Record** | | | | | | | | |
| Return on Assets % | 2.85 | 2.62 | 2.33 | 2.59 | 2.56 | 2.60 | 2.24 | 3.46 |
| Return on Equity % | 10.74 | 9.83 | 8.78 | 9.56 | 9.16 | 8.89 | 7.25 | 11.24 |
| EBITDA Margin % | 46.72 | 42.55 | 43.47 | 41.40 | 41.16 | 41.61 | 41.54 | 40.95 |
| Net Margin % | 17.21 | 14.18 | 14.75 | 17.19 | 15.38 | 14.88 | 14.81 | 21.76 |
| Asset Turnover | 0.16 | 0.16 | 0.16 | 0.15 | 0.17 | 0.17 | 0.15 | 0.16 |
| Current Ratio | 0.59 | 0.62 | 0.58 | 0.60 | 0.83 | 1.54 | 1.09 | 1.98 |
| Debt to Equity | 0.96 | 0.97 | 0.98 | 1.02 | 0.88 | 0.91 | 0.80 | 0.82 |
| Price Range | 28.16-20.91 | 28.16-20.03 | 27.88-20.03 | 25.61-17.39 | 28.95-20.60 | 25.49-22.76 | 27.45-20.45 | 27.57-22.16 |
| P/E Ratio | 20.11-14.94 | 22.17-15.77 | 24.67-17.73 | 21.52-14.61 | 26.08-18.56 | 24.28-21.68 | 32.68-24.35 | 21.88-17.59 |
| Average Yield % | 3.79 | 3.88 | 3.94 | 4.11 | 3.59 | 3.58 | 3.64 | 3.35 |

**Address:** 93 West Main Street, Clinton, CT 06413
**Telephone:** 860-669-8636
**Fax:** 860-669-9326

**Web Site:** www.ctwater.com
**Officers:** Eric W. Thornburg - Chairman, President, Chief Executive Officer David C. Benoit - Vice President, Chief Financial Officer, Treasurer

**Auditors:** Pricewaterhouse Coopers LLP
**Investor Contact:** 800-428-3985
**Transfer Agents:** Registrar and Transfer Company, Cranford, NJ

# EDUCATIONAL DEVELOPMENT CORP.

| Exchange | Symbol | Price | 52Wk Range | Yield | P/E |
|---|---|---|---|---|---|
| NMS | EDUC | $5.20 (8/31/2011) | 6.98-5.00 | 9.23 | 15.76 |

*7 Year Price Score 86.95 *NYSE Composite Index=100 *12 Month Price Score 89.80

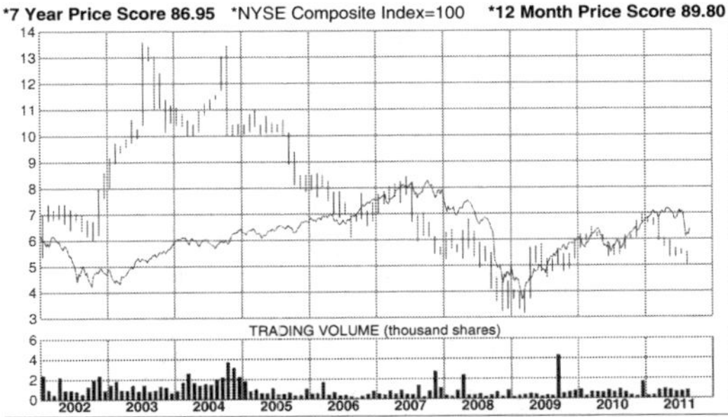


**Interim Earnings (Per Share)**

| Qtr. | May | Aug | Nov | Feb |
|---|---|---|---|---|
| 2008-09 | 0.13 | 0.08 | 0.17 | 0.00 |
| 2009-10 | 0.11 | 0.06 | 0.24 | 0.08 |
| 2010-11 | 0.05 | 0.05 | 0.20 | 0.00 |
| 2011-12 | 0.08 | ... | ... | ... |

**Interim Dividends (Per Share)**

| Amt | Decl | Ex | Rec | Pay |
|---|---|---|---|---|
| 0.15Q | 11/30/2010 | 12/08/2010 | 12/10/2010 | 12/17/2010 |
| 0.12Q | 02/28/2011 | 03/09/2011 | 03/11/2011 | 03/18/2011 |
| 0.12Q | 05/25/2011 | 06/08/2011 | 06/10/2011 | 06/17/2011 |
| 0.12Q | 08/26/2011 | 09/07/2011 | 09/09/2011 | 09/16/2011 |

**Indicated Div: $0.48**

| Valuation Analysis | | Institutional Holding | |
|---|---|---|---|
| Forecast EPS | $0.35 (09/02/2011) | No of Institutions | 10 |
| Market Cap | $20.2 Million | Shares | 904,454 |
| Book Value | $14.4 Million | % Held | 23.56 |
| Price/Book | 1.41 | | |
| Price/Sales | 0.74 | | |

**Business Summary:** Retail - General Merchandise/Department Stores (MIC: 2.1.1 SIC: 5199 NAIC: 424990)

Educational Development is a trade publisher of educational children's books produced in the U.K by Usborne Publishing Limited (Usborne). Co. also owns Kane/Miller Book Publishers, which publishes International children's books. Co. sells its children's books through two divisions. Co.'s Home Business division (Usborne Books and More or UBAM) distributes books through independent consultants who hold book showings in individual homes, and through book fairs, direct sales and Internet sales. The UBAM Consultants also distribute these titles to school and public libraries. Co.'s Publishing division markets books to bookstores, toy stores, specialty stores, museums and other retail outlets.

**Recent Developments:** For the quarter ended May 31 2011, net income increased 59.5% to US$300,200 from US$188,200 in the year-earlier quarter. Revenues were US$6.3 million, unchanged from the year before. Direct operating expenses rose 5.1% to US$2.4 million from US$2.3 million in the comparable period the year before. Indirect operating expenses decreased 9.0% to US$3.3 million from US$3.7 million in the equivalent prior-year period.

**Prospects:** Our evaluation of Educational Development Corp. as of Sep. 6, 2011 is the result of our systematic analysis on three basic characteristics: earnings strength, relative valuation, and recent stock price movement. The company has produced a positive trend in earnings per share over the past 5 quarters. Because the company lacks sufficient analyst estimate data, we place greater weight on the historical EPS trend as the measure of earnings strength. Based on operating earnings yield, the company is about fairly valued when compared to all of the companies in our coverage universe. Share price changes over the past year indicates that EDUC will perform very poorly over the near term.

| **Financial Data** (US$ in Thousands) | 3 Mos | 02/28/2011 | 02/28/2010 | 02/28/2009 | 02/29/2008 | 02/28/2007 | 02/28/2006 | 02/28/2005 |
|---|---|---|---|---|---|---|---|---|
| Earnings Per Share | 0.33 | 0.30 | 0.49 | 0.50 | 0.60 | 0.62 | 0.62 | 0.59 |
| Cash Flow Per Share | 0.69 | 0.72 | 0.11 | 1.06 | 0.67 | 0.66 | 0.37 | 1.04 |
| Tang Book Value Per Share | 3.70 | 3.75 | 3.97 | 4.14 | 4.53 | 4.17 | 3.55 | 3.25 |
| Dividends Per Share | 0.510 | 0.510 | 0.550 | 0.800 | 0.220 | 0.200 | 0.150 | 0.120 |
| Dividend Payout % | 154.55 | 170.00 | 112.24 | 160.00 | 36.67 | 32.26 | 24.19 | 20.34 |
| **Income Statement** | | | | | | | | |
| Total Revenue | 6,264 | 27,243 | 28,671 | 29,398 | 30,521 | 31,403 | 31,789 | 31,651 |
| EBITDA | 481 | 1,995 | 3,189 | 3,279 | 3,872 | 4,029 | 4,035 | 4,078 |
| Depn & Amortn | ... | 125 | 137 | 140 | 139 | 144 | 138 | 126 |
| Income Before Taxes | 481 | 1,870 | 3,052 | 3,139 | 3,732 | 3,878 | 3,814 | 3,885 |
| Income Taxes | 181 | 702 | 1,139 | 1,226 | 1,408 | 1,471 | 1,416 | 1,479 |
| Net Income | 300 | 1,168 | 1,914 | 1,913 | 2,324 | 2,407 | 2,398 | 2,406 |
| Average Shares | 3,899 | 3,890 | 3,868 | 3,797 | 3,859 | 3,875 | 3,898 | 4,088 |
| **Balance Sheet** | | | | | | | | |
| Current Assets | 15,828 | 15,758 | 16,321 | 16,984 | 17,180 | 16,708 | 15,689 | 14,758 |
| Total Assets | 18,644 | 18,705 | 19,360 | 19,941 | 20,065 | 19,702 | 18,644 | 17,981 |
| Current Liabilities | 4,255 | 4,047 | 3,863 | 3,896 | 3,268 | 4,041 | 5,305 | 5,848 |
| Long-Term Obligations | ... | ... | 75 | 150 | ... | ... | ... | ... |
| Total Liabilities | 4,255 | 4,047 | 3,938 | 4,046 | 3,268 | 4,041 | 5,305 | 5,848 |
| Stockholders' Equity | 14,389 | 14,659 | 15,422 | 15,895 | 16,797 | 15,661 | 13,339 | 12,132 |
| Shares Outstanding | 3,889 | 3,905 | 3,887 | 3,838 | 3,706 | 3,757 | 3,753 | 3,735 |
| **Statistical Record** | | | | | | | | |
| Return on Assets % | 6.96 | 6.14 | 9.74 | 9.56 | 11.66 | 12.55 | 13.10 | 12.98 |
| Return on Equity % | 8.70 | 7.77 | 12.22 | 11.70 | 14.28 | 16.60 | 18.83 | 18.26 |
| EBITDA Margin % | 7.67 | 7.32 | 11.12 | 11.15 | 12.68 | 12.83 | 12.69 | 12.89 |
| Net Margin % | 4.79 | 4.29 | 6.67 | 6.51 | 7.62 | 7.67 | 7.54 | 7.60 |
| Asset Turnover | 1.48 | 1.43 | 1.46 | 1.47 | 1.53 | 1.64 | 1.74 | 1.71 |
| Current Ratio | 3.72 | 3.89 | 4.22 | 4.36 | 5.26 | 4.13 | 2.96 | 2.52 |
| Debt to Equity | ... | ... | N.M. | 0.01 | ... | ... | ... | ... |
| Price Range | 6.98-5.30 | 6.98-5.32 | 6.19-3.15 | 6.78-3.24 | 8.44-5.25 | 8.50-6.10 | 10.98-7.65 | 13.49-10.00 |
| P/E Ratio | 21.15-16.06 | 23.27-17.73 | 12.63-6.43 | 13.56-6.48 | 14.07-8.75 | 13.71-9.84 | 17.71-12.34 | 22.86-16.95 |
| Average Yield % | 8.34 | 8.29 | 10.58 | 16.26 | 3.23 | 2.74 | 1.59 | 1.10 |

**Address:** 10302 East 55th Place, Tulsa, OK 74146-6515
**Telephone:** 918-622-4522
**Fax:** 918-665-7919

**Web Site:** www.edcpub.com
**Officers:** Randall W. White - Chairman, President, Chief Executive Officer, Treasurer Marilyn R. Welborn - Corporate Secretary, Controller

**Auditors:** HoganTaylor LLP
**Investor Contact:** 918-622-4522
**Transfer Agents:** American Stock Transfer & Trust Company, New York, NY

# FARMERS & MERCHANTS BANCORP (LODI, CA)

| Exchange | Symbol | Price | 52Wk Range | Yield | P/E |
|---|---|---|---|---|---|
| OTC | FMCB | $372.00 (8/26/2011) | 425.00-360.00 | 3.05 | 13.60 |

*7 Year Price Score N/A *NYSE Composite Index=100 *12 Month Price Score 99.32

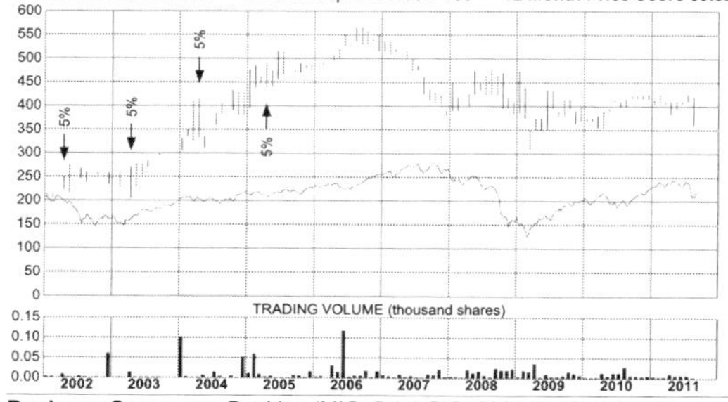


**Interim Earnings (Per Share)**

| Qtr. | Mar | Jun | Sep | Dec |
|---|---|---|---|---|
| 2008 | 7.21 | 7.50 | 7.63 | 6.35 |
| 2009 | 7.55 | 3.93 | 7.90 | 6.18 |
| 2010 | 7.75 | 5.13 | 7.95 | 6.22 |
| 2011 | 7.86 | 5.33 | ... | ... |

**Interim Dividends (Per Share)**

| Amt | Decl | Ex | Rec | Pay |
|---|---|---|---|---|
| 5.90S | 12/03/2009 | 12/09/2009 | 12/11/2009 | 01/02/2010 |
| 5.35S | 05/11/2010 | 06/09/2010 | 06/11/2010 | 07/01/2010 |
| 6.00S | 12/03/2010 | 12/09/2010 | 12/13/2010 | 01/03/2011 |
| 5.65S | ... | 05/27/2011 | 06/01/2011 | 06/30/2011 |

**Indicated Div: $11.33**

| **Valuation Analysis** | | **Institutional Holding** |
|---|---|---|
| Forecast EPS | N/A | No of Institutions N/A |
| Market Cap | $289.9 Million | Shares |
| Book Value | $181.1 Million | N/A |
| Price/Book | 1.60 | % Held |
| Price/Sales | N/A | N/A |

**Business Summary:** Banking (MIC: 5.1.1 SIC: 6021 NAIC: 522110)

Farmers & Merchants Bancorp is a bank holding company. Through its subsidiary, Farmers & Merchants Bank of Central California (the Bank), Co. provides a range of banking services to businesses and individuals located in the mid Central Valley of California. Co.'s deposit instruments include checking, savings, money market, time certificates of deposit, individual retirement accounts and online banking services. Co.'s lending products include commercial, real estate construction, agribusiness, installment, credit card, and real estate loans. As of Dec 31 2010, Co. had total assets of $1.84 billion and total deposits of $1.57 billion.

**Recent Developments:** For the quarter ended June 30 2011, net income increased 3.7% to US$4.2 million from US$4.0 million in the year-earlier quarter. Net interest income decreased 0.2% to US$18.5 million from US$18.6 million in the year-earlier quarter. Provision for loan losses was US$3.9 million versus US$5.1 million in the prior-year quarter, a decrease of 23.3%. Non-interest income rose 17.8% to US$3.0 million from US$2.5 million, while non-interest expense advanced 14.1% to US$11.2 million.

**Prospects:** Co. is experiencing lower net interest income attributable to a decrease in the net interest margin, offset somewhat by growth in average earning assets. Co. noted that the decline in net interest margin is due to a decline in average loans as a percentage of average earning assets. The decrease in average loan balances, coupled with the decrease in the yield on those loan balances due to the continuing low rate environment, is resulting in lower interest revenue from loans. Meanwhile, Co. continues to be challenged by competitor pricing for loans, which may result in greater negative pressure on future loan yields and net interest margin going forward.

**Financial Data**

| (US$ in Thousands) | 6 Mos | 3 Mos | 12/31/2010 | 12/31/2009 | 12/31/2008 | 12/31/2007 | 12/31/2006 | 12/31/2005 |
|---|---|---|---|---|---|---|---|---|
| Earnings Per Share | 27.36 | 27.16 | 27.05 | 25.57 | 28.69 | 28.05 | 25.25 | 22.24 |
| Cash Flow Per Share | 51.74 | 48.20 | 39.50 | 16.33 | 28.94 | 29.11 | 0.03 | 0.02 |
| Tang Book Value Per Share | 232.36 | 229.21 | 222.27 | 210.93 | 198.92 | 179.25 | 0.16 | 0.15 |
| Dividends Per Share | 11.650 | 11.350 | 11.350 | 11.000 | 10.650 | 9.700 | 8.550 | 7.700 |
| Dividend Payout % | 42.58 | 41.79 | 41.96 | 43.02 | 37.12 | 34.58 | 33.86 | 34.62 |
| **Income Statement** | | | | | | | | |
| Interest Income | 41,066 | 20,531 | 84,461 | 91,314 | 93,208 | 95,775 | 88,396 | 72,458 |
| Interest Expense | 4,188 | 2,165 | 9,685 | 16,331 | 24,784 | 32,225 | 24,621 | 14,032 |
| Net Interest Income | 36,878 | 18,366 | 74,776 | 74,983 | 68,424 | 63,550 | 63,775 | 58,426 |
| Provision for Losses | 4,450 | 525 | 14,735 | 15,420 | 7,998 | 1,495 | 275 | 425 |
| Non-Interest Income | 6,329 | 3,334 | 17,185 | 18,194 | 16,064 | 15,455 | 12,063 | 11,274 |
| Non-Interest Expense | 22,279 | 11,031 | 42,563 | 44,582 | 42,767 | 41,945 | 43,121 | 40,617 |
| Income Before Taxes | 16,088 | 9,739 | 33,287 | 31,328 | 36,387 | 35,565 | 32,442 | 28,658 |
| Income Taxes | 5,807 | 3,613 | 12,169 | 11,315 | 13,597 | 12,870 | 11,813 | 10,230 |
| Net Income | 10,281 | 6,126 | 21,118 | 20,013 | 22,790 | 22,695 | 20,629 | 18,428 |
| Average Shares | 779 | 779 | 780 | 782 | 794 | 809 | 817,044 | 828,537 |
| **Balance Sheet** | | | | | | | | |
| Net Loans & Leases | 1,158,859 | 1,135,286 | 1,143,741 | 1,182,905 | 1,157,330 | 1,122,486 | 1,028,813 | 955,397 |
| Total Assets | 1,846,704 | 1,861,162 | 1,841,491 | 1,781,014 | 1,684,437 | 1,519,172 | 1,411,233 | 1,352,989 |
| Total Deposits | 1,564,127 | 1,578,248 | 1,566,503 | 1,498,124 | 1,432,702 | 1,310,790 | 1,198,528 | 1,103,340 |
| Total Liabilities | 1,665,600 | 1,682,511 | 1,668,250 | 1,616,287 | 1,527,892 | 1,375,754 | 1,278,893 | 1,229,341 |
| Stockholders' Equity | 181,104 | 178,651 | 173,241 | 164,727 | 156,545 | 143,418 | 132,340 | 123,648 |
| Shares Outstanding | 779 | 779 | 779 | 780 | 786 | 800 | 811,933 | 823,651 |
| **Statistical Record** | | | | | | | | |
| Return on Assets % | 1.20 | 1.17 | 1.17 | 1.16 | 1.42 | 1.55 | 1.49 | 1.43 |
| Return on Equity % | 12.13 | 12.18 | 12.50 | 12.46 | 15.15 | 16.46 | 16.12 | 15.34 |
| Net Interest Margin % | 90.15 | 89.45 | 88.53 | 82.12 | 73.41 | 66.35 | 72.15 | 80.63 |
| Efficiency Ratio % | 47.80 | 46.22 | 41.87 | 40.71 | 39.14 | 37.71 | 42.92 | 48.51 |
| Loans to Deposits | 0.74 | 0.72 | 0.73 | 0.79 | 0.81 | 0.86 | 0.86 | 0.87 |
| Price Range | 425.00-383.00 | 425.00-355.00 | 425.00-355.00 | 475.00-310.00 | 475.00-385.00 | 535.00-381.00 | 565.00-485.00 | 515.00-395.24 |
| P/E Ratio | 15.53-14.00 | 15.65-13.07 | 15.71-13.12 | 18.58-12.12 | 16.56-13.42 | 19.07-13.58 | 22.38-19.21 | 23.16-17.77 |
| Average Yield % | 2.83 | 2.77 | 2.80 | 2.87 | 2.51 | 2.08 | 1.63 | 1.66 |

**Address:** 111 W. Pine Street, Lodi, CA 95240
**Telephone:** 209-367-2300

**Web Site:** www.fmbonline.com
**Officers:** Kent A. Steinwert - Chairman, President, Chief Executive Officer Richard S. Erichson - Executive Vice President & Senior Credit Officer

**Auditors:** Perry-Smith LLP

# FIRST CAPITAL INC.

| Exchange | Symbol | Price | 52Wk Range | Yield | P/E |
|---|---|---|---|---|---|
| NAS | FCAP | $18.48 (8/31/2011) | 18.50-14.63 | 4.11 | 13.79 |

*7 Year Price Score N/A *NYSE Composite Index=100 *12 Month Price Score 110.33

**Interim Earnings (Per Share)**

| Qtr. | Mar | Jun | Sep | Dec |
|---|---|---|---|---|
| 2008 | 0.32 | 0.32 | 0.29 | 0.35 |
| 2009 | 0.29 | (0.15) | 0.00 | 0.13 |
| 2010 | 0.36 | 0.35 | 0.33 | 0.35 |
| 2011 | 0.32 | 0.34 | ... | ... |

**Interim Dividends (Per Share)**

| Amt | Decl | Ex | Rec | Pay |
|---|---|---|---|---|
| 0.19Q | 11/19/2010 | 12/14/2010 | 12/16/2010 | 12/30/2010 |
| 0.19Q | 02/23/2011 | 03/14/2011 | 03/16/2011 | 03/30/2011 |
| 0.19Q | 05/23/2011 | 06/14/2011 | 06/16/2011 | 06/30/2011 |
| 0.19Q | 08/17/2011 | 09/14/2011 | 09/16/2011 | 09/30/2011 |

**Indicated Div: $0.76**

| Valuation Analysis | | Institutional Holding |
|---|---|---|
| Forecast EPS | N/A | No of Institutions 3 |
| Market Cap | $51.5 Million | Shares 29,237 |
| Book Value | $49.5 Million | % Held |
| Price/Book | 1.04 | 1.05 |
| Price/Sales | N/A | |

**Business Summary:** Credit & Lending (MIC: 5.4.1 SIC: 6035 NAIC: 522120)

First Capital is the holding company for its subsidiary, First Harrison Bank (the Bank). The Bank is a federally-chartered savings bank which provides a range of deposit, loan and investment products to individuals and business customers through 13 locations in southern Indiana. The Bank originates one-to-four-family residential mortgage loans, multi-family residential loans, commercial real estate and business loans and consumer loans. Co. provides a range of deposit instruments, including regular savings accounts, certificates of deposit and retirement savings plans. At Dec 31 2010, Co. had total assets of $452.4 million and total deposits of $378.0 million.

**Recent Developments:** For the quarter ended June 30 2011, net income decreased 4.7% to US$945,000 from US$992,000 in the year-earlier quarter. Net interest income decreased 0.1% to US$4.1 million from US$4.2 million in the year-earlier quarter. Provision for loan losses was US$425,000 versus US$420,000 in the prior-year quarter, an increase of 1.2%. Non-interest income fell 4.8% to US$955,000 from US$1.0 million, while non-interest expense was unchanged at US$3.4 million.

**Prospects:** Our evaluation of First Capital Inc. as of Sep. 6, 2011 is the result of our systematic analysis on three basic characteristics: earnings strength, relative valuation, and recent stock price movement. The company has generated a negative trend in earnings per share over the past 5 quarters. Because the company lacks sufficient analyst estimate data, we place greater weight on the historical EPS trend as the measure of earnings strength. Based on operating earnings yield, the company is undervalued when compared to all of the companies in our coverage universe. Share price changes over the past year indicates that FCAP will perform very poorly over the near term.

| Financial Data (US$ in Thousands) | 6 Mos | 3 Mos | 12/31/2010 | 12/31/2009 | 12/31/2008 | 12/31/2007 | 12/31/2006 | 12/31/2005 |
|---|---|---|---|---|---|---|---|---|
| Earnings Per Share | 1.34 | 1.35 | 1.39 | 0.28 | 1.27 | 1.20 | 1.30 | 1.29 |
| Cash Flow Per Share | 3.72 | 2.95 | 2.01 | 0.94 | 1.77 | 2.23 | 1.30 | 1.97 |
| Tang Book Value Per Share | 15.82 | 15.35 | 15.22 | 14.62 | 14.99 | 14.22 | 12.30 | 12.68 |
| Dividends Per Share | 0.760 | 0.750 | 0.740 | 0.720 | 0.710 | 0.680 | 0.649 | 0.564 |
| Dividend Payout % | 56.72 | 55.56 | 53.24 | 257.14 | 55.91 | 56.67 | 49.93 | 43.66 |
| **Income Statement** | | | | | | | | |
| Interest Income | 10,249 | 5,099 | 21,834 | 22,969 | 25,686 | 27,085 | 26,211 | 23,659 |
| Interest Expense | 2,058 | 1,052 | 5,502 | 8,388 | 10,745 | 13,699 | 12,741 | 10,343 |
| Net Interest Income | 8,191 | 4,047 | 16,332 | 14,581 | 14,941 | 13,386 | 13,470 | 13,316 |
| Provision for Losses | 925 | 500 | 2,037 | 4,289 | 1,570 | 558 | 810 | 563 |
| Non-Interest Income | 1,878 | 923 | 3,906 | 3,373 | 3,573 | 3,524 | 3,430 | 2,961 |
| Non-Interest Expense | 6,623 | 3,252 | 12,762 | 13,473 | 11,846 | 11,349 | 10,510 | 10,112 |
| Income Before Taxes | 2,521 | 1,218 | 5,439 | 192 | 5,098 | 5,003 | 5,580 | 5,602 |
| Income Taxes | 677 | 319 | 1,561 | (586) | 1,529 | 1,591 | 1,872 | 1,914 |
| Net Income | 1,837 | 896 | 3,865 | 766 | 3,569 | 3,412 | 3,708 | 3,688 |
| Average Shares | 2,787 | 2,787 | 2,786 | 2,784 | 2,815 | 2,836 | 2,848 | 2,848 |
| **Balance Sheet** | | | | | | | | |
| Net Loans & Leases | 289,721 | 287,824 | 298,925 | 312,555 | 323,629 | 334,721 | 335,850 | 322,453 |
| Total Assets | 444,979 | 449,228 | 452,378 | 455,534 | 458,625 | 453,179 | 457,105 | 438,354 |
| Total Deposits | 369,169 | 374,633 | 378,003 | 374,476 | 355,891 | 328,151 | 331,143 | 317,264 |
| Total Liabilities | 395,456 | 400,989 | 404,485 | 409,590 | 411,103 | 407,443 | 413,016 | 396,397 |
| Stockholders' Equity | 49,523 | 48,239 | 47,893 | 45,944 | 47,522 | 45,736 | 44,089 | 41,957 |
| Shares Outstanding | 2,785 | 2,787 | 2,787 | 2,761 | 2,794 | 2,814 | 3,113 | 2,846 |
| **Statistical Record** | | | | | | | | |
| Return on Assets % | 0.82 | 0.82 | 0.85 | 0.17 | 0.78 | 0.75 | 0.83 | 0.85 |
| Return on Equity % | 7.63 | 7.90 | 8.24 | 1.64 | 7.63 | 7.60 | 8.62 | 8.92 |
| Net Interest Margin % | 80.47 | 79.37 | 74.80 | 63.48 | 58.17 | 49.42 | 51.39 | 56.28 |
| Efficiency Ratio % | 55.22 | 54.00 | 49.58 | 51.15 | 40.49 | 37.08 | 35.46 | 37.99 |
| Loans to Deposits | 0.78 | 0.77 | 0.79 | 0.83 | 0.91 | 1.02 | 1.01 | 1.02 |
| Price Range | 18.50-14.19 | 16.80-14.19 | 16.64-13.75 | 18.27-12.17 | 16.89-13.00 | 18.65-15.17 | 19.25-15.81 | 19.09-15.15 |
| P/E Ratio | 13.81-10.59 | 12.44-10.51 | 11.97-9.89 | 65.25-43.46 | 13.30-10.24 | 15.54-12.64 | 14.81-12.16 | 14.80-11.75 |
| Average Yield % | 4.81 | 4.90 | 4.93 | 4.70 | 4.77 | 3.95 | 3.70 | 3.30 |

**Address:** 220 Federal Drive N.W., Corydon, IN 47112
**Telephone:** 812-738-2198

**Web Site:** www.firstcapital.com
**Officers:** J. Gordon Pendleton - Chairman William W. Harrod - President, Chief Executive Officer

**Auditors:** Monroe Shine & Co., Inc.
**Investor Contact:** 812-738-2198
**Transfer Agents:** Registrar and Transfer Company, Cranford, NJ

# FIRST KEYSTONE CORP.

| Exchange | Symbol | Price | 52Wk Range | Yield | P/E |
|---|---|---|---|---|---|
| OTC | FKYS | $19.30 (8/29/2011) | 20.20-15.90 | 4.97 | 11.03 |

***7 Year Price Score 98.15** *NYSE Composite Index=100 ***12 Month Price Score 110.59**

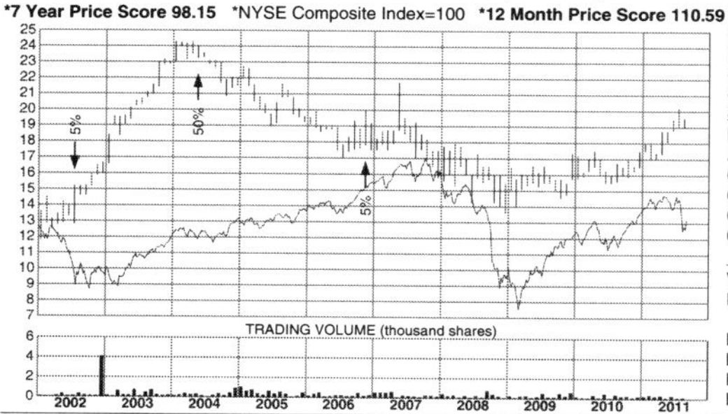


**Interim Earnings (Per Share)**

| Qtr. | Mar | Jun | Sep | Dec |
|---|---|---|---|---|
| 2008 | 0.32 | 0.34 | 0.41 | 0.32 |
| 2009 | 0.39 | 0.39 | 0.39 | 0.29 |
| 2010 | 0.40 | 0.83 | 0.45 | 0.37 |
| 2011 | 0.46 | 0.47 | ... | ... |

**Interim Dividends (Per Share)**

| Amt | Decl | Ex | Rec | Pay |
|---|---|---|---|---|
| 0.24Q | 12/01/2010 | 12/10/2010 | 12/14/2010 | 12/31/2010 |
| 0.24Q | 02/23/2011 | 03/04/2011 | 03/08/2011 | 03/31/2011 |
| 0.24Q | 05/25/2011 | 06/10/2011 | 06/14/2011 | 06/30/2011 |
| 0.24Q | 08/25/2011 | 09/09/2011 | 09/13/2011 | 09/30/2011 |

**Indicated Div: $0.96**

| Valuation Analysis | | Institutional Holding |
|---|---|---|
| Forecast EPS | N/A | No of Institutions |
| | | 1 |
| Market Cap | $105.1 Million | Shares |
| Book Value | $84.3 Million | 124,349 |
| Price/Book | 1.25 | % Held |
| Price/Sales | N/A | 2.19 |

**Business Summary:** Banking (MIC: 5.1.1 SIC: 6022 NAIC: 522110)

First Keystone is a bank holding company. Through its subsidiary, First Keystone Community Bank (the Bank), Co. provides banking, trust and related services in its Northeastern and Central Pennsylvania market area. The Bank's commercial banking activities include accepting time, demand, and savings deposits and making secured and unsecured commercial, real estate and consumer loans. The Bank also provides personal and corporate trust and agency services, including trust investment accounts, investment advisory services, mutual funds, estate planning, and management of pension and profit sharing plans. As of Dec 31 2010, Co. had total assets of $796.6 million and deposits of $626.9 million.

**Recent Developments:** For the quarter ended June 30 2011, net income increased 9.9% to US$2.5 million from US$2.3 million in the year-earlier quarter. Net interest income increased 10.7% to US$6.9 million from US$6.2 million in the year-earlier quarter. Provision for loan losses was US$300,000 versus US$400,000 in the prior-year quarter, a decrease of 25.0%. Non-interest income fell 24.1% to US$1.1 million from US$1.4 million, while non-interest expense advanced 4.5% to US$4.5 million.

**Prospects:** Co.'s results are benefiting from improved net interest income, as well as growth in its net interest margin. In addition, Co. noted a decline in total non-performing assets as compared to year end 2010, where it increased due to higher unemployment and the downturn of the housing industry. Co. is also seeing loan growth as compared to the year end 2010, driven by commercial loans secured by real estate, as well as tax exempt real estate and other loans. However, Co. noted slower growth in loans as loan demand remains weak and borrowers are generally paying down debt.

**Financial Data**

| (US$ in Thousands) | 6 Mos | 3 Mos | 12/31/2010 | 12/31/2009 | 12/31/2008 | 12/31/2007 | 12/31/2006 | 12/31/2005 |
|---|---|---|---|---|---|---|---|---|
| Earnings Per Share | 1.75 | 2.11 | 1.65 | 1.46 | 1.39 | 1.31 | 1.35 | 1.48 |
| Cash Flow Per Share | ... | ... | 2.97 | (0.50) | 0.58 | 1.99 | 0.92 | 1.34 |
| Tang Book Value Per Share | 11.78 | 10.82 | 10.78 | 10.12 | 9.19 | 9.55 | 11.52 | 11.34 |
| Dividends Per Share | 0.950 | 0.940 | 0.930 | 0.920 | 0.890 | 0.880 | 0.849 | 0.781 |
| Dividend Payout % | 54.29 | 44.55 | 56.36 | 63.01 | 64.03 | 67.18 | 62.86 | 52.90 |
| **Income Statement** | | | | | | | | |
| Interest Income | 18,677 | 9,347 | 38,154 | 37,726 | 37,638 | 31,899 | 28,577 | 26,382 |
| Interest Expense | 4,979 | 2,516 | 12,742 | 15,565 | 18,116 | 17,785 | 14,972 | 11,621 |
| Net Interest Income | 13,698 | 6,831 | 25,412 | 22,161 | 19,522 | 14,114 | 13,605 | 14,761 |
| Provision for Losses | 600 | 300 | 2,575 | 800 | 700 | 150 | 500 | 750 |
| Non-Interest Income | 2,022 | 963 | 5,758 | 4,299 | 4,046 | 4,199 | 3,788 | 3,782 |
| Non-Interest Expense | 8,776 | 4,304 | 17,272 | 16,444 | 13,923 | 10,645 | 9,515 | 9,583 |
| Income Before Taxes | 6,344 | 3,190 | 11,323 | 9,216 | 8,945 | 7,518 | 7,378 | 8,210 |
| Income Taxes | 1,305 | 694 | 2,362 | 1,279 | 1,394 | 1,391 | 1,188 | 1,363 |
| Net Income | 5,039 | 2,496 | 8,961 | 7,937 | 7,551 | 6,127 | 6,190 | 6,847 |
| Average Shares | ... | ... | 5,444 | 5,442 | 5,442 | 4,680 | 4,578 | 4,622 |
| **Balance Sheet** | | | | | | | | |
| Net Loans & Leases | 407,790 | 404,136 | 403,950 | 401,375 | 403,172 | 371,557 | 248,086 | 230,917 |
| Total Assets | 805,036 | 809,283 | 796,601 | 758,330 | 714,898 | 681,207 | 525,920 | 512,399 |
| Total Deposits | 623,100 | 626,349 | 626,895 | 580,569 | 504,633 | 493,041 | 384,020 | 362,796 |
| Total Liabilities | 720,689 | 730,088 | 717,541 | 684,163 | 645,751 | 610,283 | 472,533 | 458,956 |
| Stockholders' Equity | 84,347 | 79,195 | 79,060 | 74,167 | 69,147 | 70,924 | 53,387 | 53,443 |
| Shares Outstanding | 5,445 | 5,444 | 5,444 | 5,440 | 5,440 | 5,440 | 4,526 | 4,605 |
| **Statistical Record** | | | | | | | | |
| Return on Assets % | 1.18 | 1.16 | 1.15 | 1.08 | 1.08 | 1.02 | 1.19 | 1.36 |
| Return on Equity % | 11.44 | 11.89 | 11.70 | 11.08 | 10.75 | 9.86 | 11.59 | 12.83 |
| Net Interest Margin % | 73.60 | 73.08 | 66.60 | 58.74 | 51.87 | 44.25 | 47.61 | 55.95 |
| Efficiency Ratio % | 43.05 | 41.75 | 39.33 | 39.13 | 33.40 | 29.49 | 29.40 | 31.77 |
| Loans to Deposits | 0.65 | 0.65 | 0.64 | 0.69 | 0.80 | 0.75 | 0.65 | 0.64 |
| Price Range | 19.50-15.50 | 17.95-15.50 | 17.50-15.50 | 17.35-14.01 | 17.95-13.55 | 21.75-15.80 | 20.00-17.00 | 22.76-18.95 |
| P/E Ratio | 11.14-8.86 | 8.51-7.35 | 10.61-9.39 | 11.88-9.60 | 12.91-9.75 | 16.60-12.06 | 14.81-12.59 | 15.38-12.81 |
| Average Yield % | 5.56 | 5.65 | 5.68 | 5.88 | 5.56 | 4.87 | 4.59 | 3.81 |

**Address:** 111 West Front Street, Berwick, PA 18603
**Telephone:** 570-752-3671

**Web Site:** www.firstkeystonecorporation.com
**Officers:** Robert E. Bull - Chairman Robert J. Wise - Vice-Chairman

**Auditors:** J. H. Williams & Co., LLP
**Investor Contact:** 570-752-3671
**Transfer Agents:** Registrar and Transfer Company, Cranford, NJ

# FIRST ROBINSON FINANCIAL CORP.

| Exchange | Symbol | Price | 52Wk Range | Yield | P/E |
|---|---|---|---|---|---|
| OTC | FRFC | $32.30 (8/8/2011) | 35.50-32.30 | 2.79 | 10.03 |

*7 Year Price Score N/A *NYSE Composite Index=100 *12 Month Price Score N/A

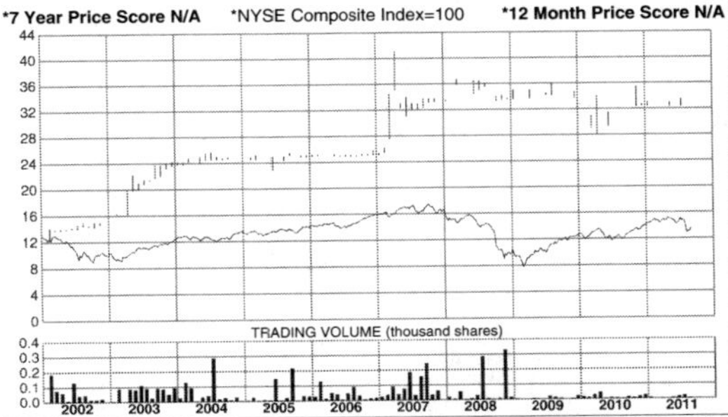


**Interim Earnings (Per Share)**

| Qtr. | Jun | Sep | Dec | Mar |
|---|---|---|---|---|
| 2008-09 | 0.38 | 0.54 | 0.44 | 0.41 |
| 2009-10 | 0.38 | (0.08) | (1.10) | 0.72 |
| 2010-11 | 0.97 | 0.94 | 1.22 | 0.12 |
| 2011-12 | 0.94 | ... | ... | ... |

**Interim Dividends (Per Share)**

| Amt | Decl | Ex | Rec | Pay |
|---|---|---|---|---|
| 0.75A | 05/20/2008 | 05/29/2008 | 06/02/2008 | 06/16/2008 |
| 0.80A | 05/19/2009 | 05/29/2009 | 06/02/2009 | 06/16/2009 |
| 0.85A | 05/18/2010 | 05/28/2010 | 06/02/2010 | 06/16/2010 |
| 0.90A | 05/17/2011 | 05/31/2011 | 06/02/2011 | 06/16/2011 |

**Indicated Div: $0.90**

| Valuation Analysis | | Institutional Holding |
|---|---|---|
| Forecast EPS | N/A | No of Institutions N/A |
| Market Cap | $13.8 Million | Shares |
| Book Value | $12.8 Million | N/A |
| Price/Book | 1.08 | % Held |
| Price/Sales | N/A | N/A |

**Business Summary:** Credit & Lending (MIC: 5.4.1 SIC: 6035 NAIC: 522120)

First Robinson Financial is the bank holding company for First Robinson Savings Bank, N.A. (the Bank), which serves the Crawford County and surrounding counties in Illinois and Knox County and in Indiana. The Bank acquires retail deposits from the general public and invests those funds in one- to four-family residential real estate loans as well as consumer, commercial, agricultural real estate and commercial business and agricultural finance loans. The Bank's deposits include statement savings, negotiable order of withdrawal accounts, certificate accounts, money market and non-interest bearing accounts. At Mar 31 2011, Co. had total assets of $208.8 million and deposits of $176.4 million.

**Recent Developments:** For the quarter ended June 30 2011, net income decreased 3.6% to US$401,000 from US$416,000 in the year-earlier quarter. Net interest income increased 18.4% to US$1.6 million from US$1.4 million in the year-earlier quarter. Provision for loan losses was US$255,000 versus US$45,000 in the prior-year quarter, an increase of 466.7%. Non-interest income rose 2.2% to US$646,000 from US$632,000, while non-interest expense advanced 4.4% to US$1.4 million.

**Prospects:** Despite higher non-interest expense, provision for loan losses and income tax provision, Co. is seeing an increase in net interest income and non-interest income. In detail, Co. attributes its net interest income growth to higher interest income, reflecting an increase in interest income from loans receivable and the increase in interest earned on deposits, offset by lower interest income on taxable securities and tax-exempt securities. Further, non-interest income improved due to increases in net gain on sale of loans, charges and fees on loans, and other non-interest income, offset in part by lower charges and fees on deposit accounts as well as the sale of foreclosed property.

| **Financial Data** (US$ in Thousands) | 3 Mos | 03/31/2011 | 03/31/2010 | 03/31/2009 | 03/31/2008 | 03/31/2007 | 03/31/2006 | 03/31/2005 |
|---|---|---|---|---|---|---|---|---|
| Earnings Per Share | 3.22 | 3.25 | (0.07) | 1.77 | 2.06 | 2.04 | 1.91 | 1.65 |
| Cash Flow Per Share | 7.68 | 6.60 | 2.13 | 2.15 | 2.83 | 3.21 | 3.63 | 3.41 |
| Tang Book Value Per Share | 29.96 | 29.88 | 27.80 | 28.28 | 26.31 | 24.52 | 22.92 | 21.94 |
| Dividends Per Share | 0.900 | 0.850 | 0.800 | 0.750 | 0.650 | 0.550 | 0.500 | 0.430 |
| Dividend Payout % | 27.95 | 26.15 | ... | 42.37 | 31.55 | 26.96 | 26.18 | 26.06 |
| **Income Statement** | | | | | | | | |
| Interest Income | 2,098 | 8,309 | 7,802 | 7,605 | 7,309 | 6,852 | 5,963 | 5,440 |
| Interest Expense | 465 | 2,417 | 3,231 | 3,132 | 3,139 | 2,657 | 1,848 | 1,348 |
| Net Interest Income | 1,633 | 5,892 | 4,571 | 4,473 | 4,170 | 4,195 | 4,115 | 4,092 |
| Provision for Losses | 255 | 735 | 1,297 | 220 | 175 | 60 | 158 | 200 |
| Non-Interest Income | 646 | 2,569 | 2,233 | 1,708 | 1,572 | 1,242 | 1,074 | 1,113 |
| Non-Interest Expense | 1,406 | 5,630 | 5,460 | 4,875 | 4,133 | 3,861 | 3,531 | 3,612 |
| Income Before Taxes | 618 | 2,096 | (152) | 1,082 | 1,430 | 1,514 | 1,500 | 1,372 |
| Income Taxes | 217 | 701 | (122) | 291 | 459 | 501 | 516 | 514 |
| Net Income | 401 | 1,395 | (30) | 791 | 971 | 1,013 | 984 | 858 |
| Average Shares | 427 | 428 | 417 | 447 | 471 | 495 | 514 | 520 |
| **Balance Sheet** | | | | | | | | |
| Net Loans & Leases | 119,949 | 120,518 | 100,151 | 86,757 | 76,246 | 71,070 | 65,506 | 66,815 |
| Total Assets | 202,293 | 208,831 | 182,989 | 164,419 | 133,809 | 112,274 | 109,428 | 111,445 |
| Total Deposits | 171,025 | 176,352 | 149,312 | 140,088 | 103,898 | 86,773 | 86,202 | 88,968 |
| Total Liabilities | 189,494 | 196,066 | 170,944 | 152,112 | 121,933 | 100,384 | 98,012 | 99,989 |
| Stockholders' Equity | 12,799 | 12,765 | 12,045 | 12,307 | 11,876 | 11,890 | 11,416 | 11,456 |
| Shares Outstanding | 427 | 427 | 433 | 435 | 451 | 484 | 498 | 522 |
| **Statistical Record** | | | | | | | | |
| Return on Assets % | 0.71 | 0.71 | N.M. | 0.53 | 0.79 | 0.91 | 0.89 | 0.80 |
| Return on Equity % | 11.07 | 11.25 | N.M. | 6.54 | 8.15 | 8.69 | 8.60 | 7.66 |
| Net Interest Margin % | 77.84 | 70.91 | 58.59 | 58.82 | 57.05 | 61.22 | 69.01 | 75.22 |
| Efficiency Ratio % | 51.24 | 51.76 | 54.41 | 52.35 | 46.54 | 47.70 | 50.18 | 55.12 |
| Loans to Deposits | 0.70 | 0.68 | 0.67 | 0.62 | 0.73 | 0.82 | 0.76 | 0.75 |
| Price Range | 35.50-32.30 | 35.50-28.10 | 36.00-29.00 | 36.50-33.25 | 41.05-31.00 | 34.50-24.90 | 25.50-22.75 | 25.75-24.00 |
| P/E Ratio | 11.02-10.03 | 10.92-8.65 | ... | 20.62-18.79 | 19.93-15.05 | 16.91-12.21 | 13.35-11.91 | 15.61-14.55 |
| Average Yield % | 2.70 | 2.63 | 2.41 | 2.14 | 1.93 | 2.13 | 2.02 | 1.75 |

**Address:** 501 East Main Street, Robinson, IL 62454
**Telephone:** 618-544-8621
**Fax:** 618-544-7506

**Web Site:** www.frs-1.com
**Officers:** Scott F. Pulliam - Chairman Rick L. Catt - President, Chief Executive Officer

**Auditors:** BKD LLP
**Investor Contact:** 618-544-8621
**Transfer Agents:** Register & Transfer Company, Cranford, NJ

# 1ST SOURCE CORP.

| Exchange | Symbol | Price | 52Wk Range | Yield | P/E |
|---|---|---|---|---|---|
| NMS | SRCE | $22.75 (8/31/2011) | 23.85-16.22 | 2.81 | 13.54 |

***7 Year Price Score 90.92** *NYSE Composite Index=100 ***12 Month Price Score 112.91**

**Interim Earnings (Per Share)**

| Qtr. | Mar | Jun | Sep | Dec |
|---|---|---|---|---|
| 2008 | 0.38 | 0.30 | 0.18 | 0.51 |
| 2009 | 0.20 | 0.19 | 0.21 | 0.19 |
| 2010 | 0.33 | 0.25 | 0.39 | 0.25 |
| 2011 | 0.43 | 0.61 | ... | ... |

**Interim Dividends (Per Share)**

| Amt | Decl | Ex | Rec | Pay |
|---|---|---|---|---|
| 0.16Q | 10/21/2010 | 11/03/2010 | 11/05/2010 | 11/15/2010 |
| 0.16Q | 01/20/2011 | 02/02/2011 | 02/04/2011 | 02/15/2011 |
| 0.16Q | 04/21/2011 | 05/04/2011 | 05/06/2011 | 05/16/2011 |
| 0.16Q | 07/21/2011 | 08/03/2011 | 08/05/2011 | 08/15/2011 |

**Indicated Div: $0.64**

| **Valuation Analysis** | | **Institutional Holding** |
|---|---|---|
| Forecast EPS | N/A | No of Institutions |
| | | 92 |
| Market Cap | $550.8 Million | Shares |
| Book Value | $505.6 Million | 15,708,141 |
| Price/Book | 1.09 | % Held |
| Price/Sales | N/A | 63.47 |

**Business Summary:** Banking (MIC: 5.1.1 SIC: 6022 NAIC: 522110)

1st Source is a bank holding company. Through its subsidiaries, Co. provides a range of financial products and services. Co.'s banking subsidiary, 1st Source Bank (the Bank), provides commercial and consumer banking services, trust and investment management services, as well as insurance to individual and business clients in Indiana and Michigan. The Bank's Specialty Finance Group provides financing services for new and used private and cargo aircraft, automobiles and light trucks for leasing and rental agencies, medium and heavy duty trucks, construction equipment, and environmental equipment. As of Dec 31 2010, Co. had total assets of $4.45 billion and total deposits of $3.62 billion.

**Recent Developments:** For the quarter ended June 30 2011, net income increased 90.7% to US$14.9 million from US$7.8 million in the year-earlier quarter. Net interest income increased 3.7% to US$37.6 million from US$36.2 million in the year-earlier quarter. Provision for loan losses was US$67,000 versus US$5.8 million in the prior-year quarter, a decrease of 98.8%. Non-interest income rose 4.0% to US$21.4 million from US$20.6 million, while non-interest expense declined 9.3% to US$35.9 million.

**Prospects:** Our evaluation of 1st Source Corp. as of Sep. 6, 2011 is the result of our systematic analysis on three basic characteristics: earnings strength, relative valuation, and recent stock price movement. The company has enjoyed a very positive trend in earnings per share over the past 5 quarters. Because the company lacks sufficient analyst estimate data, we place greater weight on the historical EPS trend as the measure of earnings strength. Based on operating earnings yield, the company is undervalued when compared to all of the companies in our coverage universe. Share price changes over the past year indicates that SRCE will perform in line with the market over the near term.

**Financial Data**

| (US$ in Thousands) | 6 Mos | 3 Mos | 12/31/2010 | 12/31/2009 | 12/31/2008 | 12/31/2007 | 12/31/2006 | 12/31/2005 |
|---|---|---|---|---|---|---|---|---|
| Earnings Per Share | 1.68 | 1.32 | 1.21 | 0.79 | 1.37 | 1.28 | 1.72 | 1.46 |
| Cash Flow Per Share | 6.48 | 4.68 | 3.85 | 2.15 | 2.66 | 3.59 | 3.73 | 2.17 |
| Tang Book Value Per Share | 16.97 | 16.25 | 16.44 | 15.56 | 14.86 | 13.82 | 16.21 | 15.03 |
| Dividends Per Share | 0.630 | 0.620 | 0.610 | 0.590 | 0.580 | 0.560 | 0.535 | 0.445 |
| Dividend Payout % | 37.50 | 46.97 | 50.41 | 74.68 | 42.34 | 43.75 | 31.08 | 30.43 |
| **Income Statement** | | | | | | | | |
| Interest Income | 95,083 | 47,210 | 200,626 | 200,412 | 235,308 | 253,587 | 208,994 | 168,532 |
| Interest Expense | 20,639 | 10,350 | 53,129 | 72,200 | 103,148 | 134,677 | 102,561 | 70,104 |
| Net Interest Income | 74,444 | 36,860 | 147,497 | 128,212 | 132,160 | 118,910 | 106,433 | 98,428 |
| Provision for Losses | 2,265 | 2,198 | 19,207 | 31,101 | 16,648 | 7,534 | (2,736) | (5,855) |
| Non-Interest Income | 40,377 | 18,953 | 86,691 | 85,530 | 84,003 | 70,619 | 76,585 | 68,533 |
| Non-Interest Expense | 74,419 | 38,476 | 154,505 | 151,123 | 153,114 | 140,312 | 126,211 | 123,439 |
| Income Before Taxes | 38,137 | 15,139 | 60,476 | 31,518 | 46,401 | 41,683 | 59,543 | 49,377 |
| Income Taxes | 12,664 | 4,531 | 19,232 | 6,028 | 13,015 | 11,144 | 20,246 | 15,626 |
| Net Income | 25,473 | 10,608 | 41,244 | 25,490 | 33,386 | 30,539 | 39,297 | 33,751 |
| Average Shares | 24,263 | 24,279 | 24,239 | 24,163 | 24,388 | 23,810 | 22,830 | 23,052 |
| **Balance Sheet** | | | | | | | | |
| Net Loans & Leases | 3,033,147 | 2,965,558 | 2,983,749 | 3,004,914 | 3,218,436 | 3,124,839 | 2,643,735 | 2,404,734 |
| Total Assets | 4,354,951 | 4,412,376 | 4,445,281 | 4,542,100 | 4,464,174 | 4,447,104 | 3,807,315 | 3,511,277 |
| Total Deposits | 3,523,316 | 3,609,007 | 3,622,745 | 3,652,464 | 3,514,542 | 3,469,663 | 3,048,284 | 2,745,587 |
| Total Liabilities | 3,849,357 | 3,921,909 | 3,958,898 | 3,971,780 | 4,010,510 | 4,016,600 | 3,438,411 | 3,165,701 |
| Stockholders' Equity | 505,594 | 490,467 | 486,383 | 570,320 | 453,664 | 430,504 | 368,904 | 345,576 |
| Shares Outstanding | 24,211 | 24,303 | 24,172 | 24,111 | 24,362 | 24,376 | 22,759 | 22,996 |
| **Statistical Record** | | | | | | | | |
| Return on Assets % | 1.11 | 0.95 | 0.92 | 0.57 | 0.75 | 0.74 | 1.07 | 0.95 |
| Return on Equity % | 8.99 | 7.89 | 7.81 | 4.98 | 7.53 | 7.64 | 11.00 | 10.04 |
| Net Interest Margin % | 78.51 | 78.08 | 73.52 | 63.97 | 56.16 | 46.89 | 50.93 | 58.40 |
| Efficiency Ratio % | 51.87 | 58.15 | 53.78 | 52.85 | 47.95 | 43.28 | 44.19 | 52.07 |
| Loans to Deposits | 0.86 | 0.82 | 0.82 | 0.82 | 0.92 | 0.90 | 0.87 | 0.88 |
| Price Range | 21.22-15.99 | 20.85-15.99 | 20.61-14.36 | 23.63-13.88 | 27.00-15.00 | 32.36-16.66 | 33.28-23.33 | 23.64-17.88 |
| P/E Ratio | 12.63-9.52 | 15.80-12.11 | 17.03-11.87 | 29.91-17.57 | 19.71-10.95 | 25.28-13.02 | 19.35-13.56 | 16.19-12.25 |
| Average Yield % | 3.33 | 3.37 | 3.46 | 3.45 | 2.87 | 2.33 | 1.92 | 2.12 |

**Address:** 100 North Michigan Street, South Bend, IN 46614
**Telephone:** 574-235-2000

**Web Site:** www.1stsource.com
**Officers:** Christopher J. Murphy - Chairman, President, Chief Executive Officer Wellington D. Jones - Vice-Chairman, Executive Vice President

**Auditors:** Ernst & Young LLP
**Investor Contact:** 574-235-2702
**Transfer Agents:** 1st Source Bank

# GREENE COUNTY BANCORP INC

| Exchange | Symbol | Price | 52Wk Range | Yield | P/E |
|---|---|---|---|---|---|
| NAS | GCBC | $17.53 (8/31/2011) | 19.96-16.28 | 3.99 | 14.14 |

*7 Year Price Score 117.06 *NYSE Composite Index=100 *12 Month Price Score 101.47

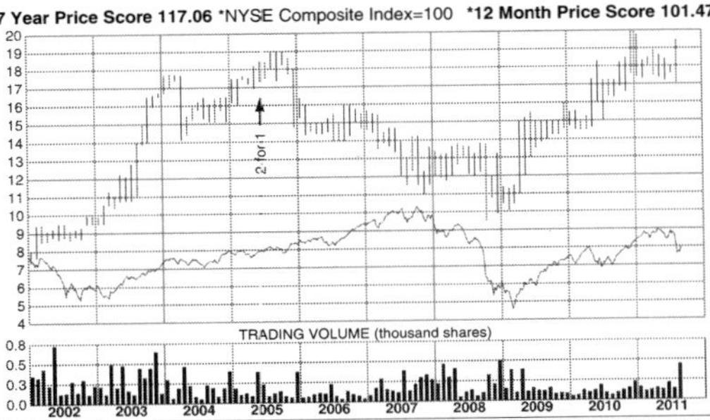


**Interim Earnings (Per Share)**

| Qtr. | Sep | Dec | Mar | Jun |
|---|---|---|---|---|
| 2007-08 | 0.14 | 0.15 | 0.16 | 0.20 |
| 2008-09 | 0.20 | 0.25 | 0.28 | 0.26 |
| 2009-10 | 0.29 | 0.29 | 0.30 | 0.30 |
| 2010-11 | 0.32 | 0.32 | 0.30 | ... |

**Interim Dividends (Per Share)**

| Amt | Decl | Ex | Rec | Pay |
|---|---|---|---|---|
| 0.20Q | 10/20/2010 | 11/09/2010 | 11/12/2010 | 12/15/2010 |
| 0.175Q | 01/20/2011 | 02/11/2011 | 02/15/2011 | 03/01/2011 |
| 0.175Q | 04/19/2011 | 05/11/2011 | 05/13/2011 | 06/01/2011 |
| 0.175Q | 07/20/2011 | 08/11/2011 | 08/15/2011 | 09/01/2011 |

**Indicated Div: $0.70**

| Valuation Analysis | | Institutional Holding |
|---|---|---|
| Forecast EPS | N/A | No of Institutions 4 |
| Market Cap | $72.7 Million | Shares |
| Book Value | $46.7 Million | 49,250 |
| Price/Book | 1.56 | % Held |
| Price/Sales | N/A | 1.18 |

**Business Summary:** Credit & Lending (MIC: 5.4.1 SIC: 6036 NAIC: 522120)
Greene County Bancorp operates as the federally chartered holding company of The Bank of Greene County (the Bank), a federally chartered savings bank. The Bank's principal business consists of accepting retail deposits from the general public in the areas surrounding its branches and investing those deposits primarily in one to four-family residential mortgage loans, commercial real estate loans, consumer loans, home equity loans and commercial business loans. In addition, the Bank invests a portion of its assets in investment securities, mortgage-backed and asset-backed securities. As of June 30 2010, Co. had total assets of $495.3 million and total deposits of $421.7 million.

**Recent Developments:** For the quarter ended Mar 31 2011, net income was unchanged at US$1.2 million versus US$1.2 million the year-earlier quarter. Net interest income increased 6.6% to US$4.9 million from US$4.6 million in the year-earlier quarter. Provision for loan losses was US$343,000 versus US$307,000 in the prior-year quarter, an increase of 11.7%. Non-interest income was unchanged at US$1.1 million, while non-interest expense advanced 8.1% to US$3.8 million.

**Prospects:** Our evaluation of Greene County Bancorp Inc. as of Sep. 6, 2011 is the result of our systematic analysis on three basic characteristics: earnings strength, relative valuation, and recent stock price movement. The company has produced a positive trend in earnings per share over the past 5 quarters. Because the company lacks sufficient analyst estimate data, we place greater weight on the historical EPS trend as the measure of earnings strength. Based on operating earnings yield, the company is undervalued when compared to all of the companies in our coverage universe. Share price changes over the past year indicates that GCBC will perform very poorly over the near term.

| Financial Data (US$ in Thousands) | 9 Mos | 6 Mos | 3 Mos | 06/30/2010 | 06/30/2009 | 06/30/2008 | 06/30/2007 | 06/30/2006 |
|---|---|---|---|---|---|---|---|---|
| Earnings Per Share | 1.24 | 1.24 | 1.21 | 1.18 | 0.99 | 0.65 | 0.54 | 0.54 |
| Cash Flow Per Share | 2.14 | 2.22 | 1.88 | 1.60 | 1.28 | 1.19 | 1.06 | 1.08 |
| Tang Book Value Per Share | 11.27 | 11.10 | 11.14 | 10.80 | 9.81 | 8.86 | 8.53 | 8.10 |
| Dividends Per Share | 0.900 | 0.895 | 0.690 | 0.685 | 0.680 | 0.700 | 0.480 | 0.450 |
| Dividend Payout % | 72.58 | 72.18 | 57.02 | 58.05 | 68.69 | 107.69 | 88.89 | 83.33 |
| **Income Statement** | | | | | | | | |
| Interest Income | 18,041 | 12,042 | 5,976 | 23,083 | 22,482 | 19,534 | 16,985 | 14,825 |
| Interest Expense | 3,429 | 2,350 | 1,179 | 5,366 | 6,752 | 7,344 | 6,442 | 4,137 |
| Net Interest Income | 14,612 | 9,692 | 4,797 | 17,717 | 15,730 | 12,190 | 10,543 | 10,688 |
| Provision for Losses | 1,179 | 836 | 353 | 1,273 | 2,018 | 581 | 279 | 200 |
| Non-Interest Income | 3,563 | 2,461 | 1,100 | 4,616 | 6,097 | 4,577 | 3,941 | 3,112 |
| Non-Interest Expense | 11,061 | 7,245 | 3,528 | 13,611 | 13,557 | 12,301 | 11,037 | 10,528 |
| Income Before Taxes | 5,935 | 4,072 | 2,016 | 7,449 | 6,252 | 3,885 | 3,168 | 3,072 |
| Income Taxes | 2,020 | 1,396 | 692 | 2,564 | 2,167 | 1,165 | 909 | 829 |
| Net Income | 3,915 | 2,676 | 1,324 | 4,885 | 4,085 | 2,720 | 2,259 | 2,243 |
| Average Shares | 4,172 | 4,163 | 4,152 | 4,134 | 4,121 | 4,157 | 4,193 | 4,179 |
| **Balance Sheet** | | | | | | | | |
| Net Loans & Leases | 296,651 | 296,165 | 299,394 | 295,582 | 267,902 | 238,440 | 207,280 | 190,093 |
| Total Assets | 560,444 | 531,356 | 529,481 | 495,323 | 460,536 | 379,608 | 325,826 | 307,565 |
| Total Deposits | 498,849 | 465,854 | 463,444 | 421,732 | 398,729 | 321,431 | 284,176 | 268,250 |
| Total Liabilities | 513,713 | 485,444 | 483,548 | 450,820 | 420,272 | 343,341 | 290,411 | 273,984 |
| Stockholders' Equity | 46,731 | 45,912 | 45,933 | 44,503 | 40,264 | 36,267 | 35,415 | 33,581 |
| Shares Outstanding | 4,145 | 4,135 | 4,123 | 4,118 | 4,105 | 4,095 | 4,151 | 4,145 |
| **Statistical Record** | | | | | | | | |
| Return on Assets % | 1.00 | 1.03 | 1.00 | 1.02 | 0.97 | 0.77 | 0.71 | 0.74 |
| Return on Equity % | 11.47 | 11.66 | 11.48 | 11.53 | 10.68 | 7.57 | 6.55 | 6.76 |
| Net Interest Margin % | 82.01 | 80.70 | 80.27 | 76.75 | 69.97 | 62.40 | 62.07 | 72.09 |
| Efficiency Ratio % | 53.74 | 50.05 | 49.86 | 49.14 | 47.44 | 51.02 | 52.74 | 58.69 |
| Loans to Deposits | 0.59 | 0.64 | 0.65 | 0.70 | 0.67 | 0.74 | 0.73 | 0.71 |
| Price Range | 19.96-14.50 | 19.96-14.46 | 18.31-14.25 | 18.31-13.50 | 15.50-9.50 | 14.25-11.00 | 16.00-13.35 | 19.00-14.34 |
| P/E Ratio | 16.10-11.69 | 16.10-11.66 | 15.13-11.78 | 15.52-11.44 | 15.66-9.60 | 21.92-16.92 | 29.63-24.72 | 35.19-26.56 |
| Average Yield % | 5.19 | 5.41 | 4.40 | 4.55 | 5.64 | 5.53 | 3.24 | 2.71 |

**Address:** 302 Main Street, Catskill, NY 12414
**Telephone:** 518-943-2600
**Fax:** 518-943-4328

**Web Site:** www.tbogc.com
**Officers:** Martin C. Smith - Chairman Donald E. Gibson - President, Chief Executive Officer

**Auditors:** ParenteBeard LLC
**Transfer Agents:** Computershare Trust Company, N.A., Canton, MA

# HARLEYSVILLE SAVINGS FINANCIAL CORP

| Exchange | Symbol | Price | 52Wk Range | Yield | P/E |
|---|---|---|---|---|---|
| NMS | HARL | $14.24 (8/31/2011) | 15.56-13.20 | 5.34 | 9.49 |

*7 Year Price Score 95.86 *NYSE Composite Index=100 *12 Month Price Score 98.32

**Interim Earnings (Per Share)**

| Qtr. | Dec | Mar | Jun | Sep |
|---|---|---|---|---|
| 2007-08 | 0.21 | 0.28 | 0.29 | 0.43 |
| 2008-09 | 0.38 | 0.33 | 0.24 | 0.36 |
| 2009-10 | 0.33 | 0.32 | 0.36 | 0.35 |
| 2010-11 | 0.33 | 0.29 | 0.53 | ... |

**Interim Dividends (Per Share)**

| Amt | Decl | Ex | Rec | Pay |
|---|---|---|---|---|
| 0.19Q | 10/20/2010 | 11/08/2010 | 11/10/2010 | 11/24/2010 |
| 0.19Q | 01/26/2011 | 02/07/2011 | 02/09/2011 | 02/23/2011 |
| 0.19Q | 04/20/2011 | 05/09/2011 | 05/11/2011 | 05/25/2011 |
| 0.19Q | 07/20/2011 | 08/08/2011 | 08/10/2011 | 08/24/2011 |

**Indicated Div: $0.76**

**Valuation Analysis**

| | |
|---|---|
| Forecast EPS | N/A |
| Market Cap | $53.4 Million |
| Book Value | $56.6 Million |
| Price/Book | 0.94 |
| Price/Sales | N/A |

**Institutional Holding**

| | |
|---|---|
| No of Institutions | 11 |
| Shares | 236,575 |
| % Held | 6.49 |

**Business Summary:** Credit & Lending (MIC: 5.4.1 SIC: 6036 NAIC: 522120)

Harleysville Savings Financial is a bank holding company for Harleysville Savings Bank (the Bank). The Bank is engaged in accepting deposits from the general public and business customers through deposit programs and investing such deposits in first mortgage loans secured by residential properties. The Bank originates consumer loans, mainly home equity loans and lines of credit. The Bank is also engaged in the general commercial banking business, and provides commercial loans and commercial real estate loans. The Bank's primary market area includes Montgomery County, and, to a lesser extent, Bucks County. At Sep 30 2010, Co. had total assets of $857.1 million and deposits of $528.1 million.

**Recent Developments:** For the quarter ended June 30 2011, net income increased 51.3% to US$2.0 million from US$1.3 million in the year-earlier quarter. Net interest income increased 2.1% to US$4.8 million from US$4.7 million in the year-earlier quarter. Provision for loan losses was US$165,000 versus US$150,000 in the prior-year quarter, an increase of 10.0%. Non-interest income rose 199.2% to US$1.5 million from US$508,000, while non-interest expense advanced 5.6% to US$3.4 million.

**Prospects:** Co.'s near-term outlook appears encouraging. In detail, Co. is experiencing growth in net interest income, primarily driven by a reduction in interest expense. In addition, Co. noted an increase in non-interest income, mainly due to a Bank Owned Life Insurance benefit. Co. is also seeing an improvement in its interest rate spread as it continues to increase the number of relationships with customers wanting to establish their checking and savings accounts with a locally owned and managed community bank. Accordingly, Co. anticipates that its interest rate spread will continue to improve as high cost liabilities reprice over the coming quarters.

**Financial Data**

| (US$ in Thousands) | 9 Mos | 6 Mos | 3 Mos | 09/30/2010 | 09/30/2009 | 09/30/2008 | 09/30/2007 | 09/30/2006 |
|---|---|---|---|---|---|---|---|---|
| Earnings Per Share | 1.50 | 1.33 | 1.36 | 1.36 | 1.31 | 1.20 | 0.83 | 1.08 |
| Cash Flow Per Share | 1.56 | 2.13 | 2.23 | 1.42 | 1.14 | 1.74 | 0.95 | 1.03 |
| Tang Book Value Per Share | 15.09 | 14.74 | 14.63 | 14.47 | 13.82 | 13.23 | 12.65 | 12.59 |
| Dividends Per Share | 0.760 | 0.760 | 0.760 | 0.760 | 0.730 | 0.690 | 0.680 | 0.640 |
| Dividend Payout % | 50.67 | 57.14 | 55.88 | 55.88 | 55.73 | 57.50 | 81.93 | 59.26 |
| **Income Statement** | | | | | | | | |
| Interest Income | 28,216 | 18,722 | 9,430 | 40,018 | 41,343 | 43,076 | 40,289 | 39,091 |
| Interest Expense | 14,475 | 9,739 | 4,975 | 21,747 | 24,886 | 29,016 | 28,806 | 26,366 |
| Net Interest Income | 13,741 | 8,983 | 4,455 | 18,271 | 16,457 | 14,060 | 11,483 | 12,725 |
| Provision for Losses | 490 | 325 | 150 | 600 | 400 | 85 | ... | ... |
| Non-Interest Income | 2,453 | 933 | 501 | 1,987 | 1,471 | 1,730 | 1,890 | 1,300 |
| Non-Interest Expense | 9,888 | 6,502 | 3,161 | 12,702 | 11,527 | 10,094 | 9,216 | 8,568 |
| Income Before Taxes | 5,816 | 3,089 | 1,645 | 6,956 | 6,001 | 5,611 | 4,157 | 5,457 |
| Income Taxes | 1,518 | 779 | 429 | 1,948 | 1,285 | 1,232 | 911 | 1,255 |
| Net Income | 4,298 | 2,310 | 1,216 | 5,008 | 4,716 | 4,379 | 3,246 | 4,202 |
| Average Shares | 3,771 | 3,758 | 3,731 | 3,685 | 3,610 | 3,663 | 3,896 | 3,903 |
| **Balance Sheet** | | | | | | | | |
| Net Loans & Leases | 509,467 | 501,180 | 504,787 | 510,093 | 498,391 | 476,858 | 419,053 | 385,450 |
| Total Assets | 857,579 | 856,478 | 856,681 | 857,140 | 830,007 | 825,675 | 773,544 | 775,638 |
| Total Deposits | 531,102 | 531,272 | 531,647 | 528,100 | 466,601 | 425,513 | 424,035 | 429,254 |
| Total Liabilities | 801,028 | 801,469 | 802,477 | 803,789 | 779,868 | 778,466 | 726,503 | 727,166 |
| Stockholders' Equity | 56,551 | 55,009 | 54,204 | 53,351 | 50,139 | 47,209 | 47,041 | 48,471 |
| Shares Outstanding | 3,747 | 3,731 | 3,704 | 3,687 | 3,627 | 3,567 | 3,717 | 3,849 |
| **Statistical Record** | | | | | | | | |
| Return on Assets % | 0.65 | 0.58 | 0.59 | 0.59 | 0.57 | 0.55 | 0.42 | 0.54 |
| Return on Equity % | 10.30 | 9.27 | 9.53 | 9.68 | 9.69 | 9.27 | 6.80 | 8.75 |
| Net Interest Margin % | 50.12 | 48.72 | 47.24 | 45.66 | 39.81 | 32.64 | 28.50 | 32.55 |
| Efficiency Ratio % | 30.74 | 34.35 | 31.83 | 30.24 | 26.92 | 22.53 | 21.85 | 21.21 |
| Loans to Deposits | 0.96 | 0.94 | 0.95 | 0.97 | 1.07 | 1.12 | 0.99 | 0.90 |
| Price Range | 15.72-14.01 | 15.72-13.35 | 15.72-13.12 | 15.72-12.30 | 15.90-10.50 | 14.50-10.70 | 19.26-13.40 | 18.25-16.16 |
| P/E Ratio | 10.48-9.34 | 11.82-10.04 | 11.56-9.65 | 11.56-9.04 | 12.14-8.02 | 12.08-8.92 | 23.20-16.14 | 16.90-14.96 |
| Average Yield % | 5.06 | 5.10 | 5.24 | 5.37 | 5.57 | 5.30 | 4.11 | 3.69 |

**Address:** 271 Main Street, Harleysville, PA 19438
**Telephone:** 215-256-8828
**Fax:** 215-256-0510

**Web Site:** www.harleysvillesavings.com
**Officers:** Edward J. Molnar - Chairman Ronald B. Geib - President, Chief Executive Officer

**Auditors:** ParenteBeard LLC
**Investor Contact:** 215-256-8828
**Transfer Agents:** Registrar and Transfer Company, Cranford, NJ

# JUNIATA VALLEY FINANCIAL CORP

| Exchange | Symbol | Price | 52Wk Range | Yield | P/E |
|---|---|---|---|---|---|
| OTC | JUVF | $17.60 (8/29/2011) | 18.00-16.55 | 5.00 | 15.30 |

***7 Year Price Score 84.33** *NYSE Composite Index=100 ***12 Month Price Score 102.69**

**Interim Earnings (Per Share)**

| Qtr. | Mar | Jun | Sep | Dec |
|---|---|---|---|---|
| 2008 | 0.32 | 0.32 | 0.33 | 0.34 |
| 2009 | 0.32 | 0.27 | 0.30 | 0.29 |
| 2010 | 0.27 | 0.26 | 0.30 | 0.30 |
| 2011 | 0.29 | 0.26 | ... | ... |

**Interim Dividends (Per Share)**

| Amt | Decl | Ex | Rec | Pay |
|---|---|---|---|---|
| 0.21Q | 10/19/2010 | 11/10/2010 | 11/15/2010 | 12/01/2010 |
| 0.21Q | 01/18/2011 | 02/11/2011 | 02/15/2011 | 03/01/2011 |
| 0.21Q | 04/19/2011 | 05/12/2011 | 05/16/2011 | 06/01/2011 |
| 0.22Q | 07/19/2011 | 08/11/2011 | 08/15/2011 | 09/01/2011 |

**Indicated Div: $0.88**

| Valuation Analysis | | Institutional Holding |
|---|---|---|
| Forecast EPS | N/A | No of Institutions |
| | | 2 |
| Market Cap | $74.6 Million | Shares |
| Book Value | $50.5 Million | 17,600 |
| Price/Book | 1.48 | % Held |
| Price/Sales | N/A | 0.41 |

**Business Summary:** Banking (MIC: 5.1.1 SIC: 6022 NAIC: 522110)

Juniata Valley Financial is a bank holding company. Through its subsidiary, The Juniata Valley Bank (the Bank), Co. provides retail and commercial banking services and other financial services in central Pennsylvania. Banking services include on-line banking, an automatic teller machine network, checking accounts, savings accounts, money market accounts, fixed rate certificates of deposit, club accounts, secured and unsecured commercial and consumer loans, construction and mortgage loans, safe deposit facilities, credit loans with overdraft checking protection, student loans as well as trust services. As of Dec 31 2010, Co. had total assets of $435.8 million and deposits of $376.8 million.

**Recent Developments:** For the quarter ended June 30 2011, net income was unchanged at US$1.1 million versus US$1.1 million the year-earlier quarter. Net interest income decreased 5.1% to US$3.8 million from US$4.0 million in the year-earlier quarter. Provision for loan losses was US$116,000 versus US$282,000 in the prior-year quarter, a decrease of 58.9%. Non-interest income was unchanged at US$1.0 million, while non-interest expense was unchanged at US$3.3 million.

**Prospects:** While provision for loan losses benefited from a reduction in overall outstanding loan balances, Co.'s overall results reflects a decline in net interest income. In detail, the increase in deposits, in addition to the low general rate environment, contributed to the reduction in the cost to fund earning assets. Co. is also seeing lower non-interest income driven by a reduction in customer service fees as a result of regulations enacted in Jul 2010 that prohibit banks from charging certain fees for services provided to customers that overdraw deposit accounts, partially offset by an increase in other non-interest income, driven by higher fees derived from electronic payment activity.

| **Financial Data** (US$ in Thousands) | 6 Mos | 3 Mos | 12/31/2010 | 12/31/2009 | 12/31/2008 | 12/31/2007 | 12/31/2006 | 12/31/2005 |
|---|---|---|---|---|---|---|---|---|
| Earnings Per Share | 1.15 | 1.15 | 1.14 | 1.18 | 1.31 | 1.22 | 1.11 | 1.00 |
| Cash Flow Per Share | 1.55 | 1.57 | 1.60 | 1.08 | 0.97 | 1.61 | 1.20 | 1.14 |
| Tang Book Value Per Share | 11.38 | 11.23 | 11.20 | 11.13 | 10.62 | 10.46 | 10.16 | 10.46 |
| Dividends Per Share | 0.840 | 0.830 | 0.820 | 0.780 | 0.740 | 0.950 | 0.660 | 1.110 |
| Dividend Payout % | 73.04 | 72.17 | 71.93 | 66.10 | 56.49 | 77.87 | 59.46 | 111.00 |
| **Income Statement** | | | | | | | | |
| Interest Income | 10,128 | 5,088 | 21,574 | 23,268 | 25,230 | 26,723 | 24,663 | 22,707 |
| Interest Expense | 2,381 | 1,183 | 5,502 | 7,279 | 9,057 | 11,060 | 10,111 | 8,015 |
| Net Interest Income | 7,747 | 3,905 | 16,072 | 15,989 | 16,173 | 15,663 | 14,552 | 14,692 |
| Provision for Losses | 204 | 88 | 741 | 627 | 421 | 120 | 54 | 28 |
| Non-Interest Income | 2,025 | 1,024 | 3,974 | 4,397 | 4,591 | 4,232 | 3,830 | 3,323 |
| Non-Interest Expense | 6,477 | 3,178 | 12,720 | 12,619 | 12,008 | 12,209 | 11,245 | 11,680 |
| Income Before Taxes | 3,091 | 1,663 | 6,545 | 6,914 | 7,781 | 7,533 | 7,083 | 6,307 |
| Income Taxes | 761 | 424 | 1,630 | 1,808 | 2,057 | 2,099 | 2,081 | 1,741 |
| Net Income | 2,330 | 1,239 | 4,915 | 5,106 | 5,724 | 5,434 | 5,002 | 4,566 |
| Average Shares | 4,240 | 4,259 | 4,300 | 4,345 | 4,385 | 4,444 | 4,492 | 4,568 |
| **Balance Sheet** | | | | | | | | |
| Net Loans & Leases | 289,128 | 294,549 | 295,278 | 308,911 | 312,522 | 295,678 | 303,246 | 295,300 |
| Total Assets | 452,004 | 444,740 | 435,753 | 442,109 | 428,084 | 420,146 | 415,931 | 410,802 |
| Total Deposits | 393,553 | 386,417 | 376,790 | 377,397 | 357,031 | 359,457 | 355,169 | 343,467 |
| Total Liabilities | 401,518 | 394,837 | 385,777 | 391,506 | 379,599 | 371,574 | 368,145 | 363,683 |
| Stockholders' Equity | 50,486 | 49,903 | 49,976 | 50,603 | 48,485 | 48,572 | 47,786 | 47,119 |
| Shares Outstanding | 4,236 | 4,238 | 4,257 | 4,337 | 4,341 | 4,409 | 4,457 | 4,503 |
| **Statistical Record** | | | | | | | | |
| Return on Assets % | 1.10 | 1.12 | 1.12 | 1.17 | 1.35 | 1.30 | 1.21 | 1.13 |
| Return on Equity % | 9.74 | 9.86 | 9.77 | 10.31 | 11.76 | 11.28 | 10.54 | 9.39 |
| Net Interest Margin % | 76.23 | 76.75 | 74.50 | 68.72 | 64.10 | 58.61 | 59.00 | 64.70 |
| Efficiency Ratio % | 54.61 | 52.00 | 49.79 | 45.61 | 40.27 | 39.44 | 39.47 | 44.87 |
| Loans to Deposits | 0.73 | 0.76 | 0.78 | 0.82 | 0.88 | 0.82 | 0.85 | 0.86 |
| Price Range | 18.00-16.55 | 18.00-16.25 | 18.00-16.25 | 19.00-16.00 | 22.00-19.00 | 23.75-20.00 | 24.50-21.00 | 25.50-21.10 |
| P/E Ratio | 15.65-14.39 | 15.65-14.13 | 15.79-14.25 | 16.10-13.56 | 16.79-14.50 | 19.47-16.39 | 22.07-18.92 | 25.50-21.10 |
| Average Yield % | 4.94 | 4.85 | 4.76 | 4.56 | 3.60 | 4.58 | 2.93 | 4.72 |

**Address:** Bridge and Main Streets, Mifflintown, PA 17059
**Telephone:** 717-436-8211

**Web Site:** www.JVBonline.com
**Officers:** Philip E. Gingerich - Chairman Timothy I. Havice - Vice-Chairman

**Auditors:** ParenteBeard LLC
**Investor Contact:** 717-436-8211
**Transfer Agents:** Registrar and Transfer Company, Cranford, NJ

# NATIONAL BANKSHARES INC. (VA)

| Exchange | Symbol | Price | 52Wk Range | Yield | P/E |
|---|---|---|---|---|---|
| NAS | NKSH | $25.91 (8/31/2011) | 32.28-23.21 | 3.71 | 11.17 |

*7 Year Price Score 115.11 *NYSE Composite Index=100 *12 Month Price Score 95.56

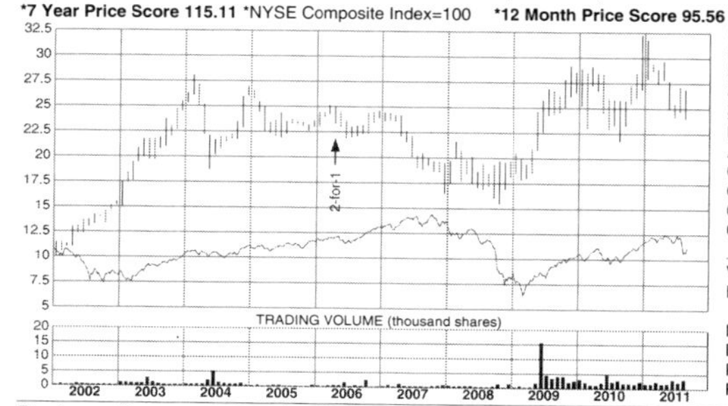


**Interim Earnings (Per Share)**

| Qtr. | Mar | Jun | Sep | Dec |
|---|---|---|---|---|
| 2008 | 0.46 | 0.50 | 0.52 | 0.48 |
| 2009 | 0.49 | 0.48 | 0.54 | 0.54 |
| 2010 | 0.54 | 0.58 | 0.58 | 0.55 |
| 2011 | 0.58 | 0.61 | ... | ... |

**Interim Dividends (Per Share)**

| Amt | Decl | Ex | Rec | Pay |
|---|---|---|---|---|
| 0.43S | 11/12/2009 | 11/19/2009 | 11/23/2009 | 12/01/2009 |
| 0.44S | 05/12/2010 | 05/20/2010 | 05/24/2010 | 06/01/2010 |
| 0.47S | 11/10/2010 | 11/17/2010 | 11/19/2010 | 12/01/2010 |
| 0.48S | 05/11/2011 | 05/19/2011 | 05/23/2011 | 06/01/2011 |

**Indicated Div: $0.96**

| Valuation Analysis | | Institutional Holding |
|---|---|---|
| Forecast EPS | $2.41 (09/02/2011) | No of Institutions 58 |
| Market Cap | $179.8 Million | Shares 1,834,639 |
| Book Value | $136.3 Million | |
| Price/Book | 1.32 | % Held 24.33 |
| Price/Sales | N/A | |

**Business Summary:** Banking (MIC: 5.1.1 SIC: 6021 NAIC: 522110)

National Bankshares is a financial holding company. Co. operates mainly through its wholly-owned bank subsidiary, the National Bank of Blacksburg (NBB), which provides a range of retail and commercial banking services to individuals, businesses, non-profits and local governments from its headquarters in Blacksburg, VA and 24 branch offices throughout southwest Virginia. NBB has telephone and internet banking and it operates 25 automated teller machines in its service area. Co. also owns National Bankshares Financial Services, Inc., which provides non-deposit investment products and insurance products. As of Dec 31 2010, Co. had total assets of $1.02 billion and deposits of $884.6 million.

**Recent Developments:** For the quarter ended June 30 2011, net income increased 5.5% to US$4.2 million from US$4.0 million in the year-earlier quarter. Net interest income increased 6.7% to US$10.1 million from US$9.5 million in the year-earlier quarter. Provision for loan losses was US$753,000 versus US$852,000 in the prior-year quarter, a decrease of 11.6%. Non-interest income was unchanged at US$2.1 million, while non-interest expense advanced 5.8% to US$6.0 million.

**Prospects:** Our evaluation of National Bankshares Inc. (VA) as of Sep. 6, 2011 is the result of our systematic analysis on three basic characteristics: earnings strength, relative valuation, and recent stock price movement. The company has produced a positive trend in earnings per share over the past 5 quarters and while recent estimates for the company have remained steady, NKSH has posted better than expected results. Based on operating earnings yield, the company is undervalued when compared to all of the companies in our coverage universe. Share price changes over the past year indicates that NKSH will perform very poorly over the near term.

**Financial Data**

| (US$ in Thousands) | 6 Mos | 3 Mos | 12/31/2010 | 12/31/2009 | 12/31/2008 | 12/31/2007 | 12/31/2006 | 12/31/2005 |
|---|---|---|---|---|---|---|---|---|
| Earnings Per Share | 2.32 | 2.29 | 2.24 | 2.06 | 1.96 | 1.82 | 1.80 | 1.76 |
| Cash Flow Per Share | 3.15 | 2.92 | 2.68 | 2.15 | 2.28 | 2.23 | 2.02 | 2.20 |
| Tang Book Value Per Share | 18.06 | 17.65 | 16.97 | 15.79 | 13.91 | 12.94 | 11.57 | 10.66 |
| Dividends Per Share | 0.950 | 0.910 | 0.910 | 0.840 | 0.800 | 0.760 | 0.730 | 0.710 |
| Dividend Payout % | 40.95 | 39.74 | 40.63 | 40.78 | 40.82 | 41.76 | 40.56 | 40.34 |
| **Income Statement** | | | | | | | | |
| Interest Income | 24,940 | 12,465 | 49,139 | 50,487 | 50,111 | 50,769 | 47,901 | 45,380 |
| Interest Expense | 4,725 | 2,379 | 11,158 | 15,825 | 18,818 | 21,745 | 18,564 | 14,180 |
| Net Interest Income | 20,215 | 10,086 | 37,981 | 34,662 | 31,293 | 29,024 | 29,337 | 31,200 |
| Provision for Losses | 1,553 | 800 | 3,409 | 1,634 | 1,119 | 423 | 49 | 567 |
| Non-Interest Income | 4,024 | 1,934 | 8,347 | 8,804 | 9,087 | 8,760 | 8,802 | 7,613 |
| Non-Interest Expense | 12,109 | 6,084 | 23,127 | 23,853 | 22,023 | 20,956 | 21,670 | 21,898 |
| Income Before Taxes | 10,577 | 5,136 | 19,792 | 17,979 | 17,238 | 16,405 | 16,420 | 16,348 |
| Income Taxes | 2,337 | 1,112 | 4,223 | 3,660 | 3,645 | 3,730 | 3,788 | 3,924 |
| Net Income | 8,240 | 4,024 | 15,569 | 14,319 | 13,593 | 12,675 | 12,632 | 12,424 |
| Average Shares | 6,946 | 6,957 | 6,949 | 6,945 | 6,935 | 6,985 | 7,024 | 7,061 |
| **Balance Sheet** | | | | | | | | |
| Net Loans & Leases | 585,078 | 579,657 | 568,779 | 583,021 | 569,699 | 518,435 | 495,486 | 487,162 |
| Total Assets | 1,034,857 | 1,026,558 | 1,022,238 | 982,367 | 935,374 | 887,647 | 868,203 | 841,498 |
| Total Deposits | 892,187 | 885,895 | 884,583 | 852,112 | 817,848 | 776,339 | 764,692 | 745,649 |
| Total Liabilities | 898,549 | 892,893 | 893,051 | 860,291 | 825,266 | 782,847 | 771,448 | 749,559 |
| Stockholders' Equity | 136,308 | 133,665 | 129,187 | 122,076 | 110,108 | 104,800 | 96,755 | 91,939 |
| Shares Outstanding | 6,937 | 6,935 | 6,933 | 6,933 | 6,929 | 6,952 | 6,980 | 7,019 |
| **Statistical Record** | | | | | | | | |
| Return on Assets % | 1.58 | 1.57 | 1.55 | 1.49 | 1.49 | 1.44 | 1.48 | 1.52 |
| Return on Equity % | 12.15 | 12.16 | 12.39 | 12.33 | 12.62 | 12.58 | 13.39 | 13.88 |
| Net Interest Margin % | 81.19 | 80.91 | 77.29 | 68.66 | 62.45 | 57.17 | 61.25 | 68.75 |
| Efficiency Ratio % | 41.37 | 42.25 | 40.23 | 40.23 | 37.20 | 35.20 | 38.22 | 41.32 |
| Loans to Deposits | 0.66 | 0.65 | 0.64 | 0.68 | 0.70 | 0.67 | 0.65 | 0.65 |
| Price Range | 32.28-21.76 | 32.28-21.76 | 32.28-21.76 | 29.21-17.91 | 21.64-15.50 | 24.49-16.48 | 25.15-21.90 | 26.84-21.88 |
| P/E Ratio | 13.91-9.38 | 14.10-9.50 | 14.41-9.71 | 14.18-8.69 | 11.04-7.91 | 13.46-9.05 | 13.97-12.17 | 15.25-12.43 |
| Average Yield % | 3.55 | 3.41 | 3.47 | 3.53 | 4.30 | 3.62 | 3.09 | 3.00 |

**Address:** 101 Hubbard Street, P.O. Box 90002, Blacksburg, VA 24062-9002
**Telephone:** 540-951-6300

**Web Site:** www.nationalbankshares.com
**Officers:** James G. Rakes - Chairman, President, Chief Executive Officer F. Brad Denardo - Executive Vice President

**Auditors:** Yount, Hyde & Barbour, P.C.
**Transfer Agents:** The National Bank of Blacksburg

# NORWOOD FINANCIAL CORP.

| Exchange | Symbol | Price | 52Wk Range | Yield | P/E |
|---|---|---|---|---|---|
| NMS | NWFL | $25.01 (8/31/2011) | 29.75-24.83 | 4.64 | 10.29 |

*7 Year Price Score 90.95 *NYSE Composite Index=100 *12 Month Price Score 96.75

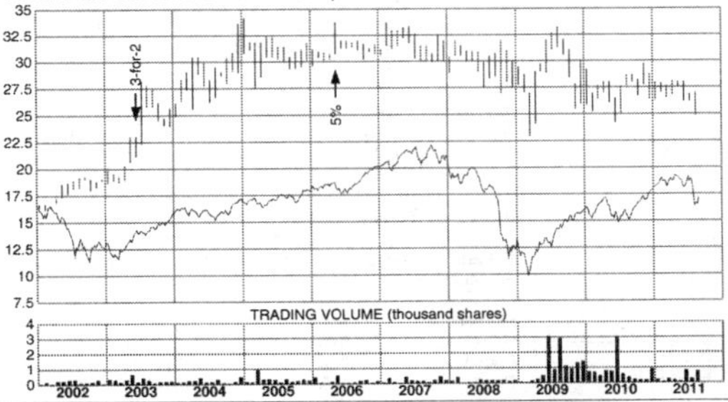


**Interim Earnings (Per Share)**

| Qtr. | Mar | Jun | Sep | Dec |
|---|---|---|---|---|
| 2008 | 0.64 | 0.62 | 0.58 | 0.57 |
| 2009 | 0.63 | 0.63 | 0.64 | 0.65 |
| 2010 | 0.65 | 0.66 | 0.68 | 0.65 |
| 2011 | 0.60 | 0.50 | ... | ... |

**Interim Dividends (Per Share)**

| Amt | Decl | Ex | Rec | Pay |
|---|---|---|---|---|
| 0.28Q | 09/14/2010 | 10/13/2010 | 10/15/2010 | 11/01/2010 |
| 0.29Q | ... | 01/12/2011 | 01/14/2011 | 02/01/2011 |
| 0.29Q | 03/08/2011 | 04/13/2011 | 04/15/2011 | 05/02/2011 |
| 0.29Q | 06/14/2011 | 07/13/2011 | 07/15/2011 | 08/01/2011 |

**Indicated Div: $1.16 (Div. Reinv. Plan)**

| **Valuation Analysis** | | **Institutional Holding** |
|---|---|---|
| Forecast EPS | N/A | No of Institutions 25 |
| Market Cap | $82.3 Million | Shares 409,068 |
| Book Value | $84.6 Million | % Held 14.76 |
| Price/Book | 0.97 | |
| Price/Sales | N/A | |

**Business Summary:** Banking (MIC: 5.1.1 SIC: 6022 NAIC: 522110)

Norwood Financial is the holding company for Wayne Bank (the Bank). The Bank is an independent community bank with five offices in Wayne County, three offices in Pike County and three offices in Monroe County. In addition, the Bank operates 11 automated teller machines. The Bank provides personal and business credit services and trust and investment products and real estate settlement services to the consumers, businesses, nonprofit organizations, and municipalities. The Bank primarily serves the Pennsylvania counties of Wayne, Pike and Monroe, as well as the counties of Lackawanna and Susquehanna. As of Dec 31 2010, Co. had total assets of $537.0 million and deposits of $393.9 million.

**Recent Developments:** For the quarter ended June 30 2011, net income decreased 18.4% to US$1.5 million from US$1.8 million in the year-earlier quarter. Net interest income increased 10.1% to US$5.3 million from US$4.8 million in the year-earlier quarter. Provision for loan losses was US$430,000 versus US$150,000 in the prior-year quarter, an increase of 186.7%. Non-interest income fell 2.3% to US$993,000 from US$1.0 million, while non-interest expense advanced 23.9% to US$3.9 million.

**Prospects:** Our evaluation of Norwood Financial Corp. as of Sep. 6, 2011 is the result of our systematic analysis on three basic characteristics: earnings strength, relative valuation, and recent stock price movement. The company has managed to produce a neutral trend in earnings per share over the past 5 quarters. Because the company lacks sufficient analyst estimate data, we place greater weight on the historical EPS trend as the measure of earnings strength. Based on operating earnings yield, the company is undervalued when compared to all of the companies in our coverage universe. Share price changes over the past year indicates that NWFL will perform poorly over the near term.

| **Financial Data** (US$ in Thousands) | 6 Mos | 3 Mos | 12/31/2010 | 12/31/2009 | 12/31/2008 | 12/31/2007 | 12/31/2006 | 12/31/2005 |
|---|---|---|---|---|---|---|---|---|
| Earnings Per Share | 2.43 | 2.59 | 2.64 | 2.55 | 2.41 | 2.30 | 2.07 | 1.92 |
| Cash Flow Per Share | 2.94 | 2.92 | 3.11 | 2.18 | 2.60 | 1.34 | 4.57 | 2.49 |
| Tang Book Value Per Share | 22.56 | 24.83 | 24.45 | 23.25 | 21.45 | 20.27 | 18.67 | 17.07 |
| Dividends Per Share | 1.140 | 1.130 | 1.120 | 1.080 | 1.000 | 0.920 | 0.820 | 0.686 |
| Dividend Payout % | 46.91 | 43.63 | 42.42 | 42.35 | 41.49 | 40.00 | 39.61 | 35.64 |
| **Income Statement** | | | | | | | | |
| Interest Income | 12,645 | 6,026 | 25,687 | 26,835 | 28,095 | 29,255 | 25,949 | 21,768 |
| Interest Expense | 2,546 | 1,245 | 6,023 | 7,726 | 9,694 | 11,983 | 9,766 | 6,505 |
| Net Interest Income | 10,099 | 4,781 | 19,664 | 19,109 | 18,401 | 17,272 | 16,183 | 15,263 |
| Provision for Losses | 650 | 220 | 1,000 | 1,685 | 735 | 315 | 220 | 350 |
| Non-Interest Income | 2,201 | 1,208 | 4,064 | 5,392 | 4,087 | 3,524 | 3,583 | 3,548 |
| Non-Interest Expense | 7,470 | 3,534 | 12,753 | 13,471 | 12,240 | 11,341 | 10,957 | 10,623 |
| Income Before Taxes | 4,180 | 2,235 | 9,975 | 9,345 | 9,513 | 9,140 | 8,589 | 7,838 |
| Income Taxes | 1,036 | 575 | 2,662 | 2,282 | 2,836 | 2,629 | 2,679 | 2,341 |
| Net Income | 3,144 | 1,660 | 7,313 | 7,063 | 6,677 | 6,511 | 5,910 | 5,497 |
| Average Shares | 2,939 | 2,770 | 2,766 | 2,766 | 2,769 | 2,826 | 2,850 | 2,859 |
| **Balance Sheet** | | | | | | | | |
| Net Loans & Leases | 459,379 | 344,348 | 351,239 | 358,021 | 345,171 | 327,215 | 311,739 | 287,221 |
| Total Assets | 703,795 | 530,926 | 537,005 | 529,696 | 504,296 | 480,610 | 454,356 | 433,556 |
| Total Deposits | 538,289 | 397,120 | 393,865 | 391,473 | 359,635 | 370,000 | 358,103 | 340,603 |
| Total Liabilities | 619,160 | 462,351 | 469,307 | 465,225 | 445,606 | 424,791 | 402,125 | 385,448 |
| Stockholders' Equity | 84,635 | 68,575 | 67,698 | 64,471 | 58,690 | 55,819 | 52,231 | 48,108 |
| Shares Outstanding | 3,292 | 2,761 | 2,768 | 2,772 | 2,736 | 2,753 | 2,797 | 2,818 |
| **Statistical Record** | | | | | | | | |
| Return on Assets % | 1.09 | 1.36 | 1.37 | 1.37 | 1.35 | 1.39 | 1.33 | 1.30 |
| Return on Equity % | 9.04 | 10.74 | 11.07 | 11.47 | 11.63 | 12.05 | 11.78 | 11.72 |
| Net Interest Margin % | 80.34 | 79.34 | 76.55 | 71.21 | 65.50 | 59.04 | 62.36 | 70.12 |
| Efficiency Ratio % | 51.71 | 48.85 | 42.87 | 41.80 | 38.03 | 34.60 | 37.10 | 41.96 |
| Loans to Deposits | 0.85 | 0.87 | 0.89 | 0.91 | 0.96 | 0.88 | 0.87 | 0.84 |
| Price Range | 29.75-25.00 | 29.75-24.18 | 29.75-24.18 | 33.25-22.95 | 32.00-27.00 | 33.75-29.90 | 33.75-29.59 | 34.18-27.48 |
| P/E Ratio | 12.24-10.29 | 11.49-9.34 | 11.27-9.16 | 13.04-9.00 | 13.28-11.20 | 14.67-13.00 | 16.30-14.29 | 17.80-14.31 |
| Average Yield % | 4.17 | 4.17 | 4.15 | 3.69 | 3.36 | 2.91 | 2.64 | 2.22 |

**Address:** 717 Main Street, Honesdale, PA 18431
**Telephone:** 570-253-1455
**Fax:** 570-253-3278

**Web Site:** www.waynebank.com
**Officers:** John E. Marshall - Chairman Lewis J. Critelli - President, Chief Executive Officer

**Auditors:** S.R. Snodgrass, A. C.
**Investor Contact:** 570-253-1455
**Transfer Agents:** Illinois Stock Transfer Company, Chicago, IL

# OHIO VALLEY BANC CORP.

| Exchange | Symbol | Price | 52Wk Range | Yield | P/E |
|---|---|---|---|---|---|
| NMS | OVBC | $17.38 (8/31/2011) | 22.96-16.12 | 4.83 | 13.07 |

***7 Year Price Score 80.39** *NYSE Composite Index=100 ***12 Month Price Score 91.26**

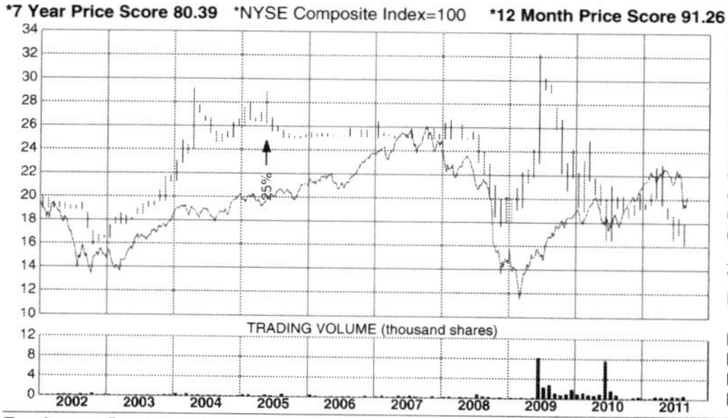


**Interim Earnings (Per Share)**

| Qtr. | Mar | Jun | Sep | Dec |
|---|---|---|---|---|
| 2008 | 0.48 | 0.43 | 0.47 | 0.39 |
| 2009 | 0.51 | 0.35 | 0.43 | 0.38 |
| 2010 | 0.48 | 0.37 | 0.10 | 0.33 |
| 2011 | 0.51 | 0.39 | ... | ... |

**Interim Dividends (Per Share)**

| Amt | Decl | Ex | Rec | Pay |
|---|---|---|---|---|
| 0.21Q | 10/19/2010 | 10/27/2010 | 10/29/2010 | 11/10/2010 |
| 0.21Q | 01/25/2011 | 02/02/2011 | 02/04/2011 | 02/10/2011 |
| 0.21Q | 04/19/2011 | 04/27/2011 | 04/29/2011 | 05/10/2011 |
| 0.21Q | 07/22/2011 | 08/02/2011 | 08/04/2011 | 08/10/2011 |

**Indicated Div: $0.84**

| **Valuation Analysis** | | **Institutional Holding** |
|---|---|---|
| Forecast EPS | N/A | No of Institutions 18 |
| Market Cap | $69.5 Million | Shares 218,686 |
| Book Value | $70.8 Million | |
| Price/Book | 0.98 | % Held 5.47 |
| Price/Sales | N/A | |

**Business Summary:** Banking (MIC: 5.1.1 SIC: 6022 NAIC: 522110)

Ohio Valley Banc is a financial holding company. Co. has one banking subsidiary, The Ohio Valley Bank Co. (the Bank), as well as a subsidiary that engages in consumer lending to individuals with higher credit risk history and an insurance agency that facilitates the receipts of insurance commissions. Co. accepts deposits in checking, savings, time and money market accounts and makes personal, commercial, floor plan, student, construction and real estate loans. The Bank also invests in U. S. Government and agency obligations, interest-bearing deposits in other financial institutions and other investments. At Dec 31 2010, Co. had total assets of $851.5 million and deposits of $694.8 million.

**Recent Developments:** For the quarter ended June 30 2011, net income increased 5.7% to US$1.6 million from US$1.5 million in the year-earlier quarter. Net interest income was unchanged at US$8.2 million versus the year-earlier quarter. Provision for loan losses was US$759,000 versus US$721,000 in the prior-year quarter, an increase of 5.3%. Non-interest income rose 10.7% to US$1.7 million from US$1.5 million, while non-interest expense was unchanged at US$7.0 million.

**Prospects:** Our evaluation of Ohio Valley Banc Corp. as of Sep. 6, 2011 is the result of our systematic analysis on three basic characteristics: earnings strength, relative valuation, and recent stock price movement. The company has produced a positive trend in earnings per share over the past 5 quarters. Because the company lacks sufficient analyst estimate data, we place greater weight on the historical EPS trend as the measure of earnings strength. Based on operating earnings yield, the company is undervalued when compared to all of the companies in our coverage universe. Share price changes over the past year indicates that OVBC will perform very poorly over the near term.

**Financial Data**

| (US$ in Thousands) | 6 Mos | 3 Mos | 12/31/2010 | 12/31/2009 | 12/31/2008 | 12/31/2007 | 12/31/2006 | 12/31/2005 |
|---|---|---|---|---|---|---|---|---|
| Earnings Per Share | 1.33 | 1.31 | 1.28 | 1.67 | 1.77 | 1.52 | 1.27 | 1.64 |
| Cash Flow Per Share | 4.23 | 3.71 | 3.09 | 1.24 | 2.32 | 2.73 | 2.87 | 2.46 |
| Tang Book Value Per Share | 17.38 | 17.04 | 16.72 | 16.38 | 15.51 | 14.79 | 14.07 | 13.60 |
| Dividends Per Share | 0.840 | 0.840 | 0.840 | 0.800 | 0.760 | 0.710 | 0.670 | 0.632 |
| Dividend Payout % | 63.16 | 64.12 | 65.63 | 47.90 | 42.94 | 46.71 | 52.76 | 38.54 |
| **Income Statement** | | | | | | | | |
| Interest Income | 22,842 | 12,025 | 46,514 | 47,623 | 51,533 | 54,947 | 52,421 | 46,071 |
| Interest Expense | 5,485 | 2,822 | 13,547 | 16,932 | 20,828 | 26,420 | 23,931 | 18,137 |
| Net Interest Income | 17,357 | 9,203 | 32,967 | 30,691 | 30,705 | 28,527 | 28,490 | 27,934 |
| Provision for Losses | 3,703 | 2,944 | 5,871 | 3,212 | 3,716 | 2,252 | 5,662 | 1,797 |
| Non-Interest Income | 5,346 | 3,659 | 6,154 | 7,747 | 6,211 | 5,236 | 5,830 | 5,522 |
| Non-Interest Expense | 14,079 | 7,098 | 26,643 | 26,309 | 23,343 | 22,583 | 21,199 | 21,359 |
| Income Before Taxes | 4,921 | 2,820 | 6,607 | 8,917 | 9,857 | 8,928 | 7,459 | 10,300 |
| Income Taxes | 1,333 | 787 | 1,511 | 2,272 | 2,729 | 2,631 | 2,061 | 3,283 |
| Net Income | 3,588 | 2,033 | 5,096 | 6,645 | 7,128 | 6,297 | 5,398 | 7,017 |
| Average Shares | 4,000 | 4,000 | 3,984 | 3,983 | 4,018 | 4,131 | 4,230 | 4,278 |
| **Balance Sheet** | | | | | | | | |
| Net Loans & Leases | 616,891 | 622,988 | 631,936 | 643,158 | 622,592 | 630,366 | 615,752 | 610,399 |
| Total Assets | 838,290 | 874,288 | 851,514 | 811,988 | 781,108 | 783,418 | 764,361 | 749,719 |
| Total Deposits | 681,554 | 726,725 | 694,781 | 647,644 | 592,361 | 589,026 | 593,786 | 562,866 |
| Total Liabilities | 767,485 | 804,855 | 783,386 | 745,467 | 718,052 | 721,907 | 704,079 | 690,448 |
| Stockholders' Equity | 70,805 | 69,433 | 68,128 | 66,521 | 63,056 | 61,511 | 60,282 | 59,271 |
| Shares Outstanding | 4,000 | 4,000 | 4,000 | 3,984 | 3,983 | 4,074 | 4,193 | 4,264 |
| **Statistical Record** | | | | | | | | |
| Return on Assets % | 0.64 | 0.61 | 0.61 | 0.83 | 0.91 | 0.81 | 0.71 | 0.95 |
| Return on Equity % | 7.63 | 7.63 | 7.57 | 10.26 | 11.41 | 10.34 | 9.03 | 12.11 |
| Net Interest Margin % | 75.38 | 76.53 | 70.88 | 64.45 | 59.58 | 51.92 | 54.35 | 60.63 |
| Efficiency Ratio % | 55.83 | 45.26 | 50.59 | 47.51 | 40.42 | 37.52 | 36.39 | 41.40 |
| Loans to Deposits | 0.91 | 0.86 | 0.91 | 0.99 | 1.05 | 1.07 | 1.04 | 1.08 |
| Price Range | 22.96-16.47 | 22.76-16.47 | 24.99-16.47 | 32.28-18.00 | 26.65-17.65 | 26.49-25.00 | 25.89-25.00 | 29.00-24.99 |
| P/E Ratio | 17.26-12.38 | 17.37-12.57 | 19.52-12.87 | 19.33-10.78 | 15.06-9.97 | 17.43-16.45 | 20.39-19.69 | 17.68-15.24 |
| Average Yield % | 4.37 | 4.30 | 4.19 | 3.23 | 3.27 | 2.82 | 2.66 | 2.42 |

**Address:** 420 Third Avenue, Gallipolis, OH 45631
**Telephone:** 740-446-2631

**Web Site:** www.ovbc.com
**Officers:** Jeffrey E. Smith - Chairman, Chief Executive Officer Thomas E. Wiseman - President, Chief Operating Officer

**Auditors:** Crowe Horwath LLP
**Transfer Agents:** Ohio Valley Banc Corp

# ORRSTOWN FINANCIAL SERVICES, INC.

| Exchange | Symbol | Price | 52Wk Range | Yield | P/E |
|---|---|---|---|---|---|
| NAS | ORRF | $14.30 (8/31/2011) | 29.28-14.30 | 6.43 | 46.13 |

*7 Year Price Score 74.55 *NYSE Composite Index=100 *12 Month Price Score 80.30

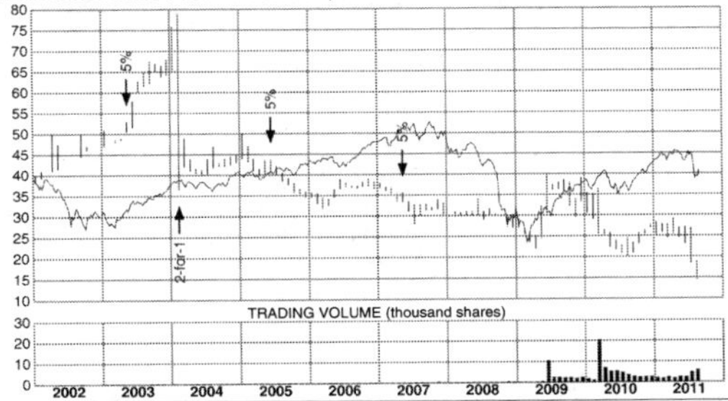


**Interim Earnings (Per Share)**

| Qtr. | Mar | Jun | Sep | Dec |
|---|---|---|---|---|
| 2008 | 0.48 | 0.54 | 0.46 | 0.46 |
| 2009 | 0.45 | 0.51 | 0.58 | 0.44 |
| 2010 | 0.50 | 0.47 | 0.61 | 0.55 |
| 2011 | 0.48 | (1.33) | ... | ... |

**Interim Dividends (Per Share)**

| Amt | Decl | Ex | Rec | Pay |
|---|---|---|---|---|
| 0.225Q | 10/28/2010 | 11/09/2010 | 11/12/2010 | 11/24/2010 |
| 0.23Q | 01/27/2011 | 02/09/2011 | 02/11/2011 | 02/23/2011 |
| 0.23Q | 04/28/2011 | 05/11/2011 | 05/13/2011 | 05/25/2011 |
| 0.23Q | 07/28/2011 | 08/10/2011 | 08/12/2011 | 08/24/2011 |

**Indicated Div: $0.92**

| Valuation Analysis | | Institutional Holding | |
|---|---|---|---|
| Forecast EPS | $0.25 (09/02/2011) | No of Institutions | 60 |
| Market Cap | $114.6 Million | Shares | 2,217,765 |
| Book Value | $153.4 Million | % Held | 34.68 |
| Price/Book | 0.75 | | |
| Price/Sales | N/A | | |

**Business Summary:** Banking (MIC: 5.1.1 SIC: 6022 NAIC: 522110)

Orrstown Financial Services is the bank holding company for Orrstown Bank (the Bank). Through the Bank, Co. is engaged in providing banking and bank related services in South Central Pennsylvania, principally Franklin, Perry and Cumberland Counties and in Washington County, MD. The Bank provides lending services such as commercial loans, residential loans, commercial mortgages and various forms of consumer lending, as well as deposit services such as checking, savings, time and money market deposits. The Bank also provides investment and brokerage services through its Orrstown Financial Advisors division. At Dec 31 2010, Co. had total assets of $1.51 billion and deposits of $1.19 billion.

**Recent Developments:** For the quarter ended June 30 2011, net loss amounted to US$10.6 million versus net income of US$3.9 million in the year-earlier quarter. Net interest income increased 13.4% to US$12.8 million from US$11.3 million in the year-earlier quarter. Provision for loan losses was US$21.2 million versus US$5.0 million in the prior-year quarter, an increase of 324.6%. Non-interest income fell 30.4% to US$5.2 million from US$7.5 million, while non-interest expense advanced 14.1% to US$9.7 million.

**Prospects:** Our evaluation of Orrstown Financial Services Inc. as of Sep. 6, 2011 is the result of our systematic analysis on three basic characteristics: earnings strength, relative valuation, and recent stock price movement. The company has suffered a very negative trend in earnings per share over the past 5 quarters. However, while recent estimates for the company have been lowered by analysts, ORRF has posted results that fell short of analysts expectations. Based on operating earnings yield, the company is overvalued when compared to all of the companies in our coverage universe. Share price changes over the past year indicates that ORRF will perform very well over the near term.

| Financial Data (US$ in Thousands) | 6 Mos | 3 Mos | 12/31/2010 | 12/31/2009 | 12/31/2008 | 12/31/2007 | 12/31/2006 | 12/31/2005 |
|---|---|---|---|---|---|---|---|---|
| Earnings Per Share | 0.31 | 2.11 | 2.17 | 1.98 | 1.94 | 1.86 | 1.80 | 1.69 |
| Cash Flow Per Share | 3.33 | 3.32 | 3.26 | 1.92 | 2.21 | 1.97 | 2.14 | 1.74 |
| Tang Book Value Per Share | 16.58 | 17.77 | 17.50 | 13.96 | 13.01 | 11.65 | 10.53 | 10.03 |
| Dividends Per Share | 0.910 | 0.900 | 0.890 | 0.880 | 0.870 | 0.820 | 0.743 | 0.673 |
| Dividend Payout % | 293.55 | 42.65 | 41.01 | 44.44 | 44.85 | 44.09 | 41.27 | 39.95 |
| **Income Statement** | | | | | | | | |
| Interest Income | 30,862 | 15,325 | 58,423 | 53,070 | 52,313 | 53,106 | 44,788 | 32,415 |
| Interest Expense | 5,664 | 2,937 | 12,688 | 16,500 | 19,408 | 22,986 | 17,371 | 9,537 |
| Net Interest Income | 25,198 | 12,388 | 45,735 | 36,570 | 32,905 | 30,120 | 27,417 | 22,878 |
| Provision for Losses | 24,425 | 3,195 | 8,925 | 4,865 | 1,450 | 750 | 390 | 144 |
| Non-Interest Income | 10,285 | 5,076 | 23,793 | 17,894 | 15,417 | 13,306 | 11,083 | 9,059 |
| Non-Interest Expense | 19,161 | 9,439 | 37,552 | 32,176 | 28,287 | 24,921 | 21,628 | 17,397 |
| Income Before Taxes | (8,103) | 4,830 | 23,051 | 17,423 | 18,585 | 17,755 | 16,482 | 14,396 |
| Income Taxes | (1,307) | 1,003 | 6,470 | 4,050 | 5,482 | 5,197 | 4,850 | 4,409 |
| Net Income | (6,796) | 3,827 | 16,581 | 13,373 | 13,103 | 12,558 | 11,632 | 9,987 |
| Average Shares | 8,000 | 8,026 | 7,639 | 6,740 | 6,750 | 6,735 | 6,475 | 5,918 |
| **Balance Sheet** | | | | | | | | |
| Net Loans & Leases | 976,766 | 970,376 | 950,966 | 870,007 | 813,328 | 695,823 | 613,307 | 455,958 |
| Total Assets | 1,531,290 | 1,512,393 | 1,511,722 | 1,196,432 | 1,051,783 | 884,979 | 809,031 | 601,460 |
| Total Deposits | 1,260,206 | 1,207,373 | 1,188,377 | 915,170 | 757,368 | 646,356 | 638,719 | 462,822 |
| Total Liabilities | 1,377,849 | 1,349,720 | 1,351,238 | 1,085,546 | 948,436 | 788,855 | 719,643 | 544,150 |
| Stockholders' Equity | 153,441 | 162,673 | 160,484 | 110,886 | 103,347 | 96,124 | 89,388 | 57,310 |
| Shares Outstanding | 8,013 | 7,991 | 7,985 | 6,443 | 6,316 | 6,419 | 6,441 | 5,711 |
| **Statistical Record** | | | | | | | | |
| Return on Assets % | 0.17 | 1.20 | 1.22 | 1.19 | 1.35 | 1.48 | 1.65 | 1.79 |
| Return on Equity % | 1.59 | 10.81 | 12.22 | 12.48 | 13.10 | 13.54 | 15.86 | 18.74 |
| Net Interest Margin % | 82.45 | 80.84 | 78.28 | 68.91 | 62.90 | 56.72 | 61.22 | 70.58 |
| Efficiency Ratio % | 46.86 | 46.27 | 45.67 | 45.34 | 41.76 | 37.52 | 38.71 | 41.95 |
| Loans to Deposits | 0.78 | 0.80 | 0.80 | 0.95 | 1.07 | 1.08 | 0.96 | 0.99 |
| Price Range | 29.28-20.26 | 28.39-20.26 | 36.42-20.26 | 39.80-22.00 | 33.96-27.00 | 38.00-28.10 | 39.00-31.80 | 50.00-34.50 |
| P/E Ratio | 94.45-65.35 | 13.45-9.60 | 16.78-9.34 | 20.10-11.11 | 17.51-13.92 | 20.43-15.11 | 21.67-17.67 | 29.59-20.41 |
| Average Yield % | 3.62 | 3.63 | 3.39 | 2.68 | 2.90 | 2.48 | 2.08 | 1.68 |

**Address:** 77 East King Street, P.O. Box 250, Shippensburg, PA 17257
**Telephone:** 717-532-6114

**Web Site:** www.orrstown.com
**Officers:** Joel R. Zullinger - Chairman Jeffrey W. Coy - Vice-Chairman

**Auditors:** Smith Elliott Kearns & Co.
**Transfer Agents:** Registrar and Transfer Company, Cranford, NJ

# REPUBLIC BANCORP, INC. (KY)

| Exchange | Symbol | Price | 52Wk Range | Yield | P/E |
|---|---|---|---|---|---|
| NMS | RBCA A | $17.80 (8/31/2011) | 24.37-16.00 | 3.46 | 4.07 |

*7 Year Price Score 96.62 *NYSE Composite Index=100 *12 Month Price Score 92.89

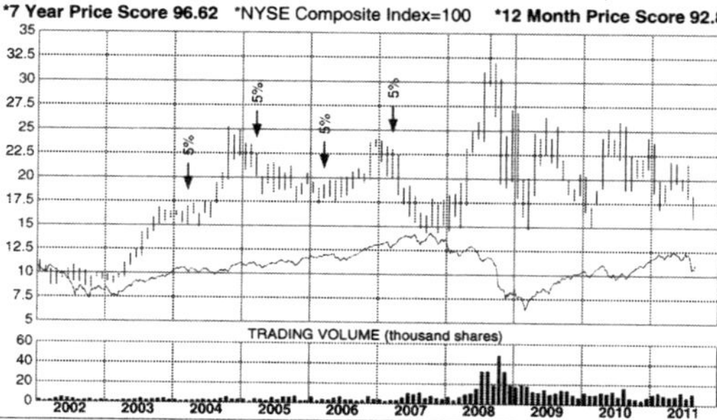


**Interim Earnings (Per Share)**

| Qtr. | Mar | Jun | Sep | Dec |
|---|---|---|---|---|
| 2008 | 0.96 | 0.31 | 0.22 | 0.03 |
| 2009 | 1.24 | 0.33 | 0.27 | 0.18 |
| 2010 | 2.14 | 0.40 | 0.35 | 0.21 |
| 2011 | 3.40 | 0.41 | ... | ... |

**Interim Dividends (Per Share)**

| Amt | Decl | Ex | Rec | Pay |
|---|---|---|---|---|
| 0.143Q | 11/17/2010 | 12/15/2010 | 12/17/2010 | 01/21/2011 |
| 0.143Q | 01/19/2011 | 03/16/2011 | 03/18/2011 | 04/15/2011 |
| 0.154Q | 05/09/2011 | 06/15/2011 | 06/17/2011 | 07/15/2011 |
| 0.154Q | 07/20/2011 | 09/14/2011 | 09/16/2011 | 10/21/2011 |

**Indicated Div: $0.62 (Div. Reinv. Plan)**

| Valuation Analysis | | Institutional Holding |
|---|---|---|
| Forecast EPS | $4.28 (09/02/2011) | No of Institutions 104 |
| Market Cap | $372.6 Million | Shares 4,897,950 |
| Book Value | $445.7 Million | |
| Price/Book | 0.84 | % Held |
| Price/Sales | N/A | 22.86 |

**Business Summary:** Banking (MIC: 5.1.1 SIC: 6022 NAIC: 522110)

Republic Bancorp is a bank holding company. Co.'s subsidiaries include Republic Bank & Trust Company and Republic Bank, Republic Funding Company and Republic Invest Co. At Dec 31 2010, Co. operated 43 banking centers, primarily in the retail banking industry, and conducted its operations predominately in metropolitan Louisville, KY, central Kentucky, northern Kentucky, southern Indiana, metropolitan Tampa, FL, metropolitan Cincinnati, OH and through an Internet banking delivery channel. Co.'s lending activities include mortgage lending, commercial lending, construction lending, and consumer lending. At Dec 31 2010, Co. had total assets of $3.62 billion and total deposits of $2.30 billion.

**Recent Developments:** For the quarter ended June 30 2011, net income increased 3.2% to US$8.7 million from US$8.4 million in the year-earlier quarter. Net interest income decreased 4.4% to US$26.8 million from US$28.1 million in the year-earlier quarter. Credit for loan losses was US$439,000 versus a provision for loan losses of US$3.0 million in the prior-year quarter. Non-interest income rose 24.9% to US$15.4 million from US$12.3 million, while non-interest expense advanced 15.7% to US$28.5 million.

**Prospects:** Our evaluation of Republic Bancorp Inc. (KY) as of Sep. 6, 2011 is the result of our systematic analysis on three basic characteristics: earnings strength, relative valuation, and recent stock price movement. The company has suffered a very negative trend in earnings per share over the past 5 quarters and while recent estimates for the company have remained steady, RBCAA has posted results that fell short of analysts expectations. Based on operating earnings yield, the company is undervalued when compared to all of the companies in our coverage universe. Share price changes over the past year indicates that RBCAA will perform poorly over the near term.

**Financial Data**
(US$ in Thousands)

| | 6 Mos | 3 Mos | 12/31/2010 | 12/31/2009 | 12/31/2008 | 12/31/2007 | 12/31/2006 | 12/31/2005 |
|---|---|---|---|---|---|---|---|---|
| Earnings Per Share | 4.37 | 4.36 | 3.10 | 2.02 | 1.62 | 1.20 | 1.35 | 1.63 |
| Cash Flow Per Share | 6.01 | 7.40 | 4.27 | 3.47 | 2.86 | 1.88 | 1.34 | 2.25 |
| Tang Book Value Per Share | 20.81 | 20.55 | 17.25 | 14.70 | 12.88 | 11.76 | 11.04 | 10.46 |
| Dividends Per Share | 0.583 | 0.572 | 0.561 | 0.517 | 0.473 | 0.424 | 0.363 | 0.306 |
| Dividend Payout % | 13.34 | 13.12 | 18.10 | 25.59 | 29.20 | 35.36 | 26.86 | 18.79 |
| **Income Statement** | | | | | | | | |
| Interest Income | 127,082 | 92,623 | 193,473 | 212,605 | 202,142 | 199,097 | 176,540 | 155,619 |
| Interest Expense | 16,282 | 8,652 | 36,661 | 48,742 | 72,418 | 104,619 | 88,242 | 62,940 |
| Net Interest Income | 110,800 | 83,971 | 156,812 | 163,863 | 129,724 | 94,478 | 88,298 | 92,679 |
| Provision for Losses | 17,643 | 18,082 | 19,714 | 33,975 | 16,205 | 6,820 | 2,302 | (562) |
| Non-Interest Income | 102,680 | 87,312 | 87,658 | 57,621 | 45,854 | 37,792 | 31,700 | 30,503 |
| Non-Interest Expense | 71,344 | 42,818 | 126,323 | 121,485 | 107,486 | 87,256 | 74,862 | 70,581 |
| Income Before Taxes | 124,493 | 110,383 | 98,433 | 66,024 | 51,887 | 38,194 | 42,834 | 53,163 |
| Income Taxes | 44,418 | 38,971 | 33,680 | 23,893 | 18,235 | 13,281 | 14,718 | 18,098 |
| Net Income | 80,075 | 71,412 | 64,753 | 42,131 | 33,652 | 24,913 | 28,351 | 35,065 |
| Average Shares | 20,994 | 20,991 | 20,960 | 20,884 | 20,824 | 20,840 | 21,078 | 21,570 |
| **Balance Sheet** | | | | | | | | |
| Net Loans & Leases | 2,218,222 | 2,149,742 | 2,152,161 | 2,245,353 | 2,289,025 | 2,384,338 | 2,289,670 | 2,049,647 |
| Total Assets | 3,104,570 | 3,395,744 | 3,622,703 | 3,918,768 | 3,939,368 | 3,165,359 | 3,046,787 | 2,735,556 |
| Total Deposits | 1,826,044 | 2,024,711 | 2,302,692 | 2,602,481 | 2,743,369 | 1,968,812 | 1,692,722 | 1,602,565 |
| Total Liabilities | 2,658,827 | 2,955,309 | 3,251,327 | 3,602,748 | 3,663,446 | 2,916,499 | 2,809,439 | 2,521,982 |
| Stockholders' Equity | 445,743 | 440,435 | 371,376 | 316,020 | 275,922 | 248,860 | 237,348 | 213,574 |
| Shares Outstanding | 20,935 | 20,937 | 20,935 | 20,807 | 20,628 | 20,296 | 20,592 | 20,408 |
| **Statistical Record** | | | | | | | | |
| Return on Assets % | 2.94 | 2.78 | 1.72 | 1.07 | 0.94 | 0.80 | 0.98 | 1.34 |
| Return on Equity % | 22.63 | 22.95 | 18.84 | 14.23 | 12.79 | 10.25 | 12.57 | 17.12 |
| Net Interest Margin % | 77.86 | 90.66 | 81.05 | 77.07 | 64.17 | 47.45 | 50.02 | 59.56 |
| Efficiency Ratio % | 57.25 | 23.80 | 44.93 | 44.96 | 43.34 | 36.83 | 35.95 | 37.92 |
| Loans to Deposits | 1.21 | 1.06 | 0.93 | 0.86 | 0.83 | 1.21 | 1.35 | 1.28 |
| Price Range | 25.97-16.87 | 25.97-16.87 | 25.97-15.11 | 27.20-14.76 | 34.98-14.55 | 23.94-14.32 | 24.05-17.33 | 23.54-17.37 |
| P/E Ratio | 5.94-3.86 | 5.96-3.87 | 8.38-4.87 | 13.47-7.31 | 21.59-8.98 | 19.95-11.93 | 17.81-12.84 | 14.44-10.66 |
| Average Yield % | 2.80 | 2.67 | 2.68 | 2.47 | 2.04 | 2.32 | 1.83 | 1.52 |

**Address:** 601 West Market Street, Louisville, KY 40202
**Telephone:** 502-584-3600

**Web Site:** www.republicbank.com
**Officers:** Bernard M. Trager - Chairman A. Scott Trager - Vice-Chairman

**Auditors:** Crowe Horwath LLP

# SPAN-AMERICA MEDICAL SYSTEMS, INC.

| Exchange | Symbol | Price | 52Wk Range | Yield | P/E |
|---|---|---|---|---|---|
| NMS | SPAN | $14.37 (8/31/2011) | 15.90-13.33 | 3.06 | 10.26 |

***7 Year Price Score 108.14** *NYSE Composite Index=100 ***12 Month Price Score 100.80**

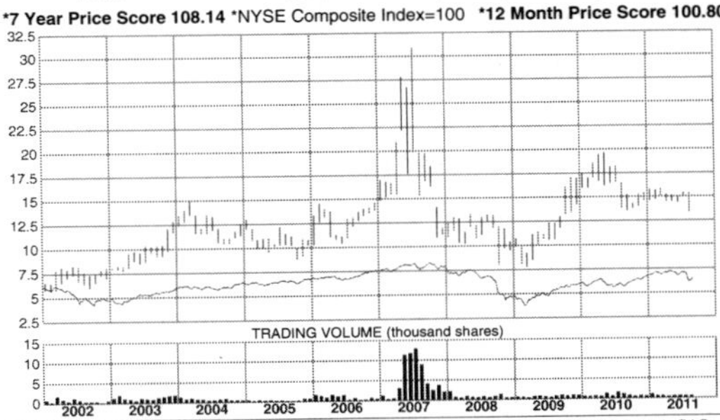


**Interim Earnings (Per Share)**

| Qtr. | Dec | Mar | Jun | Sep |
|---|---|---|---|---|
| 2007-08 | 0.36 | 0.48 | 0.41 | 0.45 |
| 2008-09 | 0.32 | 0.38 | 0.41 | 0.57 |
| 2009-10 | 0.40 | 0.44 | 0.33 | 0.42 |
| 2010-11 | 0.25 | 0.37 | 0.36 | ... |

**Interim Dividends (Per Share)**

| Amt | Decl | Ex | Rec | Pay |
|---|---|---|---|---|
| 0.10Q | 11/10/2010 | 11/22/2010 | 11/24/2010 | 12/03/2010 |
| 0.10Q | 02/18/2011 | 02/24/2011 | 02/28/2011 | 03/09/2011 |
| 0.11Q | 04/29/2011 | 05/16/2011 | 05/18/2011 | 06/03/2011 |
| 0.11Q | 07/29/2011 | 08/16/2011 | 08/18/2011 | 09/02/2011 |

**Indicated Div: $0.44**

| Valuation Analysis | | Institutional Holding |
|---|---|---|
| Forecast EPS | $1.37 (09/02/2011) | No of Institutions 23 |
| Market Cap | $40.2 Million | Shares 845,956 |
| Book Value | $23.6 Million | % Held 28.36 |
| Price/Book | 1.70 | |
| Price/Sales | 0.76 | |

**Business Summary:** Medical Instruments & Equipment (MIC: 4.3.1 SIC: 3842 NAIC: 339113)

Span-America Medical Systems manufactures and distributes therapeutic support surfaces, mattress overlays, patient positioners, seating cushions, skin care products and fall prevention products for the medical market and pillows, mattress pads and various foam products for the custom products market throughout the U.S. and Canada. Co. is engaged in two segments: medical and custom products. In the medical segment, Co. manufactures polyurethane foam mattress overlays, therapeutic support surfaces, patient positioners, seating products and Selan® skin care products. In the custom products segment, Co. manufactures two product lines: consumer bedding products and industrial foam products.

**Recent Developments:** For the quarter ended July 2 2011, net income increased 8.2% to US$1.0 million from US$945,275 in the year-earlier quarter. Revenues were US$13.7 million, up 4.0% from US$13.2 million the year before. Operating income was US$1.5 million versus US$1.4 million in the prior-year quarter, an increase of 10.6%. Direct operating expenses rose 6.2% to US$9.0 million from US$8.5 million in the comparable period the year before. Indirect operating expenses decreased 4.2% to US$3.2 million from US$3.3 million in the equivalent prior-year period.

**Prospects:** Our evaluation of Span-America Medical Systems Inc. as of Sep. 6, 2011 is the result of our systematic analysis on three basic characteristics: earnings strength, relative valuation, and recent stock price movement. The company has enjoyed a very positive trend in earnings per share over the past 5 quarters. Because the company lacks sufficient analyst estimate data, we place greater weight on the historical EPS trend as the measure of earnings strength. Based on operating earnings yield, the company is undervalued when compared to all of the companies in our coverage universe. Share price changes over the past year indicates that SPAN will perform poorly over the near term.

| Financial Data (US$ in Thousands) | 9 Mos | 6 Mos | 3 Mos | 10/02/2010 | 10/03/2009 | 09/27/2008 | 09/29/2007 | 09/30/2006 |
|---|---|---|---|---|---|---|---|---|
| Earnings Per Share | 1.40 | 1.37 | 1.44 | 1.59 | 1.67 | 1.70 | 1.06 | 1.10 |
| Cash Flow Per Share | 1.51 | 1.43 | 0.93 | 1.38 | 2.45 | 1.90 | 2.32 | 0.95 |
| Tang Book Value Per Share | 7.65 | 7.40 | 7.11 | 6.95 | 6.77 | 5.47 | 4.16 | 8.22 |
| Dividends Per Share | 0.410 | 1.400 | 1.400 | 1.400 | 0.360 | 0.340 | 5.300 | 0.195 |
| Dividend Payout % | 29.29 | 102.19 | 97.22 | 88.05 | 21.56 | 20.00 | 500.00 | 17.73 |
| **Income Statement** | | | | | | | | |
| Total Revenue | 38,856 | 25,161 | 11,707 | 52,356 | 55,867 | 59,265 | 60,689 | 51,557 |
| EBITDA | 4,792 | 3,046 | 1,263 | 7,529 | 7,661 | 8,225 | 5,329 | 5,379 |
| Depn & Amortn | 603 | 396 | 194 | 743 | 764 | 656 | 892 | 814 |
| Income Before Taxes | 4,188 | 2,650 | 1,070 | 6,786 | 6,893 | 7,461 | 4,334 | 4,565 |
| Income Taxes | 1,399 | 883 | 353 | 2,280 | 2,188 | 2,542 | 1,460 | 1,510 |
| Net Income | 2,789 | 1,767 | 717 | 4,506 | 4,684 | 4,869 | 2,874 | 3,055 |
| Average Shares | 2,843 | 2,837 | 2,830 | 2,841 | 2,803 | 2,868 | 2,864 | 2,771 |
| **Balance Sheet** | | | | | | | | |
| Current Assets | 19,027 | 17,811 | 16,425 | 16,845 | 16,281 | 13,331 | 13,096 | 18,186 |
| Total Assets | 29,217 | 27,843 | 26,745 | 27,212 | 26,835 | 24,113 | 23,969 | 31,012 |
| Current Liabilities | 4,798 | 4,192 | 4,070 | 4,977 | 5,424 | 5,283 | 5,650 | 4,848 |
| Long-Term Obligations | ... | ... | ... | ... | ... | 700 | 3,700 | ... |
| Total Liabilities | 5,616 | 5,024 | 4,915 | 5,834 | 6,261 | 6,780 | 10,181 | 6,495 |
| Stockholders' Equity | 23,601 | 22,820 | 21,830 | 21,379 | 20,573 | 17,332 | 13,788 | 24,517 |
| Shares Outstanding | 2,794 | 2,782 | 2,757 | 2,757 | 2,712 | 2,759 | 2,775 | 2,660 |
| **Statistical Record** | | | | | | | | |
| Return on Assets % | 14.49 | 14.13 | 15.05 | 16.72 | 18.09 | 20.31 | 10.48 | 10.27 |
| Return on Equity % | 18.09 | 17.19 | 18.91 | 21.54 | 24.31 | 31.38 | 15.05 | 13.30 |
| EBITDA Margin % | 12.33 | 12.11 | 10.79 | 14.38 | 13.71 | 13.88 | 8.78 | 10.43 |
| Net Margin % | 7.18 | 7.02 | 6.12 | 8.61 | 8.38 | 8.22 | 4.74 | 5.93 |
| Asset Turnover | 1.92 | 1.89 | 1.90 | 1.94 | 2.16 | 2.47 | 2.21 | 1.73 |
| Current Ratio | 3.97 | 4.25 | 4.04 | 3.38 | 3.00 | 2.52 | 2.32 | 3.75 |
| Debt to Equity | ... | ... | ... | ... | ... | 0.04 | 0.27 | ... |
| Price Range | 18.17-13.52 | 19.67-13.52 | 19.67-13.52 | 19.67-13.38 | 13.53-7.77 | 18.43-10.26 | 30.91-13.27 | 14.59-8.85 |
| P/E Ratio | 12.98-9.66 | 14.36-9.87 | 13.66-9.39 | 12.37-8.42 | 8.10-4.65 | 10.84-6.04 | 29.16-12.52 | 13.26-8.05 |
| Average Yield % | 2.72 | 8.84 | 8.59 | 8.50 | 3.42 | 2.73 | 29.10 | 1.66 |

**Address:** 70 Commerce Center, Greenville, SC 29615
**Telephone:** 864-288-8877
**Fax:** 864-288-8692

**Web Site:** www.spanamerica.com
**Officers:** James D. Ferguson - President, Chief Executive Officer Robert E. Ackley - Vice President

**Auditors:** Elliott Davis, LLC
**Transfer Agents:** American Stock Transfer & Trust Company

# TOMPKINS FINANCIAL CORP

| Exchange | Symbol | Price | 52Wk Range | Yield | P/E |
|---|---|---|---|---|---|
| ASE | TMP | $38.85 (8/31/2011) | 42.20-36.43 | 3.71 | 12.33 |

*7 Year Price Score N/A *NYSE Composite Index=100 *12 Month Price Score 100.17

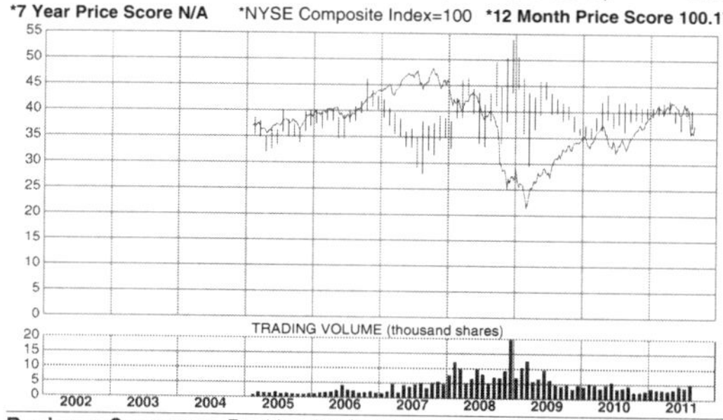


**Interim Earnings (Per Share)**

| Qtr. | Mar | Jun | Sep | Dec |
|---|---|---|---|---|
| 2008 | 0.70 | 0.66 | 0.74 | 0.67 |
| 2009 | 0.72 | 0.69 | 0.78 | 0.77 |
| 2010 | 0.78 | 0.83 | 0.69 | 0.81 |
| 2011 | 0.80 | 0.85 | ... | ... |

**Interim Dividends (Per Share)**

| Amt | Decl | Ex | Rec | Pay |
|---|---|---|---|---|
| 0.34Q | 10/27/2010 | 11/03/2010 | 11/05/2010 | 11/15/2010 |
| 0.34Q | 01/26/2011 | 02/02/2011 | 02/04/2011 | 02/15/2011 |
| 0.34Q | 04/27/2011 | 05/04/2011 | 05/06/2011 | 05/16/2011 |
| 0.36Q | 07/20/2011 | 08/03/2011 | 08/05/2011 | 08/15/2011 |

**Indicated Div: $1.44**

| Valuation Analysis | | Institutional Holding |
|---|---|---|
| Forecast EPS | $3.30 (09/02/2011) | No of Institutions 103 |
| Market Cap | $427.2 Million | Shares 3,640,250 |
| Book Value | $298.5 Million | % Held 36.73 |
| Price/Book | 1.43 | |
| Price/Sales | N/A | |

**Business Summary:** Banking (MIC: 5.1.1 SIC: 6022 NAIC: 522110)

Tompkins Financial is as a financial holding company that operates three banking subsidiaries, an insurance subsidiary, and a financial planning, wealth management and broker-dealer subsidiary. Co. has two business segments: banking, which consists of accepting deposits from the areas served by its banking subsidiaries' banking offices and using those deposits to originate a range of commercial loans, consumer loans, real estate loans, and leases; and financial services, which consists of its trust, financial planning and wealth management, broker-dealer services, and risk management operations. As of Dec 31 2010, Co. had total assets of $3.26 billion and total deposits of $2.50 billion.

**Recent Developments:** For the quarter ended June 30 2011, net income increased 4.0% to US$9.4 million from US$9.1 million in the year-earlier quarter. Net interest income decreased 0.5% to US$28.0 million from US$28.1 million in the year-earlier quarter. Provision for loan losses was US$1.0 million versus US$1.4 million in the prior-year quarter, a decrease of 28.6%. Non-interest income rose 6.0% to US$12.0 million from US$11.3 million, while non-interest expense advanced 2.6% to US$25.2 million.

**Prospects:** Our evaluation of Tompkins Financial Corp. as of Sep. 6, 2011 is the result of our systematic analysis on three basic characteristics: earnings strength, relative valuation, and recent stock price movement. The company has produced a positive trend in earnings per share over the past 5 quarters and while recent estimates for the company have remained steady, TMP has posted better than expected results. Based on operating earnings yield, the company is undervalued when compared to all of the companies in our coverage universe. Share price changes over the past year indicates that TMP will perform very poorly over the near term.

**Financial Data**

| (US$ in Thousands) | 6 Mos | 3 Mos | 12/31/2010 | 12/31/2009 | 12/31/2008 | 12/31/2007 | 12/31/2006 | 12/31/2005 |
|---|---|---|---|---|---|---|---|---|
| Earnings Per Share | 3.15 | 3.13 | 3.11 | 2.96 | 2.78 | 2.45 | 2.53 | 2.52 |
| Cash Flow Per Share | 5.11 | 4.95 | 6.00 | 2.23 | 5.78 | 3.52 | 3.46 | 3.52 |
| Tang Book Value Per Share | 22.74 | 21.57 | 20.85 | 20.31 | 16.12 | 16.27 | 15.21 | 15.41 |
| Dividends Per Share | 1.360 | 1.360 | 1.329 | 1.236 | 1.200 | 1.127 | 1.041 | 0.969 |
| Dividend Payout % | 43.17 | 43.45 | 42.74 | 41.77 | 43.14 | 45.93 | 41.20 | 38.45 |
| **Income Statement** | | | | | | | | |
| Interest Income | 68,841 | 34,287 | 144,062 | 146,795 | 140,783 | 132,441 | 121,041 | 106,707 |
| Interest Expense | 13,347 | 6,745 | 32,287 | 39,758 | 50,393 | 58,412 | 48,184 | 31,686 |
| Net Interest Income | 55,494 | 27,542 | 111,775 | 107,037 | 90,390 | 74,029 | 72,857 | 75,021 |
| Provision for Losses | 2,915 | 1,910 | 8,507 | 9,288 | 5,428 | 1,529 | 1,424 | 2,659 |
| Non-Interest Income | 24,505 | 12,492 | 46,159 | 46,213 | 46,035 | 44,049 | 41,091 | 30,783 |
| Non-Interest Expense | 50,380 | 25,216 | 99,045 | 96,617 | 87,056 | 78,056 | 71,910 | 62,122 |
| Income Before Taxes | 26,704 | 12,908 | 50,382 | 47,345 | 43,941 | 38,493 | 40,614 | 41,023 |
| Income Taxes | 8,466 | 4,102 | 16,420 | 15,383 | 13,810 | 11,991 | 12,716 | 13,207 |
| Net Income | 18,173 | 8,773 | 33,831 | 31,831 | 29,834 | 26,371 | 27,767 | 27,685 |
| Average Shares | 11,016 | 10,955 | 10,864 | 10,759 | 10,718 | 10,759 | 10,999 | 11,000 |
| **Balance Sheet** | | | | | | | | |
| Net Loans & Leases | 1,892,355 | 1,886,309 | 1,882,526 | 1,890,468 | 1,798,859 | 1,425,515 | 1,311,970 | 1,257,672 |
| Total Assets | 3,287,598 | 3,278,894 | 3,260,343 | 3,153,260 | 2,867,722 | 2,359,459 | 2,210,837 | 2,106,870 |
| Total Deposits | 2,572,008 | 2,612,517 | 2,495,873 | 2,439,864 | 2,134,007 | 1,720,826 | 1,709,420 | 1,683,010 |
| Total Liabilities | 2,989,055 | 2,998,142 | 2,988,387 | 2,909,704 | 2,649,813 | 2,162,264 | 2,021,217 | 1,925,649 |
| Stockholders' Equity | 298,543 | 280,752 | 271,956 | 243,556 | 217,909 | 197,195 | 189,620 | 181,221 |
| Shares Outstanding | 10,997 | 10,899 | 10,842 | 9,703 | 10,615 | 10,498 | 10,807 | 10,824 |
| **Statistical Record** | | | | | | | | |
| Return on Assets % | 1.07 | 1.05 | 1.05 | 1.06 | 1.14 | 1.15 | 1.29 | 1.36 |
| Return on Equity % | 12.22 | 12.81 | 13.13 | 13.80 | 14.33 | 13.63 | 14.98 | 15.72 |
| Net Interest Margin % | 80.89 | 80.33 | 77.59 | 72.92 | 64.21 | 55.90 | 60.19 | 70.31 |
| Efficiency Ratio % | 54.04 | 53.90 | 52.07 | 50.06 | 46.60 | 44.23 | 44.35 | 45.18 |
| Loans to Deposits | 0.74 | 0.72 | 0.75 | 0.77 | 0.84 | 0.83 | 0.77 | 0.75 |
| Price Range | 42.20-36.13 | 43.44-36.13 | 43.44-35.00 | 52.68-29.55 | 53.91-32.88 | 42.20-27.91 | 46.18-34.64 | 40.17-32.03 |
| P/E Ratio | 13.40-11.47 | 13.88-11.54 | 13.97-11.25 | 17.80-9.98 | 19.39-11.83 | 17.22-11.39 | 18.25-13.69 | 15.94-12.71 |
| Average Yield % | 3.43 | 3.43 | 3.43 | 3.03 | 2.87 | 3.13 | 2.63 | 2.69 |

**Address:** The Commons, P.O. Box 460, Ithaca, NY 14851
**Telephone:** 607-273-3210

**Web Site:** www.tompkinstrustco.com
**Officers:** James J. Byrnes - Chairman James W. Fulmer - Vice-Chairman

**Auditors:** KMPG LLP
**Investor Contact:** 888-503-5753x2319
**Transfer Agents:** American Stock Transfer & Trust Company, New York, NY

# TRI CITY BANKSHARES CORP.

| Exchange | Symbol | Price | 52Wk Range | Yield | P/E |
|---|---|---|---|---|---|
| NBB | TRCY | $15.45 (8/31/2011) | 21.25-15.45 | 7.77 | 9.90 |

***7 Year Price Score 95.44** *NYSE Composite Index=100 ***12 Month Price Score 90.23**

**Interim Earnings (Per Share)**

| Qtr. | Mar | Jun | Sep | Dec |
|---|---|---|---|---|
| 2008 | 0.34 | 0.30 | 0.30 | 0.30 |
| 2009 | 0.28 | 0.29 | 0.25 | 1.66 |
| 2010 | 0.53 | 0.47 | 0.30 | 0.71 |
| 2011 | 0.26 | 0.29 | ... | ... |

**Interim Dividends (Per Share)**

| Amt | Decl | Ex | Rec | Pay |
|---|---|---|---|---|
| 0.30Q | 04/14/2010 | 04/22/2010 | 04/26/2010 | 05/06/2010 |
| 0.30Q | 04/14/2010 | 06/30/2010 | 07/02/2010 | 07/12/2010 |
| 0.30Q | 07/14/2010 | 09/30/2010 | 10/04/2010 | 10/14/2010 |
| 1.20Q | 10/25/2010 | 11/26/2010 | 11/30/2010 | 12/10/2010 |

**Indicated Div: $1.20**

| Valuation Analysis | | Institutional Holding | |
|---|---|---|---|
| Forecast EPS | N/A | No of Institutions | N/A |
| Market Cap | $137.6 Million | Shares | N/A |
| Book Value | $119.3 Million | | |
| Price/Book | 1.15 | % Held | N/A |
| Price/Sales | N/A | | |

**Business Summary:** Banking (MIC: 5.1.1 SIC: 6022 NAIC: 522110)

Tri City Bankshares is a holding company. Through its subsidiary, Tri City National Bank (the Bank), Co. is engaged in providing a range of consumer and commercial banking services to individuals and businesses. The services provided include demand deposit accounts, money market deposit accounts, negotiable of withdrawal accounts, time deposits, safe deposit services, direct deposits, notary services, money orders, night depository, travelers' checks, cashier's checks, savings bonds and secured and unsecured consumer, commercial, installment, real estate and mortgage loans. As of Dec 31 2010, Co. had total assets of $1.14 billion and total deposits of $1.02 billion.

**Recent Developments:** For the quarter ended June 30 2011, net income decreased 36.5% to US$2.7 million from US$4.2 million in the year-earlier quarter. Net interest income decreased 15.6% to US$12.4 million from US$14.7 million in the year-earlier quarter. Provision for loan losses was US$1.9 million versus US$950,000 in the prior-year quarter, an increase of 102.1%. Non-interest income fell 5.3% to US$3.7 million from US$3.9 million, while non-interest expense declined 8.4% to US$10.1 million.

**Prospects:** Co.'s decrease in net interest income is primarily due to lower interest rates on earning assets as well as a volume shift from loans to lower-yielding investment securities. Furthermore, Co. noted that reinvestment in existing rate environment produces relatively low-yielding investments which also negatively affected its net interest margin. In addition, Co.'s earnings are being adversely affected by the increase in the provision for loan losses, as well as a decline in noninterest income, reflecting a reduction in other income and service charges on deposits. Meanwhile, Co. continues to focus its efforts on providing products that will encourage further deposit growth going forward.

| **Financial Data** (US$ in Thousands) | 6 Mos | 3 Mos | 12/31/2010 | 12/31/2009 | 12/31/2008 | 12/31/2007 | 12/31/2006 | 12/31/2005 |
|---|---|---|---|---|---|---|---|---|
| Earnings Per Share | 1.56 | 1.74 | 1.61 | 2.48 | 1.24 | 1.13 | 1.06 | 1.05 |
| Cash Flow Per Share | 0.57 | (0.08) | 0.81 | 1.09 | 1.47 | 1.28 | 1.22 | 1.25 |
| Tang Book Value Per Share | 13.08 | 12.76 | 12.49 | 13.21 | 12.17 | 11.94 | 11.73 | 11.36 |
| Dividends Per Share | 1.500 | 2.100 | 2.100 | 1.380 | 1.040 | 1.000 | 0.880 | 0.780 |
| Dividend Payout % | 96.15 | 120.69 | 130.43 | 55.65 | 83.87 | 88.50 | 83.02 | 74.29 |
| **Income Statement** | | | | | | | | |
| Interest Income | 26,437 | 12,843 | 61,929 | 44,387 | 43,451 | 45,067 | 40,924 | 36,026 |
| Interest Expense | 2,508 | 1,328 | 5,713 | 6,953 | 9,518 | 12,574 | 10,592 | 7,631 |
| Net Interest Income | 23,930 | 11,516 | 56,216 | 37,433 | 33,934 | 32,493 | 30,332 | 28,395 |
| Provision for Losses | 3,320 | 1,400 | 6,930 | 3,706 | 1,300 | 480 | 240 | 175 |
| Non-Interest Income | 7,080 | 3,376 | 16,477 | 36,601 | 12,885 | 11,265 | 10,420 | 9,472 |
| Non-Interest Expense | 20,429 | 10,332 | 43,079 | 34,616 | 29,202 | 28,017 | 26,425 | 24,486 |
| Income Before Taxes | 7,260 | 3,160 | 22,684 | 35,712 | 16,317 | 15,261 | 14,087 | 13,206 |
| Income Taxes | 2,322 | 874 | 8,374 | 13,635 | 5,293 | 5,284 | 4,804 | 4,257 |
| Net Income | 4,938 | 2,286 | 14,310 | 22,077 | 11,024 | 9,977 | 9,284 | 8,949 |
| Average Shares | 8,904 | 8,904 | 8,904 | 8,904 | 8,903 | 8,847 | 8,734 | 8,529 |
| **Balance Sheet** | | | | | | | | |
| Net Loans & Leases | 712,810 | 725,353 | 737,302 | 781,846 | 593,701 | 580,521 | 528,947 | 510,891 |
| Total Assets | 1,109,058 | 1,123,715 | 1,141,687 | 1,125,709 | 792,933 | 790,027 | 770,014 | 742,308 |
| Total Deposits | 982,974 | 1,002,045 | 1,018,447 | 987,984 | 677,678 | 665,804 | 661,428 | 639,291 |
| Total Liabilities | 989,785 | 1,007,094 | 1,027,353 | 1,004,313 | 683,997 | 683,260 | 665,981 | 643,507 |
| Stockholders' Equity | 119,273 | 116,620 | 114,335 | 121,396 | 108,936 | 106,767 | 104,033 | 98,801 |
| Shares Outstanding | 8,904 | 8,904 | 8,904 | 8,904 | 8,904 | 8,884 | 8,801 | 8,615 |
| **Statistical Record** | | | | | | | | |
| Return on Assets % | 0.95 | 1.07 | 1.26 | 2.30 | 1.39 | 1.28 | 1.23 | 1.24 |
| Return on Equity % | 8.59 | 9.91 | 12.14 | 19.17 | 10.19 | 9.47 | 9.15 | 9.35 |
| Net Interest Margin % | 91.32 | 89.66 | 90.78 | 84.33 | 78.10 | 72.10 | 74.12 | 78.82 |
| Efficiency Ratio % | 58.38 | 63.70 | 54.94 | 42.74 | 51.84 | 49.74 | 51.47 | 53.82 |
| Loans to Deposits | 0.73 | 0.72 | 0.72 | 0.79 | 0.88 | 0.87 | 0.80 | 0.80 |
| Price Range | 21.25-17.25 | 21.25-17.50 | 21.25-17.50 | 19.01-10.05 | 20.00-12.25 | 20.50-19.00 | 22.00-19.00 | 23.50-19.00 |
| P/E Ratio | 13.62-11.06 | 12.21-10.06 | 13.20-10.87 | 7.67-4.05 | 16.13-9.88 | 18.14-16.81 | 20.75-17.92 | 22.38-18.10 |
| Average Yield % | 8.20 | 11.35 | 11.22 | 9.19 | 6.08 | 5.06 | 4.44 | 3.87 |

**Address:** 6400 South 27th Street, Oak Creek, WI 53154
**Telephone:** 414-761-1610
**Fax:** 414-423-2291

**Web Site:** www.tcnb.com
**Officers:** Ronald K. Puetz - Chairman, President, Chief Executive Officer Robert W. Orth - Executive Vice President

**Auditors:** Baker Tilly Virchow Krause,
**Transfer Agents:** Robert W. Baird, Milwakee, WI

# YORK WATER CO

| Exchange | Symbol | Price | 52Wk Range | Yield | P/E |
|---|---|---|---|---|---|
| NMS | YORW | $17.83 (8/31/2011) | 18.04-14.74 | 2.94 | 24.09 |

***7 Year Price Score 106.45** *NYSE Composite Index=100 ***12 Month Price Score 103.94**

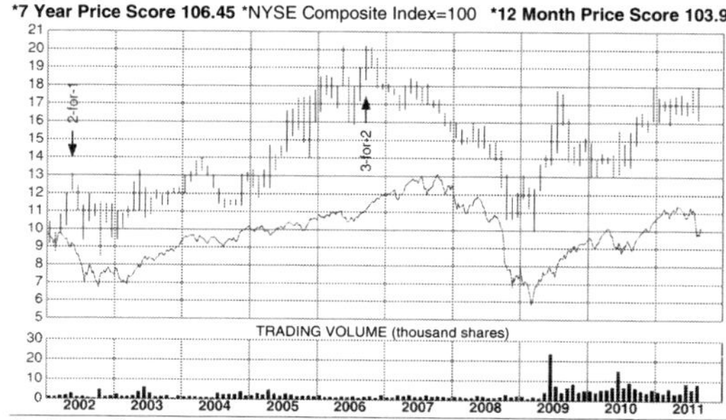


**Interim Earnings (Per Share)**

| Qtr. | Mar | Jun | Sep | Dec |
|---|---|---|---|---|
| 2008 | 0.11 | 0.13 | 0.15 | 0.17 |
| 2009 | 0.13 | 0.17 | 0.18 | 0.16 |
| 2010 | 0.15 | 0.18 | 0.21 | 0.17 |
| 2011 | 0.17 | 0.19 | ... | ... |

**Interim Dividends (Per Share)**

| Amt | Decl | Ex | Rec | Pay |
|---|---|---|---|---|
| 0.131Q | 11/22/2010 | 12/29/2010 | 12/31/2010 | 01/14/2011 |
| 0.131Q | 01/25/2011 | 02/24/2011 | 02/28/2011 | 04/15/2011 |
| 0.131Q | 04/25/2011 | 06/28/2011 | 06/30/2011 | 07/15/2011 |
| 0.131Q | 08/22/2011 | 09/28/2011 | 09/30/2011 | 10/14/2011 |

**Indicated Div: $0.52 (Div. Reinv. Plan)**

| **Valuation Analysis** | | **Institutional Holding** |
|---|---|---|
| Forecast EPS | $0.76 (09/02/2011) | No of Institutions 71 |
| Market Cap | $227.2 Million | Shares 3,405,490 |
| Book Value | $93.4 Million | % Held 24.90 |
| Price/Book | 2.43 | |
| Price/Sales | 5.63 | |

**Business Summary:** Water Utilities (MIC: 3.2.1 SIC: 4941 NAIC: 221310)

York Water is engaged in the business of impounding, purifying, and distributing water. Co. operates within its franchised territory, which covers 39 municipalities within York County, PA and seven municipalities within Adams County, PA. Water service is supplied through Co.'s own distribution system. Co. obtains its water supply from the south branch and east branch of the Codorus Creek. Co. has two reservoirs, Lake Williams and Lake Redman, as well as a 15-mile pipeline from the Susquehanna River to Lake Redman that provides access to an additional supply. As of Dec 31 2010, Co.'s service territory had an estimated population of 182,000.

**Recent Developments:** For the quarter ended June 30 2011, net income increased 4.9% to US$2.5 million from US$2.3 million in the year-earlier quarter. Revenues were US$10.5 million, up 7.2% from US$9.7 million the year before. Operating income was US$5.2 million versus US$5.0 million in the prior-year quarter, an increase of 2.3%. Direct operating expenses rose 10.9% to US$1.8 million from US$1.6 million in the comparable period the year before. Indirect operating expenses increased 13.4% to US$3.5 million from US$3.1 million in the equivalent prior-year period.

**Prospects:** Our evaluation of York Water Co. as of Sep. 6, 2011 is the result of our systematic analysis on three basic characteristics: earnings strength, relative valuation, and recent stock price movement. The company has managed to produce a neutral trend in earnings per share over the past 5 quarters and while recent estimates for the company have remained steady, YORW has posted results that fell short of analysts expectations. Based on operating earnings yield, the company is about fairly valued when compared to all of the companies in our coverage universe. Share price changes over the past year indicates that YORW will perform very poorly over the near term.

**Financial Data**

| (US$ in Thousands) | 6 Mos | 3 Mos | 12/31/2010 | 12/31/2009 | 12/31/2008 | 12/31/2007 | 12/31/2006 | 12/31/2005 |
|---|---|---|---|---|---|---|---|---|
| Earnings Per Share | 0.74 | 0.73 | 0.71 | 0.64 | 0.57 | 0.57 | 0.58 | 0.56 |
| Cash Flow Per Share | 1.33 | 1.19 | 1.17 | 1.35 | 1.02 | 0.89 | 0.68 | 0.89 |
| Tang Book Value Per Share | 7.33 | 7.24 | 7.19 | 6.92 | 6.14 | 5.97 | 5.84 | 4.85 |
| Dividends Per Share | 0.521 | 0.518 | 0.515 | 0.506 | 0.489 | 0.475 | 0.454 | 0.424 |
| Dividend Payout % | 70.41 | 70.96 | 72.54 | 79.06 | 85.79 | 83.33 | 78.28 | 75.71 |
| **Income Statement** | | | | | | | | |
| Total Revenue | 20,097 | 9,645 | 39,005 | 37,043 | 32,838 | 31,433 | 28,658 | 26,805 |
| EBITDA | 12,078 | 5,817 | 24,005 | 21,493 | 18,440 | 17,477 | 15,974 | 15,058 |
| Depn & Amortn | 2,446 | 1,219 | 4,592 | 4,412 | 3,622 | 3,227 | 2,522 | 2,238 |
| Income Before Taxes | 7,052 | 3,303 | 14,507 | 12,091 | 10,059 | 10,106 | 9,287 | 9,216 |
| Income Taxes | 2,455 | 1,164 | 5,578 | 4,579 | 3,628 | 3,692 | 3,196 | 3,383 |
| Net Income | 4,597 | 2,139 | 8,929 | 7,512 | 6,431 | 6,414 | 6,091 | 5,833 |
| Average Shares | 12,720 | 12,695 | 12,626 | 11,695 | 11,298 | 11,225 | 10,475 | 10,359 |
| **Balance Sheet** | | | | | | | | |
| Current Assets | 11,444 | 10,118 | 8,793 | 7,146 | 7,347 | 6,812 | 6,698 | 5,124 |
| Total Assets | 264,762 | 261,740 | 259,931 | 248,837 | 240,442 | 210,969 | 196,064 | 172,296 |
| Current Liabilities | 5,803 | 5,439 | 5,331 | 14,605 | 14,196 | 21,360 | 5,923 | 24,650 |
| Long-Term Obligations | 85,006 | 85,031 | 85,132 | 73,227 | 83,612 | 58,465 | 61,095 | 39,835 |
| Total Liabilities | 171,398 | 169,631 | 168,674 | 161,915 | 170,676 | 143,697 | 130,703 | 121,881 |
| Stockholders' Equity | 93,364 | 92,109 | 91,257 | 86,922 | 69,766 | 67,272 | 65,361 | 50,415 |
| Shares Outstanding | 12,743 | 12,714 | 12,692 | 12,558 | 11,367 | 11,264 | 11,201 | 10,399 |
| **Statistical Record** | | | | | | | | |
| Return on Assets % | 3.61 | 3.61 | 3.51 | 3.07 | 2.84 | 3.15 | 3.31 | 3.55 |
| Return on Equity % | 10.25 | 10.26 | 10.02 | 9.59 | 9.36 | 9.67 | 10.52 | 11.85 |
| EBITDA Margin % | 60.10 | 60.31 | 61.54 | 58.02 | 56.15 | 55.60 | 55.74 | 56.18 |
| Net Margin % | 22.87 | 22.18 | 22.89 | 20.28 | 19.58 | 20.41 | 21.25 | 21.76 |
| Asset Turnover | 0.16 | 0.16 | 0.15 | 0.15 | 0.15 | 0.15 | 0.16 | 0.16 |
| Current Ratio | 1.97 | 1.86 | 1.65 | 0.49 | 0.52 | 0.32 | 1.13 | 0.21 |
| Debt to Equity | 0.91 | 0.92 | 0.93 | 0.84 | 1.20 | 0.87 | 0.93 | 0.79 |
| Price Range | 17.96-13.52 | 17.96-13.01 | 17.96-13.01 | 17.80-9.95 | 16.04-10.61 | 18.45-15.50 | 20.23-15.87 | 17.79-11.79 |
| P/E Ratio | 24.27-18.27 | 24.60-17.82 | 25.30-18.32 | 27.81-15.55 | 28.14-18.61 | 32.37-27.19 | 34.89-27.36 | 31.77-21.05 |
| Average Yield % | 3.21 | 3.36 | 3.49 | 3.61 | 3.48 | 2.75 | 2.51 | 2.88 |

**Address:** 130 East Market Street, York, PA 17401
**Telephone:** 717-845-3601

**Web Site:** www.yorkwater.com
**Officers:** Jeffrey R. Hines - President, Chief Executive Officer Bruce C. McIntosh - Vice President, Secretary, Assistant Treasurer

**Auditors:** ParenteBeard LLC
**Investor Contact:** 717-845-3601
**Transfer Agents:** American Stock Transfer & Trust Company, New York, NY

# WEYCO GROUP, INC

| Exchange | Symbol | Price | 52Wk Range | Yield | P/E |
|---|---|---|---|---|---|
| NMS | WEYS | $22.75 (8/31/2011) | 26.64-21.87 | 2.81 | 18.65 |

*7 Year Price Score 98.39 *NYSE Composite Index=100 *12 Month Price Score 99.46

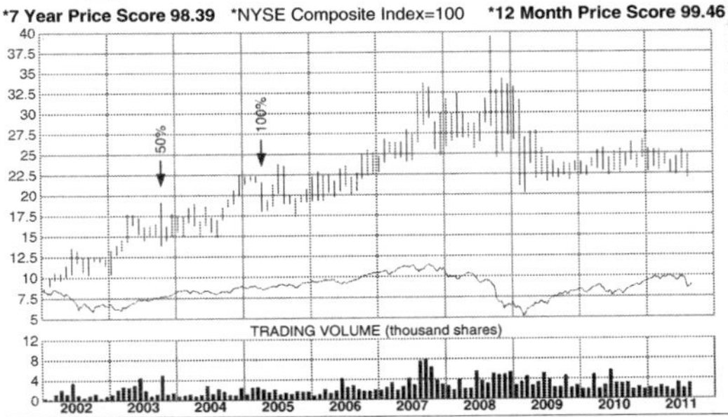


**Interim Earnings (Per Share)**

| Qtr. | Mar | Jun | Sep | Dec |
|---|---|---|---|---|
| 2008 | 0.43 | 0.34 | 0.37 | 0.30 |
| 2009 | 0.22 | 0.19 | 0.29 | 0.41 |
| 2010 | 0.34 | 0.11 | 0.30 | 0.45 |
| 2011 | 0.30 | 0.17 | ... | ... |

**Interim Dividends (Per Share)**

| Amt | Decl | Ex | Rec | Pay |
|---|---|---|---|---|
| 0.16Q | 11/01/2010 | 11/30/2010 | 12/02/2010 | 01/03/2011 |
| 0.16Q | 02/21/2011 | 03/10/2011 | 03/14/2011 | 04/01/2011 |
| 0.16Q | 04/27/2011 | 05/27/2011 | 06/01/2011 | 07/01/2011 |
| 0.16Q | 08/01/2011 | 08/30/2011 | 09/01/2011 | 10/01/2011 |

**Indicated Div: $0.64**

| **Valuation Analysis** | | **Institutional Holding** |
|---|---|---|
| Forecast EPS | N/A | No of Institutions |
| | | 53 |
| Market Cap | $250.4 Million | Shares |
| Book Value | $166.4 Million | 4,980,881 |
| Price/Book | 1.50 | % Held |
| Price/Sales | 1.04 | 38.38 |

**Business Summary:** Retail - General Merchandise/Department Stores (MIC: 2.1.1 SIC: 5131 NAIC: 424310)

Weyco Group is a distributor of men's casual, dress and fashion shoes. Co.'s brands of shoes include Florsheim, Nunn Bush, Stacy Adams, Umi, Brass Boot and Nunn Bush NXXT, as well as SAO by Stacy Adams, and Florsheim by Duckie Brown. Co. has two reportable segments: North American wholesale, which includes marketing to shoe specialty stores, department stores and clothing retailers in the U.S. and Canada, as well as licensing agreements with third parties; and North American retail, which consists of its 35 Co.-owned retail stores in the U.S. and an Internet business. Co.'s other category includes its wholesale and retail operations in Australia, South Africa, Asia Pacific, and Europe.

**Recent Developments:** For the quarter ended June 30 2011, net income increased 111.7% to US$2.3 million from US$1.1 million in the year-earlier quarter. Revenues were US$56.6 million, up 16.1% from US$48.7 million the year before. Operating income was US$2.7 million versus US$1.7 million in the prior-year quarter, an increase of 62.1%. Direct operating expenses rose 12.7% to US$33.9 million from US$30.1 million in the comparable period the year before. Indirect operating expenses increased 17.4% to US$19.9 million from US$17.0 million in the equivalent prior-year period.

**Prospects:** Our evaluation of Weyco Group Inc. as of Sep. 6, 2011 is the result of our systematic analysis on three basic characteristics: earnings strength, relative valuation, and recent stock price movement. The company has produced a positive trend in earnings per share over the past 5 quarters. Because the company lacks sufficient analyst estimate data, we place greater weight on the historical EPS trend as the measure of earnings strength. Based on operating earnings yield, the company is about fairly valued when compared to all of the companies in our coverage universe. Share price changes over the past year indicates that WEYS will perform very poorly over the near term.

| **Financial Data** (US$ in Thousands) | 6 Mos | 3 Mos | 12/31/2010 | 12/31/2009 | 12/31/2008 | 12/31/2007 | 12/31/2006 | 12/31/2005 |
|---|---|---|---|---|---|---|---|---|
| Earnings Per Share | 1.22 | 1.16 | 1.19 | 1.11 | 1.45 | 1.91 | 1.81 | 1.62 |
| Cash Flow Per Share | 0.64 | 0.08 | 0.01 | 3.36 | 1.38 | 2.09 | 0.83 | 3.35 |
| Tang Book Value Per Share | 10.96 | 11.37 | 14.06 | 13.54 | 13.02 | 13.00 | 11.72 | 10.86 |
| Dividends Per Share | 0.640 | 0.640 | 0.630 | 0.590 | 0.530 | 0.420 | 0.340 | 0.265 |
| Dividend Payout % | 52.46 | 55.17 | 52.94 | 53.15 | 36.55 | 21.99 | 18.78 | 16.36 |
| **Income Statement** | | | | | | | | |
| Total Revenue | 121,696 | 65,146 | 229,231 | 225,305 | 221,432 | 232,617 | 221,047 | 209,469 |
| EBITDA | 9,075 | 5,568 | 21,826 | 21,134 | 27,109 | 36,641 | 35,664 | 32,916 |
| Depn & Amortn | 1,425 | 703 | 2,700 | 2,948 | 2,631 | 2,484 | 2,206 | 2,263 |
| Income Before Taxes | 8,599 | 5,365 | 21,297 | 20,010 | 26,432 | 35,963 | 34,791 | 31,351 |
| Income Taxes | 2,809 | 1,863 | 7,171 | 6,940 | 9,407 | 13,062 | 12,935 | 11,950 |
| Net Income | 5,309 | 3,372 | 13,668 | 12,821 | 17,025 | 22,901 | 21,856 | 19,401 |
| Average Shares | 11,239 | 11,366 | 11,493 | 11,510 | 11,757 | 12,012 | 12,094 | 11,965 |
| **Balance Sheet** | | | | | | | | |
| Current Assets | 108,707 | 114,658 | 111,488 | 111,259 | 101,477 | 97,836 | 101,222 | 92,647 |
| Total Assets | 258,399 | 263,151 | 223,435 | 207,153 | 190,640 | 190,152 | 189,623 | 175,498 |
| Current Liabilities | 55,626 | 52,991 | 27,719 | 20,277 | 16,823 | 21,103 | 32,914 | 29,913 |
| Total Liabilities | 91,993 | 88,570 | 50,989 | 42,857 | 31,983 | 29,394 | 41,450 | 38,930 |
| Stockholders' Equity | 166,406 | 174,581 | 172,446 | 164,296 | 158,657 | 160,758 | 148,172 | 136,568 |
| Shares Outstanding | 11,006 | 11,353 | 11,356 | 11,333 | 11,353 | 11,534 | 11,714 | 11,574 |
| **Statistical Record** | | | | | | | | |
| Return on Assets % | 5.96 | 5.60 | 6.35 | 6.45 | 8.92 | 12.06 | 11.97 | 11.69 |
| Return on Equity % | 8.32 | 7.72 | 8.12 | 7.94 | 10.63 | 14.83 | 15.35 | 15.14 |
| EBITDA Margin % | 7.46 | 8.55 | 9.52 | 9.38 | 12.24 | 15.75 | 16.13 | 15.71 |
| Net Margin % | 4.36 | 5.18 | 5.96 | 5.69 | 7.69 | 9.84 | 9.89 | 9.26 |
| Asset Turnover | 1.04 | 0.99 | 1.06 | 1.13 | 1.16 | 1.23 | 1.21 | 1.26 |
| Current Ratio | 1.95 | 2.16 | 4.02 | 5.49 | 6.03 | 4.64 | 3.08 | 3.10 |
| Price Range | 26.64-22.32 | 26.64-22.29 | 26.64-22.19 | 33.21-20.19 | 39.44-24.55 | 33.71-22.78 | 25.50-19.25 | 23.85-17.38 |
| P/E Ratio | 21.84-18.30 | 22.97-19.22 | 22.39-18.65 | 29.92-18.19 | 27.20-16.93 | 17.65-11.93 | 14.09-10.64 | 14.72-10.73 |
| Average Yield % | 2.66 | 2.65 | 2.64 | 2.42 | 1.83 | 1.56 | 1.55 | 1.31 |

| | | |
|---|---|---|
| **Address:** 333 W. Estabrook Boulevard, P.O. Box 1188, Milwaukee, WI 53201 **Telephone:** 414-908-1600 | **Web Site:** www.weycogroup.com **Officers:** Thomas W. Florsheim - Chairman, Chief Executive Officer John W. Florsheim - President, Chief Operating Officer, Assistant Secretary | **Auditors:** Deloitte & Touche LLP **Transfer Agents:** American Stock Transfer & Trust Company, New York, NY |